Y0-EHY-330

Short Story Criticism

Guide to Thomson Gale Literary Criticism Series

For criticism on	Consult these Thomson Gale series
Authors now living or who died after December 31, 1999	*CONTEMPORARY LITERARY CRITICISM (CLC)*
Authors who died between 1900 and 1999	*TWENTIETH-CENTURY LITERARY CRITICISM (TCLC)*
Authors who died between 1800 and 1899	*NINETEENTH-CENTURY LITERATURE CRITICISM (NCLC)*
Authors who died between 1400 and 1799	*LITERATURE CRITICISM FROM 1400 TO 1800 (LC)* *SHAKESPEAREAN CRITICISM (SC)*
Authors who died before 1400	*CLASSICAL AND MEDIEVAL LITERATURE CRITICISM (CMLC)*
Authors of books for children and young adults	*CHILDREN'S LITERATURE REVIEW (CLR)*
Dramatists	*DRAMA CRITICISM (DC)*
Poets	*POETRY CRITICISM (PC)*
Short story writers	*SHORT STORY CRITICISM (SSC)*
Literary topics and movements	*HARLEM RENAISSANCE: A GALE CRITICAL COMPANION (HR)* *THE BEAT GENERATION: A GALE CRITICAL COMPANION (BG)* *FEMINISM IN LITERATURE: A GALE CRITICAL COMPANION (FL)* *GOTHIC LITERATURE: A GALE CRITICAL COMPANION (GL)*
Asian American writers of the last two hundred years	*ASIAN AMERICAN LITERATURE (AAL)*
Black writers of the past two hundred years	*BLACK LITERATURE CRITICISM (BLC)* *BLACK LITERATURE CRITICISM SUPPLEMENT (BLCS)*
Hispanic writers of the late nineteenth and twentieth centuries	*HISPANIC LITERATURE CRITICISM (HLC)* *HISPANIC LITERATURE CRITICISM SUPPLEMENT (HLCS)*
Native North American writers and orators of the eighteenth, nineteenth, and twentieth centuries	*NATIVE NORTH AMERICAN LITERATURE (NNAL)*
Major authors from the Renaissance to the present	*WORLD LITERATURE CRITICISM, 1500 TO THE PRESENT (WLC)* *WORLD LITERATURE CRITICISM SUPPLEMENT (WLCS)*

ISSN 0895-9439

Volume 91

Short Story Criticism

Criticism of the Works of Short Fiction Writers

Jessica Bomarito
Jelena Krstović
Project Editors

Detroit • New York • San Francisco • New Haven, Conn. • Waterville, Maine • London • Munich

Short Story Criticism, Vol. 91

Project Editors
Jessica Bomarito and Jelena Krstović

Editorial
Kathy D. Darrow, Jeffrey W. Hunter, Michelle Lee, Thomas J. Schoenberg, Noah Schusterbauer, Lawrence J. Trudeau, Russel Whitaker

Data Capture
Frances Monroe, Gwen Tucker

Indexing Services
Factiva®, a Dow Jones and Reuters Company

Rights and Acquisitions
Margaret Abendroth, Margaret Chamberlain-Gaston, Edna Hedblad

Imaging and Multimedia
Dean Dauphinais, Leitha Etheridge-Sims, Lezlie Light, Mike Logusz, Dan Newell, Christine O'Bryan, Kelly A. Quin, Denay Wilding, Robyn Young

Composition and Electronic Capture
Gary Oudersluys

Manufacturing
Rhonda Dover

Associate Product Manager
Marc Cormier

For more information, contact
Thomson Gale
27500 Drake Rd.
Farmington Hills, MI 48331-3535
Or you can visit our internet site at
http://www.gale.com

LIBRARY OF CONGRESS CATALOG CARD NUMBER 88-641014

ISBN 0-7876-8888-6
ISSN 0895-9439

Printed in the United States of America
10 9 8 7 6 5 4 3 2 1

Contents

Preface

Short Story Criticism (*SSC*) presents significant criticism of the world's greatest short-story writers and provides supplementary biographical and bibliographical materials to guide the interested reader to a greater understanding of the authors of short fiction. This series was developed in response to suggestions from librarians serving high school, college, and public library patrons, who had noted a considerable number of requests for critical material on short-story writers. Although major short-story writers are covered in such Thomson Gale series as *Contemporary Literary Criticism* (*CLC*), *Twentieth-Century Literary Criticism* (*TCLC*), *Nineteenth-Century Literature Criticism* (*NCLC*), and *Literature Criticism from 1400 to 1800* (*LC*), librarians perceived the need for a series devoted solely to writers of the short-story genre.

Scope of the Series

SSC is designed to serve as an introduction to major short-story writers of all eras and nationalities. Since these authors have inspired a great deal of relevant critical material, *SSC* is necessarily selective, and the editors have chosen the most important published criticism to aid readers and students in their research.

Approximately three to six authors, works, or topics are included in each volume, and each entry presents a historical survey of the critical response to the work. The length of an entry is intended to reflect the amount of critical attention the author has received from critics writing in English and from foreign critics in translation. Every attempt has been made to identify and include the most significant essays on each author's work. In order to provide these important critical pieces, the editors sometimes reprint essays that have appeared elsewhere in Thomson Gale's Literary Criticism Series. Such duplication, however, never exceeds twenty percent of an *SSC* volume.

Organization of the Book

An *SSC* entry consists of the following elements:

- The **Author Heading** cites the name under which the author most commonly wrote, followed by birth and death dates. Also located here are any name variations under which an author wrote, including transliterated forms for authors whose native languages use nonroman alphabets. If the author wrote consistently under a pseudonym, the pseudonym will be listed in the author heading and the author's actual name given in parentheses on the first line of the biographical and critical introduction. Uncertain birth or death dates are indicated by question marks. Single-work entries are preceded by the title of the work and its date of publication.

- The **Introduction** contains background information that introduces the reader to the author and the critical debates surrounding his or her work.

- The list of **Principal Works** is ordered chronologically by date of first publication and lists the most important works by the author. The first section comprises short-story collections, novellas, and novella collections. The second section gives information on other major works by the author. For foreign authors, the editors have provided original foreign-language publication information and have selected what are considered the best and most complete English-language editions of their works.

- Reprinted **Criticism** is arranged chronologically in each entry to provide a useful perspective on changes in critical evaluation over time. All short-story, novella, and collection titles by the author featured in the entry are printed in boldface type. The critic's name and the date of composition or publication of the critical work are given at the beginning of each piece of criticism. Unsigned criticism is preceded by the title of the source in which it appeared. Footnotes are reprinted at the end of each essay or excerpt. In the case of excerpted criticism, only those footnotes that pertain to the excerpted texts are included.

- Critical essays are prefaced by brief **Annotations** explicating each piece.

- A complete **Bibliographical Citation** of the original essay or book precedes each piece of criticism. Source citations in the Literary Criticism Series follow University of Chicago Press style, as outlined in *The Chicago Manual of Style,* 15th ed. (Chicago: The University of Chicago Press, 2006).

- An annotated bibliography of **Further Reading** appears at the end of each entry and suggests resources for additional study. In some cases, significant essays for which the editors could not obtain reprint rights are included here. Boxed material following the further reading list provides references to other biographical and critical sources on the author in series published by Thomson Gale.

Indexes

A **Cumulative Author Index** lists all of the authors that appear in a wide variety of reference sources published by Thomson Gale, including *SSC.* A complete list of these sources is found facing the first page of the Author Index. The index also includes birth and death dates and cross references between pseudonyms and actual names.

A **Cumulative Nationality Index** lists all authors featured in *SSC* by nationality, followed by the number of the *SSC* volume in which their entry appears.

An alphabetical **Title Index** lists all short-story, novella, and collection titles contained in the *SSC* series. Titles of short-story collections, separately published novellas, and novella collections are printed in italics, while titles of individual short stories are printed in roman type with quotation marks. Each title is followed by the author's last name and corresponding volume and page numbers where commentary on the work is located. English-language translations of original foreign-language titles are cross-referenced to the foreign titles so that all references to discussion of a work are combined in one listing.

In response to numerous suggestions from librarians, Thomson Gale also produces an annual paperbound edition of the SSC cumulative title index. This annual cumulation, which alphabetically lists all titles reviewed in the series, is available to all customers. Additional copies of this index are available upon request. Librarians and patrons will welcome this separate index; it saves shelf space, is easy to use, and is recyclable upon receipt of the next edition.

Citing *Short Story Criticism*

When citing criticism reprinted in the Literary Criticism Series, students should provide complete bibliographic information so that the cited essay can be located in the original print or electronic source. Students who quote directly from reprinted criticism may use any accepted bibliographic format, such as University of Chicago Press style or Modern Language Association (MLA) style. Both the MLA and the University of Chicago formats are acceptable and recognized as being the current standards for citations. It is important, however, to choose one format for all citations; do not mix the two formats within a list of citations.

The examples below follow recommendations for preparing a bibliography set forth in *The Chicago Manual of Style,* 15th ed. (Chicago: The University of Chicago Press, 2006); the first example pertains to material drawn from periodicals, the second to material reprinted from books:

Morrison, Jago. "Narration and Unease in Ian McEwan's Later Fiction." *Critique* 42, no. 3 (spring 2001): 253-68. Reprinted in *Short Story Criticism.* Vol. 57, edited by Jelena Krstovic, 212-20. Detroit: Gale, 2003.

Brossard, Nicole. "Poetic Politics." In *The Politics of Poetic Form: Poetry and Public Policy,* edited by Charles Bernstein, 73-82. New York: Roof Books, 1990. Reprinted in *Short Story Criticism.* Vol. 57, edited by Jelena Krstovic, 3-8. Detroit: Gale, 2003.

The examples below follow recommendations for preparing a works cited list set forth in the *MLA Handbook for Writers of Research Papers,* 6th ed. (New York: The Modern Language Association of America, 2003); the first example pertains to material drawn from periodicals, the second to material reprinted from books:

Morrison, Jago. "Narration and Unease in Ian McEwan's Later Fiction." *Critique* 42.3 (spring 2001): 253-68. Reprinted in *Short Story Criticism.* Ed. Jelena Krstovic. Vol. 57. Detroit: Gale, 2003. 212-20.

Brossard, Nicole. "Poetic Politics." *The Politics of Poetic Form: Poetry and Public Policy.* Ed. Charles Bernstein. New York: Roof Books, 1990. 73-82. Reprinted in *Short Story Criticism.* Ed. Jelena Krstovic. Vol. 57. Detroit: Gale, 2003. 3-8.

Suggestions are Welcome

Readers who wish to suggest new features, topics, or authors to appear in future volumes, or who have other suggestions or comments are cordially invited to call, write, or fax the Associate Product Manager:

Associate Product Manager, Literary Criticism Series
Thomson Gale
27500 Drake Road
Farmington Hills, MI 48331-3535
1-800-347-4253 (GALE)
Fax: 248-699-8054

Acknowledgments

The editors wish to thank the copyright holders of the excerpted criticism included in this volume and the permissions managers of many book and magazine publishing companies for assisting us in securing reproduction rights. Following is a list of the copyright holders who have granted us permission to reproduce material in this volume of *SSC*. Every effort has been made to trace copyright, but if omissions have been made, please let us know.

COPYRIGHTED MATERIAL IN *SSC*, VOLUME 91, WAS REPRODUCED FROM THE FOLLOWING PERIODICALS:

America, v. 136, March 26, 1977; v. 191, October 4, 2004. Copyright 1977, 2004 www.americamagazine.org. All rights reserved. Both reproduced by permission of America Press. For subscription information, visit www.americamagazine.com.—***American Literature,*** v. 35, May, 1963; v. 48, January, 1977; v. 52, May, 1980. Copyright, 1963, 1977, 1980 Duke University Press. All rights reserved. Used by permission of the publisher.—***The Antioch Review,*** v. 63, spring, 2005. Copyright © 2005 by the Antioch Review Inc. Reproduced by permission of the Editors.—***Book World-The Washington Post,*** v. 28, February 8, 1998 for "By Literature Possessed" by Tamsin Todd; v. 29, May 22, 1999 for "Running Hot and Cold" by Dennis Drabelle. Copyright © 1998, 1999, Washington Post. Both reproduced by permission of the authors.—***Canadian Literature,*** v. 84, spring, 1980 for "The Revolt against Instinct: The Animal Stories of Seton and Roberts" by Robert H. MacDonald. Reproduced by permission of the author. —***Critique,*** v. 40, summer, 1999; v. 45, winter, 2004. Copyright © 1999, 2004 by Helen Dwight Reid Educational Foundation. Both reproduced with permission of the Helen Dwight Reid Educational Foundation, published by Heldref Publications, 1319 18th Street, NW, Washington, DC 20036-1802.—***The Commonweal,*** v. 70, June 5, 1959. Reproduced by permission.—***The Dalhousie Review,*** v. 73, winter, 1993-94 for review of "*The Vagrants of the Barren and Other Stories*, by Charles G. D. Roberts" by J. E. Baker. Reproduced by permission of the publisher and the author. —***The Explicator,*** v. 48, fall, 1989. Copyright © 1989 by Helen Dwight Reid Educational Foundation. Reproduced with permission of the Helen Dwight Reid Educational Foundation, published by Heldref Publications, 1319 18th Street, NW, Washington, DC 20036-1802.—***Hecate,*** v. 29, 2003. Reproduced by permission.—***The Independent,*** October 17, 1998. Copyright © 1998 Independent Newspapers (UK) Ltd. Reproduced by permission.—***Journal of Canadian Studies,*** v. 22, spring, 1987. Reproduced by permission.—***The Journal of Commonwealth Literature,*** v. 29, 2004. Copyright 2004 by Sage Publications, www.sagepub.co.uk. Reproduced by permission of Sage Publications, Thousand Oaks, London and New Delhi.—***London Review of Books,*** v. 9, June 15, 1987; v. 14, November 19, 1992. Both appear here by permission of the London Review of Books.—***Modern Fiction Studies,*** v. 35, summer, 1989. Copyright © 1989 The Johns Hopkins University Press. Reproduced by permission.—***The Modern Language Review,*** v. 99, January, 2004. Copyright © Modern Humanities Research Association 2004. Reproduced by permission of the publisher.—***The Nation,*** v. 278, June 14, 2004. Copyright © 2004 by The Nation Magazine/The Nation Company, Inc. Reproduced by permission.—***The New Republic,*** v. 209, August 2, 1993. Copyright © 1993 by The New Republic, Inc. Reproduced by permission of The New Republic.—***New Statesman & Society,*** v. 5, November 6, 1992. Copyright © 1992 New Statesman, Ltd. Reproduced by permission.—***New Statesman***, v. 85, April 14, 1973; v. 92, July 2, 1976. Copyright © 1973, 1976 New Statesman, Ltd. Both reproduced by permission.—***New York Review of Books,*** v. 46, June 10, 1999. Copyright © 1999 by NYREV, Inc. Reproduced with permission from The New York Review of Books.—***The Observer,*** March 16, 1973; January 22, 1998. Copyright Guardian Newspapers Limited 1973, 1998. Both reproduced by permission of Guardian News Service, LTD.—***Saturday Review,*** v. 42, June 13, 1959; v. 47, March 7, 1964; v. 51, December 14, 1968. All reproduced by permission. —***The Scotsman,*** September 26, 1998 for "Rays of Hope in the Heat and Dust" by Angus Wolfe Murray. Reproduced by permission of the author.—***The Spectator,*** May 19, 1973; April 11, 1987; v. 281, November 14, 1998; v. 293, November 29, 2003. Copyright © 1973, 1987, 1998, 2003 by The Spectator. All reproduced by permission of The Spectator.—***Studies in American Fiction.*** 2001. Copyright © 2001 by Studies in Short Fiction. Reproduced by permission.—***Studies in American Fiction,*** v. 30, autumn, 2002. Copyright © 2002 Northeastern University. Reproduced by permission.—***Studies in Canadian Literature,*** v. 5, spring, 1980. Copyright by A. C. Morrell Reproduced by permission of the editors.—***Studies in Short Fiction,*** v. 12, fall, 1975; v. 18, winter, 1981; v. 21, winter, 1984; v. 24, winter, 1987; v. 25, summer, 1988; v. 25, winter, 1988; v. 27, spring, 1990; v. 27, summer, 1990; v. 28, spring, 1991; v. 33, 1996; v. 36, fall, 1999 Copyright © 1975, 1981, 1984, 1987, 1988, 1990, 1991, 1996, 1999 by Studies in Short Fiction. All reproduced by permission.—***Tennessee Studies in Literature,*** v. XIII, 1968. Copyright © 1968 by The University of Tennessee Press. Reproduced by permission of The University of Tennessee Press.—***The Women's Review of Books,*** v. xxi, July, 2004 for "The Failure to Communicate" by Jewelle Gomez. Reproduced by permission of the author.—***Times Literary Supplement,*** April 16, 1973; June 25, 1976; April 10, 1987; April 10, 1998; October 2, 1998; October 31, 2003. Copyright © 1973, 1976, 1987, 1998, 2003 by The Times Supplements Limited. All reproduced from The Times Literary Supplement by permission.—***Twentieth-Century Literature,*** v. 23, February, 1977; v. 45, winter, 1999. Copyright 1977, 1999, Hofstra University Press. Reproduced by permission.—***Women's Studies,*** v. 33, 2004. Copyright © Taylor & Francis Inc. Reproduced by permission of Taylor & Francis Group, LLC., http://www.taylorandfrancis.com.—***World Literature Today,*** v. 74, winter, 2000. Copyright © 2000 by World Literature Today. Reproduced by permission of the publisher.

COPYRIGHTED MATERIAL IN *SSC,* VOLUME 91, WAS REPRODUCED FROM THE FOLLOWING BOOKS:

Bentley, D. M. R. From "'The Thing Is Found to Be Symbolic': *Symboliste* Elements in the Early Short Stories of Gilbert Parker, Charles G. D. Roberts, and Duncan Campbell Scott," in ***Dominant Impressions: Essays on the Canadian Short Story.*** Edited by Gerald Lynch and Angela Arnold Robbeson. University of Ottawa Press, 1999. © University of Ottawa Press, 1999. All rights reserved. Reproduced by permission of the University of Ottawa Press.— Campbell, Jane. From ***A. S. Byatt and the Heliotropic Imagination.*** Wilfrid Laurier University Press, 2004. © 2004 Wilifid Laurier University Press. Reproduced by permission.—Crane, Ralph J. From ***Ruth Prawer Jhabvala,*** 1992. Copyright © 1992 by Twayne Publishers. All rights reserved. Reproduced by permission of Thomson Gale.—Gooneratne, Yasmine. From ***Silence, Exile and Cunning: The Fiction of Ruth Prawer Jhabvala.*** Orient Longman, 1983. © 1983 Orient Longman Limited. Reproduced by permission.—Jacobson, Dan. From an Afterword in ***Inklings: Selected Stories by Dan Jacobson.*** Weidenfeld and Nicolson, 1973. Copyright © 1973 Dan Jacobson. All rights reserved. Reproduced by permission of the author.—Kelly, Kathleen Coyne. From ***A. S. Byatt.*** Twayne Publishers, 1996. Copyright © 1996 by Twayne Publishers. All rights reserved. Reproduced by permission of Thomson Gale.—Love, Glen A. From an Introduction to ***Winesburg, Ohio.*** Edited by Glen A. Love. Oxford University Press, 1997. Copyright © 1997 by Oxford University Press. Used by permission of Oxford University Press, Inc.—Rideout, Walter B. From "Talbot Whittingham and Anderson: A Passage to Winesburg, Ohio," in ***Sherwood Anderson: Dimensions of His Literary Art.*** Edited by David D. Anderson. Michigan State University Press, 1976. Copyright © 1976 Michigan State University Press. Reproduced by permission.—Roberts, Sheila. From ***Dan Jacobson.*** Twayne Publishers, 1984.Copyright © 1984 by G. K. Hall & Company. All rights reserved. Reproduced by permission of Thomson Gale.—Stouck, David. From "Anderson's Expressionist Art," in ***New Essays on* Winesburg, Ohio.** Edited by John W. Crowley. Cambridge University Press, 1990. Copyright © 1990 Cambridge University Press. Reprinted with the permission of Cambridge University Press.—Sucher, Laurie. From ***The Fiction of Ruth Prawer Jhabvala: The Politics of Passion.*** St. Martin's Press, 1989. © Laurie Sucher 1989. All rights reserved. Reproduced with permission of Palgrave Macmillan.—Ware, Martin. From an introduction in ***The Vagrants of the Barren and Other Stories of Charles G. D. Roberts.*** Edited by Martin Ware. The Tecumseh Press, 1992. Copyright © by The Tecumseh Press Ltd., 1992. All rights reserved. Reproduced by permission.

PHOTOGRAPHS APPEARING IN *SSC,* VOLUME 91, WERE RECEIVED FROM THE FOLLOWING SOURCES:

Byatt, A. S., photograph. © Jerry Bauer. Reproduced by permission.—Jacobson, Dan, photograph by Mark Gerson. Reproduced by permission of Mark Gerson.—Jhabvala, Ruth Prawer, photograph. The Kobal Collection. Reproduced by permission.

Thomson Gale Literature Product Advisory Board

The members of the Thomson Gale Literature Product Advisory Board—reference librarians from public and academic library systems—represent a cross-section of our customer base and offer a variety of informed perspectives on both the presentation and content of our literature products. Advisory board members assess and define such quality issues as the relevance, currency, and usefulness of the author coverage, critical content, and literary topics included in our series; evaluate the layout, presentation, and general quality of our printed volumes; provide feedback on the criteria used for selecting authors and topics covered in our series; provide suggestions for potential enhancements to our series; identify any gaps in our coverage of authors or literary topics, recommending authors or topics for inclusion; analyze the appropriateness of our content and presentation for various user audiences, such as high school students, undergraduates, graduate students, librarians, and educators; and offer feedback on any proposed changes/enhancements to our series. We wish to thank the following advisors for their advice throughout the year.

Barbara M. Bibel
Librarian
Oakland Public Library
Oakland, California

Dr. Toby Burrows
Principal Librarian
The Scholars' Centre
University of Western Australia Library
Nedlands, Western Australia

Celia C. Daniel
Associate Reference Librarian
Howard University Libraries
Washington, D.C.

David M. Durant
Reference Librarian
Joyner Library
East Carolina University
Greenville, North Carolina

Nancy T. Guidry
Librarian
Bakersfield Community College
Bakersfield, California

Heather Martin
Arts & Humanities Librarian
University of Alabama at Birmingham, Sterne Library
Birmingham, Alabama

Susan Mikula
Librarian
Indiana Free Library
Indiana, Pennsylvania

Thomas Nixon
Humanities Reference Librarian
University of North Carolina at Chapel Hill, Davis Library
Chapel Hill, North Carolina

Mark Schumacher
Jackson Library
University of North Carolina at Greensboro
Greensboro, North Carolina

Gwen Scott-Miller
Assistant Director
Sno-Isle Regional Library System
Marysville, Washington

Winesburg, Ohio

Sherwood Anderson

The following entry presents an overview of the criticism on Anderson's collection of short stories *Winesburg, Ohio: A Group of Tales of Ohio Small Town Life* (1919). For a discussion of Anderson's complete short fiction career, see *SSC,* Volumes 1 and 46.

INTRODUCTION

Winesburg, Ohio is regarded as a classic American short story collection. A series of stories focused on the inhabitants of a small Ohio town, *Winesburg* chronicles their struggles to make emotional connections and express their feelings. Critics agree that it was in *Winesburg* that Anderson was most successful in conveying his ideas about loneliness, interpersonal communication, and artistic expression. Several of the individual stories appeared in periodicals before 1919, but Anderson soon realized that the pieces were unified by setting, theme, and character, creating a hybrid form that would later be viewed as an innovation in the development of the American short story form. The work has been recognized as a profound influence on the work of several leading twentieth-century American writers including Ernest Hemingway, William Faulkner, Thomas Wolfe, and John Steinbeck.

PLOT AND MAJOR CHARACTERS

The stories in *Winesburg* are unified by the common setting of Winesburg; the character of George Willard, a young reporter and the protagonist of the book; the themes of loneliness and frustrated self-expression; and the folksy, poignant tone of the stories. All of the action takes place in Winesburg, Ohio, a small rural community, at the end of the nineteenth century. In the first piece of the collection, "The Book of the Grotesque," an anonymous old writer has a bedtime vision of people who become obsessed with pursuing various "truths" to the point that they become "grotesque." These hallucinations prefigure the stories of the characters in *Winesburg*. In the next story, "Hands," Wing Biddlebaum, a frightened old man, attempts to act as mentor to young George Willard; when he becomes animated in conversation, his hands move wildly and expressively, which seems to upset him. George senses that Wing is ashamed of his hands and that they are somehow the reason for his isolation from the rest of the town. It is revealed that as a schoolteacher in another town years before, Wing's physical expressiveness was mistaken for sexual perversion and he was beaten and driven out of town. In "Paper Pills," an old physician, Dr. Reefy, writes his thoughts on bits of paper. Unable or unwilling to share his inner vision with others, he then crumples them up and throws them away. "Mother" explores the frustrated life of George's mother, Elizabeth Willard, and her inability to communicate her feelings and hopes for George's success. "Respectability" chronicles the downfall of Wash Williams, a skilled telegrapher who is the dirtiest and ugliest man in town. When his vile mother-in-law sabotages his troubled marriage, Wash comes to hate all women.

The longest story in the volume, "Godliness," recounts the tale of Jesse Bentley, a tough, demanding farmer who alienates his family with his unforgiving ways.

Misunderstanding figures prominently in "The Teacher." The town's schoolteacher, Kate Swift, a lonely, plain woman, awkwardly attempts to express her faith in and hopes for George, which are initially mistaken for a sexual overture. Kate also appears in "The Strength of God." The Reverend Curtis Hartman spies on the naked teacher as she relaxes, unaware, in her bedroom. Although overcome with guilt, he is unable to stop. One night, when he sees her praying in anguish, he becomes convinced that God has visited him in Kate's unclothed form. In "Drink," the quiet Tom Foster becomes intoxicated and confesses to George his sexual desire for Helen White, his dreams, and his private suffering. "Queer" is the story of Elmer Cowley, an eccentric and unsuccessful merchant in Winesburg. Viewed as an outsider, Elmer tries to express himself to George. When that fails, he leaves Winesburg in spectacular fashion, shouting his victory over the town from the top of a train car. In "Sophistication," George and Helen White walk together in town and have a special moment of mutual love and acceptance. Finally, in "Departure," the last story of *Winesburg,* George is ready to go forth to Chicago to start his new life. Critics consider George's departure as a symbol of a new age and a new century.

MAJOR THEMES

One of the first American authors to explore the unconscious in his fiction, Anderson in *Winesburg* expresses his self-professed desire to "see beneath the surface of lives"; his portrayal of the psychological motivations of ordinary people is an accomplishment that has often prompted comparisons to the work of Anton Chekhov and Fyodor Dostoevsky. Loneliness and alienation are major thematic concerns in the stories of *Winesburg*; critics contend that the work is informed by Anderson's theory that materialism, industrialization, and urbanization in the modern era led to a degeneration of communal bonds and a growing sense of isolation for individuals. As repressive small-town mores and gender roles hinder full artistic and human expression, people in Winesburg are also isolated by intolerance, insensitivity, circumstance, and personal weakness. Critics note that people's inability to communicate the full spectrum of their hopes, dreams, and fears sometimes causes violent and socially unacceptable behavior—usually aided by alcohol, desperation, or misunderstanding. Happiness is fleeting in *Winesburg* and most characters are doomed to unhappy marriages or profound loneliness punctuated by brief moments of love, empathy, and spiritual epiphany. Understanding is another dominant theme of the stories; as George encounters the diverse inhabitants of Winesburg and begins to understand the wide range of human experience, he becomes more aware of human failings but is more open to what the world holds. He eventually becomes mature enough to leave Winesburg and begin his new life in Chicago.

CRITICAL RECEPTION

Winesburg is one of the most critically discussed books within the American short story tradition. Upon its publication, it established Anderson's reputation as an important new voice in American literature. Early critics derided the book as depressing and obsessed with sex; other reviewers, however, praised it for its honesty and depth of psychological insight into the lives of ordinary people in a small, rural town. It has been interpreted from a variety of perspectives: as commentary on social and sexual mores in small town America; as an allegory of the sociopolitical changes that were occurring at the turn of the twentieth century; and as a naturalistic study of biological and social determinism. Feminist readings explore the role of women in the stories, particularly the ways in which gender roles and sexual mores work to stifle the full potential of the female characters. Similarities between Anderson's life and the characters and events in *Winesburg* have been a recurring topic of critical examination as well. For example, commentators view Winesburg as based on Anderson's hometown, Clyde, Ohio; trace parallels between Anderson and the book's protagonist, George Willard; consider the prominence of the father-son relationship in the book; and contend that the characters in *Winesburg* are based on people Anderson met in a Chicago apartment house. Commentators have also regarded the book as a coming-of-age tale; as George comes into contact with various inhabitants of Winesburg, he grows in understanding and compassion and therefore becomes initiated into adult life. Critics have discussed the influences on Anderson's stories, including the impressionistic styles of Gertrude Stein, Edgar Lee Masters's *Spoon River Anthology,* and James Joyce's *Dubliners.* The stories in *Winesburg* have been frequently anthologized and the collection is regarded as Anderson's most important literary achievement. It is also recognized as a masterpiece of twentieth-century American literature.

PRINCIPAL WORKS

Short Fiction

Winesburg, Ohio: A Group of Tales of Ohio Small Town Life 1919

The Triumph of the Egg: A Book of Impressions from American Life in Tales and Poems 1921

Horses and Men: Tales, Long and Short, from Our American Life 1923

Death in the Woods, and Other Stories 1933

The Sherwood Anderson Reader 1947

The Short Stories of Sherwood Anderson 1962
Certain Things Last: The Selected Short Stories of Sherwood Anderson 1992

Other Major Works

Windy McPherson's Son (novel) 1916
Marching Men (novel) 1917
Mid-American Chants (poetry) 1918
Poor White (novel) 1920
Many Marriages (novel) 1923
A Story Teller's Story: The Tale of an American Writer's Journey through His Own Imaginative World and through the World of Facts, with Many of His Experiences and Impressions among Other Writers (autobiography) 1924
Dark Laughter (novel) 1925
Tar: A Midwest Childhood (autobiography) 1926
A New Testament (poetry) 1927
Beyond Desire (novel) 1932
Kit Brandon (novel) 1936
Buck Fever Papers (journalism) 1971
Sherwood Anderson: Selected Letters (letters) 1984

CRITICISM

Epifanio San Juan Jr. (essay date May 1963)

SOURCE: San Juan, Epifanio, Jr. "Vision and Reality: A Reconsideration of Sherwood Anderson's *Winesburg, Ohio*." *American Literature* 35, no. 2 (May 1963): 137-55.

[*In the following essay, San Juan analyzes Anderson's narrative technique in* Winesburg, Ohio *and refutes Lionel Trilling's charge that the stories hold "very little of the stuff of actuality" (see Further Reading).*]

The profound impact of Sherwood Anderson's ***Winesburg, Ohio*** on the fictional art of America after its appearance in book form in 1919 has become part of literary history. Just why it then exerted, and perhaps still exerts, so much influence, and to what in particular one may attribute its power and significance, remain persistent questions over which critical arguments of every kind have accumulated. Beyond doubt the answers ultimately involve the matter of Anderson's craft: the form, technique, and style of his narrative art.

On this point Lionel Trilling persuasively contends that a marked discrepancy between life as Anderson conceives it and the language he uses to convey to us this conception vitiates the exemplary integrity of his fiction. Consequently, the moments of enlightenment and conversion, as Anderson celebrates them in ***Winesburg, Ohio,*** fail as acts of will to crystallize into acts of the intelligence. For Trilling, therefore, Anderson's stories, though dealing with many emotions, have "few sights, sounds, smells, very little of the stuff of actuality" that give moral value to the organic act of living.[1] Ultimately Anderson's predilection for insensate abstractions is said to betray a distasteful lack of real sensory, as well as social, experience in his work.

Is it verifiably true, one may legitimately inquire, that Anderson's fiction betrays an absence (to use Henry James's phrases) of the "quality of felt life" or "the solidity of specification" that is necessary for any piece of fiction to be "interesting," that is, a significant impression of one of the myriad forms of reality? A more analytic approach seems to be called for if we are to appreciate more intensively the personal vision of life and experience that Anderson projected in his fiction.[2] A new consideration of ***Winesburg, Ohio*** seems to me at this point necessary, especially because of its intrinsic significance—by which is meant just those positively enduring qualities that Edmund Wilson spoke of with cogent percipience:

> We are soothed as well as disturbed by the feeling of hands thrust down among the inner organs of life—hands that are delicate and clean but still pitiless in their explorations. . . . Anderson functions with a natural ease and beauty on a plane in the depths of life—as if under a diving bell submerged in the human soul—which makes the world of the ordinary novelist seem stagy and superficial. . . . [Anderson] has shown an almost perfect instinct that fashions, from what seems a more intimate stratum of feeling and imagination than our novelists usually explore, visions at once fresh and naive and of a slightly discomfiting strangeness.[3]

In the introductory chapter of ***Winesburg, Ohio*** entitled **"The Book of the Grotesque,"** Anderson presents initially the theoretical motivations that underlie his basic theme: "That in the beginning when the world was young there were a great many thoughts but no such thing as a truth. Man made the truths himself and each truth was a composite of a great many vague thoughts. All about in the world were the truths and they were all beautiful."[4] According to Anderson, man makes his truths. But "the moment one of the people . . . took one of the truths to himself, called it his truth, and tried to live his life by it," he became a grotesque and the truth he embraced became a "falsehood." That is, anyone who identifies himself absolutely with fixed schematic ways of doing, feeling, and thinking, and tries to direct his life according to these "vague thoughts" will inevitably distort the inner self and its potentialities, since the inner self has the unexercised capacity to demonstrate a range of *virtù* greater than any experienced situation could afford, or demand of it. Consequently, his truths, falsifying his nature, should, if he does not stick to any one formulation of them, ideally lead to an intenser enlargement of life and not to a constricted compass of response and possibilities for the qualification of motives; he should ideally initiate a greater intensity of critical self-awareness, cognizant of the fact that to any one point of view there exist horizons and landscapes that are closed to it; hence, he has imperative need for constant inquiry, perpetual examination of principles, and endless pursuit of other modes, more organic and integrative, of self-expression.

The consensus of critical opinion about Anderson's protagonists so far has been generally negative, owing perhaps to the notion that there is in them a marked absence of any positive force or direction in the way they conduct their revolt against the milieu. Among others, Trilling bewails Anderson's success with the simple idea of "instinct-versus-reason" conflict as applied to characterization. In allowing this idea to remain simple and fixed, Anderson (Trilling points out) is logically led to adopt a one-sided outlook manifest in the compulsive, repetitive quality of his characters' behavior.[5] And yet, despite this anomalous confusion of the author and his characters in a single point of view, could we, for instance, call Doctor Parcival (in **"The Philosopher"**) a flat, unrealized character?

The truth is, I submit, that Doctor Parcival incarnates the intensest energy and amplitude of imagination which Anderson prized above all other qualities that we find solidified in the static normative values of any given society, revealed here in the choric comments of such typical Winesburg conformists as Tom Willard and Will Henderson. No doubt Doctor Parcival's tales defy category and summary: "they begin nowhere and end nowhere." Apart from this inherently ironical temper, his varied suppositions of his past life testify to the triumph of possibility and free initiative against the doctrine-bound moralizing and deterministic orientation of the average Winesburg citizen:

> "I was a reporter like you here," Doctor Parcival began. "It was in a town in Iowa—or was it in Illinois? I don't remember and anyway it makes no difference. Perhaps I am trying to conceal my identity and don't want to be very definite. . . . I may have stolen a great sum of money or been involved in a murder before I came here. There is food for though in that, eh?"[6]

The exploratory tenor of the Doctor's recollections, his susceptibility to enlarge on facts until they assume fabulous proportions, leads, in effect, to his transcending the limitations of the social environment, and its stultifying, because static, assumptions. When he refuses to examine the dead child, terror overwhelms him; nevertheless his imagination anticipates all possible futures, even the worst, dwelling tentatively and experimentally, so to speak, on concrete details as rope and lamp-post in this passage:

> "What I have done will arouse the people of this town," he declared excitedly. "Do I not know human nature? Do I not know what will happen? Word of my refusal will be whispered about. Presently men will get together in groups and talk of it. They will come here. We will quarrel and there will be talk of hanging. Then they will come again bearing a rope in their hands. . . . It may be that what I am talking about will not occur this morning. It may be put off until tonight but I will be hanged. Everyone will get excited. I will be hanged to a lamp-post on Main Street."[7]

On this wealth of suppositions, this inexhaustible fund of hypothetical plotting and spontaneous prophecies of the future, Doctor Parcival transcends any dogmatic judgment that Winesburg may for the moment decree and impose. Spiritually he transcends the realm of facts and contingencies of human finitude by positing as many alternatives of personal fate as he could, finally subsuming all of them under a ruling insight: "everyone in the world is Christ and they are all crucified." With Christ goes the possibility for resurrection, renewal, and affirmation. And by force of his emotional convictions, this idea ceases to be a cold abstraction and becomes in him a living dynamic truth.

Equalling Doctor Parcival's imaginative resources, we have the poetic sensitivity of Tom Foster (in **"Drink"**), the grotesque, on whom the spicy odor of coffee could induce thoughts of "things and places far away." Lying on the grass a little drunk, he is overcome by the abundance of sensory impressions impinging on his consciousness:

> of mornings in Winesburg and of how the stones in the graveled driveway by Banker White's house were wet with dew and glistened in the morning light . . . of the nights in the barn when it rained and he lay awake hearing the drumming of the raindrops and smelling the warm smell of horses and of hay.[8]

It seems sufficient then for Tom Foster to simply "stand in the shadow of the wall of life," never daring to assert himself, doing nothing but receiving impressions of unending novelty, however horrible or terrifying. Thus, once tempted by a woman, he "never forgot the smell of the room" where the temptation took place, nor the greedy look of the woman's eyes that sickened him and "left a scar on his soul." "Scar" here exemplifies how Anderson tends to portray the depth of his characters' experiences in terms of physical wounds or of physiological reactions.[9] Having the unique ability "to be part of and yet distinctly apart from the life about him," Tom exhibits the temperament of a poet, his concern being solely with the process of his thought, its aesthetic qualities: "He let himself think of Helen White and only concerned himself with the manner of his thoughts." Subsequently he begins to visualize his thoughts and feelings: he is "a little tree without leaves standing out sharply against the sky"; Helen White is "a flame dancing in the air," then "a strong terrible wind coming out of the darkness of a stormy sea"; then he is "a boat left on the shore of the sea by a fisherman." Tree, flame, wind, boat—these details and figures so beautifully suggestive of isolation provide a fit medium of self-expression which makes the flux of Tom Foster's experience a rich raw material for the creative understanding of his life. At such moments he is most alive to the world which gives shape and body to his dreams.

According to H. E. Bates, Anderson's fiction endeavors to present "a picture rather than . . . an ephemeral play"; that is, "to present significant form than to dazzle the eye with colour."[10] What predominates in ***Winesburg, Ohio*** is precisely the complex of pictorial representation that stems from the writer's concentrated attention and exploitation of the sensuous potentialities of his material. For Anderson, form is essentially an organic element which follows the contours of an image, of a symbolic cluster of sensory impressions aimed toward delivering an objective immediate presentation of a character's inner struggles, the specific quality of inwardness that constitutes the "roundness" of his personality. Writing in the *Notebook,* Anderson implicitly defines form as rhythm: "The rhythm you are seeking in any of the arts lies just below the surface of things in nature. To get below the surface, to get the lower rhythms into your hands, your body, your mind, is what you seek."[11] Thus, Kate Swift's impulsive eagerness (in **"The Teacher"**) to "open the door of life" to George Willard takes possession of her to such a degree that "it became something physical." Anderson frequently tends to embody abstractions in some organic or physical act, thereby capturing just the exact rhythm and movement of body and speech on which drama in fiction depends.

The rhythmic movement of Anderson's sentences and the variations of sense in the repetitions of phrases in syntactically varying contexts may be illustrated in George Willard's endeavor to define his ultimate decision in **"Sophistication."** Here the process of groping toward a climactic resolution is imitated and dramatized in the tempo and cadence of each unit of his soliloquy:[12]

> "I'll go to Helen White's house, that's what I'll do. I'll walk right in. I'll say that I want to see her. I'll walk right in and sit down, that's what I'll do," he declared, climbing over a fence and beginning to run.[13]

Walking along Main Street, George listens to the fiddlers tuning their instruments: "The broken sounds floated down through an open window and out across the murmur of voices and the loud blare of the horns of the band . . . the sense of crowding, moving life closed in about him."[14] Four pages later, after George has discovered the meaninglessness of life, "the fiddlers, their instruments tuned, sweated and worked to keep the feet of youth flying over a dance floor." Through qualified repetitions, the development and changes in the character's attitudes are thus immediately conveyed. Similarly, Gertrude Stein's prose functions on the premise, implicit in Anderson's aesthetic, that "repetition is an essential strategy in composition; it guarantees similarity and forces the consciousness upon the nature of the thing seen while at the same time it provides the avenue along which movement and change may occur."[15]

The effective repetition of figurative patterns functions also as a method for attaining unity in the story. As a particular instance, the focus on Dr. Reefy's hands (in **"Paper Pills"**) becomes the integrating center of his poignantly pathetic crisis in life. His hands, resembling "unpainted wooden balls," have the habit of putting down his thoughts in scraps of paper which then become "little round hard balls" in his pockets. The story of his courtship is then compared to "twisted little apples" which in turn evoke the image of his gnarled knuckles, and therefore the hands that write down his thoughts. What is the implication of this circularity or continuity of images? Dr. Reefy refuses, in effect, to be a sentimentalist, for thoughts—do they not compose the truths Anderson spoke of in **"The Book of the Grotesque"**?—become to him literally transformed into useless paper pills.

It may be said that life in ***Winesburg, Ohio*** often tends to move in a circular pattern either by force of habit and custom or by force of sympathetic obedience to the cycle of the seasons, to the life of the instincts and impulses in man. When George Willard (in **"Sophistication"**) takes the "backward view of life,"

> a door is torn open and for the first time he looks out upon the world, seeing, as though they marched in procession before him, the countless figures of men who before his time have come out of nothingness into the world, lived their lives, and disappeared again into nothingness.[16]

This mood of bitter nihilism and despair extends to the interpretation of the people's gaiety during Fair time: "In the street the people surged up and down like cattle confined in a pen." After retrospective meditations comes the introspective search for the existential dimension of life, arriving finally at an insight as potently illuminating in application as the spectacle of the tragic human condition offered us by Pascal, Kierkegaard, or Kafka. George then formulates with impressionistic clarity his need for understanding, invoking nature to furnish metaphoric equivalents for life:

> With a little gasp he sees himself as merely a leaf blown by the wind through the streets of his village. He knows

> that in spite of all the stout talk of his fellows he must live and die in uncertainty, a thing blown by the winds, a thing destined like corn to wilt in the sun. He shivers and looks eagerly about.[17]

The strain of "cornfed mysticism" often alluded to by Anderson's critics[18] has its roots here in the cycle of the season to which George, on the April morning of his departure, responds in a ritual of walking again on Trunion Pike to complete the circle of his maturity in Winesburg, showing his appreciation of the vibrant chiaroscuro of light and shade, the trilling resonance of melody in nature which, preserved in memory, would serve as the nourishment for his "growing passion for dreams":

> He had been in the midst of the great open place on winter nights when it was covered with snow and only the moon looked down at him; he had been there in the fall when bleak winds blew and on summer evenings when the air vibrated with the song of insects.[19]

Throughout the stories we encounter the constant recurrence of phrases and sentences, constant repetitions intended to contribute to the organic unity of the narrative rendition. Consider these examples: "Things went to smash" (in **"Loneliness"**), "You dear! You dear! You lovely dear!" (in **"Death"**), or Elmer Cowley's habitual refrain: "I'll be starched. . . . I'll be washed and ironed and starched!" (in **"Queer"**)—all these indicate the particular obsessions of the characters who frequently repeat them when subject to great emotional pressures that prove resistant to personal solutions: thus, they are in their contexts epiphanic. Consequently, the first repetition asserts Enoch Robinson's resigned acceptance of defeat, the second articulates Mrs. Willard's grasping after some impossible fulfilment of her most cherished hopes; the third suggests the impulse to search for order, the urgent need in Elmer Cowley to devise some means of escaping the deadening effect of petty business routine.

Besides such specific functions of delivering the exact fluctuation of emotion and thought through rhythmical repetition, Anderson's technique of recurring tonalities also serves to dramatize indirectly the behavior of his characters through the skilful variations of sentence-length or duration. Note how, in the following passage, the first words may be taken as stage directions. Obviously most of the sentences begin with the "I," emphasizing the speaker/first person as actor, followed by significant alterations carefully signalized by new beginnings: "One night . . . ," "When she . . . ," "A look . . . ," "Maybe she . . . ," "That's how. . . ." One may also observe how the sense of the passage evolves climactically until a dialectical turnabout is reached when the speaker declares that he, paradoxically enough, wants and does not want to be understood:[20]

> The old man sprang to his feet and his voice shook with excitement. "One night something happened. I became mad to make her understand me and to know what a big thing I was in that room. I wanted her to see how important I was. I told her over and over. When she tried to go away, I ran and locked the door. I followed her about. I talked and talked and then all of a sudden things went to smash. A look came into her eyes and I knew she did not understand. Maybe she had understood all the time. I was furious. I couldn't stand it. I wanted her to understand but, don't you see, I couldn't let her understand. I felt that then she would know everything, that I would be submerged, drowned out, you see. That's how it is. I don't know why.[21]

Anderson's craftsmanship shows itself once more in the careful laying out of his scenes so as to communicate the maximum amount of emotional charge to the dramatic confrontation of characters. Moreover, he shows an astonishing deftness at establishing an orderly progression of events in which a concretely drawn perspective is visually and aurally animated, rendering setting, mood, atmosphere, and tone through particular details that forcefully appeal to the senses. The movement of this passage (examples may be easily multiplied) has a thematic purposiveness which contributes toward introducing the principal dramatic interest of **"Tandy,"** in particular the somber mystery of the stranger's words, his identity, as he is situated in what seems to be a timeless stage:

> It was late evening and darkness lay over the town and over the railroad that ran along the foot of a little incline before the hotel. Somewhere in the distance, off to the west, there was a prolonged blast from the whistle of a passenger engine. A dog that had been sleeping in the roadway arose and barked. The stranger began to babble and made a prophecy concerning the child that lay in the arms of the agnostic.[22]

In the story **"Sophistication,"** Anderson successfully renders a skilful modulation of mood from the serious didactic reflections like this: "One shudders at the thought of the meaninglessness of life while at the same instant, and if the people of the town are his people, one loves life so intensely that tears come into the eyes,"[23] to the suspense-filled confrontation of the "two oddly sensitive" souls when George Willard announces: "I have come to this lonely place and here is this other," and then finally to the spontaneous lighthearted frolic of two persons, lovers in fact, whose egos have finally dissolved into the affections of their natural selves—a token of maturity: "They stopped kissing and stood a little apart. . . . They were both embarrassed and to relieve their embarrassment dropped into the animalism of youth. They laughed and began to pull and haul at each other."[24]

In "A Note on Realism," Anderson enunciated part of the aesthetic implications of his prose style, his peculiar manipulation of language, his personal beliefs as to the selection of facts and details in fiction: "The life of reality is confused, disorderly, almost always without apparent purpose, whereas in the artist's imaginative life there is purpose. There is determination to give the tale, the song, the painting Form."[25] In a letter to a friend, he confessed his aspiration "to try to develop, to the top of my bent, my own capacity to feel, see, taste, smell, hear. I wanted, as all men must want, to be a free man, proud of my own manhood, always more and more aware of earth, people, streets, houses, towns, cities. I wanted to take all into myself, digest what I could."[26] Trilling's accusation that Anderson's fiction lacks "the stuff of actuality" seems to me a gross mistake not only in the light of Anderson's lifelong preoccupation with sensory experience, its qualities and values, but also in the face of the testimony of ***Winesburg, Ohio*** and its "prose of reality." Of Anderson's artistic end we may say that, like Hemingway, he has always sought the real thing, the sequence of motion and fact which make the real emotion so that, as a result, the act being described is "no sooner done than said," becoming "simultaneous with the word, no sooner said than felt."[27] But let us consider the evidence itself, "the solidity of specification" in ***Winesburg, Ohio.***

Anderson's power of visualization contributes in a large measure to the full realization of his characters' personalities. We see this in Tom Foster's grandmother (in **"Drink"**) with her hands twisted out of shape so that "when she took hold of a mop or a broom handle the hands looked like the dried stems of an old creeping vine clinging to a tree." Belle Carpenter's sensuality (in **"An Awakening"**) and her callous nature are epitomized in a few bold strokes: dark skin, gray eyes, and thick lips. Joe Welling's face (in **"A Man of Ideas"**) inscribes itself in memory for one striking particularity: "The edges of his teeth that were tipped with gold glistened in the light"—an impression which convincingly sums up his unfeeling nature, and his devotion to the pursuit of material wealth. Tom Willard's hands (in **"The Philosopher"**) appear as though "dipped in blood that had dried and faded," a statement which may be construed to connote the sufferings and pain he has inflicted upon George and Mrs. Willard and of which he is so pathetically unaware.

Thus, in order to render and organize the inarticulate sensibilities of his characters, Anderson exploits natural scenery as an objective fact whose emotive charge or connotativeness may act as an index or correlative key to the affective or psychic situation of the characters. In **"Drink,"** for example, the stage for Tom Foster's exuberant flights of imagination are set by the spring season evoked through a graphic delineation of setting: "The trees . . . were all newly clothed in soft green leaves . . . and in the air there was a hush, a waiting kind of silence very stirring to the blood." Scenery also functions as a reconciling force among conflicting interests, thereby destroying the isolation of selves and liberating the hidden undiscovered self. In **"The Untold Lie,"** Ray Pearson and Hal Winters become all alive to each other upon perceiving the beauty of the country in the failing autumnal light. In a sad distracted mood, Ray Pearson feels the spirit of revolt rising within him against all crippling commitments that make life ugly. The open spacious field stimulates in him a desire to "shout or scream," to do something "unexpected and terrifying," resisting the claims of the identity that Winesburg society has forced upon him on account of his past, his habitual failings, utterly ignoring the qualitative worth of his infinite cravings, his endless dreams.

We see, then, that objective details and situations, particularly those with a density of texture and a load of emotional suggestiveness, usually appear in strategic places as a focus for all those qualities which the characters are supposed to represent or demonstrate in word and action. Generally, they may be construed as preparations for any idiosyncratic display of feeling or as tactfully placed amplifications of a given mood or tone; in effect, their presence serves as a contributing element toward accomplishing a total unity of effect. Let us examine some representative examples.[28]

Observe how the sense of waste and moral inertia in the lives of Elmer Cowley and his father is immediately suggested to us by an apparently insignificant detail: "beside the mass of the coal stood three combs of honey grown brown and dirty in their wooden frames" (in **"Queer"**). Loneliness and isolation prevail once more when George Willard and Helen White (in **"Sophistication"**) sit on a half-decayed, unpainted old grandstand whose "boards are all warped out of shape." George senses that "on all sides are ghosts, not of the dead but of living people." Spiritual emptiness in the lives of Henry Carpenter and her daughter (in **"An Awakening"**) is evoked by the bleak landscape and the dilapidated condition of their house, "a gloomy old house far out at the end of Buckeye Street,"[29] surrounded by pine trees with no grass beneath them. A vivid auditory image is given to integrate the barren, sordid features of the environment and, indirectly, of their lives—possibly the formula to evoke just the right psychological response: "A rusty thin eavestrough had slipped from its fastenings at the back of the house and when the wind blew it beat against the roof of a small shed, making a dismal drumming noise that sometimes persisted all through the night."[30] That "dismal drumming"—an unforgettable touch—foreshadows Belle Carpenter's gesture of smearing her father's pressing-board as a sign of her hatred, for their relation indeed has, as it were, fallen into ruins. The experience of defeat embodies itself most forcefully in the faded wallpaper and ragged carpets of Tom Willard's shabby hotel, inside of which one may observe the ghostly figure of his wife "doing the work of a chambermaid among beds soiled by the slumbers of fat travelling men." There is actually nothing aerial or phantom-like about Mrs. Willard; for her association with soiled beds, and her gaunt face marked with smallpox scars stamp her figure so indelibly in our minds. And yet, being in her youth "stage-struck," she could assume still another role, even though melodramatic and theatrical, to cure the paralysis of her will. Thus, no ghostly worn-out figure "should come striding down the stairway before the startled loungers in the hotel office. The figure would be silent—it would be swift and terrible. As a tigress whose cub had been threatened would she appear, coming out of the shadows, stealing noiselessly along and holding the long wicked scissors in her hand."[31] Such comparison of her deeper self with a tigress signifies an imaginative transcendence on her part from her sordid plight, as suggested earlier by the fugitive cat pursued by the wrath of the baker, and with which she identifies herself: "In the alley the grey cat crouched behind barrels filled with torn paper and broken bottles above which flew a black swarm of flies."[32] Such an image, which provokes her tears, seems like "a rehearsal of her own life, terrible in its vividness."[33]

To illustrate further how Anderson manipulates imagery to suggest the development of a character's sensibility, consider how the scene of the meeting between Enoch Robinson and George Willard in **"Loneliness"** is described. Enoch, whose every act is punctuated with the refrain "Nothing ever turns out for Enoch" exhibits a "child-mind" inclined to inventing "shadow-people"; thus, having lost control of reality, he could now play only with the "essences" of his fancy. Against this dream-world Anderson opposes the stark chaos of the actual world which provides the ironic counterpoint to Enoch's fancies and his pleas for understanding: "All you have to do is to believe what I say, just listen and believe, that's all there is to it"—or is it? To be sure, this hunger for belief leads to disillusionment if the resistance of facts to ideals is not recognized and properly managed for one's designs:

> It rained on the evening when the two met and talked, a drizzly wet October rain. The fruition of the year had come and the night should have been fine with a moon in the sky and the crisp sharp promise of frost in the air, but it wasn't that way. It rained and little puddles of water shone under the street lamps on Main Street. In the woods in the darkness beyond the Fair Ground water dripped from the black trees. Beneath the trees wet leaves were pasted against tree roots that protruded from the ground. In gardens back of houses in Winesburg dry shriveled potato vines lay sprawling on the ground. Men who had finished the evening meal and who had planned to go uptown to talk the evening away with other men at the back of some store changed their minds.[34]

Whereas the rain gladdens George, who, though saddened by thinking about his lot, does not weep, since it is unmanly to weep, Enoch, on the other hand, feels the danger of being "submerged, drowned" in the event that George succeeds in understanding his motives.

At this point, the importance of irony emerges more clearly as a technique for integrating fact and fancy, for balancing reality and dream, an irony which lies precisely at the center of Anderson's narrative art. We have already seen (in the above passage) how ironic counterpointing may throw into sharp relief the particular predicament of a person whose inner self can appropriate no medium by which it may subdue the facts of the external world. In ***Winesburg, Ohio,*** irony as a device assumes in general 1) the form of an objective situation running counter to the subjective interpretation of it by the character concerned, and 2) the form of utterances whose implications run counter to the surface meaning and tone of the words themselves. Let us illustrate the first.

Like almost all the protagonists in the book, Seth Richmond (in **"The Thinker"**) wants love and freedom, but his passion evaporates in endless efforts at rationalization. This dilemma Anderson skillfully objectifies in the contrast between Seth's mental vacillations and the spontaneous productive activity of the bees amid the sensuous, extravagant forms and colors of nature. With the bees everywhere about him, "he stood in a mass of weeds that grew waist-high in the field that ran away from the hillside. The weeds were abloom with tiny purple blossoms and gave forth an overpowering fragrance. Upon the weeds the bees were gathered in armies, singing as they worked. Seth imagined himself lying on a summer evening, buried deep among the weeds beneath the tree."[35]

Without the aid of a strong will, Seth could never affirm through sustained action any serious purpose in life. The scene suggests just those positive qualities that, conveyed through the description of an external landscape, prove antithetical to the internal state of the character concerned. An ironical effect is produced when, earlier, Seth the indecisive "thinker" finally resolves to see Helen:

> Seth raised the knocker and let it fall. Its heavy clatter sounded like a report from distant guns. "How awkward and foolish I am," he thought. "If Mrs. White comes to the door, I won't know what to say."[36]

Obviously the determined or decisive quality of the guns' report (the bees were referred to as "armies" above) directly mocks the wavering or hesitant gestures that he displays here in the rhythmical movement and tone of his language.

In **"Respectability,"** Wash Williams has a deeply sensitive and poetic nature despite the ugliness of his features. In the house of his wife's mother (his wife has been guilty of adultery before he visits her), he observes that everything looks "stylish" and respectable. But respectability, symbolized by "plush chairs and couch," pales into insignificance beside the fierce, trembling hatred of Wash, his raw and tender feelings: "I ached to forgive and forget." But the mother outrageously treats him as though he were a seducer. The distinctly human aspect of Wash William's personality is finally rendered in the humor and gentle irony of the ending: "I didn't get the mother killed. . . . I struck her once with a chair and then the neighbors came in and took it away. She screamed so loud, you see, I won't ever have a chance to kill her now. She died of a fever a month after that happened."[37]

Now let us illustrate the second type of irony. In **"A Man of Ideas,"** Joe Welling, despite his occupation as Standard Oil agent with a life of simple mechanical routine, is described as "a tiny little volcano that lies silent for days and then suddenly spouts fire." In the thick of baseball fights, he would be making "fierce animal cries," acting as though possessed by a malignant spirit. Posing to himself the question "What is Decay?" he ruthlessly begins pursuing facts to their absurd limits, arriving at the conclusion that "The World is On Fire!" Clearly, Joe Welling's routine existence becomes the object of critical parody conducted by his own creative self—his animal cries, his clever syllogisms and systematic deductions working toward the fantastic distortion of practical reality from which his public mask virtually derives substance. Whereas Joe Welling is a victim of candid naïveté and lack of critical self-awareness, Dr. Parcival exhibits the utmost degree of critical awareness possible, using comic understatement in order to immunize himself from any propensity for mawkish sentimentality. At the outset, he explains his eccentricity by attributing to his character "many strange turns." Visiting his father's corpse in the asylum, he is delighted in being treated like a king; then he pronounces over his father's body this slightly cynical prayer: "Let peace brood over this carcass." His comic spirit, detached and ironical, finally assumes a grim, intensely self-wounding edge when he speaks of his brother's attitude of superiority which is climaxed by the ridiculous manner of his death. One feels here how Dr. Parcival, to prevent any future caricature of his attitudes, adopts in anticipation an utterly conscious self-critical stance:

> "I want to fill you with hatred and contempt so that you will be a superior being," he declared. "Look at my brother. . . . He despised everyone, you see. You have no idea with what contempt he looked upon mother and me. And was he not our superior? You know he was. . . . I have given you a sense of it. He is dead. Once when he was drunk he lay down on the tracks and the car in which he lived with the other painters ran over him."[38]

(Contextually viewed, whenever Dr. Parcival lauds himself—as, for instance, "a man of distinction"—this is usually expressed with a muted tone of self-hatred, self-doubt.) This critical self-awareness is perhaps implied by the description of his "black irregular teeth" and his strange uncanny eyes: "The lid of the left eye twitched; it fell down and snapped up; it was exactly as though the lid of the eye were a window shade and someone stood inside the doctor's head playing with the cord."[39]

It seems to me thus far that the fundamental dilemma of George Willard, the central hero of the book, involves chiefly a search for order—primarily, an order between intention and act, thought and deed, dream and reality. We may discern this problem dramatized in the relationship of the three characters in **"An Awakening"** whose intentions are never fulfilled through appropriate modes of action. For instance, Belle Carpenter submits to George Willard's demands when, in fact, she loves Ed Handby. Ed Handby himself suffers from a particular deficiency epitomized by his having large fists yet a soft and quiet voice—that is, great physical strength coupled with impotency at verbal expression. Since society does not afford the means or the manners for the communication of passion, Ed Handby, like Elmer Cowley (in **"Queer"**), can express himself only through bodily force; thus, when he comes to woo Belle, his actions prove menacingly brutal.

George Willard senses this malaise of dissociation when he asserts that men are not responsible for what they do with women, implying thereby a lack of order or governing law to sanction any definite harmonious kind of relationship between the sexes. Although the ardent exercise of his intellect delights him, it leads him nowhere. In his walk he comes to a place resembling "old world towns of the middle ages" that all at once excites his fancy, arousing thoughts of a former existence and perhaps of lost innocence and purity. A strong impulse drives him to a dark alley where he smells the rank odor of manure from cows and pigs. His senses aroused, he now feels oddly detached from all life, feeling "unutterably big" and heroic amid the putrid squalor of the Winesburg slums. The density and massive "thickness" of life has thus released him from all self-centered, limiting speculations, infusing fervent vitality in him which only words like "death, night, sea, fear, loveliness" can transmit. Now a "twice-born soul" (in William James's sense), George acquires a sense of increased masculine power in his passage through the dark alleyway—possibly an initiation into the mysterious realm of instinct and impulse. Anderson believes that in youth there are always two forces in conflict: the warm, unthinking little animal, and the thing that reflects and remembers, that is, the sophisticated mind. The reflective force reduces one to stasis in which the will is inert until the moment of liberation when sensations regenerate the spirit. Just as the rank smell of animal refuse awakens him from mental stupor, the rubbish and the nail lead into a crystallization of an act:

> George went into a vacant lot and, as he hurried along, fell over a pile of rubbish. A nail protruding from an empty barrel tore his trousers. He sat down on the ground and swore. With a pin he mended the torn place and then arose and went on. "I'll go to Helen White's house, that's what I'll do."[40]

In this connection, we may cite the kindred experience of Kate Swift (in **"The Thinker"**) who, like many others, becomes transfigured in her nocturnal wanderings. Despite her face which "was covered with blotches," "alone in the night in the winter streets she was lovely." Night and winter exalt her to the rank of a goddess: "her features were as the feature of a tiny goddess on a pedestal in a garden in the dim light of a summer evening."

Just this transformation of fact in art into what William Faulkner calls "the exactitude of purity" seems to be Sherwood Anderson's significant achievement. It is Faulkner, too, who is the only one to elucidate with vigorous precision Anderson's basic artistic motivation when he describes him "fumbling for exactitude, the exact word and phrase within the limited scope of a vocabulary controlled and even repressed by what was in him almost a fetish of simplicity, to milk them both dry, to seek always to penetrate to thought's uttermost end."[41] Style is then ultimately the primary end of Anderson's art, an art practiced by a man whose epitaph is: "Life not death is the great adventure." To what extent Anderson's style exactly mirrors his personality, his vision of reality, Henry Miller makes an appreciative testimony:

> The style was as free and natural . . . as the glass of ice water which stands on every table in every home and restaurant. . . . His way of stringing the words together, of breaking off, of fumbling and faltering, of searching and stumbling, all this was exactly as I had experienced it in his writing. His stories were like ripe fruit dropping from an overladen tree. . . . He was all there and giving of himself in his easy steady way ("easy does it!"), giving what was ripe and ready to fall to the ground, not straining, not pumping it up, not wondering if it were just the right quality or not.[42]

After examining Anderson's method of characterization and the values it upholds, his handling of patterns of imagery, the rhythm of his prose, his modes of irony, I should like to conclude by affirming Faulkner's intelligent appreciation and interpretation of Anderson's art, and asserting that, contrary to Trilling's judgments, Sherwood Anderson exemplifies the artist "to whom nothing is lost," and whose major work, ***Winesburg, Ohio,*** successfully "renders the look of things, the look that conveys their meaning," thus converting "the very pulses of the air into revelations."

Notes

1. Lionel Trilling, *The Liberal Imagination* (New York, 1950), pp. 20-31 *passim.*
2. One of the recent sympathetic revaluations of Anderson's achievement, Irving Howe's *Sherwood Anderson* (New York, 1951), touches on the waste-land symbolism of *Winesburg,* but does not probe far into the dramatic structure and organization of the stories.
3. Edmund Wilson, *The Shores of Light* (New York, 1952), pp. 93, 233.
4. All quotations are from the edition of Malcolm Cowley, Compass Books edition, published by the Viking Press, New York, 1958, p. 24 (hereinafter referred to as *Winesburg*).
5. Trilling, p. 23.
6. *Winesburg,* p. 51.
7. *Ibid.,* p. 56.
8. *Ibid.,* p. 217.
9. See Frederick J. Hoffman, *Freudianism and the Literary Mind* (Baton Rouge, La., 1945), pp. 245 ff. Hoffman endeavors to refute critics who have charged Anderson with indiscriminate misinterpretations of Freudian doctrines by proving that Anderson discovered his insights through personal experience.
10. *The Modern Short Story* (Boston, 1956), pp. 164, 165.
11. *Sherwood Anderson's Notebook* (New York, 1926), p. 185.
12. On Anderson's lyricism, see the acute essay on *Winesburg* by Waldo Frank in *Story,* XIX, 29-33 (Sept.-Oct., 1941).
13. *Winesburg,* p. 238.
14. *Ibid.,* p. 237.
15. Frederick J. Hoffman, *Gertrude Stein* (Minneapolis, 1961), p. 20.
16. *Winesburg,* p. 234.
17. *Ibid.,* p. 234.
18. See, for instance, Alfred Kazin, *On Native Grounds* (New York, 1956), pp. 166 ff.
19. *Winesburg,* p. 245.
20. Compare my description of Anderson's dramatization of speech here with the analytic remarks of Stephen Spender on American diction in *The Making of a Poem* (New York, 1962), pp. 166-173.
21. *Winesburg,* p. 176.
22. *Ibid.,* p. 144
23. *Ibid.,* pp. 240-241.

24. *Ibid.*, p. 242.
25. *Sherwood Anderson's Notebook,* pp. 75-76.
26. Quoted from "The Selected Letters of Sherwood Anderson," ed. H. M. Jones, *Atlantic Monthly,* CXCI, 32 (June, 1953).
27. Harry Levin, "Observations on the Style of Ernest Hemingway," *Hemingway and His Critics,* ed. Carlos Baker (New York, 1961), p. 110.
28. Some articles of recent date have touched here and there on the stylistic techniques of *Winesburg, Ohio*; most of them are repetitive. A novel interpretation of the speech habits of Anderson's characters is proposed by John J. Mahoney, "An Analysis of *Winesburg, Ohio,*" *Journal of Aesthetics and Art Criticism,* XV, 245-252 (Dec., 1956).
29. *Winesburg,* p. 179.
30. *Ibid.*
31. *Ibid.*, p. 47.
32. *Ibid.*, p. 41.
33. *Ibid.*
34. *Ibid.*, p. 174.
35. *Ibid.*, p. 140.
36. *Ibid.*, pp. 137-138.
37. *Ibid.*, p. 127.
38. *Ibid.*, p. 55.
39. *Ibid.*, p. 49.
40. *Ibid.*, p. 238.
41. William Faulkner, "Sherwood Anderson," *Atlantic Monthly,* CXCI, 28 (June, 1953).
42. Henry Miller, "Anderson the Story Teller," *Story,* XIX, 72, 74 (Sept.-Oct., 1941).

Chris Browning (essay date 1968)

SOURCE: Browning, Chris. "Kate Swift: Sherwood Anderson's Creative Eros." In *The Merrill Studies in* Winesburg, Ohio, compiled by Ray Lewis White, pp. 74-82. Columbus, Ohio: Charles E. Merrill Publishing Co., 1971.

[*In the following essay, originally published in 1968, Browning discusses the character Kate Swift as Anderson's portrait of an ideal woman and a symbol of the creative Eros.*]

Critics have approached Sherwood Anderson's ***Winesburg, Ohio,*** from varying perspectives. They have discussed it in terms of the Freudian psychology it contains,[1] of the themes of loneliness and frustration,[2] and of men and women whose ability to function in their society is inadequate.[3] They have analyzed its style and structure as a novel,[4] but they have had little to say about the individual characters of the book other than as illustrations of the "grotesque" theme. It is true that some of the people in the novel are, as Burbank says, "characterized by various types of psychic unfulfillment or limitation owing in part to the failure of their environment to provide them with opportunities for a rich variety of experience . . . ,"[5] but it is equally true that Anderson advises that not all the grotesques are horrible; "some [are] almost beautiful."[6] One of these beautiful ones is the teacher, Kate Swift. In this woman, Anderson has drawn a portrait of his ideal woman, giving to her all the qualities he desired, in fact, required, in his own women: intelligence, education, energy and passion for life, independence of spirit. But even more than the ideal woman in human relationships, he presents her as the symbol for the continuity of life, in both the creative and spiritual realms. She becomes what Ludwig Lewisohn calls "the creative Eros."[7] Hoffman describes this creative force as deriving from the body of woman: "The body of woman is beauty itself, from which all other kinds of beauty are derived. . . . The origin of all art is religion; the purpose of both is to give man's inner world its outer symbols and to explain and justify God's ways and nature. At the root of all this ultimate knowledge and beauty is the creative Eros, the body of woman become a spiritual symbol and a biological source of strength."[8] Although Anderson wrote before Lewisohn, he illustrates beautifully in Kate Swift this same philosophy of woman as a creative force. Filled with an overweening hunger to transmit her knowledge of the true significance of life, she not only epitomizes the women Anderson loved and needed in his own life; but she is an active creative force, a creative Eros, in the lives of George Willard and the Reverend Curtis Hartman. In the two chapters of the novel in which Kate Swift appears, she furnishes the creative stimulus to these people, and her body is the instrument through which each gains the desired knowledge of life.

One has only to compare Kate Swift with the women who played important roles in Anderson's life to see that he has given to her the qualities he loved in his mother and in his four wives. Both Schevill and Burbank agree that Anderson was intensely devoted to his mother. He idealized her and often "embellished [her] with romance and mystery. She possessed great inner wisdom and [he] credited her with instilling her own penetrating insight and sympathetic understanding of people" in him.[9] In tribute to this inheritance he dedicated his novel to her: "To the memory of my mother, Emma Smith Anderson, whose keen observations on the life about her first awoke in me the hunger to see beneath the surface of lives. . . ."[10] To show that Kate

Swift serves this same function in the life of George Willard, Anderson has her encourage the young journalist also to look beneath the surface: "The thing to learn is to know what people are thinking about, not what they say" (p. 163). Burbank says that Anderson, in the **"Mother"** and **"Death"** chapters of the novel, presents his mother as "the prototype of the lonely person whose inner beauty shines forth in a strangely twisted fashion,"[11] but the inner beauty which he reveals in Kate Swift is more nearly the image he had of his mother. Anderson does not give the teacher a beauty that is readily apparent; she is "not known in Winesburg as a pretty woman" with her complexion "covered with blotches that indicated ill health" (p. 160). But she possesses an ethereal, but very real, loveliness for those with insight to see and appreciate. "Alone in the night in the winter streets she was lovely. Her back was straight" with pride, "her shoulders square" with courage, "and her features were as the features of a tiny goddess on a pedestal" with their reflection of her glowing spirit (p. 160). Anderson could have used the same terminology to describe his reverence for his mother. He saw the beauty in his mother, and George Willard, in the novel, is to see the beauty in Kate Swift.

Physical beauty was not the most important quality which Anderson desired in a woman. None of his four wives was considered beautiful, but each had character and personality traits that were very necessary to complement him as a man. Anderson suffered all his life from an acute awareness of his lack of formal education and he felt inferior because of it. He admired culture and refinement in women, and each of his four wives had these qualities in abundance. Cornelia Lane, his first wife, was a "well-educated, young woman of prosperous family, who seemed a personification of the qualities he lacked: social refinement, cultural ease, personal assurance."[12] His second wife, Tennessee Mitchell, was a music teacher and an enthusiastic suffragette; and her intellect inspired admiration in Anderson's Chicago and New York intellectual friends.[13] His third wife, Elizabeth Prall, was "a gently aristocratic person, daughter of an academic family, representing to Anderson established culture."[14] His fourth wife, Eleanor Copenhaver, was also well-educated, widely traveled, and through her interest in social reform, caused Anderson to broaden his own interests and activities, even to participation on an international scale.[15] In Kate Swift, Anderson embodies all these characteristics which appealed to him in women. She is a teacher: therefore she is well-educated, conversant with literature, art, and music. She is a cosmopolite since she has lived in New York and traveled extensively in Europe. She is an independent spirit; she smokes, and goes her own way with dignity even when her way differs radically from the custom in Winesburg. She is filled with the great wonder of living; she is "the most eagerly passionate soul among them" (p. 160). In these attributes, Kate Swift reflects those qualities which attracted Anderson to women and revitalized his own joy in life.

Kate Swift is, however, more than just the physical and mental projection of Anderson's ideal woman. She is also the symbol of creativity in the lives of George Willard and the Reverend Curtis Hartman. In this, as in the physical realm, she represents Anderson's own need for women. He could not go long without feminine companionship and readily admitted that he needed the impulse to love in order to work. He often described love as his "hope for renewed creative instinct."[16] Kate Swift, as a teacher, tries to make her students aware of the creative element in life through an intimate knowledge of the arts. She talks to them of Charles Lamb, Benvenuto Cellini, and the German music teacher, but the children, although drawn to her, miss the essence of what she is trying to tell them. This accounts, in part perhaps, for the "grief" that wars with the "hope" in her and creates the conflict of emotion that often drives her from the confines of her room to walk in the country or to kneel, naked and weeping, beside her bed after she thought she had failed to communicate with George Willard.

When young George was a student in Kate Swift's class, she recognized the latent genius in him, and her excitement was almost beyond containment. She is on fire to make him conscious that there is a greater world than that of Winesburg and a fuller life than that of the flesh. She feels she must not only encourage his talent but she must also prepare him for disappointment, for those who feel most acutely and love most sincerely are also the most vulnerable to hurt. "You will have to know life," she declares and her voice trembles with earnestness (p. 163). George is slow to understand her interest, however, and he translates it into physical desire. "He began to have lustful thoughts and pulling down the shade of his window closed his eyes and turned his face to the wall. He took a pillow into his arms and embraced it, thinking first of the school teacher, who by her words had stirred something within him . . ." (p. 158). On another occasion, she is moved "to have him understand the import of life, to learn to interpret it truly and honestly," and she embraces him, kissing him on the cheek (p. 165). At still a later meeting, she actually lets him take her in his arms for a moment, "so strong was her passion that it became something physical" (p. 165).

Burbank uses this behavior as the basis for listing Kate Swift as "an outcast or spiritual recluse" who is defeated by "the insensitivity and unresponsiveness of others."[17] Later in the same work, he concludes that she is defeated because "there is no man of her sensibility in Winesburg."[18] Kate Swift is far from defeated, however, and her behavior stems from more than mere physical desire. What she feels is an emotion beyond words, beyond physical passion; she is reaching for the imagination, the essence of creativity. D. H. Lawrence wrote that the "imaginative vision . . . includes physical, intuitional perception" and that "real imaginative awareness is largely physical."[19] Kate Swift looks at George and sees in him "a man ready to play the part of a man" (p. 165), and she lets him take her in his arms. As soon as the physical contact is made, however, the inspired rapport is broken, and she leaves George violently. George might look like a man, but she realizes he is not yet mature enough to understand more than the sexual promise of her actions and she feels that to limit this vast, soaring emotion to mere physical expression is a spiritual violation.

Although these scenes are described in sexual language, "the man's appeal to the lonely woman" (p. 163), and later "the passionate desire to be loved by a man . . . swept like a storm over her body" (p. 165), Anderson is following the tradition of Whitman and D. H. Lawrence—using sexual imagery to symbolize the compulsion to create or the fusion of the physical and spiritual natures. Kate Swift's excitement has its beginning as she thinks of George's potential to understand life; her passion grows out of her "great eagerness to open the door of life to the boy . . ." and it is only as she pours out her desire to him that he shall find this fulfillment that her passion becomes so strong that "it [becomes] something physical" (p. 164). The physical awareness, then, is the original stimulus of the creative imagination, but it is not all of it. Kate Swift realizes this, which accounts for her withdrawal and her subsequent grief because she thinks she has failed to reach George.

Howe names Kate Swift as one of the "communicants seeking individual expression" through George Willard, and he concludes that because George admitted that he'd missed something she was trying to tell him, he was unable to "save" Kate.[20] It is true that George is not fully aware of Kate's meaning, but Kate is able to understand George. She understands that he is not yet mature enough to grasp the full significance of all she said to him. It would be "ten years" before he would understand what she really meant. Contrary to Howe, then, Kate seems the mature one, the one who "saves" because she does not allow herself to accept a compromise, and at the same time does not confuse George's creative awakening by submitting to him physically. She is wrong in thinking that she has made no impression on George, for he is aware for the first time "of the marked beauty of her features"—a beauty which he could see only with eyes of spiritual awareness (p. 164). After he recovers from feeling "the baffled male," he realizes that he has "missed something Kate Swift was trying to tell" him (p. 166). It is this realization that sends him questing, perhaps, because his mind becomes "carried away by his growing passion for dreams," and he eventually leaves Winesburg to "paint the dreams of his manhood" (p. 247). This was what Kate Swift had been trying to tell him, and as his creative Eros, she has provided the initial stimuli which will lead ultimately to his creative maturity.

Kate Swift, although unconsciously, is also the creative Eros in the life of the Reverend Curtis Hartman. The minister, dedicated to a spiritual call to serve God, often "wondered if the flame of the spirit really burned in him and dreamed of a day when a strong sweet new current of power would come like a great wind into his voice and his soul and the people would tremble before the spirit of God made manifest in him" (p. 148). The desire to be a power for God is strong in the minister, but his motive in wanting the power is selfish and un-Christian; therefore, his message and his personality lack force. Then, from his prayer room in the church, he looks into Kate Swift's bedroom and sees her lying in her bed, reading and smoking. At first, he is shocked by the sight of the woman, and she becomes for him a symbol of all those he wants to save. He forgets his preoccupation with self and thinks of how he may reach this "woman who [is] gone in secret sin" (p. 149). His effectiveness in the pulpit increases as he forgets his gestures and his voice and concentrates on her. She has made him concerned about the sinful behavior of mankind, and he is offering God as the means of forgiveness for the sin. But he is more concerned with sin than with love, and he has more to learn from Kate Swift.

In the beginning, he looked at her body and saw only sin. Then by accident, he sees her again, and her bare shoulders and white throat excite carnal desire in his heart. The very room where he has prayed for an increase of God's power in him becomes his battleground against temptation and lust. There is, deep within him, a nameless longing, a gnawing hunger to know the true meaning of life and he equates this longing with the physical body of the woman he sees in the bedroom. But because he lusts for her, her body becomes more than objective universal sin; it becomes his personal sin. After a fall and winter in which the Reverend Hartman resists, succumbs, and resists again the desire to look upon Kate Swift's body, he decides to give full expression to his lustful thoughts. He goes to the bell tower, helpless at last before the carnal forces of his nature, but instead of finding satisfaction in the pleasures of the flesh, he experiences a revelation about mankind and his relationship to his Creator. Through his little peephole in the window, the minister sees Kate Swift, not in bed, not smoking, not as an object of carnal desire, but as a symbol of suffering humanity, kneeling naked and weeping before God in an attitude of abject supplication. He sees in her need the need of all men. In her naked body he sees the individual self in its search for vital mysteries and her body becomes for him a symbol of the spirit, for, as D. H. Lawrence believed, the "soul and the body are one."[21] The minister suddenly sees this relationship, and he is delivered from the merely physical desire he has felt earlier. He smashes the window, representing the evil of his temptation, and runs into the streets, aware that he has truly found what he has prayed for. "What he took to be a trial of his soul was only a preparation for a new and beautiful fervor of the spirit" (p. 155). Because he has looked on Kate Swift's body, he recognizes the sinful nature of man; he learns humility through his own temptation; and he experiences compassion for all men, even as God commanded. So, even though unwittingly on her part, Kate Swift becomes for the Reverend Hartman "an instrument of God, bearing the message of truth" (p. 155). Spiritual perception, the ultimate function of the creative Eros, is the minister's reward.

So Kate Swift, the creative Eros, is Anderson's ideal of both woman and Woman. She is drawn with tenderness and understanding because she personifies all the women Anderson loved; and she is also an extension of his own search for the beauty in and meaning of life. Anderson said "that always, every minute, day and night, I am after something—some abstract pure beauty,"[22] and he gives that beauty to Kate Swift. It is not a beauty readily seen by the villagers who look on the exterior alone, but a beauty apparent to those who have the insight to recognize the "goddess-like" qualities she exhibits. Anderson's philosophy was that "life, not death, is the great adventure,"[23] and he endows Kate with this same intense passion for knowledge and understanding. Hers is not a tranquil disposition. She is often driven by her emotions to walk "half the night fighting out some battle raging within," but her life had been and "was still adventurous." Behind her composed exterior "the most extraordinary events transpired in her mind" (p. 162). This is a woman of great soul, with a consuming desire to impart the richness of her own spirit to those who are capable of sharing the joys and pains of creating.

Anderson's own creative effort, as Howe suggests, was expended "to refract an enlargement of consciousness" in his readers,[24] and Kate Swift, in a similar effort, seeks to arouse, first in her students and later in George Willard, a hunger for a richer understanding of life. She succeeds in awakening George's interest which eventually motivates him to active pursuit of the Dream. The climax of Kate's function as the creative Eros comes when the Reverend Hartman experiences the revelation of Truth through her body and is freed from the shackles of superficial religiosity, making it possible for him to find the spiritual fulfillment he prayed for. The realization which the Reverend Hartman gains is the ambition Anderson himself cherished—a full understanding of and participation in the vital activities of life. All these emotions and functions which woman contributes to man, and Woman contributes to Mankind, are lovingly and sensitively combined by Anderson in Kate Swift.

Notes

1. Frederick J. Hoffman, *Freudianism and The Literary Mind* (Baton Rouge, Louisiana, 1945).
2. S. K. Winthur, "The Aura of Loneliness in Sherwood Anderson," *Modern Fiction Studies,* V (1959), pp. 145-152.
3. Rex Burbank, *Sherwood Anderson* (New York, 1964), p. 72. James Schevill, *Sherwood Anderson: His Life and Work* (Denver, Colorado, 1951), p. 103.
4. Burbank, pp. 61-67.
5. *Ibid.,* p. 68.
6. Sherwood Anderson, *Winesburg, Ohio,* Compass Books edition (New York, 1965), p. 23. All subsequent references are to this edition.
7. Hoffman, p. 294. Quoted by Hoffman from Ludwig Lewisohn, *Stephen Escott,* p. 216.
8. *Ibid.,* p. 295.
9. Burbank, p. 27.
10. Anderson, dedication page.
11. Burbank, p. 28.
12. Irving Howe, *Anderson* (New York, 1951), p. 38.
13. *Ibid.,* p. 81.
14. *Ibid.,* p. 145.
15. *Ibid.,* p. 216.
16. Schevill, p. 171.
17. Burbank, p. 72.
18. *Ibid.,* p. 73.
19. D. H. Lawrence, *Selected Literary Criticism,* Compass Books edition, 1966 (New York, 1923), p. 59.
20. Howe, pp. 103-104.
21. Lawrence, p. 406.
22. Schevill, p. 302.
23. *Ibid.,* p. 343.
24. Howe, p. 153.

Joan Zlotnick (essay date fall 1975)

SOURCE: Zlotnick, Joan. "Dubliners in Winesburg, Ohio: A Note on Joyce's 'The Sisters' and Anderson's 'The Philosopher'." *Studies in Short Fiction* 12, no. 4 (fall 1975): 405-07.

[*In the following essay, Zlotnick explores the influence of James Joyce's "The Sisters" on Anderson's "The Philosopher."*]

Sherwood Anderson was one of the first American authors to know and admire the works of James Joyce, whom he met during his European travels in the twenties. He freely acknowledged the influence of Joyce's writing on his own, particularly the influence of *Ulysses* on *Dark Laughter.* Anderson's debt to Joyce is not, however, limited to the fragmentary prose style of this one novel: a far greater debt is evident in ***Winesburg, Ohio,*** published just five years after *Dubliners.* Although Joyce's influence is discernible throughout the work, it is particularly evident in **"The Philosopher,"** which is strikingly similar to "The Sisters."

The form of ***Winesburg, Ohio*** is very close to that of *Dubliners.* Both are "collections" of stories, many of which were published separately, either prior to or after publication in the collection. The stories are loosely bound together by the similarity in setting, the repetition of particular motifs, the re-introduction of characters, and the repeated use of certain literary techniques. Together, each collection of stories provides a moral and psychological history of its drab and oppressive community and its inhabitants, most of whom have long ago suffered a paralysis of the spirit.

There is no autobiographical character like George Willard in *Dubliners,* no "artist" type whose struggle to flee from the place of his birth provides a narrative framework for the tales; there are, however, several unnamed young boys, sensitive and artistic, temperamentally like the young Joyce, who suffer disillusionment and seek escape from communities that repress and oppress, that warp and destroy life.

Joyce's Dubliners are every bit as grotesque as Anderson's. Some, like Maria, the protagonist in "Clay," whose nose is so long that it nearly touches the tip of her chin, are as physically grotesque as Anderson's Wash Williams, but almost all of them are emotionally grotesque as a result of their having denied or been denied love. The themes of sexual repression, spinsterhood, barrenness, alienation, and entrapment resound throughout *Dubliners* and ***Winesburg, Ohio,*** where religion teaches people that life is little more than endurance.

The Alice Hindmans and Elizabeth Willards have their counterparts and perhaps their prototypes in Joyce's women, married and unmarried, who endure lives of emotional privation and the men are, like James Duffy, unable to love another human being, or, like Little Chandler, trapped in a loveless marriage, or, like Father Flynn, brought to the brink of madness by a sense of religious obligation.

There is in many of the characters, Dubliners and Ohioans alike, pent up emotion that cannot be expressed naturally and must therefore break loose in apparently senseless and violent behavior, for example, when Farrington (Joyce's "Counterparts") beats his son or when the Reverend Hartman (Anderson's **"The Strength of God"**) smashes his fist through a church window.

A similar cast of characters, motifs of entrapment, denial, and frustration, and the structural similarities of the books indeed suggest that Anderson was influenced by Joyce. An examination of **"The Philosopher"** and "The Sisters" will indicate that Anderson's debt to Joyce is even more extensive.

The relationship between Dr. Parcival and George Willard in **"The Philosopher"** is almost identical with that of Father Flynn and the unnamed boy in "The Sisters." Both the doctor and the priest, who have ceased to perform their traditional functions, are aging and physically repulsive. Father Flynn's garments are faded and soiled, and "when he smiled he used to uncover his big discolored teeth and let his tongue lie upon his lower lip—a habit which . . . made . . . [the] boy feel uneasy."[1] Dr. Parcival is a "fat unclean looking man";[2] "his teeth were black and irregular and there was something strange about his eyes."[3] Priest and doctor alike are attracted to the sensitive and uninitiated youths, to whom they have an almost compulsive need to talk, and eventually to confess. Dr. Parcival, like Father Flynn, mystifies, confuses, and seeks to shape the future of George Willard, who, like the boy in "The Sisters," is both attracted to and repulsed by the older man who has become a surrogate father to him. In both cases, the boys have unsatisfactory father figures at home, men so lacking in sensitivity, imagination, and intellectual curiosity that they cannot relate to the youths.

Like Father Flynn, whom we find laughing in the confessional, Dr. Parcival is considered "mad" by the members of his community when he refuses to attend to the body of a dead girl, and his ultimate "confession" to George suggests that his early religious training has warped him in much the same way it did Father Flynn. It is George's discovery of the secret nature of Dr. Parcival that constitutes the major action of the story. Like the protagonist in "The Sisters," he has an epiphany, a moment of insight or illumination, that will have a significant impact on his future life.

Although the epiphany of George Willard, like that of his counterpart in "The Sisters," will help to set him free, few of the other inhabitants of Dublin or Winesburg will be so lucky. Indeed, both *Dubliners* and ***Winesburg, Ohio*** bear testimony to the often irreversible effects of repressive middle-class life. The setting may change from provincial Dublin to Middle America, but Anderson is in effect re-telling Joyce's story of spiritual impoverishment on a personal and communal level. In so doing, he is at once attesting to the "international" nature of the problem and to his own considerable debt to Joyce.

Notes

1. *The Portable James Joyce,* ed. Harry Levin (New York: Viking Press, 1947), p. 23.
2. Sherwood Anderson, *Winesburg, Ohio* (New York: Viking Press, 1958), p. 42.
3. Anderson, p. 38.

Walter B. Rideout (essay date 1976)

SOURCE: Rideout, Walter B. "Talbot Whittingham and Anderson: A Passage to *Winesburg, Ohio.*" In *Sherwood Anderson: Dimensions of His Literary Art,* edited by David D. Anderson, pp. 41-60. East Lansing: Michigan State University Press, 1976.

[*In the following essay, Rideout analyzes the relationship of* Winesburg, Ohio *to Anderson's unpublished novel* Talbot Whittingham, *arguing that some of the stories' themes and characters are prefigured in this earlier work.*]

One of the puzzling aspects of Sherwood Anderson's literary career has been the apparent suddenness with which, so near the beginning of it, he made a kind of aesthetic quantum jump from his apprentice novels, *Windy McPherson's Son* and *Marching Men,* published in 1916 and 1917 respectively, to his masterpiece, ***Winesburg, Ohio,*** published in 1919. It is even more puzzling when one goes behind publication dates to composition dates; for though he had written some kind of draft of both novels before he abandoned his career as an independent businessman early in 1913, he made his last revisions in each novel manuscript after he had begun writing the Winesburg stories in the autumn of 1915. The lateness of these last revisions can of course be explained by his difficulties in finding a publisher for the novels, for it was not until February 28, 1916, that the John Lane Company contracted with the author to publish *Windy McPherson's Son* and gave him a month in which to put his manuscript in final shape.[1] Nevertheless, the question remains: how could Anderson "jump" from the first two novels, with their promise and yet their deficiencies, to the mature artistry of ***Winesburg, Ohio***? Ultimately, the question is as unanswerable as the similar one of how William Faulkner could leap from his first three uneven novels to the extraordinary achievement of *The Sound and the Fury*; however, in Anderson's case at least part of the answer can be learned from his attempts, just before beginning the Winesburg stories, to create an artist figure resembling himself, especially, but not solely, in his unpublished fourth novel named for that figure, *Talbot Whittingham.* In that novel and figure he can be seen making a passage to ***Winesburg, Ohio.***

Since few people have had the opportunity to read this unpublished novel, the text of which is now available through the efforts of Gerald Nemanic,[2] it is necessary first to describe it in some detail. *Talbot Whittingham,* which seems to have been written between, roughly, the spring of 1914 and the early summer of 1915, is the one full-length novel among the many manuscript fragments concerning a man by that name which Anderson produced over perhaps as much as two decades.[3] The man in the fragments is not always the same person, but the large amount of Whittingham material suggests that at least originally this character had some special significance for its author. That significance may readily be surmised. Whereas, when published, *Marching Men* would describe the development of a largely invented labor leader and *Windy McPherson's Son* that of an only partially invented businessman, *Talbot Whittingham* traces the growth of a writer, one who despite obvious differences in external life seems often a projection of his creator's inner existence.

Although the brief Book 1 of the *Talbot Whittingham* manuscript is missing, some of its events can be reconstructed from references in the remaining four books and from a report that Anderson's friend Marietta Finley, a professional manuscript reader, prepared in "about 1916."[4] Talbot, son of an "umbrella-thief" father and a musician mother, spends his childhood in "a stuffy little apartment in New York," where the mother tries to create a salon from "an indiscriminate lot of art hangers-on" and achieves only an "abnormal, sickly atmosphere." One night the boy listens intently as a drunken youth urges him to be an artist, explaining that it is the artist alone who, though he may not understand "the law of life," knows that there is such a law which orders the mystery of existence. (Only Jesus of Nazareth, the omniscient narrator comments, would have understood this law, though a sense of it comes at times to the artist "in flashes" because of his desire to communicate with others through artistic "form.") When Talbot is twelve, his father disappears, and his mother, having discovered "her affinity in the person of a wealthy Breakfast Food man," commits him to the care of her former patron, Billy Bustard, a shy, middle-aged baker in the small Ohio town of Mirage, a name in keeping with the sardonic tone in which Book 1 appears to have been at least partly narrated.

Book 2 describes, in a series of episodes, Talbot's life in Mirage from age twelve to eighteen as he begins to develop toward what he eventually will become, a "master artist." Talbot, the narrator explains, has a "double nature." On the one hand, he is self-centered, arrogant, and manipulative of others, especially of Billy

Bustard, who supports him in a lazy life with a large monthly allowance; on the other hand, he is imaginative, inquisitive and sensitive about life, and sometimes inwardly insecure despite his outward self-assurance. Thus he embodies in surrogate form the conflict between the success-seeking and the dreamy Anderson of the author's Clyde years. Through his relationships with various inhabitants of Mirage, Talbot begins to mature. Bruce Harvey, a man totally devoted to horses and harness-racing, urges him to be hard and relentless as a driver in the race of life. With a strong, imaginative girl named Jeanette Franks he vies as a teller of wild adventure tales until she enters sexual maturity, becomes pregnant by the local barber, and is forced into marriage with him. Another girl, Lillian Gale, provides Talbot with his first sexual conquest, and Kit Donahue, a tough, virginal waitress, gets drunk with him one night while "they were trying to get at an understanding of each other and, through each other, of all men and women" who must live in the "modern world." Then Billy Bustard's brutal old father, Tom, returns to Mirage, rather like Huck Finn's Pap to St. Petersburg, demands money from his son, and tells Talbot to get out. Frightened by the man's threats, Talbot borrows Bruce Harvey's revolver, deliberately kills Tom, is exonerated on the false grounds that he was defending his benefactor, and with a gift of $1,500 from the embarrassed Billy leaves Mirage on the advice of the town's one Socialist, who shrewdly perceives that secretly the boy regards the murder as his "passport to manhood."

Books 3 and 4 detail the sequence of experiences in Chicago that over several years leads Talbot further toward an artist's career. On the train from Mirage to Chicago he meets and is attracted to a frank, courageous young woman who has left schoolteaching in an Indiana town for a try at becoming a painter; but once in the city Talbot, living on Billy's gift, forgets her and responds to his double nature, satisfying his aggressiveness by acting as a sparring partner at a boxing academy and his curiosity about human beings by standing "at street crossings and looking at people," the latter being a "passion with Talbot all of his days" and "his way of going to school." Soon he begins the daily practice of writing down some of his thoughts, and in a dark street one rainy night he has a visionary experience. Suddenly "all the men and women he had ever known seemed to press in about him" and "with their eyes and their hands" to plead with him to be their voice: "'Do not think of your own life but lend your brain and your young courage to us. Help us that we may make ourselves understood; that all men and women may make themselves understood.'" Shortly thereafter, however, he joyfully beats two men in a fight over a dancehall girl but by chance again meets the woman from Indiana. The latter explains to him bitterly that she has failed as an artist both because the modern woman is still too hampered by her traditional social role and because women will perhaps always be prevented by their biological role from achieving what the male as true artist can achieve, even if his dedication destroys him—the expression through himself of "the very spirit of his times and people."

Despite these steps on the way, however, Talbot's journey toward becoming a master artist is not direct. Through an acquaintance named Billows Turner, a gifted if eccentric advertising man, he drifts with the moneymaking spirit of the times into the advertising firm of Lester & Leach. Here he is financially successful, but he soon begins seriously to question "the meaning of his life." He becomes involved at the office in a long-standing quarrel between an exponent of Christ's teachings and a disciple of Nietzsche. The former insists equally on Jesus's "idea of infinite pity" and his tough-minded saying (from Luke 9:60), "Let the dead bury the dead"; the latter dismisses Christianity as sentimentality and, briefly taking Talbot on a drinking spree before hurrying nervously home to his wife, lectures his saloon audiences on the necessity of an "army of individualists," of "natural men" dedicated to following their instincts, whether to become artists or murders. Continuing the spree on his own, Talbot late that evening wildly accosts six separate people and attempts to make each perceive that he or she is a "grotesque," having been made so by the ugliness and deadness of life. Then he stalks a drunken merchant through the streets of Chicago's North Side with the purpose of killing him, obscurely feeling that this extreme act will somehow clarify his own confusion.[5] About to assault the businessman, however, he suddenly conceives of another bizarre way by which he can objectify to his maddened satisfaction Christ's "terrible saying," "Let the dead bury the dead"; and he at once goes to Turner's house to obtain his assistance in the scheme, a mass sale of inexpensive cemetery lots that will let Talbot view crowds of the living paying money toward their deaths. When carried out, the sale is very profitable for Talbot, but paradoxically it also softens the hatred he has developed against human beings as physically ugly and spiritually dead.

Book 5, the time of which is set eleven years after Talbot's first coming to Chicago, consists solely of two contrasting meetings between him and a woman. In the first he dines at a restaurant with Adelaide Brown, a wealthy dilletante more interested in artists than their art, who, as Talbot has told her, has "never done anything bold and beautiful" in her life. Just as he has cruelly forced her to admit that she does not have the courage to enter an affair with him, he catches sight of the Indiana woman, now named for the first time as Lucile Bearing, entering the restaurant with a little foreign-looking man as escort. Talbot sends Adelaide away and turns to Lucile, who, his artist's nature recognizes, has been defeated by life and yet has had the courage to accept that defeat. Seating her at a restaurant table and ignoring her angry escort, he describes to Lucile his frequent daydream of seeing her enter a long room out of a misty night, lovely of feature and with droplets of mist in her hair and on her coat that sparkle in the flames of the fireplace. The three people leave the restaurant, and as they walk toward Lucile's apartment through a misty evening, the escort becomes increasingly enraged, suddenly draws a revolver, shoots her, and runs off. Though wounded, Lucile continues to walk with Talbot to her apartment. Talbot insists on entering the apartment first, finds it, as he had hoped, a replica of the setting in his daydream, and, when the dying Lucile enters, perceives this woman who has accepted defeat to be as beautiful in actuality as in his fantasy. Then as the fireplace dances on the droplets of mist in her hair, Lucile, appearing to have "grown suddenly younger, taller and straighter," smiles at him for a moment and falls to the floor dead.

Such a summary of the book's action suggests why Anderson seems never to have submitted the manuscript to a publisher. As he himself presumably recognized, the novel has serious flaws. Not only is the ending contrived and melodramatic, but Lucile Bearing, who is given only three scenes in the narrative, functions largely as a mechanical device for charting the development of Talbot's understanding as an artist, her unselfish death being apparently so placed as to balance out in both the novel's structure and its ethical concerns Talbot's selfish act of murder. Almost as mechanical is the Jesus-Nietzsche debate. The values ascribed to Jesus in a series of references throughout the manuscript are affirmed at the end when Talbot links his perception of the beauty hidden in defeat with his recognition that Christ wanted men and women to live in the present, not the past; but Anderson's handling of concepts is simplistic and obvious, and the "defeat" of Nietzscheanism is an easy, even unfair one. Perhaps the major defect of the novel is the uncertain presentation of the protagonist. In the long Book 2 set in Mirage, Talbot's double nature is awkwardly reflected in an inconsistent tone. Instead of being a coherent, though complex, personality, Talbot is at times described, sardonically, as one who exploits Billy Bustard, contrives a leadership image of himself among his fellows, and murders Tom Bustard with no sense of guilt, while at other times he is described, sympathetically, as one who is sensitive toward others and puzzled about life. In the Chicago books the tone shifts again as the narrator moves waveringly from a detached, somewhat condescending attitude toward Talbot to, as he comes closer to his creator's age and condition, an open approval of him, exemplified by pronouncements like, "Such men as Whittingham know everything. They confound us with the strength and insight of their glances."

Talbot Whittingham reveals much, perhaps more than intended, about Anderson's feelings and attitudes at this point in his life. The explicit assignment of a double nature to Talbot suggests how aware he was of having been himself inwardly divided in his Clyde years and later, while the psychic melodrama of such scenes as Talbot's stalking of the merchant or his sale of the burial lots is probably a gauge of the frenzied hatred of self and others that would sweep over Sherwood from time to time in reaction to his advertising job. The "argument" of the novel, too, reflects Anderson's own conviction that entering the artist's vocation could resolve divisions, conflicts, frustrations within the self; yet in the form in which he embodies this argument there is a curious ambivalence that seems to result as much from uncertainty of concept or attitude as from the inadequate technical skill of an apprentice novelist.

Overtly the argument of the book leads toward a particular conception of the artist. In this conception the artist is connected with others, shares a common humanity with them, indeed can create his art only out of their lives and his understanding of their lives. This is what is asserted in Talbot's visionary moment in the Chicago night when all the people he has known seem to plead to him to be their voice, in Lucile Bearing's anguished admission that a man, if not a woman, can express the very spirit of his times and people, and in Talbot's ultimate penetration into the meaning of the grotesque. It is implied also in the series of admiring references to Jesus running through the novel and in the rejection of the Nietzschean view. This admiration of Jesus as one whose sayings and life were works of art, furthermore, is not only Talbot's or the omniscient narrator's; it was Anderson's as well. George Daugherty, Anderson's friend at the Critchfield advertising agency, recalled that while Sherwood was living in the lodging house at 735 Cass Street his "passing interest in Nietzsche . . . [was] awakened" and that "he bought a New Testament, applied himself to it, and informed the copy department that he 'was sold on Jesus Christ'." Daugherty's memory of Anderson's interest in Jesus at that time is confirmed by the fellow lodger Jack, whose drunkenness first from liquor then from life would prompt the story **"Drink"** in ***Winesburg, Ohio,*** and who later reminded Sherwood that in their Cass Street days he had "personally told [Jack that] Jesus was a great poet."[6]

But there are elements in *Talbot Whittingham* that contradict this argument. Talbot's deliberate murder of Tom Bustard is closer to Nietzsche's will to power than to Jesus's infinite pity, and far from ever feeling guilt for his act Talbot instances it to Adelaide Brown in his mature years as a "bold and beautiful" thing to have done.[7] And if he treats Adelaide Brown with what the narrator calls the "strange cruelty that is a part of such natures" as Talbot's, certainly his disregard in the book's concluding scene for the dying Lucile Bearing would appear, in realistic terms, self-regarding to the point of inhumanity were not that scene so obviously a maneuver by the author to provide Talbot and the reader with a climactic revelation. Especially noteworthy in a novel ostensibly asserting the closeness of artist and other men and women is Talbot's actual isolation from others. Such family ties as he originally had are permanently broken when he comes to Mirage at twelve; he establishes few close relationships among the townspeople and even these are abruptly severed by his act of murder; he forms no more than acquaintanceships among the men he works with in Chicago; his attitudes toward most of the women he meets in the city—the dancehall girl, a woman at his rooming house, Adelaide Brown—vary from mere tolerance to contempt, and that toward Lucile Bearing is essentially exploitative, however Anderson might have wished it to be regarded. Perhaps Talbot's isolation reflects Anderson's own intense desire to be free of family and business impediments in order to devote himself to writing, but in terms of the "meaning" of the novel it is as though the author of *Talbot Whittingham* were caught between competing conceptions of the artist. On the one hand, the artist is a being beyond good and evil in his personal life, the "master artist" whose gifts set him apart from other human beings; on the other hand, the artist is one who, in Lucile Bearing's words, must "give his life" in order to "make the world understand in him what there is in all men and women and what, in their own persons, they cannot understand." Perhaps Anderson himself recognized the warring impulses in the book as yet another reason for his dissatisfaction with it. At any rate, *Talbot Whittingham* would not be submitted for publication, and in practical terms Anderson was faced either with finding an approach and a form that would reveal the essence of his artistic development more successfully, or with abandoning this subject.

Actually what he was looking for was there, almost realized, not yet recognized, in the unpublished and unpublishable manuscript. The chief significance of *Talbot Whittingham* is its attempt to handle materials that would eventuate in two of his best books. Early in the 1920s he would return to the characters in the manuscript as the basis for some of the tales that would make up ***Horses and Men*** (1923). The bold imaginative girl Jeanette Franks foreshadows the attractive and pathetic May Edgely of "'Unused'." The Bruce Harvey scenes, with their emphasis on the satisfaction that "horse talk" and harness racing provided townsmen in Anderson's youth, look toward **"I'm a Fool,"** while a few details, such as Talbot's desire to be with horses in a barn on a stormy night, reappear in that highly personal tale **"The Man Who Became a Woman."** Particularly obvious is the resemblance of the final scene in *Talbot Whittingham* to its more successful reworking as **"The Man's Story."** The fact that this last tale would remain one of Anderson's favorites suggests that his unpublished novel had indeed a psychic value for him much exceeding its aesthetic achievement. That psychic value is especially manifested in the striking relationships between the Mirage section, significantly the longest by far of the five books, and ***Winesburg, Ohio,*** the various tales of which would begin almost to flood from his imagination only a few months after he had written *Talbot Whittingham.*

There is, to begin with, the close similarity of setting. Although the name "Mirage" is satiric rather than, like "Winesburg," evocative, it refers to the same kind of small town in the same part of Ohio. Mirage is a rural community connected to the outside world by trains but with an essentially preindustrial economy. There are a town hall, a Main Street, a hotel for travelers, a fairgrounds, a cemetery; just outside the town begin the fields, meadows, patches of woods. As Winesburg would, in fact, Mirage much resembles Clyde in its geography. Though Clyde has no Pennsylvania Street, it has, as does Mirage (and Winesburg), a Buckeye Street; the Main Streets of Clyde and Mirage slope downward from the town hall to the railroad tracks; in each case the cemetery lies beyond the tracks in the north part of town. The inhabitants of Mirage, furthermore, bear Clyde names in many instances and some exhibit Clyde characteristics. Barley Miller, son of the Mirage butcher, presumably received his first name from Barley Mann, son of the Clyde butcher, and his last from such a Clyde citizen as Harkness Miller; Salty Adair, Mirage's shoemaker, may get his name from "Body" Adare, in whose saloon young Sherwood, when he was a newsboy, used to sell off his last newspapers for the day; Bruce Harvey—the real Frank Harvey was a partner in Harvey and Yetter's livery stable—habitually howls out an Indian war cry in the excitement of a harness race as did Clyde's George Crosby. So close is the Mirage milieu to remembered folkways that, as though his reader were a fellow townsman, Anderson could refer to fictitious community landmarks without bothering to describe them, simply to "Turner's Grocery" or "the alley that turns out of Main Street by Nichols Tailor Shop." Only lightly masked by invented names, his home town stood in the eye of Sherwood's memory, a background against which to move the part-imagined, part-remembered character of Talbot Whittingham.

Occasionally the distance between townsman-author and townsman-character narrows suddenly in the manuscript. At one point the omniscient narrator drops his intermittently sardonic tone and, as though he were writing a first draft of *Sherwood Anderson's Memoirs,* asserts that Talbot's boyhood in Mirage "was for him the great romantic epic of his life, the period about which he was never afterward sure, a time when fancy took on a reality that was truth and that left a mark on the growing man and artist that was never afterward effaced." Thereupon the narrator interrupts his narrative with an essay in praise of the American village, beginning with the statement that Talbot "was, in later life, like most of us who live in cities, a man who looked lovingly back upon his days in an American small town." With Whitmanesque expansiveness Talbot's individual experience becomes generalized, since men from Michigan, Pennsylvania, Vermont, and Ohio and "western fellows who have looked out over the prairies" share in common the townsman past: "'Tis a thing in the blood of Americans, this memory of village life." Then suddenly the abstract essay turns into a single lyric scene which in its selection and composition of detail, its diction, even its sentence rhythms is fully in the yet-to-be-achieved ***Winesburg*** manner.

> The young and vigorous looking man we see walking before us in the street and who is going in at the door of the great store there, half running forward, working his way through the crowd, was such a fellow and walked with such a girl but five short years ago. On an evening he went with the girl along a street over a hill and a bridge into a country road. With the girl he climbed over a fence into a field. There was a pile of brush and he set it afire. The dew wet his shoes and made a dark band at the bottom of the girl's skirt. The fire did not burn well and the young man tramped it out. With the girl he went to lean against a fence. When a team passed on the road they crouched, hiding. There was no reason for concealment but they did not want to be disturbed. They were silent, their minds alive and filled with vague thoughts. The young man thought he would cut a noble figure in the world. His thoughts were vague, now they are quite definite. Next year he thinks perhaps he may own an automobile and have a beautiful woman to live in his house. His thoughts have lost color. They are now the thoughts of a thousand young men we shall see going in at the store doors.

The stylistic manner is maintained only momentarily; yet in other ways as well the long Mirage section of *Talbot Whittingham* shows that, unbeknown to himself, Anderson was going toward ***Winesburg, Ohio.*** The novel as a whole traces into early middle age the development of a writer, and that second book shows how a town and its people influence the writer's adolescent years. Foreshadowings of particular ***Winesburg*** tales occur in other books of *Talbot* besides the second: out of her defeat is born in Lucile Bearing what a drunken young man, apparently borrowed from the missing Book 1, prophesies in **"Tandy"** for Tom Hard's little daughter, "the quality of being strong to be loved"; and Talbot's vision in Chicago of "all the men and women he had ever known" pleading to him to interpret their lives resembles the old writer's vision in **"The Book of the Grotesque,"** the prefatory tale of ***Winesburg, Ohio.*** But in the Mirage section, episodic as it is in structure like a series of stories, appear several meetings with individual human beings that help shape Talbot, as similar meetings in Winesburg will shape George Willard. Though Bruce Harvey is not an isolate like ***Winesburg***'s Wing Biddlebaum and though his message differs from Wing's, each is fond of the young protagonist of his respective book and seeks to guide him; and Talbot's relationship with Kit Donahue will share with that of George Willard and Helen White in **"Sophistication"** a common interest in how men and women may understand each other in the "modern world." Most strikingly of all, the chapter describing Talbot's sexual initiation with Lillian Gale prefigures that of George with Louise Trunnion in **"Nobody Knows."**

A final aspect of *Talbot Whittingham* points directly toward ***Winesburg, Ohio***—Anderson's concern with what he was already calling the "grotesque." Although he twice uses the term in the Mirage section, only midway into Book 4 does he begin to attach a special meaning to it. Appropriately, that special meaning appears during his night drinking spree when he runs through the Chicago streets distraught with the conviction that he is "trying to live in a dead world filled with dead men and women." Life, Talbot believes, has "twisted and maimed" the minds and personalities of the six people he accosts, making them "grotesques," mere reflections of the world's own deadness and ugliness. The only one of the six to be described at length is a woman who works in a restaurant where, persecuted by male customers, she has become obsessed with a single desire, literally to "beat down men" with an iron bar in order to begin life anew, "to stand for something," to "make her protests felt and understood." This Chicago woman would have been at home in Winesburg. Talbot's confrontation with her and the other five "grotesques" saves him that night, the author asserts, "perhaps from insanity"; for in his agitation he senses that by roughly touching the six persons, each of whom he tells is "alive but . . . not beautifully alive," he will be able to find and restore "Something sweet and precious [that] has gone out of the world." The full meaning of grotesqueness only comes to Talbot much later, however, when by perceiving the courageous beauty Lucile Bearing exhibits beneath her outward defeat, he understands that "Everything is grotesque and the beautiful is beyond the grotesque." It is the duty of the artist to break through the grotesque, which Talbot now likens to a wall surrounding each person and thing, and to discover the beauty behind it. Grotesqueness, in sum, is a universal but outward condition of the world which both defeats men's dreams and separates them as individuals; beauty is a universal but inward condition which exists beyond defeat, binds individuals into a community, and when liberated by the artist's insight, emerges out of defeat in the form of art.

In *Talbot Whittingham,* then, Anderson had told the story of an artist much resembling his inward self, had reawakened and set down memories of his home town, and had worked out a theory of the grotesque, all apparently by the late spring of 1915. But even after completing his novel he continued to "play in his fancy" with the novel's main figure, attempting to use him now as an even more direct means of self-examination. He started but seems not to have progressed far with a novel entitled *The Golden Circle,* the very first page of which confirms the intensely personal significance of the Whittingham persona for his creator.[8] Talbot is first seen standing "at the window of a room on the second floor of a frame house in the town of Winesburg, Ohio." So the evocative name has already replaced the earlier sardonic one; and the close relationship of the fictional Winesburg with the real Clyde, of Talbot Whittingham with Sherwood Anderson is drawn tighter when the description of the frame house and its setting is seen exactly to tally with 129 Spring Avenue, where the Andersons lived from 1889 onward. There is even a big beech tree in the front yard with a spring at its foot. A neighbor child had drowned in the spring, and a white-faced Mrs. Whittingham had pulled the body out.[9] Anderson was openly relying on his own psychic past, for in a clear-sighted but sympathetic way he portrays seventeen-year-old Talbot as one who continues to envy another Winesburg boy his skill at baseball while turning for compensation to the reading of books and to flamboyant daydreams so intense that they take on the vividness of actuality.

For some unknown reason *The Golden Circle* was left unfinished. Another attempt to search the author's self by means of the Talbot persona was the likewise unfinished, perhaps hardly begun, *Talbot the Actor.* Here Whittingham is introduced as a young man on the last evening of his yearlong stay in Springfield, Ohio, during which he had lived at a boarding house run by an older woman, had attended the local college, had given a speech at Commencement exercises on the Jews in modern society, and had so held the audience's attention that an enthusiastic business executive had offered him an advertising solicitor's job on the spot.[10] So many other events prior to Anderson's own Springfield year are so direct from memory that one pays particular attention to what Talbot's former army friend Bert had told him before they parted one evening "on the docks in the city of Cienfu[e]g[o]s, in Cuba," that Talbot "was always an actor." This last evening in Springfield, while he waits until time to meet a passionate town girl with whom he is having an affair, Talbot as usual is absorbed in thinking of himself, of the contradictory impulses making up his "subconscious life," impulses that he visualizes as separate people conflicting within him in a kind of psychodrama. One person is "a white bearded old man," always sternly and honestly judging others and Talbot himself, but a "laughing lustful thing" within Talbot struggles with this puritanical judge and always comes out victorious. This laughing, lustful "poet" person Talbot revealingly visualizes as a figure who physically resembles the young Sherwood Anderson, a handsome, slender youth with "black hair and burning eyes," a youth always "running, through the world, among people, through streets of towns, over hills," though to what goal Talbot does not know. Sometimes, however, this "white and pure" youth, dancing like a white streak through the world, turns abruptly into "a grotesque ugly thing." Such a metamorphosis had happened in the terrible period just before Talbot had gone into the army, when for two years he had been "a young laborer in factories" and had devoted himself to hating people. Talbot likes to think, and knows that he likes to think, of the poet rather than the grotesque ugly youth as his true self, though "One could be quite satisfied if the poet was within him occasionally." Yet other persons exist within the "highly organized" Talbot, who, the narrator comments, is becoming a type in the modern world: one is "the figure of a small white faced woman hurrying with quick frightened footsteps through of [*sic*] life as though wanting to escape from it quickly and another of a general, very pompous and empty headed [;] he continually strutted before people."

This self-analysis by the fictional Talbot Whittingham is striking, since seen in the closely autobiographical context of the novel fragment it confirms Anderson's capacity for both imaginative self-dramatization and for a ruthlessly honest introspection. It also confirms his interest just prior to beginning the Winesburg stories, in dealing with the inner life of a character and in discovering fictional devices for expressing that inner life. In addition the person's self-analysis suggests how closely Anderson's observation of his own psychic mechanisms was related to the creative act itself. So Talbot's emphasis on the youthfulness of his poet-self points back to the "boyishness" that repeatedly characterizes the mature artist in *Talbot Whittingham* and forward to the "young thing" within him that saves the old writer in **"The Book of the Grotesque,"** the introductory tale of ***Winesburg,*** all of these instances expressing Anderson's sense of being, in terms of his own writing career, still a youth. In such ways both *The Golden Circle* and *Talbot the Actor* fragments show him, to use one of his favorite words, groping toward his master work.

Anderson's several versions of how he wrote the first story of ***Winesburg*** conflict with each other in details and even with obvious facts, including his specific reference in most versions to the first story as being **"Hands,"** actually the second written after **"The Book of Grotesque"**; but most of the accounts agree in suggesting that at the moment he was feeling especially harassed by his advertising job. He may also have been feeling frustrated by his failure as yet to place one of his longer works with a publisher, and he could well have been dispirited that, though he had been writing steadily through the summer and into the early fall, so much of this writing did not appear to be getting anywhere. Putting aside the inconclusive experiments with

Talbot Whittingham, he had started a story about a George Bollinger and an Alice Hassinger who, though each is married to another, fall desperately in love; but he could not get them beyond the point where they admit what is happening between them. Adding the pages of this failed effort to the growing pile of discarded sheets on his big worktable in the room at the top of his Cass Street rooming house, he next drove his pencil across some thirty-three sheets of yellow paper in an effort to tell about a Trigant Williams, who as a boy in an Ohio River town lacked the courage to approach a promiscuous little girl from a rural slum, but who, with the town "fixed" in his memory even in adulthood, later became "a pagan." Then Anderson abruptly dropped Trigant Williams and tried another approach to the theme of the artist through describing the boyhood of a Paul Warden, who in one scene rejects formal Christianity because it lacks the sense of the erotic and mystical which, Paul feels, Christ himself must have had, and who in high school shows sufficient skill at drawing that a teacher encourages him to "protect your imagination." Yet the Paul Warden story did not seem to head in the right direction either, and Anderson broke it off on a final page containing a single sentence: "Paul was in a house in the city of Chicago."

That sentence may have been the last push to his imagination that he needed; for one evening in the fall of 1915 he came back wearily from the advertising office to his room in Cass Street and was seized with yet another story idea which by conscious design would allow him to unite the image of an old writer in a house in Chicago with that of a young man developing his artistic imagination in a small Ohio town named Winesburg. Turning over on his worktable the big pile of discarded sheets, Anderson took the top one—on its reverse was that sentence, "Paul was in a house in the city of Chicago"—and began to write about an old writer in a room like his own whose mind, like that of the first Talbot Whittingham, was filled with a procession of people, all the people he had ever known, all of them grotesques, who had helped a young artist to maturity and kept an old one young. He began to write ***Winesburg, Ohio.***

Notes

1. Information from a reproduction of a copy of the Memorandum of Agreement between the John Lane Company and Sherwood Anderson, generously furnished by John Ryder of The Bodley Head, founded by John Lane.

2. See Gerald Carl Nemanic, "*Talbot Whittingham*: An Annotated Edition of the Text Together with a Descriptive and Critical Essay" (Doctoral dissertation, University of Arizona, 1969); available from University Microfilms. Quotations in my article are from this edition with the permission of Eleanor Copenhaver Anderson and Gerald Nemanic. Although Nemanic and I of necessity differ in our approaches to the novel, I am glad to acknowledge my indebtedness to his introductory essay for several suggestions.

3. The evidence concerning dates of composition of Anderson's first four novels is fragmentary, vague, contradictory, and too complicated to be rehearsed here. Mr. Nemanic tentatively dates the writing of *Talbot Whittingham* as extending from "possibly" late 1912 to "probably" 1915 or 1916. Partly on the grounds that Anderson probably completed his third novel, the also unpublished *Mary Cochran,* in the winter of 1914, I tentatively date *Talbot Whittingham* as being written within the shorter period of time. It is certain, however, that Anderson had written all or substantially all of this fourth novel before he began the Winesburg tales.

4. Nemanic, "*Talbot Whittingham,*" p. 12, fn. 21. Mr. Nemanic quotes a letter to him from William A. Sutton, who reported what Miss Finley (Mrs. E. Vernon Hahn) told him. The text of this report is given in Sutton, *The Road to Winesburg: A Mosaic of the Imaginative Life of Sherwood Anderson* (Metuchen, N.J.: The Scarecrow Press, 1972), pp. 584-88. Quotations in this paragraph are from the report except for those in the parenthesis, which are from the edited text.

5. A suggestion of how closely Anderson seems to be projecting through Talbot's action his own periods of emotional stress is the curious fact that in a novel little given to naturalistic detail the route of the hunted and hunter is traced by street names so exactly that an actual murder would have been committed in full view from Anderson's room in the lodging house at 735 Cass Street on Chicago's Near North Side. He had taken up residence there in the fall of 1914 and there began writing the Winesburg stories a year later.

6. George H. Daugherty, "Anderson, Advertising Man," *Newberry Library Bulletin,* Second Series, No. 2 (Dec. 1948): 37; letter from Bronson Gobe to Sherwood Anderson, July 15, 1921. Of Anderson's "passing interest in Nietzsche," Daughterty further states: "The only thing in the Overman's philosophy that we ever heard him quote was the assertion to the effect: This is true—but the opposite is also true, which fitted in admirably with Anderson's well-known theory of the relation of truth and romance."

7. Talbot's killing of Tom Bustard may be an echo of H. G. Wells's *Tono-Bungay* (1910), which it is likely Anderson had read in the summer of 1913. Although the circumstances differ widely and George Ponderevo, the narrator of *Tono-Bungay,*

feels guilt when he commits the murder, by the time he has come to write his "autobiographical" novel, he can refer to the act with a detachment surprisingly like Talbot's: "It is remarkable how little it troubles my conscience and how much it stirs my imagination, that particular memory of the life I took." (*Tono-Bungay,* [NY: Scribner's, 1925], Atlantic Edition, vol. 12, p. 298.)

8. In "How Sherwood Anderson Wrote *Winesburg, Ohio*" (*American Literature,* 23 [Mar. 1951]: 7-30), William L. Phillips astutely argued that *The Golden Circle,* and the other uncompleted fictions here discussed, preceded *Winesburg* and formed the pile of discarded sheets on the blank back sides of which Anderson wrote many of the *Winesburg* tales. Though the argument is generally persuasive, these original pieces of writing must be dated cautiously. At least one story, narrated in the first person by an advertising man named Sidney Melville, was certainly written well after the first *Winesburg* tales were composed, since on page 7 Melville says of a party that "now that prohibition has come, everyone got a little drunk." The Eighteenth Amendment did not come into effect, of course, until Jan. 19, 1919.

9. See Sutton, *Road to Winesburg,* pp. 505-507, for accounts of the actual incident involving Anderson's mother and the neighboring Wyatt child.

10. Except for the fact that Anderson had attended Wittenberg Academy, not Wittenberg College, these events are almost unchanged autobiography from his Springfield year, 1899-1900.

David Stouck (essay date January 1977)

SOURCE: Stouck, David. "*Winesburg, Ohio* as a Dance of Death." *American Literature* 48, no. 4 (January 1977): 525-42.

[*In the following essay, Stouck elucidates the Dance of Death theme in* Winesburg, Ohio *and speculates on how Edgar Lee Masters's treatment of death in his* Spoon River Anthology *may have influenced Anderson's stories.*]

Sherwood Anderson's implied purpose in ***Winesburg, Ohio*** is "to express something" for his characters, to release them from their frustration and loneliness through his art. This motive is revealed in the prayer of Elizabeth Willard (mother of the nascent artist George Willard), who, sensing the approach of her death, says: "I will take any blow that may befall if but this my boy be allowed to express something for us both" (p. 40).[1] The view of art, however, in this book does not suggest the fulfillment of that prayer. Artists, like the old man in the introductory sketch and like Enoch Robinson in **"Loneliness,"** are among those least capable of expressing themselves to others, either in their life gestures or in their art. The old man in **"The Book of the Grotesque"** is a pathetic figure preoccupied with fantasies about his failing health. He has a vision of people in a procession and a theory about the "truths" that make them grotesques; but he does not publish the book he is writing about these people, for he realizes it would represent only *his* truth about them, that it is not possible to express the truth for someone else. Enoch Robinson, the pathologically shy painter, tries to reach out to others through his work, but his paintings fail to make even his fellow artists experience what he has thought and felt.

The central insight in the book concerning human relationships is that each man lives according to his own "truth" and that no one can understand and express fully that truth for someone else. Or, put another way, every human being in this world is ultimately alone. In desperate reaction to this vision Elizabeth Willard, near the end of her life, seeks out death as her companion:

> The sick woman spent the last few months of her life hungering for death. Along the road of death she went, seeking, hungering. She personified the figure of death and made him now a strong black-haired youth running over hills, now a stern quiet man marked and scarred by the business of living. In the darkness of her room she put out her hand, thrusting it from under the covers of her bed, and she thought that death like a living thing put out his hand to her. "Be patient, lover," she whispered. "Keep yourself young and beautiful and be patient."
>
> (p. 228)

In this one vivid paragraph are telescoped many of the book's central concerns: the suffering mother, frustration and loneliness, life as unending movement, the search for love, and the power of death. Describing death as Elizabeth Willard's lover, Anderson suggests not only a central theme but perhaps a principle of structure in his book—namely, the medieval concept of life as a Dance of Death.

I

Anyone familiar with Anderson's writing is aware of the frequency of the word death in his titles. In ***Winesburg, Ohio*** **"Death"** is the title of a key sequence concerning Elizabeth Willard. **"Death in the Woods"** is the title of one of Anderson's most accomplished short stories and was made the title of a collection of stories published in 1933. One of the best stories in that collection is titled **"Brother Death,"** a story of a boy who must die young but who, unlike his older brother, never has to part with his imagination. "Death" and "A Dying

Poet" are two of the titles in *A New Testament* and "Death on a Winter Day" is a chapter title from *No Swank*. In the ***Sherwood Anderson Reader*** we find a magazine piece titled "A Dead Dog" and a sequence from the unedited memoirs published as "The Death of Bill Graves." The suggestion in these titles that Anderson was more than casually preoccupied with the theme of death is quickly borne out by an examination of his novels, stories, and memoirs.

In almost every book Anderson published the death of a beloved character is of crucial significance and casts the protagonist's life in a wholly different perspective. And on a more philosophical level Anderson saw modern man, alienated from creativity by mechanized factory work and by a repressive Puritan ethic, caught up in a form of living death. These two forms of death—the death of an individual and the death of a society—correspond to the distinction in late medieval art between a dance of Death and the dance of the dead. Holbein's *Dance of Death,* artistically the most sophisticated expression of this theme, depicts Death claiming various individuals and leading them away singly from this life. The more popular representations, such as the relief on the cemetery at Basel, depicted the dead either in a procession or dancing with the living. One of the popular beliefs associated with the Dance of Death was that the dead appeared to warn the living of their fate.[2] Such images and themes, as will be shown, were a part of Anderson's imagination throughout his career as a writer.

The death of Sherwood Anderson's mother when the author was eighteen likely determined, more than any other experience, the persistent preoccupation with death in his fiction. The mother's death is recorded several times in Anderson's writings, in both semi-autobiographical and fictional form. For some of Anderson's protagonists the death of the mother changes radically the course of their lives and initiates an unending quest to find a home and a place in the world. In *Windy McPherson's Son* Sam's mother dies when the hero is still a youth and he seeks in the motherly Mary Underwood someone to fill that role. His later attachments to women follow the same pattern. When he marries Sue Rainey he envisions a whole family of children, for he wants himself to be part of a family with Sue mother to them all. Because Sue cannot give birth to living children, the marriage fails for a long time, and Sam becomes an alcoholic, guilt-ridden over the deaths of motherly women he has known. Only after he has found three children to adopt does he go back and resume his life with Sue. In the more ideological novel *Marching Men,* the death of Beaut McGregor's mother has a similar profound effect on the course of the protagonist's life. The death of Beaut's mother is imaged as a Dance of Death in the manner of Holbein. Death personified comes unexpectedly one night up the stairs to the old woman's room, sits grim and expectant at the foot of the bed and carries the old woman away before morning. Grief stricken over the death of this humble and obscure figure, McGregor dedicates himself to a vision of mankind's purposeful march toward perfection, a march that will give the anonymous lives of people like his mother order and meaning.

In more directly autobiographical writings the mother's death initiates the youth into the world of experience and awakens him to his own mortality. In *A Story-Teller's Story* it is an experience of profound alienation for the boy; Anderson writes "for us there could be no home now that mother was not there."[3] Similarly in ***Winesburg, Ohio*** it occasions George Willard's departure from the town in which he has grown up. In *Tar: A Midwest Childhood* the mother's death spells the end of childhood and innocence. The day after his mother's funeral, Tar crawls inside a box car on a railroad siding and for the first time in his life thinks about his own death—what it would be like to be buried under a load of grain. When later he hurries up the street, forcing himself to take up his paper route again, we are told in the book's closing lines that although he did not know it he was "racing away out of his childhood."[4] In each instance the mother's death awakens the hero to the mortal view of existence and raises the difficult question of life's meaning and purpose.

Adult life in Anderson's fiction is repeatedly imaged as processional movement along a road. In *Marching Men* mankind is represented as shuffling in disorderly fashion toward death. Beaut McGregor's vision is that the procession will become orderly and dignified when men cease to serve the ambitions of individual leaders and march for the betterment of human kind. All of Anderson's writing is remarkable for its sensitivity to movement as a characteristic mark of American life. In *Poor White* it is the rapid change of America from a rural to an industrial nation; swarms of men, like the sky full of moving, agitated clouds, are seen moving from the prairies into the cities. The young, optimistic spirit of the country, we are told, made it "take hold of the hand of the giant, industrialism, and lead him laughing into the land."[5] But in *Many Marriages* those people working in factories, living side by side without communicating to each other, are represented collectively as a city of the living dead. When John Webster decides to leave his business and his timid, repressed wife, he feels he has come back from the dead. By contrast other people in the novel are imaged as moving steadily toward the throne of Death, who is also described as the god of denial. Death is personified as a general with an army made up not of the physical dead but of the living dead.

> Death had many strange tricks to play on people too. Sometimes he let their bodies live for a long time while he satisfied himself with merely clamping the lid down

> on the well within. It was as though he had said, "Well, there is no great hurry about physical death. That will come as an inevitable thing in its time. There is a much more ironic and subtle game to be played against my opponent Life. I will fill the cities with the damp fetid smell of death while the very dead think they are still alive . . . I am like a great general, having always at his command, ready to spring to arms at the least sign from himself, a vast army of men.[6]

Anderson sees America made up of lonely, frustrated individuals who cannot communicate with each other and who form a procession of the living dead. The same image occurs in ***The Triumph of the Egg*** in the long story **"Out of Nowhere into Nothing."** The heroine, Rosalind Wescott, returns from Chicago to her home town to find that her people "in spirit were dead, had accepted death, believed only in death" (p. 266).[7] The whole town, she feels, lies in the shadow of death: her mother, whose face appears death-like, sits like "a dead thing in the chair" (p. 248); and Rosalind feels she must herself run away "if she doesn't want death to overtake her and live within her while her body is still alive" (p. 185).

In *Dark Laughter,* Anderson's most Lawrentian novel, life is imaged as a dance. For the central character, Bruce Dudley, the image functions initially to suggest life's energy and potential rhythms ("Dance life . . . Pretty soon you'll be dead and then maybe there'll be no laughs"[8]), but the image acquires a darker dimension when Dudley thinks of his dead mother as having been "part of the movement of the grotesque dance of life" (p. 90).

As far as I know Anderson never referred to ***Winesburg, Ohio*** as incorporating the Dance of Death idea. The different images, however, fall together suggestively—life as a procession, life as a dance, life as a living form of death. He did frequently personify death in his writings, including in *A Story-Teller's Story* a traditional image of Death, the Grim Reaper, coming for the author (p. 404), and in the *Notebooks* an image of himself old and dying and listening to "the sound of the tramping of many feet."[9] Moreover, we do know that he conceived of the frustrated and defeated characters in his early stories as among the living dead. In a letter to M. D. Finley, December 2, 1916 (the period in which he was composing the Winesburg stories), he says:

> Men's fears are stories with which they build the wall of death. They die behind the wall and we do not know they are dead. With terrible labour I arouse myself and climb over my own wall. As far as I can see are the little walls and the men and women fallen on the ground, deformed and ill. Many are dying. The air is heavy with the stench of those who have already died.[10]

The same idea appears in *A New Testament* in "The Story Teller" where Anderson describes his tales as people dying from cold and hunger, while in his memoirs he says that dead people, such as his mother, would return to him in dreams and he concluded they wanted their stories told.[11]

Winesburg, Ohio may not have taken shape directly around the Dance of Death idea, but it was most certainly influenced by a book, Edgar Lee Masters's *Spoon River Anthology,* of which the central theme is death. Masters's poems were published in book form in the spring of 1915 (the year Anderson probably started writing the Winesburg stories), and we know that Anderson read the book shortly after its publication.[12] He professed a distaste for Masters's poems which critics have explained in the light of Masters's relationship with Anderson's second wife, but it may also reflect a literary debt that Anderson was reluctant to acknowledge.[13] However that may be, there is no denying some fundamental similarities between the two books. Both ***Winesburg*** and *Spoon River* depict in episodic fashion a cross-section of life in a small midwestern town. In both books at the deepest level there is an intransigent sense of despair. The Spoon River poems are vignettes of lives lived at cross-purposes, with recognitions after death that life has been wasted and is now forever irrecoverable. Masters's poems incorporate the medieval idea of the dead appearing to warn the living of their inevitable end. The voices of the dead, each one telling a story from the tomb, was a formal design which must surely have influenced Anderson considerably, for we have seen him speak of his Winesburg characters as each walled in by fears and already dead or dying. Anderson's characters are not presented as spirits returned from the dead, and yet in a very important sense that is what they are, for the characters in ***Winesburg, Ohio*** are people from the narrator's memory of his home town, and many of them, most significantly the mother, are in fact long dead.[14]

But what is particularly suggestive, given the fact that Anderson had seen Masters's book, is that several of Oliver Herford's illustrations for the first edition of *Spoon River Anthology* depicted the Dance of Death in various forms. Death swinging a lariat appears twice and, placed above the first of the poems, serves as a controlling visual motif throughout the collection. Death is also shown in the manner of Holbein leading away a child in one sketch and beckoning to a drunk in another. But two of the illustrations suggest actual situations in the Winesburg stories. One shows Death in bed as a lover and we are reminded of Elizabeth Willard's erotic personification of death in her last days. The other presents Death approaching an older man who has just taken a young wife, and we think of Doctor Reefy, whose young bride is snatched away from him by Death only a few months after the couple are married. Anderson may not have consciously conceived of his stories being arranged like a medieval Dance of Death, but it is hard to believe that the Masters's book with its death theme and design did not influence his imagination at some fundamental level.

II

In ***Winesburg, Ohio*** the idea of death does not signify only the grave, but more tragically it denotes the loneliness and frustration of the unlived life. As in *Poor White* we are aware in ***Winesburg, Ohio*** of movement as characteristic of American life, but here it is the restlessness of the individual who grows increasingly oppressed by his loneliness and his inability to express himself to others. In each story when the character reaches an ultimate point of insupportable frustration or recognizes that he can never escape his isolation, he reacts by waving his hands and arms about, talking excitedly, and finally running away. In a very stylized pattern almost every story brings its character to such a moment of frenzy where he breaks into something like a dance.

The introductory sketch, **"The Book of the Grotesque,"** is either ignored by critics or dismissed as a murky and confusing allegory. That Anderson intended it to carry significant weight in relation to the rest of the book is clear when we remember that **"The Book of the Grotesque"** was the publication title Anderson first gave to the whole collection of stories. In its oblique and terse fashion the sketch defines the relationship of the artist to his characters. The subject is an old man who is writing a book about all the people he has known. The first thing we notice is that the writer is preoccupied with fantasies about his failing health. When he goes to bed each night he thinks about his possible death, yet paradoxically that makes him feel more alive than at other times; thoughts of death heighten his awareness to things. In this state the old writer has a waking dream in which all the people he has known are being driven in a long procession before his eyes. They appear to the writer as "grotesques," for each of these characters has lived according to a personal truth which has cut him off from the others. These are the characters of Anderson's book. The procession they form is like a dance of the dead, for as mentioned above most of these people from Anderson's childhood are now dead. The youth in the coat of mail leading the people is the writer's imagination and also his death consciousness—his memory of the past and his awareness that loneliness and death are the essential "truths" of the human condition. We are told in this sketch that the old carpenter, who comes to adjust the height of the writer's bed and who instead weeps over a brother who dies of starvation in the Civil War, is one of the most lovable of all the grotesques in the writer's book. Just such a character apparently befriended Anderson's lonely mother in Clyde, Ohio;[15] this detail indicates both the personal and the elegiac nature of the book.

The first story, **"Hands,"** tells about Wing Biddlebaum whose unfulfilled life typifies the other life stories recounted in the book. From his little house on the edge of town Wing can watch life pass by: ". . . he could see the public highway along which went a wagon filled with berry pickers returning from the fields. The berry pickers, youths and maidens, laughed and shouted boisterously. A boy clad in a blue shirt leaped from the wagon and attempted to drag after him one of the maidens, who screamed and protested shrilly. The feet of the boy in the road kicked up a cloud of dust that floated across the face of the departing sun" (p. 27). With its archetypal images of the public highway, youths and maidens, the berry harvest, and the cosmic image of the sun, the scene Anderson has created is a tableau depicting the dance of life. By contrast Wing Biddlebaum ventures only as far as the edge of the road, then hurries back again to his little house. He lives in the shadows of the town. Yet, like the berry pickers, his figure is always in motion, walking nervously up and down his half decayed verandah. His hands especially are always moving and are compared to the beating wings of an imprisoned bird. In *Tar* Anderson tells us that likely "the memory of his mother's hands made him think so much about other people's hands" (p. 276), again creating a link between his fictional characters and dead mother. Wing's story of being accused of perverted love for the boys he teaches ends in his flight from a small Ohio town. The newspaper reporter George Willard, persona for the young Anderson, listens sympathetically to Wing as he tries to describe his pastoral dream of living like the classical teacher Socrates; but his hands, caressing George Willard, betray him and he runs away to resume his endless pacing in the shadows of his old house.

Several of the stories follow the basic pattern of **"Hands"**: a misfit in the town is telling George something of his story but cannot express himself completely; he begins to wave his hands about helplessly and breaks into a run. In **"Drink"** Tom Foster, a gentle, passive boy, is described as living "in the shadow of the wall of life." Like Wing Biddlebaum he watches the parade of life pass him by. But he conceives an affection for the banker's daughter Helen White, and one spring night he goes for a long walk and gets drunk on a bottle of whiskey. He becomes a grotesque figure moving along the road: "his head seemed to be flying about like a pinwheel and then projecting itself off into space and his arms and legs flopped helplessly about" (p. 218). He tries to tell George Willard that he has made love to Helen White, but the reporter won't listen because he too loves the banker's daughter. They take a long walk in the dark. Tom raises his voice to an excited pitch to explain that he wants to suffer because "everyone suffers," but George does not understand him.

In the story **"'Queer'"** George does not get an opportunity to understand. Elmer Cowley, oppressed by his sense of being different from everyone else, resolves that he will be like other people. He goes on a long walk in the country where he encounters the half-wit named Mook. Walking up and down and waving his arms about, he tells Mook that he won't be queer any longer, and then goes on to tell of his resolution to George Willard, whom he sees as typifying the town and representing public opinion. They go on a walk together but Elmer cannot explain himself to the reporter: "He tried to talk and his arms began to pump up and down. His face worked spasmodically. He seemed about to shout" (p. 198). Having failed to communicate to anyone, he decides to run away from the town, but as he is leaving on the train he calls George Willard down to the station to try once again to explain. Still speechless he breaks into a grotesque dance: "Elmer Cowley danced with fury beside the groaning train. . . . With a snarl of rage he turned and his long arms began to flay the air. Like one struggling for release from hands that held him he struck out, hitting George Willard blow after blow on the breast, the neck, the mouth" (pp. 200-201).

George is similarly struck at by the school teacher, Kate Swift. Like so many of the characters in the book Kate takes long walks alone at night; one night she walks for six hours. In the eyes of the town she is a conventional old maid, but inside, her passionate nature yearns for companionship and for significant achievements. She half loves George Willard, her former pupil, and in her desire to see his genius flower, she goes to the office of the newspaper to talk to him. Like George's mother she wants him to be a serious writer and to express something for the people of the town. But confused by her love for the boy, she cannot express herself adequately and winds up beating him on the face with her fists, and then running out into the darkness. That same night the Reverend Curtis Hartman, who for weeks has paced the streets at night imploring God to keep him from his sinful habit of peeping into Kate Swift's bedroom window, bursts into the office of the Winesburg *Eagle* "shaking a bleeding fist into the air" as an emblem of his triumph. He has broken the church study window through which he had "peeped," so that now it will be repaired and he will no longer be able to indulge in his sin. Over and over inarticulate characters in a moment of passion wave their hands in the air and burst into a run.

Two of the stories present a macabre vision of life's "truth." In **"The Philosopher"** Doctor Parcival tells George Willard about his childhood, but when he reaches the point of telling about his father's death in an insane asylum, he breaks off and paces distractedly about the newspaper office. Doctor Parcival is another of the book's failed artists; he is writing a book and his sole vision is that life is a form of crucifixion, a long torture and dying as it was for Christ on the cross. **"Respectability,"** the story of the cuckold Wash Williams, also involves a vision of living death. In reaction to his wife's faithlessness Williams holds the idea that all women are corrupt and dead.

Wash Williams is perhaps most remarkable for his hideous physical appearance. He is compared to "a huge, grotesque kind of monkey, a creature with ugly, sagging, hairless skin below his eyes and a bright purple underbody" (p. 121). Everything about Wash, including the whites of his eyes, looks unclean, everything except his hands which in striking contrast are well cared for. There is a medieval grotesqueness in the description of several of the characters; as in medieval art, the twisted inner nature of the people is manifested in imperfections and distortions of the physical body. Doctor Reefy in **"Paper Pills"** has a huge nose and hands; the knuckles of his hands are "like clusters of unpainted wooden balls as large as walnuts fastened together by steel rods" (p. 35). This stylized image of the doctor's physical body anticipates the description of his character as being like the sweetness of the gnarled apples left on the trees in autumn, and the image of the little balls of paper on which he has written a number of truths. Some of the characters are almost like gargoyles on medieval buildings. Doctor Parcival, who believes all men are crucified, has a yellowed mustache, black irregular teeth, and a left eye that twitches, snapping up and down like a window shade. Elmer Cowley's father has a large wen on his scrawny neck; he still wears his wedding coat which is brown with age and covered with grease spots. Elmer too is grotesque in appearance: extraordinarily tall, he has pale blond almost white hair, eyebrows, and beard, teeth that protrude, and eyes that are the colorless blue of marbles. Characteristically many of the physical portraits focus on hands. The hands of Tom Willy, the saloon keeper, are streaked with a flaming red birthmark, as if the hands had been dipped in blood that dried and faded. Tom Foster's grandmother has hands all twisted out of shape from hard work. When she holds a mop or broom handle they look like "the dried stems of an old creeping vine clinging to a tree" (p. 211). There are two half-wits in Winesburg as well: Turk Smollet, the old wood-chopper, who talks and laughs to himself as he passes regularly through the village, and Mook, the farm hand, who holds long involved conversations with the animals. Perhaps it is not accidental that George Willard thinks of the Middle Ages one night when he is walking through the town, and that the first word that comes to his lips when he looks up at the sky is "Death" (p. 184).

In some of the stories George Willard does not appear except of course as implied narrator; the characters nevertheless are pictured as breaking into a run or dance at peak moments of frustration or loneliness. Jesse Bentley in **"Godliness,"** who has a vision of being a Biblical patriarch, runs through the night imploring God to send him a son; years later when he takes his grandson to sacrifice a lamb, hoping God will send him a visible sign of His blessing, the scene ends with the flight of the grandson from Winesburg. In **"Adventure"** Alice Hindman, who has been waiting for years for the return of her lover, one night runs out naked onto the lawn in the rain. In the story of the two farm hands, entitled **"The Untold Lie,"** the moment of truth brings Ray Pearson to run across the field to save his friend, Hal Winters, from marriage.[16] Repeatedly the most vivid images in the book are those of characters in grotesque or violent motion: Louise Bentley, the estranged daughter of the Biblical patriarch, driving her horse and carriage at breakneck speed through the streets of Winesburg; Jesse Bentley's drunken brothers driving along the road and shouting at the stars; Enoch Robinson described as "an obscure, jerky little figure bobbing up and down the streets when the sun was going down" (p. 173); Hal Winters' father, Windpeter Winters, drunk and driving his team along the railroad tracks directly into the path of an onrushing locomotive. Such images seem to have coalesced to form a grotesque procession in the writer's memory.

The procession becomes a Dance of Death when the writer comes to recognize his own mortality. The death of his mother awakens George Willard to both the brevity and the loneliness of human exisence. Elizabeth Willard, perhaps more than any of the other characters, seeks some kind of release from her perpetual loneliness. As a young woman she had been "stage-struck" and, wearing loud clothes, paraded the streets with traveling men from her father's hotel. Like the other grotesques her desire to escape loneliness is expressed in movement. Once she startled the townspeople by wearing men's clothes and riding a bicycle down the main street. After she married and still found no communion with another human being, she drove her horse and buggy at a terrible speed through the country until she met with an accident. (The image of a woman hurt in an accident or disfigured in some way recurs several times to the eyes of the artist figures in the book: one of Enoch Robinson's paintings depicts a woman who has been thrown from a horse and has been hurt [p. 170], while the old writer in the introduction is crying over "a woman all drawn out of shape" [p. 23].) Eventually when her long illness comes we are told that Elizabeth went along the road seeking for death: "She personified the figure of death and made him now a strong black-haired youth running over hills, now a stern quiet man marked and scarred by the business of living" (p. 228). As a young woman she had taken several lovers before she married; now her lover is Death.

"Sophistication," the penultimate chapter, is shaped around George's growing awareness of life as a procession or dance toward death. In the background is the Winesburg County Fair: people are moving up and down the streets and fiddlers sweat "to keep the feet of youth flying over a dance floor." But in spite of the crowds George Willard feels lonely; he wants someone to understand the feeling that has possessed him since his mother's death. Significantly we are told that "memories awoke in him" and that he is becoming conscious of life's limitations. The narrator, reflecting on youth, generalizes: "There is a time in the life of every boy when he for the first time takes the backward view of life. . . . If he be an imaginative boy a door is torn open and for the first time he looks out upon the world, seeing, as though they marched in procession before him, the countless figures of men who before his time have come out of nothingness into the world, lived their lives and again disappeared into nothingness" (p. 234). At this point George sees his own place "in the long march of humanity. Already he hears death calling" (pp. 234-235). And in the last chapter he joins the procession when he leaves on the train, and Winesburg becomes a "background on which to paint the dreams of his manhood."

III

Twenty years after the Winesburg stories were written, Sherwood Anderson created a drama out of his famous collection of stories. *Winesburg, Ohio: A Play*[17] focuses more squarely on the figure of George Willard and the events, particularly the death of his mother, that precipitate his growth into manhood and nurture his desire to become a writer. The death theme running through the stories also stands out more boldly in the play. Nine scenes comprise the play and the first scene is set, like a Spoon River poem, in the Winesburg cemetery on the day of Windpeter Winters's funeral. The Winesburg people are seen formed in a procession and their conversation inevitably turns to the macabre. The young people, by contrast, create a dance of life; despite the sobriety of the occasion, they tease and jostle one another as the irrespressible life instinct demands expression. One of the sub-plots in the play involves Belle Carpenter, who has become pregnant and who goes to Doctor Reefy in Scene two to ask for an abortion. Reefy counsels against this request and says to Belle "there are always two roads—the road of life and the road of death" (p. 30). This image describes the two main narrative threads in the play: in the foreground is George's involvement with three different women in Winesburg and his sexual awakening, while in the background Elizabeth Willard makes elaborate preparations to die. Her death, as in the stories, precipitates George's departure from Winesburg, but the road of life he sets out on is also the road of death, for Elizabeth Willard, in prayer, has made her promise to come back from the dead if she sees her son becoming "a meaningless, drab figure." The fulfillment of that prayer eventually places George on the road back to Winesburg.

In his later books as well Sherwood Anderson continued to use the Dance of Death motif as a measure of life's brevity and misdirection. When Red Oliver, the principal character in the novel *Beyond Desire,* is about to be killed for his peripheral involvement in a strike, a dancing death figure appears in the form of a limping stationer who exhorts the soldiers to shoot the communist leaders of the strike.

> The little stationer of Birchfield, the man with the bad feet had followed the soldiers to the bridge. He had come limping along the road. Red Oliver saw him. He was dancing in the road beyond the soldiers. He was excited, filled with hatred. He danced in the road, throwing his arms above his head. He clenched his fists. "Shoot. Shoot. Shoot. Shoot the son-of-a-bitch." The road sloped down sharply to the bridge. Red Oliver could see the little figure above the heads of the soldiers. It seemed dancing in the air over their heads.[18]

Just before the fatal shot is fired we are told that Red "saw the absurd little stationer dancing in the road beyond the soldier" and that he asked himself whether the little man "represented something" (p. 355). Anderson seems to be asking the reader at this point to give the figure thoughtful consideration. The image is reminiscent of such Winesburg figures as Elmer Cowley and Wing Biddlebaum who claw at the air with their hands and dance about in a hopeless effort to communicate with other people. The stationer in *Beyond Desire* is an emblem of countless repressed twentieth-century men who find an outlet for their frustrations in violent mob action.

Anderson himself used the term "dance of death" when he was writing his *Memoirs.* In that posthumous volume he registered his horror at the spectacle of World War II in an entry entitled "The Dance Is On."[19] He begins, "It's a crazy dance of death now" referring to the war, but he quickly extends the image to include all the mechanical, dehumanizing forces of the modern industrial world. Anderson did not believe that modern industry was in itself negative. In *Beyond Desire* and his last novel, *Kit Brandon,* he describes the cotton mills as dancing with life, and in this entry from the *Memoirs* he points to a cloth mill and says "here is a gay dance, a purposeful dance. See the many colored cloth rolling out of the flying machines in the cloth mills." But he also saw a "monster" latent in the industrial process, an uncontrollable appetite for production and profit without reference to the needs of the human community. The monster's consuming, destructive power is imaged by Anderson in a sequence titled "Loom Dance" in *Perhaps Women* where a group of factory girls working at the loom are stricken with choreomania; they become mindless robots of production unable to stop their movements. The question Anderson puts in his *Memoirs* is "Can the dance be made, not a dance of death, but of joy and new life?" He equates the dance of life with man's ability to reach out and communicate with his fellow man: "Can men come out of their selves to others?" Although Anderson despairs at the world around him, he believes that "men never intended it to be the dance of death," rather "dreamed of making it a great new dance of life." Similarly Anderson in his epitaph insisted that "Life not Death is the great adventure."

But the qustion still to be asked is what is gained by viewing ***Winesburg, Ohio*** in the light of the recurrent death imagery in Anderson's writing. Most obviously it directs us to something dark and pessimistic in the book that recent critics, unlike the early reviewers, have either ignored or explained away.[20] In a period of rapid economic growth and expansion, Anderson was drawing attention to the tragedy of those people, like his own parents, who did not succeed, and who were alienated from each other by economic failure and by the repressive American Puritan ethic. Seeing the lives of such people as a form of living death underscores the social tragedy that the book presents, and also suggests a continuity between Anderson's early writing and those later books and stories such as *Many Marriages* and **"Out of Nowhere into Nothing"** where he envisions America as a land of the dead. As a Dance of Death ***Winesburg, Ohio*** functions as social satire to warn the living of what is happening to their lives.

The Dance of Death idea is most closely associated with the mother figure and directs us to a personal tragedy implicit in the book—the narrator's sense of filial guilt. While she lived, Elizabeth Willard and her son seldom spoke to each other; before her death Elizabeth prayed that her son would some day "express something" for them both. But the artist's central insight in the book is that all truth is relative to the individual, so that he cannot really express anything for his characters—he can only hint at their secret, repressed lives. Ironically, in attempting to give dignity to the lives of his people, the narrator has made them grotesques, and like the old writer in the introduction must be left to whimper like a small dog at the "woman drawn all out of shape" (p. 23). At best the narrator, like the author of the *Spoon River Anthology,* has erected out of love a series of tombstones for the people he once knew. The Dance of Death perspective functions then as a framework around the book reminding us that these characters are now gone, and that they were never released from the agony of their loneliness while they lived. This tragic personal emotion is described by the narrator in **"Sophistication"** when he says: "One shudders at the thought of the meaninglessness of life while at the same instance, and if the people of his town are his people, one loves life so intensely that tears come into the eyes" (p. 241).

The narrator's sympathy and love for his people makes more poignant the failure of art to expiate his filial guilt. Anderson had dedicated the book as an expression of love to his mother; we cannot help feeling that it has come too late. But this of course does not mean that ***Winesburg, Ohio*** fails as a work of art. On the contrary, seeing the book as a Dance of Death further testifies to its richness of pattern and form. The medieval Dance of Death was a highly ritualized art and it is that quality of stylized repetition which is most striking formally in Anderson's book. To see ***Winesburg, Ohio*** as a Dance of Death is not only to underscore rightly its essentially tragic nature, but also to recognize its considerable artistry.

Notes

1. This and subsequent page references to *Winesburg, Ohio* are to the "Compass Book" edition (New York, 1960).
2. For a comprehensive treatment of the historical origins of the Dance of Death see James M. Clark, *The Dance of Death in the Middle Ages and the Renaissance* (Glasgow, 1950).
3. *A Story-Teller's Story* (New York, 1924), p. 127.
4. *Tar: A Midwest Childhood* (New York, 1930) p. 346. All references are to the same text.
5. *Poor White* in *The Portable Sherwood Anderson,* ed. Horace Gregory (New York, 1949), p. 162.
6. *Many Marriages* (New York, 1923), p. 217.
7. *The Triumph of the Egg* (New York, 1921). All references are to this text.
8. *Dark Laughter* (New York, 1925), p. 68. All references are to this text.
9. *Sherwood Anderson's Notebooks* (New York, 1926), p. 22.
10. See William A. Sutton, *The Road to Winesburg* (Metuchen, N.J., 1972), pp. 446-447.
11. See *Sherwood Anderson's Memoirs: A Critical Edition,* edited by Ray Lewis White (Chapel Hill, 1969), pp. 524-526.
12. See William L. Phillip's article "How Sherwood Anderson Wrote *Winesburg, Ohio*" in *The Achievement of Sherwood Anderson: Essays in Criticism,* ed. Ray Lewis White (Chapel Hill, 1966), pp. 71-72.
13. See Sutton, pp. 299-300. Anderson's second wife, Tennessee Mitchell, had been the poet's mistress and this may have prompted Anderson's dislike of the book. But Anderson seems to have encouraged the myth that his stories were appearing in print before Masters's poems. This is demonstrably untrue and suggests Anderson was concerned about the question of originality.
14. Typically Anderson gave two different accounts about the source of his Winesburg characters. At one point in his memoirs he says that the tales came "out of some memory or impression got from boyhood in a small town," but only a couple of pages further he claims that the characters were portraits done of his fellow boarders in a cheap Chicago rooming house on Cass Street. See *Sherwood Anderson's Memoirs: A Critical Edition,* pp. 346-348. Probably both accounts are true, but certainly figures like the mother, Doctor Reefy and the old carpenter are from Clyde, Ohio. See also William L. Phillips, "How Sherwood Anderson Wrote *Winesburg, Ohio,*" pp. 69-74.
15. See *Tar: A Midwest Childhood,* pp. 71, 85.
16. Anderson told his son in a letter that "The Untold Lie" was inspired by the memory of sitting on a train once and seeing a man run across a field. *Letters of Sherwood Anderson,* selected and edited with an introduction and notes by Howard Mumford Jones and Walter B. Rideout (Boston, 1953), p. 357.
17. *Plays: Winesburg and Others* (New York, 1937). All references are to this text.
18. *Beyond Desire* (New York, 1961), p. 354. All references are to this text.
19. "The Dance Is On," *Sherwood Anderson's Memoirs: A Critical Edition,* pp. 552-553.
20. For example, in his introduction to the 1960 "Compass Book" edition Malcolm Cowley concludes that "*Winesburg, Ohio* is far from the pessimistic or destructive or morbidly sexual work it was once attacked for being. Instead it is a work of love, an attempt to break down the walls that divide one person from another, and also in its own fashion, a celebration of small-town life in the lost days of good will and innocence." And in his article "*Winesburg, Ohio*: Art and Isolation," *Modern Fiction Studies,* VI (Summer, 1960), 106-114, Edwin Fussell sees the loneliness and frustration of the characters being dissolved by the future art of George Willard, who will give these people a voice.

John O'Neill (essay date February 1977)

SOURCE: O'Neill, John. "Anderson Writ Large: 'Godliness' in *Winesburg, Ohio.*" *Twentieth-Century Literature* 23, no. 1 (February 1977): 67-83.

[*In the following essay, O'Neill considers "Godliness" within the context of the other tales in* Winesburg, Ohio, *maintaining that the story illustrates and integrates key thematic and stylistic elements of the collection.*]

In language and form, Sherwood Anderson's **"Godliness"** is simpler, less innovative than most of the other stories in ***Winesburg, Ohio.*** Perhaps this explains why it has received less attention from the critics.[1] We may consult stories like **"Hands"** and **"Paper Pills"** for insight into the experimental features of Anderson's work, aspects which make him an important figure in the development of the American short story and in the emergence of a twentieth century prose style. But when we come to assess all of Anderson's work, not just that which was innovative, it becomes equally important to understand precisely what is taking place in a story like **"Godliness,"** for here the innovative and the traditional, in language and fictional technique, are pretty thoroughly fused, as indeed they were, sometimes bewilderingly so, in Anderson's career.

"Godliness" serves an important integrative function in ***Winesburg.*** Partly because of the story's length and traditional narrative technique, it reveals in a more thorough and straightforward way the nature of the fanatical, the obsessive and the lonely, as well as other key psychological forces at work throughout the book. Jesse's "fanaticism" is provided with a history, and although the narrator offers us no clinical cause for his condition (since as we shall see, none could exist) that condition has at least fairly well defined stages, a period of evolution arranged for us as a story. In fact, Jesse's fanaticism, like the bitter loneliness of his daughter, and the terror of his grandson, exists as part of a history; in the other stories intense emotion exists more in the form of brilliantly evocative gestures, or objects symbolically freighted with pain or bewilderment. The method of **"Godliness,"** like the method of the biblical stories Anderson alludes to, is that of the exemplary tale, fiction's miniature epic; on the other hand, the method of such stories as **"Hands"** and **"Paper Pills"** is that of revelation, Andersonian epiphany, although not so bare of conventional narrative and description as the tales of James Joyce's *Dubliners.*[2]

The tone of **"Godliness"** further helps to integrate the ***Winesburg*** tales. The narrator's voice bespeaks Anderson's characteristic attitude throughout: the impressive and finely controlled combination of pity for his people and bewildered, sometimes horrified acknowledgment of the energy encased in their stunted dreams and nightmares. Anderson could, after all, sustain this highly charged, mixed tone, a fact which ought to be remembered when we discuss Faulkner's more spectacular achievement of the same kind in *As I Lay Dying* and his notable failures such as *Intruder in the Dust.* With pity and recognition Anderson creates Jesse Bentley, Louise and David Hardy, and his tone is here similar to, if more emphatic than, that with which he draws Dr. Reefy or Elizabeth Willard. So that in this respect, too, **"Godliness"** integrates by underlining and simplifying for us an element of crucial importance in most of ***Winesburg.***

The characters in **"Godliness"** focus and reinforce our overall impressions of ***Winesburg,*** for each is seen to be an amplified and dramatically simplified version of the essential types to which Anderson returns over and over again in ***Winesburg*** and indeed in the best of his stories outside this collection. The essential relations among the characters here are paradigmatic and hence illustrative and integrative versions of the relations among characters in the other stories.

Jesse Bentley is a "fanatic" who wants God to praise and approve of him. Further, Jesse wants God to guarantee that his craftily acquired wealth will not be sacked by "Philistine" farmers of Northern Ohio. He is a strong man with a warped and arrogant vision to which he, like the Reverend Curtis Hartman and Dr. Parcival, has yoked God, not entirely without a certain weirdly adolescent desire for paternal acceptance from this same God.

Jesse's daughter Louise plays out in the story the role so often given to Anderson's women, from Elizabeth Willard to the old woman of **"Death in the Woods"**: as a young woman Louise wants acceptance, love, and the chance to exploit the fact that she is intelligent (just as Elizabeth wishes to profit from her audacity and even old woman Grimes wants to exploit her one talent, feeding). Hope is denied; desperately the woman, here Louise, offers sex in the hope that what the man wants so much may satisfy her desire for love, survival, or glory. Always, and most explicitly in the case of Louise Hardy, sex is only sex, remarkably ineffective as an instrument, a means, or a symbol. Indeed, Anderson's stories, insofar as they deal with women, are almost always *about* sex—here his critics were correct—but sex treated in anything but a sensational or titillating way. His subject was the failure of sex as instrument, as symbol, as a means of exchange powerful enough to evoke something more than sensation. His women, even more than male adolescents like the hero of **"I Want to Know Why,"** believe with disastrous purity of intent in the symbolical, the instrumental power of sex.

David Hardy, the third major character, plays out, in intense and simplified terms, the experience rendered more subtly through George Willard in the other stories. Thus David, no less than Louise and Jesse, is exploited by Anderson to amplify one of the book's essential roles. (Throughout ***Winesburg*** one of Anderson's key strategies is such amplification, the sudden absurd or pathetic enlarging of a gesture, a feeling, even an object or character which, in ordinary perspective, would be normal, banal. Hence, **"Godliness"** stands in relation to the other ***Winesburg*** tales as Enoch Robinson's room, Elizabeth Willard's theatrical makeup, and Dr. Parcival's "Let peace brood over this carcass" stand in relation to other details in these stories.) David is first of all of tremendous importance to Jesse. He is the instrument by which security and peace and vindication are to be achieved. The various "grotesques" in the other stories attach a similar if usually unmentioned significance upon George Willard. They regard him as the vehicle by which a message or a feeling or a philosophy is going to get communicated—or at least expressed.[3]

So David Hardy undergoes a version of the experience of George Willard, trying both to comprehend and to protect himself from each of the grotesques. In the case of the young reporter, though, the process of initiation provoked by these stark and cryptic messages is gradual and cumulative, while the boy David Hardy is plunged directly into his grandfather's delusions. What is suggested in George Willard's case is terribly evident in David's: while the grotesques themselves awaken sympathy, their delusions threaten injury. David's terror at the sight of his grandfather approaching with a knife in hand is an enlarged and hence illustrative version of the dismay and sometimes real fear with which George Willard received the sometimes overtly menacing gestures of the grotesques.

But perhaps the most immediately important contribution made by **"Godliness"** to our sense of the scope and integrity of ***Winesburg, Ohio*** is its treatment of social and economic themes, and its fusion of sociological and psychological realities in the town. In the story **"Godliness"** Anderson is at pains to show us the historical antecedents and sociological implications of his action, as well as the points at which the acts of the grotesque or fanatic intersect with events of the region, or with even larger movements affecting the whole country. In short, a proper understanding of **"Godliness"** calls into question the critical commonplace that Anderson was relatively unconcerned with concrete social and economic aspects of Winesburg.[4]

The critics have been right, I think, to stress the fundamentally non-realistic quality of ***Winesburg.*** But what we have not yet sufficiently noticed is the degree to which **"Godliness"** ushers into the whole work certain quite specific sociological details, indeed a whole social dimension. This doesn't transform the work into realism, but rather suggests the way in which, in Anderson's view of the American midwest, social and psychological phenomena interacted. We must deal with the data of both the psychological and the social life, data presented to us not in the orderly or clinical fashion of the realistic or naturalistic novel, but rather as disparate elements of a dream or an ideal that has come unstuck in Ohio, and perhaps in all the country, around the turn of the century.

Originally, in this territory, there had been only the land, and the brute need for strength and perseverance to clear it. (Anderson knows the past of an agricultural community too well to limit himself to idyllic visions of a literary pastoral—here there are no green shores ever receding.) But there had been, at this point in Winesburg's past, a kind of convergence between primitive conditions of the land and the range of simple, intense response in the farmers who fought with it:

> On Saturday afternoons they hitched a team of horses to a three-seated wagon and went off to town . . . It was difficult for them to talk and so they for the most part kept silent. When they had bought meat, flour, sugar, and salt, they went into one of the Winesburg saloons and drank beer. Under the influence of drink the naturally strong lusts of their natures, kept suppressed by the heroic labor of breaking up new ground, were released. A kind of crude and animal like poetic fervor took possession of them. On the road home they stood up on the wagon seats and shouted at the stars.
>
> (p. 65)[5]

The atmosphere, the conditions of the land, the confluence of primitive in land and man, the maintenance of a ritual and the suggestion of a submerged poetry of religious impulse occasionally breaking through the surface of routine life—these are all elements characteristic of the society and the psychology of the region. Anderson's farmers are made to move with a certain biblical solemnity, even when their actions are violent or destructive. For example, the crimes of the Bentley men are biblical in association, like the parricide averted in the following passage, a passage in which Anderson contrives diction and sentence structure to evoke scriptural accounts of restless, violent tribes. The motif of parricide will run throughout **"Godliness"** and dominate its conclusion:

> Once Enoch Bentley, the older one of the boys, struck his father, old Tom Bentley with the butt of a teamster's whip, and the old man seemed likely to die. For days Enoch lay hid in the straw in the loft of the stable ready to flee if the result of his momentary passion turned out to be murder. He was kept alive with food brought by his mother, who also kept him informed of the injured man's condition.
>
> (p. 65)

What interrupts this cycle—brute work interspersed with outbursts of poetic fervor or murderous rage—is a superior and more mechanical type of violence, that of the Civil War. And although Anderson does not often deal directly with his town's memory of the war (a memory in any case too intimately associated for Anderson with the anecdotal irresponsibility of his father), he does occasionally refer to it in terms which suggest the mocking impersonality of the conflict. The land and the war: two conflicts which in Winesburg establish a context for the random, mysterious, absurdly mechanical violence of the grotesques. Note how Anderson's language, with its strategy of naive, even formulaic narration ("sharp turn to the fortunes of" and the chronicle of names) tends to underline the massiveness with which the war intruded: "The Civil War brought a sharp turn to the fortunes of the Bentleys and was responsible for the rise of the youngest son, Jesse. Enoch, Edward, Harry, and Will Bentley all enlisted and before the long war ended they were all killed." (pp. 65-66)

Of all the sons of Tom Bentley only Jesse survives, hidden away from the war in a college where he has been sent to train himself for the Presbyterian ministry. He is small, delicate in his movements and appearance, not at all the kind of young man who, according to the townspeople, would be capable of farming.

> By the standards of his day Jesse did not look like a man at all. He was small and very slender and womanish of body and, true to the traditions of young ministers, wore a long black coat and a narrow black string tie. The neighbors were amused when they saw him, after the years away, and they were even more amused when they saw the woman he had married in the city.
>
> (pp. 66-67)

The town mocked Jesse, its derision being a sign of resistance to change, the community's demand that the familiar be endlessly renewed, and the strange rejected. Jesse's size is a version of Wing Biddlebaum's gentleness, or the furious epithets of Elmer Cowley, or the jangled and surly gestures of any number of women, who, prowling deserted hotel corridors, driving wagons at break-neck speed, or simply hiding, are reputed to drink or drug themselves. But Jesse's dandyism is also his ticket of release from the torpid rounds of physical work—as also the various signs of frenzy and hysteria in the town are, potentially at least, the forewarnings of rebellion against the inertia that constitutes Winesburg's sense of the proper order of things. Jesse is small, delicate, his spirit quickened and animated by a vision similar in intensity, if not in scope or strength, to that which drives Faulkner's Thomas Sutpen to wrestle his "hundred" out of the Mississippi wilderness.

The common sense of the village, its main protective device and the principal source of its inertia, causes the townspeople to smile at the thought of the dandified, preacherfied young man trying to drive a straight plow line through a Northern Ohio field. Winesburg's common sense misses the native shrewdness of the man, which, in the absence of physical strength, he will have to depend on. And although religion is still very much alive in the country, Winesburg's believers do not foresee how Jesse's faith will prick him to drain land and increase crops. In this respect also, the young man represents for us, but in intense or exaggerated form, a sociological fact of key importance. The harshness of life in the middle west just after the Civil War revived and kept alive an unlovely creed, a Calvinism long since judged too unyielding and graceless for the new commercial sections of Boston, but grimly satisfying for those who found the earth as uncompromising as the Hebrews' God. But in his faith, as in his shrewdness as a farmer, Jesse outdistances his neighbors. While his neighbors merely "believed in God and in God's power to control their lives," Jesse knows that God has singled him out to rule, like Saul, and has contracted to furnish his servant Jesse with protection against the neighbor Philistines. His grandson is to shield Jesse, as David shielded Saul.

And if it can be said that in this era "the figure of God was big in the hearts of men," the hero of **"Godliness"** takes it for granted that Jesse Bentley is big in the heart of God, and that God will provide physical evidence of this fact. The sections in **"Godliness"** in which Anderson renders the "fanaticism" of his hero have something of the simplicity and the dignity of the Old Testament. Such passages establish for us the social importance of a particular kind of Calvinism and reveal how stark conditions of life could and did make a cogent metaphor out of a dying creed. Anderson's language urges us to feel how the exalted sense of God's favor could naturally flow into the sense that possession was right and that the godly man had a duty to dominate his neighbors.

> The Bentley farm was situated in a tiny valley watered by Wine Creek, and Jesse walked along the banks of the stream to the end of his own land and on through the fields of his neighbors. As he walked the valley broadened and then narrowed again. Great open stretches of field and wood lay before him. The moon came out from behind clouds, and, climbing a low hill, he sat down to think.
>
> Jesse thought that as the true servant of God the entire stretch of country through which he had walked should have come into his possession. . . . Before him in the moonlight the tiny stream ran down over stones, and he began to think of the men of old times who like himself had owned flocks and lands.
>
> (p. 72)

What is particularly impressive about the characterization of Jesse is that Anderson has managed to bring alive and set into motion that peculiar fusion of native ruthlessness and visionary exaltation that did in fact mark the new race of powerful men emerging in the country after the Civil War. Whereas the rigor and spiritual poverty of life on this land reduced most men to dumb submission, occasionally interrupted by lyric flights of drunkenness and an "animal like poetic fervor," Jesse elevates harshness and struggle to an intensity and significance offered him by the Old Testament. Shrewder than his fellow farmers, more aggressive and with more to lose in case of defeat, he seeks allies, signs of favor, tangible proof of approval and support from God the commanding general of the Righteous. Jesse is a fanatic to be sure, but neither trivial nor a fool. His story is that of power and wealth in a primitive country, which availed itself of religion as a weapon in an immediate and very pressing economic struggle.

Of course, as a number of critics have pointed out, in actual practice American Calvinism tended to identify spiritual victory with material success. The remarkable achievement of Anderson's story is not just that it illustrates this tendency, but that, by heightening and intensification, it manifests the emotional dynamic behind the process. The process was one by which God's terrible swift sword could be unleashed in battle against Philistine host disguised as neighbor farmers, or Confederate politicians. **"Godliness"** dramatizes not just the fusion of Calvinism and capitalism but the emotional and moral processes by which, in the minds of certain Americans of the period, the Old Testament became a living metaphor for the life they lived on the land.

Jesse Bentley has, of course, considerably outdistanced Melville's Captain Bildad or even Faulkner's McEachern. For him, the story provided by the scripture has ceased to be metaphor and has become simple fact, interchangeable except for accidentals with the facts of his own life. In Anderson's marvelously calm and balanced style:

> While he worked night and day to make his farms more productive and to extend his holdings of land, he regretted that he could not use his own restless energy in the building of temples, the slaying of unbelievers and in general in the work of glorifying God's name on earth.
>
> (p. 80)

And as the passage continues, Anderson's style calmly, imperturbably transmits Jesse back once again to the realm of the energetic and resourceful American business-man farmer. What such remarkable but oddly plausible transitions reflect is what the whole story reflects: the interpenetration of the ordinary with bizarre, intense modes of experience, the latter figured for us in **"Godliness"** by Jesse's willed, "fanatical" re-creation from the Old Testament. This is, as James Schevill points out, Anderson's great theme.[6] Here is the transition effected by Anderson's style:

> That is what Jesse hungered for and then also he hungered for something else. He had grown into maturity in America in the years after the Civil War and he, like all men of his time, had been touched by the deep influences that were at work in the country during those years when modern industrialism was being born. He began to buy machines that would permit him to do the work of the farms while employing fewer men and he sometimes thought that if he were a younger man he would give up farming altogether and start a factory in Winesburg for the making of machinery.
>
> (pp. 80-81)

Jesse does eventually invent a machine "for the making of fence out of wire." Anyone who finds it incredible that such inventive energy has been generated *faute de mieux*, that is, in the absence of temples to build or unbelievers to slay, will not have gauged the intense emotions which are the main subject of ***Winesburg.*** Elizabeth Willard at her dressing table; Wash Williams in his filth at the telegraph office; Doctor Parcival, the village Nietzsche; the Reverend Curtis Hartman who, like Jesse, demands and gets a heavenly sign: these key figures of Winesburg, like Jesse Bentley, busy themselves with the ordinary implements of life in nineteenth-century Northern Ohio, while waiting for the divine fire that is sure to come eventually. They invent wire-making machines until they shall be called upon to build temples, or, in Elizabeth's case, to kill her husband or, in Wash Williams' case, to rain vengeance on all women or, in that of Dr. Parcival, to be crucified. The energy for their achievements—and let us recall that by no means all of the grotesques in ***Winesburg*** are failures—comes from reservoirs of psychic energy which, directly released, can and does make them act like madmen. Jesse Bentley stumbles towards his grandson, knife in hand. Curtis Hartman bursts into the office of the village newspaper to announce God's visitation in a woman's body. The mad and the obsessive spill over into the sane, and what is revealed once again to the reader is the frightening absence of what might be called the middle ground of emotional experience, some organic functioning of shared emotions by which the most intensely energetic members of Winesburg might be saved from madness—giving up visions of the lord in an Ohio field or in Elizabeth Willard's hotel room, or in the Reverend Hartman's study.

"Godliness" dramatizes for us in a particularly vivid fashion this fusion of the ordinary and the deranged which is the chief subject of ***Winesburg.*** Further, Anderson's use of sociological and economic details of post Civil War Northern Ohio anchors the story within a specific social context. Or perhaps a better way of putting the case would be to say that realistic social and economic details are introduced into **"Godliness"** and the other stories to be charged and intensified by the energy typified by Jesse Bentley's history. The art of ***Winesburg*** consists in this: on the one hand, we are given enough sociological detail to *recognize* a character, that is, accord him or her a specific social identity, (farmer inventor, Presbyterian disciple of progress, etc.); nevertheless, we are made to feel that no society exists which could channel, transform, or even neutralize the brilliantly erratic energies of some of Winesburg's citizens. Were there such a society available, its religion would give Jesse temples to build rather than wire fence machines to invent; it would "educate" Kate Swift and Wing Biddlebaum in a union of teacher and student; Drs. Reefy and Parcival would ponder the meaning of life and Elizabeth Willard would protect her child in circumstances and in a social context which accorded some meaning or chance of success to their gestures. In ***Winesburg*** the grotesques reveal themselves supremely eager to live, to mother, philosophise, teach, worship, love. They make these gestures intensely, with great determination, but absurdly, in a kind of vacuum. Elizabeth prepares herself to mother in front of her mirror as she applies make-up for the murder of her husband; Dr. Reefy prescribes paper pills for the universal cure; Jesse Bentley and Curtis Hartman play proud Saul and lustful King David.

In Europe, wealth, land and steadily accumulated power over the land might have focused and satisfied Jesse Bentley's hunger. In Winesburg, social power, agricultural wealth, shrewdness in draining the land—these have absolutely no relevance except as poor ciphers in lieu of real gestures of energy, ambition, power: the sword, temples, a sign from God to his servant Jesse. (Curtis Hartman senses obscurely that if he lusts hard enough he will drive through and dissolve the mere body of a woman and find, as he does find, God). Dr. Parcival is an expert in what might be called the semiology of failure. In a European village he would be merely the once respectable, now sodden drunk with some mysterious disgrace in his past. But in Winesburg Dr. Parcival avails himself of the intricate social signs of failure in his own dress rehearsal for the Armageddon which he confidently anticipates, the universal crucifixion soon to occur.

One final example of Anderson's creation of the materials of "society" which do not appear to function at all, until animated by the anarchic energy of one of his principals: Louise Bentley distinguishes herself in school, and Anderson makes clear to us that in Winesburg in the 1880's a bright young woman with luck and a well-to-do father could hope to escape the limits of the role imposed on women by mid-western farm life. But Louise masters her lessons only to render service to the two girls in whose house she lives, in a dumb gesture of appeal to them for affection and acceptance. The father of the two girls, Mr. Hardy, intervenes at this point out of dissatisfaction with the dullness of his own daughters, praises Louise for her devotion to learning, and of course causes his own two daughters to despise Louise. She abandons all hope of friendship with the two Hardy sisters, but, as Anderson wryly indicates to the reader, does not give up her efforts to educate herself in the means of being loved. Finding herself in the parlor one evening when Mary Hardy is with "her young man," Louise hides in the closet while "without words Mary Hardy, with the aid of the man who had come to spend the evening with her, brought to the country girl a knowledge of men and women." (p. 93) She then puts this knowledge to use in taking "John Hardy to be her lover," a gesture which has little to do with John Hardy, even less to do with sexual desire, but everything to do with the need for affection that made Louise Bentley such a paragon in Math and American History.

The episode is a minor one in the story, but indicative of the peculiar and ironic way in which Anderson exploits social data. Rather than saying that society does not exist in Winesburg or that no such village ever existed, we ought to stress the manner in which social institutions in Winesburg have first of all only a theoretic existence—as in, for example, the formulas of Mr. Hardy—and are then animated, brought to life by the furious energy of the character whom these institutions will later crush. Education in Winesburg begins because Louise Bentley wants to be loved. Lands are drained, farms are combined, the poor and the unlucky must vacate—all because Jesse burns to build temples and smite his God's enemies. Religion begins when the empty gaze of the boy in the stained glass window (the Rev. Curtis Hartman before the revelation) falls upon Kate Swift's body.

Besides presenting us with paradigms of Winesburg and establishing the significance of social and economic data in the book, **"Godliness"** confronts the reader with character types and motifs which clearly had an enormous significance for Sherwood Anderson. Such types were for him powerhouses of feeling and creative energy. They represent no doubt fixed points in his own psychological development, but since the main lines of such development are clear enough to the attentive reader of Anderson's *Memoirs, Letters,* and the two fine studies by Howe and Schevill, I'll merely suggest the *kind* of emotional resonance which the characters in **"Godliness"** probably had for Anderson. In doing so, one links these characters with other major figures who exercised upon their creator a similar attraction. Anderson's preoccupation with such types as Jesse, David and Louise Hardy reveals at once the extraordinary generosity and sympathy with which he regarded life around him but also his tendency to close off for himself possible routes of further development as an artist.

Jesse Bentley apparently had great emblematic significance for Anderson. The character fused elements of strength, power and arrogant self-possession with a desperate need for approval and reassurance. His power is particularly manifest in his relations with his daughter Louise and with his grandson David. The first he rejects totally and absolutely, suffering no hesitation or compunction, only a brief embarrassment when Louise refers to the way in which she has been dismissed. Toward the grandson also the old man's power is absolute, and, apart from the Saul-David, the Jesse-David, and the David-Goliath Biblical parallels which the story makes explicit, the denouement suggests Abraham's willingness to sacrifice Isaac, should this be demanded. But the old man would not be capable of inspiring terror in the boy, would not have been allowed to come close enough to do so, had he not earlier introduced David into a world in which every element welcomes and comforts the boy. Hence the scene in the story, rendered from David's point of view, in which the boy wakes up on his grandfather's farm, one of the two or three passages of pastoral romanticism which mark the Winesburg stories and of course other well-known stories such as **"I Want to Know Why"** and **"The Man Who Became a Woman."** Such passages evoke a tone which, in English fiction, is found most prominently in George Eliot and D. H. Lawrence.

> At night when he went to bed after a long day of adventures in the stables, in the fields, or driving about from farm to farm with his grandfather, he wanted to embrace everyone in the house . . . There in the country all sounds were pleasant sounds. When he awoke at dawn the barnyard back of the house also awoke. In the house people stirred about. Eliza Stoughton the half-witted girl was poked in the ribs by a farmhand and giggled noisily, in some distant field a cow bawled and was answered by the cattle in the stables, and one of the farm hands spoke sharply to the horse he was grooming by the stable door. David leaped out of bed and ran to the window. All of the people stirring about excited his mind, and he wondered what his mother was doing in the house in town.
>
> (pp. 82-83)

In David's mind his grandfather is sufficiently powerful to admit him to such warmth or to kill him. The reader, who enters Jesse's mind, realizes that underneath the old man's Biblical theatrics there lies a fundamentally adolescent desire to be singled out for special approval and attention. It's not so much power or wealth that Jesse wants—these he has—but rather the certitude that his Father thinks he has done a good job. Jesse is the potent male figure, capable of evoking both terror and peace, but absurdly, "grotesquely" in need of approval himself. Potency and the indiscriminate desire to be approved of are the key elements of the portrait of his father which Anderson spent all of his creative life writing.

The combination of traits turns up in any number of Anderson's male characters, in Jerry Tillford, for example, and in Tom Appleton in **"The Sad Horn Blowers."** Perhaps they appear most strikingly in the following excerpts from a passage in *The Memoirs* where Anderson muses over his contradictory feelings towards his father. He feels contempt for the man who tries so hard for a little applause, and yet great tenderness for the suddenly quiet and strong man who swims by his side in a pond.

> I'd be up in my room and father'd be down on the porch with some of his crowd. This would be on a summer night. He'd be spinning some of his tales. Then I didn't understand but now I know he never told any lies that hurt anyone. I know now that he just wanted to give people a show, make them laugh.
>
> I was up there in my room and I was awake. I was filled often with bitterness, hearing my father go on and on with his tales, and often I wished he wasn't my father. I'd even invent another man as my father.
>
> And so naked we went into the pond. He did not speak or explain. Taking my hand he led me down to the pond's edge and pulled me in. It may be that I was too frightened, too full of a feeling of strangeness to speak. Before that night my father had never seemed to pay any attention to me.
>
> "And what is he up to now?" I kept asking myself that question. It was as though the man, my father I had not wanted as father, had got suddenly some kind of power over me.
>
> I was afraid and then, right away, I wasn't afraid. We were in the pond in the darkness. It was a large pond and I did not swim very well but he had put my hand on his shoulder. Still he did not speak but struck out at once into the darkness.
>
> In me there was a feeling I had never known before that night.
>
> It was a feeling of closeness. It was something strange. It was as though there were only we two in the world. It was as though I had been jerked suddenly out of myself . . .
>
> He had become blood of my blood. I think I felt it. He the stronger swimmer and I the boy clinging to him in the darkness. We swam in silence and in silence we dressed, in our wet clothes, and went back along the road to the town and our house.[7]

This combination of paternal strength and dependence fascinated Anderson. Jesse Bentley does not tell whoppers on the back porch; he wants God's applause and approval. His strength is revealed not as he swims naked with his son in an Ohio pond, but as he stumbles, knife in hand, toward the grandson who is certain that he is to be killed. The combination of paternal qualities yields comedy and tenderness in the *Memoirs* passage, and melodrama in **"Godliness,"** but the peculiar combination remains essentially the same.

The recurrence of certain emotional motifs in Anderson's work, similar though often quite different in tone, lead us to compare the role of David Hardy with that of George Willard. In George we recognize the figure of the young man as apprentice writer. The grotesques seek him out, sense in him some sympathy, receptiveness, or power to grow in ways not dictated by Winesburg, Ohio. To the young George Willard, the grotesques deliver their secrets and their obsessions. George, perceptive, bewildered, kind, sometimes pretentious, prepares himself to play the part of the artist, which meant for Anderson mediating between "the passion for dreams" and the harsh particularity of experience. Hence the last paragraph of ***Winesburg***:

> The young man's mind was carried away by his growing passion for dreams. One looking at him would not have thought him particularly sharp. With the recollection of little things occupying his mind he closed his eyes and leaned back in the car seat. He stayed that way for a long time and when he aroused himself and

> again looked out of the car window the town of Winesburg had disappeared and his life there had become but a background on which to paint the dreams of his manhood.
>
> (p. 247)

Now consider the manner in which David Hardy leaves Winesburg:

> With a cry he turned and ran off through the woods weeping convulsively. "I don't care," he sobbed. As he ran on and on he decided suddenly that he would never go back again to the Bentley farms or to the town of Winesburg. "I have killed the man of God and now I will myself be a man and go into the world," he said stoutly as he stopped running and walked rapidly down a road that followed the windings of Wine creek as it ran through fields and forests into the west.
>
> (p. 102)

David too had been sought out by at least one of the town's obsessed, his own grandfather. He is not to record his story, but is intended to witness the old man's triumph in God's revelation. The message David is to receive will be one of supreme force and clarity. But in his urgency Jesse terrifies the boy: "I must put the blood of the lamb on the head of the boy," says the old man, and his frantic desire to communicate becomes, in the boy's mind, indistinguishable from the threat of murder.

But at this point, the reader may well recall that messages conveyed by Winesburg's grotesques to George Willard are also frequently accompanied by abrupt, wild gestures: vaguely or overtly menacing bursts of emotion as the various figures—Wing Biddlebaum, Wash Williams, Dr. Parcival, and Elmer Cowley—transfer bits and pieces of the nightmare to George Willard. At these moments George usually registers shock, amazement, incomprehension. Perhaps David Hardy, who also receives and reacts to a message from one of the dispossessed, expresses for us some of the fear experienced by the artist, ultimately by Anderson himself, as the dark and violent underside of Winesburg, which is to say, of American life, is revealed. About being a writer Anderson entertained a number of different feelings. His George Willard suggests, potentially at least, the self-conscious craftsman, the sensitive, if sometimes posturing artist: Stephen Dedaelus of Northern Ohio. David Hardy suggests the artist who has received a message from a madman, a message that is both menacing and incomprehensible.

Louise Bentley is the third character in the story to draw her force from deep feelings and partly unresolved conflicts within the author himself. She epitomizes the other women characters in Winesburg, reflecting aspects of a woman's life that most moved Anderson. She dramatizes these aspects in almost pure form, presenting in Winesburg the kind of evocative and recapitulative image that Anderson made of Mrs. Grimes in **"Death in the Woods."** Louise is rejected, ignored, or grossly misunderstood by each of the males closest to her. She retaliates, of course, by rejecting her own son, but she's also quite correct in pointing out that since he's a male he'll at least not be neglected. Like Elizabeth Willard, Kate Swift, and Louise Trunnion, she has sought some special fulfillment (obscure but intensely desired), failed to attain it, discovered that sex is at once powerful and irrelevant to her as a means, and subsided into more or less cynical observation of the male world.

Louise is not Griselda-like in her fidelity, like Alice Hindman, though she suffers from her father a more crushing abandonment. Nor is she like Belle Carpenter and Helen White, relatively uninteresting sketches of, respectively, the manipulative and the pure woman. Her essential note is that she is ambitious, intellectually and morally superior to the men around her, used and disappointed by them. As with Jesse, the character assembles for us a series of traits so frequently encountered in Anderson's work, and so carefully underlined as to suggest, pretty clearly, their emotional significance for him. Neglect and exploitation by more or less unappreciative males were experiences which Anderson guiltily associated with his own mother. The very common theme of the attempt, doomed to disappointment, to use sex as a means of acquiring some "higher," only vaguely conceived of objective in life—this sounds like the young Anderson making excuses, unwarranted as far as one can tell—for his mother's attachment to his father.

One may thus summarize the interests of Anderson's **"Godliness"** in the hope that it will begin to receive as much attention as more innovative but no more substantial stories such as **"Hands"** and **"Paper Pills." "Godliness"** employs a traditional narrative technique to heighten and intensify character types and relationships common throughout ***Winesburg.*** It therefore both illustrates and integrates key elements of the whole work. Further, the story depends for its force on our understanding the particular effect Anderson achieved by fusing psychological and sociological detail. Finally, the characters of **"Godliness"** have considerable interest for the reader as images of those feelings which most profoundly moved Anderson as a man and as a writer.

Notes

1. The best and most extensive discussion of the story is "Godliness and the American Dream in *Winesburg, Ohio,*" by Rosemary M. Laughlin, *Twentieth Century Literature,* 13 (July 1967), 97-103. Ms. Laughlin argues that "Godliness" is "integrally attached" to the other tales in *Winesburg,* and, moreover, that "it is clearly connected with several significant streams of American literary tradition." I build on Ms. Laughlin's first major

point, advancing a case for the illustrative or paradigmatic role of the story. I am more interested in Anderson's use of sociological detail and in the personal fascination with which, throughout his career, he dealt with characters here called Jesse Bentley and Louise and David Hardy. I certainly agree with Ms. Laughlin that the story deserves more attention and praise than it has received.

2. For a discussion of different types of narrative exploited by Anderson, see "Narrative Form in *Winesburg, Ohio*" by James Mellard, *PMLA,* 83 (Oct. 1968), 1304-12. Irving Howe in *Sherwood Anderson* (Stanford: Stanford Univ. Press, 1951) argues that the structure of "Godliness" is not typical of *Winesburg.*

3. On the attempts to communicate and the success and failure of such attempts, see Barry D. Bort, "*Winesburg, Ohio:* The Escape from Isolation," *Midwest Quarterly,* 11 (Summer 1970), 443-56, and Walter R. McDonald, "*Winesburg, Ohio*: Tales of Isolation," *University Review Kansas City,* 35 (March 1969), 237-400.

4. The critics have seldom been in complete agreement, however, as to the function and significance of factual detail in Anderson's work. In general we may say that whereas the book's first critics tended to stress the accuracy of Anderson's portrait of an Ohio town, later critics considered it evident that such a town *could* not exist, and that specific details had quite another function than that of promoting verisimilitude. For an example of the first position, see the review by "M.A." in the June 25, 1919, issue of *The New Republic.* Howe's chapter "The Book of the Grotesque" in *Sherwood Anderson* represents the majority opinion of today: "no such town could possibly exist."

5. All page numbers in parentheses are to *Winesburg, Ohio: Text and Criticism,* ed. John H. Ferres (New York: Viking Press, 1966).

6. James Schevill, *Sherwood Anderson: His Life and Work* (Denver: Univ. of Denver Press, 1951), pp. 93-108.

7. *Sherwood Anderson's Memoirs: A Critical Edition,* ed. Ray Lewis White (Chapel Hill: Univ. of North Carolina Press, 1969), pp. 82-84.

Martha Curry (essay date May 1980)

SOURCE: Curry, Martha. "Sherwood Anderson and James Joyce." *American Literature* 52, no. 2 (May 1980): 236-49.

[*In the following essay, Curry investigates the influence of James Joyce's* Dubliners *on* Winesburg, Ohio.]

I

James Joyce's *Dubliners* was published in London in 1914 and in New York in 1916. Sherwood Anderson's ***Winesburg, Ohio*** was published in New York in 1919. The New York editions of both books were published by the avant-garde publisher Benjamin W. Huebsch. Despite the significant differences between *Dubliners* and ***Winesburg,*** there is a remarkable coincidence in the fact that in the opening decade of the twentieth century Joyce wrote a series of stories depicting the lives of drab, isolated, and frustrated citizens of Dublin and that in the next decade Anderson wrote stories of the same kind of people in a small Midwestern American town. An obvious question arises: was Sherwood Anderson in any way influenced by Joyce's *Dubliners* when he wrote the stories that were to become ***Winesburg, Ohio***?

There is no evidence of direct influence.[1] Anderson did not meet Joyce until he visited Paris in the spring and summer of 1921; and his close friend Harry Hansen, literary critic for the *Chicago Daily News* and after 1926 for the *New York World,* maintains that Anderson had never read Joyce until after their meeting in Paris.[2] Anderson's letters prove that, although *Dubliners* and *A Portrait of the Artist as a Young Man* had both been published in New York in 1916, the first work of Joyce's that Anderson took as a model for his own writing was neither of these but, rather, *Ulysses.* Anderson could have read the serialization of the first half of *Ulysses* in the *Little Review* between March 1918 and December 1920—the novel's serialization was stopped because of prosecution and subsequent conviction on the grounds of obscenity—or Anderson could have read the 1922 version published by Sylvia Beach in Paris. In any case, the stream of consciousness style of *Ulysses* persuaded Anderson to depart from his usual simple prose and to experiment with a new style, a style far different from that of ***Winesburg*** and his other two books of short stories, ***The Triumph of the Egg*** (1921) and ***Horses and Men*** (1923). A letter that Anderson wrote from New Orleans to his old friend George Daugherty on 15 September 1925 gives evidence of Joyce's influence. When speaking of a copy of *Ulysses* that he had lent to Daugherty, Anderson claims: "I think as a matter of prose experiment you will sense what Mr. Joyce was driving at when you read *Dark Laughter.* As I think I told you here, I very frankly took his experiment as a starting place for the prose rhythm of the book."[3]

Although we cannot be sure when, if ever, Anderson read *Dubliners,* a letter written to Anderson by Waldo Frank seems to indicate clearly that Anderson had not read any of Joyce's work before 1920—that is, two-and-a-half years after Anderson's ***Winesburg*** stories were completed and, in fact, six months after ***Winesburg*** was published as a book. Waldo Frank, novelist, critic, and co-founder and editor of *Seven Arts,* was a close friend of Anderson's in the late 1910's and early 1920's. They corresponded frequently during these years but, unfortunately, Frank omitted the date on almost half of his letters to Anderson. When Frank included an address, however, it is usually possible to ascribe approximate dates. In the letter in question, Frank is apparently introducing Anderson to the writings of James Joyce, and toward the end of the letter Frank comments: "Write me, care of my buried Past . . . care of J J Frank, 52 William Str. N Y."[4] Waldo Frank's father, Julius J. Frank, had his law offices at 52 William Street in New York from 1915 until 1920. Sometime between November 1920 and October 1921 he moved his offices to 61 Broadway. Therefore, a conservative estimate of the latest possible date for this letter would be November 1920.

How much before November 1920, however, could it have been written? Another way to date the letter is to consider the arrangement of the Frank letters preserved with the Sherwood Anderson Papers at the Newberry Library. Howard Mumford Jones, in collaboration with Walter Rideout, edited Anderson's letters in 1953; by comparing Anderson's answers with Frank's letters he was able to arrange Frank's letters in their apparent chronological order, and, thereby, to assign dates. According to Jones's arrangement, the letter immediately following the one just quoted has typed at the top: "Note New Address: 19 West 69 Street."[5] Waldo Frank's address from 1917 to 1919 was 137 East 30th Street, but by February 1920 he had moved to 19 West 69th Street. Because of the frequency of the correspondence between Frank and Anderson at this time, it seems safe to assume that very close to February 1920 Frank wrote the first letter, the one on which I place the burden of my proof that Sherwood Anderson had not read any work by James Joyce before he wrote ***Winesburg.***

The clearest indication that Anderson had not read *Dubliners* before he wrote ***Winesburg*** is a sentence in the first of these two undated letters. The excitement of Frank's discovery of Joyce and the thrill of telling Anderson about him and his style are evident in this sentence. After explaining to Anderson that he thinks only good, loving men "pass through" the colander of time, and including himself and Anderson in this group of loving men whose talents time will respect, Frank adds: "There is one other man using that glorious bastard English prose beside us who passes through. . . . A Mick, Joyce . . . you should love him too."

One more piece of evidence to disprove ***Winesburg***'s indebtedness to *Dubliners* concerns its title. Anderson had originally intended to call his series of stories after the first story, **"The Book of the Grotesque,"** and many critics conclude that it was the New York publisher of both books, Benjamin Huebsch, possibly because he recognized the effectiveness of Joyce's title, who suggested that Anderson change his title to ***Winesburg, Ohio.*** Again, however, Anderson's letters tell a different story. Since the John Lane Publishing Company brought out Anderson's first three books, Lane had first option on the manuscript of ***Winesburg.*** Two letters that Anderson wrote in 1918, however, show that he not only referred to the individual stories as "Winesburg tales," but that he also called the whole volume ***Winesburg*** even when Lane was still considering the manuscript. In April Anderson wrote to Van Wyck Brooks: "Lane's have decided to go ahead with my cornfield sons. I call them Mid-American chants. Then I am going to publish the Winesburg tales, some two dozen of them, in a book under the title ***Winesburg.***"[6] In May or early June he wrote to Waldo Frank: "***Winesburg*** has gone off to Lane. I wonder if the public will really take that book." Thirty years later William Phillips wrote an excellent dissertation on ***Winesburg,*** and at that time, that is, in 1949, Huebsch wrote Phillips claiming that he was the one who suggested the change of title to Anderson. I believe, however, that Huebsch's memory of thirty-odd years is in error. From the evidence of Anderson's letters I contend that, before Huebsch was shown the manuscript and independently of any influence from Joyce's book, Anderson had already recognized the additional unity that could be gained if he called his collected stories after the town where his fictional characters lived out their thwarted lives.

Therefore, for four reasons I conclude that Anderson was not influenced by Joyce's *Dubliners* when he wrote ***Winesburg.*** First, as early as 1918 Anderson was calling his book of collected stories ***Winesburg.*** Second, Harry Hansen, closely associated with Anderson and the other members of the "Chicago Renaissance" in the late 1910's and early 1920's, maintains that Anderson had not read any of Joyce's works until after 1921. Third, Anderson admits that the style of *Ulysses,* a book that Joyce succeeded in having published in its entirety only in 1922, prompted him to change his own prose style in *Dark Laughter,* a novel that he wrote in 1924 and published in 1925. Lastly, and most importantly, in a letter that was probably written shortly before February 1920 Waldo Frank tells his friend Sherwood Anderson that he would love the works of Joyce if he were to read them. It seems apparent, therefore, that independently of each other, James Joyce in Dublin and Trieste between 1904 and 1907 and Sherwood Anderson in Chicago between 1915 and 1916 were writing books remarkably similar in structure, narrative technique, and theme.

II

Although there is no evidence of the direct influence of *Dubliners* on ***Winesburg,*** several affinities between the two books have often been noted by critics. First,

Dubliners and ***Winesburg,*** when published in the second decade of the twentieth century, introduced British and American readers to volumes of short stories that are structurally very different from previous collections. These two books are not mere collections of isolated stories but are, as Forrest Ingram has persuasively demonstrated, among the first representatives in modern English of the genre he calls "the short story cycle." Ingram defines the short story cycle as "a set of stories so linked to one another that the reader's experience of each one is modified by his experience of the others"—a series of stories "linked to each other in such a way as to maintain a balance between the individuality of each of the stories and the necessities of the larger unit."[7] Evidence from the letters and memoirs of both Joyce and Anderson reveals that, from the time of the composition of the stories, they hoped to gather them together into unified volumes of stories.

In his initial attempt to get *Dubliners* published, Joyce wrote from Trieste on 23 September 1905 to tell William Heinemann in London that he had "almost finished a book . . . a collection of twelve short stories. . . . The book is not a collection of tourist impressions but an attempt to represent certain aspects of the life of one of the European capitals." By September 1907 the number of stories had grown to fifteen, and during those years Joyce and Grant Richards—who, rather than Heinemann, had agreed to publish the book—entered into a long and bitter correspondence over changes and deletions. This correspondence provides valuable insights into Joyce's understanding of the structural unity underlying *Dubliners.* For example, Joyce wrote to Richards on 16 June 1906, after Richards had suggested that "Two Gallants" be omitted: "I regard such an omission as an almost mortal mutilation of my work." Perhaps the clearest statement, however, of the underlying unity controlling the organization of *Dubliners* is contained in Joyce's letter to Richards on 5 May 1906:

> My intention was to write a chapter of the moral history of my country and I chose Dublin for the scene because that city seemed to me the centre of paralysis. I have tried to present it to the indifferent public under four of its aspects: childhood, adolescence, maturity and public life. The stories are arranged in this order. I have written it for the most part in a style of scrupulous meanness and with the conviction that he is a very bold man who dares to alter in the presentment, still more to deform, whatever he has seen or heard. I cannot do any more than this. I cannot alter what I have written.[8]

Sherwood Anderson, too, in his letters to friends and publishers, insisted on the unity of ***Winesburg, Ohio.*** As early as November, 1916, in a letter to Waldo Frank, he spoke of ***Winesburg*** as a whole book: "I made last year a series of intensive studies of people of my home town, Clyde, Ohio. In the book I called the town Winesburg, Ohio."[9] Three years later, after Anderson's dream of publishing ***Winesburg*** as a book had come true, he wrote to Ben Huebsch, telling him about "Mary Cochran." Anderson had been working on this novel for a number of years but never succeeded in publishing it. When describing "Mary Cochran" in a letteer to Huebsch on 12 November 1919 Anderson showed how he conceived of ***Winesburg***:

> One of these days I shall be able to give you the Mary Cochran book. It has tantalized me a good deal but is coming clear now. In its final form it will be like ***Winesburg,*** a group of tales woven about the life of one person but each tale will be longer and more closely related to the development of the central character. It can be published in fact as a novel if you wish.
>
> It seems to me that in this form I have worked out something that is very flexible and that is the right instrument for me. . . . No one I know of has used the form as I see it and as I hope to develop it in several books. Damn, man, I wish I had time to work.[10]

Although Anderson was correct when he said, "No one I know of has used the form," Joyce's *Dubliners* had been in print for five years. Nonetheless, when writing his *Memoirs* in the late 1930's, Anderson can still claim that in ***Winesburg, Ohio*** he created "my own form":

> The stories belonged together. I felt that, taken together, they made something like a novel, a complete story. There was all of this starved side of American small town life. Perhaps I was even vain enough to think that these stories told would, in the end, have the effect of breaking down a little the curious separateness of so much of life, these walls we build up about us. . . .
>
> . . . I have even sometimes thought that the novel form does not fit an American writer, that it is a form which had been brought in. What is wanted is a new looseness; and in ***Winesburg*** I had made my own form. There were individual tales but all about lives in some way connected. By this method I did succeed, I think, in giving the feeling of the life of a boy growing into young manhood in a town. Life is a loose flowing thing. There are no plot stories in life.[11]

In addition to the fact that Joyce and Anderson were among the first in the twentieth century to structure a series of stories into a cycle, they were also among the first to write what has been called the "new" short story, a story which de-emphasizes plot because it strives to be "true to life," not to literary stereotypes.[12] In his biography of his brother, Stanislaus Joyce tells us that, even before he was sixteen, James Joyce had started writing a series of prose sketches—*Silhouettes*—which "were already in the style of *Dubliners*" and were "the first faint indication of that coming revolt of his against the hypocrisy of art." Stanislaus explains his brother's motives for writing *Silhouettes*: "He had no doubt that most artists, even the greatest, belied the life they knew, and offered the world a make-believe. Literature, he said, was a parody of life." In order to avoid this parody, Joyce developed his own kind of story: "But almost from the beginning my brother followed his natural bent, which was for the plotless sketch. He came to consider a well-ordered plot in a novel or story as a meretricious literary interest, like the story in a *tableau de genre.*"[13]

Anderson, too, speaks out against the lies told in highly plotted stories. He explains his theory most explicitly in his first autobiography, *A Story Teller's Story*:

> In telling tales of themselves people constantly spoiled the tale in telling. They had some notion of how a story should be told got from reading. Little lies crept in. . . .
>
> There was a notion that ran through all story telling in America, that stories must be built about a plot and that absurd Anglo-Saxon notion that they must point a moral, uplift people, make better citizens, etc., etc. The magazines were filled with these plot stories and most of the plays on our stage were plot plays. "The Poison Plot" I called it in conversation with my friends as the plot notion did seem to me to poison all story telling. What was wanted I thought was form, not plot, an altogether more elusive and difficult thing to come at.[14]

Furthermore, in their revolt against the lies often told in literature both Joyce and Anderson turned to a similar narrative technique, namely, sharing with their readers the moment when an ordinary object or event reveals its inner significance to the artist and, through his work, to the reader. Joyce called this revelation "epiphany"; Anderson spoke of significant "moments."

The Feast of the Epiphany takes its name from the Greek word *epiphancia* which means "manifestation," and it commemorates the journey of the Magi to the Christ Child; that is, it commemorates the manifestation of Christ's divinity to the Gentile nations. As early at 1900 Joyce called the notes he jotted down from his observations of his native city and its denizens epiphanies.[15] It seems that he originally intended to publish these epiphanies as a book of their own, but he evidently saw that he could incorporate them into his early, uncompleted autobiographical novel *Stephen Hero* and later into *A Portrait of the Artist as a Young Man. Dubliners,* also, can be considered a series of stories about everyday people and events which render forth their inner significance to the artist and through him to the reader.

In *Portrait,* by means of his protagonist Stephen Daedalus, Joyce explains his understanding of the aesthetics of Thomas Aquinas, on which his theory of epiphany rests. According to Aquinas, a thing of beauty must have three qualities: *integritas* (wholeness), *consonantia* (harmony), and *claritas* (radiance). As Stephen explains, again using a scholastic term, *claritas* requires that the *quidditas* of the object be made manifest. The *quidditas*—or whatness—of an object is the quality that makes us view it as this particular object and nothing else.[16] When the intrinsic "whatness" of a person, event, or object leaps forth to the viewer, that person, event, or object is "epiphanised." Furthermore, it is important to Joyce's theory that an ordinary person, event, or object—a triviality—occasion the epiphany. Commonplace objects and events, things that the nonartist sees every day in their ordinariness and even coarseness, are capable of manifesting their inner radiance, and the artist must make this radiance clear to the reader. In *Stephen Hero,* referring to the clock of the Ballast Office in Dublin, Stephen tells his friend Cranley: "Imagine my glimpses at that clock as the gropings of a spiritual eye which seeks to adjust its vision to an exact focus. The moment the focus is reached the object is epiphanised." Earlier in this same passage from *Stephen Hero* Joyce gives us his only explicit definition of epiphany. After Stephen overhears a whispered conversation between a young woman and man, the narrator explains:

> This triviality made him think of collecting many such moments together in a book of epiphanies. By an epiphany he meant a sudden spiritual manifestation, whether in the vulgarity of speech or of gesture or in a memorable phase of the mind itself. He believed that it was for the man of letters to record these epiphanies with extreme care, seeing that they themselves are the most delicate and evanescent of moments.[17]

James Joyce was well acquainted with philosophical principles guiding the practice of narrative art; but Sherwood Anderson, even though he read rather widely in the field of fiction, was almost completely ignorant of aesthetic theory. He had an intuitive feeling for the qualities that make objects beautiful, but he could not express his intuitions in any other way than in his fiction. As was the case with Joyce, however, Anderson strove in his creative work to capture on paper the inner beauty of significant moments; unlike Joyce, though, Anderson's best work was confined to the short story genre.

The reasons why Anderson's best works are short stories or short story collections and why his stories focus on significant moments in his character's lives may lie in his ability to work well only in certain times of acute awareness. In the letter to Benjamin Huebsch of 12 November 1919, which has already been quoted, Anderson explains why he felt the best form for his stories was the one he used successfully in ***Winesburg*** and tried to use in his uncompleted "Mary Cochran." Because at the time he had to support himself by writing advertising copy, he found that he had "no chances at all for long periods of uninterrupted thought or work. I can take my character into my consciousness and live with it but have to work in this fragmentary way. These individual tales come clear and sharp. When I am ready for one of them it comes all at one sitting, a distillation, an outbreak." What follows immediately is his affirmation that: "No one I know of has used the form as I see it and as I hope to develop it in several books."[18] Of course, the form was never more fully developed than in ***Winesburg.***

The thought Anderson expresses in this letter is very similar to the statement in *A Story Teller's Story* where he describes his usual method of writing: "I, at least, could only give myself with complete abandonment to the surfaces and materials before me at rare moments, sandwiched in between long periods of failure. It was only at the rare moment I could give myself, my thoughts and emotions, to work and sometimes, at rarer moments, to the love of a friend or a woman." Later in *A Story Teller's Story* Anderson gives a more detailed description of the way a moment of insight inspired his creative imagination. During a stay in France in 1921, Anderson visited Chartres Cathedral. A scene he saw enacted on the steps of the cathedral—a scene between two women, one American and the other French, who were both in love with the same man—set his imagination to work: "All tales presented themselves to the fancy in just that way. There was a suggestion, a hint given. In a crowd of faces in a crowded street one face suddenly jumped out. It had a tale to tell, was crying its tale to the streets, but at best one got only a fragment of it." The conclusion Anderson draws is: "It was the artist's business to make it stand still, well, just to fix the moment, in a painting, in a tale, in a poem."[19]

What was the catalyst that enabled Anderson to "fix the moments" that became his ***Winesburg*** tales? Anderson's own memories of his boyhood and youth in Ohio towns, especially Clyde, came alive to him when he moved into the boarding house at 735 Cass Street in Chicago. Many of the boarders were men and women like himself, emigrants to the big city from small rural communities throughout the Midwest. They were confused, silent people whose drab lives stirred Anderson's creative imagination. When Anderson was living in the boarding house in Chicago he felt that he knew the stories of his fellow boarders, knew the hidden revelations that they would like to make, knew the moment when they suddenly had an insight into their own existence but then had grown no further. In his *Memoirs* he explains the process by which his fellow boarders stirred his memories of Clyde:

> It was as though I had little or nothing to do with the writing. It was as though the people of that house, all of them wanting so much, none of them really equipped to wrestle with life as it was, had, in this odd way, used me as an instrument. They had got, I felt, through me, their stories told, and not in their own persons but, in a much more real and satisfactory way, through the lives of these queer small town people of the book.[20]

Since the time Joyce used epiphany as a term to explain one principle of his aesthetics, literary critics have adapted it to their purposes; and in the course of the decades it has taken on two slightly different meanings. According to Joyce, the word means that the artist himself is able to see and recreate the radiant "whatness" of an object and then share with his readers this same moment of full intellectual and emotional awareness. The second meaning of the term in contemporary critical usage, however, describes the artist's treatment of his characters. When an author depicts characters who in a notable way either realize, or fail to realize, the inner significance of their lives, critics say that these characters experience, or fail to experience, an epiphany. In this secondary meaning of the word we see once again that Joyce and Anderson wrote books with notable affinities. In both *Dubliners* and ***Winesburg,*** Joyce and Anderson were able to capture a significant moment in a character's life and express that moment by means of an epiphany, a moment when the character—or at least the reader—realizes the essential truth of the situation. Furthermore, the essential truth of the character's life is often his inability to grow to full maturity. This basic theme of inability to mature or to change the circumstances of one's life is epitomized by Joyce's word "paralysis" and by Anderson's word "grotesque."

As Joyce explained to Grant Richards, he envisioned *Dubliners* as a book about paralysis. To explain his idea of paralysis Joyce again turned to a term from his Catholic background. When he was about to submit the first of his *Dubliners* stories to the periodical *The Irish Homestead,* Joyce wrote to his lifelong friend Constantine P. Curran: "I am writing a series of epicleti—ten—for a paper. I have written one. [Possibly "The Sisters."] I call the series *Dubliners* to betray the soul of that hemiplegia or paralysis which many consider a city."[21] Joyce's term *epicleti* is a corruption of the Greek word *epiclesis* or *epicleses.* The Byzantine Rite of the Mass has an easily recognizable epiclesis and the Latin Rite a brief one: the priest's petition to the Holy Spirit to descend upon the species of bread and wine and to turn them into the Body and Blood of Christ. Thus, an epiclesis is an invocation to the Holy Spirit to bless mundane reality and to change it into sacred reality. From the beginning of its composition Joyce regarded *Dubliners* as an invocation to his people to recognize the paralysis of their city and of their lives. Joyce insisted that he wrote *Dubliners* to help his fellow citizens see the futility and paralysis of their lives. For example, in the midst of his quarrel with Grant Richards, Joyce refused to omit the disputed stories and passages: "I fight to retain them because I believe that in composing my chapter of moral history in exactly the way I have composed it I have taken the first step towards the spiritual liberation of my country."[22]

Anderson's theory of the "grotesque" also concerns a person's inability to grow. The first story of ***Winesburg***, **"The Book of the Grotesque,"** forms an introduction to the whole volume and initiates one of the unifying themes, the theme which depicts the essence of starved, thwarted lives. This first story describes an old writer who once wrote a book called "The Book of the Grotesque" but never published it. The "central thought" of the book is that there are many beautiful truths in the world but no such thing as one truth. When a person "took one of the truths to himself, called it his truth, and tried to live his life by it, he became a grotesque and the truth he embraced became a falsehood." As the old writer tries to sleep at night something inside him, "like a pregnant woman," drives processions of these grotesques before the writer's eyes. "He crept out of bed and began to write. Some one of the grotesques had made a deep impression on his mind and he wanted to describe it."[23] The voice of this old writer becomes the narrative voice through the rest of ***Winesburg.***

Thus, despite many differences, *Dubliners* and ***Winesburg*** are remarkably similar works. Despite the fact that, at the time of composition, neither author knew the other or his work, the two books were written only ten years and published only five years apart. These two books are also the first examples in English of modern short story cycles. Furthermore, although Joyce's book depicts the lives of ordinary men and women who inhabit one of Europe's capitals and Anderson's depicts the lives of ordinary people of a small Midwestern town in the United States, both books provide modern man with a vivid revelation of his frustration, isolation, and paralysis.

Notes

1. Most critics assume that in writing *Winesburg* Anderson was influenced by Joyce. One recent example is Joan Zlotnick's "Dubliners in Winesburg, Ohio: A Note on Joyce's 'The Sisters' and Anderson's 'The Philosopher,'" *Studies in Short Fiction,* 12 (1975), 405-07.

2. *Midwest Portraits: A Book of Memoirs and Friendships* (New York: Harcourt, Brace and Company, 1923), p. 132.

3. *Letters of Sherwood Anderson,* ed. Howard Mumford Jones and Walter B. Rideout (Boston: Little, Brown and Company, 1953), p. 148, quoted by permission of Mrs. Eleanor Anderson and Little, Brown and Company.

4. Unpublished; Incoming Letters, Waldo Frank to Anderson, with The Sherwood Anderson Papers, The Newberry Library, Chicago. All of the Frank and Anderson letters quoted in this paper are part of the Sherwood Anderson Papers at the Newberry Library and are quoted by permission of Mrs. Eleanor Anderson, The Newberry Library, and the University of Pennsylvania Library, which houses the Waldo Frank Papers. Some of the letters, as notes indicate, are also published in the Jones and Rideout edition.

   I make two kinds of editorial changes in unpublished letters; for clarity, I underscore titles of books and I correct misspellings.

5. Another proof that this letter was written in 1920, and probably well before October, is that in it Frank speaks about the French translation of his book of essays, *Our America. Our America* was originally published by Boni and Liveright in New York in 1919; and in Paris in October 1920, the *Nouvelle Revue Française* published a translation by Hélène Boussinesq. In his letter to Anderson, Frank remarks: "In a few days now, I hope to see *Our America,* but it will not be published till the end of October. The reason is, the usual delay in France. MMe Riviere who was translating the book was taken seriously ill—and a new translator meant delay."

   The addresses of Julius J. Frank and Waldo D. Frank are in the New York City (Manhattan) phone books for 1915-22.

6. The first letter is printed in *Letters,* ed. Jones and Rideout, p. 31; the second letter is unpublished: Outgoing Letters, Newberry Library, 1918. For Huebsch's letter to Phillips, see "How Sherwood Anderson Wrote *Winesburg, Ohio,*" *American Literature,* 23 (1951), 7-30, ns. 57 and 58. This article is drawn from his dissertation: "Sherwood Anderson's *Winesburg, Ohio*: Its Origins, Composition, Technique, and Reception," University of Chicago, 1949.

7. Forrest L. Ingram, *Representative Short Story Cycles of the Twentieth Century: Studies in a Literary Genre* (The Hague: Mouton, 1971), pp. 13 and 15.

8. *Letters of James Joyce,* ed. Richard Ellmann (New York: The Viking Press, 1966), II, quoted by permission of Viking Penguin, Inc. The first letter is from pp. 108-09, the second from p. 142, and the third from p. 134.

9. *Letters of Sherwood Anderson,* ed. Jones and Rideout, p. 4.

10. Outgoing Letters of Sherwood Anderson, Newberry Library, 1919.

11. *Sherwood Anderson's Memoirs* (New York: Harcourt, Brace and Company, 1942), p. 289. This passage is omitted in the critical edition of the *Memoirs* edited by Ray Lewis White (Chapel Hill: The University of North Carolina Press, 1969).

12. See, for example, Harry Hansen, *Midwest Portraits*; Herbert E. Bates, *The Modern Short Story* (London: Thomas Nelson and Sons, 1941); Frank O'Connor, *The Lonely Voice* (Cleveland and New York: The World Publishing Company, 1962); Chester G. Anderson, *James Joyce and His World,* A Studio Book (New York: The Viking Press, 1967); Marvin Magalaner and Richard M. Kain, *Joyce: The Man, the Work, the Reputation* (New York: Collier Books, 1962); and William Peden, who in *The American Short Story* (Boston: Houghton Mifflin Company, 1964, p. 11), when speaking of the "new" short story, claims that "*Dubliners* (1914), and *Winesburg, Ohio,* published five years later, are towering landmarks and seminal forces in its development."

13. *My Brother's Keeper,* ed. Richard Ellmann (New York: The Viking Press, 1958), pp. 57, 92, 90-91, and 92.

14. *A Story Teller's Story,* ed. Ray Lewis White (Cleveland: The Press of Case Western Reserve University, 1968), p. 255.

15. Richard Ellmann, *James Joyce* (New York: Oxford University Press, 1959), p. 87.

16. *A Portrait of the Artist as a Young Man* (New York: The Modern Library, 1916), pp. 248-50. See also *Stephen Hero,* ed. Theodore Spencer; new ed. by John J. Slocum and Herbert Cahoon (London: Jonathan Cape, 1956), for a similar discussion of Aquinas' theory of beauty, pp. 217-18; it is in *Stephen Hero* that Stephen explicitly says: "*Claritas* is *quidditas,*" p. 218. Two of the earliest of the many critics who argue that Joyce based his theory of epiphany on Aquinas' theory of *claritas* are Irene Hendry Chayes, "Joyce's Epiphanies," *The Sewanee Review,* 54 (1946), 449-50; and William Y. Tindall, *James Joyce: His Way of Interpreting the Modern World* (New York: Charles Scribner's Sons, 1950), pp. 119-20.

17. *Stephen Hero,* p. 216.

18. Outgoing Letters, Newberry Library, 1919. This letter was also quoted on p. 22.

19. *A Story Teller's Story,* pp. 232 and 311-12.

20. *Memoirs,* ed. White, p. 348.

21. *Letters of James Joyce,* ed. Stuart Gilbert (New York: The Viking Press, 1966), I, 55, quoted by permission of Viking Penguin, Inc. This letter was written in the summer of 1904. Note that Joyce originally intended to write only ten stories for *Dubliners.*

22. *Letters of James Joyce,* ed. Gilbert, I, 62-3. This letter was written on 20 May 1906.

23. *Winesburg, Ohio* (New York: B. W. Huebsch, 1919), pp. 4, 5, 2, and 4.

Robert H. Sykes (essay date winter 1981)

SOURCE: Sykes, Robert H. "The Identity of Anderson's Fanatical Farmer." *Studies in Short Fiction* 18, no. 1 (winter 1981): 79-82.

[In the following essay, Sykes identifies a source for the character of Jesse Bentley in "Godliness."]

On the several occasions when Sherwood Anderson referred to his Winesburg characters, he disclaimed that any was a specifically identifiable person, insisting instead that they were imaginative figures drawn from many different sources. In a letter to Waldo Frank on November 14, 1916, he said the tales were "studies of people of my hometown" of Clyde, Ohio.[1] But in "A Writer's Conception of Realism," he said, "The book was written in a crowded tenement district of Chicago. The hint for almost every character was taken from my fellow lodgers in a large rooming house."[2] Later he wrote in his *Memoirs,* "I had got the characters of the book everywhere about me, in towns in which I had lived, in the Army, in factories and offices."[3]

At least one of the characters in Winesburg, though, can be identified as the fictional counterpart of an actual person. The life of Joseph F. Glidden of DeKalb, Illinois, gave Anderson raw material for his portrait of Jesse Bentley in the story **"Godliness."**

We get a first clue from Anderson's letter to Waldo Frank of August 27, 1917, written when he had just started the aborted novel that he later put into the Winesburg tales as **"Godliness."** He told Frank, "My new book (has) a delightful old man, Joseph Bentley by name. . . ."[4] This message shows that initially he thought of his character by the same name as the lay figure who was the model—Joseph, not Jesse.

Throughout the story, the details about Jesse dovetail too specifically with the life of Joseph Glidden to be coincidental. Anderson wrote, i.e., "The Bentley family had been in Northern Ohio for several generations before Jesse's time. They came from New York State and took up land when the country was new and land could be had at a low price."[5] Glidden also came from New York at age 33, migrating with his family from Orleans County to DeKalb.[6]

The fictional Jesse and the real-life Glidden were both educated for the ministry before reverting to farming. Of Jesse, Anderson wrote, "At eighteen he had left home to go to school . . . and eventually to become a minister of the Presbyterian Church" (p. 66). Likewise, Joseph Glidden attended Middlebury Academy and then studied "at the seminary at Lima, N. Y."[7]

Two other analogies have to do with their wives and children; each had a wife who died in childbirth, and each was survived by a daughter.[8]

In two places Anderson used the specific number of 600 acres as the size of Jesse Bentley's first farm: "When he came home to take charge of the farm, that had at that time grown to more than 600 acres . . ." (p. 66), and "He grew avaricious and was impatient that the farm contained only six hundred acres" (p. 72). In the *Biographical Record of DeKalb County* is the arresting notation about Glidden that, "In the winter after his arrival he purchased six hundred acres of land on Section 22, DeKalb Township, a mile west of the village."[9] He and Anderson's Jesse became land barons of an identical order. "Jesse at night walked beyond his own farm and through the fields of his neighbors and thought that all the land he had traversed should belong to him" (p. 72). Later we find, "The effort he had made to extend his land holdings had been successful and there were few farms in the valley that did not belong to him" (p. 80). Transaction receipts among the Glidden papers in the Archives of Northern Illinois University attest that Glidden ultimately acquired eight farms that originally surrounded his 600 acres.

Anderson differentiates Jesse from his neighbors by the fact that the old man was the only farmer among them to drain his fields. He had built modern barns "and most of the land was drained with carefully laid drain tile" (p. 64). "Great ditches had to be dug and thousands of tile laid. Neighboring farmers shook their heads over the expense" (p. 97). In this respect it is noteworthy that Glidden had a nephew who was a drainage engineer who had come to live with his uncle and drained the Glidden farms into what is now a 40-acre lake on the NIU campus. The Glidden papers there contain receipts for 51 invoices and bills for elbows, stone, brick, and drain tile.[10]

The most convincing detail, however, linking Jesse Bentley with Joseph Glidden is the reference Anderson makes to Jesse's invention, "a machine for the making of fence out of wire" (p. 81). It is for his role in the invention of barbed wire and the invention of the machine to make it that Joseph Glidden is best known to the world. After years of patent litigation, the United States Supreme Court decision on February 29, 1892, established Glidden's original patent. It is important to observe that Anderson did not say he invented barbed wire, but that he said he invented a *machine* for the making of wire fencing. Glidden's patent specifically refers to the machine he invented to hold the spur wires.[11]

In the story, we read that Jesse "had a wing built on to the old house and in a large room facing the west he had windows that looked off across the fields" (p. 68). That detail coincides with Glidden's having added to his original farm house an observatory that enabled him to scan the farm in three directions. His neighbors referred to it as the "Obscuratory."[12]

Some significant landmarks that tie the Bentley farm to the Glidden farm are the creek, the valley, and the low hill mentioned in the tale. Anderson wrote, "The Bentley farm was situated in a tiny valley watered by Wine Creek (p. 72). A forest came down to the road and through the forest Wine Creek wriggled its way over stones toward a distant river" (p. 84). The south branch of the Kishwaukee River (it's really a creek) winds across what were once the Glidden farms, through a forest and empties into the Rock River at Rockford, Illinois. The lands are indeed in a shallow valley, most of it occupied today by NIU. There was mentioned a low hill where Jesse sat down to think. This low hill doubtless corresponds to the one on which NIU's "Castle on the Hill" was built.[13]

There is something teasing about the names Anderson uses in the story and other Winesburg tales when they are set beside names in the Glidden geneology. If the *Biographical Record of DeKalb County* was his main source for facts about Joseph Glidden, which is probably true, he may have discovered in that volume the entry for George D. Bentley, who had a son named Jesse Bentley. The fictional farmer's grandson is named David, which was Glidden's father's name. An Eliza Staughton lived at the Bentley farm in the story, and an Eliza Gates lived at the Glidden farm. A more startling coincidence is the fact that Joseph Glidden's brother was named Willard, the name of the narrator of the tales. Glidden's daughter married a merchant named William H. Bush, and in the story **"Adventure,"** Alice Hindman marries a Bush Milton. Moreover, Willard Glidden had a daughter Lizzie Mary, who married a man named Albert Hindman.[14]

A nagging question asserts itself. Where or how did Sherwood Anderson come upon the facts in the life of Joseph Glidden, spurring his imagination to write **"Godliness"**? By the time he began to write the Winesburg tales, Glidden had been dead for ten years. It is possible, though, that Anderson, working for an advertising agency specializing in farm implements, had actually met the most famous farmer-inventor in Illinois. Glidden held nine patents (at least) on farm tools and conveniences. He was a heavy advertiser of these inventions, and his agent was the Long Critchfield Corporation—the same agency for which Anderson worked.[15]

Glidden had a horse collar manufactory in the basement of a hotel he owned in DeKalb and a glove factory on the first floor. Elsewhere in town he had a gate lock factory and a field roller factory. Anderson may have visited one of these, for in his *Memoirs* he wrote this of his advertising years:

> I had begun to get a little ahead. After all, the solicitors, the salesmen, had to depend upon us. We were the writers. They were compelled to send us to the factories where the goods we were to advertise were made. Sometimes we stayed at such a factory, in some town, for days.
>
> Acquaintances and sometimes something like friendships were made. There were two men in a Kentucky town, another in an Ohio town, a fourth and fifth in Illinois towns, on whose accounts I worked. I had selected these men from among all those whose accounts I was sent to write. I made it my business to cultivate them. All of them were men who had a certain flair.[16]

If one of those Illinois towns he mentions was DeKalb, which had, besides the Glidden factories, the factories of Isaac Ellwood and Jacob Haish, it is logical that he would have stayed at the Glidden House Hotel, then advertised as "the most magnificent hotel west of Chicago," and indeed the only one in DeKalb at the time. And, if he was in DeKalb, Anderson surely must have visited the horse race track located a mile from the center of town, a track owned, incidentally, by Joseph Glidden.

Notes

1. *Letters of Sherwood Anderson,* ed. Howard Mumford Jones and Walter B. Rideout (Boston: Little, Brown and Co., 1953), p. 4.
2. Quoted by Horace Gregory in his Intro. to *The Portable Sherwood Anderson,* rev. ed. (New York: Viking, 1972).
3. *Sherwood Anderson's Memoirs* (New York: Harcourt, Brace and Co., 1942), p. 295.
4. *Letters,* p. 15.
5. Sherwood Anderson, *Winesburg, Ohio,* ed. Malcolm Cowley (New York: Viking Press, 1975). All citations from "Godliness" are from this edition and hereafter are in parentheses in the text.
6. *Biographical Record of DeKalb County* (Chicago: S. J. Clarke, 1898), p. 300.
7. Ibid.
8. Ibid.
9. Ibid. The Plat Book of DeKalb County of 1892 in the present township Office of DeKalb shows the original 600 acres.
10. Archives, Swen Parsons Library, Northern Illinois University.
11. "Barbed Wire—Who Invented It?" *Iron Age,* 117 (June 1926), 1769-1774.
12. Harriet Wilson Davy, *From Oxen to Jets* (Dixon, Ill.: Rogers Prntg. Co., 1968) p. 107.
13. Earl W. Hayter, *Education in Transition* (DeKalb: Northern Illinois University Press 1974), p. 57.
14. *The Descendants of Charles Glidden of Portsmouth and Exeter, New Hampshire* comp. by George Walter Chamberlain, and ed. Lucia Glidden Strong, (Boston: 1925), p. 218.
15. Invoices and correspondence in Glidden papers.
16. *Memoirs,* p. 209.

Jim Elledge (essay date winter 1984)

SOURCE: Elledge, Jim. "Dante's Lovers in Sherwood Anderson's 'Hands'." *Studies in Short Fiction* 21, no. 1 (winter 1984): 11-15.

[*In the following essay, Elledge traces parallels between "Hands" and the Paolo-Francesca segment of Dante's* Inferno.]

Sherwood Anderson is not generally associated with Dante, although one might readily link the Italian poet to T. S. Eliot or a number of other writers. Perhaps years of reader prejudice—that the Midwest and its people do not adequately lend themselves to a serious art—coupled with Anderson's almost obsessive regionalism has created the impression that he is simply a spit-and-whittle tale-teller whose stories are quaint but gloomy pastoral episodes in a variety similar to, although far less substantial than, Joyce's *Dubliners.* While there are obvious correlations between *Dubliners* and ***Winesburg, Ohio,*** there are many specific parallels between Anderson's **"Hands,"** the introductory story in the collection, and the Paolo-Francesca segment of Dante's *The Inferno.*[1] By investigating these complementary works, one recognizes that Anderson is a sophisticated writer whose technique not only parallels Dante's but profoundly reveals the depth and complexity of Wing Biddlebaum's suffering.

Wing Biddlebaum is the first person with whom George Willard interacts in Anderson's collection, but George never initiates any conversation with Wing. In fact, he and Wing never engage in dialogue.[2] Although he intuits a correlation between Wing's hands and "'his fear . . . of everyone'" (p. 31) and although "he had been on the point of asking" Wing about his origins, his life, and especially his hands many times, "only a growing respect for Wing Biddlebaum kept him from blurting out the questions that were often in his mind" (p. 29).

Paolo and Francesca are the first souls with whom Dante speaks, but it is he who initiates the conversation, calling to them, "'O wearied souls! / if none forbid it, pause and speak to us'" (ll. 80-81). Dante's presence momentarily interrupts their tortured existence. George's meetings with the grotesques of Winesburg are also interruptions, but it is the grotesques who approach him, intruding into his life with their suffering. However, such interruptions permit George and Dante to progress toward, and finally attain, knowledge. For George this knowledge may be defined as sophistication, while for Dante it is divine revelation. George collects the secrets the grotesques impart to him, and Dante is entrusted with the confessions and grumblings of the souls he encounters. Both are writers—George a newspaper reporter, Dante a poet—who will someday record what they see and are told during their journeys.

Francesca tells Dante the story of her and Paolo's adultery, claiming that, while reading the tale of Lancelot and Guinevere together, "'one soft passage overthrew / [their] caution and [their] hearts'" (ll. 129-130). Also in an unguarded moment, when "he forgot the hands" (p. 30), Wing reveals to George his dream of "a kind of pastoral golden age" in which there figures "an old man who sat beneath a tree in a tiny garden and who talked to [young men]" (p. 30). At least a portion of the stories which Francesca and Wing tell mirror, with idyllic overtones, their actions in a previous time and place. Lancelot and Guinevere's adultery parallels Paolo and Francesca's, and Wing's old man, a teacher, is himself as he imagines he might have become if left unharassed in the Pennsylvania town.

Love is the prime reason for Paolo and Francesca's and for Wing's expulsions from previous states of happiness and is the key to their current states of suffering. It is "'love that drives / and damns'" (ll. 77-78) Paolo and Francesca, "who sinned in the flesh, . . . / who betrayed reason to their appetite" (ll. 38-39). Murdered by her husband, who was also his brother, Paolo and Francesca were expelled from the world of the living and were subsequently damned.[3] Unlike their carnal love, Wing's "love of men" (p. 31) is a Platonic love of humankind which was misinterpreted by his students' parents and his neighbors as homosexual desire. Their misinterpretation of his actions compelled them to consider murdering him. They relented and, instead, ran him out of the Pennsylvania town where he had been happy as a teacher.

The memory of what is lost is also an instrument of Wing's suffering, as it is for Paolo and Francesca. She admits to Dante that the "'double grief of a lost bliss / is to recall its happy hour in pain'" (ll. 118-119). Wing's happiest hour was teaching. He "was meant by nature to be a teacher of youth" (p. 31), and he was an ideal teacher, a miracle worker of his profession whose very touch could "carry a dream into . . . young minds" (p. 32). When he was stopped from performing his natural role, his nature was perverted, his means of self-fulfillment destroyed, and he became a grotesque. This point is emphasized when one realizes Wing's major, and perhaps only, dream in Winesburg is the fantasy of the Socratic teacher who imparted wisdom to youths gathered about him.

Dante discovered that hell is "a place stripped bare of every light / and roaring on the naked dark" (ll. 28-29), and critics agree that Winesburg is a similar place, one of darkness, over which hangs an atmosphere of "charged stillness" analogous to "the tortured air" of hell (l. 26). Because the "crisis scenes of all but five of the tales [are] in the evening," Winesburg is a modernized version of Dante's hell: the darkness, the consuming flames of sublimated passions, and the inaudible shrieks of tormented psyches. Winesburg's inhabitants are "spiritually and morally . . . as dead as the corpses whose epitaphs Edgar Lee Masters collected in the 'Spoon River Anthology'" [sic] and the "sterile, unchanging quality of their words and actions [is] a constant counterpoint to the growth and change of [George Willard]. Their repetitiveness and rigidity [implies], finally, . . . atrophy and death."[4]

In such a hellish environment Wing exists, his life as decayed as his veranda.[5] Ironically, his refuge has metamorphosed into his hell. As Paolo and Francesca, who were damned together to an eternity of being swept in a circle by wind, Wing is also characterized by movement: his incessant pacing on his veranda and the constant flutter of his hands. However, while Paolo and Francesca are driven by an external force representing their impetuous and passionate love, Wing is driven by an internal force, his uncontrollable anxiety which is the seat of his torture and suffering. After any experience even slightly threatening to his solitary and superficially peaceful existence, such as his meeting with George during which he caressed the boy, Wing runs "back to walk again upon the porch" as if it were a sanctuary (p. 28). He is often described as being on "the veranda of the house," pacing "up and down" long after "the sun had disappeared" (p. 33). Wing is the perfect example of an anxious personality whose only means of coping with his anxiety is to pace.

The movement of Wing's hands is also a manifestation of his inner turmoil. Having no students to teach, his hands constantly twitch and flutter, reminding him of the idyllic life he once led as a teacher who was "much loved by the boys of his school" (p. 31); of the violence that prefaced his expulsion from the Pennsylvania town and, simultaneously, from the teaching profession; and of the possibility that, if he is not circumspect, he may again draw upon himself the wrath of his neighbors. As his hands' fluttering reminds him of his past, he becomes more anxious, fearful, and confused, which makes his hands twitch more and, in turn, further stimulates his memory. A psychological vicious circle is created, one from which Wing has no escape and with which he torments himself.

Wing's attempts to deter his hands' movements, by striking them on objects to deaden them or by hiding them, succeed only with a conscious effort on his part. His need to censor his hands' expression is only slightly more powerful than his need to fulfill himself by teaching with caresses, and consequently, his hands are "forever active" yet "forever striving to conceal themselves" (p. 28), representing not only his inner struggle but the subsequent suffering his struggle entails. Only once does his hands succeed against him, when they "lay upon George Willard's shoulders" (p. 30).

Paolo and Francesca "add to one another's anguish . . . as mutual reminders of their sin" in the same way that George's presence adds another dimension to Wing's suffering.[6] Wing had one glimmer of hope—that George, with whom "he had formed something like a friendship" (p. 27), might have become his student, the person with whom he might realize his dream of the Socratic teacher, a dream of "a kind of pastoral golden age" (p. 30). When Wing begins "a long rambling talk" in which he becomes "wholly inspired," he drops his guard, and his hands steal "forth and lay upon George Willard's shoulders" (p. 30). For an instant, Wing is totally uninhibited, following freely his natural inclination for the first time since his arrival in Winesburg. However, Wing's hands again remind him of his happier life and he also quickly remembers Henry Bradford's warning: "'Keep your hands to yourself'" (p. 33). As a "look of horror" sweeps "over his face," Wing jambs "his hands deep into his trousers pockets" (p. 30). He is so distraught over and frightened by his loss of control that he runs away, leaving George as "perplexed and frightened" as Wing is (p. 31). Wing's hopes are shattered by the experience, and from that moment on, he is doomed to spend his life in Winesburg with "never a hope of hope" (l. 44), pacing his veranda, his hands "beating [like] the wings of an imprisoned bird" (p. 28).

Although Francesca confesses having committed the sin for which she and Paolo suffer, Wing is not only innocent of wrongdoing but is so naive that "he did not understand what had happened" to turn his neighbors against him and only intuited "that the hands must be to blame" (p. 33) for the "unspeakable things" (p. 32) of which he was accused. Understanding neither himself nor the world around him, Wing believes his hands are independent of his body and powered by a consciousness other than his, as Anderson's references to them as *the* hands, not *his* hands, implies.

The depth of Wing's suffering is revealed in the last scene of **"Hands,"** a display of the "compulsive symptomatic act" of a penitent.[7] On his knees in "the dense blotch of light beneath the table," "he began to pick up the [bread] crumbs" he had dropped and to carry "them to his mouth one by one with unbelievable rapidity." Wing's "nervous expressive fingers, flashing in and out of the light, might well have been mistaken for the fingers of the devotee going swiftly through decade after decade of his rosary" (p. 34). The phrase "decade after decade" refers not only to periods of ten years but also to the fifteen divisions of the rosary, each of which is a "decade" of ten beads. The image derived by combining both definitions is one of an eternity of suffering and penance. Several lines of one prayer of the rosary, the Pater Noster, are significant to a penitent like Wing: "Give us day by day our daily bread. / And forgive us our sins. . . ."[8]

Ironically, Wing's penance is futile and filled with pathos since he did not sin and logically can not ask to be forgiven; but because he blindly accepted the lie of his guilt, he is forced by his anxiety to seek pardon. Wing chooses to be alone in Winesburg and to suffer loneliness out of fear of harsher suffering in the future, not out of an inclination toward hermitage. If he permits himself another person's company, as he had with George, he is afraid of losing control of his hands and of being run out of Winesburg—or worse. The memory of his most recent happiest hour, his uninhibited moment with George, and the trauma which it produced prevents him from taking the risk of living a fulfilled life. Yet, because the memory of that moment is also enjoyable, he will not obliterate it.

If Wing Biddlebaum had realized he committed no wrong by following his natural mode of teaching, his torment would have ended. He would have become, in essence, his own savior. He could not. Henry Bradford's warning echoes too loudly in Wing's ears, so he devours the crumbs of a wasted life in an act of penance, suffering decade after decade in his self-created hell.

Notes

1. The texts used are Sherwood Anderson, "Hands," in *Winesburg, Ohio* (New York: Viking Press, 1960), pp. 27-34 and Dante, *The Inferno,* trans. John Ciardi (New York: New American Library, 1954). The pagination for subsequent references to "Hands" will be given in parentheses following the excerpt. The Paolo-Francesca episode is in Canto V, 11. 73-140, and the line numbers of passages quoted from it will also be given in parentheses following the passage.

2. John J. Mahoney has revealed that in *Winesburg, Ohio* there is "an extremely small amount of alternate speaking. But it is never in response to anything the previous speaker has said; hence is not

conversation" and that "one does get a good deal of the *sense* of conversation. All that is lacking is the conversation itself." ("An Analysis of *Winesburg, Ohio,*" *Journal of Aesthetics and Art Criticism,* 15 [1956], 248).

3. Ciardi, Footnote to line 74 of Canto V, pp. 63-64.
4. The passages quoted are from Glen A. Love, "*Winesburg, Ohio* and the Rhetoric of Silence," *American Literature,* 40 (1963), 45; Walter R. Rideout, "The Simplicity of *Winesburg, Ohio,*" in *Winesburg, Ohio: Text and Criticism,* by Sherwood Anderson, ed. John H. Ferres (New York: Viking Press, 1966), p. 292; Irving Howe, "The Book of the Grotesque," in *The Achievement of Sherwood Anderson: Essays in Criticism,* ed. Ray Lewis White (Chapel Hill, NC: University of North Carolina Press, 1966), p. 94; Régis Michaud, *The American Novel To-Day: A Social and Psychological Study* (Boston: Little, Brown, 1928), pp. 185-186; and Love, pp. 55-56.
5. Rosemary M. Laughlin, "'Godliness' and the American Dream in *Winesburg, Ohio,*" *Twentieth Century Literature,* 13 (1967), 98.
6. Ciardi, Footnote to line 102 of Canto V, p. 64.
7. Jarvis A. Thurston, "Anderson and 'Winesburg:' Mysticism and Craft," *Accent,* 16 (1956), 113.
8. Luke 11:3-4.

Judith Arcana (essay date winter 1987)

SOURCE: Arcana, Judith. "'Tandy': At the Core of *Winesburg.*" *Studies in Short Fiction* 24, no. 1 (winter 1987): 66-70.

[*In the following essay, Arcana discusses the thematic centrality of "Tandy" within* Winesburg, Ohio.]

All of the stories Sherwood Anderson wrote for ***Winesburg, Ohio*** are illustrations of his theory of the grotesque. **"Tandy"** was the third such illustration he wrote, preceded only by **"The Book of the Grotesque"** itself, **"Hands,"** and **"Paper Pills."**[1] He had originally intended to write a trilogy about a woman named Tandy Hard,[2] but instead used the character in ***Winesburg.*** Though **"Tandy"** was written early, it is placed very nearly at the center of the book, and is the shortest story of the collection. In this short central story, Anderson presents a statement of one of his most deeply held principles, and in doing so creates a unique variation on ***Winesburg***'s primary form. That primary form is defined in **"The Book of the Grotesque,"** the framework Anderson built around his stories of the town and people of Winesburg. In it, "the old man" dreams and writes of "the beginning when the world was young," and poses his "elaborate theory" about the creation of truth from thought, and the subsequent twisting of truth. "It was his notion that the moment one of the people took one of the truths to himself, called it his truth, and tried to live his life by it, he became a grotesque and the truth he embraced became a falsehood" (Anderson 25).[3]

All of the stories follow this form. Some tell of one such metamorphosis; others, like **"Godliness"** and **"A Man of Ideas,"** include more than one character who has "snatched up one of the truths" (Anderson 24) and made it false. But **"Tandy"** is different; in this story one of the characters—a young man already grotesque—passes his truth, and its fate, to another character—a five year old girl. The other seekers of Winesburg find their own truths as they grow through life, and twist them false. Only Tandy is captured and possessed by the truth of another. This capture and possession not only serve to demonstrate Anderson's theory of the grotesque, but also express what he felt and believed to be the essential relationship between men and women. **"Tandy"** contains ***Winesburg***'s most explicit statement of this theme: the need of men for women, and their desire to own the qualities of women, wanting to make women into "a thing to love" (Anderson 144).[4] **"Tandy"**'s brevity, its central placement in the collection, and the fact that it differs from the author's defined form in **"The Book of the Grotesque"** call our attention to the statement Anderson is making.

Throughout ***Winesburg,*** in most of his other writing, and in his own living, Sherwood Anderson struggled to understand, delineate, and express his feeling about the interplay between masculine and feminine, male and female.[5] Though he believed that industrialization and urbanization had, by the turn of the century, fractured American men and women, he thought that "more women than men retain the instincts that can redeem everyone."[6] His male characters, despite disappointment and discouragement, seek what Anderson felt men should get from women, a care-taking and nurturance that one critic has identified as "feeding."[7] Anderson's women, the feeders, have been described as "peculiarly circumscribed in their development,"[8] but this is because they do not need the depth or breadth of the male. They need only to fulfill their "responsibility for [creating] harmonious relationships between the sexes."[9]

Though this is an extremely complicated role to play, Anderson considered it instinctive and organic in women, and not, therefore, difficult in its intricacy. Despite the fact that many critics see his women and girls as crippled figures, Anderson did not.[10] He was a man who loved and honored his mother, married four women in what psychoanalysts might consider a search for her replacement, took inspiration from his sister, and declared his own creative powers, via metaphor, to be those of a pregnant and mothering woman.[11] Anderson honored women in that fatal mode we may call pedestalization—he set women apart from and above men, insisting that they had not only the power to give men life, but the obligation to sustain and uplift them as well.

This burden, this curse, is imposed upon the child in **"Tandy."** She is open, empty, and lacking love. Anderson has given her a life so bleak that he neither describes nor names her. She has no light, no color, no warmth. Her mother is dead; her father gives her "but little attention." They live in "an unpainted house on an unused road." In her father's obsession with "destroying the ideas of God that had crept into the minds of his neighbors . . . he never saw God manifesting himself in the little child." She is hungry for emotion. Though female, *she* needs feeding. She is five years old—so young that the sudden energy of the drunken stranger, directed solely to her, is both intensely fascinating and spontaneously absorbed.

The "tall, red-haired young man who was almost always drunk" forces his tragic desire onto the little girl he names Tandy. Though he is still young, the stranger has already taken up a truth and distorted it; he declares himself "addicted" to the fruitless search for his "thing to love." The search is his truth, and his devotion to its fruitlessness has made him grotesque. But, like the other grotesques in Winesburg, the drunkard's twisted spirit holds a charge of electric passion that can flash out, exposing its core of truth, still radiant and powerful.

The drunkard sees in Tandy what Sherwood Anderson sees in women—a vessel into which he can pour his desire, and out of which he may drink to sustain himself. Anderson believed in the primitive magic mother—a pitcher that changes water to wine and pours endlessly, eternally full. Though Tandy is a small child, she attracts the attention of the stranger, who sees what her father cannot see—her spirit, that manifestation of God, growing into the woman she will become. In the selfishness of a grotesque, the stranger exploits her hunger to satisfy his own.

In his intoxication, the drunkard becomes a prophet, an oracle who dazzles the child with his intensity. Like the seers of the Testaments, like the shamans of the old religion—wild with snakebite or vapors—his "body shook and when he tried to talk his voice trembled. . . . The stranger began to babble and made a prophecy. . . . [He] leaned forward and stared into the darkness as though seeing a vision." He declares his sympathetic bond with the female: "They think it's easy to be a woman, to be loved, but I know better." His eyes return to the little girl again, offering her his "understanding." "Perhaps of all men I alone understand." His glance wanders and the connection breaks again as he speaks into the darkened street. His prophecy takes its power from the core of his truth, for it is the author's own truth. Here is the compulsion of his plea, the heart of his desperation. "Tandy . . . is the quality of being strong to be loved. It is something men need from women and that they do not get."

The stranger rises to his feet, rocking back and forth, "about to fall." It seems he will wander out into the street, following his words. But he drops "to his knees on the sidewalk and raise[s] the hands of the child to his drunken lips. He kiss[es] them ecstatically. 'Be Tandy, little one.' he plead[s]. 'Be brave enough to dare to be loved.'" The drunken lips and ecstatic kiss are near-Dionysian; he rises above himself as he kneels before her. Whatever an adult might think—Tom Hard is oblivious—the child is deeply moved. She has received his gaze, his words, his passion, his truth. Into her small dry life, the drunkard has poured his wine. She was bereft; now she holds a vision. She is possessed by his prophecy; she too will become grotesque, in her inability to bear his truth, to contain it.

When, that night, her father speaks her name, she weeps bitterly as he tries to comfort her. But she is unprotected yet; her father still cannot see her. He too approaches her as if she were a woman, for Anderson describes his response in sexual terms. When she begins to weep, he "stop[s] beneath a tree and, taking her into his arms, beg[ins] to caress her." Of course he cannot comfort her, and "she g[ives] herself over to grief . . . shaking and sobbing as though her young strength were not enough to bear the vision the words of the drunkard had brought to her." Too young, too small, possessed by another's grief, Tandy cannot hold or control what the drunken stranger has forced upon her.

Despite the fact that he has written a story of the spiritual and emotional exploitation of a child whose circumstances render her particularly susceptible to abuse,[12] Anderson's interest was his major theme. His conscious intent was almost certainly that the reader should see this small girl elevated to the pedestal of "the lovely one," carrying the faith and desperate hope of the drunkard as a blessed and martyred recipient of his ecstatic annunciation. In fact, Anderson repeats this ecstasy in the story immediately following **"Tandy,"** called **"The Strength of God."** This next tale ends with the revelation that began the drunken stranger's interest in Tandy. The Reverend Curtis Hartman's bloody struggle with lust—his spying on the teacher, Kate Swift, in her bedroom—is charged with the same passion of the desperate soul. One night, after a fury of weeping and beating the pillow with her fists, the naked woman kneels to pray, releasing and relieving Reverend Hartman, who cries out, "God has manifested himself to me in the body of a woman!" (Anderson 155).

The repetition of this revelation intensifies its effect in **"Tandy."** Its location in a church and embodiment in a preacher further emphasize this view of the female as sacred. In **"Tandy,"** Sherwood Anderson varied the primary form of the theory of the grotesque to present an explicit statement of a theme so compelling to him that it was to remain central throughout the canon of his work.[13]

Notes

1. Luther Luedtke, "Sherwood Anderson, Thomas Hardy, and 'Tandy,'" *Modern Fiction Studies,* 20 (1974-75), 531-40; and William L. Phillips, "How Sherwood Anderson Wrote *Winesburg, Ohio,*" in *Sherwood Anderson: A Collection of Critical Essays,* ed. Walter B. Rideout (Englewood Cliffs: Prentice-Hall, 1974), p. 28.
2. Luedtke, p. 532.
3. This and all quotations from the text are from *Winesburg, Ohio* (New York: Viking, 1968).
4. Hereafter, quotations from "Tandy" will be unmarked; the story is so short that they are not necessary.
5. Mia Klein, "Sherwood Anderson: The Artist's Struggle for Self-Respect," *Twentieth Century Literature,* 23 (1977), Sherwood Anderson Issue, 49-51.
6. Nancy L. Bunge, "Women in Sherwood Anderson's Fiction," *Critical Essays on Sherwood Anderson,* ed. David D. Anderson (Boston: Hall, 1981), p. 248.
7. William V. Miller, "Earth Mothers, Succubi, and Other Ectoplasmic Spirits: The Women in Sherwood Anderson's Short Stories," *Critical Essays on Sherwood Anderson,* ed. David D. Anderson (Boston: Hall, 1981), 205-6.
8. Miller, p. 196 and John O'Neill, "Anderson Writ Large: 'Godliness' in *Winesburg, Ohio,*" *Twentieth Century Literature,* 23 (1977), Sherwood Anderson Issue, 68-9.
9. Bunge, p. 242.
10. See Miller, O'Neill, Bunge, and Judith Atlas, "Sherwood Anderson and the Women of Winesburg," *Critical Essays on Sherwood Anderson,* ed. David D. Anderson (Boston: Hall, 1981), pp. 250-66.
11. Klein, p. 49.
12. I. A. Richards has pointed out that though we often speak—and write—"with much conscious control and insight," just as often "we may be deeply surprised by what we have been doing," I. A. Richards, "Jakobson's Shakespeare: The Subliminal Structures of a Sonnet," *The Times Literary Supplement,* 28 May 1970, p. 590.
13. I appreciate the criticism of Professor James E. Rocks, who read this essay in its next-to-final form.

Martin Bidney (essay date summer 1988)

SOURCE: Bidney, Martin. "Anderson and the Androgyne: 'Something More Than Man or Woman'." *Studies in Short Fiction* 25, no. 3 (summer 1988): 261-73.

[*In the following essay, Bidney argues that an androgynous model of the psyche is the organizing principle of* Winesburg, Ohio *and serves as "the unifying vision tying together the remarkably varied stories."*]

No previous study of Sherwood Anderson has noted his use of the androgynous model of the psyche in ***Winesburg, Ohio.***[1] The present essay attempts to show that the androgyny myth is in fact the organizing principle of Anderson's complex book, the unifying vision tying together the remarkably varied stories. Anderson strategically places in his work three passages which metaphorically articulate his psychological and artistic ideal. The first of these orienting passages occurs in the prefatory **"Book of the Grotesque"**; the second is found in the visionary tale **"Tandy,"** at the exact center of the volume, with ten stories preceding and ten following (the preface excluded); the third appears in **"Sophistication,"** George's culminating epiphany, near the book's conclusion. We have in these three passages the beginning, middle, and end of a progress of vision: first an old writer sees the androgyne vision in quasi-scriptural figurations; then a drunkard sees it as potentially realizable in the future growth of Tandy; finally George and Helen experience it for the briefest of moments on earth.

The old writer in **"The Book of the Grotesque"** sees the androgynous potential within himself. Close reading of the relevant passage shows its central image subtly doubled—an androgyne within an androgyne: "He was like a pregnant woman, only that the thing inside him was not a baby but a youth. No, it wasn't a youth, it was a woman, young, and wearing a coat of mail like a knight."[2] "He" is "like" a "woman"—male and female fused—and the "woman" inside him, at first indistinguishable from a "youth," wears "mail like a knight." The images are arranged in a male-female symmetry: the "youth," moved aside for a moment to make way for the young woman, returns in the final image of the armored knight. Going from old man to pregnant woman to baby to youth to young woman to knight, we are left with an androgynous blur, something between Joan of Arc and Don Quixote. The coat of mail of the questing knight suggests the qualities which masculinity is held to add to the androgynous synthesis: boldness and initiative, to balance the intimacy and receptivity of the female in the Anderson world. The female within the old man looks male and wears mail.

This vision of androgynous wholeness is the "young thing within the writer" (22), the thing that "saved the old man" (25) from becoming a grotesque. It is a vision of life "in the beginning when the world was young" (24)—Genesis—and it is introduced by a conversation with a compassionate carpenter, "for the purpose of raising the bed" (24)—a play on "raising the dead," or the Apocalypse (cf. "For a time the two men talked of the raising of the bed" [21]). The carpenter—Anderson's hint at a Jesus-family theme, with messianic resonances—becomes "the nearest thing to what is understandable and lovable of all the grotesques in the writer's book" (25), for his womanly weeping endears him to the writer: it shows that he too approaches a male-female synthesis. We learn from the writer's vision that the seizing of individual truths—primal apple-greed—turns them into fallen falsehoods: the imagery of that vision informs us further that the supposed truths, but real falsehoods, of isolated maleness and femaleness are the worst consequences of the fall.

Angus Fletcher has argued that the protagonists of all allegories are "divided androgynes": for him, allegories shade into religious or mythic vision when their fixated, one-sided personae approach androgynous awareness, as in the concluding apocalypses of Blakean epics.[3] Certainly the Andersonian vision, at once spiritual and psychological, has marked affinities with the Blake-Shelley tradition of androgynous mythmaking. Albion must unite with Jerusalem, Prometheus with Asia, a male psychic/cosmic force with its female counterpart: the apocalyptic marriage means, for both world and mind, a higher version of primal wholeness.[4] Later writers have focused either on the religious expressions of this vision, as Eliade in *The Two and the One* (originally titled *Méphistophélès et l'Androgyne*), or on its psychological content, as in Jung's posited unity of male self with anima, female with animus. Psychological androgyny has been more recently reconceived by June Singer and Carolyn Heilbrun.[5] Sherwood Anderson contributes powerfully to this important tradition.

Central to the meaning of ***Winesburg, Ohio*** are the utterances of Anderson's persona, the visionary drunkard of **"Tandy."** The unnamed, and thus intriguingly mysterious, "stranger" sees a five-year-old girl whom he speculatively envisions as perhaps the future woman of his lifetime dream, the new woman who will be "strong to be loved," who will be—in a phrase of crucial import—"'*something more than man or woman*'" (145; emphasis added). It is implied that God is peculiarly manifest in this young girl: we are encouraged to believe that Tandy Hard (her new first name the drunkard's visionary gift) will be the divine woman—or man-woman, since she must transcend male and female. The mysterious stranger has a "faith" in the new "strong and courageous" being, but he fears his faith "will not be realized" (144-45). Tandy Hard can hardly "bear the vision" (146) thrust upon her.

What does it mean to be "strong to be loved"? What does it mean to say, as the drunkard says to Tandy, "'Be brave enough to dare to be loved'"? (145). Strength here seems closely allied to initiative and courage; "to be loved" implies intimacy and receptivity. Be "strong," or "dare," plus "to be loved" thus strongly suggests the formula: Be man plus woman; be the androgyne. The phrases "dare to be loved" and "strong to be loved" connect the androgynous vision of **"Tandy"** with George and Helen's initiation into maturity near the book's end. George "wanted to love and to be loved by" Helen (241). This is a clue that George—and Helen, too, who has similar feelings at the same moment—has understood, as the drunken visionary wanted Tandy Hard to understand, the need to combine and thus transcend both active and passive, boldness and vulnerability, the need "to love" and the need "to be loved." Just as Tandy has sobbed "as though her young strength were not enough to bear the vision the words of the drunkard had brought to her" (146), so too George has to try "With all his strength" to "hold and to understand the mood that had come upon him" (241).

How does one go about daring to be loved—combining strength and tenderness, boldness and vulnerability, active initiative and quiet receptivity, so as to become "'something more than man or woman'"? The people of Winesburg do not show us. Instead, they characteristically overcompensate for the frustrations of imposed or felt passivity by a blind rush into some form (often a destructive or unreasoned form) of activity. Rebelling against feeling "female"—and this applies to men as well as women—they try, desperately and ineffectually, to assert their "maleness." But afterward they fall back into their original passivity, or else their "male" and "female" qualities simply persist, together but separate, in mutual antagonism. In place of androgynous synthesis, we see a double distortion in the grotesques of Winesburg. Femaleness becomes twisted or suppressed into mere passivity, and maleness becomes brutally simplified into mere egotistic assertiveness or gestures of pointless aggression.

All of Anderson's characters in ***Winesburg*** are failed androgynes—even Tandy and George are not so much exceptions as intimations of something different, suggestions for the future social or spiritual development of our capacity for synthesis. But their failure would mean little if their inherent potential for androgyny were not correspondingly great. And just as, in Romantic mythmaking, the artist is the intensified type of humanity in general, so too in the neo-Romantic Andersonian world it is the artist who embodies the most urgent need and longing for androgynous synthesis, which is the fundamental requirement of Andersonian humanity.

The two women whose mental worlds Anderson describes most fully in ***Winesburg,*** Elizabeth Willard and Kate Swift, are also the women who correspond most fully to the designation of failed artist. Elizabeth combines the interrelated roles of failed actress and failed androgyne:

> For years she had been what is called "stage-struck" and had paraded through the streets with traveling men guests at her father's hotel, wearing loud clothes and urging them to tell her of life in the cities out of which they had come. Once she startled the town by putting on men's clothes and riding a bicycle down Main Street.
>
> (45)

Elizabeth dreams of combining male boldness and female intimacy, of "wandering over the world, seeing always new faces and giving something out of herself to all people" (46). Turned eventually by overwork into a "ghostly" shadow of her true self, she one day overhears her husband berating their son for acting like an absent-minded, "'gawky girl'": "'You're not a fool and you're not a woman. You're Tom Willard's son and you'll wake up. . . . If being a newspaper man had put the notion of becoming a writer into your mind that's all right. Only I guess you'll have to wake up to do that too, eh?'" (44). Elizabeth realizes that her husband is trying to suppress or distort the boy's androgynous potential, to make George equate "fool" and "woman" so he will think of writing not as expression of intimacy but as male-oriented journalistic pragmatism.

Because Elizabeth has been praying to God for years to let "'this boy be allowed to express something for us both'" (40)—i.e., to achieve a form of expression that would combine his truth and her own in a synthesis of male and female inwardness—she reacts vigorously to the threat her husband now poses. To defend George against the imminent destruction of his androgynous/artistic instinct—"the thing I let be killed in myself" (43)—she resolves to stab Tom with her dagger-like sewing scissors, half hoping that after the murder she too would suddenly die. But she collapses on a chair when she hears George's footsteps outside, and when he tells her of his decision to leave town to "'to go away and look at people and think'" (48), she feels too weak, perhaps too permanently repressed, to express her joy. It is wonderful that George still has a chance to become a true, uncorrupted writer, but Elizabeth's own chance at a starring role in high tragic drama has just passed her by.

Kate, too, is a failed artist/androgyne. Her frustrating internalized passivity and consequent sadomasochistic overcompensation attempts parallel those of Elizabeth. For schoolchildren she teaches, but even more for her own benefit, Kate makes up "intimate" stories about Charles Lamb, counterbalanced with anecdotes about "bragging, blustering, brave" Benvenuto Cellini (161)—a revealing choice of contrasting heroes, mild modesty and violent braggadocio respectively embodied in figures manifesting those elements seen as "female" and "male" in Winesburg society. Like Elizabeth, Kate wants George to express something in his writing for her also. In fact, she is in love with him, though most of the time she doesn't realize it, and when he fails to respond to her confused advances, she beats on his face with her fists. Aggressively but vainly, she rebels against her passive "female" role. As we see her walk distractedly through the wintry streets with her "features of a tiny goddess on a pedestal" (160), we recall the vague "gods" which timid Dr. Reefy claimed that he and Elizabeth Willard had worshiped together. Anderson uses fantasy-deities and pedestalled goddesses as ironic comments on the imprisoning idealizations practiced by imaginatively gifted but confused and inhibited people. One is amazed at the boldness of the sarcasm Anderson directs against forms of idealism which, he feels, frustrate union and thwart internal synthesis: it is no accident that Kate, on one of her walks, follows a street that "led over Gospel Hill and into Sucker Road . . ." (161).

Less imaginative than Elizabeth and Kate, and with less androgynous potential, Alice Hindman and Belle Carpenter make less determined efforts to counter the frustrations of their imposed "female" vulnerability. Alice, left behind by a man, remains faithful for two or three years to the quixotic ideal of his eventual return. But even after giving up on him, Alice lacks the initiative to seek out anyone else, except on one occasion when, seized with the wish to convert her vulnerability into defiance, she impulsively runs naked from her house to the sidewalk in the rain. When the man to whom she desperately calls turns out to be old and half deaf, she treats this fact simultaneously as a relief and as a punishment. She makes a swift retreat, physically into her home, mentally into a stoical acceptance of the supposed "fact that many people must live and die alone . . ." (120). Principled subjection to her supposed fate is Alice's form of mind-stunting idealism. Belle Carpenter seems somewhat stronger—"When black thoughts visited her she grew angry and wished she were a man and could fight someone with her fists" (179)—but after only one brief, delightful episode of defiance, when she smeared soft mud on her tyrannic father's clothes-press, she reverts to her customary passivity. She even chooses as her beloved a man who, in his bullying aggressiveness, is a mere copy of her bullying father, who had brutally abused her mother. Her only defiance of Ed Handby—a few walks with the notably unthreatening non-rival George—is of the mildest sort. Like Alice, Belle understands maleness as pure activity, femaleness as sheer passivity. Since both conceptions are badly oversimplified, neither woman can imagine a valid androgynous synthesis. What's needed is "something more" than "man" or "woman" as Winesburg grotesques like Alice and Belle understand these terms.

Louise Bentley—to conclude the roster of major Winesburg women—is highly intelligent, enough so to serve as provocation for the jealousy of the two Hardy sisters, who play the role of evil stepsisters to Louise's Cinderella. But she, too, quickly reverts from balked "male" ambition ("Be strong," "dare") back to "female" passivity ("to be loved"), and cannot begin to conceive of the needed androgynous synthesis. Frustrated in her intellectual ambition, she seeks salvation in being loved by some Prince Charming: "Sometimes it seemed to her that to be held tightly and kissed was the whole secret of life" (94). She places her faith in **"Surrender"** (the title Anderson gives to his account of her younger years), and when satisfaction in marriage fails, she, like Elizabeth Willard, resorts to futile gestures of murderous aggression: "She got a knife from the kitchen and threatened her husband's life" (74). Then she turns the sadism into masochism—or combines the two—through drugs, drink, reclusiveness, and frantic driving, aimlessly, "furiously through the quiet streets" (75). Louise conforms to the typology of the Winesburg woman, who seeks to make up for the limitations of "feminine" tenderness and receptivity through some act of "masculine" boldness or daring. Such acts prove useless: defiance is fruitless; destructive impulses boomerang.

We have seen that this pattern of impulsive but futile overcompensation takes variant forms among Winesburg women. The compensatory activity is sometimes aggressive, sometimes self-destructive (or both together), and sometimes it is still so submerged or muffled by inhibitions as to be hardly more than a pathetic gesture, mere token rebellion, followed by regressive perseveration in the behavior it was meant to counteract. The men of Winesburg, starting from the same frustrating feeling of imprisoning ("female") passivity, overcompensate in the same ways as the women, with equally disappointing results. Reactions rather than actions, their assertions of "maleness" are panicky, misguided, distortive.

The pattern shown by Elizabeth, Louise, and Kate is repeated in the lives of Elmer Cowley, Curtis Hartman, and the George Willard of "Nobody Knows." Elizabeth and Louise threatened their husbands with knives; Kate beat on George's face with her "fists" (165). The Winesburg men aren't desperate enough for knives, but Elmer and Curtis carry over the fist motif. Perennially passive Elmer finally projects years of frustration at being considered "queer" on the nearest person who might serve as embodiment of the community he feels has victimized him: Elmer hits George Willard "blow after blow on the breast, the neck, the mouth" (201). Afterward Elmer feels less "queer." But the meaningless tokenism of Elmer's revolt does nothing to free him from his lifetime of passive subjection to his supposed fate of queerness.

Rev. Curtis Hartman thinks he wins a violent victory through the strength of God. But the only God that Anderson values is the God "manifesting himself in the little child" Tandy, the potential androgyne (143). And *this* God will remain forever unknown to fearful Hartman, who tries to fight off lustful thoughts by smashing the stained glass window with a hole in the corner, through which he had seen the naked figure of Kate Swift. But it was only through such voyeurism that Hartman had ever succeeded in generating enough passion to enable him, for the first and only time, to be "something like a lover in the presence of his wife" (151). So Hartman's bloody fist indicates nothing but self-defeat, a relapse into passive celibacy-within-marriage. Hartman's brief aggressive act wholly defeats his maleness and insures the continuance of his lifelong passionless passivity.

George, too, tries to use egotistic "male" aggressiveness to counteract a deeper "female" fear. On his way to a tryst initiated by Louise Trunnion's note, George "was afraid . . . that he would lose courage and turn back" (59). Like Wash Williams, he timidly imagines that "Just to touch the folds of the soiled gingham dress" of his love object would "be an exquisite pleasure" (60). Overreacting against the idealizing timidity that makes him feel unmale and vulnerable, George finally, for the briefest moment, becomes "wholly the male, bold and aggressive," with "no sympathy" for Louise "in his heart" (61). But after this bit of cruelty, his nervous unease predictably returns: hapless, exaggerated gestures contain no promise of synthesis.

Anderson also offers several richly developed male examples of the same kind of heavily inhibited and thus merely token rebellion enacted by female personae such as Elizabeth and Belle. Tom Foster, Seth Richmond, and the George of "An Awakening" all illustrate the paradigm of pathetically inhibited, token boldness or "male" activity, followed by relapse into a "female" passivity which hardly makes much of a contrast. Maleness is as hopelessly oversimplified and misunderstood as femaleness in Winesburg.

Tom and Seth are astonishingly passive people, grotesques of overwhelming "femaleness" as Winesburg understands it, males without "mail." "So gentle" was Tom's nature "that he could not hate anything and not being able to understand he decided to forget" (215). Brought up in rough circumstances, he edits the roughness out of consciousness—or tries to. It returns in his fantasies, transformed into masochistic pleasure. When he falls "in love with Helen White," he images her as a flame to his dry and leafless tree, a stormy and "terrible" sea-wind to his solitary, abandoned boat (216). When, in a mood of rebellion, Tom resolves to imitate all those other people he sees and knows—that vast majority of mankind which "suffers and does wrong"—he decides to get drunk. Getting drunk, he feels, is the only thing he can do that would not "hurt someone else" (219); it is unaggressive. It's "like making love" because it "hurt . . . and made everything strange" (219): pleasure and meaning are seen as things painfully inflicted. Activity is possible for Tom only insofar as it feels like passivity. He wholly lacks the "male" component of the needed androgynous unity.

Seth is even more passive, more grotesquely non-"male." Tom, at least, savors a myriad of tiny joys, but Seth "sometimes wondered if he would ever be particularly interested in anything" (133). Resolved to court Helen White, Seth imagines himself "buried deep among the weeds beneath the tree," holding hands with Helen, who is buried right beside him; a "peculiar reluctance" keeps him from kissing her, and he listens instead to the "masterful song of labor" of the bees overhead (140). Like Tom, Seth cannot transcend masochistic passivity (death, burial) even in his fantasies: love itself must take this symbolic form.

In the ironically titled story **"An Awakening,"** George Willard remains unawakened because the brief experience of cosmic consciousness that makes him feel "unutterably big and remade" (185) really only conveys to him a sense of his pathetic passiveness in a mythically idealized form. Of the five "brave" words he mutters—"Death," "night, the sea, fear, loveliness" (185)—the first four entities are large, dark, threatening things. And so the final item, "loveliness," takes on the same passive-making, forbidding and man-dwarfing largeness. George's passivity has overmastered him: though he holds Belle's hand, he thinks not of her but of comfortingly abstract generalities: "lust and night and women" in the plural (188). We are prepared to see Ed Handby toss George casually aside: Belle, sensing George's passivity, would hardly consider him worth helping. Like those of Seth and Tom, George's inhibited attempt at passionate, active self-assertion is hardly more than an unwittingly transformed but, to the reader, barely disguised idealization of passivity. No "mail" is here, either.

There is one more major group of Andersonian failed androgynes, a group characterized not by some isolated, sudden act of real or idealized rebellion, but rather by a long-term split within the psyche. In these grotesques, the impulse toward rebellious "activity" is strong enough to make over at least half of the mind on a fairly permanent basis. But since the "active" impulse never truly transforms the "passivity" it so dislikes, the result is an unhappy stalemate, or an alternation of power between the two warring components within the mind. Unintegrated, the "male" and "female" components are each twisted away from a fulfilling purpose toward something self-punishing or destructive. Each person in this group embodies an unmastered war within, a battle of two deformed sub-selves, ruling out any prospect of an androgynous union.

Dr. Parcival and Jesse Bentley are physical grotesques because their disjointed or dissociated "vision" is mirrored in their abnormal eye movements. Each persona overcompensates, unwisely but too well, for a delicacy or vulnerability which is felt as a source of never-appeased irritation. The unsuccessful suppression of this "female" component is symbolized by an intermittent hampering of vision in the left (Latin, *sinister:* disapproved) eye. In Dr. Parcival's case, "The lid of the left eye twitched; it fell down and snapped up" (49), while of Jesse Bentley we learn: "At one time in his life he had been threatened with paralysis and his left side remained somewhat weakened. As he talked, his left eyelid twitched" (81). The grotesqueness of this one-sided vision is the more pathetic in that both men have an uncommonly expansive, artistic androgynous potential. "To write [a] book Dr. Parcival declared was the object of his coming to Winesburg to live" (55). Jesse, for his part, was "born an imaginative child" and had "within him a great intellectual eagerness" (71). Each man is inherently an artist: the prime object of their lives is a total "vision" (Parcival is even named after Sir Perceval or Parsifal, the Holy Grail visionary).

Both men were brought up religious and were closely attached to their mothers; later, trying to become less "odd" and "womanish," they each tried to work out a more "male" form of religious vision, accenting power and hardness. The "dream" of Parcival's mother, whom he loved obsessively, was to make him a "Presbyterian minister" (52); of Jesse's family, "only his mother had understood him, while everyone else was simply "amused" to see him, "small and very slender and womanish of body," dressed in the traditional garb of "young ministers" (66). Parcival's worshipful love of his mother proved unrequited—"'My mother loved my brother much more than she did me'" (53)—and since the brother, a domineering person, treated Mother roughly and managed the household finances like a dictatorial god, the jealous Parcival reluctantly concluded that the bossy brother was his superior. He conquered jealousy by identifying with, even deifying, his brother, a "superior" being whose capacity for "hatred and contempt" seemed to set Parcival an example of callous, proud lordliness (55). Eventually Parcival's brother, drunk, was run over by a railroad car, and it seems likely that even in Parcival's final philosophical formulation—"everyone in the world is Christ and they are all crucified" (57)—he is still identifying with his brother, this time as deified martyr. Parcival's philosophy is partly true, but hopelessly one-sided. Like Christ, we all suffer, but like Cain, we also inflict suffering, as Anderson emphasizes with his references to Parcival's fantasies of committing murder and to the mysterious bloody birthmarks, recalling the mark of Cain, on the hands of Tom Willy. Parcival's superman ethic is as absurd as his obsessive compensatory guilt at having refused to examine the dead child in the motor accident. Deifying his harsh brother has simply intensified Parcival's guilty self-pity as Mother's unloved, passive, and vulnerable child.

Jesse Bentley's overcompensation for being "womanish" and an "odd sheep" in the family takes the form of so massive an identification with the twin male power-myths of Biblical-patriarchal leadership and industrial-technological prowess that he works his wife to death "in his service" (69) and terrifies his grandson by trying to mark him out as his divinely chosen successor in a weird ritual of initiation. The power-crazed, yet somehow "wavering, uncertain stare" (99) of the old Jesse is so threatening to his grandson David that the latter fells Jesse with a slingshot as an inimical Goliath. Jesse had wanted, for his own crazed mystical reasons, to rub the boy's head with the blood of the lamb, but now poor David, thinking himself a murderer, feels more like Cain than Christ. The story of Jesse's unloved, neglected daughter Louise is called **"Surrender"**; that of Jesse's ritual assertion of power over David is called **"Terror."** Surrender and Terror—the grotesque extreme of "female" vulnerability and "male" aggression—together haunt the Bentley family like a curse of the Atreidae.

If Parcival and Jesse show us a mode of vision in which the left eye (in Jesse's case, the whole left side), felt as female or oversensitive, is partly disabled by the right eye (representing male strength, approved by society), Wing Biddlebaum and Wash Williams each show an analogous sort of mental rift, this time between regions designated as "upper" and "lower." These two men, like Parcival and Jesse, are instructive examples of failed androgynes because they, too, are inherently artists, with highly imaginative temperaments.

Wing, a boy-man of idealized and diffused sexuality, is "not unlike the finer sort of women"; a gifted, poetic teacher of young people, he rules "by a power so gentle that it passes as a lovable weakness" (31). His hands are compared repeatedly to wings, as of the Holy Spirit, for they express his aspiration to a communion of dreams. But after he is run out of town on false charges of molestation, Wing's hands change their function. No longer "pennants of promise" (31) to awaken the poetic imaginations of apathetic pupils, they are now employed in the male-approved business world of "activity": "With them Wing Biddlebaum had picked as high as a hundred and forty quarts of strawberries in a day" (29). The strawberry business is something "high," highly valued in the community, while the deeper sort of community Wing longs for is lowered, degraded in the estimation of his fellows. In terror, Wing suppresses his wish to talk to George of dreams and goes home instead to practice his frustrated communion ritual on the floor, where he picks up bread crumbs "like a priest engaged in some service of his church" (34). Male-oriented society demotes Wing's "female" values to the lowest level.

Hands[6] are central to the symbolism of rifts between "upper" and "lower" regions in the psyche of Wash Williams as well. Here hands represent the upper, approved world of rationality or male activity, while the rest of Wash's body is equated with the unconscious, with sexuality, with everything Wash has disowned and banished as "female." Wash himself was extremely "female" in Winesburg terms—passive, vulnerable, delicate, tender—throughout his marriage. His androgynous potential was great, his imaginative capacity expansive but idealizing: a religious poet, he worshiped his wife. "'When the hem of her garment touched my face I trembled'" (126). When his mother-in-law tried shock tactics, organizing an exhibition of her daughter's nudity to startle Wash out of passive idealism into active desire, she succeeded only in making Wash feel dishonored. Now he keeps his hands pure for his cerebral telegraph work, while he expresses his unconscious sense of defilement by letting himself become repellently fat, dirty, and ugly—a mirror image of the offensive wife whom he hates, as something "foul," with the "abandon of a poet" (124). Since Wash has unwittingly made himself into a mirror image of the object of his hatred, we must conclude that he unwittingly despises the female within himself as well. Yet he remains "still proud" of his ability as telegraph operator—perhaps still "the best telegraph operator in the state" (122). In the male world of business and brains, self-respect is still partially possible.[7]

Our last three examples of failed androgynes with permanently split personalities—Dr. Reefy, Enoch Robinson, and Joe Welling—each overcompensate for a "female" passivity through various forms of male hardness, futile assertion of power, or unrelenting, driving will. Reefy is an aphorist, Enoch a painter, Joe a homegrown natural philosopher. Though each is a potential artist, all remain fragmented, unrealized.

Since Enoch Robinson can never paint the ideally beautiful "wounded woman" (170) who embodies his vulnerable anima, he overcompensates through two equally futile forms of male-oriented power. He pretends to hold a job, to pay taxes, to get married—that is, in a manner which R. D. Laing has analyzed, Enoch does all these things with his "unreal self."[8] Meanwhile, with his "real" self, Enoch peoples his mental world with imaginary beings, over whom he is the male ruler, "a kind of tiny blue-eyed king" (171). But his unreal marriage falls through, and when his ex-wife visits him in his lonely room, her fleshly reality dissipates the insubstantial beings he has created. Nothing is left but the invisible wounded female who, once again, overshadows the animus-that-might-have-been. Enoch has never been able to paint this invisible woman and never will: he has not "mail" enough for an artist/androgyne.

Contrasting with Enoch's atrophied maleness is Dr. Reefy's suppressed femaleness. In Dr. Reefy were "seeds of something very fine" (35), like the truths he is always writing down on scraps of paper, but these seeds have compacted and hardened into something dead, like paper pills, or "hard balls" (38), or Reefy's own wooden-looking knuckles, or the fatal reefs in his own name. Reefy can't produce a coherent structure out of the truths he discovers because together they form a huge truth that becomes terrifying. So he repeatedly takes the fragmented scraps or paper pills out of his pocket and throws them defiantly at John Spaniard, whom he calls a "'sentimentalist.'" (36), thereby indicating that what threatens Reefy is a truth that might be construed as sentimental or overly tender (read "feminine").

Joe Welling is so passive in relation to his inspirations as to resemble an epileptic in his "seizures" (124). But, like Coleridge's unhappy ancient mariner whom in many ways he closely resembles,[9] Joe projects his extreme ("female") passivity outward as compelling, merciless power. "'In me,'" he says to the hypnotized ballplayers he coaches, "'you see all the movements of the game'" (107). These words are the motto of Joe's life: he bosses and bewitches rather than communicates. Although he rhetorically asks, "'You can't be too smart for Sarah, now can you?'" (111), Joe is really much "too smart" for his "sad-looking" financée (108), for he talks *at* her, not *to* her, showing that he cares as little for her as for anyone else. Unconsciously overcompensatory power-drive has turned Joe into a solipsist: the victim of seizures seizes total power.

Finally, a word about **"The Untold Lie."** Though adventurous Hal Winters has asked the "quiet, rather nervous" (202) Ray Pearson for advice on whether to marry the young woman whom Hal had audaciously but predictably gotten "in trouble" (205), anything Ray says "'would have been a lie'" (209). Horribly henpecked, the abjectly passive Ray cries out at one point against his life of enslavement to wife and children. The beauty of the land at sunset makes Ray want to "scream or hit his wife with his fists" in frustration (206), behavior reminiscent of Kate or Elmer or Curtis. But Ray's children have given him "pleasant evenings" (208-09) of deep value. In sum: Ray's excessive ("female") passivity has been no worse and no better, no more or less one-sided, than the assertive ("male") adventurousness for which Hal is notorious in Winesburg. Hal and Ray are each incomplete. They are the split halves of the psychological androgyne.

If, in the people of Winesburg, "feminine" receptivity is continually suppressed into forms of inertness, delusion, and fear, it cannot be said that the qualities of boldness and enterprising action defined as "masculine" receive adequate expression either. Sometimes, as with Tom, Seth, and Enoch, "male" attributes are repressed. When affirmed, "male" qualities are misused; employed in panicky reactions rather than originative actions, they too are twisted out of shape—into forms of oblivious, egotistic willfulness. The result is a lack of fertile interaction between self and anima, or animus. Instead we see recurrent confict, inner rifts. The greater the androgynous/artistic potential, the more tragic the rift. No one in Winesburg is unaffected. The day of the psychological or spiritual androgyne is not yet. But like the old man and the carpenter at the book's beginning, Anderson himself speaks implicitly of the raising of the dead.[10]

Notes

1. Sally Adair Rigsbee, however, has broken new ground with her valuable emphasis on the "crippled feminine dimension of life" in Anderson's book; see Rigsbee, "The Feminine in *Winesburg, Ohio,*" *Studies in American Fiction* 9 (Autumn 1981), 236. Her correlation of femininity, as defined in Winesburg, with the values of "vulnerability, intimacy, and tenderness" (pp. 236-37) is accurate and has also been adopted here. But she devotes no attention to masculinity, or to androgyny, in Anderson's vision.
2. Sherwood Anderson, *Winesburg, Ohio* (New York: The Viking Press, 1960), p. 22; all quotations are from this edition. For biographical background, see Robert George Kraft, "Sherwood Anderson, Bisexual Bard: Some Chapters in a Literary Biography," diss. Univ. of Washington, 1969. Rigsbee's description of the above-cited passage as depicting an "image of artistic power as a woman within a woman" is misleading: such a formulation ignores half the image-data in the passage, as my analysis makes clear.
3. Angus Fletcher, *Allegory: The Theory of a Symbolic Mode* (Ithaca: Cornell Univ. Press, 1964), p. 356, n. 61.
4. Though one cannot prove Anderson studied Blake or Shelley, for general Romantic affinities, see

Walter Göbel, *Sherwood Anderson: "Ästhetizismus als Kulturphilosophie* (Heidelberg: Carl Winter Universitätsverlag, 1982), pp. 141-52. Though Plato's Aristophanic myth of the primal androgyne in *Symposium* is a possible reference point, more immediate thematic parallels may be found in Whitman. On parallels between Blake and Whitman, see my "Structures of Perception in Blake and Whitman: Creative Contraries, Cosmic Body, Fourfold Vision," *Emerson Society Quarterly: A Journal of the American Renaissance* 28 (Winter 1982), 36-47. In Anderson's quasi-Whitmanesque *A New Testament* (New York: Boni and Liveright, 1927), p. 11, we find the following androgynous vision:

> At times, just for a moment, I am a Caesar, a Napoleon, an Alexander.
> I tell you it is true.
> If you men who are my friends and those of you who are acquaintances could surrender
> yourselves to me for just a little while.
> I tell you what—I would take you within myself and carry you around within me as though
> I were a pregnant woman.

Anderson the would-be prophet is a pregnant Napoleon. His androgynous vision, dubbed "insanity" to disarm critics, comes through clearly in paired images of a clinging vine and a phallic worm: "My insanity is a slow creeping vine clinging to a wall. / My insanity is a white worm with a fire in its forehead" (15).

5. See Mircea Eliade, *The Two and the One,* trans. J. M. Cohen (New York: Harper and Row, 1965); *Méphistophélès et l'Androgyne* (Paris: Gallimard, 1962). Also, C. G. Jung, *Aion: Researches into the Phenomenology of the Self,* trans. R. F. C. Hull (Princeton: Princeton Univ. Press, 1959), pp. 11-22; June Singer, *Androgyny: Toward a New Theory of Sexuality* (Garden City, N.Y.: Doubleday, 1977); Carolyn G. Heilbrun, *Toward a Recognition of Androgyny* (New York: Knopf, 1973).

6. For more on hands in *Winesburg,* see Carl J. Maresca, "Gestures as Meaning in Sherwood Anderson's *Winesburg, Ohio,*" *College Language Association Journal* 9 (March 1966), 279-83.

7. Not only does Wash hate his wife with the "abandon of a poet"; we can probably even identify the specific poet-mentor Anderson may have in mind. Wash's description of his wife as a "living-dead thing . . . making the earth foul by her presence" (122) recalls the lines, "The Nightmare Life-in-Death was she, / Who thicks man's blood with cold." See "The Rime of the Ancient Mariner," ll., 193-94, in *The Complete Poetical Works of Samuel Taylor Coleridge,* ed. E. H. Coleridge (Oxford: Oxford Univ. Press, 1912), I, 194.

8. R. D. Laing, *The Divided Self: An Existential Study in Sanity and Madness* (Baltimore: Penguin, 1965), *passim,* especially pp. 94-105, "The false-self system."

9. "Pouncing upon a bystander he began to talk. For the bystander there was no escape. The excited man breathed into his face, peered into his eyes, pounded upon his chest with a shaking forefinger, demanded, compelled attention" (*WQ* 103). Cf. Coleridge: "'Hold off! unhand me, grey-beard loon!'" ("The Rime of the Ancient Mariner," l. 11).

10. This would be my reply to David Stouck's sensitive but pessimistic appraisal, "*Winesburg, Ohio* as a Dance of Death," *American Literature* 48 (January 1977), 525-42.

Joseph Dewey (essay date summer 1989)

SOURCE: Dewey, Joseph. "No God in the Sky and No God in Myself: 'Godliness' and Anderson's *Winesburg.*" *Modern Fiction Studies* 35, no. 2 (summer 1989): 251-59.

[*In the following essay, Dewey underscores the significance of "Godliness" and the story of Jesse Bentley within the context of* Winesburg, Ohio *as a whole.*]

Of all the wraiths in Winesburg, none seems lonelier than Jesse Bentley. Alone of Anderson's characters, he seems unable to elicit even the sympathy of his creator. Whereas Anderson delicately balances sympathetic amusement with a most profound admiration for his other grotesques, he seems callously unambivalent toward Jesse. In the raging egocentricity of the Ohio landowner who refashions himself into some Old Testament patriarch while shamelessly indulging gross materialism, Anderson seems to express his generation's bitter condemnation of the new age "love of surfaces," the new "religion of getting on" ("To Waldo Franks" 23). To insert this lengthy lampoon of the Puritan work ethic, Anderson seems to set aside awkwardly not only his artist-hero, George Willard, but also his novel's melancholic ambience, the sense of irresistible yearning for communion that so twists the spirits of his other characters. Examined casually, Jesse does not seem to fit with them. Where they are retiring, he is assertive; where they seem frozen and static, he is a dynamo; where they are lost in self-pity, he crows of his many accomplishments; where they bottle themselves up into tiny chambers, he sees with a vision that encompasses hundreds of acres; where they nurse quiet anxieties to escape Winesburg, he thrusts his roots deeply; where they seem confused and plagued by doubts, he subscribes to a clear, teleological order; where they seem curiously infertile, he begats with Biblical intensity. Indeed, it would seem appropriate that Jesse lives far outside the corporation limits of Winesburg, a suggestion of how removed he is from Anderson's other grotesques.

Yet Anderson takes Jesse far more seriously than he would some throwaway caricature of feverish pietism. Indeed, the tales of Jesse Bentley are by far the longest in the book. In the description of the impulses that drive Jesse, Anderson points out that Jesse is driven half by greediness and half by fear. To understand Jesse's appropriateness, the reader must explore the complexity of these fears rather than the simplicity of the greed. Refusing the harsh caricature of Puritanism that figures in the work of Anderson's contemporaries, among them Dreiser and Lewis, Anderson offers a sensitive reading of the original Puritan vision that accounts not only for the intensity of Jesse Bentley's campaign to tame the Ohio wilderness but also for his place in the ongoing story of the evolution of George Willard.[1]

I

To understand Jesse Bentley, Anderson cautions early, "we will have to go back to an earlier day" (***Winesburg*** 64). Jesse Bentley reflects Anderson's fascination with the New England consciousness[2]; in journals and letters Anderson assessed the Puritan legacy, joining other early century writers who, uneasy over the loneliness implicit in the human condition unrelieved even by speculation about a possible union with some divinity, reviewed the fervor of the original Puritans and their dream of seeking the transfiguration possible in a union with God.[3]

What those Puritans sought (and what Jesse seeks two hundred years later) was confirmation of the self through communion with some greater whole, an awesome union between creation and creator, between the timebound and impotent and the fixed and omnipotent. Yet because the only dignity opened to man was such a restoration of his maimed soul with a divinity that felt no obligation to indicate its attention, the Puritan heritage often reflects anxious lives spent searching for ways to connect with an all-too-distant God, to fight the holy struggle with doubt, despair, and self-insufficiency that often eclipsed the remarkably successful struggle to coax a community from the Massachusetts wastes.

This spiritual hunger felt by Puritans struck Anderson deeply. Although he emphatically rejected the commercial misappropriation of Puritanism and its corruption into the Victorian "virtues" of sexual repression, dry intellectuality, and material acquisition, he did find use for Puritanism in its expressive hunger for communion, a hunger that so many of his Winesburg characters feel. "To the young man a kind of worship of some power outside himself is essential. One has strength and enthusiasm and wants gods to worship" (*A Story Teller's Story* 164).[4] The question that Jesse poses in the novel is one as old as Plymouth Plantation and as immediate as Winesburg itself with its deathly quiet streets: can the imperfect finite earn the infinite, feel the surety of that outside power? In the tradition of Puritan mysticism, Jesse seeks to be blasted by an excess of light. His raging prayers up and down the Wine Creek Valley capture the desperate (and thoroughly) Puritan condition of man never being at home in however splendid a world he finds or builds on earth. Jesse's neat cluster of houses gives ironic testimony to his homelessness; at heart he feels himself an outcast in a Puritan postlapsarian landscape. In an age of exploding capitalism, Jesse resists heroically the purely material. Although tempted by the success of his unending campaign to create a farm non pareil, he finds nevertheless his possessions ultimately unfulfilling. His farm is critical only as a devotion to God. Absurdly he asserts his role as God's chosen; fearfully in the fury of this assertion, he raises traditional questions of Puritan self-insufficiency but to a universe fearfully silent or, worse, fearsomely empty.

The story of Jesse Bentley, then, is not a parable against relentless acquisition or a lampoon of fanatical faith. It is the story of hunger. Jesse's dilemma is not that he is soulless but that his soul is lean and starved. Any satisfaction he may seem to take in his accumulation of land is undercut by this growing desperation for God to assent to its importance. He can dredge a farm from the swamps, drive farmhands relentlessly, work his wife to an early death, even fashion about his own head an unsteady halo—yet without that recognition, without that communion, he is denied peace. As the Puritans discovered, Jesse finds his God incomprehensible, ominously quiet even at times of greatest need. If, as Perry Miller has suggested, the central drama of the Puritan experiment was the relationship between man and his God, it was often a heartcrushingly one-sided communication.

Yet such silence seems profoundly more disturbing for Jesse. In a time when God was big in the hearts of His creation, the Puritans communed with merely a silent God; Jesse communes with an absent God. As Anderson makes clear, Jesse, driven to call on the very God he fears, uses a shofar in the age of the telephone. He is left with the agony of separation. Anderson counsels, nevertheless, a way to resist the implicit threat of being left, as Jesse is, living in a simple material world, a way, in short, to lose God but to keep the faith. When the finite, awash in temporality, find no hope of the sweet union with the infinite promised by religion, Anderson counteroffers a communion by way of art, the articulation of a sympathetic union not of man to God, maimed soul to distant perfection, but rather of man to man or, more exactly, maimed soul to maimed soul. Lovingly, George Willard, gradually educated into this power of communion, will come to gather the fragments of Winesburg's shattered souls and will give compassionate expression to that agony. In such a humane gesture there is a wondrous sort of religion, a healing of souls that offers the bittersweet consolation of human communion to relieve the aching burden of an alienation as wide as the modern cosmos itself.[5] Winesburg, then, must have its failed prophet to underscore the religious dimension of George Willard's commitment to art. In the movement from prophet to artist, in Biblical terms from king to poet, Anderson charts the course in which the art replaced religion. In *A Story Teller's Story* Anderson reveals an emerging artist desperately searching for the security and stability offered by religion. The alternative, a fragmented multiverse or a nothingness too bleak to accept, reduced Anderson to the sort of paralysis that afflicts Jesse by the close of his story. In a novel where any movement has validity, Jesse is a character moving but in all the wrong directions. When Jesse searches the hillsides all about him for validation, George learns to look no further than the nearest human heart; when Jesse looks for peace outside himself, George will learn to look inside; when Jesse looks up in frantic desperation, George will come to look about in gentle compassion.

II

Early on, Jesse Bentley determines that he will not be just another "clod" like those all around him. Such a determination echoes Elizabeth Willard's hopes for her son. "He is not a dull clod, all words and smartness" (***Winesburg*** 43). But the development from Jesse to George is a movement from ego to self. Although Jesse inherits the sense of a driving self-assertion that is so much a part of the American tradition, when his religion fails him so completely, he becomes simply an ego, a forcible will with an unbending purpose. The considerable energy of his self-assertion merely inflates his own character, and therefore he cannot bridge the way toward communion with his God. He is left in the sham resplendence of empty grandeur, alone—as Anderson points out, Jesse is the inventor of a machine that turns wire into fences. In the dazzling spectacle of the Old Testament prophet, Jesse loses the humility necessary not only for the traditional religious experience he seeks but also, as Anderson demonstrates, for an artistic one as well, the sort that George establishes as a man with Helen and as an artist later with the Winesburg citizenry. Jesse's unsympathetic disdain establishes his religion as a self-enclosing impulse, unable to furnish the communion he so desperately seeks. In the relationship with George suggested by Mrs. Willard's hope for her son, Anderson juxtaposes the urgency of Jesse's ego that diminishes the more it asserts itself with the intensity of George Willard's self that expands the more it is asserted.

When Jesse absurdly invokes notions of Puritan typology, he fancies himself the fulfillment of the Old Testament patriarchs, the encroaching neighbors as legions of Philistines, his offspring as potential Davids. He finds not only identity but community as well. When he confronts his bewildered and terrified grandson at the mock-sacrifice, Jesse tries desperately to discover a sympathetic soul who would do what the empty Ohio sky will not—validate what has become for Jesse a mission as burning as the Puritans' mission to erect a City on a Hill. Because Anderson keeps the figure of God so carefully absent, Jesse's entire project threatens to collapse into the absurdity of one man's fanaticism. But clearly Jesse wants to be possessed not so much by God as by significance. He yearns for a sign that what he has created in his hard hunger has validity. His lengthy tale is the difficult story of the insufficiency of what is simply material, coming hard on the story of George Willard's furtive initiation into the mystery of sex with his uninspired coupling with Louise Trunnion. George will find his way finally to the sophisticated touch of Helen White's hand. That Jesse wrings purpose from a religion no longer available drives him more inward than Anderson can allow. Jesse comes to feel the insuperable sense of his farm being simply that. As George moves to tap the tremendous potential of the quotidian, Jesse despairs over it, finally bankrupt. When his God does not touch his fulsome soul, it shrivels into a thin ego. The more he pursues religion, the more he is doomed. He destroys any links with humanity, turns hard eyes away from his wife, his daughter, his grandson, and ends a man alone, far from even the community of Winesburg. Jesse's spirit haunts Anderson's book of spirits. Anderson uses notions of Jesse's farm as a beehive not to suggest that, compared with the other villagers, Jesse is expansive and bustling but to suggest furious kinesis without purpose, relentlessly spent without spiritual invigoration. Ironically, Jesse's soul is finally inert—it cannot expand to the outermost sympathies there to discover the self. In his grandson, he longs to affirm his covenant with his God, his bridge between the finite and the infinite. In the spontaneous prayer session in the woods and later, more dramatically, in the aborted sacrifice of the lamb, Jesse attempts to assert his union. Unable to face the chaos implicit in a godless world, Jesse ends up lost. Anderson hints at Jesse's failings, afflicts him with approaching paralysis and a nervous twitch that marks him in moments of fervent religiosity. Jesse fails to make the transition away from the spent powers of religion toward the potential of art, but the reader can examine what Jesse does accomplish. In the Old Testament tradition that he values, Jesse begats offspring. In the stories of Jesse's daughter and his grandson, tales interwoven with Jesse's, Anderson provides the vital links between Jesse's pathetic deterioration and George Willard's grand maturation.

III

Louise Bentley, Anderson notes, inherited her father's gray eyes. In many disturbing ways, she sees the world much as her father. She longs to be recognized, to be reassured by communion, to be noticed, her significance confirmed. Like her father, she is not happy with the simpler achievements. In her hunger for education, she ransacks the Hardy family library with a spiritual urgency that leads her to feel, like her father, a radical isolation. In her fanaticism, she is abandoned at school and more cruelly by the Hardy daughters, threatened by Louise's obvious achievements. Like her father, the more isolated she feels, the more she ranges about for communion. Unlike her father, she does not look up but rather around her but not gently or lovingly as George Willard will—rather, she looks about like some ravenous animal scouring the landscape for sustenance. She settles on John Hardy for whom she has a vague distaste. When she thinks that the secrets of life are to be possessed, she says quietly to herself what her father says in a rage at the blank skies over the Winesburg countryside. Like her father, she calls "notice me" to a largely indifferent cosmos. Indeed, there are no neater or sadder parallels to Jesse's fist-waving philippics than his daughter's wild carriage ride through the night streets of Winesburg (streets, of course, that are empty) or her setting fire (harmlessly) to the Hardy house, or, finally, her marriage to John Hardy. They are messages unreceived.

Unloved and unloving, Louise is a difficult middle stage between the failing religion of her father and the emerging artistic sense of her son. Of the triptych that Anderson fashions, she fits most closely the profile of Winesburg's citizens. What Jesse seeks in God and what David shows promise of seeking in the imagination, Louise seeks in the sexual act. It is precious tender spent wastefully, like Jesse's heartfelt prayers lost in the distances between stars. Louise finds such simple vitality pitilessly stymied. She marries in desperation, fearing pregnancy; she never connects with her son. Like her father with his fence-making machine, she ends up bitter and walled-in, locked for days in her room. Her story of doorless walls grimly rearing themselves about her soul is the stuff of Anderson's grotesques. Even in her surrender, however, Louise links Jesse to David and by extension to George. In Anderson, the sexual communion is analogous to the act of writing[6]; they are both the spontaneous show of sympathetic sensibility that links souls profoundly. When Louise searches for sexual healing and settles for bloodless coupling with John Hardy, she offers the reader another example of failed communion. Naturally, the title of her story is **"Surrender."** But she surrenders more than her self, more than her sexuality. She surrenders her son to the care of her father, and in doing so, she initiates the events that will give to Winesburg its first refugee-artist.

Although David Hardy is hardly a conscious artist in the manner of the writer George Willard, he does, nevertheless, in his two stumbling flights from Winesburg foreshadow George's resolution that finally allows him to step beyond Winesburg's city limits. When Jesse's dementia at the mock-sacrifice finally breaks David's "shell of the circumstances of his life" (97), what emerges is at least the embryonic artist, one armed for manhood with both sensitivity and imagination, a concept that shares much with Anderson's notions of the artistic consciousness. From this root Jesse springs forth Anderson's neoredeemer—the prototype artist.

David has brown eyes, a suggestive detail that separates him from the failed version of his mother and his grandfather. Where they are demonstrative and forceful, he is introspective, given to talking to himself. Where Jesse betrays his faith and Louise betrays the sexual impulse, David finds his way to the imagination. As Jesse prepares the lamb for sacrifice, David uses his imagination to invest every action with significance. As Jesse and Louise move into closets of their own fashioning, David, transplanted to the farmhouse, opens up to sounds and sights, delighting in the outdoors. Gentle, expansive, imaginative, open—David prefigures Anderson's artist. Like the many citizens of Winesburg who confide in George, Jesse, on a carriage ride about the farm, is struck impulsively to trust the boy to understand the importance of his mission. Clearly, David Hardy, who ponders at odd moments what his life will offer him, is poised on a threshold.

After David strikes out at his grandfather, rejecting outright Jesse's religious enthusiasm, he flees impulsively not only the farm but Winesburg as well. His closing words lend special significance to ties he has with George Willard. "I have killed the man of God and now I will myself be a man and go into the world" (102). David prefigures George's growth from innocence to experience. He feels strong sympathy for the lamb Jesse chooses for sacrifice and blanches as Jesse approaches with the knife. Far from the "vague and intangible hunger" (96) that finally reduces his mother to bitter surrender, David's terror sparks him to action, although frenzied and unplanned. He forsakes religion, forsakes family, to embrace hesitatingly and fearfully nothing less than the world itself.

David then suggests the function of the lengthy parable of Jesse Bentley. Anderson "slays" the religiosity of

Jesse and prepares for the conversion of such destructive energy into the calmer drive of George Willard. David's journey from Winesburg begins, as it must, in fiction. He has only knocked down Jesse; he has not killed him at all. Yet the Jesse he leaves behind is a strangely quieter man. His reaction to his grandson's departure denies Jesse the anagnorisis that would confer on him the dignity of tragedy. Although he does admit he was too greedy, he adds that God has taken his boy. Jesse will not abandon his ego; still he lays claim to a potent God who would speak to him directly if only to admonish him so severely.

IV

It is fitting that a writer so convinced of the religious appointment of the artist in a world reeling from the loss of its God should center his novel on a religious zealot only figuratively slain. Like displaced Puritans, both Jesse and George, finally twin sons of different mothers, seek the reassuring communion with a potent Otherness to rescue them from the legions of the poignant but pathetic, the "clods" of Winesburg. In the passage from Jesse to George, Anderson preserves the sense of religion to define the essence of the artist in the new wasteland in which the springs of religion have dried. The progression from Jesse to David via Louise's failure is a progression from failed religion to art via the thwarting of the sexual communion; it is the triangular relationship that recalls the relationship of the Reverend Hartman, Kate Swift, and George himself. Reverend Hartman, bursting into George's office convinced that the vision of Kate Swift's naked shoulders is a sign from God, recalls Jesse's displaced energy and absurdity in trying to divine the eternal in his farmland. The reader knows that Kate will teach George the basic commandments of Anderson's humane art. Like Louise, she is frustrated sexually, despite her advances to George. She will help nurture the artist-hero by warning George to cease his word-playing and to delve into his humanity.

Finally, to deal with Jesse Bentley solely in terms of acquisition is to deal only with surfaces. His essence connects him with the village ghosts of Winesburg. In Jesse's one-way conversation with the divine, Anderson reenforces the general sense of failed communication chronic in his village. Alone in a cast of inarticulates, however, Jesse can articulate his fears of the atomistic age dawning in America, his ache to be sublime in a cosmos that denies sublimity. More than David, Jesse feels the terror of the closing tale. He tries to pull his grandson into his great arching vision of typological grandeur that could assure him that his life was not splendidly unnecessary. When he is silenced, the book reaches its nadir, a point that only George Willard's gradual ascent can salvage. That he is condemned to search for a God long laid to rest damns him to ineffectuality and prepares the reader for George's eventual assertion of the power of invention rather than invective.

Whereas Jesse prays for God's touch and Louise craves a warming touch of sexual possession, David stumbles toward the new fictive diety. David is, finally, hardier than his family. It is surely no accident that Anderson chooses Jesse as the name for his modern Puritan. Typologically, Jesse corresponds to the Old Testament patriarch, the prosperous sheep-farmer who gives to Israel his son David, the maker of songs, the harper-king. When Jesse confesses that God has taken his boy, he inadvertently suggests what has indeed taken place. But what has taken David is not Jesse's raging omnipotent figure but rather the new god that Anderson offers for the seemingly hopeless disorder of the early century—the god of art. When so much seemed blasted away into a moral wasteland, writers such as Anderson recognized a similar dilemma in the soul-shaking loneliness felt by that generation of Puritans who faced the merciless physical wasteland on a thin strip of land between ocean and wilds. The comfort that those Puritans found in their religion Anderson fuses into his faith in a compassionate art.

To understand the mystery and interiority of George Willard's conversion from hack journalist to artist, one must go by way of Jesse Bentley. George reshapes that feverish frenetic search for spiritual communion to produce his knowing sophistication. For readers who have long puzzled over where George Willard is in the lengthy dissertation on Jesse Bentley, his farm, and his family, the answer can only be suggested. George is present in the rage of Jesse's eyes turned upward toward vacancy; he is in the desperation of Louise's spread fingers grasping the edges of private walls; and, finally, he is in the stumbling resolution of David Hardy's churning feet as he disappears out of the Wine Creek Valley.

Notes

1. Although evidence in Anderson's letters and in his memoirs indicates that the story of Jesse Bentley figured prominently in the creation of the tales, critical reactions to the story have ranged from Irving Howe's early dismissal of it to John A. McAleer's sympathetic defense but apparent inability to "fit" the Bentley story into the scheme of George Willard. Ralph Ciancio suggests that of all the characters Jesse does not seem able to elicit Anderson's sympathy, Rosemary Laughlin's brief explication helps readers understand the story but does not make a place for the tale in Anderson's larger work. Of recent criticism, John O'Neill best treats the subject although he suggests only a unity of tone rather than specific thematic ties between

Jesse and the rest of the work. He does make a persuasive argument for the relationship between David and George but does not make any such claims for ties between Jesse and George. Indeed, O'Neill dismisses Jesse's hunger for his God as "fundamentally adolescent" (78).

2. Both Anthony Hilfer and Norman Pearson look at the ties between Anderson and Puritanism. They suggest that Anderson reacted particularly to the writings of Waldo Franks (*Our America*) and of Van Wyck Brooks (*The Wine of the Puritans*), works that treated the influence of the Puritans in harsh, negative terms.
3. Sacvan Bercovicz analyzes the Puritan notions of the self in the American literary tradition. D. Sebastian's unpublished dissertation presents a summary of the Puritan influence at the time of Anderson, a survey that includes Adams, Robinson, Dreiser, London, Crane, Masters, and Lewis.
4. In the letter to Waldo Franks, Anderson writes, "a curious notion came over me. Is it not likely that when the country was new and men were often alone in the fields and forests they got a sense of bigness outside themselves that has now been lost? I don't mean the conventional religious thing . . . the people, I fancy, had a savagery superior to our own. Mystery whispered in the grass." In *A Story Teller's Story* Anderson records a moment of his own experience when such a tie to Otherness was destroyed, leaving him in a paralysis that recalls Jesse: "There was no God in the sky, no God in myself, no conviction in myself that I had the power to believe in God, and so I merely knelt in the dust in the silence and no words came to my lips" (270).
5. One of the most complete examinations of Anderson's theories of the relationship between religion and art is found in D. Sebastian who makes the points that for Anderson the beauty of art came from humanistic rather than aesthetic impulses and that the finest expression possible for the artist was sympathy.
6. The often explicit and somewhat obsessive tie Anderson found between sexual communion and the writing act is summed up in Sebastian, although Benjamin T. Spenser and Maxwell Geismar trace the fascination to parts of Anderson's *Midwestern Chants.*

Works Cited

Anderson, Sherwood. *A Story Teller's Story.* Garden City: Garden City Publishing, 1924.

———. "To Waldo Franks." 27 August 1917. Letter 22. *The Letters of Sherwood Anderson.* Ed. Howard Mumford Jones. Boston: Little, 1953. 23.

———. *Winesburg, Ohio.* 1919. New York: Viking, 1969.

Bercovicz, Sacvan. *The Puritan Origins of the Self.* New Haven: Yale UP, 1975.

Ciancio, Ralph. "The Sweetness of Twisted Apples: The Unity of Vision in *Winesburg, Ohio,*" *PMLA* 87 (1972): 994-1006.

Geismar, Maxwell. *The Last of the Provincials: The American Novel from 1915-1925.* Boston: Houghton, 1947. 223-286.

Hilfer, Anthony. *The Revolt from the Village.* Chapel Hill: U of North Carolina P, 1969.

Howe, Irving. *Sherwood Anderson.* New York: Sloane, 1951.

Laughlin, Rosemary. "'Godliness' and the American Dream in *Winesburg, Ohio.*" *Twentieth Century Literature* 13 (1967): 97-103.

McAleer, John A. "Christ Symbolism in *Winesburg, Ohio.*" *Discourse* 4 (1961): 168-181.

Miller, Perry. *The New England Mind.* New York: Macmillan, 1939.

O'Neill, John. "Anderson Writ Large: 'Godliness' in *Winesburg, Ohio.*" *Twentieth Century Literature* 23 (1977): 67-83.

Pearson, Norman Holmes. "Anderson and the New Puritanism." *Newberry Library Bulletin* 2 (1948): 52-63.

Sebastian, D. "Sherwood Anderson's Theory of Art." Diss. Louisiana State U, 1972.

Spenser, Benjamin T. "Sherwood Anderson: American Mythopoeist." *American Literature* 41 (1969): 1-18.

Gwendolyn Morgan (essay date fall 1989)

SOURCE: Morgan, Gwendolyn. "Anderson's 'Hands'." *Explicator* 48, no. 1 (fall 1989): 46-7.

[*In the following essay, Morgan examines Anderson's use of hand imagery in the story "Hands."*]

As Malcolm Cowley notes in his introduction to ***Winesburg, Ohio,*** a major influence of Sherwood Anderson on American literature lies in the tightness and precision of his style, a legacy admitted by such other writers as Wolfe and Hemingway. It is with surprise, then, that we note an artistic problem in the imagery of **"Hands."** This story, considered one of his best crafted, takes as its major symbol the hands of the central character, for "the story of Wing Biddlebaum is a story of hands" (28). Ever active, they are the expression of all Wing feels and thinks, indeed the very index of his humanity. This is succinctly expressed in the passage that describes Wing's method of communicating his vision and his affection to his students:

> Here and there went his hands, caressing the shoulders of the boys, playing with tousled heads. As he talked his voice became soft and musical. There was a caress in that also. In a way the voice and the hands, the stroking of the shoulders and the touching of the hair were a part of the schoolmaster's effort to carry a dream into the young minds. By the caress that was in his fingers he expressed himself. . . . Under the caress of his hands doubt and disbelief went out of the minds of the boys and they began also to dream.
>
> (31-2)

An inconsistency appears when the hands that are representative of such sensitivity and affection are compared to the most inhuman of all symbols in Anderson's writing—machinery:

> Wing Biddlebaum talked much with his hands. The slender expressive fingers, forever active, forever striving to conceal themselves in his pockets or behind his back, came forth and became *the piston rods of his machinery of expression.*
>
> (my emphasis)

There are indeed points in the story at which Wing's hands express his dehumanized, "grotesque" condition, but this is not such an instance: the conversations with George are the only moments when the protagonist regains any measure of his humanity. Thus, the analogy to piston rods would seem inapproprate here. The problem appears to stem from Anderson's attempt to have the hands reflect Wing's progress toward his "grotesque" condition as well as the hidden emotional depths of his character. The first level of symbolism bleeds into the second and produces a stylistic inconsistency.

In Wing's days as a teacher, the hands expressed concern and gentleness, summarized in the first passage quoted above. It was misinterpretation of those hand movements by a a narrow-minded community that led to his ostracism. The character's consequent fear of human contact is afterward reflected in his tendency to hide his hands, and his final dehumanization represented by his employment as a berry picker who worked with mechanical speed and precision (29). Wing's progress from open emotional expression and altruistic concern, in Pennsylvania, to his grotesque isolation and repression, in Winesburg, is, for his hands, a change from soft, fluttering contact with human beings to quick, darting movements that are nothing but the means to earn a living. The symbolism is tight and effective, characteristic of Anderson's work.

For the most part, Anderson is also successful in employing the hand imagery to represent Wing's inner being. The pounding of his fists on tables, walls, or fence posts mirrors his earnestness and enthusiasm during conversations with George Willard (29). His anxiety is expressed through rubbing his hands together (28), his affection for George through a caress (30). When Wing's fears make it necessary for him to withdraw into himself, he thrusts his hands into his pockets (30), and his generally reticent nature is represented by "their inclination to keep hidden away" (29). It is also through hands that Wing's essential warmth and humanness are contrasted with the brutality and narrow-mindedness of others. Wing's gentleness is expressed in the soft, fluid movements of his hands; the hostility of the lynch mob that drives him from Pennsylvania is reflected in "hard knuckles [which] beat down into the frightened face of the schoolmaster" and hands that carry lanterns and ropes and throw sticks and mud (32-3).

That Anderson took pains to make the symbolic import of Wing Biddlebaum's hands comprehensive is thus clear. That Wing's inner nature is above all emotional is evident in the fluidity and naturalness of his hand movements. Their activity is at various times compared with "the beating of the wings of an imprisoned bird" (28), "fluttering pennants" (31), wriggling fish (28), and the devout fingering of a devotee's rosary (34). Only when Wing suppresses his humanity in his role as outcast field laborer do they behave in a mechanistic and inhuman fashion. Thus it is surely an oversight on the author's part when Anderson blurs his imagery by bringing the mechanistic to bear on the emotional, transforming the highly expressive fingers into "piston rods" and the means for expressing the human essence of this very human character into "machinery."

Works Cited

Anderson, Sherwood. "Hands." *Winesburg, Ohio.* New York: Penguin, 1976.

Cowley, Malcolm. Introduction. *Winesburg, Ohio.* By Sherwood Anderson. New York: Penguin, 1976.

Martin Bidney (essay date spring 1990)

SOURCE: Bidney, Martin. "Refashioning Coleridge's Supernatural Trilogy: Sherwood Anderson's 'A Man of Ideas' and 'Respectability'." *Studies in Short Fiction* 27, no. 2 (spring 1990): 221-35.

[*In the following essay, Bidney finds similarities between "Respectability" and "A Man of Ideas," arguing that both stories "turn out to be epiphanies of distorted love."*]

The poet-philosopher Joe Welling, solipsistic yet inspired, and the monstrously ugly yet mysteriously attractive Wash Williams, courtly lover turned morose misogynist, are two of the most profoundly conceived visionary grotesques in Sherwood Anderson's ***Winesburg, Ohio.*** They are almost antitypes of human nature: Joe, shielded in his private world of enthusiastic self-absorption from all disappointment or dismay; Wash, so vulnerable in his self-abasingly idealistic wife-worship that a sudden revelation of the facts of life induces a lifelong trauma. At a deeper level the antithesis between self-absorption and self-abasement is greatly qualified: Joe and Wash turn out to be alike in surprising ways. The two men are both inspired seers, for even Wash's love-turned-hate still invests him at moments with visionary power, though he and Joe are equally comic-grotesque in the fanaticism of their fixations. Deep down, Wash is irremovably attached to his tarnished ideal, and Joe is transfigured by his love for making discoveries about every detail in the surrounding world (though he can't get over the fact that they are *his* discoveries). So **"Respectability,"** the story of Wash, and **"A Man of Ideas,"** the tale of Joe, both turn out to be epiphanies of distorted love. But they have far more in common than this.

Taken together, the two stories constitute a richly detailed refashioning of Coleridge's great trilogy of "supernatural" poems.[1] In **"A Man of Ideas"** Anderson re-envisions "Kubla Khan"; in **"Respectability"** he recreates "Christabel"; and both stories rework imagery and episodes from "The Rime of the Ancient Mariner." Anderson's rethinkings or reimaginings are surprisingly specific and comprehensive, forming a carefully woven texture of borrowed and analogous images, close paraphrases of Coleridgean wordings, and outright quotations of phrases and epithets. One does not ordinarily expect this sort of thing from Anderson, whose relaxed approach and ambling stylistic gait in ***Winesburg*** do not alert the reader in any obvious way to complex allusive patterns. But the element of surprise in Anderson's allusive strategy increases the power that these tales possess to release their meanings through a series of delayed-reaction effects. Wash and Welling (their names allied by the theme of water—an initial hint at some of the "Ancient Mariner" parallels we will look at later) are intensely alive in their own right, psychological portraits attesting to Anderson's originality and boldness of conception. Yet as meditations on three of Coleridge's profoundest lyrics, they gain still further depth by acquiring greater psychological complexity and fuller mythic resonance.

Before beginning the analysis of Coleridgean image- and motif-patterns in the two stories, it may be useful to suggest a possible motive for Anderson's decision to single out the tales of Joe Welling and Wash Williams for such unusual allusive texturing (no other stories in ***Winesburg*** receive anything like a comparable treatment). Names may provide a clue. It is probably no accident that the novel's central questing protagonist, the aspiring writer George Willard, has a surname that not only resembles those of the grotesque imaginers Welling and Williams, but is situated alphabetically between them. Willard's eventual development is but vaguely adumbrated in ***Winesburg,*** but Anderson may be offering both his hero and his readers a context of paired symbolic indicators. If all goes well, Anderson hints, Willard may some day be situated in fact where his name appears to place him symbolically: somewhere between the self-absorbed inspiration of Joe Welling, reminiscent of the "Kubla Khan" visionary, and the self-transcending poetic idealism (so tragic when disabused) of innocent, Christabel-like Wash Williams. Situated at the midpoint, Willard may avoid the hazards of the two extremes.[2]

That both Welling and Williams are deeply troubled seers is indicated by the oddly but revealingly symbiotic way in which their stories interrelate through shared reworkings of Coleridge's "Rime of the Ancient Mariner," the story of still another darkly ambivalent visionary, prophet and outcast, grotesquely punished and yet exalted by the inseparability of love and torment. Willard, even if he avoids the extremes of Welling and Williams, may not avoid the existential problems they share—these problems are perhaps our common lot. But however that may be, the central position symbolically hinted by his name may help us relate Willard, the central Andersonian portrait of the very young artist, to mainstream Romantic visionary tradition. For I do not think one can find anywhere a more ingenious re-creation of Coleridge's "supernatural" trilogy than Anderson offers in his neo-Romantic psychological portraits of Welling and Williams.

Ambitious and intelligent, Joe resembles the poet-persona of "Kubla Khan" in the inclusiveness of his many-sided vision, even if at times he unwittingly parodies the Coleridgean seer in the unabashed boastfulness of his self-dramatization as wonder-worker. In the Coleridge lyric, it is impossible to distinguish the visionary marvel created by Kubla Khan, the "sunny pleasure-dome with caves of ice" (l. 36), from the vision of the poet-persona who narrates the lyric, and who claims he himself can "build," or rebuild, "that dome in air" (l. 46) with some help from an Abyssinian muse. Kubla Khan becomes blended with his modern recreator, as the dream-filled skull of the poet-persona becomes the new pleasure-dome. We shall see that Joe Welling internalizes the visionary landscape of "Kubla Khan" as thoroughly as the Coleridgean persona had done.

As Coleridge's seer-persona blends with the dome-building Kubla Khan in the final lines of the lyric, he presents a self-portrait that is strongly echoed in Anderson's presentation of Joe. The shaman-like prophet is possessed:

> I would build that dome in air,
> That sunny dome! those caves of ice!
> And all who heard should see them there,
> And all should cry, Beware! Beware!
> His flashing eyes, his floating hair!
> Weave a circle round him thrice,
> And close your eyes with holy dread,
> For he on honey-dew hath fed,
> And drunk the milk of Paradise.
>
> (ll. 46-54)

As the shaman's frenzy arouses fear, so too the citizens of Winesburg watch Joe, the visionary eccentric, "with eyes in which lurked amusement tempered by alarm. They were waiting for him to break forth, preparing to flee" (***WO*** [***Winesburg, Ohio***] 104). The amusement can only "lurk," cannot become fully manifest, for the "alarm" keeps it in check. Joe's "seizures" are "overwhelming" and "could not be laughed away" (104). Like Coleridge's shaman, Joe is overcome by uncontrollable powers as if in an epileptoid attack. "He was beset by ideas and in the throes of one of his ideas was uncontrollable"; he "was like a man who is subject to fits, one who walks among his fellow men inspiring fear because a fit may come upon him suddenly and blow him away into a strange uncanny physical state in which his eyes roll and his legs and arms jerk" (103). The Coleridgean "Beware! Beware!" motif is underlined: Joe is possessed. "Uncanny" is the best characterization of Joe's fear-inspiring "fits," as of the Coleridgean shaman's visionary possession.

The "flashing eyes" motif is equally pronounced in the portrayal of Joe, whose "eyes began to glisten" when he started telling George Willard, the young newspaperman, what a "marvel" Joe himself would be as a newspaper reporter (the "sunny pleasure-dome," too, was a "miracle," as Coleridge tells us [l. 35]). Even when the light in Joe's eyes becomes less bright, it remains visionary: "With a strange absorbed light in his eyes he pounced upon Ed Thomas" (104). At other times, the motif of a flashing gleam is transferred half-humorously to Joe's teeth: "The edges of his teeth that were tipped with gold glistened in the light" (103) as Joe pounces on another bystander; as he speaks to George of his latest marvel of insight, "A smile spread over [Joe's] face and his gold teeth glittered" (106). Joe even manages to allude glancingly to Coleridge's "dome in air" when he tells George, "I just snatched that idea out of the air" (106).

What sort of ideas or visionary insights does Joe snatch from the air? Very much the sort that the Coleridgean seer embodies in his air-built "sunny" dome with "caves of ice": ideas of opposites or contrasts, which in combination add up to an inclusive world-view. The central symbol in the Coleridge poem is the river that runs through the lyric landscape. Called Alph by Coleridge to recall alpha, the letter of beginnings, it meanders and descends "Through caverns"(l. 4) till it reaches the "lifeless ocean" (l. 28), the ocean of endings. It sums life up from beginning to end. Or, since it is a "sacred river" (l. 5) and since God himself is described as "Alpha and Omega, the beginning and the end" (Rev. 21:6)—God adds, "I will give unto him that is athirst of the fountain of the water of life freely"—we may see the river as including all the life of man, as conceived in religious tradition, from genesis to apocalypse. In **"A Man of Ideas"** Joe Welling offers three visionary insights, corresponding respectively to the three stages of the Coleridgean river's course: the alpha of beginnings, the meanderings and cavern-descent of midlife and aging, and the apocalypse of endings, the lifeless ocean.[3]

Altering Coleridge's order, Anderson has placed Joe's genesis-vision last, but let us begin with it, so as to conform to the mythic pattern's own inherent logic. Anderson's story ends with a monologue, delivered by Joe to his startled future in-laws, Tom and Edward King, in which a hypothetical new creation, a marvellous imaginary genesis, is sketched out. Joe speculates that if all the world's vegetables and crops were "by some miracle swept away,"[4] a new genesis or quasi-magical regeneration of the vegetable world could nevertheless come to pass:

> Now here we are, you see, in this county. There is a high fence built all around us. We'll suppose that. No one can get over the fence and all the fruits of the earth are destroyed, nothing left but these wild things, these grasses. Would we be done for? . . . More than one fat stomach would cave in. But they couldn't down us. I should say not.
>
> (110)

Of course we wouldn't be defeated, for we are in Joe's miracle-place, in his personal visionary territory. The "high fence" recalls the "walls and towers" that "girdled round" the Kubla Khan garden, and the fenced-in area of Joe's creative vision will likewise prove extremely "fertile ground" ("Kubla Khan" ll. 6-7). Joe explains: "We'd begin, you see, to breed up new vegetables and fruits," simply using the surviving wild grasses in the fenced-in area as our evolutionary starting-point, and "soon we'd regain all we had lost," even if the "new things" wouldn't be "the same as the old" (111). "There would be a new vegetable kingdom you see" (111). Like Kubla Khan, Joe becomes a visionary monarch or emperor, creator of a "kingdom."

As metaphorical kingdom-maker, Joe is imperial, but he is still more than this: he is an Eden-maker. One plant species particularly absorbs Joe's attention and excites his wonder: "'Take milkweed now,' he cried. 'A lot might be done with milkweed, eh? It's almost unbelievable. I want you to think about it'" (111). It is not clear at first what makes milkweed such a marvel, but the secret lies in Coleridge's lines in "Kubla Khan": "For he on honey-dew hath fed, / And drunk the milk of Paradise" (ll. 53-54). Milkweed is metaphorically milk of paradise, for by its means we may accomplish a new genesis, which means a new Eden. (The fenced-in, or walled-in, area where the new genesis is imagined to take place is appropriate to the edenic typology: a *hortus conclusus.*) Joe is dreaming of a new plant kingdom, so the milk of paradise is suitably metamorphosed into milkweed (honey-dew, conveniently, also has a secondary meaning relating to the regenerate vegetable world of Joe's vision: it is a kind of melon). Milkweed, an image felt as "almost unbelievable" in its potential for evolving meaning, ends Joe's story on the same note of awestruck wonder as Coleridge's poem.

Next we come to the downward course of Coleridge's visionary river, which has its wonder-inducing counterpart in bright-eyed Joe's first childlike monologue, this time delivered to helpless Ed Thomas in the Winesburg drugstore. Like the genesis vision of a plant kingdom springing forth from edenic grasses or paradisal milkweed, this too is a victory of unschooled visionary science. Joe's account of the discovery begins in wonder and leads to a deeper wonder. Joe says he could "hardly believe" his "own eyes" when he first noticed that, even though there hadn't been any rain in Winesburg for ten days, the water in Wine Creek had risen to within eleven and a half inches of the flooring of Trunion Bridge: "Thoughts rushed through my head. I thought of subterranean passages and springs. Down under the ground went my mind, delving about" (105). Or, as Coleridge puts it, ". . . Alph, the sacred river ran / Through caverns measureless to man" (ll. 3-4); and again, "Through wood and dale the sacred river ran, / Then reached the caverns measureless to man" (ll. 26-27). There was still no cloud in the sky, or rather only the tiniest of clouds ("no bigger than a man's hand" [105]), so Joe's thoughts had to be directed below (though he finally realized it must have rained over in Medina County). Exploring imagined underground caverns within the local landscape, Joe had blended his ranging, meandering mind with the descending, now subterranean river. "Thoughts rushed" through his head like a rushing river; then "Down under the ground went" his riverlike "mind, delving about" the hidden caverns of a geographic landscape now hardly separable from his mental topography. The Coleridgean allusion helps us see Joe, like the Kubla Khan visionary, as a seeker of the mind's subterranean passages.

Joe's third vision is, appropriately, apocalyptic, a vision of endings: "The world is on fire" (106). Of course, Heraclitus used this same insight to express the interdependence of birth and death, coming into being and passing away, as mutually counterbalancing processes sustaining the cosmos. Joe, however, stresses only one side of the Heraclitean fire philosophy—fire as death or, as Joe calls it, "decay": "Decay you see is always going on. It don't stop" (106). This is the omega of Joe's alpha, the "lifeless ocean" (1. 28)—death, the terminus of decay, and the beginning of yet more decay—toward which the Coleridgean river leads, the termination of the life-vision. But Joe, like the Coleridgean poet-persona, is a seer, and even this vision of all-consuming fire (which, if it were only "decay," would leave the earth "lifeless" indeed) is experienced not as desolation but as apocalypse or revelation (however tinged with the comic-grotesque). Joe claims that if he ran such apocalyptic visions as headlines in the local newspaper, "I'd be a marvel. Everybody knows that" (107). If Kubla Khan's sunny pleasure-dome is a "miracle of rare device," Joe's vision of cosmic fire, like Joe himself, is (in its childlike way) assuredly a "marvel"—one need only recall the cosmic, world-consuming fires in Revelation.

Since Joe experiences, after his own fashion, the three major moments of the "Kubla Khan" river vision (genesis, visionary descent, and apocalypse), Anderson appropriately describes Joe's visionary speech in river-like or water-like terms. "Words rolled and tumbled from his mouth" (103); "His personality . . . overrode the man to whom he talked, swept him away, swept all away" (104); "Joe Welling was carrying the two men in the room off their feet with a tidal wave of words" (110). The mention of rising water in Wine Creek also hints at a water-into-wine context of miraculous doings. And the wine motif is introduced early in the story, whose second sentence reads: "The house in which [Joe and his mother] lived stood in a little grove of trees, beyond where the main street of Winesburg crossed Wine Creek" (103), the creek that gives Winesburg its name. The wine motif is strongly implied in "Kubla Khan," too, for the Coleridgean shaman—frenzied, possessed, ecstatic and dangerous—is readily identifiable as a Dionysian or Bacchic seer, a devotee of the wine god: one may think of the "Bacchic maidens" in Plato's *Ion,* who are said to "draw milk and honey from the rivers when they are under the influence of Dionysus but not when they are in their right mind" (Abrams 355, n. 9). If Wine Creek was indeed intended to refer to the maenad-like or Bacchic visionary transport of Joe Welling the Coleridgean river-seer, Anderson may want us to see Joe as the archetypic Winesburg citizen, epitome of all the town's solitary dreamers.

It certainly bears re-emphasizing that Joe is no mere copy or uncritical re-envisioning of Coleridge's poet-persona, but a highly original Andersonian meditation on that persona. In part, Joe Welling is a semi-parodic, comic or tragicomic grotesque. This guiding idea can lead us to some observations about Anderson's telling divergences or deviations from the Coleridge prototype. For instance, even though the name "Welling" suggests the "mighty fountain" (l. 19) welling up from the "chasm" (l. 17) as the river Alph wends its way through the landscape of "Kubla Khan," Joe is also explicitly compared to a volcano, "a tiny little volcano that lies silent for days and then suddenly spouts fire" (103). True, the Coleridgean fountain is itself quite volcano-like, eruptive: amid its "swift, half-intermitted burst / Huge fragments vaulted like rebounding hail, / Or chaffy grain beneath the thresher's flail" (ll. 20-22). One thinks of the Grim Reaper; Coleridge's vision, with its goal of inclusiveness as well as intensity, is replete with imagery of destruction as well as creation. But when we learn that Joe's mother was a "grey, silent woman with a peculiar ashy complexion" (103), it's hard to avoid concluding that she got that way from living with a grotesquely monomaniacal verbal volcano. Joe's fiancée, too, though "tall and pale," has "dark rings under her eyes" (108), and it's equally easy to see these dark circles as a parodic allusion to Coleridge's verse "Weave a circle round him thrice" (l. 51). The circles under poor Sarah's eyes are always close to the image of the tirelessly voluble Joe, an image that will be continually reflected in those eyes as long as Sarah doesn't close them with holy dread, or weary satiety.

Though her doubly regal name ("Sarah" is usually translated "princess") suggests that Sarah King would be a suitable mate for the imperial, khanlike Joe, as his fiancée she will be so bedevilled by his incessant self-promotion that we are equally entitled to wonder: could Sarah be the unfortunate Coleridgean "woman wailing for her demon lover" (l. 16)? Anderson playfully encourages us to pose such questions when he slyly notes that Joe's "passionate eager protestations of love" were "heard coming out of the *darkness by the cemetery wall,* or up from the *deep shadows* of the trees . . ." (108-09; emphasis added). Anderson never forces points like these; Sarah just happens to live near the cemetery, so Joe has to go near there when he takes her for a walk. But the voice heard coming up from the cemetery wall and from the deep shadows clearly suggests that Joe is as much comic-grotesque chthonic demon lover as khan-like maker of visionary decrees. Sarah, for her part, tall and pale and lean and sad, is not exactly Coleridge's muse-like Abyssinian maid, but she may well spend more time than she likes in the abyss of Joe's absorbing or devouring self-preoccupation.

For the "holy dread" that this fascinating seer inspires is twofold. It can arise from deep empathy, as when George Willard finds himself "Shaking with fright and anxiety" as he waits to see whether Joe will be able to confront the menacing-looking Tom and Edward King without suffering grievous bodily harm. Joe is fearless, and his unworldliness combined with physical vulnerability arouses in George a response compounded of amusement and terror—a "terror that made his body shake" from empathetic identification (109). Yet there is also the kind of terror that strikes the baseball players who fall victim to Joe's series-winning but alarming enchantments as spellbinding coach: "The players of the opposing team . . . watched and then, as though to break a spell that hung over them, they began hurling the ball wildly about," while Joe's players scamper home to the accompaniment of "fierce animal-like cries" from their coach (107). Joe hypnotizes everybody with his incessant shouts of "Watch me! In me you see all the movements of the game!" Alarmingly, he seeks total control. "He is a wonder," everyone agrees (107), accepting Joe's own self-estimation as "marvel." A wonder, but a holy terror.

That is why any visionary monologue from Joe may well leave its hearer "A sadder and a wiser man" or woman (Rime, l. 624). Like that of Coleridge's Ancient Mariner, Joe's narrative compulsion both charms and repels his captive audience: "Pouncing upon a bystander he began to talk. For the bystander there was no escape. The excited man breathed into his face, peered into his eyes, pounded upon his chest with a shaking forefinger, demanded, compelled attention" (103). Compare Coleridge:

> He holds him with his skinny hand,
> "There was a ship," quoth he.
> "Hold off! unhand me, grey-beard loon!"
> Eftsoons his hand dropped he.
>
> He holds him with his glittering eye—
>
> (ll. 9-13)
>
> The Wedding-Guest sat on a stone:
> He cannot choose but hear;
> And thus spake on that ancient man,
> The bright-eyed Mariner.
>
> (ll. 17-20)

We have mentioned the transfixing stare and glistening eyes of Joe in connection with the "flashing eyes" of the "Kubla Khan" visionary, but the "glittering eye" of the Mariner is equally apposite. Joe's compulsion to narrate is not impelled by guilt like the Mariner's; rather, his never-expiated (because never recognized) flaw is self-absorption.

Joe's implicit evangel—his message concerning the miraculousness of simple things about us—is not far removed from the Ancient Mariner's injunction to love well "All things both great and small" (l. 615). Yet, like the glassy-eyed Mariner, Joe tells his tale in a kind of seizure or fit; he talks *at* his targeted listeners rather than *to* them. Each seer's spoken message, being inseparable from the message conveyed by his behavior, is both enlightening and sobering, joyful and frighteningly melancholy. The symbolically two-sided miracles experienced by the Mariner are perhaps typified by a single revealing example: at one point in his tale, rain is described as pouring down from "one black cloud," the single solitary cloud in the sky, hardly enough (one would think) to produce the wide "river" of "lightning" that issues from it (ll. 320, 325-26). A similar cloud shadows Joe's narrative. Telling of his attempts to discover why the water was so high in Wine Creek though it hadn't rained in town for ten days, Joe says he surveyed the almost empty sky till he finally found a single solitary cloud, "a cloud in the west down near the horizon, a cloud no bigger than a man's hand" (105). The illuminations conveyed by Joe and his Coleridgean tale-telling prototype, the Ancient Mariner, are never free, even at their brightest, from the shadow of a darkening cloud. Neither man can escape the specter of self-preoccupation. From this point of view, Joe's beleaguered fiancée, Sarah King, is typologically more Wedding-Guest (captive audience) than prospective bride.

If Joe Welling is a self-confident, many-sided "man of ideas" (a phrase that also happens to epitomize neatly the intellectual range and diversity of the polymathic S. T. Coleridge), Wash Williams is an extremely vulnerable, shame-plagued man obsessed with a single idea: his traumatically violated "respectability" (Coleridge's own addiction-induced problems with shame and dubious respectability may come to mind here as well). Wash's obscure sense of sinfulness allies his personal nightmare with that of the guilt-ridden Mariner, but since Wash has thoroughly repressed his guilt, projecting it outward as hate, we had best postpone the Mariner parallels for a little while. Wash quite simply hates women—all women—and the ineradicable trauma that gives rise to his murderous loathing of half the human race has its typological roots in Coleridge's "Christabel."

Four motifs link Wash's experience to that of Christabel. Originally, Wash is innocent, virginal, worshipful. He undergoes a sexual trauma. The exhibition of female nakedness that brings on the shock becomes allied in his mind with the source of all evils. But finally, and paradoxically, he cannot help resembling, in the most blatant and dramatic way, the very being he both fears and hates. That is because Wash's story, like that of Christabel, is a tale of unavowed love, love of a kind so distorted through suppression and denial that the force which generates it is manifested as something demoniacally threatening and foul. If Joe Welling's capacity for love was crippled by hypertrophy of the ego, Wash Williams' love is distorted through his extreme vulnerability to terrifying internal rebellions against the fragile structure of his idealism. For, as Coleridge sums it up in "Christabel," "to be wroth with one we love / Doth work like madness in the brain" (ll. 412-413).

The virginal "maiden" (l. 388) Christabel is as "lovely" (l. 23) as she is pious, "Like a youthful hermitess, / Beauteous in a wilderness, / Who, praying always, prays in sleep" (ll. 320-322), and the baleful Geraldine, who will administer such an irreparable shock to her innocence, is likewise "Beautiful exceedingly!" (l. 68). So too Wash, when young, was "a comely youth," who with "a kind of religious fervor" had been careful to "remain virginal until after his marriage" to a similarly attractive woman, "tall and slender" with "blue eyes and yellow hair" (123, 125). Wash was the most worshipful of courtly lovers to his young wife: he "kissed her shoes and the ankles above her shoes" (126). Christabel doesn't grovel before Geraldine's feet in this way; after all, Geraldine is simply a mysteriously abandoned lady whom Christabel has happened to meet at midnight in a forest where she has gone to pray for her distant lover. Yet Coleridge's imagery, too, focuses on a foot fixation: Geraldine's "blue-veined feet unsandaled were" (l. 63); Christabel's bedroom lamp is "fastened to an angel's feet" (l. 183); after the seduction, the blood "Comes back and tingles in her feet" (l. 325). In any event, Wash and Christabel are total innocents; neither knows anything of physical love. Wash doesn't understand why his wife has acquired three other lovers even though he worships her so unreservedly. And Christabel suspects no possible evils when she urges lonely Geraldine to come home with her and "share your couch with me" (l. 122).

There is also a "couch in the room" (***WO*** 126) of Wash's mother-in-law's house, where Wash has been summoned for a dramatic display presentation: Wash's mother-in-law wants to have her daughter march into the room naked and to observe how Wash will react. Of course, Wash suspects nothing; he has simply responded to his mother-in-law's invitation (even though he had dismissed his wife earlier for her accumulated infidelities) because he wants his wife back. "I hated the men I thought had wronged her," he says (127), just as Christabel guilelessly and sympathetically accepts Geraldine's story about being helplessly abducted by "five warriors" (l. 81). When Wash begins to tell George about the shock Wash is about to receive, Wash's "voice became soft and low" (127). In strikingly similar fashion, when Christabel is walking in the woods toward the place where Geraldine will be, "The sighs she heaved were soft and low" (l. 32). Both Coleridge and Anderson deftly use the phrase "soft and low" to help build up a mood of suspense before the shocking event to ensue.

It is the same shocking event in both cases: a revelation of nakedness to unexpecting eyes. Wash hears his wife's mother outside the door, "taking the girl's clothes off"; then she pushes his naked wife through the door and stands "in the hallway waiting, hoping we would—well, you see—waiting" (127). Wash is so horrified that although he doesn't succeed in murdering his mother-in-law on the spot, he does hit her with a chair (rescued by the neighbors, she dies of fever a month later). As for Christabel, when Geraldine drops her silken robe, the revelation is literally unspeakable: "Behold! her bosom and half her side—/ A sight to dream of, not to tell! / O shield her! shield sweet Christabel!" (ll. 252-54). Christabel provides no model for Wash's violent response; she conforms to the myth of passive womanhood and has no defense against Geraldine's demoniacal seduction. But there is a parallel in the two protagonists' repression: Christabel is cursed by being made permanently unable to speak of the evil that has happened to her, and Wash, too, nurses his shock and dismay mostly in silence, consistently shunning contact with all other human beings (until at long last he feels able to tell his story to George).

Though in one respect, Wash's trauma is a comic-grotesque version of Christabel's (nothing worse has been inflicted on Wash than a view of the nakedness of his own lawfully wedded wife), his fate is tragic, too. The psychological damage Wash undergoes is immense because he feels he has lost his "respectability." He was made to learn too much too fast. He can never forgive the grossness of his mother-in-law's pedagogic technique, for it has summoned up within him the sexual awareness that his idealistic mentality had so powerfully repressed for so long. He feels defiled, shamed—but of course he wants to repress that feeling, too. So he defensively projects the feeling of pollution and shame onto his mother-in-law, his wife, all women. He is not dirty; *they* are.

So Wash is now convinced that women are evil: "'Bitches,' he called them" (122). Men he simply pities because they are controlled by these self-same "bitches": "'Does not every man let his life be managed for him by some bitch or other?' he asked" (122). The "bitch" motif is repeatedly sounded in "Christabel," too:

> And what can ail the mastiff bitch?
> Never till now she uttered yell
> Beneath the eye of Christabel.
> Perhaps it is the owlet's scritch:
> For what can ail the mastiff bitch?
>
> (ll. 149-153)

Anderson's coarse allusive humor accentuates the comic-grotesque mood of Wash's tale.[5] But surely there is enough, too, of Coleridgean "sorrow and shame," "rage and pain" (ll. 674, 676). Wash, in hating what he loves, has come to hate not only women but "life, and he hated it whole-heartedly, with the abandon of a poet" (122). (In view of the "Christabel" parallels that we have seen and the "Ancient Mariner" parallels that we have yet to look at, the word "poet" is doubly apropos.) When Bracy the bard has a dream revealing the evil potential of Geraldine, he laments to Christabel's father, "This dream it would not pass away—/ It seems to live upon my eye!" (ll. 558-59). Trying to rid himself of analogous visions of traumatic horror, Wash says to George, "Already you may be having dreams in your head. I want to destroy them" (125). Good dreams may lead to bad ones; better not to dream. But Wash is enough of a poet to know that this is impossible.

In fact, it is impossible for Wash to stop loving what he hates: he deeply loved his wife after his courtly, idealistic fashion ("I ached to forgive and forget" [127]), and he can never banish either her image or the unconscious feelings of love it arouses in him still, despite his consciously willed loathing. He calls his wife "a foul thing come out of a woman more foul" (124), but in his own appearance he expresses—in fact, he physically embodies—the foulness he professes to despise: "He was dirty. Everything about him was unclean. Even the whites of his eyes looked soiled" (121). Wash calls women "creeping, crawling, squirming things," but he himself admits to George that he "crawled along the black ground" to his wife's "feet and groveled before her" (124, 126). That is to say, in his descriptive language Wash cannot help but unwittingly compare women with himself, drawing an unconscious likeness and thereby expressing an unconscious attraction. Again, the prototype for Wash's unconscious attraction to what he consciously rejects may be found in Christabel's behavior toward Geraldine. When Geraldine's eyes suddenly shrink up and turn serpent-like, Christabel "passively did imitate / That look of dull and treacherous hate" (ll. 605-06). How could such a look of hate appear in "eyes so innocent and blue" (l. 612) as those of the loving and lovely Christabel? Coleridge's explanation is plain and penetrating: he calls such unwilling imitation "forced unconscious sympathy" (l. 609). It is unconscious love (unwilling imitation, the sincerest form of unconscious flattery), love of what is consciously rejected and denied.

The two themes of supposed female foulness and of "creeping, crawling, squirming things" lead us, finally, to the parallels between **"Respectability"** and Coleridge's "Rime of the Ancient Mariner," parallels quite as striking as those with "Christabel." But here again, as in the case of **"A Man of Ideas,"** the contrast with Coleridge's Mariner is fully as important as the comparison. Joe Welling, we recall, shares the Mariner's compulsion to narrate, his obsession with cornering a captive audience, but lacks any trace of the Mariner's obsessive guilt, his never-satisfied need for expiation. Wash Williams, on the other hand, is even more guilt-ridden than the Mariner: in his obsession with a nightmarish female apparition of foulness and horror (a theme as basic to "Ancient Mariner" as to "Christabel"), he effectively incorporates the Coleridgean theme of dread. But in his great distaste for vermiform crawling creatures, he still embodies a state of mind that the Mariner, to his credit, brilliantly transcends. While the

Mariner achieves at least a momentary redemption by blessing the sea-snakes, Wash Williams never comes to satisfactory terms with the earthworms.

Let us look more closely, in turn, at the two Mariner-motifs that preoccupy Wash: female foulness and crawling creatures. When George innocently asks Wash if his wife is perhaps no longer living, Wash replies,

> She is dead as all women are dead. She is a living-dead thing, walking in the sight of men and making the earth foul by her presence. . . . My wife, she is dead; yes, surely, I will tell you, all women are dead, my mother, your mother,[6] that tall dark woman who works in the millinery store and with whom I saw you walking about yesterday—all of them, they are all dead.
>
> (124)

Wash's envenomed portrait of archetypic woman as a living-dead thing whose presence is a contamination mirrors Coleridge's famous presentation of the leprous-looking woman Life-in-Death, who wins the soul of the Ancient Mariner:

> Her lips were red, her looks were free,
> Her locks were yellow as gold:
> Her skin was white as leprosy,
> The Night-mare Life-in-Death was she,
> Who thicks man's blood with cold.
>
> (ll. 190-94)

Her "looks were free"—even this hint at wantonness may be easily related to Wash's disgust at the coarse display that has demolished his respectability. To Wash, his wife is a living-dead thing, someone who has made his life a life-in-death, as the leprous-looking woman has made the Mariner's. (Interestingly, in view of the Wash's trauma over nakedness, the next line in the Coleridge poem is "The naked hulk alongside came" [l. 195].) Or we may say that Wash's wife, though alive, is pictured as dead in his vengeful wish-fantasies, for he says, "Why I don't kill every woman I see I don't know" (124).

The connecting link between the themes of female fatality and crawling creatures in Wash's free association misogynist harangue is the specific idea of rottenness, also derived from Coleridge's "Ancient Mariner." Continuing his diatribe about women, Wash adds, "I tell you there is something rotten about them. I was married, sure. My wife was dead before she married me, she was a foul thing come out of a woman more foul" (124). Coleridge writes:

> The very deep did rot: O Christ!
> That ever this should be!
> Yea, slimy things did crawl with legs
> Upon the slimy sea.
>
> (ll. 123-26)

The theme of women's rottenness (the rotten deep related to the leprous-looking woman) merges in Wash's vision, too, with repellent "things" that "crawl": "I would like to see men a little begin to understand women. They are sent to prevent men making the world worth while. It is a trick in Nature. Ugh! They are creeping, crawling, squirming things, they with their soft hands and their blue eyes. The sight of a woman sickens me" (124). The Mariner's and Wash's nightmares each exhibit a double disgust: with a repellent female and with repulsive things that crawl.

What is the connection between these two motifs in psychological terms? Since serpentine or worm-like creatures, things that squirm and creep and crawl and feel soft or slimy, are not female symbols but quite evidently phallic emblems, what is the connection between this emphatic disgust at male sexuality and the equally obvious odium directed at a fatal female? The combination, for both Wash and the Mariner, would seem to indicate a *repudiation of sexuality as a whole.* But the Mariner impressively recovers from this. In one of the most dramatic visionary conversions of Romantic literature, he learns to bless the water-snakes; they are transfigured for him, and his albatross/cross, his burden of guilt, drops away. For Wash, no such deliverance is available. He even fantasizes about killing women, as the Mariner killed the albatross (and, indirectly, the two hundred crewmen). We might say that Wash's equivalent of the Mariner's albatross (a white bird, an emblem of innocence and purity) is Wash's now-dead ideal of women's purity, but Wash can't bring himself to admit that he had anything at all to do with "killing" it.

The reason for Wash's refusal to implicate himself is that Wash cannot separate the phallic worm-image from his trauma over the "rotten" female. For it is Wash's trauma-inducing wife who first tried to give him some lessons about the facts of life, and she also played flirtatious games with the metaphors of *worms* and *seeds.* As Wash worked in the garden, his wife "ran about laughing and pretending to be afraid of the worms"; then when planting time came, Wash tells George, "she handed me the seeds that I might thrust them into the warm, soft ground" (126). Wash never quite gets the point of this metaphoric sexual instruction, except on the unconscious level. He senses that his hands, which planted the seeds, are somehow connected with the traumatic sexual awakening occasioned later by his wife's sudden display of her nakedness, and that is why even now Wash takes "care of his hands" (121), the one part of his body that he wants to keep symbolically clean. (He also uses his hands to do telegraph work, a cerebral occupation, suggesting careful, conscious control.) But the sexuality he has rejected expresses itself in the rest of his body: he calls women foul and rotten, yet in keeping the rest of his body bad-smelling and dirty, he symbolically shows an unconscious affirmation of likeness, of attraction, to the women he supposedly rejects. Clean hands vs. dirty body, clean and lofty idealism vs. hidden or repressed ("dirty," "rotten") wishes—Wash is locked into a never-resolvable conflict, a nightmare worse than the Mariner's, a nightmare more like that of the spellbound Christabel, also enchained by a love she cannot admit or confess to herself.

Water, a symbol of the unconscious mind that controls the ungovernable behavior of the symbolically named Wash and Welling, unites them with each other and with Coleridgean Mariner-thematics as well. Like the Ancient Mariner, both Wash and Welling convey and embody visions of deeply problematic or troubled love. Wash's visionary fervor is not so different from Welling's: both are problematic poets. (We recall that "There was something almost beautiful" in Wash's voice as he told his "story of hate"—he had become "a poet"; "Hatred had raised him to that elevation" [125].) Wash's story of traumatic disillusionment is a tale of hate, but it hides an unavowed love, an unconfessed attraction to sexuality, to the women he maligns. At the deepest level, Wash still aches to forgive and forget. His hate hides love. Joe is also an embodied conflict or contrast: his insight conceals his blindness. Joe's loving visionary absorption in daily epiphanies makes him resemble a force of nature, oblivious to the individual personalities of his captive auditors, whom he lectures and hypnotizes into silence. In creating these profoundly moving, impressively complex psychological portraits, Anderson has proved himself no mere copyist of Coleridge, but one of the strongest remakers of that poet's rewarding, troubling legacy.

Notes

1. I find in the critical literature no detailed analyses of these two stories, nor any attempt to look at them from a Coleridgean perspective. Goebel (148, 151) mentions Coleridge, but only with reference to Anderson's supposed kinship to Emerson. Pickering (37-38) compares Anderson's Enoch Robinson to Coleridge's Ancient Mariner, but misreads Coleridge; Pickering sees the Mariner's blessing the water-snakes as a loss rather than a gain in creative power. My earlier article on Anderson contains two brief footnotes on Coleridge (Bidney 271, n.7; 272, n.9).

2. This ties in well with the approach to Willard's development that we find in Shilstone's essay (*passim*).

3. Compare Knight (97): names in "Kubla Khan" are "so lettered as to suggest first and last things: Xanadu, Kubla Khan, Alph, Abyssinian, Abora. 'A' is emphatic; Xanadu, which starts the poem, is enclosed in letters that might well be called eschatological; while Kubla Khan himself sits alphabetically central with his alliterating k's. Wordsworth's line of first, and last, and midst, and without end, occurring in a mountain-passage (*The Prelude,* VI.640), of somewhat similar scope, may be compared."

4. It's odd that Joe calls it a miracle instead of a disaster. But "miracle" certainly underlines the Coleridgean motif, "miracle of rare device" ("Kubla Khan" l. 35). And the word also expresses Joe's sense of the primacy of his own miraculous state of visionary transport over any mere material event in the external world.

5. In view of Faulkner's well-known admiration for Anderson, we may perhaps speculate that Eupheus Hines, in *Light in August* (e.g., 141), borrows some vocabulary ("womansinning and bitchery") from Wash. In other respects, the two characters differ greatly, but they are alike in that each is his own worst enemy.

6. Wash's emphasis on mothers in this context of accusation recalls Schapiro's analysis (61-92) of "Christabel" as embodying regressive narcissistic conflicts between "good" and "bad" mother-images. Beres (*passim*) applies similar categories (derived from Melanie Klein and others) to the study of Coleridge's "Ancient Mariner."

Works Cited

Abrams, M. H., et al., ed. *The Norton Anthology of English Literature.* 5th ed. 2 vols. New York: Norton, 1962. Vol. 2.

Anderson, Sherwood. *Winesburg, Ohio.* Ed. Malcolm Cowley. New York: Viking, 1958 (orig. pub. W. B. Huebsch, 1919).

Beres, David. "A Dream, a Vision, and a Poem: A Psychoanalytic Study of the Origins of 'The Rime of the Ancient Mariner.'" *International Journal of Psychoanalysis* 32 (1951): 97-116.

Bidney, Martin. "Anderson and the Androgyne: 'Something More Than Man or Woman.'" *Studies in Short Fiction* 25 (1988): 261-273.

Coleridge, Samuel Taylor. *Complete Poetical Works.* Ed. Ernest Hartley Coleridge. 2 vols. Oxford: Clarendon P, 1912. Vol. 1.

Faulkner, William. *Light in August.* Ed. Noel Polk. New York: Random House, 1987.

Goebel, Walter. *Sherwood Anderson: Aesthetizismus als Kulturphilosophie.* Heidelberg: Carl Winter Universitaetsverlag, 1982.

Knight, G[eorge] Wilson. *The Starlit Dome.* London: Methuen, 1941.

Pickering, Samuel. "*Winesburg, Ohio:* A Portrait of the Artist as a Young Man." *Southern Quarterly* 16 (1977): 27-38.

Schapiro, Barbara. *The Romantic Mother: Narcissistic Patterns in Romantic Poetry.* Baltimore: Johns Hopkins UP, 1983.

Shilstone, Frederick W. "Egotism, Sympathy, and George Willard's Development as Poet in *Winesburg, Ohio.*" *West Virginia University Philological Papers* 28 (1982): 105-113.

Lynda Brown (essay date summer 1990)

SOURCE: Brown, Lynda. "Anderson's Wing Biddlebaum and Freeman's Louisa Ellis." *Studies in Short Fiction* 27, no. 3 (summer 1990): 413-14.

[*In the following essay, Brown considers Mary E. Wilkins Freeman's "A New England Nun" as a source for "Hands."*]

Sherwood Anderson's Winesburg stories are generally believed to have been influenced by Edgar Lee Masters's group portrait of villagers in *Spoon River Anthology* (1915). But in at least one Winesburg story, Anderson seems far more indebted to Mary E. Wilkins Freeman. While Anderson acknowledged his indebtedness to some writers—Mark Twain, Theodore Dreiser, and Gertrude Stein, for instance—he was silent about his indebtedness to others and confessed in *A Story Teller's Story* that he had often taken material from other writers "without being detected" (333). Freeman's name does not appear on any of Anderson's various lists of literary mentors, but striking similarities between **"Hands,"** the first tale in ***Winesburg, Ohio*** (1919), and "A New England Nun," the title story in *A New England Nun and Other Stories* (1891), suggest that Freeman's New England eccentries might well be an unacknowledged and heretofore undetected source for Anderson's midwestern "grotesques." In particular, Wing Biddlebaum, Anderson's fat little man with the strangely restless hands, and Louisa Ellis, Freeman's fastidious spinster, have a surprising affinity.

Each story begins with the placement of the central character in a rural setting at the close of the day. Freeman's "A New England Nun" begins: "It was late in the afternoon, and the light was waning . . . now and then a farm-wagon tilted by, and the dust flew; some blue-shirted laborers with shovels over their shoulders plodded past" (109).[1] In the opening scene of Anderson's **"Hands,"** Wing Biddlebaum walks upon his veranda, from which he can see "a wagon filled with berry pickers returning from the fields." One of the berry pickers "clad in a blue shirt leaped from the wagon" and "kicked up a cloud of dust that floated across the face of the departing sun" (27). Setting suns, wagons, blue shirts, and dusty roads are all common enough that these similarities would not be remarkable if it were not for more arresting correspondences in the endings of the stories.

At the close of "A New England Nun," Louisa Ellis has chosen a life of celibacy and solitude: "She gazed ahead through a long reach of future days strung together like pearls in a rosary" and "sat, prayerfully numbering her days, like an uncloistered nun" (125). Anderson's Wing Biddlebaum also lives a solitary, celibate life. In the last scene of **"Hands,"** Biddlebaum picks bread crumbs from his "cleanly washed floor" (reminiscent of Louisa's spotless home) and carries "them to his mouth one by one with unbelievable rapidity." In this repetitive action, he looks "like a priest engaged in some service of his church. The nervous expressive fingers, flashing in and out of the light, might well have been mistaken for the fingers of the devotee going swiftly through decade after decade of his rosary" (34). In each story, the rosary is metaphorical rather than literal, and in both instances the metaphor is used to suggest a succession of routine acts through a long period of time. Through Freeman's use of the word "nun" and Anderson's use of the word "priest," the writers emphasize the austere, chaste lives of their principal characters.

A further similarity in the stories makes coincidence seem unlikely. In each story, an image of fluttering wings or hands is associated with a fear of sexuality. In "A New England Nun," the "little yellow wings" of Louisa's canary beat "against the wires" of its cage whenever Joe Dagget comes into the room (111). Through this image, Freeman reinforces the idea that the presence of Louisa's fiancé is disruptive not only of the canary's tranquillity but of the virginal orderliness Louisa has come to cherish. In short, the fluttering of wings in Freeman's story is associated with the sexuality the New England spinster shuns. It seems significant that Anderson chose to compare the restless movement of Biddlebaum's hands with "the beating of the wings of an imprisoned bird" and that the nickname of his character was derived from the resemblance between his fluttering hands and wings (28). Equally significant, Anderson—as though taking a cue from Freeman—associates the bird-like movement of Wing's hands with a fear of sexuality. In another town under another name, Wing had been a teacher of young boys, and when he touched their heads with his restless, expressive hands, the gesture was interpreted as an indication of homosexuality. The parents of the boys, fearing homosexuality, had run Biddlebaum out of town, forcing him to flee to Winesburg, where he now lives as a recluse.

When Anderson wrote **"Hands"** in 1915, he was in rebellion against the Victorian standards of taste and form that Freeman exemplifies, yet he must have responded positively to Freeman's sensitive depiction of obscure, provincial people similar to those he would so vividly portray in the Winesburg tales. In Louisa Ellis, Anderson likely saw "strange, beautiful qualities" (29) akin to those he created in the character of Wing Biddlebaum, and from Freeman's artistic treatment of social aberrance, he may have gained inspiration for his own.

Note

1. Alice Hall Petry calls attention to parallels in the opening of Freeman's story and Gray's "Elegy" in her "Freeman's New England Elegy." *Studies in Short Fiction* 21 (1984): 68-70.

Works Cited

Anderson, Sherwood. *A Story Teller's Story.* New York: Viking, 1969.

———. "Hands." *Winesburg, Ohio.* New York: Viking, 1960. 27-34.

Freeman, Mary E. Wilkins. "A New England Nun." *Selected Stories of Mary E. Wilkins Freeman.* Ed. Marjorie Pryse. New York: W. W. Norton, 1983. 109-25.

David Stouck (essay date 1990)

SOURCE: Stouck, David. "Anderson's Expressionist Art." In *New Essays on Winesburg, Ohio,* edited by John W. Crowley, pp. 27-51. Cambridge: Cambridge University Press, 1990.

[*In the following essay, Stouck describes the stories in* Winesburg, Ohio *as expressionistic in nature, contending that Anderson's goal for his fiction was "to give outward expression to the intense private feelings of both the artist and the characters he created."*]

In the introductory sketch in ***Winesburg, Ohio*** the narrator tries to describe what is inside an old writer as he lies on his high bed. Is it a baby, a youth, a young woman wearing a coat of mail like a knight? He cannot say (p. 22). In the first story, **"Hands,"** the narrator is again reflecting on what is concealed from sight: "Let us look briefly into the story of the hands. Perhaps our talking of them will arouse the poet who will tell the hidden wonder story" (p. 31). And in the following piece, **"Paper Pills,"** we are told that "Winesburg had forgotten the old man, but in Doctor Reefy there were the seeds of something very fine" (p. 35). Each passage makes reference to human potential that has not yet been uncovered and released.

In the third story, **"Mother,"** we are introduced to Elizabeth Willard, a woman who is withdrawn and silent, especially in her relation to her husband. But with her son George, a young newspaper reporter, she has established a deep bond of sympathy that centers on her desire that he do something with his life that will justify her unhappy existence. She prays to God, saying she will take any blow he might inflict "if but this my boy be allowed to express something for us both" (p. 40). She prays, in effect, to be released through her son from her lonely isolation. Elizabeth Willard's prayer is important because it describes the motive behind the Winesburg stories: the artist's desire "to express something" for his characters, to break down barriers and release them from their frustration and loneliness. Equally important is the phrasing of the mother's prayer, "to express something for us both," because it suggests the formal approach Anderson took to his writing, an approach best described by the term "expressionism."

In essays and letters, Anderson stated repeatedly that the goal of his writing was to bring to the surface the hidden depths of thought and feeling in the characters he created, characters representing ordinary humanity in the America of his time. In a particularly vivid statement of these intentions, he wrote to his publisher, Ben Huebsch, that "there is within every human being a deep well of thinking over which a heavy iron lid is kept clamped." The artist's task was to tear that lid away so that "a kind of release takes place" that "cuts sharply across all the machinery of the life about him."[1] His method was to write stories that were almost plotless in the conventional sense, stories that focused instead on an intense moment of feeling. He said in *The "Writer's Book"* that a "short story is the result of a sudden passionate interest,"[2] and to Huebsch he wrote that it often would come "all at one sitting, a distillation, an outbreak."[3] That quality of a sudden insight, a revelation, an "outbreak" is what is most indelible in the Winesburg fictions—a repressed woman running naked out onto the lawn in the rain, a minister waving a bloodied fist in the air after breaking the window in the church study. The Winesburg stories accumulate power from those exaggerated, stylized gestures by which a character is revealed or through which a scream of suffering is made to be heard. "Expressionism" is the formal term especially suitable to describing Anderson's art, because in common with the dramatists and painters in that period, Anderson made it his goal to give outward expression to the intense private feelings of both the artist and the characters he created.

1

The link between Anderson and painting is important; he often described himself as a painter using the medium of words. He saw both painter and writer trying, above all else, to express human emotions. Anderson enjoyed a lifelong association with a number of painters. His older brother, Karl, with whom he was always closely associated, made his living as a portrait painter in New York; Karl was involved in bringing a portion of the famous Armory Show to Chicago's Art Institute in 1913. His second wife, Tennessee Mitchell, worked as a sculptor, and Anderson himself turned to the canvas on several occasions to express the essence of what he was experiencing. But probably more important for his writing was his friendship with Alfred Stieglitz, the photographer and art enthusiast, whose gallery "291" introduced Anderson to the best experimental painting being done in America at that time. Anderson was taken to the gallery by Paul Rosenfeld as early as 1917 (he was then writing the later Winesburg stories and had come East to meet the editor of the *Seven Arts* who was publishing them).[4] At the gallery he saw works by Marsden Hartley, John Marin, Arthur Dove, and Georgia O'Keeffe. Through Stieglitz he came to know these artists personally and commented in letters and notebooks on their work. In *A Story Teller's Story* he states that seeing the work of these modern painters "had given me a new feeling for form and color."[5]

What these painters revealed to Anderson was that representational accuracy conveyed only life's surfaces, that an artist, whether painter or writer, had to alter the perception of surface reality so that "the hidden inner truth" of the subject would emerge. In "A Note on Realism," he refers to Marin's Brooklyn Bridge paintings as examples of art being very different from reality.[6] Marin's paintings of the bridge are not photographic, but transcribe through expressionistic distortions and tiltings the hidden dynamic forces the painter felt present in all things, even man-made engineering structures. Anderson admitted a special preference for the nature paintings of Arthur Dove: "Perhaps at bottom I'm like Dove, a country man. The warm earth feeling gets me hardest."[7] Typically, Dove's paintings render the rural environment, including its flora and fauna, in a stylized way. His country landscapes are not suggestive of a visionary mystery or symbolism, but present nature as vibrantly alive, physically immanent. In his collection of critical essays titled *Port of New York,* which includes an essay on Anderson, Paul Rosenfeld writes of Dove's work in a way that describes Anderson's often stated intentions: Dove's painting of grazing cows "brings the knowledge of someone who has almost gotten into the kine themselves; and felt from within the rich animality of their being . . . and then given it out again in characteristic abstraction."[8]

Through Stieglitz, Anderson also came to know the work of Gertrude Stein. Anderson's first exposure to Stein is presumed to have been the August 1912 copy of Stieglitz's *Camera Work,* which contained Stein's experimental pieces "Henri Matisse" and "Pablo Picasso."[9] It is in the correspondence between Stein and Anderson and in his published writings about her that Anderson most fully discusses his writing in terms of painting. Although the friendship with Stein began after the publication of ***Winesburg, Ohio,*** his writing about her contains summary opinions held since first reading her work. In *A Story Teller's Story,* dedicated to Stieglitz, he describes his excitement when first reading her purely experimental prose; it reminded him of when he had once been taken into a painter's studio to be shown the painter's colors. In Stein's writing, words were separated from sense: "Here were words laid before me as the painter had laid the color pans on the table in my presence." It struck him then that "words used by the tale teller were as the colors used by the painter."[10] In a later piece about Stein, defending her against the charge of automatic writing, he observes that "word is laid against word as carefully and always instinctively as any painter would lay one color against another."[11] In her review of *A Story Teller's Story,* she pays her admirer a compliment by saying that his book does not reflect, describe, embroider, or photograph life, but expresses it "and to express life takes essential intelligence."[12] And after *Sherwood Anderson's Notebook* was published in 1926, with its chapter on the young William Faulkner, she wrote to him suggesting that he should someday "write a novel that is just one portrait,"[13] comparing his writing to the work of a painter.

Anderson was complimented indeed by Stein's review of his work, because when she said that he had succeeded in expressing life rather than merely describing it, she was including him with the modern artists whom he so much admired. The verb Stein chose was increasingly being used to describe the artistic goal of the avant-garde. The term "expressionism," however loosely applied, indicated the artist's rejection of a surface realism and the attempt instead to make mainfest the hidden essence of things. It was an attempt, in Freudian terms, to reveal the secret inner life. "What Expressionist art seeks to render visible," writes Ulrich Weisstein, "are soul states and the violent emotions welling up from the innermost recesses of the subconscious."[14] The things that are caught on canvas or on the page are the extreme moods, such as fear, despair, or ecstasy, but it is especially the soul in anguish that the expressionist desires to project—Edvard Munch's painting, *The Scream* being a classic example. Anderson, in a letter to Marietta D. Finley, describes himself working on the Winesburg stories with the same goal: "My mind is tumbling about and trying to fit itself in a mood of sustained work. That will come. You must of course know that the things you want, the warm close thing, is the cry going up out of all hearts."[15]

Critics have acknowledged that the term "realism" does not accurately describe Anderson's writing. Walter B. Rideout has written that "what Anderson is after is less a representation of 'reality' than, to [draw] a metaphor from art, an abstraction of it." He goes on to point out that in Anderson's stories, "what is important is 'to see beneath the surface of lives,' to perceive the intricate mesh of impulses, desires, drives growing deep down in the dark, unrevealed parts of the personality."[16] Similarly, Irving Howe observes that "Anderson is not trying to represent . . . the immediate surface of human experience; he is rather drawing the abstract and deliberately distorted paradigm of an extreme situation."[17] Expressionist art cannot, strictly speaking, be designated abstract, because it remains referential, content-oriented, but it does reject the methods of verisimilitude in favor of more stylized techniques—distortions (in both art and literature) of color, shape, syntax, vocabulary, oversimplification of form, exaggeration. The grotesque is often the result of these distortions. Anderson's art in ***Winesburg, Ohio*** is a particularly striking example of expressionism in literature, where the narrative yields repeatedly to a violent projection outward of "soul states" or, as Howe phrases it, "conditions of psychic deformity."[18]

Short stories are especially congenial to expressionist art, because plot (cause and effect) is pared down to its simplest form. Action in expressionist fiction is always secondary to the transmission of an inner feeling or vision of the world. For example, in *Three Lives,* Stein was concerned to "express" what she referred to as the ground nature of her characters, the essence of the personality, and was not very interested in what happened to them in their daily lives except as it manifested something of the inner life. Similarly, O'Neill's expressionist plays, such as *The Hairy Ape* and *The Emperor Jones,* consist of a few characters and a series of short scenes that dramatize vividly his vision of human nature and society's ills. In longer dramatic narratives, action becomes more important, and fully rounded characters acquire more psychological particularity, which works against the purpose of expressionist art.

But expressionism is more than a style; it is a *Weltanschauung.* Historically it was a reaction in the early twentieth century against the increasing mechanization of society. The impact of the Industrial Revolution in Western civilization was permeating all aspects of living, from the nature of one's work to the forms of one's recreation. In the American Midwest, Sherwood Anderson witnessed the transition of the small town from a rural economy to a factory-based economy. The loss he most lamented was the craftsman's relation to the world, a loss he viewed as both material and aesthetic:

> with the coming into general use of machinery men did lose the grip of what is perhaps the most truly important of man's functions in life . . . the right . . . to stand alone in the presence of his tools and his materials and with those tools and materials to attempt to twist, to bend, to form something that will be expression of his inner hunger for the truth that is his own and that is beauty.[19]

Anderson had participated in America's industrial "progress" as both an advertising man and a man with his own business. Accordingly, he knew firsthand how individuals are affected by work on an assembly line, how human relations change in a mechanized and commercial world. He told the story of "progress" in the four-part tale **"Godliness"** in ***Winesburg, Ohio*** and in *Poor White,* the novel that followed the tales. In both stories the protagonists become slaves of the machinery they use to acquire wealth; they become frustrated and life-destroying figures. Anderson describes men turning to their machines, especially big cars, to compensate for a kind of physical impotence felt when a man no longer works with his hands, no longer expresses himself by crafting things.

To counter humankind's impotence in the age of the machine, the expressionists turned to the cult of primitivism, celebrating generally, as the Fauvists did specifically, the wild beast in man. It was also an acknowledgment of Freud, who was laying bare the phantasms repressed in the depths of the human psyche. For Anderson, the cult of the primitive was a way of rebelling against the repressive work ethic of Puritanism, the specific legacy of American history. In *A Story Teller's Story,* he describes the artist as "a man with a passion" who "wants to dream of color, to lay hold of form, free the sensual in himself, live more freely and fully in his contact with the materials before him than he can possibly live in life."[20] In ***Winesburg, Ohio,*** this emerges in the descriptions of men who retain something of the child in their characters (figures such as Enoch Robinson), and in *Dark Laughter* (1925) it emerges in the celebration of the American Negro and African-American culture. Releasing "the hidden passion of people"[21] was Anderson's artistic goal as he created the characters in ***Winesburg, Ohio.*** At the same time, to make visible the inner passionate life was the program central to the expressionist movement in the arts.

2

In a letter to a Russian translator in 1923, Anderson said that the first two novels he published were written under the influence of his reading rather than from his own reactions to life.[22] Looking at *Windy McPherson's Son* (1916) and *Marching Men* (1917), one thinks indeed of realists like Howells and Dreiser, writers committed to recording the changes taking place in society from a journalistic, and in Dreiser's case pseudo-scientific, perspective. It was with the Winesburg stories that he felt he "had really begun to write out of the repressed, muddled life about [him]."[23] One might well describe the characters and situations in the first two novels as repressed and muddled—the words seem appropriate to the content of all of Anderson's work. However, there is a big change between the first two novels and the short fiction, and it is a radical stylistic change, effected in part by the influence of Gertrude Stein. The style in the Winesburg stories is not the realistic, conventional prose style of the period, but rather a vastly simplified kind of writing in which image, rhythm, and what Anderson calls "word color" stand out sharply as the crucial elements in the writing. This is because Anderson has changed his choices of words and the structuring of his sentences.

A passage from *Windy McPherson's Son* beside one from ***Winesburg, Ohio*** will reveal the change in style. Each passage describes a man living in a town in the Midwest who is remarkable for his unusual appearance. From *Windy McPherson's Son:*

> At the age of forty-five John Telfer was a tall, slender, fine looking man, with black hair and a little black pointed beard, and with something lazy and care-free in his every movement and impulse. Dressed in white flannels, with white shoes, a jaunty cap upon his head, eyeglasses hanging from a gold chain, and a cane lightly swinging from his hand, he made a figure that might have passed unnoticed on the promenade before some fashionable summer hotel, but that seemed a breach of the laws of nature when seen on the streets of a corn-shipping town in Iowa. And Telfer was aware of the extraordinary figure he cut; it was a part of his programme of life. Now as Sam approached he laid a hand on Freedom Smith's shoulder to check the song, and, with his eyes twinkling with good-humour, began thrusting with his cane at the boy's feet.[24]

From **"Paper Pills"** in ***Winesburg, Ohio***:

> He was an old man with a white beard and huge nose and hands. Long before the time during which we will know him, he was a doctor and drove a jaded white horse from house to house through the streets of Winesburg. Later he married a girl who had money. She had been left a large fertile farm when her father died. The girl was quiet, tall, and dark, and to many people she seemed very beautiful. Everyone in Winesburg wondered why she married the doctor. Within a year after the marriage she died.
>
> The knuckles of the doctor's hands were extraordinarily large. When the hands were closed they looked like clusters of unpainted wooden balls as large as walnuts fastened together by steel rods. He smoked a cob pipe and after his wife's death sat all day in his empty office close by a window that was covered with cobwebs. He never opened the window. Once on a hot day in August he tried but found it stuck fast and after that he forgot all about it.
>
> (p. 35)

The differences in these two passages reveal the emergence of Anderson's expressionistic style. The passage from *Windy McPherson's Son* (155 words) consists of four long sentences, three of which are compound-complex in construction. The same number of words from the ***Winesburg, Ohio*** passage compose ten sentences, four of which are simple, and none of which are compound-complex. The immediate effect of radically simplifying the sentences is to make their content stand out more sharply. Although we are given considerable information about John Telfer in the *McPherson* passage—he is tall, slender, fine-looking, with black hair and pointed beard, and is lazy, carefree, good-humored, and an elegant dresser—the portrait is nonetheless blurred by the arrangement of the details in a series of qualifying phrases. In the second sentence of the *McPherson* passage the details of Telfer's appearance have even less impact because of the delay in identifying the subject ("he") they modify. In the ***Winesburg*** passage the effect of the shorter sentences with so few subordinate clauses is to render the information about Dr. Reefy with clarity and conciseness. Moreover, there is a rhythm to these short declarative sentences that makes the information solid and incontrovertible, rhetorically unimpeachable statements of fact, not subject to the delays, qualifications, or elaborations in the *McPherson* paragraph.

There is also the difference in point of view. While the *McPherson* passage is propositionally a much denser text, the importance of the information is diminished by being interpreted, evaluated for the reader by an omniscient narrator. We are told that Telfer is fine-looking, but that he appears to be lazy and carefree. We are told that he cuts a strange figure in a corn-shipping town in Iowa. The omniscient narrator also informs us of Telfer's awareness of the impression he creates. The reader is a passive recipient of this information. In the ***Winesburg*** passage, on the other hand, the lexical items are not interpreted, nor is the staging of the text. The old man (Dr. Reefy) has a white beard, and huge nose and hands, but we are not told if they are attractive or ugly. Nor are we given a source of information for this portrait. The story begins, "He was an old man," presupposing in the use of a pronoun rather than a name that information has preceded. Then the speech situation shifts to "we" and later to "everyone's" point of view. Anderson risks coherence in these shifts in point of view and also in the shifts of subject, from "he" to "she" in the first paragraph to the doctor's hands as subject in paragraph two. This technique foregrounds the art of the story, making us aware of a story being told through many perspectives, rather than a scene being reported as in the *McPherson* passage. It is the difference between a formal, written description of characters and events and oral storytelling.

"How fond we both are of sentences," Stein wrote to Anderson, recommending some of her own in *The Making of Americans.*[25] The sentence was a subject they frequently discussed, and it remained central to their concept of what was new and important in their art. In 1929, Stein tells Anderson, "I am working fairly steadily on the sentence . . . I struggled all last year with grammar, vocabulary is easier, and now I think before more grammar I must find out what is the essence of a sentence."[26] And in his defense of Stein in the *Atlantic*

Monthly in 1934, Anderson talks about words and sentences as the materials of the craft and says he has "often heard sentences on the street that glow like jewels." In the same essay he praises Hemingway: "The man can make sentences. He is one of the few American writers who can."[27]

Anderson wrote frequently about the power of sentences to reveal the life within:

> There are sentences written by all writers of note in all countries that have their roots deep down in the life about them. The sentences are like windows looking into houses. Something is suddenly torn aside, all lies, all trickery about life, gone for the moment.[28]

The bedrock of simple sentences in Anderson's prose signals a paring down to the basic experiences and thoughts of the character. The essential facts about Dr. Reefy's life are telescoped into just a few short sentences in the passage cited. The repetitive rhythm of those sentences with their coordinating conjunctions allows Anderson to express an element of fatality to the doctor's life. Repetition was more crucial to Stein's delineation of character in *Three Lives,* but Anderson also uses repetition to get at the essential nature of his character. Here the detail of the doctor's huge hands is repeated and exemplified in a grotesque image of hands like clusters of unpainted wooden balls. The other item repeated is the fact of his wife's death. The old man's strange appearance and his isolation are linked by his repetition, which suggests some inner truth about the character.

Anderson also wrote about the power of individual words to reveal the life within, and once again he credits Gertrude Stein with awakening him to the expressionist power of language. He compares first reading Stein somewhere around 1915 to the excitement of exploring a new and wonderful country, a sort of Lewis and Clark expedition:

> Here were words laid before me as the painter had laid the color pans on the table in my presence. My mind did a kind of jerking flop and after Miss Stein's book had come into my hands I spent days going about with a tablet of paper in my pocket and making new and strange combinations of words. The result was I thought a new familiarity with the words of my own vocabulary. . . . Perhaps it was then I really fell in love with words, wanted to give each word I used every chance to show itself at its best.[29]

Anderson was describing the period when he began the Winesburg stories. Stein instilled in Anderson a new respect and love for good solid Anglo-Saxon words from common life. In the preface to *Geography and Plays,* he wrote that "here is one artist who has been able to accept ridicule . . . to go live among the little housekeeping words, the swaggering bullying street-corner words, the honest working, money saving words."[30] And in his essay on Stein in "Four American Impressions" he describes her as a woman in a great kitchen of words, making wonderful preserves from the words of our English speech. In this essay and elsewhere he talks about the sensuality of words. In her kitchen, he writes, Stein "is laying word against word, relating sound to sound, feeling for the taste, the smell, the rhythm of the individual word."[31] It is when words have color and smell, Anderson suggests, that they can convey "the life within."

The paragraphs cited earlier from *Windy McPherson's Son* and ***Winesburg, Ohio*** again illustrate the way Anderson dramatically sharpened his use of language by the time he wrote the Winesburg tales. Anderson's style was never what might be described as "learned." There is never an abundance of Latinate words in his vocabulary. A marked distinction between the two texts, however, can be seen in the frequent use of vague, unspecific words and phrases in the first passage and uninterpreted, clear, hard, denotative language in the second. Words and phrases like "fine looking," "something lazy and care-free," "might have passed unnoticed," "breach of the laws of nature," and "pro-gramme of life" lack specificity. They are suggestive, but not clear or focused in their reference. In the Winesburg passage there are no words or phrases that are comparably vague and suggestive; solid Anglo-Saxon nouns like "horse," "house," "knuckles," and "hands" and adjectives like "huge," "jaded," "large," "tall," "dark," and "empty" are simple and clear in reference. There are no clauses in the conditional mode ("might have passed unnoticed"), no inflated phrases like "a breach of the laws of nature" or "programme of life" that might call for explication. Words that convey simple statements of fact reveal directly the bleak, narrow confines of Dr. Reefy's existence as something innate and inescapable, whereas the unusual character of John Telfer in the first passage is never clearly defined or felt; it is something the reader is told.

"One works with words," wrote Anderson about Stein, "and one would like words that have a perfume to the nostrils, rattling words one can throw into a box and shake, making a sharp, jingling sound, words that, when seen on the printed page, have a distinct arresting effect upon the eye."[32] In the simile describing Dr. Reefy's hands, Anderson releases the physicality of the words used. The doctor's knuckles are like "clusters of unpainted wooden balls as large as walnuts fastened together by steel rods." The words are arresting because of their unusual use in this descriptive context. The words are familiar from farm and workshop ("the little housekeeping words . . . the honest working, money saving words"), but in this context they achieve a curiously poetic quality. The twisted, grotesque character to the doctor's inner life is expressed in a powerfully visible way. As Linda W. Wagner has observed, the emotional life of each character in ***Winesburg, Ohio*** is presented graphically rather than rhetorically;[33] that is, we are made to see and experience for ourselves the inner life of the character, rather than being told about it.

The result is not realism but expressionism. Reality and art are always separate, Anderson argued, and although realism may be very good journalism, it is always bad art.[34] Anderson was often told that in ***Winesburg, Ohio*** he had given an exact picture of Ohio village life, but he said that in fact the idea for his characters came from observing his fellow lodgers in a Chicago boardinghouse, not from recalling the villagers of his youth. On other occasions, however, he would credit memories of Clyde, Ohio, as the source of the book. Both statements are probably true and reveal something of his method as an expressionist writer. In his "A Note on Realism" and in his *Memoirs,* Anderson describes his method of creating character. He explains that he would try in his writing to get at "some inner truth" of a character that he had observed, but would then put that character into the physical body of another to see if the essence of the characterization remained intact.[35] Sometimes boardinghouse residents would merge with remembered figures from Clyde. In that way the character would become a denizen of Anderson's imaginative world, no longer an individual realistically observed and drawn "true to life," but a character whose essential being transcended the physical body of the prototype, assuming other external features more expressive of the individual's essential nature.

Another major change in Anderson's writing when he moved from the early novels to the Winesburg stories was a shift away from plot. As an expressionist drama, there is little development of a story line in the Winesburg tales in terms of cause and effect. Typically a story begins with a physical description of the central character, emphasizing some grotesque feature or trait. Then, usually in relation to George Willard as listener, something of the character's past history is revealed (a desertion, a death in the family, an unwanted pregnancy). The story usually ends with the character committing a desperate act (getting drunk, shouting in the streets, striking at the newspaper reporter), then fleeing temporarily from the town. By means of distortion and repetition, rather than plot, Anderson is able to reveal something about the hidden inner life of his characters and about the nature of society.

In Anderson's view, the chief obstacle to exploring fully the world of the imagination was the conventional demand for plot. Refusing to acknowledge the importance of plot in fiction became a point of honor with Anderson. Repeatedly in his writings he blames his lack of commercial success on the fact that he would not craft his stories on the formula of de Maupassant or O. Henry, writers whom he considered slick. In *A Story Teller's Story* he writes heatedly on the subject, distinguishing plot from form:

> There was a notion that ran through all story telling in America, that stories must be built about a plot and that absurd Anglo-Saxon notion that they must point a moral, uplift the people, make better citizens, etc, etc. The magazines were filled with these plot stories and most of the plays on our stage were plot plays. "The Poison Plot" I called it in conversation with my friends as the plot notion did seem to me to poison all story telling. What was wanted I thought was form, not plot, an altogether more elusive and difficult thing to come at.[36]

True form, he wrote in his defense of Stein, emerges from words and sentences. Again, drawing an analogy with painting, he wrote that words have color value, and therein lies true form.[37] Writing to Paul Rosenfeld in 1921, he said that he would not be bound by the critic's idea of form, for if he wrapped his packages up more neatly, he would lose the "large, loose sense of life" he was after. In the same letter, he added: "One thing I would like you to know is this: as far as I am concerned, I can accept no standard I have ever seen as to form. What I most want is to be and remain always an experimenter, an adventurer."[38] When he was actually writing the Winesburg stories in 1917, he called them fragments.[39]

This approach is evident in **"Tandy,"** a Winesburg piece with no plot or story line at all. Three characters appear in the sketch: an agnostic widower, his daughter, who is still a child, and a red-haired young man who has come to live in Winesburg and hopes there to overcome his alcoholism. The only character with a name is the widower, Tom Hard. He befriends the young stranger, but the latter does not stop drinking. The only event that takes place is when the drunken stranger one evening drops to the knees and tells the little girl to be "Tandy," the quality in a woman of being "brave enough to dare to be loved" (p. 145). The point of the sketch is to reveal something that is missing in human relationships—courage for sexual expression in women. It is not the study of an individual—the stranger remains nameless—but of a profound psychological need. Plot is sacrificed to the expressionist's concern to reveal another dimension to a repressive society. Like much expressionist drama, this sketch is pared down to a monologue designed to release the expressionist scream.

3

Anderson's vision of life in ***Winesburg, Ohio*** is tied directly to the expressionist form of his stories. The narrator in the introductory sketch tells us simply that there is no such thing as truth, but that there are a great many thoughts, that is, many ways of viewing life, all of which are valid. But human beings, he says, have insisted on experiencing life from just one vantage point, which becomes a position of truth. This distorted view of the world in turn distorts the viewer, who becomes a grotesque, a character "all drawn out of shape." That phrase describes the characters remembered by the old writer in the introduction and subsequently the characters in the stories that follow.

Anderson has made each of his characters memorable by means of a bizarre physical trait or a stylized gesture that isolates the individual from society. Dr. Reefy is not the only character with unusual hands. **"Hands"** is the title of the first story, the tragedy of an effeminate schoolteacher who tries to reach out to others through touch, but whose motives are misunderstood. The narrator says that the constant movement of Wing Biddlebaum's hands is like "the beating of the wings of an imprisoned bird" (p. 28). In **"Respectability,"** Wash Williams is described as monstrously ugly and dirty like a baboon; even the whites of his eyes look soiled. Yet "he took care of his hands," which are shapely and sensitive (p. 121). Hands dramatize the individual's deep need for connection to others. Even minor characters are sometimes remarkable for their hands. Tom Willy, the saloon keeper, has a flaming birthmark on his hands. When he becomes excited talking to one of his customers, he rubs his hands together, and the red deepens in color "as though the hands had been dipped in blood" (p. 50). Other characters, such as Kate Swift, the teacher, and Elmer Cowley, in **"Queer,"** make their hands into fists and beat at George Willard in a desperate desire to communicate to him some painful truth that they cannot wholly articulate. The Reverend Curtis Hartman puts his fist through the window of the church study. Hands provide a particularly striking aspect of Anderson's expressionist portraits. These hands do not participate in the public handshake or in the caress of lovers, but like the bleeding fist of Reverend Hartman, they signal the pain and the frustrated desire of these characters to make connections to others.

The eyes of the Winesburg characters are also described in a way that reveals something twisted and obsessive in their nature. The soiled whites of Wash Williams's eyes reflect his vision of the foulness of women. The tiny bloodshot eyes of the baker, Abner Groff, convey the scope of his narrow existence as he seeks revenge on a neighborhood alley cat. In the description of Dr. Parcival's eyes, Anderson uses an elaborate simile to render vividly something alien and closeted in this figure. There was something strange about his eyes, says the narrator: "The lid of the left eye twitched; it fell down and snapped up; it was exactly as though the lid of the eye were a window shade and someone stood inside the doctor's head playing with the cord" (p. 49). Dr. Parcival's refusal of medical assistance when a little girl is thrown from a buggy is like the closing of the window shade. He is left alone with the conviction that someday he will be crucified.

There is a venerable literary tradition of eyes being expressive and central to communication (the poetry of courtly love and Shakespeare's sonnets spring to mind); thus, when a character's eyes are clouded or in any way unusual, interpersonal contact is threatened. On her deathbed, Elizabeth Willard is paralyzed and can no longer speak, but her eyes remain very much alive. She communicates to her son, without the use of words, her desire that he express something for them both: "in her eyes there was an appeal so touching that all who saw it kept the memory of the dying woman in their minds for years" (p. 230). But the eyes of Jesse Bentley that flame with the passionate burning things in his nature are blind with regard to others, and as he grows older his left eyelid develops an uncontrollable twitch. Similarly, his grandson, David Hardy, has "a habit of looking at things and people a long time without appearing to see what he [is] looking at" (p. 75). One of the most alien figures in the book, the albino-like Elmer Cowley, has eyes almost bleached of any color: "his eyes were blue with the colorless blueness of the marbles called 'aggies' that the boys of Winesburg carried in their pockets" (p. 194).

The recurring attention to hands and eyes is part of the expressionist method of repetition. Stein explains her use of repetition as a way of approaching the essence of a character, for she argues that people, carefully observed, are seen to repeat themselves, and in so doing they reveal their essential or ground nature. Anderson focuses on the repetitive behavior of his characters—Dr. Reefy writing down his truths on little pieces of paper, Joe Welling talking excitedly about ideas to casual passersby, Alice Hindman taking her lonely walks. But in his larger vision of a repressed society—"everyone in America really hunger[ing] for a more direct and subtle expression of our common lives than we have ever yet had"[40]—he describes many people living in similar circumstances, enacting the same gestures, so that "the almost universal insanity of society"[41] becomes boldly clear. Even family living patterns are stylized by repetition. Boys and young men in the stories live alone with poor old women (mothers, aunts, grandmothers); they live on the margins of the town. Similarly, young women most often live alone with their fathers, or sometimes their brothers. There are no whole families in the book suggesting complete or fulfilled relationships; Anderson's vision is one of repression, loneliness, and the absence of love. As Walter B. Rideout has observed, the setting is one of the repeated elements in the story. In seventeen of the twenty-two stories, the crisis scene takes place in the evening; some kind of light—a lamp, a fire, some lingering light in the sky—partly relieves the gathering dark. Most of the tales end with the characters going off into total darkness.[42]

But even more striking in ***Winesburg, Ohio*** is the pattern of people in motion who form something like a procession of the living dead. We know that he thought about the frustrated and defeated characters in his early stories as among the living dead, for he described them in a letter to M. D. Finley, 2 December 1916, as building walls of fear around themselves, inside of which they die.[43] In an earlier letter to Finley he used the image of the procession as part of this vision:

> At times there comes over me a terrible conviction that I am living in a city of the dead. In the office dead voices discuss dead ideas. I go into the street and long rows of dead faces march past. Once I got so excited and terrified that I began to run through the streets. I had a mad impulse to shout, to strike people with my fist. I wanted terribly to awaken them.[44]

This was Anderson's vision of Puritan America. In the introductory sketch, **"The Book of the Grotesque,"** the old writer has a waking dream wherein all the people he has known are being driven in a long procession before his eyes. Afterward he creeps out of bed and writes down what he has seen, describing all the people as grotesques because they live by one truth. These are the characters of Anderson's book, originally titled **"The Book of the Grotesque"** instead of ***Winesburg, Ohio.*** The image of the procession is evoked in almost every tale by the central character breaking into a run when he or she reaches a point of insupportable frustration.

Kate Swift, the schoolteacher, is a conventional unmarried woman in the eyes of the townspeople, but, within, her passionate nature yearns for companionship and significant achievement. She takes long walks alone at night; one night she walks for six hours. She half loves her former pupil, George Willard, and in her desire to see his talent as a writer flower, she goes to the newspaper office one night to talk to him. But confused by her love for the boy, she cannot express herself adequately and winds up beating him with her fists, then running out into the darkness. That same night, Reverend Hartman, who for weeks has paced the streets at night imploring God to keep him from his sinful habit of peeping into Kate Swift's bedroom window, bursts into the Winesburg *Eagle* office, shaking a bleeding fist, having broken the window of the church study.

Repeatedly, inarticulate characters in a moment of passion wave their hands in the air and burst into a run. Tom Foster, the shy gentle boy in **"Drink,"** falls in love with the banker's daughter, Helen White. The relationship is socially impossible, and one night Tom goes for a long walk and becomes drunk on a bottle of whiskey. He becomes a grotesque figure moving along the road: "His head seemed to be flying about like a pinwheel and then projecting itself off into space and his arms and legs flopped helplessly about" (p. 218). Jesse Bentley, in **"Godliness,"** who has a vision of being a biblical patriarch, runs through the night begging God to send him a son; years later, when he takes his grandson to sacrifice a lamb, hoping God will finally send a visible sign of his blessing, the scene ends with the flight of the terrified boy from Winesburg. In **"Adventure,"** Alice Hindman, who has been waiting many years for the return of her lover, one night runs out onto the lawn in the rain naked. In the story of the two farmhands, entitled **"The Untold Lie,"** the moment of truth brings Ray Pearson to run across the fields to save his friend, Hal Winters, from marriage.

The most vivid scenes in the book are those of characters in grotesque or violent motion: Elizabeth Willard wearing men's clothes and riding a bicycle through the town's main street; Louise Bentley, the estranged daughter of the biblical patriarch, driving her horse and carriage at breakneck speed through the streets of Winesburg; Jesse Bentley's drunken brothers driving along the road shouting at the stars; Hal Winters's father, Windpeter Winters, drunk and driving his team along the railroad tracks directly into the path of an onrushing locomotive. The repetition of such images expresses powerfully the frustration and despair felt by the characters in the small Ohio town. These gestures are another form of the expressionist scream.

4

Considering ***Winesburg, Ohio*** as an expressionist work further illuminates its historical significance in American literary history. Anderson has long been recognized as an innovator in style, influenced by the vernacular of Mark Twain and responsive to the prose experiments of Gertrude Stein. What Richard Bridgman sees as innovative in Anderson's style is his ability to write in the American vernacular (and its colloquial rhythms) without the use of a child or fool as first-person narrator. Twain used Huckleberry Finn to write in a uniquely American voice; Ring Lardner used Jack Keefe. Anderson, on the other hand, actually established the simple style and its colloquial rhythms as an independent American prose medium.[45] His attempts to forge this unique American voice are seen to flower in the prose style of Ernest Hemingway. But the extent of that influence goes further than Hemingway, and I shall suggest in conclusion that Anderson's expressionist experiments were bolder than Hemingway's and consequently more far-reaching.

In the mainstream of American writing, Anderson's expressionist style represents a sharp break with both realism (including the writing of the naturalists) and impressionism. The latter term is used to describe the psychological realism of Henry James and those he influenced, that is to say, a style of writing that is always suggestive, ambiguous, and heavily dependent on symbolism. The sentences in an impressionist text are characteristically compound-complex, with many qualifying subordinate clauses, and these sentences are often cast in the conditional mode. At the heart of an impressionist novel or story is an experience, emotion, or idea that cannot be explained, only approached obliquely—in what James called a presentiment or what Willa Cather termed "the thing not named." The impressionists (Conrad and Ford were the most eloquent on the subject) acknowledge the relativity of truth, but it is also an aesthetic of evasion, an art of secrets.

Anderson also acknowledged the relativity of truth. At the center of ***Winesburg, Ohio*** there is despair over the book's central mission—"to express something" for his characters. The view of art in the book undercuts that goal. The artists in ***Winesburg, Ohio,*** like the old man in the introductory sketch and like Enoch Robinson, are among the least capable of communicating to others, either in their life gestures or in their art. One of the pivotal insights in the book is the realization that comes to Alice Hindman after her adventure on the front lawn: "that many people must live and die alone, even in Winesburg" (p. 120). But Anderson does not retreat with this insight to an art of suggestion, of half-guessed truths. He records instead the struggle to communicate, the effort and the frustration of individuals to explain who they really are. The characters in his fiction are grotesque; yet they are rendered whole in their efforts to express themselves.

"Loneliness," the story of Enoch Robinson, can be viewed as an allegorical statement about art. Robinson is a painter who is remembered in Winesburg as a quiet, dreamy youth. When he was twenty-one he went to New York City, where he attended art school and studied French, hoping some day to finish his art education in Paris. Robinson does not get to France, but it seems likely that the masters with whom he wanted to study there were from the impressionist school. This is reinforced by the description of one of the paintings he shows to a group of artist friends gathered in his room facing Washington Square. Robinson has painted a scene on a country road near Winesburg. In the picture is a clump of elder bushes, inside of which is the body of a woman thrown from a horse. A farmer passing by is shown looking anxiously about in the picture. The woman who has been hurt is at the center of the painting: "She lies quite still, white and still," thinks Robinson, "and the beauty comes out from her and spreads over everything. It is in the sky back there and all around everywhere." But the woman, in fact, is not shown in the picture at all: "I didn't paint the woman, of course. She is too beautiful to be painted" (p. 170). Robinson's painting accords with the aesthetic of the impressionist painter and the literary symbolist, where everything depends on the suggestive power of "the thing not named." But what is significant in the story is that Robinson's painting fails to communicate anything to the audience of friends. They talk of line values and composition, but experience nothing of the emotion that went into the picture. The failure of Robinson's impressionist aesthetic is paralleled in his failure to develop as a man—he remains withdrawn and childlike and retreats into the companionship of imagined people whose presences are threatened every time he comes into contact with real flesh-and-blood people. Robinson's aesthetic fails him, and he becomes "an obscure, jerky little figure, bobbing up and down on the streets of an Ohio town," but Anderson's expressionist art of simplifying, distorting, and exaggerating has rendered Enoch Robinson's character vividly. We learn as much as can be known about this character in a third-person narrative.

Sherwood Anderson argued that good writing has the strong color and form of a Cézanne painting.[46] Hemingway also liked to hold up Cézanne as an artistic model and attributed to the painter important influences on his writing. But in fact, the technical features of the Hemingway style—the choice of language, the structuring of the sentences—have their antecedent in Anderson's prose. What Hemingway learned from Anderson was the power of non-literary words, the four-letter Anglo-Saxon words with their direct appeal to the senses and their hard denotative surfaces. He also learned from Anderson that the arranging of these words in short declarative sentences could have enormous power.

> Dick Boulton looked at the doctor. Dick was a big man. He knew how big a man he was. He liked to get into fights. He was happy. Eddy and Billy Tabeshaw leaned on their canthooks and looked at the doctor. The doctor chewed the beard on his lower lip and looked at Dick Boulton. Then he turned away and walked up the hill to the cottage.[47]

In the structuring of sentences, he learned especially how effective conjunctions were instead of subordinate clauses to convey uninterpreted statements of fact. Subordination creates a hierarchical value structure in a sentence, the main clause being of greatest significance, whereas the use of conjunctions (polysyndeton) gives all the clauses equal value. Implicit in this stylistic choice is the intent to describe and the refusal to judge. This technique is fundamental to Hemingway's clear, hard, nonimpressionistic prose.[48]

Throughout his career Anderson saw himself as an experimental writer. He wrote to Van Wyck Brooks in March 1919, saying that "I want constantly to push out into experimental fields. 'What can be done in prose that has not been done?' I keep asking myself."[49] In his novels in the 1920s, he resisted the formal strictures of plot in favor of looser narrative structures that would include, as he said in the same letter to Brooks, "the purely fanciful side of a man's life, the odds and ends of thought, the little pockets of thoughts and emotions that are so seldom touched."[50] In a letter to Alfred Stieglitz, he described *Dark Laughter* as "a 'fantasy' rather than a novel," with "no realism in it."[51] Hemingway, in order to dispel the anxiety of influence he felt in relation to his literary mentor, wrote *The Torrents of Spring* (1926) to expose what he felt were the thematic weaknesses and stylistic mannerisms of Anderson's fiction. But, ironically, those elements of Anderson's prose he highlighted—the dimension of fantasy, the exaggerated comic-book characters, the loose plot structure, and especially the self-reflexive asides between author and reader—have become valued features of contemporary postmodern fiction. ***Winesburg, Ohio*** is a classic work of fiction about small-town life in the American Midwest, but as an expressionist work it has a further significance in American literary history in that it provides an important link between the modernism of the first quarter of this century and American writing today.

Notes

1. *Sherwood Anderson: Selected Letters,* ed. Charles E. Modlin (Knoxville: University of Tennessee Press, 1984), p. 32.
2. *The "Writer's Book" by Sherwood Anderson: A Critical Edition,* ed. Martha Mulroy Curry (Metuchen, N.J.: Scarecrow Press, 1975), p. 85.
3. Quoted by Martha Mulroy Curry in "Anderson's Theories on Writing Fiction," in *Sherwood Anderson: Dimensions of His Literary Art,* ed. David D. Anderson (East Lansing: Michigan State University Press, 1976), p. 94.
4. Kim Townsend, *Sherwood Anderson* (Boston: Houghton Mifflin, 1987), p. 200.
5. Sherwood Anderson, *A Story Teller's Story: A Critical Text,* ed. Ray Lewis White (Cleveland: Case Western Reserve University Press, 1968), p. 272.
6. *Sherwood Anderson's Notebook* (New York: Boni & Liveright, 1926), p. 72.
7. *Letters of Sherwood Anderson,* ed. Howard Mumford Jones and Walter B. Rideout (Boston: Little, Brown, 1953), p. 247.
8. Paul Rosenfeld, *Port of New York: Essays on Fourteen American Moderns* (New York: Harcourt, Brace, 1924), pp. 171-2.
9. *Sherwood Anderson/Gertrude Stein: Correspondence and Personal Essays,* ed. Ray Lewis White (Chapel Hill: University of North Carolina Press, 1972), p. 7.
10. Anderson, *A Story Teller's Story,* pp. 261-3.
11. White, ed., *Anderson/Stein: Correspondence,* p. 82.
12. Ibid., p. 45.
13. Ibid., p. 56.
14. Ulrich Weisstein, ed., *Expressionism as an International Literary Phenomenon* (Paris: Didier, 1973), p. 23.
15. *Letters to Bab: Sherwood Anderson to Marietta D. Finley, 1916-33,* ed. William A. Sutton (Urbana: University of Illinois Press, 1985), p. 85.
16. See Walter B. Rideout, "The Simplicity of *Winesburg, Ohio,*" in *Critical Essays on Sherwood Anderson,* ed. David D. Anderson (Boston: G. K. Hall, 1981), p. 148.
17. See Irving Howe, *Sherwood Anderson* (New York: William Sloane, 1951), p. 99.
18. Ibid.
19. *Sherwood Anderson's Notebook,* pp. 153-4.
20. Anderson, *A Story Teller's Story,* p. 217.
21. Ibid., p. 237.
22. Jones and Rideout, eds., *Letters of Sherwood Anderson,* p. 92.
23. Ibid., p. 93.
24. Sherwood Anderson, *Windy McPherson's Son* (University of Chicago Press, 1965), p. 5.
25. White, ed., *Anderson/Stein: Correspondence,* p. 49.
26. Ibid., p. 68.
27. Ibid., p. 81.
28. Anderson, *A Story Teller's Story,* p. 237.
29. Ibid., p. 263.
30. White, ed., *Anderson/Stein: Correspondence,* p. 17.
31. Ibid., p. 24.
32. Ibid., p. 16.
33. Linda W. Wagner, "Sherwood, Stein, The Sentence, and Grape Sugar and Oranges," in Anderson, ed., *Dimensions of His Literary Art,* p. 82.
34. *Sherwood Anderson's Notebook,* p. 76.
35. *Sherwood Anderson's Memoirs: A Critical Edition,* ed. Ray Lewis White (Chapel Hill: University of North Carolina Press, 1969), p. 348.
36. Anderson, *A Story Teller's Story,* p. 255.

37. White, ed., *Anderson/Stein: Correspondence,* pp. 82-3.

38. Jones and Rideout, eds., *Letters of Sherwood Anderson,* p. 72.

39. Ibid., p. 11.

40. Anderson, *A Story Teller's Story,* p. 234.

41. Jones and Rideout, eds., *Letters of Sherwood Anderson,* p. 44.

42. See Rideout, "The Simplicity of *Winesburg, Ohio,*" p. 149. Other repeated images and motifs in the book are discussed by Monika Fludernik in "'The Divine Accident of Life': Metaphoric Structure and Meaning in *Winesburg, Ohio,*" *Style* 22 (Spring 1988): 116-35.

43. Sutton, ed., *Letters to Bab,* pp. 17-18.

44. Ibid., p. 15.

45. Richard Bridgman, *The Colloquial Style in America* (Oxford University Press, 1966), p. 153.

46. White, ed., *Anderson/Stein: Correspondence,* p. 83.

47. Ernest Hemingway, *In Our Time* (New York: Scribner, 1958), p. 28.

48. Paul P. Somers, Jr., "The Mark of Sherwood Anderson on Hemingway: A Look at the Texts," *South Atlantic Quarterly* 73 (Autumn 1972): 487-503, suggests that Anderson's influence on Hemingway was chiefly in the use of colloquial language, that matters of syntax were learned from Gertrude Stein. Although it is not possible to determine this question of influence with certainty, it is clear nonetheless that Anderson demonstrated to Hemingway the usable features of Stein's literary experiments.

49. Jones and Rideout, eds., *Letters of Sherwood Anderson,* p. 46.

50. Ibid.

51. Ibid., p. 129.

Glen A. Love (essay date 1997)

SOURCE: Love, Glen A. Introduction to *Winesburg, Ohio,* by Sherwood Anderson, edited by Glen A. Love, pp. vii-xxvi. Oxford: Oxford University Press, 1997.

[*In the following introduction to his edition of* Winesburg, Ohio, *Love discusses the defining characteristics of the stories and assesses their place within American literature.*]

In his book of loosely related short stories, ***Winesburg, Ohio,*** Sherwood Anderson made his most important contribution to modern American—and world—literature. Although a handful of his other tales, for example, **'I Want to Know Why'**, **'I'm a Fool'**, **'The Egg'**, and **'Death in the Woods'**, may individually represent a higher artistic achievement than any single story in ***Winesburg,*** still the book has a collective power which is greater than the sum of its parts. It has had an enormous influence on succeeding generations of writers. It restructured the course of the American short story, turning that genre from its O. Henry emphasis upon plot to its capacity for illuminating the emotional lives of ordinary people. For these and other reasons, ***Winesburg, Ohio*** remains today as an important part of America's imaginative record.

Winesburg is one of those rare works that have their own aura. We know the book so well that even if we don't know it, we know it. Lionel Trilling, many years ago in a generally disparaging essay on Anderson, called attention to this almost palpable quality of ***Winesburg***: not just a book but 'a personal souvenir'. Trilling goes on to describe it from its outside, in the old Modern Library edition with its 'brown oilcloth binding, the coarse paper, the bold type crooked on the page'. 'Dreadfully evocative,' he concludes, as if the physical presence of the book itself were somehow enough to objectify his resentment of its hurtful appeal. And yet, he allows, 'as for the ***Winesburg*** stories themselves, they are as dangerous to read again, as paining and puzzling, as if they were old letters we had written or received'.[1]

It is this odd double quality of Anderson's stories, their almost aching personalness, together with the sense that they also touch the deepest springs of common human sympathy, that seems to hold us as readers. This reverberation inward and outward suggests the presence of myth in ***Winesburg*** and others of the author's best works, and the conception of Anderson as American mythopoeist has long been a centre of interest for critics.[2] ***Winesburg*** inevitably calls up phrases of interiority, of the buried life, of essences, of seeing beneath surfaces, of cutting to the bone. Edmund Wilson, Jr. may have given this strange invasive quality its most powerful metaphor when he wrote of Anderson's work, 'we are at once disturbed and soothed by the feeling of hands thrust down among the deepest bowels of life—hands delicate but still pitiless in their exploration'.[3]

The quality of doubleness extends into Sherwood Anderson's life as well. Born in 1876 into a growing and often poverty-stricken rural Ohio family, he seems to have cast his own parents, a loud-mouthed but ineffectual father and a quietly mysterious but insightful mother, into the figures of Tom and Elizabeth Willard, the mismated parents of George Willard, the young central character of ***Winesburg.*** Moving from town to town, the Anderson family spent Sherwood's formative years, from about 1883 to 1896, in Clyde, Ohio, the background for the fictional Winesburg, although Anderson would later claim both that the characters were drawn from his small-town boyhood and that they were portraits of fellow-roomers in a Chicago boarding-house. Later, Anderson became an advertising writer and a successful businessman, married and with children of his own. At the same time, beneath this Babbitt-like exterior, he lived his own buried life, privately writing novels and short stories. Finally, in 1912 at the age of 36, he suffered a nervous collapse and, in a legendary gesture, walked out of the paint factory of which he was general manager to become an 'artist'. Though the walkout from business was not so final and dramatic as the legend would have it—Anderson continued to rely upon ad-writing to support himself long after his symbolic revolt—he did indeed begin to realize his ambition to become a writer. After coming out with two less-than-successful novels and a volume of poetry, he published ***Winesburg, Ohio*** in 1919 at the age of 43, and became famous. Other story collections followed, as well as more novels, non-fiction, and plays. He remained a productive writer until his death in 1941, but ***Winesburg*** stands as his one truly great book.

Its stories, along with a handful of others, have led following generations of writers to consider Anderson an essential spiritual ancestor. William Faulkner wrote of him: 'He was the father of my generation of American writers and the tradition of American writing which our successors will carry on. He has never received his proper evaluation. Dreiser is his older brother and Mark Twain the father of them both.'[4] Faulkner and Ernest Hemingway, both to become Nobel Prize recipients, were, as William L. Phillips has described them, Anderson's 'prize pupils',[5] and his line of influence reaches down to the present, wherein writers like John Updike, Raymond Carver, and Joyce Carol Oates have all paid homage to Anderson's arresting experiments in style and subject. ***Winesburg, Ohio*** is linked with a group of similar works, including Sarah Orne Jewett's *The Country of the Pointed Firs,* Jean Toomer's *Cane,* Hemingway's *In Our Time,* and Faulkner's *Go Down, Moses,* to which John Crowley has called our attention as forming an important American genre: a collection of stories concerning a central character, and coalescing as something closer to a novel.[6]

Just as Anderson helped to shape the writing of his followers, so his own craft in ***Winesburg*** was influenced by the works he read and admired, like Ivan Turgenev's *A Sportsman's Sketches* (1847-51) and George Borrow's tales of gypsy life in England, *Lavengro* (1851) and *The Romany Rye* (1857). In these writers, as in American writers like his fellow mid-American Mark Twain, Anderson seems to have found the same note of concern for ordinary lives which is seen in the ***Winesburg*** tales. From Gertrude Stein's new fictional techniques in such works as *Three Lives* (1909) and *Tender Buttons* (1914), Anderson found inspiration for his own stylistic experimentation with sound and rhythm. And in the free verse poems of Edgar Lee Masters's *Spoon River Anthology,* published in 1915 while Anderson was beginning to write the ***Winesburg*** tales, Anderson must have experienced his own shock of recognition. A friend loaned him the *Spoon River* book, and Anderson read it through excitedly in a single night. Masters's poems, epitaphs of people buried in a Midwestern town cemetery in which the dead confess their secret sins, frustrations, and broken dreams, provided Anderson with a record of quite literally buried lives which seemed to validate his own vision and may have helped him shape his emerging stories.

Anderson's early published works, the big, sprawling novels *Windy McPherson's Son* (1916) and *Marching Men* (1917), and the shapeless prose poems of *Mid-American Chants* (1918), strike chords which are wonderfully concentrated in ***Winesburg***: the threatening sense of loss in much of modern life, the sickness of machine civilization, the difficulty of human communication, the alienation of men from women and of both from the earth. In ***Winesburg,*** Anderson began thinking small—narrowing and deepening his focus, distilling the conflicts which engrossed him into a successful form, a series of stories about a boy approaching maturity in an American small town, a boy whose life is touched by the truths of the frustrated and warped grotesques who wear the masks of his kindred townspeople. The linear development of the earlier novels, emphasizing character development, control of plot, and an encompassing view of subject, is rejected in ***Winesburg*** in favour of a revelation of thoughts and feelings through symbolic setting and gesture. The Winesburg subjects, both town and townspeople, undergo through Anderson's technique an arrestment and isolation, like the figures on Keats's urn. The tales are presented in a series of highly charged scenes, disquieting but also peculiarly airless, as if taking place under a Plath-like bell-jar. Their effect is cumulative rather than progressive. Alfred Kazin has praised the stories as 'moments' of revelation, but they are set in the larger moment of the book itself.[7] That moment is, historically, the watershed moment of American history, occurring in the early 1890s, the period in which the book is set. This divide, made famous by Frederick Jackson Turner and his interpretation of American history, is commonly seen as marking the end of the Western frontier and the point at which the balance in America shifts from a nation primarily rural and agrarian to one that is increasingly urban and industrial.

The 'Revolt from the Village' label of scandalous realism which ***Winesburg*** wore during the years following its publication is little noticed today. A characteristic

1919 review claimed that the book would 'shatter forever what remains of the assumption that life seethes most treacherously in cities and that there are sylvan retreats where the days pass from harvest to harvest like an idyll of Theocritus'.[8] It remained for V. F. Calverton, Maxwell Geismar, Malcolm Cowley, and others to correct the book's early reputation, and today it seems apparent that Anderson turned back, in ***Winesburg,*** to the cornfields and the village of his youth because they represented the sort of ordered, natural world where love and communication were possible. Throughout his career, the return to the village, not the revolt from it, was to become the characteristic journey of Anderson's idealized self.

This is not to say that there is no realistic component in the descriptions of town and townspeople in ***Winesburg.*** The sociological background in the novel may not be extensive, but it is essential, as critic William V. Miller argues.[9] Anderson's glimpses into the social life of rural Midwestern towns scarcely resemble the exhaustive examination of a Sinclair Lewis, whose *Main Street,* published in 1920, only a year after ***Winesburg,*** matches closely the common conception of realism as a fairly straightforward depiction of contemporary social life. We should not be surprised that ***Winesburg, Ohio,*** a title which seems to promise a slice of Midwestern realism, opens with a prologue called **'The Book of the Grotesque'**, which leads the work off into a new direction. *Main Street* invites interesting comparison and contrast with ***Winesburg*** and with Anderson's published statements on realism. Anderson's concentration upon interior life is the realm of anti-realism, or, as critic David Stouck persuasively argues, expressionism, the motivation for which Stouck finds in a letter Anderson wrote to Ben Huebsch, his first publisher: 'there is within every human being a deep well of thinking over which a heavy iron lid is kept clamped,' and it is the writer's task to release that well-spring.[10] But the most important effect of Anderson's modernist treatment of this buried life is that it becomes not a retreat into solipsism, but a world which we all have in common.

In the setting of ***Winesburg,*** in the fields and farms and the rounds of town life, are to be found the sources of the book's evocation of lost worth. Through the setting is expressed the essential unity of country life, linked to the cycle of crops, to the weather and the slow turning of the seasons. Here is a pastoral world organic and yet impervious to time. Its calmness and stillness suggest a self-sufficiency full of promise and latent with meaning. Balanced against this green world are threatening, disintegrative forces. Implicitly, there is the city, which stands on the horizon of Winesburg's scenes and events, and sometimes intrudes in episodes of the characters' lives. Always it is an emblem of irresistible progress and forces of change which threaten to alter forever the life of the town. It 'watches from the shadows | And coughs when you would kiss,' like W. H. Auden's personification of Time. It has attracted smart young village boys like Ned Currie, and it has turned back queer souls like Enoch Robinson and Doctor Parcival, just as it has accepted only the perfect, uniform apples from the Winesburg orchards, which

> have been put in barrels and shipped to the cities where they will be eaten in apartments that are filled with books, magazines, furniture, and people. On the trees are only a few gnarled apples that the pickers have rejected. . . . One nibbles at them and they are delicious. Into a little round place at the side of the apple has been gathered all of its sweetness. One runs from tree to tree over the frosted ground picking the gnarled, twisted apples and filling his pockets with them. Only the few know the sweetness of the twisted apples.
>
> (**'Paper Pills'**)

The twisted apples are, of course, the 'grotesques' of ***Winesburg***'s prologue, **'The Book of the Grotesque'.** There, the narrator tells of an old writer who dreams that all the men and women he had known had become grotesques. 'The grotesques were not all horrible. Some were amusing, some almost beautiful, and one, a woman all drawn out of shape, hurt the old man by her grotesqueness. When she passed he made a noise like a small dog whimpering'. The narrator goes on to explain the old writer's idea of grotesqueness, saying that when the world was young, people formed truths out of the errant and vague thoughts of the world.

> The old man had listed hundreds of truths in his book. I will not try to tell you of all of them. There was the truth of virginity and the truth of passion, the truth of wealth and of poverty, of thrift and of profligacy, of carefulness and abandon. Hundreds and hundreds were the truths and they were all beautiful.
>
> And then the people came along. Each as he appeared snatched up one of the truths and some who were quite strong snatched up a dozen of them.
>
> It was the truths that made the people grotesques. The old man had quite an elaborate theory concerning the matter. It was his notion that the moment one of the people took one of the truths to himself, called it his truth, and tried to live his life by it, he became a grotesque and the truth he embraced became a falsehood.

The stories which follow would seem to present illustrations of the theory of a self-imposed grotesqueness, but such is not always the case. Irving Howe, in his book on Anderson, sees a contradiction in that the grotesqueness of the characters in the stories is less a result of their 'wilful fanaticism' than of their 'essentially valid resistance' to external forces.[11] Another reading, that of Robert Dunne, claims that 'in most of the ***Winesburg*** tales the characters look back first at moments early in their lives when they began practicing their tightly held ideals and when they reached a certain decisive moment when they could have adjusted their fixed plans but did not'.[12] Another view would centre upon the 'young thing within', which, the narrator tells us, saved the old writer from grotesqueness himself. This interpretation would underscore the healing power of sexuality and art as they are presented in **'The Book of the Grotesque'**.[13] Still another reading, one which is developed more fully in the following pages, finds the grotesques victims of their inability to communicate with others, an inability rooted in the failure of words themselves. Readers continue to find in **'The Book of the Grotesque'** a brilliant example of Anderson's fictional method, less than systematic and yet at the same time compelling.

The grotesques—twisted apples, unfit for the fashionable cities—provide an explicit counterforce to the natural self-sufficiency of the setting, from which they are cut off almost as completely as from the urban world on the horizon. The silence of many of them, while it is a measure of their twisted sweetness, their significance, is not the purposeful, cornfield silence of their surroundings, but rather a threatening muteness, stretched taut over a great pressure to communicate. While they are likely to remain almost wordless until the moment at which they spill out their 'truth', a few, at the other extreme, sputter uncontrollably, like Joe Welling in **'A Man of Ideas'**, who cannot restrain himself when caught up in one of his own schemes: 'Words rolled and tumbled from his mouth. . . . Pouncing upon a bystander he began to talk'. Doctor Parcival in **'The Philosopher'** is another compulsive talker, who watches from his office window until he sees George Willard alone in the newspaper office where he works, then hurries in to tell the boy his tales. Later, in self-disgust, he says, 'What a fool I am to be talking'. A common failing of all the grotesques is suggested in the plight of Enoch Robinson in **'Loneliness'**, who 'wanted to talk, but he didn't know how'. Thus both the mute grotesques and the sputtering grotesques manifest a sickness which is in conflict with the quiet and benign setting. The verbal incapacity of these figures who cannot love, who cannot draw comfort from their surroundings, is suggestive of their crippling inner wound. One recalls Irving Howe's description of Faulkner's *Light in August* as a work which 'resembles an early Renaissance painting—in the foreground a bleeding martyr, far to the rear a scene of bucolic peacefulness, with women quietly working in the fields'.[14]

From the precarious equilibrium of these forces—rural permanence threatened by encroaching city, placid setting opposed by tortured inhabitants, the urge to communicate thwarted by verbal incapacity—is created the aura of charged stillness which characterizes the tales. The first paragraph of the opening story, **'Hands'**, quickly sets forth the elemental conflicts:

> [1] Upon the half decayed veranda of a small frame house that stood near the edge of a ravine near the town of Winesburg, Ohio, a fat little old man walked nervously up and down. [2] Across a long field that had been seeded for clover but that had produced only a dense crop of yellow mustard weeds, he could see the public highway along which went a wagon filled with berry pickers returning from the fields. [3] The berry pickers, youths and maidens, laughed and shouted boisterously. [4] A boy clad in a blue shirt leaped from the wagon and attempted to drag after him one of the maidens who screamed and protested shrilly. [5] The feet of the boy in the road kicked up a cloud of dust that floated over the face of the departing sun. [6] Over the long field came a thin girlish voice. [7] 'Oh, you Wing Biddlebaum, comb your hair, it's falling into your eyes,' commanded the voice to the man, who was bald and whose nervous little hands fiddled about the bare white forehead as though arranging a mass of tangled locks.

This opening, like the beginnings of all memorable fictions, is a microcosm of the strengths of what is to come: in this case, a portrait of an incommunicative grotesque, both defined and opposed by suggestive details of landscape and human community. The concealed artifice of Anderson's apparently artless style is worth a closer look here. One notices that the opening two sentences, both describing Wing Biddlebaum, are, in the grammatical term, periodic, with the main clause arrived at only after those details of scene—the half-decayed veranda and the field seeded for clover but gone to weeds—which suggest and prepare the reader for the half-ruined life and blighted hopes of Wing, the subject of the main clauses. The first action attributed to him ('walked nervously up and down') presages his timidity and the repetitive nature of his behaviour. In the second sentence, the reader's attention is turned from Wing toward the object of his gaze, the wagon-load of young berry-pickers. They are, of course, an extension of the felicitous landscape, their easy and uninhibited physicality etched against Wing's mute isolation, a contrast heightened by a change in grammatical structure in the next sentences (3-5) given over to the berry-pickers. Now, main clauses are shifted to the beginning of the sentences to form a 'normal' word order. The sentences become loose, rather than periodic, and the presentation flows into a more direct, straightforward narration, freed from the heavy subordination and the symbolic details which marked the opening sentences describing Wing.

Anderson's choice of the archaic 'youths and maidens' in sentence 3 suggests an idealized, even mythical, landscape, but the brief glimpse of innocence is dimmed by the cloud of dust across the sun and by a taunting cry from one of the the girl berry-pickers, a cry which carries our attention back to the figure on the veranda. In shifting attention back to Wing (6), Anderson reintroduces the periodic sentence with which Wing has previously been identified, again opening with a prepositional phrase, and again echoing the earlier suggestive detail of the field gone to weeds. In both sentences 6 and 7, normal word order is again set aside to encompass an appropriate attitude toward Wing. Subjects and verbs are reversed ('came a . . . voice', 'commanded the voice') so that Wing is made passive, one to whom things happen—and have happened. Unlike the youths and maidens who laugh and shout, scream and protest, and even command, Wing remains silent, his behaviour repetitive and acquiescent. He can only watch, or listen, or pace up and down, or fiddle with his hands in a series of compulsive and perhaps ominous movements.

As the story develops, Wing's hands increasingly draw our attention. They seem ready to give him away, fluttering nervously, aimlessly, alarmingly. 'He wanted to keep them hidden away and looked with amazement at the quiet inexpressive hands of other men who worked beside him in the fields, or passed, driving sleepy teams on country roads.' These quiet, inexpressive hands announce their oneness with the natural setting, while Wing's hands are associated with images of futility and frustration, as when they are compared to 'the beating of the wings of an imprisoned bird'. The recurring presence of *hands* throughout not only this story but many of the stories suggests other opportunities for the inquiring reader to consider Anderson's use of images in establishing patterns of meaning and unity throughout the ***Winesburg*** stories. To pursue the imagery of hands, one thinks of the knob-like knuckles of Doctor Reefy in **'Paper Pills'**, which resemble the gnarled and twisted apples rejected by the pickers; or the bleeding hand of Reverend Curtis Hartman in **'The Strength of God'**; or Kate Swift's sharp little fists, in **'The Teacher'**, beating, in frustration, upon her pupil, George Willard. Many such patterns underpin the stories, as Walter B. Rideout points out.[15] Anderson's use of light and darkness, of windows, of dreams, of countless subjects may repay close reading in ways often unanticipated, since the author often invests his images and physical details with intimations of the inner lives of his characters.

The gulf between dream and reality in Wing Biddlebaum's life establishes still another tension in the story. Wing advises George Willard to close his ears to the 'roaring of the voices', to begin to dream, and his own ideal is expressed as a dream:

> Out of the dream Wing Biddlebaum made a picture for George Willard. In the picture men lived again in a kind of pastoral golden age. Across a green open country came clean limbed young men, some afoot, some mounted upon horses. In crowds the young men came to gather about the feet of an old man who sat beneath a tree in a tiny garden and who talked to them.

The dream is one of perfect communication among human beings, set, significantly, in a 'pastoral golden age'. The Socratic instructor of youth is Wing's idealization of his own former role as teacher. But, like the contrast between Wing's inhibitions and the easy sensuality of the youths and maidens, the dream of a revered teacher is placed against the nightmarish incidents of his actual life, in which, like Socrates, he had been attacked as a corruptor of youth. A victim of homophobia in the town where he had been teaching as a young man, he had been run out after being beaten by the saloon-keeper father of one of the students, and later nearly lynched. Anderson's treatment of these events—the saloon-keeper's rage, his hard fists, the insect-like scurrying of the children, the rain, the darkness, and the stick and balls of mud which are thrown at the screaming figure of the terrified schoolteacher—emphasizes sharply the opposition between the ugly reality of misunderstanding and the ideal of perfect communication, and between the agonizingly repressed and isolated grotesque and a setting of freedom, innocence, and love.

Besides serving as an ironic opposite to the inner state of the grotesques of Winesburg, the natural world occasionally provides the needed resolution and solace. Both of the latter functions are seen in **'The Untold Lie'**, in which Ray Pearson is saddened by the autumn beauty of the Winesburg countryside. His sordid little cabin, his scolding wife, a crying child—all are brought into sharp relief by the lovely autumn twilight. 'All the low hills were washed with color and even the little clusters of bushes in the corners by the fences were alive with beauty.' Overcome by the splendour of the natural world and the squalour of his own life, he tears off his old tattered overcoat and runs across a field shouting protests 'against his life, against all life, against everything that makes life ugly'. Yet it is also the beauty of the autumn setting which results in a rare moment of contact between Ray and a younger man with whom he is working: 'There they stood in the big empty field with the quiet corn shocks behind them and the red and yellow hills in the distance, and from being just two indifferent workmen they had become all alive to each other. Here, the empty, quiet fields serve to dissolve momentarily the barrier of incommunicability which surrounds the men, and a brief but genuine awareness takes place. The silent moment becomes Ray Pearson's 'truth', while his unspoken advice to the younger man at the story's conclusion he dismisses as merely an untold lie.

George Willard, in whom Wing Biddlebaum and many of the other grotesques find the opportunity for verbal release, is, in a sense, the *genius loci* of the Winesburg landscape, the attendant spirit of the town. He provides a kind of synecdoche for the village, standing, Janus-like, between innocence and experience, youth and maturity, rural past and urban future. Many of the grotesques seem to sense the boy's connection with the spirit of life in the village, and they reach out for contact through him. That he also harbours feelings of loneliness and inadequacy seems not to occur to them; whether or not he actually shares in the aura of hope and life which interfuses the natural setting becomes less important than their belief that he does. Elmer Cowley imagines to himself that George 'belonged to the town, typified the town, represented in his person the spirit of the town' (**'"Queer"'**). Seth Richmond envies George's apparent link with the town and its people. Similarly, Wing Biddlebaum does not think of himself as a part of Winesburg although he has lived there twenty years, but with George Willard he finds the solace of human contact. 'With a kind of wriggle, like a fish returned to the brook by the fisherman, Biddlebaum the silent began to talk, striving to put into words the ideas that had been accumulated by his mind during long years of silence' (**'Hands'**).

In his position as confidant to the grotesques, and hence as a counterforce to the loneliness and verbal failure which isolates them, George Willard's identification with the ameliorative aspects of the setting is further reinforced. He is the human, and thus communicable, manifestation of the same spirit which must remain deaf and dumb in the natural world. This is not to say that he is patriarchal or wise beyond his years. He is a believable character, possessed by the lusts and self-doubts of youth, whom Anderson is careful never to allow to become too good or all-knowing.

Feminist readings of ***Winesburg,*** in this respect, have recently added important insights into our understanding of George Willard and the other characters. Nancy Bunge and Claire Colquitt, for example, have demonstrated how exploitation is the defining element in nearly all the love relationships in the stories.[16] George is a participant in this exploitation, as is revealed in the stories **'Nobody Knows'** and **'An Awakening'**. Near the end of the book, in **'Sophistication'**, George Willard may be seen as coming to a new awareness, with Helen White, of the possibility for companionable love, but the awareness may be too little and too late to overcome the permeating impression of the rest of the book that there is no way for women to construct satisfying lives for themselves. This sense of women's sexual and emotional frustration drives some of ***Winesburg***'s most powerful stories, including **'Mother'** and **'Death'** (about Elizabeth Willard); **'Surrender'** (about Louise Bentley); **'Adventure'** (about Alice Hindman); and **'The Teacher'** (about Kate Swift). At the same time, Anderson may also be recognized for his insights into these women's lives; Sally Adair Rigsbee notes that 'few other modern male writers have been able to convey with such loving sensitivity the hurt women bear or to advocate as openly as Anderson does that the relationships of men and women should be equal'.[17]

In the matter of stylistic innovation, ***Winesburg, Ohio*** reveals interesting links with modernist experimentation of the time. Along with Willa Cather's 'unfurnishing' of the novel and Ernest Hemingway's 'iceberg theory', based upon the analogy that the dignity of movement of an iceberg results from nine-tenths of it being underwater,[18] Anderson, too, is deeply involved in techniques which leave the important things unsaid. Anderson's technique in this regard is to call attention, as narrator, to the inability of words to convey meaning satisfactorily. In **'Hands'** he professes his inadequacy to the task of describing Wing's hands, saying, 'It is a job for a poet'; later, he says of Wing's sensitivity as a teacher, 'And yet that is but crudely stated. It needs the poet there'. This same refrain—the call for a 'poet', one whose godlike powers of communication will pierce the inexpressible mystery—sounds through the book, lending greater poignancy to the state of incommunicability in which both narrator and characters find themselves.

Describing Joe Welling, the narrator gropes for the right comparison: 'He was like a tiny little volcano that lies silent for days and then suddenly spouts fire. No, he wasn't like that—he was like a man who is subject to fits . . .' (**'A Man of Ideas'**). Or, in portraying Wash Williams in **'Respectability'**, the teller backtracks to correct himself: 'I go too fast. Not everything about Wash was unclean. He took care of his hands'. Sometimes the narrator seems almost to give up before the impossibility of his task as in **'The Untold Lie'**, when he says of Ray Pearson, 'If you knew the Winesburg country in the fall and how the low hills are all splashed with yellows and reds you would understand his feeling'. Or, again, in the introductory **'Book of the Grotesque'**, the voice fumbles for a time with several similes about the old writer, then concludes, 'It is absurd, you see, to try to tell you what was inside the old writer . . .'. These repeated confessions of verbal inadequacy encourage the reader to doubt the power of words and serve to intensify the verbal failures which occur between the characters in the stories.

These failures are, of course, seen most readily in the dearth of verbal communication between characters. As the tales unfold, the act of speech becomes strained and frustrated almost beyond endurance. The verbs tell this most dramatically. Characters do not simply speak; they cry, they stammer, or mutter, or sputter, or ultimately are altogether silent. Perhaps the most characteristic and important verb in the book is 'whispered'. The soliloquy-like oral discourse in ***Winesburg*** is further emphasized by the high number of reflexive pronouns following verbs of speech ('said aloud to himself', 'muttered to himself', etc.). Verbs which express the normal give and take of discourse, such as 'answered', 'replied', and 'responded', are almost totally absent in ***Winesburg.*** The unusually high proportion of verbs of strained communication seems to permeate the texture of the entire work. The aura of loneliness and frustration in ***Winesburg,*** which every reader notices, must, to a great degree, radiate outward from advice unheard or unheeded, from words shouted to empty fields and sky, or whispered in lonely rooms.

Anderson's pastoral vision, which led him in ***Winesburg*** to turn from what he had come to regard as the shrill disorder of industrialism back to the country town of his youth, was, in an important sense, valid after all. Winesburg was the right place for love, the proper setting for human communication although, as the stories reveal, it may not occur there. 'Many people must live and die alone, *even* in Winesburg', concludes one of the tales (**'Adventure'**; italics added). Thus, the leave-taking of George Willard in the book's final episode gathers more than ordinary significance. **'Departure'** is not really a story at all, but a protraction and savouring of the meaning of Winesburg for the city-bound youth, and a suggestion of the place's enduring value. On the final morning, George arises early and walks one last time on Trunion Pike, the road leading from the village out into the country. In his silent farewell to Winesburg, Anderson completes the pastoral frame begun in the opening paragraph of **'Hands'**, the first story. Here he expands earlier descriptions of setting into a diapason of countryside and seasons, reinforcing the bond between the young man and the natural world, reasserting his significant silence, his 'organic' nature, in contrast to the static quality of the grotesques.

Paradoxically, the lesson of purposeful, cornfield silence which George takes from his natural surroundings may be the beginning of the means by which the walls of thwarted communication which surround the grotesques will be finally broken down. He may become the hoped-for connector between these tortured souls and the great world. Filled with his vague dreams, he is inevitably drawn to the city, where, immersed in that destructive element, he gives promise of becoming the artist whose heightened understanding and whose craft of language may counteract the limitations of words, the one who, as Edwin Fussell says, will become the spokesman for all of the grotesques, whose 'fragmentary wisdom' he now possesses.[19]

And the sort of artist which George will become has been suggested all along. It is found in the book's dedication to Anderson's mother, the silent but insightful one, 'whose keen observations on the life about her first awoke in me the hunger to see beneath the surface of lives'. It is found in the narrator's expression of his craft in **'The Book of the Grotesque'**: 'The thing to get at is what the writer or the young thing within the writer was thinking about.' It is heard in Kate Swift's advice to George to 'know what people are thinking about, not what they say,' an admonition Anderson later repeated to his own son, John, when the young man was considering becoming a writer.[20] It is, in short, the sort of credo which is indistinguishable from Anderson's own self-conception as a writer. He presents us, finally, with an important paradox, the artist who is, at bottom, sceptical of his medium: distrustful of words, he is nevertheless driven to their use, not only to record his scepticism, but also to attempt a communication which even at its best cannot approach the power of non-words, the more perfect communication which lies wrapped within purposeful silence.

If this seems to suggest for the reader in a postmodern present something like a collapse of meaning and a retreat into interiority, then a further pondering of ***Winesburg, Ohio*** may be in order. Thomas Yingling argues from such a postmodernist perspective that the book shows Anderson attempting to shore up for his own age a great 'shibboleth' of nineteenth-century American culture, 'the notion that the commonality of life is grounded in some "universal" experience or quality of life (i.e., that beneath such negligible differences as class, ethnicity, race, and gender, we are all somehow "the same"). . . . But even if we grant that it exists, we must also insist that the "universal" is not the same as the "collective."'[21] Yingling's deconstructive reading of ***Winesburg*** brings to the front what is certainly an issue of enduring, as well as contemporary, significance. What is the fate of a ***Winesburg, Ohio,*** or any classic from the past, if contemporary ideological tests are applied to such works, which are then almost inevitably found wanting? Can the common roots of experience survive the gender and culture wars of the present and the future?

That the basic universality of human nature can be dismissed as an outworn notion, or that cultural differences have completely overridden nature in the determination of human behaviour—these are assumptions which are increasingly questioned today.[22] We seem to have more in common as human beings, as possessors of an undeniable human nature, than the proponents of difference would allow. Though we continue to suffer individually or collectively, our sufferings and our silences may still unite us. Because the universal underlies the collective, great works from the past continue to speak meaningfully to us. The Andersonian artist in ***Winesburg*** does not dissolve into interiority, but lives to touch the universal sympathy in which our shared differences are recognized. The responses of many readers through the years who have found ***Winesburg, Ohio*** a moving and engrossing experience suggest that the book will not go gently into that good night of elegy and retrospective, but that it will continue to hold its place in the conflictive present and future.

Notes

1. Lionel Trilling, 'Sherwood Anderson', in Ray Lewis White (ed.), *The Achievement of Sherwood Anderson* (Chapel Hill: University of North Carolina Press, 1966), 214.

2. David D. Anderson, 'Anderson and Myth', in David D. Anderson (ed.), *Sherwood Anderson: Dimensions of his Literary Art* (East Lansing: Michigan State University Press, 1976), 121-41.

3. Edmund Wilson, Jr., '*Many Marriages*', *The Dial,* 74 (Apr. 1923), 400.

4. William Faulkner, interview, 'The Art of Fiction XII', *Paris Review,* 12 (Spring 1956), 46.

5. William L. Phillips, 'Sherwood Anderson's Two Prize Pupils', in White (ed.), *The Achievement of Sherwood Anderson,* 202-10.

6. John W. Crowley, 'Introduction', in John W. Crowley (ed.), *New Essays on Winesburg, Ohio* (Cambridge University Press, 1990), 14-15.

7. Alfred Kazin, *On Native Grounds* (Garden City, NY: Doubleday, 1956), 169.

8. M. A., 'A Country Town', *New Republic,* 19 (25 June 1919), 257.

9. William V. Miller, 'Sherwood Anderson's "Middletown": A Sociology of the Midwestern States', *Old Northwest,* 15 (Winter 1991/2), 245-59.

10. David Stouck, 'Anderson's Expressionist Art', in Crowley (ed.), *New Essays on Winesburg, Ohio,* 28.

11. Irving Howe, *Sherwood Anderson* (New York: William Sloane, 1951), 107.

12. Robert Dunne, 'Beyond Grotesqueness in *Winesburg, Ohio*', *Midwest Quarterly,* 31 (Winter 1990), 181.

13. A. Carl Bredahl, 'The Young Thing Within: Divided Narrative and Sherwood Anderson's *Winesburg, Ohio*', *Midwest Quarterly,* 27 (Summer 1986), 422-37.

14. Irving Howe, *William Faulkner: A Critical Study* (New York: Random House, 1952), 64.

15. Walter B. Rideout, 'The Simplicity of *Winesburg, Ohio*', in David D. Anderson (ed.), *Critical Essays on Sherwood Anderson* (Boston: G. K. Hall, 1981), 146-54.

16. Nancy Bunge, 'Women in Sherwood Anderson's Fiction', in Anderson (ed.), *Critical Essays on Sherwood Anderson,* 242-9; Claire Colquitt, 'Motherlove in Two Narratives of Community: *Winesburg, Ohio* and *The Country of the Pointed Firs*', in Crowley (ed.), *New Essays on Winesburg, Ohio,* 73-87.

17. Sally Adair Rigsbee, 'The Feminine in Winesburg, Ohio', *Studies in American Fiction,* 9 (1981), 242.

18. See Glen A. Love, '*The Professor's House*: Cather, Hemingway and the Chastening of American Prose Style', *Western American Literature,* 24 (Winter 1990), 295-311.

19. Edwin Fussell, '*Winesburg Ohio*: Art and Isolation', *Modern Fiction Studies,* 6 (Summer 1960), 110. For a questioning of the equating of George Willard with the narrator of *Winesburg,* see Marcia Jacobson, '*Winesburg, Ohio* and the Autobiographical Moment', in Crowley (ed.), *New Essays on Winesburg, Ohio,* 53-72.

20. *The Portable Sherwood Anderson,* ed. Horace Gregory (New York: Viking Press, 1949), 595.

21. Thomas Yingling, '*Winesburg, Ohio* and the End of Collective Experience', in Crowley (ed.), *New Essays on Winesburg, Ohio,* 114.

22. For a thorough examination of these issues in the present century, see Carl N. Degler, *In Search of Human Nature: the Decline and Revival of Darwinism in American Social Thought* (New York: Oxford University Press, 1991).

Belinda Bruner (essay date fall 1999)

SOURCE: Bruner, Belinda. "Pedagogy of the Undressed: Sherwood Anderson's Kate Swift." *Studies in Short Fiction* 36, no. 4 (fall 1999): 361-68.

[*In the following essay, Bruner discusses the characterization of Kate Swift as a teacher and as a woman.*]

Sherwood Anderson idealizes Kate Swift as "a tiny goddess on a pedestal" (160)[1] yet seemingly discards her once she has served her purpose. Critics tend to conclude that Anderson fails his female characters; Marilyn Judith Atlas points out that Anderson denies Kate Swift the kind of "ascension" toward a new life that he affords some of the male characters of Winesburg.[2] Kate is trapped within several female types, most notably, the modest, no-nonsense schoolteacher behind whom hides a sexual wildcat. Despite Anderson's attempts to define her and George's misunderstanding of her desire, in the role of the teacher she is at her most successful. By combining character analysis with critical pedagogy[3] in the context of ***Winesburg, Ohio,*** I aim to provide a thorough reading of Kate Swift as a teacher and to remain faithful to Anderson's explanation of Kate: "She was a teacher but she was also a woman" (164-65).[4]

Kate understands and controls her sexual desire but readily demonstrates that love and learning coexist. Kate's desire "to open the door of life" to George Willard was so strong that "it became something physical"

(164) and Kate embraces that physicality as a teaching tool. Kate's readiness to teach eventually moves beyond her own awareness with the Reverend Hartman and is at its most deliberate with the young schoolchildren in her classroom. When Kate is teaching, her "biting and forbidding" character becomes passionate and beautiful; the children sit "back in their chairs and look at her" (161). She "was not known in Winesburg as a pretty woman" (160), but when she shares her passion with George he becomes "aware of the marked beauty of her features" (164). Kate does not touch the children in her classroom for they lack the maturity to understand what she carries within; instead, she walks "up and down in the schoolroom," her "hands clasped behind her back." The reader is told she is stern, "yet in an odd way very close to her pupils" (161). Indeed, the youngsters in her care often did not understand her—she sometimes made up stories that confused them, and once made a boy laugh so hard that "he became dizzy and fell off his seat" (162). After this Kate quickly resumed control of the atmosphere of the classroom.

Children are schooled in order to be trained in facts, but primarily to be taught the difference between public and personal behavior. Kate does not touch her students or seduce them into learning; rather, she is a model of restraint and public behavior. Children look at the teacher's body sensually and instinctively, and as Madeleine Grumet explains in *Bitter Milk,* intentionality, desire, and "the capacity to symbolize" (104) are learned through the gaze. Touch is retrained in school; the body must surrender in order to be educated. When the child is quiet, still and attentive, learning can begin. In the room full of children, Kate is clothed and physically inaccessible, conveying a lesson concerning public behavior. She is aware of the power of the body to send messages and uses that power appropriately. With the voyeuristic Reverend she is powerless and presents a humbling message about private behavior. With George Willard she uses her body's passion in a different way. Kate and George are on more equal ground, because they are both adults and because they regularly converse with each other. Kate enjoys speaking with George and allows her body to respond with the power of pleasure.

Teachers' bodies convey messages that alert students to the teacher's availability as a guide or confidant, the teacher's attitude toward her or his subject, or even toward the confines of the environment in which they are teaching and learning. The student comes to the classroom expecting to encounter "the subject presumed to know," which, Lacan explains, causes desire and, through transference, love. The teacher's body naturally becomes objectified as he or she stands in front of the class with something to profess. The success of the ritual of lecture depends upon the physical presence of the teacher and the student's desire. Arthur W. Frank offers the experience of his own "perpetual fascination" when students come to his office to "see" him: "I ask them what questions they have. I gradually realize they have no specific questions; they only want, quite literally, to *see* me . . . as if that contact could confer something" (29-30). Roger Simon points out that "pedagogy [is] a form of seduction" and "as a teacher, it is important to acknowledge one's eroticization, to realize that one's actions matter to students" (99). In her relationship with George, Kate Swift is direct and mature in utilizing touch and the gaze. Kate's love for George is tangible as she seeks him out, and her action strengthens her ability to teach. By contrast, Wing Biddlebaum merely paces on his veranda "hoping" George will come by; his inaction conveys fear, causing George to refrain from questioning "with a shiver of dread" (31).[5]

Kate takes responsibility for her "eroticization" and accepts the significance of her role as a teacher. Kate seeks out and touches George because "in something he had written as a school boy she thought she had recognized the spark of genius and wanted to blow on the spark" (162-63). More than once she had met George at his office or taken him out for walks during which she tried to talk to him about being a writer. Kate uses her body to communicate with George. Taking him by the shoulders she "turned him about so that she could look into his eyes. A passer-by might have thought them about to embrace" (163). Kate grabs George passionately but says with sensitivity: "I don't want to frighten you, but I would like to make you understand" (163). Kate tells George not to be afraid of living, and she has the experience to know what she is saying. Kate recognizes that her desire to teach George is accompanied by a sexual desire. She believes this is a force that can help George if he is mature enough to understand it, which at the time he is not. Still, Kate is aware of the capacities of passion: "the impulse that had driven her out into the snow poured itself out into talk" (164). She is conscious of her feelings and acknowledges them, lightly and hesitantly—"in a moment, if I stay, I'll be wanting to kiss you" (164)—but controls them, first simply, then with confusion and impatience as she sees George is not ready to understand what she means. Kate Swift possesses an awareness of Eros as a pedagogical force, and she works that force to instill in her students the desire to keep seeking even after the teacher and student have parted. She educates in the true sense of the word—she leads George out of Winesburg and she leads the Reverend Hartman out of spiritual despair. Through Kate they each create their own truth and then leave her behind. The reader sees Kate's despair as she is isolated in her passion. Kate never learns of the effect she has had on George. She knows something of the desire she aroused in him but never sees him mature: "what's the use? It will be ten years before you begin to understand what I mean when I talk to you" (164). In spite of his initial immaturity, Kate has blown on the spark in George. She inspires him to desire and explore mature love, and to read, think, and question.

George's sexual response to Kate's passion has provoked his drive to know. The reader sees this several times after George's fumbling encounter with Kate. He forwards the flame to Helen, telling her, "I've been reading books and I've been thinking" (236), likely books that Kate brought to his office. Only hours after lying on his bed fantasizing about Kate and Helen (158), he lay awake until four o'clock in the morning thinking, not fantasizing, and trying to understand. The arm that had earlier embraced a pillow now reached upward, and with his hand George groped in the darkness feeling an urgency deeper than his sexual one had been. The desire to feel like a man became the desire to know all he still needed to learn: "I have missed something. I have missed something Kate Swift was trying to tell me" (166). George recognizes that whatever he missed he will have to learn for himself. He passes the search for this unnameable thing on to Helen:

> I want you to do something, I don't know what. Perhaps it is none of my business. I want you to try to be different from other women. You see the point. It's none of my business I tell you. I want you to be a beautiful woman. You see what I want.
>
> (236-37)

In the cycle of good teaching, Helen, now, must miss what George is trying to tell her. It is probable that Helen does not see what George wants and she must discover it for herself. George's sharing with Helen is a part of Kate's legacy. Kate Swift offers herself to George and allows him to grasp what he needs.

Kate intuitively reveals enough of herself to aid the instruction of each student who is ready to learn. She exposes nothing extraordinary as she teaches young children, guarding her body and keeping a barrier between it and the bodies of the students. She does not touch her young students as Wing Biddlebaum does, and she does not have to; her presence is so commanding that the students sit back in their seats and look at her. She is not accountable for the Reverend's voyeurism because she is in her apartment, where it is appropriate to indulge in the private behavior of unbinding her body. She does not invite eroticization but she has some sense of its possibility, exhibited in the fact that she makes a conscious decision to touch George but not her current students. In fact, Kate does not touch anyone but George, though her body, dressed and undressed, is an erotic focal point for many who observe it.

George had never really looked at Kate until she made the move to touch him. When he did look, he found her to be very beautiful. Anderson makes it clear that it is the passion of her teaching that beautifies Kate, but never suggests that Kate is a desperate old maid. She has known passion and she has had adventures:

> Although no one in Winesburg would have expected it, her life had been very adventurous. It was still adventurous . . . the people of the town thought of her as a confirmed old maid and because she spoke sharply and went her own way thought her lacking in all the human feeling that did so much to make and mar their lives. In reality she was the most eagerly passionate soul among them.
>
> (162)

This passion becomes physical as her intense desire to have George understand life sweeps over her. It is emotional eagerness and a trick of light—"in the lamplight George Willard looked no longer a boy, but a man ready to play the part of a man"—(165) that causes Kate to become aroused by George. But with the Reverend Hartman it is entirely the essence of Kate that teaches, and Kate-in-the-flesh cannot respond. The Reverend sees Kate's body undressed, and lusts for her, but she has not provoked it; she does not even know he is looking at her. The Reverend never describes Kate's body as beautiful but as a spiritual diversion, as God in the body of a woman. In Hartman's case, Kate's body teaches without her knowledge, serving as a kind of blank page upon which the Reverend writes his own text. Kate's body becomes a spectacle as she appears to the Reverend as a holy vision leading him out of spiritual despair. She unconsciously teaches him that sexual desire and intellectual desire often come together. The Reverend also learns to acknowledge that the truth may set him free, even if that truth is something he considers sinful. Kate's nude body first incites lust but then leads the Reverend to pray. As with George, lust is followed by a yearning for truth.

Kate's bared body is the "strong sweet new current of power" (148) for which the Reverend has been praying. He becomes more confident in himself after seeing Kate through her window. He is more aware of temptation and his sermons are more charismatic. Even though his lust increases, he is happy to find that the Lord delivers him from temptation every time, for example, by one evening sending Aunt Swift to the window instead of Kate. The Reverend is shocked by Kate's smoking but reminds himself that she has lived an adventurous life, having spent time in Europe and New York City. This is one way that he begins to have more compassion for human imperfection. His own imperfection, that of lust for a woman, is manifested by the hole he makes in his window. The image that is cracked away, the heel of the boy looking into the face of Christ, is a pagan symbol but an apt one: the Reverend's Achilles' heel. He prays: "Please, Father, do not forget me. Give me power to go tomorrow and repair the hole in the window" (152). When God does not move him to do so, he decides that God must be testing him with a temptation.

As he continues to contemplate the test, he decides that he deserves to know passion and that he will not be a hypocrite. He considers leaving the ministry and seeking women:

> Man . . . has no right to forget that he is an animal . . . I will besiege this school teacher . . . if I am a creature of carnal lusts I will live then for my lusts . . . I will see this woman and will think the thoughts I have never dared to think.
>
> (154)

This time when the Reverend goes to wait and watch for Kate, she appears naked and weeping, and kneels down to pray, looking like "the figure of the boy in the presence of the Christ on the leaded window" (155). The Reverend smashes the whole window with his fist and runs into the street. He goes to George Willard to tell of his message from God brought to him in the body of a woman:

> God has appeared to me in the person of Kate Swift, the school teacher, kneeling naked on a bed. Do you know Kate Swift? Although she may not be aware of it, she is an instrument of God, bearing the message of truth.
>
> (155)

The Reverend's comments suggest that the objectified teacher may be holding the truth and yet unaware of her role. Kate is humiliated for a greater good and is cast as a martyr by Anderson's simple imagery. The fragile, beautiful vision is used to portray truth and then smashed like a fallen idol. Now the Reverend knows that even the naked and carnal pray, that he can lust and still serve God. He has also learned not to try to patch up a hole but to replace the entire spectacle. He credits God through the body of Kate for his insight, but in reality he has learned this truth by and for himself.

The Reverend's voyeuristic act is not unlike that of a student. The student, or the observer, processes many ideas and thinks through many fantasies of which the teacher is unaware. The teacher is a vulnerable object, moving, breathing, speaking for the class before her, his or her body a tablet upon which students will write their story of a night, a semester, a lifetime. A strong and generous person should take this position, with an awareness of the power not only to manipulate and suggest, but also the humility of being formed and designed, of being part of the student's learning material. Kate is seductive and compelling as a manifestation of her ability to educe—to lead people out of their delusions toward an understanding of their real lives. A teacher must be able to know when a student is ready for such learning. Wing Biddlebaum dreams that he is on a pedestal toward which young men come to sit and learn. Wing is afraid of that dream. Kate embodies it, and suffers perhaps as much as Wing because she never learns of the stories she brings out in people, the places to which she leads. Her seduction arouses, empowers, and ennobles others, but humiliates Kate. She is the teacher who makes herself available at her own risk:

> During the afternoon the school teacher had been to see Doctor Welling concerning her health. The doctor had scolded her and had declared she was in danger of losing her hearing. It was foolish for Kate Swift to be abroad in the storm, foolish and perhaps dangerous. The woman in the streets did not remember the words of the doctor and would not have turned back had she remembered.
>
> (164)

She is walking through the storm when she decides to have another talk with George Willard. Her lack of regard for herself is typical as she reaches out again in George's interest. When Kate has a care for herself she loses power as a teacher. With the children, a moment of happiness for Kate means that a boy like Sugars McNutts (puns intended) becomes unruly. When Kate allows herself to experience personal pleasure in her relationship with George, George becomes confused. In each instance, Kate must deny herself in order to maintain her effectiveness as a teacher. In her dealings with George she must deny herself even basic personal caution. As she weathers the literal storm and her desire, Kate Swift is a martyr to the cause of unrequited teaching.

Like many teachers, Kate never sees the fruit of her work. Shortcomings that have been noted about Kate Swift's character may be essential aspects of her role as a teacher. If Anderson has failed to complete Kate's story, it is because the essence of what occurred was for those who objectified Kate or took her to be an answered prayer. In presenting keen observations about life, Anderson chances upon a truth of passionate dedication and self-sacrifice, the teacher Kate Swift.

Notes

1. Page references are from the 1976 Penguin edition of Anderson's *Winesburg, Ohio* except where otherwise noted.
2. Atlas concludes that "by exploring the lives of the women in Winesburg we explore the biases of a period . . . and an author" (264-65). Chris Browning maintains that Kate Swift is Anderson's "portrait of his ideal woman" (141) while William V. Miller explores Anderson's craft and the "bewildered understanding of women" (208) that seems to motivate his creation of frustrated females. For additional discussion of Anderson's female characters, see Arcana, Bunge, and Rigsbee.

3. Since Freire's injunction to educators to behold the political and sociological conditions under which our students learn, there have been a series of developments. These range from the 1982 *Yale French Studies* special issue on teaching as a literary genre, in which Paul de Man derides the personal aspects of teaching, to Jane Gallop's 1995 conference on teaching and the personal. Works of note in addition to these proceedings include those by Laurie Finke; bell hooks; Barry Kanpol; and Jane Tompkins on teacher angst.
4. Students of Anderson biography will appreciate Browning's discussion of the women who may have influenced Anderson's characterization of Kate. Ray Lewis White, in his critical edition of *Winesburg, Ohio,* mentions Trillena White as a possible source for the teacher Kate (139).
5. In a separate work I compare the teaching methods of Kate Swift and Wing Biddlebaum. Here it will suffice to enter that both teacher characters suffer Christ-like fates.

Works Cited

Anderson, David D., ed. *Critical Essays on Sherwood Anderson.* Boston: Hall, 1981.

Anderson, Sherwood. *Winesburg, Ohio.* New York: Penguin, 1976.

Arcana, Judith. "Tandy: At the Core of Winesburg." *Studies in Short Fiction* 24 (1987): 66-70.

Atlas, Marilyn Judith. "Sherwood Anderson and the Women of Winesburg." D. Anderson 250-66.

Browning, Chris. "Kate Swift: Sherwood Anderson's Creative Eros." *Tennessee Studies in Literature* 8 (1968): 141-48.

Bunge, Nancy. "Women in Sherwood Anderson's Fiction." D. Anderson 242-49.

Finke, Laurie A. "The Pedagogy of the Depressed: Feminism, Poststructuralism, and Pedagogical Practice." *Teaching Contemporary Theory to Undergraduates.* Ed. Dianne F. Sadoff and William E. Cain. New York: MLA, 1994 154-68.

Frank, Arthur W. "Lecturing and Transference: The Undercover Work of Pedagogy." Gallop 28-35.

Freire, Paulo. *Pedagogy of the Oppressed.* Trans. Myra Bergman Ramos. New York: Seabury P, 1970.

Gallop, Jane, ed. *Pedagogy: The Question of Impersonation.* Bloomington: Indiana UP, 1995.

Grumet, Madeleine R. *Bitter Milk: Women and Teaching.* Amherst: U of Massachusetts P, 1988.

hooks, bell. "Passionate Pedagogy: Erotic Student/Faculty Relationships." *Z Magazine* Mar. 1996: 45-51.

Kanpol, Barry. *Critical Pedagogy: An Introduction.* Westport, Connecticut: Bergin and Garvey, 1994.

Lacan, Jacques. *The Four Fundamental Concepts of Psychoanalysis.* Ed. Jacques-Alain Miller. Trans. Alan Sheridan. New York: Norton, 1973.

Man, Paul de. "The Resistance to Theory." *Yale French Studies* 63 (1982): 3-20.

Miller, William V. "Earth-Mothers, Succubi, and Other Ectoplasmic Spirits: The Women in Sherwood Anderson's Short Stories." D. Anderson 196-209.

Rigsbee, Sally Adair. "The Feminine in *Winesburg, Ohio.*" *Studies in American Fiction* 9 (1981): 233-44.

Simon, Roger I. "Face to Face With Alterity: Postmodern Jewish Identity and the Eros of Pedagogy." Gallop 90-105.

Tompkins, Jane. "Pedagogy of the Distressed." *College English* 52 (1990): 653-60.

White, Ray Lewis, ed. *Sherwood Anderson's* Winesburg, Ohio. Athens: Ohio UP, 1997.

Marc C. Connor (essay date autumn 2001)

SOURCE: Connor, Marc C. "Fathers and Sons: *Winesburg, Ohio* and the Revision of Modernism." *Studies in American Fiction* 29, no. 2 (autumn 2001): 209-38.

[*In the following essay, Connor examines the central and recurring motif of the father-son relationship in the stories of* Winesburg, Ohio.]

> The American had finally denied too many fathers to survive except as the fatherless man.
>
> —Leslie Fiedler

> One of the strangest relationships in the world is that between father and son.
>
> —Sherwood Anderson

Sherwood Anderson's ***Winesburg Ohio*** opens with the author's famous dedication to the memory of his mother, "whose keen observations on the life about her first awoke in me the hunger to see beneath the surface of lives."[1] It has become a commonplace of ***Winesburg*** criticism to see Anderson's work as the fulfillment of what one critic describes as "the debt Anderson felt toward his mother."[2] As Anderson's biographer Kim Townsend states, in ***Winesburg, Ohio*** Anderson "had done what George Willard had set out to do; he had justified his mother's faith."[3] Yet with the exception of George Willard's mother, who plays a prominent role in two of the twenty-two ***Winesburg*** tales, the figure of the mother is conspicuously absent from the book: the dominant figure throughout the tales—more dominant even than George Willard himself, the apparent central character—is the figure of the father, and the crucial relationship in ***Winesburg, Ohio*** is that of the father and the son. An overarching pattern exists throughout the ***Winesburg*** tales: a father-figure places an overwhelming burden on his son; the son is either unable or unwilling to assume this burden; the son then rejects his father and flees Winesburg. The unfolding of this pattern forms the book's primary narrative, for George Willard's response to this pattern determines either the hopefulness or the despair with which we read the conclusion of ***Winesburg, Ohio.***

This pattern mirrors Sherwood Anderson's own life: for years Anderson felt a bitter resentment toward his father, and as he grew older he struggled to come to terms with this relationship. Townsend states that "if Anderson wanted anyone to blame for his having so little sense of family, there was—clearly—his father" (9). According to all accounts Irwin Anderson was a lazy man who preferred telling anecdotes of his Civil War days to providing for his family, and he became the model for Tom Willard in the ***Winesburg*** stories, a man who "always thought of himself as a successful man, although nothing he had ever done had turned out successfully," and whose wife "he took as a reproach to himself" (44, 39). The young Sherwood Anderson resented his father not only for his failings as a provider, but also because Irwin "left Anderson to face his mother's pain alone" (Townsend, 5). Sherwood Anderson saw the effect his father's shiftlessness and adultery had on his mother, and, as he explained in his semi-fictional autobiography *Tar: A Midwest Childhood,* he internalized the pain and guilt himself: "It was as though she had been struck a blow and when you looked at her you felt at once that your hand had delivered the blow."[4] When Anderson's mother died, his father seemed to feel little or no remorse, and this confirmed Anderson's hatred for the man. At the age of nineteen Anderson left his hometown for Chicago and never laid eyes on his father again.

Consequently the struggle between fathers and sons in ***Winesburg, Ohio,*** when it has received attention, has been read as a portrayal of Anderson's hatred toward his own father. As Marcia Jacobson asserts, in ***Winesburg, Ohio*** Anderson "found a way to dramatize his continuing hostility to his father";[5] similarly, Townsend speculates that the son who desires to kill his father to avenge his mother's life of hardship in *Windy McPherson's Son,* the novel that preceded ***Winesburg,*** is drawn directly from Anderson's own patricidal fantasies. But more than a son's resentment toward his father is at work here: at the heart of this struggle with the father that so dominates the ***Winesburg*** tales is the struggle for expression. The principal burden placed on the son in this book is to express the essence of his father's life, to tell the tale of his father that his father is unable to tell. Hence the father-son struggle that dominates ***Winesburg, Ohio*** is simultaneously Sherwood Anderson's own struggle with his self-imposed vocation as a writer.

In this respect, Anderson seems to be participating in the great myth of the American author as Adamic hero, struggling to create his work and his self in opposition to the fathers, biological and literary, who have come before him. The Adamic myth, first adumbrated by such major critics of American literature in the 1950s as R. W. B. Lewis and Lionel Trilling, and recently reasserted by Eric Sundquist and Harold Bloom, asserts, in Sundquist's words, that for the strong American writer "what is at issue is the authority generated by dependence upon, or independence of, a genealogy; and it is precisely in the very personal terms of such a question that authorship may find its own power." The American writer struggles heroically against his fathers in order to create his work of art; the father challenges the writer to create both himself and his poem—"filial anxiety prompts the writer's participation and challenges his power of independent self-representation"—and thereby makes the creation possible *if* the writer has sufficient power to overcome the father-figure.[6]

This wholly masculine model of creation has been well examined by Nina Baym, who points out that a theory of "American authors . . . obsessed with *fathering* a tradition of their own, with becoming their 'own sires,'" necessarily excludes any writer who seeks a different model of literary creation—most notably, women writers. Such a model, she argues, is both limiting and destructive, and perhaps reflects more of the anxieties of the critics than of the writers themselves.[7] But a closer examination of ***Winesburg, Ohio*** reveals that Anderson seeks neither to defeat the father-figure nor to follow a model of creation defined by agonistic struggle. Rather, the search in ***Winesburg*** is for a *reconciliation* between father and son: only by coming to terms with the figure of the father can Anderson—like his avatar, George Willard—achieve his identity as an artist. Thus the struggle with the father is resolved by the book's end, enabling both father and son to survive, and making possible the work of art without the ritualistic slaying demanded by the Adamic model of creation. Consequently, the debt owed to the mother by the writer of ***Winesburg, Ohio*** is misleading, for the real debt is to the father, who both demands and, in the end, makes possible the son's ascendance to the writer's vocation. Anderson thereby offers a model for artistic creation that differs in crucial ways from that of his strongest contemporaries and descendants in modern American letters, most notably Hemingway and Faulkner; and suggests that a more complex view of artistic creation, one that connects modernity to its own past, is needed to accommodate perhaps the most important early modern writer in American fiction.

The father-son pattern in ***Winesburg, Ohio*** begins with the first full story, **"Hands,"** which establishes the paradigmatic structure of most of the tales: a bizarre figure—almost always an older man—who is excluded from the community has a moment of intense emotion as he attempts to communicate something to young George Willard; this "grotesque" hopes to express his deepest desire or most private secret; but the communication fails, and the story ends with the figure still excluded and his anguish unrelieved. These grotesques all want something from George Willard—they share the desire that George's mother expresses in **"Mother"**: that "my boy be allowed to express something for us both" (40), what Edwin Fussell has called "the representative prayer of all the grotesques."[8] In **"Hands,"** Wing Biddlebaum attempts to give George crucial advice that Wing feels will save George much suffering: "You must begin to dream. From this time on you must shut your ears to the roaring of the voices" (30). But this advice of a father-figure to a son places a terrible burden on the son: to express something not just for himself, but for the father as well, and ultimately for their entire community. As Malcolm Cowley describes this pattern: "All the grotesques hope that George Willard will some day speak what is in their hearts and thus re-establish their connection with mankind."[9] This pattern is repeated three stories later, in **"The Philosopher,"** when Dr. Parcival becomes "intent upon convincing the boy of the advisability of adopting a line of conduct that he was himself unable to define" (50). This desire to advise George transforms into an overwhelming urge to convince George to express Parcival's own life: "You must pay attention to me," the doctor cries to George at the story's end; "If something happens perhaps you will be able to write the book that I may never get written" (56). Again, the son is called upon to express and finally redeem the father's life, and this burden leads directly to the dominant pattern of flight followed by all of the sons of Winesburg.

The story in ***Winesburg*** concerned most directly with the relations of father to son is the longest tale, **"Godliness."** This story also seems most disconnected and distinct from the rest of the collection: it does not feature George Willard, it is told in four parts, and it is not interrelated with any of the other stories or characters in the book. However, in its vivid representation of the struggle between the father and the son, **"Godliness"** forms the defining pattern of the entire collection.[10] The story opens with the suggestion of patricide, as Enoch Bentley strikes his father and nearly kills him. This act pervades the rest of the story, which deals chiefly with Enoch's brother Jesse, who in taking over the family farm and turning it into a thriving success commits his own version of patricide: "When his father, who was old and twisted with toil, made over to him the ownership of the farm and seemed content to creep away to a corner and wait for death, [Jesse] shrugged his shoulders and dismissed the old man from his mind" (69). Having eliminated his father, Jesse turns his thoughts towards sons, and in his Puritanical zeal to mirror the Old Testament Patriarchs becomes obsessed with fathering a line of sons who will confirm him in both his religious and worldly drives. "Send me a son," he cries, "to be called David who shall help me to pluck at last all of these lands out of the hands of the Philistines and turn them to Thy service and to the building of Thy kingdom on earth" (73).

Ironically, Jesse's wife bears him a daughter and dies shortly thereafter. But this daughter bears a son, David, who becomes for Jesse the son for whom he has always yearned, and who renews Jesse's burning desire to justify himself to God. Yet this justification becomes an awful burden for David, whom Jesse's fevered imagination transforms into the Biblical ruler about to initiate the glories of the Davidic kingdom. Jesse's fervent prayers terrify David, who becomes convinced "that he was in the presence not only of his grandfather but of someone else, someone who might hurt him, someone who was not kindly but dangerous and brutal" (85). David denies the paternal link, feeling that this transformed fanatic is not his grandfather, that "something strange and terrible had happened . . . a new and dangerous person had come into the body of the kindly old man" (86). David flees from the woods, and when Jesse catches up with him the boy pleads, "Take me away. There is a terrible man back there in the woods." This moment expresses the terrifying demon that lurks behind the father-figure throughout the ***Winesburg*** stories.

This scene foreshadows the more extreme confrontation that concludes the story as a whole, when Jesse again takes David, who is now fifteen, back into the woods to attempt once more the confirmation of holiness that has been denied the old man. Convinced that the Lord demands a blood sacrifice, Jesse takes along a lamb "as a burnt offering," which soon becomes identical with David himself—when Jesse approaches with a long knife, it is unclear whether the lamb or the boy will constitute his offering. As Clarence Lindsay argues, at this point Jesse "shows every sign of actually sacrificing his grandson, a metaphor for all parental relations in this novel."[11] The fantasy that Jesse has sustained—that he is father to the boy who will be a divine king—is transformed into a different Biblical paradigm, that of Abraham and Isaac: Jesse is preparing to sacrifice his "son" in order to confirm his own state of "godliness." David's reaction is again one of terror—he turns and flees, releasing the lamb as well, and when Jesse nearly overtakes him, David fires a stone from his slingshot that hits Jesse "squarely in the head" and drops him "almost at the boy's feet." Thus **"Godliness"** ends precisely where it begins—with the son striking down the threatening father. (And continuing Anderson's vicious irony, here David finally *does* typify his Biblical namesake, not as the great king but rather as the boy who struck down the menacing giant—Jesse himself.)

David is certain he has killed his grandfather, but sobs that he does not care and determines to leave Winesburg:

> As he ran on and on he decided suddenly that he would never go back again to the Bentley farms or to the town of Winesburg. "I have killed the man of God and now I will myself be a man and go into the world," he said stoutly as he stopped running and walked rapidly down a road that followed the windings of Wine Creek as it ran through fields and forests into the west.
>
> (102)

David enacts the defining gesture of the Winesburg sons: faced with an impossible burden imposed by his father—both to fulfill and redeem the father's own existence—he strikes down his father and flees his hometown. This is the most overt example of a pattern repeated in varying forms throughout the collection, until finally George Willard will both fulfill and triumph over this pattern at the book's end. Indeed, Jesse himself fits this pattern, not only as a father, but as a son as well. As John O'Neill points out, Jesse has "a certain weirdly adolescent desire for paternal acceptance from this same God," that is, he too is a son trying desperately to please a father whose burden is too great. "It's not so much power or wealth that Jesse wants—these he has—but rather the certitude that his Father thinks he has done a good job." Significantly, O'Neill concludes that this is the fundamental pattern that consumed Anderson himself throughout his career: "Potency and the indiscriminate desire to be approved of are the key elements of the portrait of his father which Anderson spent all of his creative life writing."[12]

Throughout ***Winesburg, Ohio*** sons flee their fathers. In **"The Thinker,"** Seth Richmond's dead father—another portrait of Irwin Anderson—was a womanizer and a gambler who squandered his family fortune and left his wife and child with little support after his violent death. Hence Seth responds to the burden of being "as good a man as [his] father" (129) by retreating into isolation, "feeling himself an outcast in his own town" (137). He determines to flee Winesburg because he feels that, unlike George Willard, he does not fit into the life of the town: "George belongs to this town," he thinks. "It's different with me. I don't belong . . . I'm going to get out of here" (137). Similarly, in **"Queer"** Elmer Cowley burns with rage and shame at his foolish and pathetic father who seems so "queer" to his son. Determined not to follow his father's example—"I will not be queer—one to be looked at and listened to," he declares. "I'll be like other people" (194)—Elmer is still unable to express what he feels and suffers; he tries to explain his emotions to his father, but his father's response only enrages him more: "He was waiting for some word of understanding from his father but when Ebenezer spoke his words only served to reawaken the wrath in the son and the young man ran out of the store without replying" (193). In his need to escape his father's legacy of frustrated expression and bizarre behavior, Elmer determines to leave Winesburg: "The idea that he thought might put an end to all of his unhappiness was very simple. 'I will get out of here, run away from home'" (199). Yet when he is waiting for the train and trying one final time to tell George Willard of his sufferings, he can only repeat the meaningless words of his father: "'I'll be washed and ironed. I'll be washed and ironed and starched,' he muttered half incoherently" (200). Despite his burning desire to leave his father and avoid his fate, Elmer is denied any original expression; like a determined figure, he cannot escape, but can only repeat, the words of his father. He ends his story in mute rage, striking blow after blow on George Willard, acting out his inability to express on the "spokesperson" for the town.

"The Strength of God" repeats this desire to evade the paternal burden. The Reverend Hartman, like Jesse Bentley, desires a transfiguring experience of the holy to demonstrate his divine purpose and fire the zeal of his congregation, and also to confirm approval from his divine Father. Yet in his efforts to peep at Kate Swift, Hartman breaks out a corner of the church's stained-glass window that depicts Christ laying his hand upon a child's head; by breaking off a corner of the boy's heel, Hartman in effect wounds the child-figure, a metaphor for the crippling of sons that all the Winesburg fathers inflict. And Hartman is not only the terrifying, zealous father; he is also, like Jesse Bentley, a terrified son, for the father he so fears is God. In his temptation, Hartman mutters the prayer that is the plea of all the Winesburg sons: "Please, Father, do not forget me" (152).

The second version of this story belongs to Kate Swift, who, although a woman, actually follows the father-son pattern of the other stories. The schoolteacher is translated into a masculine figure—Kate's aunt attributes the teacher's independence and eccentric behavior to her similarity to Kate's father—and Kate acts toward George Willard exactly as do all the various father-figures George encounters throughout his maturation. She urges George to "stop fooling with words," to stop being "a mere peddler of words"—like Wing Biddlebaum in **"Hands,"** Doctor Reefy in **"Paper Pills,"** and Doctor Parcival in **"The Philosopher,"** Kate demands that George become the writer she cannot, demands that George "express something for us both." Though Kate embraces George towards the story's end and arouses his sexual feelings, she then stiffens and strikes him with her fists, a masculine response that prefigures the crucial beatings George later suffers in **"Queer"** and **"An Awakening."** Again George, like all the Winesburg sons, is given an overwhelming task by a fatherly figure: to create, to express, to tell the stories of the grotesques of his childhood town.

Anderson's use of a woman character as the father-figure expands the scope of the father-son conflict in ***Winesburg, Ohio*** to include the community as a whole. This fits with the overall trajectory of the book, which focuses increasingly upon George Willard and his relation to the entire town. George becomes in the final third of the book not only the central character to whom stories are told, but also the central actor who carries the narrative burden of the book. This parallels George's process of maturing, from his early entry into masculine sexual experience in **"Nobody Knows"** to his growing vocation as a writer in the later stories. As the book progresses, George—like all the Winesburg sons—tries to distance himself from his father. In **"An Awakening,"** a crucial story poised between George's adolescence and his emergence as a man, George enacts the most powerful attempt in ***Winesburg, Ohio*** to overthrow the father figure.

The story presents George's rivalry with the bartender Ed Handby for the affections of Belle Carpenter, and the action begins as George walks alone through town at night and ponders the "law" that governs human existence:

> "The law begins with little things and spreads out until it covers everything. In every little thing there must be order, in the place where men work, in their clothes, in their thoughts. I myself must be orderly. I must learn that law. I must get myself into touch with something orderly and big that swings through the night like a star. In my little way I must begin to learn something, to give and swing and work with life, with the law."
>
> (183)

Faced with a weak, vacillating, and yet demanding father, George is attempting to understand the law of life, the structure and rule given by the father that George feels is missing in his own life. George is trying to comprehend and master that "law" on his own—that is, he is attempting to *father himself,* to free himself from the greatest debt a son owes his father, the debt of origin.

George's thoughts generate in him both fear and excitement: "his body began to tremble. He had never before thought such thoughts as had just come into his head and he wondered where they had come from. For the moment it seemed to him that some voice outside of himself had been talking as he walked" (183-84). George's sense of self-created power increases, and, crucially, he turns to words to release his energy and virility:

> He felt unutterably big and remade by the simple experience through which he had been passing and in a kind of fervor of emotion put up his hands, thrusting them into the darkness above his head and muttering words. The desire to say words overcame him and he said words without meaning, rolling them over on his tongue and saying them because they were brave words, full of meaning. "Death," he muttered, "night, the sea, fear, loveliness."
>
> (185)

George uses words as Adam does, as if naming the creation and all he sees and feels. Full of his own puissance, he then—like Adam after awaking in the Garden—desires a companion: "If there were only a woman here I would take hold of her hand and we would run until we were both tired out," he thinks. He goes to see Belle, "half drunk with the sense of masculine power," and says to her: "You've got to take me for a man or let me alone. That's how it is" (187). George begins his seduction of her, when Ed Handby appears and easily beats George into unconsciousness and takes Belle. When George wakes "his heart was sick within him. He hated himself and he hated the fate that had brought about his humiliation." At the very moment when George feels most independent and free from all debt to a father-figure, Ed Handby—an older man—beats him and takes the woman away. The father-figure reasserts power over the son precisely when the son is most sure of his own power (and this completes the Edenic parallel: just when Adam takes the fruit to rival his Father, the Father appears and inflicts a humiliating punishment on His son). The story concludes with George "hoping to hear again the voice outside himself that had so short a time before put new courage into his heart." But he can now hear nothing, and as he makes his way homeward his town seems to him "utterly squalid and commonplace" (188-89). George's ambition of self-authorship, of mastering the "brave words" he fleetingly envisioned, is dashed by the father-figure, thereby poisoning George's relation to his town. As long as the father and the son struggle, the son is sundered from the community, and hence the community's story remains untold.

This is George's state of mind going into the triad of stories that concludes ***Winesburg, Ohio***: **"Death," "Sophistication,"** and **"Departure."** Like the other Winesburg fathers, George's father compels his son to flee the town. When pressed by his father to give up his dreams of writing, George tells his mother that he will have to leave town, that "something father said makes it sure that I shall have to go away" (48). As the stories progress, George's efforts to father himself and thereby defeat his father are frustrated, and so the burden of fatherhood still oppresses George. To fulfill his vocation as a writer he must come to terms with that burden; and the final three stories, which tell simultaneously of George's maturation and his departure, focus on that effort. Yet George's concluding departure differs radically from those undertaken by the other Winesburg sons: rather than a forced flight, George embarks on a positive leave-taking, made possible only by his gradual reconciliation with his father.

"Death" is often seen as the pivotal story in ***Winesburg*** because it deals with the death of George's mother. As Cowley observes, "George Willard is released from Winesburg by the death of his mother," and he can now leave the small town and begin his career as a writer.[13] This reading fits with Anderson's own life—as he writes in *A Storyteller's Story,*[14] "for us there could be no home now that mother was not there"—and of course it supports the link between Anderson's storytelling art and his mother. But in the margins of this story another narrative develops that diminishes the father figure: masculine failure is connected to both George's father and grandfather, thereby reducing the father from the demonic, threatening figure of the earlier stories to a man who is all too human. Consequently, the father's role begins to transform from the terrifying opponent whom the son must overcome to a merely human progenitor with whom the son may be reconciled. Through this startling shift, the need for expression changes from an overwhelming burden to a positive gift, making possible George Willard's liberation and artistic vocation at the end of the book.

"Death" concludes the story of George's mother, and tells of her near-affair with Doctor Reefy, the frustrations of her repressed girlhood, her passionate desire to have "a real lover," and her effort "in all the babble of words that fell from the lips of the men with whom she adventured . . . to find what would be for her the true word" (224). Like all the Winesburg grotesques, Elizabeth's desires take the form of frustrated written expression. But **"Death"** also tells of Elizabeth's own father, who disapproves of her marriage to Tom Willard and regrets his own inability to provide for her. On his death-bed, Elizabeth's father reveals to her that he has put away eight hundred dollars for Elizabeth, provided she promises not to marry Tom and to go away from Winesburg: "Hide it away," he tells her. "*It is to make up to you for my failure as a father*" (225, emphasis mine). He leaves the money as recompense for his insufficiency as a father; and he foresees what Elizabeth was to learn on her wedding night: that Tom Willard would not be able to satisfy her romantic desires. Elizabeth states to Doctor Reefy of her marriage: "It did not turn out at all. As soon as I had gone into it I began to be afraid. Perhaps I knew too much before and then perhaps I found out too much during my first night with him" (226). Tom Willard's inadequacies as a lover echo the repeated failures of masculinity, particularly in the sexual realm, that pervade ***Winesburg, Ohio*** (Reverend Hartman's inability to achieve sexual satisfaction with either his wife or Kate Swift, Wing Biddlebaum's terror of touch in **"Hands,"** and especially the impotency and sexual failure of Wash Williams in **"Respectability,"** perhaps the darkest of all the ***Winesburg*** tales). Thus this story directly presents paternal failure in George's grandfather, and reveals masculine failure in George's father, thereby diminishing these figures. The eight hundred dollars—George's legacy, his patrimony—is *not* handed down to George: Elizabeth suffers a paralyzing stroke and dies before she can tell George of the money. Thus the legacy of the father is symbolically severed, and George's liberation from the burden handed down from father to son begins. Though he will have to make his own way in the world without the money, the way will be his own.[15]

Immediately after his mother's death, George meets Doctor Reefy—yet another failed writer in Winesburg, unable to communicate his written words to another. The pattern demands that Reefy will place on George once again the burden of expression, will require George to put into words the meaning and desires of the older man's life. Yet for the first time this is precisely what does *not* happen; rather, Reefy resists the effort to impose that burden on George: "The doctor arose and started to go out. He put out his hand as though to greet the younger man and then awkwardly drew it back again. The air of the room was heavy with the presence of the two self-conscious human beings, and the man hurried away" (230). Paradoxically, this failure of communication signals not continued repression, but liberation, as George is freed from the father's burden. Hence the father-figure, not the son, retreats, leaving the son literally untouched by the paternal demand.

Yet ***Winesburg, Ohio*** does not end at this moment, for although George is being released from the burden of the father, he is still alienated from his community, and thus is not yet able to render his own stories of his boyhood town. The penultimate story, **"Sophistication,"** provides the positive understanding of expression that George still lacks. One of the final stories Anderson penned for the collection,[16] **"Sophistication"** is markedly distinct from the typical ***Winesburg*** pattern: rather than failed expression, it depicts successful communication; rather than the inability of man and woman to come together, it shows George and Helen achieving union; rather than paralysis and stasis, the story is filled with images of motion, activity, and regeneration; and most importantly, rather than the predatory, repressive nature of the Winesburg community, **"Sophistication"** reveals a harmony within and even a reverence for the vanishing Ohio town that Anderson both despised and loved. Thus, within this story George—and Sherwood Anderson as well—begins to take the steps that will bring him peace with his father, and carry him to his vocation as a writer. Consequently this story serves as the true climax to ***Winesburg, Ohio.***

In **"Sophistication"** George responds to the death of his mother by growing from boyhood to manhood and achieving a state of mind that is reflective, that looks beyond the self and sees the nature of the world, and becomes aware of one's place within that world: "The sadness of sophistication has come to the boy. With a little gasp he sees himself as merely a leaf blown by the wind through the streets of his village. He knows that in spite of all the stout talk of his fellows he must live and die in uncertainty, a thing blown by the winds, a thing destined like corn to wilt in the sun" (234). And yet, remarkably, George responds to this insight not by turning inward and isolating himself—the pattern of all the Winesburg grotesques—but by turning outward and seeking communion with another person: "With all his heart he wants to come close to some other human, touch someone with his hands, be touched by the hand of another . . . He wants, most of all, understanding" (235). George's desire for the "touch" of another—such a powerful contrast from the opening story, **"Hands,"** and its terror of human contact—is testament to the extent of his growth and maturation by this point.

George's yearnings are mirrored by Helen White's dissatisfaction with Winesburg, which for Helen becomes a crisis of *meaning*: "It seemed to her that the world was full of meaningless people saying words" (239). When the two come together, they are at first unable to speak; yet this apparent failure of communication is transformed by the more "sophisticated" view of the young couple and by their feelings of love towards their community. Sitting in silence with Helen, George's alienation vanishes and his healing begins: as he and Helen touch hands and he puts a hand on her shoulder, "the presence of Helen renewed and refreshed him," and he begins "to think of the people in the town where he had always lived with something like reverence." Each feels the same thought of fellowship, a concept that appears for the first time in the stories and that responds to the most primary need of the Winesburg grotesques: "I have come to this lonely place and here is this other" (241).[17] George and Helen are renewed and regenerated, "like two splendid young things in a young world," and the story concludes with them walking together back into town, prepared to make their way in the world before them: "For some reason they could not have explained they had both got from their silent evening together the thing needed. Man or boy, woman or girl, they had for a moment taken hold of the thing that makes the mature life of men and women in the modern world possible" (243). Thus George finally understands his home town, because he has shed the tyranny of the father and embraced a human ideal of love and sympathy.

"Sophistication" seems the most controversial of the ***Winesburg*** stories, precisely because it determines the way the collection as a whole is read. Jacobson asserts that in this story "the distance between artistic aspiration and achievement . . . becomes more troublesome," that is, George's vocation seems to her more doubtful by the story's end.[18] Similarly, Colquitt argues that "the fledgling writer has not achieved the negative capability necessary for the artist . . . he does not understand the meaning of what people say." Yet this is a difficult reading to sustain in the face of the clearly successful moment of communication between George and Helen, and the obvious development of George's sympathy and awareness that this story dramatizes. Colquitt asserts that the county fair that is the site of George and Helen's meeting is "not of significant narrative interest."[19] But this misses one of the principal points of this story: George and Helen come together at this village ritual precisely as the representatives of their entire community, and the joining of their hands at the story's end stands for the potential gathering of all the grotesques within their town.

Curiously, critics of ***Winesburg, Ohio*** from the 1950s to the 1980s seem to have viewed **"Sophistication"** as a redemptive moment of successful communication, and thus crucial in the overall tone of the book; only more recently have scholars tended to see this story as dramatizing a failure rather than a triumph of expression.[20] This tendency parallels another new direction in ***Winesburg*** scholarship of focusing intensely on the primary female figures, Helen and George's mother. Thus Colquitt concludes that George at the end is still weighed down by the command to express the life of his mother: "The narrative suggests . . . that George's chief burden as a writer will be to give meaning to his mother's life."[21] The increased attention on the women of Winesburg has shed much light on the stories; but these readings miss the crucial narrative of reconciliation between George and his father, a narrative that in the end enables George to shake off his filial obligation, achieve a communion with another individual, and eventually emerge as a writer.

Only after **"Sophistication"** can the true conclusion of ***Winesburg, Ohio*** take place, for now George is able to express the longings, frustrations, and passions of his hometown grotesques, and hence set off on his journey to become a writer. **"Departure"** opens in the springtime, with George waking early and "thinking of the journey he was about to take and wondering what he would find at the end of his journey," looking out over the land that surrounds Winesburg and feeling that "to look across it is like looking out across the sea" (244). His world seems to him limitless and vast as he prepares for that archetypal American journey westward toward possibility and challenge. This vastness is available to George because he has escaped his father's shadow. Tom Willard carries his son's bag to the train station, and the narrator observes that "the son had become taller than the father." No longer a threatening

King Hamlet bequeathing to his son an impossible task, Tom Willard is now reduced to "an American Polonius" (Townsend, 30), giving his son petty advice about keeping his eyes on his money and not appearing "green" to the city folk. Yet curiously, when George boards the train he is concerned with precisely the words of his father: "His mind was occupied with a desire not to appear green" (246). Even in departure, the voice of the father still lingers; yet here, for the first time in ***Winesburg, Ohio,*** the movement from father to son is not a violent overthrow but rather a gentle passing. Such a moment is remarkable in American fiction: rather than the son's violent flight from the father in order to make his way in the world—the great Adamic pattern as practiced by Huck Finn, Nick Adams, Jay Gatsby, Thomas Sutpen, and so many other American sons—George Willard achieves a peaceful, even loving, departure from his father as he moves into the world beyond Winesburg.

The community itself gathers to bid George farewell: the clerks call out their goodbyes, and more than a dozen people gather at the platform. Even a woman who "had never before paid any attention to George" approaches him and, speaking for the entire Winesburg community, "voiced what everyone felt": "Good luck." As the train pulls out and George reflects on "the adventure of his life," he does not think of anything particularly grand, but muses instead on "little things": the town idiot, Turk Smollet; a beautiful woman who once stayed at his family's hotel; the Winesburg lamp lighter; Helen White mailing off a letter.[22] George's final thoughts are precisely the stuff of the ***Winesburg*** tales, the odd doings of a small Ohio town. Hence when he rouses himself to find that Winesburg is literally behind him, he realizes that he is fulfilling the original wish of Wing Biddlebaum, that he follow his "inclination to be alone and to dream" (30); for as George looks out the train window he realizes that "the town of Winesburg had disappeared and his life there had become but a background on which to paint the dreams of his manhood" (247). The end of the book suggests that George *will* ultimately fulfill the wishes of his grotesques, that he will give form, expression, and meaning to their isolated lives, precisely because he has escaped this fate as a burden and embraced it as a vocation.

The conclusion of ***Winesburg*** is remarkable not for what happens, but for what does *not* happen: there is no climactic confrontation between George and Tom Willard; rather, we see only the gradual easing of the fatherly burden, the steady development of George from boy to man, and the transformation of the terrified flight of the son into a generous, even loving, departure. It is curious that the strongest theme in the book should be resolved in so subtle a manner—George's reconciliation with his father is so understated that most readers have scarcely noticed it. This hidden narrative of reconciliation between father and son makes George's vocation as a writer possible—without it, George would remain paralyzed and unable to express himself, like all the other Winesburg isolates. Yet of even greater importance, this same reconciliation occurs within ***Winesburg, Ohio*** between Sherwood and Irwin Anderson, enabling Anderson himself to shake off the burden of debt and guilt that he felt toward his own father, and consequently to emerge as the crucial early modernist storyteller that he was to become.

There was another side to Sherwood Anderson's father that emerged only later in Anderson's career, but that clearly haunted the young writer's mind when he was composing ***Winesburg, Ohio.*** In a famous passage of *Sherwood Anderson's Memoirs* he describes his father taking him swimming, when the two shared a few hours in which neither seemed to judge or disappoint the other. Anderson describes it as "a feeling I had never known before that night. It was a feeling of closeness . . . as though there were only we two in the world. It was as though I had been jerked suddenly out of myself, out of a world of the school boy, out of a world in which I had been ashamed of my father, out of a place where I had been judging my father."[23] At such rare times Anderson felt a kinship towards his father because Irwin Anderson served as a model to his son for telling stories. Townsend states that the elder Anderson "always . . . could gather a group around him and tell stories about the Civil War," that he frequently read to his son, and "of course he also had his own stories to tell" (10-11). Though to the young Sherwood this often seemed part of his father's foolish boasting, nevertheless it became the source for Anderson's own desire to tell tales, to be what he later called "the storyteller." If his mother bequeathed to Anderson "the hunger to see beneath the surface of lives," his father granted him the desire and skill to transform those observations into the stuff of art. Hence Anderson's attitude towards his father was really two-fold: he rejected his father, based on feelings of shame, resentment, and guilt; and he felt a closeness to his father, and an appreciation for—perhaps even an envy of—the man's ability to transform life into story.

This dual attitude of condemnation and praise pervades ***Winesburg, Ohio,*** beginning with the prefatory vignette that bears Anderson's original title for the collection, **"The Book of the Grotesque."** This opening tale presents an ancient writer who has composed tales dealing with "all the men and women the writer had ever known"—a figure representative of Anderson himself, the true author of the tales of the grotesques. This old man is visited by a carpenter who "had been a soldier in the Civil War" and soon "got on the subject of the war"—a veiled allusion to Anderson's father, for, as O'Neill has suggested, the Civil War was always "intimately associated for Anderson with . . . his father."[24]

Thus ***Winesburg*** opens with a writer being visited by his father. Immediately after this visit, the writer begins to dream, and in his dream "the procession of grotesques passed before the eyes of the old man, and then, although it was a painful thing to do, he crept out of bed and began to write" (23). The resulting book he titles **"The Book of the Grotesque"**—the work Anderson himself had composed. Hence ***Winesburg, Ohio*** opens with a myth of creation in which the father of the writer makes possible the composition of the tales. And this opening concludes with a benediction to the father, as the narrator states that the old carpenter "became the nearest thing to what is understandable and lovable of all the grotesques in the writer's book" (24). This praise of the father parallels the dedicatory gesture towards the mother, but is offered in a much more subterranean fashion; for the achievement of this praise is precisely the burden of the book.[25]

Anderson scholars generally agree that he gradually came to terms with the memory of his father, but they locate this development in the post-***Winesburg*** writings. David Anderson states that the period immediately following the publication of ***Winesburg, Ohio***—the decade of the 1920s that witnessed Anderson's greatest fame and the publication of a remarkable eleven books—"marked his coming to terms with his identity as a writer-craftsman and with the image of his father that had haunted him since his youth." Similarly, Jacobson notes that Anderson's "autobiographical" writing of this period (*A Story Teller's Story* [1924], *Sherwood Anderson's Notebook* [1926], and *Tar: A Midwest Childhood* [1926]) all "concerns itself in some way with the relationship between father and son." These works suggest that the legacy of storytelling was handed down to Anderson not by his mother, but by his father; thus Jacobson concludes that "in these books [Anderson] recognizes the extent to which he is his father's son."[26]

Significantly, Anderson opens *A Story Teller's Story* by speaking of his father, whom he describes as "a house-and-barn painter"; "However," he goes on, "he did not call himself a house-painter. The idea was not flashy enough for him. He called himself a 'sign-writer.'" He then describes the exciting escapades of illicitly painting signs on a farmer's fence, and how his father would magnify the thrill by telling "a story of the Civil War." "Father," he concludes, "was made for romance." One of Anderson's main narratives in *A Story Teller's Story* is his father's failure as a writer, and Anderson's own calling to fill this role successfully: "I was in my whole nature a tale teller. My father had been one and his not knowing had destroyed him." Anderson makes the claim in 1924—five years after the publication of ***Winesburg, Ohio***—that his vocation as a writer is exactly a fulfillment of his paternal destiny:

> I am the tale teller, the man who sits by the fire waiting for listeners, the man whose life must be led into the world of his fancies, I am the one destined to follow the little, crooked words of men's speech through the uncharted paths of the forests of fancy. *What my father should have been, I am to become.*[27]

Nearly all critics argue that Anderson's reconciliation with his father occurs after the publication of ***Winesburg, Ohio,*** and that ***Winesburg*** continues the narrative of father-son strife that Anderson begins in *Windy McPherson's Son.* Jacobson argues:

> ***Winesburg*** . . . came before Anderson was ready to acknowledge how much he was his father's son: George, like Windy McPherson, albeit less violently, defines himself in opposition to his father. It is probable that Anderson needed success as a writer—needed, that is, to outdo his father as a storyteller—before he could define himself as his father's son. Because that success had not yet come to Anderson, ***Winesburg*** emerged as a book shaped by his ongoing struggle with his father.[28]

While Jacobson is absolutely right to link Anderson's development as a storyteller with his "ongoing struggle with his father," she misses the *resolution* of this struggle, and the subsequent emergence of Anderson *as* a "successful" writer, within the structure of ***Winesburg*** itself.

Winesburg, Ohio marks the oft-noted emergence of Sherwood Anderson as a major American writer. *Windy McPherson's Son,* a less mature work, was published three years earlier, and Anderson's maturation as a writer is simultaneous with his rejection of the earlier book's overt motif of patricide. The father-son struggle is reconfigured in ***Winesburg*** into a constant engagement with the grotesques—father-figures all—of George Willard's hometown. Hence the one story that does overtly treat of patricide is **"Godliness,"** a story that, as remarked earlier, is distinct from the rest of the book, most obviously in its distance from George Willard, who plays no role in the tale. The motif of patricide is distanced from George precisely because it has no central role in the structure of ***Winesburg, Ohio,*** which deals not with the son's killing of the father, but rather with the reconciliation achieved between father and son, from which the son receives the gift of storytelling. Anderson suggests that this was his own experience after that rare feeling of closeness he once had with his father, which concludes with Anderson stating that his father "had become blood of my blood . . . For the first time I had come to know that I was the son of my father. He was a story teller as I was to be. It may be that on the night of my childhood I even laughed a little . . . knowing that, no matter how much as a story teller I might be using him, I would never again be wanting another father."[29]

In the opening ***Winesburg*** tale, the old Civil War soldier becomes "the nearest thing to what is understandable and lovable of all the grotesques in the writer's book." Hence each new grotesque presented in the tales—man or woman, child or adult—is another version of this father-figure, another version of Irwin Anderson. The struggle of each grotesque to get George Willard to tell his story, to "express something for us both," is really the repeated cry of Anderson's own father to see his son become "the tale teller" that Anderson's father wanted to be, but could not be. Hence when George Willard takes a peaceful departure from Winesburg, he embodies the successful passing-on of this fatherly legacy to the son; the pattern of overwhelming burden and flight is translated in the end to an acceptance and fulfillment of the father's charge. This is the import of the claim made by Fussell, that while it is certainly true that each grotesque shows a "pathetically eager need to draw sustenance from George Willard," it is equally true that "many of them come to him convinced that it is *they* who have something to give."[30] The reconciliation between Anderson and his father that critics see in Anderson's later work actually occurs in his greatest work, and is precisely what makes ***Winesburg, Ohio*** such a triumph.

This reconciliation in ***Winesburg*** explains the trajectory of Anderson's overall career, which, ever since the great evaluative essays of Trilling, Howe, and Cowley in the 1940s and 1950s, has been viewed as a sharp decline from the triumph of ***Winesburg*** to the mediocre novels of the 1920s to the minor works of the 1930s.[31] Such a view depends first of all on seeing Anderson's most important work as his novels, when in fact, as Maxwell Geismar and others have pointed out, Anderson "was a natural-born short-story writer, completely as original in this genre as he was unsuited for the novel form."[32] But more importantly, the reconciliation with his father that Anderson achieves in ***Winesburg*** allows him to portray his father in subsequent writings in a loving and comic light, and to focus his emotional energy on his relation with his mother, a relation that carried its own attendant guilt and demanded an expiation in writing comparable to that achieved with his father in ***Winesburg.*** Ultimately these twin reconciliations in his fiction enabled Anderson to develop his mature aesthetic, which proffers a powerful revision of American modernism and seeks to return it to an older American tradition, rooted in the community and the land.

"The Egg," one of Anderson's most famous stories, was composed in 1918 while ***Winesburg*** was awaiting publication. The story is definitively post-***Winesburg*** in its comic depiction of the father, who, as Judy Small has pointed out, is portrayed with a "creative sympathy" that shows his marked contrast with the fathers depicted in *Windy McPherson's Son* and especially ***Winesburg.***[33] With the grand agon with the father resolved at the end of ***Winesburg, Ohio,*** Anderson is now able to portray a ridiculous, rather pathetic, but quite sympathetic man. The central riddle in the story is the egg itself—the question of generation: "The hens lay eggs out of which come other chickens and the dreadful cycle is thus made complete." The hen-egg cycle is also the father-son cycle: what the father is, the son will become, willingly or not. The father in **"The Egg,"** like the father-figure in **"The Book of the Grotesque,"** speaks Anderson's own aesthetic ideal: a love for the grotesques of this world. "The Grotesques were," the father declares to his son, "valuable. People, he said, liked to look at strange and wonderful things." By the story's end, the son has learned the very lesson Anderson himself learned in the writing of ***Winesburg***: "I wondered why eggs had to be and why from the egg came the hen who again laid the egg. The question got into my blood. It has stayed there, I imagine, because I am the son of my father."[34] The story suggests a writer who is at peace with his father, has outgrown the child's rebellion against his parents, and, as Michael West remarks, is working "to love his parents maturely."[35] Such a tale—unthinkable within ***Winesburg, Ohio***—is made possible by the reconciliation Anderson depicted and achieved in ***Winesburg***; furthermore, its portrayal of a loving and supportive mother shows a movement toward the mother-figure that will occupy Anderson for the rest of his career.

After reconciling with his father, Anderson now had to deal with his failures toward his mother. In the 1920s and 1930s Anderson wrote a number of stories that focus on mother-figures, the greatest of which is **"Death in the Woods."**[36] Anderson first began work on the story as early as 1916 (when he was in the midst of the ***Winesburg*** tales) and did not publish the final, revised version until 1933, indicating the complexity and depth of emotion he associated with the mother-figure.[37] **"Death in the Woods,"** with its portrait of a nameless, overworked mother for whom "every moment of every day . . . was spent feeding something," is suffused with the love and guilt Anderson felt toward his mother, and it simultaneously pays homage to her and condemns both the father and the son who never cared for the mother as they should have. The old woman is merely an orphan, "one of the nameless ones," but she takes on mythic dimensions in the story, evolving into a type of the nurturing earth-mother who survives despite the brutality and neglect of her husband, and also of her son; for, the narrator informs us, "when the son grew up he was just like his father." Here Anderson is pursuing the logic of his identification with his father: if he is indeed the son of his father, then he must share the burden of guilt for the mistreatment and abandonment of his mother. And Anderson had done the same thing to his own wife and children, walking out of their lives the same day he walked out of his factory office and commenced his mythic journey as the archetype of the modern artist.

The death in **"Death in the Woods"** is also a rebirth, both of the land and of the poet's ability to portray that land as the sustaining force of his life and art. When the dogs run about the dying body of the old woman, it is "a kind of death ceremony" in which the natural world honors and claims as its own this woman whom the human world has rejected. Through her death she is rejuvenated into a "charming young girl"; and when the boy-narrator sees her lifeless body, it appears to him "white and lovely, so like marble." The old woman's body is transformed into a classical monument to her effort to feed and nurture during her life. For the boy, this scene becomes "the foundation for the real story I am now trying to tell," the story of the author's gratitude to his own mother; for her body, by returning to the land to fertilize and sustain it, despite its abuse and neglect at the hands of its fathers and sons, becomes the source of the writer's aesthetic.[38] Thus, even in the condemnation of the son we see an expiation, as the mother grants the final aesthetic vision Anderson held at the end of his life, in which the land, the community, death, and life are all combined in a regenerative cycle. This vision would constitute the final reconciliation between the son and both his parents in one of his final stories, **"Corn Planting."**

"Corn Planting" is perhaps unique among Anderson's work in its depiction of a strong and loving marriage, a man and woman "who make a go of marriage" and as a result "grow more and more alike." The contrast between the Hutchensons in **"Corn Planting"** and the Willards in ***Winesburg*** indicates how far Anderson traveled in his imaginative relation to his parents in the twenty years between the stories. The Hutchensons' son, Will, is a portrait of Anderson as he wished he had been: a responsible, loving son, succeeding at the Art Institute in Chicago, and dutifully sending money and letters home to his parents who treasure the letters almost as if they were the beloved boy himself. When the son is killed, the parents respond in what seems an odd way to the narrator: together, late at night, they go into their fields to plant corn. But the narrator realizes that they are reconciling themselves to the larger cycles of birth, death, and regeneration into which their son's life fits, the same cycle that defines the land that they have tended all their lives:

> It was the first time in my life I ever understood something, and I am far from sure now that I can put down what I understood and felt that night—I mean something about the connection between certain people and the earth—a kind of silent cry, down into the earth, of these two old people, putting corn down into the earth. It was as though they were putting death down into the ground that life might grow again—something like that.[39]

This ending expresses the mature aesthetic vision Anderson achieved in the last stage of his career, and that he had been working toward since at least the first ***Winesburg*** tales: an emphasis on the American land—the soil itself—and the rich characters that come from it and return to it. As Benjamin Spencer has compellingly argued, Anderson, like Whitman and Twain, felt "impelled . . . toward the mythic, toward the archetypal and the elemental, rather than toward the urban and sociological."[40] This aesthetic opposes the dominant strains of modernism in the 1920s and 1930s, which were increasingly cosmopolitan and international. Anderson, in contrast, looked back to the great nineteenth-century writers he so admired—Thoreau, Emerson, and particularly Whitman and Twain, similar writers of the soil and probably his two strongest precursors—as opposed to the modern writers who ironically followed in Anderson's own wake. Thus David Anderson suggests that Anderson's most significant achievement was not his influence on the writers who followed him, but rather his difference from them, his effort "to re-establish in the mainstream of American literature the vernacular tradition and the subject matter that had come out of the Old West with Mark Twain and Huckleberry Finn two generations earlier, only to fall by the northeastern American wayside."[41] Consequently, a more accurate model for understanding Anderson's career is not that of a writer who produced one fine book and then declined, but rather a writer who rejected the direction taken by so many of the modernist writers, and instead looked back to a different aesthetic tradition that was distinctively American and oriented toward the land, the small town, and the ordinary folk who lived there. The treatment of the father-son struggle in ***Winesburg, Ohio*** shows the decisive step in this direction. For only after reconciling with the father-figure and moving toward a vision of harmony and understanding, rather than alienation and isolation, could Anderson achieve his mature vision.

Anderson has long been considered a crucial precursor to the major American modernists, particularly Hemingway and Faulkner; but in his vision of reconciliation between father and son, he shows a significant contrast with their work. The father-son trope dominates the work of both Hemingway and Faulkner; the long struggle with the father in the Nick Adams stories, and the epic father-son conflicts in *The Sound and the Fury* and *Absalom, Absalom!* offer only the most striking examples. But whereas Anderson shows in ***Winesburg, Ohio*** a reconciliation with the father, Hemingway and Faulkner tended for years to follow the grand pattern of strife and alienation between father and son, and they begin to express a reconciliation between father and son only in their later works. Hemingway's "Fathers and Sons," the final story (chronologically) in the Nick Adams sequence, and the relation between Santiago and the boy in *The Old Man and the Sea* point toward such a reconciliation; similarly, Faulkner's *Go Down, Moses* tends away from alienation and toward reconciliation, particularly in the central relationship of the book, the father-son relation between Isaac McCaslin and Sam Fathers. Intriguingly, these are the works in which both authors look most closely to the land itself as their governing aesthetic.

Late in their careers, both Hemingway and Faulkner expressed a renewed appreciation for Anderson's influence upon their writing. Hemingway's parody of Anderson in his 1926 novel *The Torrents of Spring* caused a rift between the two that would never heal.[42] But in *A Moveable Feast,* his retrospective on the Paris years, Hemingway professed again his admiration for Anderson's ability to craft a story. "I liked some of his stories very much," Hemingway wrote. "They were simply written and sometimes beautifully written and he knew the people he was writing about and cared deeply for them."[43] As Hemingway approached his own reconciliation with the fathers of his past (even finally emulating his father's act of suicide), his appreciation of Anderson returned, if indeed it ever left. Similarly, as Faulkner moved from the father-son agon to a more conciliatory vision, his attitude toward Anderson became increasingly appreciative. His 1953 lecture, "Sherwood Anderson: An Appreciation," praised Anderson's style and influence on the modernists, in particular Anderson's sustaining of the older traditions of Melville and Twain.[44] Hemingway and Faulkner may well have rejected their teacher too soon, since he pointed the way to the vision they would, years later, themselves achieve.[45]

Modernity itself commences in the ritual slaying of the father. Pound's defining dictum, "make it new," offers the archetypal modernist impulse: the severing of all ties with the past, what Paul de Man calls the "parricidal . . . desire to wipe out whatever came earlier, in the hope of reaching at last a point that could be called a true present, a point of origin that marks a new departure." Hence in the definitive modernist novel, Joyce's *Portrait of the Artist as a Young Man,* Stephen Dedalus struggles to reject his own, inadequate human father, and replace him with a mythic father. But modernity found itself unable to dispose of the historical past: as de Man argues—in a passage that expresses precisely Anderson's argument in **"The Egg"**—modernity "discovers itself to be a generative power that not only engenders history, but is part of a generative scheme that extends far back into the past."[46] Like the son who must admit the reality of his father, modernity must admit its inevitable entanglement in the past that begot it. This is a wisdom that Sherwood Anderson understood, though his more famous contemporaries took much longer to realize.

Consequently, in regard to the Adamic theory of literary creation that is so central to American fiction, Anderson also offers a powerful revision. Refusing both the "seizure of authority" enacted through "the crime of patricide" and the subsequent "sense of guilt" that "pay[s] homage to the fallen ancestor,"[47] Anderson instead suggests that by achieving atonement with the father, one can chart a path to a healing, nurturing aesthetic that involves one's self, one's community, and one's land.[48] Anderson seeks to resolve the grand agon—what Bloom famously describes as "battle between strong equals, father and son as mighty opposites, Laius and Oedipus at the crossroads"[49]—and in its place he offers reconciliation, regeneration, the gentle, commending touch of a father who loves his son, crafted by a son who honors his father. Anderson returns again to Whitman, the greatest American poet of reconciliation, whose lovely blessing of father to son in "Song of Myself" could stand as Anderson's own view of the proper relation between fathers and sons:

> Sit a while dear son,
> Here are biscuits to eat and here is milk to drink,
> But as soon as you sleep and renew yourself in sweet clothes,
> I kiss you with a good-by kiss and open the gate for your egress hence.
>
> Long enough have you dream'd contemptible dreams,
> Now I wash the gum from your eyes,
> You must habit yourself to the dazzle of the light and of every moment of your life.
>
> Long have you timidly waded holding a plank by the shore,
> Now I will you to be a bold swimmer,
> To jump off in the midst of the sea, rise again, nod to me, shout,
> and laughingly dash with your hair.[50]

Notes

I am grateful to William Gleason, who offered very helpful direction to this essay while in its early stages. My epigraphs come from Leslie Fiedler's *Love and Death in the American Novel,* revised ed. (New York: Doubleday, 1992), 78; and Sherwood Anderson's essay "Discovery of a Father," *Reader's Digest* 35 (Nov. 1939), 21-25.

1. Sherwood Anderson, *Winesburg, Ohio,* ed. Malcolm Cowley, revised ed. (New York: Viking, 1960), v. Hereafter cited parenthetically.

2. Clare Colquitt, "Motherlove in Two Narratives of Community: *Winesburg, Ohio* and *The Country of the Pointed Firs,*" in *New Essays on* Winesburg, Ohio, ed. John W. Crowley (Cambridge: Cambridge Univ. Press, 1990), 73-97.

3. Kim Townsend, *Sherwood Anderson* (Boston: Houghton Mifflin, 1987), 114. Hereafter cited parenthetically.

4. Sherwood Anderson, *Tar: A Midwest Childhood* (New York: Boni and Liveright, 1926,) 100. This passage is also quoted in Townsend, 10.

5. Marcia Jacobson, "*Winesburg, Ohio* and the Autobiographical Moment," in *New Essays on* Winesburg, Ohio, 56; Townsend, 29.

6. Eric Sundquist, *Home As Found: Authority and Genealogy in Nineteenth-Century American Literature* (Baltimore: Johns Hopkins Univ. Press, 1979), xii, xviii. See also R. W. B. Lewis, *The American Adam: Innocence, Tragedy, and Tradition in the Nineteenth Century* (Chicago: Univ. of Chicago Press, 1955).

7. Nina Baym, "Melodramas of Beset Manhood" in her *Feminism and American Literary History* (New Brunswick: Rutgers Univ Press, 1992), 3-18.

8. Edwin Fussell, "*Winesburg, Ohio:* Art and Isolation," *Modern Fiction Studies* 6, no. 1 (1960), 106-14.

9. Malcolm Cowley, Introduction, *Winesburg, Ohio,* 15.

10. Even on the level of narrative, the story differs from the rest of the collection. As John O'Neill observes, "Godliness" employs the method of the exemplary tale or miniature epic (akin to the Biblical tales that "Godliness" parallels in other ways), whereas most of the other stories are structured around epiphany and revelation, more bare of conventional narrative. Yet "Godliness" is of a piece with the other stories in that "the essential relations among the characters here are paradigmatic and hence illustrative and integrative versions of the relations among characters in the other stories." See John O'Neill, "Anderson Writ Large: 'Godliness' in *Winesburg, Ohio,*" *Twentieth Century Literature* 23, no. 1 (1977), 67-83.

11. Clarence Lindsay, "The Community in *Winesburg, Ohio:* The Rhetoric of Selfhood," *Midamerica* 15 (1988), 39-47. However, the act of sacrificing one's children is reserved for the *fathers* of Winesburg. The paradigmatic act of the mothers is to sacrifice *themselves* (as does Tom Foster's mother in "Drink," David Hardy's mother in "Godliness," and of course George Willard's mother).

12. O'Neill, 68, 78-79.

13. Cowley, 14.

14. Sherwood Anderson, *A Story Teller's Story* (New York: B. W. Huebsch, 1924), 127.

15. It is particularly appropriate that this severing of the fatherly tie should come from George's mother, because Elizabeth, like Kate Swift, is linked throughout the stories with masculine imagery, as when in "Mother" we are told that she once "startled the town by putting on men's clothes and riding a bicycle down Main Street" (45). Thus Elizabeth's "prayer" to her son that he "express something for us both" parallels the burden placed by fathers throughout the book.

16. William Phillips reports that the final three stories were all apparently written after most of the collection was completed, probably with the intention of bringing together many of the major themes and characters throughout *Winesburg* and thereby making the book "something more than a mere collection of short stories." Hence these final stories suggest the culmination of the motifs that run throughout the book. See William Phillips, "How Sherwood Anderson Wrote *Winesburg, Ohio,*" *American Literature* 23 (1951), 7-30. Fussell makes this same point when he claims that the true climactic story is "Sophistication," whereas the final story, "Departure," is remarkable precisely in its being "pointedly *anti*-climactic" (Fussell, 112).

17. I see this brief sentence as a response to the loneliness that dominates the book, as expressed most poignantly in the conclusion of Alice Hindman's story, "Adventure." Abandoned to a solitary life in Winesburg, Alice "began to practice the devices common to lonely people," and the story ends with her realization that she must "force herself to face bravely the fact that many people must live and die alone, even in Winesburg" (115, 120). Just as Alice embodies the loneliness of the entire community, so too George and Helen's communion assuages that communal loneliness, even if only temporarily. This sort of intertextual dialogue within *Winesburg* has not received sufficient scholarly attention.

18. Jacobson, 66.

19. Colquitt, 81, 84.

20. For example Fussell, writing in 1960, claims that in "Sophistication" the near-universal loneliness of the Winesburg grotesques is for a moment assuaged, and George realizes his artistic role (114); and Walter Rideout, in 1962, states that "Sophistication" "records in all ways a triumph," in which "George and Helen share a brief hour of absolute awareness" after which for George "the way of the artist lies clear before him"; "The Simplicity of *Winesburg, Ohio,*" *Shenandoah* 13 (1962), 20-31. The "negative" reading of "Sophistication," and hence of the collection as a whole, begins perhaps with Samuel Pickering's 1977 essay, "*Winesburg, Ohio*: A Portrait of the Artist as a Young Man," *Southern Quarterly* 16 (1977), 27-38, which claims that the book depicts the *failure* of George's artistic aspirations, and argues that "the happy ending of the artist painting the dreams of his manhood is deceptive." For an overview of

these shifts and changes in Anderson criticism, see David Anderson, "Sherwood Anderson and the Critics," *Critical Essays on Sherwood Anderson,* ed. David Anderson (Boston: G. K. Hall, 1981), 1-17.

21. Colquitt, 86. For other views of the revaluation of the women in Anderson's book, see Marilyn Judith Atlas, "Sherwood Anderson and the Women of Winesburg," and Nancy Bunge, "Women in Sherwood Anderson's Fiction," *Critical Essays on Sherwood Anderson,* ed. David Anderson, 250-66 and 242-49, and Sally Adair Rigsbee, "The Feminine in *Winesburg, Ohio,*" *Studies in American Fiction* 9 (1981), 233-44.

22. Critics have noted that Helen and George fail to bid goodbye to one another in the final pages, and suggest that this indicates a failure in their relationship. Yet the fact that Helen is mailing a letter in her final appearance seems to me another revision of the American trope of failed expression: unlike Melville's Bartleby or Pynchon's Oedipa Maas, George and Helen do send the letter, they do achieve, however momentarily, "the thing that makes the mature life of men and women in the modern world possible."

23. *Sherwood Anderson's Memoirs: A Critical Edition,* ed. Ray Lewis White (Chapel Hill: Univ. of North Carolina Press, 1967) 84. Anderson describes this moment in slightly different form in "Discovery of a Father."

24. O'Neill, 71.

25. "The Book of the Grotesque" was the very first part of *Winesburg* to be composed (see Phillips, 280, and Townsend, 110), and thus the genesis of the entire book is contained in this story of debt toward and praise of Anderson's father.

26. David Anderson, "Sherwood Anderson and the Critics," 2; Jacobson, 69-70.

27. Anderson, *A Story Teller's Story,* 3, 308, 19.

28. Jacobson, 70.

29. *Sherwood Anderson's Memoirs,* 84-88. Anderson's sense of debt to his father's storytelling prowess is further suggested in *A Storyteller's Story* when, having interrupted a tale, Anderson states that "I am too good a son to my father to leave such a tale hanging forever thus, in the air" (45).

30. Fussell, 387.

31. Lionel Trilling first put forth his thesis that Anderson never developed beyond a certain emotional adolescence in his essay "Sherwood Anderson" in *Kenyon Review* 3 (Summer 1941), 293-302; Howe's view of Anderson as a minor writer with a few lasting works first appeared in his 1948 essay in *Partisan Review* 15 (April 1948), 492-99, and was treated in greater detail in his book-length study *Sherwood Anderson* (New York: William Sloane & Associates, 1951); Cowley, while viewing Anderson's work more charitably, still relegated it to a lesser position than the other major modernists in his writings on Anderson from the late 1930s through the 1960s. For Cowley's numerous reviews and essays on Anderson, see Ray Lewis White's *Sherwood Anderson: A Reference Guide* (Boston: G. K. Hall, 1977).

32. Maxwell Geismar, Introduction, *Sherwood Anderson: Short Stories,* ed. Maxwell Geismar (New York: Hill and Wang, 1962), xi.

33. Judy Jo Small, *A Reader's Guide to the Short Stories of Sherwood Anderson* (NY: G.K. Hall & Co., 1994), 237-38.

34. Sherwood Anderson, "The Egg," in *Sherwood Anderson: Short Stories,* 20-29.

35. Michael West, "Sherwood Anderson's Triumph: 'The Egg,'" *American Quarterly* 20 (1968), 675-93.

36. Other mother-stories include "Motherhood," "Out of Nowhere into Nothing," and "Like a Queen," as well as the essays in *Perhaps Women* and his last novel, *Kit Brandon.*

37. The first published version of the story appeared in the *American Mercury* in 1926; Anderson revised it once for *Tar: A Midwest Childhood* (1926), and again for *Death in the Woods and Other Stories* (1933). For the composition and publication history of "Death in the Woods," see Small, 347-52.

38. Sherwood Anderson, "Death in the Woods," in *Sherwood Anderson: Short Stories,* 121-32. For a reading of the mother as a Demeter-Persephone figure, which is certainly complementary to the reading I am suggesting here, see Mary Rohrberger, "The Man, the Boy, and the Myth: Sherwood Anderson's 'Death in the Woods,'" *Midcontinent American Studies Journal* 3 (Fall 1962), 48-54.

39. Sherwood Anderson, "The Corn Planting," in *Sherwood Anderson: Short Stories,* 199-203. The story was first published in book form in Paul Rosenfeld's *The Sherwood Anderson Reader* in 1947.

40. Benjamin Spencer, "Sherwood Anderson: American Mythopoeist," *American Literature* 41, no. 1 (1969), 1-18.

41. David Anderson, "Sherwood Anderson's Grotesques and Modern American Fiction," *Midwestern Miscellany* 13 (1984), 53-65.

42. On Hemingway's parody and Anderson's response, see Townsend, 227-32. Geismar states that this parody signaled the rift between not just two writers, but two generations of American literature: "The post-World War I American writers belonged to the 'modern world' of either international or expatriated artists, as you like; but their lack of *place* or of communal ties, or of native belief and roots, was to show up clearly in their later careers, or lack of careers" (xii-xiii).
43. Ernest Hemingway, *A Moveable Feast* (New York: Macmillan, 1964), 27-28.
44. William Faulkner, "A Note on Sherwood Anderson," *Essays, Speeches, and Public Letters,* ed. James B. Meriweather (New York: Random House, 1965), 3-10.
45. Even Fitzgerald, who in 1925 proclaimed Anderson as "one of the very best and finest writers in the English language today," then later that year described *Dark Laughter* as "lousy" (Townsend, 227), moves in his work from the father-son conflict to the desire to overcome that conflict. *The Great Gatsby* offers another archetypal modernist rejection of the father, in Jay Gatsby's insistence that he is self-fathered, that he "sprang from his own Platonic conception of himself." *The Great Gatsby* (New York: Scribner's, 1953), 99. But *Tender is the Night,* published after a decade of Fitzgerald's desperate personal and professional sufferings, depicts Dick Diver's realization that his father, "this earliest and strongest of protections" who had been "his moral guide," had called Dick to be a better person; his father's death prompts Dick's wish that "he had always been as good as he had intended to be." Dick's poignant statement at his father's funeral indicates his—and Fitzgerald's, and even the twentieth century's—longing for a reconciliation with the father who had been too easily taken for granted: "Good-by, my father—good-by, all my fathers." *Tender is the Night* (New York: Simon & Schuster, 1995), 203-205. Note also Fitzgerald's similar response to his own father's death in an unfinished essay, "The Death of My Father," in Matthew Bruccoli, *Some Sort of Epic Grandeur* (New York: Carroll and Graf, 1993), 366.
46. Paul de Man, "Literary History and Literary Modernity," in *Blindness and Insight: Essays in the Rhetoric of Contemporary Criticism,* 2nd edition, revised (Minneapolis: Univ. of Minnesota Press, 1983), 142-65.
47. Sundquist, xii.
48. Crucially, this aesthetic is not a wholly masculine domain. Certainly Willa Cather's best novels, particularly *O Pioneers!* (1913) and *My Antonia* (1918), reflect a similar interest in the land, the community, and the preservation of parent and child; and Edith Wharton's *The Age of Innocence* (1920) reveals a similar, and supposedly anti-Modernist, interest in reconciliation between the past of one's forebears and the present of one's self. One might conclude that Anderson's model of creation is curiously androgynous; the old writer in "The Book of the Grotesque" is, after all, described as "like a pregnant woman," and this was one of Anderson's favorite metaphors for describing the composition of the *Winesburg* stories: "He said he felt 'like a woman, having my babies, one after another, but without pain,' and (not limiting himself to one sex) like a Rabelaisian man too, the stories having 'fairly gushed from his pen'" (Townsend, 109). For an intriguing argument that "the androgyny myth is . . . the organizing principle of Anderson's complex book," see Martin Bidney, "Anderson and the Androgyne: 'Something More than Man or Woman,'" *Studies in Short Fiction* 25, no. 3 (1988), 261-73.
49. Harold Bloom, *The Anxiety of Influence: A Theory of Poetry* (Oxford: Oxford Univ. Press, 1973), 11.
50. Walt Whitman, "Song of Myself," section 46, lines 1225-33, in *Leaves of Grass,* ed. Sculley Bradley and Harold W. Blodgett (New York: Norton, 1973), 84.

Mark Whalan (essay date autumn 2002)

SOURCE: Whalan, Mark. "Dreams of Manhood: Narrative, Gender, and History in *Winesburg, Ohio.*" *Studies in American Fiction* 30, no. 2 (autumn 2002): 229-48.

[*In the following essay, Whalan argues that Anderson's depiction of gender relations in* Winesburg, Ohio *was influenced by his "often overlooked sense of unease about the effect of the First World War on white American masculinity."*]

Gender—or what he called the "man-woman thing"—was a career-long obsession for Sherwood Anderson. In assessments of his most famous text, ***Winesburg, Ohio*** (1919), the failure of heterosexual relationships has often been cited as the reason for the "grotesque" nature of several of Winesburg's inhabitants, and his three novels of the 1920s—*Poor White* (1920) *Many Marriages* (1923) and *Dark Laughter* (1925)—can read as quest narratives, with their male protagonists searching for an elusive heterosexual happiness. Yet what early critics perceived as Anderson's radical sexual politics (one anonymous early reviewer claimed his fiction was "of a character which no man would wish to see in the hands of a daughter or sister") has in the past thirty years more often been seen as a restrictive conventionality.[1] Anderson's frequent insistence on the absolute differentiation between men and women relied on binaries such as activity/passivity, or culture/nature, which feminist criticism has long identified with patriarchal culture, and recent critics have not been slow to remark on this aspect of his work.[2] Yet criticism engaging with the gender politics of ***Winesburg, Ohio*** has tended to ignore the fact that it was written during the First World War—a war that provoked a period of what Kaja Silverman has called "historical trauma" that problematized the "dominant fictions" of personal (and specifically gender) identity.[3] It is this "trauma," I shall argue, that was implicated in many of the formal innovations of ***Winesburg, Ohio,*** a text that marks a distinctly different approach to the relationship between narrative and gender than is evident in the rest of Anderson's writing. Often celebrated as a timeless text exhibiting universal truths about isolation, small-town life, and male adolescence, ***Winesburg, Ohio*** connects with Anderson's often-overlooked sense of unease about the effect of the First World War on white American masculinity.

For much of his writing life Sherwood Anderson was fascinated by history. In his letters, autobiographical writings, and fiction, he often produced accounts of the coming of industrialism, the Civil War, and the expansion of the frontier. He considered writing a biography of Grant, in collaboration with Gertrude Stein; he also discussed writing a history of the Mississippi. This interest was most clear in shaping his thoughts on national identity and Americanness, but was also central to his ideas of gender identity. As he wrote in his *Memoirs,* in one of his most reductive and starkly binaristic statements about gender difference: "In reality women have no desire to DO. Doing is for them a substitute. Their desire is to BE. There was never a real woman lived who did not hunger to be beautiful. The male desires not to be beautiful but to create beauty."[4] According to such a misogynist logic, which predicates masculinity on agency and action and femininity on passivity and absence, "history" as a narrative of change and development inevitably comes to be gendered as masculine. In ***Winesburg, Ohio,*** indeed, the central character George Willard's progress into manhood is dependent on his developing an historical sense, as "there is a time in the life of every boy when he for the first time takes a backward view of life. Perhaps that is the moment when he crosses the line into manhood."[5] The "backward view" of placing the self in an historical perspective and therefore becoming both an inheritor and a progenitor marks the beginning of George's "manhood." Although the category of "manhood" and his identification with this category is always problematic for George, this moment nonetheless marks the empowerment of being inducted into a temporal order and invested with the potential for historical agency.

The simultaneous conferral of manhood and historical agency is evident in several of Anderson's works, yet it was constituted within a specifically martial framework in Anderson's important pre-war novel *Marching Men.* In the section from ***Winesburg, Ohio*** quoted above, the "backward view" fills George with feelings of his own insignificance and provides a reminder to him of his own mortality. Yet in *Marching Men,* which was composed at some point between 1906 and 1913, Anderson couched the relation between what becomes constituted as history and masculinity in terms that are remarkably self-aggrandizing, aggressive, and mili-taristic.[6] The storyline focuses on Beaut MacGregor, a miner's son who migrates to Chicago and organizes its workingmen into the "Marching Men," a group somewhere between a labour union and a militia. Yet the "Marching Men" have no overt political or social agenda: MacGregor explains that the movement is about "the thing that can't be put into words," and that "for a time men will cease to be individuals. They will become a mass, a moving all powerful mass."[7] This they do by marching in their thousands through the streets of Chicago, much to the consternation of the city's authorities and industrialists, but not in support of any concrete proposals for labour reform—merely for the experience of marching. Christopher Looby has described such moments of depersonalization and massification as "a kind of fantasy upon which military *esprit de corps* thrives, a fantasy of selfless absorption into a powerful collective body," yet the objective of this in Anderson's novel seems less about military objectives or class politics than about gender politics.[8] This agenda is implicitly revealed as the collective body of the "Marching Men" becomes aggressively hyper-masculinized to a degree unachievable by an individual—a process that produces a sense of exhilaration in the men involved. Indeed, Anderson's exaltation of the collective male military body often drifts close to an endorsement of a totalitarian and proto-Fascistic politics. It was the following type of extremism that he was to re-assess as the Great War unfolded:

> In the heart of all men lies sleeping the love of order. How to achieve order out of our strange jumble of forms, out of democracies and monarchies, dreams and endeavours is the riddle of the Universe and the thing that in the artist is called the passion for form . . . The long march, the burning of the throat and the stinging of dust in the nostrils, the touch of shoulder against shoulder, the quick bond of a common, unquestioned, instinctive passion that bursts in the orgasm of battle, the forgetting of words and the doing of the thing, be it winning battles or destroying ugliness, the passionate massing of men for accomplishment—these are the signs, if they ever awake in our land, by which you may know you have come to the days of the making of men.[9]

The imposition of order by masculine force, the links between this epistemology and the act of writing, the analogies among military conquest, creativity, and phallic sexual gratification—all features problematized in ***Winesburg, Ohio***—are put forward with a deeply disturbing sincerity in this passage. Indeed, Anderson's misogyny and stress on war as restorative rather than destructive, as what Fillipo Tomasso Marinetti called the "great healthgiver of the world," recall the manifestos of the Italian Futurists that became central to Fascist aesthetics after World War One.[10] As David Forgacs has noted, "the discourse of Fascism is full of imagined acts of violence which heal and restore order where there had been a perceived state of disease and disorder," and commonly the source of disease and disorder was represented as a woman.[11] The kind of imaginary violence that Anderson indulges in here celebrates the fullness of a masculinity established through the wounding of an unnamed and objectified other, a passive victim of a phallic assault. The "Marching Men" of the novel's title, established in a homo-social system that crucially obliterates all difference between them, thus become an undifferentiated, absolute aesthetic correlate to a passive other, a distinctly feminized antagonist. It is this dynamic, the novel suggests, that produces history—the "making of men" within a martial order. As John Ditsky notes with considerable discomfort, "it is hard to agree with the notion that Anderson clearly rejects the lock-step totalitarianism he portrays so prophetically."[12]

However, as Forgacs goes on to discuss, imaginations of violence are very different from the actualities of warfare, and during the First World War a sense of this discordance led several Futurists to retract their pre-war positions of militaristic misogyny.[13] It is no surprise that the war presented a challenge to Anderson's teleological historiography of masculine power, to the totalizing narrative made possible by the "love of order" which he believed formed the most significant moments of historical reality. Yet rather than simply abandoning his faith in this historical model, Anderson oscillated in his opinions about the value and meaning of war, opinions undoubtedly affected by his own memories of military service during the Spanish-American war. During his service in 1898-1899 Anderson was most affected by the imaginary of violence rather than actual combat; he trained extensively in the South before sailing to Cuba four weeks after the armistice, and consequently never saw action. Indeed, his nostalgic recollections of marching and drilling resemble the passage quoted from *Marching Men* above; as he remembered wistfully, "one's individuality became lost and one became part of something wholly physical, vast, strong, capable of being fine and heroic, capable of being brutal and cruel."[14] He also fondly remembered his military service for its promotion of male homosociality, a homosociality in which the tempering regulation of "homosexual panic" never seemed to intrude:

> Suppose a man spend certain months not thinking consciously, letting himself be swept along by other men, with other men, feeling the weariness of a thousand other men's legs, desiring with others, fearing with the others, being brave sometimes with the others. By such experience can one gain knowledge of the others and of oneself too? Comrades loved![15]

Such fond nostalgia for his military service often coexisted with a misogynistic cast to his celebrations of martial violence; in *A Story Teller's Story* Anderson refers to Spain as a "poor old woman" facing America, the "young and swaggering giant of the west."[16] Even more disturbing is his account of the gang-rape of a local woman by four soldiers in his company during their posting in the South (*Memoirs,* 188-89). The collectivization of men and the attendant heightening of their sense of power, invulnerability, and masculinity was central to Anderson's romantic memorialization of his time in the army; yet in all his descriptions, the figure of a defeated feminized antagonist to this masculine force is rarely absent.

These experiences colored Anderson's perspective on the First World War, at times leading him to see it as a glorious opportunity for young men to escape the hollow and basely materialistic experience of working life in America. He wrote to his friend Marietta Finley in November 1916:

> I made a picture of trains coming in at the railroad stations in Chicago, and bearing young men from the cornfields, strong bright eyed young men, thousands of them, walking over the bridges and into the loop district and to spiritual death. The bodies live but the thing that made them bright eyed and eager dies. I should prefer my sons to die in the war and terror of a Verdun.[17]

In many ways this letter evinces sentiments of war as an adventure, a thrilling and potentially noble opportunity that sidestepped the grubby materialism of American life—an attitude held by many of the early American volunteers, according to ex-servicemen such as John Dos Passos and Malcolm Cowley. Indeed, a martial ideal of male civic virtue, the opportunities the armed services gave for escaping what Michael C. C. Adams has called "civic claustrophobia," and the persistence of a romance of chivalry around the military figure made war attractive to many men in the United States. Moreover, as Adams and T. Jackson Lears have remarked, it offered an alternative to a bourgeois domesticity often perceived as effeminate.[18]

A romanticized martial ideal that offered a transcendence of materialistic and capitalistic values, and that offered heroic masculinities based on *esprit de corps* and battlefield courage, undoubtedly held a strong attraction for Anderson, especially during the initial phases of the war. Counterbalancing this, however, were the experiences and opinions of the intellectual circles upon which he relied for publication. This was most obvious in his dealings with *The Seven Arts,* which had published several of his Winesburg stories and championed him as one of the most significant of a group of emerging American artists. *The Seven Arts* would eventually collapse due to a withdrawal of funds; the magazine's financial backer balked at its controversial antiwar stance, particularly evident in the essays of Randolph Bourne—a stance that also caused it to be placed under surveillance by United States intelligence services. Waldo Frank was then the assistant editor of *The Seven Arts,* and had glowingly praised the "Promise of Sherwood Anderson" in its first number. Frank's correspondence with Anderson during the war continually refers to his own fear of imprisonment for his conscientious objection, and criticizes the herdlike mentality and the attention of the intelligence services which he felt was preventing open debate on the war. Anderson was sympathetic towards Frank, and also worried when, in 1918, his friend and colleague Paul Rosenfeld was drafted and agreed to serve. These concerns crystallised in another letter to Marietta Finley, one markedly different in tone and feeling from that of November 1916:

> I had some dreams when the war began. I saw in fancy men marching shoulder to shoulder and doing big deeds. Instead, as you know men have gone into the ground and there is only the horrible, mechanical guns and the deafness and the stench of decaying bodies.
>
> Well, I won't go on! Thinking of it has driven me near to madness.[19]

Rather than making a romantic escape from the mechanised modes of production of industrial capitalism, the soldiers now find themselves at the mercy of its military counterpart: in the same letter Anderson calls the war "industrialism gone mad." Indeed, Anderson himself had "escaped" from working in a factory to enlist in the Spanish American war, and in 1924 would complain that instead of the "democracy" of that conflict the Great War involved the "standardization of men" and the ethos that "everything must be made as machine-like and impersonal as possible."[20] The Great War condemns bodies to decay in death instead of promoting the integrity and impenetrability of the clean, healthy male body. Rather than buttressing masculinity through the bonds of martial homosociality, the war engulfs men in the feminized, womb-like trenches of passivity and death.

It was between these two positions that Anderson oscillated throughout the war. He wrote to Waldo Frank on December 7, 1917, that "As an antidote to the war I now read history. Histories of Poland, Russia, Austria, Italy, France. One gets the sense of the long line of events. The present sinks into nothingness."[21] He also advised Finley to read history as an "antidote." This surely reflects his hope that the narrative continuity of these histories, and their chronicles of individual accomplishment and brilliance, would sustain his faith in a male subjectivity that relied heavily on those foundations. On the other hand was the "madness" of the opposite position, as in his sobered letter to Marietta Finley; in another letter he remarked of the war that "In me always . . . there has been the sense of a persistent outcry of little distracting voices. Now it is as though they have begun to shout madly and meaninglessly."[22] This tension—between the cacophony of "meaninglessness" and the "antidote" of his favourite *meaningful* narratives from history—would trouble his thought about historiography and the role of narrative within identity formation throughout the duration of the war. Moreover, because Anderson believed so absolutely in the gendering of subject and object, this anxious reassessment of how to order experience through narrative became an explicitly masculine problem.

If Anderson's reading during periods of the Great War served to circumvent—or at least negotiate—a crisis in his gendered views about narrative, then similar negotiations are evident in his writing during the war, and particularly in ***Winesburg, Ohio.*** According to William L. Phillips, Sherwood Anderson wrote the stories of ***Winesburg, Ohio*** one after the other between late 1915 and early 1916, yet they were not collected for publication until 1919.[23] The stories—and crucially the principles that governed their collection and organization—were thus in development at precisely the time Anderson was confronting the implications of the war in Europe. Indeed, ***Winesburg, Ohio***'s interest in militarism, the connections between social order, gender, and narrative, and the ways in which the short story cycle form brings the reading dynamic of the text into contact with these issues, all suggest that the Great War is a crucial, but often overlooked, historical context for Anderson's most famous work.

However, arguing for the uniqueness of ***Winesburg, Ohio***'s negotiation of these issues within Anderson's thirty-eight year-long publishing career is problematic, since the tension between narrative or semantic significance and "meaninglessness" that troubled Anderson about the Great War is one that structures much of his fiction. Indeed, although evident in its crudest form in *Marching Men,* the search for order or meaning, as many critics have noted, runs throughout Anderson's corpus. Claire Colquitt has linked this quest to Anderson's politics of gender, observing that the desire for control through art in his writing is explicitly masculine.[24] Yet the short story cycle form—which several critics have argued is defined by the tension between an overarching aesthetic design and the autonomy of individual stories that disturb that design—was not a form to which he would return after ***Winesburg, Ohio.***[25] Moreover, the anti-social, monologistic, tyrannical and even absurd nature of the desire for control through art is pushed to the forefront in ***Winesburg, Ohio*** to a degree that does not appear in Anderson's other work.

Such absurdity is particularly evident in the story **"An Awakening."** Early in the story, George Willard indulges in exactly the type of despotic and militaristic fantasies of social order that Beaut MacGregor pursued with such sincerity in *Marching Men.* On the night streets of Winesburg, George fantasizes about being a military inspector admonishing his men: "Everything must be in order here. We have a difficult task before us and no difficult task can be done without order" (101). In his mind, he decides that "in every little thing there must be order, in the place where men work, in their clothes, in their thoughts. I myself must be orderly. I must learn that law" (101). Entry into the knowledge of this law offers George the alluring possibility of imposing order on an otherwise random environment. Later in the story George's desire for order is explicitly codified as narrative in its basis:

> For a year he had been devoting all of his odd moments to the reading of books and now some tale he had read concerning life in old world towns of the middle ages came sharply to his mind so that he stumbled forward with the curious feeling of one revisiting a place that had been a part of some former existence.
>
> (102)

By placing himself and his environment within this narrative sequence, George becomes even more "excited" by the sense of his own power in controlling previously unconnected phenomena; he feels "unutterably big and remade by the simple experience" (102). This heady sense of empowerment only intensifies George's desire to create order through narrative, which centers on the objectified body of Belle Carpenter, whom he has arranged to see later that evening. George hopes to "achieve in her presence a position he had long been wanting to achieve" (102). The *double-entendre* of this quotation exemplifies well the way in which Belle simultaneously becomes an object of sexual desire and a figure in a set of linguistic relations, able to be repositioned and re-contextualised by George to achieve a narrative—and sexual—consummation. George feels a "sense of masculine power" in his walk with Belle up the hill to the fairground, a power grounded in his certainty that masculinity has the ability to write the script. At one point, quite independently of any indication of desire on her part, he suddenly decides "that Belle Carpenter was about to surrender herself to him" (103).

However, George's self-aggrandisement and egoism is ridiculed when Ed Handby throws him into the bushes, grabs Belle Carpenter, and marches her away. Indeed, "George Willard did not understand what happened to him that night on the hillside. Later, when he got to his room, he wanted to weep and then grew half insane with anger and hate" (104). "Insanity" seems here to indicate George's fear that he has gone beyond the limits of acceptable difference, limits beyond which (as Sander Gilman and others have shown) negative stereotypes of race, sexuality and (often mental) illness overlap and reinforce one another.[26] It also seems to confirm Eve Kosofsky Sedgwick's thesis that fear of being shamed by acting in an "inappropriate" gender role is a highly effective psychological mechanism in policing a wide range of social behaviors.[27] The story clearly ridicules the possibility of one individual imposing "his story" upon others; stories and agencies interact in more complex ways than George allows for. While ridiculing its simplicity, however, **"An Awakening"** also suggests the inevitability of George's impulse; his self-conception relies on narration as a mode of empowerment and gender identification. When the objectification and inscription of this narration are disturbed, George is faced with the "half insanity" of a breakdown in the normative practices of gender that structure his subjectivity. Moreover, the trope of madness as indicative of a threat to gender normativity recalls the voices that Anderson felt were shouting "madly and meaninglessly" at him as he realized what was happening to American men in the Great War. In both the letter and **"An Awakening,"** "madness" for Anderson seems to denote aberrant sexuality, perverse desire, or the failure to conform to a certain set of parameters within which he believed normative male subjectivity to exist.

The futile search for an often aestheticized pattern of order and significance on the part of Winesburg's male inhabitants is staged repeatedly throughout ***Winesburg, Ohio.*** Moreover, just as Anderson's militaristic fantasies of empowerment were often predicated on the destruction of a feminized "other," his fantasies of imaginative expression and creative production often focused on artistic control of the female body. This is most obvious in the two stories of ***Winesburg*** that have perhaps the closest sequential and thematic links, **"The Strength of God"** and **"The Teacher."** The stories focus on successive attempts by both George Willard and the Reverend Curtis Hartman to interpret the body of the local schoolteacher, Kate Swift. In **"The Strength of God,"** Hartman, working in the bell-tower of the church and looking at Kate Swift's "white shoulders and bare throat," is troubled by his own "carnal desire" but attempts to regain a sense of control and knowledge by placing this body in a Biblical narrative of trial; "The Lord has devised this temptation as a test of my soul and I will grope my way out of darkness into the light of righteousness" (82-84). However, his interpretation of Kate Swift's body on his crucial night of decision in the middle of winter provides him with "what he took to be the way of life for him" (85). Having sat in the cold tower for hours with soaking feet waiting for Kate Swift to reappear, uncertain of God and of himself, Hartman's epistemological crisis takes on a physical dimension. He had "come near dying with cold"; drifting into unconsciousness, several times he needs "by an exercise of will power to force himself back into consciousness" (85). He is at risk of the ultimate loss of control and reduction to passivity, that of death—the analogue to the selflessness that Gilbert and Gubar find nineteenth-century patriarchal society prescribed as the ultimate feminine virtue.[28] However, at this moment Kate Swift becomes readable and seemingly available as an object of knowledge as Hartman sees her praying naked on her bed. This scene presents her as a signifier in a narrative of transcendental truth, as a remasculinized Hartman explains to a bewildered George Willard:

> "I did not understand," he said. "What I took to be the trial of my soul was only a preparation for a new and more beautiful fervour of the spirit. God has appeared to me in the person of Kate Swift, the schoolteacher, kneeling naked on a bed. . . . Although she may not be aware of it, she is an instrument of God, bearing the message of truth."
>
> (85)

In Hartman's re-formed narrative perspective on his own life, Kate Swift's naked body has become a symbol of God's truth, a narrative that both the reader and George see as delusional. However, it is the only mode by which Hartman is able to rescue himself from crisis. The "signing" of Kate's body enables him to control its threatening potential; as Peter Brooks says, "Signing or marking the body signifies its passage into writing, its becoming a literary body, and generally also a narrative body, in that the inscription of a sign depends on and produces a story."[29] Through Kate's inscription as an "instrument of god" Hartman both reads and writes her body into a narrative that re-establishes his sense of self-control and masculine identity.

The following story, **"The Teacher,"** focuses instead on George Willard's fantastical appropriation of Kate Swift, who once again acts as an object of both sexual desire and curiosity. For the men of the town she presents an enticing and disturbing narrative vacuum, as her enigmatic presence and character provoke desires for a seemingly inseparable sexual and authorial control over her. Indeed, shortly after his muttered intention to "find out about you. You wait and see" (86) George embraces a pillow and thinks of Kate; his fantasy of her embodiment is inseparable from his desire to control knowledge of her. **"The Teacher"** is also the story in which the fantasy of male control through the exercise of imaginative power seems closest to being realized, as Kate's status as a doubly seen and objectified body seems to impel her to actions over which she has no control: "It was past ten o'clock when Kate Swift set out and the walk was unpremeditated. It was as though the man and the boy, by thinking of her, had driven her forth into the wintry streets" (88). Here, the lines of division between the author in control of what actually occurs in his material, the narrator, and the aspiring author-character George are as thin as anywhere in the text. The fantasy of being able to write one's own life story, and write other people in and out of it at will, is momentarily indulged in during a moment in which the imperative of wish fulfilment seems to override the literary codes of realism. However, this intrusive generic rupture with realism also serves as a reminder of the textuality of the story, and thus the legitimation of this fantasy is called into question just as it receives its most forceful articulation.

Another voice enters the fantastical scramble for appropriation in the next paragraph with the narrator's imaginative re-creation of Kate Swift:

> At the age of thirty Kate Swift was not known in Winesburg as a pretty woman. . . . Alone in the night on the winter streets she was lovely. Her back was straight, her shoulders square and her features were as the features of a tiny goddess on a pedestal in a garden in the dim light of a summer evening.
>
> (88)

In such transformations, which recur consistently in Sherwood Anderson's fiction, Colquitt finds that Anderson's real subject is not the nature of beauty or femininity but "the transforming power of artistic genius."[30] By using the image of a woman transformed into a work of art, "the narrator/artist can effectively ignore the political realities facing [women] by making one woman's life a poetical whole."[31] Once again, however, this masculine strategy of control is revealed as flawed. At the end of the story George's quest for knowledge has been frustrated; "He could not make it out. Over and over he turned the matter in his mind" (91). Similarly, "When he became drowsy and closed his eyes, he raised a hand and with it groped about in the darkness. 'I have missed something Kate Swift was trying to tell me,' he muttered sleepily" (91). George gropes in the darkness for Kate's body and the legibility of that body, both of which have eluded him.

The structure of the two stories also contributes to articulating this strategy of corporeal reading as flawed; as J. Gerald Kennedy has noted, "By splitting a potentially single narrative into two stories, Anderson accentuates the solipsistic quality of his characters' lives."[32] Splitting the "potentially single narrative" also accentuates the polyvalency of Kate Swift's body by separating the different "readings" of it; only briefly do Hartman's and George's readings come into the same fictional space. And when they do, it is the spectre of "madness" that is again invoked: George believes "the town had gone mad" (91). Once again, when disparate desires and narratives are brought into contact with each other, the situation is represented as confusing and threatening. Moreover, Anderson only seems able to classify the disruption this causes to the narrative basis of normative masculine subjectivities by denoting it "insane." This struggle for control is staged throughout these two stories, and in considering whether Kate is "an instrument of God," George's belief that "she might be in love with him" (86) or the narrator's comment that her "eagerly passionate soul" (89) transforms her into a statuesque "tiny goddess" (88), Kate's status as a subject recedes to the point of invisibility, as she is inscribed and re-inscribed into various systems of male interpretation. Yet their juxtaposition shows up each of these systems as inadequate and impoverishing, reducing a character to a simplistic semantic value. Moreover, if we as readers attempt to recover the "real" Kate Swift from these inscriptions, we replicate the masculine and appropriative strategy of George, Curtis Hartman, and the narrator. Kate's status as existing only in the perspective of others is thereby foregrounded, as is the dubious nature of the voices that struggle over her.

The investment of heterosexual masculinity in the process of narration is obvious in several other stories. This is particularly true of **"Hands,"** where it is contrasted to the socially peripheral status of homosexuality through the contrast between George Willard and Wing Biddlebaum, and also in the penultimate story of the collection, **"Sophistication."** When George, the aspiring writer, leaves Winesburg he perceives it as a "background on which to paint the dreams of his manhood," an aestheticization of experience that imagines Winesburg as a memorialized and geographical whole (138). Anticipating the phallocentrism of all notions of unified identity or aesthetics postulated by Cixous and Irigaray, George's problem of aesthetically unifying both Winesburg and his own conception of self is predicated on the essentialized difference of Helen White, the local banker's daughter and the woman with whom he forms his most meaningful erotic relationship. In their encounter in **"Sophistication,"** "what he felt was reflected in her" (134), and the elemental feature of their mutual experience is that "I have come to this lonely place and here is this other" (135). It is her essential "otherness," the binary polarization between masculine and feminine reinforced by this encounter, that "renewed and refreshed him" (135).

This "renewal" is a misnomer, however, as it refers to something George has never in fact possessed—namely, the absolute masculinism that he has struggled to achieve throughout the cycle. This fiction of recapitulation is completed through a reflection of difference. Anderson's image of reflection here evokes the tradition of feminist thought on the necessity of "femininity" for the definition of boundaries of "masculinity," a tradition that has often used the mirror as its figure for this operation. One thinks, for example, of Virginia Woolf's observation that women have "served all these centuries as looking-glasses possessing the magic and delicious power of reflecting the figure of the man at twice its natural size," or Irigaray's later description of masculine specularization, which makes women serve as a "mirror entrusted by the masculine 'subject' with the task of reflecting and redoubling himself."[33] George's legitimation within the world of art and the story's correspondent "refreshing" of a unitary masculinity necessitate this mirroring function on the part of Helen: what at first seems to be the only legible body in the entire text therefore becomes an exercise in narcissism. With this epistemology, George totalizes Winesburg and essentializes gender. Yet if this is a precarious state of totality and security with which to end the text, it is all the more so as we are told that Winesburg is a painted background; once again (as with Belle Carpenter and Kate Swift) Anderson cannot invoke his conception of female subjectivity without drawing attention to the framing structures of representation within which these subjectivities exist.

Moreover, this masculinized practice of interpretation not only is implicit in the attempts of ***Winesburg, Ohio***'s male characters to inscribe the female body into a self-serving system of signification, but is also implicated in the generic structure of the text. As a short story cycle, ***Winesburg, Ohio*** invites the reader to make connections among its parts, to engage in a process of finding similarities. J. Gerald Kennedy has argued that "lacking a continuous narratorial presence, the [short story] sequence—like the decentred modernist novel—places the reader in a strategic position to draw parallels, to discern whatever totalizing meanings may inhere in the composite scheme," and that this process "enhances the pleasure of the text." This may go some way to explaining why the task of establishing the unity of ***Winesburg, Ohio*** has always attracted critics, especially those grounded in "the holistic assumptions of New Criticism."[34] Unifying features have been seen to include George as the *Bildungsroman* protagonist, the universal application of the theory of Grotesquerie established in **"The Book of the Grotesque,"** the myth of androgyny, the structural pattern of the Dance of Death, or the importance of "feminine" qualities.[35]

However, I think it is fair to these critics to state that none of their explanations of unity can be applied consistently across all the twenty-one stories that make up ***Winesburg, Ohio,*** just as my own arguments have gravitated towards certain stories and not mentioned others. Discussions that focus on George Willard often have no place for analysis of **"Tandy"** or **"The Untold Lie"**; those analyzing the category of grotesquerie often omit discussion of Joe Welling in **"A Man of Ideas"** or Tom

Foster in **"Drink."** It is therefore a feature of ***Winesburg, Ohio*** that although it invites interpretation, and even very obviously encodes a textual place for a model reader to engage in interpretation, it ultimately frustrates such an exercise across the entire text through the diversity of its individual text units. The structure of the text seems to problematize its own logic, namely the ability of narrative under masculine control to provide continuity and order.

Winesburg, Ohio thus engages directly with what Robert M. Luscher feels to be the "quest for coherence" implicit in reading all short story cycles.[36] However, although the text does seem to endorse George's search for knowledge and control, it focuses on his frustrations and self-aggrandizement more than on his successes. This pattern can also be replicated by the reader who, attracted by the text's invitations, attempts to impose a totalizing meaning onto the text. Luscher's comment that "our desire for unity and coherence is so great that we often use our literary competencies to integrate apparently unrelated material" seems particularly apt for the mode of reading suggested by the textual strategies of ***Winesburg, Ohio,*** strategies that invite totalization but simultaneously frustrate it—and thus draw the reader's attention to the problematics of their reading endeavour.[37] As I have shown, such a strategy can only function by exclusion and a wilful blindness to contradiction and plurality.[38]

The book Anderson wrote immediately after ***Winesburg, Ohio,*** *Poor White* (1920), is, like *Marching Men* (1917), notable by its contrast with ***Winesburg.*** *Poor White* narrates the coming of industrialism to the Midwest, nostalgically chronicling the destruction of older patterns of labor and community involved in that process. Yet it does so with a more confident and controlling narrative voice than is evident in ***Winesburg, Ohio,*** with none of the fragmentation or reluctance to endorse totalizing conceptualization to be found in the earlier text. *Poor White* also takes a mythopoetic approach to historicism, seeing a national "mood" or character as determining social and economic change; it is a narrative animated by the assumption that there is a teleology to these changes, a national "destiny." Moreover, it was the narrative coherence of *Poor White* that led Anderson to boast of its veracity as a social document; he later commented that *Poor White* was "a source to which practically all of the historians of the period go. It is already used in most of our colleges and universities *to tell the story* to the present generation of American youth."[39] Once again, *Poor White* deals with the formation of masculinity, of boys growing into men (particularly through their encounters with women); this was a fascination that extended through much of Anderson's career, and he rarely depicted it as anything other than a complex, clumsy, fraught experience. However, the narrative fragmentations of ***Winesburg, Ohio***—and its embattled attempt to cement a patriarchal masculinity through a politics of representation—are absent from *Poor White,* and indeed were elements that Anderson was never to repeat.

That this is so suggests that Anderson's often fraught re-assessment of the relation between martial service and narratives of male empowerment and subjectivity in 1916 and 1917 must be reconnected with the narrative strategies and formation of gender subjectivities in ***Winesburg, Ohio.*** Kaja Silverman has discussed the relation of historical trauma to male subjectivity, arguing that history is a "force [that] disrupts the equilibrium of the dominant fiction, generating temporary irregularities and even radical change within textual practice."[40] This "dominant fiction" is inseparable from the operations of patriarchal culture; it is "the mechanism by which a society 'tries to institute itself as such on the basis of closure, of the fixation of meaning.'"[41] It is the "dominant representational and narrative reservoir" of a culture that is able to conceal the fact that male subjectivity is founded on lack; it is within this set of dominant fictions that "the paternal signifier 'grows' into an organ, and becomes available to the male subject as his *imago.*"[42]

History, for Silverman, is thus a force of rude intrusion, one that by definition troubles representational practice in the products of the "dominant fiction" and therefore precipitates crisis within male subjectivities. It is precisely this quality of disturbance that characterizes the narrative and semiotic practices of ***Winesburg, Ohio***; the text carefully lays out the mutually constitutive nature of patriarchal masculinity, narrative, and social order, only to remark consistently on the fragile and precarious nature of this process. Later, in his recollection of the war, Anderson stated that "It was a time of too much 'greatness.' . . . It was a flood. It was to me terrible, unbearable. . . . I wanted passionately now not to think of great soldiers, statesmen, writers, but of being first of all little" (*Memoir,* 448). The fragmentation of experience depicted in ***Winesburg, Ohio*** can, therefore, be read as a questioning of the value of narrative continuity, the aesthetic of unification, and the possibility of masculine narrative control prompted by the seemingly meaningless slaughter of the war.

Floyd Dell, Anderson's first significant literary contact in Chicago, remarked in 1961 that the "non-heroic" mood of ***Winesburg, Ohio*** "turned out to be the postwar mood of many critics and writers."[43] Dell's view that Anderson's text exhibited a profound reaction to the war is an assessment that has been lost in much subsequent criticism. This is despite the fact that two of Anderson's admirers in the 1920s, Ernest Hemingway in *In Our Time* (1925) and William Faulkner in *The Unvanquished* (1933), would use the short story cycle as a form for questioning many of the romantic and patriarchal myths that surround war. Anderson's wartime story cycle does not end, as Duane Simolke suggests, with George able not only to "transcend the dominant social ideology of gender roles" but also to "transcend gender."[44] Rather, it shows George's dogged adherence to a set of aesthetic and representational systems of order and narration that he uses to mediate his experiences and identification in relation to women. The inconsistency, inadequacy, and narcissism of these systems is foregrounded again and again, but George's only alternative is marginalization, or the "half insanity" brought about by being rejected by Belle Carpenter. As George leaves Winesburg on a train, like the thousands of young American men who left their homes in 1917 in response to the American military mobilization, "the dreams of his manhood" await him. Yet the fact that that Anderson's dreams for the manhood of America's military had turned into the "stench of decaying bodies" illustrates what a precarious business dreaming of manhood could be.

Notes

1. Anon., "Sordid Tales," *The New York Evening Post,* July 19, 1919: III, 3; repr. in *Winesburg, Ohio,* ed. Ray Lewis White and Charles Modlin (New York: Norton, 1996), 164.
2. See Marilyn Judith Atlas's "Sherwood Anderson and the Women of Winesburg," and also Nancy Bunge's "Women in Sherwood Anderson's Fiction," both included in *Critical Essays on Sherwood Anderson,* ed. David D. Anderson (Boston: G. K. Hall, 1981); Clare Colquitt's "Motherlove in Two Narratives of Community: *Winesburg, Ohio* and *The Country of the Pointed Firs,*" *New Essays on* Winesburg, Ohio, ed. John W. Crowley (Cambridge: Cambridge Univ. Press, 1990), 73-97; and Susan Sontag, "Notes on Camp," *Against Interpretation and Other Essays* (New York: Picador, 2001), 275-92.
3. Kaja Silverman, "Historical Trauma and Male Subjectivity," *Psychoanalysis and Cinema,* ed. E. Ann Kaplan (New York: Routledge, 1990), 110-27, 118.
4. *Sherwood Anderson's Memoirs: A Critical Edition,* ed. Ray Lewis White (Chapel Hill: Univ. of North Carolina Press, 1969), 554. Hereafter cited parenthetically as *Memoirs.*
5. Sherwood Anderson, *Winesburg, Ohio,* ed. Ray Lewis White and Charles Modlin (New York: Norton, 1996), 130. Hereafter cited parenthetically.
6. Sherwood Anderson, *Marching Men, 1917,* ed. Ray Lewis White (Cleveland: Press of Case Western Reserve Univ., 1972). White's introduction to *Marching Men* considers the date of its composition.
7. *Marching Men,* 182-83.
8. Christopher Looby, "'As Thoroughly Black as the Most Faithful Philanthropist Could Desire': Erotics of Race in Higginson's *Army Life in a Black Regiment,*" *Race and the Subject of Masculinities,* ed. Harry Stecopoulos and Michel Uebel (Durham NC: Duke Univ. Press), 71-115, 85.
9. *Marching Men,* 48.
10. See David Forgacs, "Fascism, Violence and Modernity," *The Violent Muse: Violence and the Artistic Imagination in Europe, 1910-1939,* ed. Jana Howlett and Rod Mengham (Manchester: Manchester Univ. Press, 1994), 5-21, especially 10-15; see also Sandra M. Gilbert and Susan Gubar, *No Man's Land: The Place of the Woman Writer in the Twentieth Century,* Vol. I (New Haven: Yale Univ. Press, 1988), 22. Anderson's position here partially validates claims that many of the emergent modernisms of this period were expressly misogynistic, geared to gendering modernism as masculine. This is the argument of Ann Douglas in *Terrible Honesty: Mongrel Manhattan in the 1920s* (London: Papermac-MacMillan 1995), which contends that the impulse of much of American modernism was "matricidal," aimed at supplanting a "feminized" Victorian literary culture. See also Gilbert and Gubar's chapter "Tradition and the Female Talent: Modernism and Masculinism" in *No Man's Land.*
11. Forgacs, 5.
12. John Ditsky, "Sherwood Anderson's Marching Men: Unnatural Disorder and the Art of Force," *Twentieth Century Literature* 23 (1977), 102-114, 104.
13. Forgacs (13) cites as one example Giovanni Papini, who converted to Catholicism during the war in a crisis of guilt over his earlier opinions.
14. Sherwood Anderson, *A Story Teller's Story,* 1924 (New York: Viking, 1969), 272.
15. *A Story Teller's Story,* 274.
16. *A Story Teller's Story,* 277.
17. *Letters to Bab: Sherwood Anderson to Marietta D. Finley, 1916-1933,* ed. William A. Sutton (Urbana: Univ. of Illinois Press, 1985), 14-15.
18. Many historians have examined the links between the First World War and gender identity. Important for my understanding have been Michael C. C. Adams, *The Great Adventure: Male Desire and the Coming of World War One* (Bloomington: Indiana Univ. Press, 1990); Paul Fussell, *The Great War and Modern Memory* (London: Oxford Univ.

Press, 1975); Donald J. Mroezek, "The Habit of Victory: The American Military and the Cult of Manliness," *Manliness and Masculinity: Middle-Class Masculinity in Britain and America, 1800-1940,* ed. J. A. Mangan and James Walvin (Manchester: Manchester Univ. Press, 1987), 220-41; T. Jackson Lears, "The Destructive Element: Modern Commercial Society and the Martial Ideal," in his *No Place of Grace: Antimodernism and the Transformation of American Culture 1880-1920* (Chicago: Univ. of Chicago Press, 1994); Joanna Bourke, *Dismembering the Male: Men's Bodies, Britain and the Great War* (London: Reaktion, 1996) and Sheila Rowbotham, *A Century of Women: The History of Women in Britain and the United States* (London: Penguin, 1999), 69-118.

19. *Letters to Bab,* 64.
20. *A Story Teller's Story,* 281.
21. *Letters of Sherwood Anderson,* ed. Howard Mumford Jones and Walter B. Rideout (Boston: Little, Brown and Co., 1953), 27.
22. *Letters of Sherwood Anderson,* 15.
23. William L. Phillips, "How Sherwood Anderson Wrote *Winesburg, Ohio,*" *Sherwood Anderson: A Collection of Critical Essays,* ed. Walter B. Rideout (Englewood Cliffs: Prentice-Hall, 1974), 18-38, 24.
24. Colquitt, "Motherlove," 86.
25. See, for example, Forrest L. Ingram's *Representative Short Story Cycles of the Twentieth Century: Studies in a Literary Genre* (The Hague: Mouton, 1971), 19: and Susan Garland Mann's *The Short Story Cycle: A Genre Companion and Reference Guide* (New York: Greenwood Press, 1989), 15.
26. See Sander Gilman's *Difference and Pathology: Stereotypes of Sexuality, Race and Madness* (Ithaca: Cornell Univ. Press, 1985).
27. Sedgwick discusses the operation of what she calls "homosexual panic" within these terms; as she notes, "no man must be able to ascertain that he is not (that his bonds are not) homosexual. In this way, a relatively small exertion of physical and legal compulsion potentially rules great reaches of behaviour and filiation." "The Beast in the Closet: James and the Writing of Homosexual Panic," *Sex, Politics and Science in the Nineteenth-Century Novel,* ed. Ruth Bernard Yeazell (Baltimore: Johns Hopkins Univ. Press, 1986), 147-186,151.
28. See Toril Moi's *Sexual/Textual Politics: Feminist Literary Theory* (London: Routledge, 1995), 58.
29. Peter Brooks, *Body Work: Objects of Desire in Modern Narrative* (Cambridge: Harvard Univ. Press, 1993), 3.
30. Clare Colquitt, "The Reader as Voyeur: Complicitious Transformations in 'Death in the Woods,'" *Modern Fiction Studies* 32 (1986), 175-190, 189. Similar episodes occur in Anderson's stories "Death," "The New Englander," and "Like a Queen."
31. Colquitt, "Reader as Voyeur," 189.
32. J. Gerald Kennedy, "From Anderson's Winesburg to Carver's *Cathedral:* The Short Story Sequence and the Semblance of Community," *Modern American Short Story Sequences: Composite Fictions and Fictive Communities,* ed. J. Gerald Kennedy (Cambridge: Cambridge Univ. Press, 1995), 194-215, 199.
33. See Virginia Woolf, *A Room of One's Own,* ed. Morag Shiach (Oxford: Oxford Univ. Press, 1998), 45; and Luce Irigaray's "This Sex Which Is Not One," trans. Claudia Reeder, *New French Feminisms: An Anthology,* ed. Elaine Marks and Isabelle de Courtrivron (Brighton: Harvester, 1981), 99-106, 104.
34. Kennedy, 196, 195.
35. The "unifying" function within *Winesburg, Ohio* of the theory of grotesquerie advanced in "The Book of the Grotesque" is argued for in Ralph Ciancio's "Unity of Vision in *Winesburg, Ohio,*" *PMLA* 87 (1972), 994-1006; and also in Malcolm Cowley's influential introduction to *Winesburg, Ohio* in the Viking-Compass edition of 1960 (Harmondsworth: Penguin, 1976), 1-15; and in Judith Arcana's "'Tandy' at the Centre of Winesburg," *Studies in Short Fiction* 24 (1987), 66-70. The myth of androgyny as a unifying principle for the text is offered by Martin Bidney in his "Anderson and the Androgyne: 'Something more than Man or Woman,'" *Studies in Short Fiction* 25 (1988), 261-73; a similar role for the "dance of death" is argued for by David Stouck in his "*Winesburg, Ohio* as a Dance of Death," *American Literature* 48 (1977), 525-42. Sally Aidair Rigsbee has argued that "feminine" principles provide the text with coherence in "The Feminine in Winesburg, Ohio," *Studies in American Fiction* 9 (1981), 233-44.
36. Robert M. Luscher, "The Short Story Sequence: An Open Book," *Short Story Theory at a Crossroads,* ed. Susan Lohafer and Jo Ellyn Clarey (Baton Rouge: Louisiana State Univ. Press, 1989), 148-167, 156.
37. Luscher, 155.
38. This foregrounding of the reading process provoked by *Winesburg, Ohio*'s use of the short story cycle genre recalls Wolfgang Iser's comments on

the formal strategies of modernism; he remarked that "they are often so fragmentary that one's attention is almost exclusively occupied with the search for connections between the fragments; the object of this is not to complicate the 'spectrum' of connections, so much as to make us aware of the nature of our own capacity for making links. In such cases, the text refers back directly to our own preconceptions—which are revealed by the act of interpretation that is a basic element of the reading process." "The Reading Process," repr. in *Modern Literary Theory: A Reader,* 2nd ed., ed. Philip Rice and Patricia Waugh (London: Edward Arnold, 1992), 77-83, 80.

39. Anderson to B.G. Braver-Mann, January 13, 1934, emphasis mine. See *Sherwood Anderson: Selected Letters,* ed. Charles E. Modlin (Knoxville: Univ. of Tennessee Press, 1984), 177.

40. Silverman, 118.

41. Silverman, 115. Silverman quotes here from Ernesto Laclau, "The Impossibility of Society," *Canadian Journal of Political and Social Theory* 7 (1983), 24.

42. Silverman, 110

43. Floyd Dell, "On Being Sherwood Anderson's Literary Father," *Newberry Library Bulletin* 5, 315-21, 320.

44. Duane Simolke, *Gender, Isolation and Industrialism: New Readings of* Winesburg, Ohio (San Jose: ToExcel, 1999), 64-65.

FURTHER READING

Criticism

Anderson, David D., ed. *Critical Essays on Sherwood Anderson.* Boston: G. K. Hall & Co., 1981, 302 p.

Includes several critical essays on *Winesburg.*

Campbell, Hilbert H. "The 'Shadow People': Feodor Sologub and Sherwood Anderson's *Winesburg, Ohio.*" *Studies in Short Fiction* 33, no. 1 (1996): 51-8.

Finds parallels between "Adventure" and several stories in Feodor Sologub's *The Old House and Other Tales.*

Crowley, John W., ed. *New Essays on* Winesburg, Ohio. Cambridge: Cambridge University Press, 1990, 133 p.

Collection of critical essays on *Winesburg, Ohio.*

Dunne, Robert. "Getting the 'Thing Needed': The Modern Grotesque in *Winesburg, Ohio.*" In *A New Book of the Grotesques: Contemporary Approaches to Sherwood Anderson's Early Fiction,* pp. 43-110. Kent, Ohio: The Kent State University Press, 2005.

Contends that by "working within fragmentary tales, employing a style of narration that constantly questions the veracity of what is narrated, and focusing on characters who are incapable of effective articulation in their quest for meaning, Anderson creates in *Winesburg* an exemplary precursor to postmodernism."

Gold, Herbert. "*Winesburg, Ohio*: The Purity and Cunning of Sherwood Anderson." In *Twelve Original Essays on Great American Novels,* edited by Charles Shapiro, pp. 196-209. Detroit: Wayne State University Press, 1958.

Describes Anderson as "one of the purest, most intense poets of loneliness."

Love, Glen A. "*Winesburg, Ohio* and the Rhetoric of Silence." *American Literature* 40, no. 1 (March 1968): 38-57.

Considers the theme of silence in the stories of *Winesburg, Ohio* related to another recurring theme in Anderson's work—"the loss of human significance in America with the onset of urban, machine civilization."

Modlin, Charles E., and Ray Lewis White, eds. Winesburg, Ohio: *An Authoritative Text, Backgrounds, and Contexts, Criticism, by Sherwood Anderson.* New York: W. W. Norton & Co., 1996. 234 p.

Includes several important reviews and essays on *Winesburg, Ohio.*

Papinchak, Robert Allen. "*Winesburg, Ohio.*" In *Sherwood Anderson: A Study of the Short Fiction,* pp. 20-7. New York: Twayne Publishers, 1992.

Provides a thematic overview of the stories in *Winesburg, Ohio.*

Rideout, Walter B., ed. *Sherwood Anderson: A Collection of Critical Essays.* Englewood Cliffs, N.J.: Prentice-Hall, Inc., 1974, 177 p.

Collection of several important critical essays on *Winesburg, Ohio.*

Scruggs, Charles. "The Reluctant Witness: What Jean Toomer Remembered from *Winesburg, Ohio.*" *Studies in American Fiction* 28, no. 1 (spring 2000): 77-100.

Judges the influence of *Winesburg, Ohio* on Jean Toomer's *Cane.*

Sias, Michael. "Anderson's 'Hands'." *Explicator* 58, no. 1 (fall 1999): 30-1.

Explores the hand imagery in "Hands."

Small, Judy Jo. "*Winesburg, Ohio.*" In *A Reader's Guide to the Short Stories of Sherwood Anderson,* pp. 5-206. New York: G. K. Hall & Co., 1994.

Provides critical introductions to the stories in *Winesburg, Ohio.*

Sutton, William A. *The Road to Winesburg: A Mosaic of the Imaginative Life of Sherwood Anderson.* Metuchen, N.J.: Scarecrow Press, Inc., 1972, 645 p.

Elucidates the close relationship between Anderson's life and his work.

Trilling, Lionel. *The Liberal Imagination,* pp. 20-31. New York: Viking Press, 1950.

Brief commentary on *Winesburg* that downplays the stories' realism.

White, Ray Lewis, ed. *The Achievement of Sherwood Anderson: Essays in Criticism.* Chapel Hill: The University of North Carolina Press, 1966, 270 p.

Includes several seminal critical essays on *Winesburg, Ohio.*

———, ed. *The Merrill Studies in* Winesburg, Ohio. Columbus, Ohio: Charles E. Merrill Publishing Co., 1971, 113 p.

A compilation of critical essays on *Winesburg, Ohio.*

———, ed. *Sherwood Anderson's* Winesburg, Ohio *with Variant Readings and Annotations.* Athens: Ohio University Press, 1997, 230 p.

Traces the origin, composition, and publication history of *Winesburg, Ohio.*

Additional coverage of Anderson's life and career is contained in the following sources published by Thomson Gale: *American Writers*; *American Writers: The Classics,* Vol. 2; *Authors and Artists for Young Adults,* Vol. 30; *Beacham's Encyclopedia of Popular Fiction: Biography & Resources,* Vol. 1; *Concise Dictionary of American Literary Biography,* Vols. 1917-1929; *Contemporary Authors,* Vol. 121; *Contemporary Authors New Revision Series,* Vol. 61; *Dictionary of Literary Biography,* Vols. 4, 9, 86; *Dictionary of Literary Biography Documentary Series,* Vol. 1; *DISCovering Authors*; *DISCovering Authors 3.0*; *DISCovering Authors: British*; *DISCovering Authors: Canadian Edition*; *DISCovering Authors Modules: Most-Studied Authors, Novelists*; *Encyclopedia of World Literature in the 20th Century,* Ed. 3; *Exploring Short Stories*; *Gay & Lesbian Literature,* Ed. 2; *Literature Resource Center*; *Major 20th-Century Writers,* Eds. 1, 2; *Major 21st-Century Writers,* 2005; *Novels for Students,* Vol. 4; *Reference Guide to American Literature,* Ed. 4; *Reference Guide to Short Fiction,* Ed. 2; *Short Stories for Students,* Vols. 4, 10, 11; *Short Story Criticism,* Vols. 1, 46; *Twayne's United States Authors*; *Twentieth-Century Literary Criticism,* Vols. 1, 10, 24, 123; and *World Literature Criticism.*

A. S. Byatt
1936-

(Full name Antonia Susan Drabble Byatt) English novelist, critic, essayist, short story writer, and editor.

INTRODUCTION

Byatt is regarded as a proficient and erudite short fiction writer. Best known for her award-winning novel, *Possession* (1990), she has also received favorable critical attention for her inventive stories that combine fantasy and realism, as well as for her exploration of such themes as loss, love, aging, identity, and the role of memory. Critics often note her interest in artistic expression, the creative process, and the relationship between art and life.

BIOGRAPHICAL INFORMATION

Byatt was born on August 24, 1936, in Sheffield, England. Her father, John Drabble, was a judge; her sister, Margaret Drabble, also became a writer. In 1957 Byatt received her B.A. from Newnham College, Cambridge University. She then embarked on graduate studies at Bryn Mawr College and Somerville College, Oxford. She left Oxford in 1959 and taught part-time at the University of London. She also began working on her first novel, *The Shadow of a Sun,* which was published in 1964. A year later, *Degrees of Freedom* was published. The book is a critical examination of the novels of Iris Murdoch, whom critics identify as a key influence on Byatt's work. In 1976 Byatt published a second work of criticism on Murdoch, *Iris Murdoch.* She has edited works by George Eliot and Robert Browning and has written critical studies of such subjects as William Wordsworth, Samuel Taylor Coleridge, and Victorian poetry. Her novels have been popular with critics and readers alike. Her best-known novel, *Possession,* was a best-seller and earned Byatt a Booker Prize and Best Book in Commonwealth Prize. It was also made into a film in 2002. Byatt has contributed book reviews and commentary to such publications as the London *Times, New Statesman, Encounter, New Review,* and *American Studies.* She lives in London.

MAJOR WORKS OF SHORT FICTION

Byatt's short fiction is characterized by her imaginative, masterfully crafted stories that explore memory, death, and the relationship of art to life. In her first collection, *Sugar and Other Stories* (1987), Byatt explores the nature of time, identity, and loss. In "Precipice-Encurled," Byatt bases her story on an incident from the life of Robert Browning. In 1882 Browning and his sister cancel a visit to friends at a villa in the Apennines when the friends' houseguest, a young painter, is swept off a cliff to his death. This tragic accident cuts short two promising romantic relationships and illustrates the intrusion of outside events on the life of imagination and emotion. Two of Byatt's longer stories, "Morpho Eugenia" and "The Conjugial Angel," were published in 1992 as *Angels and Insects.* Both stories are set in Victorian England, copy mid-nineteenth-century literary English, and treat themes of determinism, individual freedom, and love. In "Morpho Eugenia," William Adamson, an entomologist, works for Rev. Harald Alabaster, an anti-Darwinian activist. While living at his estate and aiding Alabaster with his work, he falls in love with the reverend's lovely and remote daughter, Eugenia. When he finds that Eugenia is involved in an incestuous relationship with her brutal older brother, Edgar, Adamson leaves the estate and continues his entomology work. Set in 1870, "The Conjugial Angel" chronicles a circle of bereaved people, including the sister of the poet Alfred Lord Tennyson, who engage in a séance and mesmerism to make contact with their dead loved ones.

In Byatt's next short story collection, *The Matisse Stories* (1993), she exhibits the influence of her favorite painter, Henri Matisse, and his vivid visual style on her work. In "Medusa's Ankles," Susannah, a successful academic, meditates on aging, identity, desire, and vulnerability after she has a disastrous trip to the hairstylist. The five stories in *The Djinn in the Nightingale's Eye* (1994) are fairy tales that explore the relationship between fantasy and reality and focus on the act of storytelling; two of the stories appeared earlier as part of the novel *Possession.* Published in 1998, *Elementals* contains both realistic and fantastic tales that illuminate the deep connections between literature and life. For example, an ice princess is pursued by a desert prince in "Cold." An artist, the prince creates for her a glass castle encased in ice. Although they are by their very natures unsuited for one another, the two lovers create a way to express their love. Critics note that Byatt also deftly fuses fantasy and realism in her latest collection of short fiction, *Little Black Book of Stories* (2003). In "The Thing in the Wood," Penny and Primrose, two young girls who had been sequestered in the countryside during World War II, are reunited years later and confront the monster in the woods that had terrified and traumatized them years earlier. In "A Stone Woman," a woman transforms from flesh to stone, which she finds both horrifying and redemptive.

CRITICAL RECEPTION

Byatt has garnered significant critical attention for her short fiction. Reviewers have often considered her stories in relation to her novels; a few critics have expressed a preference for her longer fictional works, contending that she is a more provocative and effective writer of longer works. Scholars have discussed Byatt as a postmodern Victorian writer and have analyzed the use of historical characters, events, and language in her fiction. In some instances, her recreation of Victorian literary style has also initiated discussions regarding the role of the postmodern novel and the connection between history and contemporary fiction. Most reviewers find her short fiction highly intelligent, carefully crafted, and finely detailed. For some readers, the density of her work is satisfying, but for others her fiction is detached, self-conscious, and didactic. There have been several feminist examinations of individual works, focusing in particular on Byatt's depiction of the female artist. Critics have also investigated the role of death in her short fiction and novels, as well as her treatment of the creative process and the power of art to transform human experience.

PRINCIPAL WORKS

Short Fiction

Sugar and Other Stories 1987
Angels and Insects: Two Novellas 1992
The Matisse Stories 1993
The Djinn in the Nightingale's Eye: Five Fairy Stories 1994
Elementals: Stories of Fire and Ice 1998
Little Black Book of Stories 2003

Other Major Works

The Shadow of a Sun (novel) 1964
Degrees of Freedom: The Novels of Iris Murdoch (criticism) 1965
The Game (novel) 1967
Wordsworth and Coleridge in Their Time (nonfiction) 1970; also published as *Unruly Times: Wordsworth and Coleridge in Their Time,* 1989
Iris Murdoch (criticism) 1976
The Virgin in the Garden (novel) 1978
Still Life (novel) 1986
Possession: A Romance (novel) 1990
Passions of the Mind: Selected Writings (nonfiction) 1991
Babel Tower (novel) 1996
The Biographer's Tale (novel) 2000
A Whistling Woman (novel) 2002

CRITICISM

Anne Duchêne (review date 10 April 1987)

SOURCE: Duchêne, Anne. "Ravening Time." *Times Literary Supplement* (10 April 1987): 395.

[*In the following mixed review of* Sugar and Other Stories, *Duchêne finds the short stories in the collection to be uneven in quality.*]

This is A. S. Byatt's first collection of short stories [***Sugar and Other Stories***]; there are eleven, of which seven have already appeared elsewhere. She has also, apart from her critical work, published four novels. These have shown her to be clever and composed, to have a clear and careful eye, a clean and careful pen, and to be unabashed by being beautifully schooled—indeed, highly academic: Cambridge recurs, as a natural centre, planets like Wordsworth and George Eliot and Forster revolve in her firmament. She has somewhat exquisite anxieties about the relationship of literature and art to life, and now and then abruptly and disconcertingly addresses the reader directly ("I had intended writing this novel in such-and-such a way, but . . ."). Under the polished surface and the occasionally professorial fidgeting, though, there runs a turbulent vein of more common speculation, about the nature of time, identity and death. Not surprisingly, in her novels, so many impulses and ideas only order themselves slowly into a pattern. The shift into the short story, at once more primitive and more delicate—the scratch on a stone, the painting of an egg-shell—must be difficult, one imagines, for a writer of such rigorous standards.

Before any critical cavilling begins, then, it must be reported that two of these stories are very fine indeed, and between them encompass virtually all this author's abiding concerns. **"Precipice-Encurled"** is an immensely elegant story, of literary provenance, based on Robert Browning's once not arriving, in the 1880s, at a hired summer-castle in the Apennines, to which English admirers had invited him. There is a shy Victorian maiden, up at the castle, and a young artist-lover who falls to his death; down in Venice and on the plains, late-Romantic energies are shading off into Jamesian urbanities, while Browning broods on Elizabeth, on death, and on the medium Sludge ("*At* the back is something simple, undifferentiated, indifferently intelligent, live"). The addition of a latter-day research student, introduced as underpinning, seems almost needless: the story really does float like a cloud above a precipice.

The title-story, **"Sugar"**, is of another, more powerful order. It takes up the author's habitual preoccupation with the peculiar properties of being a daughter, and uses her frequent tripartite current of grandmother-mother-daughter narrator. It centres on the death of the father, an English judge, in Amsterdam (which in turn allows digressions into Van Gogh, who, as readers of her last novel *Still Life* will remember, has absorbed much of the author's thinking recently). It is called **"Sugar"** partly because the narrator as a child was shown round her grandfather's sweet-making factory in Pontefract; but really because it is about the ravening of time and the puniness of memory's attempts to withstand it, and how our progenitors have to take on the stature of myth if they are not to melt away completely. The story is told in brilliant, firm detail and with unwavering control, rolling the generations together in headlong, deliquescent paragraphs. The roaring of time becomes like an avalanche or dam-burst, drenching and destroying, while the narrator struggles to stand on a few pieces of memory's rubble. This is supremely a short story which does not aspire to the condition of the novel.

Several of the other stories do, in comparison with these two, seem like reworkings of episodes from the novels. **"Rose-Coloured Teacups"** ravels up the grandmother-mother-daughter theme, in six pages, slightly unavailingly; **"The Next Room"** has a daughter, newly bereaved, fighting the persistence of her parents in her own present; **"Racine and the Tablecloth"** describes the despoiling of a clever schoolgirl by an hysterical headmistress, with precision but many *longueurs.*

Others merely bring a highly literary lady-writer's perception of what is happening inside her into conjunction with something untoward happening outside. One story (**"On the Day That E. M. Forster Died"**) involves her in a grisly encounter in Jermyn Street with a friend from Cambridge years before; another has her offering increasingly uneasy shelter to a disturbed student. **"Loss of Face"** allows a more cheerful interlude when she flies out, primed to speak of Milton and George Eliot, to a Far Eastern academic congress, and becomes confused among professors called Sun and professors called Moon.

Two more interesting stories stand apart. **"In the Air"** is a quite terrifying foray into the Pinter-land of menace. A widow walking her dog, another woman, blind, with her guide-dog, and a youth with a knife meet on a common, and take tea together. It is a quite flawless study in female panic, of the kind now sadly familiar. Lastly, the rogue story, **"The Dried Witch"**, is interesting because the author here throws out all her usual domestic and cultural supports, and imagines in a Far Eastern village a widow, bleached by solitude into irresponsibility, who is pegged out to be dried by the sun, in the standard village test of the jinx, the *iettatura.* Apart from the grandly baleful moment of death, the conscientious exoticism makes rather a dry bundle of twigs, and curiously diminishes the authorial presence.

It is a brave experiment. But otherwise, apart from the three triumphant pieces (including **"In the Air"**), one has to hope these stories of very familiar turn and rather uneven value have not impeded the sequel promised to *Still Life*: there are so many faithful admirers who want to know what happens to Felicia after Cambridge.

Anita Brookner (review date 11 April 1987)

SOURCE: Brookner, Anita. "Fear in a Handful of Pages." *The Spectator* (11 April 1987): 35-6.

[*In the following review, Brookner praises the veracity and strength of the stories in* Sugar and Other Stories, *but asserts that Byatt's style is better suited to the longer form of the novel.*]

The circumscribed life of the writer comes through with alarming strength in this collection of stories [***Sugar and Other Stories***]. A. S. Byatt is of course better known as the author of voluminous and impressive novels, constructed almost on Victorian lines, which entrap somewhere in their strong north-country narrative drive a fascination with pictures and an ability to describe them in minute but suggestive particulars. Somewhere, in the story called **'Sugar'**, which is in fact a fragment of autobiography to do with her father's death, she mentions, casually, yet with the truth she brings to all her observations, her fear of art. This seems to me more interesting than the fragment which surrounds it, yet 'fragment' will hardly do for the rock-like solidity of the memoir, with its intimations of cold, discomfort and Victorian restrictions, and its bleak attempt to recall without fantasy a family background, a family history.

Indeed, A. S. Byatt's determination to tell the truth, and the honourable discomfort that this engenders, militate against the setting up and resolution of situations or the transcription of incidents which are the essence of the short story. It is, on the other hand, the setting forth of histories which cannot be truncated that makes a novel. People who express a desire to write (and genuinely cannot) tend to say everything in four pages and get discouraged. Real writers set out on a journey the end of which cannot be entirely foreseen. Novelists waiting for another novel to form experience restlessness, the desire to get something down. These stories seem to me what A. S. Byatt has decided to work on in a dry time. They form a distinguished collection—for everything she writes is distinguished—but they cannot be said to add anything to the art of short-story writing, which seems to have been perfected, for the present time at least, by the two Canadian writers, Alice Munro and Mavis Gallant.

Only in one story **'In the Air'**, does the form appear to have been respected. Mrs Sugden is a widow and nervous. (There is a great deal of fear in this collection.) Every day she forces herself to go out with her dog, Wolfgang, for a long walk on the common. She knows that some day she will encounter violence, an irrational attack, some kind of threat. Therefore she is more than relieved to see the blind lady, Miss Tillotson, walking, unafraid, for her accustomed two hours. Except that on this occasion Miss Tillotson is being followed by an extravagant young man with overblown features and pink shoe laces who occasionally imitates an aeroplane. Catching up with Miss Tillotson, Mrs Sudgen reasons that there is safety in numbers. The young man introduces himself as Barry, unemployed. Miss Tillotson, who cannot see him and who has been in social work all her life, is not much affected, but Mrs Sugden recognises him as the enemy. Forced to walk as a trio, for Barry has no reason to leave them alone, they ritually encompass the common. Miss Tillotson invites Mrs Sugden, who has by now taken her arm, to tea, to which Barry assents enthusiastically. This is authentically terrifying. The problem is that even if Mrs Sugden leaves Miss Tillotson, one of them is going to be alone with Barry.

The gathering horror of this story, with its anxiety truly embodied in a character and a circumstance, makes an impact which none of the other stories match because in a sense they contain neither. Death is present, almost overwhelmingly, in the suicide of an awkward boy, in an accident on a mountain side, in the announcement, on a newsvendor's placard, of E. M. Forster's demise, admittedly at the age of 91. It is a world of misadventure, in which events are announced by quotations from Ruskin, Browning, or Henry James. The story, **'Precipice-Encurled'**, is in fact about Browning, whose journey to Florence was aborted by the death in a storm of a young house guest at the villa in which he himself was intending to stay. In **'The Next Room'**, ghostly voices alert Joanna Hope to the fact that her much tolerated parents will not leave her alone, even though she has seen her mother through the crematorium ('they must wait for the smoke') and put her house on the market. In **'The Dried Witch'**, a story that takes place in Indonesia, the witch of the title, A-Oa, is put to death by being tied to a tree and left for three days in the broiling sun. The ghost of a dead child appears, but not to his mother who longs to see him.

With the exception of silly, vulnerable (and lifelike) Mrs Sugden, the narrator of most of these stories is a strong, clever woman, doomed to exorcise her fears by writing. The girl heroine of **'Racine and a Tablecloth'** outwits her mediocre but steel-willed headmistress by continuing to be clever despite warnings, perhaps no longer familiar to schoolchildren, that mediocrity encapsulates the higher virtues. The girl manages to write her examination answers in spite of the minor breakdown she is so obviously suffering. Lecture tours are undertaken, surveys prepared, the London Library visited on a daily basis, problem children welcomed. It is a strenuous and uncomfortable world, kept cool and practical by very real Victorian virtues.

One returns to the memoir called **'Sugar'**. On his way back from a journey in Europe, A. S. Byatt's father was taken ill at Schiphol airport and forced to spend some time in an Amsterdam hospital. Visiting him daily, the author passed her free time in the Van Gogh museum at Otterlo. She has used Van Gogh to great effect in her novel, *Still Life,* attracted by that lucid pictorial intelligence, that socially uncontainable behaviour, and that obsession with the light of the sun, the white or yellow light that makes northern visitors drunk.

There is something of this dichotomy of light and dark in **'Sugar'**, although the dark wins. It is the dark not of her father's death, which was accomplished with good humour and good manners, but of the less explicable extravagances of her mother and her paternal grandfather. Dark houses, by no means as reassuring as the Hoogstraten on the jacket, cold winds, an inefficient embroidery of repressive or irritating fact by a mother who had a gift for anecdote but not for fiction, and above all the remembered leap of the infant A. S. Byatt into her father's arms, a leap which she cannot remember as ending in safety, or indeed ending at all, leave an aftertaste of considerable sadness in the reader. The exercise is a strong one, but finally it is less about the events themselves than about the strenuous attempt to get them down. The facts are got down, wrestled down, almost, in an heroic narrative that eschews all temptation to fantasy. That fear of art, so fleetingly but determinedly mentioned, might explain the unadorned writing. It might, on the other hand, allude to a more primitive fear, one more widely shared than is generally acknowledged. Will writing make it go away? Surely this is a theme for a novel, a long novel, which, equally surely, A. S. Byatt must some day write.

Francis Spufford (review date 25 June 1987)

SOURCE: Spufford, Francis. "The Mantle of Jehovah." *London Review of Books* 9, no. 12 (25 June 1987): 22-3.

[*In the following review, Spufford identifies loss as the central theme of* Sugar and Other Stories *and examines Byatt's stories within the context of her novels.*]

To keep a single vision single, or perhaps to conserve their own energy, writers who deal in strong feelings and violent flavours most often choose narrow canvases. Not, however, A. S. Byatt. Her writing has been synoptically intense. It has been so, anomalously, in a genre (the English social novel) which makes comparisons with other violently-flavoured writers, outside the genre, seem silly. You could, of course, draw a contrast simply in terms of range of Bad Moments covered: Norman Mailer has preferred to steer clear of the peculiar pains of childbirth, and Andrea Dworkin has chosen not to dwell on the distinctive horror an uneasy Christmas dinner can become, while Byatt can and has handled both as elements in her continuing series of novels.

That series began with *The Virgin in the Garden* in 1981, and proceeded with *Still Life* in 1985; more is promised. In the meantime comes a book of short stories, ***Sugar,*** more distinct in method than in concerns. Several of the pieces in it can be seen as out-takes from the long movement of the series, where her subject is a biography of what was recently called this country's 'cultivated class': from its post-war beginnings in a fusion of the lettered gentry and the old-style educationally-mobile working-class, through its maturity in the long warm years of the grammar schools, to (presumably—Ms Byatt's fictions have not taken the story so far) its present state of bewilderment. Both novels have had framing themes: in the one case, Elizabethan drama, and in the other Van Gogh. She has had much to say about, respectively, virginity and the implications of *nature morte,* whether through her plot or at one discursive remove from it. But though the characters' lives are cultured, and revealingly cultural, the strongest impression you are likely to take from the novels is of the desperate fragility of experience, the way it is likely to break down into biological or sexual or mental hurts that gain force from their close conjunction with the shapes of the culture. The catastrophes of the mind and flesh meet the flesh and mind's most deliberate creations. For Byatt, and so for the reader, verse drama joins to the rupture of virginity, Suez joins to sexual terror, Leavis to tainted love.

The end of the Prologue to *The Virgin in the Garden* declares the double—or complicatedly single—intention. Daniel, a priest, leaves an exhibition at the National Portrait Gallery which has gathered, retrospectively and iconically, many of the concerns of the main action of the book, set 16 years earlier, to which we are about to be introduced. Daniel has to see someone:

> Someone was a woman whose son had been damaged in a smash. He had been a beautiful boy and still was, a walking unreal figure of a beautiful boy, a wax doll inhabited alternately by a screaming daemon and a primitive organism that ate and bulged and slept, amoeba-like. His father had been unable to bear it and had left. The woman had been a good teacher, and now was not, had had friends, and now did not, had had a pleasant body, and now did not.

Much of what is going on at this moment of particular intensity can be taken as more widely typical. The use of biological terminology, the brutally physical clinching words like 'bulged', and especially the ruthless parallelism, all enforce the truth of the view we are being given of a life. Elsewhere the truth of pain is enforced in other ways, but enforcement remains a constant factor. She is consistently willing to risk excess in language and metaphor so long as the effect achieved is, in her terms, appropriately strong. It is as if a sort of honesty acts on her as the most potent and compelling of principles, with the making of this sort of fiction as its necessary praxis. C.S. Lewis observed with partisan savagery that the prospect of near-universal damnation worried the bright young Calvinists of the 1590s no more than the imminent liquidation of the bourgeoisie worried the bright young Marxists of the 1930s: and something of the same disregarding fire burns in A. S. Byatt so far as her readers' more evasive sensibilities are concerned. A propos of pastoral calls on the sick, the character Stephanie remarks to the curate Daniel, 'Conventions . . . can make a slow, bearable way of getting into—bits of life. You can't always rush people to extremes. In case people can't stand them.' 'Extremes exist,' replies Daniel, firmly enough to win this fictional argument, and for us to take this as the sufficient answer to our own bruised query, as the final Byatt word.

We encounter extremes, all right, and not only of suffering. The novels are rich in less spectacular kinds of thinking and feeling that have been pushed towards some absolute. Because Daniel hides his force beneath a fat exterior and an uncontentious attitude to theology, we are told that no one notices that he is a fanatic. For a priest to have a vocation is unremarkable, though probably only Byatt would have credited him with quite this kind of extreme commitment: it is rather stranger that a young merchant banker should manifest the signs of a vocation, a complete 'directedness' to his imagination. In language appropriate to his class and period (1957 or so), he eulogises the Thames as the emblem of trade. What the banker has so obviously, other characters have in quieter ways: an animating idea. But we are a long way from the grounds of Lewes's complaint that Mr Micawber was no more alive than a galvanised frog's leg. Byatt's people are not mechanical, or predictable, though they are rather more coherent than most fictional characters. In that, they resemble the novels as a whole, in which extremity sometimes seems as much to enable coherence as coherence is used as a device to indicate extremity. We are on paradoxical ground. While both the novels put forward experience as contingent and fissile, both exploit the full powers of omnipotent authorship to give authority to contingency.

The power of what results is undeniable. Extremes exist, but in life we rely on the inarticulacy of the extreme to keep it muted and bearable. With monumental clarity Byatt takes her readers to places in the soul they had not imagined could be so well-lit for their observation. If at times one cannot believe, quite, in the normality of her characters, their disease is that useful ailment, a disease of lucidity. Other writers may give us a madness, or a wedding-night, or the reading of a poem, but only Byatt consistently delivers intellectual madnesses, love-making as reflective as it is tumultuous, poems considered with painful experience and the whole resources of a mind. It is extraordinary to read. When, in *Still Life,* Daniel and Stephanie, who have been married for some time, go to bed certain of each other yet conscious of passions blunted by circumstance and possibilities dissipated, the critical words of Stephanie's abandoned profession 'wandered loose and unused. Peripateia. Anguish. Morphology . . . Men have died and worms have eaten them, but not for love nor yet for constriction of vocabulary.' Byatt gains for her reader something analogous to the astonishment an adolescent feels at the scale and complexity of newly-glimpsed grown-up feelings, without the shallowness. Can it all be so big? Sometimes it can.

And sometimes it surely cannot. Ms Byatt, for example, believes in appropriating the more brutally reductive parts of the male vocabulary for talking about sex, partly from a conviction, I think, that an action involving power should register its language, and presumably, also, to borrow the confident potency of such words for her own ends. They do, after all, make for instant focus of a sort. A female character being capably, ruthlessly and benevolently brought to her first orgasm is described as being 'searched': the association of the wound is intended. You could call the effect penetrating, though you might well rather not. You are more likely to object, not on grounds of taste, but because of the clarity the technique so violently claims. In this instance, and in others, it can seem that potency or coherence are being taken as proofs of truth without its being acknowledged that truth does not necessarily reside in what can, no matter how impressively, be clearly seen. Fervent lucidity is a dangerous technique: once belief is called into question, the stylisation of the characters begins to seem dubious. Agitation and worry follow. One begins to wonder whether, despite the unequivocally realistic premises of the writing, Byatt has not moved surreptitiously into fantasy—a willed fantasy about psychology, a shadow-play rather than a drama. How far can one second her use of authorial omnipotence? Surely no other writer since Hardy has so comprehensively donned the mantle of Jehovah smiting the Egyptians with plagues, so thoroughly used the prerogative of blighting, distorting and crushing lives.

A naked madman stands in a school pond decked in flowers, cutting gashes in himself with a knife; he has been thinking a little too much about ley-lines. A major and sympathetic character is killed suddenly, all too believably, by a badly-wired fridge. Damaged people damage others without intending to, or intending to, while the undamaged walk away. Malign chance works overtime. More pressing than discomfort at individual horrors is the sense that experience is being ordered inhumanely. When the man I have mentioned goes Lear-crazy, one of the characters actually thinks how shaking it is for madness to take such a literary, utterly revealing form, so far beyond ordinary incoherence. On that occasion one's nervousness has been recognised, pre-empted, and itself patterned into the book, but the reader is likely to feel it as a much more abiding reservation—as a reason, ultimately, to withhold the assent which the novels demand while granting them great respect.

One of the great pleasures of the novels is Byatt's passion for describing, at length, people looking at things: at pictures, at architecture, at objects. They see so well one is grateful for one's borrowed eyes. They make connections, they speculate, they observe extravagantly. There could be little better company in which to consider bakelite or a statue of Actaeon or Van Gogh's *Reapers,* few more impressive guides than Byatt, for though the intensity of the looking does contribute to the books' worrying stylisation, the set-pieces of looking—taken simply as pieces of prose—vindicate her largesse of language. ***Sugar*** is equally interested in seeing, but there are no set-pieces; the stories break up and diffuse the acts of regard. The title piece, narrated by a woman sojourning in Amsterdam while her father dies slowly in hospital there, interlaces passages of memory and regret with visits to the Rijksmuseum, taking from the pictures single private observations and pursuing, from moment to moment, wholly private associations. She traces out, with fine concentration, the various walls of her childhood on which a Vermeer and a Van Gogh print have hung. The contrasts drawn—between the then of the pictures and the now of the dying father, between the stillness of the gallery and a sudden whiff of teargas on the street outside—come across as serious, satisfactory, unflip, unfacile because Byatt so obviously has no easy patterning to lay on them, no 'theoretical' impulsion to distinguish them, only hard thinking, which is the wrong word for the narrative compound of feeling, event, reflection. In Byatt's case, that compound comes closer to resembling thinking than for most writers. She preserves the shapes of the pictures seen, and makes their description a shape in the story, without any forcing of the story's concerns onto the pictures. Here, response modestly remains response. Which is appropriate, since this story, like most of the others in the volume, concerns the difficulties of extracting meaning from experience—a shift, as it were, from a biographical to an autobiographical view of lives, in terms of *point d'appui.*

Sugar is about losses: of possibilities, of parents, of children, of love, of ideas, of the ability to reach certain delicate and composed states of feeling, of equilibrium, of hope, even of one's saving diseases. On a Victorian family holiday in Italy, a young woman outwardly reconciled to flattened, self-forgetting spinsterhood suddenly sees the new prospect of a new sort of life; the young painter she has fallen in love with climbs into the Appennines the next day, achieves a remarkable sketch, glimpses *his* calling for the first time, and falls to his death in a gust of wind. A novelist named Mrs Smith rejoices in the long uncluttered perspectives of her middle age and conceives a plan for a long novel rather like *The Virgin in the Garden*; in the street she meets precisely the person to take the bloom off her elation, and then contracts a cancer which ensures she'll not have time enough for the novel. And so on. Yet the tone is never apocalyptic: it is, on the contrary, deeply sympathetic, close to the perceptions of the characters, elegantly and scrupulously attentive to their struggles. Only the title story is written in the first person, but many of the others deliver the workings of a mind to us with an intimacy that approaches that of the directly first-person view and shares, importantly, its formal restrictions. Intimate loss reduces people; loss viewed intimately places limits on stories. With the loss of present certainties comes a difficulty in retrieving the authentic shape of what has been lost. The narrator of **'Sugar'** (the story) can handle her own scruples, folding them back again and again into the tissue of her memory until they become part of her impression of her father. His return home on leave during the war:

> This event was a storied event, already lived over and over, in imagination and hope, in the invented future . . . More things come back as I write; the gold-winged buttons on his jacket, forgotten between then and now. None of these words, none of these things recall him. The gold-winged, fire-haired figure in the doorway is and was myth, though he did come back, he was there.

Elsewhere Byatt herself makes frequent authorial interventions and interruptions, in propria persona, to weigh and consider, to sift the value of what is known in formal almost essay-like deliberations; and to remind us, as if that too were an aspect of difficulty, that these are stories, constructed things it is proper to halt with reservations and deconstructions. A suggestion of metafiction, of uncertainties found to be themselves fictionally productive? Not quite. Byatt's interruptions may seem to have the ludic touch, but they lack the centrifugal ludic conviction. This 'uncertain' manner complements and to some extent continues her previous certainties; the change is less substantial than it appears. A certain amount of dovetailing is discernible.

The first story in ***Sugar,*** **'Racine and the Tablecloth'**, recounts the school life of a scholarship girl, Emily, who wants to be understood. By being understood she means something quite precise. For five years or so she is quietly persecuted by a genteel mistress in a feud that is the worse for being totally unacknowledged. At home in the Potteries Emily has an aunt whose life has been given over, at the expense of herself, to looking after other people and doing embroidery. Caught in a vice only she feels between the example of the aunt and the criticisms of the teacher, Emily does what she does best, which is academic work. She has an angular, precocious brilliance; the Racine set text excites her and bores the other girls. She comes remorselessly first in everything except maths and domestic science. But none of this is the occasion for praise, which she might not want anyway; the ethos of the school runs more to ladylike accomplishment, incarnated in the mistress. What Emily wants is for none of these circumstances to matter, for her best work to be taken dryly and dispassionately for what it is, for its care and its intentions and its insights to be comprehended. Having opted sensibly for atheism, she proceeds to invent with one corner of her mind a God called the Reader 'whose nature was not to love but to understand'. Emily does not manage to keep the jaws of the vice apart: why, after all, should she have that kind of strength? Lectured at on the evils of the competitive spirit just before her A levels, she bursts into tears which last for three days. When the mistress comes to her bedside and makes a horribly blanketing protestation of concern, Emily is forced more or less to apologise: 'it felt,' in a nice phrase, 'like a recantation without there having been an affirmation to recant.' She does her papers all right, and excels, but can no longer believe in the possibility of that dry, fair academic Light in which it is possible to work unhurt.

The story is set very definitely in Emily's past, and whether Emily can remember correctly what happened is a kind of issue in it. Could Miss Crichton-Walker really have called Emily depraved? Upon such unanswered questions hangs the larger question of whether Emily has grown to be able to understand what happened. To save urgency from being dissipated, to give importance to that understanding, Byatt attaches the live irony of a brief epilogue in which we see Emily failing—under the restraint of her own scarring—to prevent her daughter's academic hopes from being blighted in the same way. Though for different reasons: in the present the snuffer-out of the Light takes the form of a deputy head castigating Emily for her middle-class academic prejudices. Already, in that neat ironic arrangement, you can see one of the real limits to the influence of uncertainty in the story. Meticulous measurements of memory aside, the narration follows the certainties of balanced images, revealing metaphors and, above all, convinced authorial judgments. However many hints of metatextuality there may be, you will find no flirtation here with theories that question the propriety of authorial knowledge. No writer could be farther than Ms Byatt from the dissociations of the Nouveau Roman. In **'Racine and the Tablecloth'** description and commentary are always united. Each incident is given a permeating and graceful significance that cannot be called imposed because it is not in the nature of the writing to recognise intrinsically inimical differences between characters and landscapes, objects and humans. There is a non-stop play of metaphor, like a thinking fountain. One notes, too, her distance from those writers who have seen the worst misery of boarding-school as the fearful lack of proportion it imposes on children—a promising direction for a fiction about uncertainty.

In his radio play *Where are they now?* Tom Stoppard gives a character the satisfying chance to complain, with hindsight, of 'the momentous trivialities and tiny desolations', the 'hollow fear of inconsiderable matters'. But Byatt is not having any. While she concurs with, and captures beautifully, the desperate, vulnerable privacies of children, and their susceptibility to atmosphere, she insists on the immutability of the line of a life established by such hollow fears. Emily does not escape her school, and what it did to her. The fears, in fact, were not hollow, the losses not temporary. And Byatt, as ever, shows herself to be supremely good at establishing the absolute nature of some feelings, of which loss is one. ***Sugar*** has, in fact, the same confidence as the novels in what a writer can show, with a strategically diminished confidence in what a character can know: a less worrying version of extreme coherence.

'Precipice-Encurled', the story containing the accident in the Appennines, also gives us (a passage of immaculate ventriloquism) Browning musing on the creation of characters for his dramatic monologues. What, he asks, lies behind the individual diversities of man? What lies at the back of him, Browning? '"The best part of my life," he told himself, "the life I have lived most intensely, has been the fitting, the infiltrating, the inserting the self of another man or woman, explored and sleekly filled out, as fingers swell a glove."' Perhaps that is because at the back of the *him* that he puts at the back of his characters, he has, at 'my best times', something close to a generic (or divine) creative intelligence: 'something simple, undifferentiated, indifferently intelligent, live'. This is, of course, meant as a homage—as well as possessing an organic importance in the story—but it is tempting to imagine that Byatt sees herself (at her best times) putting on those gloves and wriggling her fingers, because, looking at ***Sugar,*** it seems that whatever she does we come back to the multivalent power of the articulate voice, the commanding word. Long live (with reservations) Jehovah.

Keith Cushman (review date winter 1988)

SOURCE: Cushman, Keith. Review of *Sugar and Other Stories,* by A. S. Byatt. *Studies in Short Fiction* 25, no. 1 (winter 1988): 80-1.

[*In the following mixed review of* Sugar and Other Stories, *Cushman compares Byatt's fiction to that of her sister, Margaret Drabble.*]

Antonia Byatt doesn't advertise it, but she is the older sister of Margaret Drabble. She has published four novels as well as two critical studies: *Wordsworth and Coleridge in Their Time* and a book about Iris Murdoch. ***Sugar*** is her first collection of stories.

It's not fair to compare Byatt's fiction to that of her sister, but the comparison is inevitable. Though both writers are extremely literary, their literariness differs in kind. Drabble habitually constructs her novels on the concealed foundation of earlier novels by such writers as George Eliot, Bennett, and Woolf. But Drabble rarely *seems* literary. Her fiction is warm and disarmingly direct, and she establishes an agreeably intimate bond with her reader.

In contrast, Byatt's literariness expresses itself in her detached, self-conscious manner. Her fiction presents an icy surface to the world. Byatt's stories are filled with sensitive women who brood about time, identity, family, art, and life's incertitude. The stories are tightly written and richly nuanced. But they mostly seem too solemn and inward and, in the bargain, over-educated.

Byatt populates these stories with literary people. An unhappy scholarship girl reads Racine and does battle with a difficult headmistress. A novelist takes into her home a troubled boy who is like a character she had created. **"Loss of Face,"** which takes place at a Far Eastern academic conference, is a Bech story without Updike's sense of humor. The stylish **"Precipice-Encurled"** features the aged Robert Browning. In another story Mrs. Smith encounters a now-mad friend from Cambridge on Jermyn Street on the day E. M. Forster died. The story reads like a dark footnote to *Mrs. Dalloway*: "How precarious it was, the sense of self in the dark bath of uncertainty." Literature can only distract us from the unshakable facts of time and death.

The title-story, originally published in the *New Yorker,* is the most impressive. The death of the narrator's father is the central event of **"Sugar."** In beautifully flowing, modulated prose, the narrator thinks back on parents and grandparents, great-aunts and great-uncles, and briefly on the little sister she shared a room with. As a child the narrator was impressed by the long ropes of processed sugar she saw in her grandfather's candy factory. But the sugar in the title really refers to memory and the way we "select and confect" from our past to give our lives shape and meaning, to save ourselves. Time is so all-consuming that we must convert our parents and grandparents into myths if we are not to lose them altogether:

> More things come back as I write; the gold-winged buttons on his jacket, forgotten between then and now. None of these words, none of these things recall him. The gold-winged, fire-haired figure in the doorway is and was myth, though he did come back, he was there, at that time, and I did make that leap. After things have happened, when we have taken a breath and a look, we begin to know what they are and were, we begin to tell them to ourselves. Fast, fast these things took and take their place beside other markers, the teapot, the horse trough, real apples and plums, a white ankle, the coalscuttle, two dolls in cellophane, a gas oven, a black and white dog, gold-winged buttons, the melded and twisting hanks of brown and white sugar.

"Sugar" is lovely, but Byatt fails to duplicate its powerful though understated emotional impact elsewhere in the collection.

Sugar and Other Stories is the work of a skillful, polished writer. But though there is often much to admire in this book, I didn't always find a great deal to like.

Jane Campbell (essay date spring 1991)

SOURCE: Campbell, Jane. "'The Somehow May Be Thishow': Fact, Fiction, and Intertextuality in Antonia Byatt's 'Precipice-Encurled'." *Studies in Short Fiction* 28, no. 2 (spring 1991): 115-23.

[*In the following essay, Campbell provides a stylistic and thematic overview of "Precipice-Encurled," focusing on Byatt's merging of fact and fiction in the story as well as on her inclusion, as embedded text, of other authors' works.*]

Antonia Byatt's collection of short stories, ***Sugar*** (1987), continues her exploration of the struggle of language with things. In the title story, the last in the volume, the narrator recalls, on the occasion of her father's dying, the versions of family history that have been handed down. The central metaphor is of narration as confecting. As a small girl the narrator was shown by her grandfather, a candy manufacturer, how the stripes in the humbug candy were produced: "It's the air that does it," he tells her. "Nothing but whipping in air. There's no difference between the two stripes in a humbug but air" (**"Sugar"** 244). Self-consciously reflecting on her own confections as she "whips in air," the narrator struggles for accuracy, at the same time acknowledging its impossibility: "The real thing, the true moment, is . . . inaccessible" (248).

In this collection one story stands apart from the others, both in its use of literary history and biography and in its formulation of the problems of confection. Entitled **"Precipice-Encurled,"** it immediately precedes **"Sugar."** Its title comes from Robert Browning's poem "De Gustibis—," in which the poet declares, "What I love best in all the world / Is a castle, precipice-encurled, / In a gash of the wind-grieved Apennine" (14-16). Ostensibly, the story tells of an occasion in 1882, in the last decade of Browning's life, when the poet and his sister Sarianna (his companion after his wife's death) fail to carry out their plan of visiting friends at a villa in the Apennines. What prevents them is the death of their friends' house guest, a young English painter named Joshua Riddell. Intent on capturing the appearance of an approaching storm, Joshua is swept from his perch on a cliff and dashed to pieces. The young painter and the old poet, the reader is made to feel, would have understood each other: they share a passion for accuracy about the most minute and insignificant details of the human and natural worlds. The plot thus embodies one of Browning's favorite themes, opportunity missed. This narrative itself is enclosed in, and encloses, two more stories on the same theme—stories of unfulfilled love. Joshua's death cuts short a tender relationship with his host's daughter Juliana, and (according to the hypothesis of another of Byatt's characters, a twentieth-century scholar) Browning is falling in love with Mrs. Bronson, his hostess during his visits to Venice, who returns his affection but remains unaware of his passion. The Brownings plan to visit Mrs. Bronson later that year but are prevented, by flooded roads and illness, from reaching Venice, although they do so in 1883. Both love stories are left without conclusions; the image of Mrs. Bronson, waiting for Browning, begins the story, and Joshua's unfinished portrait of Juliana ends it.

The plot thus represents the intrusion of destructive chance happenings into the life of imagination and emotion. The title refers to the precariously occupied spaces of love and art, and the narrative method demonstrates the hazards of creativity. Through Browning's and Joshua's work and in its own movement, the story shows the creative mind's encircling, assimilating work—and the inevitable escape of "the real thing" from the mind's grasp. In the words Juliet Dusinberre has used of Byatt's novel *The Virgin in the Garden,* this short story "seems to declare that the real is beyond form" (61).

It is the epigraph, however, rather than the title, that provides the most telling clue to the story's special qualities:

> What's this then, which proves good yet seems untrue?
> Is fiction, which makes fact alive, fact too?
> The somehow may be thishow.

The lines, with some interesting omissions and a significant change in punctuation, are from Browning's *The Ring and the Book:*

> Well, now; there's nothing in nor out o' the world
> Good except truth: yet this, the something else,
> What's this then, which proves good yet seems untrue?
> This that I mixed with truth, motions of mine
> That quickened, made the inertness malleolable
> O' the gold was not mine,—what's your name for this?
> Are means to the end, themselves in part the end?
> Is fiction which makes fact alive, fact too?
> The somehow may be thishow.
>
> (I.693-700)

Byatt uses Browning's words to hint slyly at her own way of using biography. At the center of her story, surrounded by documented details of Browning's life and quotations from his work, and by an unnamed work of twentieth-century scholarship, Byatt has placed an example of "fiction which makes fact alive." By adding the comma where Browning did not use one, she suggests that fiction-making is inevitable whenever the imagination is at work on facts. The story of Joshua and Juliana (which even the dust jacket of ***Sugar*** encourages us to read as fact, "an almost unremembered incident on Browning's Italian travels") is invented. The facts are that the Brownings had been invited by the Cholmondeleys (not the Fishwicks) to visit them on the island of Ischia (not in the Apennines); their visit was canceled because the Cholmondeleys' guest, Miss Wade, accidentally fell from a ledge while sketching the sunset, and died of her injuries.

On the other hand, the scholar and the hostess, who both may appear to be invented, are real. Although, unlike Mrs. Bronson, he is never named by Byatt, the scholar is Michael Meredith. His book *More than Friend* (1985) contains, after a long introductory essay, the Browning-Bronson letters, edited with meticulous attention to facts—including the proposed visit to Ischia and the death of Miss Wade (xii, 15n3). The craftsmanship with which Byatt mixes fact and fiction is so skillful that a reviewer of Byatt's most recent novel, *Possession,* praises **"Precipice-Encurled"** for its achievement as historical fiction; in comparing the story with the novel, the reviewer says that for the story the details of Browning's life were "all *there;* the art was in the gathering and sorting" (Karlin 18). It is, however, the "something else" that was *not* "there" that gives life to the story. By calling into question the existence of the boundary line between fact and fiction, Byatt daringly shows both the impossibility of originality and, conversely, the inevitability, in all writing, of invention and "confection." Embedded in her story are additional texts. Meredith's book, which provides Byatt's starting point, itself contains other texts as appendices: Mrs. Bronson's two published reminiscences of Browning, and a memoir by an American acquaintance, Daniel Sargent Curtis. Several other works are intertextually present, including Browning's poems, James's *Aspern Papers* and "The Private Life," Christopher Smart's *Song to David,* Andrew Marvell's "Mower's Song," Shakespeare's *As You Like It,* and Ruskin's *Modern Painters.* The workings of the imagination with these texts are part of Byatt's subject.

The four-part structure represents the encircling work of the imagination as it appropriates its material. The first two parts are very short. The story opens with the "lady," Mrs. Bronson (she is not named until the fourth part), sitting in her house in Venice, waiting for Browning. This part appears reliably factual: there are descriptions of the lady as she appears in portraits and photographs and details of her life—the number of her servants, the names of her dogs, and her love of delicate objects, together with the information that Henry James gave her a small role in *The Aspern Papers* and planned to make her the central character in a novel. Yet even here fiction creeps in, as the narrator speculates on the party to which the lady's daughter may have gone on the afternoon when her mother "sits, or might be supposed to sit" in the window—and on the umbrella the daughter may have taken with her. The narrator also interprets the lady's expression as shown in "the portraits, more than one, tallying" (Meredith reproduces three portraits and two photographs) as "an indefinable air of disappointment" (185).

In the second section, set in the twentieth century, the scholar is introduced, working with letters and other documents to construct his story. He "combs" the facts—including Browning's poem "Inapprehensiveness," which the scholar interprets as a confession of Browning's love—in the direction of the hypothesis of the old poet's "dormant passion" for the lady. The scholar's work borders on fiction as he gives a shape, "subtle, not too dramatic," to the facts, as his imagination curls around the woman whom "he likes because he now knows her, has pieced her together" (187). After recording Browning's missed visit to Mrs. Bronson in 1882, he writes, "He was in danger of allowing the friendship to cool," and the narrator adds possible interpretations: "perhaps anxious on her behalf, perhaps on the poet's, perhaps on his own" (188). As Mrs. Bronson and Browning have been enclosed by the scholar's biography the scholar is now enclosed by Byatt's narrative—and both the scholar and the narrator are "piecing together" their subjects.

Browning, who has been at the periphery of the first and second sections, is at the center of the third. In his hotel room in the mountains he reflects upon his two selves—his expansive public self, which pursues facts in the outer world, and his creative private self, which uses these facts, and which he imagines as "a brilliant baroque chapel at the center of a decorous and unremarkable house" (189). The stream of his associations leads him to the idea that Descartes would be a suitable subject for a poem and he thinks of how he could "inhabit" the philosopher, making the "paraphernalia" of Descartes's world spin around "the naked cogito." "The best part of my life," he thinks, "has been the fitting, the infiltrating, the inventing the self of another man or woman, explored and sleekly filled out, as fingers swell a glove." Yet he himself, who gives "coherence and vitality" to these other selves, is "just such another concatenation" (191). He reviews his favorite characters—the Duchess, Karshish the Arab physician, the risen Lazarus, David, Christopher Smart—noting that they have all shared his own "lively and indifferent interest in everything" (193). These thoughts take him to Sludge the Medium through whom, following his principle of giving "true opinions to great liars," he has expressed his own vision of the creative intelligence "at the back" of the universe: "something simple, undifferentiated, intelligent, alive" (193-94). His reverie is interrupted by Sarianna who tells him of a fellow guest, Mrs. Miller, who wears "an aviary on her head" (194); the next day Browning's public self autographs Mrs. Miller's birthday book and tells her of the proposed visit to the Fishwicks, and she recites the lines about the precipice-encurled castle. In this section, Browning is both enclosed by Byatt's narrator and encloses other creative selves, and his imaginative piecing together of fact and fiction mirrors Byatt's.

The fourth section, much the longest, presents the—literally—precipice-encurled heart of the story. As she and her family prepare for Browning's visit, Juliana wonders what the poet will "make" of them. The process of creativity is the subject of this section, but this process is either, like Joshua's, broken off in the middle or, like Browning's as imagined by Juliana, never begun. Joshua begins to sketch Juliana's "extremely pleasant" but unremarkable face, feels their souls meet, and they kiss. The next morning, after spending the night wrestling alone with the conflict between his new love and his responsibility to the "empty greenness" of his "primitive innocence, before," Joshua goes up the cliff to paint; he wants to look at "the land beyond habitation" (204). Remembering Ruskin's words about mountains and a painting by Monet, he perches in an "eyrie" on the precipice and begins to work. He is alternately "miserable" at his "failures of vision" and "supremely happy" as he experiences self-oblivious absorption, "unaware of himself and wholly aware of rock formations, sunlight and visible empty air" (209). As the sky suddenly darkens he resolves to try to follow Monet's example, painting light itself and "the act of seeing" (210). Losing his footing as the ice pellets strike him, "still thinking of Ruskin and Monet" (211), he falls to his death. The narrator then records the impact of the death on Browning, who reflects briefly on the unknown young man: "his imagination . . . reached after him and imagined him, in his turn . . . reaching after the unattainable" (212). When Mrs. Miller asks if he will compose a poem about the death, he replies that he is left "mute" by such events; he does, however, write a poem about Mrs. Miller, "clothed with murder" in her hat of birds' wings (213). In the twentieth century, the scholar is at first hopeful that Browning will now visit Mrs. Bronson, then disappointed, as he reads more letters. The last image is of the unfinished sketch that "Aunt Juliana" keeps pressed in the family Bible, of "a young girl who looked out of one live eye and one blank, unseeing one, oval like those on monumental sculpture" (214).

With this image the encircling process is concluded, but all the narratives—and all the creative experiences they examine—are left incomplete, and all hold within them potential subjects that are not mined by any artist. Mrs. Bronson's story is described by the scholar, Meredith, as "the novel Henry James missed" (xxv); Descartes never becomes the subject of a poem by Browning, nor does Browning ever 'make' anything of the Fishwicks or of Joshua; Joshua never completes either of his sketches.

In its use of fact and fiction the story produces an effect of *trompe l'oeil.* The scholar, who to the uninitiated reader appears imaginary (as Mrs. Bronson herself may) is real. Joshua (the Riddell/riddle), who seems real to the same reader, is imaginary. The impression of the reader who does not have a prior knowledge of the facts is that the scholar, in his eagerness to reclaim Mrs. Bronson—to do what James had merely planned to do—and to construct a love story for Browning's old age, has missed the poignant story of youthful ambition and young love that Browning also missed. In fact, there was no story to miss. Byatt, marginalizing both the scholar and his subject, and altering the facts of Browning's itinerary in 1882, creates a story for the fourth section of **"Precipice-Encurled"** that has more apparent authenticity than any other part. The question "what, then, is real?" can also be asked from another perspective. Noting that the story of male creative endeavor (supported, in Browning's case, by the quiet, loyal sister) is framed by the images of two passive women, and that Byatt has changed a female sketcher to a male (because in the late nineteenth century only males could take art seriously?), we may recognize a feminist subtext that plays with sexual stereotypes. The story offers multiple perspectives.

"A good scholar may permissibly invent, he may have a hypothesis, but fiction is barred," observes the narrator (187-88). Her own procedures explore and threaten the line between scholarly invention and fiction. She moves from dependence on Meredith to innovative use of James to bolder manipulation, finally departing from fact—and other texts—altogether. She also shows that both Meredith and—much more daringly—Browning combine fact and fiction. Browning imagined Smart noticing not only the whale and the polyanthus, which Smart did include in his *Song to David,* but also the blossoms of Virgin's Bower, which he did not (Browning "Parleying with Christopher Smart" 195-98; Smart *Song to David* 310, 456-57). Starting with the account of the raising of Lazarus in John 11:1-44, he imagines the life of Lazarus afterward, about which John is silent—and encloses this story in that told by Karshish, whom Browning has also imagined. The narrator's work in this third section parallels Browning's. When Sarianna opens the door of her brother's room, the windows are described in the words used by James' narrator in "A Private Life" when, coming upon the poet Claire Vawdrey (modeled on Browning), writing in the dark, he sees "a couple of vague, star-lighted apertures" (194; "Private Life" 205)—and concludes that there are two Vawdreys, the public and the private. Mrs. Miller is an invention of Byatt's, but the French words uttered by Browning when he hears about her are a version of those that he is recorded as having said on a different occasion.[1] When, in Byatt's story, Browning writes in Mrs. Miller's birthday book, there is more unacknowledged borrowing from James. In "A Private Life," however, it is the narrator who cannot remember his own birthday; in **"Precipice-Encurled"** it is Browning. Immediately after this there is explicit reference to James' dislike of Browning's lack of discrimination, and an image from James is used literally when Mrs. Miller nods "under the wings of the dove" (195). The language of the fourth section is the most original and independent, movingly creating the feelings of Joshua and Juliana and the moments just before Joshua's death. The narrator then parries Meredith's "hypothesis" about the personal reference of "Inapprehensiveness" with a "fiction" of her own, making Mrs. Miller's hat the stimulus behind "The Lady and the Painter."[2] The point is clear: that while Meredith's hypothesis may have more basis in fact, the truth about the subjects of both poems—like the truth about Lazarus, Smart, Mrs. Bronson and Browning himself—remains beyond reach.

Browning wrote that Smart "pierced the screen / Twixt thing and word" ("Smart" 113-14). These are brave words, but Browning knew, and Byatt again demonstrates, that the screen is impenetrable. On the contrary, her story both openly and covertly—and disturbingly—displays the predatory activity of the imagination as it raids other texts in its fruitless attempt to get to the "thing." More optimistically, Byatt also shows the fertility of language. In her novel *Still Life* her narrator confesses, "I had the idea that this novel could be written innocently, without recourse to other people's thoughts, without, as far as possible, recourse to simile or metaphor. This turned out to be impossible" (108). In **"Precipice-Encurled"** Byatt shows why the experiment must always fail. The scholar, dutifully retracing Browning's steps to Asolo, hears the sounds of the place through Browning's words, as he listens to the "contumacious grasshopper" (*Sordello* VI.787). Even Joshua, the painter, sees through others' words, recognizing the accuracy of Milton's description of the fallen leaves in Vallombrosa (199; *Paradise Lost* I.300-304), experiencing first love through Marvell's Mower: "She / What I do to the grass, did to my thoughts and me" (203; Marvell wrote "did," not "does"), and applying to himself Shakespeare's description of lovers who "no sooner looked but they loved" (202; *As You Like It* V.ii.37). Even when painting and sketching he sees through

Ruskin's language. When he tries to reach beyond language, remembering simply Monet's canvas and sketching the unmediated subject, he dies. On one level, his death is paradigmatic.

Byatt has praised Iris Murdoch's sense of "a contrary tug of value between attempts at form and attempts to live with the knowledge that [in Murdoch's words] 'what *does* exist is brute and nameless, it escapes from the scheme of relations in which we may imagine it to be rigidly enclosed, it escapes from language and science, it is more and other than our descriptions of it'" (*Murdoch* 14). In **"Precipice-Encurled"** the language of incompleteness and shattering, like the structure, testifies to the failure of enclosure. On the precipice, Joshua sketches a broken snail shell, "the arch of its entrance intact, the dome of the cavern behind shattered to reveal the pearly interior revolution" (209). In a few moments he himself has vanished in a "shattering of bone and brain" (211). Despite the many invocations of enclosure, epitomized by Browning's fantasy that the "pothooks and spider traces" of his handwriting contain the world (189), the broken shell more accurately images the story Byatt tells. Yet if fiction stops short of holding reality it also extends it. It is like Monet's "Vétheuil in Fog," which so startled Joshua: "You could see, miraculously, that if you could see the town. which you could not, it would be reflected in the expanse of river at the foot of the canvas, which you also could not see" (210). Like Browning's resuscitation of his source, the "Yellow Book," in *The Ring and the Book,* Byatt's fiction has made fact alive. "The somehow may be this-how."

Notes

1. Curtis, "Robert Browning 1879 to 1885," in Meredith, Appendix C, 167, records that on being shown the first proposition for a Browning Society Browning responded, "Il me semble que cela frise le ridicule." Byatt substitutes "ce genre de chose" for "cela."
2. Before Meredith, Betty Miller had interpreted "Inapprehensiveness" as expressing Browning's feelings for Mrs. Bronson: see Meredith ixxvi,n71. Meredith's argument is more extended, however. Mrs. Bronson, "Browning in Asolo," in Meredith, Appendix A, 132, quotes Browning as saying that "The Lady and the Painter" was composed during a drive from Bassano to Asolo and was suggested by "the birds twittering in the trees."

Works Cited

Browning, Robert. *Complete Works.* Ed. Roma A. King, Jr. 9 vols to date. Athens, OH: Ohio UP and Baylor UP, 1969-.

Byatt, A. S. *Iris Murdoch.* Harlow: Longman, 1976.

———. *Still Life.* London: Chatto and Windus, 1985.

———. *Sugar and Other Stories.* London: Chatto and Windus, 1987.

Dusinberre, Juliet. "Forms of Reality in A. S. Byatt's *The Virgin in the Garden.*" *Critique* 24.1 (1982): 55-62.

James, Henry. "The Private Life." *The Complete Tales of Henry James.* Ed. Leon Edel. Vol. 8. Philadelphia: Lippincott, 1963. 12 vols. 1961-1964.

Karlin, Danny. "Prolonging Her Absence." Rev. of *The Wimbledon Prisoner* by Nigel Williams, *The Other Occupant* by Peter Benson, and *Possession* by A. S. Byatt. *London Review of Books* 8 March 1990: 17-18.

Marvell, Andrew. *The Poems and Letters of Andrew Marvell.* Ed. H. M. Margoliouth. 2nd ed. Vol. 1. Oxford: Clarendon, 1952. 2 vols.

Meredith, Michael, ed. *More than Friend: The Letters of Robert Browning to Katharine de Kay Bronson.* Waco, TX: Armstrong Browning Library of Baylor U, Wedgestone, 1985.

Milton, John. *Paradise Lost.* Ed. Alastair Fowler. London: Longman, 1971.

Shakespeare, William. *As You Like It.* Ed. Richard Knowles. New York: MLA, 1977.

Smart, Christopher. *Poetical Works.* Vol. 2. Ed. Marcus Walsh and Karina Williamson. Vol. 2. Oxford: Clarendon, 1983. 4 vols. 1980-1987.

Kathryn Hughes (review date 6 November 1992)

SOURCE: Hughes, Kathryn. "Repossession." *New Statesman & Society* 5, no. 227 (6 November 1992): 49-50.

[*In the following review, Hughes discusses the eroticism and erudition of the two novellas that make up* Angels and Insects.]

Angels and Insects comprises two novellas, both resolutely mid-Victorian in tone and content. Whereas in *Possession* Byatt allowed herself the safety net of a modern narrative to enclose her Victorian tale, here she plunges straight in, obliged to get it exactly right from the start. And, of course, she does, pulling off that tricky business of finding a format that refers to the prose of George Eliot *et al* without falling into pointless archivism.

In the process Byatt manages to make explicit much that was censored from her predecessors' text. Hence the eroticism that runs through both tales. In **"Morpho**

Eugenia", Eugenia Adamson, white and humid, commits incest (a play on the "insects" of the title) with her brute of a brother while her husband William sniffs delicately at the arid and spinsterish Miss Crompton. In **"The Conjugal Angel"**, the spiritualist seance becomes a place of social and sexual possibility, where conventional morality is revealed as nothing more than a thin skin stretched over an insistent pulse of desire.

The first of the novellas is set in a country house, a perfectly enclosed system where servants scurry around unseen below stairs while the Alabaster family lounges languidly above. Meanwhile, out in the extensive grounds, colonies of ants accurately reproduce these social relations, with workers busying themselves about their bloated and repellent queens.

Byatt's account uses the contemporary storm over Darwin to make neat connections between insect and human society while at the same time nodding in homage to *The French Lieutenant's Woman*—the text that pioneered the contemporary novel's obsession with rifling the dressing-up box of its own past.

The second story, **"The Conjugal Angel"**, sets itself a more difficult task by mixing fictional and real characters in an attempt to sort out, among other things, whether Tennyson and his friend Arthur Hallam were actually at it. Byatt helpfully provides the relevant ambiguous stanzas from "In Memoriam". The results are gruesome, with a rotting Hallam appearing to the terrified Sophy Sheeky, nursery governess turned medium.

But still there is a problem. Byatt's novel makes the familiar point about the status of historical record as literary text, fit to be unravelled and made anew. Others will have difficulties with the idea of taking real people and inventing things about them. Hallam, always a shadowy figure, has now, for good or ill, become the Hallam of A. S. Byatt.

Byatt's incursions into Victorian literature have always been set apart by the range and depth of her learning. Fowles cheerfully admitted to plundering anthologies for his sources; Byatt, one feels, simply skims hers from the surface of a vast storehouse. The problem is that she sometimes overestimates her readers' fortitude. Once again, she peppers her narrative with extracts from historical and fictional sources to produce a text constantly interrupted by indentations, italics and print switches over which the eye yearns to skip.

There are signs, too, that the longing for authenticity in her work is on the point of taking it over completely: ***Insects and Angels*** comes furnished with line drawings, engravings and, as a final touch, a smart red ribbon of a bookmark.

John Barrell (review date 19 November 1992)

SOURCE: Barrell, John. "When Will He Suspect?" *London Review of Books* 14, no. 22 (19 November 1992): 18-19.

[*In the following review, Barrell argues that the novellas in* Angels and Insects *are heavily didactic, overly constructed, Victorian in style, and distant yet claustrophobic.*]

I don't quite know what to say about ***Angels and Insects.*** It consists of a pair of novellas, **'Morpho Eugenia'** and **'The Conjugial Angel'**, which, like *Possession,* are set in Victorian England, and written in a free imitation of mid-19th-century literary English. My doubts are the obvious ones. It's not that I can't make up my mind about whether or not the work they do, of re-creation and creative imitation, is well done—much of the time it's very well done, as well as I can imagine it could be. But even when it is, I'm not sure of the point of doing it, or of doing it more than once (just to see if it can be done). The idea behind these novellas seems to be something like the converse of the adage that if a thing is worth doing it's worth doing well: if a thing can be done well, it must be worth doing. But the more successfully Byatt re-creates the Victorian novel of ideas, the more she persuades us of the irredeemable pastness of the past she re-creates, and the more the ideas she deals with, of determinism, individual freedom, the nature of life after death, seem to announce that these are no longer our concerns, at least not in this way, in these contexts, in these words and forms. The book seemed far more remote from me than any Victorian fiction, partly no doubt because of my awareness of the factitiousness of the enterprise, but also because that awareness was continually reinforced by the inevitable factitiousness of the style, which becomes Victorian at the cost of using too many formulas and too few resources, like Latin prose written by a thoroughly competent Latinist.

It is possible I suppose to see this not as a problem but as the whole point, and this may be how Byatt thinks of it. The point would be, I take it, to labour in vain in order to establish that the labour *is* vain—that the attempt to invent Victorian fictions will invite and enable us to reflect on the impossibility of doing so; to realise that the past is indeed a foreign country, and that the closer we seem to approach it the further it will recede. But this is not an idea so difficult to grasp or to exemplify as to account for the dedication with which Byatt in recent years has embraced her task. And if this were the point, it would make redundant the occasional displays of deliberate verbal bad manners: a dog 'farts', a man has a 'prick', a woman in bed 'asks for more'. These anachronisms, by reminding us of what Victorian novels could not say, certainly serve to establish the distance between 1870 and 1992, but they do so unnecessarily when the same point will be made by the most faithful obedience to Victorian proprieties.

Then again it may be that moments like these are supposed to function like the table I once saw in Jane Austen's house, which was advertised by its explanatory card as the very one at which Miss Austen is reputed to have written *Persuasion,* except that (as the card very candidly acknowledged) it could not have been made before 1847. The idea behind this confession was perhaps that it would act as a magnet for our suspicions, leaving us with nothing but the fullest confidence in the authenticity of the other features of the house, the Laura Ashley wallpapers, the glass cabinet with its dingy Regency dolls.

Perhaps I am striving too hard to see the 'point' of these novellas, when their only point is to be enjoyable fictions, but I don't think so. They are both urgently didactic, with a striking, and strikingly single-minded, drive to deliver a message—the need to believe in the freedom of the will in an apparently deterministic universe, for example, or the importance of seeking our happiness on earth and not in an uncertain heaven. There is a moral to each novella, thoroughly appropriate to the story, but the appropriateness depends to a large extent on the reconstructed language and context of Victorian religious anxiety, so that the more pressing the message, the less it seems to press upon us. These Victorian novellas of ideas are resolutely novellas of Victorian ideas.

To put it another way, or it may be to make a related point, that appropriateness of moral to story, story to moral, is largely the result of the impressive intelligence with which the thread of the narrative is so inextricably interwoven with the discourses which combine to give it meaning—Victorian religion, science, elegiac poetry, ethics, social description. There is an extraordinary density of signification: the discussions about whether the order of the universe is the product of blind chance or of design, or about the nature of death or the existence of the spirit world, the numerous quotations, the stories within the stories, the description of landscapes, of rooms, of people, of clothes, of social events, all contribute with a fascinating efficiency to the construction of meaning. I began sidelining what seemed to be the salient instances of connectedness, but gave up when I found an almost unbroken pencil line running down every page. And I soon began to feel a relentlessness about the intelligence with which these novellas are constructed; they induced claustrophobia; there is no room in them to discover anything except what has been put there to be discovered; every road is signposted, and to the same destination. The tone of my review is in places a reflection, no doubt, of the relief I felt on emerging from this book; it can be taken as a tribute, however backhanded, to the complexity of its organisation.

The ending of **'Morpho Eugenia'** made me think of Michael Heseltine. The story opened up the deep mines of the realist novel only to shut them down with the ruthless logic of allegory and fable. William Adamson, the son of a Yorkshire Methodist butcher, is an entomologist who has spent ten years in the Amazon rainforest, studying butterflies, moths, ants and termites. On his return to England, he had expected to be able to finance his future research from the sale of the specimens he had collected, and from the royalties on a book about his experiences and studies. But on the voyage home he is shipwrecked, most of his specimens are lost, and at the start of the novella he has washed up penniless at Bredely Hall, the Gothic mansion of the Rev. Harald Alabaster, a baronet, liberal churchman and anti-Darwinian collector of zoological specimens, who is attempting to write a lengthy vindication of the argument from design.

At Bredely he meets Alabaster's sad and beautiful daughter Eugenia, whose fiancé, a soldier, has recently died. He falls in love with her at first sight; or perhaps what he falls for are the qualities enshrined in her name—her breeding, so much more distinguished than his own, her whiteness, so gleamingly different from the Amerindian women he occasionally coupled with in Brazil. 'I shall die if I cannot have her,' he tells his diary; and so when her father invites him to extend his stay at Bredely, as a kind of paid guest, he accepts with enthusiasm. Adamson's duties are to catalogue the baronet's own vast and still unpacked collection of specimens and to act as a sounding-board for his confused attempts to refute the theory of evolution; there are vague promises of funding for future field-work. In addition he agrees (he can hardly refuse) to help with the scientific education of the younger Alabaster children, which is conducted by the knowing Matty Crompton, a poor dependant and unofficial governess.

He is of course in no position to propose to Eugenia, but he does find an opportunity to tell her that if only he could, he would. To his amazement and delight, Eugenia brushes his scruples aside; her father raises no objections; and in no time the pair are married. Adamson's life, however, is very little changed by the gratification of his greatest desire. Husband and wife continue to live at Bredely; Adamson continues to feel a less than free and accepted member of the family, and finds himself performing the same duties as before. Plans for a return to the Amazon are indefinitely postponed; and except for the few weeks each year when Eugenia is not pregnant, the couple enjoy little more mutual intimacy than before their marriage. Adamson's closest relationship is with Matty, the only person in the house with whom he is on a footing, socially and intellectually. Together they begin an elaborate study of the local population of ants, with the idea—it is Miss Crompton's originally—that Adamson will write a book about them, at once popular and path-breaking. Conversation and research with Matty Crompton are all that console him for the futility of his new life.

But when will he suspect? The reader has been encouraged to suspect since early in the story, when Adamson sees but does not overhear a conversation between Eugenia and Edgar, her brutal elder brother, which leaves her in tears. Suspicion becomes a racing certainty in the following twenty or so pages, when Edgar reveals the depth of his anger at the approaching marriage, when Eugenia in her bridal bed seems to know much more than she should, and when she insists on christening her first-born Edgar. Her terrible secret, however, is for many years safe from her husband, born too soon to be wise in the way of readers of 20th-century detective fiction, and disabled, by his scientific training, from recognising any but ocular proof. It is not until ten pages from the end that he returns from hunting to discover his wife in bed with her brother. They had been at it for years; when Eugenia's fiancé had found out, he shot himself.

In the final scene, Adamson is in mid-Atlantic, bound once again for Brazil, his fare paid by the advance on his book; beside him on deck is Miss Crompton, the plain Jane who, true to the values of the Victorian novel, has stepped out of her protective covering and revealed herself as a much worthier partner for the hero than the flashy object of his earlier impetuous desire. She, too, has emerged as a writer who can rely on her pen to pay for her liberation. Her first effort was an insect-fable, in which she had suggested to Adamson, at tedious length, the possibility of escape.

It is the fact that Adamson is so slow on the uptake which delays the denouement of the novella long enough to allow the development of the themes, arguments, descriptions, writings, which announce the story's meaning. There is (for example) an extended opposition between Paradise and the Inferno which poses continually the question of which is which and where it is better to be. During his long years in Brazil, Adamson had repeatedly dreamed of the peaceful English countryside, staring at the grotesquely luxuriant, mosquito-infested rain-forest and seeing, as if in the calenture, the green meadows of England with their abundant but chastely-tinted flowers. In the landscape around Bredely he seems to have found his English Paradise, complete with Eugenia as an English Eve with whom Adamson can pretend to be a still unfallen Adam. As he begins, however, to become accustomed to his new life at Bredely, the household begins to be revealed to him as a universally coercive system, in which the Alabaster family has become so dependent upon its largely invisible army of servants that its own paradisal idleness is as much forced as is their labour. Worse still, the system persuades those whom it enslaves to identify its ends as theirs, so that it takes much tactful prompting by Miss Crompton, as well as the discovery that his Eve had been seduced by the serpent Edgar, for Will to see that this paralysis of the Will can be shaken off only by a decision to return to the Inferno he has left, the place of thorns and thistles, west of Eden, where there is real work to be done.

Adamson's sense of the Bredely household as a system which operates by itself, independently of the organising will of any of its members, develops mainly from the study he undertakes with Miss Crompton of the ants that live in the nearby woods, the meticulousness of which testifies—as does so much else in these novels—to the meticulousness of Byatt's own Victorian researches. The pair are especially interested in the *Formica sanguinea,* the red ants who capture ants of other species and make them their slaves. Bredely, Adamson seems to understand, exists only for breeding. It is organised round the red bedroom of its queen, the obese and languid Lady Alabaster, who spends the day in idle deshabille, while endless lines of maidservants dressed in black scuttle back and forth from the kitchen bearing sweetmeats and beverages. By the end of the book, Eugenia, too, has become a mere breeding creature, an incestuous red ant queen, and the authorial voice gives her a thorough dressing-down. This seemed a bit harsh, for I don't imagine Eugenia would have agreed to do the sex-scenes if Byatt hadn't insisted that, like everything else in ***Angels and Insects,*** they were absolutely integral to the plot.

By one of the arguments that Adamson considers, the house is no more matriarchal than patriarchal; like a nest of ants—perhaps, he speculates, like a mill, or like society itself—the house is run by no one and for no one's individual benefit, but by the spirit of the system itself. The division of labour includes everyone, the mill-owners as well as the mill-hands, the queens and the drones like Harald Alabaster and Adamson as well as the countless army of subterranean workers. What Adamson still has to learn, however, and he finally learns it from Miss Crompton, is that the analogy between the forms of organisation discovered among the social insects, and human forms of social organisation, is fatally deceptive. The analogy will do for the likes of the amoral Eugenia, who uncomprehendingly defends her incest as 'natural'; but for a moral being like Adamson it offers no insight into how humans *should* behave, and to believe in it is merely the symptom of a diseased will.

It is not clear to me whether Adamson and Matty ever reached the Amazon. They sailed on the *Calypso,* whose captain, Arturo Papagay, is missing presumed dead in the second novella, **'The Conjugial Angel'**, following the wreck of that very ship—though he turns up in the final pages, to the great delight of his semiphoney spiritualist wife, who much prefers flesh and blood to ectoplasm. She has been attempting, with the aid of Sophy Sheekhy, a medium, and several members of the New Jerusalem Church, to raise the spirit of Arthur Henry Hallam, he of *In Memoriam,* with whom Emily Jesse, Tennyson's now married and elderly sister, had once had an understanding. In the interstices of their attempts, the novel reflects on the persistence of mourning, partly by means of a reading of Tennyson's poem. When a message from Hallam finally arrives, it assures Mrs Jesse that she and he will be one angel in the hereafter. But Mrs Jesse, most of whose life has been spent waiting, anxiously, guiltily, for just such a promise, realises at once that she wants no part of it, has not done so for years. She wants her present husband, also a seafarer, stolid, loyal, selfless; she wants him now and she wants him after death. The spiritualist group collapses, to nearly everyone's apparent relief.

And certainly to mine: I enjoyed **'The Conjugial Angel'** much less than its companion-piece. Perhaps I preferred **'Morpho Eugenia'** because I read it in almost ideal conditions. I have rented a London flat for the summer and autumn, convenient for the British Library, and after four visits from a pest-control company it is still infested with bedbugs. When the landlord provided me with a new bed, I tied grease bands round the legs, on which several specimens of the species *Cimex lectularius* are now displayed. It was on this bed that I read ***Angels and Insects,*** and I responded with more sympathy to Byatt's account of a house run and overrun by insects than to her reflections on life after death; the only after-life I look forward to at present will begin when my lease expires.

By the time I got to the second novella, the relentless coherence of Byatt's narrative method had come to seem less fascinating—it had become all too familiar. But it was the style that finally wore me down. Its Victorianness is achieved mainly by a series of variations on a sentence whose verbs, like ants, are continually trying to move more luggage—more clusters of adjectives, more relative clauses—than they can comfortably bear. This is good for evoking the oppressive heaviness we associate with some aspects of Victorian life; with the formal interiors, for example, all that plush and polished wood, all those warm colours. Victorians could live in those rooms, no doubt, because they could also be elsewhere, in the chill bedroom or dank shrubbery. But wherever we go in ***Angels and Insects,*** inside or out, upstairs or down, it is too often a version of the same sentence that leads us there and tells us what to see, think and feel. **'The Conjugial Angel'** is set in Margate, and reminded me of a dismally wet afternoon I spent there as a child, trailing behind a great-aunt who was showing my grandmother the sights; each called the other 'Ma'. My great-aunt, too, was particularly attached to one sentence: every thirty yards or so she would stop and say: 'And this is the 'igh Street, Ma.' When my grandmother finally broke her silence, she spoke for us both: 'Bugger the 'igh Street, Ma.'

Michael Levenson (review date 2 August 1993)

SOURCE: Levenson, Michael. "The Religion of Fiction." *New Republic* 209, no. 5 (2 August 1993): 41-4.

[*In the following review, Levenson deems Byatt a "postmodern Victorian," contending that* Angels and Insects *shows "the reach and the promise of the Byattian project of resuming the incomplete work of the past."*]

Suppose that our modernizing century has been, on the whole, a mistake. Suppose that what it called liberation—in the arts, but also in politics, in religion, in philosophy—was only a new confinement; that its craving for revolution, with all its ferocities and its ambitions, made this modernity cruelly unjust to those who came before. Suppose, finally, that the older, nearly forgotten path of slower (call it evolutionary) growth, interrupted by our great-grandparents, the whooping young modernists, remains for us to resume.

A. S. Byatt frequently gets called a postmodernist. Fine. She does go in for smart parodies of earlier narrative forms; she enjoys literary gamesmanship; and like many teasing contemporaries, she breaks up her stories with stories about her stories. But you miss a good deal of what is most interesting in Byatt, and what is most significant in the movement of which she is a part, if you ignore the way her postmodernity finds its ground in something else, something older, namely an earnest attempt to get back before the moderns and revive a Victorian project that has never been allowed to come to completion. What you have in Byatt is an odd-sounding but perfectly intelligible creature, the postmodern Victorian. She knows where we live and when; she knows her Joyce and Woolf and Beckett; but she is undeterred in the belief that the road into the twenty-first century winds exactly through the middle of the nineteenth.

Just over thirty years ago, Iris Murdoch published an essay called "Against Dryness," which built an image of the modern novel as diminished, depleted and thin, failing badly in two opposed ways: through an excessively tight formalism, which produced overly polished jewels of authorial control; and through loose journalistic rambles, the lazy, loopy meander through anything crossing the path of reverie. Different as they were, the two forms shared a cult of the brave, lonely ego—solitary, adventurous, free—aiming to fulfill its private destiny. Lost was the older, thicker sense of the ego in community, of a novel full of many separate beings, of a world beyond the self. Authenticity, sincerity, self-assertion: these were for Murdoch the meager modern legacy, bequeathed by a philosophy of subjectivity and a politics of happiness. Against this dryness, this fetish for the lonely, authentic self spreading the feathers of its "brave naked will," Murdoch invoked Jane Austen, Leo Tolstoy and George Eliot, who produced thick social fictions that never forgot "that other people exist."

In a formulation that Byatt calls "electrifying," Murdoch praised the "hard idea of truth" at the expense of the "facile idea of sincerity." Byatt, who wrote a critical study of Murdoch early in her own career, returns frequently, even obsessively, to "Against Dryness," citing her favorite phrases as if to remind herself of what she believes. Murdoch has been her literary mother. The two of them alone are enough to count as a distinct contemporary lineage, nourished on the conviction that, our modernist complacencies aside, our Victorian origins are unresolved, unsurpassed.

Three years ago *Possession* gave Byatt big international success. It not only brought her fame, it gave her career a new roundness. Much of the earlier fiction was quickly and finely reprinted. Scattered essays were collected. Translations, introductions and interviews crowded her life. After two decades of writing, her work assumed a more vivid shape for her readers, and still more interestingly, it seemed to assume a more vivid shape for Byatt herself. Now, in the long middle of her career, her intentions seem sharper, her future more interesting than it has been before.

The two novellas that make up ***Angels and Insects*** are not yet that future, but they are signposts. Taken together, they show the reach and the promise of the Byattian project of resuming the incomplete work of the past. In the first of them, **"Morpho Eugenia,"** the Victorian scientist William Adamson, a student of ants, beetles and butterflies, comes home to England after years in the rainforests of South America. Most of his specimens having been lost in a shipwreck, Adamson, estranged and friendless, faces personal catastrophe. But then the Reverend Harold Alabaster, a wealthy baronet and an amateur naturalist, invites Adamson into his grand mansion, where the shattered scientist is given free rein first to rethink his studies and then to marry Eugenia, the beautiful daughter of the house.

Adamson finds himself back inside the mid-Victorian matrix, with its class rigidities, its religious panic, its moral agitation. He looks for solace in the insects. Turning his practiced eye to a colony of ants living on the grounds of the estate, he initially finds an alternative to his tense family life, but the longer he looks, the more clearly he sees his own world reflected in the mirror held up by the little bugs. Adamson fights those analogies. He doesn't want to know himself as a drone recruited to serve his more powerful conquerors, the country-house aristocracy with its endless appetite for blood, money and horsemanship.

But his denials aside, **"Morpho Eugenia"** is intent on forcing the thought that seen from a height, watched across centuries, we humans creep and crawl, scratch and burrow like any other low creature moving close to the surface of the planet. Are we little more, too little more, than the insects? When we watch the ants, making war, making love, carrying crumbs, building ant cities, stealing ant babies, can we keep from growing dizzy? The old shudder of Darwinism is what Byatt's story wants to give.

And why shouldn't we still shudder? What have we become that we have forgotten the shock of our origins? Byatt has accepted from Murdoch, who accepted it from George Eliot, the urgent literary imperative to make struggle against fantasy. This is Byatt's version of their realist credo: "That there is a hard reality, not ourselves, which is not amenable to our planning, plotting and power-strategies." So **"Morpho Eugenia"** thrashes Adamson's self-deceptions, his blindness to class and domestic violence, his cult of innocence and beauty, forcing him into the rude perception that what we call civilization is a fancy name for our animal contrivances.

A natural history of the ant colonies is what Adamson writes, but Byatt makes clear that a "natural history" of humanity is what any strong novel must be. It must disregard the fantasies of species-pride that we use to cheer ourselves up. It must face up to the Darwinian nightmare, well expressed by Tennyson when he enters the second novella, **"The Conjugial Angel,"** as a shambling, frightened old man:

> Men now saw what he saw, the earth heaped and stacked with dead things, broken bright feathers and shriveled moths, worms stretched and sliced and swallowed, stinking shoals of once bright fish, dried parrots and tigerskins limply and glassily snarling on hearths, mountains of human skulls mixed with monkey skulls and snake skulls and asses' jawbones and butterfly wings, mashed into humus and dust, fed on, regurgitated, blown in the wind, soaked in the rain, absorbed.

If that were all, it would be bad to be alive. But it is a first principle of the natural history of humanity, as Byatt inherits it from Eliot, that you must tell all, where "all" includes not only the bad moments when we know ourselves to be beasts among the beastly, but also the moments of shivering insight when we feel that we float like angels under the eye of a winking mystery.

If it were only a matter of finding an open space between the Angels and the Insects, being human would be easy. What makes it hard in Byatt's world is that we are hybrid beings who go wrong when we seek purity of any kind. In **"Morpho Eugenia,"** Adamson must free himself from class indignity and sexual humiliation by seeing the insect in the human, where this means understanding the natural cruelties beneath the myth of Victorian family harmony. Only if we know ourselves as partly animal can we be fully human. This implies, among other things, that to exaggerate our creepy crawliness is as dangerous as to ignore it, and further along this line of thought, that our human chances depend on knowing that we two-legged insects are also fallen angels.

Thus the perspective in the second novella turns upward, not to transcend this world but to bring higher visions down into the earthly mix. The events of **"The Conjugial Angel"** take place in the mid-1870s, a little more than ten years after the time of **"Morpho Eugenia."** Byatt the precise Victorianist knows that the brief period saw some large changes, including, for instance, the great vogue of drawing-room spiritualism, with its séances and mediums, its dark closets and mumbled voices and apparitions. She has described this as "the religion of a materialist age," part of a craving to confirm a threatened faith through visible proof of the life immortal. Bowing under the worldly pressures of science and industry. Darwin and advertising, a more desperate band of seekers looked to find spirits as material as any other commodity in the new commercial age.

They fought death with all means available, with "animal magnetism" and "aethereal telegraphy"—and then also with poetry. No Victorian death was more extravagantly resisted, not even the death of Prince Albert, than that of Arthur Henry Hallam. In 1833 he was gone at twenty-two. Seventeen years later Tennyson published "In Memoriam," the more than 100 lyrics of his long mourning for this friend. From this point, Hallam's untimely death became the type for all inexplicable suffering and for the fragility of faith under the heavy tramp of science. "Next to the Bible," said Queen Victoria, "'In Memoriam' is my comfort."

But of course Hallam's death caused other, less literary, less public, griefs. The conceit of **"The Conjugial Angel"** is to ponder the case of Tennyson's sister Emily, engaged to marry Hallam after knowing him just four weeks, and condemned to represent the Bereaved Lover frozen into a pose of "perpetual maidenhood" (her brother's phrase). After nine years of mourning for Hallam, she married a Captain Jesse, and **"The Conjugial Angel"** imagines what it must have been for Emily Tennyson Jesse to endure the sniffy opinion that she should never have married, but should have burned always for the young god Hallam. What must it have been to be married to another when "In Memoriam" appeared with all its steadfast, untainted fidelity? What must it have been to age with the memory of an absurdly short romance, longing to settle emotional accounts with the ghost of the young lover?

Building on the fact that the aging Emily Tennyson Jesse attended séances and dallied with the spiritualists, Byatt imagines her way into this spiritually edgy world. She invents a circle of initiates who yearn really to see what they hope they believe. A second leading character in **"The Conjugial Angel,"** Mrs. Lilias Papagay, has drifted into the séance business, looking first for word on her lost husband and then finding a tidy profit in hosting respectable sessions with the ghosts. Byatt neatly tags her as "an intelligent, questioning kind of woman, the kind who, in an earlier age, would have been a theologically minded nun, and in a later one would have had a university training in philosophy or psychology or medicine." But Byatt, I suspect, rather likes Mrs. Papagay just where she is, neither devout nun nor rational psychologist, caught in the twisted branches of sex and money, even as she yearns to see an angel in the sunset.

For Byatt, those twisted branches, this yearning, are ours, too. She has described late Victorian spiritualism as "part of a whole shift in religious feeling," and she sees us in our own late century as living in the same spiritual swamp. But this perception is entirely without scorn. Byatt may not believe in the truths of religion, but she unquestionably believes in the belief. And so she takes pleasure in recalling George Eliot's religious progress from "evangelical Anglican" to "resolutely anti-Christian" rationalist and then finally to the larger, more generous humanism that "saw Christian belief and morality as forms of human experience that must be studied and valued as part of our natural history." This is what Byatt appears to want for herself: she wants to be the natural historian of a post-Christian spiritual life.

All through Byatt's writing life, she has reflected on the way we earthly beings dream of spirit. She is a Realist, a post-Christian, a sometime academic living in skeptical times. These may seem heavy drags on the religious turn, but for Byatt these are simply the latest natural conditions for our spirit-hunger. It's no use whining. Her point is not to confirm religious truth, but to enlarge the religious sense, which locates value not in the infinite but in the yearning for the infinite, not in God but in the search for God. In a more than clever analogy, Byatt has drawn a connection between the "afterlife" of the Bible and the "afterlife" of the nineteenth-century novel. We live in the shadow of both. But the task, as she sees it, is not to get out from under the shadow into the white modern light. It is to respect and to love our old shadowy needs, to keep faith with faith, and with realist fiction.

The insight—you might even call it the revelation—that seems to have clarified for Byatt through the writing of *Possession* is that a novel might not only be about the act of faith; it can itself be the act. Soon after *Possession* appeared she wrote a long essay on the persistence of belief in nineteenth-century culture, in which she took the French historian Michelet as a beautiful instance, beautiful because in choosing a name for his history, Michelet rejected "Narrative" and "Analysis" in favor of "Resurrection." To write history (or, by extension, historical fiction) is to resurrect the dead, it is to raise Lazarus: this thought is made for Byatt. It leads quickly to her own elevated vision for the contemporary novelist, who through strenuous imagining might herself raise the dead, and it encourages her in the proud thought that what religion was, literature can now be.

At the end of **"The Conjugial Angel,"** when the ghost of Hallam appears to appear, Byatt's reader must experience an unnerving double response. The first instinctive mockery of those who see ghosts gives way to a second, less cozy recognition that we novel readers are always seeing ghosts. Every character is an apparition. Whenever we lend solidity to the stories we follow, we are living proof of a visionary capacity almost always undervalued. Byatt's purpose is to push this fact about fiction into the foreground of consciousness, so that reading novels becomes the training of vision.

She asks no one to believe in God, and she doesn't tell us to pray. But lately she wants to remind us at every turn that our species has an entrenched habit of looking into the sky, and however little that may tell us about the sky and beyond, it tells us a good deal about our believing, hoping, fearing selves. We do want thicker characters alive in many dimensions. We do want to summon the fading impalpable past. Many of our most disbelieving friends call certain things "sacred." Some of the most worldly among us throw embarrassed upward glances at the highest blue.

Kathleen Coyne Kelly (essay date 1996)

SOURCE: Kelly, Kathleen Coyne. "Short Stories." In *A. S. Byatt,* pp. 36-62. New York, N.Y.: Twayne Publishers, 1996.

[*In the following excerpt, Kelly discusses Byatt's short stories in the context of thematically and stylistically linked groups.*]

Byatt's short stories appear in two collections: ***Sugar and Other Stories*** (1987) and ***The Matisse Stories*** (1994). Both collections, especially ***The Matisse Stories,*** can be read as a sequence: that is, while each story stands on its own, each can be read in connection with the others. However, Byatt's tales may be distinguished from other, more formal short-story sequences in that characters are not carried over from one story to the next, such as in Hemingway's *Nick Adams Stories* and Jamaica Kincaid's *Annie John.* Rather, what holds the stories together in Byatt's collections is a repetition of emphasis and theme.

To foreground certain thematic links, I have grouped the eleven stories in ***Sugar*** in twos and threes instead of discussing them sequentially as they appear in the text (though my groupings do often follow the order in which they were published). ***The Matisse Stories*** contains only three stories (**"Medusa's Ankles," "Art Works,"** and **"The Chinese Lobster"**); these are much more consciously linked together than those in ***Sugar,*** and I take them up in the order in which they appear.

Sugar and Other Stories

"Racine and the Tablecloth" and "Rose-Coloured Teacups"

"Racine and the Tablecloth" is about the slow smothering of female intellect under the weight of societal disapproval. It is hard to resist reading it as a piece of alternative autobiography. That is, this story of a curious and able girl, forced by cultural and historical circumstance to suppress her intellectual ambitions, could have been Byatt's story. In fact, **"Racine"** may well be the story of Byatt's mother, who, like so many women before the 1960s in the United States and in England, was forced to sacrifice meaningful work for husband and children.

There are three main characters in **"Racine and the Tablecloth"**: Emily Bray, the schoolgirl who is our heroine and protagonist; the headmistress Martha Crichton-Walker, who functions as "the clash of principle, the essential denial of an antagonist";[1] and the "Reader," Emily's imaginary, objective—and therefore presumably just—audience. The narrator, another important presence, often directly addresses her own "reader"—that is, us—as she develops the narrative.

Emily is a brilliant student who arrives at an exclusive and expensive private boarding school at midyear—timing that serves to set an already lonely and isolated girl apart. She is shy, unhappy, and, if the schoolmistress Miss Crichton-Walker is correct in her criticisms, rather grubby—very much like Anna Severell in *The Shadow of the Sun.* But as the child of working-class parents, Emily is also like Oliver Canning in *Shadow.* She comes to the school on scholarship and is very self-conscious about the class differences between herself and her classmates. Emily's passion is the work of the 19th-century French poet Racine; her reading of his works transports her, takes her away from her trying existence at school.

Miss Crichton-Walker is neat, severe, judgmental, "firmly benign and breastless" (***SOS*** [***Sugar and Other Stories***], 2). The lines of battle are drawn between

Emily and the schoolmistress, who seems intent on breaking what little spirit Emily reserves to herself. (Crichton-Walker is based, says Byatt, on a teacher she knew, "a destroyer, knocking down academic success.")[2] The narrator describes an early confrontation between the two: "Emily Bray saw that there were two outsiders in the room [of students]. There was herself, set aside from the emotion that was swimming around, and there was Miss Crichton-Walker, who wanted them all to be sharing something" (3). Though the headmistress is grudgingly respectful of Emily's intellectual gifts, she finds ways to criticize her, as in her description of the girl's handwriting as "aggressive" (5).

Just as a younger girl might invent an invisible companion for herself, someone to play with, Emily imagines an "ideal Reader" (***SOS,*** 6). "He was dry and clear, he was all-knowing but not messily infinite. . . . Emily was enabled to continue because she was able to go on believing in the Reader" (6). She imagines this Reader, not the headmistress or her other teachers, as the true audience for her work: "In another place, the Reader walked in dry, golden air, in his separate desert, waiting to weigh her knowledge and her ignorance" (29). Emily is much better equipped to come to terms with the Reader's judgments than she is with Miss Crichton-Walker's, whose opinion of Emily's scholarship is so colored by her own feelings.

Toward the end of the story, the narrator directly addresses the reader: "Who won, you will ask, Emily or Miss Crichton-Walker, since the Reader is mythical and detached, and can neither win nor lose?" (***SOS,*** 30). We learn that Emily marries "young and hastily" and settles down to the small rewards and trials of homemaking, raising two "clever daughters" (30). But Emily is not able to evade the Crichton-Walkers of the world, for the pattern of her school life is repeated in her daughter Sarah's life. Sarah wants to study French and mathematics, yet an adviser at her school tries to discourage her and attempts to enlist Emily in his plans. The story ends with the following comment: "What Sarah made of herself, what Sarah saw, is Sarah's story. You can believe, I hope, you can afford to believe, that she made her way into its light" (32).

There is a lurking malevolence in **"Racine and the Tablecloth,"** embodied in Miss Crichton-Walker and the deputy head at Sarah's school. This evil permeates all the small rituals of public-school life, based as many are on class and privilege. (What we call private school in the United States is called public school in England.) Moreover, this evil is gender-biased: Emily, and then her daughter, are expected to fit into roles fixed by gender rather than by ability and inclination.

But **"Racine"** does not foreground the issue of gender; rather, it reads like a parable, a story with a hidden message. For example, the narrator tells us of an April Fool's joke in which Emily and her classmates, in concert with the boys at the neighboring school, switch their assigned pews in church. This is certainly a harmless prank by today's standards, but it is rich in meaning for the story, in which gender is so proscribed. In a way, **"Racine"** is a variation on the story Byatt tells in *Still Life,* in which she explores the split future of two sisters: Stephanie, who stays home, and Frederica, who goes off to Cambridge.

"Rose-Coloured Teacups" is another story of women who are squeezed out of their ambition and their rightful place in academe. Byatt builds her narrative on three levels: the central character, Veronica, imagines her mother at university in the 1920s, then remembers herself there in the 1950s, and goes on to imagine a future when her emphatically modern daughter Jane will attend the same university. Both Veronica and her mother attended university in high hopes; both gave up their ambitions once they married. Will Jane break this chain of despair?

The story opens with a scene in which three women are drinking tea from pink luster cups in their college rooms. This scene is "imagined not remembered" by Veronica, who escapes into this picture of peace when her own domestic life threatens to overwhelm her (***SOS,*** 38). Moreover, it is, as the narrator says, "a curious form of mourning, but compulsive, and partly comforting" (36). Veronica mourns her mother, and her own lost ambition.

Like rose-colored glasses, which soften the harshness of reality, the teacups symbolize a period of innocence, of hope, in the insulated world of the university—"a safe place" (***SOS,*** 38). Veronica is aware of her romanticizing of her mother's past when, in reflecting on the scene she has imagined, she feels that she is "overdoing the pink." "She did not like pink," we are told (36). The truth is that "her mother had wanted her to be at the college and had felt excluded, then, by her daughter's presence there, from her own memories of the place. The past had been made into the past, discontinuous from the present. It had been a fantasy that Veronica would sit in the same chairs, in the same sunlight and drink from the same cups" (37).

The teacups also come to be associated in Veronica's mind with her mother's "miserable disappointed face" and her own feeling at university as, in a "daze of defeat and anguish," she carelessly packs up the cups, thus breaking them. The reason for her violent feelings is long forgotten, however important it may have been at the time (***SOS,*** 37). Two cups and one saucer are all that remain.

This story—imagined, remembered, experienced—of three generations of women ends with a very masculine intrusion into the 1920s room of Veronica's mother.

Several "young men in blazers and wide flannels, college scarves and smoothed hair, smiling decorously," come to tea (***SOS***, 38). One of these men is Veronica's father. The present, the story suggests, is irrevocably bound up in the past, and the choices of one generation resonate into the next.

"Loss of Face," "On the Day E. M. Forster Died," and "Precipice-Encurled"

"Loss of Face," "On the Day E. M. Forster Died," and **"Precipice-Encurled"** are loosely linked by the fact that the main characters are writers. Each writer—a literary scholar in the first, a novelist in the second, and Robert Browning in the third—reflects intensely on writing itself and on writing as a vocation.

In the first story, a Milton and George Eliot scholar, Celia Quest, attends an academic conference in an unnamed Eastern country. Confined to a hotel for the most part of her stay—the city is, at the moment, in "fear of turbaned terrorists"—Celia feels disoriented, out of touch, as if she has not left her Western home at all (***SOS***, 113). I use the word *disoriented* deliberately, for Byatt, from the beginning, plays with the word *orientation* and its connotations of "East" and "direction." For example, the hotel and its elevators are compared to an "orientation maze"—it seems to be uniquely non-Western and therefore rather bewildering (112). Byatt gave a number of lectures in India, China, Korea, and Hong Kong in the early 1980s. She may well have drawn upon her experiences in these places for this story; we might imagine that, like Celia, she felt cocooned in a self-conscious Westernness.

One of the themes in **"Loss of Face"** is the collision of cultures. For example, how can people from different backgrounds come to a common understanding of a literary text? What happens when one culture reads the canonical texts of another's and for good or ill assimilates some of the values inherent in such texts—and in the privileging of such texts? Byatt is aware of an Anglophone audience for her work beyond England and has commented on the difficulties of crossing cultural barriers: "I am a European writer as well as being a local English one. I am at the moment exercised by the problem of communicable detail—can an Italian or a Californian or an Indian take any interest in or appreciate the nuances of an English bus queue? How many readers will have read Milton's *Paradise Lost* or . . . *The Aeneid*? How many who have not will be annoyed to find them in my books?" (McTighe, 71).

These questions are Celia's as well: how can her non-English-speaking audience "hear Milton's transitions from Latinate complexity to Anglo-Saxon plain speech?" (***SOS***, 114). But Byatt does not have to go far from home in order to worry about readers being able to read Milton: Celia's own English students, we learn, are stubbornly resistant to *Paradise Lost*.

At one point, Celia visits the "Folk Village"—a static representation of how life used to be in this imaginary Asian country: "Here was collected everything that was poised silently to vanish away" (***SOS***, 120). By including this episode, Byatt seems to be drawing a parallel between this monument to the past (romanticized as it may be) and the "monuments" of canonical English literature (Celia, we are told, thinks of art "as a work of rescue" [120]). **"Loss of Face"** is of two minds: it criticizes Western notions of cultural superiority at the same time that it upholds the innate greatness of English literature.[3]

The title **"Loss of Face"** is double-pronged, first as a metaphor signifying the loss of status through defeat or humiliation, and second as a reference to the unfortunate inability of many Westerners to distinguish differences in Asian faces. Asians literally "lose" their faces in Western eyes. However, the narrator tells us that Celia can distinguish a Chinese face from a Japanese, and that she realizes that the "uniformity of the black hair, to Western eyes, creates an illusion of greater similarity" (***SOS***, 115). In fact, after spending time in China, Celia "found herself seeing her compatriots as unfinished monsters, pallid meat topped by kinky, lusterless, unreal hair" (115). In spite of this, at the end of the tale, Celia "misreads" an Asian face, which results in her own loss of face.

After Celia gives her lecture on Milton, on his figures of virtue ("Milton was very sure what virtue was" [***SOS***, 113]), an Asian scholar, Professor Sun, politely and inexorably disagrees with her interpretation. She is interested in a uniquely English aesthetic, while he is more interested in a materialist, contextualized reading that would problematize this aesthetic by introducing class into the mix. Later, at the official conference banquet, after Celia has had quite a long conversation with her dinner companion to the left, she "made the mistake of asking his name" (126). She has failed to recognize this same Professor Sun.

The professor is understandably hurt and angry. He had broken a characteristic reserve—and taken quite a risk, given the political situation of his country—to declare that "I think perhaps we should be studying Third World Literature. We should think about imperialism" (***SOS***, 125). Celia had replied: "I am told I should [study Third World Literature]. But Milton and George Eliot are my roots, I do not want them to vanish from the world" (126).

At the end of **"Loss of Face,"** as Celia broods on her mistake, Byatt expands the metaphor of face to include culture and cultural relativism: how does one move from "sketched universals" to the "exact particular" (***SOS***, 126)? How does one achieve a balance between the universal and the particular? What do we lose when we exalt one over the other?

"On the Day E. M. Forster Died" opens with a declaration: "This is a story about writing. It is a story about a writer who believed, among other things, that time for writing about writing was past" (***SOS,*** 129). The narrator—an explicit "I"—says further that "it seems worth telling this story about writing, which is a story, and does have a plot, is indeed essentially plot, overloaded with plot, a paradigmatic plot which, I believe, takes it beyond the narcissistic consideration of the formation of the writer, or the aesthetic closure of the mirrored mirror" (130).

Mrs. Smith, the main character, is a writer, wife, and mother. She believes (as she has been taught) that the novel is indeed "salvation," that the "bright books of life were the shots in the arm, the warm tots of whisky which kept her alive and conscious and lively" (***SOS,*** 130). Surely this is Byatt speaking as well. The moment of the story is, as the title indicates, the day in 1970 when E. M. Forster died. The location is the London Library; as Mrs. Smith contemplates her next writing project, "a fantastically convoluted, improbably possible plot reared up before her like a snake out of a magic basket" (132). In an excited, expansive mood after outlining her novel, Mrs. Smith (we never learn her first name) walks down Jermyn Street, reads the headlines, and learns that Forster is dead. Her immediate reaction: "Now I have room to move, now I can do as I please, now he can't overlook or reject me" (135). Of course, she realizes that he did not know that they were in any sort of competition; in fact, it is not a real competition, but an expression of Bloomian anxiety of influence. (See *Still Life* [129ff] for an account of Frederica Potter going to a tea party over which Forster presides.)

"On the Day E. M. Forster Died," written by a writer about writing, about a writer writing, is crossed with another story of "deathly music-machines and lethal umbrellas" (***SOS,*** 145). Mrs. Smith encounters Conrad, a friend of a friend, who commandeers her into coffee. She does not like him very much. But Conrad appeals to Mrs. Smith because he is full of information "about things she knew too little about" (137). He recently has had a conversion experience and become a music student. Mrs. Smith sees him as "a man submitted to a new discipline . . . for the sake of an ideal vision," and because of this ideal vision, because of the music, Mrs. Smith forgives him much (139-40).

However, on this day, the day E. M. Forster died, she notices that he looks sick and is rather dirty—that he smells "of mortality" (***SOS,*** 141). He tells a tale of danger and espionage and asks for her help. He is obviously afraid and agitated, and Mrs. Smith becomes afraid of his madness. She thinks: "How precarious it was, the sense of self in the dark bath of uncertainty, the moment of knowing, the certainty that music is the one thing needful" (145). Mrs. Smith, of course, has her own version of the "one thing needful": her projected novel. Conrad's madness serves as a kind of warning or foreshadowing of what can happen to anyone when something unexpected rears up and displaces one's true work.

The narrator adds a coda to the story: we learn that, after her encounter with Conrad, Mrs. Smith discovers that she has cancer. Her response, part denial, part mourning for what is not to be written, is to stare "out of the window and [try] to think of short tales, of compressed, rapid forms of writing, in case there was not much time" (***SOS,*** 146).

"Precipice-Encurled" begins realistically, with a description of a woman sitting in a window overlooking a canal in Venice: "She is a plump woman in a tea gown. She wears a pretty lace cap and pearls." However, we next read: "These things are known, highly probable" (***SOS,*** 185). Byatt, as she does in ***Angels and Insects,*** thus begins to weave a story around real Victorians. The narrator tells us that this woman (who remains unnamed until the end of the story) "is the central character in no story, but peripheral in many, where she may be reduced to two or three bold identifying marks" (186). But Byatt gives her a story in which she can emerge more fully into our imagination—and a story in which the imagination is a central theme.

The woman, an actual historical person, is Katherine Kay Bronson (Mrs. Arthur Bronson), who met Robert Browning in 1880. They remained close friends until Browning's death. He dedicated his last book of poems, *Asolando* (1889), to her. Mrs. Bronson often took his social affairs in hand when he stayed in Venice and lent him the use of her palazzo. She is, the narrator tells us, "an enthusiast: she collects locks of hair, snipped from great poetic temples" (***SOS,*** 186). Mrs. Bronson, interested in Browning's comfort, solicitous of his welfare, also collected whatever bon mots fell from his lips in order to record them for posterity. Here, locks of hair and famous words are given equal weight.

This is one thread of the story. Another is the tale of the imaginary scholar who finds a letter of Sarianna Browning, Robert's sister. Following a ghost of a trail of evidence, the scholar speculates that Browning, at 77 (the last year of his life), might have begun to fall in love with Mrs. Bronson, the accomplished cultivator of poets and society. The (unnamed) scholar, like Mrs. Bronson, is also a sum of hypothetical scenarios: we see him "*perhaps* turning over browned packets of . . . notes" (***SOS,*** 187, emphasis mine). He believes that a "good scholar may permissibly invent, he may have a hypothesis, but fiction is barred" (187-88). It is Byatt, of course, who invents—as she invents the scholar himself—and who lets loose the possibilities of fiction. She takes her cue from the epigraph to the story, lines taken from Browning's *The Ring and the Book*:

> What's this then, which proves good yet seems untrue?
> Is fiction, which makes fact alive, fact too?
> The somehow may be thishow.
>
> (185)

The categories of fiction (Byatt's story) and fact (the particulars of Robert Browning's and Mrs. Bronson's lives) are thus intermixed, effectively destabilizing both.

Mrs. Bronson's story, and the story of the scholar who pursues her, wraps around yet another story, that of Juliana Fishwick and the painter Joshua Riddell, in which is embedded the portrait of Browning, the heart of **"Precipice-Encurled."** Here, Browning ruminates on his life, acquaintance, and accomplishments—or rather, Byatt creates a Browning to ruminate so (***SOS,*** 188-94, 212-14). "The best part of my life, he told himself, the life I have lived most intensely, has been the fitting, the infiltrating, the inventing the self of another man or woman, explored and sleekly filled out, as fingers swell a glove" (191). In other words, Browning believes he has lived most intensely when he is creating fictional characters. We are told that "writing brought to life in him a kind of joy in greed" (192). Byatt transfers her own comments about herself as a "greedy reader" to Browning—who is, of course, one of the writers she has read so greedily. Browning's meditations establish a genealogy for Byatt's own forays into fiction writing.

The Fishwicks provide the context for the excursus on Browning. They have rented the Villa Colomba and invited young Joshua Riddell and Browning to visit. Their daughter Juliana is goodhearted but not a beauty; she is too plump, the narrator tells us, for that year's fashions. She is innocent, feeling love as "vaguely aflame, diffusely desirous" (***SOS,*** 203). Joshua Riddell, intended by his family for "the Bar, the House of Commons, the judiciary," has plans of his own: "He meant to be a great painter. He meant to do something quite new, which would have authority. He knew he should recognize this, when he had learned what it was, and how to do it" (196). Joshua, as we see, has a different kind of innocence.

Juliana and Joshua begin to fall in love, but like Browning's and Mrs. Bronson's relationship, it is never to be: Joshua goes to the mountains to paint and, absorbed alternately in Ruskin and in Juliana, ignores the signs of a coming storm and falls to his death. The Fishwicks give up the villa, and Browning's visit is put off. Browning heads back to London and never sees Mrs. Bronson again.

The title, taken from Browning's "De Gustibus" ("What I love best in all the world / Is a castle, precipice-encurled") is in part an allusion to Riddell's precipice and to the villa itself, perched as it is in the mountains. But "precipice" is also a symbol: Riddell teeters on the dangerous edge of commitment, either to art or to love. Through Joshua, Byatt develops a meditation on an aesthetic with an emphasis on the visual, on the representation of light and color. John Ruskin is pressed into service, for according to him, "clarity of vision was the essence of truth, virtue, and good art" (***SOS,*** 206). The "clarity of vision" Joshua experiences on the mountain leads him to reject Juliana. Monet is invoked as well; the narrator tells us how, in *Vétheuil in the Fog,* Monet "had painted, not the thing seen, but the act of seeing" (210). Once again, Byatt makes a metaphor for her own writing.

At the end of **"Precipice-Encurled,"** one theme that emerges is that of loss, of possibilities and potentialities never realized. Joshua's death is described as "the vanishing between instants of all that warmth and intelligence and aspiration" (***SOS,*** 211). The story of Joshua is, in a way, a nonstory, a story that didn't happen—in both real life *and* in fiction. The stories of Mrs. Bronson and Juliana, who never marries, are nonstories as well: "An opportunity has been missed. A tentative love has not flowered" (214). In essence, **"Precipice-Encurled"** is a path not taken.

"The Changeling," "The July Ghost," "The Next Room," and "The Dried Witch"

In spite of Mrs. Smith in **"On the Day E. M. Forster Died"** (she is "a writer who believed, among other things, that time for writing about writing was past"), **"The Changeling"** is a *mise-en-abîme,* in which Henry James both influences Byatt's writing and, through her, Byatt's imaginary author. It is a Gothic tale that evokes the ambiguity and darkness of *The Turn of the Screw.* Josephine Piper is a writer whose subject "was fear. Rational fear, irrational fear, the huge-bulking fear of the young not at home in the world" (***SOS,*** 151). Her most famous book is *The Boiler-Room,* in which the central character, the disturbed and antisocial Simon Vowle, has created a sanctuary behind the furnace in his boarding school. In real life, Josephine sees many such troubled boys: she and her son "had tried to fill the bedrooms, surround the dining room table, with guests whom . . . they called the Lost Boys" (148).

At the urging of her friend Max, she takes in Henry Smee, who is, he says, very much like Simon Vowle. It seems to Josephine upon first meeting him that he does indeed look like the Simon she created in her book. He is silent and withdrawn, having, the narrator says, "a habit of stasis" (***SOS,*** 150). Josephine begins to be afraid of him, "to listen in fear for his door to open again, for him to begin his slow, deliberate, desperate-seeming descent" (151).

The secret of the story, what remains hidden under the cover of Josephine's writing, is that Josephine herself is the one who is full of fear: she has crafted a life to suppress this fact. The exact nature of Josephine's fear is not made clear—it may simply be a fear of fear. Josephine's mother was agoraphobic; Josephine spent her childhood worrying that fear may be hereditary (***SOS,*** 153). Her husband left her because, she believes, "he had found her out"—he had seen through her defenses (157). She had tried carefully to shield her son Peter from her fears, but Josephine realizes too late that he may have had other, different fears that she was too blind to see. Her son, instead of following in her footsteps to university, "spent all his time helping a group who brought soup to ragged sleepers in parks and subways . . . who were not above taking what they saw as necessities from supermarkets" (157). It is significant that Byatt names the son Peter, deliberately invoking Peter Pan: Peter himself is truly Josephine's lost boy.

When Henry Smee reads *The Boiler-Room,* he asks Josephine: "How do you *know* about Simon. . . . The world is more terrible than most people ever let themselves imagine. Isn't it?" (***SOS,*** 155). But she is afraid to tell the truth about how she has come to her knowledge. One night, when Josephine comes home, she finds Henry in her room, examining himself in the mirror. She screams: "Get out, get out of my house, I can't bear any more of this, I can't bear your creeping" (159). He reacts oddly, sinisterly: he smiles "a small circumscribed and satisfied little smile"—as if he had intended to push her to this point (159). When Henry leaves the house, Josephine's writing block clears. He commits suicide several weeks later.

The theme of unhappy school days appears more than once in Byatt's fiction. The imaginary Simon is based on Josephine's own school experience, for she often used the boiler room for sanctuary while in school: "She had been saved . . . by the solitary and sensuous pleasure of writing out her fear" there (***SOS,*** 154). Before Josephine, Byatt herself fled to the boiler room of her school in order to make space for writing. "Simon Vowle was an exorcism" (154), the narrator tells us. The question is for whom.

Like the other stories in this cluster, **"The July Ghost"** centers on a woman who lives alone. Its subject is genuine grief that is bottled up, unreleased, and, when catharsis is offered, mediated through another's experience.

Imogen is a woman too sensible to see her own son's ghost when he appears in her garden; she can only be solaced by his presence secondhand. It is her lodger who can see the ghost. It is not so much that he has an ability or a sense that she lacks; rather, she has too much grief to be able to take comfort in such a visitation. It took Byatt herself many years before she could write about her son and his death. She transmutes some of her own powerful feelings into this tale.

The story begins with the voice of the (unnamed) lodger: "I think I must move out of where I am living" (***SOS,*** 40). He then proceeds to tell the story of the ghost to an American woman he meets at a party. This conversation, part flirtation, is a frame-story for the story of Imogen and her son. In fact, he met Imogen under similar circumstances: he had said these exact words to her at a different party weeks earlier. His lover, Anne, had just left him, and he could not stand to be in the flat they had shared. Imogen had invited him to stay with her.

At Imogen's house, the lodger sits in the back garden to read and write. He is often disturbed by the children who have taken over the Commons on which the garden wall abuts. They lose their balls over the wall and scramble to the top to retrieve them. Imogen tells him that "there aren't many safe spaces for children, round here," and that the Commons is "an illusion of space. . . . Just a spur of brambles and gorsebushes and bits of football pitch between two fast four-laned main roads." She adds, "No illusions are pleasant" (***SOS,*** 43).

These remarks prepare us for the appearance of a very particular boy in the garden. The lodger first notices him sitting in a tree (***SOS,*** 44). As the boy returns day after day, the lodger begins to converse with him, though the child never replies. However, when the lodger meets him coming out of the kitchen door, he decides he must tell Imogen. She explains that the boy might be a friend of her son's, who was killed in a car accident while trying to reach the Commons two years earlier. Once he describes the boy's physical appearance, including his clothes, she reacts oddly. In a "precise conversational tone," she says that "the only thing I want, the only thing I want at all in this world, is to see that boy" (46). She sits down "neatly as always," and faints. For the boy is her son. While she thinks she is "too rational" to see ghosts (46), she says, "I can't stop my body and mind waiting. . . . I can't let go" (47).

However, the version of this tale that he tells the American woman has no ghost; he talks about a boy who was *like* Imogen's dead son and begins to explain their relationship in terms of a mutually shared grief—his for Anne, hers for the boy. He revises the truth because "there was a sense he could not at first analyse that it was improper to talk about the boy—not because he might not be believed . . . because something dreadful might happen" (***SOS,*** 49).

The lodger comes to like the boy more and more; he asks him if there is anything that he can do for him. The boy, it seems, does try to tell him something. It seems that "what he required was to be re-engendered, for him, the man, to give to his mother another child, into which he could peacefully vanish" (*SOS,* 52). The lodger realizes he could be mistaken: "The situation was making him hysterical. . . . He could not spend the rest of the summer, the rest of his life, describing non-existent tee-shirts and blond smiles" (52). When the lodger comes to her bedroom, Imogen seems to understand his intent and acquiesces. However, once they begin to make love, she cannot: "Sex and death don't go. I can't afford to let go of my grip on myself" (54). The boy is obviously grieved by this failure.

The story ends with the lodger returning to Imogen's house to collect his things. When he goes to his room, the boy is sitting on his suitcase. The lodger tries to explain to him why he must leave, saying "I can't get through. Do you want me to stay?" At this, "as he stood helplessly there, the boy turned on him again the brilliant, open, confiding, beautiful desired smile" (*SOS,* 56). We are left wondering what the lodger will do next.

"The Next Room" is about a woman who had set out on her career, her gladly chosen lifework, but put her dreams and ambitions aside for 20 years in order to care for a demanding, selfish, invalid mother. Joanna Hope's work as a surveyor in Third World countries required that she travel; however, after her father died and her mother became ill, she had to stay in the London office. Once her mother dies, however, the 59-year-old Joanna discovers that she has not really broken free, for she keeps hearing the voices of her parents in the next room, querulous, angry, and constant.

The story opens with Joanna attending the cremation of her mother, feeling "an emotion to which, firmly and with shame, she put a name. It was elation" (*SOS,* 58). Joanna returns home, begins gingerly to plan her new life, and reflects on the presence and absence of both her parents: a hairbrush, a dressing gown, a gardening jacket, a tweed hat. Joanna's way of remembering her parents, her organizing image, is what she calls "the jigsaw": "a set of images, strip-cartoon pictures, patches of colour, she seemed to snip out with mental scissors and fit together awkwardly with overlaps or gaps, labelling this for reference 'my mother'" (61).

Joanna's relationship with her father, we are told, was mediated through her mother, who was "a great requirer" (*SOS,* 62). Because of this, Joanna feels that she never really knew or understood him. His place in her mental jigsaw is more ambiguous: "There were things now, that constituted sharp corners and jagged edges, that she had never brought out to look at. . . . Many of these pieces were to do with her vanished father, who had begun to vanish long before he had in fact choked gently to death" (62). But examining this and other memories that make up the jigsaw makes her uncomfortable. As her mother so often did, Joanna switches on the television, in time to listen to a Native American describe his people's relationship with the dead: "We can hear the spirit-voices of our ancestors, close to us, not gone away, in the grass and trees and stones we know and love. You send your ancestors away in closed boxes to your faraway Heaven" (65). The TV, instead of deflecting her thoughts, only gives shape to the question of, "Where had her mother gone, particles and smoke?" (66).

We next learn that Joanna's mother had told her about a curious state she would often find herself in between waking and dreaming, in which she heard her own parents "quarrelling dreadfully in the next room, ever so close . . . they might turn on me and draw me into it at any minute . . . they are waiting for me—I almost said, lying in wait, but that would be an awful thing to say" (*SOS,* 71-72).

These two incidents make explicit what Byatt has been hinting at all along: that the border between the living and the dead is more permeable than we think. It is no surprise, then, when Joanna begins to hear voices in the next room, in her fitful sleep induced by painkillers. She hears "aggrieved voices, running on in little dashes like a thwarted beck clucking against pebble-beds. . . . They had the ease of long custom and the abrasiveness of new rage" (*SOS,* 74). Even when the realtor comes, "the voices hissed and jangled. It was as though these brick walls were interwoven with some other tough, indestructible structure, containing other rooms, other vistas, other jammed doors. Like a dress and its lining, with the slimmest space between" (75).

Joanna escapes to Durham on business and stays at a hotel reputedly haunted by two ghosts. But her own familial voices are all that she hears, for they "were attached . . . to her own blood and presence" (*SOS,* 83).

I group **"The Dried Witch"** with these stories because, in spite of its very different setting, it has certain generic similarities to them. It is a British version of Shirley Jackson's "The Lottery," in which a small village holds a ritual lottery in order to choose a scapegoat each year. In Jackson's story, the scapegoat is then stoned to death. **"The Dried Witch"** owes its ambiance to the fairy tale in which the figure of the old crone is capable of inspiring fear, respect, and pity. The place and time of the story are never specified, but certain Asian resonances and the un-English names of the characters signal that the story occurs "once upon a time" and far away.

A-Oa (a name that hints at "Alpha-Omega") is an aging widow who, frustrated by the restrictive customs of her village and her own "dryness," becomes a witch. The villagers turn on her and condemn her to a painful death.

"The Dried Witch," like all fairy tales, can be read allegorically: it is the story of anyone who deviates from the norms of his or her community and of the price that must be paid.

More specifically, this story is a fable about women who are seen as transgressing social boundaries. In many cultures, the old woman is viewed as frightening—as taboo—because she has lost her sexual attractiveness and ability to bear children. She is a threat because she no longer has a place in the hierarchy. At the same time, she is often a repository of lore that can benefit the whole community. Such a woman is often labeled a witch, "a term invented for women who contest the patriarchal orders of theological or medical knowledge."[4] And finally, **"The Dried Witch"** is an allegory of the artist, the writer—the woman writer—who cannot win for losing: she suffers when her gifts dry up; she is penalized by the community when her talents are too much in view.

A-Oa suffers from dryness—a literal, physical dryness, and a figurative, spiritual, or creative dryness. "There was an age when a woman might become a jinx, and she had perhaps arrived there" (***SOS,*** 86). But A-Oa was not always old and dry. In the early days of her marriage, in her hope for children, in her "running blood," A-Oa had viewed the elder village witch "with a mixture of repugnance, fear, and something approaching pity." For "the old woman, in her . . . dry black cloths seemed unnecessary, waste, fragile." But now A-Oa herself is "waste, fragile," and seeks a charm against dryness.[5] The elder witch promises "power over wet and dry, to heal or, if need be, to harm. You will be respected and feared. Unless you come against some more powerful magic" (93).

The "more powerful magic" is that of the shopkeeper Kun, who represents male power and retribution. He is a great extorter and blackmailer; he knows secrets about the villagers, and "how to make himself necessary" (***SOS,*** 88). A jinx, on the other hand, is not "necessary" in the conventional sense; she is feared, able to "dry up a child, or cause crops to fail, or pigs to be barren. A jinx could cause a tree to burst into flames" (88).

As A-Oa begins to work small cures, she gains respect and a title: "Mother." A young man of the village, "the beautiful, gleaming Cha-Hun," comes for a love charm (***SOS,*** 97). He stands on her doorstep, asking permission to enter. "'I am too old to forbid you,' said A-Oa drily, meaning that there would have been a time when it would have been sinful and punishable for him to enter a house alone with a woman who was no kin of his, but that now it was not, for she was no woman, she was something else" (98). This passage illustrates the rigid hierarchies that govern village life. Cha-Hun desires his absent brother's wife. He says he will give his life to possess her. But it is A-Oa who will be put to death if the pair are caught in adultery. And it is very likely that they will be caught, for Kun follows Cha-Hun wherever he goes. A-Oa realizes that he is sexually interested in the boy, as he was in her own missing husband. (Most of the men were conscripted into the army years ago.) A-Oa, in spite of the danger, agrees to provide the potion, because of "the force of his youth . . . [and] the girl's youth, that blazed and would not be denied" (101).

Of course, A-Oa is caught and punished. The motif of dryness takes on a frightening reality as the villagers chant: "We sun the jinx. We put the jinx to dry in the sun" (***SOS,*** 107). She is bound to a tree stump and left to die. What follows is an excruciating description of her suffering, and how she comes to accept it. At the very end, in a final gathering of will and affirmation, she sets the thorn trees alight around her.

"In the Air"

Mrs. Sugden is a retired schoolteacher who watches too much TV and feels guilty about it. Her most meaningful human contact is her daily call to get the recorded weather forecast. Otherwise, her main companion is a sheepdog named Wolfgang. **"In the Air"** is a dismal story about one woman's obsession with "the man"—a stalker of women on the Common where Mrs. Sugden walks Wolfgang every day (***SOS,*** 162). "The man," we learn, exists only in Mrs. Sugden's imagination: "He was black, he was white, he was brown, he was dirty grey, he was a thin youth with acne or an ageing bullet-headed stroller in leather jacket and trainers. He carried a briefcase, a plastic bag of junk from rubbish bins, a knife" (163). He is, in sum, potentially anyone. "Every day," we are told, "she feared him a little more, every day the mental encounter took another step into the vividly realised" (163).

At first, one might be tempted to dismiss Mrs. Sugden's unhealthy fantasies as a projection outward onto "the man" of her own fears about sexuality, her body, and its natural aging. Byatt/the narrator is aware of this possibility. However, Mrs. Sugden represents a point, extreme as it may be, on a scale along which most women are ranged in society. "Mrs. Sugden, a sensible woman, knew he was an obsession, but did not know how to exorcise him." She is aware of very real assaults on women in her neighborhood. "Why should he not wait for, or at the least, accidentally notice her too?" (***SOS,*** 163). She wonders: "Were little girls always violated and old women struck down in their thin blood, or is it more now, is it really more, and different?" (167-68).

One day, Mrs. Sugden watches a blind woman being stalked by a gangling young man in a blue track suit. He circles her, making grotesque gestures ("'mopping and mowing,' said Mrs. Sugden's fairytale vocabulary to her" [***SOS,*** 173]). This brings Mrs. Sugden out of her isolating fear: she must reach out and help someone else who is in danger and literally blind to it. She introduces herself to Eleanor Tillotson, and they walk together. Eleanor tells Mrs. Sugden: "There isn't much I could do, if I was worried. Just live a little less, in a smaller circle" (177). The young man, Barry, stops to ask the time; he is intrusive, asking questions of Eleanor too directly, Mrs. Sugden feels, and getting himself, along with Mrs. Sugden, invited to Eleanor's for tea.

We see Barry through Mrs. Sugden's eyes: "Gold curls, damp or greasy, clustered on his forehead. His features were all exaggerated, like his movements. His mouth was large. . . . His nose was full and snuffing, with curling nostrils and huge dark holes" (***SOS,*** 175). Mrs. Sugden feels he is playing with both of the women; he knows her fear, but he is blocked by Eleanor's fearlessness. At one point in Eleanor's flat, he suggests to Mrs. Sugden that one could move the furniture around: "She'd be all over the place, wouldn't she, she wouldn't know what to do with herself?" (182).

What is fascinating about the crafting of this story is how the reader's initial doubts about Mrs. Sugden and her fears are gradually turned into real alarm. While we pity Mrs. Sugden at first for her loneliness, we finally identify with her helplessness. The story ends ominously: as Barry and Mrs. Sugden stand on the sidewalk after tea, he takes out a knife and begins to play idly with it. He says, "Goodbye then. We'll see each other again, for sure. Up and down. I'm around a lot. I'll look out for you specially" (***SOS,*** 184).

"Sugar"

Proust provides the intertext for **"Sugar,"** which reads like a remembrance of things past in Byatt's own life; this feeling is enhanced by her use of an unnamed first-person narrator. Byatt has always made known her admiration for Proust. As she says in the 1989 introduction to **"Sugar,"** she appreciates his ability to "narrate what was his own life . . . because what he wrote contained its own precise study of the nature of language, of perception, of memory, of what limits and constitutes our vision of being" (*PM* [*Passions of the Mind*], 16). This indeed is the theme of **"Sugar."**

The fulcrum of the story is a hospital room in Amsterdam in which the narrator's father lies dying of cancer. From this locale—spatial and mental—the narrator ranges backward in time and place as she reflects upon her family: her mother, who "was not a truthful woman" (***SOS,*** 215); her father, a judge, a Yorkshireman, "a late-convinced Quaker, a socialist-turned democrat" (217); and her father's father. The narrator recounts bits of history about her father's family. Her grandfather owned a candy factory and expected his children to follow him into the business. The narrator's father, however, saved his money and defiantly went to Cambridge to read law—as did Byatt's own father, who refused to go into his father's candy business.[6]

Byatt examines the idea of family myth, of tradition and history, and how such things are altered by family members. The narrator says, as she sits by her father's sickbed, that she "needed an idea of the past, of those long-dead grandparents" (***SOS,*** 219). This idea, she knows, can never be the result of an absolute truth, but only a result of the truth that belongs to memory, defective and self-serving as it is.

Her mother, for example, seemed to want to alter memory; she "lied in small matters, to tidy up embarrassments, and in larger matters, to avoid unpalatable truths" (***SOS,*** 215). At one point, the narrator gives the following example of her mother's art: "My mother's accounts of my grandmother's selflessness were like pearls, or sugar-coated pills, grit and bitterness polished into roundness by comedy and my mother's worked-upon understanding of my grandmother's real meaning" (229). This passage is worth taking apart: the narrator/daughter can learn only at secondhand about her grandmother, who died when the narrator was young. Her mother mediates the meaning of her grandmother's life. Her mother, however, often shaped her "accounts" into polished narratives, each with an internal logic of its own. Through long use and retelling, these stories have accrued layers of significance that drain the original moments of their pain or embarrassment. The pearl, begun as a grain of irritation in an oyster shell, is an apt and vivid image of these stories and their layers. It also invokes the notion of pearls cast before swine—which, of course, cannot appreciate their worth. The sugar-coated pills point to the title and to the family business, as well as serving as a parallel to pearls.

The mother is not the only player in this familial collusion, which is both painful and necessary, as the daughter realizes, "for the sake of peace" (***SOS,*** 215). At one point, she asks her father, "Have you ever thought . . . how much of what we think we know is made out of her stories? One challenges the large errors. . . . But there are all the *little* trivial myths that turn into memories" (240-41).

We might see **"Sugar"** as strategically placed at the end of Byatt's collection of short stories as a commentary on the deeply personal that these stories often represent—and often do *not* represent. As the narrator of **"Sugar"** observes: "After things have happened, when we have taken a breath and a look, we begin to know what they are and were, we begin to tell them to ourselves" (***SOS,*** 248). However, any such telling involves a certain amount of self-deception. This particular story began, Byatt says, "as a kind of temptation. I had been thinking about the problem of the relations between truth, lies and fiction all my life" (14). This problem is well illustrated by the title of the story: **"Sugar"** resonates beyond the particular memories the narrator/Byatt has of the candy factory and becomes a sign for art itself: "I saw that much of my past might be [my mother's] confection" (240), the narrator says. She/Byatt goes on to say that "I have inherited much from her. I do make a profession out of fiction. I select and confect. What is all this, all this story so far, but a careful selection of things that can be told, things that can be arranged in the light of day?" (241).

It is hard to resist the clear sound of Byatt's own voice here, as if she has dropped the mask of the narrator. Compare this statement to Byatt's scholarly voice in her commentary on the story: "If fiction does not eat up life, reality, truth, it rearranges it so that it is forever unrecognisable except in terms of the fixed form, the set arrangement" (15). Byatt captures the essence of **"Sugar"** and of her fiction generally in this statement. Whatever the autobiographical origins of her work may be, they are always transformed into art. Byatt retains a sense of ambivalence about these metamorphoses: "the relations between truth, lies and fiction" are continually problematized, a process that is both exhilarating and exhausting.

The Matisse Stories

"Medusa's Ankles," "Art Work," and "The Chinese Lobster"

The Matisse Stories is Byatt's tribute to Henri Matisse's method and to his palette. Matisse, we are told, is Byatt's favorite painter; she aspires to write in the same way that he painted (Kellaway, 45). According to one reviewer, "Byatt is attempting literally to paint with words, to convey physical sensations from the taste of food to the weight of heartache."[7] Indeed, Byatt says she has a vivid visual sense: "I see any projected piece of writing or work as a geometric structure: various colours and patterns"—quite like, one might add, Matisse's later collages.[8] Matisse experimented with translating pure color into form; in ***The Matisse Stories,*** Byatt uses color in much the same way. In each story, colors often serve as objective correlatives to both theme and character.

In **"Medusa's Ankles,"** a middle-aged woman's routine visit to her hairdresser becomes anything but routine. Susannah is to be interviewed on TV and has more than her usual share of anxiety about her aging looks. She had initially chosen Lucian's shop because of the Matisse on the wall, a reclining voluptuous nude—which has since been replaced by contemporary black-and-white photographs of models. However, Susannah continues to see Lucian because she has come "to trust him with her disintegration" (***MS*** [***Matisse Stories***], 7). Apparently, the fact that Susannah is intelligent, a successful academic with a specialty in classics, provides no protection against the effects of age. In the strange between-world of the beauty parlor, in which one becomes disconnected from one's identity on the way to arriving someplace—or becoming someone—else, Susannah contemplates her face, both itself and symbol:

> She looked at her poor face, under its dank cap and its two random corkscrews, aluminum clamped. She felt a gentle protective rage towards this stolid face. She remembered . . . looking at her skin, and wondering how it could grow into the crepe, the sag, the opulent soft bags. This was her face, she had thought then. And this, too, now, she wanted to accept for her face . . . this greying skin, these flakes, these fragile stretches with no elasticity, was her, was her life, was herself.
>
> (19)

In a reversal of the usual relationship between hairdresser and client (patient?), Susannah does not confide in Lucian; he, however, tells her all about his personal life. On this particular day, Lucian tells her about making the decision to leave his wife for a younger woman. Susannah, married herself, identifies with Lucian's wife throughout his chatter—an identification that the narrative of **"Medusa's Ankles"** suppresses, only to foreground it at the very end of the story. At one point, Lucian says: "I don't want to put the best years of my life into making suburban old dears presentable. . . . I want something more." Susannah is, of course, one of the "old dears." To make matters worse, he complains about his wife: "She's let herself go. It's her own fault. She's let herself go altogether. She's let her ankles get fat, they swell over her shoes, it disgusts me, it's impossible for me" (***MS,*** 21).

When Lucian's assistant does something disastrous to Susannah's hair, she flies into a rage: "She could only see dimly, for the red flood was like a curtain at the back of her eyes, but she knew what she saw. The Japanese say demons of another world approach us through mirrors as fish rise through water, and, bubble-eyed and trailing fins, a fat demon swam towards her, turret-crowned, snake-crowned, her mother fresh from the dryer in all her embarrassing irreality" (***MS,*** 23). "'It's horrible,' said Susannah. '*I look like a middle-aged woman with a hair-do.*' She could see them all looking at each other, sharing the knowledge that this was exactly what she was" (24). The result is worth quoting at length:

> Susannah seized a small cylindrical pot and threw it. . . . It burst with a satisfying crash and one whole mirror became a spider-web of cracks, from which fell, tinkling, a little heap of crystal nuggets. In front of Susannah was a whole row of such bombs or grenades. She lobbed them all around her. Some of the cracks

> made a kind of strained singing noise, some were explosive. She whirled a container of hairpins about her head and scattered it like a nailbomb. She tore dryers from their sockets. . . . She broke basins with brushes. . . . She silenced the blatter of the music with a well-aimed imitation alabaster pot of Juvenescence Emulsion, which dripped into the cassette which whirred more and more slowly in a thickening morass of blush-coloured cream.
>
> (25-26)

Lucian is astonishingly understanding and soothing about the whole incident. When Susannah goes home, and before she washes her new hairdo out—and this is the twist of the story—her estranged husband comes home and notices her for the first time in years: "And he came over and kissed her on the shorn nape of her neck, quite as he used to do" (28).

In this story, Susannah has tapped into the power of Medusa, the woman-monster out of mythology whose hair is a mass of deadly writhing snakes and who is capable of turning to stone anyone who looks at her. As such, Medusa is traditionally viewed as ugly and repugnant—all that is the opposite of youth, beauty, and desire. She also symbolizes, via Freud, the threat of castration and the power of woman. In a way, Medusa, here with the "fat ankles" of middle age, lies latent within the *Rosy Nude* of Matisse that Lucian initially hung in his shop.

The French feminist Hélène Cixous, in her famous essay "The Laugh of the Medusa," turns the Medusa figure into something positive and affirming for women: "And she's not deadly. She's beautiful and she's laughing."[9] By doing so, Cixous contests the power men have traditionally wielded through their control of myth and challenges women to rewrite myth in their own "true" image. As *Possession: A Romance* makes clear, Byatt has read Cixous; we might read **"Medusa's Ankles"** as a response to Cixous, in which Byatt accepts Cixous's revision of Medusa but wants to keep—and honor—the terrible aspect of her beauty and the edge to her laugh.

"Art Work" begins with a meditation on Matisse's *Le Silence Habité des Maisons* ("the inhabited silence of the house"). In this painting, a mother and child sit at a table while the child turns the pages of a book. Byatt asks of the painting, and of her readers, "Who is the watching totem under the ceiling?" (***MS,*** 32).

Byatt goes on to create her own vision of the "inhabited silence" of a contemporary London household: the Dennison house, filled with domestic sounds, including washing machine, dryer, television, the electric train that son Jamie plays with, and the suppressed sound of pop music coming through "the earphoned head" of daughter Natasha, whose "face has the empty beatific intelligence of some of Matisse's supine women" (***MS,*** 34). At this point, we step into another Matisse painting: Natasha's bedspread "is jazzy black forms of ferns or seaweeds on a scarlet ground, forms that the textile designer would never have seen without Matisse. Her arms and legs dangle beyond the confines of the ruffled rectangle of this spread, too gawky to be an odalisque's, but just as delicious in their curves" (34-35).

Debbie, mother, wife, design editor of a women's magazine, sits at her typewriter writing about new colors in kitchen plastics, such as the one she describes as a "peculiarly luscious new purple, like bilberry juice with a little cream swirled in it" (***MS,*** 38). Debbie has given up her own artistic ambitions as a wood engraver to allow her husband Robin to pursue his painting. The narrator tells us that Debbie's "fingers remembered the slow, careful work in the wood, with a quiet grief that didn't diminish but was manageable. She hated Robin because he never once mentioned the unmade wood engravings" (54). Robin, who at first seems to be the main candidate for the "watching totem under the ceiling" in the Dennison vignette, presides over the third floor, converted into an art studio. He has appropriated the best space and light in the house—and colonized his family's lives as well; their desires are always made subordinate to his.

However, it is Mrs. Brown, the black housekeeper from Guyana, who is the central character and the true totem of the house—and of art. We first meet her as she moves a vacuum cleaner "up and down the stairs, joining all three floors" (***MS,*** 38). Sheba Brown is thus seen as one who can cross over from one milieu to another. She is a genius of juxtaposition in other ways as well: "Mrs. Brown's clothes were, and are, flowery and surprising—jumble-sale remnants, rejects and ends of lines, rainbow-colored pullovers made from the ping-pong-ball-sized unwanted residues of other people's knitting" (40). When Robin fails to interest the Florimel Gallery in mounting an exhibit of his works, it is Mrs. Brown who succeeds. The Dennison family discovers that her sartorial confusions are just a prelude to the larger collages she makes out of the discards of other people's lives. If we see her against a larger canvas than that of the Dennison family, Sheba Brown can be imagined as a recycler of culture, reversing the flow of Western appropriation of the Third World.

Sheba Brown and Robin are locked in an allegorical battle over the possession of culture in small: Robin constantly complains about what he sees as Mrs. Brown's cleaning interferences in his studio. At one point, Mrs. Brown had apparently gathered the detritus of her cleaning—paper clips, a dead flower, matches, and so on—and placed it in a decorated ceramic bowl that Robin was using as a model for color. In fact, Robin has several such "fetishes" that serve as his inspiration for color—a tin soldier, a butter dish, and other such miscellaneous items. Mrs. Brown tends to rearrange these things; Robin is compulsive about what can and cannot be touched. The colors must be arranged just so. These fetishes are the way Robin attempts to come to terms with what he feels is the crushing obligation to live up to the magisterial color in Matisse's paintings.

Robin, an exacting neorealist, hates Mrs. Brown; he sees her as "chaotic and wild to look at" and thinks that she represents "filth" (***MS,*** 58). Mrs. Brown obviously has none of Robin's inhibitions about color as she goes about in her "magenta and vermilion coverall over salmon-pink crêpe pantaloons, or in a lime-green shift with black lacy inserts" (59). Her philosophy, diametrically opposed to the classically trained Robin's, is that "they're all there, the colors, God made 'em all and mixes 'em all in His creatures, what exists goes together somehow or other" (60).

Debbie, trying to manage family, a self-absorbed husband, and a job that stifles her own creativity, depends upon Mrs. Brown to keep her house running smoothly. It is clear to her, the mediator in the battle between Robin and Mrs. Brown, that Robin makes "resolute attempts to unsettle, humiliate, or drive away Mrs. Brown, without whom all Debbie's balancing acts would clatter and fall into wounding disarray" (***MS,*** 54-55). Debbie also knows that "Mrs. Brown has her own modes of silent aggression," and that the battle is not one of Robin's imagination (48).

When Debbie sees Mrs. Brown's exhibit at the Florimel Gallery, quite by accident, it is as if the gallery had been transformed into a "brilliantly colored Aladdin's cave" (***MS,*** 77). Here are all the castoffs that Mrs. Brown has collected and now rearranged into tapestries and soft sculptures—including clothing from Debbie's own family. Her work is highly symbolic. Made up of the bits and pieces of domestic life, it serves as a running commentary on women and their subjugation. For example, she has made a mulberry-colored dress that once belonged to Debbie into the scales of a huge dragon that threatens a woman rag doll, bound and chained with twisted bras and petticoats.

Debbie feels betrayed. She also feels "a kind of subdued envy that carries with it an invigorating sting" (***MS,*** 82). As a result, Debbie goes back to her woodcuts and achieves commercial success with them. Robin turns his grief and his rage at Mrs. Brown into art and begins painting differently, with a "loosed, slightly savage energy" (90). In the work of both husband and wife, Mrs. Brown's face appears—as good and bad fairies in Debbie's woodcuts, as Kali the Destroyer in Robin's. But Kali, the Hindu goddess of death, has her positive aspect as well, for out of death new life is born.

"The Chinese Lobster" is, in part, a meditation on Matisse's place as a painter in a world vastly different from the one in which he painted. While Matisse's greatness is never in doubt in the tale, how one might appreciate or appropriate his paintings is. The argument about Matisse centers on gender—his own exploitation of the women in his family, his representation of women in his art, and what it is like to "read" his paintings as a woman and as a man.

Professor Gerda Himmelblau, dean of students at a London college, must investigate a charge of sexual harassment brought by a female student against Peregrine Diss, a famous and imposing art critic who is a visiting professor at the school. Perry Diss is the quintessential older male professor, passionate about "his" art (he lays claim to most of the great Western tradition) and unable to cope with a postmodern world that seems intent on destroying everything he loves. Gerda Himmelblau attributes his eloquent crankiness to "the possibly crabbed view of a solitary intellectual" (***MS,*** 98). She also recognizes—and for her this is more important—that he "loves [paintings], like sound apples to bite into, like fair flesh, like sunlight" (98).

Gerda herself has a strong aesthetic sense, as we learn in the narrator's description of her clothes: she wears "suits in soft, dark, not-quite-usual colours—damsons, soots, black tulips, dark mosses—with clean-cut cotton shirts, not masculine . . . in clear colors: palest lemon, deepest cream, periwinkle, faded flame" (***MS,*** 99).

The student peggi nollet (she spells her name entirely in lower case) is a different picture altogether. She is writing her dissertation, titled "The Female Body and Matisse," and she is also engaged in the studio work required for graduation. In the stained and rumpled letter she sends to Gerda about Perry Diss, she writes that he "is a so-called EXPERT on the so-called MASTER of MODERNISM, but what does he know about Woman or the internal conduct of the Female Body, which has always until now been MUTE and had no mouth to speak?" (***MS,*** 100). Peggi recounts a conversation that she had with him: "He said Matisse was full of love and desire toward women (!!!!!) and I said '*exactly*' but he did not take the point" (102). One of her pieces is titled *The Resistance of Madame Matisse,* which peggi describes as showing Madame Matisse and her daughter "being *tortured* by the Gestapo in the War whilst *he* sits by like a Buddha cutting up pretty paper with scissors. They wouldn't tell him they were being tortured in case it disturbed his *work.* I felt sick when I found out that. The torturers have got identical scissors" (104). She goes on to relate how Diss comes to her studio to see her work-in-progress. He does not like it, of course. According to peggi, Diss said she had too many clothes on, and that she ought to wear brighter colors—and then he "began kissing and fondeling me and stroking intimate parts of me" (104; peggi's spelling is atrocious throughout this missive). Peggi is also suicidal, and this incident pushes her into deeper despair. What is more, after the reader gets Perry Diss's account of the incident, one might conclude that she is delusional as well.

Just as peggi and Gerda Himmelblau differ in taste and appearance, so do Perry Diss and peggi—a fact that aligns Himmelblau against peggi and seems to substantiate his denial of harassment. He is elegant, with a head of white hair and startling blue eyes. Himmelblau thinks of him as "both fastidious, and marked by ancient indulgence and dissipation" (***MS,*** 109). Peggi, on the other hand, is described by Diss in far less respectful terms: "Her skin is like a *potato,* and her body is like a *decaying potato*. . . . I do not think her hair can have been washed for some years" (115). She reworks prints of Matisse by changing the outlines of the female bodies with some unknown substance, which Diss thinks is blood or feces. How could he be interested in her sexually if she creates such desecrations of Matisse?

As we learn more about peggi, it becomes rather clear that Diss is innocent. However, sexual harassment is not about attraction; it is about power. We might imagine that, if Diss can assert his physicality against peggi's—and her physical body can be extended to include her art—perhaps Diss can ensure that his own aesthetic values triumph.

Gerda Himmelblau and Perry Diss have a conversation over a Chinese lunch, which serves as a kind of visual and sensual counterpoint to their conversation. The two share an aesthetic, highly stylized visual and gastronomic experience as they proceed slowly from course to course. This makes them almost conspiratory—or at the least, members of the same club that excludes the peggi nollets of the world. Peggi's greatest sin, for both Perry and Gerda, is that she cannot *see* Matisse. Why Matisse? asks Perry. Answers Gerda: "Because he paints silent bliss. *Luxe, calme et volupté*" (***MS,*** 121). In other words, Matisse is everything peggi is not. But this sympathetic union also causes Gerda to identify against peggi when Diss calls her a "poor little bitch" (109). Gerda, in the midst of investigating a sexual harassment charge, cannot or will not confront this; she can only manage, "in her head, wincing," to think, "Don't say 'bitch'" (110).

This story, only partially about sexual harassment, real or imagined, is complicated further by the fact that Gerda also identifies against the disturbed and suicidal peggi in another, more fundamental way. Gerda's best and only friend, Kay, the only person she has ever really loved, committed suicide a few years before. Her daughter killed herself as well: "Over the years Kay's daughter's pain became Kay's, and killed Kay" (***MS,*** 127-28). Gerda now feels that "she is next in line" (129).

The very issue that might incline Gerda toward peggi instead strengthens the bond she has with Perry Diss. She notices scars ("well-made *efficient* scars" [***MS,*** 130]) on his wrists; she becomes aware of an undercurrent in their conversation; both know, and know the other knows, the despair that leads one to suicide. Finally, "Gerda Himmelblau sees, in her mind's eye, the face of Peggi Nollett, potato-pale, peering out of a white box with cunning, angry eyes in the slits between puffed eyelids. She sees golden oranges, rosy limbs, a voluptuously curved dark-blue violin case in a black room. One or the other must be betrayed" (132-33).

In the end, Gerda Himmelblau decides to pass peggi on to another adviser and hopes the charge of sexual harassment will evaporate. It is an ambiguous compromise for peggi, but out of it comes a tentative reprieve for Gerda. As she and Perry Diss part, she realizes that "something has happened to her white space, to her inner ice, which she does not quite understand" (***MS,*** 133). Perry Diss has touched her, both through their shared but unspoken grief and through his assertion of a shared aesthetic.

Notes

1. A. S. Byatt, *Sugar and Other Stories* (Harmondsworth, Eng.: Penguin, 1988), 1; hereafter cited in the text as *SOS.*

2. Quoted in Sarah Booth Conroy, "The Magic Brew of A. S. Byatt" [interview], *Washington Post Book World* (29 November 1991): D9; hereafter cited in the text.

3. One narrative comment is especially telling in this respect. Conversation at the conference is apparently dominated by "serious oriental questions about Kristeva's views on Desire and Harold Bloom's map of misreading" (*SOS,* 112). This suggests, however inadvertently, that the "oriental" audience is able to ask questions only, that it cannot provide answers or incisive readings of Julia Kristeva and Harold Bloom. This is, the story seems to imply, partially the result of a repressive government, partially a cultural characteristic. Byatt's choice of literary theorists is interesting, for Kristeva's "views on Desire" focus on desire toward the other; in this case, the East as constructed as different or other. (The East as other and the problems that arise from such an equation dominate a good deal of postcolonial scholarship and critique.) And Bloom argues that certain poets must somehow get around or conquer their predecessors in order to avoid the paralyzing effects of what he calls the anxiety of influence. In other words, in order to find a voice, one must silence, or as he says, misread, those who have come before. Postcolonial discourse is especially con-

cerned with critiquing, modifying, and/or replacing the aesthetic influences and conventions of Western European literature and art.

4. Griselda Pollock, *Vision and Difference: Femininity, Feminism, and Histories of Art* (New York and London: Routledge, 1988), 144.

5. Byatt's use of the word *dryness* recalls Iris Murdoch's critical essay "Against Dryness" (see chap. 1).

6. A. S. Byatt, interview with Juliet A. Dusinberre, in *Women Writers Talking,* ed. Janet Todd (New York and London: Holmes & Meier, 1983), 188; hereafter cited in the text.

7. Sue Kelman, "The Painted Words of A. S. Byatt," *The Toronto Star* (19 March 1994): K12.

8. "Still Life/Nature Morte," in *PM,* 7.

9. Cixous's essay has been widely anthologized. First published in 1975, it can be found in *New French Feminisms: An Anthology,* ed. Elaine Marks and Isabelle de Courtivron, trans. Keith Cohen and Paula Cohen (New York: Schocken Books, 1981), 245-64.

Emily Perkins (review date 22 January 1998)

SOURCE: Perkins, Emily. "Naming Nîmes." *The Observer* (22 January 1998): 14.

[*In the following review, Perkins asserts that in* Elementals *Byatt's "exquisitely formed stories brim with fine detail."*]

'She did not sleep that night, but lay awake, still and calm, visited by hypnagogic moons and stars and waves lapping on seashores, or skies lit with flaring curtains of blue and crimson lights, as though she had stepped, or fallen, into some world of mythical absolutes.' This is Patricia Nimmo, a middle-aged English woman, who has fled her violently altered life for a hotel in Nîmes.

'Crocodile Tears', the first story in A. S. Byatt's elegant new collection [***Elementals***], charts her bewildered journey through the glacial landscape of grief. One of Nîmes's origin myths concerns Antony and Cleopatra; Patricia met her husband Tony when he played Lepidus in a student production of Shakespeare's play. How we mourn the dead, and what we owe them, is the question asked here.

Byatt knows that 'there's beggary in the love that can be reckoned'—she does not do more than outline the couple's long marriage. What we see are the externals of Patricia's grief, swathed in cold sheets of numbness. Her indifference is in danger of overwhelming curiosity. This is never a state the collection falls prey to. The exquisitely formed stories brim with fine detail. They are tales more than stories, narratives strewn with symbols, clues—objects as intriguing as Atalanta's golden apples. These are images to pause over—a palace carved from glass, say, or an amulet of Thor's hammer—and to turn this way and that. The descriptions of place, as seen and as experienced, are beautiful: 'She remembered Nîmes, like a hot blue and golden ball, containing creamy stone cylinders and cubes.'

Much of the collection is concerned with art and mystery. In **'A Lamia in the Cevennes'**, the painter Bernard struggles to capture air and water on canvas. His swimming-pool is visited by a snake-like Lamia, 'a darkness spangled with living colours', who lets him paint her in return for a transformative kiss. The sinister currents under this parable are neutralised, at least for Bernard, who is too practical to become trapped by the siren's charms. He believes in the integration of art and 'cold philosophy': science does not interfere with an appreciation of Otherness; it is Bernard's courage to embrace both that makes him an artist, and that saves him.

If the above stories seem almost too highly polished, too frostily beautiful to engage emotionally, some grit is allowed into **'Jael'**, a story of violent treachery, and the heat is turned up. This is a compelling and subtle investigation into self-deception, the failure of memory, the betrayal of art by commercialism and the fragility of power. The contemporary risk of dismissing lessons from classical myth and the Scriptures as 'dead cultural baggage' is illustrated with piercing force.

The myriad facets to the stories in ***Elementals*** may deal in fundamentals, but they reach far beyond the material. What it is to be warm-blooded—to be, unlike the crocodile of Nîmes, 'quick'—this is the larger question at the collection's source. Blood, dust, love, the supernatural—all are strands threaded through these timeless fables. A recurring device is the story within a story, illustrating with classical allusion the mythical absolutes available to make poetry out of our experience.

Tamsin Todd (review date 8 February 1998)

SOURCE: Todd, Tamsin. "By Literature Possessed." *Book World—The Washington Post* 28, no. 6 (8 February 1998): 4-5.

[*In the following favorable review, Todd maintains that "if* Imagining Characters *suggests that literary criticism and fiction share some of the same concerns, then* The Djinn in the Nightingale's Eye *is a demonstration of this idea."*]

It's a curious fact on university campuses that the two kinds of people professionally concerned with literature—literary critics and creative writers—rarely talk to each other. Poets and fiction writers, under the auspices of writing programs, study things like character and craft and voice, while critics, housed in English and comparative literature departments, talk about literary theory and cultural studies. They publish in different journals, attend different conferences and, when they find themselves at the same parties, peer at each other with suspicion.

All of which makes A. S. Byatt a bit of an anomaly. Byatt—professor of English at University College, London, and a Booker Prize-winning novelist for *Possession*—successfully straddles these fields. How does she do it? For one thing, she doesn't subscribe to all this separatism. She believes that literary critics and creative writers, despite their different professional interests, do have a lot to say to each other. As she says in *Imagining Characters,* a new collection of conversations about major women writers, conversation about books should be "a form of shared reading—a pleasure and a way of learning which has almost vanished."

Imagining Characters is, in part, an effort to reconcile these two kinds of literary study. In scintillating conversations with clinical psychologist Ignes Sodre, Byatt guides readers through six English and American novels, speaking as both a literary critic and as a writer. Wearing her academic hat, she talks lucidly about culture, narrative structure and literary history, making reference to a range of critics and theorists. She riffs on differences between American and European novels ("I think the image of the good suffering person, whom you can hold on to to make yourself good, underlies what Toni Morrison can do with a novel and European novelists have lost") and discovers interesting thematic connections ("*The Professor's House,* like *Monsfield Park, Daniel Deronda* and in some ways *Villette,* is about the relations between human beings and the houses that contain them").

But she also talks about writing from a writer's point of view. Why, she asks, do writers write? How do they go about making stories? What differentiates a good book from a bad one? The result is a dazzling display of knowledge, insight and intelligence.

The book is modeled on Socratic dialogues with Sodre playing student to Byatt's Socrates. Sodre asks questions ("I would be really interested in hearing you talk about how something gets transformed in a writer's mind from the raw material—the basic stuff that's inside you—emotional experience, unconscious processes and things you think and know about—into producing a creative work of art"), and Byatt performs. Sodre is the perfect foil for Byatt: intelligent, knowledgeable and willing to listen.

Byatt's enthusiasm for literature is infectious. Books have long been important in her life; she describes herself as a "lonely child who escaped into books." For Byatt, novels aren't merely objects for academic study: Like George Eliot, whom she frequently quotes, Byatt believes novels are life-models and teachers. She talks frankly about her personal reaction to books and characters, revealing, for example, that Daniel Deronda's mother is "of all the characters in fiction . . . the one who I felt I was, as opposed to feeling I ought to be or wanted to be, or might have been."

The title of this book is a bit misleading, since Byatt and Sodre talk more about stories and storytelling than characters. More perplexing is the somewhat random selection of "major texts" discussed. The 19th-century roster is sound (Austen, Bronte, Eliot); but where is Virginia Woolf? And what makes Iris Murdoch's *An Unofficial Rose* a major text, on par with *Beloved* and *Mansfield Park*? Still, *Imagining Characters* makes a powerful argument for the importance of reading and thinking about novels.

If *Imagining Characters* suggests that literary criticism and fiction share some of the same concerns, then ***The Djinn in the Nightingale's Eye*** is a demonstration of this idea. The five stories in this magical little book sound like conventional fairy tales. They have fairy-tale beginnings ("There was once a little tailor . . ."; "Once upon a time, in a kingdom between the sea and the mountains . . .") and feature tailors, sailors, princesses, talking animals, and dragons. But these are not traditional fairy tales. A princess worries about fulfilling her destiny because she is "by nature a reading, not a traveling, princess." A story in which a village is destroyed by giant worms turns out to be a story not about devastation but about the way the village people turn the devastation into tales. These are stories about making stories, about how stories begin and end, and about the relation between fantasy and reality.

Byatt's writing is crystalline and splendidly imaginative. Moonlight splits "into dull little needles of bluish light on the moss." A cockroach bends his segments "voluptuously." In the glorious opening to the 75-page title story, the familiar world is momentarily suspended and transformed into something fantastic: The story begins, "Once upon a time, when men and women hurtled through the air on metal wings, when they wore webbed feet and walked on the bottom of the sea . . . when folk in Norway and Tasmania in dead of winter could dream of fresh strawberries, dates, guavas and passion fruits and find them spread next morning on their tables. . . ."

The best stories in this collection are **"The Glass Coffin,"** which appeared in Byatt's novel *Possession,* and the title story, a complex and intriguing tale about an encounter between a scholar and a genie. These perfectly formed tales are intelligent without being pedantic. In other tales, the writing occasionally tends toward the didactic. "You are a born storyteller," an old lady unnecessarily tells the princess in **"The Story of the Eldest Princess."** "You had the sense to see you were caught in a story, and the sense to see that you could change it to another one."

There is joy in these two books. Byatt reminds us of the pleasure we took in the first stories we read, and then provides us with that pleasure. She gives us good reason to read.

Katy Emck (review date 10 April 1998)

SOURCE: Emck, Katy. "The Consolations of a Kindly Genie." *Times Literary Supplement* (10 April 1998): 25.

[*In the following review, Emck contends that* Elementals *contains "stories about seeing which really make you see more sharply, and stories about seeing which take the idea of art a little too seriously, while failing to deliver the consolations of fiction."*]

A. S. Byatt is as interested in the way things look in a short story as in what happens. Colour, shape, texture, shine and the very chemical composition of substances are lovingly detailed in her work. At times, her descriptions are as vivid and etched as illustrations from a book of fairy tales. She includes mythical creatures and beasts—djinns, dragons, a Lamia—as much for their visual resonance as for their story value.

In her new collection, ***Elementals,*** Byatt is pointed about her visual obsession. The tales are full of artists whose work is so minutely described as to make us forget we are in a story and think we are standing before "the thing itself". In one of them, the actual look of a real-life Lamia is the point of the narrative. In an ironic take on Keats's "Lamia", Byatt writes of a painter who finds a glittering serpent in his swimming-pool and falls in love with it; not because he finds it erotic, but because he finds it aesthetic. He is not interested in women, but in art, and is disappointed when the snake turns into a woman and he has nothing to paint.

And who are we to criticize, asks Byatt, for: "He was happy, in one of the ways in which human beings are happy." Both the aestheticism and the wry generosity towards disconnected human beings seem typical of Byatt. One of the main messages of this intriguing collection of stories is that people must be as they are, and the way they are frequently defies what we think of as normal and "human", which are probably rather narrowly defined anyway.

In **"Cold"**, the longest and best of the tales, Byatt describes a princess who defies the requirement of softness. She is a spiky, pallid icicle princess who is happiest when dancing naked in the snow and is almost killed by her family's concerned insistence on fires, warm clothes and nourishing stews. **"Cold"** brings together the two modes which have shaped Byatt's short stories to date; namely, the fairy tale and the preoccupation with art and artists. In it, Byatt evokes the marvels of dreams rather than reality. What more could one want of a fairy tale; or of art? **"Cold"** is a love story in which the ice princess is paradoxically wooed by a desert prince who is also a consummate artist. He sends her a castle enclosed in ice:

> Solid walls of light glittered and, seen through their substance, trapped light hung in bright rooms like bubbles. . . . From the dense, invisible centre little tongues of rosy flame (made of glass) ran along the corridors, mounted, gleaming, in the stairwells and hallways, threaded like ribbons round galleries. . . .

His fantastic glass creations capture the essence of the ice princess's nature, even though they are made from materials which are inimical to it; namely, fire and the sands of the desert.

In this original and moving love story, Byatt finds a chemical metaphor for love's potential to obliterate the self—the ice princess is almost melted by her love for the desert prince. The story is imbued with feminist, postmodernist knowingness about women and love in fairy tales. But it ends up as a celebration of the power of love and art to provide new life and new answers to old and apparently insoluble conundrums.

One of the things that makes Byatt so enjoyable to read is that she is not afraid of wish-fulfilment. In the title story of her last collection, ***The Djinn in the Nightingale's Eye,*** she generously provides a middle-aged academic who has just been left by her husband with a genie who is not only sexy and entertaining but also in love with her, Byatt's stories usually offer reprieve from death and despair. At the same time they suggest that the release from suffering is provisional and cannot last for ever. For all their play with "colour" and fantasy, they retain a wry realism.

This is certainly the case with **"Crocodile Tears"**, which is about a woman who, when her husband drops down dead in an art-dealer's, reacts by fleeing to southern France. Patricia's façade of touristic insensibility is shattered by Nils, another northerner abroad, a Norwegian who claims he too is mourning a spouse's death. They are two more Byatt characters who do not feel, or act, as they ought, because they are "frozen". They are living on a kind of psychological margin, haunted by reality-warping "suppressed terrors . . . flickering frames of the continuum". At the end, however, there is a mood of forgiveness and reprieve which suggests that the northerners' mutually shared "altered state" in the crackling heat of a southern climate really has unfrozen them. **"Crocodile Tears"**, like several other tales in this book, is about slipping out of everyday reality into another, more "elemental" dimension of being. Byatt captures the sense of dislocation with typical painterly verve:

> Time had become like a coloured cave of light in which planets rolled like plates, and fish leaped, and toothed reptiles floated and paddled.

In describing the peregrinations of Patricia and Nils round Nîmes, **"Crocodile Tears"** alludes to great swaths of cultural history. However, there seems no real need for this. Byatt's cultural compendiousness, and her fiction's use of art to provide alternative ways of seeing, work better when they are more tightly focused.

Elementals contains two splendid little parables in praise of art. One is about Velázquez's great painting "Christ in the House of Martha and Mary". The other, more daring story is about an illustration of one of the Bible's most gratuitously violent tales, the story of Jael. It marvellously conjures up the triviality and boredom of an all-girls' school in the 1950s and the intense satisfaction of painting an illustration to the story of **"Jael"** with a lot of red blood in it. The combination of undemonstrative wit and disconcerting honesty is excellent.

Contained in ***Elementals*** are stories about seeing which really make you see more sharply, and stories about seeing which take the idea of art a little too seriously, while failing to deliver the consolations of fiction. Sometimes, like the character in **"Jael"**, one really does want more colour and sensationalism. Yet throughout all these tales, there is a kindly, tolerant spirit that confronts anger, death and terror but is inventive in finding consolations for life's shortcomings. In **"Cold"**, Byatt's ability not only to conjure up a magical environment but to describe it in minute detail creates an utterly captivating story. The marvellous creations of the glassblower-prince provide solutions which are simultaneously a question of art and a question of love. In fact, the two can hardly be separated; a beguiling vision indeed.

Katie Grant (review date 14 November 1998)

SOURCE: Grant, Katie. "Tricks of the Light." *The Spectator* 281, no. 8889 (14 November 1998): 54.

[*In the following laudatory assessment, Grant perceives the stories in* Elementals *to be like little jewels that should be viewed from various angles.*]

Opening this little collection of short stories [***Elementals***] is like opening a jewellery box. You extricate a brooch which is, as a concept, essentially a workaday object. It is the coloured gem which is attached to the clasp that, in different lights, transforms the mundane into something magical. This is the art of the lapidarist and this is also the art of A. S. Byatt.

In **'Crocodile Tears'**, the first story of the six, she gives us Patricia Nimmo, a suddenly widowed, unremarkable, middle-aged home counties lady. This perfectly ordinary woman in unfortunate but not unusual circumstances is transformed into something extraordinary as Byatt reveals her in her contrasting lights. **'Crocodile Tears'** is a tale of warmth and cold, of clarity and obscurity, of the commonplace and the bizarre. It never becomes so fanciful that it loses its sense of the real, yet it is written with a detachment which, despite the detailed, factual descriptions of place and colour, make it as mysterious as a fable or a fairy story.

The following tales—'Stories of Fire and Ice', as the author calls them—reach a climax of fancy in **'Cold'**, an unashamed imaginative flight ripe for interpretation by budding literary critics. Then we are slowly brought back to earth until in **'Jael'** we are, or at least we think we are, listening to the schoolgirl reminiscences of a maker of advertisements. This penultimate story chills the spine even more than imagining the naked rompings of Princess Fiammarosa in the snow. Byatt then adds, as a sort of coda, what she imagines the story to be behind the painting by Velazquez entitled 'The Kitchen Scene with Christ in the House of Martha and Mary'. This is a faultless short story, told in such a matter-of-fact tone that one must read carefully to take in the build-up of detail which makes the final dénouement so perfect.

It is part of Byatt's talent that she uses the same formula, the mixing of fact and fancy, for both her novels and her short stories to equal effect. That the short stories, in my opinion, seem more memorable is a tribute rather than a criticism. In the spirit of Pascal, when Byatt has time to make her writings shorter, they gain in zest. She is obsessed by obsession but often needs no more than a dozen or so pages, rather than several hundred, to infect the reader.

Obsession for Byatt is a quest for knowledge of some kind. *Possession* and ***Angels and Insects*** are as much living encyclopaedias as novels and it is not necessarily always to her novels' advantage that they display the sort of intricate familiarity with obscure subjects that is more usually to be found in dusty academic tomes. However, in her short stories the lists—of, for example, painting techniques in **'A Lamia in the Cevennes'**—

never overwhelm. Byatt uses her methodological expertise as the warp and her imagination as the weft. The result is a rare balance.

If Byatt does not paint herself, maybe she should, for everything in her world is coloured and textured. Descriptions of both are a vital part of the developing stories. Patricia throws off her confident bright yellow home counties suit and buys a white silk jersey dress of falling pleats, gold slippers, 'a honeycomb cotton robe, in aquamarine', and a 'gold-and-silver striped toothbrush' when she arrives in Nîmes, a place of 'warm cream and gold stone' and 'white places where she blinked and saw water'. Bernard, the painter, wrestles to capture 'recalcitrant blue' and 'amiable, non-natural aquamarine' but ends up capturing an enchanted spirit trapped in a snake's body, a 'miraculous black velvet rope'. The ice princess, whose rosy flush gives way to milky paleness 'like white rose petals', is only truly herself when she is encased in a 'crackling skin of ice' that breaks into 'spiderweb-fine veined sheets' as she dances.

This is a happy book whose stories benefit from being taken out and reread from different angles. Whatever the angle, they glitter. Byatt has done it again.

Heidi Hansson (essay date winter 1999)

SOURCE: Hansson, Heidi. "The Double Voice of Metaphor: A. S. Byatt's 'Morpho Eugenia'." *Twentieth Century Literature* 45, no. 4 (winter 1999): 452-66.

[*In the following essay, Hansson provides a reading of "Morpho Eugenia" as a postmodern romance, focusing on the function of allegory and metaphor in the story.*]

> Analogy is a slippery tool.
>
> —A. S. Byatt (100)

The double voice of postmodern fiction presents a challenge because it requires that we question the way we read and interpret not only postmodern literature but also literature as a whole.[1] This doubleness is particularly noticeable in works that openly display their affiliation with generic conventions or older works, such as J. M. Coetzee's *Foe* (1986), which rewrites *Robinson Crusoe,* Peter Ackroyd's *Hawksmoor* (1985), which is structured like a detective story, or A. S. Byatt's *Possession* (1990), Lindsay Clarke's *The Chymical Wedding* (1989), John Fowles's *The French Lieutenant's Woman* (1969), and Susan Sontag's *The Volcano Lover* (1992), which all build on romance conventions. Such doubleness resembles allegory, insofar as allegory defines the moment when one text is read through the lens of another (Owens pt. 1, 68). By thus allying themselves with previous texts in their genres and by fusing conventional and postmodern narrative strategies, these literary hybrids destabilize our interpretations of traditional works, and, at least in the case of the postmodern romances, manage both to reread their tradition and revitalize its twentieth-century appearance.[2] Thus the multiple narrative voices, the open contradictions, and the consistent resistance to totalizing answers in a postmodern romance like *Possession* can be seen as continuing the allegorical mode of the "high" romances of the late Middle Ages and the Renaissance, as questioning the apparent uniformity of women's popular romances, and as restoring those complex and sophisticated qualities that formerly characterized the romance but seem to have disappeared from its twentieth-century manifestations.

Even though *Possession* in its parodies of scholars influenced by French feminism and Lacanian psychoanalysis contains a fair amount of critique of poststructuralist and postmodern attitudes, it signals its own postmodernity through devices like fluctuating narrative perspectives, paradox, ambiguity, and self-reflexivity. The short stories in Byatt's ***The Djinn in the Nightingale's Eye*** (1994) can also be categorized as postmodern fictions, especially through the inclusion of magic and fairy-tale structures in apparently realistic tales, and the disjunctive narrative style of *Babel Tower* (1996) is another example of Byatt's interest in postmodern literary techniques. Works like these, which openly display their postmodern links, need to be approached in a way that can acknowledge the multiple meanings produced. Works that at least on the surface look like straightforward narratives might appear to be another matter. But are they? Consider the novella **"Morpho Eugenia"** in Byatt's ***Angels and Insects.*** In contrast to *Possession,* **"Morpho Eugenia"** is firmly set in the past, and there is no visible twentieth-century perspective in the telling. The story is mainly told by an omniscient narrator, and even though it is interspersed with fictional texts ostensibly written by the various characters in the novella, these do not represent different voices and shifting perspectives to the extent they do in *Possession.*

"Morpho Eugenia" opens like a women's historical romance and continues like a Victorian novel about love, marriage, society's expectations, nineteenth-century hypocrisy, social injustices, Darwin, and religion. Because the stories in ***Angels and Insects*** are set in the 1860s and 1870s and deal with Victorian concerns, reviewers have described the diptych as "resolutely mid-Victorian in tone and content" (Hughes 49), and A. S. Byatt as "a Victorianist Iris Murdoch" (Butler). The postmodern connection is consequently overlooked. One reviewer, however, sees continuities between the Victorian novel and postmodernism when he refers to Byatt as a "postmodern Victorian" who finds the grounds of her postmodernity in "an earnest attempt to get back before the moderns and revive a Victorian project that has never been allowed to come to completion" (Levenson 41). Like the great nineteenth-century novelists, Byatt is a storyteller who continues the Victorian tradition of describing the individual in society, but it does not automatically follow that she exercises her storywriter's authority to present total world visions.[3] **"Morpho Eugenia"** appears to be double-voiced only in its extensive use of analogy in comparing the world of the Victorian household with that of insects, but even though the narrative seems stable enough, a struggle is going on within the text itself, so that at times narrative and language seem to be at cross-purposes. To read the novella as a postmodern romance—or as a postmodern Victorian novel, if such a hybrid can exist—helps to account for the ambiguities this gives rise to.

The prominence of comparisons, analogies, and metaphors places the novella in the tradition of allegorical writing, a quintessentially medieval or Renaissance genre. But allegory is also characteristic of postmodernism (Owens pt. 2, 64). In Deborah Madsen's words, "[a]llegory flourishes at times of intense cultural disruption, when the most authoritative texts of the culture are subject to revaluation and reassessment" (135). Such reassessment takes place when a photographer like Sherrie Levine takes pictures of famous photographs or when Coetzee's *Foe,* Marina Warner's *Indigo* (1992), and Peter Carey's *Jack Maggs* (1998) reappraise *Robinson Crusoe, The Tempest,* and *Great Expectations.* Works like these stand in an allegorical relationship to the subjects they appropriate, but it is not altogether clear which of the works involved represents the literal and which the figurative meaning of an allegory. The hierarchical relation between the texts is unstable, since it is equally possible to read the modern works through the filters of their predecessors as the reverse.

A characteristic of the late twentieth century, as well as of postmodern literature, is that certainties are continuously called into question, and thus allegory becomes a suitable form for expression. The model is certainly not alien to postmodernism: on the contrary, allegory is a classic example of double discourse, as well as a textual mode that—like postmodern literature—avoids establishing a center within the text, because in allegory the unity of the work is provided by something that is not explicitly there. This last point is where postmodern allegories differ from traditional ones, however, because most allegories depend on the existence of a recognized and more or less universally accepted frame of reference outside the text. But where, for example, a Protestant allegorist like John Bunyan could presuppose his reader's knowledge of the Bible, the postmodern allegorist can take no referent for granted. As a consequence, postmodern allegory is notoriously unstable, and a conventional allegorical interpretation of a work like **"Morpho Eugenia"** becomes impossible, because no single key can explain the meaning of the analogies.

The question is: who is in charge of decoding the allegory? In contrast to symbols, which are generally taken to transcend the sign and express universal truths, allegories and metaphors divide the sign, exposing its arbitrariness (Smith 106). Thus the allegorical impulse in contemporary literature can be seen as a reflection of the postmodern emphasis on the reader as coproducer, since it invites the reader's active participation in meaning making. But allegories can also be manifestations of authorial power: relentlessly didactic works that resolutely direct the reader's interpretations. Viewed in this way, allegory is reactionary (Smith 120). If allegory requires the presence of a fixed, culture-specific, author-controlled referent, the notion of a postmodern allegorical form is contradictory indeed. If, on the other hand, allegories serve to destabilize the relation between word and meaning, between form and essence, such texts become very suitable expressions of the postmodern distrust of accurate representation. In **"Morpho Eugenia"** the reader can discover several meanings in dialogue with each other, and the hierarchical relation between a monologic "message" and the allegorical form that obscures it collapses. This is precisely the mark of postmodern allegory.

The comparisons between, for instance, people and insects in Byatt's novella are quite explicit, so much so that one reviewer accuses Byatt of "applying the message with a trowel" (Lesser), and another sighs that "she follows the reader around with a cowhorn, instructing him in thought and reaction, rather than rendering an action and letting the reader enjoy the illusion of freedom in his engagement with the text" (Tate 60). The description of the clash between an aristocratic society and a new, work-oriented one seems to invite a political reading, and the feminization of the insect metaphors suggests a reading in terms of gender struggle. But the apparent transparency of the comparisons is illusory, and the meanings of the analogies remain unsteady. Byatt uses common, even trite, metaphors, but she uses the same metaphor in several different ways, which draws attention to language itself and means that readers will have to reevaluate their interpretation of the text over and over again. Both the figurative—or the hackneyed—meanings and the literal meanings are present at the same time, and so metaphors and analogies become more than embellishments: they become tools for emphasizing the double voice that is an integral part of language.

Metaphors are indeed highly appropriate postmodern devices, because they are obvious vehicles for ambiguity. A living metaphor always carries dual meanings, the literal or sentence meaning and the conveyed or utterance meaning. In **"Morpho Eugenia"** the strain between the figurative and the literal meaning is constantly underscored, since ants and butterflies appear both as insects and as metaphors for human behavior. As Brian McHale puts it, the hesitation between literal and conveyed meaning typifies postmodern metaphorical writing:

> Postmodernist writing seeks to foreground the ontological *duality* of metaphor, its participation in two frames of reference with different ontological statuses. This it accomplishes by aggravating metaphor's inherent ontological tensions, thereby slowing still further the already slow flicker between presence and absence. All metaphor *hesitates* between a literal function (in a secondary frame of reference) and a metaphorical function (in a "real" frame of reference); postmodernist texts often *prolong* this hesitation as a means of foregrounding ontological structure.
>
> (McHale 134)

Using analogy displays the metaphor's reference to the "real" world, and as a consequence, Byatt's technique of offering metaphorical descriptions in the form of analogies ensures that the postmodern vacillation between literal and figurative meanings is constantly present in **"Morpho Eugenia."** But metaphors are unstable not only because they hover between two frames of reference: their figurative meanings are also shaky. A metaphor induces comparison, but since the grounds of similarity are not forever given, metaphors serve to emphasize the freedom of the reader as opposed to the authority of the writer. This becomes particularly clear in **"Morpho Eugenia."** Because ants and butterflies are present both literally and metaphorically, the reader is forced to take a closer look at what is embedded in the familiar comparisons of women with butterflies or human societies with ant communities. Metaphors invite thought because they enforce the understanding that there are at least two sides to everything. **"Morpho Eugenia"** may at times seem overloaded with metaphors, but since the interplay between metaphorical and literal meaning destabilizes both the novella and the metaphors themselves, this is one of the clearest signs of its postmodernity.

* * *

> "Things Are Not What They Seem"
>
> —A. S. Byatt (119)

"Morpho Eugenia" takes its title from a butterfly, and the controlling metaphors belong to the worlds of ants, bees, and butterflies. William Adamson, a naturalist recently back from the Amazon, is welcomed into the Alabaster household at Bredely Hall. At the beginning of his visit, the young ladies present at a ball appear to him as butterflies, shimmering in "shell-pink and sky-blue, silver and citron" (3). Very soon his interest focuses on one of them, Eugenia, who, like all the other members of the Alabaster family, is a "pale-gold and ivory" creature, almost always dressed in white (4). By contrast, William himself is "sultry-skinned, with jaundice-gold mixed into sun-toasting" (3), and Eugenia's whiteness, so easily interpreted as betokening innocence, tempts him by its difference from the "olive-skinned and velvet-brown ladies of doubtful virtue and no virtue" he knew in Pará and Manáos (5). After a period of silent longing, William proposes to Eugenia among a cloud of butterflies he has raised for her in the conservatory, and they marry and settle at Bredely Hall.

Eugenia is compared to the butterfly that shares her name, the shimmering satiny-white Morpho Eugenia. The butterfly image is quite automatically understood as a rather common metaphor for feminine beauty and flightiness, but as William points out, it is the male butterflies who exhibit bright colors and whirl about in the sunlight, whereas the females are drab-colored and timid. Obviously the butterfly metaphor in **"Morpho Eugenia"** cannot be read traditionally, and the title of the novella gives a clue: *morpho* is the Greek word for "form," which suggests that the title could be read as "the form of Eugenia." What is most significant about the form of a butterfly is that it changes, that it undergoes meta*morpho*sis, and this is indeed what Eugenia—and William's conception of her—does. As the story progresses, William realizes that Eugenia's whiteness is not a reflection of her purity and innocence but instead signals degeneration and the impurity of incest. **"Morpho Eugenia"** becomes a story about a fall from innocence to experience and knowledge, where William has to realize that "things are not what they seem." Beneath the orderly surface of life at Bredely Hall are a dysfunctional family and a section of society—the country aristocracy—that has lost its sense of direction and purpose. William becomes like Psyche in the inset Psyche and Cupid story, where Psyche can keep her husband only if she promises "*never to try to see him*" (42). If William is allowed to see Eugenia and her world for what they are, his marriage, like Psyche's, will disintegrate.[4]

This seems to identify Eugenia as the villain of the story, but the unstable nature of the butterfly metaphor counteracts a single interpretation. At Bredely Hall, butterfly specimens are beautifully laid out in display cases, which emphasizes their status as objects, and in many ways Eugenia and her sisters are objects too, with no other aspiration in life than to make themselves beautiful for a prospective husband. In the world of insects, the use of beauty as a way of attracting the other sex is reserved for the male, but as the Alabaster relative Matty Crompton observes, "this appears to be the *opposite* to human societies, when it is the woman whose success in that kind of performance determines their lives" (40). Eugenia is a victim of a society that has no use for her except as the breeder of the next generation, and to secure her place in this society she has to make herself the object of men's admiration.

Bredely Hall represents a fraction of a society that, according to the history books, was male dominated. In **"Morpho Eugenia"** Byatt suggests, however, that at least that society's domestic life was controlled by women:

> Houses such as this were run for and by women. Harald Alabaster was master, but he was, as far as the whirring of domestic clocks and wheels went, a *deus absconditus,* who set it all in motion, and might at a pinch stop it, but had little to do with its use of energy.
>
> (76)

That women have been relegated to the domestic sphere and as a result have been able to exert their power over household matters is no revolutionary insight. What gives the observation new life are the analogies with bee and ant societies. One reviewer expresses his disaffection with the device thus: one "must endure the elaborate comparison of insect and human societies, an idea that I might not be alone in finding hackneyed" (Tate 60-61). This comment fails to acknowledge that in the novella, as in nature, ant and bee communities are predominantly female.[5] Everything is run by and determined by females, down to the sex of the embryos. The male ants and the drones are sex objects, just like the male butterflies that flaunt their brilliant colors to attract the females, and fertilization of the females is the sole justification for their existence. When Byatt describes such a male-dominated society as the nineteenth-century English aristocracy through resolutely gendered metaphors of bees, ants, and butterflies, one of the results is to challenge the conventional picture of this society.

In most Victorian fiction, marriage "means the end of sexual adventures but the beginning of social responsibility" (Belsey 120), and this principle appears to be pared down to its essence at Bredely Hall.[6] But marriage seems to mean nothing more than a socially acceptable way to secure the propagation of the species, and once conception has occurred, the pretense of love is not required. The men at Bredely Hall lead the lives of male ants or drones whose existence is directed solely to "the nuptial dance and the fertilization of the Queens" (103), and the women become "egg-laying machines, gross and glistening, endlessly licked, caressed, soothed and smoothed—veritable Prisoners of Love" (102). Their ability to produce young gives them their value, and in such a society love becomes "an instinctual response leading to the formation of societies which [gives] even more restricted and functional identities to their members" (116).

Pregnancy and motherhood metamorphose women's lives, but sometimes this metamorphosis is of a Kafkaesque kind. Eugenia experiences pregnancy as a period of cocooning, but she emerges from her cocoon not reborn as a butterfly but as something resembling an ant queen. With each pregnancy she becomes more and more like the Queen of the Wood Ants:

> She was swollen and glossy, unlike the matt workers, and appeared to be striped red and white. The striping was in fact the result of the bloating of her body by the eggs inside it, which pushed apart her red-brown armour-plating, showing more fragile, more elastic, whitish skin in the interstices.
>
> (39)

Like the ant communities it is compared with, the aristocratic society to which the Alabasters belong has no other purpose than to guarantee its own perpetuation. That this involves inbreeding is also highlighted by the comparison. As soon as Eugenia is pregnant, William is shut out of her bedroom to be let in again only when it is time to produce another baby. Quite soon it is clear to the reader that Eugenia has an incestuous relationship with her half-brother, and that William's children, who are so "true to type—veritable Alabasters," may not be William's at all (106).[7] In an ant or bee society, incest is the rule, of course, because there are no other insects in the nests than those produced by the queen.

William finds out about Edgar's and Eugenia's relationship by a message nobody admits to having sent:

> "And *someone* sent for me to come back to the house, today, when I was not wanted. When I was anything but wanted."
>
> "*I* didn't send for you," she said. "If that is what you are thinking. There are people in a house, you know, who know everything that goes on—the invisible people, and now and then *the house* simply decides that something must happen—I think your message came to you after a series of misunderstandings that at some level were quite deliberate."
>
> (154-55)

Matty Crompton implies that the house itself wants to put a stop to the incestuous relationship, that the invisible people at Bredely Hall work in conjunction toward what they believe is right. Certainly the household, as well as the rest of nineteenth-century society, would agree on Edgar's and Eugenia's guilt, but Byatt offers Eugenia's side of things as well:

> "I *know* it was bad," said Eugenia. "I know it was bad, but you must understand it didn't *feel* bad—it grew little by little, out of perfectly innocent, natural, *playful* things—which no one thought wrong—I have never been able to speak to any other living soul of it, you must forgive me for speaking to you—I can see I have made you angry, though I tried to make you love

> me—if I could have spoken to anyone, I might have been brought to see how wrong it was. But—*he* thought it wasn't—he said—people like making rules and others like breaking them—he made me believe it was all perfectly *natural* and so it was, it was natural, nothing in us rose up and said—it was—*un*natural."
>
> (158-59)

Eugenia may appear primarily as a self-indulgent breeding machine, but she is also the victim of a hypocritical society where sex is not talked about, and where women are not encouraged to acknowledge their sexual feelings. To a certain extent, Eugenia's incestuous relationship with her brother is an act of rebellion, a way of eluding the constrictions of her society. There are two sides to everything, and what makes it impossible to come to a final conclusion about how to interpret incest in the novella is that the union between Edgar and Eugenia produces children, whereas their sister, who marries "outside the nest," remains childless.

To fill his days, William Adamson agrees to help Matty Crompton and the girls in her charge to make a study of the "social insects." Together they set up a glass bee hive and a glass tank for ants in the schoolroom. The formicary becomes a miniature reflection of life at Bredely Hall. The Victorian household is filled with servants who occupy the place of the worker ants:

> The servants were always busy, and mostly silent. They whisked away behind their own doors into mysterious areas into which he had never penetrated, though he met them at every turning in those places in which his own life was led. . . . They were as full of urgent purpose as the children of the house were empty of it.
>
> (74)

Harald Alabaster believes that the social insects exercise both altruism and self-sacrifice; by implication these virtues govern the lives of his servants as well. William slowly arrives at another conclusion, both about the ants and the household: "most social systems work by mutual aggression, exploitation, the sacrifice of the many not for the whole, but for the few" (Butler). He is gradually brought to realize that his situation at Bredely Hall in many ways equals that of the Wood Ants who are enslaved by the Blood-red Ants. The slaves lose all sense of their origin and identify completely with the inhabitants of their new nest, to the point where they take part in slave raids against members of their own species. "Men are not ants," however, and William does not have to be trapped in the analogy (106). Disenchanted with Eugenia, and supplied with the proceeds from the book about ants he has written together with Matty Crompton, he finally breaks out and leaves for the Amazon with Matty as his companion. Ultimately the development and choices of the individual matter, and as a consequence a reading that tries to explain the analogies in universal terms collapses.

* * *

> Names, you know, are a way of weaving the world together, by relating the creatures to other creatures and a kind of *metamorphosis,* you might say, out of a *metaphor* which is a figure of speech for carrying one idea into another.
>
> —A. S. Byatt (131-32)

Discussing her story "Things Are Not What They Seem" with William, Matty expresses a fear that it might contain "too much *message*" (141). In certain ways the same is true of **"Morpho Eugenia"**: as a reader, one sometimes feels that there is just too much message, or too many messages. The novella both begs for interpretation and resists it. The frequent analogies invite an allegorical reading that is continually thwarted by the instability of the novella's abundant metaphors and symbols. At times, the political drift of the narrative appears to be antifeminist, from the role reversal that places William Adamson in the Cinderella position, through the misogynistic descriptions of pregnant women and William's final repudiation of his wife and his life at Bredely Hall. The accentuation on ant and bee communities as female societies does not counteract such a reading, because the emphasis on this could also be taken to imply that it is the women who tie themselves, each other, and men to fixed gender roles.

On the other hand, the insect analogies are used to describe a society usually thought of as completely male dominated, which is a challenge with rather feminist overtones. An important feminist project has been to reveal that language and linguistic expression are not innocent, and in **"Morpho Eugenia"** Byatt shows that this is true of metaphor as well. Discussing "gynocentric writing," Mary Daly demonstrates that, for instance, hyphenation may operate as a means of exposing the veiled meanings in words, to dis-cover language, as it were (24). Judicious installation of hyphens can reveal hidden meanings in words and invites the reader to look at common words in new ways, as in the examples "his-tory," "mis-take," and "re-member." Similarly, Byatt's revitalization of common metaphors points to a feminization of language, so that when the ant hill is presented as a society run and perpetuated by the female of the species, an overlooked component in the familiar metaphorical connection of human and ant societies is laid bare. As a result, an internal struggle occurs in the story between the level of narrative and the level of language. This instability creates a tension in the novella that renders any single political interpretation difficult.

Metaphors and analogies, like proverbs, are often given universal significance, and largely go unquestioned. What makes metaphorical expressions interesting, however, is that they are double signs. The discrepancy between the literal meaning of the words and the utterance meaning of the statement, that is, what is being conveyed, gives life to the metaphor. As a consequence, metaphors die or lose their value when the utterance meaning is so automatic it no longer carries dual meaning, and this is when they need to be reetymologized.[8]

Commonly used metaphors may retain their double meaning—presumably nobody would take the "people are ants" metaphor literally—but when their figurative meanings have become hackneyed, these, too, demand re-examination. What exactly are the grounds of similarity? In which ways do people resemble ants? Female gendered, the metaphor obtains new life, but the analogy's more conventional meanings are also present. The meanings of metaphors and analogies are always in flux, and Byatt draws attention to this in **"Morpho Eugenia"** when she uses identical linguistic figures in quite divergent ways.

The main metaphors in **"Morpho Eugenia"** are all inherently contradictory. The "people are butterflies" metaphor contains meanings like beauty, fickleness, and metamorphosis, as well as the observation that the perceived similarities between women and butterflies are actually illusory, because only male butterflies flaunt their beautiful colors. The "people are ants" metaphor is questioned in the same way: ants are insignificant, they specialize, they form rigid societies, but they are also predominantly female, unlike the human society to which they are compared. By gendering the metaphors, Byatt has enhanced their instability. Does this mean that these expressions should be taken as separate words, as homonyms, words that sound the same but mean different things? I do not think so. I would suggest that the ambiguity is there to provoke thought and to offer questions without finally providing the answers. Thus, the lavish use of metaphor draws attention to the extent to which we are unaware of the attitudes we perpetuate through language itself. The "people are ants" metaphor, for instance, functions as a provocation and questions the male-dominated society it describes. It also questions the kind of separatist feminism that advocates single-sex communities, in that it describes a feminine society that is both thoroughly hierarchical and extremely rigid. More conventionally, it functions as a means of "forcing the thought that seen from a height, watched across centuries, we humans creep and crawl, scratch and burrow like any other low creature moving close to the surface of the planet" (Levenson 42).

The rather blatant clue given in the name "Alabaster" emphasizes the significance of references to color, "white" in particular, in **"Morpho Eugenia."** To William, Eugenia's whiteness symbolizes an innocence tied up with his dreams of England and precious by its contrast to the brown colors of the Amazon. The "white lilies" and the "snowy bedspread" (8) in his bedroom suggest an English cleanness very different from "the earth-floored hut" that used to be his home in the jungle (12). On his wedding night, he is "afraid of smutching her [Eugenia], as the soil smutched the snow in the poem" (67). If the color white is seen as an image of purity, the color brown becomes an image of dirt, impurity, perhaps guilt, in consequence. If, on the other hand, "brown" represents health and vigor, the meaning of "white" has to change.

When Matty Crompton is introduced into the story, the darkness of her features is foregrounded:

> She stood in the shadows in the doorway, a tall, thin dark figure, in a musty black gown with practical white cuffs and collar. Her face was thin and unsmiling, her hair dark under a plain cap, her skin dusky too.
>
> (27)

Matty has "a quick step" (36) and her movements are "quick and decisive" (96), a contrast both in coloring and manner to the languid Eugenia. Her similarity to William with his "mane of dark, shining hair" (9) is obvious, and as William's fondness for Matty grows, the whiteness of the Alabasters takes on a more sinister meaning.

One of William's tasks in the Alabaster household is to organize Harald Alabaster's collection of insects and other specimens, which he does, but with diminishing enthusiasm, because William "wanted to observe life, not dead shells, he wanted to know the processes of living things" (73). Bredely Hall is a dying society, and William realizes this as he tries to complete his apparently endless chore. William's reaction as he looks at Harald Alabaster's hands illustrates that "white" stands for death, too:

> The hands were ivory-coloured, the skin finely wrinkled everywhere, like the crust on a pool of wax, and under it appeared livid bruises, arthritic nodes, irregular tea-brown stains. William watched the hands fold the wavering papers and was filled with pity for them, as for sick and dying creatures. The flesh under the horny nails was candlewax-coloured, and bloodless.
>
> (90)

"White" and "dark" are thus contrasted with each other throughout **"Morpho Eugenia,"** but the meaning of the contrast changes.

England, finally, is white, and the Amazon brown, with everything this might suggest of racism and colonialism. At the beginning, the novella seems to take an imperialist perspective, but such an interpretation collapses as the reversal of the relation between "white" and "dark" becomes clear. **"Morpho Eugenia"** could very well be interpreted as a story about Eden and the fall, particularly since William's last name is Adamson.

But where is Eden? In Brazil, William thought of England as paradise, but in England, the Amazon is "the innocent, the unfallen world, the virgin forest, the wild people in the interior who are as unaware of modern ways—modern evils—as our first parents" (30). On the other hand, the Amazon is unsafe—there is unchecked growth, unbridled sex, strong feelings, snakes and dangerous insects—but it is alive. If the comparisons between Bredely Hall and the female societies of ants and bees suggest an antifeminist politics, this is countered by the contrast with the Amazon, a place-name with explicit feminist connotations.

* * *

> You may argue anything by analogy, Sir, and so consequently nothing.
>
> —A. S. Byatt (89)

Analogy is a precarious device, because it gives the appearance of universality, and if William Adamson is taken to represent "man in general" as his last name seems to suggest, it would seem as if the reader is asked to find an authoritative answer about man's place in society in the text. But political readings of **"Morpho Eugenia"** break down because everything seems to contradict everything else. The narrative points one way, an allegorical interpretation of the analogies another, and the fluctuating meanings of the metaphors in yet other directions. This ambivalence is a feature of postmodern literature, since postmodern art is concerned with problematizing, not offering solutions. As Linda Hutcheon points out:

> Most of the issues raised by postmodernism are actually doubly encoded. Most are by definition ambivalent, though it is also true that there are few notions which cannot be formulated in opposing political terms.
>
> (205)

The metaphors and analogies in **"Morpho Eugenia"** embody these "opposing political terms," and thus the politics of the story remain unclear. As a postmodern allegory, **"Morpho Eugenia"** does not guide the reader toward the disclosure of a final answer but operates on several levels at the same time, introducing meanings that conflict with one another, replacing the monologic message of conventional allegory with dialogue. Postmodern allegorical writing speaks in at least two voices, both of which need to be heard.

Notes

1. I use the term *postmodern* rather than *postmodernist,* avoiding the association between a postmodern aesthetic and the philosophies and literatures of "high" modernism, whether this relation is viewed as a continuation or a replacement of modernist ideas. Even though I believe that "postmodernism" is best seen as a phenomenon of the late twentieth century, the existence of a postmodern allegorical form suggests a connection between postmodern attitudes and literature from the Renaissance and before.
2. See Hansson for a more thorough discussion of postmodern romances and their relationship to the chivalric, historical, and women's popular subcategories of the genre, as well as to some influential individual romances.
3. This is not to say that Victorian novels are necessarily authoritarian, or that the worldviews they present are absolute. One effect of Byatt's reworking of the genre is to indicate that there is considerable ambiguity in the Victorian models.
4. The reference to Psyche is yet another way in which the butterfly metaphor is expanded, since Psyche, as a personification of the human soul, is often represented as a butterfly.
5. The observation that the societies of bees and ants are female societies is overlooked in all the reviews quoted in this article, despite the emphasis on it in the novella.
6. The similarity between the sounds of the words "breeding" and "Bredely Hall" is certainly not coincidental.
7. "Morpho Eugenia" is the "insect" novella in the diptych *Angels and Insects,* and to a certain extent the story can be read as an elaborate pun on "insect" and "incest."
8. For a discussion of dying metaphors, see, for instance, Traugott.

Works Cited

Belsey, Catherine. *Desire: Love Stories in Western Culture.* Oxford: Blackwell, 1994.

Butler, Marilyn. "The Moth and the Medium." Rev. of *Angels and Insects* by A. S. Byatt. *Times Literary Supplement* (16 Oct. 1992): 22.

Byatt, A. S. *Angels and Insects.* 1992. London: Vintage, 1993.

Daly, Mary. *Gyn/Ecology: The Metaethics of Radical Feminism.* Boston: Beacon, 1978.

Hansson, Heidi. *Romance Revived: Postmodern Romances and the Tradition.* Uppsala: Swedish Science P, 1998.

Hughes, Kathryn. "Repossession." Rev. of *Angels and Insects* by A. S. Byatt. *New Statesman and Society* (6 Nov. 1992): 49-50.

Hutcheon, Linda. *A Poetics of Postmodernism: History, Theory, Fiction.* 1988. New York: Routledge, 1992.

Lesser, Wendy. "Séance and Sensibility." Rev. of *Angels and Insects* by A. S. Byatt. *New York Times Book Review* (27 June 1993): 14.

Levenson, Michael. "The Religion of Fiction." Rev. of *Angels and Insects* by A. S. Byatt. *New Republic* (2 Aug. 1993): 41-44.

Madsen, Deborah L. *Rereading Allegory: A Narrative Approach to Genre.* New York: St. Martin's, 1994.

McHale, Brian. *Postmodernist Fiction.* 1987. London: Routledge, 1994.

Owens, Craig. "The Allegorical Impulse: Toward a Theory of Postmodernism." Part 1. *October* 12 (1979): 67-86.

———. "The Allegorical Impulse: Toward a Theory of Postmodernism." Part 2. *October* 13 (1980): 59-80.

Smith, Paul. "The Will to Allegory in Postmodernism." *Dalhousie Review* 62.1 (1982): 105-22.

Tate, J. O. "Dress for Success." Rev. of *Angels and Insects* by A. S. Byatt. *National Review* (23 Aug. 1993): 60-61.

Traugott, Elisabeth Closs. "'Conventional' and 'Dead' Metaphors Revisited." *The Ubiquity of Metaphor: Metaphor in Language and Thought.* Ed. Wolf Paprotté and René Dirven. Amsterdam: Benjamins, 1985. 17-56.

Dennis Drabelle (review date 22 May 1999)

SOURCE: Drabelle, Dennis. "Running Hot and Cold." *Book World—The Washington Post* 29, no. 18 (22 May 1999): 3.

[*In the following review, Drabelle commends the whimsical and imaginative aspects of the stories in* Elementals.]

Anyone who enjoyed A. S. Byatt's book of original fairy tales, ***The Djinn in the Nightingale's Eye***—and who wouldn't?—will warm to this collection of six more fanciful stories [***Elementals***]. Byatt, also the author of the bibliomanic, Booker-winning novel *Possession,* has the right stuff for whimsy: a roving imagination; an uncanny ability to create ageless, read-aloud prose while at the same time playing with language; and a fascination with the variety and uses of art.

She even has the moxie to write almost unrelievedly happy stories. **"Cold"** is about Fiammarosa, an ice princess who lives in "a temperate kingdom." The girl seems content enough but oh so lethargic. One day her father asks her if she's ill. "I feel much as usual, she said. Much as I always feel. She spoke, he thought, with a desperate patience. He closed the window, to keep out the draught." But it turns out that Fiammarosa craves shivery temperatures and wilts in even moderate heat. Once her parents surround her with coolness, she blossoms.

When Fiammarosa comes of age, suitors from a number of countries ply her with courtship gifts. Wouldn't you know it, she falls in love with the one, Prince Sasan, who hails from the hottest land of all, a desert monarchy. "Human beings are adaptable, said the icewoman. If I use my intelligence, and my willpower, she said, I shall be able to live there; I shall certainly die if I cannot be with the man on whom my heart is set." How she and her prince work out their climactic differences is the pith of this captivating story.

If **"Cold"** harks back to both the Brothers Grimm and *The Thousand and One Nights,* **"A Lamia in the Cevennes"** is redolent of classical mythology by way of Keats. Disaffected with Thatcherite Britain, a British artist moves to southern France. There he buys a place, has a swimming pool built, and becomes engrossed in capturing its exact shade of blue.

The problem of the blue pool resolves itself only after it is invaded by a lamia: a talking water snake who is actually a woman imprisoned in a reptile's body and desperate to give the hero a spell-breaking kiss. Somehow her presence enables the artist to fix that blue on canvas. But he knows his Greek mythology and his Keats (see the long, late poem "Lamia"). Wary of becoming snake-food, he promises to liberate the woman in good time but strings her along while he daubs away and eludes her forked tongue. Each night, Byatt writes, "he saw to his locks; he was not about to be accidentally kissed in his sleep." In the end both the artist and the lamia get their wish.

"Christ in the House of Martha and Mary" is also about an artist—or, rather, about the relationship between an artist and one of his models, Dolores, a squatty, homely cook who complains about her station in life and resents Concepcion, a lovely fellow-servant. When the painter depicts them side-by-side in the same work, the question is how Dolores will react to this stark juxtaposition of beauty and brawn. But once again we have a story with a happy ending, at which Byatt has already hinted in a lecture the painter has given Dolores: "the important lesson—as long as you have your health—is that the divide is not between the servants and the served, between the leisured and the workers, but between those who are interested in the world and its multiplicity of forms and forces, and those who merely subsist, worrying or yawning."

If I'm less bullish on **"Crocodile Tears,"** about the awkward friendship between a newly widowed English exile and a Scandinavian gentleman with a secret, and on **"Jael,"** about leaders of rival girl cliques in an English school, it's only because they pale slightly in the same volume with the three fine stories I've described. And **"Jael"** is memorable if only for an iconoclastic observation its narrator makes about her pre-TV childhood: "I know young people have a worked-up nostalgia for an imaginary time when families communicated, people made things, played games, instead of passively watching. Now and then we did. . . . But mostly—apart from books—I remember this smeared, fuggy, limited light of boredom, where you couldn't see very much or very far, and the horizon was unimaginable."

For me the book's only failure is **"Baglady,"** a one-note, Twilight Zone-ish story of a rich woman traumatized by a visit to a shopping mall. But this is only a scratch on an otherwise lustrous surface. **"Lamia"** ends by blatantly summing up its protagonist's state of mind: "He was happy, in one of the ways in which human beings are happy." That can hardly be improved upon as a description of how readers will feel on finishing ***Elementals.***

Gabriele Annan (review date 10 June 1999)

SOURCE: Annan, Gabriele. "Letting Go." *New York Review of Books* 46, no. 10 (10 June 1999): 28-9.

[*In the following review of* Elementals, *Annan asserts that Byatt's "combination of playfulness and stern agnosticism has something in common with the fables of Voltaire and other Enlightenment writers."*]

Elementals is a collection of A. S. Byatt's short stories. It was published in Britain last year, and so was *The Oxford Book of English Short Stories,* introduced by A. S. Byatt. An introduction of that kind can hardly help being at least a little pronunciamental (and in her photograph on the dust cover of the Oxford book Byatt looks positively vatic). It was brave of her to allow such a coincidence to happen. So the questions are: What are her proclaimed standards, and how will she measure up to them?

The first paragraph of her introduction to the Oxford book of stories ends on a note of inviting pseudo-discouragement:

> Do we have anything to compare with Maupassant and Chekhov, Shen Tsung-Wen and Calvino, Borges and Kafka? Or, to keep to your own language, with Patrick White, Samuel Beckett, R. K. Narayan, Raymond Carver, and the great Alice Munro? I feared being marooned amongst buffers and buffoons, bucolics, bullies, and Blimps.

Well, with stories by Dickens, Kipling, D. H. Lawrence, V. S. Pritchett, Ian McEwan, and Angela Carter, among many others, obviously it hasn't turned out as bad as that. Later on, "reading in bulk," she found herself "developing a dislike for both the 'well-made tale' and the fleeting 'impression'"—she is hostile in fact to the generally accepted conventions that short stories should concentrate on a minimum of characters and incidents and have a single story line. She discovers that "I like stories in which energy overcomes inhibition." This sounds spunky and promising.

Elementals is subtitled *Stories of Fire and Ice.* There are six of them, and each is preceded by a reproduction of a work of art—a black-and-white reproduction so small that it comes across as a light-hearted rococo squiggle: and this sets the tone of the collection. Or one of the tones: the other is didactic, and also rationalist. The combination of playfulness and stern agnosticism has something in common with the fables of Voltaire and other Enlightenment writers; and of the six stories, the three most striking ones belong to that genre.

The illustrations include reproductions of two pictures, one by the contemporary artist Darren Haggar, the other a detail from a large canvas by Velázquez. There are also a Matisse etching, a "School of Rembrandt" print, a Roman coin, and a seventeenth-century Venetian glass goblet. The story that goes with the goblet, **"Cold,"** is a fairy tale set in a mythological age. It is about an ice princess who feels happy only when she can dance naked and unseen in the snow. In summer she stays indoors. There is the usual fairy-story lineup of suitors, but to her parents' surprise she turns down the Norseman who could have given her what her temperament and physique crave, and chooses instead a dusky prince from a scorching desert country. She gives birth to twins, one fair like her, the other dark like her husband. He has to travel a lot, so the princess sometimes feels lonely. She also longs to "roam amongst fjords and ice-fells, [but] this was not unusual, for no one has everything she can desire." So she studies the flora of her new country and becomes a serious botanist in correspondence with other botanists all over the world. There seem to be two morals: the first is that interracial marriage works; the second is a version of the Protestant work ethic. Both are so simple and obvious that it's hard to believe there's not another hidden meaning somewhere.

"A Lamia in the Cévennes" is also a fairy story. It is set in the 1980s, and that gives it an amusing Angela Carterish edge of incongruity. The plot is so neat, shapely, and satisfying that it falls into the spurned category of "well-made tale," and is all the better for it. It is introduced by the Matisse etching—of a siren from an illustrated volume of Ronsard's poems. "In the mid-1980s," the story begins. "Bernard Lycett-Kean decided that Thatcher's Britain was uninhabitable, a land of dog-eat-dog, lung-corroding ozone and floating money, of which there was at once far too much and far too little." Bernard abandons Britain and buys a small house in the Cevennes. He is a painter whose work is described by Byatt as so lusciously Matisse-like that it is no surprise when it sells well enough for Bernard to afford a large, beautiful swimming pool with a stone rim and a dolphin mosaic on its floor. The color and feel of the water in different weathers and Bernard's delight in swimming in it are rendered with the same sensual virtuosity and pleasure as the winter scenes in **"Cold."** "*Volupté,*" Bernard quotes to himself. "*Luxe, calme et volupté.*" Byatt is good at sensual pleasure: not sex so much as look and taste, and the feel of textures on the skin. The *volupté* passages, in both fairy tales, are stunning, if overlong.

One day Bernard sees a large snake in the bottom of the pool. He notices it has human eyelashes and teeth, and soon it snuggles up to him, lets him paint it, and tells him, in Cévegnol French, that it is a Lamia: if he kisses and promises to marry it, it will turn into a beautiful woman. He looks "Lamia" up in Keats and also remembers that the anthropologist Mary Douglas (Byatt never misses a chance at cultural name-dropping) "says that *mixed* things, neither flesh nor fowl, so to speak, always excite repulsion and prohibition." So he refuses.

Not so a friend of his who comes to stay, uninvited and unwelcome. Raymond spends the night with the Lamia, and next day she appears at breakfast in the shape of a sexy lady with a lot of makeup. Bernard is delighted when his friend takes her away. He prefers science to myth, and "would rather have the optical mysteries of waves and particles in the water and light of the rainbow than any old gnome or fay." He starts painting a butterfly poised on the breakfast table. The colors pose a demanding problem. "There is months of work in it. Bernard attacked it. He was happy, in one of the ways in which human beings are happy." Another proclamation of the work ethic.

"Christ in the House of Martha and Mary" is an undisguised morality tale, but Byatt's moral isn't the same as Christ's: very nearly the opposite, in fact. The story is preceded by a detail from Velázquez's painting of the same title in the London National Gallery. The left foreground of this painting is occupied by a cross, dumpy young kitchen maid pounding garlic in a mortar, while a handsome older servant advises or admonishes her. In the background behind the two women. Christ can be seen with Mary at his feet and Martha standing indignantly behind her. This much smaller scene represents a well-known art-historical puzzle: Is it a mirror image of something taking place on the viewer's side of the frame? Or is it set in a space beyond an opening in the kitchen wall? Or is it a painting hanging on the wall?

In any case, in ***Elementals*** you don't get to see the whole painting, because the illustration for Byatt's story shows only the still life in the right-hand foreground: fish, eggs, garlic, and an oil jar. Unfortunately, its tactile beauty quite fails to come across in the black-and-white reduction. For the two servants in the left foreground you have to rely on Byatt's description. She calls the younger one Dolores and the elder Concepción. Dolores is angry because she is plain and a servant and has to wait on her spoiled and pretty young mistress. "You are all brawn, and you should thank God for your good health in the station to which he has called you," says Concepción. "Envy is a deadly sin." "It isn't envy," says Dolores. "I want to live. I want time to think. Not to be pushed around."

Concepción has a young artist friend (the National Gallery painting is an early Velázquez) who often visits the kitchen, to paint and also to eat her delicious food. He too lectures Dolores: cooking is as creative as painting, he says, and "the divide is not between the servant and the served, between the leisured and the workers, but between those who are *interested* in the world and its multiplicity of forms and forces, and those who merely subsist, worrying or yawning."

When he has finished his painting of Christ with Martha, Mary, Concepción, and Dolores, the painter invites Concepción and Dolores to see it in his studio. Concepción thinks that Dolores will be offended by her portrait, but the girl sees the point and laughs with pleasure that someone should have "looked so intently" at her.

> The momentary coincidence between woman and image vanished, as though the rage was still and eternal in the painting and the woman was released into time. The laughter was infectious, as laughter is: after a moment Concepción, and then the painter, joined in. He produced wine, and the women uncovered the offering they had brought, spicy tortilla and salad greens. They sat down and ate together.

This is the last paragraph of the book: the combination of complex art interpretation, sermon, biblical diction, with a touch of Julia Child (or more probably the English cookery expert Elizabeth David, who was a writer as much as a cook) sums up some of its more important ingredients. Still, I'm not certain that the combination of so many pungent flavors makes a good dish: and anyway the pulpit tone sounds sanctimonious coming from such a rationalist writer.

In her acknowledgments Byatt describes the Velázquez story as ekphrastic, or descriptive. She is not just ekphrastic, though, but also eclectic. She likes trying out different styles: the desert prince's palace in **"Cold"** is richly described à la Wilde, the encounter with the Lamia sounds like Calvino, and **"Baglady"**—about a woman who loses her sense first of where and then of who she is in a foreign shopping mall—is a Kafkaesque nightmare of displacement.

"Crocodile Tears" strikes out in the opposite direction. It's about a lonely English widow and a lonely Norwegian widower who happen to meet in a hotel in Nîmes and decide to stay together. Byatt upgrades this magazine romance by embedding it in a highbrow travelogue full of obscure and fascinating information about the history, prehistory, natural history, and especially art history of Nîmes. She describes works of art with love and understanding (she began her considerable academic career teaching literature to art students at the prestigious Central School of Art in London). In **"Crocodile Tears"** she ranges from Roman coins to Sigmar Polke, illuminating many other kinds of art in the centuries between. When the National Portrait Gallery invited her to be painted, she chose the English painter and critic Patrick Heron to do it: an adventurous choice compared to many of her neighbors' on those walls.

Byatt is best known for her gigantic Booker Prize-winning novel *Possession.* When it appeared in 1990, the *Sunday Times* called it "a cerebral extravaganza of a story [which] zigzags across an imaginative terrain bristling with symbolism and symmetries, shimmering with myth and legend, and haunted everywhere by presences of the past." The description fits ***Elementals*** pretty well. Some readers are inspired by Byatt's scope, energy, virtuosity, verve, and nerve, and entranced by the cornucopia of recherché pleasures she pours out for them; others see this as overwhelming, an avalanche, showoff and hectoring. Both sides have a point. Whatever else, she lives up to her ideal that energy should overcome inhibition. Or perhaps she doesn't have inhibition.

Margaret Pearce (essay date summer 1999)

SOURCE: Pearce, Margaret. "'Morpho Eugenia': Problems with the Male Gaze." *Critique* 40, no. 4 (summer 1999): 399-411.

[*In the following essay, Pearce points out some problems with Adamson's reductive point of view in "Morpho Eugenia" and considers light and dark imagery in the novella.*]

In **"Morpho Eugenia,"** the first novella of ***Angels and Insects,*** A. S. Byatt unravels the man-is-hero story by telling the story from a male protagonist's point of view. Byatt does this to illustrate the corrupted power he wields from his narrative vantage point of "the male gaze." William Adamson views the world as if he were subject, and all others are objects, gazed upon by him, observed by him. He represents the other characters through a masculine, unitary gaze, centering himself in the story while trying to create closure and unity all around him. Adamson not only sees everything in a binary opposition of white against black, beautiful against ugly; he names and labels everything and everyone around him, and he speaks for others. This is a "system of power that authorizes certain representations while blocking, prohibiting or invalidating others" (Owens 59). Adamson's narration of events in **"Morpho Eugenia"** is what Craig Owens calls a Master Narrative:

> What function did these narratives play other than to legitimize Western man's self-appointed mission of transforming the entire planet in his own image? And what form did this mission take if not that of man's placing of his stamp on everything that exists—that is, the transformation of the world into a representation, with man as its subject? In this respect, however, the phrase *master narrative* seems tautologous, since all narrative [. . .] may be narrative of mastery.
>
> (Owens 65-66)

If Adamson's reductive narrative perspective is to be overcome, it is not enough to replace him with a female narrator. If a previously peripheral female character were to overthrow Adamson, she would merely be in his position of master in the narrative. A reversal of the hierarchy is not the solution because in order to "prevent this counter-stance from freezing into a dogma (in which the dominance-submission patterns remain unchanged), the strategy of mere reversal needs to be displaced further, that is to say, neither simply renounced nor accepted as an end in itself" (Trin 39-40). Thus Byatt, to decentralize Adamson, does not replace him with another central narrative. Instead she subverts his gaze by clearly illustrating its reductive repercussions. Then she demonstrates how Adamson is actually manipulated, not an observer so much as one observed.

William Adamson, an entomologist, is "a scientist and an observer" (6). His profession is one in which he discovers, names, and categorizes insects, especially butterflies. Throughout the novella, he applies that way of seeing to the people around him, especially the women. The story begins with Adamson as a spectator, watching the guests at the Alabaster ball. He studies the Alabasters as if they were part of his insect collection: he reduces people to categories, compares them to the insects he knows, and separates everybody into roles. Adamson's reductive point of view is clearly illustrated in the way he applies binary distinctions by constantly contrasting white images against black: Eugenia and her family represent a "white world" of class distinction, wealth, luxury, and beauty; whereas the servants, including Matty, are relegated to the shadows and the dark hours of the morning during which they perform their duties. Toni Morrison, in her book *Playing in the Dark,* asks what are the consequences of creating what she calls "literary whiteness" and "literary blackness"? Although Morrison speaks specifically of American writing and the use of what she calls Africanist motifs, her theories can be applied to **"Morpho Eugenia"** in which the colors of black and white help Adamson to control his understanding of the world. Morrison's theory of "Africanism" is the use of darkness and blackness (especially when associated with people) to contrast with whiteness or goodness. That contrast is "a way of talking about and a way of policing matters of class, sexual license, and repression, formations and exercises of power, and meditations on ethics and accountability. Through the simple expedient of demonizing and reifying the range of color on a palette [. . .] Africanism makes it possible to say and not say, to inscribe and erase. [. . .] It provides a way of contemplating chaos and civilization, desire and fear [. . .]" (7). Now living in Bredely Hall with the fair-skinned, golden-haired Alabaster family, Adamson separates himself from the counterculture that flourishes in the Amazonian jungle of dark-skinned natives.

"Morpho Eugenia" opens at a ball that the Alabasters are giving at Bredely Hall. Adamson, feeling out of place, recalls how in the jungle "his whiteness itself had given him automatic precedence at table. Here he seemed sultry-skinned, with jaundice-gold mixed into sun-toasting" (3). Color is a way of talking about a multitude of social differences, and in this story whiteness is equated with wealth and breeding. Having just come to Bredely Hall from a shipwreck, Adamson's world is chaos because, as he says, "I am penniless and with no prospects" (13-14). He uses white and black differences to order his life and to order and understand his position in the Alabaster household. The jungle now represents all that he disdains because the dark images of the jungle dirty the brilliantly anticipated cleanliness of "civilization." Darkness reminds him of savagery; white symbolizes, for him, class standing and breeding; and, when Eugenia becomes a central figure, innocence and beauty as well.

As Adamson dances with Enid, he recalls the dances he had in the jungle with "olive-skinned and velvet-brown ladies of doubtful virtue and no virtue" (5). As his continued descriptions of the jungle suggest, darkness, for Adamson, represents an otherness that is incompatible with the sexually repressed lifestyle of upper-class, white Victorians. While he dances with Eugenia, Adamson's memories of the dance rituals in the jungle arouse sexual and erotic imagery: "He remembered the palm-wine dance, a swaying circle which at a change in rhythm broke up into hugging couples who then set upon and danced round the one partnerless scapegoat dancer. He remembered being grabbed and nuzzled and rubbed and cuddled with great vigour by women with brown breasts glistening with sweat and oil, and with shameless fingers" (6-7). He repels those images because he feels that they soil his new surroundings. The whiteness of Bredely Hall symbolizes virginity, unattainability, and power. He refuses to allow the sexuality with which he associates the jungle to tarnish his new world and his prospects in it.

The Alabasters are, as their name suggests, "pale-gold and ivory creatures, with large blue eyes and long pale silky lashes" (4). The entire family is described as a "homogeneous group" of symbolically "gold and white colouring" (4). In comparison to himself, everything and everyone seems very pale. That color difference, more than class difference, increases Adamson's feeling of being alien from the Alabasters. He not only must borrow a dress suit from one of the young Alabaster men (he never owned one even before his belongings were lost at sea), but he feels like a minority group of one, marginalized within a sea of "pale people," unable to fit in despite his appropriate attire (4). Paradoxically, Eugenia's very difference makes Adamson love her almost at first sight.

Adamson loves Eugenia for her whiteness. She represents the purity and beauty that he dreamed about while in the jungle, the things he hoped to find when he returned. At first, her difference from him makes him feel distant from her, unable to know her. He chooses instead to dance with her younger sister Enid. Adamson sees Enid's whiteness as "milky-wholesome and so airily untouchable" (5). The similar whiteness of the sisters, of the entire family, might have made Eugenia indistinguishable from her homogeneous family; however, Adamson's interest in her overflows when he discovers that she is unhappy. Eugenia has recently lost her fiancé, in circumstances that remain mysterious throughout much of the story. Adamson, perhaps thinking he might console her, as the family seems unable to do, asks Eugenia to dance. While they dance, she remains "distant [. . .]—or at least that was how he saw [her]" (6). The distance seems to make him want her more. She is now more than white against his tan: she is wealthy against his poverty, graceful against his awkwardness, virtuous against his vice, sad against his happiness, and female against his male. She is also cold, perhaps distracted; but Adamson sees her as distant from his grasp, from his passion. Because of the distinctions between them, Adamson makes Eugenia into a fantasy, one he desires ultimately to control. For if darkness represents chaos and whiteness represents order or civilization, then Adamson will need to control Eugenia. In other words, Eugenia is not only a fantasy: she is symbolic of the civilization men have constructed and tamed for their own needs. He needs to conquer and possess Eugenia and her characteristics to become a part of the white, civilized, ordered world he desires.

As Adamson dances with Eugenia, he has "[h]er presence within his grasp—that was how he thought of it" (6). He imagines a type of hold or control he might have over her. The desire for control is heightened by his seeing her as the embodiment of whiteness:

> He looked *down* from his height at her *pale* face and saw her large eyelids, blue-veined, almost translucent, and the thick fringes of *white*-gold hairs on their rims. [. . .] Her shoulders and bust rose *white* and *flawless*

> from the froth of tulle and tarlatan like Aphrodite from the foam. A simple row of pearls, soft *white* on soft *white* with a shimmering *difference*, rested on her collarbone.
>
> (6; emphasis added)

For Adamson, Eugenia's whiteness makes her a goddess, something he cannot dream of having, and yet cannot live without. As he says later, "I shall die if I cannot have her" (13). In his dreams he desires control: after the ball is over, Adamson dreams "that he was pursuing a flock of golden birds through the forest, which settled and preened and allowed him to approach, and then rose and wheeled away, crying in high voices, only to settle again, just out of reach" (14). He not only wants control of Eugenia, he wants to fly with the golden flock. Adamson is driven to be a part of, and to control, the things the Alabasters represent: order, routine, harmony, and money.

Because Adamson desires to become part of the order of things, he possesses only contempt for anything separate from that order, anything that is darkness against the Alabaster whiteness. He writes in his journal about a time in the jungle when he was cured by a woman of color. However, his binary way of seeing the world cannot accept that he was once in the control of someone to whom he believes himself superior. He writes,

> In my delirium in the boat, it is true, and earlier under the ministrations, or torments, of that filthy *hag* in whose house I cured *myself* of the fever, I did dream from time to time of a kindly female presence, as something deeply needed, unreasonably forgotten, as though the phantom were weeping for me as I was weeping for her.
>
> (13)

Adamson cannot accept the kindness and healing skill of a marginalized "other" if he must be under her control. To emphasize that, he imagines a scenario he would prefer: to be in the arms of a white female. The "filthiness" of the old woman compounds the image of darkness that Adamson understands her to represent. By contrast, Eugenia's distance and whiteness is antithetical to the closeness, the grabbing, nuzzling, rubbing, cuddling, and color of the women in the jungle. It seems as though Adamson desires Eugenia mostly for what she is not: she is not close; she is not filthy; she is not dark-skinned; and most important, she is not his.

Finally, on the night of their wedding, Adamson sees Eugenia as a white creature, so white that "even her nipples must be white" (66). He had not wanted to corrupt this whiteness with his knowledge of sex: "He was [. . .] afraid of smutching her, as the soil smutched the snow in the poem. He did not come to her pure. He had learned things—many things—in the raffish dancing places in Pará, in the sleep-time after dancing in the villages of the mulattoes [. . .]" (67).

Perhaps the most evident way in which Adamson seeks control is the way in which he names Eugenia. By naming and representing his world, Adamson creates a master narrative that is difficult to challenge. Because a central narrative implies power, Adamson can relegate characters to a peripheral position in the story, thus offering the reader only his perspective. Therefore, naming gives Adamson power. It follows, then, that he comes to brand Eugenia at the very beginning of the story: "*You* would be Morpho Eugenia. It means beautiful, you know. Shapely" (21). Furthermore, by calling her "Morpho Eugenia," he names her after a butterfly; thus, in a sense, Adamson has captured Eugenia and placed her in a category that he can label, name, and thereby possess. Adamson wants only to see her as a beauty, delicate, fragile, exotic, and dead like the butterfly specimens he brings with him to Bredely Hall. Throughout the story, Adamson emphasizes the way in which Eugenia possesses the same coloring as the Morpho butterflies: "the blue pools of her eyes" are the same "iridescent blue" (21; Davies 140) of the butterfly. But because Adamson sees Eugenia only as a beauty, he does not allow the reader to know her as anything more than a unifaceted, vacuous character whose only attribute is aesthetic.

When Adamson marries Eugenia, he sees her transform from the beautiful Morpho Eugenia into a queen ant. Early in their marriage, Adamson expects many things: "increasing affection and budding and crowing babes, [. . .] ripe orchards and heavy-headed cornfields, gathered in on hot nights. [. . .] Certainly he expected some kind of intimate new speech to develop between himself and his wife, and expected her, vaguely, to initiate it. Women were expert in emotional matters" (69). But when Eugenia begins to have children, she disappears "into a world of women" (70). She spends most of the year in "her white nest" where she prepares for her babies while she slowly grows larger (70). The wetnurse, Peggy, suckles all the children, and Adamson feels relief when that allows Eugenia to return to him for further conjugal sex: "the existence of Peggy had restored Eugenia's body to use" (71). Only when they are making love can Adamson feel remote pleasure with his wife. But when Eugenia continues to have children again and again, Adamson realizes that "he was not happy. He had perhaps never been exactly happy, though he had had what he desired" (72). He believes she has been reduced to a breeding machine, with no other purpose but to procreate. And because that is not part of his vision of Eugenia, he is no longer happy with her.

While he describes the Queen ant and her workers, he seems also to be comparing her with Eugenia: the Queens "must snap off their wings, like a young girl stepping out of her wedding veils, and scurry away to find a safe place to found a new nest-colony. [. . .

A]nd in due course, as the workers take over the running of the nursery and the provision of food, they will forget that they ever saw the sun, or thought for themselves, or chose a path to run on, or flew in the midsummer blue. They become egg-laying machines, gross and glistening, endlessly licked, caressed, soothed and smoothed" (102). Furthermore, when Adamson discusses the worker ants, he is clearly outlining his own miserable state: "their whole existence is directed *only* to the nuptial dance and the fertilisation of the Queens. [. . .] And after their day of glory, they are unnecessary and unwanted. They run hither and thither, aimlessly, draggle-winged" (103).

When Adamson discovers Eugenia in bed with her half-brother Edgar, he gains and loses control over the situation. He loses control of a fixed image he has of Eugenia, but he also gains control because his husband role gives him unilateral power over what is to happen. In other words, while he loses control over Eugenia, he gains control over his own destiny: to finally leave what has become an unhappy situation for him. Adamson becomes the namer and the labeler in the cruelest fashion: He says, "It is like a whorehouse" in the bedroom (150). He refuses to touch Eugenia as if, this time, *she* will soil *him*. He refuses to look at Eugenia, demanding that she dress quickly and cover up, so that he will not have to look at the evidence that she is not "Morpho Eugenia." Eugenia tries to tell her story, haltingly. Because she neither accuses Edgar nor blames herself, Adamson cannot categorize the situation; he cannot immediately label Eugenia. Finally, because he cannot understand her, he chooses to leave her. He feels Eugenia has betrayed him with whore-like behavior, but he does not realize that "lady and whore are both bred to please," that, in fact, she has been an object of pleasure for both Edgar and Adamson (Trinh 97).

Nevertheless, even in the last moments he spends with Eugenia, Adamson tries desperately to retain his original vision of her. Having decided to leave her, he still manages to tell her, "Morpho Eugenia. You are very lovely—" (159). Earlier, he silences Eugenia, saying, "You cannot wish to attract any more attention" (151). Of course, that is the very thing Eugenia wants: she wants to be seen as who she is; she wants to speak for herself; she does not want to be "Morpho Eugenia," wife, mother, virtuous angel. And before Adamson leaves her, Eugenia tries to break out of his categorical, reductive perception of her one last time: "I would like to be different," she says (159). But Adamson "could not take that seriously" because that would not conform to his aesthetic vision of her (159). Adamson has not endowed his construct of Eugenia with a mind or much of a personality. Even as he leaves, he can only understand that she is beautiful and nothing else, noting that she breathes "a pretty little sigh of relief" before he goes (159).

Adamson liberates himself from what he imagines is a limited social standing by controlling Eugenia's ability to speak. He creates a world where he can label as "other" those who do not conform to his categories. By desiring what he believes is perfection, Adamson places himself at the apex of his hierarchical world when he obtains Eugenia for a wife; and then discards her. He has moved from the margins to the center of the story by marginalizing Eugenia. He begins painfully aware of his social standing and dependence in the Alabaster household, and he moves into a dominant location where he can be central to the story by silencing those who threaten to marginalize him. In other words, he categorizes and silences Eugenia because she reminds him that he is not as "white" as she is, not as civilized or wealthy.

However, although Adamson views himself as the master of his narrative, he is, in fact, manipulated himself. He recognizes himself as a worker ant in the community at Bredely Hall, but he does not notice the way in which that community observes and controls him. The family, with Harald Alabaster as the conductor, maneuver Adamson into marrying Eugenia and thereby covering any signs of her relationship with Edgar (and of any possible offspring that might and will come from that liaison). Eugenia herself wants to marry Adamson, perhaps to avoid marrying after her younger sister, or for other less obvious reasons. Matty Crompton suggests that Adamson write a book, which leads Matty to publish her own work and gain financial independence. The servants, often represented by Matty because they are, on the whole, "invisible people," play a crucial role in ultimately helping Adamson discover Eugenia in bed with Edgar (155). The insect analogy that runs throughout **"Morpho Eugenia"** strengthens the reading that Adamson is manipulated: the running debate on determinism in insect society suggests that humans also live in predestined ways. The insect analogy also reminds us of other manipulations occurring within the story: the ongoing struggle between the servants and the Alabasters, worker ants and their rulers, slaves and their masters.

Ironically, Matty Crampton, the one person whom Adamson sees as an ally, turns out to be the most manipulative of all. The short story she gives to Adamson to read clearly illustrates her understanding of the relationships and events within Bredely Court. The title, "Things Are Not What They Seem," refers not only to the events in the story but also alludes to the situation between Edgar and Eugenia. The story tells a tale partially similar to Adamson's: Seth is shipwrecked on an island where he is enslaved by a fairy named Mrs. Cottitoe Pan Demos, "which means, 'for all the people'" (122). Seth must cooperate with the fairy, "for the good of the household," as Adamson must continue with Eugenia to make everyone happy (123). Finally, Seth is saved by a worker ant and other insects that "have other purposes" and "are not subject to the laws of the Garden and will leave it." Those insects are clearly allusions to the invisible servants in the household (one of whom sends Adamson the note that brings him back to discover Eugenia in bed with her half-brother) and to Matty Crompton, who by her unclassified position in the household is not subject to the laws of Bredely Hall and does leave it at the end of **"Morpho Eugenia"** (130).

Adamson, however, does not realize the extent of Matty's knowledge, even after having read the story. To him, the story is just a "flight of imagination" (140). He further suggests that children will enjoy the story and even attempts to read into it a religious allegory.

Nevertheless, Matty uses Adamson to pave her route to the literary world. Although he does not understand her story, she continues her attempt to make the breadth of her knowledge known to him through a game of anagrams. To communicate with Adamson, Matty must make her message even simpler and more direct than her story. Thus she chooses a word he will understand: when he passes her cards spelling the word INSECT, she rearranges the cards, passing them back to him as INCEST. Thus, she reveals her knowledge about Eugenia and Edgar. She communicates to Adamson by rearranging (or manipulating) the letters of his chosen word.

It is clear that "[n]aming is the means whereby we attempt to order and structure the chaos and flux of existence which would otherwise be an undifferentiated mass. By assigning names we impose a pattern and a meaning which allows us to manipulate the world" (Spender 163). Despite the fact that "women have been excluded from naming and definition," Matty undermines the chief namer in the story and takes the chance to name something herself (Cameron 13). When Adamson meets a young housemaid, he calls her "his beetle-sprite" (96). Although Adamson has attempted, again, to reduce a person to an insect-like category, Matty thwarts the attempt and renames her Amy. By naming the young woman, Matty diminishes Adamson's power to aestheticize people. Moreover, in her small, cell-like room, Matty voices her desires and names herself. She suggests a way in which Adamson can leave Bredely Hall. She wants to go to South America, and she has made enough money from her publication to buy two tickets for them aboard a ship. Adamson objects; the jungle is "*no place* for a woman," he says (156). But instead of allowing him to silence her, Matty Crompton makes him look at her, makes him see her as a woman, not a sexless worker ant. She replies that he does not know who she is or what she is. Rather than letting him perceive her from his own perspective, Matty names herself: "'My name', she said, 'is Matilda. Up here at night there is no Matty. Only Matilda. *Look at me*'" (157). She refuses to let Adamson believe that all her work to ensure their safe passage to South America is simply to fulfill his wishes. She insists that she has made those plans because she wants to travel, and he will be her escort until they arrive. She does not wish to travel with him because she adores him; she tells him, "You need not heed me, once the voyage is over" (157). Adamson attempts several times to convince her that she is unprepared for life in the jungle, but she perseveres, repeatedly voicing her desires: "It is *what I will do*" (157).

At first, Adamson seems to be a hero in Matty's life. When he finally turns to her, Matty gains an opportunity to break away from the labels imposed upon her in the Alabaster household. Although Adamson reduces Eugenia to a mere symbol, a butterfly, a queen bee, a breeding machine, appropriates her act of creation (her giving birth), and reduces it to a mechanism; Matty Crompton re-appropriates the many things that Adamson has undermined: she begins creating herself by writing and manages to make Adamson her partner in the writing. Adamson is supposedly Eugenia's partner in marriage and birthing, but he does not include himself in her creative acts. By contrast, he and Matty Crompton become partners writing a book. He helps her to create; and through her writing, she manages to make herself central in his life and, more important, in his story. However, that synopsis of Matty Crompton's role in **"Morpho Eugenia"** is derived purely from Adamson's biased view of it.

In the beginning, Adamson hardly notices Matty Crompton; therefore, the reader does not realize that her name appears as early as the first page of the story. At the ball, Lady Alabaster tells Adamson, "I shall ask Matty to find you a pretty partner, unless you can pick one out for yourself" (3). Other people speak of her and about her for several pages until Adamson finally notices her himself: "There was a thin Miss Crompton, usually known as Matty, who, although not the governess—that was Miss Mead—nor the nursery nurse—that was Dacres—seemed to be in some way employed in the care of the younger members of the family" (22). She holds little importance for him until she almost forces herself into his world. In his first perception of Matty Crompton, Adamson likens her to himself: neither he nor Matty have officially defined roles in the household; they both belong to the same class of educated workers; they both are poor and financially dependent on the Alabasters; and they are both intellectual people who enjoy scientific pursuits. In the household, they are designated labels that carry varied status or influence: Matty is a servant and Adamson is a son-in-law, not a son. Their powerlessness helps to bring them together. Adamson immediately familiarizes himself with her by referring to her only as Matty, whereas whenever she is not with Adamson, she is referred to as Matty Crompton. Adamson does not seem to feel the necessity of giving Matty a surname, a name that would recognize her family and hence her status, because he thinks she has none. Moreover, by calling her Matty, Adamson gives himself the prerogative of familiar naming; whereas by calling him only Mr. Adamson, Matty clearly respects that status.

Matty makes various attempts to escape from the confines imposed upon her by Bredely Hall and by Adamson himself. She begins by trying to give herself a voice. When Adamson first meets with Matty Crompton, he paraphrases what she says so that we cannot hear her own words: "She spoke quietly, clearly, with little expression. [. . .] What was that he had in his hand? It looked quite alarming" (27). "The practice of speaking for others is often born of a desire for mastery, to privilege oneself as the one who more correctly understands the truth about another's situation. [. . .] And the effect of the practice of speaking for others is often [. . .] erasure and a reinscription of sexual, national, and other kinds of hierarchies" (Alcoff 29). However, while Adamson is visiting Lady Alabaster in her parlor, Matty Crompton interrupts him, asking him if he would help with the lessons in the schoolroom. By cutting off his own words, she compels him to listen to her. At first, Adamson feels coerced, but as Matty Crompton revitalizes his interest in living ants rather than dead butterflies, he realizes that the work has put "him in the way of purposeful activity again" (76). However, simply watching Adamson regain his interest in his studies is not enough for Matty Crompton. She works side by side with him, studying ant colonies, naming them, collecting specimens, making sketches. Her devotion to entomology sparks Adamson's respect, and he begins to call her *Miss* Crompton. Miss Crompton also convinces Adamson to begin writing a book about his work with the ant colonies. However, she proposes that she become his assistant. Thus she moves herself from assistant to accomplice. They keep their project a secret between themselves, a bond that ties Adamson and Matty closer together and drives a wedge between Adamson and his wife. Working with Adamson, Matty Crompton gains the knowledge she desires to have. She firmly believes that "[w]e should not live in ignorance of the rest of the world" (81).

Signs of Matty's intent to manipulate Adamson do not appear until late in the story, when Adamson begins to recognize her as an intellectual (and social) equal. When he says she is "very much in her own control," Adamson does not know the extent of that control. Soon Matty begins to suggest, plan, and rewrite a book Adamson is to draft (92). "Perhaps you should write your own book," Matty suggests (92). When Adamson hesitates, she defines the book for him: "I believe if you were to write a *natural history* of the colonies over a year—or two years, if you were to feel the need was absolute—you would have something very interesting to a very general public, and yet of scientific value. You could bring your very great knowledge to bear on the particular lives of these creatures—make comparisons—bring in their Amazonian relatives—but told in a *popular* way with anecdotes, and folklore, and stories of how the observations were made" (93). Although she then suggests that she might be Adamson's "*assistant*" it is clear that she is in charge (93). As the book takes form, Matty rewrites parts of it, brightening Adamson's rather turgid style, ensuring the success of the book (109). Even though Matty is Adamson's closest friend in **"Morpho Eugenia,"** he does not see her intent in getting the book published. She wants the financial independence that she ultimately achieves by publishing her own book of fairy tales. In the last scene of **"Morpho Eugenia,"** while Matty is going toward her future, Adamson is escaping, an escape he envisioned (and foreshadowed) at the beginning of the story when he imagines "a ship in flight, with the green water churning away from the bows, and the spray racing" (20).

Matty also introduces us (and Adamson) to another level of determination that occurs in the story when she says, "There are people in a house, you know, who know everything that goes on—the invisible people, and now and then *the house* simply decides that something must happen" (155). It is not Matty who sends Adamson the note that brings him back to the house to discover Eugenia with Edgar; therefore, we (and he) become aware of all the others in the house who are aware of what is going on. While the Alabasters try to keep Adamson ignorant and tied to Bredely Hall, the servants (Matty among them) help to orchestrate the events that lead to his leaving Bredely. As Matty says, "The will of the mill owners is not the Spirit of the Nest" (40). In other words, the Alabasters are not the masters of the servant-slaves. When Adamson says that "the workers [ants] are known to control the access of the males to the Queens, choosing which shall be admitted to their presence and which shall be kept at bay," we begin to perceive the control exerted by the almost invisible world of servants (101). While the queen is destined "to enjoy love, to burn with jealousy and anger, to be incited to vengeance, and to pass her time without labour," the worker is "zealous for the good of the community, a defender of the public rights. [. . .] laborious, industrious, patient, ingenious, skilful" (85-86). Thus it is no wonder that the masters of Bredely Hall are not as much in control as they might think.

One remarkable aspect of the story of the servants is that Adamson views the invisible community of workers at Bredely as mostly women. When thinking of Matty, he first "came to the conclusion that Matty Crompton was required to 'make herself useful' without any demeaning named post. Women were better at making themselves useful, he supposed" (76). He understands that "amongst the nations both of the bees and of the ants, there is only *one* true female, the Queen, and that the work of the community is carried on by barren females, or nuns, who attend to the feeding, building, and nurturing of the whole society and its city" (85). Thus it seems logical to Adamson to understand the invisible worker world at Bredely to be mostly women, "nuns" who do not reproduce. When he finally finds "a very different population [at Bredely] from the daylight one," they must obviously be, for Adamson, "a host of silently hurrying, black-clad young women, carrying buckets of cinders, buckets of water, boxes of polishing tools, fistfuls of brooms and brushes and carpet beaters" (49). However, if Adamson attempts to control the women in his life by placing them in social categories, continually naming and labeling them, he clearly fails with the servants at Bredely for they are the one(s) who send him the fateful note. When he arrives at the Hall, he runs into a nameless maid and her attitude itself undermines Adamson's illusory authority and control over the situation: "There was something odd about the girl's manner. Something furtive, apprehensive, and also excited" (148).

Byatt shows how "[b]eing aware of the limitations that are inherent in the language we possess, being sensitive to its falseness and its distortions is [. . .] a beginning (Irigaray 65). Therefore, by illustrating Adamson's delusions of control and the traps into which he falls, Byatt reveals the insipid quality of the male gaze and its characteristic behavior of distorting and marginalizing other stories. At the end of **"Morpho Eugenia,"** "William and Matilda are standing on [the] deck [of the *Calypso,* bound for South America], leaning over the rails, watching the ship's nose plunge down and on" (159). Although Matty has engineered her escape from Bredely Hall, Byatt does not conclude that all will be well for her. Now the symbols and signs of darkness, once part of Adamson's reductive categorization of the world, appear again: "The sky is a profound blue-black," "[t]he sea is a deep blue-black," and "William's *brown* hand grips her *brown* wrist on the rail" (159, 160). The darkness now represents fear of the unknown as they travel toward the Amazon. Even as the story closes, Adamson names a butterfly that has flown aboard, and he tells Matilda that "they are strong fliers" (160). He is obviously still locked in his system of naming, still imparting knowledge to Matty as if he were the authority, while her concerns are only with "emotion" (160). As they sail away, Matty and Adamson "look out with renewed interest at the points of light in the dark around them" (160). Byatt does not send her characters into rays of light—they are sailing into the dark, watching the lights, which may (or may not) represent the possibility of hope. Although Spender says that "[w]here women have renamed part of the world it is clear that values have shifted and, with them, the balance of power" (184), no shift occurs until the second novella in ***Angels and Insects,* "The Conjugial Angel."** In the end, all that Byatt may insist upon in **"Morpho Eugenia"** is:

> The woman is both "inside" and "outside" male society, both a romantically idealized member of it and a victimized outcast. She is sometimes what stands between man and chaos, and sometimes the embodiment of chaos itself. This is why she troubles the neat categories of such a regime, blurring its well-defined boundaries. Women are represented within male-governed society, fixed by sign, image, meaning, yet because they are also the "negative" of that social order there is always in them something which is left over, superfluous, unrepresentable, which refuses to be figured there.
>
> (Eagleton 190)

And that is why the story ends where it does, in the ambiguous dark, with two people sailing into an unfamiliar and possibly perilous future.

Works Cited

Alcoff Linda. "The Problem of Speaking for Others," *Cultural Critique* 29 (1991-2): 5-32.

Byatt, A. S. "Morpho Eugenia," *Angels and Insects.* London: Chatto, 1992.

Cameron, Deborah, ed. *The Feminist Critique of Language: A Reader.* London: Routledge, 1990.

Davies, R. G. "Insects (Class Insecta)," *The New Larousse Encyclopedia of Animal Life.* London: Hamlyn, 1980.

Eagleton, Terry. *Literary Theory: An Introduction.* Minneapolis: U of Minnesota P, 1983.

Irigaray, Luce. "Women's Exile," Trans. Couze Venn, *Ideology and Consciousness* 1 May 1977: 62-76.

Morrison, Toni. *Playing in the Dark: Whiteness and the Literary Imagination.* Cambridge: Harvard UP, 1992.

Owens, Craig. *Beyond Recognition: Representation, Power, and Culture.* Ed. Scott Bryson et al. Berkeley: U of California P, 1992.

Spender, Dale. *Man Made Language,* 2nd ed. London: Routledge, 1985.

Trinh, T. Minh-ha. *Woman, Native, Other: Writing Postcoloniality and Feminism.* Bloomington: Indiana UP, 1989.

Caroline Webb (essay date 2003)

SOURCE: Webb, Caroline. "Forming Feminism: Structure and Ideology in *Charades* and 'The Djinn in the Nightingale's Eye'." *Hecate* 29, no. 1 (2003): 132-41.

[In the following essay, Webb argues that despite drawing on the form of The Thousand and One Nights, *Janette Turner Hospital's* Charade *and Byatt's "The Djinn*

in the Nightingale's Eye," respectively, display complex narratives of the female experience that subvert the traditional fairytale.]

Some months ago I gave a paper on a postmodern work by a female author and, during the subsequent discussion, several people took issue with the ways in which the author portrayed female characters. Their implication was that these portraits of characters and their narrative destinies were in themselves sufficient to dismiss the author as conservative and anti-feminist. (I apologise to the participants for oversimplifying these comments.) The discussion made me question how we locate feminism—and anti-feminism—in fictional texts, especially texts by women.

In 1929 Virginia Woolf noted the importance of breaking the expected sequence of events in a text; she saw conventional narrative expectations as shaped by the patriarchal order.[1] In the late twentieth century, feminist theorists such as Luce Irigaray and Hélène Cixous speculated on ways in which particular formal strategies can represent phallogocentricity or enact an *écriture féminine*;[2] in this period a number of scholarly articles were themselves written in forms intended to represent the feminine.[3] But even in the blossoming feminist studies of Woolf's own writing, for example, the post-1970s assessment of her political agenda has been accompanied by diminishing attention to the *forms* of her fictions, although both are acknowledged to be radical.[4] Novelist A. S. Byatt has said that we think in narratives, not—or not only—in the 'moments' described by Modernists.[5] Her claim resonates with contemporary developments in psychology and sociology; narrative itself is thus identified as a particularly important object of study. In this article I consider how formal narrative elements can shape not only the content of fictional works, as they inevitably do, but the politics of the text as a whole.

In many postmodern texts, patterns of allusions act as genre encodings: they invite us to look for, and more especially *at,* the structure belonging to the work, or works, to which they allude. Recognizing its play with that structure is crucial to an understanding of the postmodern text and its meaning. Feminist values are encoded in different ways at these structural levels of postmodern fictional texts. I examine here two works—Janette Turner Hospital's novel *Charades* (1988) and A. S. Byatt's novella **'The Djinn in the Nightingale's Eye'** (1994)—that allude, among other works, to *The Thousand and One Nights.* Both works generate structures derived in part from their source-text that provide, I would argue, a shared message about features of female lives and storytelling that goes beyond messages derivable directly from their very different plots.

To begin with the content of *Charades.* Its opening chapter provides us with a vision of the woman as Other, when a strange girl appears late at night in a Nobel-winning physicist's office at MIT in Boston. The perspective of this opening, as of much prepostmodern fiction, is a masculine one: although both figures are described in the third person, the 'girl' (as she is called here) is seen from the outside—'"And the connecting link is Katherine Sussex," she says, quite cool and businesslike'—while the man's perceptions and internal responses are provided to the reader, 'He has a sense of her jotting down data in a logbook somewhere' (p. 7).[6] Moreover, her sudden appearance and disappearance are presented almost supernaturally, preparing the man, and the reader, to see her stereotypically, as a male construction: 'When he shakes himself clear of shock and looks again, the girl has vanished. Of course he is certain he has invented her. Or that he has fallen asleep at the desk and Rachel, his ex-wife, has spooked another dream' (p. 7).

Although the reference to the girl's mental 'logbook' may make her seem an unusually rational image of the female, the conjunction with her vanishing may make her seem a version of the recording angel, 'spooking' the physicist Koenig's guilt. This beginning, then, sets us up for a conventionally male-focused narrative. And the early characterizations of women in the narrative appear to confirm not only the masculine focus but phallogocentric assumptions, given that we seem to have a group of familiar female stereotypes. As the girl Charade begins to tell her stories she refers to her mother, Bea, as 'the Slut of the Tamborine Rainforest' (p. 16); it emerges that Bea is the unwed mother of some ten children, and a kind of mother goddess to boot. In the section entitled 'K: The Variorum Edition,' Bea appears as an essence of stereotypic femininity: from the age of six she is a natural flirt with full awareness of the power of her body over males. Katherine Sussex, meanwhile, whose story is told in 'K: The Variorum Edition,' is unconfident and easily enthralled, whether by Bea's stories or by the brooding presence of Verity Ashkenazy; she is the passive woman, shy, apparently docile, her considerable academic success masked by her own self-deprecation. Katherine's early passivity—she is barely able to speak when addressed by Nicholas Truman, object of her adolescent sexual longings—seems to fit with the description of her as seduced, in effect and in fact, by a stranger, Koenig himself, with a passing resemblance to Nicholas, whom she hasn't seen for decades. Finally, Rachel Koenig and Verity Ashkenazy are both represented as the darker side of female Otherness: both function as objects of obsession because of their fascinating misery, and both are discovered to be hysterics, or worse, crazed by their experiences or crazily inventing experiences. Such characterizations merge easily with our expectations of more chauvinistic texts. A number of details within those characterizations that complicate these expectations could be further explored; the focus of this article, however, is on how the novel's allusive structure undercuts the stereotypic and provides a new understanding of its operations.

Directly following the passage in which Koenig ponders the girl's disappearance, he decides the cause of the apparition is 'not Rachel really. His own guilt, he supposes, which comes in a thousand and one different guises and plays many games' (p. 7). The number alerts us to the novel's engagement with the tale of *The Thousand and One Nights,* and particularly with its frame-story. In this frame narrative the king, Shahriyah, discovers that his wife is cuckolding him. He and his brother, who discovers that he is being similarly betrayed, wander around the countryside and confirm that fornication and adultery are happening everywhere; Shahriyah then goes back home and starts a new programme of serial marriages, marrying a new wife each day and cutting off her head in the morning so that she cannot betray him. The clever Scheherezade manages to stave off her execution by telling stories in the night, breaking off at an exciting moment when dawn comes. Each morning Shahriyah decides that he will wait just one more day so that he can hear the end of the current story (or stories—a lot of the tales have embedded narratives).

Hospital's central male character is named Koenig, German for King, formally placing him as the Sultan figure. When he fumbles over the girl's name, Charade Ryan, she explains that his difficulty arises because he as an American mispronounces the word 'charade' (Americans say 'sha-rayd'): 'The proper way, well the Brit way . . . is the way I say my name' (p. 17). She thus draws attention to the *sound* of the word, '*Shuhrahd*' (p. 17), and its similarity to 'Shahrazad' or its more familiar form 'Scheherezade.' As in *The Thousand and One Nights,* Koenig is accustomed to liaisons with many different women—he is a Nobel Prize-winner, and they feel 'an *aura* about him' (p. 17)—but finds himself sleeping with Charade for over a year. We see almost nothing of their sex together, despite chapters headed 'The First Night,' 'The Second Night'; instead what we are given (and all Koenig seems to remember) is Charade's endless monologues. I say 'all Koenig seems to remember' because for most of the novel their relationship is, as I have noted, shown from his point of view. Charade in that sense remains mysteriously Other.

But if this point of view implies that the novel replicates *The Thousand and One Nights* in its assumption that the man's goals—the King's goals—structure the nature of events, this is far from being the case. In *The Thousand and One Nights* the woman tells stories for her life—tells them to the man and for the man's purposes. She is caught within his structure and seeking desperately to change it with her stories. Although she is telling the tale for her own interests her interests depend on his pleasure. In *Charades,* however, the woman tells stories for *her life*; that is, to find out the sense of her life by finding the truth of her origins. In telling stories she is using the man; he is necessary as a listener (especially as she sees him as version of her putative father), but her telling is for herself, and once she herself discovers the truth of her identity she leaves him without even telling him what she has discovered. Conversely Koenig tells his 'Kynges Tale,' one of the sections of the novel, for her, fearful of losing her—much more Scheherezadic, as Charade is not just a necessary listener but the whole reason for the telling. Thus the patriarchal success figure—male, American, Nobel-winning—is displaced by the outsider, female, Australian, vagrant, not just in Koenig's perception but in the reader's. Although Koenig remains our point of view through most of the framing narrative, Charade's stories about women, about female identity and how it is constructed, hold the narrative centre and provide its significance.

Instead of the woman operating inside a dangerously patriarchal structure, the man is held within her structure of story, and not only the routine of his life but his own conception of himself is changed by this. Following Charade's departure, we are told, Koenig repeatedly starts to ring the Australian telephone numbers she had noted down (again for her own use, not his), but does not do so because 'he thinks of Heisenberg and the indeterminacy question, and wishes to keep the ending open' (p. 345). This underlines not only the fact that Koenig has, as he himself notes, become someone else (he never needed to ring a woman before), but also the novel's intricate commentary on story and its power. Koenig's decision, according to him, is a physicist's one, 'think[ing] of Heisenberg,' about whom he and Charade have talked. But it is also a narrative decision, dependent as much on the form of Charade's conversation as on its content. 'The indeterminacy question' turns out to be intimately related to the nature of narrative in this novel (I shall come back to this), and here it is the woman's narration, not the man's, that is powerful. He tells his 'Kynges Tale' in order to keep her attention, as a substitute for saying 'I love you' (something he never says); but it is not enough to keep her. '*And with that,* as Scheherezade said to King Shahryar when the thousand-and-first night had come, *she vanished like camphor*' (p. 340; original italics).

With that sentence, appended by the frame narrator following Charade's departure, we recognize that in Hospital's feminist retelling Charade has been both subject and teller of her stories and of the novel, reversing traditional expectations. Not only is this Scheherezade independent of the King, and able to 'vanish' of her own free will, but she occupies his attention with her own story. From the reader's point of view, too, the female—

and female-centred—narrative is what controls our attention. Though men, or a man, haunt these stories, Charade's final revelation is that the real quest of her life has not been to discover her father, but to recognise her mother. With that recognition the quest ends and the narratives end. Although Hospital provides a brief coda describing Koenig's response to Charade's final disappearance, the novel effectively ends when Charade's storytelling concludes, underlining the significance not just of Charade's story but of her stories.

I noted earlier that 'the indeterminacy question' turns out to be intimately related to the nature of narrative in this novel. Modern physics turns out to be anticipated by female experience; the postmodern becomes itself feminised through Hospital's strategies of form. The patriarchal life story, traditionally told, may end in marriage or provide the trajectory of a career up to a Nobel Prize, but Charade's female life is unshaped, open-ended; it may have resolution but is not predetermined. Further, and crucially, as represented here the woman's story is multiple and intertextual, depending on the stories of other women. This is no simple love-story or narrative of quest: using the embedding and digressive techniques of Scheherezade, Hospital demonstrates the complexity and indeterminacy of the female life within the interstices of patriarchy. Moreover, unlike the masculine regime of Shahriyah, which excises—in his case by strangling—the Other with which the King cannot deal, Hospital's text is inclusive. Charade listens to Koenig's tale, as well as rendering Bea's and Katherine's—and the reader receives them all. As Hospital's story depends on *The Thousand and One Nights,* so Charade's story depends on Katherine's and Bea's (both of which are represented at length), and on the untold story of the Sleeping Beauty in a Queensland nursing home, who has moved outside story into silence. The novel's structure thus highlights the extent to which the female story is not the duologue of patriarchal romance fiction but a multiplicity of interweaving threads that can, and do, lead everywhere.

This focus on how female story itself is structured within western patriarchal discourse is shared by A. S. Byatt's novella **'The Djinn in the Nightingale's Eye.'** This work is shorter than *Charades,* but even denser with stories. Its opening, also evokes generic conventions:

> Once upon a time, when men and women hurtled through the air on metal wings, when they wore webbed feet and walked on the bottom of the sea, learning the speech of whales and the songs of the dolphins, when pearly-fleshed and jewelled apparitions of Texan herdsmen and houris shimmered in the dusk on Nicaraguan hillsides, when folk in Norway and Tasmania in dead of winter could dream of fresh strawberries, dates, guavas and passion fruits and find them spread next morning on their tables, there was a woman who was largely irrelevant, and therefore happy.
>
> (p. 95)[7]

The framing 'Once upon a time' and the representation of facts of modern life as magical locates this opening as a fairytale, while its allusion to 'houris' indicates that Byatt is drawing on the tradition of *The Thousand and One Nights* as well as European folktale—and that her narrative will be as complex as its opening sentence.

I would argue that the very choice of the fairytale form situates Byatt in a tradition of feminist (re)writers of fairytales and that, in fact, she is meditating here on the fairytale tradition and conventional shaping of female life stories. It is noteworthy that in the best-known fairytales the opening 'there was a woman . . .' such as Byatt provides here is generally followed by 'who had [some number of sons or daughters],' so that the child rather than the woman becomes the focus of the tale. Byatt, like many recent woman writers, is contemplating, among other things, the place of the woman and of female power in the fairytale tradition—western and eastern—as well as in the modern world she magically depicts.

In content terms, Byatt's protagonist, Gillian Perholt (an allusion to the eighteenth-century French fairytale collector Charles Perrault), is a figure very different from Charade Ryan. Charade was a socially marginal figure, but Gillian, a British narratologist who gives keynote lectures at conferences also attended by Todorov and Genette, seems thoroughly successful in patriarchal terms. She enacts a woman's role (the teller of old wives' tales) with a twist: she is in the tale-telling business for pleasure and profit, instead of being, as Byatt puts it, '[an] ingenious queen in fear of the shroud brought in with the dawn' (pp. 95-96), a direct allusion to Scheherezade. But shared formal energies imply a far closer relationship between *Charades* and **'The Djinn in the Nightingale's Eye.'** While characterizations and action may imply one set of political positions, attention to underlying structures reveals a shared interest in the complex form of the female life and its resistance to traditional narrative trajectories.

The novella is dense with stories, in a mode insistently ascribed to Gillian's profession; some are told separately—mostly as part of conference papers—but others are read, or intercalated in the course of an individual's narration of an idea or a life. Gillian herself, for example, gives papers on Chaucer's 'The Clerk's Tale' and a fairytale (including its telling), but we also read part of her friend Orhan's conference paper, which describes two stories from *The Thousand and One Nights,* the frame story and the story of Prince Camaralzaman and the Princess Budoor.

Both the protagonist's own retelling of 'The Clerk's Tale' and her friend's version of 'Camaralzaman and Budoor' draw the attention of Byatt's readers to the issue of narrative agency. They emphasize the concentration of the power to make things happen in persons either too involved in the action, like Chaucer's Count Walter, or too detached, like the earth spirit in 'Camaralzaman and Budoor' who recommends that two competitive djinn encourage mutual defloration of the two sleeping humans. Gillian's own meditations on how Griselda in 'The Clerk's Tale' and Shakespeare's Hermione in *The Winter's Tale* are images of 'stopped energies' (p. 121), their lives halted for years by the demands of the artist-figures, highlight the fact that Byatt's interest is not only in the agency involved in telling stories, but also in the roles available within them.

Gillian's discovery of a djinn, or genie, in a bottle of nightingale's-eye glass half-way through the novella propels the narrative into a new space, evoking a world of fairytale at odds with the portrait of Gillian as modern-day elderly professional. This move into fairytale underlines the extraordinary modernity of Gillian's situation and the extent to which she is, as she thinks early on, 'an unprecedented being' (pp. 104-05): after all, few fairytales are told about women of fifty-five. Instead, the older woman is conventionally represented as godmother or witch in tales with younger heroes. Like the earth spirit in 'Camaralzaman and Budoor' the crone figure may make something happen, but it happens to someone else: she is a 'redundant' figure, an adjective with which Byatt and Gillian make play early in the narrative, because she has no direct biological involvement in social reproduction, and, according to the social structures implied in European fairytales, can have no other direct social role. She therefore participates in other people's lives as witch if her meddling is malevolent, or 'fairy godmother' if it is helpful.

Although Gillian has early rejoiced both in her success and in her freedom following her husband's departure with a younger woman, she is haunted by the spectre of a decaying woman throughout her attendance at the conference 'Stories of Women's Lives.' It seems that what she fears is after all the decay of her body, and her identification of the spectre as 'Hermione-Griselda' (p. 123) emphasizes the extent to which she sees that decay, despite her apparent pleasure in being 'an unprecedented being,' as weighted by the fate of the aging woman in traditional literature. It is not surprising then that her first wish—the djinn tells her he will give her three, in an evocation of European folktale tradition—is to have her body as it was when she 'last really *liked* it' (p. 201), which turns out to be as it was when she was in her early thirties, rather than when it was 'terrifying' to her in its beauty, as it was when she was a young girl (p. 241).

It is in keeping with the oddity of the story as fairytale, if less so with the pattern of more modern patriarchal fictions about women, that Gillian's second wish is for the djinn, the magical agent who has his own set of tales to tell about being imprisoned by beautiful and intelligent women, to love her: she becomes a romantic heroine in her own fairytale, a most unusual role for an aging woman—unless of course she turns out to be really a beautiful girl under a curse. However, the story does not end with the happy-ever-after of heterosexual romance. Gillian gives her third wish to the djinn himself and he leaves her, with a promise to return. She responds: 'If you remember to return in my lifetime,' and he says: 'If I do' (p. 270). This would make for a rather downbeat ending; but we are then given an epilogue in which the djinn briefly visits her life again and leaves with the same promise (p. 277). Like the ending of *Charades,* this provides us with an openness, an indeterminacy, that is common in postmodern fiction, but not in either the fairytale tradition or *The Thousand and One Nights.*

If we read this novella with an eye only to its plot and the destiny of its protagonist we might think simply that Gillian, and Byatt beyond her, wants to have her cake and eat it too: to be a successful senior academic *and* have a younger woman's body *and* be able to have fantastic sex (literally) with no strings attached. But the layers of the narrative, the many stories told to and by Gillian, complicate that picture, and not just through the content of each episode. Rather, as in *Charades,* the complex form of the narrative directs us as readers to see Gillian's situation in relation to a long tradition of 'stories of women's lives.' Further, the very multiplicity of the narrative is in itself a commentary on how the female life can be told. In addition to its layers, this modern fairytale includes in itself all kinds of stories, as Byatt offers us many stories for the price of one. The narrative she provides us is fairytale; it is monster story, when the djinn first appears in giant form; it is sex, since Gillian and the djinn sleep together in appropriately magical perfection; it is a love story; it is comedy; if not tragedy, it provides pity and terror. I would argue that this very complexity arises because it is a woman's story and, contrary to Gillian's own view, Byatt sees the woman's story as, after all, multiple. Byatt is not only reminding us of changes in the historical roles of women; she is also doing her own version of narratology which, the narrator explains, requires the telling of stories.

Christien Franken has pointed out that although Byatt frequently insists that she is a novelist, and not or only incidentally a critic, she has developed a substantial record of critical publications since the 1960s.[8] Here she is doing both jobs at once: this novella is itself literary criticism. As in *Charades,* the woman's experience turns out to be multiple and indeterminate. The provisional, tentatively repeated quality of the tale's ending provides a sense of openness to which we are not accustomed in reading the more popular western fairytales. Unlike most other recent feminist rewriters of the fairytale, Byatt refuses to allow its patterns to be simply oppressive; drawing on the strategies of *The Thousand and One Nights,* if not its content, she demonstrates how the form of story itself can be feminised, made multiple rather than phallically direct, in ways implied by feminist theorists. Her metanarrative, like Hospital's, updates the feminist fairytale in form and, therefore, in meaning. For both Hospital and Byatt, the forms of *The Thousand and One Nights* enable a narrative of the female life story as multiple and complex, breaking the sequence and subverting the simplicities encoded in the traditional fairytale.

Notes

1. Virginia Woolf, *A Room of One's Own* (1929), Oxford, Oxford University Press, 1992: 119ff. Woolf describes at some length the work of a hypothetical female author who breaks the Austenian sentence and breaks the sequence, 'the expected order,' deciding approvingly that 'she wrote as a woman . . . who has forgotten that she is a woman, so that her pages were full of that curious sexual quality which comes only when sex is unconscious of itself' (p. 121).
2. Hélène Cixous, 'The Laugh of the Medusa,' *Signs* 1 (1975): 875-93. Reprinted in Robyn R. Warhol and Diane Price Herndl (eds.), *Feminisms: An Anthology of Literary Theory and Criticism,* New Brunswick, Rutgers University Press, 1991: 334-49; Luce Irigaray, *This Sex Which Is Not One,* trans. Catherine Porter with Carolyn Burke, Ithaca, NY, Cornell University Press, 1985, especially chapter 4.
3. See for example Rachel Blau DuPlessis and Members of Workshop 9, 'For the Etruscans: Sexual Difference and Artistic Production—The Debate over a Female Aesthetic,' in Hester Eisenstein and Alice Jardine (eds.), *The Future of Difference,* New York, Barnard College Women's Center / Boston, G. K. Hall, 1980: 128-57.
4. There are, of course, exceptions to this, including notably Rachel Bowlby, *Virginia Woolf: Feminist Destinations* (Oxford, Basil Blackwell, 1988) and Pamela L. Caughie, *Virginia Woolf and Postmodernism: Literature in Quest and Question of Itself* (Urbana, University of Illinois Press, 1991).
5. Nicolas Tredell, 'A. S. Byatt in Conversation,' *PN Review* 17 (1991): 24.
6. Page references in this section are to Janette Turner Hospital, *Charades,* St Lucia, University of Queensland Press, 1988.
7. Page references in this section are to A. S. Byatt, 'The Djinn in the Nightingale's Eye' (1994), in *The Djinn in the Nightingale's Eye: Five Fairy Stories,* London, Random House, 1995: 93-277.
8. Christien Franken, 'The Turtle and Its Adversaries: Gender Disruption in A. S. Byatt's Critical and Academic Work,' in Richard Todd and Luisa Flora (eds.), *Theme Parks, Rainforests and Sprouting Wastelands: European Essays on Theory and Performance in Contemporary British Fiction,* Amsterdam, Rodopi, 2000: 195-96.

Samantha Matthews (review date 31 October 2003)

SOURCE: Matthews, Samantha. "Monsters, Trolls, and Creative Writers." *Times Literary Supplement,* no. 5248 (31 October 2003): 21-2.

[*In the following review, Matthews discusses the central thematic concerns of the stories in* Little Black Book of Stories, *concluding that the collection is "a bravura performance of imaginative artistry."*]

A. S. Byatt's fifth story collection really is a little black book. It has the same elegantly compact format as its predecessors: ***The Matisse Stories*** (1993), ***The Djinn in the Nightingale's Eye: Five Fairy Stories*** (1994), and ***Elementals: Stories of Fire and Ice*** (1998). However, the title of this group of five modern folk and fairy tales is purposeful as well as reflexive, registering a unifying concern with relations between occult knowledge and everyday existence, secrets and survival, grief and the quest for resolution. As in the little black book of urban myth, words and names are spells to be conjured with, "open sesames" to imaginative spaces often correspondingly dark.

The fairytale quest into darkness is tellingly represented by the reproduction on the dust-jacket of Jóhannes S. Kjarval's painting "Forest Palace" (1918). This is a dreamed or mythic forest, columns of densely massed trees receding into obscurity and growing from a pulsingly rich crimson floor. Kjarval's blood-nourished forest invokes both the Gothic and the visceral sources of Byatt's translations of folk motifs into a contemporary and realistic idiom. As she notes in an essay on the *Arabian Nights* (a strong influence on her stories of the last decade). "Narration is as much part of human nature as breath and the circulation of the blood". As Byatt's career progresses, storytelling appears more than ever a matter of life and death for her, inseparable from the life of the body, rites of passage and an awareness of mortality. These modern fairytales do not invite the reader to escape into fantasy, but rather refigure the spiritual and psychological significance of archetypal narratives for our secular times. One story, **"Raw Ma-**

terial", explores with considerable irony the therapeutic pros and cons of creative writing; the psychotherapeutic value of reading stories is never in doubt.

In an essay, "Old Tales, New Forms", Byatt charts her development from early self-conscious realism in the tradition of the British classic novel to a strong investment in "the irrepressible life of old stories", the tales, anecdotes and folk myths of European and world literature. Although Byatt's first collection, ***Sugar and Other Stories*** (1987), roughly conformed to received ideas about the short story, by the time of her introduction to *The Oxford Book of English Short Stories* (1998), she had taken an oppositional stance to the "well-made tale" or fleeting "impression", the importance of formal unity, the single event, no redundance. The criteria for that anthology reflect those of her own stories: rules are made to be broken, stories can mutate from genre to genre, "make unexpected twists and then twist again", "pack together comedy and tragedy, farce and delicacy, elegance and the grotesque".

As a novelist, Byatt has a deserved reputation as an intellectual heavyweight, concerned with the impact of science on religious feeling and imagination, with theory and ethics, relations between graphic and textual representation, with an allusive and self-conscious style to match. As a writer of small, discrete stories, she aims rather for a "quickness and lightness of narrative", quite as artful but less overtly clever. She records the pleasure of "handling the old, worn counters of the characterless persons", of narrating "more flatly, which is sometimes more mysteriously". Her marrying of realistic and fantastic modes helps to cultivate this mystery, which should leave imaginative space for the reader to inhabit. If this is not uniformly the case, most readers will feel that Byatt's authority as master storyteller and omniscient narrator is adequate compensation.

Translation and transformation are keynotes of this volume, which is dedicated to Byatt's German and Italian translators, "precise readers" whose conversation "over the years has changed my writing, and my reading". The book's exhilarating centrepiece, **"A Stone Woman"**, is a tale about the transformation of organic and emotional materials. Ines, an ageing etymological researcher grieving for her dead mother, undergoes a physical metamorphosis after a life-threatening operation. This is not a transformation of Ovidian swiftness; Ines documents day-by-day her flesh's change into geological and mineral forms. Yet where the reader might expect her brilliantly realized and aesthetically gorgeous metamorphosis to be a simple allegory for emotional petrifaction, it is in fact only a phase in a process of liberation. An Icelandic carver encountered in a cemetery takes her to Iceland, where she becomes not a "stone woman" but a troll, happily wild and dancing, at one with the volatile and constantly changing landscape. At moments, Ines's attraction to the occult language of mineralogy feels like the author's enthusiasm shining through ("Chabazite, from the Greek for hailstones, obsidian, which, like analcime and garnet, has the perfect icositetarahedral shape"). In general, though, Byatt wears her learning lightly, adopting the role of the alchemist, combining scientific empiricism with the magician's occult arts.

The Little Black Book of Stories is shaped like a life, beginning with two small girls setting out on a journey into the unknown, and ending with a tragic elderly couple going to bed and to death. The vision of the human condition is dark; the unsettling influence of the Second World War hangs over the first and last stories. Characters are literally or psychically orphaned and homeless; they live in tawdry bedsits and caravans or imprisoned by perverse domestic circumstances. There are two violent deaths and the promise of another. Although an unwanted baby is born to redeem its parents, another longed-for baby fails to be born, and its parents are permanently marked by its absence. By contrast, the supernatural creatures, a monster, a troll and a glamorous "fetch" (a spirit of the living supposed to appear as a portent of their death) are forces for possible redemption.

The first story, **"The Thing in the Forest"**, wears its debt to fairytale self-consciously. Two urban evacuees, Penny and Primrose (the archetypal pairing of dark and fair), encounter a monster in a wood. Unable to speak of this impossible trespasser from the world of fantasy, the modern babes in the wood grow into cautious and isolated women; one is a child psychologist, the other a professional storyteller, offering children the protection they missed. The women meet again in middle age, over a picture of the creature, the "Loathly Worm", emerging from a book's shadowy spine. Finally confirmed in the reality of what they witnessed, each separately returns to the wood, and comes to an individual accommodation with her past.

Byatt's exploration of the emotional scars of war through folk motifs is beautifully restrained. The Worm is forcefully realized, a stinking, farting bricolage of rubbish and decay, yet also pitiful in its painful movement and hideous face of "pure misery". It is a postmodern monster, a thing of fragments held together by an act of the imagination, evoking the unspeakable dark forces and terrible griefs of war, but not weakened into mere symbolism. The children's experience is touched with magic and grotesquerie: their gloves on tapes hang "like a spare pair of hands", the evacuees tramp "like a disorderly dwarf regiment", and the disturbingly blacked-out station signs make them feel as disorientated as Hansel and Gretel. The story is strongest in evoking the persistence of childish fears and sufferings into maturity; the adult Penny and Primrose feel like stereotypes rather than archetypes. As in a fairytale, the story is brought full-circle; the omniscient narrator's opening words—"There were once two little girls who saw, or believed they saw, a thing in a forest", with the echo "once upon a time"—are also the closing words, as Primrose finally begins to tell her own story.

The mystery of the human body is another keynote here, in particular the flesh morbid and mortified. The Worm is "the colour of flayed flesh" and has lips "like welts from whipstrokes"; Ines's transformation begins after her navel is cut out and reconstructed in scar-tissue: respectability conceals a brutal secret history of physical abuse and mutilation. **"Body Art"**, commissioned by the Wellcome Trust, considers conflicting views of the creative body as medical, artistic and affective subject. The fairytale element here is art student Daisy Whimple, a fan of installation art, who disrupts the controlled, abstract existence of doctor Damian Becket on the gynaecological ward of an East London hospital. Daisy is a frail but streetwise sprite, all white skin, silver-dyed hair and piercings, a vegan, petty thief and would-be free spirit; she also suffered a botched abortion in Becket's ward. The ascetic and morally rigid doctor is thwarted in a developing relationship with an art historian (working with the hospital's Wellcome-like collection of historical medical equipment and specimens), by his attempts to help Daisy, who is responsible for two near-the-bone creative acts in the story. She appropriates gruesome artefacts and body-parts from the collection, to make a public installation "of the goddess Kali, who was constructed like an Arcimboldo portrait out of many elements"; good art, bad ethics. Daisy's protest against patriarchal medical science is quickly ironized by her pregnancy from a brief haison with Becket: he forces her to keep the baby, almost killing her in the process. Finally, the human body's miraculous creativity is invoked as an overwhelming force for emotional recovery, but the resolution remains ironic and provisional.

"Raw Material" gives Byatt an opportunity to display her talent for writing in another writer's voice. Jack Smollett, after a brief London success with his first novel, scrapes a living teaching creative writing in his native Derbyshire village. Byatt has a lot of not entirely good-natured fun with the self-deluding amateur writers in his class, and their melodramatic wish-fulfilment fantasies. The discovery of one real talent, a reserved and dignified elderly woman. Cicely Fox, forces Smollett to confront his own failure. Fox's two pieces are interpolated: "How We Used to Black-lead Stoves" and "Wash Day" are indeed fine pieces of writing, detailed and evocative descriptions of rituals recalled from youth, which subtly hint at darker emotional terrain. Disturbing but enigmatic revelations of her private life undermine Smollett's idealization of Fox: again Byatt teases out the awkward interrelations of art and life. The story leaves a sour taste; its denouement does not change the fact that Fox's sympathetically presented artistry is Byatt's, the only true writer in the midst of a group of satirical cameos. Perhaps it read less self-regardingly in its original context as a commission for the Ilkley Literature Festival.

The final story, **"A Pink Ribbon"**, is a return to darkness. A retired classics teacher James Ennis numbly cares for his senile wife Mado or Madeleine (another orphan). His caring gestures are covertly hostile: he carefully dresses her hair, then finishes it with a pink ribbon (a colour she hated); she watches *Teletubbies,* but the doll he gives her is the bile-green Dipsy, which he absently stabs with hairpins like a voodoo fetish. Mado's rantings register her misery ("They took her into a dark a dark darkness and lost her"), but it is not until a mysterious young woman knocks on the door, Mado's "fetch", that James can recall his wife properly.

For the "precise reader" of ***The Little Black Book of Stories,*** there are a few disconcerting moments where verbal transformations appear to owe more to inattention than to art. **"The Thing in the Forest"** ends with Primrose setting out a "circle of rainbow-coloured plastic chairs", part of a harmonizing resolution that would be more satisfying had the chairs not earlier been "bright yellow". In **"A Stone Woman"**, the Icelandic stonecutter presents Ines with "a small, carved head which contained a basilisk and two mussel shells"; a few sentences later it has become a "stone hand". The discrepancy is more visible because Ines's stony hand is the subject of the passage: Thorsteinn's gift chinks against her fingers, and when she cuts her hand it runs molten lava rather than blood.

A. S. Byatt's publishers should remember that their exacting author invites and rewards such scrutiny, for these are minor blemishes in a sophisticated and powerfully realized work, which—like the Worm. Daisy's Kali installation and Ines's mineral body—fuses seemingly irreconcilable fragments by means of a bravura performance of imaginative artistry.

Stephen Abell (review date 29 November 2003)

SOURCE: Abell, Stephen. "Making It a Just So Story." *The Spectator* 293, no. 9147 (29 November 2003): 58.

[*In the following favorable assessment, Abell finds the pieces in Byatt's* Little Black Book of Stories *to be more modern, challenging, and relevant than many of her earlier stories.*]

This new collection [***Little Black Book of Stories***] is, surprisingly for a little black book, decidedly unsexy. In fact, A. S. Byatt—unsurprisingly, perhaps, for those readers who persisted through the Victorian mumblings and fumblings of *Possession*—does bad, awkward sex rather well. Here is a gynaecologist and an art student getting together (note especially the prophylactic double negative of the last sentence):

> She put cold fingers on his lips, and then on his sex, which stirred. He touched her, with a gynaecologist's fingers, gently and found the scars of the ovarectomy, a ring pierced into her navel, little breasts with rings in the left nipple . . . She began, not inexpertly, to caress him.

Elsewhere, a wartime couple fiercely go 'at it . . . tooth and claw, feather and velvet, blood and honey'; a woman who is turning into stone allows a sculptor 'to study her ridges and her clefts', if nothing else; and a writer, pondering sex with his partner, cannot 'find the right words to describe her orgasms—prolonged events with staccato and shivering rhythms alternating oddly—and this teased and pleased him'. Indeed, throughout the five stories on offer, Byatt is able to find the right words for the not-quite-right, unblinkingly capturing a sense of the jarring, the startling and the not entirely pleasant. It is a welcome departure for the author, an erstwhile chronicler of folk tales and legends, who this time appears to have her eye on something more edgily modern, more relevant and, therefore, far more intriguing than expected.

This is not to say that the mystical element is entirely missing, rather that it has been placed in a context that renders it powerful. A notable example is **'The Pink Ribbon'**, in which a husband suffers the indignity of cleaning up and caring for his mentally ill wife until he is urged to euthanasia by a visitor who turns out to be 'the Fetch', her living ghost. James Ennis is a 'vessel of seething rage', which he releases with 'harmless acts' of mental violence against mad Madeleine and acts of outright cruelty towards her childish possessions: 'he began abstractedly to drive the hairpins into Dipsy's silver screen, in his greenish towelling tummy. He stabbed and stabbed.' The reference to Teletubbies (as if you didn't know), described by Byatt as 'little fairies and elves', neatly encapsulates how the book seeks to combine the mythic and the modern. And the effect, despite what you might think, is haunting.

Thankfully, although touching on the 'etheric' and magical, these are not at all airy-fairy tales: Byatt's prose solidly evokes the emotionally and the physically specific. So, the central—and most beautiful—piece (the self-explanatory **'A Stone Woman'**) charts the grief-stricken petrification of a middle-aged woman both as a case-study in loneliness and acceptance ('she liked to see the dark spread in the square, because then bedtime was not far away') and a taxonomic account of a physical process: 'like a shingly girdle pushing down long fibrous fingers towards her groin, thrusting out cysts and gritty coruscations towards her pubic hair'. Here, as elsewhere, the writing is dauntingly precise and realistic, even as it points to something unnatural and bizarre: 'always aiming', as Byatt herself has characterised 'good' modern prose, 'at an impossible exactness which it knows it will never achieve'.

In **'The Story of the Eldest Princess'**, a previous—and typical—Byatt fairy tale about the telling of fairy tales, the narrator-heroine smugly 'telling the story feels the pure pleasure in getting it right, making it just so'. Her new collection is instead more honestly dissatisfied, impurely accurate and therefore has a convincing 'aesthetic horror to it that is pleasing'. In it, A. S. Byatt has demonstrated that she is far more than an 'Auntie Antonia' merely capable of spinning well-worn yarns, a creator of affecting and challenging pieces of writing: when you're sitting uncomfortably, you know she's begun.

Kathleen J. Renk (essay date 2004)

SOURCE: Renk, Kathleen J. "Rewriting the Empire of the Imagination: The Post-Imperial Gothic Fiction of Peter Carey and A. S. Byatt." *Journal of Commonwealth Literature* 29, no. 2 (2004): 61-71.

[*In the following essay, Renk discusses Byatt's "The Conjugial Angel" and Peter Carey's* Jack Maggs, *contending that both authors parody the conventions of Victorian literature and the Gothic novel.*]

> My empire is of the imagination.
>
> (Ayesha, *She*[1])

After she has revealed her "magic glass," H. Rider Haggard's She-who-must-be-obeyed, a nearly immortal magician/scientist,[2] says to a British adventurer:

> There is no such thing as magic, though there is such a thing as a knowledge of the secrets of Nature. That water is my glass [. . .] it is an old secret; I did not find it.
>
> (pp. 151-2)

She suggests the narrow line between magic and science that mesmerized the Victorians. Victorians dabbled in occult practices, such as telepathy, séances and mesmerism, even while they struggled to accept Darwinian science and its earthly ramifications. They also practised spiritualism while the Empire magically spread itself around the globe.[3] Victorian anthropologist Andrew Lang's explanation of the relationship between empire and the occult casts light on the period's wedding of science and pseudo-science: "As the visible world is measured, mapped, tested, weighed, we seem to hope more and more that a world of invisible romance may not be far from us".[4] Lang implies that as the British reached the limits of exploration, after they had weighed, mapped, and claimed as their own more than their share of the globe, the only frontier left to explore and map was the invisible world.

Patrick Brantlinger argues that British adventure novels, such as *She,* can be categorized as Imperial Gothic fiction. Expressing British anxieties about declining empire, these novels betray an antithetical fascination with the science and "magical" pseudo-science of the time, while supporting a "Darwinian ideology of imperialism".[5] Outlining three main themes of the Imperial Gothic, the fear of "individual regression" or "going native", the "invasion of civilization by the forces of barbarism or demonism" and the "diminution of opportunities for adventure and heroism in the modern world",[6] Brantlinger says these themes point toward the British Empire's worries that there were no further territories to conquer and despite supposed British superiority, the Empire might regress and fall due to prolonged contact with the supposedly less-fit people.

I would like to consider the Post-Imperial Gothic elements that I locate in works by Peter Carey and A. S. Byatt. Drawing on the conventions of Victorian and especially Imperial Gothic fiction, Carey in *Jack Maggs* and Byatt in **"The Conjugial Angel"** parody the style and conventions of Victorian literature, as they also critique and satirize the Imperial Gothic novel. Byatt and Carey move beyond parody though, as they also grapple with the western divisions between magic and science and mystery and certainty. Moreover, dealing variously with the science of exploration, mapping and Darwinian classification, and the pseudo-science of mesmerism, passive and invisible writing and séances, these texts commonly critique the British male writer/conjuror who, at times, claims, names and speaks with certainty about the mysterious universe. While the Imperial Gothic novel reveals the anxieties of ebbing Empire, the Post-Imperial Gothic novel exposes how Victorian writers plundered the minds of the marginalized to create art.

Parodying Dickens's style, Carey richly recreates the London of Dickens's story of Magwitch, much in the way Jean Rhys fashions a past for Brontë's Bertha Mason. Shaping characters as Dickens would with exaggerated, singular characteristics, Carey creates a "humble" Percy Buckle, who makes plans for the "latest donkey engine",[7] reminding the reader of both Uriah Heep and the inventive Mr. Dick. The leader of a den of thieves who befriends Maggs, Silas, is obviously a Fagin character. And Carey, like Dickens, neatly summarizes the outcome of each character's life by the end of the novel. Tobias Oates, like Dickens himself, falls in love with his sister-in-law and Oates's shiftless father recalls Dickens's own scallywag father who "had the ingratiating charm of a habitual sponger".[8] In addition, Oates's lack of sympathy for the exiled, colonial criminal is reminiscent of Dickens's strong anti-colonial stance demonstrated during the Morant Bay Rebellion.[9] The great apologist for the underclass had little sympathy for the plight of the colonials.

Beyond these parallels, Carey also satirizes the Imperial Gothic novel while criticizing the writer/conjuror who plunders marginalized lives to make art. In a state of fallow, Tobias Oates mesmerizes the Australian convict, Jack Maggs, alluding to Dickens's use of mesmerism in his own fictional practice.[10] Many writers, including Tennyson and Elizabeth Barrett Browning, became interested in mesmerism, which, through the supposed operator's control of a person's magnetic fluid, purported to wipe out "disease, corruption, discord, and [even] war", much like a modern philosopher's stone. Practitioners often hoped to combine this "science" with a "Romantic utopianism" that would recreate society.[11]

However, Oates lacks this utopian intention. He mesmerizes Maggs after Maggs has convulsed, only to discover that Maggs's inner world is a treasure of exotic stories, characters and landscapes that Oates can use in his fiction. Oates says of Maggs's mind, "This Australian of ours holds his life in his Cerebrum. He carries pelicans and parrots, fish and phantoms, things the Royal Botanist would give a sov or two to hold" (p. 97). According to Buckle's cook, Oates "is looking at you [Maggs] like a blessed butterfly he has to pin down on his board" (p. 48). From Oates's point of view, Maggs is an exotic collectible that can be controlled by the writer/conjuror.

In addition to viewing Maggs as an exotic collectible, Oates wants access to his mind because of its supposed criminal tendencies. Oates says to Percy Buckle, a would-be gentleman,

> But what you have brought me here is a world as rich as London itself. [. . .] what stolen gold lies hidden in the vaults beneath his filthy streets [. . . .] It's the Criminal Mind [. . .] awaiting its first cartographer.
>
> (p. 99)

Embracing scientific language in suggesting how he will dig into the layers of Maggs's subconscious, the stolen gold, Oates assumes that he will be the first to map the alleys of the criminal mind and "he would be the archeologist of [. . .] s[its] mystery [. . .]" (p. 60).

Like the Victorians who used mesmerism as a way to understand and perhaps control the subconscious world,[12] Oates enters Maggs's subconscious replete with dark Phantoms. Like a Victorian explorer, he mesmerizes Maggs in order to "map" Maggs's world, in much the same way as he maps London's world of the poor.

Recalling his own childhood experience of London, Oates considers the ways in which his writing lays out the map of London.

> Now, each day in the *Morning Chronicle,* each fortnight [. . .] with a passion he barely understood himself, he named it, mapped it, widened its great streets, narrowed its dingy lanes, framed its scenes with the melancholy windows of his childhood.
>
> (p. 199)

Perhaps indicating how closely Maggs's world intersects with Dickens's own world of near "abandonment", this mapping of London and the mapping of the colonial criminal mind through mesmerism show the ways in which Dickens may have used mesmerism as a way to augment his fiction. According to Fred Kaplan,

> [Dickens's] fiction is a process of self-discovery parallel to and drawing upon the processes of mesmerism: the recall of the past, the free flow of feelings, the interaction between the conscious and unconscious mind [. . . .][13]

Beyond parodying Dickens and his use of mesmerism, Carey also chastizes the British male writer/conjurer. When Maggs confronts Oates about what he has written about Maggs's life, *The Death of Maggs,* and Oates's writing about other "characters," Maggs remarks:

> "You get a good laugh out of the old biddy, I must say." [. . .]
>
> "She is a comic figure, Jack." [. . .]
>
> "To the Gods we are all comic figures," Tobias said.
>
> (p. 247)

Despite including himself among the playthings of the gods, Oates does not appear to recognize the ways in which his god-like writing exploits Maggs's weaknesses and suffering or how he benefits from the suffering of these "comic figures" whom he controls in his fictional landscape.

When Maggs realizes that his world has been "plundered", that Oates has "burgled" him (p. 36), he sets out to become his own cartographer, to write his own map. Worrying that he "left a blank map" for Henry Phipps that would make it impossible for his real story to be known, he too draws on occult practices as he writes his story as a map that must be deciphered. Using a "great albatross quill" (p. 81), which recalls the Ancient Mariner's necessary story of exploration and repentance, Maggs inscribes his story backwards on a mirror with invisible ink to ensure that only his beloved son will discern his true story. His invisible writing acts as a counter "magic" against Oates's mesmeric act that attempts to steal Maggs's treasure. Yet, scrutinizing the truth-telling of writing itself, the narrator tells us "writing is a distrustful art" (p. 81). Nevertheless Maggs tells his Bounderby-like story of abandonment where Silas "[found him] in the mud flats 'neath London Bridge" (p. 83). His benefactor Silas claims to have "walked beside the sea with Mr Coleridge" (p. 105). Even though Silas seemingly promises to raise Jack's expectations, he takes him to the abortionist Ma Britten. Like Mother England who neglects the poor, she will raise Jack to be a thief. Maggs confesses "I am an old dog [. . .] who has been treated bad, and has learned all sorts of tricks he wishes he never had to know" (p. 80).

Like Magwitch, Jack Maggs is a gentleman in Australia, but in England he is an exiled criminal who risks his life in returning to the motherland. Although Anthony Hassall argues that Maggs is transformed from an Englishman to an Australian in his narrative, the transfiguration is more problematic than Hassall supposes. To a certain extent, Maggs gets his sense of an English identity from encountering a Great House during one of his "chimney cleanings". When he enters the house after "coughing and wailing and choking [him]self with fear" (p. 108), he falls into a new world, a space on the English map he never knew existed. It is filled with the "smell of apples and oranges [. . .] cinnamon [. . .] All around the room there were arm-chairs, sofas [. . .]" (p. 109). He breaks into a genteel English world that can never be his. Even though he claims, "I am a fucking Englishman" (pp. 140-1), his ideal past is linked to the sense of English identity that he discovers in entering the Great House. He longs to return "home" where his eyes first saw the "kind and beautiful interior", "which he later knew was meant by authors when they wrote of England and of Englishness" (p. 350). In this metafictional moment, Carey makes Maggs, the exiled colonial, aware of how English identity has been constructed through literature. Yet this English identity cannot be his. Maggs is never truly at home in England. England throws Maggs on the colonial refuse pile, even though his crimes are not self-willed or self-aggrandizing.

Despite his struggle with meeting Phipps's gentlemanly expectations of him and coming to terms with his own identity, Maggs's narration and mapping/writing of his own story reclaim the postcolonial voice and disconnect it from the nineteenth-century assumption that criminals and colonials are interchangeable. Maggs refutes Oates's god-like usurpation and manipulation of his story, claiming the right to write on his own behalf, to be his own cartographer.

If *Jack Maggs* is concerned with the right of the colonial to map his "own" world and mind, the Post-Imperial Gothic **"The Conjugial Angel"** is concerned with what transpires in the nineteenth-century British imperial mind in the homeland, especially within the mind of the female imperial subject. Again, like Carey, Byatt draws on Imperial Gothic's fascination with antithetical magical and scientific discourse. Yet, instead of concentrating on the connection between the practice of Victorian mesmerism and writing as Carey does, Byatt focuses on another pseudo-scientific practice, spiritualism, and the way it may have been used as a mode of alternative exploration and philosophic contemplation. Byatt's novella grapples with western divisions between magic and science and mystery and certainty as it uses spiritualism as a mode for trying to reconcile Darwinian science and religious faith. As a meditation on Tennyson's *In Memoriam,* the story struggles with where to place humanity in the now defunct Great Chain of Being. In foregrounding the nineteenth-century fascination with spiritualism that attempted to connect the living with the dead, Byatt presents the reader with the points of view of three women excluded from male-dominated intellectual debates, the literary world and exploration, thus calling into question supposed English superiority, the basis for imperialism. Although these women are excluded from the male world of letters, they ultimately use spiritualism as a way to explore worlds denied them. In this way, they embrace an alternative form of adventure and exploration.

Written after Byatt reviewed Alex Owen's *The Darkened Room: Women, Power, and Spiritualism in Late Victorian England,* **"The Conjugial Angel"** seems to be a fictionalized account of the spiritualist movement in England.[14] According to Ann Braude, the movement purported to "[provide] scientific evidence for religious truth". Like mesmerism, which was based on the scientific theory of the time, spiritualism used the language of modern science, claiming that spiritualists used a "spiritual telegraph" to communicate with the dead.[15]

Owen shows us that women were considered "natural mediums" because of the societal edict that encouraged their "self-renunciation", demonstrating the ways in which women spiritualists used their roles as mediums to create a "transgressive femininity".[16] Much like the English Civil War Prophetesses, who defied Paul's admonition to female silence as they spoke their visions to influence Cromwell, these female spiritualists used the space of mediumship that transgresses time and geography to express themselves. Owen tells us, "spiritualism validated the female authoritative voice and permitted women an active professional and spiritual role largely denied them elsewhere".[17]

American suffragettes Elizabeth Cady Stanton and Susan B. Anthony in the *History of Woman Suffrage* acknowledge that spiritualism was the "only religious sect in the world . . . that recognized the equality of women". Yet this female agency seems ordained by at least some scripture, as believers recalled *Job* 2: 28-9: "Your sons and daughters shall prophesy . . . and upon the handmaids in those days will I pour out my spirit".[18]

The three women's points of view reveal the imperial mindset that excludes them from the world of letters and adventure. The less-gifted spiritualist is Mrs Lilias Papagay, a Swedenborgian who has difficulty seeing angels in our earthly world. Nevertheless Mrs Papagay appears to be a stifled writer who turns to spiritualism and automatic writing to express herself in an uncensored fashion. Drawing on the stories told to her by her mixed-race mariner husband Arturo, Mrs Papagay has written an "aborted novel" about a shipwrecked sailor "imprisoned by [an] amorous Tahitian princess".[19] Fascinated by the exotic world Arturo describes, she has endeavoured to write because she "liked stories. She spun them from bobbins of gossip [. . .]". When she hears Mr Jesse, a sea-captain, speak of typhoons, "[s]he saw it all, she lived it all, the turmoil of the waters with the lashing crests and their howling, dissolute walls, the scream and roar of the gale [. . .]" (p. 189). Despite her imaginative genius, she thinks she is "unequal" to the task of writing. She considers her writing "rubbish" and instead chooses a substitute—automatic writing. Without an acceptable mainstream occupation, she turns to spiritualism and she "lived more and more in the passive writing" (p. 194) at the séances, which she leads. Byatt portrays Mrs Papagay in a similar way to other fictional and non-fictional Victorian women who felt the period's constraints on womanhood. Like Jane Eyre and Florence Nightingale, she "could not bear to sit and gossip of bonnets and embroidery and the eternal servant problem, she wanted life" (p. 196). The narrator discloses that:

> Mrs Papagay was an intelligent, questioning kind of woman, the kind who, in an earlier age, would have been a theologically minded nun, and in a later one would have had a university training in philosophy or psychology or medicine.
>
> (p. 195)

An embryonic "psychologist", Mrs Papagay does not seek control of human minds as Oates does in *Jack Maggs,* but connections between minds and between worlds. As if refuting Sir Arthur Conan Doyle's presumption that spiritualism was a "substitute for imperialism",[20] a duty-driven English benevolence to the heathen, non-English world, the narrator tells us that spiritualism has a social levelling, anti-imperial effect. In this way, spiritualism and the séance are put forward as a non-geographic "location" and practice where an anti-imperial world map is redrawn. Referring to Swedenborg as a "Spiritual Columbus" (p. 191) and holding the séances in a room filled with exploration technologies, including a sextant and a telescope (p. 189), suggesting the discovery of unseen worlds through the practice of spiritualism, Mrs Papagay reveals the "democracy" of this mode of travel. Byatt writes, "Mrs Papagay would not have mixed socially with the Jesses if it were not for the democracy of the spirit world" (p. 197).

Mrs Emily Jesse, the sister of Alfred Lord Tennyson, is the second woman whose point of view undercuts the imperial mindset. In noting that Emily was once engaged to Arthur Hallam, Tennyson's friend and the focus of his elegy, Mrs Jesse's story reveals that Tennyson and Hallam excluded Emily from their intellectual life. It also shows how Tennyson, like Oates stealing Maggs's story, plundered Emily's story and usurped her grief, writing her mournful tribute as his own, making her merely a "ghost" in *In Memoriam.*

Attempting to contact the dead Hallam through the spiritualists, Mrs Jesse spends a lot of time recalling Somersby, the lost world of childhood magic, while she also recollects her brief courtship by Hallam. Gazing at a William Morris sofa embroidered with "a trellis of dark boughs" and an "impossible hybrid of exotic Amazonian parrakeets and the English mistle thrush", she remembers Somersby. This idyllic spot is where the Tennyson children and their friends "had played at the Arabian Nights and the Court of Camelot [. . .]" (p. 204). The sofa's pattern suggests the conflation of British and exotic landscapes that contain colonial wealth and resources. For Emily, this artifact is a touchstone to a "lost world" of childhood magic, folktale and myth. It reminds her of the "windows of the Gothic dining-room" which recalled "ladies in the latest modes, ready to slip away to trysts, or magic casements behind which Guenevere and the Lily Maid waited with beating hearts for their lovers" (p. 204). While it further suggests the sense of loss associated with Hallam and unfulfilled love, the sofa also implies the paradise lost for women who cannot explore the Amazon, cannot venture beyond Somersby, the "beloved prison" (p. 265), as well as the lost world of an accepted female intellectual life.

Emily recalls two instances of Hallam's dismissal of her intellectual curiosity. In the first, he has written "Theodicaea Novissima," which tries to explain the existence of evil as "God's need for love—for the passion of love". Hallam supposes that God created a "Universe, full of sin and sorrow, to provide an adequate background for this passion to work itself out in". When Emily questions his thinking, he says, "I do not think women ought to trouble themselves much with theology" (p. 250).

In the second instance, Emily asks about Hallam's assumptions concerning the gendered personification of nature:

> "Why is inert Matter female and the animating Nous male, please?"
>
> "Because earth is the Mother, because all beautiful things spring from her, trees and flowers and creatures."
>
> "And Nous, Arthur?"
>
> (pp. 262-3)

Arthur's answer is built on the supposition that women are beautiful objects that men contemplate in order to "apprehend truth". Emily is not satisfied with his answer and once again he shuts her out by telling her "[w]omen shouldn't busy their pretty little heads with all this theorizing[. . .]" (p. 263).

Aside from the fact that Byatt suggests a homosexual, homosocial bond between Hallam and Tennyson, the image that Emily recalls of their fingers nearly touching represents the male linking that excludes females. The narrator states, "There were the two fingers of their trailing relaxed arms, touching earth, pointing quietly at each other" (p. 263), recalling Michelangelo's image of the male God touching the male human, and failing to touch the female. Most importantly, Tennyson's *In Memoriam* "expresse[s] *exactly* the nature of her own shock and sorrow [. . .]" (p. 268). Notwithstanding the fact that he mourned his friend and perhaps his lover, Tennyson, according to Byatt, seems to draw on Emily's grief, her psychological and physical "entombment" after Hallam's death, her widow-like mourning.

Sophy Sheekhy, the true medium, is the third character who reveals the status of the female imperial mind in this era. The epitome of self-renunciation, Sophy seems to be a container that the dead can pour themselves into. She has no life of her own and seems nearly dead, recalling Pre-Raphaelite characters like Rossetti's "Blessed Damozel", the apotheosis of the dead woman as heavenly art. Suggesting her own longing for male companionship and her loneliness, Sophy wants Hallam's ghost to come to her as she evokes Tennyson's "Mariana". "'He will not come,' she said./ She wept, 'I am aweary, aweary, / Oh God, that I were dead'" (p. 287). Sophy Sheekhy ends up embracing the dead Hallam who tries to have a vision of Tennyson. However, she is the only one who can see the frail Tennyson, whose thoughts betray his fears about the human condition and position in a post-Darwinian world:

> There it came again, the clay and the mould, and the moulding. You wrote something easily in youth [. . . .] The angels had kneaded the clay into human form in forty days. [. . .] Now there was Darwin, grubbing away at the life of the earthworm, throwing up mould and humus all over the place.
>
> (p. 313)

Yet while the aged Tennyson falters with buttoning his shirt and fails to reconcile faith and science, Sophy Sheekhy bridges the gap between the living and the dead. Representing Pistis Sophia, the angel in the garden before man, according to Hallam, she becomes the female "principle of love" that supersedes male power and hierarchy in the biblical garden, one of the bases for British imperialism.

Carey and Byatt rewrite the empire of the imagination as they rework Imperial Gothic fiction. Rather than using science and the occult as ways of expressing the anxieties of a fading Empire, they use Post-Imperial Gothic fiction as a way of critiquing the imperial mindset of the writer/conjuror who plundered the lives of the marginalized. While Carey focuses on the right of the colonial to map his own world, Byatt creates an alternate map for her female characters, one that envisions female explorers traversing a spiritual frontier. Resisting British cartography, these writers anticipate the postcolonial parrot/trickster figure in Guyanese writer Pauline Melville's *The Ventriloquist's Tale* who knows how to "dig time's grave" and who claims, without the benefit of British technology, to have "an entire map" in his head of his own world.[21] He too is his own cartographer.

Notes

1. H. Rider Haggard, *She,* New York: Signet Classic, 1994, p. 175. All subsequent references are to this edition and appear in parentheses in the text.

2. See Ioan P. Couliano, *Eros and Magic in the Renaissance,* Chicago: University of Chicago Press, 1987. According to Couliano, magic is "the means of control over the individual and the masses based on a deep knowledge of personal and collective erotic impulses" (p. xviii). In other words, the magician knows his audience's desires and uses them to his advantage, becoming as Craig Williamson says "one who fears and manipulates others". See Williamson, *A Feast of Creatures: Anglo-Saxon Riddles and Songs,* Philadelphia: University of Pennsylvania Press, 1982. Haggard's She uses her mesmeric sexuality to manipulate her audience. I also label her a "scientist", because she has bio-engineered a race of servants.

3. See Frances Yates, *The Occult Philosophy in the Elizabethan Age,* London: Routledge, 1979. Yates argues that Elizabethan magicians wanted to use white magic to create a British Empire.

4. See Patrick Brantlinger, "Imperial Gothic: Atavism and the Occult in the British Adventure Novel, 1880-1914", *Rule of Darkness: British Literature and Imperialism,* Ithaca: Cornell UP, 1988, p. 240.

5. *ibid.,* p. 227.

6. *ibid.,* p. 230.

7. Peter Carey, *Jack Maggs,* New York: Vintage, 1997. p. 67. All subsequent references are to this edition and appear in parentheses in the text.

8. See Norman and Jeanne MacKenzie, *Dickens: A Life,* New York: OUP, 1979, p.4. Anthony Hassall recognizes the strong parallels between Carey's novel and *Great Expectations* and the shift of interest from Pip to "Magwitch and Dickens himself" (128). Yet he fails to draw out the implications of these parallels and others between Dickens and the character of Jack Maggs, as well as Dickens's use of mesmerism in his own "healing" practice. See Hassall, "A Tale of Two Countries: *Jack Maggs* and Peter Carey's Fiction", A*ustralian Literary Studies,* 8, 2 (1997), 128-35.

9. Emery Neff, *Carlyle and Mill: An Introduction to Victorian Thought,* New York: Columbia UP, 1926, p. 48.

10. Fred Kaplan, *Dickens and Mesmerism: The Hidden Springs of Fiction,* Princeton, NJ: Princeton UP, 1975, p. 4.

11. *ibid.,* p. 7.

12. See *Rule of Darkness,* p. 241. This mesmeric act is much like Dickens's use of mesmerism in the case of Madame de la Rue. Dickens mesmerized her to "exorcise" a "phantom" that caused her physical pain, *Dickens and Mesmerism,* pp. 86-94. Yet mesmerism was not just thought of as a healing art; it was also a passage into an unknown world. As David de Giustino notes: "[t]o treat an audience to a demonstration of thought transference . . . was like conducting them on a tour of an unknown land. Mesmerism was the forcible opening of undiscovered territory, the inscrutable frontier", De Giustino, *Conquest of the Mind: Phrenology and Victorian Social Thought,* London: Croom Helm, 1975, p. 48.

13. *Dickens and Mesmerism,* p. 112.

14. Kathleen Coyne Kelly, "Angels and Insects: Two Novellas", *A. S. Byatt,* New York: Twayne, 1996, p.107.

15. Ann Braude, "'My Soul's Thraldom and Its Deliverance'", *Radical Spirits: Spiritualism and Women's Rights in Nineteenth-Century America,* second edn., Bloomington: Indiana UP, 1989, pp. 4-5.

16. *ibid.,* "Introduction" and p. 16.

17. Alex Owen, *The Darkened Room: Women, Power, and Spiritualism in Late Victorian England,* Philadelphia: University of Pennsylvania Press, 1990, p. 6.

18. *Radical Spirits,* pp. 2 and 6. Braude also indicates that spiritualists were also involved in radical social movements, including the abolition of slavery, marriage and labour reform, religious freedom and vegetarianism (p. 3).

19. A. S. Byatt, "The Conjugial Angel," *Angels and Insects,* New York: Vintage, 1994, p. 201. All subsequent references are to this edition and appear in parentheses in the text.

20. Arthur Conan Doyle, *The History of Spiritualism,* 1926; repr. New York: Arno, 1975.

21. Pauline Melville, *The Ventriloquist's Tale,* New York: Bloomsbury, 1997, p. 2.

Kathleen Williams Renk (essay date 2004)

SOURCE: Renk, Kathleen Williams. "A. S. Byatt, the Woman Artist, and Suttee." *Women's Studies* 33, no. 5 (2004): 613-28.

[*In the following essay, Renk maintains that in "Cold" Byatt revises the traditional European fairy tale genre to explore the conditions necessary for the creation of women's art.*]

> Woman is the Sleeping Beauty, Cinderella, Snow White, she who receives and submits. In song and story the young man is seen departing adventurously in search of a woman; he slays the dragon, he battles the giants; she is locked in a tower, a palace, a garden, a cave, she is chained to a rock, a captive, sound asleep; she waits.
>
> —Simone de Beauvoir, *The Second Sex*

* * *

> Beauty is a simple passion,
> but oh my friends, in the end
> you will dance the fire in iron shoes.
>
> —Anne Sexton, *Transformations*

* * *

> They speak together of the threat they have constituted
> towards authority, they tell how they were burned on pyres
> to prevent them from assembling in the future.
>
> —Monique Wittig, *Les Guerillères*

* * *

The model for Christabel La Motte in A. S. Byatt's *Possession,* Elizabeth Barrett Browning speaks powerfully of how women are entombed in myth and literature. Staring at her mother's portrait, Aurora Leigh muses about how woman in nineteenth-century art is represented as "[g]host, fiend, and angel fairy, witch and sprite" but never as a flesh and blood character or as a poet/artist who comprehends the scope of earthly and heavenly realms (*Aurora Leigh* Book I: 154). While Aurora Leigh argues with her cousin Romney about the existence of the woman artist, the "female Christ," she never contemplates which conditions are necessary for the production of women's art. These questions are left to twentieth-century women writers, such as Virginia Woolf and Adrienne Rich, who together advocate rooms that women lock, money, and a rewriting strategy that moves women past the negative archetypes of women's so-called nature as "fiend, angel, fairy, witch." Drawing on the matriarchal underpinnings of the traditional European fairy tale, A. S. Byatt uses the fairy tale **"Cold"** to further contemplate which conditions are necessary for the creation of women's art, arguing that the woman artist should remain aloof like the male artist, an "ice-princess" who, according to Byatt in her essay about the writing of revisionist fairy tales, defies the biological imperative of "blood, kiss, roses, birth, death, and the hungry generations" ("Ice, Snow, Glass" 164). As a rewrite of Hans Christian Andersen's "Snow Queen," **"Cold"** warns us of what may happen to a woman artist when she forgets or ignores her elemental nature; she, like the women fairy tale characters who came before her, is buried/burned alive, melted, fused, to be used at the prince's whim.[1]

Jack Zipes and Richard Todd have both noted Byatt's reworking of the fairy tale that returns it to the style of the women's "extended salon" French fairy tale and the German wonder tale. In my view, Byatt's work resonates more with the matriarchal origins of folk tales and with Christine Benedikte Naubert's eighteenth-century German tales of "powerful [pagan] sorceresses" who "reject marriage and patriarchal redemption" (Zipes, *Fairy Tales and the Art of Subversion* 156). Returning the Snow Queen to her pagan roots and redefining the Snow Queen in a positive way, Byatt offers us a glimpse of what the woman artist could be if she would only follow her calling, if she would look past the illusion of the glass/mirror, to see herself as she truly is, if she remains in her ice, a form of self-imposed creative isolation, in order to pursue what Simone de Beauvoir and Jean-Paul Sartre call the *pour-soi* condition. Drawing on the philosophy of G.W.F. Hegel, which theorizes a "self-alienated spirit" within human beings that consists of an observing and observed self, Sartre developed his contrasting concepts of the *pour-soi* and *en-soi* conditions, roughly compatible with Hegel's notion of the dual self. According to Sartre, *Being and Nothingness, pour-soi* or "being-for-itself" is the human experience of consciousness, in which creativity may unfold. In contrast, the *en-soi* condition is the repetitive, material existence shared by humans, "animals, vegetables and minerals."

In *The Second Sex,* de Beauvoir applied Sartre's theories from *Being and Nothingness* to women's lives and argued that women mostly experience the *en-soi* condition as they perform mundane repetitive acts and rarely are allowed to develop their intellectual lives and complete consciousness (Tong 174-75). For de Beauvoir, the *en-soi* condition can be described as a "permanent state of being" (de Beauvoir 538), or "the fixed, lower nature" (613), while the *pour-soi* requires the "self-knowing self" (256) that for women "would imply

[. . .] economic independence" and transcendence that didn't require male intervention or agency (668). The woman artist in **"Cold"** must not only seek a room and finances of her own but she must deliberately seek her own creative consciousness in the locale and circumstances best suited for her, as she connects with a matriarchal past; she must pursue the *pour-soi* rather than the *en-soi* condition, associated with childbearing and endless household tasks.

Fairy tale scholars, such as Jack Zipes and Cristina Bacchilega, and writers, such as Joyce Carol Oates, all acknowledge the role women writers play in both the origins of and the re-formation of the fairy tale in our contemporary world. In particular, Zipes historicizes the fairy tale's connection to both the oral female as well as the written tradition developed by women in the French salons, while Oates notes how fairy tales, despite their recording and retelling by male fairy tale collectors, such as the Grimm Brothers, Charles Perrault, and Hans Christian Anderson, were originally told by women and hence have always been a female genre. She suggests then that contemporary feminist "re-envisioned" fairy tales by writers such as Anne Sexton, Angela Carter, and A. S. Byatt reclaim the fairy tale tradition from the men who usurped it as their own. In *Postmodern Fairy Tales: Gender and Narrative Strategies,* Bacchilega argues that "within a feminist frame [. . .], fairy tales are sites of competing, historically and socially framed desires." And she further asserts that "[t]hese narratives continue to play a privileged role in the production of gender and as such are deconstructed and reconstructed in a variety of ways [. . .]" (10). One of the ways the fairy tale is re-formed is through viewing it via a contemporary feminist lens. And in terms of this contemporary tale, Oates emphasizes how recent feminist fairy tales "subvert original models," showing from a "woman's perspective [how] the romance of fairytales is an illusion, to be countered by wit, audacity, skepticism, cynicism, [and] an eloquently rendered rage."

Byatt has authored a number of these subversive fairy tales, some of which are entire collections, such as ***The Djinn in the Nightingale's Eye,*** while others appear in short story collections, such as ***Elementals,*** or are embedded within novels, such as *Possession,* or in novellas, such as **"Morpho Eugenia."** In arguing on behalf of storytelling and her reinvigoration of it as it relates to fairy tales, Byatt renounces modernism's forms. In "The Greatest Story Ever Told," which for Byatt appears to be *The Thousand and One Nights,* Byatt rejects modernist form and its effort to reveal the contents of the mind:

> Modernist literature tried to do away with storytelling, which it thought was vulgar, replacing it with flash-backs,
> epiphanies, streams of consciousness. But storytelling is
> intrinsic to biological time, which we cannot escape.
>
> (166)

The fairy tale then, as Byatt envisions it, is part of this narrative unfolding, one that is forever linked to time and the histories of women's lives.

While Annegret Maack suggests that Byatt's fairy tales offer liberation and metamorphosis for women, Jane Campbell and Caroline Webb appear to agree that Byatt's agenda is more complex than women's liberation and change. Campbell speaks of how Byatt uses the fairy tale to expose the "possibilities and limitations of women's lives in the world" (135). More self-reflexive than the oral tale that may have hinted at how women's lives were enclosed and limited by patriarchy, Byatt reveals the extent of those limitations and how the fairy tale itself shaped women's lives. Webb sees that Byatt is working in a feminist tradition that "meditates" on the fairy tale. "[Byatt contemplates] the place of women and of female power in the fairy tale tradition, as well as in the modern world she magically depicts."

While other critics have written of the value and place of Byatt's fairy tales in a postmodern era, no one has linked Byatt's work to its matriarchal underpinnings. Intrinsically different from Sexton's female fairy tale characters "trapped in their legends like puppets on strings" (Oates) or like Carter's erotically charged fairy tale protagonists, Byatt's protagonist in **"Cold"** has much in common with the characters created by German Romanticist Christine Benedikte Naubert. According to Zipes, Heide Gottner-Abendroth in *Die Gottin und ihr Heros* shows that pagan pre-Medieval folk tales were "stamped by a matriarchal mythology" and patriarchal revisions during the Middle Ages transformed the "goddess [. . .] [into] a witch, evil fairy or stepmother and the active young princess was changed into an active [male] hero" (Zipes, *Subversion* 7). Naubert resurrects this active young princess, as does Byatt. Zipes further notes that Naubert's novels and short stories, such as *Velleda* (1795) and *New German Tales* depict magical women who offer "positive rights of passage for females," which serve as a prelude to contemporary twentieth-century feminist fairy tales (Zipes, *Subversion* 156). In "The Vanished Woman of Great Influence: Benedikte Naubert's Legacy and German Women's Fairy Tales," Shawn Jarvis reminds us of the neglected Naubert who "explored the forgotten histories of women, both mythical and real" (197). According to Jarvis, Naubert's work, which had a profound influence on the women fairy tale writers of the French salons as well as E. T. A. Hoffmann, was "dismally ignored in the canonical scholarship" (209) because she refused to make the fairy tale a male adventure quest and a female captivity narrative (196). Instead her themes include "the creation of a female community outside traditional society; the mediating role of the magical wise woman; the rites of passage for females, and the rejection of patriarchal 'redemption'" (200). For example, in *Velleda,* Naubert writes of the ancient German historical figure Velleda found in "Tacitus' narration of the [Roman] war with Civilis" but Naubert makes this "soothsayer" a legendary leader of young women (198). Velleda creates a separate female community of princesses who defy their mothers and reject marriage. They prefer living with one another and Velleda to "domestic entrapment" (Jarvis 201). And Naubert commonly shows us women who draw on their own magical powers as they renounce marriage "in favor of independence" (Zipes, *Subversion* 156). Byatt's work returns us to this matriarchal foundation as it rejects Andersen's version of the ice princess.

Andersen's "Snow Queen," which Byatt says influenced her writing of **"Cold"** and other fairy tales ("Ice, Snow, Glass"), presents the reader with a female figure associated with voyeurism, deception, danger, and death. The Snow Queen lures a young boy named Kay, whose vision and perception have been distorted through fragments of a demonic mirror that have entered his eye, causing him to misperceive evil, thinking it is good. In addition, Kay has heard of the Snow Queen through the Old Grandmother's stories of the Queen "fly[ing] through the streets [and peeping] through windows," freezing the panes into artistic, ice crystal patterns that look like flowers (113). Associated with art and natural and artificial beauty as well as with a pagan prying eye that looks at children after they've said their prayers and gone to bed, the Snow Queen pulls Kay away from his cozy home associated with roses and the Infant Jesus, when she appears to Kay through the window pane one evening. Once in her clutches, Kay, because of his distorted vision, is "delighted" with the Snow Queen, who imprisons him in her icy arms. Through his association with the Snow Queen, Kay has lost his Christian perspective. He can no longer remember the Lord's Prayer but instead is fascinated with math and science. Intensely analytic, Kay has developed an icy heart and a "cold intellect" because of the demonic mirror and because of his association with a pagan ice woman (Zipes, *The Oxford Companion to Fairytales* 478). All of this could lead to his spiritual and physical death. Each of these images and themes is reworked in Byatt's tale but before I discuss her rewriting strategy and its relevance to women and art, I want to point out two more interesting and somewhat unexpected moments in Andersen's tale that lend themselves to Byatt's revision.

Although this tale is obviously, as Zipes suggests, one of the nineteenth-century fairy tales that inculcated roles for Christian boys and girls, East Indian "customs" also inform the text (*Subversion* 8-9). As Kay's friend Gerda searches for him, she encounters Tiger Lilies who do not know where Kay is but instead tell her of the Indian practice of women's self-immolation:

> 'Do you hear the drum? Rub-a-dub. It only has two notes.
> Rub-a-dub. Always the same. The wailing of women and the
> cry of the preacher. The Hindu woman in her long red garment
> stands in the pile, while the flames surround her and her dead husband.
> But the woman is only thinking of the man in the circle round, whose
> eyes burn with a fiercer fire than that of the flames which consume the body.'
>
> (121-2)

Mary Daly tells us that upper caste Hindu women were forced to commit suttee because as widows they were considered outcasts who were not permitted to remarry. To prevent them from "sexual temptation," they had to place themselves on their husband's funeral pyre. Suggesting that Indian suttee or sati is a "custom" whereby women renounce their own lives, thinking only of the men, the Tiger Lilies seem to promote the notion that Gerda and all women should give up their own lives for men, even if the drum conveys the wailing of women who most likely cry out in pain not for their dead husbands but for themselves as they are burned alive.[2]

The second moment, which is perhaps less unexpected than the first but which also seems to inform Gerda of her place in the world as a female, occurs when the hyacinths tell her of

> three beautiful sisters [. . .] These three danced hand in hand by
> the edge of the lake in the moonlight [. . .] [T]hey vanished into the wood
> [. . .] [and] three coffins glide out of the wood [. . .] and in them lie the
> maidens [. . .] Do these dancing maidens sleep, or are they dead? The
> scent of the flower says they are corpses.
>
> (123)

Even though Gerda never asks for advice or guidance from the flowers except in regard to Kay's whereabouts, she receives a warning from them about the dangers of women's ecstasy and female community. Dancing in the moonlight with your sisters or with other women will lead to death, not mere enchantment. Gerda, as a female, and other good Christian boys and girls should note this as they learn that the pagan Snow Queen beguiles them with art only to entrap them.

In many ways, **"Cold"** begins as a conventional fairy tale that uses Andersen's images of the demonic mirror and the theme of the "icy heart" yet **"Cold"** quickly progresses to a revisionist feminist version of "Snow Queen." Fiammarosa is the only female born after twelve brothers, the unlucky thirteenth who is coddled by her mother and father in order to protect her "vulnerable fragility." Quite paternalistic, her father vows that "no one shall ever hurt [Fiammarosa]" (116). Yet despite her doting parents' guardianship, Fiammarosa does not grow stronger but seems to weaken, becoming "thinner and whiter" with "sharp cheekbones" like "fine bone china." Tending her own rose garden and emotionally "attached to a little silver hand-mirror, engraved with twining roses" Fiammarosa seems to resemble the children in the Snow Queen who are surrounded by roses and later enchanted by the distorting mirror (120). Byatt breaks away from the traditional narrative, however, and begins to rewrite "Snow Queen" when we learn that despite her parent's protection, Fiammarosa cries out in pain. Her mother notices "an involuntary grimace" that seems to be "a perfectly silent howl or cry" (118). And even though her mother has discerned her anguish, she does nothing and they continue to smother Fiammorosa, going as far as locking her in the castle each night.

On the edge of puberty, Fiammarosa begins to dream of traveling "at high speeds." Much like Eve in *Paradise Lost,* she longs to fly above forests to escape the confines of her sequestered life (122). She also hears the wind "shriek," and she's drawn to look outside to the icy, cold night. Placing her "cheek against the frozen tracery," she feels a "bite, a burn, that was both painful and intensely pleasurable" feeling the pattern of ice created by the Snow Queen in Andersen's tale (122). Yet, unlike Kay, she does not see the Snow Queen outside her windowpane. Instead she becomes the Snow Queen as she is drawn into the cold by "an image of her own naked body, stretched on the couch of snow" (123).

Alluding to death and transgression in the snow, Fiammarosa sees herself in a "frozen sleep," which in a traditional tale necessitates the prince's awakening intervention. Yet Fiammarosa does not experience a frozen sleep that needs the prince's thawing kiss. Instead she follows her longing and like the princesses in the "Snow Queen" dances in ecstasy in the moonlight, flirting with an icy death. But rather than dying as the three sisters do, she becomes alive and full of "electric charge." In the ice, she realizes who she is and is for the "first time in her life, happy" (126).

> And when she was quite cold and completely alive and
> crackling with energy, she rose to her feet, and began
> a strange, leaping dance, pointing sharp fingers at
> the moon, tossing her long mane of silver hair,
> sparkling with ice-crystals, circling and bending and
> finally turning cartwheels under the wheeling sky.
>
> (126-7)

Fiammarosa is the "Snow Queen," the ice princess who has found her natural element; she is now alive and knows what she needs to make her dance and to be happy. She must remain in her natural element and be free to develop her art or she will perish.

Shortly after Fiammarosa's ice dance, she learns from her tutor Hugh that she had a Northern ice princess ancestress named Fror who was "given as a pledge for a truce" to King Beriman. Like Fiammarosa, she danced in the icy moonlight. The villagers believed she was a witch and the priests and king's council wanted to "melt her stubbornness" so they imprisoned her in a cell under the palace. She was detested because the people and the king believed she had an icy heart. Hugh thinks that the ice princess has now been reborn in Fiammarosa and he tells her "you too are framed for cold" (132). Although Fiammarosa worries that she too will develop an icy, uncaring heart, she thinks "there was more life in coldness. In solitude" (133) and she "thought she would do better, ideally, to remain unmarried. She was too happy alone to make a good wife" (136). Like Naubert's active female characters, she seeks independence from marriage.

Acknowledging her need for cold, the court creates an icy environment where she thrives. In this world, she becomes an artist/scientist but not a "cold intellect" like Kay and flourishes as she studies "snow crystals and ice formations under a magnifying glass [. . .] and studied the forms of her wintry flowers and mosses in the summer." Based on her scientific study of ice patterns, she weaves intricate, unique tapestries and she begins to write to natural philosophers (134-35).[3] She often thinks in the abstract and this "suited her." She is happy pursuing the *pour-soi* condition in which she is free to develop all of her capacities and talents rather than perennially attend to the mundane *en-soi* tasks that women must ordinarily carry out. She is the active young princess who needs no prince to awaken or complete her. Yet like all other princesses, she is expected to marry because her father believes that his daughter "needed to be softened and opened to the world." He also knows of the ice woman and wants Fiammarosa "melted smooth" so that she will not become like Fror who remained cold and jagged, an "uncaring" seeker of solitude (137).

In "Feminism and Fairy Tales," Karen Rowe points out that in conventional fairy tales when the heroine acquiesces and marries the prince, she gains social and financial security, and yet this arrangement, at its heart, is based on the commodification of women (333). Fiammarosa becomes aware of this through the reading of wonder tales and through her knowledge of the plight of her ancestress Fror, but she also learns that princesses can be "clever choosers" and she sets out to have a competition for her hand (135).

Drawing on the binary oppositions that are the basis for this story, Byatt presents two opposing princes and ways of living in the world. Prince Boris from the icy north, Fiammarosa's "natural" partner, presents her with a necklace of bear claws and Fiammarosa intuitively reaches for her neck, which suggests her fear of entrapment. The second prince, Prince Sasan, named after the shepherd/founder of ancient Iran (Horne), is a magician/artist from the desert. His envoys endow her with several enticing gifts, which artfully deceive Fiammarosa. The first is a glass palace with "hallucinatory turrets and chambers, fantastic carvings and pillars." Drawn to its ice-like appearance, she believes at first that it is a "block of [carved] ice" and she "touch[es] its cool surface with a cool finger" (141). Within the palace, Fiammarosa sees "little tongues of flame (made of glass)" and the envoy tells her that the palace represents his master's "empty" heart, which "awaits the delicate warmth of the Princess Fiammarosa" obviously misunderstanding Fiammarosa's icy nature (142) (143). Nevertheless, Fiammarosa is attracted to what she perceives to be ice, confusing the intricate glass with her natural element, seemingly enticed by the way the palace seems to encapsulate and secure the opposing forces of fire and ice. Similar to Kay's confused vision, Fiammarosa's vision is distorted by the illusory glass.

In addition to the palace, Fiammarosa receives a second gift that is also a marvel. This time she obtains a glass beehive, an image and metaphor that draws on both Byatt's fascination with the insect world, as in **"Morpho Eugenia,"** and on an element of Andersen's tale, where the Snow Queen is the Queen Bee who fabricates through her nighttime work her icy artistic patterns. Again the envoy speaks of this gift as a metaphor for his master's heart, this time representing the "garden of his heart." Fiammarosa does not seem to be allured by this metaphor though and instead scientifically studies the carving.

The ultimate gift is the last, a magical tree of paradise filled with the birds of all seasons, as well as "sharp icicles, [which catch] light and make rainbows in the air" (146). Suggesting immortality, the tree also promises that if the princess chooses Sasan, she will experience an Edenic paradise. Fiammarosa chooses Sasan when she learns that he is the glassblower who created these wonders, that he is an artist/scientist who can teach her the art of glassblowing, the melting and fusion of sand in the desert. Although the desert holds many dangers for her and despite the fact that when Sasan touches her he "leaves faint rosy marks" as if she'd been "lashed" (155) and the fact that Hugh reminds her that "glass is not ice" (148), she says "I will come with you to the desert" and "learn about glass blowing" (152). She believes that marriage to the desert prince will fulfill her artistic and scientific urge; she ignores her elemental icy nature, her need for "cold" isolation, and consents to enter the desert.

Immediately after the wedding, Fiammarosa begins to be transformed. She starts to "slop and sway where she had been solid and shining" and in experiencing sexual climax, her experience exceeds other women's sense of "melting" yet this melting is not the height of delicious passion but instead she felt as "though her whole being were becoming liquid except for some central icicle, which was running with waterdrops that threatened to melt that too, to nothing" (156). This act of passion and disregard for her nature will kill her.

The farther Fiammarosa ventures into Sasan's kingdom the more distress she feels. And even though she loses the child that she is pregnant with and nearly dies as she watches what for her is infernal glassblowing,[4] Sasan takes her further into the desert. His rationale is that the desert is "his place" as he tells her "[t]hese are the things I am made of, [. . .] grains of burning sand, and breath of air, and the blaze of light. Like glass" (173). Insisting that he must be within his own element, he dismisses the fact that entrance into his element will lead to Fiammarosa's death.

In many of her fairy tales, including and especially **"The Djinn in the Nightingale's Eye,"** Byatt plays with how the East and West might be reconciled, through conversation and the sharing of stories. Initially, Byatt seems to join East and West here too, making the artistic European ice princess the "natural" partner of the Eastern scientific sultan. Yet, if we return to our knowledge of the Far Eastern Indian practice of suttee, we can see that Fiammarosa is expected to sacrifice her nature in order to glorify her husband's, much in the way Indian women were expected to gladly seek their own death at their husband's demise.[5] Fiammarosa is not a widow and she does not die in this story, yet she is eventually taken far into the desert and locked away in a mountain after her husband has carved for her a series of nine swollen, glassblown, pregnant women that seem to represent what will become of her if she succumbs to the biological imperative and no longer pursues the "pour-soi" condition. When Fiammarosa sees the glass women, who depict the nine months of pregnancy, she "[ignores] the fiery choking in her throat" (166), the sense of suffocation that may come with pregnancy. In "Ice, Snow, Glass," when she speaks of how the queen dies when Snow White is born Byatt recognizes how a woman's child seems to "kill" her (152). And in "One Doesn't Stir Without the Other," Luce Irigaray also suggests that the mother's life dissolves or ceases when her child is born. The child narrator in Irigaray says,

> When the one of us comes into the world, the other goes
> underground. When the one carries life, the other dies.
> And what I wanted from you, Mother, was this:
> that in giving me life, you still remain alive.
>
> (67)

If Fiammarosa gives in to the biological imperative and becomes the glassblown pregnant woman, her life, her quest for the *pour-soi* condition will also cease and she will be relegated to the endless repetition of the *en-soi* condition. In light of Irigaray's assertion, she will perish.

Even though Sasan finally creates an "ice" palace for her in the middle of the mountain that includes a "field of untouched snow" where she is free to dance, she is ultimately buried alive in the mountain in the middle of a desert that she cannot cross. She can never leave and can never "roam among fjords and ice-fells" (182). She cannot create in her own icy realm. Because she has ignored her icy nature, she must be satisfied to live in this contrived illusory world. And although the narrator suggests that this entrapment is acceptable because few of us get what we want, the reader senses the bitter irony of the unfulfilled life of the cold princess who once experienced artistic freedom and is now buried within a mountain in the desert. Her vast world and potential have been stifled and her ice has been melted smooth.

Byatt's feminist version of the "Snow Queen" says a lot about what may happen to the woman artist if she ignores her need for "ice" and solitude, her need to keep herself in her natural element. Although Byatt does not suggest that childbearing, marriage, and artistry are incompatible for all women artists, she does insist that each artist know her own nature and elements, those aspects of herself that are necessary for the development of her creative capacity, her *pour-soi* condition. The woman artist might be attracted to the illusion of glass but if she is to thrive, she must see herself as she truly is and flee those who ask her to sacrifice herself in the fire or who want to melt her smooth. If she is to beguile us with her art, she must be free to sit at the top of the ice mountain and soar at will.[6]

Notes

1. Although this reading may suggest an essentialist perspective about women's "nature," I am not claiming that Byatt is saying that women artists have an essential or true nature; rather Byatt is suggesting that each woman artist must examine the conditions that enable her art. If not, she could, like Byatt's protagonist, perish.
2. Women were also thought to be partly to blame for their husband's death either in this life or in a previous incarnation, so burning their living bodies was considered just punishment for whatever they had done to bring about their husband's death. Although it was commonly believed that women willingly committed suttee, Daly notes that "[women were] often pushed, and poked with long stakes after having been bathed, ritually attired, and drugged out of [their] minds" (116). And even though suttee was outlawed in 1829, more subtle forms of widow torture still occur in India (115).
3. Thanks to my former colleague at Indiana State University, Assistant Professor of Art History Alden Cavanaugh, who pointed out that Fiammarosa's analysis of snow crystals is similar to the female scientist's in Peter Høeg's *Smilla's Sense of Snow.*
4. This scene is reminiscent of Hawthorne's "The Birth-mark," where a wife views the husband/scientist's forbidden laboratory and she collapses because of her knowledge.
5. One might criticize Byatt's metaphoric use of the horrific practice of "suttee." However, Byatt makes it clear that this tale is a warning to women who allow themselves to be beguiled by deceptive art and who, as a consequence, give up their own creative isolation.
6. In "Ice, Snow, Glass," Byatt writes of a "Norweigan [. . .] version of the Atalanta myth" where a princess straddles a mountain and throws apples at her would-be suitors who try to ascend (151). "There was something wonderful about being beautiful and shining and high up with a lap of golden fruit, something which was lost with human love, with the descent to be kissed and given away" (155). And she also speaks of how Graham Greene speculated that every artist has a "splinter of ice in his heart" (156). Byatt applies this condition to Christabel LaMotte in *Possession,* who is deeply afraid that any ordinary human happiness may be purchased at the expense of her art, that maybe she needs to be alone [. . .] on her glass eminence, an ice-maiden" (157), for "preserving solitude and distance, staying cold and frozen, may, for women as well as artists, be a way of preserving life." (158)

Works Cited

Alfer, Alexa and Michael J. Noble. *Essays on the Fiction of A. S. Byatt.* Westport: CT.: Greenwood Press, 2001.

Andersen, Hans Christian. "Snow Queen." *Andersen's Fairy Tales.* Translated by E.V. Lucas and H.B. Paul. New York: Grosset and Dunlap Pub., 1981, 110-46.

Bacchilega, Cristina. *Postmodern Fairy Tales: Gender and Narrative Strategies.* Philadelphia: U of Pennsylvania P, 1997.

Barrett Browning, Elizabeth. *Aurora Leigh.* New York: Penguin, 1995.

Beauvoir, Simone de. *The Second Sex.* New York: Vintage, 1989.

Byatt, A. S. "Morpho Eugenia." *Angels and Insects.* New York: Vintage Books, 1994.

———. "Cold." In *Elementals: Stories of Fire and Ice.* 115-82. Vintage Books, 1998.

———. *The Djinn in the Nightingale's Eye: Five Fairy Stories.* New York: Vintage Books, 1994.

———. "The Greatest Story Ever Told." *On Histories and Stories: Selected Essays.* Cambridge, MA: Harvard U. P, 165-171.

———. "Ice, Snow, Glass." *On Histories and Stories: Selected Essays.* Cambridge, MA: Harvard U P, 151-64.

———. *Possession.* New York: Vintage Books, 1991.

Campbell, Jane. "'Forever Possibilities. And Impossibilities, of Course': Women and Narrative in *The Djinn in the Nightingale's Eye.*" Alfer and Noble 135-46.

Daly, Mary. *Gyn/Ecology: The Metaethics of Radical Feminism.* Boston: Beacon Press, 1978.

Hawthorne, Nathaniel. "The Birth-mark." *Tales and Sketches.* New York: The Library of America, 1982. 764-80.

Høeg, Peter. *Smilla's Sense of Snow.* New York: Bantam Books, 1994.

Horne, Charles F. (ed). *The Sacred Books and Early Literature of the East.* Vol. VII: Ancient Persia. New York: Parke, Austin, and Lipscomb, 1917. 31 Oct., 2003. *http://www.jordham.edu/hasall/ancient/ardashir.html.*

Irigaray, Luce. "One Doesn't Stir Without the Other." *Signs: Journal of Women in Culture and Society.* Vol. 7 (no. 1) (1981): 60-67.

Jarvis, Shawn. "The Vanished Woman of Great Influence: Benedikte Naubert's Legacy and German Women's Fairy Tales." *In the Shadow of Olympus: German Women Writers Around 1800.* eds. Katherine R. Goodman and Edith Waldstein. 189-209. Albany, New York: State U of New York P, 1992.

Maack, Annegret. "Wonder Tales Hiding a Truth: Retelling Tales in *The Djinn in the Nightingale's Eye.*" Alfer and Noble 123-46.

Milton, John. *Paradise Lost.* Ed. Scott Ellege. New York: Norton, 1975.

Naubert, (Christine) Benedikte. *Veileda, Ein Zauberromen.* Leipzig: Schäfer, 1795.

Oates, Joyce Carol. "In Olden Times, When Wishing Was Having . . ." *Kenyon Review* 19: 3 and 4 (Summer/Fall 1997). 19 Feb. 2004. http://search.epnet.com/direct.asp?an=9710011678& db_afh& site_ehost.

Rich, Adrienne. "When We Dead Awaken: Writing as Re-Vision." In *Feminist Literary Theory: A Reader.* 2nd ed., 84-91. Oxford: Blackwell, 1996.

Rowe, Karen. "Feminism and Fairy Tales." *Folk and Fairy Tales.* Eds. Martin Hallett and Barbara Karasek. 2nd ed. 325-45. Broadview Press, 1996.

Sartre, Jean-Paul. *Being and Nothingness.* Trans. by Hazel Barnes. London: Methuen, 1957.

Sexton, Anne. *Transformations.* New York: Houghton Mifflin, 1972.

Todd, Richard. *A. S. Byatt.* Plymouth: Northcote House, 1997.

Tong, Rosemary Putnam. *Feminist Thought.* 2nd ed. Boulder: Westview Press, 1998.

Webb, Caroline. "Forming Feminism: Structure and Ideology in *Charades* and 'The Djinn in the Nightingale's Eye.'" *Hecate* V.XXIX; n. 1 (2003). Proquest Direct. Date accessed 2/19/04.

Wittig, Monique. *Les Guerillères.* New York: Beacon Press, 1985.

Woolf, Virginia. *A Room of One's Own.* New York: Harvest, 1989.

Zipes, Jack. *Fairytales and the Art of Subversion: The Classic Genre for Children and the Process of Civilization.* New York: Wildman Press, 1983.

———. [Ed.] *The Oxford Companion to Fairy Tales.* Oxford: Oxford U P, 2000.

Susan Poznar (essay date winter 2004)

SOURCE: Poznar, Susan. "Tradition and 'Experiment' in Byatt's 'The Conjugial Angel'." *Critique* 45, no. 2 (winter 2004): 173-89.

[In the following essay, Poznar argues that "The Conjugial Angel" embodies Byatt's interest in the artistic problems of "historical nostalgia and skepticism, realism and experiment."]

In her extensive writing on her own and other writers' fiction, A. S. Byatt foregrounds a problem that she does not overtly resolve. In her essay "People in Paper Houses: Attitudes to 'Realism' and 'Experiment' in English Post-war Fiction," she claims that many contemporary writers maintain an ambivalent posture toward "realism" and "experiment," combining "a sense that models, literature and 'the tradition' are ambiguous and problematic goods [. . .] with a profound nostalgia for [. . .] the great works of the past" (161).[1] Byatt's sympathy for, yet impatience with, much contemporary British fiction emerges when she gently accuses certain novelists of a muddled kind of compromise and contends that

> much aggressively "experimental" fiction uses [. . .] distracting devices, in part to legitimize echoes of old styles and straightforward realisms. [. . .] Through and athwart them we glimpse a plain, good, unfussy, derivative realist prose that can somehow only come about by declaring that *that* is not what it meant to be, not what it meant at all.
>
> ("People in Paper Houses" 157)

Byatt does not explain how she herself might avoid this trap and ensure that her right hand is not writing what her left hand is busy disclaiming. The student of her work cannot but wonder if Byatt does manage to negotiate the problem of combining the "realist" and the "experimental" modes. This is particularly urgent in works like *Possession* and ***Angels and Insects,*** historiographic fictions[2] that necessitate both a "realistic" representation of the historic period and an acknowledgement that a differing authorial sensibility is molding those materials. Might her historiographic fiction somehow validate the ghostly voices of the Victorian literary past within an experimental, postmodern narrative without forming a duplicitous, stitched-together sort of creature (reminiscent of the clumsily sutured cinematic Frankenstein's monster)? Can an organically whole and seamless creation be woven of these disparate materials? Or would such an achievement itself smack of bad faith? Then how might Byatt reconcile contradictory demands for the New Critically "organic" creation and the postmodern rejection of the same?

Byatt's recent historiographic metafictions maneuver adroitly around this problem, particularly in those séance scenes that witness the dialogue of the living and the dead and that stage the collision of competing voices, metaphors, and myths. The second novella in ***Angels and Insects*** (1992), entitled **"The Conjugial Angel,"** is the product of meticulous research into Victorian spiritualism, into the histories of the Hallams and the Tennysons, and into scholarly exegesis of Tennyson's *In Memoriam.* From those researches. Byatt creates a unified and compelling story of how Emily and Alfred Tennyson confront the complexities of their own grieving, of how human desires and spiritualist experiences intersect, of gender identity, of public and private mourning, and of the various "afterlives" of poetry. Her recreation of the Victorian spiritualist milieu is detailed and convincing.

Yet **"Angel"** [**"The Conjugal Angel"**] is as "aggressively 'experimental'" as any of Byatt's work, a tour de force of metanarrativity and intertextuality. It features two séance scenes, bridged by an eerie scene of tenuous communications between two living characters and Arthur Hallam's ghost. The séances are traversed by polyvocal mediumistic messages and polysemous automatic writings, glossed by the spiritualist circle's unfinished and tentative interpretations, and infused by the intertwining thoughts and memories of the séance participants, amongst whom the point of view fluidly but disconcertingly shifts. Like the shining cocoon that the medium Sophy Sheekhy perceives spinning itself around the aged Alfred Tennyson, this novella spins an intricate web of narrative and poetic lines, a continually expanding cocoon enmeshing textual threads from varied Victorian authors, from the characters' conversations about and interpretation of those texts, and from their imagined inward engagements with the texts. An earnest circle of people who are working through different problems of mourning and desire produce a changeable, meaningful collective weaving of thoughts, thematics, and images from Milton, Swedenborg, the scriptures, Keats, Tennyson, Hallam, Shakespeare, and other texts. Registering Byatt's very postmodern awareness of intersubjectivity and the presumptive "death" of the author, the narrative manipulates the reader into focusing less on the autonomous "origins" and "intentions" of particular texts than on how they intertwine, modulate one other, and proliferate.

To say that **"Angel"** evidences both Victorian and postmodern sensibilities and themes, however, does not enable us to distinguish Byatt's narrative approach from, say, John Fowles's in *The French Lieutenant's Woman.* It does not tell us how Byatt might prevent the novella's experimental devices from striking the reader as a clever veneer overlaid on an old-fashioned story.[3] The most original aspect of this novella is Byatt's approach to the simultaneously creative and theoretical dilemma outlined above. Byatt weaves her own critical threads of inquiry, through key metaphors, into this shifting, iridescent, intertextual cocoon to play with and play out the artistic problems of historical nostalgia and skepticism, realism and experiment that appear time and again in her scholarly prose. In this essay, I show that Byatt dissolves the boundary between critical and creative discourses to energize both—and to suggest fictive solutions to dilemmas that theory cannot resolve, particularly concerning narrative approach.[4] We will see, then, that Byatt's subtle self-quotation is not merely a new version of *mise en abyme* designed solely to undermine the "realist" illusion. That I have already invoked several **"Angel"** metaphors is not fortuitous because it is precisely metaphor—Byatt's revisiting and revising of her own metaphors, her revitalization of other writers' metaphors, and her critical examination of the powers and properties of metaphor in general—that grapples with these problems.[5]

In effect, **"The Conjugial Angel"** is haunted, not only by spirit voices but also by the voices of contemporary literary debate and by Byatt's own critical voices.[6] Her essays about literature form integral intertexts for **"The Conjugial Angel"** and are obliquely tested within the novella's ambiguous conversations between the living and the dead. To understand this dynamic of intertextual and metatextual experimentation, I begin by quoting the introduction to *Passions of the Mind,* as Byatt meditates on her academic training:

> More seductive than Leavis, in the world I grew up in, was T. S. Eliot, and most seductive in Eliot, to me, was his admiration for the metaphysical poets, for their mixture of intellect and passion, sense and sensuousness. My lost paradise was Eliot's elegant fiction of the undissociated sensibility, in which Donne felt his thought as immediately as the odour of a rose, unlike Tennyson and Browning (who of course, and in fact, do exactly the same, as an examination of the yew trees in *In Memoriam,* or of "Karshish," will demonstrate).
>
> (xiv)

I would note that Byatt commits a double gesture here. She immediately establishes her imaginative and intellectual assent to, and dependency on, an Eliotic literary-theoretical polarization; but nevertheless she parenthetically demurs from it. Then she immediately translates this polarization into metaphor: fallen versus unfallen paradises. She continues:

> Moved by this vision of a historical fulcrum between fallen and unfallen worlds. I embarked on a doctoral dissertation on religious allegory in the seventeenth century. This was partly because I wanted to study the sensuous metaphors of Herbert and Marvell, in which the unfallen world of the spirit was embodied in exquisite images of the fallen world of the body, and partly—the allegory bit of it—because I wanted to write novels, and was interested in narrative. [. . .] It is not too much to say that this unwritten work, with its neoplatonic myths, its interest in the incarnation, in fallen and unfallen (adequate and inadequate) language to describe reality, has haunted both my novels and my reading patterns ever since.
>
> (xiv-xv)[7]

In this matrix, the scholarly and creative, unwritten and written, metaphorical and allegorical, sensual and spiritual, "form" and "content," are all interdependent, and their relations to each other "haunt" Byatt with supernatural presence.

In part, **"The Conjugial Angel"** prompts the reader to reflect on how scholarly evaluations of artistic merit elevate or exclude writers and constructs a creative-critical refutation of Eliot's evaluation. In a review of four books on Tennyson, Byatt observes that Tennyson's

> greatness and intelligence as a poet have not received their due; he stands still in the shadow of F. R. Leavis's dismissal of his thought and his dissociated sensibility—a shadow now deepened by the encroaching shadow of Marxist characterizations of his voice as the confused voice of "essentialist humanism" disguising the ideology of bourgeois cultural and political imperialism in a claim to speak for himself and mankind.
>
> ("Insights *ad nauseum*")

In effect, Byatt restores these excluded poets to Eliot's garden, because the novella's visions and hauntings draw Tennyson and Browning into Byatt's own symbolic "patterns," as well as into the novella's literal and figurative gardens. Inside the story's séance parlor Byatt aligns different versions of the unfallen and fallen: the unfallen spirit and fallen body, language as adequate or inadequate to representing reality, writing as embodying undissociated or dissociated sensibility. Thus, the image of gardens extends to multiple critical contexts. In "Still Life/Nature morte," Byatt affirms that her earlier novel *Still Life* was explicitly concerned with the structuralist and poststructuralist assaults on transparent language:

> The play in my novel, and the novel itself, are nostalgia for a *paradis perdu* in which thought and language and things were naturally and indissoluably linked or, to use an Eliot metaphor, fused. In my experience I know what the form of a novel is when I find what I think of as the "ruling" metaphor.
>
> ("Still Life/Nature morte" 3-4)

Eliot's metaphor for the unfallen leads Byatt to the importance of metaphor for her writing; metaphor fuses body and spirit, abstract idea with its linguistic vehicle. Her more complex goal in **"Angel,"** though, is to demonstrate the simultaneous irreconcilability and interdependency of the unfallen and the fallen, whether she is treating the nature of language, human nature, or the sensibility expressed by a literary text. Then how might the novella's "ruling" metaphor negotiate both aims? A proleptic clue appears in Byatt's comments on an essay she greatly admires: Iris Murdoch's "Against Dryness" (1961). Querying which fictional forms might capture the "complexity and depth" of a "post-Christian world," she agrees with Murdoch in rejecting "what Blake might have called the single vision [. . .] of the crystalline novel [. . .]" ("Introduction" xv).[8] Yet a crucial narratological problem arises here: if indeed Byatt relies on the cohesive force of a "ruling metaphor" in each novel, how might she keep that "ruling" metaphor from reducing her novels to the "single vision" and univocality of the Blakean "crystalline" novel?[9] This question gives us a narrower angle on the tradition-experiment issue. The problem proves more manageable if we ask: how does Byatt manage metaphors that govern and characterize the metatextual séance in **"Angel,"** and how do they serve, metonymically, to delineate her own narrative solution to the quandary with which this essay opened? How will the living metaphors of the séance serve both the realistic functions of the story and its postmodern self-reflexivity? Once again, clues surface in Byatt's writing on other writers: her understanding of Paul Ricoeur's *La métaphore vive* in "Still Life/Nature morte" illumines her own approach:

> I found Ricoeur's whole discussion of the iconic element, or moment, in metaphor invaluable. [. . . H]e argues that the "voir comme" of a metaphor is both an

> experience and an act, both the reception of mental image *and* a deliberate act of understanding. It is to perceive identity and difference simultaneously and dependent on each other.
>
> ("Still Life/Nature morte" 8)

What better drama of identity and difference can one imagine than a circle of living people trying to communicate with spirits who are, at once, irrefragibly remote from and yet inexpressibly near to, the living creatures who need them? A séance itself might figure the functioning of metaphor: séances self-consciously produce images (visual, acoustic, or both) of the dead for the living; yet séances also function to interpret those images; they produce a kind of knowledge that is ordinarily and otherwise inaccessible; they unite seeming opposites to advance understanding; and they preserve an unspeakable core of paradox and mystery. They require that the participants passively receive and actively understand. What better way to trope the interdependent valences of identity and difference working within metaphor itself than by engaging human characters in contacting the beloved dead, who at once offer themselves for confident recognition and yet signal their terrible alteration in messages that demonstrate this sameness and difference? Thus, whereas Byatt uses a cluster of metaphors in a traditional way to embody themes raised by the characters' spiritualist endeavors and, further, to embody her own persistent critical concerns, the two séances, in a very postmodern move, represent the power of metaphor in general and dramatize its fissured nature and iconic dimension.

The séance as ruling metaphor is an eerie and potent self-reflexive strategy. In **"Angel,"** Byatt subjects this ruling metaphor, the séance, to interpretation by the intermingled voices that the séance invokes, so that the séance provides the arena in which issues of interpretation, intentions, and metaphoricity are themselves debated. If this were not postmodernly convoluted enough, these séances return us to the issues raised and almost always formulated in metaphoric terms in Byatt's critical works. Given the ineluctably metaphorical habit of Byatt's mind and the way the spiritual and sensuous always intertwine in her writing, it is not surprising that this "ruling" metaphor leads the reader not to abstract truths but to more metaphors: the séance metaphor generates others: angels, gardens, mirrors, birds, and so forth.[10] Insights in her works already are mediated by the metaphoric element embedded in all language, just as all spiritualist communications in this novella are mediated by female mediums whose understanding of their mediatory tasks is itself mediated by metaphors that they deploy to make themselves at home in their uncanny work. In this work, Byatt connects herself as a writer with Keats and Tennyson (and with the fictive medium Lilias Papagay) in evincing an imagination that is undeniably sensuous, engaged always with corporeal particularities so that her truths can never disengage themselves from their metaphoric expression, and her metaphors can never be reduced to the clear or "crystalline."

To study the ruling metaphor of the séance as fusing the realistic and the experimental, I must amplify earlier comments in presenting the novella both as a story with a traditional shape and themes and as a tissue of postmodern issues.

The ruling metaphor of the séance is not merely deployed for its metatextual potentiality. It enables Byatt to engage the living and dead in an interchange of insight and wisdom that liberates both from their cycles of mourning and prisons of melancholy.[11] It enables various characters to understand themselves and their associates better, to meditate on the spiritual and emotional exigencies of their age, and to arrive at crucial recognitions that will influence decisions about their lives. The séance, therefore, is a narrative agent working toward traditional forms of closure, working within a familiar thematics of loss and reparation. It demonstrates that the living cannot live without the dead, yet the dead depend no less on the living. Byatt's debt to scholars of spiritualism (such as Alex Owen, praised in the "Acknowledgements" to ***Angels and Insects***) indicates her dedication to mimesis, whereas the séances themselves, dramatic and convincing scenes that also demonstrate Byatt's understanding of high-Victorian culture, display her mimetic powers.

"Angel" assembles a spiritualist circle of fictional characters and fictionalized historic figures (blurring the line between fiction and history) in the home of Emily Jesse, née Tennyson, whose dead fiancé, Arthur Henry Hallam, was eternalized in her brother Alfred's *In Memoriam,* but whose ghost has eluded the spiritualist circle of which Emily is a central member. The séances are conducted by Sophy Sheekhy, who boards with and is assisted by Lilias Papagay, whose sailor husband has been lost at sea. Neither of the mediums is solely responsible for "authoring" the séance results; they are interdependent and complementary. (Lilias reflects that she would not be a good novelist because she cannot consciously reproduce others' experiences, though they fascinate her; Sophy would not be a good novelist because she seems not to have that strong sense of her own identity that is necessary to shape and control her fictional materials.) But together—the vital, earthy, and desiring Lilias; the passive, passionless, and permeable Sophy—they have just the incalculable, fluctuating balance of passivity and energy necessary for their venture. These two mediums of differing natures and spiritualist powers "compose" the circle's energies, anxieties, and needs; and Byatt explores all the definitions and metaphoric possibilities of the term "compose": the mediums calm the participants, coordinate them as a composer might coordinate notes or melodies, and are themselves part of the "composition" of the meeting. But the energies gathered and released by the séances work in opposite directions. On one hand, the voices that Lilias Papagay and Sophy Sheekhy channel move the plot toward resolution. They clairvoyantly announce both Mrs. Hearnshaw's pregnancy and Captain Papagay's return; they eventually transmit messages from Hallam and ultimately induce Emily to end her prolonged mourning and switch allegiance from her dead fiancé to her living husband, Captain Jesse. With their moving and apropos snippets of poetry (mainly Tennysonian), they further affirm the power of poetry to compose: to express, unify, and console the living, to consolidate human communities.

However, these supernatural, intertextual messages are ambiguous in origin and import. The séances, loci of scrambled, fragmentary, contested, and ambiguous truths, are products of a circle of participants. The supernatural spirits themselves quote the living: even in the afterlife, it seems, the soul cannot find either a separate peace or a separate voice. The mediums use spirit controls to access the beyond, further displacing the source of the supernatural communications. When they harmonize the participants' spirits, Sophy and Lilias succeed in connecting the past and present and intimating the future; but when they fail to harmonize (during the second séance), the dissonance produces further cryptic meanings. Meanwhile, the characters cannot deny that the voices, the messages may issue from within themselves. But because their own identities are manifestly constituted in their deepest "fibres" by the presence, the words, and the art of others and by memories of shared experiences, the boundaries are dissolved between individual selves, and the question of the origin of those voices and messages is complicated. Moreover, unexpected and seemingly unassimilable bits of language seem to suggest that the messages also come from some consciousness outside the circle. So this mobile séance work issues from the collective consciousness and unconscious of a community, yet is partially controlled and articulated by single individuals who are also conduits (not pure) for communications from "outside," which are not entirely outside because those mysterious invisible sources themselves are partially spoken by other living and dead voices.

In these séances, therefore, Byatt stages a riddling (one of her own favorite words) querying of the subject and its enunciations. Sophy's mediumistic voice is both hers and a mysterious Other's; the magical texts of the automatic writings belong to the dead, yet are formed by living hands with living interpolations; and the circle perceives Sophy's visions only through her verbal descriptions. There is therefore no direct access to any reality preceding enunciation. Furthermore, because the authorial and readerly functions shift among spirits, spirit controls, mediums, and séance participants, the messages are collaborative as well as intertextual, rejecting static notions of an originary authorial mind or a passive reader.

Undeniably, **"Angel"** is a variegated tissue of intertextuality, punctured by silences and gaps. It would not be an exaggeration to say that this novella is wrought almost entirely out of quotation, interpretation, and the mysterious hiatuses between: between quotation and quotation, between quotation and interpretation, and between interpretations. The texts being read, however, are fragmentary, seemingly internally inconsistent, and because they are transmitted through different vehicles, ambiguous as to origin (even as to intended recipient)—thus at first reading presenting themselves as exemplarily postmodern. Yet this pervasive intertextuality is not in the service of creating a world solipsistically constructed of nothing but language games. Byatt is not merely engaged in the by now standard game of blurring lines between the "real" and the "fictive," or of denying the transparency and adequacy of language, although, as she has reiterated in her essays, "The problems of the 'real' in fiction, and the adequacy of words to describe it" have long preoccupied her (introduction xv). As her work with George Eliot, Robert Browning, and others has amply shown and as her moving recreation of the Victorian spiritualist domain demonstrates here, Byatt is deeply committed to more traditional literary forms and will not enlist herself wholly within the ranks of the postmodern.

With this clarification of the double nature of Byatt's ruling metaphor (vitally enlisted both in her realist and postmodern aims), we may return to the "single vision [. . .] of the crystalline novel" and the question of how Byatt may, gracefully and in good faith, express a consciousness that is both Victorian and postmodern and create a fictional structure emanating from both.

In the interests of brevity, I am setting aside most of the imagery generated by those séances to focus on a single, arresting metaphor. In the first of the novella's two séances, the medium Sophy Sheekhy gazes at an uncanny crystalline creature visible only to herself and tries to describe it to the assembled company. The revelation of this creature, Sophy's responses to it, and her efforts to encompass it within language, and the automatic writings that its presence educes suggest an alternative to "single vision" and univocality and figure Byatt's historiographic metafiction itself, illuminating her strategy for addressing her aesthetic dilemma. The first séance and its crystalline creature work, both literally and figuratively, to serve both tradition and experiment.

In this first séance scene, Byatt works to recreate the magic that she perceives in the metaphysical poets and perceives through the lens of Eliot's valuations. Sophy, discerning the creature through all of her senses, experiences those unfallen moments of undissociated sensibility that Eliot and Byatt yearn for and admire in the metaphysical poets; and to some extent, she conveys that experience to the internal audience and to the reader. The birdlike creature Sophy envisions prompts physical hot and cold flashes in her, while the pen writes, "*Thou art neither cold nor hot. I would thou wert cold or hot.*" Perhaps the message is directed toward Emily Jesse, but undeniably it *makes* Sophy both hot and cold. Although this Biblical quotation concerns the lapse of the human away from the divine, its transmission by contrast evidences the possibility of communication between human and supernatural and fuses bodily sensation and spiritual appeal into an undissociated, though not unambiguous, experience, for medium and reader alike. Yet we simultaneously realize that this winged creature is not just a vibrant and active vision, but one of the myriad metaphors spun off by the ruling metaphor of the séance and one that focuses Byatt's self-reflexive use of uncontainable iconic figures:

> "It is made up of some substance which has the appearance of—I don't know how to say this—of—*plaited glass.* Of quills, or hollow tubes of glass all bound together like plaits of hair [. . .] but these are like molten glass. It appears to be very hot, it gives off a kind of bright *fizzing* sort of light. It is somewhat the shape of a huge decanter or flask, but it is a living creature. It has flaming eyes on the sides of a high glassy sort of head [. . .] And it is all eyes, all golden eyes, *inside* [. . .] it has in a way plumes [. . .] all colours—I can't do the colours [. . .] and a kind of cloak round its center [. . .] I can't see, it's all stirring about all the time, and shining and sparking and throwing off bits of light and I get the feeling, the sensation, it doesn't like me to describe it in demeaning human words and comparisons [. . .]"
>
> (232)

Language lapses here, yet this passage also celebrates its efficacy, and this efficacy is multifaceted. In her description, Sophy captures not only her sensations, but possibly also the visionary creature's; her description also links the reader to other bird and angel allusions and creates a network of figurative language. Further, this description of the creature's "crystalline" nature invokes Byatt's quoting of Murdoch's quoting of Blake's comments on "crystalline" art and thereby enables us to follow a clear path of literary references and read this creature with its penlike quills as a figure for Byatt's own artistic enterprise. More specifically, the description of this creature reveals that it is a metaphor whose many inner eyes examine itself, suggesting Byatt's fascination with and exploitation of metaphor's flexibility: it can "look" in many directions. The creature, a living vessel with an obscure core, functions as a metaphor for an elusive reality that invites and resists articulation but demonstrates finally that words can actually do many tasks, not perfectly, but wonderfully. Their imprecision is not exasperating in this séance context but delightful, as they throw off shifting meanings and connections, just as the mutable phoenixlike bird throws off its gorgeous sparks.

This iconic, metaphoric creature continually recreates itself within Byatt's matrices of meaning, and my reading does not exhaust its suggestiveness.[12] By mobilizing a metaphor that metamorphoses itself, Byatt embraces both the limitations and powers of the seance, of language, and of her own writing.

With this creature, Sophy and Byatt celebrate both evocative language, which magically captures reality, and self-reflexive language, which reveals its material origins and its artifice; indeed, throughout the novella, both author and medium demonstrate that unfallen language is not an illusion and fallen language not a cause for despair. Sophy, for instance, celebrates language as both experience and act, while remaining aware that it is composed of arbitrary signifiers detachable from any signifieds. Using imagery that doubtless evidences her imaginative digestion of the symbolic implications of the crystalline creature, she muses on

> [. . .] the equivocal repeated phrase "whether in the body, I cannot tell; or whether out of the body, I cannot tell: God knoweth." It described many of her own states and could be used, like poetry, with its repeated hum of rhythm, to induce such states. You went on saying it to yourself until it became at first *very strange,* as though all the words were mad and bristling with shiny glass hairs, and then very simple and meaningless, like clear drops of water.
>
> (221)

The complex co-functioning of these two languages, along with a vertiginous intersubjectivity and intertextuality, emerge in this later scene when Sophy uses poetry to entrance herself and summon Hallam's ghost. A brief summary of this scene demonstrates how dead and living voices, languages, and emotions inextricably intertwine and resonate, impossibly complicating the question of cause and effect relations between art and life, between language and the life it presumably reflects. The deceased Hallam enters Sophy's room when she "hum[s] in her head" lines from Keats's "Eve of St. Agnes," lines that voice the maiden Madeleine's painful voicelessness as she envisions her future bridegroom and prepares for bed. In Byatt's version, instead of materializing her own prospective bridegroom, her invitation produces Hallam (the former intended bridegroom of Sophy's acquaintance Emily Jesse), intoning the climactic "[i]nto her dream he melted" lines "in an ironic, slightly harsh voice" (288). Thus quotations from Keats, the poet beloved of and much discussed by both Hallam and Tennyson, usher in Hallam's ghost. Moreover, when Sophy with shuddering pity embraces the "baffled and impotent" Hallam, they are re-enacting parodically yet tenderly two scenes that never "really" happened: the scenes of Madeleine and Porphyro's, Hallam and Emily's erotic consummation. (One recalls that in Keats's poem the sexual union is veiled in floral metaphors.) Meanwhile, in an almost parenthetical and contrasting dose of traditional foreshadowing, the brief appearance of a brilliant parrot on the windowsill obliquely foreshadows Captain Papagay's future reunion with Lilias.[13] Sophy interprets Hallam's visit and despair through Swedenborg's teachings about the adjustments of the dead to their new state. Later in this episode, Tennyson's poetry connects both Sophy and Hallam to each other and to the elderly poet himself, and their meeting and macabre embrace apparently serve as the necessary prolegomena to the second séance's messages from Hallam to Emily. Hallam requires Sophy to recite lines from Keats's "Ode to a Nightingale" about remembering, forgetting, and the poet's apprehension of death. He requests this recitation in Keats's own words: "Darkling I listen," thereby in a sense entering into Keats's poem, and his own situation becomes a commentary on the poem. The "Ode" claims that the poet would "have ears in vain—/To thy high requiem become a sod." Yet, contradictorily, Hallam is clearly dead but nonetheless still listens to Keats, "darkling" perhaps in another sense, but not "in vain." Like the nightingale, Hallam is still audible, although he voices not ecstasy but anguish. And Keats's lines and their effects on Hallam meld almost indistinguishably into a Tennyson poem quoted earlier in the novella: "Recollections of the Arabian Nights." Someone—it is not clear whether it is Hallam's ghost, or Sophy, or perhaps Tennyson himself—recites the lines about another nightingale. This brings Sophy a vision of the living Tennyson preparing for bed and shifts the reader into Tennyson's consciousness, which is troubled by vague intimations of Hallam's and Sophy's presence and preoccupations. Thus, various lines of poetry from different sources, recited by particular characters, confirm, negate, or nuance one another, summon up other lines of poetry, and create fluctuating relations between the characters. Byatt therefore in this scene dramatizes the incalculable afterlives of poetic, metaphoric language.

This haunting, kaleidoscopic collocation of ghostly words and embraces, visions of the living and the dead, and passages of poetry "melting" and "blending" together leaves it unclear whether the poetry evokes the events or the events evoke appropriate poetry. But it unmistakably enacts that "mingling" "[a]part from place, withholding time" that both Keats's and Tennyson's poems celebrate—a mingling of texts, living and dead persons, and scenes of recognition and consummation. In this scene, Byatt multiplies the mysterious and ambiguous linkages between Sophy, Hallam, and Tennyson, with the woman medium as the necessary conduit between the two men. Byatt spins these vertiginous collisions, however, not necessarily to conclude that the dead can enlighten the living, nor that the living can find effective ways of burying their dead. Nor is she creating a kind of master-poem, eliciting some universal truth from these matrices of image and language. She is merely spinning a new and ephemeral configuration of poetry and experience shared among all three characters to suggest a complex and unending transformative circulation of imagination. Julian Gitzen notes that "Byatt is attracted to (and convincingly portrays) characters who occasionally achieve transcendent states, during which their surroundings are bathed in a radiance reminiscent of Wordsworth's 'celestial light'" (85). What is remarkable about Sophy's "transcendent" experiences, however, is that, although they have the structure of traditional mystical states, they do not transcend language or the material particularity of ordinary life. Rather, they are constituted by an enhanced awareness of the circulation of imaginative language amongst living and dead characters who, far from feeling blissfully elevated or liberated by their mystical connections, feel intensified anxiety and longing. Presumably if there is any realm in which we humans might rise above the play of textuality into pure, abstract truth, it is in the afterlife, but Byatt suggests that there, more than ever, intertextuality prevails!

If Byatt is celebrating fallen, metaphoric language (insight inextricably embedded in material signs) and rewriting transcendent, mystical experience as immanent and profoundly textual, she is not, however, thereby rejecting the abstract, impersonal formulations wherein language presents itself as objective, transparent, and unfallen. This is evident in the character of Mr. Hawkes, who is given to making philosophical pronouncements culled from his beloved Swedenborg. Byatt is not invalidating Hawkes's theories, his Logos, even though she demonstrates that his seemingly lofty and impersonal presentation of the Swedenborgian pure truth is undeniably conditioned by his personal, individual desires and needs. For instance, after the fizzing crystalline creature appears, and Emily Jesse recalls descriptions of angels from Milton and Donne, Hawkes "judiciously" discusses Swedenborg's thoughts about angels, and Papagay reflects that he "would theorise if a huge red Cherub with a fiery sword were advancing on him to burn him to the bone [. . .]" (234). Despite the humor, Hawkes's pedantic comments are not dismissed but absorbed into the metaphoric economy of the scene. The idea that "angelic offgivings" are "inserted into infants in the womb as reliques of past states of angelic conjugial love" links to the automatic writing's previous annunciation of Mrs. Hearnshaw's pregnancy, and the idea that these "offgivings" might be "reliques of past mental states stored up inwardly for future use" (233) might describe all the dynamic bits of poetry and prose that the séance participants have stored for use. Thus, although Sophy's and Lilias's silent reflections on Hawkes's theorizing strips them of their masculinist pretense to authority, they are not invalidated but integrally subsumed into the novella's imaginative and explanatory matrices. Byatt incorporates pure Logos and "crystalline" formulations into the multicolored richness of the ambiguities of the séance.

Sophy's vision of the bird-creature and her ensuing encounter with Hallam's ghost and the living Tennyson, then, are mediums for traditional and postmodern styles and views of writing, but their juxtaposition in the text does not create a jarring effect. In terms of the eponymous "conjugial angel" metaphor, the narrative "marries" the two. In these supernatural events, the novella entangles the traditional and the postmodern through a magic unavailable to the logical discourses of theory, creating a simultaneously unfallen and fallen garden, which is linked to Emily Jesse's recollections of her home at Somersby, where Alfred's and Arthur's visits were hallowed by the magic of an untroubled double consciousness. Perched on a William Morris sofa, Jesse muses on

> Mr Morris' weaving of a kind of formal, solid series of magical objects which recalled to her childhood days [. . .]. Everything was double, then—it was real and loved, here and now, it was glittering with magic and breathing out a faint cold perfume of a lost world, a king's orchard, the garden of Haroun al-Raschid [. . .]. Mr Morris' sofa acknowledged both worlds; it could be sat on, it hinted at Paradise. Emily liked that.
>
> (204-05)

I see Byatt's novella as just such an object: it evokes the vision of a garden where the ordinary and the magical coexist without exactly blending. It suspends the boundaries between Byatt's own critical and creative voices, recognizes the interdependence of opposite tendencies in contemporary critical debate, and exploits the iconic, continually self-expanding metaphor as the medium, the mediator, and the embodiment of all these dialogues.

If my analysis holds true, Byatt avoids the timid compromises that the opening quotations from *Passions of the Mind* criticized. In her fictive séances, she invites voices from "inside" and "outside" to engage in an intertextual dynamic of "realism" and "experiment." It is not merely that Byatt exploits both traditional and postmodern features in her fiction; the same could be claimed for many other writers. Rather, she manages to demonstrate the fertile imbrication of opposing positions without claiming to create either an imaginative or logical synthesis, without admitting the necessity of any such synthesis, and without apologizing for this "failure." **"The Conjugial Angel"** speaks fiction's ability to encompass contradictory theoretical stances that theory itself may not resolve.

Yet another creature that appears to Sophy, after her wincing embrace of Hallam and vision of Tennyson in his bedroom, provides a further metaphor for the novella and its strategy of conjoining opposites without synthesizing them. Sophy

> saw something, someone, standing in the bay of the window. It was larger than life, and more exiguous, a kind of pillar of smoke, or fire or cloud, in a not exactly human form. It was not the dead young man, for whom she had felt such pity, it was a living creature with three wings, all hanging loosely on one side of it. On that side, the winged side, it was dull gold and had the face of a bird of prey, dignified, golden-eyed, feather-breasted, powdered with hot metallic particles. On its other side, turned into the shadow, it was grey like wet clay, and formless, putting out stumps that were not arms, moving what was not a mouth in a thin whisper. It spoke in two voices, one musical, one a papery squeak.
>
> (328)

This bifurcated creature, in some sense, is Hallam: a reminder of the decomposing horror that Sophy accepted and embraced in the preceding chapter and the "golden" youth whose memory Emily Jesse has cherished for decades. Yet it also anticipates Sophy's image of Captain Jesse, who, receiving his wife's loving commitment, will appear like "an albatross stretching its wings, [with] its huge uncaged wings, and staring with its gold-rimmed eye" (330). Its two voices, however, connect it with the voice of the novella itself, reminding us that **"Angel"** sings with two unblended voices: the fallen, self-reflexive, ironic "papery" voice, and the unfallen, serious, "musical" voice.

This juxtaposition of unblended and complementary metaphors plays out in Byatt's alignment of fallen and unfallen gardens in the passages about the literal garden at Somersby, recollected by Emily Jesse during the séance scenes.

The Tennyson home at Somersby during Hallam's courtship of Emily Tennyson was "Alfred's dream Somersby, Arthur's visited garden Paradise" (265), when Hallam joyously joined the imaginative Tennyson youngsters, bringing the intellectual debates of Cambridge and the Apostles with him. For the two young men, it was a place (in Emily's remembered images) of joined hands and enduring tableaux of friendship, a true community. During that brief period of close friendship and romantic love, Somersby was a realm of a mutually enhancing life and art. But it also represents that garden of literary tradition that Hallam and Tennyson have entered, as they stroll amongst the flowers, discussing and reciting from Keats and Shelley, developing their theories of poetry together, commenting on "Neoplatonic mythic belief" (262) and other lofty artistic matters. Emily Tennyson, equally avid for art, however, can merely observe and overhear; her efforts to enter into their figurative garden of literature are rebuffed.

"Women shouldn't busy their pretty heads with all this theorizing. [. . .]." Hallam affirms (263). "If she was wholly truthful with herself, she remembered the sight of those two male backs [. . .] with the sensations of one excluded from Paradise" (261). Later, the Somersby garden becomes a prison with Hallam's death, when Emily feels as if she has been fully expelled from a paradise where she never really belonged because the two young men created it for themselves, two Adams whose friendly union clearly has homoerotic undertones.

Emily Jesse, remembering those days, is trying to understand how she truly can mourn—much less revisit—a garden from which she was already excluded by men who viewed the female as "inert Matter" (263), as beautiful creatures whom male poets eternalize. She also feels as if she is betraying her dead fiancé and brother by envying their bond and wishing to enter their garden. But she knows that since Hallam's death she has betrayed that garden even more radically. After the first spasms of grief at Hallam's loss, she befriended his sister Ellen, to whom she wrote "with a delicious new ease and edge, descriptions of her unpoetic world" (266). She lays claim to a very fallen garden: "She had even denied the Nightingale and its eternal preamble in the thicket, at least in Somersby" (267). It seems that she resisted endless grieving by denying that unfallen garden from which the men excluded her; older now, she realizes that she still needs and longs for that paradise. Meditating on her brother's *In Memoriam,* she admits that she "admired and idolised" it and that "[i]t made an eternal world of the bounds of the vicarage lawn and the flat Lincolnshire horizon [. . .]" (268). Much could be said about Somersby and what the various characters' fallen and unfallen visions of it imply, but suffice it to say in this context that through the medium of a longing woman, the novella subsumes both an eloquent recreation of Tennyson and Hallam's idyll and Emily's complex captivation by and rebellion against this same idyll: **"Angel"** conveys the voices of the literary nightingales that the male writers heard and the real nightingales that Emily did *not* hear. The discrepancy between the two gardens is sharply delineated, but neither is "preferred" to the other. They are suspended in balance.

* * *

Read on its own, **"The Conjugial Angel"** is coherent in terms of its internal systems of metaphor and imagery, though ambiguous in some respects. Read through the filter of certain of Byatt's critical essays, it explores the metaphors through which Byatt reads contemporary theoretical positions, to bring them to life but not to adjudicate differing positions. Thus Byatt's essays become crucial intertexts for one dimension of the novella. Sophy's visions of the crystalline creature and the bifurcated angel, I would postulate, represent Byatt's attempt to characterize an art, her art, which does not merely juxtapose the Victorian and the postmodern to oppose or to assimilate but to flicker sinuously between those two operations, to create a text that is a living creature defiant in its indefinability and anomalousness, yet potently expressive. The uncanniness of these visions expresses the uncanniness of an aesthetic maneuver that would resist the novelistic bad faith suggested at the outset of the essay without solidifying a reproducible model of narrativity for other novelists to emulate.

From another angle, Byatt's investigation of theories of language and intertextuality rebuts or eludes the criticisms of scholars who have criticized her allusiveness and academic style in other fictions. Gitzen notes that Byatt's "display of erudition" in *The Virgin in the Garden,* "has annoyed several reviewers," and admits that this is

> a potential shortcoming that assumes more troublesome dimensions in *Still Life,* where Byatt's passion for inquiry, particularly as it relates to metaphor, has temporarily usurped her role as a novelist, causing her to resort to transparent rhetorical devices, including lectures on linguistics and aesthetics by an Oxford don and a university vice-chancellor, contrived purely to argue and extend her points.
>
> (94)

Such "contrivances" are unnecessary in **"Angel"** because the characters are spiritualists and Swedenborgians accustomed to the intricacies of textual exegesis, because one main character is the sister of Tennyson and former fiancée of Arthur Henry Hallam and therefore accustomed to discussing poetics, and because most of the character are, to a lesser degree, poetry enthusiasts. The séances, likewise, provide an effective, highly dramatic forum for the collision of all sorts of voices and ideas, without the potentially clumsy formality or pedantry of the lecture hall. The very task of interpreting the supernatural messages provides a natural, convincing occasion for meditations on hermeneutics, on literary agency, and on the transmission of voice and the participation of audience in the making of meaning, amongst other issues.

I hope I have also shown that in the ironic epiphany of these supernatural creatures Byatt avoids the trap of disguising a realist world beneath a postmodern surface, for, in my view, both the realist and postmodern commitments in Byatt's work permeate it thoroughly. The intertextuality is not a surface complication but integral to the mechanisms of the narrative and affirms at once the slipperiness of language and, more surprisingly, its efficacy. The eerie séance voices and texts work toward connection and closure, while a postmodern apprehension of language, fiction, and the author function retains its authority throughout this novella. (Note that Sophy's final sentences contemplate both "the miracle of the tea" and "the inky black of the sky and the sea" [337]). The novel is exemplarily postmodern in its awareness of itself as a tissue of fallen, material signs; therefore, and yet triumphantly, it uses those signs to create epiphanic moments of undissociated sensibility for the reader.

Notes

1. She addresses this problem from a different angle also in "'The Omnipotence of Thought': Frazer, Freud and Post-Modernist Fiction" (*Passions* 109-146).

2. I am using Linda Hutcheon's term from *Narcissistic Narrative.*

3. Indeed, reviewers and scholars often treat Byatt's fiction as such: for instance, Ann Hulbert's casual observation, apropos of *Possession,* that "[h]andle it right, and you can offer old-fashioned mystery, comedy, and romance tricked out in new-fangled, self-reflexive style" (55).

4. It is fairly common for Byatt scholars to remark on the fact that "[h]er scholarly work is never far from her fiction [. . . and] her books and articles [. . .] provide a guide to her own developing history as a writer" (Kelly vii). I am arguing for a more dynamic and symbiotic relationship, not just of mutual explication but of mutual enablement and transfiguration.

5. Other scholars have explored the importance of metaphor to Byatt: witness Gitzen's remark that "[f]or Byatt the most powerful feature of language remains metaphor, that imaginative vehicle of implied or explicit comparisons" (88).

6. This could be connected to Byatt's own comments on the unique position of writers of her generation: "Writers in my life-time are the first generation to have studied set texts and then to have become set texts themselves. They are the first generation to have written, knowing that they have a sizable possible audience [. . .] of *professional* readers, from A-level students [. . .] to deconstructionists, feminists, Marxists and proponents of the Death of the Author" ("Reading, Writing, Studying [. . .]" 4).

7. Byatt already invested an earlier character. Frederica Potter, with the desire to write on seventeenth-century metaphor in *Still Life.*

8. "Crystalline" is a key metaphoric term for Byatt; she uses it in other contexts as shorthand for a kind of vision and a kind of writing. See also her comments on "George Eliot's Essays," when she uses Eliot's own comments on the novel: "Like crystalline masses it may take any form, and yet be beautiful [. . .]" ("George Eliot's Essays" 75).

9. In other critical passages, Byatt stresses her tendency to create, think, and explain through metaphor: "I don't know how much is known about the difference between those who *think* with mental imagery and those who don't. I very much do—I see any projected piece of writing or work as a geometric structure [. . .] I *see* other people's metaphors [. . .] "("Still Life/Nature morte" 7).

10. Jane L. Campbell likewise observes that Byatt's "own metaphors [. . .] suggest endless relationships rather than containment. Her least sympathetic characters are those actual or metaphorical artists who [. . .] attempt too tight a control of their own and others' narratives" (120-21).

11. Christien Franken discusses mourning and melancholia in Emily and Alfred Tennyson's lives and stresses Byatt's unconventional take on the mourning enacted in Tennyson's *In Memoriam* (*The Author as Character*).

12. I might note, for instance, that the restless and many-eyed creature, gazing both inward and outward, could represent the circle of participants in the séance.

13. "Papagei" is the German word for "parrot."

Works Cited

Byatt, A. S. *Angels and Insects: Two Novellas.* New York: Random, 1992.

———. "Insights *ad nauseum.*" *Times Literary Supplement* (14 Nov. 1986).

———. "Introduction." *Passions* xiii-xvii.

———. "George Eliot's Essays." *Passions* 109-39.

———. "'The Omnipotence of Thought': Frazer, Freud and Post-Modernist Fiction." *Passions* 109-146.

———. *Passions of the Mind: Selected Essays.* New York: Turtle Bay, 1992.

———. "People in Paper Houses: Attitudes to 'Realism' and 'Experiment' in English Post-war Fiction." *Passions* 147-68.

———. "Reading, Writing, Studying. Some Questions about Changing Conditions for Writers and Readers." *Critical Quarterly* 35, 4 (1993): 3-7.

———. *Still Life.* New York: Macmillan, 1985.

———. "Still Life/Nature morte." *Passions* 3-13.

Campbell, Jane L. "Confecting *Sugar*: Narrative Theory and Practice in A. S. Byatt's Short Stories." *Critique* 38, 2 (1997): 105-22.

Franken, Christien, "The Gender of Mourning." *The Author as Character: Representing Historical Writers in Western Literature.* Ed. Paul Franssen and Ton Hoenselaars. Madison: Associated UP, 1999.

Fowles, John. *The French Lieutenant's Woman.* Boston: Little, Brown, 1969.

Gitzen, Julian. "A. S. Byatt's Self-Mirroring Art." *Critique* 36.2 (1995): 83-95.

Hulbert, Ann. "The Great Ventriloquist: A. S. Byatt's *Possession: A Romance.*" *Contemporary British Women Writers: Narrative Strategies.* Ed. Robert E. Hosmer, Jr. New York: St. Martin's, 1993. 55-65.

Hutcheon, Linda. *Narcissistic Narrative: The Metafictional Paradox.* New York: Methuen, 1984.

Kelly, Kathleen Coyne. *A. S. Byatt.* New York: Twayne, 1996.

Murdoch, Iris. "Against Dryness: A Polemical Sketch" (1961). Rpt. in *The Novel Today.* Ed. Malcolm Bradbury, London: Fontana, 1975.

Owen, Alex. *The Darkened Room: Women, Power and Spiritualism in Late Victorian England.* London: Virago, 1989.

Ricoeur, Paul. *The Rule of Metaphor: Multidisciplinary Studies of the Creation of Meaning in Language.* Trans. Robert Czerny. Toronto: U of Toronto P, 1981.

Sarah Fishwick (essay date January 2004)

SOURCE: Fishwick, Sarah. "Encounters with Matisse: Space, Art, and Intertextuality in A. S. Byatt's *The Matisse Stories* and Marie Redonnet's *Villa Rosa.*" *Modern Language Review* 99, no. 1 (January 2004): 52-64.

[*In the following essay, Fishwick finds similarities between Byatt's* The Matisse Stories *and Marie Redonnet's* Villa Rosa, *contending that both texts focus on the image of the artist and artistic creation.*]

This article takes as its focus two texts written by contemporary European women writers and published in the mid-1990s, which draw upon the work of the French modernist artist Henri Matisse (1869-1954). These are: A. S. Byatt's ***The Matisse Stories,*** a collection of three short stories written in English and first published in 1993, and *Villa Rosa,* by the French novelist and playwright Marie Redonnet, published in 1996. Both texts incorporate protagonists who either have themselves met Matisse or have ancestors who have done so. As well as weaving direct references to Matisse's life and artistic productions into their narratives, Byatt's stories and Redonnet's tale also feature reproductions of works by Matisse in their 'peritextual' field.[1] Chatto & Windus's 1993 hardback edition of Byatt's ***The Matisse Stories*** displays a reproduction of *Le Silence habité des maisons* (1947) on the front of its dustjacket, while his *Le Nu rose* (1935) and *La Porte noire* (1942) appear on the back.[2] In addition, each of Byatt's three stories is prefaced by a line drawing by Matisse. Similarly, Flohic's hardback edition of Redonnet's *Villa Rosa* features a small-scale reproduction of Matisse's *Jeune Fille en rose* (1942) on its cover and the text is interspersed with a series of prints—thirty-seven in all—of works by Matisse. The prints, which are not reproduced in a chronological sequence, appear on the edition's left-hand pages and the novel's text on the right. The main body of the text is followed by a reproduction of a photograph taken in 1928 of Matisse and his model Zita in the artist's studio. This photograph precedes a three-page chronology of Matisse's life and achievements. Redonnet's novella is one of a series of more than twenty-five texts published since the mid-1990s by the French art-publishing house Flohic. The series, entitled 'Musées secrets', aims to explore the fertile common ground occupied by art and literature by means of short (semi-)fictional texts which are illustrated with reproductions of works of art by a single artist. As Alain Salles's article on the series published in *Le Monde* makes clear, each author selects the work or life of a celebrated artist and takes that material as the starting point for their *récit.* The series was conceived, however, with a view to avoiding the conventions of formal art criticism: 'Il ne s'agit pas d'une étude sur un peintre, mais d'un texte inspiré par son œuvre, qui fonctionne en écho avec les illustrations, soit à partir de la vie de l'artiste, soit sous la forme d'une fiction.'[3]

If I have chosen to explore Byatt's ***The Matisse Stories*** and Redonnet's *Villa Rosa* in tandem, it is not simply because they both use Matisse's work as a 'touchstone'[4] for their narratives and, like Matisse's artwork, make ample use of colour symbolism. It is also because both texts are united by a focus on the figure of the artist and the practice of artistic creation, a focus that has long been discernible in the fictional output of both writers. The texts contained in ***The Matisse Stories*** provide further evidence of Byatt's fascination with art, and painting in particular; a fascination already apparent in fictional works which predate this collection, such as *Still Life* (1985) and the short stories **'Precipice-Encurled'** and **'Sugar'**, the tenth and eleventh stories respectively in her 1987 collection ***Sugar and Other Stories.***[5] A similar interest in artistic or visual modes of representation, and what they awaken in and reveal to the individual, is apparent in Redonnet's fictional œuvre. As Aine Smith has pointed out, Redonnet's texts are populated by a whole host of characters, including writers, dressmakers, dancers, and circus performers, for whom artistic practice serves as 'a means of generating identity, or, at the very least, of elaborating a fuller, more cohesive and enduring sense of self than that which originally exists'.[6] It is worth noting, however, that, prior to *Villa Rosa* in 1996, Redonnet's interest in what the individual derives from the process of artistic creation manifests itself most prominently, not in a fictional exploration of the artist/viewer and the painted canvas but rather in a textual preoccupation with the cinematic medium and the use of photography. Redonnet's novel *Rose Mélie Rose* (1987), in particular, displays a preoccupation with the photographic image, while the cinematic image is a recurrent motif in *Silsie* (1990) and *Candy Story* (1992).

To return to Byatt's ***The Matisse Stories*** and Redonnet's *Villa Rosa,* however, both texts assemble a series of fictional characters who might be described as either 'aspiring artists' or 'scholars' of art, protagonists who experience differing degrees of success in their pursuit of self-expression and artistic excellence. The discussion that follows suggests that the Matisse-inspired creators foregrounded by Byatt and Redonnet in these two fictional narratives might more accurately be viewed as 'confectioners' and 'consumers' of art; protagonists for whom the *appropriation* and *modification* of key Matissean images and motifs play a central role in their artistic practice. Yet, what of Byatt and Redonnet's own textual appropriation of elements of Matisse's artistic vision? How might we interpret the role accorded to visual art by Matisse in both ***The Matisse Stories*** and *Villa Rosa*? It is with this question that I am principally concerned in my comparative discussion of these two texts. In her non-fictional essay *Portraits in Fiction,* published over ten years after ***The Matisse Stories*** in 2001, Byatt reflects on the textual effects produced by a writer's inclusion of depictions of paintings in his/her fictional narrative. Such depictions may, for example, Byatt asserts, operate 'as an imagined icon or unifying motif', accentuating the narrative's thematic and aesthetic concerns.[7] Paintings set down in words, Byatt suggests, can also be used to reveal a protagonist's identity, casting light on their traits, attitudes, and self-image. They act as 'temporary mirrors', allowing protagonists 'to see themselves with a difference' (*Portraits in Fiction,* p. 5). What is striking about Byatt and Redonnet's deployment of intertextual references to Matisse's artwork in their texts is that both writers use these sets of references in conjunction with two key areas within their narratives. Broadly speaking, Byatt and Redonnet deploy features of Matisse's artistic vision, first, to flesh out a fictional location or landscape and second, to shed light on the workings of the creative process in which their often troubled protagonists are engaged. Intertextual references to Matisse's artworks are used in both ***The Matisse Stories*** and *Villa Rosa* to explore the human subject's interaction with space *through the medium of art,* an exploration that is facilitated, I shall argue, by Matisse's long-established association with the richly decorated bourgeois interior. As I shall demonstrate, this focus on the interconnectedness of art and spatiality is achieved specifically by means of a focus in these texts on the key role played by artwork or art objects in the creation and modification of domestic and commercial spaces. The second half of my discussion considers a second dimension of Byatt and Redonnet's deployment of a Matissean intertext in these works. By means of an examination of Byatt and Redonnet's focus on the artistic practices of borrowing and copying, my analysis detects within Byatt's collection and Redonnet's tale a wider meditation on the notion of artistic 'originality'. This meditation, as we shall see, enables both authors to reflect on the function of artistic creativity and, ultimately, to assert its transformative power.

In each of the stories contained in Byatt's triptych ***The Matisse Stories,*** a different commercial or domestic space serves as a vibrant and richly coloured backdrop for the action. The first, **'Medusa's Ankles'**, tells of a visit to a fashionable hairdressing salon by Susannah, a respected translator, the story's middle-aged central female protagonist and the metaphorical snake-haired 'Medusa' of the title. The Matissean image of the 'Rosy Nude', featured on the back of the collection's cover or dustjacket, plays a key role in Byatt's staging of the dynamic and colour-swathed commercial space represented by the salon's interior. We learn that a reproduction of Matisse's painting *Le Nu rose* (1935) hangs in the salon, providing a theme for its decor and helping to lure weary customers into its sensual, feminized interior:

> She had walked in one day because she had seen the Rosy Nude through the plate glass. That was odd, she thought, to have that lavish and complex creature stretched voluptuously above the coat rack, where one might have expected the stare, silver and supercilious or jetty and frenzied, of the model girl [. . .]. In those days the salon was like the interior of a rosy cloud, all pinks and creams, with creamy muslin curtains here and there, and ivory brushes and combs, and here and there—the mirror-frames, the little trollies—a kind of sky blue, a dark sky blue, the colour of the couch or bed on which the rosy nude spread herself.[8]

To enhance the soft, harmonious decor the stylists wear matching pink and cream overalls (***MS*** [***The Matisse Stories***], p. 11) and coffee is served to customers 'in pink cups' accompanied by 'a pink and white wafer biscuit in the saucer' (***MS,*** p. 5). Byatt's textual enumeration of the uniform worn by the stylists and the objects habitually used in the salon suggests that they have been chosen by its head stylist and owner, Lucien, because they are both functional and aesthetically pleasing. The 'Rosy Nude', however, unlike the staff uniforms and the salon crockery, has no functional value. The print, purchased from a shop in London's Charing Cross Road, Lucien believes, 'gives the salon a bit of class' (***MS,*** p. 4). Byatt's tracking of the sale, movement, and exhibition of the Matisse print in **'Medusa's Ankles'** illuminates the manner in which objects and artefacts are routinely consumed. Moreover, the fact that Byatt's narrative invokes the perceived cultural value attached to Matisse's 'Rosy Nude'—and reproductions of it—allows her text to flag up the status of that work as a cultural commodity. In other words, Lucien's conviction that the Matisse print gives his salon an air of refinement points to the image/object's desirability on account of the symbolic value with which it is imbued. In choosing to purchase the Matisse print Lucien has sought to appropriate for his salon—and by implication, for himself—the sense of flair and sophistication denoted by the Matissean image within the cultural domain. Byatt's narrative, then, casts the reproduced image of Matisse's 'Rosy Nude' as a marker of luxury and elevated social status.

In the course of Byatt's narrative, Susannah discovers, not without some dismay, that the salon has been revamped by Lucien, and the print of Matisse's 'Rosy Nude'—for all that it signifies refinement—unceremoniously removed. The comforting pastel-themed interior is traded in for a Japanese-inspired 'monotone' look. The narrative bristles with irony as Susannah's quick eye surveys the all-new 'bleakly minimalist' workspace:[9] 'battleship-grey and maroon. Dried blood and instruments of slaughter, Susannah thought on her return' (***MS,*** p. 15). The salon's new clinical appearance denotes youthful aggression and contemporary edginess—a mood that is ironically much more in keeping with the forbidding 'stare' of the silver-tinged photographic model Susannah had expected to greet her when she visited the salon for the very first time (***MS,*** p. 3). The design, in sharp contrast to the sumptuous decor it replaces, is hard-edged and honed, even down to the black, geometric crockery and flat, spherical complimentary sweets:

> The Rosy Nude was taken down. In her place were photographs of girls with grey faces, coal-black eyes and spiky lashes, under bonfires of incandescent puce hair [. . .] The new teacups were black and hexagonal. The pink, flowery biscuits were replaced by sugar-coated minty elliptical sweets, black and white like Go counters.
>
> (***MS,*** p. 16)

Susannah's dislike of the salon's transformation is such that she thinks, momentarily, of going to another salon. Like the pink-themed Matissean decor, the decorations and objects which make up the salon's new interior would appear to have been carefully chosen to coordinate. Repeatedly purchasing material goods and installing them in his salon, Lucien's interaction with his workspace casts him in the role of 'man the designer' (*homme de rangement*) as theorized by the cultural theorist Jean Baudrillard in his analysis of technological developments and consumer goods, *Le Système des objets* (1968).[10] For Baudrillard (p. 36), this phenomenon characterizes the production of everyday space in advanced technological society and is reflected in its advertising discourse, one in which the consumer is impelled to *manipulate* and *maximize* his homespace. Described as a kind of 'active technician' (*informateur actif*) or 'engineer' of the space he inhabits, the individual does not 'consume' objects—such as furniture, gadgets, and antiques—in a literal sense but 'dominates, controls, and orders them'. In doing so, he invests material objects with symbolic value, 'personalizing' his environment and generating 'atmosphere' (*ambiance*) (pp. 37-38). Byatt's description of the salon's chameleon-like interior suggests, moreover, that Lucien has succumbed to what Roland Marchand has referred to as the '[a]esthetic of the ensemble':[11] that is, a principle promoted by modern consumer culture which works to sell increased quantities of household goods. In Byatt's narrative, then, Lucien emerges as an arch-consumer who has been 'persuaded that everything should match'.[12]

As well as illuminating the manner in which works of art are consumed and used to shape the (fabricated) environments we inhabit, in **'Medusa's Ankles'** the salon's decor also serves as a barometer for the state of mind of its central female protagonist. On overhearing the salon owner disparage his wife—whom he has recently discarded for a mistress—for having 'let herself go altogether' and dismayed by the 'hideousness' of the mass of newly coiled hair piled on top of her head by a garrulous and patronizing female stylist, Susannah is consumed by a 'red' rage: a rage fuelled by empathy for Lucien's scorned wife and despair at her own loss of youthfulness. In Byatt's tale of mental unravelling, then, the calm exuded by the salon's once cocoon-like interior is exposed as a 'sham' as Susannah trashes its newly decorated interior. In an ironic twist, on seeing his premises in total disarray, the image-conscious salon owner expresses his gratitude to Susannah: 'You've done me a good turn in a way. It wasn't quite right, the colours' (***MS,*** p. 27). Thus, Lucien's remark allows Byatt to reveal the way in which our interaction with the environments in which we live is subject to the fickle dictates of fashion mediated by the discourses of consumerism. Clearly, Byatt's salon owner is endowed with the sense of 'experimentation' with regard to his workspace much prized by advertisers.[13] Lucien's willingness to transform his living space regularly in accordance with the latest trends would seem to stem from his desire to flatter his own artistic sensibilities and cultivate an air of 'distinctiveness'.

The second piece in Byatt's collection, like **'Medusa's Ankles'**, uses references to a well-known work by Matisse as well as scholarly commentaries on his artistic productions to dramatize the living spaces inhabited by the tale's protagonists. In doing so, Byatt's text flags up the dynamics of the 'constructed' spaces we inhabit—in this case, homespace. What is more, Byatt's intertextual references to Matisse reveal the way in which textual/pictural representations of these spaces can operate as a 'window' on human spatial configurations. 'Art Work' revolves around the inhabitants of 49 Alma Road, a bourgeois family made up of Debbie and Robin, their two children, and their eccentric housekeeper, Mrs Brown. It is noteworthy that all three principal protagonists are former students of and/or active practitioners of art. Mrs Brown, by day the family's housekeeper, is revealed to be an experimental artist, whose outlandish installations mix large fabric sculptures with a multitude of household and decorative objects such as fans, cleaning equipment and items of furniture. Debbie, her employer, is a former graphic designer turned journalist for a women's style magazine, while her husband, Robin, is a struggling artist and exponent of 'neo-realist' painting. The couple, we learn, were brought together by their love of art, colour, and Matisse (***MS,*** p. 56). The narrative opens with a short, but detailed, description of Matisse's work *Le Silence habité des maisons,* interspersed with extracts from Sir Lawrence Gowing's critical commentary on Matisse's 1947 painting[14]—a critical work recommended by the central protagonist of **'Medusa's Ankles'** when the salon owner quizzes her on what he should read in order to learn more about Matisse (***MS,*** p. 9). The effect created by the opening of 'Art Work' is that of a narrator/protagonist reading Gowing's text and reflecting upon the book's black and white reproduction of the painting (***MS,*** pp. 31-32). A description of domestic life in the family home immediately follows, one that draws upon and echoes the contemplative mood of Matisse's *tableau.* The family's homespace is cast by Byatt as an 'inhabited silence', reminiscent of the reflective mood of Matisse's 1947 canvas. Inside the walls of the house there is no human noise, only mechanical noise exemplified by the 'churning hum' of the washing machine, the 'chuntering' of the tumble dryer, and the repetitive and dehumanized 'cheery squitter' of female presenters emanating from the television (***MS,*** pp. 32-33).

Similarly, Redonnet's *Villa Rosa* displays a preoccupation with the imbrication of the notions of space/place and visual art as well as an emphasis on artworks as cultural commodities.[15] *Villa Rosa* features a central male protagonist called Henri Matisse, who, we are told, was named by his maternal grandfather, Jean, in honour of a stranger, the real-life painter, whom he once befriended during a crossing of the Atlantic. On the ship's arrival in New York, Jean Matisse is given a series of ink portraits by the artist as a gift of thanks, the prompt sale of which, to a Brooklyn art collector, enables the grateful Jean to purchase a quantity of gold. This gold allows him on his retirement to buy the idyllic 'Villa Rosa' of the title, located on the island of Gore, an island apparently praised by the real-life Matisse during their conversations: 'Le peintre Henri Matisse qui un jour y avait fait escale lui en avait parlé comme du paradis.'[16] The property is later inherited by the narrative's central protagonist, the young Henri Matisse, on the death of his grandfather.

The 'Villa Rosa' serves as a locus for the action recounted in the second half of Redonnet's tale and, like Matisse's artwork, also represents, for Henri, a symbolic bond with his male ancestor and benefactor, Jean.[17] Redonnet's text suggests that Henri's experience of the villa and his new environment on his arrival in Gore is shaped by his appreciation of Matisse's landscapes: 'Il avait l'impression étrange que la Villa Rosa était un tableau d'Henri Matisse, dont il était l'habitant' (*VR* [*Villa Rosa*], p. 49). As is the case with the hairdressing salon in Byatt's **'Medusa's Ankles'** and the family home in **'Art Work'**, the fictional spaces inhabited by Redonnet's protagonists are revealed to the reader by means of direct references to Matisse's visual art. The 'Villa Rosa'—a large white house decorated with climbing roses, which overlooks the sea (*VR,* p. 43)—and its environs are cast by Redonnet as bathed in a warm, soft pink light:

> C'était son heure préférée à la Villa Rosa, quand le ciel devient rose [. . .]. Le rose du ciel imprégnait toutes les couleurs jusqu'au bleu de la mer. [Henri] peignait Rosa Bell et Tiss, nues sur la plage dans la vapeur rose du soleil couchant.
>
> (*VR,* p. 55)

The rosy sunlight, which beats down on the island, is reinforced by the inclusion in the prelude to this section of the narrative of a series of paintings of Collioure in southern France done by Matisse in 1905.[18] Redonnet represents the 'Villa Rosa' as a maternal space filled with sound and movement as well as light (*VR,* pp. 55, 57). Music is provided by Tiss, a young female violinist, and children from the nearby orphanage attend the dance classes held every morning at the villa by Rosa Bell, with whom Henri is in love and whose first name heightens the reader's sense of the blissful existence the couple enjoy in the inherited villa. According to Redonnet's narrative, their home is 'une île dans une île' (*VR,* p. 61), a refuge from tragedy which grants 'une nouvelle vie' to Henri after the loss of his adoptive mother, Désirée, and also to the children of Gore, when the island is torn apart by guerrilla conflict (*VR,* p. 51). In addition, the walls of the villa become an exhibition space for Henri's artwork. Guided by his 'ange gardien', Matisse, Henri paints 'de grandes fresques' on the walls of the dance studio in celebration of the warmth and artistic creativity that have thrived in and around the villa since his arrival, and of the presence in his life of Rosa Bell (*VR,* p. 59). Later in the narrative, the house also serves as a performance space for Rosa's solo ballet performance and a play penned by the children (*VR,* p. 67). Additionally significant in Redonnet's depiction of the 'Villa Rosa' is its status as a site of remembrance. As well as signifying community and creativity, it is, for Henri, a monument to his artistic mentor, the Chinese copyist through whom he first became acquainted with the life-affirming artwork of Henri Matisse: '[Henri] trouva les mots justes pour honorer la mémoire du vieux Chinois, grâce à qui il avait eu la révélation de la peinture d'Henri Matisse. [Henri] voulait que la Villa Rosa devienne un hymne à sa gloire' (*VR,* p. 69). In Henri's eyes, then, the 'Villa Rosa' will forever symbolize the creativity inspired in him by Matisse's vision and his faith in the cathartic power of art.

The following section of my discussion retains a focus on Byatt's and on Redonnet's incorporation of a Matissean intertext into their narratives. However, it moves away from a focus on the manner in which these two texts use references to visual art by Matisse to elucidate the way in which human subjects respond to and transform their environment. It is concerned instead with the reflections these Matisse-inspired narratives offer on the status of the work of art and role of artistic practice. I shall argue that in ***The Matisse Stories*** and *Villa Rosa* one can identify two differing approaches to, or understandings of, artistic endeavour—both of which engage with the practices of *assimilation* and *copying* of artistic styles and images by the artist. My discussion of ***The Matisse Stories*** in this section will be confined to the third and final story in Byatt's collection, **'The Chinese Lobster'**.

In embarking upon such a discussion, it is appropriate to devote some time to reviewing how the central protagonists in Byatt's story and Redonnet's novella come into contact with Matisse and his artistic legacy. Byatt's **'The Chinese Lobster'** revolves around a lunchtime meeting which takes place in a Chinese restaurant between Dr Gerda Himmelblau, a female academic, and Peregrine Diss, a high-profile professor of art. In this novella Diss is cast in the role of 'bad' or unsympathetic mentor, in sharp contrast to Redonnet's benevolent copyist. Himmelblau in her capacity as Dean of Women Students is investigating an allegation of sexual harassment made against the professor by a research student named Peggi Nollett. In this tale Matisse's representations of the female body are cast by Byatt as a source of deep antagonism between Nollett, who is writing a dissertation entitled 'The Female Body and Matisse', and Diss, her eminent research supervisor. Nollett, we learn, is also working on a series of 'mixed media' pieces, which combine commercial reproductions of works by Matisse with organic matter, such as eggs, blood, and faeces (***MS,*** p. 111). These pieces form part of her project 'of *revising* or *reviewing* or *rearranging* Matisse', conceived with a view to expressing her antipathy towards what she perceives as the sexism and brutality inherent in Matisse's vision of the female body (***MS,*** p. 103). According to Nollett, that vision distorts female corporeality and hinges upon the longstanding but highly questionable equation of female sexuality with notions of the exotic (***MS,*** p. 102). Diss, however, is appalled by her work and believes her to be guilty of obsessive and pointless desecration of 'sacred' works of art (***MS,*** p. 112). The dynamics of the case are rendered additionally complicated by the fact that, as the reader soon discovers, Peggi Nollett suffers from anorexia nervosa and acute depression (***MS,*** pp. 118-19).

According to Byatt's depiction, Professor Diss endorses a mode of artistic practice underpinned by the principles of respectful imitation and disciplined emulation. Nollett, on the other hand, views art as a medium for reworking and challenging artistic conventions and ideological positions. In their combination of materials other than paint and canvas in a kind of montage, the impact of Nollett's pieces derives precisely from their capacity to shock their audience by means of their perceived 'ugliness'. Diss complains:

> it seems to me, that if she [Nollett] could have produced *worked copies* of those—masterpieces—those shining—nevermind—if she could have *done some work*—understood the blues, the pinks, and the whites, and the oranges, yes, and the blacks too [. . .] then I would have had to feel some respect.
>
> (***MS,*** pp. 112-13)

As Hillel Schwartz explains in her 1996 study of human civilization's fascination with doubling, *The Culture of the Copy,* the technique of copying has long been an integral part of the artist's apprenticeship and the perfecting of painterly skills.[19] It is noteworthy in this respect that in *Villa Rosa* Redonnet's central protagonist Henri first encounters the work of Matisse on visiting the New York premises of an elderly Chinese copyist who produces reproductions of works by Matisse. On entering the Chinaman's shop, the young Henri becomes fascinated by one painting in particular. Entitled *Le Nu au tambourin,* the painting, unbeknownst to him, is a faithful copy of the real-life Matisse's 1926 oil painting *Nu assis au tambourin.* On learning that the artist's name is identical to his own, and the year of Matisse's death identical to that of his late grandfather, Henri becomes convinced that he is the reincarnation of the real-life Matisse—a revelation that foregrounds the theme of doubling which, as critics such as Evert Van der Starre have indicated, recurs throughout Redonnet's novels and plays (*VR,* p. 13).[20] Exchanging his tailor's craft for that of the painter, Henri sets out to fulfil his artistic 'destiny'. Before leaving for China to study the techniques of the great Chinese masters, the copyist donates his entire collection of reproductions to Henri—a bequest that only serves to fuel the latter's conviction that he *is* the reincarnated Henri Matisse (*VR*, p. 13). Further, Henri first encounters Matisse's 1939 painting *La Musique* in the form of an impressive copy shown to him by Rosa Bell. Prior to his making Rosa's acquaintance during the sea crossing to the island of Gore, the work is unknown to Henri owing to its curious omission from his collection of Matisse copies executed by the Chinese copyist (*VR*, p. 39). In Rosa, who was given the painting by a former fiancé before being jilted by him on the day of their marriage, Henri finds not only a link to his 'seul maître' (*VR*, pp. 15, 47), the Chinese copyist, but also a fresh impetus for his artistic efforts.

It is my argument that Redonnet's self-styled Henri Matisse—like Byatt's Peggi Nollett and unlike his mentor, the copyist, and Byatt's Professor Diss—embodies a highly postmodern conception of the creative process. As Hillel Schwartz explains (pp. 246-47), such a conception is governed by the principle that 'appropriation *is* creation' or 'making [viewed] *as* taking' to the extent that in post-industrial societies 'creation and imitation, invention and repetition may become as indistinct as knowing is from copying'.[21] At the heart of Redonnet's *Villa Rosa* would seem to be a repeated questioning of the notion of the 'original'. In his bid to be an inspirational painter like his namesake, Henri churns out a series of what for him are *original* works—inspired, not by 'original' artworks by Matisse, but by *copies* of artworks by Matisse done by the *copiste*: 'Ce ne serait pas une copie puisqu'il n'avait aucun don de copiste, mais un tableau original, son premier tableau' (*VR*, p. 15). Moreover, these reproductions are copied not from other painted canvases but made 'd'après des reproductions photographiques découpées dans des magazines'—that is, photographic reproductions commercially produced in the popular press (*VR*, p. 13). This episode is accompanied in the narrative by a reproduction of Matisse's *L'Atelier rouge* (1911), a *tableau* that depicts an artist's studio in which several tiny 'reproductions' of works by Matisse hang on the walls, thereby foregrounding both the painter's creative environment and the notion of a work of art within a work of art that is already a feature of Matisse's canvases. What is further striking in Redonnet's dramatization of this episode is that, although Henri is convinced that he *is* the reincarnated Matisse, the spirit of Matisse with which he believes himself to be possessed allows him to create new and original works of art: 'Il était bien la réincarnation du peintre Henri Matisse qui à travers lui commençait une œuvre nouvelle. Son tableau n'était pas une copie, mais un original. Bouleversé il l'intitula *Nouveau Nu au tambourin*' (*VR*, p. 21). In this respect, Henri's artwork resembles the clothing designed by the young dressmaker Marguerite, whom he meets in New York. Marguerite's designs are inspired by clothing and textiles depicted in Matisse's paintings but are 'reworked' (*réinventées*) by her 'à la mode de Brooklyn' (*VR*, p. 33). Redonnet, then, foregrounds a creative process in which the artistic production is never finished. Rather, it remains open-ended, modifying and assimilating self-consciously that which has gone before it to create something new yet undeniably familiar. This lack of closure typical of postmodern artistic productions is further exemplified in Redonnet's text by the unfinished, equivocal quality of the frescos painted by Henri on the walls of the 'Villa Rosa': '[Henri] décida que ses fresques étaient terminées. Elles garderaient quelque chose *d'inachevé, une incertitude, une interrogation* venue tout à la fin à laquelle il ne donnait pas de réponse' (*VR*, p. 65; emphasis added).

The exploration of the themes of inspiration and creativity instigated by both Redonnet's *Villa Rosa* and Byatt's **'The Chinese Lobster'** is inextricably linked to the anxiety and restlessness suffered by their central protagonists. In other words, both authors cast Matisse's artistic vision as the stuff of obsession. As such, Redonnet and Byatt's textual appropriation of artworks by Matisse is an integral ingredient in the meditation they offer on the nature of the creative process and the restorative power of artistic creativity. Christien Franken has detected in Byatt's fiction an emphasis on the 'transcendent potential of art', an emphasis that, according to Franken's discussion, manifests itself early on in Byatt's writing career in her fictional depiction of the writer as visionary and the troubled pursuit of *literary* excellence contained in *The Shadow of the Sun* (1964).[22] I would argue that a related interest in art and the healing potential creativity offers comes to the fore in Byatt's portrayal of the tormented visual artist in **'The Chinese Lobster'**. As the narrative progresses, the discussion between Himmelblau and the professor focuses less and less on the allegation of sexual harassment made against the latter. In fact, Diss vigorously denies Nollett's claim and Himmelblau appears to believe him. Instead, the focus of the narrative becomes Diss's failure to recognize the genuine distress and suffering articulated by Peggi Nollett's artwork. Rather, what Byatt's story does flag up is the intensity of feminine bodily anxieties in the face of the rosy 'wellbeing' signified by many of Matisse's paintings. While Diss is baffled by Noggett's vilification of Matisse, suggested in the text by his reiteration of the question '*Why Matisse?*' (***MS***, pp. 119-20) and also by his assertion that he doubts whether 'she [Nollett] has ever spent more than [half an hour] *looking at* a Matisse' (***MS***, p. 113), it is left to Himmelblau to explain the motivation behind Nollett's rage: 'Because [Matisse] paints silent bliss. *Luxe, calme et volupté.* How can Peggi Nollett bear luxe, calme et volupté?' (***MS***, p. 121).[23]

In the course of their conversation, Diss responds to Himmelblau's defence of Nollett's work by making reference to Matisse's oft-quoted assertion that art should be like an armchair—in other words, an aid to relaxation bringing calm and balance.[24] According to Diss, '[Matisse] knew the most shocking thing he could tell people about the purpose of his art was that it was designed to please and to be comfortable' (***MS***, pp. 122-23). I would argue that this view of art—adumbrated by Matisse and endorsed by Byatt's Professor Diss—is contested in this story by Byatt's female protagonists. As Himmelblau points out to Diss, 'it would be perfectly honourable to argue that this was a very *limited* view' (***MS***, p. 123). None the less, as Victoria Glendinning has commented, Diss and Himmelblau's discussion enables them to 'come to recognise their own hidden despair and self-hatred, and reassert their faith', a faith in the possibility of the kind of 'untroubled sensuality' celebrated by Matisse in his paintings.[25] In Byatt's text 'the white room' is cast as a metaphor for the depths of despair and the desire for death—a completely blank room, devoid of colour without any doors or windows:[26]

> You look around you and everything is bleached, and clear . . . You are in a white box, a white room, with no doors or windows. You are looking through clear water with no movement—perhaps it is more like being inside ice, inside the white room.
>
> (***MS***, p. 125)

What Byatt's text shows is that although Diss's and Nollett's *responses* to Matisse's artwork differ sharply, the function that artwork serves in their lives is very similar. That is, while Nollett seeks to fend off the encroaching despair of the 'white room' by transforming or 'defacing' works of art, Diss does so by looking to Matisse for colour and light: 'Matisse was the first to understand orange, don't you agree? Orange in light, orange in shade, orange on blue, orange on green, orange in black' (***MS***, p. 130). Significantly, Professor Diss goes on to tell Himmelblau of a visit he once payed to an ailing, visually impaired Matisse at the painter's Nice apartment towards the end of his life. In Byatt's rendering of that (fictional) visit, Diss is shocked to find the curtains drawn and the room inhabited by the master of colour and light 'shrouded in darkness'. Sensing the young Diss's horror, Matisse assures him that 'black is the colour of light' (***MS***, p. 131). To understand Matisse's insistence on the luminosity of the colour black, Diss maintains, one only has to look at his 1942 painting *La Porte noire*: 'It has a young woman in an armchair [. . .] and at the side is the window and the coloured light and behind—above—is the black door. Almost no one could paint the colour black as he could' (***MS***, pp. 131-32). In Redonnet's *Villa Rosa* likewise, black is symbolic of inspiration and creativity. When gripped by artistic fervour, the young Henri often experiences hallucinations. In Redonnet's *récit* these dazzling—and frequently erotically charged—visions, perhaps not unsurprisingly, are inflected by Matisse paintings and are announced by 'une tache noire vibrante', which gives way to bursts of coloured light (*VR*, p. 17). In both narratives, then, the creative force of art emerges as paramount for, as the Chinese copyist points out to Henri in *Villa Rosa,* out of the depths of frustration comes creativity: 's'obstiner dans son travail même quand il paraît sans issue parce que c'est alors que surgit la lumière' (*VR*, p. 15). Further, for both writers, art has the power to assuage suffering. While for Byatt that power derives from art's capacity to reassure *or* enrage the human subject, for Redonnet its restorative power stems from its ability to *commemorate* that which has shaped our identity—most notably in Redonnet's fictional universe our ancestors, benefactors, and mentors. Like Henri's eventual adoption of 'Monsieur Jean'—a reminder of his late grandfather's forename—as his artistic pseudonym, Redonnet's conclusion to *Villa Rosa* is further testament to her protagonists' desire to honour those from whose guidance they have benefited. In the final phase of the narrative, Henri and Rosa's idyll on the island of Gore is shattered when both Rosa and their friend Wadi, a political activist and the island's president, are murdered. Distraught at their loss, Henri flees to the 'grotte aux Images', whose name is emblematic of the proliferation of images which has been a feature of Henri's feverish artistic productions. Meanwhile, the shell of the 'Villa Rosa' sinks into disrepair. The remnants of Henri's vivid Matissean frescos, which once decorated the villa's walls, and his portrait of Rosa stand as a monument to her and the creative community they established on the island. Redonnet writes:

> Entre les plantes et les fleurs qui envahissaient les ruines, un visiteur curieux aurait pu découvrir, un peu partout, des morceaux de fresques et de tableaux, aux couleurs toujours vives. Et sur un pan de mur encore debout, il aurait découvert le portrait de Rosa Bell, intact, une pure merveille. Il aurait pu alors rêver à la Villa Rosa telle qu'elle avait dû être avant de tomber en ruines, et en réinventer l'histoire pour en sauver la mémoire.
>
> (*VR*, p. 81)

It is further significant in this extract that Redonnet's treatment of the descent into dystopia undergone by the once vibrant space of the villa emphasizes the spur to the *imagination* it will continue to offer to the 'curious visitor'.

By way of a conclusion to my comparative discussion of these two short, tragi-comic texts, it is apposite to reflect upon the reasons why two women writers writing in the 1990s might be so taken with the work of Matisse. It is clear that both Byatt and Redonnet use Matisse's work to conjure up a fictional location or 'landscape' and to communicate its mood—whether it be a hairdressing salon, an idyllic retreat, or the family home. What is more, as my discussion has demonstrated, by means of the connection they establish between visual art and the human subject's experience of his/her living space, both ***The Matisse Stories*** and *Villa Rosa* foreground the ways in which human subjects interact with the spaces they inhabit *and* the 'objects in use', which are a feature of those spaces.[27] The Matissean emphasis on the embodied human subject and his frequent depiction of homespace is such that his work serves as a highly pertinent point of reference for Byatt and Redonnet's narratives. In the case of Byatt in particular, her appropriation of Matisse's human forms would seem to reflect a fascination with the textual representation of the (female) body and how the viewer engages with those representations. As my discussion has revealed, there are further ways in which Byatt and Redonnet's deployment of intertextual references to Matisse's work shares common characteristics—characteristics that have a distinctly 'postmodern' resonance. The weaving of Matissean images into both narratives supports a sustained reflection on the status of works of art as commercial commodities whose meaning is incessantly elaborated within the cultural domain. In addition, Byatt's deliberation on how art speaks to the individual and Redonnet's fictional treatment of art as a channel for memory serves only to stress further the supremacy and endurance of the *image.* That the published versions of these narratives incorporate *reproductions* of works by Matisse into their very fabric renders their reflection on the image and the power it wields all the more compelling.

Notes

1. According to Gérard Genette's use of the term, elements of the 'peritext' include main titles and chapter headings, covers, prefaces, and notes. See Gérard Genette, *Seuils* (Paris: Seuil, 1987), pp. 10-11, 20-37. The 'peritext' combines with the 'epitext' (interviews, letters, and critical reviews) to make up what Genette refers to as the 'paratext' or, according to Graham Allen, 'those elements which lie on the threshold of the text and which help to direct and control the reception of a text by its readers' (Graham Allen, *Intertextuality* (London: Routledge, 2000), p. 103).

2. This is also true of Vintage's 1994 paperback edition of *The Matisse Stories.*

3. Alain Salles, 'Flohic, entre arts et lettres', *Le Monde,* 9 March 2001, p. 10. Other writers featured in the 'Musées secrets' series include: Tahar Ben Jelloun (on Alberto Giacometti), Sylvie Germain (on Jan Vermeer), Andrée Chedid (on Théodore Géricault), and Marie Ndiaye (on J. M. W. Turner).

4. Helen Dunmore, 'Demolish, then Rebuild with Care', *Observer,* 2 January 1994, p. 17.

5. For a useful discussion of Byatt's treatment of art and creativity in *Sugar and Other Stories* (London: Chatto & Windus, 1987), see Jane L. Campbell, 'Confecting Sugar: Narrative Theory and Practice in A. S. Byatt's Short Stories', *Critique: Studies in Contemporary Fiction,* 38 (1997), 105-22.

6. Aine Smith, 'Memory and Identity in Redonnet's Fiction', in *Women's Writing in Contemporary France,* ed. by Gill Rye and Michael Worton (Manchester: Manchester University Press, 2002), pp. 42-52 (p. 44).

7. A. S. Byatt, *Portraits in Fiction* (London: Chatto & Windus, 2001), p. 2.

8. A. S. Byatt, *The Matisse Stories* (London: Vintage), pp. 3-5. All subsequent references to this text will be given in abbreviated form (*MS*) in the main body of the article.

9. Dunmore, 'Demolish, then Rebuild with Care', p. 17.

10. (Paris: Gallimard, 1968), p. 37.

11. Roland Marchand, *Advertising the American Dream: Making Way for Modernity, 1920-40* (Berkeley: University of California Press, 1985), p. 132.

12. Peter Corrigan, *The Sociology of Consumption* (London: Sage, 1997), p. 105. On the ritualized practices involved in 'dwelling' and the 'keeping' of homespace, see Tim Dant, *Material Culture in the Social World: Values, Activities, Lifestyles* (Buckingham: Open University Press, 1999), pp. 69-76.

13. On the principle of 'experimentation' much celebrated by the discourse of advertising, see Corrigan, *The Sociology of Consumption,* p. 180.

14. Lawrence Gowing, *Matisse* (London: Thames and Hudson, 1979).

15. A number of existing essays offer stimulating insights into Marie Redonnet's treatment of the theme of place in her works of narrative fiction up until and including *Silsie* (1990). See e.g. Yvette Went-Daoust, 'Écrire le conte de fées: l'œuvre de Marie Redonnet', *Neophilologus,* 77 (1993), 387-94, and Anne-Marie Picard, 'Dans le paysage, une figure . . . presque féminine: le triptyque de Marie Redonnet', *Australian Journal of French Studies,* 31 (1994), 228-40.

16. Marie Redonnet, *Villa Rosa* (Paris: Flohic, 1996), p. 11. All subsequent references will be given in abbreviated form (*VR*) in the main body of the text.

17. The connection between inheritance and personal identity is repeatedly foregrounded by Redonnet in her fiction. However, in many of her fictional productions, unlike *Villa Rosa,* legacies (in the form of artefacts or properties) tend to be a feature of female-female relations. This is true, for example of *Splendid Hôtel* (1986) and *Rose Mélie Rose* (1987). See Elizabeth Fallaize, 'Filling in the Blank Canvas: Memory, Inheritance and Identity in Marie Redonnet's *Rose Mélie Rose*', *Forum for Modern Language Studies,* 28 (1992), 320-34.
18. These are: Matisse's *La Moulade* (1905), *La Plage rouge* (1905), *Vue de Collioure* (1905), *Paysage à Collioure* (1905).
19. Hillel Schwartz, *The Culture of the Copy: Striking Likenesses, Unreasonable Facsimiles* (New York: Zone Books, 1996), p. 247.
20. This is a feature, in particular, of texts such as Redonnet's collection of short tales entitled *Doublures* (1986), her play *Tir et Lir* (1988), as well as the novels *Rose Mélie Rose* (1987) and *Candy Story* (1992). Evert Van der Starre's discussion of doubling in Redonnet's work is featured in *Jeunes auteurs de Minuit,* edited by Michèle Ammouche-Kremers and Henk Hillenaar (Amsterdam: Rodopi, 1994), pp. 53-67. As numerous critics have pointed out, one of the ways in which this theme is signalled is by means of a play with protagonists' names. In *Rose Mélie Rose,* for example, all the female protagonists featured in the novel are named either Mélie or Rose, while in *Villa Rosa* Henri visits a cabaret bar (*Chez Lola*) where all the singers are named Lola.
21. On the blurring of the distinction between 'quoting' and assimilation effected by postmodern productions, see Fredric Jameson's critique of postmodernism, 'Postmodernism, or the Cultural Logic of Late Capitalism', *New Left Review,* 146 (1984), 53-92 (p. 55).
22. Christien Franken, *A. S. Byatt: Art, Authorship and Creativity* (Basingstoke: Palgrave, 2001), pp. 109, 40-59.
23. *Luxe, calme et volupté* was painted by Matisse in 1904. One of Matisse's best-known works, its title is taken from the refrain in Charles Baudelaire's poem 'L'Invitation au voyage', from the collection *Les Fleurs du mal* (1857). Owing much to the work of Paul Cézanne and using small blocks of rainbow-like colour, the painting depicts a group of female bathers having a picnic on the beach.
24. 'Ce que je rêve, c'est d'un art d'équilibre, de pureté, de tranquillité sans sujet inquiétant ou préoccupant, qui soit pour tout travailleur cérébral, pour tout homme d'affaires aussi bien que pour l'artiste des lettres, un lénifiant, un calmant cérébral, quelque chose d'analogue à un bon fauteuil' (Henri Matisse, 'Notes d'un peintre', *La Grande Revue,* 52 (1908), 731-45).
25. Victoria Glendinning, 'Pleasure Principles', *Times,* 30 December 1993, p. 32.
26. For a useful discussion of Byatt's treatment of the themes of death and mortality in several of her fictional works, see Sue Sorensen, 'Death in the Fiction of A. S. Byatt', *Critique,* 43 (2002), 115-34.
27. For a more detailed discussion of material objects or 'objects-in-use' and their role in social relations, see Celia Lury, *Consumer Culture* (Cambridge: Polity Press, 1996), p. 1, and Dant, *Material Culture,* pp. 1-16.

Maria Margaronis (review date 14 June 2004)

SOURCE: Margaronis, Maria. "Where the Wild Things Are." *The Nation* 278, no. 23 (14 June 2004): 24-8.

[*In the following favorable review, Margaronis discusses the stories in* Little Black Book of Stories *in relation to Byatt's Frederica novels.*]

There's a temptation to begin with death. The dark title of A. S. Byatt's ***Little Black Book of Stories*** suggests it; the phrase is also a riposte to D. H. Lawrence's description of the novel as "the one bright book of life," which was a tormenting orthodoxy of her youth. All five stories here are intimate with the uncanny, animating it in eerie, fleshly forms.

But this black book, like most of Byatt's work, is also full of colors, almost obsessively named: blues and golds, russets and purples, "shades of ink and elephant." The northern sky is "opal and gun-metal, grass-green and crimson, mussel-blue and velvet black," or "trout-dappled, mackerel-shot, turquoise, sapphire, peridot, hot transparent red." Exact, vivid descriptions bring the page to life: "They sniffed the air, which was full of a warm mushroom smell, and a damp moss smell, and a sap smell, and a distant hint of dead ashes." There is no sentiment and little mourning. Death is not so much a human event as a copula—boatman and border guard between animate and inanimate, flesh and memory, life and art.

The stories gravitate toward that boundary, blurring it or reasserting its force, in a prose that remains precise and cool. As Freud pointed out, it's the blending of the familiar with the inexplicable that sends shivers down our spines; Byatt's tales of the supernatural depend on an almost hallucinatory precision for their haunting effects. **"The Thing in the Forest,"** the first story, begins like a fairy tale, but for a crucial, small insertion of doubt—"There were once two little girls who saw, or believed they saw, a thing in a forest"—and goes on to sketch a generic group of children being evacuated from an English city during World War II: "They all had bare legs and scuffed shoes and wrinkled socks. Most had wounds on their knees in varying stages of freshness and scabbiness." The long description contains only one simile, which refers us both to the war and to the shadowy forests of the Brothers Grimm: "They were like a disorderly dwarf regiment, stomping along the platform."

The girls, Penny and Primrose, one dark, one fair, are at once fairy-tale sisters and real English children. No one has told them where they're going, or why; their sense of foreboding is transmitted by the heartbeat of the prose and by the spare and knowing use of metaphor: "the bus bumped along snaking country lanes, under whipping branches, dark leaves on dark wooden arms on a dark sky." The forest, when they enter it, is a recognizable English wood, vivid and slightly sinister to their urban senses. They hear "the chatter and repeated lilt and alarm of invisible birds, high up, further in." They admire "the stiff upright fruiting rods of the Lords and Ladies, packed with fat red berries." Out of these exact observations Byatt conjures up a vile, impossible Thing, which arrives first as a sound and smell and then as a visible worm:

> The rest of its very large body appeared to be glued together, like still-wet papier-mâché, or the carapace of stones and straws and twigs worn by caddis-flies underwater. It had a tubular shape, as a turd has a tubular shape, a provisional amalgam. It was made of rank meat, and decaying vegetation, but it also trailed veils and prostheses of manmade materials, bits of wire-netting, foul dishcloths, wire-wool full of pan scrubbings, rusty nuts and bolts . . .

The Thing is the Loathly Worm of medieval ballads and a version of the postmodern artworks Byatt likes to invent, but it is also, because it is so concretely imagined, incontrovertibly material, present, real. It moves forward relentlessly like time, like stories—and passes the two girls by.

After this the story weakens slightly, as if exhausted by the birth of its prodigy; its mystery is almost hijacked by ideas. Much later, middle-aged and unmarried, Penny and Primrose meet by chance in the same house where they had stayed as children and go back, separately, into the wood. (Here there is an uncharacteristic lapse in continuity: The season changes, overnight, from autumn into spring.) Primrose works as a children's storyteller and lives in a haze of impressions and fantasies. (Byatt's disdain for her shows through a little, cracking the narrative spell.) She follows a squirrel to a mossy tuffet in "the centre" of the wood; although she knows the worm was real she doesn't see it again. It is Penny, a child psychologist concerned with difficult truths, who stumbles on bones and fragments from the monster's meals. She goes in search of it, the horror at the heart of the world, which, in a different kind of tale, might have been called her fate: "It had trampled on her life, had sucked out her marrow, without noticing who or what she was. She would go and face it. What else was there, she asked herself, and answered herself, nothing."

The moral is that the forces shaping our lives are often inaccessible; their apprehension takes effort and accuracy, even a desperate courage, which fairy tales like Primrose's deflect. But of course **"The Thing in the Forest,"** so concrete and convincing, is itself a fairy tale. Like a Möbius strip or a mythological snake, it bites its tail and ends with the sentence that began it, spoken this time by Primrose to children sitting in a circle of little plastic chairs. The story, like the impossible worm-made-out-of-words, itself embodies a paradox, which has to do with fiction and reality.

Byatt wasn't always a writer of tales. Best known in America for *Possession,* her 1990 literary romance, she has published eight novels and six story collections as well as several books of criticism. In Britain she is a literary grande dame, though there is something equivocal about her reputation. *Possession* was a universal success; her other novels have been well reviewed, but sometimes with a polite reticence, as if they were not wholly loved. The complaint most often leveled at them is that they're too intellectually driven, weighed down with references, mired in a forgotten world where readers were assumed to know their Wordsworth and what it is that happens at the end of *A Winter's Tale.* They're certainly bookish books: Byatt is above all a passionate reader, fundamentally concerned with what it means to live in words. But they're also hungry for experience, energized by the conviction that, with a Herculean effort, the world can be made accessible to language and to thought.

Byatt began in the English realist tradition of George Eliot and Iris Murdoch—a tradition morally committed to showing the world as it is, not in the documentary sense but by revealing "the real impenetrable human person" (Murdoch's phrase) against the background of all that eludes human understanding. In an early book-length study Byatt quotes Murdoch shaking her head, as it were, pre-emptively at Primrose: "We are . . . benighted creatures sunk in a reality whose nature we are constantly and overwhelmingly tempted to deform by fantasy." For the intellectual circles of Byatt's youth in 1950s Cambridge, under the stern sign of the critic F.R. Leavis, literature was supposed to seek out truth, to fill the space left empty by religion.

What was a young writer to do with this seductive, paralyzing challenge—especially a woman writer in love with language and ideas? ("Knowledge," she wrote much later, has "its own sensuous pleasure, its own fierce well-being, like good sex, like a day in bright sun on a hot empty beach.") Frederica Potter, the semi-autobiographical heroine of Byatt's tetralogy (*The Virgin in the Garden, Still Life, Babel Tower* and *A Whistling Woman*), doesn't become a novelist at all, although she thinks she should: "I don't have any ideas. I've been educated out of it. Even thinking of it brings on a kind of panic."

Written over a period of more than twenty years, the Frederica novels are the trace of Byatt's struggle with her angel. Taken together, they are a loose, shape-shifting thing, a search for forms that grows and branches with the characters' search for ways to live their lives. Part family saga, part *Bildungsroman,* part cultural history, part novels of ideas, they have at their center the problem of how we know and describe the world—which, for Frederica, is also the problem of how to live in both her body and her mind. In Byatt's best moments, feeling and intellect go hand in hand into uncharted forest, urging each other on. Here is Frederica, in *Babel Tower,* the obsessively verbal woman making love:

> You might think, she thinks, as their bodies join, that there are two beings striving to lose themselves in each other, to become one. The growing heat, the wetness, the rhythmic movements, the hot breath, the slippery skins, inside and out, are one, are part of one thing. But we both need to be separate, she thinks. I *lend myself* to this, the language in her head goes on, with its own rhythm, *I lose myself,* it remarks with gleeful breathlessness. . . .

These lines, with their need to name and describe experience as a thinking woman, owe something to Doris Lessing, but Byatt doesn't have Lessing's strong political spin. *Babel Tower* and *A Whistling Woman* are full of sharp observations about the British 1960s (happenings, cults, the rise of television, the antipsychiatry movement), which Frederica (like Byatt) dislikes for celebrating mindless merging over clarity and precision. But the terms in which she frames them are moral and formal, not social or historical: order against chaos, truth against sincerity, science against religion. Sometimes the weight of ideas threatens to sink the project; characters turn papery, plot machinery lumbers into view. Sometimes the books risk being torn apart by the titanic, muffled struggle going on inside them: Byatt (like Frederica) constantly fights the skein of words in which she is both trammeled and at ease, trying to stub her toe on hard reality. She describes the physical world and works of art, naming colors, scrubbing out every trace of figurative language. (*Still Life,* the best of the series, began as an attempt to give up metaphor completely.) She brings in mathematics, Darwin, DNA, the life of ants and snails. And she turns the conventions of narrative form against itself—which brings us back to death.

Near the end of *Still Life* Frederica's sister, Stephanie, is fatally electrocuted by a fridge. Although her death is not entirely unprepared—Byatt can't resist laying a couple of literary clues—it is shocking nevertheless. We have lived in Stephanie's skin through first love, marriage and the birth of her two children; we know her, love her even. In the world of the novel she has come to stand for feeling, the pull of instinctive life. All our experience of fiction leads us to believe that she will live—or, if she dies, at least die meaningfully.

The accident has a terrible precedent in Byatt's own life: in 1972 her 11-year-old son was killed by a hit-and-run driver. (Her long account of Stephanie's husband's grief is painfully exact.) It also has a theological aspect: Stephanie is married to a clergyman, who is professionally bound to believe in God's care for his creation. Yet Byatt's own explanation of Stephanie's death, given in a lecture in 1999, is formal and literary: "I remember . . . being so angry with D. H. Lawrence for declaring in *Women in Love* that there were no accidents, that every man made his own fate, that I constructed a novel with at least six main characters so that I could imagine a real, unpredicted, random accident at the end of the second volume that my readers would experience as accident."

Something about this virtual murder seems to have set her free, as if she had achieved what she set out to do and had at last struck through to solid rock. Though she returned at length to Frederica and her knotty verbal self, her next book after *Still Life* was *Possession,* which juggles genre and pastiche, satire and fairy tale. The collections of stories and novellas that followed—***The Matisse Stories, Elementals: Stories of Fire and Ice, Angels and Insects, The Djinn in the Nightingale's Eye***—belong to the same stream, mixing the experience of ordinary people with the life of art and myth. In tales and fables, recalcitrant reality is not an elusive thing to be nosed out by searching sentences, but built into the structure: It is the characters' fate. Playing with stories is a way of playing with death—the thing that gives time its shape, the spoiler of plots and plans—as Scheherazade plays with the Sultan's long-deferred desire. "It should have been farce or fable, I see that now," says Gillian Perholt, the heroine of ***The Djinn,*** "and I was writing passion and tragedy and buttons done with verisimilitude. . . . I got all enmeshed in what was realism and what was reality and what was true . . . and my imagination failed."

In the story **"Raw Material"** from the ***Little Black Book,*** Byatt rewrites Stephanie's tragedy as farce, making sudden death the sting in the tail of a fable about realism. Jack Smollett, writing teacher, insists that his students avoid melodrama and write about what they know. His favorite is an elderly lady, author of detailed, Byatt-like accounts of housework in her youth, "reproduced" here in full. Her choice of words is flawless, her pleasure in them shameless; her writing glitters with "contingent quiddity." Her fellow students call her work pedantic, pompous, show-off, over-ornate, but to Smollett it's a revelation, inspiring his own stalled writing: "Miss Fox's brief essays made Jack want to write. They made him see the world as something to be written." The astonishing payoff, rendered in prose as vivid as Miss Fox's, utterly undermines his faith in his art and vindicates the students. As in **"The Thing in the Forest,"** unforeseeable, unbearable reality has the last word—but it has it in a story.

If **"Raw Material"** does a *danse macabre* on realism's grave, **"The Pink Ribbon"** goes still further. Its central consciousness belongs to James, a retired classicist, caring for "Maddy Mad Mado," his wife transformed by Alzheimer's disease; the humiliations and resentments of their life together are drawn unflinchingly. To preserve his own brain cells he reads Virgil at night—*Aeneid* VI, the descent to the underworld. As so often in Byatt, the reading permeates his life, stirring up memories of the Second World War, when the line between the quick and the dead seemed thin and provisional:

> Friends you were meeting for dinner, who lived in your head as you set off to meet them, never came, because they were mangled meat under brick and timber. Other friends who stared in your memory as the dead stare whilst they take up the final shape your memory will give them, suddenly turned up on the doorstep in lumpen living flesh, bruised and dirty . . . and begged for a bed, for a cup of tea.

In Virgil's underworld, those who will be reborn drink from the river Lethe to forget their past. Mado, too, has become a child again, and more: After a visit from a strange young woman in a red silk dress James finds himself invaded by their early love-making, "tooth and claw, feather and velvet, blood and honey."

What is most unnerving in this moving story about memory and loss is the origin of Mado herself. For Iris Murdoch's steeltrap mind was also destroyed by Alzheimer's ("like moth-eaten knitting," says James, echoing Frederica's definition of the novel as "a long thread of language, like knitting, thicker and thinner in patches"). And Murdoch in her late decline was famously soothed, like Mado, by the Teletubbies. The story is at once an act of mourning and of matricide, a murderous tribute crafted out of Byatt's own worst fears and most demanding talent, her relentless honesty. Jack Smollett could not make art out of Miss Fox's end; Byatt has no such compunctions. Bereft of memory the human body is, in more senses than one, no more or less than raw material.

Or is it? **"Body Art"** also probes the tricky seam between what's human and what's merely organic, setting an obstetrician interested in abstract painting against a young woman artist interested in bodies. The doctor has lost his Catholic faith before an awkward carving of the crucifixion; the woman has lost her fertility because of a botched abortion. Hired to help catalogue a collection of medical relics, she uses them to make a sculpture of the goddess Kali, as always meticulously described: "Her four arms were medical prostheses, wooden or gleaming mechanical artefacts, ending in sharp steel and blunt wooden fingers. . . . Her earrings were preserved foetuses, decked with beads. . . . Her crochet hooks were the tools of the nineteenth-century obstetricians, midwives and abortionists." The sculpture comes to represent the battle between doctor and artist for control of the artist's body; the story ends, unexpectedly, with the adoration of a baby: "He was overcome with dreadful love and grief. She was a person. She had not been there and now she was there, and she was the person he loved." But **"Body Art"** is no antiabortion tract. As Kali brings together creation and destruction, the birth of the baby simply shows the other face of fate. Emerging from the story's tangles as the Thing emerged from its forest, it brings with it a sudden and disarming clarity, a different confrontation with reality's mystery.

The Frederica tetralogy also ends with a surprising pregnancy, which follows a performance of *A Winter's Tale* in which Stephanie's daughter seems momentarily to reincarnate her mother. But Byatt has only limited tolerance for symbolic babies or the idea of art as consolation: For her, art is a more unyielding and inhuman thing. The central story in the ***Little Black Book*** is a countermyth to the story of Pygmalion, whose perfect statute was brought to life by Venus, and to Hermione's transformation from stone to living woman at the end of Shakespeare's play. In Byatt's version a lexicographer undone by grief finds herself turning to stone, not smoothly and generically but in specific excrescences: "flakes of silica and nodes of basalt," "bubbles of sinter," "layers of hornblende," "dikes of dolerites." Being an etymologist she searches for herself in dictionaries and relishes the "lovely words: pyrolusite, ignimbrite, omphacite, uvarovite, glaucophane, schist, shale, gneiss, tuff." As she stiffens in her mineral carapace the prose becomes encrusted with polysyllabic nouns, embodying her in lapidary sentences.

In **"A Stone Woman"** all the borders are blurred: art and nature, organic and inorganic, living and dead. Rocks, thinks the lexicographer, are often formed from things that once were living; the names of stones are full of organic metaphors: "Carnelian is from carnal, from flesh." Her metamorphosis is, as usual, painstakingly imagined from within. A sculptor takes her to Iceland to record and decorate her; red thread-worms burrow in her crevices; her slow thoughts "rumble" in her stony mind. Eventually she finds ecstatic liberation in the northern hills, running like one of Picasso's great stone women to meet the shadowy figures who live among the rocks. "Preserving solitude and distance, staying cold and frozen," Byatt once wrote, "may, for women as well as artists, be a way of preserving life."

To Lawrence's "one bright book of life," Byatt has opposed a set of crystalline stories, mined from deep structures in the human brain. In fables she has found a way to contain the paradox of realism—its necessary artifice—without giving up on reality: Her most extravagant visions depend on precise representations of a palpable world. She is an athlete of the imagination, breaking barriers without apparent effort; at a time when British writers tend to have their eyes on the Atlantic, she has placed herself in an old tradition that runs from ancient myth to Italo Calvino, from Iceland to Arabia. But still, I hope she will not turn her back on novels and their struggle with history. There's something in the messy latitude, the restless searching after truth, the vital imperfection of the Frederica books that feels especially necessary in these nightmarish, bedazzled days.

Jewelle Gomez (review date July 2004)

SOURCE: Gomez, Jewelle. "The Failure to Communicate." *The Women's Review of Books* XXI, nos. 10-11 (July 2004): 12.

[*In the following positive review of Byatt's* Little Black Book of Stories, *Gomez argues that communication is a central theme in the collection.*]

The varied ways in which human beings can be mute are difficult to convey, especially on the page. The unintelligible mutterings of the young Helen Keller were not the same as a silence emerging from ignorance. Wordless terror is different from speechless joy, yet they both might be notated on paper with an exclamation point. In her new collection of short fiction [***Little Black Book of Stories***], A. S. Byatt conveys a variety of inarticulate states successfully, and each time in an inventive manner that finds the reader eagerly leaning forward to hear better.

Several of the stories spring from the realm of speculative fiction; however, this is not an attempt by Byatt to avoid ordinary human conflict. Her approach throws into sharp relief the nuanced facets of the emotional lives of her characters. Still, at every turn, Byatt makes it clear that the elements that make the heart beat are eternally mysterious and impossible to articulate.

"A Stone Woman," the most fantastical story of the collection, is a voluptuous evocation of a drastic change that makes speech superfluous. After the death of her closest companion, her mother, a woman finds herself "flitting lightly from room to room, in the twilit apartment, like a moth." But before she can adjust to this weightlessness she begins a startling transmutation.

> She noticed . . . a spangling of what seemed like a glinting red dust, or ground glass, in the folds of her dressing-gown and her discarded underwear. It was a dull red, like dried blood, which does not have a sheen.
>
> (pp. 117-118)

Then: "One day she found a cluster of greenish-white crystals sprouting in her armpit." It's a mutation that, on the face of it, would seem to be from life to death, from motion to stasis, but in fact this proves untrue.

The transition proceeds relentlessly, more fascinating than frightening to the woman whose flesh begins to be occupied by a cascade of stones and gems.

> [A] necklace of veiled swellings above her collar-bone . . . broke slowly through the skin like eyes from closed lids, and became opal—fire opal, black opal, geyserite and hydrophane, full of watery light.
>
> (p. 120)

Making the transition is no simple task; she becomes less and less attached to the "living" world and the friend who aids her:

> He was becoming insubstantial . . . She had to cup her basalt palm around her ear to hear his great voice, which sounded like the whispering of grasshoppers.
>
> (p. 151)

Byatt's description of the metamorphosis and its effect on the woman and the one person she trusts is riveting. The author's spare language and use of Icelandic mythology evoke rich colors and textures for something—stone—that we are normally more likely to tread upon than to notice. She weighs the value of human communication against the mute world of symbiotic existence. The final triumph of this story is her exploration of the breadth of life that geological formations can represent, and the fulfillment that might be found among them. Byatt conjures a massive bulk of stones, assumed to be silent, but gives them a vibrantly articulated presence as they envelop the woman who was meant to be them.

Another story, **"Body Art,"** approaches the theme of silence more opaquely. It opens, "There was a customary banter in the Gynae Ward at St. Pantaleon's, about the race to bear the Christmas Day Baby." Dr. Damian Becket, on duty tending to mothers and their newborns, is a jumble of distractions who can barely remember when he slept last or the names of his patients. He does not, however, take his lapse lightly. He's a good obstetrician who appears to understand his personal limitations yet is unable to imagine compensating for or outgrowing them. When he meets Daisy, an erstwhile visual art student who lurks about the hospital on the verge of starvation, he's drawn to her. But he can't grasp hold of the connections that would make communication possible.

> He asked her about herself. He was not good at this. He was a good doctor, but he had no skill at talking, no ease of manner, he didn't in fact *want* to know the details of other human lives, except in so far as he needed to know facts and histories in order to save those lives. He was unaware that his conventional good looks were to a certain extent a substitute for amiability.
>
> (p. 53)

Damian becomes fascinated with the emaciated young artist who dedicates her days to decorating the hospital ward and disappears mysteriously every night. He impulsively sets about finding work and lodging for her, but his inability to bridge their communication gap leaves him bumbling unimpressively. Daisy, an acerbic, petulant, wounded child herself, is not an easy subject for rescue; she's the drowning swimmer who would sink her rescuer with her.

Although it may be that Damian's last name is coincidental, the story is, in many ways, like a Beckett play, where the pauses are the substance of the piece. It is there that the uncertainty and the possibility lie. But the characters' inability to articulate what they feel, fear, or want often poisons that space. Daisy and Damian's encounters become a comedic series of cryptic half phrases that barely touch the surface of what each of the characters wants to say.

The plot has its twists, but what stays with you are the silent turns that Byatt crafts so well. At the end of this story, what is most affecting is that none of the characters can really speak cogently, and that words would not have been able to contain the fierceness of the life inside of them anyway. Shaping her phrases like a poet, Byatt conveys the tremulous anxiety of the unspoken decisions her characters must make, decisions that will change everything.

"The Pink Ribbon" is a blend of naturalistic and speculative fiction that also depends on the inability of its central figures to communicate with each other. James, along with a home care attendant, nurses his wife, who is succumbing to Alzheimer's. The woman who'd spoken "like a radio announcer" before their marriage now answers sounds from the cupboard in "a rough Cockney voice, shrill and childish."

Their relationship has devolved into the impersonal details of care taking—but James' memories of their romantic past persist. Sadly, the state of his wife's recollections is less reliable. Their interactions around memory become the stumbling block. Can he survive if she doesn't remember him? And how can he know what she remembers if she can't talk to him? When a ghostly, attractive woman arrives at his door it is ultimately their conversations that enable James to understand what his failing wife might want to say.

In this story, as in **"The Stone Woman"** and others, Byatt uses fantasy elements to deepen the emotionality of the characters, much as Edith Wharton did in her often overlooked ghost stories. Their styles are, of course, worlds apart: Byatt has tamed the excesses of the popular minimalist style, creating lean, poetic narrative that doesn't feel obscure; Wharton reined in the stout layers of Jamesian language that might have drowned her.

Where they are similar is in how they successfully layer the fantastic over a solid undercurrent of emotional reality. Like Wharton, Byatt is able to blend the real and surreal to create sparkling, clear, and often painful vistas of humanity.

Byatt's stories are polished gems, each mined from a different universe but each about characters whose words are rendered unavailable or inadequate. Fortunately for us, Byatt herself suffers from no such affliction.

Lucy Lethbridge (review date 4 October 2004)

SOURCE: Lethbridge, Lucy. "A Way with Words." *America* 191, no. 9 (4 October 2004): 17-18.

[*In the following mixed review, Lethbridge investigates storytelling as a major thematic focus in* Little Black Book of Stories.]

In **"The Thing in the Forest,"** the opening story of A. S. Byatt's latest collection [***Little Book of Stories***], two young girls, evacuated during the last war to the English countryside, witness a monstrous creature in a sunlit wood. Rolling toward them, devouring everything in their path, comes a grotesque worm that appears to be created out of the trees and leaves themselves, to be integral to the forest even as it destroys it. "It and its stench passed within a few feet of their tree trunk, humping along, leaving behind it a trail of bloody slime and dead foliage, sucked to dry skeletons."

This story, a revisiting of the ancient English folk legend of the Loathly Worm, returns to familiar A. S. Byatt territory. With its themes of storytelling and memories woven into myths and fairy tales, it is a story about stories. And all the tales in this collection in some way return, obsessively even, to this central theme, the telling of stories, the way in which memory distorts and enriches experience, and the way in which all readers and tellers of stories are fed by the same cultural springs of ancient myth. Byatt is fascinated by words, by the sound and shape of them, by the music of lists, and by etymology and how one can unravel in a single word a hundred skeins, different histories and unexpected connections.

In **"A Stone Woman,"** Ines, a New Yorker (and a dictionary compiler), finds herself literally hardening into stone: "One day she found a cluster of greenish-white crystals sprouting in her armpit. These she tried to prise away and failed. They were attached deep within; they could be felt to be stirring stony roots under the skin surface, pulling the muscles. Jagged flakes of silica and nodes of basalt pushed her breasts upward and flourished under the fall of flesh, making her clothes crackle and rustle." Under the protection of a cemetery stonecutter, Ines goes to Iceland and, as the winter sets in, is drawn inexorably to take her part in an Icelandic folk legend about stone creatures who beckon the living into the high crags in a wild dance: ". . . figures, spinning and bowing in a rapid dance on huge, lithe, stony legs, beckoning with expansive gestures, flinging their great arms wide in invitation." In **"The Pink Ribbon,"** the elderly James, a classicist caring for his senile wife, Mado, is visited by a beautiful young woman who identifies herself as "the Fetch." She tells him she has come to take his wife: "There are many things in heaven and earth you can't see, James. The etheric body can get separated—from the clay. It can wander in churchyards. It needs to be set free. As she needs to be set free."

The stories in ***Little Black Book*** are all beautiful to look at. Byatt has a way of using words as though they are individual treasures that have been patiently sifted from a muddy riverbed. She picks them over, dwells on them, makes them jewel-like to her reader. "And now as she wandered on, she saw and recognised them, windflower and bryony, self-heal and dead nettle, and had—despite where she was—a lovely lapping sense of invisible—just invisible life swarming in the leaves and along the twigs, despite where she was, despite what she had not forgotten having seen there."

But, despite this writer's virtuosity, these stories do not really live. It is difficult to pinpoint exactly why this is. While reading them, one is impressed—often brought up short with admiration—by the author's superior literary sensibility, by the research and knowledge that are so seamlessly woven into the narrative, by the swoops of imaginative intellect that draw themes together so fascinatingly. But I for one never really cared a jot for any of the characters that inhabit them. All too often, in fact, it seemed Byatt's people, all of them clearly starting off as good, fleshed-out characters, before long became rock-hard ciphers for their creator's larger ideas. There is more than a touch of didacticism to Byatt's writing—and her characters are made into dictionary compilers, classicists, doctors, professional storytellers or stone masons, not so that we can learn about them, but so that through them Byatt can instruct us on the subject of one of her own hobbyhorses. There are flashes of humor, but they are few. In **"Raw Material"** she does an amusing parody of the list of books written by a creative writing class (and anyone who has read *Possession* will know what a superb parodist she can be), but it is rather a tired target. Unfortunately, many of the stories in ***Little Black Book*** seem to peter out as if exhausted by their own ideas. It is as if the delicate bones of plot and character were simply crushed under the weight of all that rich and lovely language.

Jane Campbell (essay date 2004)

SOURCE: Campbell, Jane. *"Sugar and Other Stories."* In *A. S. Byatt and the Heliotropic Imagination,* pp. 81-106. Waterloo, Ontario, Canada: Wilfrid Laurier University Press, 2004.

[*In the following excerpt, Campbell offers an overview of Byatt's style and themes in* Sugar and Other Stories.]

Byatt's first collection of short stories, ***Sugar and Other Stories*** (1987), extends her exploration of the relationship of art and reality. Byatt says that she turned to this form, relatively late in her career, because of her awareness of the shortness of the time for writing: "I suddenly realised that there were more and more and more things in the world that I noticed, and that I haven't got enough life to write already the novels I have thought of. . . . And so I started seeing things in this very condensed clear way, as images, not necessarily to be strung together in a long narrative, but to be thought out from" (Chevalier, "Entretien" 26). What the characters and the narrator—who are usually intimately related—make of the images is what the stories are about. The difficult process of "extracting meaning from experience" (Spufford 23), central in the four novels that preceded ***Sugar,*** is brought into sharper focus by the compression of the new form. With two exceptions, **"The July Ghost"** and **"Precipice-Encurled,"** the stories are narrated from the perspective of their female central characters. Even in the two exceptions, women characters—in each story, women who experience premature loss—are poignant presences. Several of the stories make feminist statements—concerning, for example, the discouragement of girls from academic achievement, the domination of women's lives by the needs of aging parents, and the social and cultural oppression of postmenopausal women—but Byatt's most significant feminist contribution is quieter and more pervasive. It lies in the steady, compassionate gaze she directs on the minutiae of women's lives, in the depiction of the female imagination, and in the qualities of endurance, courage, and hopefulness that her characters display in painful, often desperate situations.

In its progressive melding together of thematic and narrative strands and its steadily increasing focus on the shaping work of the imagination, the ordering of the eleven stories represents the process of confection that is Byatt's metaphor for storytelling. The first four, **"Racine and the Tablecloth," "Rose-Coloured Teacups," "The July Ghost,"** and **"The Next Room,"** are linked by the motif of parent-child relationships. Next comes a pair, **"The Dried Witch"** and **"Loss of Face,"** both set in Korea. (The nation is not named, however; the reader is left to deduce the setting from the narrator's clues.) **"The Dried Witch"** provides an implicit comment on **"Loss of Face."** Only with the seventh story does the figure of the writer become central. **"On the Day That E. M. Forster Died"** and **"The Changeling"** present two vignettes about women writers: the first is a sympathetic portrait, the second sharply critical. **"In the Air"** repeats from **"The Dried Witch"** the figure of the solitary, threatened woman, but transports her from a Korean peasant village to a British urban setting. The last two stories, **"Precipice-Encurled"** and **"Sugar,"** openly reflect on the relationship of the imagined and the real. The first features two Victorian males, a poet and a painter; the second a contemporary woman writer and her family history. With **"Sugar"** the collection comes full circle: the adult narrator shares with her dying father the same respect for justice and truth that the girl Emily in the first story projects onto her imaginary Reader. Both the child Emily in the first story and the adult in the last story contain aspects of the author. Byatt, who suffered at the Mount School from the lack of value placed on individual achievement, has also said that when she began to write, she too constructed an ideal Reader (Dusinberre, "A. S. Byatt" 188; Chevalier, "Entretien" 25). The narrator of **"Sugar,"** the only first-person narrator in the collection, is Byatt herself, "the daughter of my father, trying desperately to be accurate" (qtd. in Wachtel, "A. S. Byatt" 89). Emily's understanding, like her power, is limited; the mature woman writer who speaks in **"Sugar"** exemplifies the richness and variety of women's creativity. Taken in sequence, the stories move from the more realistic to the more metafictional end of the scale. The confecting process, the imagination's shaping activity, itself emerges gradually as the subject; simultaneously, the reader, warily addressed in **"Racine,"** is invoked more confidingly in **"Sugar."** The collection fits into the category that Patricia Waugh places at the centre of the spectrum of metafiction: "those texts that manifest the symptoms of formal and ontological insecurity but allow their deconstructions to be finally recontextualized or 'naturalized' and given a total interpretation" (*Metafiction* 19).

"Racine and the Tablecloth" is about a power struggle in a girl's school; it is also about the making of moral and literary judgments and the destructive power of language. The protagonist, Emily Bray, confronts her antagonist, the headmistress, Martha Crichton-Walker. A third figure is Emily's imaginary Reader, for whom she writes her essays: "He was dry and clear, he was all-knowing but not messily infinite. He kept his proportion and his place. He had no face and no imaginary arms to enfold or heart to beat: his nature was not love, but understanding. . . . It is not too much to say that in these seemingly endless years in that place Emily was enabled to continue because she was able to go on believing in the Reader" (6). In opposition to the silent impartiality of the Reader, Emily perceives the "essential denial" (1) of Miss Crichton-Walker, who uses language to condemn: she labels Emily's laboured handwriting "aggressive" and her essays "nastily presented": "the judgment dropped in heavily and fast, like a stone into a pond, to rest unshifted on the bottom" (5). When Emily, in an act of mild rebellion, disobeys the school's rules by walking back from church by a private shortcut, Miss Crichton-Walker finds her looking at a willow tree and calls her act of walking back alone "depraved" (or did Emily invent the word? In any case, "the word must have been in the air . . . for her to pick up" [9]).

Socially awkward, unathletic, and scholarly, Emily is a misfit among the other girls; she clings miserably to her belief that "at the end of the tunnel there was, there must be, light and a rational world full of aspiring Readers" (20). In the face of the headmistress's insistence that the academic achievement of girls must not be valued too highly—"there [is] as much lasting value, as much pleasure for others, in a well-made tablecloth as in a well-written book" (21)—Emily is determined to excel in her finals and especially to do justice to her passion, the works of Racine. She relates the tablecloth example to her great-aunt Florence, who, prevented by the needs of others from fulfilling her dream of travelling, spent her days doing embroidery until arthritis stopped that too. After this vision of her own possible fate, Emily becomes "double"; she breaks into a "feeling part" that has "given up" and a "thinking part" that "chattered away toughly" (25) as she prepares for her examinations. Crying uncontrollably except when she is actually writing the papers, she manages to achieve the highest marks in the school's records.

Near the end of this story of the oppression of women—in this case most directly by other women—the narrator asks who has won. She shows Emily as an adult, having "made up" her "account" (5) and passed judgment on Miss Crichton-Walker, appearing to win (going to university, specializing in French, marrying happily, having clever daughters, and working part-time as a translator) yet also feeling, though "in a fluctuating and intermittent way," that she has "somehow lost"

(30). The story ends by moving on to the next generation, where the pattern of thwarted female ambition threatens to repeat itself. Emily confronts authority at her daughter Sarah's school and insists that Sarah, who is good at both French and mathematics, be allowed to do both; the authority, now ironically represented in the male figure of the headmaster, accuses Emily of projecting her own "unfulfilled ambitions" on her daughter. In an updated but still sexist version of Miss Crichton-Walker's rhetoric, he says that his school cares about "the whole human being": it exists to educate Sarah "for forming personal relations, running a home, finding her place in society, understanding her responsibilities" (31). Emily, hearing the echo of Miss Crichton-Walker's "old mild voice" (31), leaves in defeat. Sarah, however, is glimpsed briefly: she has created her own (now ungendered) Reader and lays out her solution to a problem in geometry "for the absent scanning of an unfalteringly accurate mind, to whose presence she required access" (31-32). The open ending puts the reader in the position of judge, replacing the two actual authority figures and the two imagined readers, and charged with creating a future in which Sarah's heliotropic imagination can turn toward its own sun. "You can believe, I hope, you can afford to believe, that [Sarah] made her way into its light" (32), says the narrator.

"Racine and the Tablecloth" grimly demonstrates the horror of manipulation and coercion. It also shows self-reflexively that too much control will lead to a breakdown of order. By interspersing interludes of disorder and misrule with the episodes of imprisonment, Byatt demonstrates the imagination's need for openness and freedom. The girls and their counterparts at a boys' school conspire to reverse the girls' and boys' seating at church; the girls (unconsciously countering Miss Crichton-Walker's neatly allegorical, moralizing stories) concoct stories of their headmistress swinging naked in the garden. But Emily cannot participate in these carnivalesque trespasses, nor can she confront the headmistress directly through speech. As Laurent Lepaludier has shown, she must find her own form of opposition: her essays, especially her analysis of Racine's texts, provide her with "artistic discourse in its perfection" (42).[1] Emily is fascinated by Racine's control of passionate excess, holding it within "the flexible, shining, inescapable steel mesh of that regular, regulated singing verse" (17). However, in contrast to Racine's beautiful but rigid form, Byatt's form allows for indeterminacy. Despite the depressing similarity of the mother's and daughter's situations (with, in the background, two earlier generations of self-sacrificing, caregiving women, Great-Aunt Florence and Emily's mother), there is some hopefulness in this story: in the strength of the four generations of women, in Sarah's ability to excel at both a "female" and a "male" subject, and in the handing over of the ending to a non-mythical, small *r* reader whom the narrator, after a rather skittish earlier relationship, now appears willing to trust.

The second story, **"Rose-Coloured Teacups,"** is much briefer, encompassing only a few moments in the consciousness of Veronica, the main character. It again explores women's history and its repetition through four generations. Veronica, middle-aged mother of two daughters, tries repeatedly to visualize her own mother as a student, waiting with friends in a college room to entertain a group of male students—one of whom is to be Veronica's father—at a tea party. Her imagination creates the scene only to the point of the young men's arrival and the mother's smile of "pure pleasure, pure hope, almost content. She could never see any further: from there, it always began again, chairs, tablecloth, sunny window, rosy teacups, a safe place" (38). The teacups represent the irretrievable past, the fragility of loved objects, and the barriers between the generations. They had been passed on to Veronica by her mother's friend "to take back a new generation to the college" (36), but Veronica, disliking their old-fashioned prettiness, had allowed most of them to break, although she now finds the surviving pieces "exquisitely pretty" (38). Her reverie about this tea party is her only form of mourning for her mother, who had become embittered at being trapped by marriage and children. Her mother had tried to hold on to her happy past by seeing Veronica at the same college but had then felt "excluded . . . from her own memories of the place. The past had been made into the past, discontinuous from the present" (37). Now Veronica experiences the same discontinuity with her daughter Jane as Jane impatiently breaks the sewing machine on which Veronica's grandmother had made clothes for Veronica's mother. Veronica, hearing "in her mind's ear" her mother's "howling plaint" about the smashed teacups—"how *could* you"—restrains herself from reproducing that fury against the new generation, and again, as in the first story, there is the possibility of a happier future. Veronica and her sisters all "partly evaded" (37) their mother's frustrations. Veronica has not vented her mother's anger on her daughter, and the physical features of the older generations persist in benign recombination: Jane has her father's eyes and the "wide and shapely smile" (38) that Veronica has imagined as belonging to the young man at the tea party, Jane's grandfather.

"The July Ghost" and **"The Next Room"** are ironically contrasting ghost stories. In the first, a mother who (like Byatt herself) has lost her eleven-year-old son acquires a lodger who sees the boy's ghost; the mother, who longs to see the boy, cannot do so. In the second, a daughter who has faithfully nursed her widowed mother and believes herself to be free, at fifty-nine, to live her own life, finds herself pursued by the quarrelling, complaining voices of her parents. In both stories, time defeats hope and creativity, keeping pain alive. These stories also introduce another narrative thread in the collection; like **"The Dried Witch,"** they contain the weird or strange, "what haunts"—elements that, Byatt says, she wanted to use the short story form to "accommodate" (Chevalier, "Entretien" 13).

"The July Ghost" is told through the consciousness of an unnamed male character who, in the first sentence, confides to an American woman at a party, "I think I must move out of where I'm living" (39). This, it turns out, is the second time he says these words. The first time, also at a party, he says them to Imogen, who, hearing that his lover Anne has left him, suggests that he become her lodger. Near the end of the story, after the man has narrated some of his experience to his American friend, he packs his bags, intending to move to the house where she is staying. The ending itself, however, leaves his departure in question. Within this framework of repetition is the ghost story (if that is an appropriate label—it has some of the conflicting possibilities of Henry James's *Turn of the Screw*). The man repeatedly sees a boy in Imogen's garden and then (in her presence) in the house, and learns from her that her son, who was the same age and wore the same clothes, had been killed in a traffic accident two years earlier and that her prolonged, isolating grief has driven her husband away. The man tells Imogen what he has seen, and she confesses that after the boy's death she had hoped to "go mad enough" to see him again and had once half seen a "ghost of his face." But she had resolved to do no outward mourning; she had willed herself not even to dream of him: "Only my body wouldn't stop waiting and all it wants is to—to see that boy" (47). The man becomes convinced that the boy wants him to make love to Imogen in order to re-engender the boy in another child. He does not ask the boy for confirmation: "Possibly this was out of delicacy. . . . Possibly there were other reasons. Possibly he was mistaken: the situation was making him hysterical" (52). He tries to comfort Imogen with sex, but she, passive but receptive at first, becomes immobilized and begins to scream. When he sees the boy again, he uses the same expression as her husband, Noel, had used to Imogen before he left her, that he cannot "get through" (42, 55), and asks the boy to release him. Meanwhile, he has made the experience into a story, giving the American woman a "bowdlerized version" (49), which presents the boy as only the dead boy's look-alike, just as he had, earlier, given Imogen a softened, abbreviated version of his loss of Anne.

Not only Imogen and the man but also the American woman, who has come to England to get away from a love affair with her married professor and who, it seems, is about to begin an affair with her new friend, are trapped in eerie repetition. When the man, having told his version of the story, confesses that he now feels that he and Imogen are no longer helping each other and that he must leave, she says that he has to live his life. He repeats, "Yes . . . , I've tried to get through, I have my life to live" (54)—repeating Noel's words as well as the woman's. Imogen and the lodger ponder the grammar of loss. When Imogen heard her son was dead, she thought, "is dead . . . it's a continuous present tense" (47). The man, in his turn, feels that "Anne was worse lost because voluntarily absent" (48); as he prepares to make love to Imogen, he thinks of Anne and, in another linguistic formulation of loss, "what was never to be again" (53). As the man packs to leave Imogen's house, he feels that the boy may want him to stay: "as he stood helplessly there, the boy turned on him again the brilliant, open, confiding, beautiful desired smile" (56). The end, like the interpretation, is left open. Have his own experience of loss and his intuition of Imogen's needs created what he saw? Has he, as Imogen suggests, tried to do her psychic work for her? "I am too rational to go mad," she says, "so I seem to be putting it on you" (50). The story shows, in Imogen, the tension of repressed feeling and, in the man, the human need to shape experience by narratives that accommodate it; at the same time, it explores the possibility of surviving presences. The meaning of time and the function of memory (including the question of whether memories can be communicated by one person to another) are hauntingly mysterious in this story. What is indisputable is the power of loss.[2]

"The Next Room" begins with Molly Hope's cremation and her daughter Joanna's sense of relief. "She had dutifully given her mother a large part of her life"; now that her mother is "free carbon molecules and potash" (58), she hopes to be able to travel again on the foreign tours that her work had offered her before her mother's illness. Certain, like Imogen, that death ends everything and, like her, self-controlled and rational, she dismisses a toothache as psychosomatic until its persistence forces her to allow her colleague and former lover Mike to make a dental appointment for her. At this point her certainty about the finality of death begins to be countered by other versions: a television program in which a North American Indian speaks of his ancestors still living "in the grass and trees and stones we know and love" (65); a conversation with her co-worker Bridget (who has replaced her as Mike's assistant), who in Japan "had breakfast every day with the family's grandfather, who was dead" (67); most insistently of all, the "well-polished narration" (69) of the near-death experience of Bonnie Roote, a fellow patient at the dentist's. Bonnie had seen her mother's idea of heaven, a bungalow and peonies, and her dead relatives waiting, with her mother, for her. Joanna rejects Bonnie's story and her footnote, that their meeting was brought about by higher powers because of Joanna's need to hear it. She recalls her mother's complaints of hearing the quarrelling voices of Joanna's grandparents, waiting for her in the room next to her bedroom. Joanna herself now begins to repeat this experience, hearing her own parents' voices arguing. The voices persist even in a Durham hotel room, where Mike, after shattering her vision of travelling again to the desert—"the African moon faded and the horizon contracted like a brace" (76)—has sent her on an assignment. Here, one of her interviews provides a darker instance of Bonnie's comfortable belief in planned coincidences; she talks to an unemployed steelworker, now, like her, "written off" (82) by a changing society. Depressed by the evidence, Joanna is forced to revise her own version. Why should the dead be different from the living, she asks—"Why should not the worst and most tenacious aspects of our characters persist longest?" For the voices are attached not to her parents' house, but to "her own blood and presence" (83). Like the Christmas cactus "Joanna Hope," bred by her father and perpetuating the ironic family name, the individual life is determined, "bearing its eternal genes which dictate its form and future forever and forever" (83) and ensuring that she, confined, disappointed and angry as her parents and grandparents had been, will "in her turn pass, none too quietly, into that next room" (84). Having determined as a young woman to live differently from her mother, she, like her, has been trapped. The presence of the dead among the living is for Joanna a terrifying reality.

In the next two stories, the clash of cultures hinted at in **"The Next Room"** is foregrounded. Set in Korea, these stories present conflicting views of the same culture, for the first, **"The Dried Witch,"** shows a woman ritually killed by the same decadent society that in the second, **"Loss of Face,"** has become enshrined in a museum. If it were not for the harsh perspective given by the first, the second would invite us to romanticize the primitive aspect of the society. Moreover, the central figure in **"Loss of Face,"** a British woman scholar at a literary conference, aspires to a global perspective that precludes the privileging of any culture, any language, and that, inevitably, fails at a crucial moment, defeated by the limitations of her own culture.

In **"The Dried Witch"** an old woman, A-Oa, has reached the "dry" time of her life. She has lost her children, her husband has been taken by the army, and her brother-in-law, Da-Shin, with whom she had lived, sharing the only bed and forbidden to touch by the taboos (which prescribed death for the woman, presumed to be the temptress, and expulsion, rarely enforced, for the man), has mysteriously vanished. A-Oa recognizes her opposite number in Kun, an aging, effeminate old man, alone and childless like her. Both "singletons on the edge of the circle, not woven in by kin or obligation" (88), they are marginalized, but Kun, as a male, has power. Because he spies on them, the other villagers fear him; his wife has been executed for (allegedly) trying to bewitch him, and it was after Da-Shin had been followed by Kun that he disappeared. Now A-Oa sets out to make herself feared in the only way available to her: by becoming a jinx. Following the instructions of the female shaman, she sets up an altar in her kitchen, where she is safe from Kun's observation because of the taboo forbidding men to enter the woman's part of the house, and she lays out objects to dry or, if already dry, to be plumped out. She becomes accepted as a jinx and when a young man, Cha-Hun, comes to her for a charm to win (in a repetition of Da-Shin's relationship to A-Oa herself) the forbidden love of his sister-in-law An-At, she provides it, although she is "privately sure" it is "unnecessary" (104). She knows that Kun has learned of her complicity. When the young woman becomes pregnant and when Cha-Hun's young brother, A-Oa's first "cure," is found dead, the "witch" is resigned to her fate: "Let us look into this, Kun said, as she had always known he would say" (105). The lovers accuse her of putting them under a spell, and Cha-Hun, frantic to save himself, repeats, at Kun's prompting, the traditional remedy: "We sun the jinx. We put the jinx to dry in the sun" (107). A victim of Kun's manipulation of the debased collective imagination of the villagers, who take up the cry, A-Oa experiences the ultimate dryness. Tied to a stump in the burning sun, her body dies horribly. Some of her last thoughts are of An-At; she wonders if she—another victim of patriarchy—will be beheaded. Yet in the end, seeing a tree nearby burst into flames, she experiences power and creativity. Remembering the superstition that a jinx can set trees on fire, her imagination dances to the sound of the flames, and the last image, as her mind and body separate, is of freedom: "The eddies of heat . . . took her with them, away from the strapped and cracking thing, away" (111).[3]

In **"Loss of Face,"** a reconstructed version of A-Oa's village is visited by Celia Quest, a British literary scholar whose name echoes E. M. Forster's Adela Quested in *A Passage to India.* Like Adela, who wants to see the real India, Celia tries to approach the foreign culture with openness. Their hosts at the conference show the Western visitors their folk village, which preserves their vanishing past. All occupations are represented—there is even a female shaman (Celia knows from her guidebook, one of the many texts that compete for authority within the story, that the country is "Confucian, Buddhist, Catholic, residually shamanistic" [114]). Their guide, Professor Moon, explains the segregation of the women's quarters, and Celia, thinking, in terms of her own scholarship, of lares and penates, asks if there is an altar. Professor Moon avoids answering, making her aware that she has "trespassed" (121), and instead points out the contrast between the ugly Western clothes of the modern Koreans and the beautiful traditional dress of the folk dancers, and demonstrates his own skill at Korean kite flying. Celia realizes that she can never escape the language and images of her origins: she cannot help substituting Chinese kites for those he describes, and, like the Korean people themselves, is torn between two visions. When she next sees Professor Moon, she reflects that although she has been in his company for three days, she knows nothing about him; he has become for her "what she was aware of not knowing, a form of absence" (122). Meanwhile, the reader who has moved from **"The Dried Witch"** can fill in some of the blanks: the uses of a household altar, the consequences of the rigid separation of the sexes.

Celia's experience of linguistic and cultural difference in Korea is summed up in the image of the Tower of Babel, which—again pointing to the impossibility of separating ourselves from familiar landscapes—she associates with Breughel's painting. Representing fractured speech and the resulting cultural differences, the Tower of Babel duplicates itself in the two plate-glass towers where the conference takes place: the lecture tower which, following Asian superstition, has no fourth floor, and the hotel tower, which, in deference to Western fears, has no thirteenth. Further exploration of linguistic barriers occurs when Celia wonders how her Asian audience hears Milton's linguistic transitions and what they see when they read of George Eliot's sense of place. Yet these scholars can meet Celia on her intellectual ground: Professor Sun corrects her view of the English Civil War, and (unlike Celia's students) he can suspend his disbelief in Milton's "patriarchally predestined cosmology" (113). Celia is aware of the ironies involved, for both sides, in these acts of cultural appropriation. She realizes that if art is, as she believes and as T.S. Eliot implies, "a work of rescue," the decision to privilege some fragments in this way entails the failure to "canonize" others (120). She knows that there can never be a complete and universally accessible text. Yet she makes a disastrous faux pas at the concluding banquet. Seated beside what she takes to be a "younger, gentler, more shy" (123) version of Professor Sun, she assumes that he is a young lecturer and asks his name. He retrieves his name tag from his pocket and she sees in horror that "He was not like Professor Sun, he *was* Professor Sun. Not to have known him was to annihilate everything that had been said or acted, to break the frail connections that had been made" (126). She, who prided herself on enjoying difference, has failed to distinguish his face from other Korean faces. By losing his face she has herself lost face. After discussing Harold Bloom's *Map of Misreading* with her fellow scholars, she herself has misread. The title, **"Loss of Face,"** is a triple pun, for history has deprived the Koreans of their collective identity, their national face. Colonial rule has taken their language and art, and even the names they use are "versions of their names. . . . So there were many Suns and many Moons also" (115). Celia discovers that she knows neither Sun nor Moon. The real Korea, like the real India that eludes Adela Quested, remains inaccessible to her.

Flying home, thinking of the Tower of Babel, Celia finds the idea of England "irrelevant": "It was required that one think in terms of the whole world, and it was not possible" (127). Professor Sun had confided to her his belief that his people should be studying not British but Third-World literature; for Celia, the Third World is "not one, it was many" voices, like the literature of "women, or blacks, or homosexuals, voices contradicting or modifying a voice, now unheard, that had once claimed to be the best that was thought and said in the world" (125). As a woman, she does not like to be marginalized, but **"Loss of Face"** shows that both she and Professor Sun, in different ways, are being pushed to the margins of a shifting text. In the airplane, she thinks about the clash between "the human speech of particular men" and the "universals . . . the plate-glass tower, the machine gun, the deconstructive hubris of grammatologists and the binary reasoning of machines" (127). Despite the gentle humour with which Byatt describes Celia's predicament, the story is deeply pessimistic about both the survival of individual differences and the possibility of global communication.

With the next two stories, **"On the Day That E. M. Forster Died"** and **"The Changeling,"** the collection moves toward more explicitly metafictional concerns. Both are cautionary tales about women writers whose imaginative freedom is challenged by the intractable external world. However, Mrs. Smith, in the first story, is presented with a distanced sympathy, while Josephine Piper, in the second, is an alienating and alienated figure.

"On the Day" begins, "This is a story about writing" (129). Mrs. Smith is a middle-aged writer who, in 1970, believes that the "time for writing about writing was past" (129). She would not have liked the narrator's story, because Mrs. Smith "never wrote about writers. Indeed, she wrote witty and indignant reviews of novels which took writing for a paradigm of life. She wrote about the metaphysical claustrophobia of the Shredded Wheat Box on the Shredded Wheat Box getting smaller ad infinitum" (130). For her, art is an addiction, not a cure; she prefers to separate life and art and likes "things to happen" in fiction. The narrator, although "much in sympathy" with Mrs. Smith's views, nevertheless thinks her own story about writing is "worth telling"; indeed, it is "overloaded with plot, a paradigmatic plot which . . . takes it beyond the narcissistic consideration of the formation of the writer, or the aesthetic closure of the mirrored mirror" (130). This plot of the narrator's shows the failure of human plotting; in it, time and fate are triumphant.

On the day in question, Mrs. Smith has an idea for a long novel that will combine several plots. Her time has come, she thinks, to write a book that will contain the historical and biological time she has lived through.

Her planning of it, as she sits in the London Library, becomes "a growth, a form of life, her life, its own life" (133). Exhilarated, she experiences for the first time the paradox of "limitation" (for her project, huge as it is, will necessarily be limited by her own "history, sex, language, class, education, body and energy") as "release and power" (132). In the midst of her elation, however, the narrator tells the reader, "the plotting and over-plotting I wrote of . . . is . . . stalking Mrs. Smith" (135). Confident of her power to control her own plot and, with it, time, she is moving to meet the plot beyond her control. She meets an old acquaintance, Conrad, who (as his name suggests) has been involved with many plots. After a very active professional and sexual life—a psychologist, he has worked for the prison service and the army, and he has had children by several women—he was found to have tuberculosis. His active plotting abruptly suspended, he had a vision of life's finitude and decided to study music as "the most important thing." When Mrs. Smith last saw him, he was absorbed—with a concentration that parallels her own recent experience of planning her novel—in this "story of the music . . . a plot almost needing no character" (139). Now, apparently mad, he has moved into a new plot. He now knows, he tells her over lunch, that time is an illusion and that humans can live forever. Meanwhile, he must have her help, he says, in protecting the world from nuclear war by guarding a duplicate set of plans for a machine that uses music to drive its listeners mad; he is delivering the original plans to the Israeli embassy for use against the Arabs. Mrs. Smith refuses to be part of his espionage plot, escapes with the package from his frenzied attempt to force her to stay in the restaurant (their scuffle is misread by a spectator as a rape plot), and weeps for the music that Conrad has so madly misused. As the story ends, her idea for her novel is interrupted (as Conrad's earlier plots had been) by illness—a lump (ironically recalling the "growth" of her imagined text) that the surgeon says must be removed at once. She spends the three weeks before the operation trying to think of "short tales, of compressed, rapid forms of writing, in case there was not much time" (146). As the narrator promised, this plot goes beyond the "mirrored mirror" (130); it is the paradigmatic plot of the triumph of time, and it reflects not writing but life. Mrs. Smith is defeated by the biological clock that Conrad's grandiose delusion dismisses as unreal. The narrator's ominous use of tense (the present story "would not have" pleased Mrs. Smith [130]) suggests that the interruption, unlike Conrad's illness, is a final one. The irony is underscored by the reference in the title: seeing the headline announcing Forster's death after a long life, Mrs. Smith feels free to proceed as a writer: he was simultaneously "removed . . . as a measure" and made "more accessible to learn from" (136). Mrs. Smith knows that Forster believed in "recognizing the complicated energies of the world in which art didn't matter" (135)—the world that now claims her.

"The Changeling" continues Byatt's examination of the writing process. At its centre is a successful fiction writer, Josephine Piper, whose subject is fear. She specializes in the excruciating suffering of young boys. Her prototypical hero, Simon Vowle, finds a temporary haven from the horrors of boarding school life in the school's boiler room. Josephine is using her own experience here—she wrote her first stories in such a retreat—and Byatt herself did the same thing (Musil 195). The "Shredded Wheat Box" structure is shattered, however, by the entrance of Henry Smee, a recent graduate of the school, which Josephine's son Peter had also attended. He is introduced to Josephine by her friend Max McKinley, the headmaster. Max is in the habit of sending difficult and lonely boys to stay with her, and he now asks her to keep Henry—who, he says, "is Simon Vowle" (147)—until he goes to Cambridge in the autumn. Josephine sees the resemblance: "You could have used . . . the same little groups of words indifferently to describe either" (149-50). However, although the language fits Henry, the image does not encompass him; his troubling presence in her house becomes increasingly disturbing to her, and their strained relationship reaches a crisis when Henry, directed by Max, reads Josephine's story about Simon, "The Boiler Room." Reaching out for help to Josephine, who, he now knows, understands his torment (and, we are chillingly told, would have enjoyed writing about it), he is given a dismissive response, but persists: "the world is more terrible than most people ever let themselves imagine. Isn't it?" (155). After this, Josephine finds that Henry's "reading of Simon Vowle" has destroyed her freedom, for "Simon Vowle was herself, was Josephine Piper: there was no room for another" (156). Henry has given solid form to both her subject and her reader, and her writing becomes blocked. Finding Henry in her room looking in her mirror, she screams at this further invasion and orders him to leave. He does so, and kills himself. Josephine, freed from his demand that she imagine his "inside," resumes her endless task of exorcising her fear: "Her imagination tidied Henry Smee into a mnemonic" (159); "The next day she was able to start again with nothing and no one between her and the present Simon Vowle, . . . making a separate world, with no inconvenient reader or importunate character in the house" (160). All that is left of Henry is the ghost of his hands, which she appropriates for the new Simon.

"The Changeling" is a frightening study of the artistic process. Reminiscent of both *The Shadow of the Sun* and *The Game,* it explores the moral failure of the artist through irresponsible opportunism and refusal of empathy. Like Julia, the novelist in *The Game,* Josephine is the artist as consumer, attacking her human subjects with what Byatt (speaking of *The Game*) has described as "the sharp teeth and gaping jaws" of her imagination ("Sugar/Le sucre" 22). With rigid compartmentalization and iron control, Josephine pushes away the challenge of "real people" in the interests of self-preservation. In her struggle to avoid the nameless terrors of her agoraphobic mother, she entraps herself; in her frantic flight from her own fear, she avoids confronting her mother's fear, nor can she face Henry's. Henry, like Josephine's divorced husband and like her son Peter, sees through the facade of the cosy domestic household that Josephine has "made up" and forces her to acknowledge its falseness. "Perhaps she had not done wrong. She simply was wrong" (158), she reflects, while trying to understand Peter's decision to drop out of college and help the homeless. Both Henry and Peter also see through Max, who, with his urge to plot others' lives and his provision of Josephine with copy, is her accomplice and procurer. Despite his apparent sensitivity to the sufferings of adolescent boys, Max does not respond to their needs, and the narrator's statement that he reports Henry's suicide "with circumspection and tact" (159) suggests a detachment that parallels Josephine's own.

Strategically placed in relation to Byatt's developing theory of fiction, the next story, **"In the Air,"** moves away from the artistic concerns of the preceding two. Reasserting Byatt's need to imagine the lives of nonliterary characters, it explores the subject of fear—a pervasive subject in ***Sugar***—more sympathetically than Byatt allows Josephine to do. At the same time, like **"The Changeling,"** it deals with the materialization of an obsession. Mrs. Sugden, the widowed, aging central character, has found a way to "organize" (165) her fear. Living alone with her dog, Wolfgang, she is provided by the media with ample evidence that an attacker lurks in every neighbourhood, and she imagines her own future attacker in protean terms: "He was black, he was white, he was brown, he was dirty grey. . . . He had all the time in the world" (163). She knows that it is "civilized" to discuss violence more openly than in the past but her fear is increased by this openness. Fear, for her, is "in the air" (168), and it is in the open air that she expects to meet her attacker. On one of the daily walks that, steeling herself, she takes with the dog, she sees a young man who moves in an oddly exaggerated way, carries a knife, and is following a blind woman and her guide dog. Mrs. Sugden forces herself to go to the blind woman's rescue. The woman, Miss Tillotson, invites her new acquaintance home to tea, and the young man invites himself. Miss Tillotson has found her own courageous way of dealing with the ubiquitous terror; seeing the blind woman's much more vulnerable situation crystallizes Mrs. Sugden's fear. "In my position," says Miss Tillotson, "you could be afraid of everything. . . . I'd rather come out in the air" (177). As the guests leave, the young man, who has identified himself as Barry and has admitted that he "might be any kind of maniac" (182), promises that he will cross Mrs. Sugden's path again; he too likes to be out in the air. "I'm around a lot. I'll look for you, specially," he says, "tossing the blade" of his knife "in the air" (184). The atmosphere of male threat is intensified by the "jeering filth" (169) shouted by some of the small boys Mrs. Sugden passes on her walks, as well as by her knowledge that Wolfgang bites people "for his own pleasure, not for her protection" (171). Like **"The July Ghost"** and **"The Changeling,"** this story poses questions about the mind's construction of reality. Is Barry a thief, a rapist, a murderer waiting his chance, or only a sadistic bully? Has Mrs. Sugden, in her lonely, desperate, contracted life, needed her fear to materialize before it became unbearable—since "Every day she feared him a little more" (163)—and is Barry its projection?

The penultimate story, **"Precipice-Encurled,"** moves back to the world of art. Combining actual events near the end of Robert Browning's life with an invented story of a young painter, Joshua Riddell, it brings the principles of the whole collection into sharp focus. Byatt's narrative practice, blending fact and fabrication, demonstrates the duplicitous relationship of the imagination to its materials. In her essay "People in Paper Houses," Byatt observes that Julian Mitchell's novel *The New Satyricon* provides a criticism of "the relation of the novel, the writer and his world." She continues, "It plays games with truth, lies and the reader, teasing him with the knowledge that he cannot tell where veracity ends and games begin. It is the game all novelists play anyway, raised to a structural principle" (180). She is predicting her own practice in **"Precipice-Encurled,"** an art that was to be expanded to a large scale in *Possession,* ***Angels and Insects,*** and *The Biographer's Tale.*

The title of the story comes from Robert Browning's poem "De Gustibis—," in which the poet declares, "What I love best in all the world / Is a castle, precipice-encurled, / In a gash of the wind-grieved Apennine" (14-16). Ostensibly, the story tells of an occasion in 1882, in the last decade of Browning's life, when the poet and his sister, Sarianna (his companion after his wife's death), fail to carry out their plan of visiting friends at a villa in the Apennines. What prevents them is the death of their friends' house guest, a young English painter named Joshua Riddell. Intent on capturing the appearance of an approaching storm, Joshua is swept from his perch on a cliff and dashed to pieces. The young painter and the old poet, the reader is made to feel, would have understood each other: they share a passion for accuracy about the most minute and insignificant details of the human and natural worlds. The plot thus embodies one of Browning's favourite themes, opportunity missed. This narrative itself is enclosed in, and encloses, two more stories on the same theme—stories of unfulfilled love. Joshua's death cuts short a tender relationship with his host's daughter Juliana, and (according to the hypothesis of another of Byatt's characters, a twentieth-century scholar) Browning is falling in love with Mrs. Bronson, his hostess during his visits to Venice, who returns his affection but remains unaware of his passion. The Brownings plan to visit Mrs. Bronson later that year but are prevented, by flooded roads and illness, from reaching Venice, although they do so in 1883. Both love stories are left without conclusions; the image of Mrs. Bronson, waiting for Browning, begins the story, and Joshua's unfinished portrait of Juliana ends it.

The plot thus represents the intrusion of destructive chance happenings into the life of imagination and emotion. The title, **"Precipice-Encurled,"** refers to the precariously occupied spaces of love and art, and the narrative method demonstrates the hazards of creativity. Through Browning's and Joshua's work and in its own movement, the story shows the creative mind's encircling, assimilating work—and the inevitable escape of "the real thing" from the mind's grasp. In the words Juliet Dusinberre has used of *The Virgin in the Garden,* this short story "seems to declare that the real is beyond form" ("Forms of Reality" 61).

It is the epigraph, however, rather than the title, that provides the most telling clue to the story's special qualities:

> What's this then, which proves good yet seems untrue?
> Is fiction, which makes fact alive, fact too?
> The somehow may be thishow.
>
> (185)

The lines, with some interesting omissions and a significant change in punctuation, are from Browning's *The Ring and the Book*:

> Well, now; there's nothing in nor out o' the world
> Good except truth: yet this, the something else,
> What's this then, which proves good yet seems untrue?
> This that I mixed with truth, motions of mine
> That quickened, made the inertness malleolable
> O' the gold was not mine,—what's your name for this?
> Are means to the end, themselves in part the end?
> Is fiction which makes fact alive, fact too?
> The somehow may be thishow.
>
> (I.698-707)

Byatt uses Browning's words to hint slyly at her own way of using biography. At the centre of her story, surrounded by documented details of Browning's life and quotations, by his work, and by an unnamed work of twentieth-century scholarship, Byatt has placed an example of "fiction which makes fact alive." By adding the comma where Browning did not use one, she suggests that fiction making is inevitable whenever the imagination is at work on facts. The story of Joshua and Juliana (which even the dust jacket of ***Sugar*** encourages us to read as fact, "an almost unremembered incident on Browning's Italian travels") is invented. The facts are that the Brownings had been invited by the Cholmondeleys (not the Fishwicks) to visit them on the island of Ischia (not in the Apennines); their visit was cancelled because the Cholmondeleys' guest, Miss Wade, accidentally fell from a ledge while sketching the sunset and died of her injuries.

On the other hand, the scholar and the hostess, who both may appear to be invented, are real. Although, unlike Mrs. Bronson, he is never named by Byatt, the scholar is Michael Meredith. His 1985 book *More Than Friend* contains, after a long introductory essay, the Browning-Bronson letters, edited with meticulous attention to fact—including the proposed visit to Ischia and the death of Miss Wade (15 n. 3).[4] The craftsmanship with which Byatt mixes fact and fiction is so skilful that a reviewer of *Possession* praises **"Precipice-Encurled"** for its achievement as historical fiction; in comparing the story with the novel, the reviewer says that for the story the details of Browning's life were "all there, the art was in the gathering and sorting" (Karlin 18). It is, however, the "something else" that was *not* "there" that gives life to the story. By calling into question the existence of the boundary line between fact and fiction, Byatt daringly shows both the impossibility of originality and, conversely, the inevitability, in all writing, of invention and "confection." Embedded in her story are additional texts. Meredith's book, which provides Byatt's starting point, contains other texts as appendices: Mrs. Bronson's two published reminiscences of Browning and a memoir by an American acquaintance, Daniel Sargent Curtis. Several other works are intertextually present in Byatt's text, including Browning's poems, Henry James's *Aspern Papers* and "The Private Life," Christopher Smart's *Song to David,* Andrew Marvell's "Mower's Song," Shakespeare's *As You Like It,* and John Ruskin's *Modern Painters.* Byatt's imagination combines these texts and adds a new love story.

The story's four-part structure represents the encircling work of the imagination as it appropriates its material. The first two parts are very short. The story opens with the "lady," Mrs. Bronson (she is not named until the fourth part), sitting in her house in Venice, waiting for Browning. This part appears reliably factual: there are descriptions of the lady as she appears in portraits and photographs, and details of her life—the number of her servants, the names of her dogs, and her love of delicate objects, together with the information that James gave her a small role in *The Aspern Papers* and planned to make her the central character in a novel. Yet even here fiction creeps in, as the narrator speculates on the party to which the lady's daughter may have gone in the afternoon when her mother "sits, or might be supposed to sit" in the window, and on the umbrella the daughter may have taken with her. The narrator also interprets the lady's expression as shown in "portraits, more than one, tallying" (Meredith reproduces three portraits and two photographs) as "an indefinable air of disappointment" (185).

In the second section, set in the twentieth century, the scholar is introduced, working with letters and other documents to construct his story. He "combs" the facts—including Browning's poem "Inapprehensiveness," which the scholar interprets as a confession of Browning's love—in the direction of the hypothesis of the old poet's "dormant passion" for the lady. The scholar's work borders on fiction as he gives a shape, "subtle, not too dramatic" (188), to the facts, as his imagination curls around the woman whom "he likes . . . because he now knows her, has pieced her together" (187). After recording Browning's missed visit to Mrs. Bronson in 1882, Meredith writes, "He was in danger of allowing the friendship to cool," and the narrator adds possible interpretations: "perhaps anxious on her behalf, perhaps on the poet's, perhaps on his own" (188). As Mrs. Bronson and Browning have been enclosed by the scholar's biography, so the scholar is now enclosed by Byatt's narrative—and both the scholar and the narrator are "piecing together" their subjects.

Browning, who has been at the periphery of the first and second sections, is at the centre of the third. In his hotel room in the mountains, he reflects upon his two selves—his expansive public self, which pursues facts in the other world, and his creative private self, which uses these facts and which he imagines as "a brilliant baroque chapel at the centre of a decorous and unremarkable house" (189). The stream of his associations leads him to the idea that Descartes would be a suitable subject for a poem, and he thinks of how he could "inhabit" the philosopher, making the "paraphernalia" of Descartes's world spin around "the naked cogito." "The best part of my life," he thinks, "has been the fitting, the infiltrating, the inventing the self of another man or woman, explored and sleekly filled out, as fingers swell a glove." Yet he himself, who gives "coherence and vitality" to these other selves, is "just such another concatenation" (191). He reviews his favourite characters—the Duchess, Karshish the Arab physician, the risen Lazarus, David, Christopher Smart—noting that they have all shared his own "lively, indifferent interest in everything" (193). These thoughts take him to Sludge the Medium, through whom, following his principle of giving "true opinions to great liars," he has expressed his own vision of the creative intelligence "at the back" of the universe: "something simple, undifferentiated, indifferently intelligent, alive" (193-94). His reverie is interrupted by Sarianna, who tells him of a fellow guest, Mrs. Miller, who wears "an aviary on her head" (194); the next day, Browning's public self autographs Mrs. Miller's birthday book and tells her of the proposed visit to the Fishwicks, and she recites the lines about the precipice-encurled castle. In this section, Browning is both enclosed by Byatt's narrator and encloses other creative selves, and his imaginative piecing together of fact and fiction mirrors Byatt's.

The fourth section, much the longest, presents the—literally—precipice-encurled heart of the story. As she and her family prepare for Browning's visit, Juliana wonders what the poet will "make" of them. The process of creativity is the subject of this section, but this process is either, like Joshua's, broken off in the middle or, like Browning's as imagined by Juliana, never begun. Joshua begins to sketch Juliana's "extremely pleasant" (197) but unremarkable face, and feels their souls meet, and they kiss. The next morning, after spending the night wrestling alone with the conflict between his new love and his responsibility to the "empty greenness" of his "primitive innocence, before," Joshua goes up the cliff to paint; he wants to look at "the land beyond habitation" (204). Remembering Ruskin's words about mountains and a painting by Monet, he perches in an "eyrie" on the precipice and begins to work. He is alternately "miserable" at his "failures of vision" and "supremely happy" as he experiences self-oblivious absorption, "unaware of himself and wholly aware of rock formations, sunlight and visible empty air" (209). As the sky suddenly darkens, he resolves to try to follow Monet's example, painting light itself and "the act of seeing" (210). Losing his footing as the ice pellets strike him, "still thinking of Ruskin and Monet" (211), he falls to his death. The narrator then records the impact of the death on Browning, who reflects briefly on the unknown young man: "his imagination reached after him, and imagined him, in his turn . . . reaching after the unattainable" (212). When Mrs. Miller asks if he will compose a poem about the death, he replies that he is left "mute" by such events; he does, however, write a poem about Mrs. Miller, "clothed with murder" in her hat of birds' wings (213). In the twentieth century, the scholar is at first hopeful that Browning will now visit Mrs. Bronson, then disappointed as he reads more letters. The last image is of the unfinished sketch that "Aunt Juliana" keeps pressed in the family Bible, of "a young girl, who looked out of one live eye and one blank, unseeing one, oval like those of . . . [angels on] monumental sculpture" (214).

With this image, the encircling process is concluded, but all the narratives—and all the creative experiences they examine—are left incomplete, and all hold within them potential subjects that are not mined by any artist. Mrs. Bronson's story is described by the scholar, Meredith, as "the novel Henry James missed" (xxv). Descartes never becomes the subject of a poem by Browning, nor does Browning ever "make" anything of the Fishwicks or of Joshua; Joshua never completes either of his sketches.

In its use of fact and fiction the story produces an effect of *trompe l'oeil.* The scholar, who to the uninitiated reader appears imaginary (as Mrs. Bronson herself may), is real. Joshua (the Riddell/riddle), who seems real to the same reader, is imaginary. The impression of the reader who does not have a prior knowledge of the facts is that the scholar, in his eagerness to reclaim Mrs. Bronson—to do what James had merely planned to do—and to construct a love story for Browning's old age, has missed the poignant story of youthful ambition and young love that Browning also missed. In fact, there was no story to miss. Byatt, marginalizing both the scholar and his subject, and altering the facts of Browning's itinerary in 1882, creates a story for the fourth section of **"Precipice-Encurled"** that has more apparent authenticity than any other part. "A good scholar may permissibly invent, he may have a hypothesis, but fiction is barred," observes the narrator (187-88). Byatt's own procedures explore and threaten the line between scholarly invention and fiction. She moves from dependence on Meredith to innovative use of James to bolder manipulation, finally departing from fact—and other texts—altogether.

Byatt also shows that both Meredith and—much more daringly—Browning combine fact and fiction. Browning imagined Smart noticing not only the whale and the polyanthus, which Smart did include in his *Song to David,* but also the blossoms of Virgin's Bower, which he did not (Browning, "Parleyings" 195-98; Smart, *Song to David* 310, 456-57). Starting with the account of the raising of Lazarus in John 11:1-44, he imagines the life of Lazarus afterward, about which John is silent—and encloses this story in that told by Karshish, whom Browning has also imagined. The narrator's work in this third section of **"Precipice-Encurled"** parallels Browning's. When Sarianna opens the door of her brother's room, the windows are described in the words used by James's narrator in "The Private Life" when, coming upon the poet Claire Vawdrey (modelled on Browning) writing in the dark, he sees "a couple of vague, starlighted apertures" (194; "Private Life" 227) and concludes that there are two Vawdreys, the public and the private. Mrs. Miller is an invention of Byatt's, but the French words uttered by Browning when he hears about her are a version of those that he is recorded as having said on a different occasion.[5] When, in Byatt's story, Browning writes in Mrs. Miller's birthday book, there is more unacknowledged borrowing from James. In "The Private Life," however, it is the narrator who cannot remember his own birthday; in **"Precipice-Encurled,"** it is Browning. Immediately after this there is explicit reference to James's dislike of Browning's lack of discrimination, and an image from James is used literally when Mrs. Miller nods "under the wings of the dove" (195). The language of the fourth section is the most original and independent, movingly creating the feelings of Joshua and Juliana and the moments just before Joshua's death. The narrator then parries Meredith's "hypothesis" about the personal reference of "Inapprehensiveness" with a "fiction" of her own, making Mrs. Miller's hat the stimulus behind "The Lady and the Painter."[6] The point is clear: while Meredith's hypothesis may have more basis in fact, the truth about the subjects of both poems—like the truth about Lazarus, Smart, Mrs. Bronson, and Browning himself—remains beyond reach.

Browning wrote that Smart "pierced the screen / 'Twixt thing and word" ("Parleyings" 113-14). These are brave words, but Browning knew, and Byatt demonstrates, that the screen is impenetrable. **"Precipice-Encurled"** displays the predatory activity of the imagination as it raids other texts in its fruitless attempt to get to the "thing." More optimistically, Byatt also shows the fertility of language. In her novel *Still Life,* her narrator confesses, "I had the idea that this novel could be written innocently, without recourse to reference to other people's thoughts, without, as far as possible, recourse to simile or metaphor. This turned out to be impossible" (108). In **"Precipice-Encurled,"** Byatt shows why the experiment must always fail. The scholar, dutifully retracing Browning's steps to Asolo, hears the sounds of the place through Browning's words as he listens to the "contumacious grasshopper" (*Sordello* VI.787). Even Joshua, the painter, sees through others' words, recognizing the accuracy of Milton's description of the fallen leaves in Vallombrosa (199; *Paradise Lost* I.300-04), experiencing first love through Marvell's Mower: "She / What I do to the grass, did to my thoughts and me" (203; Marvell wrote "did," not "does"), and applying to himself Shakespeare's description of lovers who "no sooner looked but they loved" (202; *As You Like It* V.II.32). Even when painting and sketching, he sees through Ruskin's language. When he tries to reach beyond language, remembering simply Monet's canvas and sketching the unmediated subject, he dies. On one level, his death is paradigmatic.

In **"Precipice-Encurled,"** the language of incompleteness and shattering, like the structure, testifies to the failure of enclosure. On the precipice, Joshua sketches a broken snail shell, "the arch of its entrance intact, the dome of the cavern behind shattered to reveal the pearly interior involution" (209). In a few moments, he himself has vanished in a "shattering of bone and brain" (211). Despite the many invocations of enclosure, epitomized by Browning's fantasy that the "pothooks and spider-traces" of his handwriting contain the world (189), the broken shell more accurately images the story Byatt tells. Yet if fiction stops short of holding reality, it also extends it. It is like Monet's *Vétheuil in the Fog,* which so startled Joshua: "You could see, miraculously, that if you could see the town, which you could not, it would be reflected in the expanse of river at the foot of the canvas, which you could also not see" (210). Like Browning's resuscitation of his source, the "Yellow Book," in *The Ring and the Book,* Byatt's fiction has made fact alive. "The somehow may be thishow."

In **"Sugar,"** the author speaks for the first time as Byatt and explores, through fictionalized autobiography, her own imaginative history. Its rambling form is also its subject. Setting out to write about her paternal grandfather, the narrator finds she must describe her father's death, her mother, her other grandparents, and family history as it has been received by her, and she traces her imagination's involvement with myth from the family myth to her favourite childhood reading, the Norse myth of origin and destruction. The narrator begins by contrasting her parents as makers of fictions, and by preferring her father. A judge, he had a respect for "evidence" and a "wish to be exact, a kind of abstract need which is somehow the essence of virtue" (217). As he lay dying in an Amsterdam hospital, he tried "to construct a . . . satisfactory narrative of his life" (231). On the other hand, her mother "had a respect for truth, but she was not a truthful woman" (215). Some of her lies were told "to make a story better;" others were complaints, "fabricated evidence of nonexistent wickedness" (215-16). She told of her husband's parents, who neglected their healthy children in order to care for their crippled eldest son and who forced their son Freddie, the narrator's father, to work in the family candy factory until faced with his determination to go to Cambridge. Her version of her husband's neglected childhood focuses on the horse trough where his siblings left him as a baby and forgot him while they played. The father's own memories are more benign—of a life of freedom: "we had each other and the fields and the stables . . . we ran wild" (231). The narrator recognizes that she herself has interpreted these stories and others, of the escapes of aunts and uncles to more exciting worlds, with the help of written texts, just as her mother borrowed from the story of the Prodigal Son for her depiction of her father-in-law's response to her husband's declaration that he would go to Cambridge with the wages he had saved: he had delightedly "fallen upon your father's neck" (224), she always said. The imagination's need for shape is examined here, and the narrator begins to see her own resemblance to her mother.

Paintings, too, have contributed to the family story. There are the van Gogh prints that the narrator always associated with her mother, whose own family myth traced the family's descent to Dutch Huguenots. The prints were, in fact, her father's choice; she talks about van Gogh with him as he is dying; she is writing a novel that includes van Gogh, and she hints at a parallel between the artist and her father, both men who struggled toward accuracy of representation: "he [van Gogh] remained steadily . . . intelligent and analytic, mixing his colours, *thinking* about the nature of light, of one man's energy, of one man's death" (236). Later she "recognized with shock" (234) boats on a French beach, having seen them first in one of these prints, and she "saw that tortured and aspiring cypresses were exact truths, of their kind" (236). (Here "exact" and "of their kind" bring together the father's and the mother's versions of truth.) A paradigm of all representation, the cypresses combine factual accuracy with imaginative shaping.

The narrative progressively becomes its own subject. The narrator sees that she is herself partly her mother's invention—"I saw that much of my past might be her confection" (240)—and that she is truly her mother's as well as her father's daughter. Just as she has seen her grandfather's face in her father's, so she feels her mother's face "setting like a mask in or on my own." She is a storyteller too—"I select and confect" (241)—and, inevitably, she tells lies. In this story, she has left things out—the tear gas and police in Amsterdam—which she now returns to retrieve: "To omit them is a minor sin, and easy to correct. But what of all the others? What is the truth?" (241). Reflecting later on this story, Byatt concludes that "in some curious way" the mother became "the heroine of that story . . . the ground of the fiction" (qtd. in Wachtel, "A. S. Byatt" 89).

"Sugar" concludes with two incidents. The first modifies the narrator's mother's construction of the paternal grandfather as a stern patriarch, and shows him as a kindly man, proudly showing his grandchildren how the light streaks in humbug candy were made: "It's the air that does it. . . . Nothing but whipping in air" (244). The twisting together of the dark and light ropes of sugar to make humbugs is the dominant image of Byatt's collection, with the candy's name recalling the mother's lies, which were "sugar-coated pills, grit and bitterness polished into roundness by comedy and by . . . worked-upon understanding of . . . real meaning" (229). The candy factory is, appropriately, the subject of the first piece of writing that the narrator remembers "clearly as mine." In it—borrowing Frances Hodgson-Burnett's "spun glass" and Coleridge's "as green as emerald" (245) and thus demonstrating that we can never be free of others' language—she wrote of the texture and colours of the discarded bits of candy. The second concluding event epitomizes the whole collection by asking the central question about the dividing line between lived events and mythmaking. The narrator tries to recall her father's return from the war, "a storied event, already lived over and over, in imagination and hope" (248). She remembers the figure in the doorway of her room, herself leaping out of bed and over her sleeping sister, and the experience—"this is surely memory, and no accretion"—of "a terror of happiness." But "the real thing, the true moment, is as inaccessible as any point along that frantic leap." As she writes, other images return to her—"the gold-winged buttons on his jacket"—but neither "words" nor "things" can recall her father's reality. His return takes its place with the other "markers" of the narrative. The last sentence is a list of objects, some "storied," some experienced *and* storied (for "After things have happened . . . , we begin to know what they are and were, we begin to tell them to ourselves"), ending with the "melded and twisting hanks of brown and white sugar" (248). In this story especially, Byatt has put into action the lesson she attributes to Proust, who narrated "his own life, *beside* his life," and who showed how autobiography could contain "its own precise study of the nature of language, of perception, of memory, of what limits and constitutes our vision of things" ("Sugar / Le Sucre" 23).

In ***Sugar and Other Stories,*** Byatt successfully blends the self-reflexive and the mimetic. She shows how the imagination constructs its mosaic, and she acknowledges its limits, the dark corners where it cannot go or which it chooses not to include, "the long black shadows of the things left unsaid" (241). Situations and events recur; versions of the past are both terrifyingly powerful and frustratingly inconclusive. Repetition is sometimes oppressive and imprisoning, sometimes enriching and illuminating.

Byatt has noted that "language relates things as well as controlling them" (Dusinberre, "A. S. Byatt" 183). Her own metaphors, like the "branching and flowering" (133) pattern envisioned by Mrs. Smith, suggest endless relationships rather than containment. Her least sympathetic characters are those who, like Miss Crichton-Walker, Kun, Conrad, and Josephine, attempt too tight a control of their own and others' narratives. Her more admirable are those who, like Celia and Mrs. Smith, have the wisdom to see that no text can encompass the whole world and that no imagination can transcend its own limitations.

The stories in ***Sugar*** are deeply concerned with narrative—not only with its methods but with its uses and abuses, as exorcism, manipulation, self-projection, self-forgetfulness, rescue, paradigm. Some of the finest moments show characters experiencing creative exhilaration, as Mrs. Smith does in the library, planning her novel, and as Joshua does while sketching on his precipice. Such moments are timeless and wordless, however, and they are often doomed to premature shattering. Loss is a central fact in most of the stories, and it is often suffered by figures who are isolated—by age, gender, grief, culture, or simply difference. Opportunities are missed, or were never really there. These stories celebrate bravery, tenacity, empathy, and honesty; they show characters who, despite their obvious fictiveness, think and feel. Through their author's scrupulous attention to "what is there," they demonstrate her allegiance to the writer's goal as defined by Wallace Stevens, "accuracy with respect to the structure of reality" (qtd. in Byatt, "The Omnipotence of Thought" 121).

Barbara Beckerman Davis (review date spring 2005)

SOURCE: Davis, Barbara Beckerman. Review of *Little Black Book of Stories,* by A. S. Byatt. *The Antioch Review* 63, no. 2 (spring 2005): 398-99.

[*In the following review, Davis praises Byatt's achievement in* Little Black Book of Stories.]

The dust cover [of ***Little Black Book of Stories***] calls these tales rather than stories, because they contain so much of the magical and supernatural. And what marvelous tales they are! Two women return simultaneously to a spot in the forest where their lives changed long ago, only to bear witness to a similar event and undergo definitive personality changes; the talented and successful obstetrician, Damien Beckett becomes entangled in an unusual triangle with what he thinks is a harebrained female artist, and a professional art historian whom he increasingly covets; a talented student in a creative writing class draws her inspiration and motives for writing from unlikely sources; the younger self of a now-demented woman visits her husband to help him end the nightmare of their lives. As fantastical as these stories are, all speak to people's lives in practical and urgent ways.

My favorite concerns Ines, a cultured etymological researcher, leading a quiet life. After an operation she senses she is healing in strange ways; slowly she is turning to stone. Ines's encrustations are marvelous and varied, and Byatt's writing is virtuoso, informed of the stuff of stones. As Ines's body becomes bulkier she sets out to find an unobstrusive spot in a graveyard where she hopes to end quietly her days as a statue. Instead, she meets a sympathetic Icelandic stonecarver who winters in London where he can work outdoors. As spring returns, Ines accompanies him back to a wild and enchanted land. There he works, while her strange metamorphosis continues. Both understand that she cannot return to England: her fate is elsewhere. Apart from the glorious writing of this story, what impresses the reader is Ines's acceptance of each stage of her transformation, tinged, of course, with trepidation, amidst the ceaseless transformation of all matter; meanwhile her relationship with the stonecarver explores the depths, and also the limitations, of friendship.

FURTHER READING

Criticism

Alfer, Alexa, and Michael J. Noble, eds. *Essays on the Fiction of A. S. Byatt: Imagining the Real.* Westport, Conn.: Greenwood Press, 2001, 224 p.

Collection of critical essays on Byatt's work, including several essays that focus on her short fiction.

Messud, Claire. "The Beast in the Jungle." *New York Times Book Review* (9 May 2004): 8.

Describes the pieces in *Little Black Book of Stories* as "not just meditations on art and its place in the world" but also "thrilling Gothic tales in their own right."

Review of *Little Black Book of Stories,* by A. S. Byatt. *Publishers Weekly* 251, no. 18 (3 May 2004): 171.

Laudatory review of *Little Black Book of Stories.*

Sorenson, Sue. "Death in the Fiction of A. S. Byatt." *Critique* 43, no. 2 (winter 2002): 115-34.

Discusses Byatt's treatment of death in her novels and short fiction.

Willard, Nancy. "Dreams of Jinni." *New York Times Book Review* (9 November 1997): 38.

Positive assessment of *The Djinn in the Nightingale's Eye.*

Additional coverage of Byatt's life and career is contained in the following sources published by Thomson Gale: *Beacham's Encyclopedia of Popular Fiction: Biography & Resources,* Vol. 1; *British Writers: The Classics,* Vol. 2; *British Writers Supplement,* Vol. 4; *Contemporary Authors,* Vols. 13-16R; *Contemporary Authors New Revision Series,* Vols. 13, 33, 50, 75, 96, 133; *Contemporary Literary Criticism,* Vols. 19, 65, 136; *Dictionary of Literary Biography,* Vols. 14, 194; *DISCovering Authors 3.0*; *DISCovering Authors: Novelists, Popular Authors*; *Encyclopedia of World Literature in the 20th Century,* Ed. 3; *Literature Resource Center*; *Major 20th-Century Writers,* Eds. 1, 2; *Major 21st-Century Writers,* 2005; *Reference Guide to Short Fiction,* Ed. 2; *Twayne's English Authors*; and *20th Century Romance and Historical Writers.*

Dan Jacobson
1929-

South African-born English novelist, essayist, critic, journalist, and travel and short story writer.

INTRODUCTION

Although recognized primarily as a novelist, Jacobson has also garnered critical attention for his short stories. Set mainly in his native South Africa, his stories explore racial and class issues, his Jewish identity, the immigrant experience, and the dynamics of parent-child relationships. Critics view Jacobson as a pioneering figure in South African literature and praise his stories for their wry humor and insight into the human condition.

BIOGRAPHICAL INFORMATION

Jacobson was born in Johannesburg on March 7, 1929. When he was four years old, his family moved to Kimberley, South Africa; the drab surroundings and pervasive racism of the small mining town would later be recurring elements in Jacobson's fiction and autobiographical essays. After graduating from high school at the age of sixteen, he studied English literature at the University of the Witwatersrand, receiving his B.A. in 1948. He then traveled to Israel, where he lived on a kibbutz, and later journeyed to England. In 1951 he returned to South Africa and began writing fiction while working at a variety of jobs. He settled in England in 1954, continuing to write fiction and work as a journalist.

Jacobson's first novel, *The Trap,* was published in 1955 and was followed a year later by his next novel, *A Dance in the Sun* (1956). After a year-long fellowship in creative writing at Stanford University, during which time he wrote the novel *The Price of Diamonds* (1958), he returned to London and published his first collection of short fiction, *A Long Way from London* (1958). In 1965 he was appointed to a one-year term as visiting professor at Syracuse University. He began his career at University College, London, as a lecturer in 1974, becoming a full professor of English in 1988 and professor emeritus in 1994. Jacobson has received several awards for his fiction and autobiographical work, including the John Llewellyn Rhys award for fiction in 1959, the Jewish Quarterly-Wingate Literary Prize in 1977, and the J. R. Ackerley Award for autobiography in 1986. He has also written critical essays, travel pieces, and books on religion and culture.

MAJOR WORKS OF SHORT FICTION

Jacobson's short fiction exhibits the profound influence of his South African homeland, his background as a Jew, and his life in his adopted home of London. His stories are often set in South Africa and feature familiar racial and class issues, particularly the insidious effects of apartheid on interpersonal relationships. Many of Jacobson's short stories also address the immigrant experience as well as the role of Jews in South Africa. In his most frequently anthologized story, "The Zulu and the Zeide," an old, deaf Jewish immigrant from Lithuania living in South Africa forms a close relationship with his caretaker, a young African tribesman named Paulus. An unlikely pair, the two men find comfort in each other's company while living in a society that has marginalized them both. When the old man's son begins to resent the relationship, tragedy ensues. Critics point out that this story also touches on another important theme in Jacobson's work, the relationship between parents and children.

Another story, "Through the Wilderness," focuses on the character of Boaz, a black man who converts to Judaism and becomes a popular speaker. When the Jewish narrator of the story realizes that Boaz knows more about Judaism than he does, he reflects on the role of spirituality in his own life. In "An Apprenticeship," a young Jewish man in South Africa feels a strong bond with the black people around him because he feels that they share a history of oppression. The alienation felt by South African Jews is also explored in "A Day in the Country," a story of a Jewish family that does not challenge a group of Afrikaners who are harassing a black child for fear that they will come under scrutiny. "The Example of Lipi Lippmann" chronicles the downfall of an old Jewish man who claims that a burglar stole his life savings, intended to be used for his move to Israel. When his fellow townspeople take up a collection for him, Lipi confesses to a town elder that there had never been a burglary. Overcome by guilt, Lipi kills himself by throwing himself under a train. In "Fresh Fields," an older South African writer plagiarizes the work of a young unpublished writer, a South African native living in London. Instead of feeling deceived and betrayed, the younger writer is relieved to be rid of his past and looks forward to his future in London.

CRITICAL RECEPTION

Jacobson is a well-regarded short fiction writer. Critics underscore the humor and sadness of his stories and praise the emotional complexity of his nuanced characters as they struggle to develop their moral consciousness. Viewed as a wry, restrained observer of the human condition, Jacobson is lauded for the verisimilitude of the settings and characters in his stories. He has also been discussed as a Jewish writer, for Jewish concerns are indeed central to his fictional and autobiographical work. Some critics have deemed his South African stories more vivid and evocative than those set in London, leading them to conclude that it is his memories of his homeland and its underlying social conflicts that most drive his imagination. In fact, they assert that Jacobson's exploration of South African concerns—particularly the crippling effects of apartheid, the role of the Jew in South African society, and the divide between rich and poor—is a defining characteristic of his work and establishes his significance within the context of contemporary South African literature.

PRINCIPAL WORKS

Short Fiction

A Long Way from London 1958
The Zulu and the Zeide 1959
Beggar My Neighbour and Other Stories 1964
Through the Wilderness and Other Stories 1968
A Way of Life and Other Stories 1971
Inklings: Selected Stories 1973

Other Major Works

The Trap (novel) 1955
A Dance in the Sun (novel) 1956
The Price of Diamonds (novel) 1958
No Further West: California Visited (nonfiction) 1959
The Evidence of Love (novel) 1960
Time of Arrival and Other Essays (essays) 1963
The Beginners (novel) 1966
The Rape of Tamar (novel) 1970
The Wonder-Worker (novel) 1973
The Confessions of Josef Baisz (novel) 1977
The Story of the Stories: The Chosen People and Its God (nonfiction) 1982
Time and Time again: Autobiographies (autobiographical essays) 1985
Her Story (novel) 1987
Adult Pleasures: Essays on Writers and Readers (essays) 1988
Hidden in the Heart (novel) 1991
The God-Fearer (novel) 1992
The Electronic Elephant: A South African Journey (travel essays) 1994
Heshel's Kingdom (nonfiction) 1998
All for Love (novel) 2005

CRITICISM

Robert Gutwillig (review date 5 June 1959)

SOURCE: Gutwillig, Robert. "Range and Depth." *The Commonweal* 70, no. 10 (5 June 1959): 260-61.

[*In the following favorable assessment of* The Zulu and the Zeide, *Gutwillig claims that Jacobson is not only South Africa's best writer, but also one of the world's best short fiction writers.*]

Dan Jacobson, South Africa's best writer, has already offered abundant evidence that he is a master of that subtle, treacherous and financially unrewarding form, the short novel. *The Trap, A Dance in the Sun* and *The Price of Diamonds* were all concerned not only with inter-racial relationships or the lack thereof, but the more crucial relationships between man and man, man and wife, man and his environment, and finally the most important and difficult relationship, that of man with himself. ***The Zulu and the Zeide,*** Mr. Jacobson's first collection of short stories, gives further proof of his main interests.

Like all good story tellers, Jacobson is immediately anxious to secure his characters and their emotions to a quick and viable situation. In fourteen of the fifteen stories here he succeeds. Only the best story tellers are able to merge character and action so closely that one does not so much influence the other as reflect it. Mr. Jacobson is one of the best. The humor and sadness of his stories spring directly and lovingly from his characters and their feelings, from the situations in which they find themselves, and not from something imposed upon them by the author. Yet the personality and control of the writer is always apparent. The reader is aware that these stories are shaped and patterned; they are not true-to-life but true-to-art.

Despite the intensity of his themes and the depth of their development, Mr. Jacobson's range is extremely wide—from the South African *veld* to London coffee houses—and his characterizations varied—African servants, children and adolescents, Jewish businessmen, workers, cab drivers, old men, energetic and "inscrutable" women, *émigrés,* individuals all and still familiar contemporaries. Remarkably enough, he is apparently equally at home in urban as rural settings (I know of no other writer who is), and oddly enough, his older characters are more convincing and affecting than his younger ones.

The title story is the best of all. It is, in fact, a great story. An old, deaf Jewish grandfather, who has always been a misfit and a failure, and who is always trying to run away (not anywhere in particular, just to escape) is finally provided with a keeper—an African tribesman—by his successful and long-suffering son. Together the Zulu and the *zeide* roam the streets of Johannesburg, unable to speak to each other, and yet communicating, objects of ridicule and yet untainted, until the conclusion that is as necessary as it is revealing. It is a story in which several extremely complex relationships and emotions are handled with honesty, directness but not simplicity.

The complexity of emotion in **"The Antipodes,"** in which a woman frees herself from her lover and her own sickness. **"The Stranger,"** in which a man comes to a desolate town to die and then is impersonally raped to death by a Negro servant, and **"Stop Thief!,"** in which a father is brutally defeated by his young son, is brilliantly displayed with both economy and force. If the emotions are not as complex in **"Two Women,"** where two formerly strong men are routed by a mother and daughter, or in **"A Long Way from London,"** where a young man acts shamefully before his mother of whom he is ashamed, the final effect is no less convulsive and satisfying for it.

Even in the less successful and slighter stories where Mr. Jacobson's material is not as impressive as his technique, or when he occasionally permits himself to attenuate the action unnecessarily, there are few other writers who can evoke place so vividly or can describe a character so succinctly and finally. Dan Jacobson's stories not only fully bear rereading but actually seem to improve under the burden of renewed concentration. He is not only South Africa's best writer, which may or may not be an invidious distinction, but he is one of the best writers of short fiction anywhere.

Granville Hicks (review date 13 June 1959)

SOURCE: Hicks, Granville. "Tales of Three Lands." *Saturday Review* 42, no. 24 (13 June 1959): 13.

[*In the following excerpt, Hicks asserts that "the conflicts that dominate South African life" function to unify the stories in* The Zulu and the Zeide.]

Although he is only a year or so older than [Walter] Clemons, Dan Jacobson already has three novels to his credit, and now we have a collection of short stories, ***The Zulu and the Zeide*** (Atlantic-Little, Brown). Jacobson was born in South Africa, and all but two of his stories have South African settings. Not only are the qualities of the South African scene constantly presented to us; the conflicts that dominate South African life are always making themselves felt—conflicts between blacks and whites and conflicts between different kinds of whites.

Sometimes the racial theme is central, as in **"The Box,"** the story of a boy's realization that he has been guilty of prejudice. More often the tension is merely there in the background, one of the facts of life, and Jacobson even makes a certain comic use of it in **"After the Riots."** As a rule Jacobson moves from the particular to the general, and he does this with notable effect in the title story. An old man, grown childish, is taken care of by a Zulu who is completely new to white men's ways. The close relationship that develops between the aged Jew, who speaks only Yiddish, and the young black man, who knows only his native tongue, is a touching example of the "vagaries and contrarieties" to which Miss Lavin refers. Although the story could be laid nowhere but in South Africa, we are confronted in the end by the essentially human.

Samuel T. Bellman (review date 14 December 1968)

SOURCE: Bellman, Samuel T. "The Journey Alone." *Saturday Review* 51, no. 50 (14 December 1968): 40-2.

[*In the following review, Bellman explores the major thematic concerns of the stories in* Through the Wilderness.]

The theme of Dan Jacobson's new collection of thirteen short stories [***Through the Wilderness***] about life in South Africa (and, in a few cases, England) boils down to this: life is an obstacle course and a muddled maze. Jacobson is concerned with the kinds of people who attempt to run this difficult course, and suggests that only a very special type of person can do it successfully. Thus, in his low-keyed, self-conscious way, he is extending Hemingway's picture of life as a battle that must be fought according to the code, a contest where the winner takes nothing. Just as Lawrence emphasized the dynamics of socio-magnetic attraction and repulsion, and Fitzgerald concentrated on the dream of glory and the awakening to sodden failure, so Jacobson gives his attention to one's particular "way"—that is, not only his life-style but also his painfully complicated earthly journey over hazardous but unavoidable terrain.

The long-distance runner, what a lonely job he has, says Jacobson, as if affirming Sillitoe. Most of the story titles touch on this in one way or another: **"Through the Wilderness," "A Way of Life," "Trial and Error," "Only the Best," "The Pretenders," "Fresh Fields," "Led Astray."** In contrast to the idea of motion suggested by the stories is Jacobson's slow, ruminative manner of narration. At times he seems a latter-day Sherwood Anderson, wondering sadly why some very modest event took place. Like many other *New Yorker* contributors (two of these stories first appeared in that magazine), he details a wealth of physical minutiae and personal observation, as innocently as though he had been home in bed all the time, and then slips in a partially revealing "moment of truth" to startle, amaze, or enlighten the provincial reader. It is no disparagement of his work to call him an old-fashioned writer. The cultural-emotional lag in his stories sets them apart from much of today's frenzied, upbeat fiction. The latter often evokes the mood of a drug "trip" or a spacecraft orbiting the earth; Jacobson's work conjures up a feeling of going precariously around the neighborhood in eighty days.

The apartheid which Jacobson grew up with in South Africa, and which he treats somewhat offhandedly in a number of stories, is so much more hideous than the segregation that has existed in the American South, or anywhere else, that it defies comparison. But the basic idea of apartheid is a useful point of departure in discussing his work. In a sense Jacobson may well be suggesting that all classes, groups, or individuals are set apart from each other, self-segregated possibly, but hopelessly disunited just the same. **"Trial and Error,"** by far the best story in the book because of its dramatic effectiveness and direct emotional impact, illustrates this clearly. It deals with a young South African couple who move to a village in the English Midlands, where the husband is attached to a university. After an idyllic early period, their son is born, and before long the wife becomes deeply frustrated and unhappy with her lot. She goes to London on a holiday and falls into an affair with a mutual friend. The husband is told all in a "Dear John" letter and, understandably, his world falls completely apart. Quite unexpectedly his wife returns, saying she must have been insane. He takes her back because "his fear of being left alone was stronger than anything else he felt; stronger than his pride; stronger even than his hatred of her." They stand quietly together "as though their trouble would pass over, if only they did not move." This is a rarely beautiful story for Jacobson because it appears so immediate and unpremeditated, as if he were finally giving us more matter and less art.

Predictably, we get straight apartheid in Jacobson's stories about South Africa's blacks. In **"Through the Wilderness," "Beggar My Neighbor,"** and **"A Way of Life"** there seems such a lack of certain essential ingredients (pity? compassion? troubled awareness? innuendo?) that they read almost like schoolboy notebook jottings. The title story is about a South African Negro named Boaz who gets religion one day—Judaism, of all things—and becomes a spellbinding evangelist. He unintentionally shows up the narrator, whose own Judaism is artificial and reluctant at best. Ironically, in this labored tale filled with Biblical imagery, Boaz's death leads to the apostleship of another Negro, a sheep-stealer, who now invests the money he makes from his followers in sheep-raising. Ambiguous and over-subtle as he often is when drawing comparisons between South African blacks and Jews (as for example, in his best-known work, ***The Zulu and the Zeide***), Jacobson seems here to be catering to a jaded audience that has just finished a heavy meal.

From this viewpoint a random statement in a quite different story. **"An Apprenticeship,"** seems embarrassingly insincere and irrelevant. The young Jewish narrator, in contrasting his way of life with that of a lukewarn Methodist family, speaks of "the burden of guilt and sympathy toward the blacks which we bore as part of our Jewishness." Accomplished writer though he may be, Jacobson again and again betrays a lack of emotional depth, an unawareness that boats must sometimes be rocked, a failure to realize that once "we were slaves in Egypt" but did something about it. The story, like most in this collection, deals with painful and irremediable apartness.

"Sonia" is about an unattractive, poetry-quoting girl who, shortly before her death from a brain tumor, takes a schoolboy lover in order to achieve a brief contact with life. **"Fresh Fields,"** another excellent story, involves a young writer who is plagiarized by a famous elderly poet. And in **"Led Astray"** a young unmarried couple who are living together realize, after the birth of a neighbor's child, that they too will have to settle down and reproduce. Their hands and eyes meet, but each sees "in the other's the recognition that it was not going to be easy for them."

There seems to be no significant break-through in Jacobson's fiction, with the possible exception of the remarkable **"Trial and Error."** He is still very much the wry, restrained commentator on man's seemingly incurable tendency to segregate himself from those with whom he ought to be self-redeemingly close, since they are running the same race against formidable odds.

Julian Jebb (review date 14 April 1973)

SOURCE: Jebb, Julian. "Show of Strength." *New Statesman* 85, no. 2191 (14 April 1973): 381-82.

[*In the following laudatory review of* Inklings, *Jebb claims that the wit, accuracy, and tact of Jacobson's observations enhance his moral passion.*]

Awarded a prize or two, always respectfully and usually enthusiastically reviewed, Dan Jacobson's literary reputation is secure enough. Maddeningly secure for the author, one would imagine. Despite all the judicious praise that has been heaped on his books, from the early novellas (*The Trap, A Dance in the Sun*) up to his last novel, *The Rape of Tamar,* his work has had comparatively little impact on the bulk of the reading public. He has never written a bestseller, and few of his books are in print. It is something of a mystery why a writer so skilful, humorous, intelligent and enjoyable should not have proved more popular—a mystery which this splendid selection of his stories does little to dispel.

Inklings is not a good title, smacking as it does of the tentative and 'sensitive'. Nor does the blurb help much with its talk of 'sardonic but compassionate understanding of human motives', which gives no real indication of the strength of feeling and the power of observation which run through the book or of the way in which the author's intelligence serves to ignite the dynamite of experience. All but three of the stories are set in his native South Africa, and the majority of these in the mining town of Lyndhurst, presumably a lightly fictionalised version of Kimberley, where he was brought up. Nearly all the pieces are rooted in domestic life—a pet rabbit eats its baby, a boy falls in love with his best friend's mother—but they are set against the larger issues of race (many of the protagonists are Jews in a Black and White world). The longest and one of the most recent of the stories, which were written between 1953 and 1968, is called **'Through the Wilderness'**. It is an allegory about religion in which the narrator is caught up with orthodox Judaism on the one hand and a messianic black Israelite on the other, while his father lies dying between, wracked by a sudden onset of superstition. For so ambitious a story the imagery is curiously thin; the large gesture in which the general unpleasantness of religion is to be demonstrated declines into a scene which evokes mere distaste in the reader.

Perhaps there is a clue here, and in *The Rape of Tamar,* (altogether a finer, in fact a stunning achievement) of how Jacobson is rebelling against his reputation as an acute social ironist: for all the approval his work has gained he has been undervalued, the large moral resonance of his writing has been miniaturised by misunderstanding. Chekhov wrote that the business of the fiction writer was to deal with 'life as it is, life as it ought to be'. The fear of overdoing the second injunction has led generations of English writers to eschew moral statements for the fear of appearing either censorious or propagandist. The enormous gift of Jacobson is to combine a sophistication of vision with an unequivocal love of justice. The accuracy, wit and tact of his observation never conceal or distort his moral passion—rather, they are at its service. Here for instance he describes the parents who give their son **'The Little Pet'**:

> They had the strained and guilty air of the perpetually well-intentioned. It was their laugh that betrayed them: only two people who had lived together for some years and were keen on meeting each other on all points could have laughed so much like each other. It was a practised, accommodating, nervous laugh they both had, a laugh that never lasted long but was always quick to come again, with a rattle in their throats and a chatter between their teeth. It was a pity that little Francis, their only son, who was standing silently by did not join in the laughter too.

With other English writers the phrase 'It was a pity' would carry more strident, contemptuous overtones; in Jacobson it is a statement.

The three best stories in the collection, **'Beggar My Neighbour'**, **'The Zulu and the Zeide'** and **'Sonia'**, demonstrate very well between them the variety and depth of their author's concerns. The first is about a well-intentioned white boy who is in the end literally haunted by two small black beggar children: the guilts and ensuing rage which arise from racial conflicts encapsulated in a surprising and frightening image. **'The Zulu and the Zeide'** is a masterpiece of pathos and comedy in which a crazy old wandering Jew is tamed and finally deserted by an ignorant Zulu. It is difficult to think of a finer account of an intense relationship between two utterly different people with no language in common. **'Sonia'** is eight pages long, an astonishing lovestory about a group of boys on a visit to a holiday resort outside Cape Town and then land lady's daughter, who develops an obsessive passion for one of them. She leaves quotations from Shakespeare lying around for him, they make love and she dies of a brain tumour. Strong stuff illuminated by an intensity of irony for which one would have to look to Chekhov himself for an appropriate comparison.

Life as it ought to be *is* strong stuff, however subtly it is conveyed to the reader. It is significant that two of the finest novelists now writing in English, Jacobson himself and V. S. Naipaul, should have been born and reared outside the British Isles, the class-ridden, nostalgia haunted country house of English Literature. It sometimes looks as if they are regarded by the literate natives of this country as approved and applauded visiting ministers instead of the resident prophets that they are.

Times Literary Supplement (review date 16 March 1973)

SOURCE: "Unhistoric Lives." *Times Literary Supplement* (16 March 1973): 285.

[*In the following review, the anonymous critic lauds Jacobson's descriptive powers, range, and the genuineness of his stories in* Inklings.]

Dan Jacobson's ***Inklings,*** distilled from two earlier collections of stories (and with four substantial, hitherto uncollected pieces added in) makes a packed, various, provoking book. The first impression is of the range and genuineness of the contemporary material; the second, and truer, impression is that this density of texture springs into existence only under Mr Jacobson's intent gaze. He has a rare talent for coaxing out of his experience those living details we seldom properly perceive because in our own case they're too close, and in others' lives too often indifferent. None of these tales is padded, or forced into intensity: they speak of a steady, unashamed absorption in the unhistoric lives of which contemporary history is really made. Mr Jacobson has no heroes—his people's stories are significant because they are hampered, pressured, enriched by the concrete disabilities of their particular place and time. Their abrasive incomplete contacts are, you are made to feel, the very medium in which the common culture survives. The South African and the Jewish settings of many of the stories serve, in fact, to emphasize Mr Jacobson's concern with the merely human: beyond the ideological simplifications, he is saying, there is a constant, obstinate process of interaction—more truly terrifying than any prophetic vision of violence, and more hopeful too. As though these inevitable daily confrontations are weaving a fabric of mutual awareness, delicate but durable, something to oppose to the stupid violence of the public life.

The vividness of incident, the assurance of characterization, are persuasive; more persuasive still is Mr Jacobson's tone, his moral idiom. Most of the stories affect one less as fictions than as authentic instances of their author's judgment, and this selection will confirm his reputation as a critic of contemporary life. His tone is what readers will remember, the quality of mind that makes him a touchstone of liberal values: his deafness to the hectorings of politicians; his deliberate hard-won innocence of abstract categories; his horror of mobs, aggregations, masses; his avoidance of the crude, ready-made languages in which the fragile stuff of personal experience is mangled and exaggerated. He seems to epitomize, the tradition of literary liberalism, asserting the individual idiom against public slogans, defending quality against quantity. "Human" for him means "private".

This tone is so recognizable and so admirable that people don't often stop to analyse it. And yet the traditional claims that are made for it seem more and more doubtful. Mr Jacobson does not see people as individuals, but as particulars—his characters are the sum of their details, their background, time, place, belongings, the habitual relations of their daily experience. They are not, to put it grandly, the architects of their own lives; they don't invent, they don't imagine, or if they do we're warned to feel they're evading reality, not making it. The language of "quality" turns out, on closer inspection, to be a superfine, cautious materialism. It is as though Mr Jacobson suspects that invention and imagination come uncomfortably close to the totalitarian, abstracting tendencies he fears in the public world—and so he denies myth-making, not only to his characters, but to himself. He is too fastidious, too private, to regiment the particulars, to make them march under the banners of "symbol" or "ideas". The price of renouncing public languages is that he must do without the public language of the imagination too—and the ironic effect of *that* is to impoverish his presentation of the individual.

This is not to question Mr Jacobson's sincerity: it is precisely because he is so much "the real thing"—the authentic voice of personal judgment—that it becomes important to talk about the selectivity of his vision and to stress not only the "reality" it sustains, but also the "unreality" it dismisses. If the language of myth and symbol is discredited, then every form of public language will have been lost to the imagination.

This is a danger, perhaps, that Mr Jacobson senses: in the longest story in the book, **"Through the Wilderness"**, he *does* move tentatively into those hybrid, suspect, shared symbolisms. In it a black "Israelite", the grotesque prophet of a scattered, dying sect, re-enacts the story of Abraham and Isaac—and, with a generous heroic irony, ends up as himself the necessary sacrifice. It is one of the stories where you feel Mr Jacobson is being something more ambitious than a critic; perhaps he is emerging out of his distrust of schema, and will find or invent an imaginative system to keep the public, political systems at bay. His earlier self would, one feels, have judged that to be a betrayal; his more recent work suggests that he is no longer so sure.

Claire Tomalin (review date 16 March 1973)

SOURCE: Tomalin, Claire. "Veldtschmerz." *The Observer* (16 March 1973): 381.

[*In the following excerpt, Tomalin describes the South African stories in* Inklings *as vivid and nearly perfect.*]

Dan Jacobson has chosen 16 of his own stories written between 1953 and 1968 for this new edition [***Inklings***]; the result, though largely a reprint, is a nearly perfect collection. To carp first: the relative failures are the few tales with an English setting, temperate domestic incidents which miss the intensity of the South African ones; and it is obviously sad that Mr Jacobson's imagination has not been kindled by England. The bonus is that he continues to vivify his memories of South Africa; go home, says one expatriate author to another in **'Fresh Fields'**, and for the purposes of these stories the advice seems good.

All but four are in fact set in South Africa, and most are concerned with the discovery and growth of moral sensitivity; sometimes it is in a Jewish boy whose membership of a persecuted race causes him to look with more curiosity than his friends on the sub-caste of the Kaffirs; sometimes it is only implied in the voice of the narrator. In the very best of the stories—**'The Zulu and the Zeide'**, **'Beggar My Neighbour'**, **'A Way of Life'**—this narrator achieves a presence that measures up to Chekhov's, appalled and benign, with the same exact sense of what is blamable, the same refusal to apportion blame. The veldt and the city appear as places where boys and men live busy, humdrum, vivid lives and also as the site for perpetual collisions between alien and degraded cultures; family dramas hinge on uncertain ties between *baas* and servant; the different segments of humanity mock or parody one another's aspirations. 'Where, how, had Lena learned her honesty, punctuality and loyalty, her cheerfulness and cleanliness?' the employers of an old Negro woman ask themselves, their unanswerable question covering another: where, how, have ordinary whites learned the particular brutalities of their way of life?

Douglas Dunn (review date 19 May 1973)

SOURCE: Dunn, Douglas. "Disturbing Stories." *The Spectator,* no. 7560 (19 May 1973): 623.

[*In the following review, Dunn discusses the key thematic concerns of* Inklings *and compares Jacobson's stories with those in Susan Hill in* A Bit of Singing and Dancing.]

A number of obsessional images, sayings and themes recur in Susan Hill's excellent short stories—seaside resorts in winter, gunmetal grey skies, an ugly sea, doomed children, and characters who are often, in Philip Larkin's phrases, the "removed lives loneliness clarifies."

An elegant and masterly gloomth seems to be what Miss Hill is after. The first four stories end with death or deaths, and in two of them the victims are children. A harsh Atropos guides Miss Hill's characters, but the intrusion of Little Nell-ism is thankfully rare. It's almost as if, in most of her stories, and particularly in 'Halloran's Child', she wanted, as she wrote, to lay on sentiment so thick that her readers simply wouldn't have the chance not to be moved.

Having said that, you might wonder "Why such a genial title?" Miss Hill's stories, you might say, "are gathered as *A Bit of Singing and Dancing.* Is that just a dim irony, or what?" It certainly doesn't mean exactly as it says. The title story is on the theme of companionship and freedom. A middle-aged woman's mother dies. Her mother was fond of variety shows on television. "I like a bit of singing and dancing, it cheers you up, Esme, it takes you out of yourself a bit." After this source of advice is dead, Esme, a spinster, takes in a lodger. He has two jobs—one for summer, one for winter. During the winter he sells kitchen utensils. In the summer he does something else, which it would be unfair to reveal. But unmarried middle-class Esme, having already run more risks than ever before in taking in a lodger, is moderately affronted by the nature of the summer job. What would mother say? The story ends with Eme traipsing out mother's safe, unconscious irony about how good it is to be taken out of oneself.

Miss Hill in almost every story dramatises the dead life of our society. She writes about the lonely, the emotionally or physically crippled, the perplexed, just as William Trevor so often does. Men and women (but chiefly women) wrestle with disappointment and ruminate on the lost chances which make a new life so tempting, but so difficult, to take up. For the most part she limits herself to a middle-class milieu, nothing ostentatious, just suffocating. She is expert within that background, although capable of leaving it for the rural setting of 'The Custodian.' Short stories are often balanced over the inert nerves of those whose lives have scarcely begun. They are seldom written with the easeful and accurate mannerisms Miss Hill relies on to such good effect.

Childhood is frequently thought of as the staple source of the short story writer's inspiration. Standard themes of short stories are the conversion of childhood into adolescence, adolescence into adulthood, and the contrast of an innocent world with one not so innocent. Dan Jacobson's stories fit, like an illustration, into this pattern. His setting is, of course, South Africa; and by now the South African achievement in short story writing is the brightest in contemporary English, for there is Doris Lessing, Nadine Gordimer, and a number of black writers, as well as Mr Jacobson, whose ***Inklings*** gathers stories from two out of print collections, plus a few previously ungathered.

The peculiar and vicious social arrangements in South Africa are, to a writer, as much interesting as something to flee from or be hurt by. Stories like Mr Jacobson's thrive on subdued tensions and recognitions. His Jewish background makes these more than a simple black-white antithesis. And in order to convey the complex realities of racial and national oddities, Jacobson has devised a plain, natural prose, from which the engaging humanity of his concerns is imparted to the reader with beautiful, almost poetic, balance. Miss Hill's writing—wonderfully readable as it is—appears self-conscious by comparison.

An immense human sadness is common to both Hill's and Jacobson's stories. Within a bewildering range of imperfections and dissatisfactions, their characters find self-knowledge and the future dispiriting. There is less personal failure in Jacobson's themes; opportunities of self are more stunted by the nature of society than private indecision. Being mostly stories of childhood—Mr Jacobson's childhood—the consequences are inevitably moving. For a writer the consequence is exile. Many of the stories are set in a presumably fictional town of Lyndhurst. Adding up these stories, one gets the impression that Mr Jacobson's achievement is at least on the same level as *Winesburg Ohio,* with an apt burden of 'characters', events, detections, and a convincing portrait of 'how it is.'

Joyce Carol Oates is better known as a novelist (and such is the status of the short story, that I suppose Susan Hill and Dan Jacobson are, too). If there was a deal of death and suicide in *A Bit of Singing and Dancing,* Miss Oates's stories almost seem to seek violent, disturbing deaths as a means to rivet or shock. Unhappiness, suspicions, threats, conflicts, revenges, discontents—Miss Oates invigorates these dire though recognisably human conditions with brilliant but grim dedication. Her stories have bizarre momentum, and she is an uncompromising writer. Yet there is something almost unwholesome in her passionate engagement with such extreme situations. The quality of the writing redeems that kind of criticism, however; although such is the force of how she handles her unusual stories, that one stops to dislike oneself for appreciating them so much. Perhaps that was her intention.

Dan Jacobson (essay date 1973)

SOURCE: Jacobson, Dan. "Afterword." In *Inklings: Selected Stories by Dan Jacobson,* pp. 196-97. London: Weidenfeld and Nicolson, 1973.

[*In the following essay, which appears as an afterword to his* Inklings, *Jacobson describes what has happened to a few of the characters in his stories.*]

The first story in this collection [***Inklings***] was published in 1953; the last in 1968. They are presented here in chronological order. I have taken the opportunity to excise from them many superfluities and ineptitudes; nothing, however, has been added. The book includes everything I would wish to keep from two earlier volumes, ***A Long Way from London*** and ***Beggar My Neighbour,*** which are both out of print. The last four stories have not previously been collected in England.

Only **'The Box'** and **'A Day in the Country'** were written while I was still living in South Africa; they are also the only two which stick closely throughout to my memory of the events they describe. In every other case I can remember quite vividly the person, or incident, or set of circumstances which, years later, was to suggest the story. Such a memory would suddenly turn in its sleep and show how much life there was still in it. Then came a time for curiosity, speculation, invention, the righting or the aggravation of old wrongs, a playful or malicious juxtaposition of quite different people and incidents upon those recollected, a readiness at all stages to subject the results to rough handling, to sudden reversals and abridgements. To what end? Surprise, chiefly. Not in order to trick the reader; but rather in the hope that if I managed to surprise myself, there was a chance that the completed tale would be truly self-sufficient. It would not collapse the moment I turned my back on it; it would not need any foreword or afterword from me.

Life itself, however, has uttered its own afterwords to some of these stories; it has presented them with sequels more melodramatic or pathetic than any I might have dared to invent. For instance, a couple of years after the publication of **'A Day in the Country'**, the original of the young, aggressive, thick-armed Boer who appears in it was shot dead on a railway platform by the husband of a woman he was having an affair with. . . . The farm across which Boaz and the narrator wander in **'Through the Wilderness'**, picking up small, shining stones, looking at them and throwing them away—that farm turned out to be the site of a diamond-strike worth millions of pounds, and is now the scene of large-scale mining operations. . . . The man upon whom the character of Harry Grossman in **'The Zulu and the Zeide'** was based became, in due course, very old and difficult to cope with, senile indeed. So his children hired an African male servant to look after him, as I write of him doing for his father. But because times had changed and the family had prospered, these two did not wander about on foot, as my characters do, but instead drove about in a car, with the African at the wheel. One of their favourite drives was to 'Israel', which the old man had developed an inordinate desire to visit before his life ended. They would drive to a spot in the empty countryside around Johannesburg; the driver would point at the veld ahead of them and say, 'There's Israel,' and his employer would sit Moses-like in the seat of his car, looking out upon the promised land. . . . Readers of another story, **'The Example of Lipi Lippmann'**, written long before I had heard of this, may recognise something familiar in the situation.

But enough. If I go on I shall be accused of romancing again, or of bewailing missed opportunities. I wish to do neither. The chances these stories took are now entirely their own.

Of the previously uncollected stories, **"Led Astray"** was first published in *The New Yorker*; **"Sonia"** and **"Through the Wilderness"** in *Commentary*; and **"Another Day"** in *The Atlantic Monthly.* **"Another Day"** and **"Through the Wilderness"** were reprinted in *Penguin Modern Stories No. 6.*

Sheila Roberts (essay date 1984)

SOURCE: Roberts, Sheila. "In a Minor Key." In *Dan Jacobson,* pp. 103-21. Boston: Twayne Publishers, 1984.

[*In the following excerpt, Roberts elucidates the major themes and motifs of Jacobson's short stories.*]

The town of Kimberley in the northwest Cape, renamed Lyndhurst by Dan Jacobson in his "South African" novels, is the setting for most of his short stories. He has also written stories set in England but some of those have South African characters: for example, **"A Long Way from London," "Fresh Fields,"** and **"Led Astray."** In fact, after completing a volume of Jacobson's stories, the reader has a strong sense of having known a great variety of South Africans—blacks, whites, English, Afrikaans, Jewish, and expatriate—and understood how they interact with one another and the strategies they employ not merely to survive but also to preserve their self-respect.

The most famous of Dan Jacobson's stories, the one which has appeared in four collections and which is most frequently anthologized is **"The Zulu and the Zeide."**[1] The story deals with an old Jewish immigrant from Lithuania now living in Lyndhurst, whose son, Harry Grossman, pays a large illiterate Zulu named Paulus to accompany the old man and take care of him during his irrepressible ramblings around the town. The *zeide,* who has never got on with his son and who has never adapted to life in South Africa, becomes deeply attached to the Zulu. Although neither knows the other's language, each seems capable of talking to the other, sometimes using his hands to explain things.

Paulus eventually takes on the bathing and dressing of the old man; he trims his beard; and even carries him to bed. The closeness he established with the *zeide* becomes a source of acute irritation to the old man's son.

One day Paulus is given a free afternoon. The *zeide* calls for him but is not told by his son that the black man has the day off. Instead, Harry Grossman merely says that Paulus is away and tries to force his father to allow him to help him in the way the Zulu does. The *zeide,* who for years has had one desire in mind and that is to escape his son's house, manages to get out on his own, is knocked down by a bicycle and dies. Before Paulus is sent away permanently, Harry Grossman learns that the Zulu had cherished hopes of saving enough money to bring his wife and family from the village to Lyndhurst.

This is an engaging and moving story, one that richly deserves the fame it has earned. It also fits into the larger body of Jacobson's work because of its treatment of factors that have occupied him throughout his career; the complex relationships between fathers and sons; the immigrant experience, particularly the Jewish one; racial tension; and the frequency of human self-delusion.

Harry Grossman nurtures deep resentments against his father, dating from his boyhood when his mother had to skimp and save to send her husband from Lithuania to South Africa. His father was persuaded by friends at Bremen harbor to go with them instead to South America. He did not prosper there and had to be brought back to the old country with money borrowed from Harry's uncle, money that Harry as a teen-ager had to work to repay. Eventually the entire Grossman family emigrated to South Africa but, again, the old man had to be supported because he could not hold a job and finally gave up trying.

When the story opens, the *zeide* is obviously senile, but his senility has taken a peculiarly logical form. Understanding that his son resents him, he claims that he does not know Harry at all, and spends all his efforts trying to get out of the house.

The *zeide*'s early history of mismanaging a family's plans to emigrate was to be reused in a modified fashion in a later story of Jacobson called **"Gold from Africa,"**[2] a story which was to form the opening section of his novel *The Beginners*. In this account, Avrom Glickman, a Lithuanian Jew who has emigrated to South Africa with his sons, is financed by them, again resentfully, to return to Lithuania so that he can conduct their mother back to South Africa. Avrom, driven it seems by pity, gives his money to a destitute woman with children at Bremen station. Thus his sons have to work the harder to accumulate money to send "home" to bring both parents out. This story is based on a similar, true event which Jacobson's father was to narrate about *his* father,[3] and which obviously made a lasting impression on the writer.

Not only the opening chapter of *The Beginners* but other sections, too, take up the theme of parents or parent-figures at odds with their offspring, and this is true of parts of *The Evidence of Love, The Rape of Tamar,* and, to a lesser extent, *The Wonder-Worker.* This theme can be found in many of the short stories as well.

While resenting the way the *zeide* has failed to be a provider for his family, Harry Grossman is perversely jealous when the old man submits contentedly to the company of the Zulu and to his ministrations. Harry tries—too harshly, though—to offer himself to his father, and fails. At the end of the story, when Harry learns of Paulus's strong family feeling, he weeps, and the reader feels that Harry's new awareness can redeem him from being the unlovable and unloving man he is.

In **"The Little Pet,"**[4] another of Jacobson's parent-child stories, the end is not quite so helpful. In this tale, parents who seem ill at ease with their own little son, acquire a pregnant female rabbit for him as a pet, but they make much more of the rabbit than the child does. When the animal finally produces one runtish little brat and eats it, the adults are horrified and want to get rid of it instantly. But the little boy says to it knowingly: "I'm not cross with you. I knew you didn't like your baby."[5]

On the other hand, there is an interesting and ultimately compassionate interplay between a parent-figure and a young man in the story **"Fresh Fields."**[6] The parent-figure, an old South African writer who has lived for many years in England, is admired by the young man, also a South African and also an aspiring writer. In England, the young man seeks out Traill, the author, and is encouraged to show his work to the older man who, incidentally, has not been able to publish for some time. The young man finds out after a while that Traill is writing again, reworking the young man's material and publishing it under his own name. Traill's explanation is that the young man's work derives from his own earlier stuff in any case. Traill is, like the *zeide* and Avrom Glickman, preying off the products, literary in this instance, of his own "offspring." In this story, however, the young man does not resent the "parent." He decides to make a clean break from his literary father. He gives all his work to Traill to use and resolves to start afresh, no longer to write about South Africa as Traill has continued to do. The young man makes no accusation against Traill: instead the story ends with him living on hope, "just on hope" (***TW*** [***Through the Wilderness***], 83).

In its own distinctive way **"Fresh Fields"** links up, as does **"The Zulu and the Zeide,"** with the immigrant experience explored so extensively in Jacobson's work. The *zeide* cannot settle down to normal living in South Africa; Traill, the emigre writer, cannot write in England unless his subject is South Africa, whereas the young man hopes to do what Jacobson himself has done—successfully reject South Africa as the only setting for his work.

Part of the immigrant experience and part of the colonial experience—aspects of which Jacobson himself has undergone—involves a sense of alienation. The *zeide* has this sense and Traill has it. Fink and Gottlieb in *The Price of Diamonds* do not feel entirely that they belong to any of the various communities in Lundhurst. Joel Glickman in *The Beginners* does not achieve contentment when he tries to live in Israel and is only marginally less uncomfortable in England. Jacobson himself rejected Israel as a home in 1949, but that country was first explored by him fictively in a story called **"The Break,"**[7] though in this narrative the discontented person is an American.

Although this feeling of alienation is not confined to Jacobson's Jewish characters (the narrator of *The Dance in the Sun,* an English-speaking South African, has an intimation of it, as does Yonadab in *The Rape of Tamar*), Jacobson does generally present Jews as experiencing discomfort at their Jewishness in a country like South Africa where they have been perceived as aliens. In **"A Day in the Country"**[8] a Jewish family from Lyndhurst, out on a Sunday's excursion, and aware of their "difference," are hesitant to challenge an Afrikaner group who are frightening a black child. The sense of "difference" becomes more articulate in the story **"An Apprentice-**

ship" where a Jewish boy realizes that he envies his gentile friends, the Pallings, because

> they seemed so much safer, so much more secure than ourselves. The Palling boys did not have to read in the newspapers about the massacre of their fellow-Jews in Europe; they did not have to protest against anti-Jewish remarks made by boorish schoolmasters, or uglier things said in the playground by schoolboys; they did not have to bear a special burden of guilt and sympathy towards the blacks; they did not have to flinch inwardly when their parents mispronounced an English word.
>
> (***TW,*** 95)

To a certain extent acceptance is achieved by the Jewish immigrant if he is financially successful. In **"The Example of Lipi Lippmann"**[9] the ex-mayor of Lyndhurst is a Jew, and the story is about the embarrassment Lipi has caused, in his degrading poverty, to the wealthy and respected Jews in the town, in spite of the fact that his poverty is useful to them in their own uneasiness at the stereotypic way gentiles view them:

> In Lyndhurst, if a Gentile spoke enviously to a Jew about how rich the Jews of Lyndhurst were, how clever they were, how well they did in business, the reply was often made—"Well, it's not really true about all the Jews. Just look at Lipi Lippman!" No one, not even the biggest anti-Semite in the world could say that Lipi Lippmann was rich or clever or did well in business.
>
> Lipi Lippmann once said that the Jews of Lyndhurst should pay him to remain poor, his poverty was so useful in arguments. But the joke was received in silence; it was felt to be in bad taste. The Jews of Lyndhurst were ready to use Lipi Lippman's poverty to propitiate an envious Gentile, but they were ashamed of him nevertheless. . . .
>
> (***TW,*** 84)

So, Jews, in a sense, are damned if they do and damned if they don't. The ex-mayor, to achieve acceptance in the town, has not only had to achieve affluence, but has also had to devote himself to social and community activities: "He had also been the captain of the local golf club and the president of the local Red Cross Society; he was still chairman of the Chamber of Commerce and a member of the City Council" (***TW,*** 91). But still not entirely comfortable with his position, he has to reiterate his belief in "inter-faith relations" (***TW,*** 91). Lipi, on the other hand, despised by all because the hawking trade he plies has become a low-caste Indian one, is jeered at by Afrikaner children as *Koelie-Jood*—meaning Coolee-Jew, and is a source of shame to other Jews. One day Lipi's house is robbed when he is out. The plan he devises when he discovers the theft is a brilliant yet logical one. He lets it be known that the money-box taken from his humble home had all his savings in it, money he hoped to use to go to *Eretz Yisroel.* Guilty and remorseful, prominent Jews and gentiles in the town make a collection to provide Lipi with the needed money so that he can fulfill his dream. And the idea of the dream is not entirely inaccurate on their part: Lipi had regularly dreamed that he was in Palestine, a poignant dream of landscape and light and of "white houses, with red-tiled roofs, in the distance" (***TW,*** 89). But he had never been able to save money towards going to this dream-country.

When Lipi's lies about the burglary are believed, he is distressed and confused. He tries handing the gift money back to the ex-mayor, but is told in anger to go away and never come back. All that day Lipi wanders around the town and into the African locations. That night he throws himself under a train. We are told that "Lipi's funeral was enormous; and it was noticed that the ex-mayor of the town was among those who seemed most affected by grief at the graveside" (***TW,*** 92).

The ex-mayor, who is twenty years younger than Lipi, reacts to the old man's death in much the same way as Harry Grossman does to his father's. Again there is the implication that the younger man has realized his own callousness, so that in this story the theme of Jewishness is interlocked with that of the parent-child relationship.

The facts of Jewishness and attachment to *Eretz Yisroel* are touched on in several of the stories, sometimes strongly as in **"The Example of Lipi Lippmann"** and sometimes lightly. In **"Led Astray"** (***TW,*** 184) which is about a young couple living together in London, the young man Lewin is described as having "the face of a Russian peasant" (***TW,*** 185). Lewin admits that this is probably true, but adds that "his mind was 'all Jew'" (***TW,*** 186). His girlfriend, who is not Jewish, claims that this assertion is vulgar and they argue about it. But, all in all, nothing much is made of Lewin's Jewishness either by himself or by the narrator of the story. But the young narrator in **"Through the Wilderness"** (***TW,*** 154), an unorthodox fellow who has never taken his Hebrew lessons seriously, is brought to the point of dwelling deeply on the implications of Judaism and what it means to him when he meets an emaciated black preacher who calls himself an "Israelite" and who is convinced that he and the young man were destined to meet for the young man's spiritual benefit.

On the sixteen stories in a collection like ***Through the Wilderness,*** seven are about Jews. Of Jacobson's eight novels, four have Jewish protagonists. So when Jacobson says to an interviewer, "I suppose I'm a Jewish writer insofar as I'm a Jew. To what extent that is so, I don't really know: it varies with circumstances, depending on what I'm writing . . .,"[10] we can interpret this explanation as an attempt to resist categorization. Jacobson has never wanted to be classified as a particular kind of author, and the versatility of his work has testified to his ability to remain elusive to critical pinpointing.

Nonetheless, Jacobson has understood and expressed his own Jewish experience and the experience of Jewish immigrants living in a town like Lyndhurst in a vital and convincing way. But it is his own way, and very little can be gained, it would seem, in castigating him where the expression of that experience does not parallel what other Jewish writers have written. What Joel Glickman in *The Beginners* says could, to a large extent, be applied to Jacobson himself:

> ". . . We are trying to cure ourselves of all the false, negative ways of being set apart that we suffer from, the wrong kinds of specialness. Or loneliness . . . Loneliness, marginality—I don't know what the word is. But I know what the state is: to be a kind of demi-European at the bottom of Africa, to be a demi-Jew among Gentiles. Other people have other ways of suffering from it."
>
> (p. 194)

Jacobson's Jewish characters do not look for seclusion or exclusion; they want to be part of a larger community in the countries they emigrate to, while being allowed their individual beliefs, rituals, and habits.

Because this matter of being set apart, of being chosen or special, whether as a Jew, a genius, or a villain, has informed to varying degrees the characters in all Jacobson's fictions, as has his own ambivalent attitude to being Jewish, the reader feels (*post facto*) almost as if he could have predicted Jacobson's most recent work, an examination "in a spirit of critical speculation" (p. vii) of the scriptural myth of an all-powerful God choosing a specific people for his own purposes. This study, called *The Story of the Stories: The Chosen People and its God,*[11] allows Jacobson to argue publicly, as it were, his response to the Hebrew Scriptures (and the Christian ones to a lesser extent) and his reasons for persisting through life as a secular Jew resisting categorization.

The Story of the Stories is an exciting book. It succeeds in combining the unexpected and thought-provoking postulations of the best kind of essay with the narrative tension and calculated release of information of the novel. Jacobson involves the reader profoundly in the drama of the covenant between the people of Israel and Yahweh, managing to keep the reader intensely concerned about this reciprocal arrangement even *while* he is maintaining that the God of the Israelites is a fiction, a construct of their imaginations, an invention that helped the writers and redactors of the Scriptures "to interpret in the terms bequeathed to them *by the text itself,* everything that happened to them, and everything they hoped or feared might happen to their people in the future" (p. 5). Jacobson presents the pendulum swing of biblical events (with most of which we are already familiar) in such a skillful, suspenseful way that we must read on, curiously hopeful that the outcome will be different *this* time, that the pattern will be broken. The experience is comparable to rereading *King Lear,* with our hoping against hope, as we tend to do, that the king will on this reading, miraculously, not make a fool of himself.

Jacobson is not a theologian, nor, as he acknowledges, does he have "scholarly knowledge of the languages in which the Scriptures were originally written" (p. vii), yet *The Story of the Stories* is subtle, well informed, and serious enough to have elicited lengthy responses from Dr. Jonathan Sacks, a Rabbi,[12] from Hillel Halkin,[13] an Israeli writer and critic, and from David Lodge,[14] the novelist and literary critic. And Lodge compares Jacobson's book not unfavorably with Robert Alter's *The Art of Biblical Narrative.*[15]

I would assess that *The Story of the Stories* will enjoy its greatest popularity, not with readers in search of arguments to debunk religious beliefs, but with those who, familiar with Jacobson's other work, come to it for literary excitement. For the strange thing is that, although Dan Jacobson's arguments are cogent and rational, his eloquence and intensity are such that the reader willingly suspends disbelief—against the author's own injuctions—and is drawn into the tragic drama, identifying with the Israelites (in pity) and with Yahweh (in fear). In the author's own words, the book reads "*like* a story, as well as being an analysis *of* a story."[16]

The Painful Truth

The South African writer has traditionally seen his function as largely that of a critic of racial discrimination and the various governmental policies of apartheid (apartheid does *not* begin with the coming to power of the National Government in 1948). Much of Jacobson's work incorporates such criticism, especially *The Trap, A Dance in the Sun,* and *The Evidence of Love.* Short stories like **"A Way of Life"** (*TW,* 47) and **"Beggar My Neighbour"** (*TW,* 58) deal with the poverty and helplessness of black people and the guilt and shame of whites who recognize their plight but can only make feeble efforts to alleviate it. In this respect, Jacobson's work relates to much of the fiction by other English-speaking South Africans, particularly to a novelist like Nadine Gordimer, in that it exposes the helpless and not-quite-honest stance of the South African liberal.

In **"A Way of Life,"** for instance, when Lena, the Capons' housemaid, falls ill, a white doctor is brought in to treat her. He diagnoses a heart complaint and says that the woman must stop working, adding for the Capons' benefit:

> ". . . But you can't let yourself get too involved, you know. And I suppose she'll be able to draw some kind of sickness benefit—I'll write out anything she needs for that, if she applies."
>
> (*TW,* 55)

But there are no real social benefits for which black people are eligible. The Capons understand Lena's plight and their own dilemma, but they are not capable of thinking the problem through to its conclusion, which is that black people must be given political and civil rights so that they can make provision for their own destitute, sick, and elderly people. The narrator points out, from the Capons' point of view:

> What were they to do? The Capons were decent people, who conscientiously voted for the most liberal candidate at elections, and who talked frequently of getting out of South Africa altogether, the whole racial set-up was so distasteful to them. Not that their getting out would help people like Lena. Poor bloody Lena. What could they do with her? They couldn't pay for her upkeep indefinitely. . . .
>
> (*TW*, 56)

The Capons are, of course, unconscious of what they are revealing about themselves: their snobbish response to the racial situation as being merely "distasteful" and their voting for "the most liberal candidate," which does not involve them in calling for full electoral democracy in South Africa.

The story ends with Lena insisting on coming back to work and Leslie Capon calling out to her that she might fall ill again and then "Whose fault will it be?" (***TW***, 56). He has achieved a vague inkling that it might, in fact, be his own fault.

But because of Jacobson's long residence in England, his many visits to the United States and Israel, and more recently to Australia,[17] he has broadened his observations of human selfishness and the universal fear and dislike of "the other." Using the weapons of his superbly lucid prose and his subtle irony, he has become a critic of all the societies he has known, but without ever having become a moralizer: his sense of humor and his slightly malicious delight in human foibles and the absurdity of human self-delusion prevent him from losing his stance as an observer. As one reviewer wrote about his first collection of short stories, ***A Long Way from London,*** he mostly uses a "spare, undecorated style suited to his shrewd observation and humor, and usually, though not always, saving him from sentimentality."[18] For instance, all of these qualities and perhaps some sentimentality come into play in the story **"Led Astray."** Here the young English couple come to recognize the uncaring attitude of their relationship when a neighbor, abandoned by her husband, gives birth to a child in the apartment above theirs. And in a recently published story, **"The Summer-School Project of Jay Edward Ashridge,"**[19] a visiting university professor to the United States is made a fool of and obliquely threatened by a student in the student's fiction-writing assignment.

The young couple in **"Led Astray"** were deluding themselves that they could remain forever uninvolved in the full pain of living; the university professor deludes himself that he is creating the impression he wants to on his students. In a startlingly colorful story, **"The Pretenders"** (***TW,*** 115), an insignificant young man from Lyndhurst imagines that he can become a film star when a movie company comes to town. Unable to accept his rejection, the young man shoots the actual star but fortunately does not kill him. What is fascinating in this story is the way the towns folk shift their sympathies backwards and forwards to one or another of the characters. In **"Another Day"** (***TW,*** 140), a shocking story of black poverty and dejection, a young white boy follows a small, shabby funeral party of black people, deluding himself that there is something not immediately evident that he can find out. But he keeps his distance, learns nothing, and is mysteriously promised by the black man who pulled the funeral cart (the corpse was that of a baby) that he will see things "Another time . . . Another day" (***TW,*** 144).

From these stories the reader comes to understand how Jacobson has gained the reputation "as a masterly teller of the painful truth."[20] His short stories, unlike his later novels, may not be experimental or innovative in form (the short story is in any case the most conservative of literary genres) but there is no doubt that they are memorable in a strongly visual way. The reader cannot forget the two incongruous figures of the Zulu and the *zeide* walking hand in hand down the streets of Lyndhurst, nor that of Boaz, the black Israelite in **"Through the Wilderness"** (***TW,*** 154) who lies deathly ill while his white master prepares to sacrifice a goat for his recovery, nor that of Lipi Lippmann biting his hand and laughing hysterically when he discovers that he has been robbed of his meager possessions. Then there is the compelling scene in **"An Apprenticeship"** where a young boy is jeered at by the husband of the older woman he admires, only to retort to the husband, "You admired her too," and receive a blow. We recognize Dan Jacobson's deep understanding of human nature in the story **"Trial and Error"** (***TW,*** 102) where a young husband stands close to the wife who has left him and returned, begging, "Jennifer, don't do it again, don't do it again," while knowing full well that their incompatibility has not been resolved.

More Children

Many of Jacobson's stories are suitable for younger readers, both those which he has intentionally written for children and others, probably meant for adults, but revealing an unusually sensitive understanding of the minds of children and the way the larger world impinges on them. In the first category, stories written for children, are **"Pots and Pans for Sale,"**[21] a story about a Lithuanian boy who has the job of selling pots and pans in the streets of London, and **"The Long, Happy Life of a Ragamuffin,"**[22] about a beloved pet dog named Poker. In the second category, stories written for and enjoyed by adults, are those like **"The Box"** (***TW,*** 1), **"The Game"** (***TW,*** 40), **The Thief,"**[23] and **"A Way of Life."** The last two—**"The Thief"** and **"A Way of Life"**—were in fact published together for use in high schools in England for upper-intermediate students.[24]

"The Thief" is a particularly disturbing story because it illustrates how intensely the dehumanizing attitudes of adults toward black servants can be transferred to children. In this story the house of a wealthy white family is broken into by an "undersized, townbred"[25] African of seventeen. The police are, of course, called. But when the father of the house takes no action against the young thief, his son, only a child, screams in anger and disappointment:

> ". . . Hit the thief! Hit the thief!" he danced on his bare feet, waving his small fists in the air. "Why don't you hit the burglar? You must hit the burglar." He danced like a little devil in his light pyjamas. "Hit!" he screamed. "Hit!" His little sister joined in because she heard her brother shouting, and she added her high scream to his: "Hit the thief!"[26]

The boy has to be forcibly carried out of the room. The next day, his mother thinks with pride of her son's strong will and his aggressiveness. The reader is left despairing for a country in which such people have control.

"The Game," which has partially a similar tone to **"The Thief,"** tells of three teen-age boys who go hunting game on a farm. They see their hunting as not only "sportsmanship" but as a foreshadowing of their behavior in the war they hope to join. The narrator, who is thirteen, thinks:

> . . . There in the north there were places like Tobruk, El Alamein, Bardia, Mersa Matruh, that seemed to me, when the older ones took the rifle, just beyond the horizon that encircled us in a whitish glare of heat.
>
> (***TW,*** 45)

One deer is shot. As the oldest of the three boys is aiming at the second one, the narrator hears his brother urge the animal to "Go on, run!" (***TW,*** 45). At that moment, the implications of war seem to be clearer to the boys, and they reach a shamefaced admission that going to war is not as desirable a venture as they had been pretending. It will also be for them a final step out of the world of children into the harsh world of adults.

The ending of **"The Game"** is similar to that of **"The Box."** Here the children of the family have been on amiable terms with a young colored houseboy named Jan. The white children have as a hobby the breeding of homing pigeons and, to please them and show off a little, Jan tries to make a pigeon "hock" (pen) for the birds. He does not make it accurately, however, and without consulting him, one of the white boys breaks it up for use in the aviaries. He is astonished when Jan cries bitterly to see the destruction of his "box." Thereafter a distance is created between Jan and the white boys, widened by the white childrens' growing sense of the color barrier. The story ends on a sad note, one almost of defeat. The narrator, one of the boys, assesses that they were all saved "that self-consciousness which colour can become" (***TW,*** 7) because Jan, who has joined the army, was killed at El Adhem, near Tobruk. Thus, once again, the questions of human dignity, of giving and demanding of consideration and respect, and, more important still, the questions of social and political justice, are shelved, and people live on, as best they can, in all their blindness, vulnerability, and pain.

Dan Jacobson says that he has "virtually stopped writing stories"[27] which, in view of his considerable talent and versatility, is a great loss to the reader. Perhaps the compulsion that drove him to write those we have will in time reassert itself insistently enough to force him to return to weaving "the interplay of human relations and emotional situations common to people the world over"[28] that he has developed so adeptly and expressed so well. What makes one hopeful that Jacobson's stories will once again reappear in journals, magazines, and collections the world over is his obvious penchant for storytelling, for yarns and tales, a penchant evident even in much of his nonfiction. I have already mentioned how *The Story of the Stories,* a critical discussion of the Hebrew Scriptures, conveys "a feeling of narrative tension within it, with plot, sub-plots, doubling-back in time, denouement, etc."[29] so that it reads like a story. His earlier collection of travel articles, *No Further West,* inspired by his stay in Palo Alto in California, has a gripping, other-worldly quality about it and makes use of several novelistic devices.

The reader is charmed and his attention immediately held when, in the early pages of *No Further West,* Jacobson presents the view from an airplane traveling between New York and Los Angeles as if it were from the vantage point of the rider of the magic carpet or Peter Pan:

> . . . and we flew over the America that unrolled itself like a map beneath us. There was the North-West, fertile, industrialized, thickly-populated; there were the Great Lakes, with Chicago in tiny blocks along the side of one of the Lakes; there was the Middle West, the fields in squares and oblongs on the flat earth. There was a winding, leisurely river, brown and snake-like. . . . Then in wrinkles on the horizon, and later in warts and fissures nearer to us were the Rockies . . .

> some of the mountains were of a size that, trapped and liberated in our reaches of light and air, we could nevertheless recognize with awe.
>
> (p. 13)

The fantastic plane journey ends, but the wonderment has only begun. Jacobson describes his astonishment at his first sight of San Francisco by emphasizing (as he does throughout the Californian essays in the book) the bewilderingly vast numbers of motor cars:

> —more parked cars than I had ever seen before me in a single place, stretching in an unbroken expanse towards some kind of bridge in the distance. Over the bridge there were other cars that moved in a continual procession . . . and from the night sky broken only by the chasing headlights there came the sound of the cars—a continual rustle, a fall of sound, a whisper out of the throat of the night.
>
> (p. 14)

In fact, the whole country seems to be in perpetual, circling movement to the bemused traveler. Is San Francisco really like that? The reader asks, and immediately realizes that it is, but that he had become too accustomed to the American love-affair with the automobile to recognize it. He wonders, fascinated, how the Jacobsons, Dan, his wife, and child, are going to adapt, seeing that they are *not* accustomed to it. Of course, the newcomers don't know themselves how they are to survive.

Jacobson goes on to depict the frightening confusion of the complex clover-leaf overpasses they drive on and the fast-moving traffic on the wide Bayshore Highway where, for him, "it became too much, the imagination simply retreated and despaired, the mind was numbed" (p. 25).

Yet, when the numbed feeling passes, he achieves the instant determination to write a book for the outside world, as well as for Californians, because none of them knows what it is *like.* He is convinced that even the Californians themselves don't recognize the surreality of the things they have constructed on their earth. His description of a drive-in fast-food joint, at which they stop on their first night, is phrased with such brilliant humor and sense of stupefaction that the newcomers seem to be visitors on a strange planet.

Their amazement subsides only slightly when the Jacobsons arrive at their lodgings. Their landlady is an odd, witchlike creature with a bent body, splayed legs, and hair hanging in wisps over her forehead. "Age had withered her all right," Jacobson writes ironically, "but custom could not stale her variety" (p. 17).

The next day the author asks "in fear, in anger, in despair" . . .

> Why hadn't anyone *told* me? . . . What I saw was all new, brand-new, and of a size and populousness and a busyness that I couldn't begin to comprehend. Why hadn't anyone told me about it? Why hadn't I been warned?
>
> (p. 20)

From this moment on the reader is caught. With nose to the page and a quickening pulse, he immerses himself in the author's perplexities (comparable to those of Gulliver). *No Further West* has ceased to be a travel book (if it ever was one) and has become the suspenseful narration—almost a science-fiction—of an innocent, not merely abroad, but traveling extraterrestrially.

In Palo Alto the space is familiar, Jacobson concedes; the newness, the sandiness all remind him of South Africa. But of the town itself he says:

> . . . I had no word for it. It was a sprawl, a mess, a nightmare of repetition and disjunction and incoherence, all grown permanent and powerful.
>
> There were shops, identical houses in tracts, drive-ins, motels, factories, shopping centres, supermarkets, giant billboards, filling-stations, used-car lots all along El Camino Real. There were identical houses in tracts, drive-ins, motels, shopping-centres, supermarkets, giant billboards all along the Bayshore Highway; there were whole towns of identical houses in tracts between the Bayshore Highway and El Camino Real; and further again, and further yet, there were used-car lots and giant billboards and shopping centres and supermarkets. . . .
>
> (pp. 20-21)

And from this endlessly repeated mass, each morning the inhabitants drove off in their cars, to work or to shop, so that "the very air of the towns was filled night and day with the whisper of the traffic on the highways" (p. 23).

Trying to make sense of the new world in which he finds himself, Jacobson compares it to the other countries he has lived in, South Africa and Britain. They are, he admits, "two of the most caste-conscious societies in the Western World" (p. 24), but they are, at least, societies which possess "recognizable structures, ways of ordering people, and their towns, their dress, their manners, their speech, their relationships with one another." What is disconcerting about California to him is that it seems to have "no order, no hierarchy, no gradations, no class distinctions, no classes, no structure at all. Just people. And more people. And more people again" (p. 25).

Too many people, and too many cars, all looking the same—that is what he sees. And the cars seem designed to please the taste of "a nouveau-riche, detribalized and probably drunken Arab chieftain who had just made a fortune out of oil (and a little slave-running on the side—the side nearest his heart)" (p. 26).

The reader, concerned about the transplanted Jacobsons, is relieved by the humor of these passages and comforted when he reads that these multitudes did have faces, each one as good as the other "And their manners were alike . . . people said 'Hi!' to each other in greeting, with a sideways and backwards jerk of the head, as if shaking something free of themselves" (p. 27). They don't seem that menacing even if there is "a watchful, withdrawn quality" and "a blankness of response that could be disconcerting in the extreme" (p. 27).

Jacobson discovered what is a commonplace to the majority of Americans, which is that they live in a very mobile society. Most of the Californians he met were not originally from California. He also came to realize how transient the buildings and objects were, too; how newly established and how fragile-looking. Other writers have dealt with these aspects of American society, e.g., Alvin Tofler in *Future Shock* and Norman Mailer in *The Executioner's Song*. For the most memorable literary reconstruction of this America is in Vladimir Nabokov's *Lolita,* and it is peculiarly satisfying to notice that Nabokov, like Jacobson, considers all of us, Westerners, Easterners, the whole world, to be "American," to partake of the newness, the sameness, the shabbiness, the migrations. Jacobson says:

> For if we all regard ourselves as Americans of a kind, we do not do so with any hope or favour—America is no promised land, no golden west, but the wasteland where we live. "America"—we like to believe—is what is *dejà vu,* uprooted, nomadic, indiscriminate, faceless, shapeless; it is the uniformity that is spreading faster and faster over the whole habitable globe. . . .
>
> (p. 29)

But the confusion, the disorientation, and the helplessness experienced by Jacobson and his family did not remain unmodified. He had to give in and buy a car, even against his fixed intention to do without, and they had to find other accommodation away from the Dickensian landlady. Once reestablished, they were happier and more at peace.

As the book progresses, Jacobson's attitudes to the Californians and their way of life became increasingly tolerant. He is sardonic and yet praising of the zany grade school system; he is shocked and yet seduced by the plenty and the technical efficiency; he even comes to acknowledge the excellence of the ubiquitous popsingers, pointing out that they are always better then their foreign counterparts—the "English versions generally are poorer, thinner, quieter, weaker in every way . . ." (p. 51).

But Jacobson is not quite disarmed yet. He criticizes the way Americans simply thrust down their towns and houses, "ignoring, making null and unnoticeable the country on which they are built; and the country, for its part, seems to have nothing to do with the towns and the houses that have been placed on it" (p. 65). And he comments on the rawness, the distances, and the violence that has been done. However, he does seem to gain with each page he writes a deeper, more compassionate understanding of the place. He acknowledges:

> But when one *sees* a place like Modesto or Madera, the wonder is only that there is not more [violence] yet; and when one considers that most of these people do in fact come from elsewhere, and are new to their country, and that their loudest guides to conduct seem to be the advertisers and the radio and the television and the tabloid press, the wonder is that they aren't all continuously and desperately at war with one another, that there is so little frenzy, so few stabbings and acts of arson and bombing, that over a continent of towns like Modesto and even worse cities, there should be so much peace, so much gentleness.
>
> (p. 67)

Many non-American academics have been contemptuous, even angry, about the teaching of creative writing in American universities. Theodore Roethke's scathing short story "Last Class" comes to mind. Jacobson, who had a fellowship to Stanford for the 1957-58 academic year, points out that the current British attitude is that undergraduates are bound to write poetry and fiction, but that that is no reason why they should be given credit for their scribblings toward a degree; that to do so is merely another example of the way Americans indulge their children. But he enjoyed attending the creative writing classes and came to see their establishment in universities as an example, not of American indulgence, but of American optimism, of the belief that one can do *anything* if one puts one's mind to it; that one can learn anything and teach anything.

So, by the time he has completed two-thirds of the book, the reader relaxes with pleasure, not only in the recognition, through Jacobson's imaginative prose, of his own world, but in the certitude that the Jacobsons benefited from their stay on Planet California, and that the author himself created an exciting book about his visit to the west.

It is surely an indication of the strength of the versatile immigrant stock from which Jacobson comes that, in the matter of eight or nine months, he grew out of discomfort with America into an admiration for, of all things, American gentleness, liberality, and firmness of will. He even ended up admitting that, if the world is being Americanized, there are elements for the good in this process. We can learn from Americans, he wrote,

> . . . a new respect for our own wills, whose exercise need not always result in enmity, destruction, and despair. For none of us now is there any way of survival, but through will and awareness.
>
> (p. 127)

Notes

1. First published as "The Head of the Family," *Mademoiselle* 43 (26 July 1956).
2. *American Judaism* 12 (Winter 1962-63).
3. "Starting Out," a memoir by H. M. Jacobson (ed. Dan Jacobson) *New Review* 3 (n.d.).

4. Included in *A Long Way from London, The Zulu and the Zeide,* and *Through the Wilderness,* and also published in *Stanford Short Stories,* eds. W. Stegner and R. Scowcroft (Palo Alto: Stanford University Press, 1958), p. 17.
5. "The Little Pet," *Through the Wilderness* (Harmondsworth, 1977), p. 39; hereafter references to this edition cited in the text as *TW.*
6. First published in *Encounter* 17 (3 October 1961).
7. First published in *Commentary* 18 (October 1954).
8. First published as "Dutchman, Jew, Piccanin," *Commentary,* 16 (September 1953).
9. First published in *Commentary* 32 (November 1961).
10. Meir Mindlin, "A Talk with Dan Jacobson," *Jewish Affairs* 14 (August 1959): 22.
11. *The Story of the Stories* (New York, 1982); hereafter page references to this edition cited in the text.
12. Dr. Jonathan Sacks, BBC Broadcast, "Exorcizing the Past," September 1982.
13. Hillel Halkin, "The Wheel of History," *Commentary,* (September 1982), pp. 68-74.
14. David Lodge, "Readings and Lessons," *Times Literary Supplement* (London), 5 November 1982, pp. 1207-8.
15. Robert Alter, *The Art of Biblical Narrative* (New York: Allen and Unwin, 1982).
16. In a letter to this author dated "Boxing Day '80."
17. In a letter to this author dated 28 September 1981, Dan Jacobson wrote ". . . I've been to Australia and back: I was there for 3 months, at the University of Canberra, and enjoyed it greatly; more than I was expecting. Things in it (some of the vowel-sounds included!) were reminiscent of South Africa . . . I felt very relaxed there: in fact being there, in a "colonial" country which was like S. A. and yet so much unlike S.A., I realized just how constrained I still feel here in England, after all these years. It was a rather disheartening realisation, actually. I suppose the English *still* have the knack of making one (me) feel "one-down" somehow. The Aussies (and Americans) don't have it, to their credit."
18. Anonymous reviewer, *Cape Times,* 24 October 1958, p. 9.
19. *New Review* 5 (Autumn 1978): 23-37.
20. Anonymous reviewer, *New Statesman* 68 (October 1964).
21. *World Over,* 31 October 1958, p. 6.
22. *Country Beautiful,* 2, 10 November 1962.
23. First published in *Commentary* 21 (April 1956).
24. *Cambridge English Language Learning* (Cambridge: Cambridge University Press, 1977).
25. Ibid., p. 6.
26. Ibid., p. 7.
27. In a letter to this author dated 28 September 1981.
28. Anonymous reviewer, *Christian Science Monitor,* 11 June 1959, p. 9.
29. In a letter to this author dated "Boxing Day '82."

FURTHER READING

Criticism

Meades, Jonathan. Review of *Inklings,* by Dan Jacobson. *Books and Bookmen* 18, no. 10 (July 1973): 116.

Provides a thematic overview of the stories in *Inklings.*

Young, Dudley. "*Through the Wilderness.*" *New York Times Book Review* (24 November 1986): 66.

Contends that the stories in *Through the Wilderness* exhibit a "remarkable consistency in style, tone and subject matter."

Additional coverage of Jacobson's life and career is contained in the following sources published by Thomson Gale: *African Writers*; *Contemporary Authors,* Vols. 1-4R; *Contemporary Authors New Revision Series,* Vols. 2, 25, 66; *Contemporary Literary Criticism,* Vols. 4, 14; *Contemporary Novelists,* Ed. 7; *Dictionary of Literary Biography,* Vols. 14, 207, 225, 319; *Encyclopedia of World Literature in the 20th Century,* Ed. 3; *Literature Resource Center*; *Major 20th-Century Writers,* Ed. 1; and *Reference Guide to Short Fiction.*

Ruth Prawer Jhabvala
1927-

German-born English novelist, screenwriter, and short story writer.

INTRODUCTION

Best known for her novels and screenplays, Jhabvala is also recognized as a talented short story writer. Critics praise her complex, nuanced exploration of such themes as alienation, rebellion, cultural assimilation, and tension between traditional and modern as well as Indian and Western lifestyles in her fiction. Citing her experiences as an outsider and immigrant as a profound influence on her novels and short stories, they focus on her satirical and insightful perspective on Indian and Western life.

BIOGRAPHICAL INFORMATION

Jhabvala was born on May 7, 1927, in Cologne, Germany, to Jewish-Polish parents. When the Nazis seized political power in the 1930s, Jhabvala's immediate family escaped to England, settling in a suburb of London. In 1951 she received a master's degree in English literature from Queen Mary College at London University. She married Cyrus S. H. Jhabvala, a Parsi architect whom she had met in London, and they moved to Delhi, India, where many of her short stories are set. After the publication of her novel *The Householder* in 1960, she was approached by the independent filmmakers Ismail Merchant and James Ivory, who proposed that she write the screenplay for a cinematic adaptation of her novel. That was the first of several collaborations with the filmmakers; others include *Heat and Dust* (1983), *The Remains of the Day* (1993), and *Jefferson in Paris* (1995). She has received several prestigious awards for her novels and screenplays, many of which are adaptations of the novels of such writers as Henry James, E. M. Forster, and Jean Rhys. Jhabvala lives in New York City.

MAJOR WORKS OF SHORT FICTION

Drawn from her experiences as an outsider in Indian society, Jhabvala's short stories have been divided by critics into three main groups: stories about Indians, stories about Europeans living in India, and stories about the interaction between Indians and Westerners. Initially appearing in prominent magazines such as the *New Yorker,* her stories utilize satire to explore modern Indian life and the tension between traditional and modern values. Several stories depict repressed and alienated characters stifled by the rigidity of Indian social and cultural mores, searching for spiritual or romantic fulfillment against great odds. In "The Housewife," a matronly housewife, Shakuntala, becomes aroused by her intense passion for music, which is encouraged by her music teacher. When her teacher's wife leaves him in despair, Shakuntala risks her marriage and placid middle-class existence by offering herself to him, starting a life-changing love affair. For Jhabvala's Western characters, the search for fulfillment in India often calls for great sacrifice. In "The Young Couple," for example, Cathy and Narain, a young, happily married couple, move to Delhi to be near his family. Soon, Cathy realizes that maintaining harmony with her new family and husband will mean losing some of her individuality and freedom. Several of Jhabvala's other stories also concern a crisis of identity, particularly of American or European characters who attempt to assimilate in India and almost invariably fail. In "Miss Sahib," an aging British schoolteacher feels alienated from her English roots as well as her life in India. "Rose Petals" explores the ways in which different members of an upper-class Indian family perceive and react to the pervasive poverty that surrounds them. In "Commensurate Happiness," a pair of distant cousins—a closeted gay man and a shy woman—are pressured into marriage by family and friends. Despite nagging doubts, the two delude themselves that the marriage will be an ultimately fulfilling one. Set in India and New York City, the stories in her latest collection, *East into Upper East* (1998), further explore Jhabvala's central themes of displacement, loneliness, family dynamics, and the search for romantic fulfillment.

CRITICAL RECEPTION

Jhabvala is considered a highly accomplished short story writer. Critics praise her use of irony and satire as well as her insight into the dynamics of interfamily and intercultural relations. Some reviewers find fault with her spare dialogue, lack of dramatic intensity, and slow narrative pace, but others view her narrative technique as part of her strategy to reveal the Indian character slowly and by degree. Commentators have noted the autobiographical nature of Jhabvala's stories, particularly the ways in which she draws on her childhood as the daughter of Polish Jewish parents in pre-Holocaust Germany, her marriage and life in India, and her residence in New York and Delhi. Others examine the relationship between her stories and her novels and analyze the connection between "Myself in India," her introductory essay from her second collection of short stories, *An Experience of India,* and her short fiction. Described as a naturalistic short story writer, Jhabvala is often compared to Anton Chekhov because of her narrative preoccupation with such thematic concerns as loneliness, boredom, and the decline of society.

PRINCIPAL WORKS

Short Fiction

Like Birds, Like Fishes, and Other Stories 1963
A Stronger Climate: Nine Stories 1968
An Experience of India 1971
How I Became a Holy Mother and Other Stories 1976
Out of India: Selected Stories 1986
East into Upper East: Plain Tales from New York and New Delhi 1998

Other Major Works

To Whom She Will (novel) 1955; also published as *Amrita,* 1956
The Nature of Passion (novel) 1956
Esmond in India (novel) 1957
The Householder (novel) 1960
Get Ready for Battle (novel) 1962
A Backward Place (novel) 1965
**Shakespeare Wallah* (screenplay) 1965
**The Guru* [with James Ivory] (screenplay) 1968
A New Dominion (novel) 1971; also published as *Travelers,* 1973
Autobiography of a Princess (novel) 1975
Heat and Dust (novel) 1975
**The Europeans* [adaptor, with Ivory; from the novel by Henry James] (screenplay) 1979
**Jane Austen in Manhattan* (screenplay) 1980
A Call from the East (play) 1981
**Quartet* [adaptor, with Ivory; from the novel by Jean Rhys] (screenplay) 1981
**Heat and Dust* (screenplay) 1983
In Search of Love and Beauty (novel) 1983
**The Bostonians* [adaptor; from the novel by Henry James] (screenplay) 1984
**A Room with a View* [adaptor; from the novel by E. M. Forster] (screenplay) 1986
Three Continents (novel) 1987
Madame Sousatzka [with John Schlesinger] (screenplay) 1988
**Mr. and Mrs. Bridge* [adaptor; from the novels *Mr. Bridge* and *Mrs. Bridge* by Evan S. Connell] (screenplay) 1990
**Howard's End* [adaptor; from the novel by E. M. Forster] (screenplay) 1992
Poet and Dancer (novel) 1993
**The Remains of the Day* [adaptor; from the novel by Kazuo Ishiguro] (screenplay) 1993
**Jefferson in Paris* (screenplay) 1995
Shards of Memory (novel) 1995
**Surviving Picasso* (screenplay) 1997
A Soldier's Daughter Never Cries [adaptor, with James Ivory; from the novel by Kaylie Jones] (screenplay) 1998
The Golden Bowl [adaptor; from the novel by Henry James] (screenplay) 2000
Le Divorce [adaptor; from the novel by Diane Johnson] (screenplay) 2003
My Nine Lives (fictionalized autobiography) 2004

*The film versions of these screenplays were directed by James Ivory and produced by Ismail Merchant.

CRITICISM

William Clifford (review date 7 March 1964)

SOURCE: Clifford, William. "Life Sketches of Delhi." *Saturday Review* 47, no. 10 (7 March 1964): 37.

[*In the following positive review, Clifford contends that the stories in* Like Birds, Like Fishes *"brilliantly mirror various aspects of India today."*]

One of India's best novelists writing in English is R. Prawer Jhabvala, who was born Ruth Prawer of Polish parents in Germany, where she spent the first twelve years of her life. During the next twelve years she continued her education in England, then married a Parsi architect, with whom she has resided in Delhi for the past twelve years. Seeming to take root the day she arrived on Indian soil, Mrs. Jhabvala finished her first novel, *Amrita,* in a year and a half. Everyone said it skilfully pictured society in modern Delhi; she had completely grasped the workings of the Indian mind, while at the same time exhibiting in herself no less than the gentle irony of Jane Austen.

"I cannot," she has remarked, "imagine myself ever living—or indeed ever having lived—anywhere else. If R. K. Narayan can go on writing all those novels about Malgudi, a much smaller place, I don't see why I can't write as many as I like about Delhi." The total is now five, and each is a delight. Through the pages of *Amrita* and *The Nature of Passion* march the progressive girls and dilatory young men, the important committee-women and dishonest contractors, the esthetes and hangers-on, the poor relations and frightened underlings, the absurd but lovable characters of Delhi's upper and middle classes. *Esmond in India* has a darker coloring, concerned as it is with unhappy marriages (almost all marriages are unhappy, apparently, but some are more hysterical than others) and a search for God. *The Householder* moves to a lower economic level, but the human relationships are much the same. In *Get Ready for Battle* we return to a *nouveau riche* setting like that of the second book.

Through them all runs a rich vein of high humor. One of Mrs. Jhabvala's best effects, which she employs with great skill and welcome frequency, is to have people talking at cross purposes, paying no attention to each other, but making a meaningful and hilarious counterpoint, sometimes even harmonizing, like the singers of an operatic quartet who may or may not be singing to each other. She misses very little that goes on anywhere, at any level.

Now after five fine novels, five feasts, we are offered a book of eleven short stories [***Like Birds, Like Fishes***], like a dessert tray of sweetmeats. There's something for every taste, even a masterful story not about India but about German Jewish refugees, called **"A Birthday in London."** This and five others ran in *The New Yorker*—stories about a grandmother finding happiness for her spirit, about a widow turning to religion following the frustration of her desire for a young man, about a timid man going to apply for a job, about the young second wife of a high official; about a merchant with no sons who becomes the father of a sixth baby daughter.

Mrs. Jhabvala chooses as protagonists for the remaining five stories a little man who works his way up in a posh draper's shop, a poet who wins the Literary Academy prize, an English wife who keeps a stiff upper lip in her undisciplined Indian family, a neighboring loose woman, and a romantic vagabond who builds a brief following as a holy man. They are all life-sized and, combined, brilliantly mirror various aspects of India today.

Gabriele Annan (review date 25 June 1976)

SOURCE: Annan, Gabriele. "The Acceptance World." *Times Literary Supplement,* no. 3876 (25 June 1976): 757.

[*In the following review, Annan commends the originality and fine construction of the stories in* How I Became a Holy Mother *and finds parallels between the short fiction of Jhabvala and that of Anton Chekhov.*]

Reading reviews of Ruth Prawer Jhabvala's previous work produces a sinking feeling: how can one add to this praise without falling into cliché? Yet this volume of short stories [***How I Became a Holy Mother***] about India which follows *Heat and Dust,* the novel that won the Booker Prize last year, *is* another marvellous performance; as for clichés, coming across what must be the only one in the whole book ("sure and steady as a mountain goat") one feels a tremendous jolt because it is such a surprise to find it among 203 pages of words chosen with such imaginative accuracy.

Mrs Jhabvala has been compared with Chekhov, and her India with Chekhov's Russia. It is a valid comparison. Boredom and loneliness hang over both settings like a cloud of flies, though the Indian version of boredom is more a compound of apathy and resignation; and Mrs Jhabvala's stories have this in common with Chekhov's that they are about insignificant people in petty situations, often of disappointment, humiliation, or moral squalor. Irony ferrets out motivations which may be pathetic or disgraceful, but one is left with a feeling not of meagre depression, but of a much larger despair and pity.

Loneliness, disappointment (especially of women with men), humiliation, patience, acceptance—including the acceptance of other people's awfulness—are the main themes; and among the minor ones are the irresponsible, boisterous childishness (a young husband in dire financial straits forces his wife to play cricket with a hairbrush in their bedroom) that delighted and exasperated E. M. Forster; and an obsession with food and cramming it into other people that makes the Yiddish momma seem highly overrated in this respect.

Some of the stories are about the rich bourgeoisie (who seem to suffer endemically from poor relations); others about people who live on the margin between petty crime and minimal respectability. **"Prostitutes"**—the profession occupies a much tidier place in Indian society than in the West—is about three generations: the grandmother recently bereaved of her unloved companion; the daughter loathing her humble, ailing, elderly protector; the granddaughter at boarding school writing home for tennis rackets and new brassieres. And the man the daughter loves: charming, feckless, predatory, unfaithful and exploiting.

"On Bail" is also about a woman exploited by the man she dotes on: her husband. She slaves in a shop, he sits in coffee-houses hoping for "business contacts" and sleeping with moderately rich women for small presents. Eventually his business contacts land him in jail, and the wife is forced to borrow money from his mistress (a former college friend of hers) for his bail. The story is told in the first person by the wife, a meek, affectionate drudge: towards the end she mentions, with casual resignation, that because of Rajee's spendthrift ways she regularly has to put her hand in the till. This revelation is slipped in with such cunning that it comes like a stab at the heart; a worse stab comes on the last page, making the heart bleed as much for the irresponsible Rajee as for his sad wife.

"Picnic with Moonlight and Mangoes" is a painful tragi-comedy about humiliation. Sri Prakash is suspended from his post in the Ministry of Telecommunications for interfering with a girl who applies for a job. The girl is, in fact, a stool-pigeon for her father who lives by petty blackmail. Sri Prakash is so mortified that for weeks he never leaves his house: but eventually depression drives him out to put a bold face on it and mingle with his former cronies at the coffee-house. He half-convinces himself that they are glad to see him—until he discovers he has been excluded from their annual picnic in the grounds of a ruined palace. He ends up picnicking with his podgy seducer and her odious father in the grounds of an inferior palace—gaudy nineteenth instead of beautiful seventeenth-century: "However, in the dark it looked just the same", and he kisses the hem of Miss Nimmi's sari "worshipping all women in her, their goodness and beauty".

The remark characterizes Mrs Jhabvala's ironic manner, tragic in implication but light in touch. She is dry and matter of fact even when describing scenes sadder than this, and often she is very funny. The title story, **"How I Became a Holy Mother"**, is the joker in the pack in every sense. It is told in the first person by a Mayfair Merc who has joined an ashram. Her tone of voice is perfect: inane, but also sharp and even snide. The ashram is pretty corrupt (though much better than most, she assures the reader), and she ends up as the compulsory mate of the pretty Indian boy who has been groomed as a star swami in order to raise money abroad. Even here there is a sad undertow. Katie's acceptance of her role doing one-night meditation stands in the West is resigned rather than joyful: "We do our best. It's not very hard; mostly we just have to sit there and radiate . . . it's just a job we do, and all the time we want to be somewhere else." But they will never get to Moscow, or back to the Himalayas—or into that state of transcendental peace which they mimic and which everyone in Mrs Jhabvala's India is aware of but no one quite attains.

Susannah Clapp (review date 2 July 1976)

SOURCE: Clapp, Susannah. "Household Words." *New Statesman* 92, no. 2363 (2 July 1976): 25.

[*In the following excerpt, Clapp praises Jhabvala's ability to construct finely detailed, evocative scenes of Indian life in* How I Became a Holy Mother.]

Ruth Prawer Jhabvala's last novel, *Heat and Dust,* was a skilful but not unpredictable book: a mixture of detail about present-day and British India, with a British narrator in command at all points, alert not only to landscape and the indigenous population, but also to the absurdities of her compatriots. It worked within a tradition, which helped it towards a Booker prize.

As the tone of the title indicates, her new book is a rather different undertaking. The stories which make up ***How I Became a Holy Mother*** are wittier, more surprising, and very fine. The fact that only two have English protagonists is liable to be taken as an indication of some morally superior (because more ethnically first-hand) stance; more important, it means that Mrs Jhabvala is released from the obligation imposed by alien narrators to touch on such standard themes as the heat or snobbery. She has more space to make finer distinctions; more time for making scenes as opposed to scene-painting.

And her scene-making is uncluttered and unhurried, ranging from an eccentric's small hut on a mountain top, through a prostitute's crowded room to the rich and unhappy house of a Bombay businessman, where 'uncle and niece sat staring at each other among the marble busts and potted plants, while the snores of the sleeping family lapped around them'.

Mrs Jhabvala does not strain to present some overall personal view of India. Her attention is always directed at particular actions and reactions which are modified but not overwhelmed by their surroundings. But though she never gives the sense that a cultural exercise is taking place, she manages, by focusing on specific, undwelt-on gestures, to point to large areas of different experience. Women kneel in despair, sinking their heads onto their saris; feet and temples are massaged with eau-de-cologne in shuttered rooms; hours are spent drinking tea on verandahs. A mixture of grace and tawdriness in people and places—of mountains and a salmon-pink meditation hall festooned with flashing light-bulbs—emerges but is not used cheaply or patronisingly. Different styles and attitudes are allowed to co-exist—not unremarked, but without point-scoring. Several of these stories deal with women attached to or abandoned by unsatisfactory men. The cads are observed with some coolness: forcing his eyes to 'sparkle', one gallant enthuses to a more earnest ex-lover, 'All the discussions we had about our terrible social system. It was great.' But the irony is used to point to the men's limitations, not to any pathetic gullibility in the women, who appreciate the kind of vivacity which can enliven as well as gush. The reproving glances of outsiders are acknowledged as justifiable, but are rarely allowed the final say. These women may have been taken in, but they have also been taken, and charmed. Mrs Jhabvala has been praised for her 'compassion'. But though it's true that she deals sympathetically with adversities of temperament and circumstance, such acclaim can be misplaced. These stories never call upon sympathy before interest has been aroused, and this is in part what makes them so admirable.

America (review date 26 March 1977)

SOURCE: Review of *How I Became a Holy Mother and Other Stories*, by Ruth Prawer Jhabvala. *America* 136 (26 March 1977): 279-80.

[*In the following favorable assessment of* How I Became a Holy Mother, *the anonymous critic describes Jhabvala's narrative style as "deft, clear, often gently ironic and always eminently readable."*]

Small collections of short fiction generally do not get much attention from the reading public. This is a shame, as one especially realizes after reading a book like Ruth Prawer Jhabvala's collection of 10 marvelous stories, ***How I Became a Holy Mother.*** The author, whose name is just beginning to get the notice it deserves among American readers, is of Polish descent, was educated in England, is married to an Indian architect and has published eight novels and four books of short stories. As the stories in this latest collection show, Jhabvala is far from being a novice writer. Her style is deft, clear, often gently ironic and always eminently readable.

Most of the stories are concerned with women—upper- and lower-class, native and foreign earthy and spiritual—in contemporary India. In each case; Jhabvala describes what Joyce called an "epiphany," a moment of heightened awareness of the reality underlying a given situation, a moment of realization that always involves the reader, but only sometimes the fictional character.

The first two stories provide a study in contrasts. In **"Two More under the Indian Sun,"** a young Englishwoman married to an Indian tries, unsuccessfully, to explain to an uneasy compatriot how tremendously happy she is. In **"The Englishwoman,"** however, a woman past her prime, married for many years to an Indian, experiences the exhilaration of finally breaking with India, her husband, and his mistress, for good. Despite the contrast, there is a similar nostalgia in both these stories, a sense of the loneliness of the foreigner, of the hardship of leaving familiar ways in order to adapt to the sometimes exotic customs of an alien culture.

The moral debilitation produced by wealth, comfort and power shapes a number of other stories. Pritan, of **"In the Mountains,"** has been able to leave behind the flabbiness of her wealthy family's life in the plains for the tough, simple life of a spiritual refugee in a small town in the foothills of the Himalayas. In **"Bombay,"** on the other hand, an eccentric uncle tries unsuccessfully, to maintain his love for his favorite niece while remaining independent of the deadening influence of the family into which she has married. His ultimate dependence on her, while something of a defeat, is also, in Jhabvala's ironic vision, a source of happiness. In **"Desecration,"** Sofia, the child bride of an aging Raja whose only expression of love is the interminable verse dramas he writes for her, is less fortunate. Her dependence takes the form of sexual obsession and ends in suicide because she cannot bear to accept her husband's forgiveness.

The title story of the collection is the most comic and, perhaps, the most technically proficient. Katie, a slightly dopey but pleasant English girl, recounts how she found happiness and enlightenment in an ashram by falling in love with a young swami and following him on his rise to fame and fortune. Together they go on a world tour, with Katie embodying the Mother principle: "It's not very hard; mostly we just have to sit there and radiate."

Some of the stories first appeared in the *New Yorker,* and one could generally describe all of them—finely written as they are, with the emphasis on small details of tone and characterization rather than on plot—as typical *New Yorker* stories. If, therefore, you enjoy mastery short fiction, if you are curious about the character of modern India, if *A Passage to India* is one of your favorite books, if any or all or a combination of these conditions apply, you will find ***How I Became a Holy Mother*** a rewarding reading experience.

Yasmine Gooneratne (essay date 1983)

SOURCE: Gooneratne, Yasmine. "The Short Stories." In *Silence, Exile, and Cunning: The Fiction of Ruth Prawer Jhabvala,* pp. 234-60. Hyderabad, India: Orient Longman, 1983.

[*In the following excerpt, Gooneratne examines the major themes of Jhabvala's short fiction.*]

> 'A story is . . . like a poem . . . You can't cheat on a poem. It's one cry from the heart—just one—only that has to come out true and right.'[1]

Ruth Jhabvala's first volume of short stories, ***Like Birds, Like Fishes***[2], appeared in 1963, when she had already published five novels and was working on the cinematic version of one of them, *The Householder.* With one exception, the stories in the collection had been published earlier in American magazines[3] (incidentally confirming the impression conveyed by her novels to Western readers, of an author whose writing shed a cool, clear light on post-Independence India). The exception is the title story, which reveals Ruth Jhabvala's awakening interest in the approach to life adopted by the unfettered idealists she portrays sympathetically in her next two novels—Sarla Devi and Gautam in *Get Ready for Battle,* and Bal in *A Backward Place.* All the rest look back, chiefly at what had gripped her attention since her arrival in India in 1951: 'That's how I get to know a place, through writing'[4]. The book contains satiric studies of India committee women, social climbers and literary lions (**"The Old Lady"**, **"Lekha"** and **"The Award"**); sketches of helplessness and dispensability in Indian lower middle-class life (**"The Interview"**, **"A Loss of Faith"**); penetrating assessments of the way the Indian joint-family functions to smother individualism, yet cushion disappointment (**"The Widow"**, **"Sixth Child"**); a potted biography of a swami in the making (**"My First Marriage"**); and two deeply felt essays on loneliness and loss as experienced by individuals trapped in an alien society (**"The Aliens"**, **"A Birthday in London"**).

A second collection, ***An Experience of India***[5], was published three years later, and takes its prevailing mood and a new direction from the essay that forms an introduction to the book, "Myself in India". The studies of Indian life presented here include a portrait of Chameli, a young woman of feeling and simple affections whom circumstance and convention brand as **"A Bad Woman"**, and her own passions thrust unexpectedly into complicated tragedy; explorations of the commercial film world Ruth Jhabvala was getting to know during the making of *Bombay Talkie* and *Shakespeare-Wallah* (**"A Star and Two Girls"**, **"Suffering Women"**); and two studies of Westernised Indian women, in contrasting styles of compassionate irony (**"Rose Petals"**) and high-spirited satirical comedy (**"A Course of English Studies"**). The title story uses the cycle of response to India described in the introduction[6] as the basis for a fictional account of a Western woman's travels in India in search of self-fulfilment. It was the first to be published among the numerous studies of religious swamis and their deluded Western devotees that stud Ruth Jhabvala's novels, stories and screenplays in the ten years between 1966 and 1976. The story that seems to be the most deeply personal to the author, however, is not **"An Experience of India"**[7], but **"The Housewife"** in which a most moving exploration of the theme of artistic commitment is discreetly embedded in a domestic drama of middle-class marital infidelity.

A Stronger Climate (1968)[8] presents nine stories, six of which are about Westerners who come to India in search of a purpose in life (**"A Young Man of Good Family"**) or of spiritual, intellectual and emotional enrichment (**"A Spiritual Call"**, **"The Biography"**, **"Passion"**), only to find themselves betrayed by India (**"The Young Couple"**) or by their own capacity for self-deception (**"In Love with a Beautiful Girl"**). To these studies of 'Seekers', the author adds three studies of 'Sufferers', Westerners who have stayed too long in India, and for whom the rapture of their first encounter has turned into sour disillusionment, bewilderment, and the revulsion she describes as the third stage on her cycle of response to India (**"Miss Sahib"**, **"An Indian Citizen"**, **"The Man with the Dog"**).

Her fourth collection, ***How I Became a Holy Mother***[9], followed eight years after ***A Stronger Climate,*** and bears out Ruth Jhabvala's statement that her interest lay from the 1960s onward no longer in India as a subject, but in "Myself in India"[10]. Many of the stories are, despite their richness of observed detail and skilful characterisation, essays in self-analysis that turn over again and again themes deeply personal to their author. While the studies of Westerners in India are undertaken in a spirit of ironic amusement (**"Two More under the Indian Sun"**, **"How I Became a Holy Mother"**), the pictures of Indian life are in reality studies of different aspects of self-deception (**"Bombay"**, **"On Bail"**, **"Prostitutes"** and **"Picnic with Moonlight and Mangoes"**). Two stories are, in effect, analyses of passion and self-pity in women whom marriage has isolated from the world (**"Desecration"**, **"In a Great Man's House"**), while two others study the sensibility of female individualists who desert their comfortable middle-class lives for solitude and freedom (**"In the Mountains"** and **"The Englishwoman"**[11]).

Reference has been made elsewhere in this book to instances in which some of the stories mentioned above take up aspects of the major themes that inspire Ruth Jhabvala's eight novels and the screenplays she has written for Merchant-Ivory films. The stories selected for discussion in this chapter, however, have been chosen not so much for their importance as links between the novels and the screenplays (although that aspect has not been overlooked), as for their technical interest. The singer in **"The Housewife"**, who knows that success

> lay within her power, a little more effort and she would be there and then she could begin to set her sights on the next impossible step.
>
> (pp. 151-2)

is a recognisable projection of her creator, who has been frequently compared to Chekhov and other masters of the short story genre, but strives tirelessly in 'silence, exile and cunning' towards a personal objective and a highly individual style.

Among many stories in all four collections which examine critically or satirically the attitudes of 'modern' Indian women of the upper and middle classes, **"Lekha"** is outstanding in the range of its reference to the Indian social and cultural scene, its insight into female psychology, and its evidence of an early interest in technical experiment.[12] It is Ruth Jhabvala's first attempt, and a highly successful one, at the indirect revelation of character that we have seen in more finished and sophisticated forms in *Heat and Dust* and *Autobiography of a Princess.* As in *Heat and Dust,* a female narrator relates the story of another woman's scandalous love-affair, unconsciously laying her own soul bare as she does so. There is a clear element of social satire in this story, directed at 'Westernised' Indian women and the civil service mentality (both of which are satiric targets in the early novels, *Amrita* and *The Nature of Passion*). The narrator, who is the wife of a senior civil servant, epitomises one and reflects the other: in her opinion, eating with the fingers from a round brass tray

> may be the traditional Indian way, but it is my opinion that it is not a nice way and that it would be better for India if everyone learned to eat in the way people do in the West.
>
> (p. 171)

The husband of her young friend Lekha is described in the narrator's opening sentence as 'The head of our department—my husband's department, that is' (p. 166), and it soon becomes clear that a good deal of pushing and shoving goes on among this 'happy group' (p. 166) of senior officers and their wives to gain the favour of the head. Although the narrator describes her own attitude to the youthful and inexperienced Lekha as 'protective' and that of her arch-enemy, Mrs Nayyar, as 'possessive', there is little to choose between the two ladies in this matter.

Unlike 'Ms. Rivers' in *Heat and Dust,* the narrator of **"Lekha"** is not bent on self-analysis. On the contrary, she is perfectly satisfied with her way of life and her own personality, and the emptiness of both is only unconsciously revealed when Lekha's passionate love-affair with Govind, the narrator's bohemian brother-in-law, puts these complacent values at risk:

> I have been married now for ten years and I am fond of my husband and I have had three children by him, but we have always used restraint in our behaviour together. I pressed my face into my pillow and suddenly I began to cry . . . very bitterly.
>
> (p. 178)

The story suggests that the narrator's unadmitted but none-the-less deeply felt sense of inadequacy and lack of fulfilment is closely linked with her deracination from that spirit of India which is found in her myths and age-old festivals, dance, song and folk ways. Govind, in his conventional sister-in-law's opinion an idler who spends his time in coffee-houses, is a skilled musician possessed moreover of the dark good looks associated with the god Krishna in his aspect of the lover. Awakened to the full potential of her body and spirit by her love for him, Lekha is transformed, for the duration of their love-affair, into an avatar of Radha, the milk-maid who symbolises in Indian mythology the concept of the human soul. Their likeness to the mythological couple strikes the narrator when she first sees them together (p. 176), and on subsequent occasions she describes them in terms that, while appropriate to the human reality of their very ardent feeling for each other, suggest the presence of superhuman power:

> Suddenly she kissed me on the neck; her lips and breath were very hot.
>
> When I got home, I lay down on the bed and shut my eyes. But I could not get rid of the picture of the two of them together. . . . Oh, it was nothing really that they did; it was only the understanding between them, and something else that I can't describe—something that had come rising out of them and filled the room.
>
> (p. 177)

The old crafts and rituals have yielded their place with the narrator and her circle to the merely 'pretty' and 'nice', and a conventional style of living has been created by them which is out of touch with the power of the myths in which these rituals began. 'Christmas,' thinks the narrator, 'is such a nice festival; we always have a turkey dinner with plum pudding, and so do all our friends'—while the custom of lighting lamps on Diwali, although kept up 'because the children like it so much . . . is not in keeping with modern times' (p. 172). Similarly we hear from the head of the 'department', whose wife is about to dance to her lover's singing and drumming, that 'Government is always telling us that we must preserve and foster our cultural heritage' (p. 183).

This dilution that substitutes for the real thing is made nonsense of when the real thing actually materialises in the narrator's livingroom:

> Govind sat on the floor by the *dholak* and began to beat it with his fingers and sing, while Lekha danced. He sang:
>
> 'Bring, O bring, my beloved unto me!
> O what ecstasy shall I know with him always on the couch strewn with flowers, in the white radiance of the moon.
> O my friend, beautiful as a bird! I languish with love for my lord.
> What is this happening to me? Come, O friend!
> Ask my lord to come to me, so that flower-adorned I may dance, sing and play with him. Why this delay?'
>
> And that was what Lekha danced . . . 'I languish with love for my lord,' said her fingers. 'What is this happening to me?' said her eyes and her lips. The ankle-bells rang out as she stamped her feet. 'O what ecstasy shall I know with him always!' Govind flung back his head so that one could see the movement in his throat as he sang; his long brown fingers danced on the drum, his whole body swayed; he was smiling all the time so that his teeth and eyes flashed. 'Like a god', she had said . . . and now she was worshipping him with her dance.
>
> (pp. 183-4)

Lekha's dancing and Govind's singing at once express and transcend their physical relationship. At that moment and for the brief period of their love, the power in old myths seems to reassert itself, giving the reader an opportunity to catch the author's sense of what constitutes the true, unchanging India and what—the scuffling for priority among the civil servants and their wives, the cushions and table-runners, the 'nice', the 'pretty', the 'modern' and 'advanced', the official lip-service paid to the classical arts—is merely transient, conventional and worthless.

Although there are many portraits of Indian men of 'culture' and politicians of consequence in Ruth Jhabvala's stories (notably those of the Raja Sahib in **"Desecration"** and of the Minister in **"Rose Petals"**), her character-study of a vain literary personality in **"The Award"**[13] takes pride of place among them. A young university lecturer preparing to write a Ph.D. thesis on developments in Indian writing since Independence interviews Dev Prakash, 'the Tagore of today', on the morning of what later turns out to be the day he is awarded the Sahitya Akademi prize for his poetry. There are many contrasts in the story, some of them social: while the young lecturer supports his family of four children, a mother and a widowed aunt on Rs. 350 a month, the home of Dev Prakash's sister Usha in which the interview takes place is opulently furnished. The young man has not been able to afford new clothes for three years, and he is working for his Ph.D. to qualify himself for a position as senior lecturer in which he will earn a salary of Rs. 650, rising to Rs. 900. Everything else—even literature, to which he is genuinely responsive—must yield priority to his need to better his prospects in order to survive. In contrast, Usha's mind moves on clothes and party-giving. She ignores her brother's visitor completely:

> There was nothing studied about the way she ignored the existence of the young man; his insignificance was too real for her to have to take up an attitude about it.
>
> (p. 48)

This is the background for Ruth Jhabvala's ironic study of Dev Prakash, an amusing mixture of self-consequence and self-deception. His self-image as described by him (and later by his mistress, Aruna) to the young man is continuously contrasted with his memories of the twenty-five years he has spent in self-imposed 'exile' in London. Dev Prakash presents himself as a patriotic, self-sacrificing, sensitive soul, but the reality is that of a plump, self-indulgent poseur possessed of a (very) minor talent, who has been quick to leap upon the bandwagon of literary London's fads and fashions. The narrative moves back and forth over a time-span of twenty-five years, and with each 'flash-back', the middle-aged poet's pretensions to greatness are gently pared away.

> 'Whatever I have written, whatever little I may have achieved, my inspiration has always been: India.' Who repaid him by ignoring him, wasting him, passing him over. For twentyfive years he had been what he called in exile and even now that he had come home, he felt more exiled than ever.
>
> (p. 45)

Asked to outline his position 'in regard to other Indian writers of today', Dev Prakash (who has evidently written nothing since Independence) makes a virtue of his sterility—'Of course, I have always been something of an odd man out' (p. 46). He calls himself 'a poor scribbler', but has always enjoyed comfort and security. While in London,

> the quaintly untidy rooms he had rented in Hampstead had not betrayed the handsome allowance that was sent to him every quarter from his share of the family business.
>
> (p. 47)

In contrast, the young man interviewing him in his sister's luxurious house *is* 'a poor scribbler'. Dev Prakash does not mention that his poem, "My Country is a Rose in my Heart" is derived from Yeats, as its title instantly informs the reader. Instead, he declares that throughout his years of exile 'there was this Ache' . . . 'an unhealing wound in the heart' (pp. 48-9). His thoughts and memories, however, put this romantic sentimentality into proper perspective:

> Plump and sensuous in the tight-fitting Indian clothes he wore, with his deep dark eyes in which one could read, if one wanted to, all the sufferings of the East, he was always a success with English women; and his pa-

> triotic sentiments, which he enunciated in a low, soft voice vibrating with feeling, woke a warm glow of indignation against oppression in all the right-thinking advanced circles in which he moved.
>
> (pp. 48-9)

His companion of those days, Isabel 'a handsome no-nonsense woman with an Oxford degree who wrote sensitive novels about personal relationships' had called the poem "gooey" (p. 49); amusingly, Dev Prakash feels that her opinion of it betrayed a 'lack of depth in her', a 'failure to feel passionately'. The poem is considered 'beautiful' by the young man (in whose life there is little beauty to provide a criterion) and 'moving' by Usha, who has (like Prema in *Amrita*) a 'well of feeling in her to respond to the profound and the poetic', not to mention the 'tear-wringing emotion' that had moved her brother to write the poem (pp. 49-50).

His patriotism is similarly shown to have been little more than mere self-indulgence:

> 'Sometimes people asked me,' Dev Prakash said, 'how can you, an Indian, bear to live in exile from your country? There was only one answer I could give.' His passionate eyes gazed impressively into the distance as he quoted this answer: 'It is better than to live as a slave in one's own land'. Though this was no longer an answer he could give after Independence. He had got so used to England and his cosy, shabby rooms in Hampstead, it had been difficult to leave.
>
> (p. 50)

After Independence he had discovered that his friends and admirers 'no longer regarded him in the same light. There had even seemed to be, though of course no one had ever spoken it, an undermining undercurrent of why doesn't he go home?' (p. 50). Gently, but mercilessly, Ruth Jhabvala strips away pretension from both the man and from the quality of his mind and inspiration. Dev Prakash is a counterfeit patriot, as he is only a counterfeit poet. His heroic roles are amusingly undercut by his affectionate Indian admirers:

> 'He has suffered in his life for his country and his art,' said Aruna. 'Just think, for twentyfive years he lived in exile—twentyfive years, because he could not bear to be a slave!'
>
> 'The English winters are very cold,' said Usha. 'Every year he suffered from chilblains.'
>
> (p. 53)

Dev Prakash is longing for the award, and his affectation of unconcern is transparent. As they drink to his success, after he has been officially informed that he has won it at last, he is

> vibrating with fulfilment . . . (He had never felt in England) this oneness, this love, this union of spirit.
>
> (p. 59)

Yet all that has gone before proves that there is very little in the room of all that he 'feels'. The young man, though he talks conventionally of his pleasure at being present on such an auspicious occasion, has his sights fixed on the completion of his thesis and the obtaining of a higher salary (pp. 58-9). Usha is thinking of buying a new Banaras silk sari for Aruna's celebration garden party (p. 58), and Aruna's delight and pleasure at her hero's success is based on a mistaken view of his worth as a writer (p. 58)—his own view, which she has adopted, and now repeats:

> He is such a poet, such a fine soul, he sees everything different from ordinary people.
>
> (p. 58)

In contrast with **"The Award"**, with its picture of wealth and upper-class ease and privilege, is **"A Loss of Faith"**[14], a tale of defeated principle and thwarted hope in a lower middle-class setting. The story concerns the efforts of a salesman to build an orderly, quiet and respectable life for himself and his family, only to be thwarted by forces over which he has no control: the tradition according to which, as head of a household, he must welcome and support aged relatives and an idle elder brother; the marriage arranged for him by his mother, in which he has no real knowledge of his wife's character to begin with and no control over it when he does; and his own quiet, submissive personality and habit of obedience to what is socially considered proper. He is reduced to a position that is almost unbearable:

> There was a new why in his life that he wanted to put to someone. He could not understand how things had come to this pass: he had always worked so hard; had wanted to keep everything decent and orderly and different from what it had been in his uncle's house. Yet, in spite of his efforts, the same disorder there had been in his uncle's house, the same sense of too much and too violent a humanity, had come to swallow his own life. He felt as if everything was closing in on him—the Muslim wives fighting upstairs, the crippled astrologer and, in his own room, the monstrous shapes of his mother, his wife, his grandmother, the shrill voices, the quarrels, dirt and poverty and moneylenders who had to be cajoled. He remembered how his uncle had clutched at his head and screamed: 'They are eating me up!' and that was how he was feeling himself, devoured and eaten.
>
> (p. 40)

Deprived of order at home, the shop in which he works begins to seem 'like a deep source of orderliness and virtue, of Goodness and Truth' (p. 39). Even the salary-scale 'was to him like a law of God or Nature, incontrovertible' (p. 41). But even this is rapidly taken from him. Used to accepting other people's opinions, he begins to accept the view of life put forward by Vijay, his derelict elder brother:

> 'The world sucks the juice out of us and then spits us out like an empty, shrivelled skin,' said Vijay . . . It

> was so, he knew now; he had always worked and hoped hard, but had got nothing.
>
> (p. 42)

He loses faith and joy in his work. When he asks the proprietor of the shop in which he has worked for so long for a rise in salary, he is refused. His one act of rebellion against the life that has cheated him (and the proprietor, who is as remote from him in the shop as God seems remote from him in his life) is an unpremeditated act that surprises Ram Kumar himself. He drops the wax doll that is the shop's model, which he had hitherto loved to dress and adorn, in fragments on the floor. He finds himself

> almost enjoying this little unexpected moment, though he would no doubt have enjoyed it more if he had not known that the cost of a new doll would be taken, month by month, out of his salary.
>
> (p. 44)

The shop, the proprietor and the doll have occupied in Ram Kumar's life the respective positions of temple, God and image. As the experience of Ram Kumar illustrates, man is driven by instincts and deep compulsions he cannot explain to create the conditions in which he lives, and often to destroy them: he is the plaything, not of fate, but of tradition and his own conditioned personality. Ruth Jhabvala has ironically named her characters—'Ram Kumar' (Prince Rama, the Indian hero-King), 'Vijay' (victory)—in a story about subjection and spiritual defeat.

In her story **"The Widow"**[15], Ruth Jhabvala uses satiric irony to expose the social conventions of traditional India that can often destroy the human personality, in ways permitted and sanctified by time and religious custom. Durga has been married as a very young girl to a man much older than herself, and now a widow, has been trained by her late husband to stand up to her relatives and live the independent life of a property-owner. She has had no sexual fulfilment in marriage, and her memories of her husband are of his kindness and generosity to her, not of love—indeed, she recalls vividly

> his old-man smell, and his dried legs, when she had massaged them, with the useless rag of manhood flopping against his thigh.
>
> (p. 61)

Widowed, Durga lives as she pleases, growing 'plump and smooth with it' (p. 62). She rules her elder relatives by the power of her money and her independence, and appears to have won the battle that took place after her husband's death as to whether or not she was to be condemned to 'that perpetual mourning, perpetual expiation, which was the proper lot of widows' (p. 62). But Durga feels that 'somehow, somewhere, she had been short-changed' (p. 63). She suffers from moods of depression, and this weakness is used to advantage by an old aunt, Bhuaji, who introduces her to the cult of Krishna as a means of filling the gap in her life. The concept of Krishna as lover appeals powerfully to the sexually deprived Durga, who becomes 'dreamy and withdrawn' (p. 66) and far more tolerant of her relatives than she had formerly been. When the tenants in the upper part of Durga's house give notice and her relatives plan to move in, however, they are disappointed. Durga is not so dreamy that she is going to sacrifice a regular monthly income: and Mr Puri, his wife, two daughters and a son move in.

Disappointed by Krishna's failure to come to her in any satisfying way, Durga focuses her unfulfilled desires on the boy upstairs whose name, Govind, recalls Krishna's incarnation as a cowherd and lover of milk-maids. She rationalises her feelings, and makes out that in Govind she sees the son her late husband's impotence had robbed her of, but her response is clearly to the young man's male virility:

> His teeth were large and white, his hair sprang from a point on his forehead. Everything about him was young and fresh and strong—even his smell, which was that of a young animal full of sap and sperm.
>
> (p. 74)

Durga begins to feed Govind and to give him money, always telling herself she is acting like a mother to him (pp. 73-4). Mrs Puri takes advantage of Durga's fondness for Govind to avoid paying the rent (p. 75). The relatives regard their patroness's growing friendship with the Puris as 'both ominous and unnatural' (p. 75). Bhuaji steps in to mend matters, and by a devious course of action that reveals her creator's close observation of life within the women's quarter of an Indian joint-family, succeeds in separating Durga from the Puris and in persuading her to get rid of them as tenants (pp. 76-82). Durga, for whom life's promise has ended, and whose personality is very near disintegration, spites the memory of her dead husband by giving away her silk saris, her jewellery and her cash-box to Bhuaji and her relatives, who now move in.

The last paragraph of this story provides a memorable example of Ruth Jhabvala's early satiric style. Durga has been driven into a state of mental breakdown by the circumstances of her life and the deliberate scheming of her relatives. This is now, through the operation of irony, 'rationalised' and sanctified as being in keeping with what is right and proper behaviour for Indian widows:

> The relatives were glad that Durga had at last come round and accepted her lot as a widow. They were glad for her sake. There was no other way for widows but to lead humble, bare lives; it was for their own good. For if they were allowed to feed themselves on the

> pleasures of the world, then they fed their own passions too, and that which should have died in them with the deaths of their husbands would fester and boil and overflow into sinful channels. Oh yes, said the relatives, wise and knowing, nodding their heads, our ancestors knew what they were doing when they laid down these rigid rules for widows; and though nowdays perhaps, in these modern times, one could be a little more lenient—for instance, no one insisted that Durga should shave her head—still, on the whole, the closer one followed the old traditions, the safer and the better it was.
>
> (p. 83)

The portrait of Durga in **"The Widow"** might usefully be compared with Bibhutibhusan Banerji's treatment of Indian widowhood in his novel *Pather Panchali,* where in the greater space afforded by the novel genre, the life of Indian women is viewed in three stages—girlhood, wifehood and widowhood—and both early marriage and the treatment of widows explicitly and movingly condemned. Ruth Jhabvala's more oblique presentation creates in Durga a picture of a warm human personality first deprived, then destroyed, by the unchangeable circumstances of Indian life.

In the story **"Suffering Women"**[16], which belongs to a later period than the four already considered in this chapter, plot is less tightly structured than before, and the author's interest appears to be focused on conveying the quality of her characters' feelings and experience rather than on shaping these things to a rigid pattern of cause and effect. The story satirises the unreal values and concepts purveyed by the Indian popular film industry through the experiences of two middle-aged actresses who are close friends:

> Anjana and Sultana . . . had both played heroines in the same kind of second-grade films; both had been very popular among taxi-drivers, wrestlers and small boys queueing up for the four-anna seats on Saturday mornings. Sultana, with her tigress eyes and lithe figure, had played bold, manly parts and had been cheered out of thousands of throats as she galloped over the Khyber Pass, clutching in her arms the infant king whom she had rescued in the nick of time from his black-bearded murderers. Anjana, on the other hand, all soft bosom and melting eyes, had been made love to in trellissed bowers and danced ankledeep in meadows of white primroses. Offscreen, they were both equally romantic and had been remarkable for the number and intensity of their love affairs.
>
> (p. 172)

Anjana, now retired from her career as a movie idol, has an elderly lover, Thakkur Sahib, and a pretty teenage daughter named Kiku. Her relationship with Thakkur Sahib is still most enjoyable, in contrast with the rather unsatisfactory one Kiku has with her somewhat effeminate boy-friend Rahul, and the very unsatisfactory ones Sultana has with a succession of young lovers. Ruth Jhabvala's comic portrait of Sultana (whose apartment is continually being redecorated by a lover who plans to become an interior decorator: 'He says he needs the practice', p. 168) is softened by compassion for the vulnerability of an ageing, yet passionate woman:

> 'Well, what can I do? He's so young, so lovely. Do you know he doesn't have one single hair on his chest? Smooth, smooth, like satin. Velvet,' she said in a voice like velvet.
>
> (p. 184)

Sultana's unhappiness and the constant sight of a private nursing-home opposite her flat are permanent reminders to Anjana of the 'terrible things (that) can happen' (p. 174). Thakkur Sahib's description of his meeting with a formerly well-known and popular star named Tara Bai who now 'looks like an old beggar-woman' (p. 176) deepens her sense of foreboding, and his casual admission, 'I was glad to get rid of her' (p. 177) increases the sense of insecurity which, despite occasional moments of 'bliss', Anjana will always feel. Personal relationships—of a kind—provide her only refuge, and with all their limitations, it is only Thakkur Sahib and Sultana who give her some sense of 'safety' and of friendship.

The story **"A Spiritual Call"**[17] has close links with an 'ashram' sequence in the film *Bombay Talkie,* in which Lucia Lane briefly tries on the role of religious devotee before submitting herself to 'fate' and her passion for Vikram. Daphne is a Londoner who comes to India to seek a guru she has met in Britain and 'undergo an intensive course of spiritual regeneration' (p. 92). Her guide, whose name and personality Ruth Jhabvala was later to build into the character of Swamiji in her novel *A New Dominion,* is cheerful and serene, immaculately dressed in cream-coloured silk, his beard and shoulder-length hair shining 'in well-oiled waves'. He was not, notes the narrator, a handsome man, 'yet there was an aura of beauty about him . . . due . . . mostly of course to the radiance of his personality' (p. 94). Ruth Jhabvala's narrative tone, ostensibly straightforward, takes on ironic colouring when the Swamiji of this story is described:

> Swamiji had a very simple and beautiful message to the world. It was only this: meditate; look into yourself and so, by looking, cleanse yourself; harmony and happiness will inevitably follow. This philosophy, simple as its end-product appeared to be, he had forged after many, many solitary years of thought and penance in some icy Himalayan retreat. Now he had come down into the world of men to deliver his message, planning to return to his mountain solitude as soon as his task here was achieved. It might, however, take longer than he had reckoned on, for men were stubborn and tended to be blind to Truth.
>
> (p. 96)

Daphne's adoration of her guru conquers all her scruples, her doubts regarding his previous career (pp. 87-8) and, amusingly, even her Oxford-trained revulsion at his poor written expression (p. 98). She becomes Swamiji's secretary, and is on the way to becoming as much his slave as Evie is the other Swamiji's slave in *A New Dominion.* Conflicts develop between Daphne and Helga, a German blonde in her thirties, who accuses Daphne of 'flirting' with their guru. But all is 'resolved' in the end. Daphne, wearing the sari Swamiji has given her and tripping over it, sees Helga wearing just such another, and thinks *she* looks 'ridiculous' (p. 114). She has lost contact with reality—or else, is now on a 'higher' spiritual plane:

> She was completely happy to be going to California and anywhere else he might want her to accompany him.
>
> (p. 114)

"A Spiritual Call" belongs to that group of Ruth Jhabvala's stories in which 'her confident double-edged irony exposes with fine impartiality the neuroses of those who are seeking solace and the hypocrisy of those who are offering it'[18].

Dr Meenakshi Mukherjee, whose perceptive analysis of Ruth Jhabvala's 'swami' stories I have just quoted, has also noted the existence in this author's *oeuvre* of 'numerous case studies of Europeans under the Indian sun'.[19] In **"The Aliens"**[20] Ruth Jhabvala presented the first of her Westerners to wilt in the heat of a Delhi summer. Peggy is the middle-class English wife of a young Indian car salesman, Dev. They live with his brother's family in a large house run, as in the days when Dev's and Suraj's father was still alive, by their mother. The story, one of Ruth Jhabvala's most vivid evocations of turbulent Indian family life, is told from Peggy's point of view: that of someone puzzled, irritated, and beginning to be seriously disturbed by the experience of living in India, but battling gamely on, clinging to principles and attitudes learned in another culture. Peggy is treated ironically, her inward comparisons sometimes sounding either absurdly complacent or somewhat unreasonable. For example, when she comes in to breakfast, neither her mother-in-law nor her sister-in-law

> had had her bath yet, and consequently both looked somewhat bedraggled, with their thick long hair coming down and the crumpled saris in which they had slept all night. Peggy, on the other hand, already looked crisp and smart in her printed house-dress and with her sensible short hair neatly brushed.
>
> (p. 84)

When she comments to Dev, 'Why do they always have to quarrel and shout so loud?' Dev asks with surprise, 'Who?' (p. 87). In contrast with the uninhibited display of passion by Peggy's Indian relatives are her memories of home and England:

> No one at home ever fought like that; sometimes, of course, they had their little differences of opinion—especially on washing-days, Mum did tend to get a bit out of temper then—but they never forgot themselves. Only lower-class people forgot themselves and shouted the way they shouted in this house. She was thankful that Mum and Daddy couldn't hear them, they wouldn't know what to think. Sometimes she herself didn't know what to think.
>
> (p. 87)

Dev's family and its endless noisy quarrels are presented in a broadly comic manner, the noise exaggerated by the fact that the reader is aware that it is falling upon Peggy's already irritated ears.

It is interesting that Peggy and Dev have, despite their different nationalities, been brought up on similar social prejudices. She thinks shouting and losing one's temper betrays low social origins his mother thinks that manual labour tells the same story. The source of social 'disgrace' is different, but the conviction that such 'disgrace' exists is amusingly shared. Similarly, Peggy resents her mother-in-law's control over Dev's will and his eating habits, but her dream of a future away from this house merely substitutes her will for that of her mother-in-law:

> She thought wistfully again of a little place all to themselves. She would make a lovely home. She would do all their own cooking and have a servant only for the cleaning. She would cook roast-meat and Yorkshire pudding and sausage and mash and treacle pudding.
>
> (p. 103)

Ruth Jhabvala shows little sympathy for Peggy's insularity, but her predicament is treated with compassion. As she writes her letter to 'Mum and Daddy', keeping her frustration and growing depression bravely out of it, the intensity of her feelings and the dogged way in which she is trying to keep them under control are given full value:

> She wrote with her back very straight and her lips very tight and pressing her nib so hard that it made little holes in the paper.
>
> She didn't know this, but she looked at that moment very much like her Mum had looked twenty years ago (during the war, with Daddy away in the army) queueing up for the rations or carrying in the coal on a rainy English winter morning.
>
> (p. 106)

Peggy's heroism, unvalued of course by everyone around her, is provoked by the ceaseless domestic friction in the midst of which she must live. Ruth Jhabvala's depiction of the Indian extended family at home comes close to caricature in this story, though the exaggeration is in some measure justified because it is Peggy's sensibility that registers it. In the process there develop exchanges rich in comedy and clues as to what is going on in the minds of those involved:

> Sarla, leaning on the table with her elbow, her hair coming down over her face, never looked up except occasionally to throw dark glances at her husband; which he ignored with such insulting ease that soon she was throwing out more explicit hints: 'All morning my head has been hurting but who is there to ask are you well, are you ill, who is there to care what happens to me?'
>
> The mother-in-law stroked Suraj's shoulder and said sweetly, 'Eat, son, eat in peace,' though he hardly needed this encouragement. He leaned forward and helped himself to pickle. 'Poor boy, how hard he has been working all morning in the office.'
>
> 'Today we got our consignment of station wagons,' he said. 'They have been delayed four months.'
>
> 'Four months!' echoed the mother with exaggerated sympathy. 'So much trouble—trouble and worry, that is how it is in business.'
>
> 'And that girl with the fat legs, she is also trouble and worry?' Sarla said.
>
> 'Children who don't eat are taken away at night by the jackals,' warned the Ayah.
>
> (pp. 97-8)

Later, after the family quarrel, there is silence from the bedroom occupied by Suraj and Sarla, and Peggy knows from experience the reason for this. Her own inhibitions emerge in her disapproving thoughts and prurient speculations:

> She knew it was wicked of her, but she often thought of them lying together on the bed. Sometimes, when they came out of their room, she could see in their faces what they had been doing in there; and Sarla often had marks on her. It made her feel quite sick to think of them.
>
> (p. 103)

When Sarla exhibits her sexual fulfilment to her mother-in-law, that lady's reaction is amusingly like Peggy's:

> 'Do up your blouse,' she said crossly, 'have you no shame, with the servants walking about?' She sank down on the edge of the bed, slow and heavy like an old woman. Peggy had often noticed that, after Sarla had been with Suraj and looked the way she looked now, her mother-in-law turned herself into an old woman. She sat and sighed—'Such heat, it is too much for me to bear.'
>
> (p. 105)

This is an early instance of the Delhi heat being used by Ruth Jhabvala as a symbol of amorous passion: the mother-in-law, earlier scornful of Sarla's complaints about the heat (Sarla wants to get Suraj to accompany her on holiday in the hills, away from the lures of an overly attractive girl in his office), now—at the sight of Sarla's exposed bosom—cannot bear the heat either. Peggy's own irritations begin to seem unbearable as she gazes out of the window at 'the garden, the street beyond it, everything . . . dead and still under the white-hot sun' (p. 87).

Peggy's pale skin is considered a drawback by her Indian relations, and her 'trimness' is a source of great amusement to the physically well-endowed women of the household. Her taste in clothes—'coffee lace and taffeta skirt' . . . 'pale greens and powder blues and . . . dresses with Peter-Pan collars and little bows on them' (p. 93)—is too restrained to do herself or the family credit, and her frugal eating habits are considered a source of deprivation (of sex) to her husband and (of children) to his family (p. 94). There are connections between **"The Aliens"** and another tale published in 1968, **"The Young Couple"**, in which Naraian, like Dev, is very much under his mother's influence. Under increasing pressure, he gives up the flat he shares with his European wife Cathy, and they agree to move into the family mansion. In these stories, as in *The Nature of Passion,* the extended family is seen as octopus-like, pulling people in from the periphery to the centre, there to swallow all that is divergent or individual in them, making them part of the one organism. Nonconformists are not encouraged, and in **"The Aliens"** it is clear that Peggy's differences in appearance and opinion are being tolerated only until she can be persuaded to abandon them.

A feature of great interest in this story is Ruth Jhabvala's study of the mother-in-law, who binds her sons to her by indulging their weaknesses, especially in the matter of food. There is a contrast here with Peggy's mother, who had been 'firm', and whose memory Peggy constantly invokes to gain strength to cope with her daily trials:

> . . . good old Mum, who never complained, even when the waterpipes froze and she had to climb up in the loft and unfreeze them with hot-water bottles and her fingers all swollen with the chilblains.
>
> (p. 100)

Peggy's knowledge of England is very limited, and this limited view she applies amusingly to all that she sees, e.g., 'But he had been to England, he had had a nice education and ought to know better' (p. 101); or, 'He was a good boy—a nice steady type, with clean habits, as Mum and Doreen's mother and aunt Elsie and everyone had said; almost like one of our own boys, even if he was an Indian' (p. 102). Her family is as insular and limited in its outlook as Dev's, and the conflict between the two points of view is more comic than tragic because it is pitched at such a low level. However, the reader's sympathies are on the whole with Peggy rather than with her in-laws, partly because of her courage and determination, partly because it is only too obvious that defeat and not triumph awaits her in the future.

In **"A Birthday in London"**[21] a group of German Jews who have emigrated to Britain celebrate the birthday of Sonia Wolff, one of their number. The conversation revolves around the old days in Germany before the war and the Nazi regime, the crudeness of British Jews, and the difficulty of passing on to the children some sense of 'who they are'. They talk of travel, but as is the case with every other subject, this has a bitter undertone:

> Some people travel for pleasure . . . for kicks . . . and some travel because . . . they are kicked.
>
> (p. 135)

They appear to be living a half-life, despite their brand-new British citizenship: 'Yes, there we were all different people' (p. 128). Eating *apfel strudel* and drinking coffee is part of the celebratory ritual. Tragedy is passed over by common consent: Sonia's late father had been, we are informed, 'a large, healthy, handsome man who had loved good living and had died at Auschwitz' (p. 127). Sonia breaks down when she reflects that had fate willed otherwise, her son Werner might now have been director of the family firm, and her daughter Lilo might have enjoyed a delightful, indulged girl-hood like her own instead of knowing only the 'hard work in the Kibbutz' (p. 137). Werner's joke about it being 'time to move on, Werner' upsets her since it calls up a history of nomadic wandering. But the last word is one of hope and determined cheerfulness:

> What have you achieved in your life? And then I answer myself I have survived, I am still alive, and this is already a success story.
>
> (p. 138)

"A Birthday in London" is the only published story in which Ruth Jhabvala describes the life of expatriate German Jews in the London she knew as a child. In later stories and novels such as **"The Man and His Dog"**, and *A Backward Place* and **"An Indian Citizen"**, she depicts groups of expatriate Europeans in India clinging together for comfort and mutual support. Her own history of expatriation gives her studies of 'seekers' such as the narrator in *Heat and Dust* and 'travellers' like Lee in *A New Dominion* a special urgency and interest. It also contributes, no doubt, to the sympathetic understanding displayed by this author in stories such as **"Miss Sahib"**, **"The Aliens"**, **"The Young Couple"** and **"An Experience of India"**.

The friends and acquaintances who celebrate Sonia Wolff's birthday have been thrown together by the circumstances of their departure from Germany and their arrival and shared experiences in Britain. This, perforce, must substitute for the Jewish family, the original members of which have been lost to Auschwitz or Belsen, or are being scattered by the demands of 'Israel' or of new professions and occupations. Beneath the reminiscences that gloss over the horrors of loss, is the theme of survival. The story explains the intense interest with which Ruth Jhabvala draws the Punjabi survivors of Partition in *Amrita,* her first novel, and expands on the subject in *The Nature of Passion,* her second. It also sheds some additional light on her compassion for the helpless individuals who are moved hither and thither in her fiction by the whims of powerful and influential men. Her exploration of the theme of unfettered freedom in its Indian aspect of confidence in futurity, assurance that God will provide, is informed by this personal involvement and sympathy. She seeks there perhaps a solution to the perennial problem of the individual caught up in circumstances for which he is not responsible, and over which he has no control.

Two amusing studies on the theme of self-deception are **"A Course of English Studies"**[22] and **"In Love with a Beautiful Girl"**[23]. Nalini, the young heroine of the first story, comes from an upper class family that is in the habit of skating gracefully over Indian social realities:

> They were all great readers, and Nalini grew up on the classics. They were particularly fond of the English romantics, and of the great Russians. Sometimes they joked and said they were themselves like Chekhov characters. They . . . lived gracious lives in a big house in Delhi, but were always longing for the great capitals of Europe, London, Paris, Rome—where culture flourished and people were advanced and sophisticated.
>
> (p. 107)

However it is not social inequality that concerns Ruth Jhabvala in this story[24] but the personality of Nalini herself, and her experiences in the British midlands university to which she goes to study English literature:

> What she had (even if she didn't at the time know it) come to England for, what she expected from the place, what everything she had read had promised her, was love and a lover.
>
> A girl in such a mood is rarely disappointed.
>
> (p. 110)

The dry ironic tone of the last sentence (so reminiscent of Jane Austen when writing of her sillier heroines) sets the mood for what will inevitably follow. Nalini's romance with one of her lecturers begins, despite the fact that she is a mediocre student and he is burdened with a wife and several unkempt children. Together they shop at supermarkets and picnic furtively in a disused shed off dry Marie biscuits, providing an ironic background to all of which are constant allusions to luxurious picnics in India and the vanished glories of the Augustan Age (which happens to be Dr Norman Greaves' special field). There is also the sobering experience of Mrs Crompton, Nalini's landlady, whose divorce from her husband stands as a warning of what might await Nalini and her lover in the future.

Nalini sees Mrs Crompton's feelings about her husband as 'living . . . passion, it was the way a woman should be' (p. 125). Inspired by her landlady's story of an interview with the 'other woman', the romantic Nalini goes 'to call on Estelle Greaves' (p. 126), inviting her creator's ironic amusement at the formality, in the circumstances, of a social 'call'. Her resemblance to Shakuntala of *Esmond in India* emerges in a splendidly comic passage that follows, when she describes this visit to Norman:

> 'Why did you do it?' he said in a puzzled, tortured way. 'What-ever possessed you?'
>
> 'I wanted to clear the air,' she said grandly; and added, even more grandly, 'I can't live with a lie.'
>
> He gave a shout of exasperation; then he asked 'Is that the sort of language you used with her?'
>
> 'Oh, with her.' Nalini shrugged and pouted. 'She's just impossible to talk to. Whenever you try and start on anything serious with her, she jumps up and says the shepherd's pie is burning. Oh Norman, Norman, how do you stand it? How can you live with her and in such an atmosphere?'
>
> (p. 127)

The affair ends, and Nalini writes to her loving mother in Delhi that people in England do not have 'hearts (that) are open to each other' (p. 135). She is back with the Romantics, she adds, but feels—accompanying the comment with three exclamation marks—that they must have been Indians in a previous birth.

For Norman Greaves, the exotic Nalini has seemed 'a vision and a glory'. For Richard, a young Englishman in Delhi in **"In Love with a Beautiful Girl"**, his beloved Ruchira embodies the passion of Indian music, art and sculpture. Nalini sees Norman as a cultivated Augustan, Ruchira sees Richard as her passport to a smart and interesting social life. The two youthful heroines, though by no means copies of one another, create romantic auras about themselves and their bemused English lovers. Limited themselves, they are also totally self-absorbed and do not for a moment consider their effect on the lives of the other people around them. There is comic disappointment all round: the reality is so very different from their romantic imaginings. A further comic point is made when Nalini in her annoyance forgets grand gestures for a typically middle-class Indian row:

> 'What did you want? Some great seething scene of passion and renunciation, such as Indians like to indulge in?'
>
> (p. 129)

Norman asks this question, and a scene is exactly what he gets:

> 'Don't dare say anything bad against my country!'
>
> 'I'm not, for God's sake, saying anything bad against your country!'
>
> 'Yes, you are. And it's your wife who has taught you. I could see at one glance that she was anti-Indian.'
>
> 'Please don't let's talk about my wife any more.'
>
> 'Yes, we will talk about her. I'll talk about her as much as I like. What do you think, I'm some fallen woman that I'm not allowed to speak your wife's name? Give me my pins.' She plucked them from out of his hand and stabbed them angrily into her coil of hair. 'And I'll tell you something more. From now on everything is going to change. I'm tired of this hole and corner business. You must get a divorce.'
>
> 'A splendid idea. You're not forgetting that I have four children?'
>
> 'You can have ten for all I care. You must leave that woman! It is she or I. Choose.'
>
> Norman got up and let himself out of the hut. At the door he turned and said in a quiet voice 'You know I'm no good at these grand scenes.'
>
> (p. 129)

Two stories in Ruth Jhabvala's fourth collection are extended analyses of the innermost feelings of two women about their own personalities and their right to privacy. **"In the Mountains"**[25] concerns the way of life of an Indian woman from a conventional middle-class family (they spend their time, according to her, in 'Eating . . . (and) making money', p. 27) who has chosen to isolate herself in a small house in the mountains. Her gentle, conventional mother is upset by her daughter's individualism, but does not succeed in persuading her to abandon her mountain eyrie. A link with *Heat and Dust* is evident in the theme of self-chosen isolation, and also in the way agility in mountain climbing is used as a symbol for spiritual freedom. 'Doctor Sahib', Pritam's rather disreputable companion in her mountain life, is 'as nimble as herself' in clambering up and down the mountains on which they live. In contrast, Bobby (her associate of an earlier, romantic period in her life) is 'in very poor condition' (p. 40).

"Desecration"[26] is perhaps the most powerful story in this final collection, and centres upon the reaction of a sensitive and passionate young woman to a triple invasion: of her body and mind by her brutal and violent lover; of her heart by a love that is like a disease which 'would get worse and pass through many stages before it was finished with her' (p. 201); and of her privacy by the gossips in the township neighbouring the mansion in which she lives with her cultivated, elderly husband, the Raja Sahib. At the end of the story, when Sofia is nearing the point at which she can endure her emotional turmoil no longer and will end it in suicide, her feelings are further agitated by the realisation that the husband she has been deceiving is living in his private hell of undisclosed sickness (p. 202) and that

> there had never been anyone in the world who looked into her eyes the way he did, with such love but at the same time with a tender respect that would not reach farther into her than was permissible between two human beings.
>
> (p. 203)

And finally, **"The Housewife"**[27], a story in which is reflected the inevitable conflict that arises between a woman's artistry and her domestic and personal life. Shakuntala, a loving, faithful wife, begins after twentyfive years of contented domesticity to take singing lessons and finds that they become more important to her than anything else in her world. Her affections have hitherto been tranquilly shared among her husband, her daughter Manju and her new young grandchild, and indeed

> she loved all of them, but she could not deny to herself that her singing meant even more to her than her feelings as wife and mother and grandmother. She was unable to explain this, she tried not to think of it. But it was true that with her music she lived in a region where she felt most truly, most deeply herself. No, not herself, something more and higher than that. By contrast with her singing, the rest of her day, indeed her life, seemed insignificant. She felt this to be wrong but there was no point in trying to struggle against it. Without her hour's practice in the morning, she was as if deprived of food and water and air.
>
> (p. 138)

In the appearances and occasional failures to arrive of her singing-teacher, and in his varied responses to Shakuntala's progress are reflected the ups and downs, the triumphs and disappointments of the creative experience. Yet this analysis (and perhaps, even, self-analysis) is carefully embedded in a story of ordinary middle-class life, featuring some very ordinary middle-class characters. An interfering aunt, a mercenary daughter, feminine squabbling and the duties of a housewife are all part of the story, but they are in the nature of props, necessary parts of the setting. So is the music-master's wife and the comic by-play of aunt Phuphiji's giving him tea, and making a scene about payments. The core of the story is in the artist's alternating joy and agony as inspiration greets and deserts her:

> Shakuntala hardly noticed (Phuphiji and Manju). Her thoughts were day and night elsewhere, and she longed only to be sitting on the roof practising her singing while her teacher listened to her. But nowadays he seemed to be bored with her. He tended to stay for shorter periods, he yawned and became restless and left her before she had finished. When he left her like that, she ceased to sing but continued to sit on the roof by herself; she breathed heavily as if in pain, and indeed her sense of unfulfilment was like pain and stayed with her for the rest of the day. The worst was when he did not turn up at all. This was happening more and more frequently. Days passed and she didn't see him and didn't sing; then he came again—she would step up on the roof in the morning, almost without hope, and there he would be. He had no explanation to offer for his absence, nor did she ask for one. She began straightaway to sing, grateful and happy.
>
> (p. 156)

In this story, Ruth Jhabvala blends what is evidently a deeply felt personal testament on the subject of her art with a story of middle-class Indian domestic life. Writing is disguised as music[28], personal conflict externalised as domestic conflict involving other characters. The music master, despite his very unusual habit of materialising and disappearing is given a typical history (pp. 143-5), and partakes of afternoon tea. **"The Housewife"** married transposes into a modern setting the legendary love of Radha, milkmaid, for the god Krishna, musician and lover (an earlier version of this story, with younger lovers and a satiric, indirect exposition of a conventional narrator's character, may be seen in the short story, **"Lekha"**). With its assistance, and with that of her musical metaphor, Ruth Jhabvala explores the implications of an individual's commitment to art, especially the necessary abandonment of domestic concerns and considerations of personal safety or consequence by the woman who responds to the call of this special destiny:

> He entered her at the moment when, the structure of the raga having been expounded, the combination of notes was being played up and down, backwards and forwards, very fast. There was no going back from here, she knew. But who would want to go back, who would exchange this blessed state for any other?
>
> (p. 161)

Notes

1. R. P. Jhabvala, quoted by R. Agarwal, op. cit., p. 33.

2. R. P. Jhabvala, *Like Birds, Like Fishes* (John Murray, London: 1963). All references to stories in this collection in this chapter and throughout this book are to the 1963 edition.

3. *The New Yorker, Yale Review, Encounter* and *Kenyon Review.*

4. R. P. Jhabvala, quoted John Pym, op. cit., p. 18.

5. R. P. Jhabvala, *An Experience of India* (John Murray, London: 1966) 1968, 1971. All references to stories in this collection in this chapter and throughout this book are to the 1971 edition.

6. Quoted in Chapter I of this book.

7. The experiences of the narrator of "An Experience of India" with regard to travel around India appear to be based largely on information obtained from other Westerners in India. R. Agarwal reproduces the following exchange in his "Interview", op. cit., p. 35:

   R.A. You describe in detail the sexual habits of the Indians. What is your source of information in this regard?

   R.J. What a loaded question . . . Mostly, the many foreign girls I meet who travel around India. They certainly have some very memorable experiences in that field here. I haven't yet met one who hasn't, in the course of her travels, learned quite a bit about the sexual habits of Indians. Often more than she wanted.

8. R. P. Jhabvala, *A Stronger Climate* (John Murray, London: 1968) 1976. All references to stories in this collection in this chapter and throughout this book are to the 1976 edition. *A Stronger Climate* bears the epigraph 'They come no longer to conquer but to be conquered'.
9. R. P. Jhabvala, *How I Became a Holy Mother* (John Murray, London: 1976). All references to stories in this collection in this chapter and throughout this book are, with one exception ("The Englishwoman") to the British edition. This story, which is not included in the British edition, was published by Harper and Row in the American edition of the book (also published in 1976), and references to it in this book are therefore to the American edition.
10. "Myself in India", op. cit., p. 8.
11. See note 9 above, on "The Englishwoman".
12. See Chapter XI for further discussion of this story. "Lekha" appears in *Like Birds, Like Fishes,* pp. 166-188.
13. *Like Birds, Like Fishes,* pp. 45-59.
14. Ibid., pp. 23-44.
15. Ibid., pp. 60-83.
16. *An Experience of India,* pp. 162-87.
17. *A Stronger Climate,* pp. 90-114.
18. M. Mukherjee, op. cit., p. 5.
19. Ibid.
20. *Like Birds, Like Fishes,* pp. 84-106.
21. Ibid., pp. 132-9.
22. *An Experience of India,* pp. 106-36.
23. *A Stronger Climate,* pp. 11-32.
24. See A. Rutherford and K. H. Petersen, op. cit., p. 375.

    Q: Your novel, *Get Ready for Battle,* was your only attempt to deal with India's social problems. Can you explain why this is so?

    A. I don't know why I turned away from it. Maybe because it's just so hopeless.

    Q: Do you see any social role for the novelist in India?

    A: No, I don't think that is the role of the novelist. You'd write very poor novels if you tried to write social documents in India today.

25. *How I Became a Holy Mother,* pp. 26-47.
26. Ibid., pp. 176-203.
27. *An Experience of India,* pp. 137-161.
28. John Pym, op. cit., p. 18. quotes the following statements made by Ruth Jhabvala on her method of writing:

    Q: You try to sit down every day?

    A: I don't try. I sit. I don't know what others do. I don't put off—I know there are some who do—but I'm not like that. It's like practising the piano. I mean, if I played the piano I would play it every day, and know if I didn't play one day that I'd play worse the next. It's like that with writing.

Works Cited

Agarwal, Ramlal. "An Interview with Ruth Prawer Jhabvala", *Quest* 91 (September-October 1974), pp. 33-36.

Mukherjee, Meenakshi. "Journey's End for Jhabvala", in *Explorations in Modern Indo-English Fiction,* ed. R. K. Dhawan (Bahri Publications Pvt. Ltd. New Delhi: 1982), pp. 208-213.

Pym, John. "'Where could I meet other screenwriters?': A conversation with Ruth Prawer Jhabvala", *Sight and Sound,* London (Winter 1978), pp. 15-18.

Rutherford, Anna, and K. H. Petersen, "*Heat and Dust*: Ruth Prawer Jhabvala's Experience of India", *World Literature Written in English,* 15:2 (November 1976), pp. 373-378. Includes extracts from an interview with Ruth Jhabvala immediately after the award to her of the Booker Prize for *Heat and Dust* in 1975.

Laurie Sucher (essay date 1989)

SOURCE: Sucher, Laurie. "Difficult Adjustments: Three Stories." In *The Fiction of Ruth Prawer Jhabvala: The Politics of Passion,* pp. 143-67. New York: St. Martin's Press, 1989.

[*In the following excerpt, Sucher delineates the recurring motif of male homosexuals and their friendships with heterosexual women in Jhabvala's "A Birthday in London," "Commensurate Happiness," and "Grand-Mother."*]

Homosexual Men, Heterosexual Women

Ruth Jhabvala's latest Western-based fiction continues to develop the themes that have always concerned her as an artist. In the new setting they emerge differently, newly tailored to use the new material, as it were, yet recognisable products of the same artistic imagination. Again, she marks the clashes of generations; again, she examines her characters' paradoxical compulsions to love those who are indifferent; again, she portrays unscrupulous gurus and naïve (mostly female) disciples. I have already mentioned the new focus, perhaps reflecting the realities of the new setting, on the relationships of male homosexuals with each other and with the women who love them.

The European and American-based stories and novels do however seem bleaker in outlook, more pessimistic than the India-based fiction. The Westerners seem perhaps more alienated from one another, the author's ironies darker and unrelieved by the delight that suffuses the Indian-based tales. She herself seems at greater distance from her characters. If the author is God in relation to her characters, that is only fitting, since in the West one is at a further remove from God. 'Nothing had spoken' from the London skies, while the Indian skies seem to Judy in *A Backward Place* to reverberate with the presence of God.

There is comedy in these later tales, but it is often black. The search for authenticity, connectedness and transcendence persists in certain characters, but their paths are perhaps more circuitous and therefore more open to exploitation than the traditional and well-defined religious routes of the Indians. Often collapse and breakdown, even tragedy, occur because of a peculiarly Western devaluation of all that is named 'feminine': for example, Michael's terrible infatuation with the paramilitary 'Fourth World Movement' in *Three Continents.* Also peculiarly Western is the alienation of women from each other, which a feminist reading of these stories and novels reveals. Even more than before, emotional and spiritual integration, wholeness, fulfilment are located out of sight, above the clouds and unseeable, as they were already in *Heat and Dust.*

The later, Western-based novels and stories are peopled by women isolated from community, by which I mean the communities of other women. Even if nature offers images of healing, relief and beauty, a symbolic all-nurturant mother, real life does not. Ruth Jhabvala's searching women, disappointed by men, find themselves without any consoling or important resources, which might be supplied by affirming or central relationships among women.

For the questing female protagonist Jhabvala sees only the absence of validating or nurturing relationships. *Not with other women*: relationships between women are exploitative and manipulative, usually in one direction, though sometimes mutually. Often the 'friends' are actually rivals for the same man. Generally one—wealthier—woman bullies the other, who good-naturedly, or foolishly, tolerates her arrogance. The mother-daughter bond is conspicuously weak—daughters, usually seen from the mother's viewpoint, are selfishly obsessed with their men. When mothers are seen from the daughter's viewpoint, they are usually absent. Natasha's (adoptive) mother Marietta is mostly away. And even Marietta's first act of nurturance toward Natasha—the adoption itself—is somewhat suspect (she wishes to adopt a 'one-hundred per cent guaranteed Jewish' (p. 13) child to reaffirm her lapsed Jewishness).

Grandmothers and granddaughters generally have a closer relationship than mothers and daughters, but grandmothers are powerless to protect young women from male predation. They may even fuel the social machinery locking granddaughters into destructive marriages, as in **'Commensurate Happiness'**. In *Three Continents,* a step-grandmother (Sonya) tries to save the protagonist, but to no avail.

Not with heterosexual men: in this New-York-based fiction, a gulf that is wider than ever yawns between men and women, though the men characteristically fail to notice it, their obtuseness compounded by arrogance. The few heterosexual men in these latest works are not particularly attractive to the sensitive and artistic women who surround them, since the men's interests run exclusively to business, sport and 'dirty' jokes. These interests are shared even by Leo Kellermann, the guru-figure of *In Search of Love and Beauty,* who at least possesses a charismatic intelligence and psychological acumen, which render him attractive, if not morally sound. The one nominally heterosexual (actually bisexual) man, Crishi in *Three Continents,* is trouble, to say the least.

Not with homosexual men: though homosexual men inhabit and even *own* the urban cultural scene, their circles are closed to women in any authentic sense; they may dispense to some women a kind of love or friendship, but it is at a heavy price, usually financial (as in **'Grandmother'** or **'A Summer by the Sea'**). Jhabvala's recent focus on the relationships of homosexual men and heterosexual women probes a contemporary scene that places women at a new kind of distance from men, and that puts women at a new disadvantage.

Male homosexual characters are not new to Ruth Jhabvala's oeuvre: there was Harry, Olivia's friend in *Heat and Dust*; there was Raymond in *A New Dominion*; the stories **'Rose Petals'** (***Like Birds, Like Fishes***), **'Grandmother'**, **'Commensurate Happiness'** and

'Expiation' (the last three uncollected) present still others. The novel *In Search of Love and Beauty* expands and refines the exploration, so that we see further into the relationship of the male lovers. We also note its effects on the women who are close to it. Sister, mother, grandmother or 'patron', the woman in question may be dimly aware of the relationship; yet her reponse to it is peculiarly vague. Shrugging her shoulders, she accepts her loved one's homosexuality: but this often means accepting a kind of a second-class status for herself: *she* will never be good enough for him. Often she accepts a deep alienation in confidence: he will not talk openly about his emotional life. In some cases she refuses to acknowledge his homosexuality altogether, a manifestation of the familiar Jhabvala dynamic of interested misapprehension. (We 'read' the world to correspond with the way we wish the world to be.) While accepting his homosexuality, she often consigns herself to a kind of asexuality.

The male homosexuals in these works form part of a broad and varied culture, invisible to those who do not know how to read its signs, instantly recognisable to initiates. They are often successful and leisured, or perhaps only leisured: architects, lawyers, dealers in real estate, designers, as well as unemployed actors and dancers, part-time butlers or paid companions.

That they figure so prominently in these works is, I think, a commentary on the contemporary urban scene. The emergence of gay rights activism into politics, print and popular consciousness is both the result and the sign of an important social reality in the life of the late twentieth century, one which Jhabvala—without much company among current women authors—has chosen to highlight; in urban centres—such as Manhattan—male homosexuality seems almost more the rule than the exception. Whether this perception reflects actual numbers, or an increasing acceptability is not the issue here so much as the burgeoning importance and visibility of the 'lifestyle'.

One may read the increasing focus on male homosexuality as a kind of response to the disillusionment with heterosexual romance that is the cornerstone of Jhabvala's comedy. If demon-lovers mistreat the romantic heroine—as, of course, they do, by definition—perhaps she should look to men who might share her interests more, talk with her, understand her feelings: men who also love remote, awe-inspiring icons of power. She is quite naturally drawn to them, by virtue of shared interests and sensibilities, as Olivia is drawn to Harry.

Finally, one may see the focus on male homosexuality as a movement towards, and interest in, homosexuality *per se,* which would, of course, include female homosexuality. But lesbianism in Jhabvala's fiction is derided, ignored or viewed as revolting.

These novels and stories discount even the idea of love or support between women. Because they investigate female psychology and experience, and because they inquire into the world of male homosexuals, one might logically expect some acknowledgement of the female homosexual possibility. This appears only in the latest novel at the time of writing, *Three Continents.* Before it, there are lesbian characters, but they are very minor, and their homosexuality is viewed as comic or pathological. In the terms of these novels and stories women have three *un*satisfactory options: they may love homosexual men (who ignore them) or heterosexual men (who despise them), or they may live without love altogether. In *In Search of Love and Beauty,* Natasha, Louise and Marietta represent the three possibilities.

Adrienne Rich has argued that there exists a powerful cultural imperative to ignore the lesbian alternative, which she sees not merely as a sexual preference, but as 'woman-identified experience', or, in its broadest definition, any other 'forms of primary intensity between and among women, including the sharing of a rich inner life, the bonding against male tyranny, the giving and receiving of practical and political support'.[1] Rich questions what is generally regarded as axiomatic: the assumption of female heterosexuality. Given the reality that for all human beings the original 'search for love and tenderness in both sexes . . . [led] toward women' (that is, the mother), Rich wonders 'why in fact women would ever redirect that search'.[2] Her conclusion is that there is an active societal impulse continually working to obscure, prohibit and deny love between women. For her the *absence* of lesbian or even woman-centred love in myth and fiction 'suggests that an enormous potential counterforce is having to be restrained'.[3]

These novels and stories, in which even female friendship is discounted, certainly illustrate the premises of Rich's thesis: that is, 'the virtual or total neglect of lesbian existence',[4] coupled with the idea that 'women are inevitably, even if rashly and tragically, drawn to men: even when that attraction is suicidal'.[5] So do other Jhabvala fictions I have discussed—**'Desecration'** being the perfect illustration. And so, of course, do countless other works of literature, for 'compulsory heterosexuality' is the unexamined social norm.

The fiction of Ruth Jhabvala as a whole recreates a world illustrating Adrienne Rich's profoundly radical—that is, reaching to the root—insights. Again, to quote C. P. Snow on Ruth Jhabvala: 'life is thus and not otherwise'. By their attention to women's psychology, by their female perspectives, and by their inclusion of so many male homosexual characters, her novels and stories push us in the direction of at least *noticing* the absence of female friendships or love between women. At the core of the novel *In Search of Love and Beauty,* is a female 'friendship'—between Louise and Regi—about which the best that can be said is that with a friendship like that one needs no enemies. Bitchy Regi and tolerant Louise present a perverse image of friendship indeed, one that stands the concept on its head. There are many other examples.

For instance, from 'Myself in India', here is one passage that I hesitate to quote in this context because of its laudable, and I would even say courageous, admission of feelings that are not quite acceptable: speaking of her fictional Delhi hostess, the author dips her pen in acid:

> Our hostess . . . loves to exercise her emancipated mind, and whatever the subject of conversation . . . she has a well-formulated opinion on it and knows how to express herself. How lucky for me if I could have such a person for a friend! What enjoyable, lively times we two could have together!
>
> In fact, my teeth are set on edge if I have to listen to her for more than five minutes, yes, even though everything she says is so true and in line with the most advanced opinions of today.[6]

Her hostess, indeed, as India was her 'hostess' for some two decades! It is perhaps for remarks like these that she has been excoriated in the Indian press, which she says, liked her well enough until 'they found out that I wasn't Indian'.[7] In fact, she merely accords her 'hosts' their full humanity, which includes the possibility of their being as obnoxious as anyone else. And yet. In the light of the fiction's underlying assessment of women's relations with each other, I do quote this passage, in this context. The character—as usual, magically painted whole in a few deft strokes—could not offer friendship: poseurs never do. Perhaps, then, it is for this reason that she sets the author's teeth on edge.

But even more pointed is the Jhabvala protagonist's recoil from women who seem eager to engage in what Raymond, in *A New Dominion,* called 'undesirable revelation'. For example, Evie in that novel confides to Lee of her bliss with Swami, urging her too to live in the joy of submission. 'She was even holding my hand and pressing it ever so gently. I didn't like that much, though' (p. 158). The chapter breaks off here, in a clattering silence. The effect is one of physical revulsion, skilfully conveyed. Why, though, the overtone of awful, uninvited lesbianism? The juxtapositions here are significant. Evie's pathological realisation of an impulse inherent in all romantic lovers, and a shudder of revulsion from physical closeness with another woman.

Similarly, but more explicitly presented, is the narrator's revulsion in **'An Experience of India',** in which Evie's counterpart, Jean, confides unasked in the narrator. Again, Jean praises 'the beauty of surrender', and whispers warmly into the narrator's neck, or touches her moistly and 'ever so gently'. 'It gave me an unpleasant sensation down my spine.'

Again, the recoil from physical closeness, utterly convincingly conveyed. Is this romantic propensity for 'surrender' what is most horrible about ourselves? In a world that devalues women, while overvaluing men, in a world constructed on women's alienation for themselves and from each other, we recoil most from the threat of intimacy with another who might be like us. The Jhabvala protagonist remains alone: more so than ever, since she now situates herself among male homosexuals from whom she is fundamentally set apart because of her femaleness. This apartness is particularly ironic since love between men, for all its *difference,* and for all that it consigns those who engage in it to a subculture apart, is not that different after all: that is, it often repeats the configurations of heterosexual romance. So in a way the novels and stories of this phase continue where the demon-lover stories leave off. But women take part mostly as observers. Refugees from homosexuality, they are still aliens in the world of gay men.

Appropriately, the next three stories I wish to discuss, which lead up to the novel *In Search of Love and Beauty,* are all set within the worlds of 'real' refugees, that is, refugees from state terror, still alien in their adopted lands.

'A Birthday in London'

'A Birthday in London' was Jhabvala's first published work to be set in the West. (An uncollected story, **'Light and Reason',** 1963, was also set in England.) Appearing in ***Like Birds, Like Fishes*** (1963), it was published some twenty years before *In Search of Love and Beauty* (1983), yet it bears the seeds of the later novel. The story is little more than a poignant vignette on the theme of loss; the much later novel may be said to weave a complex design around the same fundamental idea.

'A Birthday in London' conveys the lives of the dispossessed with a Chekhovian economy, in which each detail is meaningful and revelatory. It bears interesting parallels to *In Search of Love and Beauty*: both works revolve around a mother and son whose relationship echoes the loss and alienation of all the refugees from the land that bore them. There are many other parallels, beginning with the birthday party referred to in the story's title, for birthdays also figure prominently in the novel.

In addition to their special and particular tragedies, the refugees share with everyone a more general vulnerability: that is, to time. Among many enemies to their dignity and sense of safety in the world, time is perhaps the subtlest. Its ravages go unnoticed most often, except for certain occasions, for example, birthday parties. This modern-day ritual serves as the setting not only for this story and the novel that follows it, but also for the story **'Commensurate Happiness'**. A birthday also represents the climax of the next novel, *Three Continents.* At birthday parties, time, relentless but ordinarily imperceptible, is formally acknowledged. Friends and family convene to mark the passage of a personal year. We are one year older, that much closer to our deaths; we celebrate having come through the year, and those who are there with us congratulate us, which is particularly meaningful for the refugees who have been torn from their kin. For everyone, but more so for them, beneath the celebration runs an undercurrent of regret, for the new marks of age, for the diminution of the future, for the inexorable decline—and for those whose absence is conspicuous.

There is something at once comical and touching about these birthday parties in middle or even advanced old age. Sonia, the main character in London, is a grandmother now, but she is still the 'birthday child' who makes a 'birthday wish' and receives a 'birthday letter' from her daughter Lilo in Israel (it arrives precisely on her birthday). There is 'birthday coffee' with apfel strudel, and naturally, birthday presents. It is an appealing moment. Yet the horrors of the past and the disappointments of the present loom large, contributing to the reader's poignant sense of the fragility of happiness or even consolation.

Does this party *compensate* for the losses they have endured? Well, it will have to. The idea of 'compensation' is thematic, more precisely the tragic absurdity of the concept. The refugees have lost worlds—fathers, mothers and sisters—the loss is only hinted at. What 'compensation' can there be? And when calculated in marks, pounds or dollars, how obscene is the suggestion that the balances are now cleared, and justice has been done. And yet, so it is. The money must be accepted, ugly as it is; the refugees are certainly in no position to turn it down. There is a further irony: Sonia Wolff, née Rothenstein, a widow with two grown children, receives ample 'compensation' because her deceased husband, 'Otto Wolff had been a very wealthy factory owner in Berlin'. Now 'Sonia was a rich woman again now, which was as it should be'. The others at the party, less favoured in the vanished, pre-Holocaust world, receive less 'compensation'. This is the best the world can offer: that the inequities that once prevailed shall be reestablished.

Sonia Wolff recasts the favoured Jhabvala theme of loss and disinheritance. Like so many of Jhabvala's other protagonists, Sonia, even if partially restored to her former prosperity, looks back on better, happier times: like Miss Tuhy (**'Miss Sahib'** in ***An Experience of India***), like Louise (in *In Search of Love and Beauty*), like Olivia (*Heat and Dust*), like Dr Ernst (**'An Indian Citizen'**, in ***A Stronger Climate***), like the Countess of **'How I Became a Holy Mother'**, like the poignant Nilima of the story **'Like Birds, Like Fishes'** (this title is used for the collection from which **'A Birthday in London'** is taken).

The disinherited, those who amid present squalour or loneliness think bitterly or wistfully of the ease or comfort of their former circumstances: these melancholy subjects offer in themselves a kind of personification of Jhabvala's more general themes: loss and disillusionment. There is even a kind of mytho-religious reference in the image, since it recreates the human condition: we all, all of us, come into being 'trailing clouds of glory'—which are soon blown away. Miss Tuhy of the story **'Miss Sahib'** has fallen very far, measuring out her meagre pension in a sleazy urban Indian setting. She had been a teacher, in love with India, with poetry, with feeling: and 'passionate' about the English Romantics.

The particular and modern tragedy of the German-Jewish refugees Jhabvala writes of—and, of course, one of whom she is—impinges on an event of such enormity that it shadows literally everything in modern experience. Nazism, the nightmare as reality, irretrievably altered the face of humanity: when this story was written, probably in the late fifties, the philosophical, literary and imaginative reponses to the trauma of German fascism, which have emerged and continue to emerge ever since, had only begun to take form. In this story, the name 'Auschwitz' is mentioned for the only time in Ruth Jhabvala's work to date—and characteristically woven in unobtrusively, in the usual subordinate clause. But, of course, the story is informed by that name and what it represents.

Ruth Jhabvala's work is practically devoid of direct reference to the Holocaust. She has spoken of this avoidance in her Neil Gunn Lecture, delivered in 1979 and reprinted in *Blackwood's Magazine.* **'Disinheritance'** was its title.[8]

> I don't feel like talking much about 1933 and after. Everyone knows what happened to German Jews first and to other European Jews after that. Our family was no exception. One by one all my aunts and uncles emigrated—to France, Holland, what was then Palestine, the United States. . . . My immediate family—that is, my Polish father, my mother, my brother and myself—were the last to emigrate, and also the only ones to go to England. This was 1939. I have slurred over the years 1933 to 1939, from when I was six to twelve. They should have been my most formative years, and maybe they were, I don't know. Together with the early happy German-Jewish bourgeois family years—1927 to 1933—they should be that profound well of memory and experience (childhood and ancestral) from which

> as a writer I should have drawn. I never have. I have never written about those years. To tell you the truth, until today I've never mentioned them. Never spoken about them to anyone. I don't know why not. I do know that they are the beginning of my disinheritance—the way they are for other writers of their inheritance.

This reticence is a typical response to the trauma of such loss, as many studies of political refugees and Holocaust survivors attest.[9] Refugees live *in* loss, to the extent that often even speaking of it is impossible.

The birthday party vignette, then, is particularly telling viewed as a literary portrayal of the dilemmas of survival in its specifically post-Holocaust sense—as well as the more generalised human context, in which we are all survivors. The fictionalised refugees of **'A Birthday in London'** are matter-of-fact about it: '"There is something from my dear late Papa in him [a photograph of her baby grandson]," Sonia said, sighing for her father, a large, healthy, handsome man who had loved good living and had died at Auschwitz' (p. 127). So have the families and relations of all the others: Else, Mrs Gottlob and Karl Lumbik. Each is alone; each is a survivor; each has, now, twenty years after the Holocaust, recreated herself or himself as fully as possible—which is not very fully.

Else works as a seamstress for a Mrs Davis, an 'English Jewish lady' who condescends to her. It might be more accurate to say that Mrs Davis is too ignorant—from Else's point of view—to know what is due to Else Levy, 'daughter of Oberlehrer Levy of Schweinfurt'. Mrs Gottlob, once the owner of 'Gottlob's butcher shop, where you got the finest liver-sausage in the whole of Gelsenkirchen', now keeps a rather seedy boarding house, where Sonia and Otto stayed when they arrived in London. Karl Lumbik, a much-travelled Vienna gallant, is still paying court (to Sonia). He boasts, 'Budapest, Prague, Shanghai, Bombay, London, is that bad for one lifetime?' But enforced travels are quite different from the peregrinations of the man of the world he might have been. Some, he jokes, travel 'for kicks, thank you, and some travel because—yes, because they are kicked. Is this a bad pun, Mr Werner? I am being very English now, for I am making puns so that I can apologise for them.'

Though briefly glimpsed, the refugees have weight and individuality. Though her characters may be recognisable types, they are never only that, nor are they without their petty failings. Mrs Gottlob fawns on Sonia, now that Sonia is a wealthy woman again; but before Sonia's 'compensation', Mrs Gottlob was less kind. Mr Lumbik retains his German-Jewish anti-Semitism intact: ('Do you know about Moyshe Rotblatt from Pinsk who was taken to *Tristan und Isolde*?'—we do not hear the punch line, but the lead-in tells enough). And all the refugees feel superior to the English Jews, whom they find 'uncultured'.

Compressed into some sixteen pages are the four partygoers' strategies for survival, by turns comic and heroic. Like others of Jhabvala's heroes, they are victim-survivors of circumstances ranging from the nightmare of the Holocaust to the buffetings of ordinary life, no matter where. To take the largest view, Ruth Jhabvala's fiction is a celebration of human endurance, the small heroisms of those who feel and suffer, but go on. Major and minor characters alike display this quality of quiet resistance. For example, a minor character such as Eric, the failed actor/model of *In Search of Love and Beauty*, after being turned down by Mark, 'shrugged a little bit and smiled a little bit. Probably this was the gesture with which he met every little humiliation that life offered him' (p. 179). Dr Ernst of **'An Indian Citizen'** is another version of Karl Lumbik, another elderly survivor of the Holocaust who carefully orchestrates his aimless days with small strategies for survival, such as an afternoon nap:

> Of course, a nap in the afternoon was nothing to reproach oneself with—good heavens, at his age and in this climate!—but one also had to know when to cut it short. Otherwise there was a danger of sinking too deep and giving way to the desire to sleep for ever and not have to get up at all any more and walk around and meet people. He put away his handkerchief and patted and jerked and brushed at his crumpled clothes to get them dapper again.

Despair, even suicide, is always just around the corner, having to be kept at bay. Karl Lumbik of **'A Birthday in London'** shares Dr Ernst's cheerful stoicism. But a dearth of it has brought about the death of Sonia's husband Otto, as she remembers: 'He never believed things could be well again one day. I would say to him "Otto, it is dark now but the sun will come again"; "no," he said, "it is all finished." He didn't want to live any more, you see.' Otto is a prefiguration of Bruno of the novel *In Search of Love and Beauty*, just as Sonia is a prefiguration of one of its main characters, Louise. Both Otto and Bruno are small and dark, emotionally vulnerable and deeply sensitive. Both Sonia and Louise are tall, beautiful, nurturant, but filled with regret for the lost 'beautiful times', as Sonia says. Each has a daughter who travels far away: Lilo to Israel, Marietta to India.

There are clear autobiographical references in these related pieces, which draw on Ruth Jhabvala's youth as a refugee. Like the refugees in London, she and her immediate family lost worlds: she recently counted over forty family members who perished in the Holocaust.[10] Like the families of Sonia and Louise, her mother's family in Cologne was comfortable and accomplished. Her maternal grandfather was cantor of Cologne's major synagogue.[11]

> There were aunts and uncles, all well-settled, all German patriots, all life-loving, full of energy, bourgeois virtues and pleasures, celebrating every kind of festi-

> val—all the Jewish holidays, of course, but what they really liked was New Year's Eve and, especially, the annual Cologne carnival and masked ball. We all had costumes made for that every year; one year I was a chimney-sweep, and another a Viennese pastry-cook. All this would be in the early 1930s—up to, but not including, 1933.[12]

I have already mentioned Marcus Prawer's suicide, a casualty of what his daughter called 'an epidemic' of suicides among Holocaust survivors in the London of the forties.[13]

Thus all the refugees know the temptations of suicide. Each has made his or her own compromise with it:

> 'There were many days I also didn't want to live any more,' Else said. . . . 'I would say to myself, Else, what are you doing here? Father, mother, sisters all gone, why are you still here, finish off now.' 'Who hasn't had such days?' Mr. Lumbik said. 'But then you go to the cafe, you play a game of chess, you hear a new joke, and everything is well again.'

But Otto had taken things too 'tragically'—as if it were possible to take too tragically the events he lived through. And yet, the story seems to say, it is: 'too' tragically being without the strategies for survival of those who go on, even if those strategies are denial, avoidance, stoicism and willed cheerfulness. Karl Lumbik reaffirms his resolve merely *to be*. When he asks himself what he has achieved in his life, the answer is that he has survived, he jokes, and 'this is already a success story'. In that offhand, joking remark he sums up the tragedy of the unprecedented genocidal war that wiped out the lives of millions, and with their lives all the things that they would have achieved.

At the birthday party, in 1959, two of the guests have good news: for one, Karl Lumbik has received his citizenship papers—no one can tell him again, 'Pack your bags, Lumbik! Time to move on', as he jokes: 'It is so restful, it is quite bad for my nerves.' Also, Else Levy has received her 'compensation', ten thousand marks—enough to take 'a nice holiday in Switzerland in a good hotel'.

Thus, the class differences that once prevailed have been restored. This is in contrast to the chaotic refugee years, when Sonia and Otto lived at Mrs Gottlob's rooming house, and had had to suffer her shouting at them up the stairs about 'lights that had been left burning and baths that had not been cleaned after use': all the petty indignities of poverty and unwished-for sharing. Otto would pale and Sonia would descend to placate the landlady and buffer Otto's greater sensitivity, which both clearly place first. But now Mrs Gottlob is all kindness, even obsequiousness, to Sonia. And her social inferiority is delicately suggested by the fact that she is addressed as 'Mrs Gottlob' in contrast to Sonia and Else.

The question of address comes up directly at the outset of the story, when Karl Lumbik tells Sonia to call him 'Karl'; by its end she gives in to this, his 'birthday wish'. The others notice; the change is cause for much merriment and joking. Still a gallant, Karl Lumbik feels he possesses a superior knowledge of women, especially Sonia's 'type', with which 'one had to proceed very gently and tactfully'—a view reflecting a gallant's condescension.

With the arrival of Werner, Sonia's son, the fragile glow and good feeling generated by the happy announcements will be extinguished. A handsome and animated youth, Werner treats his mother and her friends with a mixture of condescension and exasperation. He has forgotten the birthday, for which he duly apologises. But the talk of travel leads into another unexpected revelation, as Werner 'lazily' announces his intention of leaving: '"Off to Rome soon," and seeing his mother's face—"Oh come on darling, I told you I might be going."' He glosses over the surprise, but in Sonia's 'large anxious eyes' and clenched hand her shock and disappointment can be read.

This only annoys him, of course: '"Don't worry, darling," he said, trying to sound light and gay, but with an edge of exasperation all the same.' Sonia hastens to make amends, 'Of course I don't worry'. Now that there is 'enough money', he can enjoy himself doing 'a little film-work', 'a little art-photography', having his parties and girlfriends. Sonia knows that there is nothing wrong with a grown son's independence, yet she weeps: if the war had never happened, how different it would have been. Werner would have been 'Werner Wolff, Director of SIGBO, everybody would know and respect him'.

Werner's departure links up with all the other disappointments of her life, the general descent from privilege; at least she puts it in these terms, citing too her daughter's loss of advantage (which, presumably, a kibbutznik would not feel as loss):

> 'My poor Lilo—I have had such a lovely girlhood, such lovely dresses and always parties and dancing-classes and the Konservatorium in Berlin for my piano-playing. And she has had only hard work in the Kibbutz, hard work with her hands, and those horrible white blouses and shorts'—Her voice broke and she said 'My handkerchief is quite wet'.
>
> (p. 137)

In this small outburst Jhabvala brings to bear her uncanny ability to walk the fine edge of tragedy and comedy. The Kibbutz blouses may be 'horrible', but it is Werner's departure that makes Sonia cry. His presence delights her. The text makes clear her abundant good humour during the few moments that he is present, and before he makes his announcement. *In Search of Love and Beauty* repeats the relationship of Werner and Sonia, in Mark and Marietta. But many more of Ruth Jhabvala's stories and novels repeat it in its basic essence: the perils of loving and the indifference of the beloved.

The impatient departure of a loved one requires a major effort if it is to be borne gracefully. One may hardly admit it to oneself: yet there, at this level of human relations, the novelist's territory is located. Sonia's task echoes the refugees', in little: to withstand.

The refugees console each other, with reminders that they are lucky to be alive, with apfel strudel, and with flirtatious jokes. By the time Werner leaves for his date, they are laughing merrily: he 'smiled at their preoccupation: he was glad to see them having a good time' (p. 139).

This irony, the last line of the story, reveals the refugees' isolation. Certainly, their children cannot see their heroism in the face of loss. Nor is that surprising: 'We know who we are, but does my Werner know, and my Lilo?' Sonia cries. Youth in particular, with its slightly condescending affection and happy egotism, does not wish to understand; it sees only that the elders 'worry'. The currents of feeling among these five characters, glimpsed so briefly yet plumbed so deeply, the meanings of their smallest gestures being remarked and understood, make up a short text that not only illuminates the artistry of its author, but models the art of the short story as a genre, in which no word is superfluous, no detail insignificant. Like Chekhov's, whose they resemble in mood and feeling, Jhabvala's stories stand as the highest examples of their kind.

'Commensurate Happiness'

'Commensurate Happiness' is another, later, prefiguration of *In Search of Love and Beauty,* though certain characters also refer back to **'A Birthday in London'**. It is a rather astonishing vignette pinpointing the making of a marriage, and in its implications it is, if not an outright indictment of marriage and family, at least a revelation of the very imperfect reality underlying the myth of domestic bliss.

The cast comprises a comfortable German-Jewish family living in New York. There is an aged and widowed grandmother, Jeannette (who corresponds to Sonia Wolff in the story and Louise in the novel); her daughter Sandra (Lilo/Marietta) who 'had a lot of divorces and personal crises' and is thus essentially absent from the family; and the daughter's daughter Marie (Natasha), an isolated waif-like young girl. There is an overdressed female friend Wanda (Regi in the novel), who lives in an East Side apartment decorated in Bauhaus style—these elements come up again in the novel—and who has been the mistress of Jeannette's late husband (named Otto—like Sonia's husband in 'A Birthday in London').

Again there is a son, this time homosexual, unlike Werner, who had—at least his mother thought he had—'a lot of girlfriends'. This son, Hughie, corresponds to Mark, a major character in the novel. Marie is in love with Hughie as Natasha is in love with Mark. Like Mark, Hughie takes frequent trips abroad with unknown companions, who turn out to be his male lovers—again, a reworking of the issue at the heart of **'A Birthday in London'**. Hughie is sensitive and self-involved, given to unrequited love affairs with indifferent boys, and he accepts a certain comfort from Marie (as Mark does from Natasha) although once that is out of the way he is happy to dispense with her.

In the novel, Mark and Natasha are brother and sister—though only by adoption, not by blood. In this story the pair, Hughie and Marie, are cousins, a relationship that allows them to marry. Thus the plot: 'Jeanette wanted and expected Hughie and Marie to get married; Marie wanted and expected it too; and Hughie just expected it.' After years of fruitless waiting for the couple to become engaged, Wanda (the close family friend) hurries matters along. The moment comes at Wanda's birthday party, hosted by Jeannette. With supreme aplomb, Wanda toasts the engagement as if it were a *fait accompli.* Of course, it has never been mentioned. The young couple accept the ploy, and take the opportunity to 'announce' their engagement.

Like much of Ruth Jhabvala's fiction, this story is a commentary on marriage. There are two marriages in it to compare, Jeanette's and Marie's, and the reader is led to conclude that as they are similar at their inceptions, they will probably continue to resemble each other. Each marriage, desired by the bride but not by the groom, and engineered by the family, is an arrangement in which the woman, without realising it, is signed up for a lifetime of economic security at the price of emotional deprivation. Her youth and inexperience are partially to blame, but then again, the groom is clearly less than eager, a situation she could have seen had she been willing to look. Thus, women, by wishful thinking, collude in the oppressive arrangements.

Wanda indignantly justifies her high-handed intrusion thus: 'If young people don't know where they're going, the family has to take over.' She is correct: they had been waiting for her to intervene, and now Hughie will come through with a proposal—in his fashion—which poor Marie is only too happy to accept. Jeannette recalls her own engagement to Otto, which turns out to have followed a similar pattern. It too had been long in coming: 'She had adored him for four years and he had been kind to her.' It too had been prompted by the actions of interested others—aunts, in her case. However, 'It did not take Jeannette long to find out that the expectations she had had that night had been excessive. She did have happiness, but it was of a different order from what she had expected.' A flashback supplies an example of that last, drily ironic assertion. Jeannette's 'happiness' consists of an emotional abasement. It happens at another of Wanda's birthday parties, this one set a few years back, in the midst of Otto's last, fatal illness. As one of his last requests, he has asked Jeannette to host his mistress's birthday party in their home. She has complied with his wish, and he thanks her. 'In comparison with the great effort he was making just to press her hand—that seemed a very small thing to have done; and she had brought his hand up to her lips, to make him understand that it was she who was glad and grateful.' Although there is poignancy in this recollection, it is alarming that her fondest memory is that he was grateful that she tolerated his mistress! The marriage to which she urges her two grandchildren is to be drawn along similar lines, and she knows this. Still she does what she can to promote that commensurate happiness.

After Wanda's prompting, Jeannette questions Marie. Finding that Hughie has *still* not proposed, she takes up the argument, as if Hughie's recalcitrance is somehow Marie's fault.

> 'He does care for you. He loves you. As far as he can, he does. What more do you want?' she added—rather impatiently, for it seemed to her that Marie was being unreasonable in her expectations. She too would have to learn that one lived on earth and not in heaven.

When Hughie calls weakly from the next room, Jeannette pretends—although she knows better—to take it as a sign that 'he can't be five minutes without you'. Marie too knows her cousin better: 'He wants the cologne' because he has drunk too much.

Though homosexual, Hughie is by no means egalitarian in his views of the sexes. 'He resented it—to be so commingled with a girl.' But he will grudgingly accept her nurturance. As she massages his temples, he whispers (they are being listened to), 'We could, you know. If you want to.' She demurs. He covers her mouth with his hand, a symbolic muting that echoes the dynamics of their relationship.

> As soon as Hughie took his hand away Marie whispered: 'We don't have to: just because *they* want to.'
>
> '*I* want to,' Hughie said—irritably, for he always disliked it when Marie didn't at once fall in with his wishes.

And so they are married, in an arrangement in which Hughie will carry on with his love affairs under the convenient cover of their marriage, and Marie will suffer silently, with everyone's consent, her own and her family's.

For Jeannette knows, even without wishing to, about her grandson's affectional and sexual preferences. After overhearing his side of a tearful conversation with 'Chuck', she stops demanding to know the identity of his friends, a point which had greatly concerned her until then. She even loses her temper with Wanda when Wanda expresses curiosity: 'She said it was none of my business, none of her business, none of anyone's business who are Hughie's friends. This she says to me!' So reports Wanda to Marie with her customary indignation.

Jhabvala's fiction certainly endorses authentic human relationships, male homosexual ones included, to be sure. The problem that her fiction highlights, however, is that women accept a position of marginality in relation to the male homosexuals in their lives, and do not avail themselves of the same privilege of intimate relations. In exchange for Hughie's company, Marie forfeits intimacy, centrality, sexuality—love. The privileges that Hughie takes for granted, Marie never dreams of for herself.

The social and domestic machinery grinds on, and women's willed suppression of the knowledge of their own disadvantage in a male-centred society keeps it running—to women's own self-mutilation. Indeed, the 'happiness' that Jeannette has claimed, and that Marie will claim in her turn, *is* commensurate with that state of diminished expectation and resigned acceptance that is offered to the disinherited. And it is above all women who are the disinherited: from our history, from our strength and from our sense of self-worth. By showing the machinery in action, this story forces us to confront what Marie, Jeannette and Hughie might well deny.

'Grandmother' and Other Old Women

This vignette, published in the *New Yorker* in 1980, is still uncollected. Like **'Commensurate Happiness',** it is clearly preparatory for the novel *In Search of Love and Beauty*; it is set in New York, and explores the relationship between the eponymous grandmother and two young gay men. Its subject overlaps somewhat with the Merchant-Ivory-Jhabvala film *Roseland* (1977), which was set in and around the New York City dance hall frequented by elderly ladies of means and impecunious young gay men.

Minnie is one of many old women in Jhabvala's work; old age, particularly female old age, offers rich possibilities for ironic revelation of character. Behind the stereotypes and expectations limiting old women, live individual human beings who would, if we listened, prove them false: Jhabvala brings us the voices of not a few.

The old women in Jhabvala's Indian fiction to some extent escape the particular disparagement that is the lot of old age in the West, as Indian society traditionally values the last phase of life as a special period of freedom from the responsibilities of the householder and parent. Spiritual practice may now become a full-time pursuit; one learns from Jhabvala's pages that many, with full social approval, voluntarily adopt a life of itinerant begging, travelling from shrine to shrine. A number of Jhabvala's old women do achieve a spiritual strength that is associated with their devotions. **'The Old Lady'** (***Like Birds, Like Fishes***) is a character study of one such: her daily meditations fill her with such joy and satisfaction that she grows a stranger to her family—a sorry collection of irascible, dissatisfied and very worldly individuals. Maji's band of 'merry widows', in *Heat and Dust,* spend their days cavorting with one another in an all-female clan that the narrator appears to view with a kind of rueful outsiderhood. Maji herself, the adept midwife and sage, personifies a powerful female old age.

In *A New Dominion,* Banubai certainly possesses power, though there is the suggestion that her power is not all to the good. Like many another Jhabvala guru, she is too adept a manipulator not to be seriously flawed. So skilled is she at turning circumstance to her advantage that she camouflages her liaison of the moment with her advancing years: Gopi and she are chaste mother and son—it would only be ill-mannered and dirty-minded to think otherwise, as Gopi angrily accuses Raymond of doing.

Diametrically opposed to Banubai we might place another elderly lady of Jhabvala's, the Minister's wife of the beautiful vignette **'Rose Petals'** (***An Experience of India***). This character-study reveals its narrator, a dreamer. Otherwise unnamed, the Minister's wife passes her days in a kind of reposeful aimlessness, in the company of her husband's cousin Biju, homosexual and emotionally finely tuned. 'Life is only a game' for them, in painful contrast to the Minister and Mina, the grown daughter. Mina and the Minister are all earnestness, duty and busyness, as they rather self-importantly bustle from one to another committee and speech. They embody Ruth Jhabvala's deep ambivalence about, if not outright distrust of, engagement in a world fuelled by greed and corruption. The disengagement that is often characteristic of old age, then, is congenial to this writer's moral vision, which so often locates self-interest and pride officiously masquerading as good works.

Even in the stormy realm of sexual love, old women may achieve happiness in Jhabvala's fiction. The story **'The Man with the Dog'** (***A Stronger Climate***) alludes in its title to Chekhov's 'The Lady with the Little Dog'; its narrator, an Indian woman, cheerfully adores her 'old man', the Dutchman Boekelman, whom old age has now trapped in Delhi (Boekelman is one of the three elderly Europeans who, in the stories, make up the 'Sufferers' section of the collection). The elderly narrator is Boekelman's landlady, and she is also his mistress. Her grown children strenuously disapprove of the liaison, but she is one of the happiest of the tormented lovers in Jhabvala's oeuvre. She makes the connection between the erotic and the divine herself: 'Perhaps B. is a substitute for God whom I should be loving, the way the little brass image of Vishnu in my prayer-room is a substitute for that great god himself', she muses.

Boekelman's mistress no longer pays too much attention to her appearance. Nor, for that matter, does she mind her lover's missing teeth, his bald spot, and so on. Old age strips away the appurtenances of busyness, and social position, and even the physical self which helps us to maintain our dignity. The old lady and Boekelman, fighting, feigning indifference, threatening to leave each other, finally confront each other in all their frailty.

False self-importance may fall away in old age. A category of that is national pride, the absurd patriotism that so concerns 'Shammi', the old lady's officer son. Granted, Boekelman and his friends give Shammi plenty of cause: 'B.' rages peevishly against the 'damn rotten backward country' into which fate has washed him and his refugee friends (who, for their part, are also forever complaining about India). Shammi, the lieutenant-colonel who 'passionately' loves his army career, is very angry, and his mother, apologetic. She knows that Shammi 'loves talking . . . about his regiment and about tank warfare and 11.1 bore rifles and other such things, and I love listening to him. I don't really understand what he is saying, but I love his eager voice and the way he looks when he talks—just as he looked when he was a small boy and told me about his cricket.' The old woman knows how much that is thought to be serious and adult is only a more dangerous version of children's games—very much like the Minister's wife who mused that 'life is only a game'.

In contrast to their daughters and granddaughters, these old women possess a greater measure of freedom: freed now from the public scrutiny that confined ladies such as Sofia or Olivia; freed from duties to husband and children; freed, mostly, from the demands of the Romantic, according to which they re-create themselves as objects of beauty.

But one remembers Shakuntala's singing teacher's joke: 'You should burn her, that's the only thing old women are good for, burning.' These freedoms come at a heavy price, for to be a free woman is to be marginal, sacrificeable, stigmatised.

Shakuntala's teacher's remark is not without its Western equivalent. If the old are superfluous in the consumer society, old women are doubly superfluous; evidence of this appears in their poverty, but not there alone. Sentimentalised but actually held in contempt, old women are only now beginning to be acknowledged as a special underclass.[14] At worst dehumanised as ugly old witches, at best trivialised as little old ladies, women as crones are far from positions of dignity or respect which one would like to think might accompany old age. Ruth Jhabvala's probing analysis indirectly reveals these sad conditions. Her old ladies live with them. But they also manage, sometimes, to turn them to advantage, for not to be seen is to possess a certain valuable freedom. As they are for Jhabvala's unassuming writer-heroines, marginality and the invisibility that it bestows are in a sense privileged states.

A crucial factor, of course, is money. The fates of Leelavati, in *Heat and Dust,* or even, to take a non-Indian example, Miss Tuhy (**'Miss Sahib'**, ***A Stronger Climate***: *The Sufferers*) show that.

The 1980 story **'Grandmother'** presents one free old lady with the power to use her freedom, for Minnie's husband has left her plenty of money: thereby hangs the tale.

Like her Polish-Jewish grandmother, whom she has come to resemble, Minnie is 'happy, and it showed'. It shows so much that at times she has to disguise it, particularly in the company of her daughter Sandra, tall and blonde (a romantic heroine), who is much given to suffering over the neglect of her husband, Tim. Minnie, on the other hand, enjoys a companionable friendship with 'the boys', Ralph and Mickey, aspiring actors in their twenties who live together in a studio near Minnie's Upper East Side hotel. Minnie pays their rent. The narrative draws the reader into a representative scene between Minnie and the boys: Ralph plays the guitar and sings; the three of them discuss the boys' auditions; they chat about astrology. Sandra appears, weeping and railing about her troubled marriage. To Minnie's horror she even suggests moving in with her. Conveniently, she becomes pregnant and is reconciled with Tim.

Tim is also the name of Marietta's husband in *In Search of Love and Beauty.* The cool, rather distant relationship of Minnie and Sandra prefigures that of Louise and Marietta in that, like Marietta, Sandra has little interest in her mother. The young view the old as flat, two-dimensional backdrops for their own lives, assumed to possess centrality and importance. So it was with Werner and his mother. Until old age causes us to resemble our own grandparents, the old are minor characters. To be fair, Sandra has little interest in anyone, for she is preoccupied with the suffering engendered by her failing marriage; but she takes no comfort from her mother, nor, for that matter, is much offered. Minnie's advice to Sandra is rational but superfluous: 'But why do you go there!' For her part, Minnie cannot understand Sandra's frantic attachment to Tim: she 'had never been that way with Sam. When he was away, she was glad, and when he returned it was like being put back into irons'. The women have little to say to one another.

Indeed, they are at odds, while Sandra and Tim *are* united at least in their rather amused disapproval of the relationship of Minnie, Mickey and Ralph. The relationship represents a considerable financial drain, from their point of view: Minnie spends a good deal of money on Mickey and Ralph—money that would probably be theirs one day. When Sandra becomes pregnant, she and Tim hope that Minnie will become 'a proper grandmother'. She shows no sign of doing so.

The characters' names suggest that they inhabit a Disney cartoon. One hears the Klezmer music that the Disney studios appropriated. For Minnie, with her 'bright Polish-Jewish eyes that sparkled and danced' and 'skinny' Mickey, life is a game—as it was for the Minister's wife and her 'Biju'. Such creatures, while they may be subversive, are harmless. They do not outrage respectability, though they may elicit patronising laughter. Tim, normative heterosexual male, treats Ralph and Mickey 'as if they were his equals, except that the way he looked at them, his frosty blue eyes glinting with amusement, was not the way one looks at equals'. However, Tim shares one thing with Ralph and Mickey: namely, his visits to Minnie usually coincide with requests for money. But Mickey and Ralph have the grace to stay for a while, whereas Tim takes the money and runs. Yet it must be said that his departure is a relief: his attempts at small talk are oppressive monologues concerning sport, or worse, dirty jokes.

So in relation to Tim, Ralph and Mickey are an improvement. They have real charm; they treat Minnie with warmth and familiarity. Minnie loves 'her two boys'; they are the sons she never had. Ralph, though actually Muslim by birth, is 'the beautiful Jewish boy of her dreams'—a clue to Minnie's shaky grasp of reality. She enjoys their conversation about astrology and ghosts; she enjoys reassuring them about their talent and consoling them about their failed auditions; she likes to calm their domestic quarrels. She is comforted by the sight of 'lithe Ralph or skinny Mickey' stretched out on her brocade sofas; she enjoys ordering from room service for them ('one or the other of the boys was always hungry and had to call for something').

It is, in many ways, a pleasant picture. But on what, really, is this friendship based? Clearly, one must applaud Minnie's triumph over her respectable and selfish daughter and son-in-law; one must appreciate her indifference to their disapproval, her freedom to be as close as she wishes to Ralph and Mickey. But surely one must also attend to the fact that Minnie is the source of Ralph and Mickey's income, and that they would not be there if not for that. How valid, how sustaining, can a purchased friendship be? And there is no doubt that this is a purchased friendship.

Jhabvala's portrayal of this friendship of an old woman and two homosexual men is ambivalent, as is her portrayal of women's relationships with homosexual men throughout her oeuvre. By and large, it is a positive portrait: she appears to see gay men as primary sources of nurturance for her women protagonists, who have such impoverished emotional relationships with other women or with heterosexual men. But the portrayal also demonstrates the limitations of such a friendship for her woman protagonist: she will never have centrality for him, and he will never willingly reveal himself to her. The fiction is full of evasive young men and their doting mothers or sisters (Raymond, Mark, Werner, Hughie and in Jhabvala's tenth novel, Michael). Harry and Olivia's friendship in *Heat and Dust* demonstrates the pitfalls of women's reliance upon friendships with homosexual men: when pushed, Harry betrays Olivia and allies himself with the Nawab.[15]

Gay men, concerned mostly with each other, do not truly *see* the women who form friendships with them, in Jhabvala's fiction. They view them at arm's length, as images of femininity, or peripherally, as dispensers of service or advantage. For example, Mickey loves to see Minnie in her rocking chair 'just like I've seen ladies sitting on their porch with little children, reading them stories.' (Ralph comments acidly that Mickey has seen that only in the movies.) At the end of *In Search of Love and Beauty,* Eric, Regi's young homosexual escort, realises that Louise's fall will be fatal. He has worked in enough dance-halls to know that when aged ladies fall, it is often to their deaths. Yet he shrugs her death off. He has no reponse. Perhaps this is appropriate: he is employed by Regi.

Women are devalued by homosexual men in general just as they are by heterosexual men. Hughie allows Marie to comfort him but is ashamed to 'be so commingled with a girl'. Mark will not talk openly to Natasha. The basis of the relationship in **'Grand-mother'** remains Minnie's money. Without it there would be no friendship, no songs, no room service. We congratulate Minnie for having, in old age, the independence and means to do as she pleases, but we must be disturbed by the fact that her money is paramount in this friendship. In the same way, we must applaud Sofia's choice to exercise sexual freedom; but we must be disturbed by the outcome of that choice. We applaud Shakuntala's decision to be an artist, not only a housewife: but we have reason to believe that her teacher will not treat her well. The same scenario appears even more sharply etched in **'A Summer by the Sea'**.

Emotional options for Ruth Jhabvala's women are hedged with severe limitations; yet they persist in the quest for feeling, searching to know and be known. In the next novel she will focus again on the tragi-comic search for love and beauty.

Notes

1. Adrienne Rich, 'Compulsory Heterosexuality and Lesbian Existence', in *Powers of Desire: The Politics of Sexuality,* ed. Ann Snitow, Christine Stansell and Sharon Thompson (New York: Monthly Review Press, 1983) pp. 177-205; see esp. p. 192.
2. Ibid., p. 182.
3. Ibid., p. 185.
4. Ibid., p. 178.
5. Ibid., p. 200.
6. Ruth Prawer Jhabvala, 'Myself in India', in *An Experience of India* (New York: W. W. Norton, 1971) pp. 12-13.
7. Stella Dong, '*Publishers Weekly* Interviews Ruth Prawer Jhabvala', in *Publishers Weekly,* 6 June 1986, pp. 54-5.
8. Ruth Prawer Jhabvala, 'Disinheritance', *Blackwood's Magazine,* April 1979.
9. See, for example, Helen Epstein, *Children of Survivors: Conversations with Sons and Daughters of Survivors* (New York: Putnam, 1979).
10. Bernard Weinraub, 'The Artistry of Ruth Prawer Jhabvala', *New York Times Magazine,* 11 September 1983, p. 112.
11. Jhabvala, 'Disinheritance'.
12. Ibid.
13. Weinraub, 'Artistry of Jhabvala', p. 112.
14. See, for example, Barbara McDonald and Cynthia Rich, *Look Me in the Eye* (San Francisco, Cal.: Spinsters Ink, 1983).
15. As, for example, in the scene in which Harry, Olivia and the Nawab discuss British racism (*Heat and Dust,* pp. 122-3).

Ralph J. Crane (essay date 1992)

SOURCE: Crane, Ralph J. "Sufferers, Seekers, and the Beast That Moves: The Short Stories." In *Ruth Prawer Jhabvala,* pp. 93-104. New York: Twayne Publishers, 1992.

[*In the following excerpt, Crane provides a thematic analysis of Jhabvala's short stories.*]

Ruth Prawer Jhabvala has published five volumes of short stories, the first four being ***Like Birds, Like Fishes*** (1963), ***A Stronger Climate*** (1968), ***An Experience of India*** (1971), and ***How I Became a Holy Mother*** (1976). Many of the stories included in these four volumes were originally published in such magazines as the *New Yorker* (for whom Jhabvala wrote regularly), *Encounter, London Magazine,* and *Cornhill Magazine.* The fifth volume is a collection of stories selected by Jhabvala from the previous four, published under the title ***Out of India***—a delicately ambiguous title that can be taken either as an indication that the stories draw on Jhabvala's 25 years in India or as a statement about the author herself, who now lives in New York.

The tales range from beautifully written character studies like **"The Man with the Dog"** to closely observed portraits of Indian life like **"Sixth Child."** While stories like the title story of the first collection, **"Like Birds, Like Fishes,"** are concerned with Indians, stories such as those in ***A Stronger Climate*** are concerned with Europeans living in India. Marriage, particularly the problem of mixed marriage, which is the subject of **"The Aliens,"** is a common theme. Some tales, like **"An Experience of India,"** are as complete as a novel, while others, like **"Prostitutes,"** present short scenes, apparently plucked at random from everyday life, with no significant beginning or ending. These stories, in which nothing is resolved, appear to emphasize the timelessness of Indian life itself, in much the same way the presence of the punkah-wallah does in *A Passage to India.* The tone of the stories varies from satire and comedy in a piece like **"The Award"** to the moving, melancholy mood of **"Desecration."** While the majority are, like her first six novels, set in Delhi, others reach farther afield, to Bombay in **"A Star and Two Girls"** and other stories or to England in **"A Course of English Studies,"** which is set in the Midlands, and **"A Birthday in London,"** which stands apart from Jhabvala's other collected stories in that it is concerned neither with India nor with Indian characters. The stories also make use of different narrative voices, ranging from the first person (both male, as in **"The Interview,"** and female, as in **"My First Marriage"**) to various third-person perspectives, including the frequent omniscient narrator. Others, such as **"Lekha"** and **"The Man with the Dog,"** combine a first-person narrative with a limited third-person portrait of the central character.

Thus in **"Lekha,"** for instance, two distinct portraits are produced—that of the central character, Lekha, and that of the narrator, who reveals as much about herself as she does about Lekha. The social satire surrounding the descriptions of civil service parties recalls the satire of the early novels, and in particular that surrounding Chandra Prakesh and his wife in *The Nature of Passion.* While recalling the satire of earlier novels, though, **"Lekha"** also looks ahead, in its narrative technique, to later novels. As Yasmine Gooneratne explains, "It is Ruth Jhabvala's first attempt, and a highly successful one, at the indirect revelation of character that we have seen in more finished and sophisticated forms in *Heat and Dust* and Autobiography of a Princess. As in *Heat and Dust,* a female narrator relates the story of another woman's scandalous love-affair, unconsciously laying her own soul bare as she does so" (Gooneratne, 237).

While the stories stand by themselves, they also share some common ground with the novels. Marriage, as I noted, is important in a number of stories, and food is used in much the same way it is in Jhabvala's early novels. But of greater significance is Jhabvala's interest in European characters in India, an interest that becomes increasingly apparent in her novels and is reflected in her stories too.

Stories concerned with European characters appear in all Jhabvala's collections of stories, and in the second collection, ***A Stronger Climate,*** all nine stories involve Europeans in India. Divided thematically into two parts, ***A Stronger Climate*** looks at these Europeans as "seekers" and "sufferers." The seekers are all young people who have come to India in search of something, whether it be inner enlightenment, as in **"A Spiritual Call"**; information, as in **"The Biographer"**; or love (in one of its many manifestations), as in the other tales in this section. The sufferers, on the other hand, are all elderly Europeans who have stayed on after independence and are forced to live out their remaining days in India, stranded in the country just as they appear to be stranded forever in the third stage of Jhabvala's cycle of responses to India. The interest in seekers continues in ***An Experience of India*** and ***How I Became a Holy Mother,*** although these books are not exclusively concerned with Europeans. Three of the collections contain a story that focuses on a young woman on a spiritual quest, which is also the major theme of *A New Dominion* and *Heat and Dust.* The narrators of all these stories are well suited for Jhabvala's purposes—they are, as Laurie Sucher notes, "intelligent and unconventional" (Sucher, 40), which makes them ideal observers of all they see around them.

"A Spiritual Call" satirically portrays life in an ashram, as Daphne, a young English girl, follows her guru, Swamiji, to India after their initial meeting in London. Swamiji, who, not content with his simple community, wants to build "[a] tip-top, up-to-date ashram . . . with air-conditioned meditation cells and a central dining-hall" (***SC*** [***A Stronger Climate***], 99) and looks forward to his trip to America and the comforts of Mrs. Gay Fisher's California mansion complete with "swimming-pool and all amenities" (***SC,*** 107), is critically portrayed. But it is not a vicious portrait like that of the swami in **"An Experience of India."** In **"A Spiritual Call"** Ruth Prawer Jhabvala makes perhaps her clearest statement about the importance of a sari as a symbol of the adoption of Indian values: Daphne is given a sari by Swamiji, to wear as the uniform of his disciples, a symbol to denote his ownership of her, as well as her acceptance of him.

Interestingly, Daphne's role as secretary to the swami in **"A Spiritual Call"** is repeated in Evie's role in *A New Dominion,* and the swamis of both the story and the novel are writing books; in addition, Ahmed's relationship with Henry's servant, Ramu, is similar to the relationship Jhabvala later develops between Gopi and Shyam. These similarities, however, are minor given that Lee's story in the novel parallels the story **"An Experience of India"** throughout. In fact **"An Experience of India"** is unusual among Jhabvala's stories in being an obvious example of a tale later used as the basis of a novel, namely *A New Dominion.*

In **"An Experience in India,"** written in the first-person, the narrator admits she "had come to India to *be* in India. I wanted to be changed."[1] Like Lee's, her travels are unplanned, and both characters frequently accept the offers of hospitality they receive from fellow passengers on trains and buses. Moreover, after wandering for some time both characters embark on spiritual quests that lead them to an ashram and a guru.

But it is not only the character of Lee that owes much to the earlier story; the gurus are remarkably similar in both works. The one in the tale is particularly interested in the fact that Henry, the narrator's husband, is a journalist, while Swamiji in the novel is interested in Raymond because he is in the publishing business; in both cases the swami sees a way of spreading his word abroad. Jean, a young European woman in **"An Experience in India,"** can likewise be seen as a forerunner of Evie in *A New Dominion.* Jean "was quite white, waxen, and her hair too was completely faded and colourless" (***HM*** [***How I Became a Holy Mother***], 130), while Evie "was so pale and weak and blonde that she was almost invisible" (*ND* [*New Dominion*], 100). Both young women wear white cotton saris, and both are utterly humble and submissive before their gurus. Neither the narrator of the story nor Lee can easily adopt such attitudes.

The zenith of both story and novel are reached when the narrator and Lee, respectively, are raped by their gurus; however, while the rapes themselves are quite similar, the ways they are presented are quite different. The guru in **"An Experience of India,"** though initially frightening, is effectively reduced to ridicule when he asks, "How many men have you slept with?" (***HM,*** 133)—the same question that the many Indians the narrator has slept with on her travels have asked her. When he cries, "Bitch!" (***HM,*** 133) as he lies on top of her, the horror is taken out of the situation, and she is able to laugh with relief as she realizes he is no different from the men she has met on her earlier travels. Swamiji in *A New Dominion,* however, remains a frightening and cruel figure, and there is no such relief for Lee.

Both the narrator of the story and Lee in the novel leave their ashrams, but fail to find any lasting happiness afterward, and when the opportunity to go home is offered, neither is able to accept it. The narrator somewhat naively decides to stay and resume her travels, while Lee knows that she will inevitably return to the ashram. *A New Dominion* owes a great deal to the earlier story, and it is interesting to see how Jhabvala's ideas have developed from story to novel—the novel presents a far bleaker picture and perhaps reflects Jhabvala's despair of ever reaching an understanding of India that isn't in some way naive. Thus it may be that the swami's cruelty is used to show how little a Western viewpoint is capable of comprehending the nature of India. Lee's rape, like the pseudorape of Adela Quested in *A Passage to India,* is perhaps an indication of the naïveté of everything Lee, like Adela, has been thinking about India up to that point. It is too easy for Lee, and the Western reader, to leap from one view of India to another, never understanding that no simple view is adequate. As Godbole explains in *A Passage to India,* the good and the bad are indeed indivisible.

Jhabvala's dissatisfaction with India is not, however, reflected in all her stories about gurus. **"How I Became a Holy Mother,"** again a first-person narrative, gives an often-comic and altogether-more-tolerant portrait of an ashram, as signaled by the ironic tile. In this story the narrator is not destroyed and has no bad experiences. The guru is different from the earlier ones, even in his name: "this one was just called plain Master, in English" (***HM,*** 139). Unlike the guru figures in earlier stories, Master has no longings to go abroad or to build a new ashram; he is happy to let his existing one grow as the need arises, and he is quite content with his present surroundings. As he explains to Katie, the narrator: "I stand in the middle of Times Square or Piccadilly, London, and I look up and there are all the beautiful beautiful buildings stretching so high up into heaven: yes I look at them but it is not them I see at all, Katie! Not them at all!" (***HM,*** 144). What he sees in his mind's eye are the mountains and rivers surrounding the ashram, which reflect his own perfect happiness, as Katie and Vishwa (the swami's disciple who becomes the new spiritual leader) find when they begin to travel abroad and, like Master, miss the life of the ashram. The narrator's sexual experiences in the community are not the violent encounters of **"An Experience of India,"** and as a result the story presents a more positive picture of an ashram.

I have discussed these three narratives at some length and in relation to the novel *A New Dominion* because while they all treat the same theme, their different approaches illustrate Jhabvala's ability to deal with a single subject in a variety of ways. The same is true of her treatment of marriage and of all the various topics she writes about in her stories.

In **"A Birthday in London"** Jhabvala describes life for a group of German Jews living in London. [This] is the clearest description in Jhabvala's fiction of the life she must have known as a child and young adult in England. Groups of exiled Europeans similar to the one gathered here for Sonia's birthday recur in Jhabvala's Indian stories, particularly in the stories drawn together under the heading "The Sufferers" in ***A Stronger Climate,*** and in the novel *A Backward Place,* too. Later, of course, Jhabvala takes up the lives of German or Polish Jews in New York in her uncollected stories **"Commensurate Happiness"**[2] and **"Grandmother,"**[3] and again in her ninth novel, *In Search of Love and Beauty.*

"Commensurate Happiness" is another clear example of a story prefiguring a novel. Many of the characters in the story have more fully developed parallels in *In Search of Love and Beauty* in particular and in *Three Continents* too. Jeannette, the widowed grandmother, is a forerunner of Louise Sonnenblick of *In Search of Love and Beauty,* while her daughter Sandra is an earlier version of Louise's daughter Marietta. And the relationship between the cousins Hughie and Marie in the story is similar to the relationship between Mark and his adopted sister, Natasha, in *In Search of Love and Beauty* (and to the relationship between the twins Harriet and Michael Wishwell in *Three Continents.*) Wanda, also of German descent, is clearly another Regi. Jeannette's apartment crowded with inherited European furniture is seen once more in Louise's apartment; indeed, the whole family situation in the story is similar to that which occurs in *In Search of Love and Beauty.*

At the heart of the ironically titled story **"Commensurate Happiness"** lie Wanda's birthday parties (just as Regi's are important events in the novel). The earliest birthday party recalled in the story is one held for Wanda shortly before the death of Otto, Jeannette's husband. As what amounts to a final request, Otto asks that Wanda, his mistress, celebrate her birthday in his house, with his family: "So it happened that the first time Wanda was allowed to enter their home was in honour of her own birthday" (**"Happiness,"** 8). This birthday party forces the other guests, Jeannette and the young children, Hughie and Marie, to accept Otto's mistress into their family. At a later birthday party, the centerpiece of the story, Wanda takes it on herself to push the two cousins into marriage, and after her intervention the reluctant Hughie does, in his own fashion, propose to the eager Marie. The situation is, we learn, similar to that which brought about the marriage between Jeannette and Otto. When Jeannette remonstrates, Wanda justifies her actions: "That's the way it has to be done: if young people don't know where they're going, the family has to take over" (**"Happiness,"** 10). And we are immediately told that "As a matter of fact that's how it had been done with Jeannette and Otto" (**"Happiness,"** 10).

The happiness likely to be enjoyed by Hughie and Marie is commensurate to that enjoyed by Jeannette and Otto. As Jeannette had to endure Otto's affairs, so Marie will have to suffer Hughie's homosexual relationships. Jeannette is willing to accept this state of affairs, not only for herself, but for Marie too, when she supports the idea of a marriage that only Hughie seems reluctant to seal: "'He does care for you. He loves you. As far as he can, he does. What more do you want?'" she added—rather impatiently, for it seemed to her that Marie was being unreasonable in her expectations. She too would have to learn that one lived on earth and not in heaven" (**"Happiness,"** 11). Marie's so called unreasonable expectations are that her future husband should love her, and it is significant that it is another woman, her own grandmother, who scorns the expectations. The happiness Marie can expect is thus commensurate with the diminished expectations Jeannette pushes her toward, expectations that she, like Jeannette before her, is prepared to accept. In this story, in *In Search of Love and Beauty,* and in *Three Continents* Jhabvala appears to blame women who accept this course of events and by so doing help perpetuate the undervalued role women perceive for themselves in society. Such attitudes, clearly expressed in this story, suggest that Jhabvala may at times be quietly beating a feminist drum in her fiction.

In the stories **"A Birthday in London"** and **"Commensurate Happiness"** and in the novels *In Search of Love and Beauty* and *Three Continents* birthdays are important. Certainly the stories and novels celebrating birthdays are the fictions that seem closest to the author's own family circumstances. (Of course, the celebration of birthdays is very important in German culture, much more than in English culture.)

The Sufferers of the three stories **"An Indian Citizen," "Miss Sahib,"** and **"The Man with the Dog"**—Dr. Ernst, Miss Tuhy, and Boekelman, respectively—are all elderly Europeans who have stayed on in India too long. Like Lucy in Paul Scott's *Staying On* (1977), they are "alone . . . amid the alien corn, waking, sleeping, alone for ever and ever."[4] Like Scott's treatment of Tusker and Lucy Smalley, Jhabvala's treatment of these elderly "sufferers" is tender and sympathetic, yet penetrating too. It is stories like these, along with tales like **"The Aliens"** and **"The Young Couple,"** both of which portray an Englishwoman married to an Indian husband, that reflect Jhabvala's own experiences of India and her own feelings of expatriation and alienation.

There is gentle irony in **"An Indian Citizen"** and **"Miss Sahib,"** wherein the two central characters attempt to adopt India and to belong in a way vaguely reminiscent of the young seekers of the stories in the first section of ***A Stronger Climate.*** Indeed, Dr. Ernst, even though he may be an Indian citizen, remains painfully an outsider. His insistence that he has a great many Indian friends is comically undermined when he visits the dreadful Miss Chawla and even attempts to put a brave interpretation on her obvious rudeness and displeasure at seeing him: "It was foolish, he told himself, to feel hurt or slighted. She had not meant anything personal. . . . It was kind enough of her to have let him stay as long as she did. She was his good friend and esteemed and liked him as much as he did her" (***SC,*** 154). Contrary to "looking for offence where none was meant" (***SC,*** 154), as he persuades himself he is doing, Dr. Ernst is refusing to see offense where it is clearly given, turning a proverbial blind eye to what he does not want to—and cannot, if his position in India is to remain tolerable—allow himself to believe. His unfortunate position in India is cushioned, as is Etta's, by the existence of a circle of European friends that he can always turn to for comfort—literally, in the case of Maiska's flat, with its comfortable armchairs, Mozart records, and good strong coffee. Only here, in a European environment, can he truly relax and feel at home.

Miss Tuhy in **"Miss Sahib"** has no such haven to turn to when her experience of India turns sour. Like Dr. Ernst, Miss Tuhy believes India is her true home and Indians her true friends. The story traces her disillusionment with India and with her Indian friends, and draws to a conclusion that sees the sad, pathetic figure of the elderly Englishwoman realizing that she does miss England, and does want to go home, but aware too that "she no longer had the fare home to England, not even on the cheapest route" (***SC,*** 181).

The narrator of **"The Man with the Dog"** records quite clearly the reasons she (and Jhabvala) sees for elderly Europeans like Boekelman being in India, as she meditates on his friends:

> They have all of them been in India for many, many years—twenty-five, thirty—but I know they would much rather be somewhere else. They only stay here because they feel too old to go anywhere else and start a new life. They came here for different reasons—some because they were married to Indians, some to do business, others as refugees and because they couldn't get a visa for anywhere else. None of them has ever tried to learn any Hindi or to get to know anything about our India. They have some Indian "friends," but these are all very rich and important people—like maharinis and cabinet ministers, they don't trouble with ordinary people at all. But really they are only friends with one another, and they always like each other's company best.
>
> (***SC,*** 193)

In this story Jhabvala controls her first-person narrative beautifully to present a third-person portrait of Boekelman, a sad, helpless old man who has stayed in India too long, and combines it with a contrasting first-person portrait of the narrator that shows the great happiness she derives from this old man, quite contrary to the expected behavior of an Indian widow.

Jhabvala treats the subject of a would-be sufferer very differently in **"The Englishwoman,"** a story included in the American edition of ***How I Became a Holy Mother*** but omitted from the British one. It is the story of an Englishwoman, Sadie, who at age 52 and after 30 years of married life in India, decides to leave her adopted country and return "home" to England. This decision results from Sadie's taking stock of her life in a way that Jhabvala's sufferers rarely manage to do. And without overstressing the autobiographical element of this story, it appears to reflect Jhabvala's own need to return to the West after a quarter-century in India. Indeed, Sadie's explanation to her daughter "that when people get older they begin to get very homesick for the place in which they were born and grew up and that this homesickness becomes worse and worse till in the end life becomes almost unbearable"[5] echoes Jhabvala's explanation of her own desire to leave India in such pieces as **"Disinheritance,"** her Neil Gunn Memorial Lecture, in which she refers to "a terrible hunger of homesickness that I cannot describe it was so terrible, so consuming" (**"Disinheritance,"** 11).

Sadie can trace her decision to leave to a particular day 20 years earlier when her son Dev was ill. She contrasts the child's stifling sickroom, crowded with female relatives paying attention of various sorts to the patient, with her own childhood sickbeds, wherein the quiet and boredom were interrupted only by her mother bringing in her medicine. These images of the two sickrooms effectively define the differences between the two countries in Sadie's mind and lead to her realization that she is not Indian, can never become Indian, and, perhaps more significantly, has no desire to become Indian.

Sadie's inability to become Indian and the strength of her desire to return to England are mellifluously evoked in the closing sentences of the story. There the moonlit Indian scene in her garden is transformed into the memory-lit landscape of the English downs, fresh, cold, wet, and with a freedom in the wind the strength of which Sadie has never felt in India. It is a wonderful image, and one that underlines perfectly Jhabvala's interest in place and belonging, an interest in inheritance that is perhaps best understood by the disinherited—by characters like Sadie or by Jhabvala herself.

The stories concerned solely with Indian characters, like the early novels, demonstrate Jhabvala's delight in India and show that she is indeed an "outsider with unusual insight" (Agarwal 1973, 11). **"The Widow"** illustrates this position well. In this story Durga has refused to accept the traditional role of widow—"the cursed one who had committed the sin of outliving her husband and was consequently to be numbered among the outcasts"[6]—and has refused to be condemned "to that perpetual mourning, perpetual expiation, which was the proper lot of widows" (***LBLF*** [***Like Birds, Like Fishes***], 58) and is the wish of some of her more orthodox relatives.

Durga's life has been one of emptiness, in her marriage to an old and impotent man and now in widowhood, and in a quest for satisfaction—or, more particularly, sexual satisfaction—Durga first turns to dreams of the god Krishna and, when this fails to fill the void inside her, then turns her attention to Govind, the son of her tenants. Durga is drawn to Govind not only by her unfulfilled maternal feelings, but also by her unsatisfied sexual desires: "His teeth were large and white, his hair sprang from a point on his forehead. Everything about him was young and fresh and strong—even his smell, which was that of a young animal full of sap and sperm" (***LBLF,*** 69). Durga's feelings for Govind, which she demonstrates through gifts of money and promises of more presents, are, like her earlier passion for Krishna, destined to remain unrequited. When this passion too ends in disappointment for Durga, after she surrenders to her passion for Govind and is repelled, she is finally defeated and prepared to give in to her relatives and the traditional role of a widow.

In her portrayal of Durga's widowhood and in her depiction of the scheming of both Durga's relatives and her tenants, the Puris, Jhabvala demonstrates just how well she had observed life in an Indian joint family.

The irony present in her early novels is evident in the close of this story, where the scheming of the relatives and Durga's breakdown are justified in the final paragraph:

> The relatives were glad that Durga had at last come round and accepted her lot as a widow. They were glad for her sake. There was no other way for widows but to lead humble, bare lives; it was for their own good. For if they were allowed to feed themselves on the pleasures of the world, then they fed their own passions too, and that which should have died in them with the deaths of their husbands would fester and boil and overflow into sinful channels. Oh yes, said the relatives, wise and knowing, nodding their heads, our ancestors knew what they [were] doing when they laid down these rigid rules for widows; and though nowadays perhaps, in these modern times, one could be a little more lenient—for instance, no one insisted that Durga should shave her head—still, on the whole, the closer one followed the old traditions, the safer and the better it was.
>
> (***LBLF,*** 78)

This paragraph is interesting for it shows that Jhabvala is sensitive to the traditional status of widows and the way in which they were seen by their relatives, yet the very reasons concealed behind that traditional view are what Jhabvala is subverting in this ironic story. In this masterful paragraph she subtly questions the motives of Durga's relatives; when she writes, "it was for their own good," she is, of course, referring to the good of widows, but in the context of this story she could also be referring to Durga's relatives. And similarly, the closing line of the story leaves up in the air the question, Better for whom?

The most disturbing of all Jhabvala's stories is **"Desecration,"** which draws to a close her fourth collection, ***How I Became a Holy Mother.*** This tale, told very deliberately in a third-person voice, though clearly from Sofia's point of view, relates the story of a young Muslim girl who is married to Raja Sahib, an elderly Hindu landowner who always treats her with great kindness. Sofia's disaffection with her life has similarities with the sense of constraint Olivia Rivers feels in the Anglo-Indian world of *Heat and Dust.* In a search for fulfillment Sofia has an affair with the superintendent of police, Bakhtawar Singh, and is drawn down into a state of emotional turmoil that causes her to commit suicide in the hotel room in which she had been meeting her lover.

In one sense the story of the affair is archetypal: the sensitive, educated woman who by marriage at least belongs to a higher class is drawn into a sordid affair with a brutal, uneducated man from a lower class. Her quest for passion and sexual fulfillment causes Sofia to become reckless; to be talked about by everyone in the village as her affair becomes widely known; and masochistically to pursue Bakhtawar Singh and submit to him in an act of sexual union that gives the story both its apogee and its title. When Bakhtawar Singh hears an old man saying the Muhammadan prayers in the next room, he urges Sofia to pray too:

> She knelt naked on the floor and began to pray the way the old man was praying in the next room, knocking her forehead on the ground. Bakhtawar Singh urged her on, watching her with tremendous pleasure from the bed. Somehow the words came back to her and she said them in chorus with the old man next door. After a while, Bakhtawar Singh got off the bed and joined her on the floor and mounted her from behind. He wouldn't let her stop praying, though. "Go on," he said, and how he laughed as she went on. Never had he had such enjoyment out of her as on that day.
>
> (***HM,*** 266)

But even this act of gross violation is not enough to cool Sofia's passion; rather, she still attempts to persuade him to meet her more often. Nor is her passion cooled by the voices of the village, which are discussing her behind her back. Only when she reads out the drama her husband has just written for her and comes across the line "Oh, if thou didst but know what it is like to live in hell the way I do!" (***HM,*** 268) does her position become clear to her. Her husband's hell is both the pain of an unexplained illness and the pain of the love he feels for Sofia, while her hell is the hell she suffers as a result of her longing for Bakhtawar Singh, a longing that causes her heart to physically ache like a disease that "would get worse and pass through many stages before it was finished with her" (***HM,*** 267). It is a hell made worse by the look the Raja Sahib gives her: "There had never been anyone in the world who looked into her eyes the way he did, with such love but at the same time with a tender respect that would not reach farther into her than was permissible between two human beings" (***HM,*** 268). This is a respect Bakhtawar Singh does not give her; rather, the act of desecration he commits while she prays is the embodiment of the desecration he has committed by violating her as a human being.

Unlike Jhabvala's other stories, there are no deft touches of comedy in this story, no subtle ironic nuances to relieve the tragedy of the story, and nothing to diminish its power.

Ruth Prawer Jhabvala's vision of India as presented in her short stories appears to be influenced, even controlled, by the cycle she describes in her important essay "Myself in India." In **"An Experience of India,"** the title story of the volume in which her revealing essay appeared as an introduction, the narrator passes through all three stages of the cycle Jhabvala describes in "Myself in India." As the story ends, the cycle can be seen to be renewing itself as India reasserts its hold over the narrator; she, like Jhabvala, is "strapped to a wheel" ("Myself in India," 9) that will control her responses to India. The Indian beast is an animal that appears to stop thrashing beneath Ruth Prawer Jhabvala only when she leaves India and moves to New York.

Notes

1. Ruth Prawer Jhabvala, "An Experience of India," in *How I Became a Holy Mother* (Harmondsworth, England: Penguin, 1981); 120, hereafter cited in text as *HM.* The stories in this collection were originally published by John Murray as *An Experience of India* (London, 1971) and *How I Became a Holy Mother* (London, 1976).
2. Ruth Prawer Jhabvala, "Commensurate Happiness," *Encounter* 54, no. 1 (1980): 3-11; hereafter cited in text as "Happiness."
3. Ruth Prawer Jhabvala, "Grandmother," *New Yorker,* 17 November 1980, 54-62.
4. Paul Scott, *Staying On* (1977; reprint, London: Granada, 1978), 255.
5. Ruth Prawer Jhabvala, "The Englishwoman," in *How I Became a Holy Mother* (New York: Harper & Row, 1976), 24. This story is not included in British editions.
6. Ruth Prawer Jhabvala, "The Widow," in *Like Birds, like Fishes* (1963; reprint, London: Granada, 1984), 58; hereafter cited in text as *LBLF.*

Tone Sundt Urstad (essay date 1996)

SOURCE: Urstad, Tone Sundt. "Protecting One's Inner Self: Ruth Prawer Jhabvala's 'Rose Petals'." *Studies in Short Fiction* 33, no. 1 (1996): 43-9.

[*In the following essay, Urstad considers the various reactions to overwhelming poverty portrayed in the story "Rose Petals."*]

There is an exploring quality about Ruth Prawer Jhabvala's work—both as a novelist and as a writer of screenplays—that has often been noted by critics (Gooneratne; Bailur; Crane). It probably stems from the fact that she was—in her own words—"practically born a displaced person" (Gooneratne 1) and so has always had to make an effort to understand a world not quite her own. Born of Jewish parents in Germany before the second World War, she became a permanent foreigner, first in England, then in India, now in America. Looking back at the years she spent living with her Indian husband in his country, she once wrote:

> Sometimes I wrote about Europeans in India, sometimes about Indians in India, sometimes about both, but always attempting to present India to myself in the hope of giving myself some kind of foothold . . . I described the Indian scene not for its own sake but for mine.
>
> (Hayman 37)

In her short story **"Rose Petals"** she seems to have set out to explore how sympathetically drawn characters can be seen to be living isolated, privileged lives surrounded by poverty on all sides, do absolutely nothing to try to rectify obvious wrongs, and yet still retain their basic humanity. And in so doing she has raised the issue that worried her most while she lived in India and that slowly changed her attitude toward her adopted country from one of initial wonder and excitement into a battle that she knew she could not win ("Myself in India" 16).

In her article "Myself and India" Prawer Jhabvala has outlined certain ways of dealing with the proximity of overwhelming poverty: "The first and best is to be a strong person who plunges in and does what he can as a doctor or social worker." The second is quite simply to accept the situation as it is. In this connection—she comments wryly—a belief in reincarnation helps:

> It appears to be a consoling thought for both rich and poor. The rich man stuffing himself on pilao can do so with an easy conscience because he knows that he has earned this privilege by his good conduct in previous lives; and the poor man can watch him with some degree of equanimity for he knows that next time round it may be *he* who will be digging into the pilao while the other will be crouching outside the door with an empty stomach.

The third way consists in trying to escape from it all by retreating into one's own isolated world. Most of us choose the third solution, which is also Ruth Prawer Jhabvala's way of dealing with the problem, since she is in her own words "not a doctor, nor a social worker nor a saint nor at all a good person":

> I do my best to live in an agreeable way. I shut all my windows, I let down the blinds, I turn on the air-conditioner; I read a lot of books, with a special preference for the great masters of the novel. All the time I know myself to be on the back of this great animal of poverty and backwardness.
>
> (10-11)

It is precisely this question of a leisured, privileged private life in the midst of terrible poverty that is raised in **"Rose Petals,"** in which diametrically opposed attitudes toward social problems and life in general, are expressed in terms of a basic opposition in lifestyle between two pairs of characters. On the one hand we have the Minister, who has chosen an active life in politics, and his daughter Mina who is following in his energetic footsteps. On the other hand we have the Minister's wife, who is the narrator, and the Minister's cousin Biju, both of whom lead intensely private, self-indulgent lives of leisure.

Surrounding the Minister's family—but at a safe distance—is an outer world of poverty and injustice. Through their repeated references to the underprivileged, the characters create an uneasy consciousness of this threatening world, of which we get only one short glimpse. The car gets stuck, and safely cocooned inside, Biju and the narrator witness the demolition of some slum dwellings:

> Out of the car window we could see a squad of demolition workers knocking down the hovels made of old tins and sticks and rags, and the people who lived in the hovels picking up what they could from among the debris. They didn't look angry, just sad, except for one old woman who was shaking her fist and shouting something that we couldn't hear. She ran around and got in the way of the workers till someone gave her a push and she fell over. When she got up, she was holding her knee and limping but she had stopped shouting and she too began to dig among the debris.
>
> (61)

Their reaction to the scene is an indirect one: Biju "didn't say anything that time, but later in the day he was making a lot of jokes about the Revolution and how we would all be strung up on lamp-posts or perhaps, if we were lucky, sent to work in the salt-mines" (61-62).

There is more than a touch of Chekhov about Biju and the Minister's wife, two aristocratic people without the will or the wish to change their way of life, who sit around joking uneasily about the Revolution ("I don't know whether we really thought it would come. I think often we felt it ought to come, but when we talked about it it was only to laugh and joke" [61]). With no occupation in life, Biju and the Minister's wife spend much of their time together, largely cut off from the rest of the world. Significantly, Biju only reads the restaurant and cinema advertisements in the newspapers, together with the local news (54). He shies away from long and difficult plays, preferring lightweight musicals like *My Fair Lady* and *Funny Girl* (56). Both characters are subject to occasional bouts of melancholy, they both need pills to be able to sleep, and Biju has terrible nightmares about sudden personal catastrophes.

Although the Minister and Mina are extremely active members of society, they are not allowed to monopolize the moral high ground, because all of their actions are seen through the clear-sighted eyes of the narrator, who is not blind to her husband's pomposity and who recognizes in her daughter the earnestness of youth. Through her comments on her own life and the lives of the people whom she loves she comes across as a sympathetic character: unpretentious, observant and with an ironic sense of humor.

All through her story there are good-natured little digs at the Minister. To start with there is the way in which she never refers to him by name. All of the other characters—except the Minister's wife—have names, but, as she is the narrator, this is quite natural. Even Bobo Oberoi, who is only mentioned in passing as playing God the father in a play, gets a name, but not the Minister: to his daughter he is "daddy," to her friends he is "Sir," to Biju and even to his wife he is simply "the Minister" (with a capital letter), an indication that to them he has ceased to be a private individual and has become the public figure. This distinction ties in with his own view of himself: "When I think of my old age . . . I think mainly: what will I have achieved? That means, what sort of person will I be? Because a person can only be judged by his achievements" (62). By that token, his wife and his cousin can hardly be said to exist at all.

There is also the question of why the Minister is serving his country—for self-sacrificing or for selfish reasons. We are told that he likes being a Minister, that he starts the morning by making "an important face" and that he keeps up his air of pomposity for the rest of the day. It is true that he is very energetic. Exploiting two separate meanings of the verb "to serve," Prawer Jhabvala turns the scene in which the Minister serves imaginary tennis balls across an imaginary net into a metaphor for how he "serves" his country. When Biju proclaims the ball "Out," the Minister snaps "Absolutely in" (62); but in this case Biju is likely to be metaphorically correct, because it is more than hinted that the Minister, for all his activity, is perhaps not accomplishing a whole lot. His wife relates how even before he entered politics "doors banged behind him, his voice was loud and urgent like a king in battle even when he was only calling the servant for his shoes" (57). Temperamentally he is simply a very restless man who brings to politics the kind of energy he wasted in his youth on trips to Japan to study hotel management, or to Russia to observe the process of manufacturing steel; he never converted any of his houses into a hotel, never built the intended factory, and only introduced a new fertilizer to find that it killed off most of the crop (57). The scene in which he and Biju throw paper planes describes him well: he throws one "into the air with a great swing of his body like a discus thrower; but it falls down on the carpet very lamely" (68).

As a politician he is "keen to move with the times" (56), a kind way of saying that his opinions change with the newest fashions. One day the most important thing for India is doctors, the next day it is economists and political scientists. In the mornings his wife watches how he "struggles into his cotton tights; he still has not quite got used to these Indian clothes but he wears nothing else now. There was a time when only suits made in London were good enough for him. Now they hang in the closet, and no one ever wears them" (53). At a given point in his career, the Minister has clearly adopted a more Nationalistic stance as reflected in his substitution of traditional Indian clothes for the European garb associated with British colonialism. As so often in Prawer Jhabvala's works, clothes are important metaphors: although the Minister has changed his political spots his new political opinions are not entirely congenial since he still has to "struggle" into the new clothes every morning. And Mina, for all her patriotic views, still smells of Palmolive soap when she bends over to kiss her mother (53).

The Minister thinks in slogans and theories. Everything becomes an issue with him. He is not at all sensitive to people, either individually or collectively. To his mind the Revolution will not come simply because the Indian Parliamentary system is "the best mode of government" (61). Like his wife and Biju, he has no religious beliefs, but, unlike them, he makes a big noise about his views, lecturing his wife's aunt on how religion is "retarding the progress of the people" (66).

The contrast between the lifestyles of Mina and the Minister on the one hand and Biju and the Minister's wife on the other is suggested by the descriptions of what we might call their body language. The Minister, for example, is always active, on his feet, serving imaginary tennis-balls, throwing paper planes. His wife, on the other hand, always describes herself as sitting in chairs, reclining on sofas, lying in bed, details that underline the sedentary, uneventful life she leads. The same is true of Biju, except for the scene in which he dances a modern dance all alone in the garden and when he throws paper planes, although with far less energy than the Minister. Biju also enjoys mingling with the guests. However, none of these pursuits are what Mina would call "constructive" (55).

In terms of the three solutions to the problem of living in close proximity to mass poverty set forward by Ruth Prawer Jhabvala, Biju and the narrator have clearly chosen the third: they have withdrawn into a world of their own (that neither character is religious is specifically mentioned). Their withdrawal is emphasized by the imagery associated with them. Practically all the scenes take place within the confines of a room ("like two fish in an aquarium") or a private garden at night. Mina and her father are forever coming into or leaving these enclosed areas. The scene with the music box, for instance, takes place in their shooting box (a word with connotations of restriction):

> He [Biju] wound the music box again, and the sad little tune played. The thought of being together like this for ever—always in some beautiful room with a view from its long windows of water or a lawn or hot summer nights in a garden full of scents and overlaid with moonlight so white that it looked like snow—the thought of it was sad and yet also quite nice.
>
> (61)

In this description we find another element that helps to underline the secluded and protected quality of their lives—the association of subdued light with Biju and the Minister's wife. When she stays in bed in the morning the light streams into her bedroom filtered through the golden-yellow silk curtains, so that the light itself is honey-coloured. When they are in the garden the moon shines "with a silver light." The clear light of day is never allowed to reach them, except when the narrator, as the wife of a Minister, is forced out into the world to give speeches, and when she wants to tease herself and lifts the yellow silk curtain to let the sharp light—and the truth—into the room. For the disarming thing about this character is that she sees clearly that the beauty of her existence, within the confines of her little world, is artificially created. Looking back to her days as a beauty she says:

> If I don't look too closely and with the curtains drawn and the room all honey coloured, I don't appear so very different from what I used to be. But sometimes I'm in a mischievous mood with myself. I stretch out

> my hand and lift the yellow silk curtain. The light comes streaming in straight on to the mirror, and now yes I can see that I look very different from the way I used to.
>
> (54)

The minister on the other hand is associated with bright light. It is he who energetically draws the curtains apart when his wife is ill, thereby "dispelling the soothing honey-coloured light in which Biju and I have been all day," and it is "a great harsh beam" from the Minister's car that breaks into the scene when Biju dances alone in the garden, in an elegant imitation of the newest dance of the young (67, 64). This is not the bright light of truth but of rationality, for the Minister has no redeeming quality of introspection; he has far too shallow a personality for that. When he looks in the mirror he likes what he sees, and his wife comments, "I wonder—doesn't he remember what he was? How can he like that fat old man that now looks back at him?" (60).

The opposition between the two poles within **"Rose Petals"** is not just a question of a private versus a public life. It is also an opposition between profundity and superficiality, between feeling and rationality. When Biju plays the music box again and again, in a beautiful room of red and gold full of images that suggest the passing of time and even death—the ormolu clock, the light reflected from the lake that made the walls appear to be "swaying and rippling as if waves were passing over them," the prints of Venice—both Biju and the narrator think about time, aging, and death. The Minister refers to the tune made by the music box as "that damned noise" (60). He sees old age as something you face "head-on . . . a challenge that, like everything else, has to be faced and won" (62), as if he thought he had a chance of winning a battle against time and death.

It is this capacity for deep feeling and appreciation for what is beautiful that makes the Minister's wife and Biju see what the Minister can never see. When they accidentally witness the eviction of the poverty-stricken from their homes the Minister, who makes so many political speeches about serving India, is completely oblivious to what is going on and is only interested in the car. For him the suffering of the poor has become reduced to political slogans about "the changing times and building up India and everyone putting their shoulder to the wheel" (56).

What tones down the opposition between the two poles, and what holds this little world together is the all-pervading love—but not in any sense a blind love—that the narrator brings to all the members of her family: her daughter, Biju and even her husband. Her tolerance toward them all is akin to her tolerance toward herself:

> There is a Persian poem. It says human life is like the petals that fall from the rose and lie soft and withering by the side of the vase. Whenever I think of this poem, I think of Biju and myself. But it is not possible to think of the Minister and Mina as rose petals. No, they are something much stronger. I'm glad! They are what I have to turn to, and it is enough for me.
>
> (68)

This passage appears at the very end of the short story, but the title **"Rose Petals"** has, of course, been there right from the start. Rose petals are of no obvious practical use, but they are things of great beauty and sophistication, associated with exclusiveness, fragrance, fragility and an airy lightness. They are also—like all things—transient, and when they "lie soft and withering by the side of the vase" their hour of dissolution is near. All these associations suit the lives led by the narrator and Biju, so that long before we reach the ending we have already made the connection between them and the central metaphor of the short story.

That this early realization does not detract from the enjoyment of the rest of the narrative, is due to Ruth Prawer Jhabvala's restrained prose style, which is more subtle than it would appear to be on the surface. In the following passage, for example, she achieves two things simultaneously: she changes the direction of the story, and at the same time brings out the difference in character between Mina and her mother and Biju when she asks them whether they have no wish to do something constructive. Biju answers in the negative, and so Mina goes on to say,

> "Well you ought to. Everybody ought to. There's such a lot to do! In every conceivable field." She licks crumbs off the ends of her fingers—I murmur automatically, "Darling use the napkin"—and when she has got them clean she uses them to tick off with: "Social. Educational. Cultural—that reminds me: are you coming to the play?"
>
> (55)

The charm and delicacy of this moment of social comedy—affectionate, ironic and forgiving—is typical of Prawer Jhabvala. In such vignettes she achieves, momentarily, that accepting synthesis of vision that in her own person she could not achieve, when faced with what she has called "the horrors" of daily life in India ("Myself in India" 10).

Works Cited

Bailur, Jayanti. *Ruth Prawer Jhabvala: Fiction and Film.* New Delhi: Arnold, 1992.

Crane, Ralph J. *Ruth Prawer Jhabvala.* Twayne's English Authors Series 494. New York: Twayne, 1992.

Gooneratne, Yasmine. *Silence, Exile and Cunning: The Fiction of Ruth Prawer Jhabvala.* London: Sangam, 1983.

Hayman, Ronald. *The Novel Today. 1967-1975.* Harlow: Longman, 1976.

Jhabvala, Ruth Prawer. *How I Became a Holy Mother and Other Stories.* Harmondsworth, UK: Penguin, 1981.

———. "Introduction: Myself in India." Jhabvala, *How I Became* . . . 9-16.

———. "Rose Petals." Jhabvala, *How I Became* . . . 53-68.

Angus Wolfe Murray (review date 26 September 1998)

SOURCE: Murray, Angus Wolfe. "Rays of Hope in the Heat and Dust." *The Scotsman* (26 September 1998): 14.

[*In the following favorable review of* East into Upper East, *Murray lauds Jhabvala's depiction of privileged, upper-class society in the stories of the collection.*]

Ruth Prawer Jhabvala is perhaps best known for her eighth novel, *Heat And Dust,* and as Merchant Ivory's resident screenwriter. It would be hard to underestimate the quality of her film work, especially now that studio scripts are shredded by rewrite teams on a regular basis.

Born of Polish parents in Germany before the war, she married an Indian architect and spent more than two decades in that continent. Now she lives in the United States. These stories [in ***East Into Upper East***] are roughly shared between New Delhi and New York. What connects them is sympathy for older women and scepticism of love's binding truths. Men, on the whole, are rich, fat and unfaithful. Occasionally they are foolish and, once, violent. Women are rich, manipulative, overweight and abandoned. Occasionally they are saintly, and quite possibly lesbian.

Prawer Jhabvala's understanding of the upper-class milieu cuts through stereotype to the basis of privilege's failure to mend the damage of emotional deprivation. She shares, with Chekhov, a fascination with society in decline. Many of her heroines live in homes too big for them, in circumstances beyond their comprehension (or means). The rich ones are shielded by flunkies, hangers-on and genetic defects. The poor ones live off their wits, or invent jobs as spiritual healers.

A pattern emerges: a cast of three or four interlocking lives that contradict and influence one another, their real feelings caught between the lines. Her writing is unpolluted by fashion's exhaust and has the imprint of a previous golden age, before sentences lost verbs. Her style has clarity, with a notice on every page: "Leave adjectives at the door". She writes so well, you never want to leave.

The Indian stories are aware of social position, the importance of money as a power tool, the shadow of the Raj across the ancient city, people living in denial, whether it's the nature of a bad brother (**"Expiation"**) or the relationship between a dance teacher and the wife of an aged former diplomat who lives in a corrugated hut on the roof of his house (**"Husband And Son"**). Often the action is in the telling, rather than the tale. **"Independence"** is about New Delhi's former aristocracy coming to terms with new peasant politics, as well as intimations of heartbreak.

Tragedy and passion, idealism and ambition are all here. Time brings change and change leaves a residue of flotsam and jetsam, which is what interests Prawer Jhabvala. How do you get through life without losing the hope that buoyed those idyllic years? Is the future a succession of missed opportunities and unrequited love affairs (**"Development and Progress"**)?

The American stories are closer to the money—and class. Women find themselves manipulated by other women (**"Great Expectations"**, **"Parasites"**, **"Fidelity"**), out of a sense of loneliness or because they are too cushioned by wealth to recognise the falsehood of easy friendship. Husbands inevitably are off with 24-year-old secretaries, and in **"Broken Promises"** the daughter of an estranged Manhattan couple endeavours to keep the flame of desire alive in the face of her mother's selfish demands.

Prawer Jhabvala marvels at the human capacity for self-deceit and sympathises with those who join the ladies' lunch circuit as a way of filling the day before cocktails. Everyone is watching everyone, and everyone is watching the money. The fascination lies in the weave of these emotional tapestries.

East Into Upper East reminds us of how stories should be told. Human experience becomes a survival course in which men and women take separate routes. When decisions are avoided, situations dissolve into shallow defeat, like when the wife accompanies her husband to their beach house in **"A Summer by the Sea"**, so that he can surround himself with beautiful young men and she doesn't question it, or feel threatened. Because nothing is said.

Prawer Jhabvala's gift for the unspoken wraps every story in a web of subtlety. The women on the western side are more susceptible to strong influence, as if needing to submerge in other philosophies, other dreams. In the East, lines are more firmly drawn. There is a confidence of purpose, even though corruption undermines political integrity.

The author walks through dusty rooms in the old houses and you feel the warmth of her nostalgia, although there is not a hint of regret, nor a whiff of sentimentality. There are moments, as there are in every life, when the light shines brightly.

But to expect joy to be unbounded is to expect hunger to be eradicated, or lovers to remain faithful. The failure of hope is not a tragedy. As she surveys the ruins of what might have been, Prawer Jhabvala marvels at the tenacity of the human spirit.

Sarah Curtis (review date 2 October 1998)

SOURCE: Curtis, Sarah. "Antique Furnishings." *Times Literary Supplement,* no. 4983 (2 October 1998): 26.

[*In the following review, Curtis commends the humor and intensity of emotion in the stories of* East into Upper East.]

Ruth Prawer Jhabvala is one of those writers whose name immediately conjures up an image, in her case a double image. We see the heat and dust of India, particle by particle, usually through sympathetic and sometimes sentimental Western eyes. Almost simultaneously, we remember the Merchant-Ivory adaptations of E. M. Forster and the other films she has scripted with their heavy period detail. This collection of fourteen short stories [***East into Upper East***], six set mostly in India, seven in wealthier enclaves of America and one in London, shows how easy it is to think the settings are the dominant feature of her work and how misleading such a judgment is. The exotic or familiar backgrounds, lovingly depicted, are a hallmark of her novels and of the work of Merchant-Ivory, but what matters in her books is the intensity of the emotions that she transmits.

Five of the Indian stories and two of the best of those set in America were first published in the *New Yorker* or other magazines. There is no new ground in these or the other stories. As in her eleven novels, Jhabvala sticks to what she is interested in—the personal rather than the public, the small picture rather than the wide screen—and she draws from the whole of her heritage, her childhood in Germany as the daughter of Polish Jews, her marriage since 1951 to an Indian architect and her residence in New York as well as Delhi since the 1970s. She writes about the intricacies of relationships in families and between friends or lovers, about possessive love and about alienation: her people are nearly always trying to discover where they belong.

In **"Two Muses"**, for example, a young woman recalls her grandfather Max (shades of the narrator of *Heat and Dust* tracing the history of her step-grandmother) and the two women who underpinned his life. He is an appallingly egotistical German refugee writer of alleged genius who settled in Hampstead. His wife, Lilo, is his beauteous, grand, distant inspiration, and his dashing mistress, Netta, is the practical force who makes their existence in exile possible, organizing his work, taking a job as a dentist's receptionist to pay the bills. To illustrate the difference between the women, their complementary natures and two aspects of Germany, Lilo's furniture in their Hampstead flat is solidly Biedermeier and Netta's in her nearby flat in St John's Wood is tubular Bauhaus. In Jhabvala's novel *In Search of Love and Beauty* (1983), Regi had that same tubular furniture in the smart Park Avenue flat where she entertained her circle of fellow refugees from Austria and Germany. The characters surround themselves with the past from which they have been displaced. The background indicates where they stand but is not central to the argument.

The stifling feel of the past is also important in **"Fidelity"**, symbolized by Sophie's heavily curtained apartment which she inherited from her parents, including fixtures and fittings from her German grandparents. Sophie grew up with the idea that you had to keep the sunlight out to stop the upholstery from fading. She is long separated from her philandering husband, Dave, but he still telephones almost daily. In some ways Sophie is like an Anita Brookner heroine. She is rich, buys a lot of clothes, likes cakes and is essentially a quiet person. By contrast, Dave is a vital force, full of charm and tricks. To underline their difference, he and his sister are Sephardic Jews, to Ahkenazic Sophie, "exotic, semi-oriental". Michael, her nephew, like many Jhabvala characters, asserts his identity and shows his confusion by heading East and then spending time with Sufis in upstate New York and Hasidim in Brooklyn. The story is about the ties that bind them all as Sophie is secretly dying of cancer, and about the way they continue to manipulate and depend on each other until death parts them. It escapes being mawkish because the observation is acute and it is funny.

The welcome element of humour often has an ironic tinge. Jhabvala is a storyteller who does not take sides, but does expose her characters' weaknesses. This works well in **"Broken Promises"**, where she explores the confrontation of values between a mother and daughter. Donna, the rich mother, has lunch parties with Tarot readings and suffers from a weak heart. Reba, the daughter, is a strong young woman, a vegetarian conservationist living in a woodland cabin. She is a lesbian, and her lover works in her mother's neighbourhood gourmet cheese shop. "Reba's more the intellectual type", Donna tells her friends when they are discussing their daughters. The contrasts between the generations are schematic, and both women are daft, but their dilemmas and the interaction between them, Reba's struggle for freedom and Donna's dazed acceptance of what happens, are credible.

Less successful is her study, in **"Bobby"**, of a lesbian relationship torn apart by the psychotic son of one of the women. Once again, the details of the story are beguiling, with everyone's lifestyle carefully delineated, but what is important is the ties that bind the characters. Claire is more attached to Bobby than Madeleine, who has to take him, too, if she wants to keep Claire. The reasons why otherwise sane people stick to untenable situations are dissected more subtly in **"A Summer by the Sea"**, when a wife says of her bisexual husband: "No one ever tells me that it's wrong for me to love Mother for the way she is and not for how she is supposed to be."

Such themes are perhaps more obvious in the Western stories, but if the ethnic (and sometimes too folksy) settings of the East are stripped away, the preoccupations of Jhabvala are the same. Sinister intruders who attach themselves to unaccountably gullible people are the subject of **"Parasites"**, **"Temptress"**, and **"Great Expectations"** in the American stories. Similarly, it is a stranger who is the catalyst in the opening (and perhaps most memorable) story of the collection, **"Expiation"**, which is about the seduction into crime and murder of the youngest boy in a simple merchant family. There is nothing crude about the deadpan narration by Bablu's older brother, wondering why the boy was different from the start and why he chafed at the normal bonds of attachment, as if waiting to be taken away to another life. The story could be transposed to the Upper East Side or Islington, despite the particularities of Indian life which give it poignancy. This universality is perhaps why Jhabvala's Indian stories, moving as they usually are, seem the product of an observer rather than an insider.

Can the contrasts between the old and the new, whether in changing India or the rushing world of America, the mutual dependence of husband and wife in any culture, the universal anger of adolescence and the disappointments of age, be fully explored in the short story? Jhabvala is concerned with stating emotional dilemmas rather than developing arguments, so the form has always suited her well. In many stories of this collection, a stream of incidents brings the initial situation to a breathless but satisfactory conclusion. In others which are quieter and more reflective a resolution is not the point.

Carole Angier (review date 17 October 1998)

SOURCE: Angier, Carole. "Dutiful in Delhi but Moonstruck in Manhattan." *The Independent* (17 October 1998): 16-17.

[*In the following review, Angier finds the stories of* East into Upper East *rich in emotional insight but devoid of imagery, irony, and playfulness.*]

More people know Ruth Prawer Jhabvala for her Merchant Ivory screenplays than for her books, which are many. That is not a comment about her, but about us and our 90-minute (at most) culture. And yet I wonder if it does not reflect something about her after all. Many of these stories of New York and New Delhi [in ***East into Upper East***] are quite brilliant: acute, profound, moving. But they are also quite strange.

They are called "plain tales", to echo Kipling, and at first I thought: they are plain. They are very plainly divided into Indian and American sections, as the very plain title shows; and the Indian ones, which come first, despite Ruth Prawer Jhabvala's reputation, also seemed to me very plain.

Was that the right word? The two which are (mainly) about the coming of modern India are subtle in their regret for the past; the other four, (mainly) about love, are deeply acquainted with its mystery, its imperiousness, its strange sacrifices. I particularly liked **"A New Delhi Romance"**, in which the son of an ambitious mother and a reckless father falls recklessly in love, but in the end is more his mother's than his father's son. Not "plain", then, but what? They reminded me of a wonderful writer I was once meant to show around London. She hardly looked up; all she wanted to talk about was people, which she did with great brilliance.

These tales are hugely rich in emotional insight, but contain almost nothing else at all. We know if people are fat or thin, dark or fair; we see the insides of their houses and apartments. But they seem marooned in their tiny bits of New York (or New Delhi), in their families, in their obsessive loves. And the language in which they are described is equally single-minded. There are few images, almost no similes or metaphors, and no playfulness or irony at all.

A remark in one Indian story—that a daughter "was learning far more about herself and her relationship with her mother than was good for her"—is the only remotely tongue-in-cheek observation I could find. Maybe hot, analytical Ruth Prawer Jhabvala does need cool, visual James Ivory after all.

Given this quirk, these are marvellous stories. Especially the American ones, which seem to me richer than the Indian (although this difference may be more in my reading than her writing). Here, too, are two great themes. One is, again, love, and the sacrifices we make willingly for it—even when it is unreturned (**"A Summer by the Sea"**), or dangerous (**"Bobby"**), or costs us everything (**"Great Expectations"**); even unto death (**"Fidelity"**).

The other is a strange and interesting theme about the privileged Western rich, who have forgotten how to live, and who depend on the (often Eastern) poor for their spiritual and emotional renewal. Some of these exploit them, for money (**"Great Expectations"**,

"Parasites") and/or for sex (there are some pretty dark remarks about gurus). Some both love and exploit them, like Netta in **"Two Muses"**; and some simply love them, as truly as Jhabvla's other lovers.

The parasites, as the story of that title neatly shows, are the rich. In these New York stories, Ruth Prawer Jhabvala struck me as a kinder kinkier (many of these lovers are lesbian) version of Anita Brookner.

Ramlal Agarwal (review date winter 2000)

SOURCE: Agarwal, Ramlal. Review of *East into Upper East: Plain Tales from New York and New Delhi,* by Ruth Prawer Jhabvala. *World Literature Today* 74, no. 1 (winter 2000): 158.

[*In the following favorable assessment of* East into Upper East, *Agarwal designates Jhabvala "one of the best short-story writers in the world."*]

Ruth Prawer Jhabvala is known for many reasons: for her Merchant-Ivory screenplays, two of which earned Academy Awards (*A Room with a View* and *Howards End*), for her novels, one of which (*Heat and Dust*) won the Booker Prize; but, above all, as one of the best short-story writers in the world. In her short stories Jhabvala is mainly concerned with exploring the comic and the tragic aspects of the love-hate relationship between the East and the West. In a 1974 interview with the present reviewer, Jhabvala says, "Perhaps I do tend to see the ridiculous aspects first, both in situations and in characters. But I don't think I just sit and laugh at them. Especially not in my later books. On the contrary, I am beginning to feel that what is ludicrous on the surface may be tragic underneath."

Jhabvala's latest collection of short stories, ***East into Upper East,*** confirms the practice she professed in the interview years ago. The stories present the terrible restlessness and decay beneath the material superfluity in the West and the greed and deceit beneath the Indian spirituality as it is manifested by Indian godmen and holy mothers. The stories are divided into two parts, the first containing six stories set in India and the other offering eight stories set on the Upper East Side of New York City. The stories set in India deal with the changing role of women in post-Independence Delhi, the seat of power, politics, sex, and big fortunes and misfortunes. The other eight stories depict Indians raiding American life and culture. In her earlier stories and novels Jhabvala's Indian women characters were docile, stupid, possessive, and bickering, but in the present collection they are scheming, permissive, and ambitious. In her earlier works Jhabvala depicted Westerners living in India; in the present collection she depicts Indians living in America.

"Farid and Farida" is about a couple who move from New Delhi to London, which, they think, will offer them a "wider horizon." In London they live in a decaying one-room flat, hoping to move to a better one when they start making money. Farid fails to churn out profits from his ventures in ready-made garments, handcrafted Indian jewelry, Indian lampshades, bedcovers, et cetera, and turns to drink. Farida takes over from Farid the responsibility of running the family by selling Indian cocktail delicacies which she herself prepares. She is generously helped by her former lover Sunil, now a successful businessman in London. But eventually the oily smells and difficulties in distribution and payment collection lead her to return to India. There she lives the life of a recluse. Word spreads that she is a holy woman, and people living in the vicinity start visiting her with generous offerings. Farid, unable to carry on in London, rejoins her, but without revealing to her devotees his relationship with her. One day Sunil turns up. He tells her how they could cash in on her role as a holy mother in London, and soon takes her back there, notwithstanding Farid's opposition.

Much in the same line is **"The Temptress,"** which deals with the Western craze for Indian holy men, particularly in America. There was a time when Westerners came to India and conquered it. Now it is Indians' turn to go to the West and return the favor.

Jhabvala is a consummate artist, and her threadbare language, matter-of-fact style, drab details, and slow pace are all part of her fictional strategy to reveal her insights into the Indian psyche degree by degree. Not many Indian critics of Indian writing in English share the present reviewer's perception and think that her work is derogatory. Jhabvala enjoys this and keeps smiling up her sleeve.

FURTHER READING

Criticism

Agarwal, Ramlal G. *Ruth Prawer Jhabvala: A Study of Her Short Fiction.* New Delhi: Sterling Publishers Private, Ltd., 1990, 126 p.

Critical study of Jhabvala's short fiction.

Gray, Paul. "Tributes of Empathy and Grace." *Time* 127 (12 May 1986): 90.

Commends the humor and spare prose of the stories collected in *Out of India.*

Mason, Deborah. "Passage to America." *New York Times Book Review* (19 November 1998): 20-2.

Favorable review of *East into Upper East.*

Mollinger, Mehta. Review of *How I Became a Holy Mother and Other Stories,* by Ruth Prawer Jhabvala. *Library Journal* 101 (1 December 1976): 2511.

Praises the balance between comedy and tragedy in the stories of *How I Became a Holy Mother and Other Stories.*

Rees, Jasper. "Becoming Other." *Times Literary Supplement,* no. 4366 (24 April 1987): 434.

Contrasts Jhabvala's depiction of India in *Out of India* with that of Satyajit Ray in his *Stories.*

Shahane, Vasant A. "Mode in Miniature: Short Stories." *Ruth Prawer Jhabvala,* pp. 142-75. New Delhi: Arnold-Heinemann, 1976.

Discusses the defining characteristics of Jhabvala's short stories, contrasting them with her longer fictional works.

Shepherd, Ron. "'Yes, Something Is Wrong': Obscure Irritant in Ruth Prawer Jhabvala's Short Stories." In *Passages to Ruth Prawer Jhabvala,* edited by Ralph J. Crane, pp. 95-102. New Delhi, India: Sterling Publishers Ltd., 1991.

Detects a sense of discomfort and irresolution in Jhabvala's short fiction, arguing that "there exists in her work a darker, more insistent, more despairing, and more chaotic side than has been generally acknowledged so far."

Varadarajan, Tunku. "India without the Heat and the Dust." *The Times* (12 November 1998): 43.

Maintains that there is little in *East and Upper East* that is memorable or challenging, regarding it as "the perfect comfort food for those who want a break from big ideas, for those who want a break for once from those fat, ambitious Indian books which seem to sit on every bookshelf."

Wiehe, Janet. Review of *Out of India,* by Ruth Prawer Jhabvala. *Library Journal* 111, no. 7 (15 April 1986): 95.

Offers a brief positive review of *Out of India.*

Additional coverage of Jhabvala's life and career is contained in the following sources published by Thomson Gale: *British Writers Supplement,* Vol. 5; *Contemporary Authors,* Vols. 1-4R; *Contemporary Authors New Revision Series,* Vols. 2, 29, 51, 74, 91, 128; *Contemporary Literary Criticism,* Vols. 4, 8, 29, 94, 138; *Contemporary Novelists,* Ed. 7; *Dictionary of Literary Biography,* Vols. 139, 194; *DISCovering Authors: British*; *DISCovering Authors Modules*: NOV; *Encyclopedia of World Literature in the 20th Century,* Ed. 3; *The International Dictionary of Films and Filmmakers: Writers and Production Artists,* Eds. 3, 4; *Literature Resource Center*; *Major 20th-Century Writers,* Eds. 1, 2; *Major 21st-Century Writers,* Ed. 2005; *Reference Guide to Short Fiction,* Ed. 2; *Reference Guide to World Literature,* Ed. 2; *Twayne's English Authors*; and *20th Century Romance and Historical Writers.*

Charles G. D. Roberts
1860-1943

(Full name Charles George Douglas Roberts) Canadian poet, short story writer, novelist, historian, critic, and essayist.

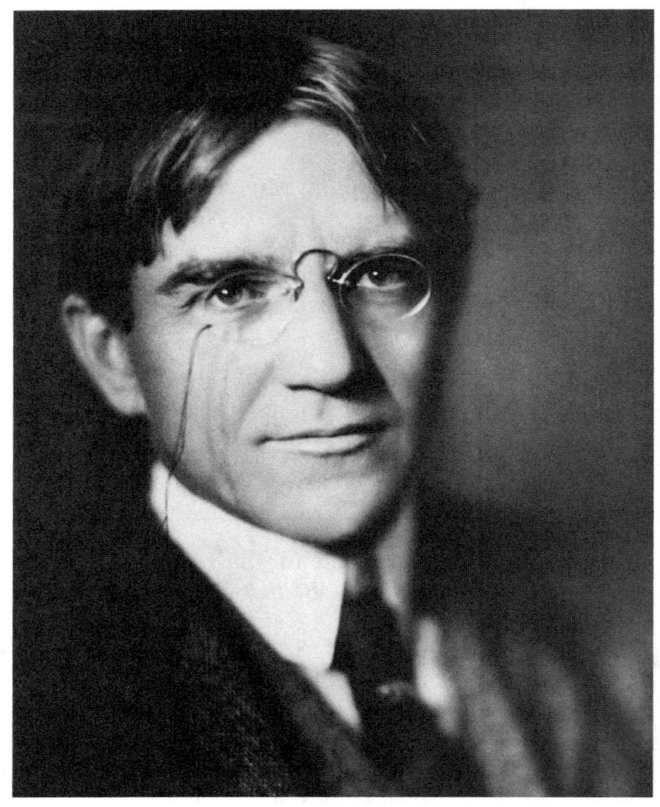

INTRODUCTION

Called "the father of Canadian literature," Roberts is acclaimed as a notable author of poetry, historical romance, Canadian history, and realistic animal stories. In these tales, he explores the symbiotic relationship between humans and animals, glorifies the beauty and cruelty of the natural world, and celebrates the primal struggle for survival, often under harsh and challenging conditions. Roberts's stories were commercially popular and influential in the first half of the twentieth century.

BIOGRAPHICAL INFORMATION

Roberts was born on January 10, 1860, in Douglas, New Brunswick, Canada, a beautiful natural landscape that figures prominently in his later poetry and fiction. His father, a minister, provided his son's early education. Roberts later attended the Collegiate School in Fredericton. A driven and bright student, he then attended the University of New Brunswick, receiving his B.A. with honors in mental and moral science and political economy in 1879. He went on to earn his M.A. in 1881. His first book of poetry, *Orion, and Other Poems* (1880), was published while he was still a student. The volume garnered praise from Matthew Arnold and Oliver Wendell Holmes. He continued to write poetry and novels, also working as editor of *This Week* magazine for a brief period. He was appointed professor of English literature at King's College in Nova Scotia in 1885. Two years later, Roberts moved to New York and began to write short stories, particularly the realistic animal tales that were published in such collections as *The Watchers of the Trails* (1904) and *Kings in Exile* (1909). At first the stories were not well received, but with the tremendous success of Ernest Thompson Seton's *Wild Animals I Have Known*—which was in part inspired by Roberts's stories—he attained some commercial success. As a result, he began to focus more on his animal stories than on his poetry. Roberts lived in New York and London for thirty years. During World War I, he volunteered as a trooper in the British Legion of Frontiersmen. He received the first Lorne Pierce medal for imaginative literature in 1926, an award given by the Royal Society of Canada. In 1927 he returned to Canada and began composing verse again. In 1935 he was knighted by King George V. He died on November 26, 1943.

MAJOR WORKS OF SHORT FICTION

Roberts's animal stories are characterized by his close observation of animal behavior, an emphasis on natural science, and a belief that animals possess personality, higher reasoning, and even a sense of morality. Critics have categorized his numerous animal stories into three groups: stories that trace an animal's growth and development from birth to death; stories that chronicle the epic conflict between man and animals; and stories that focus on a dramatic encounter between two animals. In the first type of animal story, Roberts follows the struggle of animals to survive in a ruthless world of predators and harsh climatic conditions from birth, through mating and propagation of the species, and death. For example, in "Queen Bomba of the Honey-Pots" Roberts chronicles the life of a bumblebee; in "The Last Barrier," he relates the life story of an Atlantic salmon.

Told from the human perspective, the stories in the second group focus on the effort of a person, usually male, to confront and overcome opposition from the natural world. In most stories, that means killing an animal predator and then reflecting on the moral and spiritual consequences of such an act. In "King of Beasts," a man shipwrecked on the shore of an isolated Sumatran jungle kills a majestic tiger that is hunting him. Conscience haunts the protagonist of "The Bear That Thought He Was a Dog" when he decides to raise the infant cub of the bear he reluctantly killed. The moral implications of hunting are also explored in "The Vagrants of the Barren," another well-regarded story. When a caribou herd saves a man's life, the man kills only one of the animals for food, instead of several. In an autobiographical group of stories about the "Boy," the narrator stops and beats some boys for torturing small kittens and regrets snaring rabbits as a child; as he matures, he reflects on his love and respect for the natural world as well as on the interdependence between man and nature. The protagonist of "The Stone Dog," is menaced by a large stone dog that comes to life to protect a treasure.

In the third and best known category of stories, Roberts focuses on a short but eventful period in the life of an animal as it faces a formidable obstacle, usually a conflict with a predator. Often a celebration of courage and heroism, these stories portray the circumstances and aftermath of the conflict in a realistic manner. In several stories, captive animals yearn for freedom. For example, in "The Summons of the North," a polar bear dies of a heart attack in the zoo when a snowstorm reminds him of what he has lost. A captive buffalo is killed in "Last Bull" when the animal escapes and threatens a group of children.

CRITICAL RECEPTION

Roberts's animal stories are regarded among his most popular and enduring works despite the fact that critics often focus on his verse and neglect his short fiction. As a result, there are few substantial examinations of his numerous short stories. Commentators have discussed Roberts's debt to Charles Darwin's theory of evolution and the influence of nineteenth-century scientific ideas on the genre of the nature story. Recent criticism has explored the symbolism in several of Roberts's stories, also noting the influence of his stories on Seton. By depicting animals that act not purely from instinct, but also with the aid of reason, both authors attracted the condemnation of such naturalists as John Burroughs, who labeled Seton and Roberts shams. Yet Roberts's stories were undeniably popular with readers in his own time and are perceived by modern critics as a significant contribution to Canadian literature.

PRINCIPAL WORKS

Short Fiction

Earth's Enigmas: A Book of Animal and Nature Life 1896; revised edition, 1903
The Kindred of the Wild: A Book of Animal Life 1902
The Watchers of the Trails: A Book of Animal Life 1904
The Haunters of the Silences 1907
Kings in Exile 1909
Neighbours Unknown 1910
More Kindred of the Wild 1911
Babes of the Wild 1912; also published as *Children of the Wild,* 1913
They Who Walk in the Wild 1924; also published as *They That Walk in the Wild,* 1924
Eyes of the Wilderness 1933
The Last Barrier and Other Stories 1958
The Lure of the Wild: The Last Three Animal Stories 1980
The Vagrants of the Barren and Other Stories 1992

Other Major Works

Orion, and Other Poems (poetry) 1880
In Divers Tones (poetry) 1886
Autochthon (poetry) 1889
The Book of the Native (poetry) 1896
The Forge in the Forest, Being the Narrative of the Acadian Ranger, Jean de Mer (novel) 1896
A History of Canada for High Schools and Academies (history) 1897
New York Nocturnes and Other Poems (poetry) 1898
The Heart of the Ancient Wood (novel) 1900
Barbara Ladd (novel) 1902
The Book of the Rose (poetry) 1903
Red Fox: The Story of His Adventurous Career (novel) 1905
The Heart That Knows (novel) 1906
Canada in Flanders. 3 vols. (history) 1918
New Poems (poetry) 1919
The Vagrant of Time (poetry) 1927
The Iceberg and Other Poems (poetry) 1934
Twilight over Shaugamauk and Three Other Poems (poetry) 1937

Canada Speaks of Britain and Other Poems of the War (poetry) 1941
Selected Poetry and Critical Prose (essays and poetry) 1974
Collected Poems (poetry) 1985

CRITICISM

The Nation (review date 19 May 1910)

SOURCE: Review of *Kings in Exile,* by Charles G. D. Roberts. *The Nation* 90, no. 2342 (19 May 1910): 511-12.

[*In the following review, the anonymous critic characterizes Roberts's animal stories as "a queer mixture of legitimate natural history and highly melodramatic episodes in which animal intelligence is ridiculously exaggerated, together with some good descriptive writing mingled with much that is obviously fantastic and overdrawn."*]

This is another collection of animal stories [***Kings in Exile***] done much after Mr. Roberts's usual fashion. That is to say, their substance is sometimes a queer mixture of legitimate natural history and highly melodramatic episodes in which animal intelligence is ridiculously exaggerated, together with some good descriptive writing mingled with much that is obviously fantastic and overdrawn. Mr. Roberts is fond of depicting with absurd minuteness the supposed cerebrations of wild animals in captivity, and of domesticated creatures turned loose in the woods to shift for themselves. These themes he has already worn fairly threadbare, but that does not deter him from working into the present volume the stories of **"Last Bull,"** who is a bison confined in a zoölogical park where he bewails his fate and finally meets a tragic end; of **"The Gray Master,"** which tells the same kind of tale about a timber wolf, and other yarns of the same general character. Perhaps the most ingenious one is the tale of the man who, while planning to rob an eagle's nest, tumbled over a cliff and lodged on a ledge where he stayed for about two weeks in the company of one of the young eagles which he had knocked out of the nest in his fall and with which he shared the fish, flesh, and fowl brought to the eaglet by its male parent. As an illustration of Mr. Roberts's faculty for lugging queer natural history into his stories, there is in this last story the episode of its hero's discovery that the "black eagle," of which he had seen only one specimen, was nothing but an immature bald eagle, of which he had seen many—an observation which loses its force when one remembers that the bald eagle does not get its full plumage until its second or third year at the earliest, and that, therefore, "black eagles" (as a matter of fact, the immature bald eagle is *brown,* not black) are, in the nature of the case, much more common than those with the white head and tail.

New Statesman (review date 6 September 1929)

SOURCE: "The Psychology of Animals." *New Statesman* 23 (6 September 1929): 626.

[*In the following review, the anonymous critic assesses the stories in* They That Walk in the Wild *as "sensitively planned and vividly written."*]

There is no true literature of animals. All the jungle books, from *Genesis* to *Kim,* have dealt with them necessarily from an alien point of view, without objectivity of comment. When philosophy or psychology succeeds in establishing the precise interrelations of mind and the senses we shall perhaps be nearer to a discovery of the mysterious tie, crudely traced out in the biological theories of evolution, which binds the two main divisions of organic life. At present, however, the literary naturalist is credible only when he confines his interpretative fancy within the strait-waistcoat of scientific observation. When Mr. Roberts says that "faint ancestral memories began to stir in the young puma's brain," he is not only ignoring a current theory of the automatic behaviour of animals; he is anthro-pomorphising with all the extremism, and none of the deliberateness, of Æsop, La Fontaine or Mr. Pat Sullivan, the brilliant screen-draughtsman of "Felix the Cat." Indeed, it is difficult to imagine any other method of translating the psychology of animals into terms comprehensible to our own. One may therefore take pleasure in Mr. Roberts's ambition "to help a little forward toward a wider, more tender and more imaginative perception of their essential kinship with ourselves" while remaining sceptical of the means by which he proposes to bring it about—"to present them, in their actions and their motives, from their own point of view rather than ours."

The episodes he relates [in ***They That Walk in the Wild***] of these creatures of the Canadian backwoods are sensitively planned and vividly written. As we read them we feel like hidden wild-life photographers, biding our time until every jungle bush or arctic boulder yields a beast—until that uncanny, graceful, ravenous parade begins, from which an ancestor's itch for uprightness (the unsightly skill of the winner of a sack-race) has expelled us for ever. Schopenhauer once said that men are the devils of the world, and animals the tormented souls. Modern sensibility has gone further in this direction; all of us who have ever comraded a dog, cherished a cat or paid an attentive visit to the Zoo, have had moods in which the metaphysical position of mankind seemed stripped even of a diabolistic primacy. Mankind, to such a mood, appears an unaccountable *parvenu* species marooned in a middle element; despised for its æsthetic imperfections by the denizens of the earth, and disowned, because of its moral shortcomings, by the deity beyond the sky. Mr. Roberts is, as a rule, strikingly successful in conveying, and implanting in the reader, some such respect for the integrity of the untamed animal. He describes the attack on a walrus herd by an arctic bear and a giant swordfish in such a manner that we can share the feelings of all, without attaching our sympathies to any one of the protagonists. This is the most convincing of all his narratives; some are marred by sentimentalism, others by psychological inconsistencies arising from the anthropomorphic intention which has been quoted. For instance, Mr. Roberts seems to allow no individuality to the members of the hive of Bomba, his Queen-Bee, and yet, in another section, after an exciting account of an eagle swooping down to steal fish from a cormorant, he declares that

> Few other birds there were in his colony who would have had the mettle, bold as they were, to face the Eagle as the Black Fisherman had done.

Why should individual character be given to a bird and denied to a bee? The analytical methods of the novelist—the measurement of mental processes by foot-rules of cause and effect—are partial and approximate in their estimation even of human beings. The minds of animals are a dim world to logical enquiry: perhaps we shall never be able to perceive "their essential kinship with ourselves," except by the monistic light of imagination.

> What the hammer? What the chain?
> In what furnace was thy brain?
> What the anvil? What dread grasp
> Dare its deadly terrors clasp?

Blake's very choice of metaphor emphasises the inhumanity of his tiger, and, by forcing our imaginations to accept this fact, brings the beast closer to our humanity.

H. K. G. (review date December 1933)

SOURCE: H. K. G. Review of *Eyes of the Wilderness,* by Charles G. D. Roberts. *The Canadian Forum* 14, no. 159 (December 1933): 116.

[*In the following review, the critic considers* Eyes of the Wilderness *inferior to Roberts' earlier collections of animal stories.*]

Long ago Mr. Roberts won for himself, and maintained, an enviable reputation as a writer of animal stories. It was not for nothing that W. H. Hudson, the greatest naturalist-writer in English, referred to his work with interest and commendation. What Hudson accomplished through scrupulous observation and record and an almost intuitive insight—the penetration of the springs of animal life—Roberts attempted with a large degree of success through the medium of fiction—fiction that was faithful at once to the exacting art of narrative and to nature. His skill to call up the atmosphere and homely details of a backwoods farm, the dusky silence of the deep bush, the sunlit reaches of marshland, or the shining vitality of a river, and to spin a convincing, absorbing tale of the furtive, eager life that each contains, often transcended mere ability and could only have been the happy result of sure knowledge, deep affection, and a vigorous imagination.

But Mr. Roberts' gift as an animal writer was at best limited. It failed to develop the variety and continuous change of growth. Having run its certain gamut of pictures and adventures there was nothing for it but repetition, with the inevitable consequences. It is therefore with disappointment but no surprise that, after a long silence, one picks up this new volume [***Eyes of the Wilderness***] to find that the old magic has departed. The familiar settings are there, and many of the characters that were once instinct with life and vigour, but they now refuse to come alive. The descriptions, once firm and brief as the bold strokes of a charcoal drawing, have become faint pencillings, and the creatures move dimly and mechanically about their exciting affairs. The old manner and the old mannerisms are there, too ('Spring came late that year to the upper Ottanoonsis'), but the zest which made us pardon their repetition has gone and leaves them lifeless forms. Besides, in ***Eyes of the Wilderness*** man bulks more largely than in most of the earlier books, and Mr. Roberts has never been happy in drawing human characters. The best that one can say for these stories is that they are competent and that they will entertain many new readers. But those who knew the old Roberts had better leave them alone. And how bare the book looks without the inimitable illustrations of Charles Livingston Bull!

Robert H. MacDonald (essay date spring 1980)

SOURCE: MacDonald, Robert H. "The Revolt against Instinct: The Animal Stories of Seton and Roberts." *Canadian Literature* 84 (spring 1980): 18-29.

[*In the following essay, MacDonald discusses the animal stories of Roberts and Ernest Thompson Seton as a revolt against Darwinian determinism.*]

In his introduction to ***Kindred of the Wild***—a chapter that stands as a succinct apologia for the animal story—Sir Charles Roberts in 1902 explained the particular inspiration of the new genre practised by Ernest Thompson Seton and himself. Animals and men, he said, were not so separate as had been supposed, for animals, far from being mere creatures of instinct, could and did reason, and what is more, frequently displayed to the discerning observer signs not only of their psychologies, but also of something which might appeal to man's spiritual self. "We have come face to face with personality, where we were blindly wont to predicate mere instinct and automatism." The animal story, Roberts concluded, was thus a "potent emancipator," freeing us from "shop-worn utilities" and restoring to us the "old kinship of earth," a spiritual and uplifting union with nature.[1]

These statements can be labelled "romantic," or "transcendental," and dismissed as a rather sentimental defence of the "inarticulate kindred" of the wild, who are distinguished from Black Beauty and Beautiful Joe only by the fact that they live in the woods. I propose, however, to take Roberts at his word, and to examine his and Seton's stories in the light of his crucial distinction between instinct and reason. The animal story, I shall show, is part of a popular revolt against Darwinian determinism, and is an affirmation of man's need for moral and spiritual values. The animal world provides models of virtue, and exemplifies the order of nature. The works of Seton and Roberts are thus celebrations of rational, ethical animals, who, as they rise above instinct, reach towards the spiritual. This theme, inspired as it is by a vision of a better world, provides a mythic structure for what is at first sight, realistic fiction.

At the popular level, the chief implication of Darwin's theories of evolution and the principle of natural selection had been to diminish the distinction between man and the animals. We were descended from the apes, and if the apes were mere brutes, could we be very much different? All creatures, it seemed, owed their present form to certain inherited characteristics, which together with environmental influences, dictated their ability to survive. Nature was amoral; life was a power-struggle in which only the fittest survived. Instinct, to a large extent, seemed to govern animal behaviour; there was little place in nature for ethics or spirituality. Though man traditionally had been separated from the animals by his unique power of reason, could it not now be that man himself was little more than a brute beast?

By 1900 one of the most important controversies in the biological sciences was the question of animal behaviour: did animals act instinctively, or were they capable of learning? What was the nature of an animal's knowledge: was it inherited, or was it acquired? Were animals capable of reason? Did they learn from experience, did they teach each other? The weight of opinion, at least from the biologists, seemed to favour instinct and inheritance.[2] In their reaction to this controversy (and in a larger sense to the whole impetus of Darwinism), Seton, Roberts and their fellow nature writers rescued their public from the awful amorality of Darwinian nature. They reassured their readers, not so much that man was superior to animals, but that animals were superior in themselves, that they could reason, that they could and did educate their young, and that they possessed and obeyed laws of their own. Judging by the commercial success of their stories, this was a popular and much-needed antidote to Darwinian pessimism.

"The life of a wild animal," said Seton in *Wild Animals I Have Known* (1899), *"always has a tragic end."* By that he meant that all animals die, and since most of them prey upon each other, they frequently die violently. Both Seton and Roberts refused to evade this unpleasant fact: kill or be killed is the natural law. To this extent they were both Darwinians: nature was indeed red in tooth and claw, and only the best escaped for a time. Thus "Kneepads," the mountain ewe who took to kneeling as she grazed, was an easy prey for the mountain lion, and Red Fox's weaker and stupider siblings met an early death.[3] Survival does indeed go to the fittest.

In their biographies of animal heroes, both men repeatedly illustrate this central fact of the evolutionary theory. Their animals are not ordinary animals, but superior animals, distinguished by their size, skill, wisdom and moral sense. These animals have all learned to cope with a hostile environment; they endure. They are the leaders of their kind. Thus Wahb is the largest and most intelligent grizzly, Krag the noblest mountain sheep, Lobo a giant among wolves, Raggylugs a most sagacious rabit, and so on. From the first Red Fox is the pick of his litter, larger, livelier, more intelligent, and, curiously, redder. Seton's comment on the old crow, Silverspot, will serve to characterize all these heroes: "once in awhile there arises an animal who is stronger or wiser than his fellow, who becomes a great leader, who is, as we would say, a genius, and if he is bigger, or has some mark by which men can know him, he soon becomes famous in his country, and shows us that the life of a wild animal may be far more interesting and exciting than that of many human beings."

Both Seton and Roberts took pains to establish that everything they wrote was within the bounds of truth. Their animal biographies were frequently "composite" biographies; that is, they included everything that had been done, or might have been done, by a crow, or a wolf, or a fox, but they contained nothing that was not possible. Thus Seton, in his preface to *Wild Animals I Have Known,* acknowledges having "pieced together some of the characters," but claims that there was, in at least three of the lives, "almost no deviation from the truth." Roberts, introducing Red Fox, makes the same point saying that in the life of his hero, "every one of these experiences has befallen some red fox in the past, and may befall other red foxes in the future." He has been, he assures his readers, "careful to keep well within the boundaries of fact." We may take these statements at face value: by and large, both men were astute and careful observers of nature, and in most of their writing give realistic, though fictionalized, descriptions of animal life.[4] Both also claim that though they have given their animals language and emotions, these are, within the demands of the genre, realistic, and not anthropomorphized.

However it is not realism that entirely inspires the art of Seton and Roberts, whatever strength that lends to their work, but certain ideas which frame and condition the realism, and which give to it symbolic form. The animal heroes may live and die in the wild, being only interesting specimens of their race, but their biographies, as literature, belong in the world of myth.[5] What matters is not that everything that is told *could* have happened to a fox, or a grizzly, but that it *did* happen, and that, for the author, the life of the animal was organized according to certain basic ideas, and that in its living it demonstrated certain fundamental truths. At the heart of the myth that gives structure to the work of both Seton and Roberts is their belief that animals are rational and ethical beings, and that they rise above instinct. This is demonstrated most clearly in the ways the animals train their young to survive, and the ways in which their young respond to the challenge.[6]

Seton's story of the cottontail rabbit, Raggylugs, will serve to illustrate. The young rabbit Raggylugs is "unusually quick and bright as well as strong," and he has in his mother Molly an extremely intelligent and valiant tutor, a "true heroine," a devoted mother who finally gives her life so that her son may survive. Here, as we might expect, are the superior animals, models of intelligence and mother love. Molly's first duty is to train her son, to educate him in the skills of life. His first duty, as a successful and superior animal, is to obey. "Molly was a good little mother and gave him a careful bringing up . . . he did as he was told." Rag learns the essential rabbit lessons, to "lay low," to "freeze," and to regard the briarbush as his best friend. "All the season she kept him busy learning the tricks of the trail, and what to eat and drink and what not to touch. Day by day she worked to train him; little by little she taught him. . . ." In some of his lessons he shows himself "a veritable genius," and he even goes on to take a "post-graduate course" in how to use water. On the one occasion he is disobedient—he sits up to watch his mother lose a dog—he is severely punished, being cuffed and knocked over by Molly.

Throughout this story Seton's emphasis is on the intelligence and skill of the successful animal, the "tricks" it uses to outwit its enemies, and the way in which it is able to educate its young. Molly shows her son how to run a dog into a barbed-wire fence, how to avoid snares, and how to use water as a last resource. Animals are not mere creatures of instinct, behaving according to a set of inherited responses, but capable, within their own terms, of intelligent reasoning, of teaching and learning, and of knowing right from wrong. Rabbits, for instance, have their own language: they "have no speech . . . but they have a way of conveying ideas by a system of sounds, signs, scents, whisker-touches, movements, and example that answers the purpose of speech. . . ."

It is worth pausing here to answer some questions: is Seton not right—do animals not have some very definite ability to communicate in a language of their own, and are they not capable of some kind of inductive reasoning? Do they not, in fact, educate their young, and is there not more to animal behaviour than a set of instinctive reactions?

The modern ethologist would almost certainly approach these problems with caution, for the whole question of animal behaviour has become one of immense complexity. In 1900 there seemed to be a straightforward contrast to be made between instinctive and learned behaviour; now the first point to be made is that rigid alternatives are simplistic.[7] Even the terms have changed. The "nature or nurture" controversy has been replaced by a discussion of innate or acquired characteristics, and behaviour is now classified as "environmentally stable" or "environmentally labile." The discovery of imprinting, the process by which certain animals when young respond as a species to certain stimulae, has been contrasted to "adaptive" learning. The mental processes of animals are not simple, but they are clearly not always automatic, or mechanical, or, in the old sense, simply instinctive. Apes have been taught to communicate with humans using the American Sign Language: the higher mammals, it has been argued, have mental experiences and probably even a conscious awareness.[8]

In spite of the complexity of the problems, certain generalizations may be made. Many animals are able to learn from experience. Many animals do teach their young, chiefly by example.[9] Some animals are capable of inductive reasoning. Some other animals may be able to adapt their behaviour, by a process of trial and error, and though it might appear that they act rationally, they do not always seem to comprehend what they are doing. Considered in general terms, however, the observations and speculations of the nature writers are closer in many ways to current scientific thinking than those of their more sceptical, behaviourist contemporaries. Animals have complex means of communicating with one another: Seton's description of rabbit language, a "system of sounds, signs, scents, whiskertouches" and so on, is not fanciful, though modern naturalists might argue with the details. What matters is not the scientific accuracy of Seton's nature stories—although that itself is an interesting question—but the ideas which give his work symbolic form. By the lights of his day he played down instinct; his animals are rational creatures who educate their offspring to be obedient and successful. As such, they are intended to be models for human edification, and nature, though full of sudden and "tragic" death, is an ordered and in many ways superior world.

Seton, as a careful naturalist, frequently describes instinctive (or innate) behaviour in animals. In most cases, he regards it as an inherited substratum, a built-in defence against the early dangers of life. He speaks of an animal's "native instincts," which are supplemented by the twin teachers of life, experience and the example of fellow animals.[10] The little mountain lambs in *Lives of the Hunted,* surprised and chased by a hunter just after birth, are able to dodge and escape, for "Nature had equipped them with a set of valuable instincts." Instinct, however, takes an animal only just so far. Its role in survival is subsidiary to reason. In the story of the Don Valley partridge, for instance, Seton tells us that the partridge chicks soon graduate from instinctive to rational behaviour: "their start in life was a good mother, good legs, a few reliable instincts, and a germ of reason. It was instinct, that is, inherited habit, which taught them to hide at the word from their mother; it was instinct that taught them to follow her, but it was reason which made them keep under the shadow of her tail when the sun was smiting down. . . ." And, Seton concludes, "from that day reason entered more and more into their expanding lives."[11]

Roberts treats instinct in much the same way, as a valuable though necessarily limited body of inherited knowledge. Thus Red Fox, as befits a superior animal, has an extra amount: "he seemed to inherit with special fulness and effectiveness that endowment of ancestral knowledge which goes by the name of instinct." At the same time, of course, we are told that he is more intelligent, that he can reason, and that he is "peculiarly apt in learning from his mother." Instinct is, too, a latent skill, which can surface when necessary: in the story of **"Lone Wolf"** (***Neighbours Unknown***), the tame circus wolf who escapes to the wilds, Roberts shows us its hero rediscovering "long buried memories" of how a wolf kills. "It was as if all his life Lone Wolf had been killing bulls, so unerring was that terrible chopping snap at the great beast's throat." These are perhaps unexceptionable ideas, yet elsewhere in Roberts' work there is the definite implication that instinct is a primitive force which must be controlled and subdued by reason. This is especially true when applied to man himself (though as the highest of the "kindred" what is true for man is also true for animals). In **"The Moonlight Trails"** (***Kindred of the Wild***), we are told of a boy who loves animals and is sensitive to their feelings, who accompanies the hired man on an expedition to the woods to snare rabbits. As they set the snares the boy is moved by the primitive lust of the hunter; he feels "stirrings of a wild, predatory instinct." When they return in the morning to see what they have caught the boy is still at first in the grip of the hunting passion, but when he sees the cruel tragedy of death his more civilized feelings come to the surface. "We won't snare any more rabbits, Andy," he tells the hired man.

The gap between man and the animals, Roberts insists, is very narrow. Animals "can and do reason."[12] *Red Fox* illustrates this thesis: the whole novel is a celebration of one animal's cunning and sagacity. We are repeatedly told of Red Fox's cunning, his "nimble wits," his ingenious and deliberate schemes for evading his enemies, his prodigious memory, his ability to study a situation, to make plans, to reason. We hear how he outwits "the Boy," how he leads the hounds to their destruction, how he fools his enemy Jabe Smith. His qualities are quite obvious: "look at that cool and cunning eye," says one of his American captors. "He's got brains."

In his early education, Red Fox shows that instinct is subservient to reason. Red Fox must learn both from his mother and from experience. "It is possible (though some say otherwise!) to expect too much of instinct," Roberts tells us, and explains how a successful fox will learn his lessons, "partly by example and partly no doubt by a simple language whose subtleties evade human observation." Yet we notice that when instinct gets Red Fox into trouble, it is instinct that rescues him. His nose tells him to dig in a bees' nest for honey, and when they sting him, he runs blindly for a thicket, and automatically cools his smarting nose in the mud. These are inconsistencies: Roberts' dominant theme is the supremacy and efficacy of his hero's reason. The vixen's instructions to leave men alone have "their effect on [Red Fox's] sagacious brain," whereas his stupider brother thinks he knows better, and pays the price with his life. This incident, one should note, is at the same time an apt illustration of Darwinian theory, for it is the better animal that survives.

The intelligent young animal is also the obedient young animal. In the School of the Woods, obedience is a primary virtue. The child must obey the parent. "For a young animal," Seton said, "there is no better gift than obedience,"[13] and he demonstrated this again and again by showing us the fate of the disobedient, the young lambs who do not come when they are called, and are caught and killed, or the foolish partridge chicks who refuse to stay close to mother. The fate of Red Fox's siblings again makes the point: the weak and the foolish will not survive, but the disobedient bring trouble upon all.

The essential argument of this article should be clear by now: the fiction of both Seton and Roberts is inspired by their desire to present a moral and coherent order in the life of the wild, which is part of the greater order of the cosmos. That many of their observations of animal life are accurate is undeniable—animals do learn, they are intelligent in their way, and they are probably even capable of reason. Yet what is important in Seton and Roberts is the way the details are presented. Animals, we are told, are very much like ourselves. They obey certain laws, they demonstrate qualities we would do well to admire, they are our own kin. They inhabit what is often clearly a mythic world; they are symbols in our own ontological system. Nowhere is this more obvious than in the context of morality.

Each animal, first of all, must learn to obey the laws of its kind. Morality is not a human invention, but an integral part of all nature. "It is quite common," says Seton in *Lives of the Hunted,* "to hear conventionality and social rules derided as though they were silly man-made tyrannies. They are really important laws that, like gravitation, were here before human society began, and shaped it when it came. In all wild animals we see them grown with the mental growth of the species." The higher the animal, the more clearly developed the moral system. The better the animal—the more successful, or superior specimen—the more moral the animal. Thus superior animals fight fair, but the weak, the cowards, and the mean may well resort to dirty tricks. Krag the mountain sheep, whose strength, and size, and curling horns make him appear like a "demi-god" to his ewes, has to beat off two other rams to defend his rights to his harem. One ram fights fair and meets Krag horn to horn; the other fights foul, and attacks from the side. It is important that in this moral world the immoral ram "works his own destruction," running himself over a two hundred foot cliff to his death.

These animal laws would appear to be somewhat flexible, coloured as they are by the vision of the human observer, since occasionally even a "good" animal will break the rule of his kind to preserve himself or another. This is always done for a reason: the law may be broken in the name of the higher good. We are told, in "Raggylugs," that "all good rabbits forget their feuds when their common enemy appears." Rag's rival, the stranger, ignores this basic rule of rabbit society, trying to drive Rag into the reach of a goshawk. This is bad. Yet one sentence later we find Rag playing the same game to save himself and his mother, as he successfully lures old Thunder the hound into the nest of "the stranger." This, we infer, is good.

It is at moments like this that it is most evident that the animal story belongs not to the world of natural science, but to the world of literature. There are good animals and bad animals, and we, as readers, are always expected to be on the side of morality. Seton, however, is usually careful not to denigrate a species: each animal, of whatever kind, has some quality that a man might admire. Even the hated rat is courageous.[14] Roberts, on the other hand, lets his sympathies show: there are some species who exhibit only the worst. Such are lynx. In **"Grey Lynx's Last Hunting"** we are shown a portrait of animal cruelty, selfishness and marital hatred, whose appropriate outcome is the sordid death of the male, killed by his savage and mad mate. Both writers, in their desire to make a moral point, cross from realism into romance. Seton has a story of wolves who lynch an apparent cheat and liar,[15] and Roberts the fanciful tale of a society of animals who voluntarily resolve not to kill "within eyeshot" of a sensitive and disapproving child.[16]

Throughout Roberts' work there is an insistence on the meaning, the vitality, the harmony and the morality of the struggle of life, and in Seton, of the fairness and ultimate order of nature. Perhaps the most dramatic illustration of their essentially similar moral philosophy is Seton's short *The Natural History of the Ten Commandments* (1907), in which he finds that the Mosaic laws are not "arbitrary laws given to man, but are fundamental laws of all highly developed animals." Animals, in their own way, observe the last six of the ten commandments, and in their occasional willingness to "throw themselves on the mercy of some other power," manifest the beginnings of a spiritual life. Man, obeying the first four commandments, acknowledges the Deity; the higher animals acknowledge man.

This is an idea which, in its implications of a natural cosmic order, testifies to the true symbolic role of the animals. There is an obvious correspondence here to the writing of Seton's contemporary, Kipling, and especially to the society of *The Jungle Books* (1917). Roberts, in his preface to ***The Kindred of the Wild,*** praised the Mowgli stories, though, noting that the animals were "frankly humanized," distinguished them as a different and a separate kind of fiction from Seton's and his own. Yet the difference is one of degree, rather than kind: Kipling's jungle animals are also rational creatures, who live in a balanced and reasonably harmonious society, provided they obey the rules of their kind. There are good and superior animals such as Bagheera the panther and Baloo the bear, and evil animals such as Shere Khan the tiger and the whole tribe of monkeys. The evil are punished and the good survive. The laws of the jungle must be obeyed. Man, in the shape of Mowgli himself, is superior to all the other animals.[17]

In their insistence on certain social principles—for instance the all-important rule that the young must obey the old, and that obedience is both a necessity and a duty—Seton, Roberts and Kipling all use their animal stories to exemplify clear and precise morality. The first law an animal learns, Seton tells us, is obedience, and it is with the Fifth Commandment, "Against Disobedience," that he begins his examination of the Mosaic code of nature. This is the law "which imposes unreasoning acceptance of the benefits derivable from the experience of those over us."[18] We remember from *Red Fox* "how sternly Nature exacts a rigid observance of her rules," and how Red Fox himself is always obedient to his mother, for "it was no small part of his intelligence that he knew how much better his mother knew than he." Obedience for Kipling is the first law of the jungle; every cub of the wolf pack must learn it:

> Now these are the Laws of the Jungle, and many and mighty are they;
>
> But the head and the hoof of the Law and the haunch and the hump is—Obey!

It could be argued that the evidence for the success of this moral philosophy, and the public acceptance of an anti-Darwinian optimism, can be found in the popularity of the nature writers. Both Seton's and Roberts' nature stories went through edition after edition at the beginning of the century, and one would suspect that Kipling's *Jungle Books* were read to generations of young listeners. All three writers supported the status quo; a child, if he paid attention to the moral lessons, would surely be improved. There is, however, one other means of estimating the popular encouragement given the nature writers, and that in a surprising though socially significant place—the Boy Scouts. The Scouts were also trained to be superior animals, to be brave, helpful, and especially, obedient. The third and most important part of the Scout Promise was obedience to the Scout Law. Curiously, their founder, General Robert Baden-Powell, used the work of the nature writers, and of Kipling, when he came to write the manual for his movement, *Scouting For Boys.*

"Any naturalist," Baden-Powell told his scouts, "will tell you that animals largely owe their cleverness to their mothers."[19] Older animals taught younger animals, and they taught them to obey. Instinct was not half as important as training. Seton was closely associated with the scouting movement from the first, having in fact organized a "woodcraft" group for the boys of America, and in *Scouting For Boys,* Baden-Powell used many of his ideas. Baden-Powell also recommended several of Seton's books to his readers, but when it came to the crucial questions of education, of training and obedience, and the naturalists' models of good conduct, he turned not to Seton or Roberts but to the American writer, William Long. Long's work has now sunk without trace; reading him one can see why he would appeal to a straightforward moralist like Baden-Powell. Much more sentimental and didactic than his contemporaries, and, one would guess, a less careful observer of animal life, Long made no pretense at Darwinism, but preferred to see in the school of the woods "no tragedies or footlight effects of woes and struggles, but rather a wholesome, cheerful life to make one glad and send him back to his own school with deeper wisdom and renewed courage."[20] He was quite clear on the unimportance of instinct, and he had no doubt at all about the necessity for obedience: "when one turns to animals, it is often with the wholesome, refreshing sense that here is a realm where the law of life is known and obeyed. To the wild creature obedience is everything. It is the deep, unconscious tribute of ignorance to wisdom, of weakness to power."

In *Scouting For Boys* Baden-Powell quoted Long at some length. "The Old Wolf" himself was a military man, and he believed in old-fashioned virtues; the scouting movement, though encouraging individual initiative, was authoritarian, its aim to turn out patriots and model citizens. It was important that boys be well trained, and if, in the stories of the nature writers, they had models of good behaviour, these were models that would naturally appeal to boys. Even the scout patrols were named after animals. When it came time to form the junior organization, Baden-Powell went to Kipling, and with his permission took his inspiration from *The Jungle Book.* Significantly, the first "law" of the Wolf Cubs was "the Cub gives in to the old Wolf."[21]

We have in this last detail the clue to the stories of animal heroes. Animals are not so much animals as emblems, symbols of a more perfect world. Baden-Powell called himself the "Old Wolf," and Seton used the wolf paw mark as his signature. To each, the wolf was a superior creature, a star in an ordered and moral universe. The animal stories thus are best considered mythopoeically: Old Silverspot, Seton's crow, drilling his troops and training his youngsters, could well be a model for General Baden-Powell. Red Fox, in his bravery and intelligence, might stand as a shining example to any young scout.

Seen in this light, the lives of the animals resemble, in their structure, the life of the mythic hero: they are born, go through early trials, win their kingdom and die. Some, like Seton's Krag, who returns after death to haunt his murderer, even have an apotheosis. Fate in the shape of a Darwinian catastrophe ensures in the evitable death of the hero a technical tragedy, though the prevailing note in both Seton and Roberts is one of life ever renewed. Man, especially in Seton's stories, may be part of a corrupt and decadent postlapsarian world. In Roberts, man's ignorance and callousness are crimes against nature, though innocence and goodness are often represented by a child or youth, the sensitive girl or boy who knows and loves the creatures of the woods. In Roberts also, the landscape is often magical or enchanted.

In all these details it is clear that the animal tales of both Seton and Roberts take their inspiration and structure as much from literature as from life. In their use of the conventions of the romance, in their echoing of a mythic pattern, and in their quite definite symbolic treatment of animal character, both men translate the indiscriminate facts of nature into the ordered patterns of art. At the centre of their fiction is their belief in moral and rational animals, which in its extensiveness and pervasive force, takes on the quality of an organizing myth. It is ironic that at a time when the forces of instinct, intuition and the unconscious were being rediscovered in man, the power of the Logos was found in the kingdoms of the brute beasts.

Notes

1. *The Kindred of the Wild* (1902; rpt. Boston: Page, 1921), pp. 15-29.
2. For a summary of the history of the concept of instinct see W. H. Thorpe, *Animal Nature and Human Nature* (New York: Doubleday, 1974), pp. 134 ff.
3. "Kneepads" appears in Seton's *Lives of the Hunted* (1901), "Red Fox" in Roberts' *Red Fox* (1905). Roberts wrote over two hundred stories: I have chosen to refer only to those that are (1) best known, and (2) written from the animal's point of view, or (3) contain some statement on or illustration of the instinct problem.
4. Both Seton and Roberts were embroiled in a controversy on the realism of their stories, having, in 1903, come under attack from the naturalist, John Burroughs. W. J. Keith argues that the problem of realism is important: "the stories are convincing only in so far as they can be accepted as at least possible within the world of nature" (*Charles G. D. Roberts* [Toronto: Copp Clark, 1969], p. 93). This is a reasonable view, to which it is worth adding that it depends on the genre—if the author's intention *is* realism, and not romance. A difficult case is presented by, for example, *The Heart of the Ancient Wood,* which, to use Northrop Frye's terms, falls into the mode of romance. In this tale a loving, intelligent, maternal bear named Kroof protects the child Miranda, and eventually rescues Miranda and her mother from a pair of wicked men. Did Roberts expect his readers to take this fairytale as "realistic" fiction?
5. See Joseph Gold, "The Precious Speck of Life," *Canadian Literature,* No. 26 (Autumn 1965), pp. 22-32. In this important and provocative article, Gold argues for an archetypal and mythic interpretation of Roberts' animal stories. He sees the essential myth in Roberts as that of the vitality and persistence of life in its cycles. Roberts, he states, left a body of work "consistently arranged about a clear idea of the order of life itself."
6. These were the very points on which Seton and Roberts were challenged by John Burroughs, when he returned to the attack in 1905, in his book *Ways of Nature.* See Keith, pp. 91-92.
7. See Thorpe, pp. 151 ff. For more extensive discussion, see R. F. Ewer, *Ethology of Mammals* (London: Elek, 1973).
8. See Donald R. Griffen, *The Question of Animal Awareness* (New York: Rockefeller Univ. Press, 1976).
9. See Ewer, pp. 277-78.
10. "Badlands Billy," in *Animal Heroes* (New York: Grosset and Dunlap, n.d.), pp. 124-25.
11. Twenty-three years later Seton retreated from this position, and declared that "although an animal is much helped by its mother's teaching, it owes still more to the racial teaching, which is instinct. . . ." See his foreword to *Bannertail* (London: Hodder and Stoughton, 1922).
12. *Kindred,* p. 23.
13. *Lives of the Hunted,* p. 43.
14. See "The Rat and the Rattlers," *Mainly About Wolves* (London: Methuen, 1937), pp. 171-79.
15. "The Wolf and the Primal Law," *Mainly About Wolves,* pp. 121-31. Here, as so often in Seton, it is man himself who is the villain.
16. *The Heart of the Ancient Wood,* p. 128.
17. For a discussion of the educational and moral didacticism of *The Jungle Books* see Shamsul Islam, *Kipling's "Law"* (London: Macmillan, 1975), pp. 122-31.
18. *Natural History,* p. 7.
19. R. S. S. Baden-Powell, *Scouting For Boys* (London: Cox, 1908), p. 124.
20. *School of the Woods: Some Life Studies of Animal Instincts and Animal Training* (Boston: Ginn, 1902), p. 21.
21. *The Wolf-Cub's Handbook* (1916; rpt. London: Pearson, 1923), p. 39.

A. C. Morrell (essay date spring 1980)

SOURCE: Morrell, A. C. "Symbolism and Spatial Patterning in Four Short Stories by Charles G. D. Roberts." *Studies in Canadian Literature* 5 (spring 1980): 138-51.

[In the following essay, Morrell analyzes Roberts' expression of fear through symbolism and spatial patterning in "The Stone Dog," "In the Accident Ward," "The Barn on the Marsh," and "The Hill of Chastisement."]

Charles G. D. Roberts' reputation in Canada in this century has changed almost decade by decade into the shape currently required by critics. He was early regarded as the dignified founding father of a truly Canadian literature; then dismissed in the 1940s as hopelessly Victorian in style and attitude. He has been acclaimed in the 1960s, principally by Joseph Gold, as a philosopher and myth-maker of the first rank;[1] then in the 1970s defended by Robin Matthews in the terms of Canadian nationalism.[2] All of these attitudes are attempts to portray Roberts' work as a monolith either to be toppled in the interests of modernity or to be admired from afar. In this decade, monuments are sceptically regarded, and attempts are being made to document fully the lives of Canadian writers. The Roberts Collected Letters should soon appear; they will reveal more of Roberts the man than has been possible to know heretofore.

It is not only in personal reminiscences and letters that the human Roberts can be found. In his poetry and stories he is often an intensely personal and expressive writer. His distinctive way of seeing, especially his organization of landscape detail, his response to people and animals, his moods, fears, loves and hates are recorded throughout the work itself. In order to prove my point, I shall examine the symbolism in a group of visionary stories, all of which appeared in ***Earth's Enigmas.*** **"The Stone Dog," "In the Accident Ward"** and **"The Barn on the Marsh"** were included in the 1896 edition; **"The Hill of Chastisement"** was added to the 1903 edition.[3] These stories leave the same impression as do poems such as "The Herring Weir," "The Flight," "One Night," and "The Footpath": they record fear, fear of life in the form of sexual guilt, and most especially, fear of death. I shall examine how these fears are communicated through symbols and spatial patterning and, also, whether the fears are adequately resolved in the tone and form of the endings.

The four stories are autobiographical. In the "Prefatory Note" to the 1903 edition of ***Earth's Enigmas,*** Roberts writes:

> Most of the stories in this collection attempt to present one or another of those problems of life or nature to which, as it appears to many of us, there is no adequate solution within sight. Others are the almost literal transcript of dreams which seemed to me to have a coherency, completeness and symbolic significance sufficiently marked to justify me in setting them down.[4]

And Pomeroy emphasizes that **"The Stone Dog," "In the Accident Ward"** and **"The Hill of Chastisement"** came from dreams. **"The Barn on the Marsh"** was based on an actual experience of Roberts' early youth, when he and his father discovered their neighbour hanged in his barn.[5] I stress the fact of autobiography for two reasons: first, so that my reading of these works will not seem entirely fanciful; and, more importantly, because they are self-admittedly Roberts' own dreams and visions, organized into symbols and spatial patterns by his unconscious mind, we may come to recognize similarities in other works and so have a method by which to comprehend Roberts' work as the production of a man, rather than as some vague, grand, philosophical system.

In all the works under consideration we are presented with the startlingly similar spatial image of the path. The writer walks along it in fear and trembling. Its direction may be downward, to a nearly-sunken door in a wall, or along a mountain path from a cave; it may be upward, from a gate up a hill path; or it may be a level path leading past an old barn: each is essentially the same organization of space and experience. It is well known that we can see objects, plants, animals, and landscapes in terms of ourselves, both our mental activities and our body parts. Depending on how this perceived correspondence is communicated, we term it pathetic fallacy, personification, or anthropomorphism. All have their basis in a projection outward from primary human sensation and experience into an identification with other aspects of the world. Some writers regard this process as being very primitive, that is, as something we do which preliterate people did in their attempts to order and explain their world.[6] Roberts consistently uses this identification device, whether as metaphor (naked hills, dead cities, choked stairs) or as image, which, because of its physical associations, becomes symbolic. It is this usually barely-understood symbolism which gives his works their peculiar power. In these four stories, and in many of the other stories and poems, the path leads to, from, or past a doorway or gate which may be open or closed. This is the imagery of vagina and uterus; Roberts' most consistent effort is re-entry, his most consistent failure expulsion. Death is encountered on all of the paths. Such works attempt to exorcise, by veiling them in symbols, both the anxiety caused by realization that the path from the womb leads inevitably to the tomb, and the guilt occasioned by a desire to regain permanently the protected original environment. Guilt is increased by the intuition that what is desired is a return to pre-life, which, as it would obliterate individual consciousness, is an equivalent of death. The imaginative connection commonly made between sex and death, especially for the male in so far as he views the sexual act as an attempt to re-enter the womb and orgasm as a momentary metaphorical death, can mean that that guilt is thereby doubled and transferred to all sexual activity. Proof that Roberts is expressing such fears and desires must come from the works themselves.

"The Stone Dog" is the dream most consciously shaped into a perfectly unified story. It has all the proper ingredients of the horror tale: a rational, ordinary man is placed in a strangely disquieting setting; a local folk belief in buried treasure behind a locked door is related; there is an attempt to overcome irrational foreboding and to open the door; supernatural forces accompanied by the terrific storm intervene to prevent the treasure being discovered; and a return to the ordinary daylight world is experienced in which, however, traces and proofs of the terror remain.

The narrator finds himself alone at sunset in an unknown landscape which is "gray" and "desolate." He is filled with "a vague apprehensiveness": the marshes give off a "sick metallic odor," the weeds smell disagreeably, there is a "chill, damp smell of mouldering stone-work," his eyes and ears are strained with watchfulness. Under these impressions and the "weird fantasies" which oppress him, he explores the fountain which supports the stone dog and its vicinity. The area is characterized by débris, weeds and a stagnant pool, and farther afield by "inexorable sterility." The dog appears to be sleeping, except that its half-open eyes seem to watch the approaches to the doorway in the wall. It is a realistic piece of sculpture:

> In its gathered limbs, though relaxed and perfectly at rest, a capacity for swift and terrible action seemed to hold itself in reserve, and a breath almost appeared to come from the half-opened jaws . . .[7]

From the fountain, the narrator turns to the sunken doorway. Seven "steep narrow stairs of brick work" lead down to it, and the rusty iron doorhandle is "curiously wrought of two dragons intertwisted neck and tail." We might well stop at this point to note that the dog, who watches the doorway and contains power in reserve, is an echo of Cerberus, the Greek guardian dog of the underworld; and that dragons in Eastern mythology are benevolent symbols of fertility, power and creativity, often figuring as the custodians of hidden treasure.[8]

The narrator is irresistibly attracted to this door, and intends to open it, although he has not yet heard about the treasure that is supposed to lie behind it. This, so far, is a picture of a man in conflict. He is afraid, yet wants to descend, force open and enter. As he grasps the handle, "a chill of terror crept tingling" through his frame. He decides to wait until the next day to try the door again; as he withdraws, he feels the dog's eyes "piercing" him.

He is, all the next morning, obsessed with "the spell of the dead outskirts, of the shadowless dead marshes, of that mysterious and inscrutable dog." He returns, playfully splashes water over the dog, and is reassured to see the drops rolling off the stone "like quicksilver." The area is still perceived as unhealthy: "a greenish mist steamed up, and seemed to poison the sunlight streaming through it." "The twisting dragons of the doorhandle attracted me as I drew near." He descends the steps, hears the water of the fountain behind him cease murmuring, as it had the day before; a "chilly sweat" breaks out on him and he turns round suddenly to see the head of the dog turned directly toward him, "and its eyes, now wide open, flamed upon me with strange and awful whiteness." The narrator calms himself by returning to the fountain, where he finds the dog in its original position. Having persuaded himself that he is the victim of baseless fears, he turns for the third time to the locked door. Again, the sound of the fountain stops, but he steels himself, chips away at the soft stone with his knife, and jerks hard on the bolt which gives a little, with a clatter of falling stucco. But he is horrified and turns to find:

> There, at the very top of the steps, crouched the dog, its head thrust down close to my face. The stone jaws were grinning apart. A most appalling menace was in the wide, white eyes. I know I tugged once more upon the bolt, for a great piece of the door and arch crumbled and came away; and I thought, as the head closed down, that I made a wild spring to get past the crouching form. Then reason and consciousness forsook me.

The demon-guardian of the place has done its work well.

The rest of the story consists of a partial rationalization of the experience. The narrator awakens in a "darkish, garlicky hut, with the morning sunlight streaming in the open door," and hears the history of the fountain and doorway from the muleteer who found him "lying, in a stupor, face down, across the basin of the fount, and directly beneath the jaws of the dog." A storm had come up in the night, and then an earthquake which toppled many old walls. The muleteer had gone back to the place at sunrise, hoping to find the reputed treasure revealed by the disturbance. But though the fountain and dog were untouched, the whole wall had fallen and buried the steps and doorway in masses of ruin. The narrator returns to his lodgings and though his clothing is not torn, only dusty, his shoulder is green and livid, "bruised on either side with deep prints of massive teeth."

Although the narrator has been returned to the daylight, rational world, the story does not negate what he believed he experienced. The terror the place inspires in the local people, the storm and earthquake which leave the stone dog intact, and the teeth marks in his flesh convince the narrator, so that he has "ceased to regard as necessarily absurd whatever I find it difficult to explain." This on the one hand completes aesthetically the traditional horror story; on the other the dream experience organizes unconscious desires and fears into a symbolic whole. Roberts' intense desire to enter an old room, to find the buried treasure of fertility and creativity is in itself terrifying, and his effort to do so is prohibited by the guardian of that place. Such symbols as the stone dog are projections from Roberts' own mind. Within himself, a figure of great strength and ferocity lurks. The fear that this figure will literally tear him to pieces if he follows his urge to return to the womb or to the female principle has been confirmed by the dream. The story insists upon the reality of this unresolved personal conflict.

"In the Accident Ward" is a straightforward recounting of a dream and of waking. It lacks the artistic completeness of **"The Stone Dog"** or, indeed, of **"The Barn on the Marsh"** or **"The Hill of Chastisement." "In the Accident Ward"** is a slight piece, valuable only because it, too, uses certain symbols which are central to Roberts' work.

The parts of the story, dream and waking, are not well fused. It begins, like **"The Stone Dog,"** with landscape description, but this beginning is brief. The use of landscape is symbolic rather than scene-setting. The grass is gray, "of a strange and dreadful pallor." The sky above the hill is also "gray and thick, with the color of a parched interminable twilight." The narrator stands in the middle of a "blood-red road of baked clay" and prepares to ascend the hill obliquely by a "narrow footpath, red as blood." Behind him the road descends into "a little blood-red hollow . . . crossed by an open gate." He looks back at this gate, through which he has emerged, and sees gray leopards and a small ape standing on tip-toe and eyeing him with a "dreadful curiosity." These beasts withdraw at an incomprehensible whispered word. As the dreamer looks to the summit of the hill, he sees, "cleaving the gasses in flight as swift as an arrow," a figure, all gray, being pursued by a tall and terrible second figure, who is the "Second Death." The fleeing ghost falls at the narrator's feet, clasping his knees in "awful fear." The dreamer himself no longer fears; he reaches out and grasps the pursuing horror by the throat.

> I heard the being laugh, and the iron grip of my own strong and implacable fingers seemed to close with a keen agony upon my own throat, and a curtain seemed to fall over my eyes.[9]

This ends the dream section of the story. In it, we see an opposite spatial arrangement and movement from **"The Stone Dog."** The open-gated hollow has been passed through. The dreamer would be prevented from re-entering by the animals (recalling the function of the stone dog) but since he has no intention of trying, they are called off. He is left alone on the blood red path of life, gazing upward to the empty horizon across a sterile landscape of long gray grass. The figures which initially terrorize him are a ghost and Second Death. His attempt to kill Second Death turns into suicide, proving that such figures as the stone dog and Second Death are projections from the unconscious which cannot be destroyed. The movement in this dream is paranoiac. Vicious animals behind, death ahead: after birth, there is grayness all around and uphill bloody struggle with the fear of death as a companion until the end. This dream documents not the birth trauma, not an attempt to return to the womb, but the agony of moving alone through an uncompromisingly bleak life at the mercy of self-destructive impulses.

The ending is both aesthetically and psychologically inadequate. The dreamer regains consciousness in an accident ward. The bandages, the sharp pain at his throat, the memory of the collision calm him. He allows the "terrible scene," that is, the dream, to slip from his grasp and hears the doctor say, "He'll sleep now for a couple of hours." The dream world has been vanquished by the reassuring facts of disaster and pain. The ending denies the dream's symbolic truth. It is impossible to know now whether the waking portion of the story was tacked on later, when Roberts came to prepare it for publication, or whether it is a direct account of the strange way the gradually-waking mind will attempt to make sense of what has gone before. In either case, it is apparent that Roberts found the dream's organization of setting and internal figures too frightening to accept.

The autobiographical **"The Barn on the Marsh"** is important because it repeats, in Roberts' waking life, the fears and symbols of his dreams. The tale begins when Roberts was seven years old. His father, the rector, delighted in gardening early in the morning and insisted on the child's participation.

> Weeding, and especially such thorough, radical weeding as alone would satisfy the rector's conscience, was my detestation . . . But I never found courage to betray my lack of sympathy in all its iciness. The sight of the rector's enthusiasm filled me ever with a sense of guilt, and I used to weed quite diligently, at times.[10]

Several points must be made briefly here. Roberts does not call his father "father" but "the rector," emphasizing the man's moral and spiritual function. He roots up and casts away evil growths in the garden: weeding satisfies the rector's conscience, not his aesthetic sense. His son is being taught to reject sin, shown 'the right way' through this metaphorical activity. And the son feels guilty: his father's approach to life is essentially antipathetic to him. Late in life, Roberts' dreams of his father always included their walking together in a garden or across a beautiful landscape (Pomeroy, pp. 339-40).

One morning, the rector, probably digging vigorously, breaks his hoe off at the handle. The driven and guilty child responds in this way:

> I stopped work with alacrity, and gazed with commiserating interest, while I began wiping my muddy little fingers on my knickerbockers in bright anticipation of some new departure which should put a pause to the weeding.

The new departure is a trauma which permanently imprints itself and all the details which preceded it on the boy's mind. They go together to their neighbour's barn to repair the hoe, and find him just inside the barn door, hanging dead, his face distorted and purple.

The narrative now skips ahead to a time when Roberts is eighteen, a college student visiting his old neighbourhood on holiday. He has the habit of calling on friends who live two miles from the old rectory. They "possessed some strange charm which would never permit me to say good-night at anything like a seasonable hour." He takes the road across the marsh, where the old barn now stands, as a short-cut home. It was not a pleasant road in wet weather, "but good enough for me at all times in the frame of mind in which I found myself." This frame of mind was occasioned by, as we may guess, and Pomeroy confirms, the company of young women. They were the daughters of Sheriff Botsford.

In spite of his high spirits, the description of the landscape turns sombre. The road he walks is bordered on either side by a high rail fence; the Lombardy poplars are "ghostly and perishing"; the miles of "naked marsh" stretch away to the "lonely, shifting waters of the Basin"; small black clouds "stream dizzily" across the moon's face; the barn "with its big doors opening toward the road" stands beyond the fence. Until this night, he has given only impersonal remembrance to associations the old barn has for him. On this occasion, Roberts is self-absorbed, "scarce noticing even the strange play of the moon-shadows over the marshes": just the right conditions for visions or visitations. A short way past the barn, he experiences a "creeping sensation" about his skin, and "a thrill of nervous apprehension" makes him stop suddenly and look behind. We have seen this pattern of behavior, this fear of something watching or lurking behind him, in both **"The Stone Dog"** and **"In the Accident Ward"**: also, here again, he is on a path. Hanging in the opening of the barn doors, swaying almost imperceptibly in the wind, hangs the body of the neighbour.

The rest of the story details Roberts' inner struggle between horror and common sense. He approaches the apparition gradually. Peering through the fence rails only confirms that the neighbour, his every feature distinct and horrible in its distortion, indeed hangs there. Roberts climbs the fence, the clouds thicken over the face of the moon, the light fades rapidly. Sickened but resolute, he walks up to "the swaying thing" and touches it with his walking stick. It is a piece of wood and iron, some portion of a mowing-machine or reaper which had been repainted then hung up across the doorpole to dry. Roberts is relieved and leaves. But as he climbs the fence:

> I gave a parting glance toward the yawning doorway of the barn on the marsh. There, as plain as before I had pierced the bubble, swung the body of my neighbour. And all the way home, though I would not turn my head, I felt it at my heels.

This story ends with a rational debunking of the vision. A piece of machinery, after all, not a man, hangs in the doorway. But the concluding sentences quoted above emphasize the difference between rational and irrational, factual truth and imaginative truth: for Roberts, the hanging man is an inescapable reality.

Pomeroy comments that this experience shows Roberts' subordination of imagination to reason as a prevailing characteristic throughout his entire life (p. 26). Her superficial interpretation overlooks both the ending and the story's symbolic organization. Roberts was self-absorbed in the sort of reverie which would recall all the childhood associations to the barn. Guiltily pleased that the rector was thwarted by the broken hoe, the child had wiped his muddy hands on his trousers. The next sight he recalls is the hanging man. For children, irrational conjunctions of cause and effect order the universe. The hanged neighbour was hanged *because of* the child's guilty feelings: he was rehanged because Roberts was at that later moment experiencing a similar guilt associated with a desire for pleasure and silent defiance of the rector's admonitions to "weed" diligently. The fact that Roberts was returning from the Botsford girls demonstrates the way in which sexual guilt (which does not necessarily follow only sexual activity *per se*) can subsume all guilt. Also, as in the other stories under discussion, great emotional intensity is expressed in connection with this spatial patterning of road and doorway. The feminine image of open doors contains the image of guilt, the hanging man: this can draw Roberts away from the path and inspire uncomprehended fear as he goes on his way.

"The Hill of Chastisement" is another account of a dream. Unlike **"In the Accident Ward"** its impact is not weakened by a denying conclusion, and unlike **"The Stone Dog"** it is not shaped into a unified horror story. It is presented in itself, without comment; here, the symbols which express Roberts' unconscious fears are gathered together and summed up in devastating culmination.

It is night. The dreamer dwells in a cave-mouth, midway up the steep slope of a hill, doing penance for an unnamed sin. The scene is described in body metaphors. The hill, "naked and rocky," has "terrific ribs"; from the abyss comes a silently rolling smoke, "full-bosomed and in haste"; grinning faces flame through the smoke, as "the white faces of the drowned gleam up through a black water."[11] This is a vision of hell. The faces expect the narrator's rejection from the cave; they lie in wait. Frantically, he lashes himself "more fiercely with the knotted leather scourge," throws himself down with prayers and cries at "the low stone barrier which cut me off from the sanctuary of the inner cave."

Within this sanctuary sits an old man, "a saint":

> . . . in a glory of clear and pure light, so penetrating that it revealed the secrets of my breast, yet so strictly reserved that no least beam of its whiteness escaped to pierce the dread of the outer gloom. He sat with grave head bowed continually over a book that shone like crystal, and his beard fell to his feet.

This figure in the womb-like sanctuary, with shining book and knowledge of the dreamer's guilt, is a reappearance of the rector.

The narrator suddenly grows aware that he must go out to "tread the rough path which ran from the cave mouth, skirting the gulf of faces." This path encircles the hill, coming again to the cave from the other side. He knows that if he could return to the cave from that other side, "the holy eyes would lift and look upon me from the sanctuary of light." Here again is the symbol of the road of life, which it is necessary to travel in order to arrive at the peace and safety of the afterlife, associated with the cave or womb of prelife, where Roberts and his father will surely meet again.

The dreamer sets forth trembling, the gloom deepens and the thin laughter from the faces in the smoke grows shriller. He tries to run, but his hope becomes blotted out "under a sense of nameless desolation," for far across the smoke and faces he sees a peaceful evening country-side with secure cottages, their windows warm with the hearth-fire lights. As if the cottage walls were made of glass, his eyes pierce them to see within safety and love: his forsakenness overwhelms him. So far, this is a picture of terrorized guilt and despondency. Behind him forever are the safety of the womb, the forgiveness and love of the father; alone on a dark rocky path he is surrounded by mocking faces; in the distance he can see the peace and security of home life available to others but denied to him. He does not yet yield, but drags himself forward by the rough edges of the rocks, hearing "all the air full of the thin laughter of the faces." He comes upon a heap of stones with the base of a wooden pillar rising out of it. Believing it a hillside calvary, a last refuge of such lost ones as himself, his heart almost breaks with joy as he clings to the base of the wooden upright. The cruelly ironic conclusion deserves full quotation:

> As I grasped my sanctuary, the air rang with loud laughter; the faces, coming out of the smoke, sprang wide-eyed and flaming close about me; a red flare shattered the darkness. Clutching importunately, I lifted up my eyes. My refuge was not a calvary. I saw it clear. It was a reeking gibbet.

Here again is the hanged man. As was hinted in **"The Barn on the Marsh,"** the hanged neighbour, having first been associated with Roberts' guilt feelings, became a totally internalized figure, that part of him which was perpetually sinful and in fear of punishment. **"The Hill of Chastisement,"** incidentally, makes an imaginative association of Christ on the cross, dying for the sins of humanity, with the common criminal hanged for his crime. Expecting forgiveness, the dreamer finds retribution. We may see in this a deep disbelief that the promises of Christianity have any power to ease the pain of rejection and regret or to prevent shameful death. Also, we may see here a comment on Roberts' father, and his father's faith, made in the light of hard psychological experience.

A full study of Roberts' use of symbolism has yet to be made. There is a remarkable coherency throughout the *oeuvre* of symbols, spatial patterning, movement through landscape, and themes of loss and death. A few poems which are similar in symbolic organization and meaning to the stories I have discussed are: "The Flight" (1880), a mysterious rendering of a woman's flight from murder up a mountain to join her company of witches and devils in the circle of torchlight; "One Night" (1880), a horrified recognition of death and evil as part of oneself followed by the suggestion of Christian redemption; "The Footpath" (1884), an association of a path which leads to an old house with a lost love; and "The Herring Weir" (1893), in which the black trail made by the cart leading from a house on the hill to the water's edge represents Roberts' paralyzed apprehension of certain death, both in the natural world and for himself. These examples can, no doubt, be multiplied. We may also suppose that the poems and stories which detail the fortuitous rescue of a child from imminent death represent the same feelings of helplessness and despair which have been temporarily denied by Roberts' insistence on a happy ending.

A happier dream, using much the same symbolism as the visionary stories, is recorded by Pomeroy as occurring late in Roberts' life. He used to tell this "humorous dream" as a joke on himself:

> I was driving alone through a level land in a two-wheeled "sulky." Although it was broad daylight, the level landscape on either hand was a cold grey and the road we travelled a vivid red. (His dreams were always colourful.) Presently we came to a hill and the path led straight up, almost perpendicularly, to the top. The horse stopped, but I said, "The tracks go up this steep and where others go, we can go." So up went the horse as easily as a fly up a window-pane. We travelled the same grey land for a little while and then the track led perpendicularly down to a level some twenty-five or thirty feet lower. Again the horse stopped, but again I said, "Old fellow, others have gone this way. Where they have gone, we can go." He obediently went, and without any difficulty whatever we made the descent and continued our journey through the same flat landscape. At length, however, we came to a perpendicular precipice of several thousand feet and looked over a wide and beautiful green country. Again the horse stopped. Again I said, "Where others have gone we can

> go." Still the horse balked and craned his neck over the precipice. Impatiently I said, "Come along. Let's get going," and flicked him gently with the whip. Instead of going, he turned squarely around between the shafts, stuck a huge gaunt head over the dash-board, eyed me sternly, and said, "No you don't, Charlie." Then I woke up.
>
> (Pomeroy p. 340)

The first thing we notice in "The Precipice Dream" is the similarity of the landscape to that in **"In the Accident Ward."** Here, he is not alone on the path: that symbol is no longer terrifying. The hostile animals of **"The Stone Dog"** and **"In the Accident Ward"** have been transformed into the friendly companion and helper, the horse. The self-flagellation of **"The Hill of Chastisement"** has been modified into "gentle" urging of an animal. Interestingly, the horse repeats the function of the dragons of **"The Stone Dog."** They symbolized fertility and creativity: the horse recalls Pegasus. Poets have long claimed the winged steed for their companion and said his second name was Inspiration. "In thoughts, in dreams, sufficiently fearless minds may ride the wide-plumed animal to any heights."[12] Roberts' horse does not much resemble Pegasus, we may say, being in the main a docile, agreeable creature. But at the precipice, Inspiration saves the poet from certain death. The "beautiful green country" stands in sharp contrast to the grey landscape and red path of the first part of the dream. It is an echo of the peaceful evening countryside seen from afar in **"The Hill of Chastisement,"** representing something infinitely desirable and, still, infinitely unattainable. It is Heaven, haven: but he will have to die to reach it. This dream voices Roberts' acceptance that his time has not yet come.

This late dream is an assertion of the importance and life-giving powers of Roberts' creative activities. The hidden treasure of **"The Stone Dog"** has been found, the destructive inner figures harnessed, all re-incorporated into one benign force for self-preservation and continued creative power.

Far from being the philosopher and myth-maker who serenely stands apart from struggle, pain and death in the natural world, accepting and artistically documenting, Roberts used his creative gifts to express, within the framework of natural history and consistent symbolism, his intense, moment-to-moment involvement with life. He was able to allay desolating fears of living and of death by expressing them. That Roberts' dreams accomplished this ordering for him is the best evidence we have to support a search for similar patterning in the wholly "made" or consciously contrived works.

Notes

1. Joseph Gold, "The Precious Spark of Life," *Canadian Literature,* No. 26 (Autumn 1965), 22-32.
2. Robin Matthews, "Charles G. D. Roberts and the Destruction of the Canadian Imagination," *Journal of Canadian Fiction,* I, 1 (Winter 1972), 47-56.
3. The publishing history of Roberts' stories indicates that between 1887 and 1900, he wrote animal stories, historical romances, backwoods tales and visionary stories. The fashion for animal stories was set by Ernest Thompson Seton in 1898: from 1900 Roberts published only backwoods and animal stories. The vogue neatly coincided with one of the two types of tales he wrote supremely well. If that vogue had turned to the visionary and psychological, he would have supplied them to the public with equal facility and success.
4. Charles G. D. Roberts, "Prefatory Note" to *Earth's Enigmas* (Boston: L. C. Page and Co., 1910), p. 5.
5. E. M. Pomeroy, *Sir Charles G. D. Roberts: A Biography* (Toronto: Ryerson Press, 1943), pp. 10-11, 140.
6. Otto Rank, *Art and Artist* (New York: Alfred A. Knopf, 1932), pp. 230-231, 258.
7. Roberts, "The Stone Dog," *Earth's Enigmas,* p. 247.
8. Alexander Eliot, *Myths* (New York: McGraw-Hill Bok Company, 1976), pp. 180, 181.
9. Roberts, "In the Accident Ward," *Earth's Enigmas,* p. 121.
10. Roberts, "The Barn on the Marsh," *Earth's Enigmas,* p. 221.
11. Roberts, "The Hill of Chastisement," *Earth's Enigmas,* pp. 197, 198.
12. Eliot, p. 160.

Thomas R. Dunlap (essay date spring 1987)

SOURCE: Dunlap, Thomas R. "'The Old Kinship of Earth': Science, Man, and Nature in the Animal Stories of Charles G. D. Roberts." *Journal of Canadian Studies* 22, no. 1 (spring 1987): 104-20.

[*In the following essay, Dunlap considers the role of science in Roberts's animal stories, arguing that their "ideology . . . owed as much to nineteenth-century biology, particularly to Darwinian evolution, as it did to Romanticism or the Canadian wilderness."*]

Since the 1890s, when Ernest Thompson Seton and Charles G. D. Roberts developed the genre, "realistic" animal stories have been popular with the public and ignored by the critics. This has certainly been the case with Charles G. D. Roberts, who wrote about two hundred animal stories over a period of thirty years, but is remembered, if at all, as one of the Confederation poets. His prose, critics thought, was just work he did for money. In 1965 Joseph Gold rejected this view, arguing that Roberts's animal stories were not potboilers but the "only sustained attempt" ever made to create a "coherent view of the world which man inhabits" using the material of the Canadian wilderness. They showed an articulated ideology and mastery of technique which should, Gold said, place Roberts in the front rank of Canadian literature.[1]

Later critics, if they have not fully shared Gold's views, have at least seen the stories as an important reflection of Canada and late Victorian culture. W. J. Keith and Margaret Atwood pointed out that Canadians invented and have dominated the field, and Atwood believed that the genre was the "key to an important facet of the Canadian psyche."[2] James Polk saw the stories as an attempt to mediate between man and nature; Robert MacDonald viewed them as part of a popular revolt against Darwinian determinism; and John Wadland found in the fiction of one of the preeminent animal story writers, Ernest Thompson Seton, a critique of modern North American civilization.[3]

Contemporaries, and the authors themselves, would have agreed that the stories were more than popular literature. The "nature-faking" controversy that Burroughs set off in 1903 attracted the attention of the serious part of the popular press, of scientists, and of many educated North Americans, all arguing about "correct" natural history and its use in building in the young a "healthy" interest in the outdoors.[4] Roberts believed that the "animal story, as we now have it is a potent emancipator. . . . It helps us to return to nature, without requiring that we at the same time return to barbarism. It leads us back to the old kinship of earth, without asking us to relinquish by way of toll any part of the wisdom of the ages, any fine essential of the 'large result of time.'" Our life in nature, "far behind though it lies in the long upward march of being," is nevertheless a touchstone, a life to which we can and must return for refreshment and even wisdom, and the animal story will be our guide.[5]

Modern critical work has, while recognizing the importance of the animal story, neglected or distorted a vital element—the science that made the stories plausible as realistic fiction and shaped their form and message. In his biography of Roberts, W. J. Keith described Roberts's picture of life in nature as "Darwinian" but did not discuss the nature of this debt to Darwin. Joseph Gold showed that Roberts found order in an apparently purposeless universe in the ceaseless round of life and death that drove the world, and proved convincingly that Roberts placed man as an "ambivalent beast." But he did no more than Keith to show the relationship of this to nineteenth-century biology. Both critics referred to Darwin's theories only in the vague adjective "Darwinian."[6] Others even denied this much connection; Robert MacDonald saw Seton's and Roberts's stories as a revolt against Darwinian determinism.[7]

These all missed an important element in the stories. The ideology of Roberts's animal stories owed as much to nineteenth-century biology, particularly to Darwinian evolution, as it did to Romanticism or the Canadian wilderness. Science, by Roberts's own admission, justified the stories as realistic fiction. The key feature of the genre, and a mark of Roberts's stories—the use of a point of view interior to the animal—was plausible only if one accepted the animal psychology of the period, and that science had been stimulated by Darwinian ideas. Major elements of the world view owed much to Darwinian ideas: the constant struggle of one animal with another; the ambiguous place of man in the natural world; and that central order Gold found in the stories—death as the price of life, necessary to the continuance of the world. Roberts was not revolting against a Darwinian determinism; far from it. He used the new biology, fusing it with older, Romantic conceptions to make an emotionally satisfying and scientifically correct vision of nature and of man's place in it. He constructed a new nature myth for an industrial, urban society that sought the authority of science for its views of humanity and of the world around it.[8]

The general neglect of science's role in shaping the nature story is only partly due to a general tendency to ignore science in the historical or literary analysis of fiction and the difficulties of showing how general scientific theories affect individual work. An important source of confusion is the focus on animal stories as a genre, ignoring individual differences between authors. In Roberts's case the problem is compounded by a tendency to lump him with Seton. The two men wrote very different kinds of stories, based on different views of nature. This confusion, for example, vitiates much of MacDonald's argument in "The Revolt Against Instinct." His analysis applies best to Seton and to *Red Fox,* which is not typical of Roberts's animal fiction. Seton concentrated on individual and individualized animals, gave them names, made them the heroes of their life stories, and found in them human virtue: "Lobo stands for Dignity and Love-constancy; Silverspot, for sagacity; Redruff for Obedience. . . ."[9] Roberts's animals, almost with exception, were not named (or at best were given generic names); his stories were incidents rather than accounts of animal life histories; and he did not deal with human virtue in the animal kingdom.

That the two authors agreed on the tragic nature of life in the wild has tended to obscure their profound differences. Seton rejected, on an emotional level, the bleaker implications of Darwinism and celebrated an anthropomorphic nature that reflected and ratified human ideas of virtue and morality—most prominently in *The Ten Commandments in the Animal World* but also in his stories.[10] Roberts did not. He used, as Gold said, the materials of the Canadian wilderness to create a "coherent view of the world which man inhabits," but the stories also used Darwinian science, in elements from the ideology to the plots and incidents within them.[11]

The Animal Story—Fiction Shaped by Science

> There is no fundamental difference between man and the higher mammals in their mental faculties . . . [even] the lower animals . . . manifestly feel pleasure and pain, happiness and misery . . . [and] [o]nly a few persons now dispute that animals possess some power of reasoning.
>
> —Charles Darwin (1871)[12]

The realistic animal story Seton and Roberts invented in the 1890s differed from earlier nature literature in its authors' insistence that not only the natural history but the mental life they ascribed to animals was scientifically accurate. The modern animal story, Roberts said, was "a psychological romance constructed on the framework of natural science."[13] We have, he went on, tried to explain animal behaviour on the basis of instinct and coincidence, but we have stretched these to their limits and they have failed. We now believe that "animals can and do reason." They have a mental life, like our own but simpler, and "the gulf dividing the lowest of the human species from the highest of the animals has . . . been reduced to a very narrow psychological fissure."

It was this claim—that animals "can and do reason"—that made the stories credible as realistic fiction. Without the "framework of natural science" they were fantasy, entertaining but inconsequential; with it they were powerful, emotionally compelling (so far as art made them so) dramas of the natural world surrounding man and a means of explaining man's place in it. It was the animal psychology stimulated by Darwin that furnished the "framework." Though there had been, since the late eighteenth century, a growing belief that animals felt pain and had an emotional life, even advocates of humane treatment for animals did not claim that the creatures thought. Jeremy Bentham, in his classic plea for humane treatment, brushed that aside as irrelevant. "The question is not," he said, "Can they *reason*? nor Can they *talk*? but, Can they *suffer*?"[14] Darwin changed all that. If man has evolved from the animals, if his bodily form is found among them, then so must his mind. *The Origin of Species* implicitly raised this issue; *The Descent of Man* did so directly. Darwin devoted two chapters of the latter work to the evidence that animals could think; boldly said that there was "no fundamental difference" between the minds of men and animals; and declared that it was "in a high degree probable" that under the proper conditions animals "would inevitably acquire a moral sense or conscience."[15] The question indeed was: Can they reason?

The animal psychologists who filled this previously dead field found more than traces of intellect and emotional development in the non-human world.[16] W. Lauder Lindsay, for example, in his popular *Mind in the Lower Animals,* credited protozoa with "a whole series of mental phenomena"—will and purpose, choice, ingenuity, observation, and feeling. Fish showed "conjugal and parental love, fidelity, self-sacrifice, [and] feelings of indignation and disgust." In the higher reaches of the animal kingdom (among dogs in contact with civilized humans) there were rudimentary moral feelings, a sense of religion, and an elementary understanding of money.[17]

These were the views of an enthusiastic amateur, but respected scientists like David Romanes, a friend of Darwin, agreed. Romanes was conscious of the difficulties of inferring mental processes from observed behaviour; he took pains to set out criteria of mind and mental activity; he explained animal behaviour by action on the lowest level of consciousness possible, but he reached conclusions much like Lindsay's. Refined emotions, powers of reasoning, the ability to discriminate among objects—animals had them all.[18]

The taxonomy of mental life then in use almost forced these conclusions. It had only two categories—reason (the use of thought to arrive at conclusions from observation) and instinct (conceived of as a stereotyped response to a particular situation); instinct became untenable when people began seriously to observe animals. Even simple ones showed reactions that could not be fit into the category without stretching it all out of recognition. And once instinct failed, the conclusion was inescapable: animals did think. With that, the gap between man and animal was "reduced to a very narrow psychological fissure." With popular acceptance of these views, the way was open for realistic animal stories that viewed their subjects from within.[19] More sophisticated theories would shift the focus of inquiry, but for Roberts and his contemporaries the result of scientific study was a license to depict animals with many human qualities, abilities, and emotions.

Animals Like Man

Making animals the central figures of fiction, realized from within, implied that they felt and thought, but Roberts used plots and incidents to reinforce that conclusion. Evidence of animal emotion runs through the stories. His subjects are curious, interested, brave, angry, or fearful. In some cases the emotions are the result of the constitution of the species; the weasel has an "inherited bloodlust" which drives him to spasms of slaughter.[20] Roberts even appeals to a kind of racial memory. "Last Bull," a zoo buffalo, has never known freedom, but he is restless. He escapes, and is killed by the keeper when he charges a group of children. Dying, "he saw once more, perhaps—or so the heavy-hearted keeper would have us believe—the shadowy plains unrolling under the wild sky, and the hosts of his vanished kindred drifting past into the dark."[21]

Roberts shows other reactions that are "higher," and more "human." Captive animals yearn for freedom. **"Lone Wolf"** looks for "delights which he had never known, for a freedom which he had never learned or guessed."[22] In **"The Summons of the North"** a captured polar bear dies, apparently of a heart attack, during the first snowstorm he experiences in the zoo.[23] Animals defend their young, even at the sacrifice of their lives. This is Romanticism, certainly, but Romanticism justified by science. Without animal psychology, the pathos of captivity dissolves into fantasy, and the self-sacrifice of mother love gains its emotional power only as a conscious, not instinctive, reaction.[24]

Animals also think. Sometimes Roberts is tentative in his assessments: a bear, if he is "capable of reflection—a point on which the doctors differ with some acrimony—he perhaps reflected that. . . ." The "Boy," an autobiographical figure, surveys a beaver dam and smiles as "he thought how inadequate what men call instinct would be to such a piece of work as this."[25] More often, and more characteristically, Roberts takes a bolder stand. **"The Ringwaak Buck"** has instinct as his "first, and most important, source" of knowledge. Beyond that is

> . . . experience, which teaches varying lore, according to variation in circumstances and surroundings. . . . But, after instinct and experience have accounted for everything that can reasonably be credited to them, there remains a considerable and well authenticated residuum of instances where wild creatures have displayed a knowledge which neither instinct nor experience could well furnish them with. In such cases observation and inference seem to agree in ascribing the knowledge to parental teaching.[26]

So too does *Red Fox* begin with lessons from that "inexorable instructress, Nature," which supplement "that endowment of ancestral knowledge which goes by the name of instinct. But at the same time he was peculiarly apt in learning from his mother."[27] An Arctic fox, a "Master of Supply," caches his food in frozen ground, using knowledge "which he could only have arrived at by the strictly rational process of putting two and two together—he understood the efficacy of cold storage."[28]

Men Like Animals

Attributing emotions and thought to animals was not, for Roberts, a literary device or a concession to anthropomorphism. It was a recognition that the mental life of animals resembled that of man. The opposite was also true: man was an animal, a creature of nature. Roberts pursued this theme in several ways—emphasizing the common emotional life of man and animals; portraying man as an animal, or civilized man as the inheritor of more "primitive" "instincts"; and emphasizing the ties that bound man, as they did animals, to the economy of life and death that drove the world. All these themes were affected by Romanticism and a glorification of the primitive, but they also drew on scientific theories.

Man and animal shared an emotional life. "Insofar as man is himself an animal," Roberts said, "he is subject to and impelled by many emotions which he must share with not a few other members of the animal kingdom."[29] The aim of the stories was to show that animals felt—that they suffered, feared, and rejoiced like people. Roberts made this point in all the stories, but most dramatically in **"The Kill."** Here he inverted the usual hunting story, telling it from the point of view of the hunted, wounded, and ultimately slain moose, replacing the usual emotions of excitement and ultimate triumph with the animal's suffering, pain, fear, and death.[30]

Science reinforced other similarities. Darwinian biology, blurring the boundaries between man and the animals, encouraged racial classifications based on purported distance from the beasts and theories about the survival of primitive features among civilized men. Scientists, including the new animal psychologists, found considerable overlap between the lower races of man and animals. Lindsay, for example, found that savages lacked parental feeling, a moral sense, feelings of shame and self-control, and were clumsy with their hands. In his classification, as one modern critic pointed out, an Englishman's bulldog stood higher, and closer to his master, than did the Eskimos.[31] Romanes found that the "lower races" of man were much like animals and that human and animal development overlapped considerably, with some animals reaching the mental state of young children.[32]

From this it was only a short step to the theory of recapitulation, most often associated with G. Stanley Hall, a psychologist whose work "suggested that children would wholly mature only if they were encouraged to relive the history of the human race."[33] Seton was struck with this idea and incorporated its implications into the program of the Woodcraft Indians.[34] Roberts made no explicit reference to it, but recapitulation was an important element in the earliest story, **"The Moonlight Trails,"** he wrote about the "Boy." The Boy is civilized, from the "best house in Far Bazziley," the minister's son, of a "different class from the other boys of the settlement." He is kind-hearted, and has more than once thrashed his playmates "for torturing, with boyish playfulness and ingenuity, superfluous kittens"; he defends even snakes, which the others killed on sight. But when the hired man, Andy, suggests that they set some snares for rabbits, "[t]he wild spirit of adventure, the hunting zest of elemental man, stirred in his veins at the idea." He never would have allowed a rabbit to be tortured, we are told, but the idea of snaring the creatures fired "a side of his imagination so remote from pity as to have no connection with it whatever along the nerves of sympathy or association." They set the snares, the Boy thinking of nothing but the hunt. "His tenderness of heart, his enlightened sympathy with the four-footed kindred, much of his civilization, in fact, had vanished for the moment, burnt out in the flame of an instinct handed down to him from his primeval ancestors."[35]

He is, at the end, sickened by the dead bodies, and vows never to snare anything again, but he does not abandon the woods or repudiate his primitive drives and abilities. He "had a pet theory that the human animal was more competent, as a mere animal, than it gets the credit of being; and it was his particular pride to outdo the wild creatures at their own game."[36] Nor is the Boy the only example of primitive life in the animal stories. As Keith and Gold have pointed out, Roberts was fascinated with the backwoodsmen, the lumberjacks, trappers, and hunters of his youth, and they appear in his stories as figures of man's ability to live, in one sense, within and without nature.[37] Roberts showed man as an animal—a very Darwinian animal—in a story about a castaway on the New Guinea coast. The man, civilized, helpless, out of his element, nevertheless establishes his dominion over the jungle. He is sustained by the "old faith in man as the master animal" and by his wild heritage. In the end he kills a tiger, thus taking his rightful place as the "King of Beasts" (and is then rescued, bringing his saga to an appropriately civilized conclusion).[38] In the struggle for survival, man—even civilized man—is the fitter animal.

Frequently Roberts emphasized the links that bound man with the animals in a common natural economy—the round of life and death which was the fabric of the world—and here his ideas were closely tied to popular conceptions of a dark, Darwinian world in which the price of life is the death of others.[39] The theme dominates his first story, **"Do Seek Their Meat from God."**[40] Like **"The Kill,"** it inverts a literary form for effect, which may account for the baffled reactions of several editors. The story begins with two "panthers" (eastern mountain lions) leaving their cubs in the den and setting out on a night's hunt. They hear a child crying and move toward the sound. The child, we learn, has been seeking his playmate, but the family has, that very day, abandoned their farm, leaving only the empty cabin with a broken door. The child's father, coming home from town, almost passes by, thinking it is only the "squatter's brat" crying. Then, moved by pity, he decides to see what is wrong.

So far we see the standard wilderness adventure, man against beast, with everything set for a confrontation between father and panthers at the cabin—but Roberts pauses here to disabuse the reader of his prejudices, and to drive home the moral implicit in the title.[41] "Theirs," he says, "was no hideous or unnatural rage, as it is the custom to describe it. They were but seeking with the strength, the cunning, the deadly swiftness given them to that end, the food convenient to them." The father and the panthers arrive at the clearing together, and he kills them, one in hand-to-hand combat. Only when he finds the child does he realize it is his own son he has saved. This is a melodramatic climax, but the story does not end there. It ends "not many weeks afterward" when the farmer, following a bear that has killed one of his sheep, finds a wild animal's den, and, in the back, "the dead bodies, now rapidly decaying, of two small panther cubs."[42]

Another early story, **"When Twilight Falls on the Stump Lots,"** shows that man's participation in this round of life and death is not limited to pioneer life; it is part of all existence. A hungry mother bear, seeking food in the early spring, attacks a cow and her calf. Driven off and gored, she dies on the way back to the den. Her cubs are "spared . . . some days of starving anguish" when two foxes find them. The story ends with the calf, whose "fortune was ordinary. Its mother, for all her wounds, was able to nurse and cherish it through the night; and with morning came a searcher from the farm and took it, with the bleeding mother, safely back to the settlement. There it was tended and fattened, and within a few weeks found its way to the cool marble slabs of a city market."[43]

Man Outside Nature

Roberts's stories tied man to the natural world but they also showed him separated from it. He was more than the "King of Beasts," more than a superior animal; he had a life above nature, beyond its round of life and death. Polk saw Roberts's ambivalence as "the romantic dilemma—nature good but uncivilized, civilization good but unnatural."[44] This is true, but it is the Romantic dilemma in a particular setting. Roberts had not only to reconcile his experience of the Canadian wilderness with Romantic ideas about nature, but to accommodate his vision of nature to that of science. Darwinism, fortunately, lent itself to the vision of man within, but not part of, nature. It showed him as a creature of the animal kingdom but it also, in its emphasis on change, suggested that he had "evolved" beyond nature. People could, and did, see in science a warrant for struggle, even struggle within society, and for the conquest of nature, but others could find warrant for the Romantic identification of man with the great world of nature and arguments for the humane treatment of animals.[45] Roberts's depiction of man as an "ambivalent beast," to use Gold's phrase, was one supported by science.[46]

Roberts emphasized man's divided nature in several ways, beginning with his defense of the animal story. Its particular virtue, he wrote, was that it allowed us to go back to nature "without requiring that we at the same time return to barbarism." The animal story lifted man out of himself and out of his ordinary life. Man had to go back to nature, be freed "from the mean tenement of self." The stories allowed him to do that without paying "by way of toll any part of the wisdom of the ages."[47]

The form of the stories reinforced this ambiguity. Roberts commonly framed bloody dramas of the struggle for existence with Romantic descriptions of the beauties of nature. **"When Twilight Falls on the Stump Lots"** begins with a lyrical description of the spring. **"The Watchers in the Swamp,"** a chronicle of danger faced and defeated by a pair of nesting bitterns, begins and ends with the song of a hermit thrush, one of the most beautiful sounds of the woods. **"The Sentry of the Sedge Flats"** is a string of deaths and near-deaths, ending with a peregrine carrying off a mink from the body of a heron the mink has just killed. "Some ten minutes later a splendid butterfly, all glowing orange and maroon, came and settled on the back of the dead heron, and moved its radiant wings in the tranquil light."[48] This is not an exposé, Roberts showing first the Romantic vision, then the "real" reality, the struggle for life. The animal story is not natural history muck-raking. Both the struggle and the Romantic vision are real; it is man's heritage to see them both and to know both.

Roberts also makes it clear that man, even when acting as an animal, is not natural. The hero of **"King of Beasts"** forges tools, and his victory, his crowning, does not lead him to life in the jungle. He is a king who cannot live in his kingdom. On a deeper level, too, man's skills as a hunter, his primitive heritage, are not part of the order of nature. In a story about moose hunting, for instance, we have two hunters, an older man wielding a birchbark horn to call a bull, the other a young man after his first moose. The older man is a master woodsman, able to outdo the animals at their own game and to "slay the cunning kindred of the wild by a craft finer than their own."[49] He can mimic with complete fidelity the call of the cow moose, that "noble and splendid call, vital with all the sincerity of response and love and elemental passion," and he uses that skill to lure the bull to his death. The final call, which overcomes the animal's suspicions, contains all the "yearning of all the mating ardour that had triumphed over insatiable death and kept the wilderness peopled from the first. . . ." The story is entitled **"A Treason of Nature."**[50]

Roberts addressed the theme of man's separation from nature in a less direct fashion as well, in some dozen stories dealing with man's animals—strayed, lost, or feral—and the wildlings he captured. They have a consistent theme: man has made a separate world.[51]

Domesticated animals are strangers. They may win a battle, as the cock in **"Cock Crow"** or the black-faced ram enjoying his day of freedom, but they cannot survive in the wild. The ox in **"Strayed,"** escaping from a winter lumber camp, looking for the pastures of summer, falls victim to a panther. The surviving ox in **"Brothers of the Yoke,"** the horses in **"A Stranger to the Wild"** and **"In the Unknown Dark,"** and the central figure in **"How a Cat Played Robinson Crusoe"** are glad to return to man, for life in the wild is beyond them.[52]

More striking, man can command his animals. **"The Freedom of the Black-Faced Ram,"** a day-long adventure, ends when he is found by a man. He comes when called, for there was in the man's voice "an authority . . . which [the ram] could not withstand," and without whom the world was "empty and desolate."[53] This is true even for the bitches who, in two stories, run off with wolves and raise a litter of half-bred whelps (the two are actually one, Roberts having thriftily recycled plot material by changing the locale and some of the action).[54] The climax of both stories comes when the wolf, the bitch, and the cubs attack man, and the bitches cannot resist his shouted order. In **"The Passing of the Black Whelps"** the grown cubs tear their mother apart for this treason and are themselves killed by their wolf father and the man. In **"The Invaders"** the bitch survives, better and stauncher, the old hunter says, for her fling with the wild. In both stories the half-breed offspring are worse than either parent, with an implacable hostility to man and treacherous dispositions—another indication of the unnatural nature of the crossing of wild and tame.

Roberts does show one animal living in the wild, in **"The Alien of the Wild,"** but only to show that there is no place for him. A bull, the calf of a runaway cow, survives, and in his prime defeats a bull moose—but the cow moose flees. He leaves the wilderness, but is no more at home in the settlement. His mother's owner, who realizes whose calf he is, finds him in a pasture, but is forced to shoot when the bull threatens a group of children. He spits out an epitaph over the dead animal that might serve for all who seek to enter the wild world: "'Spiled,' said he. 'Clean spiled all round! The woods, they wa'n't no place for you, so ye had to quit 'em. But they spiled you fer the habitations of man. It's a born stranger and alien you was, an' there wa'n't no place fer ye neither here nor there.'"[55]

Even wild animals, once captured, are tainted. In **"The Return to the Trails"** a bear, captured as a cub, escapes but, "having lost the habit of hibernation," he is "ruined . . . for the life of nature. . . . When man has snatched away from Nature one of her wild children, Nature, merciless in her resentments, is apt to say, 'Keep him! He is none of mine!' And if the alien, his heart aching for his own, insists upon returning, Nature turns a face of stone against him."[56] The bear eventually stumbles into a lumber camp, where the frightened boss shoots him. The same fate befalls **"Mishi,"** a panther raised by man and released in the woods by a train wreck. He is incapable of living in the wild, but, when he finds his way to a settlement and befriends some children, their father, who does not realize the animal is tame, shoots him. Kehonka, the farm-raised Canada goose, longing for the wilderness he has never known, joins the spring migration, but his ignorance and clumsiness betray him. He is taken by a fox, that "discourager of quests."[57]

The Creative Tension

Man's separate world would seem to mock Roberts's statement that the animal story will "lead us back to the old kinship of earth," but our kinship, for Roberts, does not involve a complete identification with nature. Indeed, he explicitly rejected that in an early novel, *The Heart of the Ancient Wood.*[58] The vision of a Romantic life in nature, the book says, can come only at the sacrifice of full humanity and of a real understanding of nature. The heroine, Miranda, has been raised by her mother, self-exiled from her town, in the heart of the ancient wood. She grows up "with no human companion but her mother . . . [and] the quiet folk of the wood insensibly moulded her, and the great silences, and the wide wonder of the skies at night, and the solemnity of the wind." She has "an elvish or a faun-like strangeness: as if a soul not all human dwelt in her human shape." Her powers of observation and her night vision are far better than other people's, and she can move through the woods as quietly as the animals themselves. The old she-bear, Kroof, adopts her, is her guide and protector, and presides over her initiation into "the full fellowship of the folk of the ancient woods."

She is separated from nature only by her inability to appreciate the silent struggle which goes on around her. Marked off by her red kerchief and surrounded by a charmed circle, the "Pax Mirandae," she sees little of the bloodshed of the wood, and comes to regard "the folk of the ancient wood as a gentle people, living for the most part in voiceless amity. Her seeing eyes quite failed to see the unceasing tragedy of the stillness. . . . She little dreamed that for most of them, the very price of life itself was the ceaseless extinguishing of life."[59] The plot concerns the efforts of a trapper, young Dave, to win Miranda back to humanity. In the end, she must not only recognize the place of death in the life of nature, she must participate in it; she has to shoot the old she-bear to save Dave. The last scene has Miranda, her mother, and Dave burying the dead bear, and with it Miranda's life in nature. Buried, too, is Roberts's fling with allegory, "elvish" people raised in the woods, and tutelary deities in the form of animals.[60]

Miranda's "solution," or young Dave's solution, one Roberts endorsed, was a balance between the life of civilization and the world of nature, a balance reached by the tension between two worlds, not by a resolution. Dave appreciates and understands the cruelty and death that lie below the surface of the life of the ancient woods, but he is not repelled by them. He has a place within nature, but also one outside it. Roberts developed this tension in three linked stories about "the Boy."[61] He appears, in **"The Moonlight Trails,"** as a child, stirred by primitive instincts "handed down to him from his primeval ancestors."[62] His first lesson is that these are not enough, that there is a life in nature, that the animals deserve our sympathy and our kindness. The story begins with a description of the hares dancing in the snow-covered clearing in the moonlight. It "seemed the play of care-free children . . . a spontaneous expression of the joys of life." The hares have sentries, and danger is present, but it does not affect the joy of the dance. Roberts then introduces the Boy and describes his expedition with the hired man, Andy, to set the snares. The tracks in the sunlight reveal "to the boy's eyes, though not to the man's, . . . a formal and intricate pattern. . . ." "What fun they must have been having," he exclaims.[63]

They set the snares and the scene shifts to the glade the next night, as the innocent celebration is converted into a *danse macabre.* One of the rabbits is caught, to hang kicking in the air. "[T]hen at the next entrance, there shot up into the brilliant air another like horror; and at the next, in the same breath, another." The rabbits flee in terror. Andy and the Boy return at daylight. They find two rabbits and, at the third snare, only a head—a fox could reach this one. "To [the Boy's] untrained eye the trampled snow, the torn head, and the blood spots told the story in part; and as he looked a sense of the tragedy of it began to stir achingly at the roots of his heart. . . . Then, turning his gaze upon Andy's capture, he was struck by the cruel marks of the noose . . . [and noticed] for the first time, the half-open mouth, the small, jutting tongue, the expression of the dead eyes." He tears down the snares, throws down the rabbits, and starts home, vowing never again to go rabbit-snaring.[64]

We see him next in **"The Boy and Hushwing,"** somewhat older and now a master of woodcraft. "Impatient and boyish in other matters, he had trained himself to the patience of an Indian in regard to all matters pertaining to the wood-folk." He is, though, more than a master woodsman—which he proves by catching alive the great horned owl. He knows and appreciates the workings of nature. He has no grudge against Hushwing "for his slaughter of the harmless hare and grouse, for did not the big marauder show equal zest in the pursuit of mink and weasel, snake and rat?" Even toward that "embodied death, the malignant weasel," he has no antagonism, "making allowance as he did for the inherited bloodlust which drove the murderous little animal to defy all the laws of the wild kindred and kill, kill, kill, for the sheer delight of killing."[65] The story, which is in large part a natural history of the great horned owl, ends with the bird's (contrived) escape.

The great test of the Boy's woodcraft—and expiation for the snaring done in **"The Moonlight Trails"**—comes when he matches wits with a lynx in **"The Haunter of the Pine Gloom."** He begins with observation and trailing, but when the old female acquires a mate and kits and takes to killing stock, the Boy has to hunt them down. He has renounced killing in the woods but his commitment is not absolute; man may protect his own (he may too, as Gold argues, hunt for trophies). The Boy kills a lynx in *House in the Water* to protect "his" beaver.[66] He kills two of the cubs, and the others, except for the old female, flee. She is cunning, and he finally resorts to a snare, something (we are reminded) he has not done since the rabbit expedition of his youth. The story ends with the body of the lynx hanging in a tree at night as the rabbits gambol on the snow below. "And because it was quite still, they never saw the body of their deadliest foe, hanging stark from the branch above them."[67]

Conclusion

Roberts's vision of nature struck a chord with the late Victorian reading public. In 1892 he had difficulty placing **"Do Seek Their Meat from God,"** but by the end of the decade he could sell everything he could write. *Outing* alone printed five of his stories in a two-year period (1901-1903), and up to World War I he published almost annually books filled with stories which first appeared in magazines. Roberts's production and popularity fell off after that. The stories, Gold has said, "went out of fashion and print through the aftermath of the Great War, in the Twenties, and in the Depression of the thirties," a circumstance he attributed to a change in audience. There were no longer "the post-Victorians looking for adventure in print" but "survivors of the hideous experience of war and depression and more war."[68] A complementary reading is possible. Roberts's stories were less in demand because the general educated public, to which he spoke, had assimilated Darwinism. This argument gains more force when we consider that nature essays and nature stories did not go out of fashion, but shifted focus. Especially after 1940, with such works as Rachel Carson's *Under the Sea Wind,* Sally Carrigher's *One Day on Beetle Rock,* Fred Bodsworth's *The Last of the Curlews,* and Farley Mowat's *Never Cry Wolf,* new themes appeared—the intricate connections within the web of life and man's enormous destructive powers—themes that reflected and explained our new knowledge of the science of ecology and of human impact on the ecosystem.[69]

Viewing Roberts in this light, as an author explaining and giving emotional content to a scientific view, also makes it apparent why he was so popular beyond Canada. The issues he addressed in his fiction were part of the situation of Western civilization. Science was providing a new understanding of nature and man's place in it. Industrialization was giving man new powers, making humans, for the first time, independent of nature, or at least not immediately exposed to its dangers. That the Canadian wilderness was not conquered, even that it could not be conquered, was irrelevant. The civilization of which Canada was a part and Canada itself were insulated from the horrors of life in nature. That, with our new understanding of nature, compelled a new perspective. It was Roberts's genius to subsume older Romantic ideas about nature within the framework of the popular notion of a Darwinian struggle; to show within that seeming chaos continuity, order, and a place for man; to explain nature to his generation; and to give emotional content to a scientific explanation of man and nature in a coherent world view.

Notes

1. Joseph Gold, "The Precious Speck of Life," *Canadian Literature,* no. 26 (Autumn 1965), 22-32. See also Gold's introduction to a collection of Roberts's work, *King of Beasts* (Toronto: Ryerson, 1967).

2. Margaret Atwood, *Survival: A Thematic Guide to Canadian Literature* (Toronto: Anansi, 1972), 73. W. J. Keith, *Charles G. D. Roberts* (Toronto: Copp Clark, 1969), 87-114, develops this view of the stories as a distinctly Canadian genre and Roberts's contributions to it.

3. James Polk, "Lives of the Hunted," *Canadian Literature,* no. 53 (Summer 1972), 51-59; Robert H. MacDonald, "The Revolt Against Instinct," *Canadian Literature,* no. 84 (Spring 1980), 18-29; John Wadland, *Ernest Thompson Seton* (New York: Arno, 1978).

4. There is a basic bibliography in Loren Owings, *Environmental Values, 1860-1972* (Detroit: Gale Research Company, 1976), 212-15. See John Burroughs, "Real and Sham Natural History," *Atlantic Monthly,* 91 (March 1903), 298-309. On the educational aspects of the genre see President Theodore Roosevelt's attacks on distortions in natural history: Edward B. Clark, "Roosevelt on the Nature Fakirs," *Everybody's Magazine,* 16 (June 1907), 770-74; Theodore Roosevelt, "Nature Fakers," *Everybody's Magazine,* 17 (September 1907), 427-30. Both articles are in *The Works of The-*

odore Roosevelt, National Edition (New York: Charles Scribner's Sons, 1926), Vol. 5, 367-83. Peter Finley Dunne made fun of the controversy in "Mr. Dooley on the Call of the Wild," *New York Times,* 2 June 1907, section 5, 1.

5. Roberts, "The Animal Story," *The Kindred of the Wild* (Boston: Page, 1902), 24.

6. Typical is the judgement in a review of a collection of Roberts's stories: that he used in his fiction two worlds, one "associated with romance," the other the world "observed by Darwin, of unmitigated, elemental struggle within nature itself." John Lennox, "Roberts, Realism, and the Animal Story," *Journal of Canadian Fiction,* 2 (Summer 1973), 121-23. Gold, "That Precious Speck of Life," and "The Ambivalent Beast," in Carrie MacMillan, *The Proceedings of the Sir Charles G. D. Roberts Symposium* (Sackville, NB: Centre for Canadian Studies, Mount Allison University, 1984), 77-86. W. J. Keith, "A Choice of Worlds: God, Man and Nature in Charles G. D. Roberts," in George Woodcock, ed. *Colony and Confederation: Early Canadian Poets and Their Background* (Vancouver: University of British Columbia Press, 1974), 87-102, discusses the stories seriously and notes the lack of conventional religious sentiment, even the absence of God, but does not see this in relation to Darwin.

7. MacDonald, "Revolt Against Instinct."

8. This analysis is drawn from a reading of about 130 of Roberts's stories from the following collections: *Kindred of the Wild* (1902); *Earth's Enigmas* (1895, rpr. Boston: Page, 1902); *Watchers of the Trails* (Boston: Page, 1904); *Red Fox* (Boston: Page, 1905); *Haunters of the Silences* (Boston: Page, 1907); *The House in the Water* (Boston: Page, 1908); *Kings in Exile* (New York: Macmillan, 1910); *Feet of the Furtive* (New York: Macmillan, 1913); *Hoof and Claw* (New York: Macmillan, 1914); *The Secret Trails* (New York: Macmillan, 1916); *Wisdom of the Wilderness* (Toronto: Ryerson, 1948); stories circa 1920; *Neighbors Unknown* (1924, rpr. Toronto: Macmillan, 1933); *King of Beasts* (Toronto: Ryerson, 1967), stories from 1910-1915.

9. Ernest Thompson Seton, *Lives of the Hunted* (New York: Charles Scribner's Sons, 1901), 11. See also the introduction to Seton's *Wild Animals I Have Known* (New York: Charles Scribner's Sons, 1898).

10. Ernest Thompson Seton, *The Ten Commandments in the Animal World* (New York: Doubleday, Page, 1923).

11. Gold, "The Precious Speck of Life," 22.

12. Charles Darwin, *The Descent of Man,* 2nd ed. (New York: H.M. Caldwell, 1874), 81, 84, 90.

13. Roberts, *Kindred of the Wild,* 23, 24.

14. Bentham, *An Introduction to the Principles of Morals and Legislation,* 1789, quoted in Peter Singer, *Animal Liberation* (New York: Random House, 1975), 8.

15. Darwin, *Descent of Man,* 113.

16. Two of the annual meetings of the British Association for the Advancement of Science in the 1870s were devoted to this topic, and by the end of the decade there was a new school of animal psychologists on the scene. On this development see James C. Turner, *Reckoning with the Beast* (Baltimore: Johns Hopkins University Press, 1980), Chapter Four.

17. W. Lauder Lindsay, *Mind in the Lower Animals: Volume I. Mind in Health, Volume II. Mind in Disease* (New York: D. Appleton and Company, 1880), 52, 70, 75, 79.

18. George J. Romanes, *Animal Intelligence* (New York: D. Appleton, 1883, rpr. Washington: University Publications of America, 1977).

19. It was not until the end of the century, when a new generation of psychologists, led by Lloyd Morgan and Edward Thorndike, began to lay new foundations for an experimental psychology, that scientists began to find other ways to characterize the mental processes of animals, ways which did not require animals' reasoning. See, for example, Edward L. Thorndike, *Animal Intelligence* (1911; rpr. New York: Hafner, 1965), and "Do Animals Reason?," *Popular Science Monthly,* 55 (August 1899), 480-90. It was this school's conclusions that allowed John Burroughs, in the nature-faking controversy, to allow animals a degree of thought while reserving the higher mental powers, and a special place, for man. See John Burroughs, *Ways of Nature* (Boston: Houghton Mifflin, 1905), vi, 64, 161, 171, as well as his "Do Animals Think?," *Harper's,* 110 (February 1905), 354-58, and his "Do Animals Reason?," *Outing,* 45 (March 1905), 758-59. Burroughs's main target, the Reverend William J. Long, maintained that animals did think, appealing against Thorndike and the new school of experimental psychologists to Romanes, Lindsay, and others of the school that flourished in the 1880s. Peter Rabbit (William J. Long), "Do Animals Think?," *Harper's,* 111 (June 1905), 59-62, and "The Question of Animal Reason," *Harper's,* 111 (September 1905), 588-94. These developments came too late to affect Roberts, whose ideas of animal psychology seem to have been formed some years earlier, and there is no evi-

dence that he changed his mind as a result of the nature-faking attacks.

20. "The Boy and Hushwing," *Kindred of the Wild,* 176. See also the mink in "When the Tide Came over the Marshes," *Haunters of the Silences,* 235-42, and the fisher, "Mustela of the Lone Hand," *Wisdom of the Wilderness.*

21. *Kings in Exile,* 23.

22. *Ibid.,* 243-44. Animals' dèsire for freedom is a recurring theme, the motif of the collection, *Kings in Exile.*

23. *Haunters of the Silences.*

24. "When Twilight Falls over the Stump Lots," "Wild Motherhood," "The King of the Mamozekel" (*Kindred of the Wild*); "The Freedom of the Black-Faced Ram" and "The Keeper of the Water-Gate" (*Watchers of the Trails*); and "From the Teeth of the Tide" (*House in the Water*) illustrate the theme of wild mothers and children. Self-sacrifice and mother love are common in Roberts's stories, and these instances might be multiplied.

25. "In the Year of No Rabbits," *Feet of the Furtive,* 52-70; *House in the Water,* 27.

26. *Haunters of the Silences,* 175. Seton had similar views; see "Tito, The Story of the Coyote that Learned How," *Lives of the Hunted,* 274-75. For a discussion of Seton's similar views see Wadland, *Ernest Thompson Seton,* 217-18.

27. *Red Fox,* 28, 30.

28. *Hoof and Claw,* 56-57.

29. *Red Fox,* viii.

30. *Watchers of the Trails,* 197-208.

31. This last is a paraphrase of a sentence from Peter H. Klopfer, *Introduction to Animal Behavior: Ethology's First Century* (Englewood Cliffs, NJ: Prentice-Hall, 1974), 20. See also Turner, *Reckoning with the Beast,* 63-68.

32. Romanes, *Mental Evolution in Man* (New York: D. Appleton, 1889).

33. Wadland, *Ernest Thompson Seton,* 335.

34. *Ibid.,* 335-79.

35. *Kindred of the Wild,* 46.

36. *Ibid.,* 202.

37. Gold, "The Ambivalent Beast"; Keith, "A Choice of Worlds."

38. The story is in the collection *King of Beasts.*

39. Gold, "That Precious Speck of Life."

40. The story was first published in *Harper's Magazine,* 86 (December 1892), 120-22. It is available in a collection, *The Last Barrier and Other Stories* (Toronto: McClelland and Stewart, 1965), 1-6. Page numbers in the text are from the magazine version.

41. The title comes from Psalm 104, verse 21, part of a psalm extolling the order of the world established by the Creator. Roberts used a quotation from a similar passage in Job 38:41 or Ps. 147:9 for the title of another early story, "The Young Ravens That Call on Him," published in *Earth's Enigmas.* That, too, extolls the order of the world and the oversight of the Creator. W. J. Keith, "A Choice of Worlds," 98, sees the titles as ironical comments, for the meat the panthers seek is man and the young ravens (eagles in the story) feed on a lamb whose cries have gone, presumably, unheard.

42. "Do Seek their Meat From God," 122.

43. *Kindred of the Wild,* 283-84.

44. Polk, "Lives of the Hunted," 52.

45. Donald Worster, *Nature's Economy* (San Francisco: Sierra Club, 1977), Chapters Six-Nine; Turner, *Reckoning with the Beast,* Chapter Four.

46. Gold, "The Ambivalent Beast."

47. *Kindred of the Wild,* 29.

48. *Wisdom of the Wilderness,* 106-24.

49. *Kindred of the Wild,* 193.

50. *Ibid.,* 180-96.

51. Those considered here are: "The Freedom of the Black-faced Ram," "The Passing of the Black Whelps," "The Return to the Trails," and "The Alien of the Wild," from *Watchers of the Trails*; "Cock-crow," and "Brothers of the Yoke," from *The Secret Trails*; "Strayed," *Earth's Enigmas*; "Stranger to the Wild," and "In the Unknown Dark," *Haunters of the Silences*; "The Homesickness of Kehonka," *Kindred of the Wild Kings in Exile*; "How a Cat Played Robinson Crusoe," *Neighbors Unknown*; "The Invaders" and "The Spotted Stranger," *The Feet of the Furtive.*

52. *The Secret Trails,* 154-78; *Watchers of the Trails,* 4-22; *Earth's Enigmas,* 66-75; "Brothers of the Yoke," *The Secret Trails,* 115-35; "How a Cat Played Robinson Crusoe," *Neighbors Unknown,* 175-92. An exception to the general helplessness of domestic animals is "The Black Boar of Lonesome Water," *The Secret Trails,* 1-32, who seems on its way to adapting to the wild when recaptured, but this is more a comic tale of the backwoods than an animal story proper.

53. *Watchers of the Trails,* 22. See also "Stranger to the Wild," and "In the Unknown Dark," in *Haunters of the Silences,* 108-31, 268-81.

54. "The Passing of the Black Whelps," *Watchers of the Trails,* 323-48, and "The Invaders," *The Feet of the Furtive,* 71-94.

55. *Watchers of the Trails,* 108.

56. *Ibid.,* 58-59.

57. "Mishi," *King of Beasts.* The implications—that it is the children who realize the real nature of the animal—may be worked out by the interested. "The Homesickness of Kehonka," *Kindred of the Wild.* The only successful case of return is very contrived. In "The King of the Flaming Hoops," a panther, captured as a cub, escapes from the circus and finds his way back to the cave in which he was born. *Kings in Exile,* 27-68. I am ignoring here several "pet" stories—"The Moose that Knocked at the Door," and "Red Dandy and McTavish," in *Feet of the Furtive*; "Brannigan's Mary," and "The Bear that thought He was a Dog," in *Hoof and Claw*; and "Back to the Water World," and "Lone Wolf," in *Kings in Exile,* in which the wildlings become tame. These stories seem to be outside the genre of "animal story." The main emphasis is human interest and animal point of view is not used.

58. *The Heart of the Ancient Wood* (New York: Lippincott, 1900).

59. *Ibid.,* 124. In the introduction to *The Watchers of the Trails,* viii, Roberts commented on his childhood in similar terms. He had, he said, an intimate knowledge of the wild kindreds, for he had "chanced to live much among them during the impressionable periods of his life," and might "claim to have had the intimacies of the wilderness as it were thrust upon him."

60. On an earlier draft an anonymous critic wrote here: "Almost makes one want to allude to Marian Engel's *Bear*" (New York: Atheneum, 1976). Yes, it does. Working out the significance of the bears and comparing their roles will be left, to borrow a phrase from the mathematics textbooks, as an exercise for the reader.

61. "The Moonlight Trails," "The Boy and Hushwing," and "The Haunter of the Pine Gloom," in *Kindred of the Wild.* Though the Boy appears in *Red Fox* and *The House in the Water,* he undergoes no psychological development; he is there to observe the natural history incidents Roberts wants shown and seen.

62. *Kindred of the Wild,* 46.

63. *Ibid.,* 35, 46.

64. *Ibid.,* 47, 52.

65. *Ibid.,* 176.

66. Gold, "Ambivalent Beast," 82-83.

67. *Kindred of the Wild,* 237.

68. Gold, "The Ambivalent Beast," 80.

69. Rachel Carson, *Under the Sea Wind* (Boston: Houghton Mifflin, 1941); Sally Carrigher, *One Day on Beetle Rock* (New York: Alfred Knopf, 1944); Fred Bodsworth, *The Last of the Curlews* (New York: Dodd, Mead, 1954); Farley Mowat, *Never Cry Wolf* (Boston: Little, Brown, 1963).

Martin Ware (essay date 1992)

SOURCE: Ware, Martin. Introduction to *The Vagrants of the Barren and Other Stories of Charles G. D. Roberts,* edited by Martin Ware, pp. ix-xxviii. Ottawa, Canada: The Tecumseh Press, 1992.

[*In the following essay, Ware examines themes and style in Roberts's animal stories and assesses his contribution to Canadian literature.*]

This selection presents the reader with a small sampling of the best of the more than two hundred and thirty animal stories written by Charles G. D. Roberts over a span of almost fifty years (1886-1935). Recently readers have been more and more drawn to the best of his animal stories—for their story-telling and artistic power, for the modest precision of their representation of animals, and for the challenge offered by their interpretation of animal psychology. It would be fair, I think, to say that there has been a growing consensus that his animal stories represent his most valuable contribution to the literature of Canada and of the English-speaking world. This is not to suggest that the reader should overlook his poetry, his translations, and his prose idylls. It is simply to recognize that his main writing energies went into his animal stories, and that in the best of these (perhaps about five dozen[1]), we recognize a distinctive voice and a distinctive achievement.

The task of making a representative selection of these stories is a daunting one. Beginning in 1892, Roberts started to publish them in Canadian, British and American periodicals and magazines, and for most of the next thirty years, new stories were constantly appearing, sometimes as many as sixteen in a single year. He adopted the practice of periodically making collections in book form of recent work, and tried as best he could to link the stories in each single volume according to a principle of thematic unity: the stories of ***Earth's Enigmas*** (1896), for example, are almost all concerned with the mysterious cruelty of fate, and ***The Kindred of the Wild*** (1902) pieces centre on the strange parallels between the lives of animals and lives of humans. Indeed each of the more than ten U.S. published collections of his work has a distinctive focus, and so the thematic concerns of his work are remarkably diverse. As well, there is considerable variety in the tone and form of the stories that he wrote over the years. This inevitably means that it would be very difficult to bring together a relatively brief selection of his stories which would adequately represent his overall achievement. And no guidance is to be had from Roberts himself, because, perhaps for copyright reasons, he never issued a representative selection of his animal stories in his own lifetime.

This selection of fourteen stories cannot be said to be significantly more rounded than the seven or more selections published since his death.[2] Each of these has had a thematic, or a geographical, or an aesthetic focus, and none makes any claim to offer a selection based on comprehensive principles. In my selection, which I have entitled ***The Vagrants of the Barren,*** the first three stories are Arctic stories; and the title story, which comes second last, places man within the pattern of wintry imperatives of an essentially Arctic world. The Arctic, it seems to me, represented a kind of absolute zero of Roberts' imagination, a place where, as he writes in "The Master of Supply," it often seems as if "the incalculable cold of outer space were invading the outpost of the world" (*infra,* p. 8). His Arctic animal stories are closely linked with the long poem of his old age, "The Iceberg," which depicts "the immeasurable desolation" of the primeval Arctic where "Forever no life stirred."[3] Yet just as in the poem, the bulk of the iceberg will outrage "the silence" of the Arctic sea "with mountainous surge and thunder," so in the animal stories, Roberts emphasizes again and again the suddenness of Arctic happenings. As he writes in **"The Keepers of the Nest,"** the coming of the Arctic spring was so sudden that "all the forces of the cold were routed in one night" (*infra,* p. 21). The "implacable savagery, the deathly cold of the Arctic winter" is a constant symbol in these stories for the life-extinguishing and life-threatening forces which call forth all the capacities and energies of those they threaten. The first three Arctic stories offer an appropriate point of departure for this selection by providing a backdrop to Roberts' celebration in his stories of the life instinct which not only drives individual animals to preserve life either for themselves or their tribe, but also makes them, in Fred Cogswell's words, "glory in the activity of the moment."[4] The locales of the stories range from the Arctic tundra to the Tantramar Marshes, and from these to the backwoods of the Saint John River Valley and to the mythical Ottanoonsis country (probably a fictionalized version of the highlands not far from the Restigouche River). The diversity of the chosen stories is as wide-ranging as possible—in terms of the animal protagonists, of the forms of the stories and their date of composition, and of their prevailing tone. But in virtually all of them, we see that the workings of inexorable necessity, so immediately apprehensible in the Arctic stories, can sometimes be averted by chance aberrations or by an animal's sudden adoption of a course of action which defies expected patterns. In Roberts' fictional animal world, the principle of indeterminacy is at work.

One of the main values of Roberts' animal stories lies in the way they give powerful imaginative expression to the lonely struggle for life in the Canadian wilderness. In a recent documentary Irving Layton has referred to Canadians' confrontation from the beginning of their history with a nature "raw in tooth and claw" which is "one vast warring turbulence."[5] The isolated villages and settlements often seemed to be no more than mere dots, surrounded by vast tracts of tundra or bushland, more the domain of the wild beasts than of man, and the settlers never enjoyed the feeling of nature mastered, which Americans have with the triumphant movement of their pioneering "frontier" from East to West. Canadians, it has been said, have always felt that their settlements and now their cities are mere specks "beleaguered by darkness"; and critics have added that the country's outstanding writers have ventured into the threatening circle, and made their peace with the wild beasts literally or symbolically associated with it. To borrow Irving Layton's words, we cannot escape the apparent "nothingness of the cosmos," its marvellous fertility and ceaseless savagery. From the first, the best Canadian artists have been imbued with an awareness of "the double hook of beauty and terror" and a restless metaphysical questioning. Roberts, in his animal stories, was surely one of the first and remains one of the most gifted writers to have articulated this outlook. We find in his work numerous variants of the universal metaphysical symbols of the life-giving cup of blood, or the eagle clutching the dove in its talons, as a glance at the conclusion of **"By the Winter Tide"** or of the title story will indicate.

The realistic animal story as developed by Roberts and his fellow Canadian and contemporary, Ernest Thompson Seton, has its place in the literature of the English-speaking world as the ultimate development of the romantic lyric of nature. Roberts himself was very much an heir of nineteenth-century romanticism. He himself edited a volume of Wordsworth's poetry, and he would have heartily endorsed the latter's exclamation "How exquisitely . . . / The external world is fitted to the mind."[6] As a writer, he aspired to be a "dawn-clear" reflector of the life of nature.[7] With Wordsworth, he might well have said that nature was "all in all," but his was not the benign nature "which never did betray / The heart which loved her."[8] Joseph Gold has pointed out in a seminal article that the Wordsworthian sentiment with which Roberts had most affinity was that of the "Mutability Sonnet": "Truth fails not, but her outward forms that bear / The longest date do melt like frosty rime."[9] For both Roberts and Wordsworth the metaphysical symbol of the snake with its tail in its mouth had decisive significance. Plants and animals are constantly dying that another generation may live: life is continually dissolving and renewing itself in unexpected ways. It was the role of the Canadian backwoods boy, far closer than the English dreamer to the raw reality of the natural struggle, to chronicle the often violent and painful but sometimes noble and reassuring process by which life is sacrificed that life may be sustained.

Roberts wrote the stories selected for this volume out of deep familiarity and personal knowledge of the animals, birds and fish that provide his subjects. In response to a reader who found it difficult to believe that a first-rate writer could also be a woodsman, Roberts wrote:

> It is right that I should tell you that I, for my part, am perhaps more than an 'amateur' woodsman—having spent my childhood and boyhood on a backwoods farm, shared in all the work of the woodsman and never been to school til I was fourteen. Then til the age of twenty-five, I managed to spend a good deal of time in the woods—the real backwoods, and ever since I have been making frequent returns to the life to which I am native.[10]

For the first thirteen years of his life (1860-1873), Roberts spent endless hours exploring the glebe farm and surrounding woods attached to his father's Westcock parsonage, and roaming the "miles on miles" of the long salty reaches of the Tantramar Marches which join New Brunswick to Nova Scotia. Then after his father's move to St. Anne's Church in Fredericton, he devoted weeks each year to long camping and canoeing trips into the back country; and after his appointment in 1885 as a Professor at King's College, Windsor, his main release from academic and domestic routine was provided by wilderness expeditions, often enough in pleasant female company. For years he had innumerable opportunities not only to study, but to know as a fellow creature the moose, bear, lynx, cougar, porcupine, fox, beaver, muskrat, eagle, goose, duck, deer, otter, weasel, hare and bat which he was later to depict with such skill.

In turning to the animal story, Roberts had innumerable memories on which to draw. He also had some knowledge of the range of animal stories available in the world's literature. His prefatory essay "The Animal Story" to his first widely acclaimed collection ***The Kindred of the Wild*** (1902) makes it evident that he thought carefully about his own adaptation of the animal story, and its place in the evolution of the genre as a whole. He was quite clear that the realistic story as developed by himself and his fellow Canadian Ernest Thompson Seton represented "a culmination" and a return to origins. In "The Animal Story" he argues that the first manifestations of the form were to be found in primitive man's realistic accounts of successful hunts. While interesting in terms of Roberts' own turn to realism, this view is questionable in the light of the animism, transformations, and supernatural influences that we find in a great many of the animal and etiological tales of aboriginal peoples. There is a greater degree of continuity than Roberts suggests between primitive animal tales (with their manitous and magic) and classical mythic tales (with their centaurs and unicorns). Roberts' account of the presentation of animals in classical and Christian literature is largely one of the growing alienation between man and animals. As human reason is elevated to a supreme position, so animals sink in the scale of esteem, and in literature a mode of abstraction comes to prevail. As Roberts suggests, the animals of classical fable and myth become more and more the vehicles for human qualities; in Aesop's work, Raynard the Fox and Isegrim the Wolf (the fabled embodiments of craftiness and cruelty) become "alien to the truths of wild nature" (***KW*** [***The Kindred of the Wild***], 20). Christianity, he goes on, only exacerbated the situation: "While militant, fighting for its life against the forces of paganism, its effort was to set man at odds with the natural world . . . the inarticulate kindred reaped small comfort from the Dispensation of Love." Roberts acknowledges the softening influence of the gentle friars and hermits, Francis of Assisi, Anthony of Padua and Colomb of the Bees, but his argument requires him to avoid dwelling on the animal stories associated with these and other great Christian saints. His emphasis, rather, is consistent with the way in which medieval writers in their bestiaries and allegorical writing ignored animals in themselves, so as to use animal images to signify moral qualities and human passions.

In concentrating on animals in themselves as the subjects of his stories and rejecting some aspects of the classical tradition, Roberts was both one of the last romantics, and one of the first writers to be radically influenced by Darwin. His birth followed the 1859 publication of *On the Origin of Species by Natural Selection* within little more than a month, and his work was profoundly conditioned by Charles Darwin's theory of evolution, and particularly by the great man's desire to bridge the rift between man and animals, to assuage the alienation. Where many of Darwin's readers were disgusted to discover their kinship with hairy beasts, walking on all fours and sporting fluffy tails, Roberts rejoiced in this newly discovered kinship.[11] This faith in the kinship of man with the creatures of the wild is the rock on which the project of his animal stories rests, though the associated Darwinian ideas of the struggle for survival and the effects of natural selection in evolving princely creatures are important supporting notions.

In the last thirty or forty years of the nineteenth century, the Darwinian sense of man's kinship with the animals combined with the Victorian delight in tear-squeezing melodrama (so evident in passages of Dickens and Hardy) to give rise to a vogue for sentimental animal stories by such writers as Ouida and Alfred Ollivant. The best known of these tales is Anna Sewell's *Black Beauty* (1877) with its wrenching account of a high-spirited mare's sufferings at the hands of a cruel cabby. In Canada, Sewell's fervent admirer Marshall Saunders won a large public with her melodramatic and moralizing story of a homely dog, *Beautiful Joe* (1894). The American Dudley Warner with his finely told *A Hunting of the Deer* shifts the focus to a wild animal, but the preoccupation remains with an animal's sufferings, and the tone is of the tear-inducing variety. Rudyard Kipling more than anyone else was responsible for energizing the animal story, and so paving the way for Roberts and Seton with the immense success of his *Jungle Books* (1894/5)—though the stories contained in these are in no sense realistic. Kipling's hero, the wild boy Mowgli, is no genuine wolf child, and the speaking animals echo Indian folk wisdom more than they do genuine animal compulsions. What Kipling did do was to create a taste for well-told exuberant tales, filled with the struggle and suspense of animal life. The English-speaking public's taste had been whetted for stories of the wild, and the stage was set for the appearance of the genuine animal story, as shaped by two gifted Canadians—Ernest Thompson Seton and Charles G. D. Roberts.

Roberts included three animal stories in ***Earth's Enigmas*** (1896), but it was not until the publication of Seton's *Wild Animals I Have Known* (1898) that the vogue became really established. The international success of ***Kindred of the Wild*** (1902) confirmed the popularity of a new kind of story, which for years to come commanded widespread interest and admiration. Roberts characterized it as "a psychological romance constructed on a framework of natural science" (***KW,*** 24). Basing the imaginative picture on the empirical observations of naturalists, Roberts and Seton strove to give an accurate representation of an animal's attempts to answer the imperatives of its nature in the quest for food, the nurture and protection of the young, the escape from predators, the winning of a mate, or the preservation of its freedom from man. At the same time, as romancers (and Seton was much more the romancer than Roberts) they aimed to suggest "the motive beneath the action" and to capture "the varying elusive personalities of the animals" (***KW,*** 24). Moved by the Darwinian faith in the kinship of man and animals, their purpose, as far as possible, was to create an animal's eye view of experience, which they regarded as different in kind but not in quality to that of human beings.

Seton took considerable liberties in depicting the animal heroes in his stories. The fact that he was briefly provincial naturalist for Manitoba has misled some critics into suggesting that in his tales he was the more empirical and scientific of the two writers. A perusal of his stories gives the lie to this, and shows that a modest adherence to the minutiae of nature was not his forte. As a born raconteur, he excelled in heightening the facts of natural history, in boldly divining individuality and burgeoning mental capacities in his animal heroes, and evolving highly dramatic plots. Like the man himself, Seton's stories are larger than life, large in their power to awaken our fascination about the hidden psyches of animals, and large in their tragic sense of animal magnificence as it is confronted by the near certainty of violent death. Whatever the doubts the scientist may advance, Seton's delightful account of the extraordinary capacity of the veteran crow "Silverspot" to meaningfully use a wide variety of calls, of his strange propensity to collect treasures, and of his uncanny control of the fledglings raises endlessly intriguing questions.[12] And there is a dark classical simplicity in his depiction of the epic hunt by the remorseless trapper Scotty MacDougall of the Kootenay ram Krag, "majestic as a bull, graceful as a deer, with horns that rolled around his head like thunder-clouds about a peak."[13]

Where Seton is an expansive first-person presence in his stories, explaining how a fox cub learns from a vixen, or slanting a grouse story towards the conservationist, or pointing up the pathos in the persecution of a killer wolf, Roberts' hallmark is restraint. He keeps out of his stories, and is careful not to outdo the "modesty of nature." Unlike Seton, Roberts plots his stories very lightly. He will typically introduce his animal protagonist by setting a scene which offers a series of casual impressions of animals going about their own business. It is as if Blue Fox, in **"The Master of Supply,"** registers the caribou browsing, the bold indifference of the Trumpeter Swans, the "clamouring" ducks, the twittering of the juncos and snow buntings, and the lemming mice squeaking and scurrying along their runways (*infra,* p. 9). Roberts lets his reader share Blue Fox's vigilance, and the latter's quick recognition of an airborne shadow—"slow moving deliberate wings"—and he delays, as the fox might, before identifying the bird as dangerous (the predatory Arctic Hawk-Owl). We find the same casualness punctuated by surprise in many of the stories, notably in **"The Keeper of the Water Gate"** and **"The Homeless One."**

Part of the reader's faith in the truth of Roberts' representations of the wild creatures can be ascribed to the forms in which he focuses his stories.[14] The simplest of these is "the anecdote of observation" (***KW,*** p. 21), which he describes as a story which treats "of a single incident" that lies "within the scope of a single observation" (***Watchers of the Trails,*** p. viii). Of the stories included in this selection, **"The Wolf of the Pool"** offers the clearest example of this form. The effect of such stories is to make us see with the astonished eyes of the exploring observer facets of wilderness life which we have scarcely imagined before. In **"The Little Wolf"** we are taken into the submarine depths of a pond, and invited to pay microscopic attention to "a fantastic looking creature," the back of whose head is almost covered "by two dully staring globes of eyes" (*infra,* p. 101). These are partially veiled by "a shield-like mask," which hinges back in a most sinister fashion when edible creatures appear in view. The story in such 'anecdotes' exists for the observations, and their capacity to quicken the reader's imaginative recognition of the strange otherness of living beings. These stories depend for their effect on the intensity and brevity of the observations.[15]

Closely connected to 'the anecdote' is a form much favoured by Roberts which he calls "the piece of animal biography" (***WT*** [***Watchers of the Trails***], p. viii). This, as he goes on, "follows the wild creature through wide intervals of time and space." Though the writer must necessarily build it up "from observations detached and scattered," he can by artfully linking discrete episodes make his story "not less true to nature than the transcript of an isolated fact." **"The Keepers of the Nest," "The Master of Supply,"** and **"The Keeper of the Water Gate"** are most clearly instances of "the piece of animal biography." In each case, the story follows a creature or creatures though episodes that are widely scattered in time, but each is unified by a couple of main motifs or images. The great whistling swans who are "The Keepers of the Nest" triumph again and again through their mastery of the elements of air and water; while in **"The Master of Supply"** it is Blue Fox's gregarious siting of his lair and his provident digging of cold storage caches that etch themselves in the reader's imagination. With **"The Keeper of the Water Gate,"** the muskrat's cunningly angled submarine tunnel to his nest figures again and again as an indicator of his preferred strategy for survival. These partial animal biographies, like Roberts' 'anecdotes,' tend not so much to highlight the narrative sequence, as to set the reader to musing on the extraordinary as it manifests itself in the ordinary lives of the wild creatures.

The 'piece' of animal biography ought, I think, to be distinguished from the rounded animal biography or complete chronicle (*infra,* p. 81). Where the more fragmentary 'piece' lays emphasis on some distinctive facet of an animal's life, the fuller 'biography' makes it possible for us to gain an impression of the emergent individuality of its animal hero, as the reader may confirm by looking closely at **"The Homeless One," "The King of the Mamozekel,"** and **"Queen Bomba of the Honey-Pots."** Each of these stories offers a cumulative account of an animal's experience in such a way that we almost inevitably see the animal modifying his or her survival strategy in the light of remembered experience. In **"The Homeless One"** there is one episode where the big buck is marshalled down 'rabbit' runways by a huge goshawk behaving in a very peculiar manner (*infra,* p. 41). On this occasion, the snowshoe hare just manages to evade the hawk's mate hovering over the outlet; but when he later encounters a fox with comparable intent, he makes a much prompter escape. Similarly, in **"The King"** the old bull moose at the last discovers the fortitude to overcome his fear of ambushing bears which has plagued him all his life. To use Roberts' words, "In the wilderness world . . . history has a way of repeating itself" (*infra,* p. 97); but a major theme of his stories is that animals do not always repeat themselves. His animal biographies force us to recognize the possibility that animals are capable of applying intelligence to memory, and as a result modifying their instinctive behaviour patterns. Fred Cogswell has good reason for calling these stories "existential," for in the 'biographies' we see their animal protagonists remaking themselves at particular critical moments in their lives.[16]

In his "Introduction" to ***Kindred of the Wild*** (one of his first collections), Roberts mentions "the adventure story" as being the framing form for some of the pieces included. While there are some drawbacks to shaping animal happenings in terms of this form, there are significant advantages as well. The form is considerably less episodic and haphazard than the biographical and anecdotal forms that Roberts tended to prefer, and so might be thought of as less appropriate to reflecting the chance patterns of animal life. However, when Roberts offers an account of one animal hunting another, or trying to escape man, or protecting its young from predators, the episode frequently contains within itself the constituent elements of the adventure story. These include unity of action, a strong element of suspense, and a bold and simple rendering of the protagonist; and while these may be simple, they are adapted by Roberts with thoroughly satisfying effects in **"Mothers of the North," "Lord of the Air,"** and **"By the Winter Tide."**

In the last mentioned of these, every detail of the story contributes to our sense of the inexorability of the fate awaiting the little muskrat, but we continue to hope throughout that he will be delivered from his adventure, and somehow escape the glaring eyes of the great white owl perched above him.[17] Roberts' depiction of setting helps to create the story's mood of suspense. The panorama is laid out in a series of precariously ephemeral planes: the moonscape, the precarious blue-white radiance of the marshes, the mile-on-mile of the Tantramar mud flats, and beyond them all the line of the swift Fundy tide. With the inexorable approach of the flood, a sinister shape "floats over the dyke top" (*infra,* p. 29).

Roberts' language here lures us into seeing the great white owl with his "flaming eyes" as being almost as inescapable as the tide.

The main convention of the adventure story makes us cling to the hope that the little creature will miraculously escape. And Roberts' employment of a further convention of the adventure story makes this matter to us, for he presents the muskrat's inner reaction to the emergency in the simplest, and yet the most sympathetic, terms. Simple characterization is a standard convention in the adventure story, but it happens to be more appropriate to the rendering of animals than of human beings. Roberts shows us action and reaction in the muskrat primarily through images. The little creature's hope of submarine escape arises when "the first frothy rivulets" trickle through the ice cakes to touch his feet, and this hope is given force by his longing for "the narrow safe hole, the long, ascending burrow, and the soft warm-lined chamber that was his nest" (*infra,* p. 31). The very simplicity of the images which embody the longing make Roberts' rendering credible. Without them we would not be able to identify as strongly as we do with the warm little speck of consciousness in the centre of the cold-blue radiance of the story's cruel landscape. Any excess of sentiment in us is checked by Roberts' laying stress on the fact that the would-be predator, the great white owl, is driven by a compelling necessity, "the face of his hunger."

W. H. Magee in a very useful article has argued that Roberts' unique contribution to the animal story was to capture the nonhuman aspect of a creature's experience.[18] On a more questionable line, he has gone on to suggest not only that Roberts is at his best when his theme is an animal's quest for prey or provender, but also that he seldom writes really well "with any want for his heroes but food." This is surely to fail to do justice to Roberts' handling of some of the other great compulsions of an animal's nature. In **"The Lord of the Air"** he treats the great bird's untameable instinct for freedom with absolute conviction. The picture he gives of the eagle's "watchtower," a lightning struck pine, which is hummed about by the untrammelled winds, and which gives unmatchable vistas of valley brims stretching endlessly to the horizon, conveys a superb impression of the eagle's utterly unfettered freedom. And when we see the bird at "the supreme altitude" of his immense spiral, we share for an instant the feeling of superiority to every creature and circumstance in creation. The story depends for its final effect on irony. In the slight heightening of the language, the very occasional introduction of a phrase associated with pomp ("he sailed away majestically"; "the stone . . . was a provision of destiny for his convenience"), Roberts reveals the habit-bound complacency which will betray the eagle to the designs of the trapper. Then when we see the terrible constriction placed on the freedom of the bird—he is chained by a rusty dog-chain to a perch in a rude shack—we become aware of the far greater complacency in the bird's jailers. The dimension of their ignorance is the bird's hunger for freedom, the extent of his gaze from chained entrapment to distant mountaintop. In the dénouement the men's ignorance turns out to be comic when the eagle works free, and leaves them like Laurel and Hardy grasping a broken chair and a useless silver chain, while the great bird mounts to his native element, and the men seem nothing more than grotesque dwarves.

The narrative point of view which Roberts adopts in his stories is admirably suited to conveying the inexorable nature of the evolutionary struggle. It can best be described as "the intimate omniscient," for while the principal attention is directed to the external setting and action, the picture will often come to centre momentarily on the animal in itself—through emotionally charged descriptive details, and a presentation of the creature's simple thoughts. Furthermore Roberts will quite frequently employ the equivalent of a split scene focus, divided between protagonist and antagonist to enhance our understanding of the dynamics of the conflict. In **"Mothers of the North"** Roberts gives us a parallel picture of the two mothers—the emaciated polar bear making scarcely enough milk to keep her cub alive, and the walrus anxiously coaxing her wounded calf to nurse. We are made to see the source of the walrus' protective feeling in the description of "the truculence" of her calf's sprouting tusks which is "belied by the mildness of its baby eyes." We see the same material solicitude reflected in the description of the bear whose eyes "film" when her cub whimpers at the too thin stream of milk. For a time the story's focus centres on one of the mothers, and we follow the actions and reactions of the polar bear mother, who has caught the scent of the walruses, knows that they are at their ease, recognizes them as formidable adversaries, yet is driven by hunger to hunt them. At the crisis, however, we again have a double picture, when we see the bear as she must appear to the walrus, and the walrus as she must appear to the bear. Roberts' narrative technique is designed to enable him to offer the most balanced and objective account possible of the inevitable conflict at the heart of nature.

It is only in the stories where human beings figure significantly that Roberts adopts the limited third person narrative perspective which allows him to offer a fairly full picture of the inner life of the protagonists as well as to depict the external action in which they participate. In **"Vagrants of the Barren"** we follow the story by following the movements of its hero, Pete Noel, but at the same time come to know a great deal about his thoughts and feelings. Even here, we are not confined to seeing the story from the standpoint of a single figure, because, as we will see, Roberts offers his characteristic double perspective at the moment of the story's concluding crisis.

When attending to the external appearance and actions of Pete Noel, Roberts uses metaphoric and descriptive language which underline the veteran woodsman's animal affinities. This is a story very much in key with the purely 'animal' stories. When burnt out of his shack, Noel "in the deprivation of his tree roof" has been taken back "appreciably nearer to the elemental brute" (*infra,* p. 148). We see him devouring the charred remnant of a side of bacon "with as much ceremony as a hungry wolf," and later after a hard day's trek, he 'claws' himself a deep sleeping hole (*infra,* p. 149). His one hope is to find an animal and kill it for the nourishment which will give him the strength to endure; and his opportunity arises when a herd of caribou appear on the ridge above his sleeping hole. Roberts now draws attention again and again to the parallels between Noel and a hunting beast. To prevent the caribou from scenting his man "taint," he must painstakingly get upwind of them, which he does "by slipping furtively from rampike to rampike, now creeping, now worming his way like a snake" (*infra,* p. 152). When the caribou subsequently take alarm, Noel doggedly trails them, his eyes "automatically" downwards, and when he loses the trail in a sudden storm, he plunges into it with a grim animal courage. Finally, in the last extremity of hunger and exhaustion, he literally falls on the caribou; he now reacts with the fury of a beast at bay, his unsheathed knife being the human equivalent of the sharp antlers with which the floundering caribou prods at him (*infra,* p. 157). The external perspective offered by Roberts thus compels us to see Noel as a hunting creature, almost indistinguishable in attributes to many of the animal denizens of his stories.

The inner aspect of the third person narrative perspective, which allows us to discover a good deal about the thoughts and feelings running through Noel's mind, significantly modifies this picture. What Roberts emphasizes here in his protagonist is the reflective habit of mind of an equable philosophic temperament. Even as his lonely home is being consumed by the flames, the woodsman, far from giving way to understandable spasms of anguish and dismay, is taking stock of his means of survival and figuring on turning the catastrophic flames to advantage. Noel's defiant reflective powers, which both here and subsequently hold his impulses in check, are presented in different terms than those of the animals. In Roberts' work, the wild creatures are shown as having memories which work through relatively simple image patterns, but these memories only comparatively rarely impel them to modify instinctive behaviour, and then only in fairly predictable ways. By contrast, Noel's reflective powers are forcibly counterpointed to his impulses, and permit a very strong awareness of the human self. This is most apparent when in his sleeping trench under the icy stars, he weighs the full strength of his silent adversary (Nature in her cruel and predatory phase). At this point he becomes self consciously aware of "the indomitable man-spirit" within him (*infra,* p. 150).

What Roberts means by this expression becomes clear at critical moments during Noel's struggle for survival. When he works his way up on the caribou, only to discover that they have moved off some distance, his impulses tempt him to rush off in pursuit. But a voice within him which blends resolution, restraint and calculation tells him that the exercise of intelligent patience is his best hope, even if it is a forlorn one. Later when all seems lost, and the storm has swallowed the animals' trail and all signs of refuge, he finds his way in terms of the direction of the wind, and its relation to what he remembers of the lay of the land. In the overwhelming confusion of the storm, he knows that the caribou will "forget both their cunning and the knowledge that they are being hunted," but for himself he does not forget these things.

To this point, the heart of the story lies in Noel's subjective experience, as this reaches us through the intimate aspect of the third person technique. As the story moves to its conclusion, however, Roberts offers us his characteristic double perspective. The homeless woodsman is tempted to make good his loss by preying on the stormbound herd, but the moment his hand touches his first victim's flank, he is powerless to act. The flow of sympathy from beast to man and from man to beast breaks the hard shell of Noel's self-absorption. At the point where Roberts writes "when his hand strayed down the muzzle, the animal gave a terrified snort at the dreaded man smell so violently invading his nostrils," we recognize that both the author and his protagonist have the imaginative capacity to live within the hide of the caribou, if only for an instant (*infra,* p. 157). A single sentence here serves to provide a surprisingly strong counterpoint to the human tone and perspective of much of the story.

The human perspective of the protagonist is more radically undercut in **"The Ledge on Bald Face,"** which can best be described as an ironic parable. It should serve to remind the reader of how ardently Roberts desired to achieve "a purely objective" presentation in his best work. Here the veteran woodsman, Joe Peddler, in his attempt to cross a high and perilous ledge, presumes that he can "take full measure of these splendid breadths of sunlit, wind-washed space" (*infra,* p. 161). Throughout his long climb across the brow of the mountain, which conceals layer on layer of geologic time, he persists in nursing the conviction that his right to life is almost as superior to those of the animals he meets, as he is to "the interminable leagues of cedar swamp" far below (*infra,* p. 159). As he perseveres in striding into the glare of the sun, we are brought to see the utter delusion in his pride in his eagle perspective. The eagles circling about the heights know what he does not: that the 'Law' requires that creatures cross the ledge with the sun behind them and not in front of them, so that they will avoid "unnecessary—and necessarily deadly . . . struggle" (*infra,* p. 160).

Roberts' achievement in this story is to make it a closely observed and credible story of a knowledgeable woodsman's exploration of a new trail through the high country; and at the same time to incorporate into it his recognition of the qualities of his protagonist which make him an unlikely exemplar of the inner forces that set man against the possibilities and necessities of nature. For, though the story may be the unfolding of an enthralling adventure for its human protagonist, it is also a record of understated but sustained terror for the wild creatures who are following nature's primitive imperative by crossing the ledge with the sun behind them. Joe Peddler is able to overcome them with his bold confidence, and sends one bear scurrying, followed by his mocking laughter (a potent means of human domination as we see in the "Mrs. Gammit" story). He is able to dominate a second bear by the steady authority of his voice, and to compel him to retrace his footsteps. If we are to take the story as parable, the picture of Peddler driving the bear forward suggests the way man in general is herding the animals the wrong way down a perilous and deadly path.

The overall effect of Roberts' animal stories is to remind us of what Joe Peddler knows and has forgotten, and to impress on our imaginations what we see Pete Noel experiencing so comprehensively. For these stories serve to restore "confidence in the reality of the universal and original impulses" and to reemphasize "the distinction between the essentials and the accessories of life."[19]

Notes

1. Terry Whalen's view, "Charles G. D. Roberts," *Canadian Writers and their Works: Fiction Series,* Vol 1, ed. by Robert Lecker et al. (Toronto: ECW Press, 1989), 174.
2. The seven are: E. H. Bennett, ed., *Forest Folk* (Toronto: Ryerson, 1949); *Thirteen Bears* (Toronto: Ryerson, 1947); *Seven Bears* (Richmond Hill: Scholastic, 1977); Alec Lucas, ed., *The Last Barrier and Other Stories* (Toronto: McClelland & Stewart, 1958); Joseph Gold, ed., *King of Beasts and Other Stories* (Toronto: Ryerson, 1967); *Eyes of the Wilderness,* Copyright Joan Roberts, illustrated by Brian Carter (Toronto: McGraw-Hill Ryerson, 1980); and John Coldwell Adams' edition of the three last unpublished stories *The Lure of the Wild* (Ottawa: Borealis, 1980).
3. From "The Iceberg," reprinted in W. J. Keith, ed., *Selected Poetry and Critical Prose: Sir Charles G. D. Roberts* (Toronto: University of Toronto Press), 207.
4. Fred Cogswell, "Charles G. D. Roberts (1860-1943)," in *Canadian Writers and their Works: Poetry Series,* Vol 2, ed. by Robert Lecker et al. (Toronto: ECW Press, 1983), 209.
5. "Poet: Irving Layton Observed," Canadian National Film Board Documentary.
6. "The Excursion: Preface," ll. 66, 68.
7. Quoted from Roberts' poem "The Marvellous Work," 1.22.
8. "Lines Composed a Few Miles above Tintern Abbey," ll. 75, 122-3.
9. Wordsworth, "The Mutability Sonnet," quoted in J. Gold, "The Precious Speck of Life," *Canadian Literature,* No. 26 (Aut 1965), 22-32.
10. Letter to *Century Magazine,* 26 Oct. 1908.
11. For a colourful characterization of Darwinian theories, see J. Travers Lewis, *Agnosticism* (Kingston, 1883) and *Second Lecture on Agnosticism* (Ottawa, 1884). These were Bishop Lewis' contributions to a pamphlet campaign that he undertook against W. D. LeSueur who was championing Darwinian ideas.
12. "Silverspot, the Story of a Crow," reprinted in *Selected Stories of Ernest Thompson Seton,* ed. by Patricia Morley (Ottawa: University of Ottawa Press, 1977), 19-32.
13. "Krag, the Kootenay Ram," *ibid.,* 129-66.
14. W. J. Keith has set the terms for the discussion of the types of Roberts' animal stories, though the account given here differs in some respects from his. See W. J. Keith, "Stories of Wild Life," *Charles G. D. Roberts* (Toronto: Copp Clark, 1969).
15. "The Little Wolf of the Pool" had a companion piece "The Little Wolf of the Air." Roberts combined the two and rewrote the story which he called "In a Summer Pool." This has recently been published in *The Lure of the Wild: the last three animal stories by Sir Charles G. D. Roberts,* ed. by John Coldwell Adams (Ottawa: Borealis Press, 1980).
16. Cogswell, 219.
17. For a story about an Arctic Owl driven south by hunger, see "The Odyssey of the Great White Owl," in *The Lure of the Wild,* 11-21.
18. W. H. Magee, "The Animal Story: A Challenge in Technique," *Dalhousie Review* XLIV (1961), 161 ff.

19. Roberts' words as a young man in his twenties, "Introduction" to *Poems of Wild Life* (1888), reprinted in W. J. Keith, ed., *Selected Poetry and Critical Prose: Sir Charles G. D. Roberts* (Toronto: University of Toronto Press, 1974), 266.

J. E. Baker (review date winter 1993-94)

SOURCE: Baker, J. E. Review of *The Vagrants of the Barren and Other Stories,* by Charles G. D. Roberts. *Dalhousie Review* 73, no. 4 (winter 1993-94): 560-62.

[*In the following review, Baker contends that the judicious selection of stories in* The Vagrants of the Barren *allows readers to discover and assess Roberts's career as a short fiction writer.*]

This collection of animal stories [***The Vagrants of the Barren***] represents a recent trend in Canadian literary criticism's reappraisal of Roberts's significance to Canadian literature, presenting him to a new generation of readers. Long out of vogue, particularly since the advent of the 1960s generation of literary critics, Roberts's animal stories are here made accessible for readers in the 1990s. With the public's interest in ecology growing more insistent by the day, a re-reading of Roberts can prove surprisingly fresh for readers of David Suzuki's day. The basics for such a reappraisal are well provided by Ware, whose expertise is self-effacingly tucked away in the bibliography where we learn that his 1980 PhD thesis from Dalhousie, *Canadian Romanticism in Transition,* contains a discussion of the evolution of Roberts's vision, including his Darwinian ideas.

Ware says at the outset that his selection was "daunting" and that his choices represent

> the best of the more than two hundred and thirty animal stories written by Roberts over a span of almost fifty years (1886-1935) . . . and that in the best of these [perhaps about five dozen, by Terry Whalen's calculations], we recognize a distinctive voice and a distinctive achievement.

Ware further points out that

> recent readers have been more and more drawn to the best of [Roberts's] animal stories—for their storytelling and artistic power, for the modest precision of the representation of animals, and for the challenge offered by their interpretation of animal psychology.

This challenge is one addressed specifically in the "Critical Discussions" section of his bibliography: he delineates specifically the so-called (by US President Theodore Roosevelt) "Nature Fakir" controversy concerning the work of Roberts and his contemporary, Ernest Thompson Seton, by means of a sequence of relevant periodical titles. This is the sort of useful information to be found in the critical apparatus of Ware's book. Such bibliographical headings as "Early Discussions (before 1965)," "Recent Discussions (since 1964)," and "Scientific Discussions of the Kinship of Man and Animals" serve to produce a context for a contemporary appreciation of Roberts.

Ware's selections are judiciously chosen in that each represents an aspect of Roberts's work that is strikingly his own. For example, one of the shortest, **"By the Winter Tide,"** is almost a version of "Tantramar Revisited" in focussing closely on the details of the area of one of the "Two Rivers" (the other being the St. John) Roberts had known, and been formed by, from childhood:

> Had it been daylight, the chaotic icefield would have shown small beauty, every wave-beaten floe being soiled and streaked with rust-coloured Tantramar mud. But under the transfiguring touch of the moon the unsightly levels changed to plains of infinite mystery—expanses of shattered, white granite, as it were, fretted and scrawled with blackness—reaches of loneliness older than time. So well is the mask of eternity assumed by the mutable moonlight and the ephemeral ice.

Such a passage does much to support Fred Cogswell's claim (in *Charles G. D. Roberts,* 1983) that Roberts's prose, in "the more imaginative portions of his animal stories, was as much a fulfilment of his poetic urges as it was a fulfilment of his drive towards freedom from convention." In the same volume, Cogswell says "the most serviceable tasks that can be performed for Roberts are the provision of an adequate biography" (this has now been done, by John Colwell Adams) "the publication of his letters, and the production of well-edited editions of his complete poems and the various volumes of his prose fictions." He notes "these events are not likely to occur rapidly unless more Canadian scholars are convinced that Roberts is worth such attention." The publication of Ware's collection is timely in hastening such conviction. His collection makes accessible to scholar and general reader alike an affordable and approachable number of Roberts's stories, culled by their editor's sure hand and given context by his Introduction and Notes.

D. M. R. Bentley (essay date 1999)

SOURCE: Bentley, D. M. R. "'The Thing Is Found to Be Symbolic': *Symboliste* Elements in the Early Short Stories of Gilbert Parker, Charles G. D. Roberts, and Duncan Campbell Scott." In *Dominant Impressions: Es-*

says on the Canadian Short Story, edited by Gerald Lynch and Angela Arnold Robbeson, pp. 27-51. Ottawa, Canada: University of Ottawa Press, 1999.

[*In the following essay, Bentley explores the connection of the early stories of Roberts, Gilbert Parker, and Duncan Campbell Scott to the* symboliste *movement.*]

> It is a very simple matter. Find the idea in the thing in Nature and put the idea in the thing in Art, and the problem is solved.
>
> —Richard Hovey, "The Passing of Realism" (1895)

In the essay entitled "Modern Symbolism and Maurice Maeterlinck" that serves as the introduction to the first series of his translations of Maeterlinck's *Plays* (1894), Richard Hovey makes the bold but not untenable assertion that in their symbolic practices Bliss Carman, Gilbert Parker, and Charles G. D. Roberts are akin to "Mallarmé in France [and] Maeterlinck in Belgium." With an eye very likely on Mallarmé's *L'Après-midi d'un faune* (which he had recently used as a basis for "The Faun. A Fragment" in *Songs from Vagabondia* [1894]) as well as on the poems and plays of Maeterlinck, Hovey defines "[t]he symbolism of today" as a literary mode characterized by evocative suggestion rather than explicit statement:

> It by no means . . . involves a complete and consistent allegory. Its events, its personages, its sentences rather imply than definitely state an esoteric meaning. The story, whether romantic . . . or realistic . . . , lives for itself and produces no impression of being a masquerade of moralities; but behind every incident, almost behind every phrase, one is aware of a lurking universality, the adumbration of greater things. One is given an impression of the thing symbolized rather than a formulation.
>
> (5)

In Hovey's view, Parker's "The Stone" in *Pierre and His People* (1892) and Roberts's **"The Young Ravens That Call upon Him"** in the May 1894 number of *Lippincott's Monthly Magazine* are North American instances of a type of "symbolism [that is] suggestive rather than cut-and-dried": in Parker's work "the Man and the Stone exist primarily for their own simple terrific story" but "are lifted up at the same time into Titanic primitive types" and, similarly, Roberts's "tales of animals are symbolic . . . not with the artificial symbolism of 'Aesop's Fables' . . . , but by revealing in the simple truth of animal life a universal meaning. The symbol is not invented; the thing is found to be symbolic" (6-7). "[I]t promises well for the literature that is to be," adds Hovey, "that the strongest of the young writers of to-day have a tendency to myth-making" that reveals itself in their adherence to this modern "symbolic principle" (7, 8).

As motivated as they doubtless were by a desire to give European symbolism a local habitation and to publicize the names of some of his best literary friends (see Macdonald 157), Hovey's remarks are nevertheless valuable for the light that they shed on the early short stories of Parker, Roberts, and—to substitute a third short-story writer for a friend and collaborator—Duncan Campbell Scott. If not quite as strikingly as *Pierre and His People* and ***Earth's Enigmas. A Book of Animal and Nature Life*** (1896) (where **"The Young Ravens That Call upon Him"** was first published in book form), Scott's *In the Village of Viger* (1896) displays the *symboliste* "traits and methods" that Hovey admired (7), particularly the evocation of "esoteric meaning" and a reliance on "types." Nor should this be at all surprising, for *In the Village of Viger,* like *Pierre and His People,* ***Earth's Enigmas*** and, of course, Hovey's own preference for "primitive types" and naturally symbolic animals, participates in two of the discourses that shaped Canadian almost as much as American writing in the 1880s and '90s: (1) the discourse of anti-modernity that valorized pre- and undercivilized spaces as realms of emotional and spiritual intensity anterior or adjacent to the materialistic and artificial world of the modern city; and (2) the related discourse of therapeutics that encouraged writers to produce books set in such spaces that would medicine the minds and nervous systems of the victims of modernity (see Lears, and Bentley "Carman and Mind Cure"). Hovey's closing observation about his Canadian *confrères* carries the imprint of both discourses in its insistence that "[t]heir work is saner, fresher, and less morbid" than its British equivalents and that "[t]he clear air of the lakes and prairies of Canada blows through it" (8). A "romantic" or a "realistic" work set in the Northwest, the animal world, or a French-Canadian village, Hovey implies, would allow the reader to experience vicariously the health-giving properties of these environments. If such a work also contained evocations of "universal" and "esoteric" meaning, so much better (for) the reader.

Of the circumambient presence of these ideas in late nineteenth- and early twentieth-century Canadian literature there can be no doubt. As demonstrated elsewhere (see Bentley, "Carman and Mind Cure"), the *Vagabondia* volumes of Carman and Hovey (1894, 1896, 1901) are programmatically therapeutic, as are the collections of poems and essays that Carman published between Hovey's untimely death in 1900 and the First World War. By 1885-87 in "Heat" and "Among the Timothy," Archibald Lampman was offering poetic renditions of what the Canadian novelist James Macdonald Oxley was calling "wise idleness"—"quietly absorbing something through the eye or ear that for the time at least drowns the petty business and worries of life" (56)—as a cure for minds disturbed by the enervating conditions of modern life. "I confess that my design for instance in writing 'Among the Timothy' was not in the first place to describe a landscape," Lampman told Hamlin Garland in 1889, "but to describe the effect of a few hours spent among the summer fields on a mind in a troubled and despondent condition" (qtd. in Doyle 42).[1] That Scott, who wrote and published the first of the Viger stories in the late 1880s, shared his friend and mentor's faith in "wise idleness" as a cure for—to quote "Among the Timothy"—the "aching mood" induced by "blind gray streets [and] the jingle of the throng" (*Poems* 14)—becomes very clear in the second of the two poems that preface *In the Village of Viger,* where the reader is invited to see the stories that follow as a therapeutic equivalent of "a few hours spent among . . . summer fields":

> Whoever has from toil and stress
> Put into ports of idleness,
> And watched the gleaming thistledown
> Wheel in the soft air lazily blown . . .
> . . . . .
> Might find perchance the wandering fire,
> Around St. Joseph's sparkling spire.
> And wearied with the fume and strife,
> The complex joys and ills of life,
> Might for an hour his worry staunch,
> In pleasant Viger by the Blanche.

As explicit as this about the therapeutic benefits of short fiction is Roberts's account of the emancipatory effects of the modern animal story at the conclusion of his Introduction to ***The Kindred of the Wild: A Book of Animal Life*** (1902): "It frees us for a little from the world of shop-worn utilities, and from the mean tenement of self of which we do well to grow weary. It helps us to return to nature, without requiring that we at the same time return to barbarism. It leads us back to the old kinship of earth . . . [t]he clear and candid life. . . . It has ever the more significance, it has ever the richer gift of refreshment and renewal, the more human the heart and spiritual the understanding which we bring to the intimacy of it" (29, and see Lucas vi). Parker is silent on the therapeutic aspect of his short stories, but his insistence in his introductory Note to *Pierre and His People* that, despite the impact of the railway and other manifestations of modernity on the Canadian west, life in "the far north . . . is much the same as it was a hundred years ago" (1: xv)[2] could well indicate his awareness of the regenerative properties ascribed to remote times and places by contemporary therapeutical discourse. Certainly, the extreme enthusiasm of W. H. Henley for the Pierre stories (see Adams 67-68) aligns them with the school of thought, soon to be espoused by Theodore Roosevelt, that strong doses of (masculine) strenuosity were needed to cure British and American culture of their (feminine) effeteness.[3]

Like their American and British counterparts, Canadian practitioners of literary mind cures may have disagreed about whether "wise idleness" (rest) or atavistic exertion (exercise) was the best prescription for the diseases of modernity, but none appears to have doubted that the writer and the reader's capacity to see beyond "things" to "greater things" was crucial to the efficacy of book therapy. In his Introduction to the Imperial Edition of *Pierre and His People,* Parker claims that the text from the Bible that he quotes in the opening short story—"*Free among the Dead like unto them that are wounded and lie in the grave, that are out of remembrance*" (1: 24; Psalm 88.5)—"became in a sense, the text for all the stories which came after" and describes the collection's unifying subject-matter as characters "wounded by Fate" and "The soul of goodness in things evil" (1: x-xi). In the prefatory poem to *In the Village of Viger,* "the wandering fire"—the Will-o'-the-wisp that distracts people from their workaday world—may be glimpsed "Around St. Joseph's sparkling spire." And in the Introductory to ***The Kindred of the Wild,*** the modern animal story brings its richest gifts of "refreshment and renewal" to those who have the most "humane . . . heart and spiritual . . . understanding." To the extent that they invoke orthodox Christianity as an interpretive context, all of these statements are somewhat misleading, for situations and occurrences abound in the short stories of Parker, Scott, and Roberts that clearly intimate the existence of occult forces in the human and natural worlds and impress upon the reader a disquieting (and presumably, enriching) sense of the mystery of the universe. As discussions of each collection will quickly show, superstition, the supernatural, and an emphasis on the uncanny are common features of *Pierre and His People, In the Village of Viger,* and ***Earth's Enigmas*** (which Roberts initially considered calling "Riddles of the Earth" [*Collected Letters* 183]). "As the visible world is measured, mapped, tested, weighed," wrote Andrew Lang in 1905, readers increasingly turn to literature to feel "the stirring of ancient dread in their veins" (qtd. in Lears 172, and see Bentley, "UnCannyda"). What more efficacious prescription for the rationalism, materialism, and "spiritual blindness" (Lears 173) of modern life than a dose of the immaterial, the inexplicable, and the affecting?

As Parker constructs "the Far North" in his Note to *Pierre and His People* and his Introduction to his *Works,* it is a veritable pharmacopoeia for the anaemia of modern life—a hinterland of "adventure," "isolation and pathetic loneliness," "poignant mystery, solitude, and primitive incident" salubriously remote from "cities . . . towns" and "the fertile field of civilization" (1: xv; 3: vii-ix). "In these . . . stories it was Mr. Parker's good fortune to be first in an unoccupied field," wrote Carman in 1894; in "[t]he unknown vastness of the Canadian Northwest . . . [a] region stretching far away into the land of perpetual night and everlasting snow, touched with the glamour of uncivilized romance and the mysticism of an earlier race, he found . . . a canvas large enough for the elemental scenes he wished to portray" (qtd. in Adams 61).[4] Since Parker's main interest lay less in local colour and Jamesian portraiture than in types and archetypes, or, in his terms, "reincarnat[ions]

[of] the everlasting human ego and its scena" (2: ix), the settings and characters of the short stories in *Pierre and His People* are usually presented through minimalist description and portentous allusions that invite the reader to consider their "symbolic" or "universal" significance. Encouraging this movement from "the thing" to "the greater thing" are anonymous and omniscient narrators who not only enter minds and appear simultaneously at different places but also—and this is crucial to the evocation of "mystery" in the stories—contrive to be both knowledgeable and reticent about the hidden forces that appear to be shaping the "primitive incident[s]" and "elemental scenes" that they are describing. The result of this is that—to adapt an observation by James L. Kugel in *The Techniques of Strangeness in Symbolist Poetry*—many of the short stories in *Pierre and His People* exude "a certain aura of mystery . . . due to missing information which, it is implied, is necessary for full comprehension. In other words, the [narrator] creates . . . strangeness by not telling everything, or, more precisely, by implying that not everything has been told" (38).

A good case in point is "The Patrol of the Cypress Hills," the story that begins the collection and sets the tone of what is to follow in a variety of ways, including the incorporation of the text from Psalm 88.5 that seemed to Parker "to suggest the lives and the ends of the workers of the pioneer world" (Works 1: x). Despite the geographical specificity of its title, the setting of "The Patrol of the Cypress Hills" is more suggestive than precise: the frontier is a realm of "breadth . . . vastness, and . . . pure air"; the "[s]now is hospitable-clean . . . restful and silent"; the "sun [comes] up like a great flower expanding. First the yellow, then the purple, then the red, and then a mighty shield of roses" (1: 7, 13, 23). The principal character, the Kiplingesque Sergeant Fones of the Northwest Mounted Police, is "part of the great machine of Order" and, according to his commandant "'the best soldier on the patrol,'" but he is also described by the narrator as a "little Bismarck" and, when mounted on his "stout bronco," likened by an Irish private to "the Devil and Death" (1: 8, 7, 11). Moreover, he is the subject of numerous unanswered questions: "But what of Sergeant Fones? . . . But was Sergeant Fones such a one? . . . What was Sergeant Fones' country? No one knew. Where had he come from? No one asked him more than once" (1: 6, 7, 8). Compounding these ambiguities and uncertainties are allusions to the myth of the Minotaur (1: 12-13), gestures toward the parable of the prodigal son (1: 23), references to "unknown" and "unreckoned forces" (1: 19, 20), and a series of puzzling parallels or coincidences ("And Sergeant Fones in the barracks said just then . . . 'Exactly' . . . What did it mean?" [1: 19-20]) whose cumulative effect is to surround the characters and events of the story with an "aura" of mystery and foreboding and, more than this, to suggest that they are fulfilling some unknown and unknowable design.

When Sergeant Fones is finally found dead on Christmas Day, "[m]otionless, stern, erect . . . upon his horse, beside a stunted larch tree" with "[t]he bridle rein . . . still in [his] frigid fingers, and a smile upon his face" (1: 23), the reader shares the bafflement of the narrator and the other characters, not merely because of the enigmatic nature of the Sergeant's death and smile, but also because Parker has thwarted any single or straightforward interpretation of his fate by presenting him as neither a simple, allegorical figure with a specific meaning nor as a complex, rounded character with justifying motivations. If intentions can be judged by results, then the purpose of "The Patrol of the Cypress Hills" is to suggest that the events and relationships of human life are indeed governed by "unseen" and "unreckoned forces." In the pensive and incomplete "'I felt sometimes'" that one of the characters utters "silently" to herself over the dead body of Sergeant Fones may perhaps be read a metonymy of the gnomonic qualities of a story that leaves the reader with an abiding sense that there is much in human nature that cannot be expressed in words, explained in rational terms, or reduced to materialistic laws of cause and effect.

Many of the qualities of "The Patrol of the Cypress Hills" are also present in the story that Hovey praises for its mythopoeic presentation of "Titanic primitive types." In the opening paragraphs of "The Stone," the reader is quickly inducted into a realm where human beings—in this case the inhabitants of a small settlement named Purple Hill—live in the shadow of "portentous" "Nature" in the form of a "mighty and wonderful" Stone that, according to "Indian legends" to which "white men pay little heed," "one whom they called The Man Who Sleeps" will one day dislodge from its "jutting crag" to crush those who have "dared [to] cumber his playground" in the village below (*Works* 1: 205-207). From the outset, the narrator prepares the way for the inevitable fulfillment of the Indian legend by emphasizing the strange logic of The Stone's relationship to the villagers: the terrain seems to have been designed to facilitate the prophesied catastrophe ("the hill hollow[s] and narrow[s] from The Stone to the village, as if giants had made . . . [a] path" [1: 205]); The Stone itself is uncanny in its appearance and apparent behaviour ("[a]t times . . . it . . . [seems] to rest on nothing. . . . But if one look[s] long, especially in summer, when the air throb[s], it evidently rock[s] upon . . . [its] toe" [1: 205-206]); the "first man"—later The Man—who settled in the valley had "a strange feeling" about The Stone, and his daughter goes "mad, and g[ives] birth to a dead child" at the thought that it "would hurtle down the hill at her great moment and destroy her and her child" (1: 206-207). As to what force or power has created this portentous situation, the narrator offers only alternatives: "Nature," "God or Fate" (1: 207).

Of one thing, however, the narrator is certain: the destruction of the village is a consequence of the selfishness, cruelty, unjustness, and evil of its inhabitants, whose most heinous sins of omission and commission include the acts that drive The Man into exile in "a rude hut" near The Stone and, finally, provoke him to enact his revenge: the death of his sick wife by starvation "because none . . . remembered . . . her and her needs"; the "lynching" of his only son for a crime that someone else was found to have committed; and the attempted murder of Pierre by dropping him over "the edge of a hill" (1: 207-209). As Pierre wakens from "the crashing gloom which succeeded [his] fall," he is confronted by "a being whose appearance [is] awesome and massive—an outlawed god" who has grown in his long exile to resemble not just a "Titan" and a "god" but also an Old Testament prophet and the immense Stone with which he had come to be identified. "Indeed, The Stone seemed more a thing of life . . . : The Man was sculptured rock. His white hair was chiselled on his broad brow, his face was a solemn pathos petrified, his lips were curled with an iron contempt, and incalculable anger" (1: 209).

In the nights following his rescue, Pierre first hears and then watches as The Man chips away at the "toe" of The Stone with the "eagerness of an avenging giant" (1: 210). Initially resolving to be the "cynical and approving spectator of an act of exquisite retaliation," Pierre gradually comes to harbour doubts about the justice of destroying the entire village: "had all those people hovering about those lights below done him harm? . . . [A] few—and they were women—would not have followed his tumbril to his death with cries of execration. The rest would have done so,—most of them did so,—not because he was a criminal, but because he was a victim, and because human nature as it is thirsts inordinately at times for blood and sacrifice—a living strain of the old barbaric instinct" (1: 211-212). As he continues to think "now doubtfully, now savagely, now with irony" about what is about to occur, Pierre suddenly sees the "fitness" for his situation of Abraham's final plea to God in Genesis 18.32 to spare the city of Sodom: "'*Oh, let not the Lord be angry, and I will yet speak but this once: Peradventure ten righteous shall be found there*'" (1: 212). To this, The Man's reply is a Jehovistic "'I will not spare it for ten's sake'" and a resolute "'*Now!*'" (1: 212). With the moon temporarily behind a cloud, "a monster spr[ings] from its pedestal upon Purple Hill, and, with a sound of thunder and an awful speed, race[s] upon the village below. The boulder of the hillside crumble[s] after it" (1: 213). When "[t]he moon sh[ines] out again for an instant," Pierre sees "The Man st[anding] where the Stone had been but when he reache[s] the place The Man [is] gone. Forever!" (1: 213). Melodramatic though this is, it leaves the reader disquietened and querying. Has The Man fled the scene or jumped to his death? Was his destruction of the village just or unjust? Was its ultimate cause God, Fate, (human) Nature or some combination of the three? Which of Pierre's attitudes to the event—doubt, savageness, or irony—is most appropriate, and what ethical weight should be given to the references to the "tumbril[s]" of the Reign of Terror and the persistence of "the old barbaric instinct" in his analysis of the villagers' behaviour? It is not difficult to see why Hovey singled out "The Stone" for special mention: arguably more than any other story in *Pierre and His People,* it raises momentous questions and frustrates full comprehension, leaving the reader with something like the "strange feeling" that prompted The Man to pay his first visit to The Stone.

As their collective title suggests, the short stories in ***Earth's Enigmas*** are also designed to generate feelings of mystery and puzzlement in the reader. In a Prefatory Note to the 1903 edition of the collection, Roberts both confirms this intention and emphasizes it by referring to the non-rational aspects of the bulk of the volume's contents:

> Most of the stories in this collection attempt to present one or another of those problems of life or nature to which, as it appears to many of us, there is not adequate solution within sight. Others are the almost literal transcript of dreams which seemed to me to have a coherency, completeness, and symbolic significance sufficiently marked to justify me in setting them down.[5] The rest are scenes from that simple life of the Canadian backwoods and tide-country with which my earlier years made me familiar.
>
> (5)

While the stories in Roberts's third category are not without interest as therapeutic conduits to a "simple life" remote from the vexing complexities of modernity,[6] those that show the clearest affinities with the *symboliste* mode are the "problem" and "dream" pieces. **"The Young Ravens That Call upon Him"** (which Hovey mentions) is here, as are the very similar **"Do Seek Their Meat from God"** (the first story in the collection) and the eerily supernatural **"The Perdu,"** a story that Francis Sherman, probably primed by Roberts, pronounced "more symbolic than tales of realism are likely to be" (qtd. in Pomeroy 140). Almost half a century after their first appearance in book form in 1896, Roberts used Elsie Pomeroy's "almost autobiographical record" of his life and work (*Collected Letters* 629) to call attention to the "grim symbolism" of the "dream" stories in ***Earth's Enigmas*** and to lament the "explanatory conclusion" and "practical explanation" that were added to two of them—**"The Stone Dog"** and **"In the Accident Ward"**—to satisfy "the market" (Pomeroy 140-141). He also has Pomeroy proclaim **"The Hill of Chastisement"** probably the most powerful of the dream pieces (141), very likely because its "grim symbolism" is not divested of its affectiveness by rational explanation.

"The Hill of Chastisement" may well have been generated by a dream, as Roberts claimed, but this does not prevent it from also being the product of literary influences. Of these the most obvious are the macabre poems and short stories of Edgar Allan Poe,[7] whose influence Roberts would have felt both directly in any number of collections and anthologies and indirectly through the work of Dante Gabriel Rossetti and various other writers. Since **"The Hill of Chastisement"** was one of the stories added to ***Earth's Enigmas*** in 1903, some eight years after Roberts informed Carman on January 8, 1895 that he already had a copy of the first series of Hovey's translations of Maeterlinck's plays ("I have Dick's 'Maeterlinck.' Fine essay, admirable translation" [Boone, *Collected Letters* 190]), those other writers doubtless included the playwright whose work Hovey explicitly likens in his introductory essay to "Poe's ghastly tales" (11). A juxtaposition of excerpts from Hovey's translations of the opening and closing stage directions of two of Maeterlinck's most Poeian plays, *Les Aveugles* ("The Blind") and *L'Intruse* ("The Intruder"), with the equivalent parts of **"The Hill of Chastisement"** highlights their similarities:

> An ancient Norland forest, with an eternal look, under a sky of stars. In the centre, and in the deep of the night, a very old priest is sitting, wrapped in a great black cloak. The chest and the head, gently upturned and deathly motionless, rest against the trunk of a giant oak. . . . The dumb, fixed eyes no longer look out from the visible side of Eternity and seem to bleed with immemorial sorrows and with tears. The hair, of a solemn whiteness, falls in stringy locks, stiff and few, over a face more illuminated and more weary than all that surrounds it in the watchful stillness of that melancholy wood. The cave-mouth wherein I dwelt, doing night-long penance for my sin, was midway of the steep slope of the hill. The hill, naked and rocky, rose into a darkness of gray mist. Below, it fell steeply into the abyss, which was full of the blackness of a rolling smoke. . . .
>
> In the heart of the sanctuary, far withdrawn, sat an old man, a saint, in a glory of clear and pure light. . . . He sat with grave head bowed continually over a book that shone like crystal, and his beard full to his feet.
>
> * * *
>
> Here suddenly a wail of fright is heard in the child's room, on the night; and this wail continues, with gradations of terror until the end of the scene. . . .
>
> At the moment a hurrying of headlong heavy steps is heard in the room on the left.—Then a deathly stillness.—They listen in a dumb terror, until the door opens slowly, and the light from the next room falls into that in which they are waiting. The Sister of Charity appears on the threshold, in the black garments of her order. . . .
>
> * * *
>
> As I grasped my sanctuary, the air rang with loud laughter; the faces, coming out of the smoke, sprang wide-eyed and flaming close about me; a red flare shattered the darkness. Clutching importunately, I lifted up my eyes. My refuge was not a calvary. I was it clear. It was a reeking gibbet.
>
> (Maeterlinck, *Plays* 265, 258-259; Roberts, ***Earth's Enigmas*** [1903] 197-198, 202-203)

Different as they are in certain respects, these passages share a common vocabulary of elemental space, pervasive darkness, terrified illumination, and religious types ("The Priest" and "The Sister of Charity" [Maeterlinck, *Plays* 263, 211], "a saint" and a penitent). It is, of course, impossible to state with absolute certainty that **"The Hill of Chastisement"** is primarily indebted to "The Blind" and "The Intruder" rather than to Poe or, say, Rossetti,[8] but the many qualities that the story shares with the plays, not least the "mastertone [of] . . . terror—terror . . . of the churchyard" that Hovey sees as Maeterlinck's distinguishing "mood" (11), do conspire with the external evidence to make this a distinct possibility.

But what about the animal stories in ***Earth's Enigmas***? Were they written, as Hovey also claims of the *symboliste* work of Carman and Parker, "without any communication from France of Belgium" (8)? At first glance the answer seems to be yes, for **"Do Seek Their Meat from God"** was published in *Harper's Monthly Magazine* in December 1892 and **"The Young Ravens That Call upon Him"** in *Lippincott's* in May 1894, the former eighteen months before and the latter a month after Carman, in his role as literary advisor to the Chicago publishing house of Stone and Kimball, persuaded Hovey to translate the first series of Maeterlinck's *Plays* in April 1894 (see Macdonald 155). Yet Roberts may have known *Les Aveugles* and *L'Intruse* in the original or in a translation that preceded Hovey's, for both plays had been available in French and English since the early 1890s[9] and, as indicated by Lampman's comments on "The Belgian Shakespeare" in his *At the Mermaid Inn* column for March 12, 1892 (34-35), their author's fame had spread to Canada well before the publication of **"Do Seek Their Meat from God."** Perhaps Roberts's attention was drawn to Maeterlinck's plays by Hovey in September and early October 1892 when, after returning from a year and a half in England and France, Hovey wrote and holidayed with Roberts and Carman in Windsor, Nova Scotia. "I like [Hovey] *immensely,*" Roberts wrote on September 11, "we get on most excellently together. We are both getting lots of work done" (*Collected Letters* 152). It is quite possible that **"Do Seek Their Meat from God"** and **"The**

Young Ravens That Call upon Him" (especially the latter) were written or at least revised at this time or later. Certainly, the Fall of 1892 was a productive time for Roberts in fiction as well as poetry: in early June he had complained of "*not* [having] turned the corner in short story writing yet" but by late October he was possessed of enough material and confidence to contemplate assembling the collection of stories that eventually became ***Earth's Enigmas*** (*Collected Letters* 149, and see 155 and 159). "I am much gratified by your praise of **'Do Seek Their Meat from God,'**" he told James Elgin Wetherell on December 14. "I have a few more sketches of a somewhat similar scope and carefully finished; and these I hope to print soon in book form" (*Collected Letters* 161).

Whether by coincidence or indebtedness, the initial descriptions of **"Do Seek Their Meat from God"** and **"The Young Ravens That Call upon Him"** resonate strongly with the opening stage directions of "The Blind." In the play, the initial directions concerning the "ancient Norland forest" and the "very old priest" are followed by instructions that specify the location of "six old men" and "six women" "[o]n the right" and "[o]n the left" of a set consisting of "stones, stumps . . . dead leaves . . . an uprooted tree and fragments of rocks" (Maeterlinck, *Plays* 265). "Tall funereal trees,—yews, weeping willows, cypresses,—cover [the old men and the women] with their faithful shadows," continue the directions, and "[i]t is unusually oppressive, despite the moonlight that here and there struggles to pierce for an instant the glooms of the foliage" (266). A similarly gloomy and blasted setting appears briefly at the beginning of **"The Young Ravens That Call upon Him"** ("It was just before dawn, and a grayness was beginning to trouble the dark above the top of the mountains. . . . The veil of cloud that hid the stars hung a hand-breadth above the naked summit. . . . Just under the brow, on a splintered and creviced ledge, was the nest of the eagles" [***Earth's Enigmas*** (1903) 56]), but much more similar is the scene that opens **"Do Seek Their Meat from God"**:

> One side of the ravine was in darkness. The darkness was soft and rich, suggesting thick foliage. Along the crest of the slope tree-tops came into view—great pines and hemlocks of the ancient unviolated forest—revealed against the orange disk of a full moon just rising. The low rays slanting through the moveless tops lit strangely the upper portion of the opposite steep,—the western wall of the ravine, barren, unlike its fellow, bossed with great rocky projections, and harsh with stunted junipers. Out of the sluggish dark that lay along the ravine as in a trough, rose the brawl of a swollen, obstructed stream.
>
> Out of the shadowy hollow behind a long white rock, on the lower edge of that part of the steep which lay in the moonlight, came softly a great panther. In common daylight his coat would have shown a warm fulvous hue, but in the elvish decolorizing rays of that half hidden moon he seemed to wear a sort of spectral gray. He lifted his smooth round head to gaze on the increasing flame, which presently he greeted with a shrill cry. That terrible cry, at once plaintive and menacing, with an undertone like the first protestations of a saw beneath the file, was a summons to his mate, telling her that the hour had come when they should seek their prey. From the lair behind the rock, where the cubs were being suckled by their dam, came no immediate answer. Only a pair of crows, that had their nest in a giant fir-tree across the gulf, woke up and croaked harshly their indignation. These three summers they had built in the same spot, and had been nightly awakened to vent the same rasping complaints.
>
> (***Earth's Enigmas*** [1963] 11-13)

As is the case with the stage directions to "The Blind," the interplay of darkness and moonlight plays a major part in what Hovey would call the "impression" (5) created by this description: at first the moon is a portentously "orange disk," then its "slanting" rays "strangely" light the "western wall of the ravine," and, finally, its "elvish decolorizing rays" turn the panther's coat "a sort of spectral gray." As in "The Blind," Roberts's setting is elemental, apparently blighted, and shadowed by trees that, if not exactly "funereal," are certainly ominous in their appearances and associations—"great pines and hemlocks" "stunted junipers" and "a giant fir-tree." To judge by its lighting and *flora,* Roberts's "ancient unviolated forest" could easily be an adaptation of Maeterlinck's "ancient Norland forest." Of course, Roberts's characters are not people but animals (or, as Misao Dean calls them "(m)animals"), though even here the tone of terror and foreboding so central to Maeterlinck's plays has its equivalent: the cry of the panther is "shrill, terrible, . . . plaintive and menacing," and it is ominously answered by "a pair of crows"—two corbies, so to say—that have been nesting in "the same spot" for, in the words of Pierre in "The Patrol of the Cypress Hills"—"the magic number" of "three summers" (Parker, *Works* 1: 17). As Sherman observes of **"The Perdu," "Do Seek Their Meat from God"** is "more symbolic than tales of realism are likely to be." "It is one of Roberts's most notable contributions to Literature," Hovey would maintain, for in it "[t]he problem of the struggle for existence, of the preying of life on life, is treated with an inexorable fidelity to fact, a Catholic sympathy, a sense of universality and mystery, and a calm acceptance that reaches the level of 'pathos' in the highest Greek usage of the word" (qtd. in Pomeroy 107).

As any reader of Roberts's short stories well knows, the portents that darken the beginnings of **"The Young Ravens That Call upon Him"** and **"Do Seek Their Meat from God"** are amply fulfilled: in the former, the eagle kills a newborn lamb to feed its starving young, leaving its distraught mother remote from her flock and susceptible to a similar fate; and, in the latter, the panthers attempt to kill a small boy to feed their starving cubs but are shot by the boy's father, who later finds the "rapidly decaying" bodies of their cubs in their lair (***Earth's Enigmas*** [1903] 27). As any reader of Roberts's short stories also well knows, such plot lines are unsentimentally Darwinian and Spencerian in their depiction of the struggle for survival and the survival of the fittest. But **"The Young Ravens That Call upon Him," "Do Seek Their Meat from God,"** and other stories like them in ***Earth's Enigmas*** and subsequent collections do not merely provide their readers with a simple evolutionary explanation of occurrences in the human and natural worlds; rather—to quote Roberts's Prefatory Note to ***Earth's Enigmas*** again, this time with some interpretive inflections—they strive "to present one or another of those *problems* of life or nature to which, as it appears to many of us, there is no adequate solutions *within* sight." Both **"The Young Ravens That Call upon Him"** and **"Do Seek Their Meat from God"** have biblical titles[10] that work with the spatial and temporal patterns and coincidences of the stories to suggest that the solution to their enigmas, the answer to such questions as why did the ewe drop her lamb where and when she did and what made the father, despite his selfish instincts, heed the cries of the child that turns out to be his own, may lie *out of sight,* beyond full human comprehension in an "immaterial reality" whose intellectual or theological expression is such terms as Fate and God and whose emotional or "poetic expression" (or so Hovey argues) is "modern symbolism" (4-5).[11]

Although the animal stories of ***Earth's Enigmas*** differ from the pastoral tales of *In the Village of Viger* in offering vicarious atavism rather than "wise idleness" as a cure for the ills of modernity, the dream pieces and Canadian "scenes" that constitute the remainder of the collection have a considerable amount in common with Scott's short stories. Perhaps the most striking commonality lies in the geographical settings and contingent spiritual assumptions that are present in **"The Perdu"** and the village of Viger. By Roberts's own description, "a mystic psychological thing" (*Collected Letters* 144), **"The Perdu"** is set somewhere in French Canada beside the "narrow, tideless, windless, backwater" of its title, a stretch of river whose name seems to strangers to have a certain "occult appropriateness" and whose remoteness from "modern noises" and "the stream of modern ideas" has encouraged the persistence in the local people of "superstitions," "strange and not-to-be understood" mysteries, and a "sense of unseen but thrilling influences" (***Earth's Enigmas*** [1903] 124-136). Akin to fantastic realism in its accreditation of two radically different epistemes, the story centres on a couple of visionary children, one of whom, Reuben, learns the ways of the modern world while the other, Celia, remains by the Perdu and, fulfilling the couple's earlier vision of "'a pale green hand'" sinking in the water (140), drowns as he is returning to marry her. None of Scott's stories is quite as uncanny as **"The Perdu"** but *In the Village of Viger* is, of course, also set in a part of French Canada where "modern noises and . . . ideas," though increasingly perceptible, have yet to alter the local ways ("on still nights . . . you c[an] hear the rumbles of . . . street-cars and the faint tinkle of their bells" and the time is coming for "Viger to be named in the city papers" [(1996) 3]), and, as a result, many of the village's inhabitants, particularly the elderly, retain such "pre-modern" characteristics as a belief in ghosts and a capacity for second sight.[12] Indeed, the further the reader travels into the collection (and, thus, away from modernity), the more the stories demand an acceptance of the irrational and the inexplicable: in "Sedan," Paul Latulipe knows without being told that the French have been defeated at the battle of 1870 for which the story is named ([1996] 37-38): in "The Tragedy of the Seig-niory," Louis Bois is "as superstitious as an old wife" and gradually comes to believe that a dog is a human "spirit in canine form" ([1996] 57, 59); and in the final paragraphs of the final story, Paul Farlotte, an eccentric school teacher who lives in a cottage that has "the air of having been secured from the inroads of time" and is frequently "greeted with visions of things that had been, or that would be, and s[ees] figures where, for other eyes, hung only impalpable air" ([1996] 79, 81), learns from a "vision" of his mother's death in France:

> He saw a garden much like his own, flooded with the clear sunlight[;] in the shade of an arbor an old woman in a white cap was leaning back in a wheeled chair, her eyes were closed, she seemed asleep. A young woman was seated beside her holding her hand. Suddenly the old woman smiled, a childish smile, as if she were well pleased. "Paul," she murmured, "Paul, Paul." A moment later her companion started up with a cry; but she did not move, she was silent and tranquil. Then the young woman fell on her knees and wept, hiding her face. But the aged face was expressably calm in the shadow, with the smile lingering upon it, fixed by the deeper sleep into which she had fallen.
>
> . . . . .
>
> Later in the day he told Marie that his mother had died that morning, and she wondered how he knew.
>
> ([1996] 89)

When Hovey wrote in "Modern Symbolism and Maurice Maeterlinck" that "[i]t would be interesting to trace the connection between English Pre-Raphaelitism and the new movement" (8) he was probably not thinking of **"The Perdu"** and certainly not of "Paul Farlotte," but both short stories would have confirmed the line of descent that he suggests, Roberts's with the debt of its "orange lilies" and "nameless spell" (126, 132) to such poems as "The Wind" and "The Blue Closet" in William Morris's *The Defence of Guenevere, and Other Po-*

ems (1858)[13] and Scott's with its echoes of the vision in which the artist Chiaro is visited by his own soul in the form of a beautiful woman at the climax of Rossetti's "Hand and Soul" (1850).[14]

When viewed chronologically on the basis of their publication in magazines and newspapers between 1887 and 1893, the stories in *In the Village of Viger* not only show the increasing emphasis on supernatural themes that is discernible in the sequence of the collection, but also suggest that, like Hovey and Roberts, Scott may have felt the impact of Maeterlinck at the time of the meteoric rise to fame that Lampman recorded in *At the Mermaid Inn* early in March 1892. All of the *Viger* stories published in *Scribner's Magazine* in October 1887 and March 1891—"The Desjardins," "Josephine Labrosse," "The Little Milliner," and "the Wooing of Monsieur Cuerrier"—depict a world of realistic material and psychological causes and effects, but those published in *Scribner's* in October 1893—"The Bobolink," "The Pedler," and "Sedan"—contain events and characters that are *symboliste* as well as supernatural. Two further stories in the collection—"The Tragedy of the Seigniory" and "Paul Farlotte"—anticipate and fulfil this movement from realism to spiritualism: the former was first published in April 1892 in the Boston periodical *Two Tales,* and the latter did not appear prior to its publication in 1896 in the Viger collection itself (see Groening 501-502). It is in two of the short stories first published in 1892—"The Bobolink" and "The Pedler"—that Scott first employs the two hallmarks of the *symboliste* mode—evocative suggestion and character types—that three years later would stamp his poetic masterpiece, "The Piper of Arll," as an unmistakable product of Hovey's modern "symbolic principle."

Perhaps reflecting the direct influence of *Les Aveugles,* the central characters of both "The Bobolink" and "The Pedler" are blind and mysterious. In "The Bobolink," the questions of "the little blind daughter of . . . Moreau" often leave the "old man" who calls her "'my little fairy'" at a loss for words and "mystefied" and, in "The Pedler," the "inscrutable" "green spectacles" of the blind pedlar who once brought his "magical baskets" to Viger every spring are as much a source of consternation to the villagers as his furious behaviour when by accident they are removed during a wind storm ([1996] 76-78). At the conclusion of "The Pedler," its central character disappears with the storm, leaving suspicions that he was a thief or the Devil and providing a basis for "tradition" and fantasy since "there are yet people in Viger who, when the dust blows, . . . see the figure of the enraged pedler, large upon the hills, striding violently along the fringes of the storm" ([1996] 74, 78). Consistent with the medicinal purposes of *In the Village of Viger,* this is more quaint and distracting than uncanny or terrifying. By the same token, the decision of the old man and the blind girl to release their caged bird at the conclusion of "The Bobolink" leaves the reader, like the old man himself, pensive and saddened by the evidence of change and loss rather than shocked or deeply troubled by the enigmas of life and death:

> "He's gone," she said, ". . . Where did he go, Uncle?"
>
> "He flew right through that maple-tree, and now he's over the fields, and now he's out of sight."
>
> "And didn't he even once look back?"
>
> "No, never once."
>
> They stood there together for a moment, the old man gazing after the departed bird, the little girl setting her brown, sightless eyes on the invisible distance. Then, taking the empty cage, they went back to the cabin. From that day their friendship was not untinged by regret; some delicate mist of sorrow seemed to have blurred the glass of memory. Though he could not tell why, old Etienne that evening felt anew his loneliness, as he watched a long sunset of red and gold that lingered after the footsteps of the August day, and cast a great color into his silent cabin above the Blanche.
>
> ([1996] 54)

Whether or not "The Pedler" and "The Bobolink" were written under the influence of *Les Aveugles,* they certainly reflect a sensibility that would find the essays in Maeterlinck's *Le Trésor des humbles* (1896) congenial and inspirational (see Bentley "Duncan Campbell Scott and Maurice Maeterlinck") and, in 1904, would praise their author to Pelham Edgar as "*the* modern Mystic" who is constantly "endeavouring to awaken the wonder-element in a modern way" by "expressing the almost unknowable things which we all feel" (Scott, *More Letters* 24; emphasis added).

In the final analysis, it may not be possible to locate precisely the points of intersection and the sets of parallels that enmesh the *symboliste* aspects of the early short stories of Parker, Roberts, and Scott. Perhaps, as Hovey argues, the Canadian writers arrived at "the symbolic principle . . . without any communication with France of Belgium." Perhaps the (social) landscape and (intellectual) climate in Canada in the 1890s did, indeed, generate independent manifestations of "modern symbolism." Such views have their appeal, but against them stands a good deal of evidence that, thanks in part to Hovey himself, the work of the French and Belgian *symbolistes,* particularly Maeterlinck, was far from unavailable or unknown to Canadian writers from the early '90s onwards. There may not be conclusive proof that the stories of Roberts and Scott were written under the influence of *Les Aveugles* and *L'Intruse,* but there is certainly enough internal and circumstantial evidence to allow this to stand as a plausible hypothesis. But what about Parker's stories? Published as they were in periodicals and book form in the very early '90s, are they at least an independent manifestation of "modern symbolism," or do they, too, reflect the work of Maeterlinck, and was Parker himself, like Hovey, a channel though which *symbolisme* reached Canadian writers? Some support for this second proposition can be gleaned from the fact that Parker was living in London, writing the Pierre stories, and attempting to embark on a career as a playwright at precisely the time of Maeterlinck's rise to prominence in the English-speaking world. A fervent admirer of one of the presiding doyens of British theatre in the '90s, Herbert Beerbohm Tree, Parker was unlikely to have missed the opportunity of seeing the production of Gérard Harry's translation of *L'Intruse* that opened at the Haymarket Theatre with Tree in the leading rôle on January 27, 1892. Nor did he. "Mr. Tree's playing of the Grandfather in 'L'Intruse,'" he recalled in 1895, was "subtle, . . . poetic . . . fanciful and deep . . . for here came out" the "eerie quality" that is "entirely his own" ("Herbert Beerbohm Tree" 121, 118). Since Parker wrote quickly and had an eager publisher in W. H. Henley, "The Stone" could easily have been written between the end of January and its appearance in Henley's *National Observer* on February 20, 1892. (Parker would later recall that he sent an earlier story, "Antoine and Angelique," to Henley "almost before the ink was dry" and that "The Stone" "brought a telegram of congratulations" [*Works* 1: xi].) To secure the net of influence with such tight knots is not essential, however, since the Henley circle within which Parker moved included several artists and writers, such as James McNeill Whistler, William Butler Yeats, and Henley himself, who had produced works imbued or consistent with the *symboliste* aesthetic by the early '90s. *Pierre and His People* may not be of the same stature as *The Wanderings of Oisin* (1889) and *The Countess Cathleen* (1892), but it resembles Yeats's early work in its application to local and resonantly national subjects and settings of an increasingly international mode of writing, a set of "traits and methods" with roots, not only in France and Belgium, but also, like the French and Belgian *symbolistes* themselves, in Poe, the Pre-Raphaelites, and American and British transcendentalism.

On the other side of the Atlantic, it was the local and national elements in Parker's work that assured his quick rise to prominence in Canada. In a letter to Carman on March 19, 1892, several months before the appearance of *Pierre and His People* and probably on the basis of the five Pierre stories (including "The Patrol of Cypress Hills") that were published in *The Independent* between January 1891 and March 1892 (see Adams 230), Roberts told Carman of his liking for "Parker's work" and within the year he was asking his cousin for Parker's address in England and wondering whether he could be persuaded to review *Songs of the Common Day*, and *Ave: an Ode for the Shelley Centenary* (1893) in a British periodical (*Collected Letters* 144, 159, 163).[15] When Parker paid a brief visit to Canada in the late Fall and early Winter of 1892 to spend time with his family in Belleville and to gather material for more Canadian stories and "'a novel on Quebec,'" he was warmly received in Ottawa, Montreal, and Quebec by John Bourinot, William Van Horne, and James MacPherson LeMoine (see Adams 72-74). Among those who met him in Ottawa was Scott, who reported in his *At the Mermaid Inn* column for January 7, 1893 that "*Pierre and His People* ha[d] gone into its second edition" and that Parker was sure to meet similar success with a forthcoming novel (*Mrs. Falchion* [1893]) and stage production (*The Wedding Day* [n.d.]) (227). Neither Roberts nor Scott appears to have been as enthusiastic about the other's fiction as about Parker's but they certainly knew one another's short stories both before and after their appearance in book form and may well have been engaged in a process of mutual influence: perhaps it was the presence of Scott's "The Tragedy of the Seigniory" in one of the copies of *Two Tales* that Carman sent him in May 1892 that prompted Roberts to send a story to the Boston periodical (see *Collected Letters* 148) and perhaps it was the presence of two of Roberts's poems, "Her Fan" and "Her Glove Box," in the May 18 and July 13, 1895 issues of *The Truth* (New York) that led to the appearance there on December 14 of the same year of "The Piper of Arll." The famous line that led from Roberts's *Orion, and Other Poems* (1880), through Lampman and Scott, to John Masefield is surely more sensuous and tangled than it might first appear.

These days it is extremely unfashionable to attend to the sorts of literary-historical issues raised by the relationships among the short stories of Parker, Roberts, and Scott and between this ensemble of short fiction and the *symboliste* movement. To cast an eye over the lines and intersections and parallels that connect and divide the French, Belgian, English, American, and Canadian practitioners of Hovey's "modern symbolism" is not only to perceive part of the web that constitutes Canadian literature, but also to uncover some of the Canadian tendrils of the root-system from which Anglo-American modernism was already beginning to grow as the nineteenth century waned into the twentieth. *Pierre and His People*, ***Earth's Enigmas***, and *In the Village of Viger* are all minor works, but individually and collectively they grow in richness if not in stature with an awareness of the background, functions, and presentiments of their symbolic practices.

Notes

1. The two fairy stories, "Hans Fingerhut's Frog Lesson" and "The Fairy Fountain," that Lampman wrote in the mid- to late 1880s are also therapeutic in nature, as are several of his other "nature" poems. In a letter of January 25, 1892 concerning "Comfort of the Fields," which eventually ap-

peared in *Lyrics of Earth* (1895), Carman told Lampman that "it comes with tender, enduring, and most intimate solace; taking on itself the office of hands that are no longer near to soothe. It is a very sweet and wise thing and has fallen on my heart with abundance of relief beyond the requital of words. May the dear wood-gods give you ten-fold reward . . . for this gentle service rendered to an unworthy fellow vagrant" (Lampman Papers).

2. It is just possible that this statement was in Scott's mind when he concluded the opening verse paragraph of "At Gull Lake: August 1810" (1935) with the lines "All proceeds in the flow of Time / As a hundred years ago" (*Selected Poetry* 96).

3. In his Introduction to *The Lane that Had No Turning* (1899) in the Imperial Edition of his *Works,* Parker contrasts the "almost domestic simplicity" of the later stories, a quality "in keeping with the happily simple and uncomplicated life of French Canada," to the "more strenuous episodes of the Pierre series" (9: ix). Many of Carman and Hovey's *Vagabondia* poems offer vicarious strenuosity as a mental medicine, as do most of the pieces in *The Rough Rider, and Other Poems* (1909), which Carman dedicated to Roosevelt.

4. Carman's comment that the Canadian Northwest "furnished [Parker] with good hunting, only to be equalled in . . . Kipling's India" (qtd. in Adams 61) brings into view the imperialistic dimension of Parker's claim in the Introduction to *Pierre and His People* in the Imperial (!) Edition that "what *Pierre* did was to open up a field which had not been opened before, but which other authors have exploited since with success and distinction. *Pierre* was the pioneer of the Far North in fiction" (1: xiii). For a discussion of a much earlier instance of the imperial and literary appropriation of the Canadian Northwest, see the chapter on Henry Kelsey's "Now Reader Read . . ." in Bentley, *Mimic Fires* 13-24.

5. One of the "dream" pieces in *Earth's Enigmas,* "The Stone Dog," is also one of Roberts's earliest stories (see Pomeroy 140). In a letter of January 31, 1892, Roberts tells Carman that he has "taken to writing in dreams once more" because "the Muse ha[s] deserted [his] waking hours" (Boone, *Collected Letters* 144).

6. There is a good deal of evidence to indicate that for several years beginning in the summer of 1890, Roberts suffered from bouts of weariness and depression of the sort usually attributed at the time to the effects of modernity but, in his case, apparently the result of domestic tension and excessively hard work on such projects as *The Canadian Guide-Book* (1891). "Now th[at] book is done," he told Carman on May 7, 1891, "I am setting myself to rest and recuperate for a week or two" (*Collected Letters* 133). In subsequent letters to various writers he appears to have diagnosed himself as a victim of the "nervous exhaustion" or "neurasthenia" that one of the principal theorists of the mind-cure movement, Dr. George Miller Beard, ascribed to modern American civilization. See, for example, his letter of August 8, 1891 to William Morton Paine: "Your last letter came while I was away in the wilds, with birch and paddle, trying to recuperate. As I was utterly used up, very nervous and miserable in every way, I went quite out of reach of all work. . . . [F]or the last twelve months I had been dull and oppressed (with a sort of nervous prostration, the after effect of *Grippe*). . . . Thank you for being interested in my poor guide-book, written in the midst of great depression" (*Collected Letters* 134, and see also 139, 144-145, and 153). On May 20, 1893, he would describe his recent stay with Hovey's parents in Washington, D.C. as "sick leave" and on October 10 of the same year he would write that he was "feeling better, but . . . still far from being out of the wood[s]" (*Collected Letters* 173, 186).

7. Roberts may have been thinking of Poe's well-known formal strictures when writing to Carman in April 1892 of the "absolute unity of effect" and the "*unity* complete in all respects" that he felt he had achieved in "A Tragedy of the Tides," a short story published in *The Independent* on May 26, 1892 and in *Current Literature* in July 1900 (*Collected Letters* 146).

8. Rossetti's "The Orchard Pit" and "St. Agnes of Intercession" had been available since 1886 in the two volumes of his *Collected Works.*

9. Roberts's first reference to Hovey is in a letter to Carman on May 24, 1892: "Glad to hear of Hovey. Shall do him up one of these days in 'Modern Instances'" (*Collected Letters* 148). None of the "Modern Instances" columns that Roberts published in the *Dominion Illustrated* in February, April, May, and August 1892 deals with Hovey, but in "The Genius of Richard Hovey" in the commemorative issue of *The Criterion* that was published shortly after Hovey's death he provides an astute and generous assessment of his friend's work.

10. Mary Vielé's translations of *Les Aveugles* and *L'Intruse* were published in 1891 in Washington, D.C., where Hovey was born in 1861 and his parents still lived. (Roberts, in fact, stayed with them during his "sick leave" in April and May 1893 [see *Collected Letters* 168-174].) The one transla-

tion of a Maeterlinck play other than Hovey's that almost certainly came to Roberts's attention, albeit after the publication of "Do Seek Their Meat from God," was that of *Les Aveugles* by Charlotte Porter and Helen A. Clarke in the 1893 volume of *Poet-Lore* (Boston). Among the contents of the four issues of the magazine in which Porter and Clarke's translation appeared are two vignettes, "In Great Eliza's Golden Time" and "The Mistress of the Red Lamp," by Archibald MacMechan, a correspondent of Roberts since at least the Fall of 1892. By 1893 the two were exchanging poems, short stories, and encouraging comments: on May 30, Roberts thanked MacMechan for sending him a lyric that he "like[d] greatly" and for his "kind words of the 'Perdu'" and on November 24 he thanked him "for sending . . . *Poet-Lore,* with that thoroughly exquisite pastel," adding that "Carman thinks it the best English pastel he has seen" (*Collected Letters* 173, 177). (The *OED* cites the April 22, 1893 number of *The Critic* (New York) for the use of "pastel" as a literary term: "The French pastel is really a little study [without a definite beginning or end] of a trifling topic which lacks complexity, and needs little more than a moderate space.") In addition to anticipating Hovey's "The Blind" both technically and chronologically, Porter and Clarke's "The Sightless" is prefaced by an essay by Charlotte Porter that not only conveys a sense of Maeterlinck's importance for many of his contemporaries (his "work . . . stands . . . at the doorsill of that change in world insight and impulse which means a new era"), but also provides an astute analysis of the *symboliste* mode ("the worn literary words of the past . . . [are] symbols fresh-minted for new offices and strange effects" such as the use of "suggestion" to awaken the "inward intelligence" of the audience) (151-154).

11. The former alludes to Job 38.41 ("Who provideth for the raven his food? when his young ones cry unto God, they wander for lack of meat") and the latter to Psalm 104.21 ("The young lions roar after their prey, and seek their meat from God"). See also Job 38.39 ("Wilt thou hunt the prey for the lion, or fill the appetite of the young lions . . . ?"), Psalm 147.9 ("He giveth to the beast his food, and to the young ravens which cry"), and Luke 12.24 ("Consider the ravens: for they neither sow nor reap; which neither have storehouse nor barn; and God feedeth them: how much more are ye better than the fowls?"). It is not fortuitous that most of these quotations raise large question about the relationship among humans, animals, and God.

12. Hovey's distinction in "Modern Symbolism and Maurice Maeterlinck" between "the natural, . . . the ethical, [and] . . . the poetic mind" (4) reflects his Delsartean or unitrinian belief that human beings consist of three components—body, mind, and spirit—that need to be brought into harmony to assure well-being (see Macdonald 62-79 and 75-78, and Bentley "Carman and Mind Cure"). See Gerald Lynch, "The One and the Many: English-Canadian Short Story Cycles" (97-98) for an excellent discussion of the formal characteristics and setting in *In the Village of Viger* and the same author's "'In the Meantime': Duncan Campbell Scott's *In the Village of Viger*" for another excellent discussion of the work as a cycle and as a reflection of Scott's attitudes to progress and community.

13. Roberts recommended "The Wind" to Carman in a letter of October 25, 1884 and, a month later, endorsed his cousin's opinion of "The Gilliflower of Gold" ("[i]t is splendid") and "Concerning Geffray Teste Noire" ("[a] curious and to me very touching though confused thing") (*Collected Letters* 47). Almost needless to say, the "pale green hand" that emerges from the water in "The Perdu" echoes the "arm/Clothed in white samite" that takes Excalibur in Tennyson's *Morte d'Arthur* (1842) (*Poems* 592).

14. Chiaro's soul appears to him in a pulsing "light" and dressed in "green and gray raiment, fashioned to that time." After she has finished likening his career to a "garden," he falls "slowly to his knees. . . . The air brooded in sunshine, and though the turmoil was great outside, the air within was at peace. But when he looked in her eyes, he wept." As he works later to fulfill his soul's instructions, Chiaro's face "gr[ows] solemn with knowledge" and, "[h]aving finished, . . . [he] lay[s] back where he s[its] and slips into a sleep that is death" (Rossetti, *Works* 553-555).

15. In his letter of November 30, 1892, Roberts also asks for the address of William Sharp (*Collected Letters* 159), a writer and editor with whom he had corresponded since the late '80s and to whom Hovey would pay the compliment in "Modern Symbolism and Maurice Maeterlinck" of linking his *Vistas* (1894) with Oscar Wilde's *Salomé* (1893) as English manifestations of the *symboliste* mode. (Of course, Roberts made much of the fact that he caroused with Wilde during his visit to Fredericton in October 1882 [see Pomeroy 42-43]). On January 7, 1895, Carman responded to Hovey's suggestion that *Vistas* and *Salomé* "might perhaps not have been written had the authors been less familiar with the contemporary literature of the Continent" (8) with his own assessment of Maeterlinck: "Yes, I see Sharp's indebtedness to Maeterlinck. . . . But Maeterlinck himself does not get me yet. It is trying to make literature with-

out the use of the adjective. One Stevensonian adjective, one Meredithian phrase gives more effect, more shiver than all of *The Intruder.* This method of iteration omits the use of surprise in getting its effect. A child could drill me into madness by asking questions, but I only find Maeterlinck tiresome. It does not take hold. But, mind you, this is only a first opinion. I will have to try him again and tell you how he works" (*Letters* 83, and see 91). Sharp's review of Gérard Harry's *The Princess Maleine* and *The Intruder* in the March 19, 1892 number of *The Academy* (London) reveals a thorough knowledge of Maeterlinck's works, influences, and critical history in Belgium, France, and England. "A new method is coming into literature," Sharp asserts, "and Maeterlinck is one of those who deserve honour as pioneers in a difficult path" (271). An earlier review by Sharp, "Ruysbroeck and Maeterlinck" in the March 16, 1892 number of *The Academy,* discusses both Maeterlinck's translation of *Les Ornamentes des noces spirituelles* by Ruysbroeck L'Admirable and *Ruysbroeck and the Mystics,* a translation of Maeterlinck's work by Jane T. Stoddart, whose "An Interview with M. Maurice Maeterlinck" precedes Roberts's "Three Good Things" in the May 1895 number of *The Bookman* (New York). See also Helen A. Clarke's "Maeterlinck and Sharp."

Works Cited

Adams, John Coldwell. *Seated with the Mighty: A Biography of Sir Gilbert Parker.* Ottawa: Borealis, 1979.

At the Mermaid Inn: Wilfred Campbell, Archibald Lampman, Duncan Campbell Scott in The Globe 1892-93. Ed. Barrie Davies. Literature of Canada: Poetry and Prose in Reprint. Toronto: U of Toronto P, 1979.

Beard, George Miller. *American Nervousness, Its Causes and Consequences: A Supplement to Nervous Exhaustion (Neurasthenia).* New York: G. P. Putnam's Sons, 1881.

Bentley, D. M. R. "Carman and Mind Cure: Theory and Technique." In *Bliss Carman: A Reappraisal.* Ed. Gerald Lynch. Reappraisals: Canadian Writers 16. Ottawa: U of Ottawa P, 1990. 85-110.

———. "Duncan Campbell Scott and Maurice Maeterlinck." *Studies in Canadian Literature* 21:2 (1996): 104-119.

———. *Mimic Fires: Accounts of Early Long Poems on Canada.* Kingston and Montreal: McGill-Queen's UP, 1994.

———. "UnCannyda." *Canadian Poetry: Studies, Documents, Reviews* 37 (Fall/Winter, 1995): 1-16.

Bithell, Jethro. *Life and Writings of Maurice Maeterlinck.* 1913. Port Washington, N. Y.: Kennikat, 1972.

Boone, Laurel, Ed. *The Collected Letters of Charles G. D. Roberts.* Fredericton, N. B.: Goose Lane, 1989.

Carman, Bliss. *Letters.* Ed. H. Pearson Gundy. Kingston and Montreal: McGill-Queen's UP, 1981.

———. *The Rough Rider, and Other Poems.* New York: Kennerly, 1909.

Carman, Bliss, and Richard Hovey. *Songs from Vagabondia.* Boston: Copeland and Day, 1894.

C[larke], Helen A. "Maeterlinck and Sharp." *Poet-Lore* 7 (1895): 157-161.

Dean, Misao. "Political Science: Realism in Roberts's Animal Stories." *Studies in Canadian Literature* 21:1 (1996): 1-16.

Doyle, James. "Archibald Lampman and Hamlin Garland." *Canadian Poetry: Studies, Documents,* Reviews 16 (Spring/Summer, 1985): 38-46.

Groening, Laura. "Duncan Campbell Scott: an Annotated Bibliography." In *The Annotated Bibliography of Canada's Major Authors.* Vol. 8. Eds. Robert Lecker and Jack David. Toronto: ECW Press, 1994. 469-576.

Hovey, Richard. "Impressions of Maurice Maeterlinck and the Theatre de L'Oeuvre." *Poet-Lore* 7 (1895): 446-50.

———. "Modern Symbolism and Maurice Maeterlinck." In *Plays.* By Maurice Maeterlinck. Trans. Richard Hovey. 1894, 1896. Chicago and New York: Herbert S. Stone, 1902. New York: Kraus Reprint, 1972.

———. "The Passing of Realism." *The Independent* 47 (August 22, 1895): 1125.

Kugel, James L. *The Techniques of Strangeness in Symbolist Poetry.* New Haven and London: Yale UP, 1971.

Lampman, Archibald. Papers. W. A. C. Bennett Library, Burnaby, B. C.

———. *Poems.* Ed. Duncan Campbell Scott. Toronto: George N. Morang, 1900.

Lears, T. J. Jackson. *No Place of Grace: Antimodernism in American Culture, 1880-1920.* N. Y.: Pantheon Books, 1981.

Lucas, Alec. Introduction. *The Last Barrier, and Other Stories.* By Charles G. D. Roberts. Ed. Alec Lucas. New Canadian Library 7. Toronto: McClelland and Stewart, 1958. v-x.

Lynch, Gerald. "'In the Meantime': Duncan Campbell Scott's *In the Village of Viger.*" *Studies in Canadian Literature* 17:2 (1993): 70-91.

———. "The One and the Many: English-Canadian Short Story Cycles." *Canadian Literature* 130 (Autumn 1991): 91-104.

Macdonald, Allan Houston. *Richard Hovey, Man and Craftsman*. Durham, N. C.: Duke UP, 1957.

MacMechan, Archibald. "In Great Eliza's Golden Time." *Poet-Lore* 5 (1893):431-432.

———. "The Mistress of the Red Lamp." *Poet-Lore* 5 (1893): 488-490.

Maeterlinck, Maurice. "Alladine and Palomides." Trans. Charlotte Porter and Helen A. Clarke. *Poet-Lore* 7 (1895): 281-301.

———. *Les Aveugles*. Bruxelles: Paul Lacomblez, 1890.

———. *Pelléas and Mélisande*. Trans. Erving Winslow. New York and Boston: Thomas Y. Crowell, 1894.

———. *Pelleas and Melisande and The Sightless*. Trans. Laurence Alma Tadema. The Scott Library. London: W. Scott, [1895].

———. *Plays* [First Series: "Princess Maleine," "The Intruder," "The Blind," "The Seven Princesses"; Second Series: "Alladine and Palomides," "Pelléas and Mélisande," "Home," "The Death of Tintagiles"]. Trans. Richard Hovey. 2 vols. Chicago: Stone and Kimball, 1894, 1896. The Green Tree Library. Chicago and New York: Herbert S. Stone, 1902. New York: Klaus Reprint, 1972.

———. *The Princess Maleine*. Trans. Gérard Harry. London: Heinemann, 1890.

———. *The Princess Maleine, a Drama in Five Acts; and The Intruder, a Drama in One Act*. Trans. Gérard Harry and William Wilson. New York: J. W. Lovell, 1892.

———. *Blind. The Intruder*. Trans. Mary Vielé. Washington, D. C.: W. H. Morrison, 1891.

———. "The Seven Princesses." Trans. Charlotte Porter and Helen A. Clarke. *Poet-Lore* 6 (1894): 29-32, 87-93, 150-161.

———. "The Sightless." Trans. Charlotte Porter and Helen A. Clarke. *Poet-Lore* 5 (1893): 159-163, 218-221, 273-277, 442-452.

Morris, William. 1858. *The Defence of Guenevere*. London: Scolar Press, 1979.

Oxley, J. Macdonald. "Busy People." *Man, a Canadian Home Magazine* (Ottawa) 1 (December 1885): 55-57.

Parker, Gilbert. "Herbert Beerbohm Tree: A Study." *Lippincott's Monthly Magazine* 55 (January 1895): 117-122.

———. *Pierre and His People*. London: Methuen, 1892.

———. *Works*. Imperial Edition. 23 vols. New York: Charles Scribner's Sons, 1912.

Pomeroy, E. M. *Sir Charles G. D. Roberts: A Biography*. Toronto: Ryerson, 1943.

Porter, Charlotte. "Maurice Maeterlinck: Dramatist of a New Method." *Poet-Lore* 5 (1893): 151-159.

Roberts, Charles G. D. *The Canadian Guide-Book: The Tourist's and Sportsman's Guide to Eastern Canada and Newfoundland*. London: William Heinemann, 1892.

———. *Earth's Enigmas. A Book of Animal and Nature Life*. Boston: Lamson, Wolffe, 1896.

———. *Earth's Enigmas*. Boston: L. C. Page, 1903.

———. "The Genius of Richard Hovey." *The Criterion* 23 (April 1900): 9-10.

———. *The Kindred of the Wild. A Book of Animal Life*. 1902. Boston: L. C. Page, 1935.

Rossetti, Dante Gabriel. *Collected Works*. Ed. William M. Rossetti. 2 vols. London: Ellis, 1886.

———. *Works*. Ed. William M. Rossetti. London: Ellis, 1911.

Scott, Duncan Campbell. *At the Mermaid Inn:* see *At the Mermaid Inn*

———. *In the Village of Viger*. 1896. Intro. Tracy Ware. New Canadian Library. Toronto: McClelland and Stewart, 1996.

———. *More Letters*. Ed. Arthur S. Bourinot. Ottawa: Arthur S. Bourinot, 1960.

———. *Selected Poetry*. Ed. Glenn Clever. Ottawa: Tecumseh, 1974.

Sharp, William. Rev. *The Princess Maleine and The Intruder*. By Maurice Maeterlinck. Trans. Gérard Harry. *The Academy* 41 (March 19, 1892): 270-272.

———."Ruysbroeck and Maeterlinck." Rev. *Les Ornamentes des noces spirituelles*. By Ruysbroeck L'Admirable. Trans. Maurice Maeterlinck; and *Ruysbroeck and the Mystics*. By Maurice Maeterlinck. Trans. Jane T. Stoddart. *The Academy* 47 (March 16, 1895): 232-233.

———. *Vistas*. Green Tree Library. Chicago: Stone and Kimball, 1894.

Stoddart, Jane T. "An Interview with M. Maurice Maeterlinck." *The Bookman*. New York (May 1, 1895): 246-248.

Tennyson, Alfred Lord. *Poems*. Ed. Christopher Ricks. Annotated English Poets. London: Longman, 1969.

FURTHER READING

Biography

Adams, John Coldwell. *Sir Charles God Damn*. Toronto, Canada: University of Toronto Press, 1986, 235 p.

Biography of Roberts.

Criticism

Lucas, Alec. Introduction to *The Last Barrier and Other Stories,* by Charles G. D. Roberts, pp. v-x. Toronto, Canada: McClelland & Stewart Ltd., 1958.

Surveys the major influences on Roberts's short stories and outlines the critical reaction to his work.

Polk, James. "Sir Charles G. D. Roberts." In *Wilderness Writers,* pp. 62-99. Toronto, Canada: Clarke, Irwin & Co., Ltd., 1972.

Critical study of Roberts's career.

Whalen, Terry. "Roberts and the Tradition of American Naturalism." In *The Sir Charles G. D. Roberts Symposium,* edited by Glenn Clever, pp. 127-42. Ottawa, Canada: University of Ottawa Press, 1983.

Compares Roberts's notion of naturalism in fiction with that of Jack London.

Additional coverage of Roberts's life and career is contained in the following sources published by Thomson Gale: *Children's Literature Review,* Vol. 33; *Contemporary Authors,* Vol. 188; *Dictionary of Literary Biography,* Vol. 92; *Literature Resource Center*; *Reference Guide to English Literature,* Ed. 2; *Reference Guide to Short Fiction,* Ed. 2; *Something about the Author,* Vols. 29, 88; *St. James Guide to Children's Writers,* Vol. 5; and *Twentieth-Century Literary Criticism,* Vol. 8.

How to Use This Index

The main references

Calvino, Italo 1923-1985 .... **CLC 5, 8, 11, 22, 33, 39, 73; SSC 3, 48**

list all author entries in the following Thomson Gale Literary Criticism series:

AAL = *Asian American Literature*
BG = *The Beat Generation: A Gale Critical Companion*
BLC = *Black Literature Criticism*
BLCS = *Black Literature Criticism Supplement*
CLC = *Contemporary Literary Criticism*
CLR = *Children's Literature Review*
CMLC = *Classical and Medieval Literature Criticism*
DC = *Drama Criticism*
FL = *Feminism in Literature: A Gale Critical Companion*
GL = *Gothic Literature: A Gale Critical Companion*
HLC = *Hispanic Literature Criticism*
HLCS = *Hispanic Literature Criticism Supplement*
HR = *Harlem Renaissance: A Gale Critical Companion*
LC = *Literature Criticism from 1400 to 1800*
NCLC = *Nineteenth-Century Literature Criticism*
NNAL = *Native North American Literature*
PC = *Poetry Criticism*
SSC = *Short Story Criticism*
TCLC = *Twentieth-Century Literary Criticism*
WLC = *World Literature Criticism, 1500 to the Present*
WLCS = *World Literature Criticism Supplement*

The cross-references

See also CA 85-88, 116; CANR 23, 61; DAM NOV; DLB 196; EW 13; MTCW 1, 2; RGSF 2; RGWL 2; SFW 4; SSFS 12

list all author entries in the following Thomson Gale biographical and literary sources:

AAYA = *Authors & Artists for Young Adults*
AFAW = *African American Writers*
AFW = *African Writers*
AITN = *Authors in the News*
AMW = *American Writers*
AMWR = *American Writers Retrospective Supplement*
AMWS = *American Writers Supplement*
ANW = *American Nature Writers*
AW = *Ancient Writers*
BEST = *Bestsellers*
BPFB = *Beacham's Encyclopedia of Popular Fiction: Biography and Resources*
BRW = *British Writers*
BRWS = *British Writers Supplement*
BW = *Black Writers*
BYA = *Beacham's Guide to Literature for Young Adults*
CA = *Contemporary Authors*
CAAS = *Contemporary Authors Autobiography Series*
CABS = *Contemporary Authors Bibliographical Series*
CAD = *Contemporary American Dramatists*
CANR = *Contemporary Authors New Revision Series*
CAP = *Contemporary Authors Permanent Series*
CBD = *Contemporary British Dramatists*
CCA = *Contemporary Canadian Authors*
CD = *Contemporary Dramatists*
CDALB = *Concise Dictionary of American Literary Biography*

CDALBS = *Concise Dictionary of American Literary Biography Supplement*
CDBLB = *Concise Dictionary of British Literary Biography*
CMW = *St. James Guide to Crime & Mystery Writers*
CN = *Contemporary Novelists*
CP = *Contemporary Poets*
CPW = *Contemporary Popular Writers*
CSW = *Contemporary Southern Writers*
CWD = *Contemporary Women Dramatists*
CWP = *Contemporary Women Poets*
CWRI = *St. James Guide to Children's Writers*
CWW = *Contemporary World Writers*
DA = *DISCovering Authors*
DA3 = *DISCovering Authors 3.0*
DAB = *DISCovering Authors: British Edition*
DAC = *DISCovering Authors: Canadian Edition*
DAM = *DISCovering Authors: Modules*
DRAM: *Dramatists Module;* ***MST:*** *Most-studied Authors Module;*
MULT: *Multicultural Authors Module;* ***NOV:*** *Novelists Module;*
POET: *Poets Module;* ***POP:*** *Popular Fiction and Genre Authors Module*
DFS = *Drama for Students*
DLB = *Dictionary of Literary Biography*
DLBD = *Dictionary of Literary Biography Documentary Series*
DLBY = *Dictionary of Literary Biography Yearbook*
DNFS = *Literature of Developing Nations for Students*
EFS = *Epics for Students*
EXPN = *Exploring Novels*
EXPP = *Exploring Poetry*
EXPS = *Exploring Short Stories*
EW = *European Writers*
FANT = *St. James Guide to Fantasy Writers*
FW = *Feminist Writers*
GFL = *Guide to French Literature,* Beginnings to 1789, 1798 to the Present
GLL = *Gay and Lesbian Literature*
HGG = *St. James Guide to Horror, Ghost & Gothic Writers*
HW = *Hispanic Writers*
IDFW = *International Dictionary of Films and Filmmakers: Writers and Production Artists*
IDTP = *International Dictionary of Theatre: Playwrights*
LAIT = *Literature and Its Times*
LAW = *Latin American Writers*
JRDA = *Junior DISCovering Authors*
MAICYA = *Major Authors and Illustrators for Children and Young Adults*
MAICYAS = *Major Authors and Illustrators for Children and Young Adults Supplement*
MAWW = *Modern American Women Writers*
MJW = *Modern Japanese Writers*
MTCW = *Major 20th-Century Writers*
NCFS = *Nonfiction Classics for Students*
NFS = *Novels for Students*
PAB = *Poets: American and British*
PFS = *Poetry for Students*
RGAL = *Reference Guide to American Literature*
RGEL = *Reference Guide to English Literature*
RGSF = *Reference Guide to Short Fiction*
RGWL = *Reference Guide to World Literature*
RHW = *Twentieth-Century Romance and Historical Writers*
SAAS = *Something about the Author Autobiography Series*
SATA = *Something about the Author*
SFW = *St. James Guide to Science Fiction Writers*
SSFS = *Short Stories for Students*
TCWW = *Twentieth-Century Western Writers*
WLIT = *World Literature and Its Times*
WP = *World Poets*
YABC = *Yesterday's Authors of Books for Children*
YAW = *St. James Guide to Young Adult Writers*

Literary Criticism Series Cumulative Author Index

Alexie, Sherman (Joseph, Jr.) 1966- .... **CLC 96, 154; NNAL; PC 53**
See also AAYA 28; BYA 15; CA 138; CANR 65, 95, 133; CN 7; DA3; DAM MULT; DLB 175, 206, 278; LATS 1:2; MTCW 2; MTFW 2005; NFS 17; SSFS 18

al-Farabi 870(?)-950 .... **CMLC 58**
See also DLB 115

Alfau, Felipe 1902-1999 .... **CLC 66**
See also CA 137

Alfieri, Vittorio 1749-1803 .... **NCLC 101**
See also EW 4; RGWL 2, 3; WLIT 7

Alfonso X 1221-1284 .... **CMLC 78**

Alfred, Jean Gaston
See Ponge, Francis

Alger, Horatio, Jr. 1832-1899 .... **NCLC 8, 83**
See also CLR 87; DLB 42; LAIT 2; RGAL 4; SATA 16; TUS

Al-Ghazali, Muhammad ibn Muhammad 1058-1111 .... **CMLC 50**
See also DLB 115

Algren, Nelson 1909-1981 ..... **CLC 4, 10, 33; SSC 33**
See also AMWS 9; BPFB 1; CA 13-16R; 103; CANR 20, 61; CDALB 1941-1968; CN 1, 2; DLB 9; DLBY 1981, 1982, 2000; EWL 3; MAL 5; MTCW 1, 2; MTFW 2005; RGAL 4; RGSF 2

al-Hariri, al-Qasim ibn 'Ali Abu Muhammad al-Basri 1054-1122 .... **CMLC 63**
See also RGWL 3

Ali, Ahmed 1908-1998 .... **CLC 69**
See also CA 25-28R; CANR 15, 34; CN 1, 2, 3, 4, 5; EWL 3

Ali, Tariq 1943- .... **CLC 173**
See also CA 25-28R; CANR 10, 99

Alighieri, Dante
See Dante
See also WLIT 7

al-Kindi, Abu Yusuf Ya'qub ibn Ishaq c. 801-c. 873 .... **CMLC 80**

Allan, John B.
See Westlake, Donald E(dwin)

Allan, Sidney
See Hartmann, Sadakichi

Allan, Sydney
See Hartmann, Sadakichi

Allard, Janet .... **CLC 59**

Allen, Edward 1948- .... **CLC 59**

Allen, Fred 1894-1956 .... **TCLC 87**

Allen, Paula Gunn 1939- .... **CLC 84, 202; NNAL**
See also AMWS 4; CA 112; 143; CANR 63, 130; CWP; DA3; DAM MULT; DLB 175; FW; MTCW 2; MTFW 2005; RGAL 4; TCWW 2

Allen, Roland
See Ayckbourn, Alan

Allen, Sarah A.
See Hopkins, Pauline Elizabeth

Allen, Sidney H.
See Hartmann, Sadakichi

Allen, Woody 1935- .... **CLC 16, 52, 195**
See also AAYA 10, 51; AMWS 15; CA 33-36R; CANR 27, 38, 63, 128; DAM POP; DLB 44; MTCW 1; SSFS 21

Allende, Isabel 1942- ... **CLC 39, 57, 97, 170; HLC 1; SSC 65; WLCS**
See also AAYA 18; CA 125; 130; CANR 51, 74, 129; CDWLB 3; CLR 99; CWW 2; DA3; DAM MULT, NOV; DLB 145; DNFS 1; EWL 3; FL 1:5; FW; HW 1, 2; INT CA-130; LAIT 5; LAWS 1; LMFS 2; MTCW 1, 2; MTFW 2005; NCFS 1; NFS 6, 18; RGSF 2; RGWL 3; SATA 163; SSFS 11, 16; WLIT 1

Alleyn, Ellen
See Rossetti, Christina

Alleyne, Carla D. .... **CLC 65**

Allingham, Margery (Louise) 1904-1966 .... **CLC 19**
See also CA 5-8R; 25-28R; CANR 4, 58; CMW 4; DLB 77; MSW; MTCW 1, 2

Allingham, William 1824-1889 ...... **NCLC 25**
See also DLB 35; RGEL 2

Allison, Dorothy E. 1949- .... **CLC 78, 153**
See also AAYA 53; CA 140; CANR 66, 107; CN 7; CSW; DA3; FW; MTCW 2; MTFW 2005; NFS 11; RGAL 4

Alloula, Malek .... **CLC 65**

Allston, Washington 1779-1843 .... **NCLC 2**
See also DLB 1, 235

Almedingen, E. M. .... **CLC 12**
See Almedingen, Martha Edith von
See also SATA 3

Almedingen, Martha Edith von 1898-1971
See Almedingen, E. M.
See also CA 1-4R; CANR 1

Almodovar, Pedro 1949(?)- .... **CLC 114; HLCS 1**
See also CA 133; CANR 72; HW 2

Almqvist, Carl Jonas Love 1793-1866 .... **NCLC 42**

al-Mutanabbi, Ahmad ibn al-Husayn Abu al-Tayyib al-Jufi al-Kindi 915-965 .... **CMLC 66**
See Mutanabbi, Al-
See also RGWL 3

Alonso, Damaso 1898-1990 .... **CLC 14**
See also CA 110; 131; 130; CANR 72; DLB 108; EWL 3; HW 1, 2

Alov
See Gogol, Nikolai (Vasilyevich)

al'Sadaawi, Nawal
See El Saadawi, Nawal
See also FW

al-Shaykh, Hanan 1945- .... **CLC 218**
See also CA 135; CANR 111; WLIT 6

Al Siddik
See Rolfe, Frederick (William Serafino Austin Lewis Mary)
See also GLL 1; RGEL 2

Alta 1942- .... **CLC 19**
See also CA 57-60

Alter, Robert B(ernard) 1935- .... **CLC 34**
See also CA 49-52; CANR 1, 47, 100

Alther, Lisa 1944- .... **CLC 7, 41**
See also BPFB 1; CA 65-68; CAAS 30; CANR 12, 30, 51; CN 4, 5, 6, 7; CSW; GLL 2; MTCW 1

Althusser, L.
See Althusser, Louis

Althusser, Louis 1918-1990 .... **CLC 106**
See also CA 131; 132; CANR 102; DLB 242

Altman, Robert 1925- .... **CLC 16, 116**
See also CA 73-76; CANR 43

Alurista .... **HLCS 1; PC 34**
See Urista (Heredia), Alberto (Baltazar)
See also CA 45-48R; DLB 82; LLW

Alvarez, A(lfred) 1929- .... **CLC 5, 13**
See also CA 1-4R; CANR 3, 33, 63, 101, 134; CN 3, 4, 5, 6; CP 1, 2, 3, 4, 5, 6, 7; DLB 14, 40; MTFW 2005

Alvarez, Alejandro Rodriguez 1903-1965
See Casona, Alejandro
See also CA 131; 93-96; HW 1

Alvarez, Julia 1950- .... **CLC 93; HLCS 1**
See also AAYA 25; AMWS 7; CA 147; CANR 69, 101, 133; DA3; DLB 282; LATS 1:2; LLW; MTCW 2; MTFW 2005; NFS 5, 9; SATA 129; WLIT 1

Alvaro, Corrado 1896-1956 .... **TCLC 60**
See also CA 163; DLB 264; EWL 3

Amado, Jorge 1912-2001 ... **CLC 13, 40, 106; HLC 1**
See also CA 77-80; 201; CANR 35, 74, 135; CWW 2; DAM MULT, NOV; DLB 113, 307; EWL 3; HW 2; LAW; LAWS 1; MTCW 1, 2; MTFW 2005; RGWL 2, 3; TWA; WLIT 1

Ambler, Eric 1909-1998 .... **CLC 4, 6, 9**
See also BRWS 4; CA 9-12R; 171; CANR 7, 38, 74; CMW 4; CN 1, 2, 3, 4, 5, 6; DLB 77; MSW; MTCW 1, 2; TEA

Ambrose, Stephen E(dward) 1936-2002 .... **CLC 145**
See also AAYA 44; CA 1-4R; 209; CANR 3, 43, 57, 83, 105; MTFW 2005; NCFS 2; SATA 40, 138

Amichai, Yehuda 1924-2000 .. **CLC 9, 22, 57, 116; PC 38**
See also CA 85-88; 189; CANR 46, 60, 99, 132; CWW 2; EWL 3; MTCW 1, 2; MTFW 2005; WLIT 6

Amichai, Yehudah
See Amichai, Yehuda

Amiel, Henri Frederic 1821-1881 .... **NCLC 4**
See also DLB 217

Amis, Kingsley (William) 1922-1995 ...... **CLC 1, 2, 3, 5, 8, 13, 40, 44, 129**
See also AITN 2; BPFB 1; BRWS 2; CA 9-12R; 150; CANR 8, 28, 54; CDBLB 1945-1960; CN 1, 2, 3, 4, 5, 6; CP 1, 2, 3, 4; DA; DA3; DAB; DAC; DAM MST, NOV; DLB 15, 27, 100, 139; DLBY 1996; EWL 3; HGG; INT CANR-8; MTCW 1, 2; MTFW 2005; RGEL 2; RGSF 2; SFW 4

Amis, Martin (Louis) 1949- .... **CLC 4, 9, 38, 62, 101, 213**
See also BEST 90:3; BRWS 4; CA 65-68; CANR 8, 27, 54, 73, 95, 132; CN 5, 6, 7; DA3; DLB 14, 194; EWL 3; INT CANR-27; MTCW 2; MTFW 2005

Ammianus Marcellinus c. 330-c. 395 .... **CMLC 60**
See also AW 2; DLB 211

Ammons, A(rchie) R(andolph) 1926-2001 ...... **CLC 2, 3, 5, 8, 9, 25, 57, 108; PC 16**
See also AITN 1; AMWS 7; CA 9-12R; 193; CANR 6, 36, 51, 73, 107; CP 1, 2, 3, 4, 5, 6, 7; CSW; DAM POET; DLB 5, 165; EWL 3; MAL 5; MTCW 1, 2; PFS 19; RGAL 4; TCLE 1:1

Amo, Tauraatua i
See Adams, Henry (Brooks)

Amory, Thomas 1691(?)-1788 .... **LC 48**
See also DLB 39

Anand, Mulk Raj 1905-2004 ...... **CLC 23, 93**
See also CA 65-68; 231; CANR 32, 64; CN 1, 2, 3, 4, 5, 6, 7; DAM NOV; EWL 3; MTCW 1, 2; MTFW 2005; RGSF 2

Anatol
See Schnitzler, Arthur

Anaximander c. 611B.C.-c. 546B.C. .... **CMLC 22**

Anaya, Rudolfo A(lfonso) 1937- ...... **CLC 23, 148; HLC 1**
See also AAYA 20; BYA 13; CA 45-48; CAAS 4; CANR 1, 32, 51, 124; CN 4, 5, 6, 7; DAM MULT, NOV; DLB 82, 206, 278; HW 1; LAIT 4; LLW; MAL 5; MTCW 1, 2; MTFW 2005; NFS 12; RGAL 4; RGSF 2; TCWW 2; WLIT 1

Andersen, Hans Christian 1805-1875 .... **NCLC 7, 79; SSC 6, 56; WLC**
See also AAYA 57; CLR 6; DA; DA3; DAB; DAC; DAM MST, POP; EW 6; MAICYA 1, 2; RGSF 2; RGWL 2, 3; SATA 100; TWA; WCH; YABC 1

Arden, John 1930- .... **CLC 6, 13, 15**
See also BRWS 2; CA 13-16R; CAAS 4; CANR 31, 65, 67, 124; CBD; CD 5, 6; DAM DRAM; DFS 9; DLB 13, 245; EWL 3; MTCW 1

Arenas, Reinaldo 1943-1990 .... **CLC 41; HLC 1**
See also CA 124; 128; 133; CANR 73, 106; DAM MULT; DLB 145; EWL 3; GLL 2; HW 1; LAW; LAWS 1; MTCW 2; MTFW 2005; RGSF 2; RGWL 3; WLIT 1

Arendt, Hannah 1906-1975 .... **CLC 66, 98**
See also CA 17-20R; 61-64; CANR 26, 60; DLB 242; MTCW 1, 2

Aretino, Pietro 1492-1556 .... **LC 12**
See also RGWL 2, 3

Arghezi, Tudor .... **CLC 80**
See Theodorescu, Ion N.
See also CA 167; CDWLB 4; DLB 220; EWL 3

Arguedas, Jose Maria 1911-1969 .... **CLC 10, 18; HLCS 1; TCLC 147**
See also CA 89-92; CANR 73; DLB 113; EWL 3; HW 1; LAW; RGWL 2, 3; WLIT 1

Argueta, Manlio 1936- .... **CLC 31**
See also CA 131; CANR 73; CWW 2; DLB 145; EWL 3; HW 1; RGWL 3

Arias, Ron(ald Francis) 1941- .... **HLC 1**
See also CA 131; CANR 81, 136; DAM MULT; DLB 82; HW 1, 2; MTCW 2; MTFW 2005

Ariosto, Lodovico
See Ariosto, Ludovico
See also WLIT 7

Ariosto, Ludovico 1474-1533 ... **LC 6, 87; PC 42**
See Ariosto, Lodovico
See also EW 2; RGWL 2, 3

Aristides
See Epstein, Joseph

Aristophanes 450B.C.-385B.C. .... **CMLC 4, 51; DC 2; WLCS**
See also AW 1; CDWLB 1; DA; DA3; DAB; DAC; DAM DRAM, MST; DFS 10; DLB 176; LMFS 1; RGWL 2, 3; TWA

Aristotle 384B.C.-322B.C. .... **CMLC 31; WLCS**
See also AW 1; CDWLB 1; DA; DA3; DAB; DAC; DAM MST; DLB 176; RGWL 2, 3; TWA

Arlt, Roberto (Godofredo Christophersen) 1900-1942 .... **HLC 1; TCLC 29**
See also CA 123; 131; CANR 67; DAM MULT; DLB 305; EWL 3; HW 1, 2; IDTP; LAW

Armah, Ayi Kwei 1939- . **BLC 1; CLC 5, 33, 136**
See also AFW; BRWS 10; BW 1; CA 61-64; CANR 21, 64; CDWLB 3; CN 1, 2, 3, 4, 5, 6, 7; DAM MULT, POET; DLB 117; EWL 3; MTCW 1; WLIT 2

Armatrading, Joan 1950- .... **CLC 17**
See also CA 114; 186

Armitage, Frank
See Carpenter, John (Howard)

Armstrong, Jeannette (C.) 1948- .... **NNAL**
See also CA 149; CCA 1; CN 6, 7; DAC; SATA 102

Arnette, Robert
See Silverberg, Robert

Arnim, Achim von (Ludwig Joachim von Arnim) 1781-1831 .. **NCLC 5, 159; SSC 29**
See also DLB 90

Arnim, Bettina von 1785-1859 ...... **NCLC 38, 123**
See also DLB 90; RGWL 2, 3

Arnold, Matthew 1822-1888 ..... **NCLC 6, 29, 89, 126; PC 5; WLC**
See also BRW 5; CDBLB 1832-1890; DA; DAB; DAC; DAM MST, POET; DLB 32, 57; EXPP; PAB; PFS 2; TEA; WP

Arnold, Thomas 1795-1842 .... **NCLC 18**
See also DLB 55

Arnow, Harriette (Louisa) Simpson 1908-1986 .... **CLC 2, 7, 18**
See also BPFB 1; CA 9-12R; 118; CANR 14; CN 2, 3, 4; DLB 6; FW; MTCW 1, 2; RHW; SATA 42; SATA-Obit 47

Arouet, Francois-Marie
See Voltaire

Arp, Hans
See Arp, Jean

Arp, Jean 1887-1966 .... **CLC 5; TCLC 115**
See also CA 81-84; 25-28R; CANR 42, 77; EW 10

Arrabal
See Arrabal, Fernando

Arrabal (Teran), Fernando
See Arrabal, Fernando
See also CWW 2

Arrabal, Fernando 1932- ... **CLC 2, 9, 18, 58**
See Arrabal (Teran), Fernando
See also CA 9-12R; CANR 15; DLB 321; EWL 3; LMFS 2

Arreola, Juan Jose 1918-2001 .... **CLC 147; HLC 1; SSC 38**
See also CA 113; 131; 200; CANR 81; CWW 2; DAM MULT; DLB 113; DNFS 2; EWL 3; HW 1, 2; LAW; RGSF 2

Arrian c. 89(?)-c. 155(?) .... **CMLC 43**
See also DLB 176

Arrick, Fran .... **CLC 30**
See Gaberman, Judie Angell
See also BYA 6

Arrley, Richmond
See Delany, Samuel R(ay), Jr.

Artaud, Antonin (Marie Joseph) 1896-1948 .... **DC 14; TCLC 3, 36**
See also CA 104; 149; DA3; DAM DRAM; DFS 22; DLB 258, 321; EW 11; EWL 3; GFL 1789 to the Present; MTCW 2; MTFW 2005; RGWL 2, 3

Arthur, Ruth M(abel) 1905-1979 ..... **CLC 12**
See also CA 9-12R; 85-88; CANR 4; CWRI 5; SATA 7, 26

Artsybashev, Mikhail (Petrovich) 1878-1927 .... **TCLC 31**
See also CA 170; DLB 295

Arundel, Honor (Morfydd) 1919-1973 .... **CLC 17**
See also CA 21-22; 41-44R; CAP 2; CLR 35; CWRI 5; SATA 4; SATA-Obit 24

Arzner, Dorothy 1900-1979 .... **CLC 98**

Asch, Sholem 1880-1957 .... **TCLC 3**
See also CA 105; EWL 3; GLL 2

Ascham, Roger 1516(?)-1568 .... **LC 101**
See also DLB 236

Ash, Shalom
See Asch, Sholem

Ashbery, John (Lawrence) 1927- .. **CLC 2, 3, 4, 6, 9, 13, 15, 25, 41, 77, 125, 221; PC 26**
See Berry, Jonas
See also AMWS 3; CA 5-8R; CANR 9, 37, 66, 102, 132; CP 1, 2, 3, 4, 5, 6, 7; DA3; DAM POET; DLB 5, 165; DLBY 1981; EWL 3; INT CANR-9; MAL 5; MTCW 1, 2; MTFW 2005; PAB; PFS 11; RGAL 4; TCLE 1:1; WP

Ashdown, Clifford
See Freeman, R(ichard) Austin

Ashe, Gordon
See Creasey, John

Ashton-Warner, Sylvia (Constance) 1908-1984 .... **CLC 19**
See also CA 69-72; 112; CANR 29; CN 1, 2, 3; MTCW 1, 2

Asimov, Isaac 1920-1992 ..... **CLC 1, 3, 9, 19, 26, 76, 92**
See also AAYA 13; BEST 90:2; BPFB 1; BYA 4, 6, 7, 9; CA 1-4R; 137; CANR 2, 19, 36, 60, 125; CLR 12, 79; CMW 4; CN 1, 2, 3, 4, 5; CPW; DA3; DAM POP; DLB 8; DLBY 1992; INT CANR-19; JRDA; LAIT 5; LMFS 2; MAICYA 1, 2; MAL 5; MTCW 1, 2; MTFW 2005; RGAL 4; SATA 1, 26, 74; SCFW 1, 2; SFW 4; SSFS 17; TUS; YAW

Askew, Anne 1521(?)-1546 .... **LC 81**
See also DLB 136

Assis, Joaquim Maria Machado de
See Machado de Assis, Joaquim Maria

Astell, Mary 1666-1731 .... **LC 68**
See also DLB 252; FW

Astley, Thea (Beatrice May) 1925-2004 .... **CLC 41**
See also CA 65-68; 229; CANR 11, 43, 78; CN 1, 2, 3, 4, 5, 6, 7; DLB 289; EWL 3

Astley, William 1855-1911
See Warung, Price

Aston, James
See White, T(erence) H(anbury)

Asturias, Miguel Angel 1899-1974 .... **CLC 3, 8, 13; HLC 1**
See also CA 25-28; 49-52; CANR 32; CAP 2; CDWLB 3; DA3; DAM MULT, NOV; DLB 113, 290; EWL 3; HW 1; LAW; LMFS 2; MTCW 1, 2; RGWL 2, 3; WLIT 1

Atares, Carlos Saura
See Saura (Atares), Carlos

Athanasius c. 295-c. 373 .... **CMLC 48**

Atheling, William
See Pound, Ezra (Weston Loomis)

Atheling, William, Jr.
See Blish, James (Benjamin)

Atherton, Gertrude (Franklin Horn) 1857-1948 .... **TCLC 2**
See also CA 104; 155; DLB 9, 78, 186; HGG; RGAL 4; SUFW 1; TCWW 1, 2

Atherton, Lucius
See Masters, Edgar Lee

Atkins, Jack
See Harris, Mark

Atkinson, Kate 1951- .... **CLC 99**
See also CA 166; CANR 101; DLB 267

Attaway, William (Alexander) 1911-1986 .... **BLC 1; CLC 92**
See also BW 2, 3; CA 143; CANR 82; DAM MULT; DLB 76; MAL 5

Atticus
See Fleming, Ian (Lancaster); Wilson, (Thomas) Woodrow

Atwood, Margaret (Eleanor) 1939- ... **CLC 2, 3, 4, 8, 13, 15, 25, 44, 84, 135; PC 8; SSC 2, 46; WLC**
See also AAYA 12, 47; AMWS 13; BEST 89:2; BPFB 1; CA 49-52; CANR 3, 24, 33, 59, 95, 133; CN 2, 3, 4, 5, 6, 7; CP 1, 2, 3, 4, 5, 6, 7; CPW; CWP; DA; DA3; DAB; DAC; DAM MST, NOV, POET; DLB 53, 251; EWL 3; EXPN; FL 1:5; FW; GL 2; INT CANR-24; LAIT 5; MTCW 1, 2; MTFW 2005; NFS 4, 12, 13, 14, 19; PFS 7; RGSF 2; SATA 50; SSFS 3, 13; TCLE 1:1; TWA; WWE 1; YAW

Aubigny, Pierre d'
See Mencken, H(enry) L(ouis)

Aubin, Penelope 1685-1731(?) .... **LC 9**
See also DLB 39

Author Index

Auchincloss, Louis (Stanton) 1917- .. **CLC 4, 6, 9, 18, 45; SSC 22**
See also AMWS 4; CA 1-4R; CANR 6, 29, 55, 87, 130; CN 1, 2, 3, 4, 5, 6, 7; DAM NOV; DLB 2, 244; DLBY 1980; EWL 3; INT CANR-29; MAL 5; MTCW 1; RGAL 4

Auden, W(ystan) H(ugh) 1907-1973 . **CLC 1, 2, 3, 4, 6, 9, 11, 14, 43, 123; PC 1; WLC**
See also AAYA 18; AMWS 2; BRW 7; BRWR 1; CA 9-12R; 45-48; CANR 5, 61, 105; CDBLB 1914-1945; CP 1, 2; DA; DA3; DAB; DAC; DAM DRAM, MST, POET; DLB 10, 20; EWL 3; EXPP; MAL 5; MTCW 1, 2; MTFW 2005; PAB; PFS 1, 3, 4, 10; TUS; WP

Audiberti, Jacques 1899-1965 .... **CLC 38**
See also CA 25-28R; DAM DRAM; DLB 321; EWL 3

Audubon, John James 1785-1851 . **NCLC 47**
See also ANW; DLB 248

Auel, Jean M(arie) 1936- .... **CLC 31, 107**
See also AAYA 7, 51; BEST 90:4; BPFB 1; CA 103; CANR 21, 64, 115; CPW; DA3; DAM POP; INT CANR-21; NFS 11; RHW; SATA 91

Auerbach, Erich 1892-1957 .... **TCLC 43**
See also CA 118; 155; EWL 3

Augier, Emile 1820-1889 .... **NCLC 31**
See also DLB 192; GFL 1789 to the Present

August, John
See De Voto, Bernard (Augustine)

Augustine, St. 354-430 .... **CMLC 6; WLCS**
See also DA; DA3; DAB; DAC; DAM MST; DLB 115; EW 1; RGWL 2, 3

Aunt Belinda
See Braddon, Mary Elizabeth

Aunt Weedy
See Alcott, Louisa May

Aurelius
See Bourne, Randolph S(illiman)

Aurelius, Marcus 121-180 .... **CMLC 45**
See Marcus Aurelius
See also RGWL 2, 3

Aurobindo, Sri
See Ghose, Aurabinda

Aurobindo Ghose
See Ghose, Aurabinda

Austen, Jane 1775-1817 ...... **NCLC 1, 13, 19, 33, 51, 81, 95, 119, 150; WLC**
See also AAYA 19; BRW 4; BRWC 1; BRWR 2; BYA 3; CDBLB 1789-1832; DA; DA3; DAB; DAC; DAM MST, NOV; DLB 116; EXPN; FL 1:2; GL 2; LAIT 2; LATS 1:1; LMFS 1; NFS 1, 14, 18, 20, 21; TEA; WLIT 3; WYAS 1

Auster, Paul 1947- .... **CLC 47, 131**
See also AMWS 12; CA 69-72; CANR 23, 52, 75, 129; CMW 4; CN 5, 6, 7; DA3; DLB 227; MAL 5; MTCW 2; MTFW 2005; SUFW 2; TCLE 1:1

Austin, Frank
See Faust, Frederick (Schiller)

Austin, Mary (Hunter) 1868-1934 . **TCLC 25**
See also ANW; CA 109; 178; DLB 9, 78, 206, 221, 275; FW; TCWW 1, 2

Averroes 1126-1198 .... **CMLC 7**
See also DLB 115

Avicenna 980-1037 .... **CMLC 16**
See also DLB 115

Avison, Margaret (Kirkland) 1918- .. **CLC 2, 4, 97**
See also CA 17-20R; CANR 134; CP 1, 2, 3, 4, 5, 6, 7; DAC; DAM POET; DLB 53; MTCW 1

Axton, David
See Koontz, Dean R.

Ayckbourn, Alan 1939- ...... **CLC 5, 8, 18, 33, 74; DC 13**
See also BRWS 5; CA 21-24R; CANR 31, 59, 118; CBD; CD 5, 6; DAB; DAM DRAM; DFS 7; DLB 13, 245; EWL 3; MTCW 1, 2; MTFW 2005

Aydy, Catherine
See Tennant, Emma (Christina)

Ayme, Marcel (Andre) 1902-1967 ... **CLC 11; SSC 41**
See also CA 89-92; CANR 67, 137; CLR 25; DLB 72; EW 12; EWL 3; GFL 1789 to the Present; RGSF 2; RGWL 2, 3; SATA 91

Ayrton, Michael 1921-1975 .... **CLC 7**
See also CA 5-8R; 61-64; CANR 9, 21

Aytmatov, Chingiz
See Aitmatov, Chingiz (Torekulovich)
See also EWL 3

Azorin .... **CLC 11**
See Martinez Ruiz, Jose
See also DLB 322; EW 9; EWL 3

Azuela, Mariano 1873-1952 .. **HLC 1; TCLC 3, 145**
See also CA 104; 131; CANR 81; DAM MULT; EWL 3; HW 1, 2; LAW; MTCW 1, 2; MTFW 2005

Ba, Mariama 1929-1981 .... **BLCS**
See also AFW; BW 2; CA 141; CANR 87; DNFS 2; WLIT 2

Baastad, Babbis Friis
See Friis-Baastad, Babbis Ellinor

Bab
See Gilbert, W(illiam) S(chwenck)

Babbis, Eleanor
See Friis-Baastad, Babbis Ellinor

Babel, Isaac
See Babel, Isaak (Emmanuilovich)
See also EW 11; SSFS 10

Babel, Isaak (Emmanuilovich) 1894-1941(?) . **SSC 16, 78; TCLC 2, 13, 171**
See Babel, Isaac
See also CA 104; 155; CANR 113; DLB 272; EWL 3; MTCW 2; MTFW 2005; RGSF 2; RGWL 2, 3; TWA

Babits, Mihaly 1883-1941 .... **TCLC 14**
See also CA 114; CDWLB 4; DLB 215; EWL 3

Babur 1483-1530 .... **LC 18**

Babylas 1898-1962
See Ghelderode, Michel de

Baca, Jimmy Santiago 1952- . **HLC 1; PC 41**
See also CA 131; CANR 81, 90, 146; CP 7; DAM MULT; DLB 122; HW 1, 2; LLW; MAL 5

Baca, Jose Santiago
See Baca, Jimmy Santiago

Bacchelli, Riccardo 1891-1985 .... **CLC 19**
See also CA 29-32R; 117; DLB 264; EWL 3

Bach, Richard (David) 1936- .... **CLC 14**
See also AITN 1; BEST 89:2; BPFB 1; BYA 5; CA 9-12R; CANR 18, 93; CPW; DAM NOV, POP; FANT; MTCW 1; SATA 13

Bache, Benjamin Franklin 1769-1798 .... **LC 74**
See also DLB 43

Bachelard, Gaston 1884-1962 ...... **TCLC 128**
See also CA 97-100; 89-92; DLB 296; GFL 1789 to the Present

Bachman, Richard
See King, Stephen

Bachmann, Ingeborg 1926-1973 .... **CLC 69**
See also CA 93-96; 45-48; CANR 69; DLB 85; EWL 3; RGWL 2, 3

Bacon, Francis 1561-1626 .... **LC 18, 32**
See also BRW 1; CDBLB Before 1660; DLB 151, 236, 252; RGEL 2; TEA

Bacon, Roger 1214(?)-1294 .... **CMLC 14**
See also DLB 115

Bacovia, George 1881-1957 .... **TCLC 24**
See Vasiliu, Gheorghe
See also CDWLB 4; DLB 220; EWL 3

Badanes, Jerome 1937-1995 .... **CLC 59**
See also CA 234

Bagehot, Walter 1826-1877 .... **NCLC 10**
See also DLB 55

Bagnold, Enid 1889-1981 .... **CLC 25**
See also BYA 2; CA 5-8R; 103; CANR 5, 40; CBD; CN 2; CWD; CWRI 5; DAM DRAM; DLB 13, 160, 191, 245; FW; MAICYA 1, 2; RGEL 2; SATA 1, 25

Bagritsky, Eduard .... **TCLC 60**
See Dzyubin, Eduard Georgievich

Bagrjana, Elisaveta
See Belcheva, Elisaveta Lyubomirova

Bagryana, Elisaveta .... **CLC 10**
See Belcheva, Elisaveta Lyubomirova
See also CA 178; CDWLB 4; DLB 147; EWL 3

Bailey, Paul 1937- .... **CLC 45**
See also CA 21-24R; CANR 16, 62, 124; CN 1, 2, 3, 4, 5, 6, 7; DLB 14, 271; GLL 2

Baillie, Joanna 1762-1851 ...... **NCLC 71, 151**
See also DLB 93; GL 2; RGEL 2

Bainbridge, Beryl (Margaret) 1934- . **CLC 4, 5, 8, 10, 14, 18, 22, 62, 130**
See also BRWS 6; CA 21-24R; CANR 24, 55, 75, 88, 128; CN 2, 3, 4, 5, 6, 7; DAM NOV; DLB 14, 231; EWL 3; MTCW 1, 2; MTFW 2005

Baker, Carlos (Heard) 1909-1987 .... **TCLC 119**
See also CA 5-8R; 122; CANR 3, 63; DLB 103

Baker, Elliott 1922- .... **CLC 8**
See also CA 45-48; CANR 2, 63; CN 1, 2, 3, 4, 5, 6, 7

Baker, Jean H. .... **TCLC 3, 10**
See Russell, George William

Baker, Nicholson 1957- .... **CLC 61, 165**
See also AMWS 13; CA 135; CANR 63, 120, 138; CN 6; CPW; DA3; DAM POP; DLB 227; MTFW 2005

Baker, Ray Stannard 1870-1946 .... **TCLC 47**
See also CA 118

Baker, Russell (Wayne) 1925- .... **CLC 31**
See also BEST 89:4; CA 57-60; CANR 11, 41, 59, 137; MTCW 1, 2; MTFW 2005

Bakhtin, M.
See Bakhtin, Mikhail Mikhailovich

Bakhtin, M. M.
See Bakhtin, Mikhail Mikhailovich

Bakhtin, Mikhail
See Bakhtin, Mikhail Mikhailovich

Bakhtin, Mikhail Mikhailovich 1895-1975 .... **CLC 83; TCLC 160**
See also CA 128; 113; DLB 242; EWL 3

Bakshi, Ralph 1938(?)- .... **CLC 26**
See also CA 112; 138; IDFW 3

Bakunin, Mikhail (Alexandrovich) 1814-1876 .... **NCLC 25, 58**
See also DLB 277

Baldwin, James (Arthur) 1924-1987 . **BLC 1; CLC 1, 2, 3, 4, 5, 8, 13, 15, 17, 42, 50, 67, 90, 127; DC 1; SSC 10, 33; WLC**
See also AAYA 4, 34; AFAW 1, 2; AMWR 2; AMWS 1; BPFB 1; BW 1; CA 1-4R; 124; CABS 1; CAD; CANR 3, 24; CDALB 1941-1968; CN 1, 2, 3, 4; CPW; DA; DA3; DAB; DAC; DAM MST, MULT, NOV, POP; DFS 11, 15; DLB 2, 7, 33, 249, 278; DLBY 1987; EWL 3;

EXPS; LAIT 5; MAL 5; MTCW 1, 2; MTFW 2005; NCFS 4; NFS 4; RGAL 4; RGSF 2; SATA 9; SATA-Obit 54; SSFS 2, 18; TUS

Baldwin, William c. 1515-1563 .... **LC 113**
See also DLB 132

Bale, John 1495-1563 .... **LC 62**
See also DLB 132; RGEL 2; TEA

Ball, Hugo 1886-1927 .... **TCLC 104**

Ballard, J(ames) G(raham) 1930- . **CLC 3, 6, 14, 36, 137; SSC 1, 53**
See also AAYA 3, 52; BRWS 5; CA 5-8R; CANR 15, 39, 65, 107, 133; CN 1, 2, 3, 4, 5, 6, 7; DA3; DAM NOV, POP; DLB 14, 207, 261, 319; EWL 3; HGG; MTCW 1, 2; MTFW 2005; NFS 8; RGEL 2; RGSF 2; SATA 93; SCFW 1, 2; SFW 4

Balmont, Konstantin (Dmitriyevich) 1867-1943 .... **TCLC 11**
See also CA 109; 155; DLB 295; EWL 3

Baltausis, Vincas 1847-1910
See Mikszath, Kalman

Balzac, Honore de 1799-1850 ... **NCLC 5, 35, 53, 153; SSC 5, 59; WLC**
See also DA; DA3; DAB; DAC; DAM MST, NOV; DLB 119; EW 5; GFL 1789 to the Present; LMFS 1; RGSF 2; RGWL 2, 3; SSFS 10; SUFW; TWA

Bambara, Toni Cade 1939-1995 .... **BLC 1; CLC 19, 88; SSC 35; TCLC 116; WLCS**
See also AAYA 5, 49; AFAW 2; AMWS 11; BW 2, 3; BYA 12, 14; CA 29-32R; 150; CANR 24, 49, 81; CDALBS; DA; DA3; DAC; DAM MST, MULT; DLB 38, 218; EXPS; MAL 5; MTCW 1, 2; MTFW 2005; RGAL 4; RGSF 2; SATA 112; SSFS 4, 7, 12, 21

Bamdad, A.
See Shamlu, Ahmad

Bamdad, Alef
See Shamlu, Ahmad

Banat, D. R.
See Bradbury, Ray (Douglas)

Bancroft, Laura
See Baum, L(yman) Frank

Banim, John 1798-1842 .... **NCLC 13**
See also DLB 116, 158, 159; RGEL 2

Banim, Michael 1796-1874 .... **NCLC 13**
See also DLB 158, 159

Banjo, The
See Paterson, A(ndrew) B(arton)

Banks, Iain
See Banks, Iain M(enzies)
See also BRWS 11

Banks, Iain M(enzies) 1954- .... **CLC 34**
See Banks, Iain
See also CA 123; 128; CANR 61, 106; DLB 194, 261; EWL 3; HGG; INT CA-128; MTFW 2005; SFW 4

Banks, Lynne Reid .... **CLC 23**
See Reid Banks, Lynne
See also AAYA 6; BYA 7; CLR 86; CN 4, 5, 6

Banks, Russell (Earl) 1940- .... **CLC 37, 72, 187; SSC 42**
See also AAYA 45; AMWS 5; CA 65-68; CAAS 15; CANR 19, 52, 73, 118; CN 4, 5, 6, 7; DLB 130, 278; EWL 3; MAL 5; MTCW 2; MTFW 2005; NFS 13

Banville, John 1945- .... **CLC 46, 118**
See also CA 117; 128; CANR 104; CN 4, 5, 6, 7; DLB 14, 271; INT CA-128

Banville, Theodore (Faullain) de 1832-1891 .... **NCLC 9**
See also DLB 217; GFL 1789 to the Present

Baraka, Amiri 1934- .... **BLC 1; CLC 1, 2, 3, 5, 10, 14, 33, 115, 213; DC 6; PC 4; WLCS**
See Jones, LeRoi
See also AAYA 63; AFAW 1, 2; AMWS 2; BW 2, 3; CA 21-24R; CABS 3; CAD; CANR 27, 38, 61, 133; CD 3, 5, 6; CDALB 1941-1968; CP 4, 5, 6, 7; CPW; DA; DA3; DAC; DAM MST, MULT, POET, POP; DFS 3, 11, 16; DLB 5, 7, 16, 38; DLBD 8; EWL 3; MAL 5; MTCW 1, 2; MTFW 2005; PFS 9; RGAL 4; TCLE 1:1; TUS; WP

Baratynsky, Evgenii Abramovich 1800-1844 .... **NCLC 103**
See also DLB 205

Barbauld, Anna Laetitia 1743-1825 .... **NCLC 50**
See also DLB 107, 109, 142, 158; RGEL 2

Barbellion, W. N. P. .... **TCLC 24**
See Cummings, Bruce F(rederick)

Barber, Benjamin R. 1939- .... **CLC 141**
See also CA 29-32R; CANR 12, 32, 64, 119

Barbera, Jack (Vincent) 1945- .... **CLC 44**
See also CA 110; CANR 45

Barbey d'Aurevilly, Jules-Amedee 1808-1889 .... **NCLC 1; SSC 17**
See also DLB 119; GFL 1789 to the Present

Barbour, John c. 1316-1395 .... **CMLC 33**
See also DLB 146

Barbusse, Henri 1873-1935 .... **TCLC 5**
See also CA 105; 154; DLB 65; EWL 3; RGWL 2, 3

Barclay, Alexander c. 1475-1552 .... **LC 109**
See also DLB 132

Barclay, Bill
See Moorcock, Michael (John)

Barclay, William Ewert
See Moorcock, Michael (John)

Barea, Arturo 1897-1957 .... **TCLC 14**
See also CA 111; 201

Barfoot, Joan 1946- .... **CLC 18**
See also CA 105; CANR 141

Barham, Richard Harris 1788-1845 .... **NCLC 77**
See also DLB 159

Baring, Maurice 1874-1945 .... **TCLC 8**
See also CA 105; 168; DLB 34; HGG

Baring-Gould, Sabine 1834-1924 ... **TCLC 88**
See also DLB 156, 190

Barker, Clive 1952- .... **CLC 52, 205; SSC 53**
See also AAYA 10, 54; BEST 90:3; BPFB 1; CA 121; 129; CANR 71, 111, 133; CPW; DA3; DAM POP; DLB 261; HGG; INT CA-129; MTCW 1, 2; MTFW 2005; SUFW 2

Barker, George Granville 1913-1991 .... **CLC 8, 48**
See also CA 9-12R; 135; CANR 7, 38; CP 1, 2, 3, 4; DAM POET; DLB 20; EWL 3; MTCW 1

Barker, Harley Granville
See Granville-Barker, Harley
See also DLB 10

Barker, Howard 1946- .... **CLC 37**
See also CA 102; CBD; CD 5, 6; DLB 13, 233

Barker, Jane 1652-1732 .... **LC 42, 82**
See also DLB 39, 131

Barker, Pat(ricia) 1943- ...... **CLC 32, 94, 146**
See also BRWS 4; CA 117; 122; CANR 50, 101; CN 6, 7; DLB 271; INT CA-122

Barlach, Ernst (Heinrich) 1870-1938 .... **TCLC 84**
See also CA 178; DLB 56, 118; EWL 3

Barlow, Joel 1754-1812 .... **NCLC 23**
See also AMWS 2; DLB 37; RGAL 4

Barnard, Mary (Ethel) 1909- .... **CLC 48**
See also CA 21-22; CAP 2; CP 1

Barnes, Djuna 1892-1982 .... **CLC 3, 4, 8, 11, 29, 127; SSC 3**
See Steptoe, Lydia
See also AMWS 3; CA 9-12R; 107; CAD; CANR 16, 55; CN 1, 2, 3; CWD; DLB 4, 9, 45; EWL 3; GLL 1; MAL 5; MTCW 1, 2; MTFW 2005; RGAL 4; TCLE 1:1; TUS

Barnes, Jim 1933- .... **NNAL**
See also CA 108, 175; CAAE 175; CAAS 28; DLB 175

Barnes, Julian (Patrick) 1946- . **CLC 42, 141**
See also BRWS 4; CA 102; CANR 19, 54, 115, 137; CN 4, 5, 6, 7; DAB; DLB 194; DLBY 1993; EWL 3; MTCW 2; MTFW 2005

Barnes, Peter 1931-2004 .... **CLC 5, 56**
See also CA 65-68; 230; CAAS 12; CANR 33, 34, 64, 113; CBD; CD 5, 6; DFS 6; DLB 13, 233; MTCW 1

Barnes, William 1801-1886 .... **NCLC 75**
See also DLB 32

Baroja (y Nessi), Pio 1872-1956 .... **HLC 1; TCLC 8**
See also CA 104; EW 9

Baron, David
See Pinter, Harold

Baron Corvo
See Rolfe, Frederick (William Serafino Austin Lewis Mary)

Barondess, Sue K(aufman) 1926-1977 .... **CLC 8**
See Kaufman, Sue
See also CA 1-4R; 69-72; CANR 1

Baron de Teive
See Pessoa, Fernando (Antonio Nogueira)

Baroness Von S.
See Zangwill, Israel

Barres, (Auguste-)Maurice 1862-1923 .... **TCLC 47**
See also CA 164; DLB 123; GFL 1789 to the Present

Barreto, Afonso Henrique de Lima
See Lima Barreto, Afonso Henrique de

Barrett, Andrea 1954- .... **CLC 150**
See also CA 156; CANR 92; CN 7

Barrett, Michele .... **CLC 65**

Barrett, (Roger) Syd 1946- .... **CLC 35**

Barrett, William (Christopher) 1913-1992 .... **CLC 27**
See also CA 13-16R; 139; CANR 11, 67; INT CANR-11

Barrett Browning, Elizabeth 1806-1861 ... **NCLC 1, 16, 61, 66; PC 6, 62; WLC**
See also AAYA 63; BRW 4; CDBLB 1832-1890; DA; DA3; DAB; DAC; DAM MST, POET; DLB 32, 199; EXPP; FL 1:2; PAB; PFS 2, 16, 23; TEA; WLIT 4; WP

Barrie, J(ames) M(atthew) 1860-1937 .... **TCLC 2, 164**
See also BRWS 3; BYA 4, 5; CA 104; 136; CANR 77; CDBLB 1890-1914; CLR 16; CWRI 5; DA3; DAB; DAM DRAM; DFS 7; DLB 10, 141, 156; EWL 3; FANT; MAICYA 1, 2; MTCW 2; MTFW 2005; SATA 100; SUFW; WCH; WLIT 4; YABC 1

Barrington, Michael
See Moorcock, Michael (John)

Barrol, Grady
See Bograd, Larry

Barry, Mike
See Malzberg, Barry N(athaniel)

Barry, Philip 1896-1949 .... **TCLC 11**
See also CA 109; 199; DFS 9; DLB 7, 228; MAL 5; RGAL 4

Bart, Andre Schwarz
See Schwarz-Bart, Andre

Bishop, John Peale 1892-1944 ..... **TCLC 103**
See also CA 107; 155; DLB 4, 9, 45; MAL 5; RGAL 4

Bissett, Bill 1939- .... **CLC 18; PC 14**
See also CA 69-72; CAAS 19; CANR 15; CCA 1; CP 1, 2, 3, 4, 5, 6, 7; DLB 53; MTCW 1

Bissoondath, Neil (Devindra) 1955- .... **CLC 120**
See also CA 136; CANR 123; CN 6, 7; DAC

Bitov, Andrei (Georgievich) 1937- ... **CLC 57**
See also CA 142; DLB 302

Biyidi, Alexandre 1932-
See Beti, Mongo
See also BW 1, 3; CA 114; 124; CANR 81; DA3; MTCW 1, 2

Bjarme, Brynjolf
See Ibsen, Henrik (Johan)

Bjoernson, Bjoernstjerne (Martinius) 1832-1910 .... **TCLC 7, 37**
See also CA 104

Black, Robert
See Holdstock, Robert P.

Blackburn, Paul 1926-1971 .... **CLC 9, 43**
See also BG 1:2; CA 81-84; 33-36R; CANR 34; CP 1; DLB 16; DLBY 1981

Black Elk 1863-1950 .... **NNAL; TCLC 33**
See also CA 144; DAM MULT; MTCW 2; MTFW 2005; WP

Black Hawk 1767-1838 .... **NNAL**

Black Hobart
See Sanders, (James) Ed(ward)

Blacklin, Malcolm
See Chambers, Aidan

Blackmore, R(ichard) D(oddridge) 1825-1900 .... **TCLC 27**
See also CA 120; DLB 18; RGEL 2

Blackmur, R(ichard) P(almer) 1904-1965 .... **CLC 2, 24**
See also AMWS 2; CA 11-12; 25-28R; CANR 71; CAP 1; DLB 63; EWL 3; MAL 5

Black Tarantula
See Acker, Kathy

Blackwood, Algernon (Henry) 1869-1951 .... **TCLC 5**
See also CA 105; 150; DLB 153, 156, 178; HGG; SUFW 1

Blackwood, Caroline (Maureen) 1931-1996 .... **CLC 6, 9, 100**
See also BRWS 9; CA 85-88; 151; CANR 32, 61, 65; CN 3, 4, 5, 6; DLB 14, 207; HGG; MTCW 1

Blade, Alexander
See Hamilton, Edmond; Silverberg, Robert

Blaga, Lucian 1895-1961 .... **CLC 75**
See also CA 157; DLB 220; EWL 3

Blair, Eric (Arthur) 1903-1950 .... **TCLC 123**
See Orwell, George
See also CA 104; 132; DA; DA3; DAB; DAC; DAM MST, NOV; MTCW 1, 2; MTFW 2005; SATA 29

Blair, Hugh 1718-1800 .... **NCLC 75**

Blais, Marie-Claire 1939- .... **CLC 2, 4, 6, 13, 22**
See also CA 21-24R; CAAS 4; CANR 38, 75, 93; CWW 2; DAC; DAM MST; DLB 53; EWL 3; FW; MTCW 1, 2; MTFW 2005; TWA

Blaise, Clark 1940- .... **CLC 29**
See also AITN 2; CA 53-56, 231; CAAE 231; CAAS 3; CANR 5, 66, 106; CN 4, 5, 6, 7; DLB 53; RGSF 2

Blake, Fairley
See De Voto, Bernard (Augustine)

Blake, Nicholas
See Day Lewis, C(ecil)
See also DLB 77; MSW

Blake, Sterling
See Benford, Gregory (Albert)

Blake, William 1757-1827 . **NCLC 13, 37, 57, 127; PC 12, 63; WLC**
See also AAYA 47; BRW 3; BRWR 1; CDBLB 1789-1832; CLR 52; DA; DA3; DAB; DAC; DAM MST, POET; DLB 93, 163; EXPP; LATS 1:1; LMFS 1; MAICYA 1, 2; PAB; PFS 2, 12; SATA 30; TEA; WCH; WLIT 3; WP

Blanchot, Maurice 1907-2003 .... **CLC 135**
See also CA 117; 144; 213; CANR 138; DLB 72, 296; EWL 3

Blasco Ibanez, Vicente 1867-1928 . **TCLC 12**
See Ibanez, Vicente Blasco
See also BPFB 1; CA 110; 131; CANR 81; DA3; DAM NOV; EW 8; EWL 3; HW 1, 2; MTCW 1

Blatty, William Peter 1928- .... **CLC 2**
See also CA 5-8R; CANR 9, 124; DAM POP; HGG

Bleeck, Oliver
See Thomas, Ross (Elmore)

Blessing, Lee (Knowlton) 1949- .... **CLC 54**
See also CA 236; CAD; CD 5, 6

Blight, Rose
See Greer, Germaine

Blish, James (Benjamin) 1921-1975 . **CLC 14**
See also BPFB 1; CA 1-4R; 57-60; CANR 3; CN 2; DLB 8; MTCW 1; SATA 66; SCFW 1, 2; SFW 4

Bliss, Frederick
See Card, Orson Scott

Bliss, Reginald
See Wells, H(erbert) G(eorge)

Blixen, Karen (Christentze Dinesen) 1885-1962
See Dinesen, Isak
See also CA 25-28; CANR 22, 50; CAP 2; DA3; DLB 214; LMFS 1; MTCW 1, 2; SATA 44; SSFS 20

Bloch, Robert (Albert) 1917-1994 .... **CLC 33**
See also AAYA 29; CA 5-8R, 179; 146; CAAE 179; CAAS 20; CANR 5, 78; DA3; DLB 44; HGG; INT CANR-5; MTCW 2; SATA 12; SATA-Obit 82; SFW 4; SUFW 1, 2

Blok, Alexander (Alexandrovich) 1880-1921 .... **PC 21; TCLC 5**
See also CA 104; 183; DLB 295; EW 9; EWL 3; LMFS 2; RGWL 2, 3

Blom, Jan
See Breytenbach, Breyten

Bloom, Harold 1930- .... **CLC 24, 103, 221**
See also CA 13-16R; CANR 39, 75, 92, 133; DLB 67; EWL 3; MTCW 2; MTFW 2005; RGAL 4

Bloomfield, Aurelius
See Bourne, Randolph S(illiman)

Bloomfield, Robert 1766-1823 ..... **NCLC 145**
See also DLB 93

Blount, Roy (Alton), Jr. 1941- .... **CLC 38**
See also CA 53-56; CANR 10, 28, 61, 125; CSW; INT CANR-28; MTCW 1, 2; MTFW 2005

Blowsnake, Sam 1875-(?) .... **NNAL**

Bloy, Leon 1846-1917 .... **TCLC 22**
See also CA 121; 183; DLB 123; GFL 1789 to the Present

Blue Cloud, Peter (Aroniawenrate) 1933- .... **NNAL**
See also CA 117; CANR 40; DAM MULT

Bluggage, Oranthy
See Alcott, Louisa May

Blume, Judy (Sussman) 1938- .... **CLC 12, 30**
See also AAYA 3, 26; BYA 1, 8, 12; CA 29-32R; CANR 13, 37, 66, 124; CLR 2, 15, 69; CPW; DA3; DAM NOV, POP; DLB 52; JRDA; MAICYA 1, 2; MAICYAS 1; MTCW 1, 2; MTFW 2005; SATA 2, 31, 79, 142; WYA; YAW

Blunden, Edmund (Charles) 1896-1974 .... **CLC 2, 56; PC 66**
See also BRW 6; BRWS 11; CA 17-18; 45-48; CANR 54; CAP 2; CP 1, 2; DLB 20, 100, 155; MTCW 1; PAB

Bly, Robert (Elwood) 1926- .... **CLC 1, 2, 5, 10, 15, 38, 128; PC 39**
See also AMWS 4; CA 5-8R; CANR 41, 73, 125; CP 1, 2, 3, 4, 5, 6, 7; DA3; DAM POET; DLB 5; EWL 3; MAL 5; MTCW 1, 2; MTFW 2005; PFS 6, 17; RGAL 4

Boas, Franz 1858-1942 .... **TCLC 56**
See also CA 115; 181

Bobette
See Simenon, Georges (Jacques Christian)

Boccaccio, Giovanni 1313-1375 ... **CMLC 13, 57; SSC 10, 87**
See also EW 2; RGSF 2; RGWL 2, 3; TWA; WLIT 7

Bochco, Steven 1943- .... **CLC 35**
See also AAYA 11; CA 124; 138

Bode, Sigmund
See O'Doherty, Brian

Bodel, Jean 1167(?)-1210 .... **CMLC 28**

Bodenheim, Maxwell 1892-1954 .... **TCLC 44**
See also CA 110; 187; DLB 9, 45; MAL 5; RGAL 4

Bodenheimer, Maxwell
See Bodenheim, Maxwell

Bodker, Cecil 1927-
See Bodker, Cecil

Bodker, Cecil 1927- .... **CLC 21**
See also CA 73-76; CANR 13, 44, 111; CLR 23; MAICYA 1, 2; SATA 14, 133

Boell, Heinrich (Theodor) 1917-1985 ..... **CLC 2, 3, 6, 9, 11, 15, 27, 32, 72; SSC 23; WLC**
See Boll, Heinrich (Theodor)
See also CA 21-24R; 116; CANR 24; DA; DA3; DAB; DAC; DAM MST, NOV; DLB 69; DLBY 1985; MTCW 1, 2; MTFW 2005; SSFS 20; TWA

Boerne, Alfred
See Doeblin, Alfred

Boethius c. 480-c. 524 .... **CMLC 15**
See also DLB 115; RGWL 2, 3

Boff, Leonardo (Genezio Darci) 1938- .... **CLC 70; HLC 1**
See also CA 150; DAM MULT; HW 2

Bogan, Louise 1897-1970 .... **CLC 4, 39, 46, 93; PC 12**
See also AMWS 3; CA 73-76; 25-28R; CANR 33, 82; CP 1; DAM POET; DLB 45, 169; EWL 3; MAL 5; MAWW; MTCW 1, 2; PFS 21; RGAL 4

Bogarde, Dirk
See Van Den Bogarde, Derek Jules Gaspard Ulric Niven
See also DLB 14

Bogosian, Eric 1953- .... **CLC 45, 141**
See also CA 138; CAD; CANR 102; CD 5, 6

Bograd, Larry 1953- .... **CLC 35**
See also CA 93-96; CANR 57; SAAS 21; SATA 33, 89; WYA

Boiardo, Matteo Maria 1441-1494 .... **LC 6**

Boileau-Despreaux, Nicolas 1636-1711 . **LC 3**
See also DLB 268; EW 3; GFL Beginnings to 1789; RGWL 2, 3

Boissard, Maurice
See Leautaud, Paul

Bojer, Johan 1872-1959 .... **TCLC 64**
See also CA 189; EWL 3

Bok, Edward W(illiam) 1863-1930 .... **TCLC 101**
See also CA 217; DLB 91; DLBD 16

Boker, George Henry 1823-1890 . **NCLC 125**
See also RGAL 4
Boland, Eavan (Aisling) 1944- .. **CLC 40, 67, 113; PC 58**
See also BRWS 5; CA 143, 207; CAAE 207; CANR 61; CP 1, 7; CWP; DAM POET; DLB 40; FW; MTCW 2; MTFW 2005; PFS 12, 22
Boll, Heinrich (Theodor)
See Boell, Heinrich (Theodor)
See also BPFB 1; CDWLB 2; EW 13; EWL 3; RGSF 2; RGWL 2, 3
Bolt, Lee
See Faust, Frederick (Schiller)
Bolt, Robert (Oxton) 1924-1995 ...... **CLC 14; TCLC 175**
See also CA 17-20R; 147; CANR 35, 67; CBD; DAM DRAM; DFS 2; DLB 13, 233; EWL 3; LAIT 1; MTCW 1
Bombal, Maria Luisa 1910-1980 .... **HLCS 1; SSC 37**
See also CA 127; CANR 72; EWL 3; HW 1; LAW; RGSF 2
Bombet, Louis-Alexandre-Cesar
See Stendhal
Bomkauf
See Kaufman, Bob (Garnell)
Bonaventura .... **NCLC 35**
See also DLB 90
Bonaventure 1217(?)-1274 .... **CMLC 79**
See also DLB 115; LMFS 1
Bond, Edward 1934- .... **CLC 4, 6, 13, 23**
See also AAYA 50; BRWS 1; CA 25-28R; CANR 38, 67, 106; CBD; CD 5, 6; DAM DRAM; DFS 3, 8; DLB 13, 310; EWL 3; MTCW 1
Bonham, Frank 1914-1989 .... **CLC 12**
See also AAYA 1; BYA 1, 3; CA 9-12R; CANR 4, 36; JRDA; MAICYA 1, 2; SAAS 3; SATA 1, 49; SATA-Obit 62; TCWW 1, 2; YAW
Bonnefoy, Yves 1923- . **CLC 9, 15, 58; PC 58**
See also CA 85-88; CANR 33, 75, 97, 136; CWW 2; DAM MST, POET; DLB 258; EWL 3; GFL 1789 to the Present; MTCW 1, 2; MTFW 2005
Bonner, Marita .... **HR 1:2**
See Occomy, Marita (Odette) Bonner
Bonnin, Gertrude 1876-1938 .... **NNAL**
See Zitkala-Sa
See also CA 150; DAM MULT
Bontemps, Arna(ud Wendell)
1902-1973 .. **BLC 1; CLC 1, 18; HR 1:2**
See also BW 1; CA 1-4R; 41-44R; CANR 4, 35; CLR 6; CP 1; CWRI 5; DA3; DAM MULT, NOV, POET; DLB 48, 51; JRDA; MAICYA 1, 2; MAL 5; MTCW 1, 2; SATA 2, 44; SATA-Obit 24; WCH; WP
Boot, William
See Stoppard, Tom
Booth, Martin 1944-2004 .... **CLC 13**
See also CA 93-96, 188; 223; CAAE 188; CAAS 2; CANR 92; CP 1, 2, 3, 4
Booth, Philip 1925- .... **CLC 23**
See also CA 5-8R; CANR 5, 88; CP 1, 2, 3, 4, 5, 6, 7; DLBY 1982
Booth, Wayne C(layson) 1921-2005 . **CLC 24**
See also CA 1-4R; CAAS 5; CANR 3, 43, 117; DLB 67
Borchert, Wolfgang 1921-1947 .... **TCLC 5**
See also CA 104; 188; DLB 69, 124; EWL 3
Borel, Petrus 1809-1859 .... **NCLC 41**
See also DLB 119; GFL 1789 to the Present
Borges, Jorge Luis 1899-1986 ... **CLC 1, 2, 3, 4, 6, 8, 9, 10, 13, 19, 44, 48, 83; HLC 1; PC 22, 32; SSC 4, 41; TCLC 109; WLC**
See also AAYA 26; BPFB 1; CA 21-24R; CANR 19, 33, 75, 105, 133; CDWLB 3; DA; DA3; DAB; DAC; DAM MST, MULT; DLB 113, 283; DLBY 1986; DNFS 1, 2; EWL 3; HW 1, 2; LAW; LMFS 2; MSW; MTCW 1, 2; MTFW 2005; RGSF 2; RGWL 2, 3; SFW 4; SSFS 17; TWA; WLIT 1
Borowski, Tadeusz 1922-1951 .... **SSC 48; TCLC 9**
See also CA 106; 154; CDWLB 4; DLB 215; EWL 3; RGSF 2; RGWL 3; SSFS 13
Borrow, George (Henry)
1803-1881 .... **NCLC 9**
See also DLB 21, 55, 166
Bosch (Gavino), Juan 1909-2001 ..... **HLCS 1**
See also CA 151; 204; DAM MST, MULT; DLB 145; HW 1, 2
Bosman, Herman Charles
1905-1951 .... **TCLC 49**
See Malan, Herman
See also CA 160; DLB 225; RGSF 2
Bosschere, Jean de 1878(?)-1953 ... **TCLC 19**
See also CA 115; 186
Boswell, James 1740-1795 ... **LC 4, 50; WLC**
See also BRW 3; CDBLB 1660-1789; DA; DAB; DAC; DAM MST; DLB 104, 142; TEA; WLIT 3
Bottomley, Gordon 1874-1948 ..... **TCLC 107**
See also CA 120; 192; DLB 10
Bottoms, David 1949- .... **CLC 53**
See also CA 105; CANR 22; CSW; DLB 120; DLBY 1983
Boucicault, Dion 1820-1890 .... **NCLC 41**
Boucolon, Maryse
See Conde, Maryse
Bourdieu, Pierre 1930-2002 .... **CLC 198**
See also CA 130; 204
Bourget, Paul (Charles Joseph)
1852-1935 .... **TCLC 12**
See also CA 107; 196; DLB 123; GFL 1789 to the Present
Bourjaily, Vance (Nye) 1922- .... **CLC 8, 62**
See also CA 1-4R; CAAS 1; CANR 2, 72; CN 1, 2, 3, 4, 5, 6, 7; DLB 2, 143; MAL 5
Bourne, Randolph S(illiman)
1886-1918 .... **TCLC 16**
See also AMW; CA 117; 155; DLB 63; MAL 5
Bova, Ben(jamin William) 1932- ...... **CLC 45**
See also AAYA 16; CA 5-8R; CAAS 18; CANR 11, 56, 94, 111; CLR 3, 96; DLBY 1981; INT CANR-11; MAICYA 1, 2; MTCW 1; SATA 6, 68, 133; SFW 4
Bowen, Elizabeth (Dorothea Cole)
1899-1973 . **CLC 1, 3, 6, 11, 15, 22, 118; SSC 3, 28, 66; TCLC 148**
See also BRWS 2; CA 17-18; 41-44R; CANR 35, 105; CAP 2; CDBLB 1945-1960; CN 1; DA3; DAM NOV; DLB 15, 162; EWL 3; EXPS; FW; HGG; MTCW 1, 2; MTFW 2005; NFS 13; RGSF 2; SSFS 5; SUFW 1; TEA; WLIT 4
Bowering, George 1935- .... **CLC 15, 47**
See also CA 21-24R; CAAS 16; CANR 10; CN 7; CP 1, 2, 3, 4, 5, 6, 7; DLB 53
Bowering, Marilyn R(uthe) 1949- .... **CLC 32**
See also CA 101; CANR 49; CP 4, 5, 6, 7; CWP
Bowers, Edgar 1924-2000 .... **CLC 9**
See also CA 5-8R; 188; CANR 24; CP 1, 2, 3, 4, 5, 6, 7; CSW; DLB 5
Bowers, Mrs. J. Milton 1842-1914
See Bierce, Ambrose (Gwinett)
Bowie, David .... **CLC 17**
See Jones, David Robert
Bowles, Jane (Sydney) 1917-1973 ..... **CLC 3, 68**
See Bowles, Jane Auer
See also CA 19-20; 41-44R; CAP 2; CN 1; MAL 5
Bowles, Jane Auer
See Bowles, Jane (Sydney)
See also EWL 3
Bowles, Paul (Frederick) 1910-1999 . **CLC 1, 2, 19, 53; SSC 3**
See also AMWS 4; CA 1-4R; 186; CAAS 1; CANR 1, 19, 50, 75; CN 1, 2, 3, 4, 5, 6; DA3; DLB 5, 6, 218; EWL 3; MAL 5; MTCW 1, 2; MTFW 2005; RGAL 4; SSFS 17
Bowles, William Lisle 1762-1850 . **NCLC 103**
See also DLB 93
Box, Edgar
See Vidal, (Eugene Luther) Gore
See also GLL 1
Boyd, James 1888-1944 .... **TCLC 115**
See also CA 186; DLB 9; DLBD 16; RGAL 4; RHW
Boyd, Nancy
See Millay, Edna St. Vincent
See also GLL 1
Boyd, Thomas (Alexander)
1898-1935 .... **TCLC 111**
See also CA 111; 183; DLB 9; DLBD 16, 316
Boyd, William (Andrew Murray)
1952- .... **CLC 28, 53, 70**
See also CA 114; 120; CANR 51, 71, 131; CN 4, 5, 6, 7; DLB 231
Boyesen, Hjalmar Hjorth
1848-1895 .... **NCLC 135**
See also DLB 12, 71; DLBD 13; RGAL 4
Boyle, Kay 1902-1992 .... **CLC 1, 5, 19, 58, 121; SSC 5**
See also CA 13-16R; 140; CAAS 1; CANR 29, 61, 110; CN 1, 2, 3, 4, 5; CP 1, 2, 3, 4; DLB 4, 9, 48, 86; DLBY 1993; EWL 3; MAL 5; MTCW 1, 2; MTFW 2005; RGAL 4; RGSF 2; SSFS 10, 13, 14
Boyle, Mark
See Kienzle, William X(avier)
Boyle, Patrick 1905-1982 .... **CLC 19**
See also CA 127
Boyle, T. C.
See Boyle, T(homas) Coraghessan
See also AMWS 8
Boyle, T(homas) Coraghessan
1948- .... **CLC 36, 55, 90; SSC 16**
See Boyle, T. C.
See also AAYA 47; BEST 90:4; BPFB 1; CA 120; CANR 44, 76, 89, 132; CN 6, 7; CPW; DA3; DAM POP; DLB 218, 278; DLBY 1986; EWL 3; MAL 5; MTCW 2; MTFW 2005; SSFS 13, 19
Boz
See Dickens, Charles (John Huffam)
Brackenridge, Hugh Henry
1748-1816 .... **NCLC 7**
See also DLB 11, 37; RGAL 4
Bradbury, Edward P.
See Moorcock, Michael (John)
See also MTCW 2
Bradbury, Malcolm (Stanley)
1932-2000 .... **CLC 32, 61**
See also CA 1-4R; CANR 1, 33, 91, 98, 137; CN 1, 2, 3, 4, 5, 6, 7; CP 1; DA3; DAM NOV; DLB 14, 207; EWL 3; MTCW 1, 2; MTFW 2005
Bradbury, Ray (Douglas) 1920- .... **CLC 1, 3, 10, 15, 42, 98; SSC 29, 53; WLC**
See also AAYA 15; AITN 1, 2; AMWS 4; BPFB 1; BYA 4, 5, 11; CA 1-4R; CANR 2, 30, 75, 125; CDALB 1968-1988; CN 1, 2, 3, 4, 5, 6, 7; CPW; DA; DA3; DAB; DAC; DAM MST, NOV, POP; DLB 2, 8;

Bryant, William Cullen 1794-1878 . **NCLC 6, 46; PC 20**
See also AMWS 1; CDALB 1640-1865; DA; DAB; DAC; DAM MST, POET; DLB 3, 43, 59, 189, 250; EXPP; PAB; RGAL 4; TUS

Bryusov, Valery Yakovlevich 1873-1924 .... **TCLC 10**
See also CA 107; 155; EWL 3; SFW 4

Buchan, John 1875-1940 .... **TCLC 41**
See also CA 108; 145; CMW 4; DAB; DAM POP; DLB 34, 70, 156; HGG; MSW; MTCW 2; RGEL 2; RHW; YABC 2

Buchanan, George 1506-1582 .... **LC 4**
See also DLB 132

Buchanan, Robert 1841-1901 .... **TCLC 107**
See also CA 179; DLB 18, 35

Buchheim, Lothar-Guenther 1918- .... **CLC 6**
See also CA 85-88

Buchner, (Karl) Georg 1813-1837 .... **NCLC 26, 146**
See also CDWLB 2; DLB 133; EW 6; RGSF 2; RGWL 2, 3; TWA

Buchwald, Art(hur) 1925- .... **CLC 33**
See also AITN 1; CA 5-8R; CANR 21, 67, 107; MTCW 1, 2; SATA 10

Buck, Pearl S(ydenstricker) 1892-1973 .... **CLC 7, 11, 18, 127**
See also AAYA 42; AITN 1; AMWS 2; BPFB 1; CA 1-4R; 41-44R; CANR 1, 34; CDALBS; CN 1; DA; DA3; DAB; DAC; DAM MST, NOV; DLB 9, 102; EWL 3; LAIT 3; MAL 5; MTCW 1, 2; MTFW 2005; RGAL 4; RHW; SATA 1, 25; TUS

Buckler, Ernest 1908-1984 .... **CLC 13**
See also CA 11-12; 114; CAP 1; CCA 1; CN 1, 2, 3; DAC; DAM MST; DLB 68; SATA 47

Buckley, Christopher (Taylor) 1952- .... **CLC 165**
See also CA 139; CANR 119

Buckley, Vincent (Thomas) 1925-1988 .... **CLC 57**
See also CA 101; CP 1, 2, 3, 4; DLB 289

Buckley, William F(rank), Jr. 1925- . **CLC 7, 18, 37**
See also AITN 1; BPFB 1; CA 1-4R; CANR 1, 24, 53, 93, 133; CMW 4; CPW; DA3; DAM POP; DLB 137; DLBY 1980; INT CANR-24; MTCW 1, 2; MTFW 2005; TUS

Buechner, (Carl) Frederick 1926- . **CLC 2, 4, 6, 9**
See also AMWS 12; BPFB 1; CA 13-16R; CANR 11, 39, 64, 114, 138; CN 1, 2, 3, 4, 5, 6, 7; DAM NOV; DLBY 1980; INT CANR-11; MAL 5; MTCW 1, 2; MTFW 2005; TCLE 1:1

Buell, John (Edward) 1927- .... **CLC 10**
See also CA 1-4R; CANR 71; DLB 53

Buero Vallejo, Antonio 1916-2000 ... **CLC 15, 46, 139; DC 18**
See also CA 106; 189; CANR 24, 49, 75; CWW 2; DFS 11; EWL 3; HW 1; MTCW 1, 2

Bufalino, Gesualdo 1920-1996 .... **CLC 74**
See also CA 209; CWW 2; DLB 196

Bugayev, Boris Nikolayevich 1880-1934 .... **PC 11; TCLC 7**
See Bely, Andrey; Belyi, Andrei
See also CA 104; 165; MTCW 2; MTFW 2005

Bukowski, Charles 1920-1994 ... **CLC 2, 5, 9, 41, 82, 108; PC 18; SSC 45**
See also CA 17-20R; 144; CANR 40, 62, 105; CN 4, 5; CP 1, 2, 3, 4; CPW; DA3; DAM NOV, POET; DLB 5, 130, 169; EWL 3; MAL 5; MTCW 1, 2; MTFW 2005

Bulgakov, Mikhail (Afanas'evich) 1891-1940 ..... **SSC 18; TCLC 2, 16, 159**
See also BPFB 1; CA 105; 152; DAM DRAM, NOV; DLB 272; EWL 3; MTCW 2; MTFW 2005; NFS 8; RGSF 2; RGWL 2, 3; SFW 4; TWA

Bulgya, Alexander Alexandrovich 1901-1956 .... **TCLC 53**
See Fadeev, Aleksandr Aleksandrovich; Fadeev, Alexandr Alexandrovich; Fadeyev, Alexander
See also CA 117; 181

Bullins, Ed 1935- .... **BLC 1; CLC 1, 5, 7; DC 6**
See also BW 2, 3; CA 49-52; CAAS 16; CAD; CANR 24, 46, 73, 134; CD 5, 6; DAM DRAM, MULT; DLB 7, 38, 249; EWL 3; MAL 5; MTCW 1, 2; MTFW 2005; RGAL 4

Bulosan, Carlos 1911-1956 .... **AAL**
See also CA 216; DLB 312; RGAL 4

Bulwer-Lytton, Edward (George Earle Lytton) 1803-1873 .... **NCLC 1, 45**
See also DLB 21; RGEL 2; SFW 4; SUFW 1; TEA

Bunin, Ivan Alexeyevich 1870-1953 ... **SSC 5; TCLC 6**
See also CA 104; DLB 317; EWL 3; RGSF 2; RGWL 2, 3; TWA

Bunting, Basil 1900-1985 ...... **CLC 10, 39, 47**
See also BRWS 7; CA 53-56; 115; CANR 7; CP 1, 2, 3, 4; DAM POET; DLB 20; EWL 3; RGEL 2

Bunuel, Luis 1900-1983 ... **CLC 16, 80; HLC 1**
See also CA 101; 110; CANR 32, 77; DAM MULT; HW 1

Bunyan, John 1628-1688 ..... **LC 4, 69; WLC**
See also BRW 2; BYA 5; CDBLB 1660-1789; DA; DAB; DAC; DAM MST; DLB 39; RGEL 2; TEA; WCH; WLIT 3

Buravsky, Alexandr .... **CLC 59**

Burckhardt, Jacob (Christoph) 1818-1897 .... **NCLC 49**
See also EW 6

Burford, Eleanor
See Hibbert, Eleanor Alice Burford

Burgess, Anthony . **CLC 1, 2, 4, 5, 8, 10, 13, 15, 22, 40, 62, 81, 94**
See Wilson, John (Anthony) Burgess
See also AAYA 25; AITN 1; BRWS 1; CDBLB 1960 to Present; CN 1, 2, 3, 4, 5; DAB; DLB 14, 194, 261; DLBY 1998; EWL 3; RGEL 2; RHW; SFW 4; YAW

Burke, Edmund 1729(?)-1797 .... **LC 7, 36; WLC**
See also BRW 3; DA; DA3; DAB; DAC; DAM MST; DLB 104, 252; RGEL 2; TEA

Burke, Kenneth (Duva) 1897-1993 ... **CLC 2, 24**
See also AMW; CA 5-8R; 143; CANR 39, 74, 136; CN 1, 2; CP 1, 2, 3, 4; DLB 45, 63; EWL 3; MAL 5; MTCW 1, 2; MTFW 2005; RGAL 4

Burke, Leda
See Garnett, David

Burke, Ralph
See Silverberg, Robert

Burke, Thomas 1886-1945 .... **TCLC 63**
See also CA 113; 155; CMW 4; DLB 197

Burney, Fanny 1752-1840 .... **NCLC 12, 54, 107**
See also BRWS 3; DLB 39; FL 1:2; NFS 16; RGEL 2; TEA

Burney, Frances
See Burney, Fanny

Burns, Robert 1759-1796 ... **LC 3, 29, 40; PC 6; WLC**
See also AAYA 51; BRW 3; CDBLB 1789-1832; DA; DA3; DAB; DAC; DAM MST, POET; DLB 109; EXPP; PAB; RGEL 2; TEA; WP

Burns, Tex
See L'Amour, Louis (Dearborn)

Burnshaw, Stanley 1906- .... **CLC 3, 13, 44**
See also CA 9-12R; CP 1, 2, 3, 4, 5, 6, 7; DLB 48; DLBY 1997

Burr, Anne 1937- .... **CLC 6**
See also CA 25-28R

Burroughs, Edgar Rice 1875-1950 . **TCLC 2, 32**
See also AAYA 11; BPFB 1; BYA 4, 9; CA 104; 132; CANR 131; DA3; DAM NOV; DLB 8; FANT; MTCW 1, 2; MTFW 2005; RGAL 4; SATA 41; SCFW 1, 2; SFW 4; TCWW 1, 2; TUS; YAW

Burroughs, William S(eward) 1914-1997 .. **CLC 1, 2, 5, 15, 22, 42, 75, 109; TCLC 121; WLC**
See Lee, William; Lee, Willy
See also AAYA 60; AITN 2; AMWS 3; BG 1:2; BPFB 1; CA 9-12R; 160; CANR 20, 52, 104; CN 1, 2, 3, 4, 5, 6; CPW; DA; DA3; DAB; DAC; DAM MST, NOV, POP; DLB 2, 8, 16, 152, 237; DLBY 1981, 1997; EWL 3; HGG; LMFS 2; MAL 5; MTCW 1, 2; MTFW 2005; RGAL 4; SFW 4

Burton, Sir Richard F(rancis) 1821-1890 .... **NCLC 42**
See also DLB 55, 166, 184; SSFS 21

Burton, Robert 1577-1640 .... **LC 74**
See also DLB 151; RGEL 2

Buruma, Ian 1951- .... **CLC 163**
See also CA 128; CANR 65, 141

Busch, Frederick 1941- ... **CLC 7, 10, 18, 47, 166**
See also CA 33-36R; CAAS 1; CANR 45, 73, 92; CN 1, 2, 3, 4, 5, 6, 7; DLB 6, 218

Bush, Barney (Furman) 1946- .... **NNAL**
See also CA 145

Bush, Ronald 1946- .... **CLC 34**
See also CA 136

Bustos, F(rancisco)
See Borges, Jorge Luis

Bustos Domecq, H(onorio)
See Bioy Casares, Adolfo; Borges, Jorge Luis

Butler, Octavia E(stelle) 1947- .. **BLCS; CLC 38, 121**
See also AAYA 18, 48; AFAW 2; AMWS 13; BPFB 1; BW 2, 3; CA 73-76; CANR 12, 24, 38, 73, 145; CLR 65; CN 7; CPW; DA3; DAM MULT, POP; DLB 33; LATS 1:2; MTCW 1, 2; MTFW 2005; NFS 8, 21; SATA 84; SCFW 2; SFW 4; SSFS 6; TCLE 1:1; YAW

Butler, Robert Olen, (Jr.) 1945- ...... **CLC 81, 162**
See also AMWS 12; BPFB 1; CA 112; CANR 66, 138; CN 7; CSW; DAM POP; DLB 173; INT CA-112; MAL 5; MTCW 2; MTFW 2005; SSFS 11

Butler, Samuel 1612-1680 .... **LC 16, 43**
See also DLB 101, 126; RGEL 2

Butler, Samuel 1835-1902 .... **TCLC 1, 33; WLC**
See also BRWS 2; CA 143; CDBLB 1890-1914; DA; DA3; DAB; DAC; DAM MST, NOV; DLB 18, 57, 174; RGEL 2; SFW 4; TEA

Butler, Walter C.
See Faust, Frederick (Schiller)

Canfield, Dorothea F.
See Fisher, Dorothy (Frances) Canfield

Canfield, Dorothea Frances
See Fisher, Dorothy (Frances) Canfield

Canfield, Dorothy
See Fisher, Dorothy (Frances) Canfield

Canin, Ethan 1960- .... **CLC 55; SSC 70**
See also CA 131; 135; MAL 5

Cankar, Ivan 1876-1918 .... **TCLC 105**
See also CDWLB 4; DLB 147; EWL 3

Cannon, Curt
See Hunter, Evan

Cao, Lan 1961- .... **CLC 109**
See also CA 165

Cape, Judith
See Page, P(atricia) K(athleen)
See also CCA 1

Capek, Karel 1890-1938 .... **DC 1; SSC 36; TCLC 6, 37; WLC**
See also CA 104; 140; CDWLB 4; DA; DA3; DAB; DAC; DAM DRAM, MST, NOV; DFS 7, 11; DLB 215; EW 10; EWL 3; MTCW 2; MTFW 2005; RGSF 2; RGWL 2, 3; SCFW 1, 2; SFW 4

Capote, Truman 1924-1984 . **CLC 1, 3, 8, 13, 19, 34, 38, 58; SSC 2, 47; TCLC 164; WLC**
See also AAYA 61; AMWS 3; BPFB 1; CA 5-8R; 113; CANR 18, 62; CDALB 1941-1968; CN 1, 2, 3; CPW; DA; DA3; DAB; DAC; DAM MST, NOV, POP; DLB 2, 185, 227; DLBY 1980, 1984; EWL 3; EXPS; GLL 1; LAIT 3; MAL 5; MTCW 1, 2; MTFW 2005; NCFS 2; RGAL 4; RGSF 2; SATA 91; SSFS 2; TUS

Capra, Frank 1897-1991 .... **CLC 16**
See also AAYA 52; CA 61-64; 135

Caputo, Philip 1941- .... **CLC 32**
See also AAYA 60; CA 73-76; CANR 40, 135; YAW

Caragiale, Ion Luca 1852-1912 ...... **TCLC 76**
See also CA 157

Card, Orson Scott 1951- .... **CLC 44, 47, 50**
See also AAYA 11, 42; BPFB 1; BYA 5, 8; CA 102; CANR 27, 47, 73, 102, 106, 133; CPW; DA3; DAM POP; FANT; INT CANR-27; MTCW 1, 2; MTFW 2005; NFS 5; SATA 83, 127; SCFW 2; SFW 4; SUFW 2; YAW

Cardenal, Ernesto 1925- .... **CLC 31, 161; HLC 1; PC 22**
See also CA 49-52; CANR 2, 32, 66, 138; CWW 2; DAM MULT, POET; DLB 290; EWL 3; HW 1, 2; LAWS 1; MTCW 1, 2; MTFW 2005; RGWL 2, 3

Cardinal, Marie 1929-2001 .... **CLC 189**
See also CA 177; CWW 2; DLB 83; FW

Cardozo, Benjamin N(athan) 1870-1938 .... **TCLC 65**
See also CA 117; 164

Carducci, Giosue (Alessandro Giuseppe) 1835-1907 .... **PC 46; TCLC 32**
See also CA 163; EW 7; RGWL 2, 3

Carew, Thomas 1595(?)-1640 . **LC 13; PC 29**
See also BRW 2; DLB 126; PAB; RGEL 2

Carey, Ernestine Gilbreth 1908- ...... **CLC 17**
See also CA 5-8R; CANR 71; SATA 2

Carey, Peter 1943- .... **CLC 40, 55, 96, 183**
See also CA 123; 127; CANR 53, 76, 117; CN 4, 5, 6, 7; DLB 289; EWL 3; INT CA-127; MTCW 1, 2; MTFW 2005; RGSF 2; SATA 94

Carleton, William 1794-1869 .... **NCLC 3**
See also DLB 159; RGEL 2; RGSF 2

Carlisle, Henry (Coffin) 1926- .... **CLC 33**
See also CA 13-16R; CANR 15, 85

Carlsen, Chris
See Holdstock, Robert P.

Carlson, Ron(ald F.) 1947- .... **CLC 54**
See also CA 105, 189; CAAE 189; CANR 27; DLB 244

Carlyle, Thomas 1795-1881 ..... **NCLC 22, 70**
See also BRW 4; CDBLB 1789-1832; DA; DAB; DAC; DAM MST; DLB 55, 144, 254; RGEL 2; TEA

Carman, (William) Bliss 1861-1929 ... **PC 34; TCLC 7**
See also CA 104; 152; DAC; DLB 92; RGEL 2

Carnegie, Dale 1888-1955 .... **TCLC 53**
See also CA 218

Carossa, Hans 1878-1956 .... **TCLC 48**
See also CA 170; DLB 66; EWL 3

Carpenter, Don(ald Richard) 1931-1995 .... **CLC 41**
See also CA 45-48; 149; CANR 1, 71

Carpenter, Edward 1844-1929 .... **TCLC 88**
See also CA 163; GLL 1

Carpenter, John (Howard) 1948- ... **CLC 161**
See also AAYA 2; CA 134; SATA 58

Carpenter, Johnny
See Carpenter, John (Howard)

Carpentier (y Valmont), Alejo 1904-1980 . **CLC 8, 11, 38, 110; HLC 1; SSC 35**
See also CA 65-68; 97-100; CANR 11, 70; CDWLB 3; DAM MULT; DLB 113; EWL 3; HW 1, 2; LAW; LMFS 2; RGSF 2; RGWL 2, 3; WLIT 1

Carr, Caleb 1955- .... **CLC 86**
See also CA 147; CANR 73, 134; DA3

Carr, Emily 1871-1945 .... **TCLC 32**
See also CA 159; DLB 68; FW; GLL 2

Carr, John Dickson 1906-1977 .... **CLC 3**
See Fairbairn, Roger
See also CA 49-52; 69-72; CANR 3, 33, 60; CMW 4; DLB 306; MSW; MTCW 1, 2

Carr, Philippa
See Hibbert, Eleanor Alice Burford

Carr, Virginia Spencer 1929- .... **CLC 34**
See also CA 61-64; DLB 111

Carrere, Emmanuel 1957- .... **CLC 89**
See also CA 200

Carrier, Roch 1937- .... **CLC 13, 78**
See also CA 130; CANR 61; CCA 1; DAC; DAM MST; DLB 53; SATA 105

Carroll, James Dennis
See Carroll, Jim

Carroll, James P. 1943(?)- .... **CLC 38**
See also CA 81-84; CANR 73, 139; MTCW 2; MTFW 2005

Carroll, Jim 1951- .... **CLC 35, 143**
See also AAYA 17; CA 45-48; CANR 42, 115; NCFS 5

Carroll, Lewis ..... **NCLC 2, 53, 139; PC 18; WLC**
See Dodgson, Charles L(utwidge)
See also AAYA 39; BRW 5; BYA 5, 13; CDBLB 1832-1890; CLR 2, 18; DLB 18, 163, 178; DLBY 1998; EXPN; EXPP; FANT; JRDA; LAIT 1; NFS 7; PFS 11; RGEL 2; SUFW 1; TEA; WCH

Carroll, Paul Vincent 1900-1968 ...... **CLC 10**
See also CA 9-12R; 25-28R; DLB 10; EWL 3; RGEL 2

Carruth, Hayden 1921- ..... **CLC 4, 7, 10, 18, 84; PC 10**
See also CA 9-12R; CANR 4, 38, 59, 110; CP 1, 2, 3, 4, 5, 6, 7; DLB 5, 165; INT CANR-4; MTCW 1, 2; MTFW 2005; SATA 47

Carson, Anne 1950- .... **CLC 185; PC 64**
See also AMWS 12; CA 203; DLB 193; PFS 18; TCLE 1:1

Carson, Ciaran 1948- .... **CLC 201**
See also CA 112; 153; CANR 113; CP 7

Carson, Rachel
See Carson, Rachel Louise
See also AAYA 49; DLB 275

Carson, Rachel Louise 1907-1964 .... **CLC 71**
See Carson, Rachel
See also AMWS 9; ANW; CA 77-80; CANR 35; DA3; DAM POP; FW; LAIT 4; MAL 5; MTCW 1, 2; MTFW 2005; NCFS 1; SATA 23

Carter, Angela (Olive) 1940-1992 ...... **CLC 5, 41, 76; SSC 13, 85; TCLC 139**
See also BRWS 3; CA 53-56; 136; CANR 12, 36, 61, 106; CN 3, 4, 5; DA3; DLB 14, 207, 261, 319; EXPS; FANT; FW; GL 2; MTCW 1, 2; MTFW 2005; RGSF 2; SATA 66; SATA-Obit 70; SFW 4; SSFS 4, 12; SUFW 2; WLIT 4

Carter, Nick
See Smith, Martin Cruz

Carver, Raymond 1938-1988 ..... **CLC 22, 36, 53, 55, 126; PC 54; SSC 8, 51**
See also AAYA 44; AMWS 3; BPFB 1; CA 33-36R; 126; CANR 17, 34, 61, 103; CN 4; CPW; DA3; DAM NOV; DLB 130; DLBY 1984, 1988; EWL 3; MAL 5; MTCW 1, 2; MTFW 2005; PFS 17; RGAL 4; RGSF 2; SSFS 3, 6, 12, 13; TCLE 1:1; TCWW 2; TUS

Cary, Elizabeth, Lady Falkland 1585-1639 .... **LC 30**

Cary, (Arthur) Joyce (Lunel) 1888-1957 .... **TCLC 1, 29**
See also BRW 7; CA 104; 164; CDBLB 1914-1945; DLB 15, 100; EWL 3; MTCW 2; RGEL 2; TEA

Casal, Julian del 1863-1893 .... **NCLC 131**
See also DLB 283; LAW

Casanova, Giacomo
See Casanova de Seingalt, Giovanni Jacopo
See also WLIT 7

Casanova de Seingalt, Giovanni Jacopo 1725-1798 .... **LC 13**
See Casanova, Giacomo

Casares, Adolfo Bioy
See Bioy Casares, Adolfo
See also RGSF 2

Casas, Bartolome de las 1474-1566
See Las Casas, Bartolome de
See also WLIT 1

Casely-Hayford, J(oseph) E(phraim) 1866-1903 .... **BLC 1; TCLC 24**
See also BW 2; CA 123; 152; DAM MULT

Casey, John (Dudley) 1939- .... **CLC 59**
See also BEST 90:2; CA 69-72; CANR 23, 100

Casey, Michael 1947- .... **CLC 2**
See also CA 65-68; CANR 109; CP 2, 3; DLB 5

Casey, Patrick
See Thurman, Wallace (Henry)

Casey, Warren (Peter) 1935-1988 .... **CLC 12**
See also CA 101; 127; INT CA-101

Casona, Alejandro .... **CLC 49**
See Alvarez, Alejandro Rodriguez
See also EWL 3

Cassavetes, John 1929-1989 .... **CLC 20**
See also CA 85-88; 127; CANR 82

Cassian, Nina 1924- .... **PC 17**
See also CWP; CWW 2

Cassill, R(onald) V(erlin) 1919-2002 .... **CLC 4, 23**
See also CA 9-12R; 208; CAAS 1; CANR 7, 45; CN 1, 2, 3, 4, 5, 6, 7; DLB 6, 218; DLBY 2002

Cassiodorus, Flavius Magnus c. 490(?)-c. 583(?) .... **CMLC 43**

Cassirer, Ernst 1874-1945 .... **TCLC 61**
See also CA 157

Chapman, John Jay 1862-1933 .... **TCLC 7**
See also AMWS 14; CA 104; 191
Chapman, Lee
See Bradley, Marion Zimmer
See also GLL 1
Chapman, Walker
See Silverberg, Robert
Chappell, Fred (Davis) 1936- .... **CLC 40, 78, 162**
See also CA 5-8R, 198; CAAE 198; CAAS 4; CANR 8, 33, 67, 110; CN 6; CP 7; CSW; DLB 6, 105; HGG
Char, Rene(-Emile) 1907-1988 .... **CLC 9, 11, 14, 55; PC 56**
See also CA 13-16R; 124; CANR 32; DAM POET; DLB 258; EWL 3; GFL 1789 to the Present; MTCW 1, 2; RGWL 2, 3
Charby, Jay
See Ellison, Harlan (Jay)
Chardin, Pierre Teilhard de
See Teilhard de Chardin, (Marie Joseph) Pierre
Chariton fl. 1st cent. (?)- .... **CMLC 49**
Charlemagne 742-814 .... **CMLC 37**
Charles I 1600-1649 .... **LC 13**
Charriere, Isabelle de 1740-1805 .. **NCLC 66**
See also DLB 313
Chartier, Alain c. 1392-1430 .... **LC 94**
See also DLB 208
Chartier, Emile-Auguste
See Alain
Charyn, Jerome 1937- .... **CLC 5, 8, 18**
See also CA 5-8R; CAAS 1; CANR 7, 61, 101; CMW 4; CN 1, 2, 3, 4, 5, 6, 7; DLBY 1983; MTCW 1
Chase, Adam
See Marlowe, Stephen
Chase, Mary (Coyle) 1907-1981 .... **DC 1**
See also CA 77-80; 105; CAD; CWD; DFS 11; DLB 228; SATA 17; SATA-Obit 29
Chase, Mary Ellen 1887-1973 .... **CLC 2; TCLC 124**
See also CA 13-16; 41-44R; CAP 1; SATA 10
Chase, Nicholas
See Hyde, Anthony
See also CCA 1
Chateaubriand, Francois Rene de 1768-1848 .... **NCLC 3, 134**
See also DLB 119; EW 5; GFL 1789 to the Present; RGWL 2, 3; TWA
Chatelet, Gabrielle-Emilie Du
See du Chatelet, Emilie
See also DLB 313
Chatterje, Sarat Chandra 1876-1936(?)
See Chatterji, Saratchandra
See also CA 109
Chatterji, Bankim Chandra 1838-1894 .... **NCLC 19**
Chatterji, Saratchandra .... **TCLC 13**
See Chatterje, Sarat Chandra
See also CA 186; EWL 3
Chatterton, Thomas 1752-1770 .... **LC 3, 54**
See also DAM POET; DLB 109; RGEL 2
Chatwin, (Charles) Bruce 1940-1989 .... **CLC 28, 57, 59**
See also AAYA 4; BEST 90:1; BRWS 4; CA 85-88; 127; CPW; DAM POP; DLB 194, 204; EWL 3; MTFW 2005
Chaucer, Daniel
See Ford, Ford Madox
See also RHW
Chaucer, Geoffrey 1340(?)-1400 .. **LC 17, 56; PC 19, 58; WLCS**
See also BRW 1; BRWC 1; BRWR 2; CDBLB Before 1660; DA; DA3; DAB; DAC; DAM MST, POET; DLB 146; LAIT 1; PAB; PFS 14; RGEL 2; TEA; WLIT 3; WP
Chavez, Denise (Elia) 1948- .... **HLC 1**
See also CA 131; CANR 56, 81, 137; DAM MULT; DLB 122; FW; HW 1, 2; LLW; MAL 5; MTCW 2; MTFW 2005
Chaviaras, Strates 1935-
See Haviaras, Stratis
See also CA 105
Chayefsky, Paddy .... **CLC 23**
See Chayefsky, Sidney
See also CAD; DLB 7, 44; DLBY 1981; RGAL 4
Chayefsky, Sidney 1923-1981
See Chayefsky, Paddy
See also CA 9-12R; 104; CANR 18; DAM DRAM
Chedid, Andree 1920- .... **CLC 47**
See also CA 145; CANR 95; EWL 3
Cheever, John 1912-1982 ..... **CLC 3, 7, 8, 11, 15, 25, 64; SSC 1, 38, 57; WLC**
See also AAYA 65; AMWS 1; BPFB 1; CA 5-8R; 106; CABS 1; CANR 5, 27, 76; CDALB 1941-1968; CN 1, 2, 3; CPW; DA; DA3; DAB; DAC; DAM MST, NOV, POP; DLB 2, 102, 227; DLBY 1980, 1982; EWL 3; EXPS; INT CANR-5; MAL 5; MTCW 1, 2; MTFW 2005; RGAL 4; RGSF 2; SSFS 2, 14; TUS
Cheever, Susan 1943- .... **CLC 18, 48**
See also CA 103; CANR 27, 51, 92; DLBY 1982; INT CANR-27
Chekhonte, Antosha
See Chekhov, Anton (Pavlovich)
Chekhov, Anton (Pavlovich) 1860-1904 .... **DC 9; SSC 2, 28, 41, 51, 85; TCLC 3, 10, 31, 55, 96, 163; WLC**
See also AAYA 68; BYA 14; CA 104; 124; DA; DA3; DAB; DAC; DAM DRAM, MST; DFS 1, 5, 10, 12; DLB 277; EW 7; EWL 3; EXPS; LAIT 3; LATS 1:1; RGSF 2; RGWL 2, 3; SATA 90; SSFS 5, 13, 14; TWA
Cheney, Lynne V. 1941- .... **CLC 70**
See also CA 89-92; CANR 58, 117; SATA 152
Chernyshevsky, Nikolai Gavrilovich
See Chernyshevsky, Nikolay Gavrilovich
See also DLB 238
Chernyshevsky, Nikolay Gavrilovich 1828-1889 .... **NCLC 1**
See Chernyshevsky, Nikolai Gavrilovich
Cherry, Carolyn Janice 1942-
See Cherryh, C. J.
See also CA 65-68; CANR 10
Cherryh, C. J. .... **CLC 35**
See Cherry, Carolyn Janice
See also AAYA 24; BPFB 1; DLBY 1980; FANT; SATA 93; SCFW 2; SFW 4; YAW
Chesnutt, Charles W(addell) 1858-1932 .... **BLC 1; SSC 7, 54; TCLC 5, 39**
See also AFAW 1, 2; AMWS 14; BW 1, 3; CA 106; 125; CANR 76; DAM MULT; DLB 12, 50, 78; EWL 3; MAL 5; MTCW 1, 2; MTFW 2005; RGAL 4; RGSF 2; SSFS 11
Chester, Alfred 1929(?)-1971 .... **CLC 49**
See also CA 196; 33-36R; DLB 130; MAL 5
Chesterton, G(ilbert) K(eith) 1874-1936 . **PC 28; SSC 1, 46; TCLC 1, 6, 64**
See also AAYA 57; BRW 6; CA 104; 132; CANR 73, 131; CDBLB 1914-1945; CMW 4; DAM NOV, POET; DLB 10, 19, 34, 70, 98, 149, 178; EWL 3; FANT; MSW; MTCW 1, 2; MTFW 2005; RGEL 2; RGSF 2; SATA 27; SUFW 1
Chettle, Henry 1560-1607(?) .... **LC 112**
See also DLB 136; RGEL 2
Chiang, Pin-chin 1904-1986
See Ding Ling
See also CA 118
Chief Joseph 1840-1904 .... **NNAL**
See also CA 152; DA3; DAM MULT
Chief Seattle 1786(?)-1866 .... **NNAL**
See also DA3; DAM MULT
Ch'ien, Chung-shu 1910-1998 .... **CLC 22**
See Qian Zhongshu
See also CA 130; CANR 73; MTCW 1, 2
Chikamatsu Monzaemon 1653-1724 ... **LC 66**
See also RGWL 2, 3
Child, L. Maria
See Child, Lydia Maria
Child, Lydia Maria 1802-1880 .. **NCLC 6, 73**
See also DLB 1, 74, 243; RGAL 4; SATA 67
Child, Mrs.
See Child, Lydia Maria
Child, Philip 1898-1978 .... **CLC 19, 68**
See also CA 13-14; CAP 1; CP 1; DLB 68; RHW; SATA 47
Childers, (Robert) Erskine 1870-1922 .... **TCLC 65**
See also CA 113; 153; DLB 70
Childress, Alice 1920-1994 . **BLC 1; CLC 12, 15, 86, 96; DC 4; TCLC 116**
See also AAYA 8; BW 2, 3; BYA 2; CA 45-48; 146; CAD; CANR 3, 27, 50, 74; CLR 14; CWD; DA3; DAM DRAM, MULT, NOV; DFS 2, 8, 14; DLB 7, 38, 249; JRDA; LAIT 5; MAICYA 1, 2; MAICYAS 1; MAL 5; MTCW 1, 2; MTFW 2005; RGAL 4; SATA 7, 48, 81; TUS; WYA; YAW
Chin, Frank (Chew, Jr.) 1940- .... **AAL; CLC 135; DC 7**
See also CA 33-36R; CAD; CANR 71; CD 5, 6; DAM MULT; DLB 206, 312; LAIT 5; RGAL 4
Chin, Marilyn (Mei Ling) 1955- .... **PC 40**
See also CA 129; CANR 70, 113; CWP; DLB 312
Chislett, (Margaret) Anne 1943- ...... **CLC 34**
See also CA 151
Chitty, Thomas Willes 1926- .... **CLC 11**
See Hinde, Thomas
See also CA 5-8R; CN 7
Chivers, Thomas Holley 1809-1858 .... **NCLC 49**
See also DLB 3, 248; RGAL 4
Choi, Susan 1969- .... **CLC 119**
See also CA 223
Chomette, Rene Lucien 1898-1981
See Clair, Rene
See also CA 103
Chomsky, (Avram) Noam 1928- ..... **CLC 132**
See also CA 17-20R; CANR 28, 62, 110, 132; DA3; DLB 246; MTCW 1, 2; MTFW 2005
Chona, Maria 1845(?)-1936 .... **NNAL**
See also CA 144
Chopin, Kate .... **SSC 8, 68; TCLC 127; WLCS**
See Chopin, Katherine
See also AAYA 33; AMWR 2; AMWS 1; BYA 11, 15; CDALB 1865-1917; DA; DAB; DLB 12, 78; EXPN; EXPS; FL 1:3; FW; LAIT 3; MAL 5; MAWW; NFS 3; RGAL 4; RGSF 2; SSFS 2, 13, 17; TUS
Chopin, Katherine 1851-1904
See Chopin, Kate
See also CA 104; 122; DA3; DAC; DAM MST, NOV
Chretien de Troyes c. 12th cent. - . **CMLC 10**
See also DLB 208; EW 1; RGWL 2, 3; TWA
Christie
See Ichikawa, Kon

DA3; DAM MULT, POET; DLB 5, 41; EXPP; MAICYA 1, 2; MTCW 1, 2; MTFW 2005; PFS 1, 14; SATA 20, 69, 128; WP

Clinton, Dirk
See Silverberg, Robert

Clough, Arthur Hugh 1819-1861 .. **NCLC 27, 163**
See also BRW 5; DLB 32; RGEL 2

Clutha, Janet Paterson Frame 1924-2004
See Frame, Janet
See also CA 1-4R; 224; CANR 2, 36, 76, 135; MTCW 1, 2; SATA 119

Clyne, Terence
See Blatty, William Peter

Cobalt, Martin
See Mayne, William (James Carter)

Cobb, Irvin S(hrewsbury)
1876-1944 .... **TCLC 77**
See also CA 175; DLB 11, 25, 86

Cobbett, William 1763-1835 .... **NCLC 49**
See also DLB 43, 107, 158; RGEL 2

Coburn, D(onald) L(ee) 1938- .... **CLC 10**
See also CA 89-92

Cocteau, Jean (Maurice Eugene Clement)
1889-1963 ...... **CLC 1, 8, 15, 16, 43; DC 17; TCLC 119; WLC**
See also CA 25-28; CANR 40; CAP 2; DA; DA3; DAB; DAC; DAM DRAM, MST, NOV; DLB 65, 258, 321; EW 10; EWL 3; GFL 1789 to the Present; MTCW 1, 2; RGWL 2, 3; TWA

Codrescu, Andrei 1946- .... **CLC 46, 121**
See also CA 33-36R; CAAS 19; CANR 13, 34, 53, 76, 125; CN 7; DA3; DAM POET; MAL 5; MTCW 2; MTFW 2005

Coe, Max
See Bourne, Randolph S(illiman)

Coe, Tucker
See Westlake, Donald E(dwin)

Coen, Ethan 1958- .... **CLC 108**
See also AAYA 54; CA 126; CANR 85

Coen, Joel 1955- .... **CLC 108**
See also AAYA 54; CA 126; CANR 119

The Coen Brothers
See Coen, Ethan; Coen, Joel

Coetzee, J(ohn) M(axwell) 1940- ..... **CLC 23, 33, 66, 117, 161, 162**
See also AAYA 37; AFW; BRWS 6; CA 77-80; CANR 41, 54, 74, 114, 133; CN 4, 5, 6, 7; DA3; DAM NOV; DLB 225; EWL 3; LMFS 2; MTCW 1, 2; MTFW 2005; NFS 21; WLIT 2; WWE 1

Coffey, Brian
See Koontz, Dean R.

Coffin, Robert P(eter) Tristram
1892-1955 .... **TCLC 95**
See also CA 123; 169; DLB 45

Cohan, George M(ichael)
1878-1942 .... **TCLC 60**
See also CA 157; DLB 249; RGAL 4

Cohen, Arthur A(llen) 1928-1986 ...... **CLC 7, 31**
See also CA 1-4R; 120; CANR 1, 17, 42; DLB 28

Cohen, Leonard (Norman) 1934- ...... **CLC 3, 38**
See also CA 21-24R; CANR 14, 69; CN 1, 2, 3, 4, 5, 6; CP 1, 2, 3, 4, 5, 6, 7; DAC; DAM MST; DLB 53; EWL 3; MTCW 1

Cohen, Matt(hew) 1942-1999 .... **CLC 19**
See also CA 61-64; 187; CAAS 18; CANR 40; CN 1, 2, 3, 4, 5, 6; DAC; DLB 53

Cohen-Solal, Annie 1948- .... **CLC 50**
See also CA 239

Colegate, Isabel 1931- .... **CLC 36**
See also CA 17-20R; CANR 8, 22, 74; CN 4, 5, 6, 7; DLB 14, 231; INT CANR-22; MTCW 1

Coleman, Emmett
See Reed, Ishmael (Scott)

Coleridge, Hartley 1796-1849 .... **NCLC 90**
See also DLB 96

Coleridge, M. E.
See Coleridge, Mary E(lizabeth)

Coleridge, Mary E(lizabeth)
1861-1907 .... **TCLC 73**
See also CA 116; 166; DLB 19, 98

Coleridge, Samuel Taylor
1772-1834 ...... **NCLC 9, 54, 99, 111; PC 11, 39, 67; WLC**
See also AAYA 66; BRW 4; BRWR 2; BYA 4; CDBLB 1789-1832; DA; DA3; DAB; DAC; DAM MST, POET; DLB 93, 107; EXPP; LATS 1:1; LMFS 1; PAB; PFS 4, 5; RGEL 2; TEA; WLIT 3; WP

Coleridge, Sara 1802-1852 .... **NCLC 31**
See also DLB 199

Coles, Don 1928- .... **CLC 46**
See also CA 115; CANR 38; CP 7

Coles, Robert (Martin) 1929- .... **CLC 108**
See also CA 45-48; CANR 3, 32, 66, 70, 135; INT CANR-32; SATA 23

Colette, (Sidonie-Gabrielle)
1873-1954 .... **SSC 10; TCLC 1, 5, 16**
See Willy, Colette
See also CA 104; 131; DA3; DAM NOV; DLB 65; EW 9; EWL 3; GFL 1789 to the Present; MTCW 1, 2; MTFW 2005; RGWL 2, 3; TWA

Collett, (Jacobine) Camilla (Wergeland)
1813-1895 .... **NCLC 22**

Collier, Christopher 1930- .... **CLC 30**
See also AAYA 13; BYA 2; CA 33-36R; CANR 13, 33, 102; JRDA; MAICYA 1, 2; SATA 16, 70; WYA; YAW 1

Collier, James Lincoln 1928- .... **CLC 30**
See also AAYA 13; BYA 2; CA 9-12R; CANR 4, 33, 60, 102; CLR 3; DAM POP; JRDA; MAICYA 1, 2; SAAS 21; SATA 8, 70; WYA; YAW 1

Collier, Jeremy 1650-1726 .... **LC 6**

Collier, John 1901-1980 . **SSC 19; TCLC 127**
See also CA 65-68; 97-100; CANR 10; CN 1, 2; DLB 77, 255; FANT; SUFW 1

Collier, Mary 1690-1762 .... **LC 86**
See also DLB 95

Collingwood, R(obin) G(eorge)
1889(?)-1943 .... **TCLC 67**
See also CA 117; 155; DLB 262

Collins, Billy 1941- .... **PC 68**
See also AAYA 64; CA 151; CANR 92; MTFW 2005; PFS 18

Collins, Hunt
See Hunter, Evan

Collins, Linda 1931- .... **CLC 44**
See also CA 125

Collins, Tom
See Furphy, Joseph
See also RGEL 2

Collins, (William) Wilkie
1824-1889 .... **NCLC 1, 18, 93**
See also BRWS 6; CDBLB 1832-1890; CMW 4; DLB 18, 70, 159; GL 2; MSW; RGEL 2; RGSF 2; SUFW 1; WLIT 4

Collins, William 1721-1759 .... **LC 4, 40**
See also BRW 3; DAM POET; DLB 109; RGEL 2

Collodi, Carlo .... **NCLC 54**
See Lorenzini, Carlo
See also CLR 5; WCH; WLIT 7

Colman, George
See Glassco, John

Colman, George, the Elder
1732-1794 .... **LC 98**
See also RGEL 2

Colonna, Vittoria 1492-1547 .... **LC 71**
See also RGWL 2, 3

Colt, Winchester Remington
See Hubbard, L(afayette) Ron(ald)

Colter, Cyrus J. 1910-2002 .... **CLC 58**
See also BW 1; CA 65-68; 205; CANR 10, 66; CN 2, 3, 4, 5, 6; DLB 33

Colton, James
See Hansen, Joseph
See also GLL 1

Colum, Padraic 1881-1972 .... **CLC 28**
See also BYA 4; CA 73-76; 33-36R; CANR 35; CLR 36; CP 1; CWRI 5; DLB 19; MAICYA 1, 2; MTCW 1; RGEL 2; SATA 15; WCH

Colvin, James
See Moorcock, Michael (John)

Colwin, Laurie (E.) 1944-1992 .... **CLC 5, 13, 23, 84**
See also CA 89-92; 139; CANR 20, 46; DLB 218; DLBY 1980; MTCW 1

Comfort, Alex(ander) 1920-2000 .... **CLC 7**
See also CA 1-4R; 190; CANR 1, 45; CN 1, 2, 3, 4; CP 1, 2, 3, 4, 5, 6, 7; DAM POP; MTCW 2

Comfort, Montgomery
See Campbell, (John) Ramsey

Compton-Burnett, I(vy)
1892(?)-1969 .... **CLC 1, 3, 10, 15, 34**
See also BRW 7; CA 1-4R; 25-28R; CANR 4; DAM NOV; DLB 36; EWL 3; MTCW 1, 2; RGEL 2

Comstock, Anthony 1844-1915 ...... **TCLC 13**
See also CA 110; 169

Comte, Auguste 1798-1857 .... **NCLC 54**

Conan Doyle, Arthur
See Doyle, Sir Arthur Conan
See also BPFB 1; BYA 4, 5, 11

Conde (Abellan), Carmen
1901-1996 .... **HLCS 1**
See also CA 177; CWW 2; DLB 108; EWL 3; HW 2

Conde, Maryse 1937- ..... **BLCS; CLC 52, 92**
See also BW 2, 3; CA 110, 190; CAAE 190; CANR 30, 53, 76; CWW 2; DAM MULT; EWL 3; MTCW 2; MTFW 2005

Condillac, Etienne Bonnot de
1714-1780 .... **LC 26**
See also DLB 313

Condon, Richard (Thomas)
1915-1996 .... **CLC 4, 6, 8, 10, 45, 100**
See also BEST 90:3; BPFB 1; CA 1-4R; 151; CAAS 1; CANR 2, 23; CMW 4; CN 1, 2, 3, 4, 5, 6; DAM NOV; INT CANR-23; MAL 5; MTCW 1, 2

Condorcet .... **LC 104**
See Condorcet, marquis de Marie-Jean-Antoine-Nicolas Caritat
See also GFL Beginnings to 1789

Condorcet, marquis de Marie-Jean-Antoine-Nicolas Caritat
1743-1794
See Condorcet
See also DLB 313

Confucius 551B.C.-479B.C. ..... **CMLC 19, 65; WLCS**
See also DA; DA3; DAB; DAC; DAM MST

Congreve, William 1670-1729 ... **DC 2; LC 5, 21; WLC**
See also BRW 2; CDBLB 1660-1789; DA; DAB; DAC; DAM DRAM, MST, POET; DFS 15; DLB 39, 84; RGEL 2; WLIT 3

Conley, Robert J(ackson) 1940- .... **NNAL**
See also CA 41-44R; CANR 15, 34, 45, 96; DAM MULT; TCWW 2

Connell, Evan S(helby), Jr. 1924- . **CLC 4, 6, 45**
See also AAYA 7; AMWS 14; CA 1-4R; CAAS 2; CANR 2, 39, 76, 97, 140; CN 1, 2, 3, 4, 5, 6; DAM NOV; DLB 2; DLBY 1981; MAL 5; MTCW 1, 2; MTFW 2005

Difusa, Pati
See Almodovar, Pedro
Dillard, Annie 1945- ...... **CLC 9, 60, 115, 216**
See also AAYA 6, 43; AMWS 6; ANW; CA 49-52; CANR 3, 43, 62, 90, 125; DA3; DAM NOV; DLB 275, 278; DLBY 1980; LAIT 4, 5; MAL 5; MTCW 1, 2; MTFW 2005; NCFS 1; RGAL 4; SATA 10, 140; TCLE 1:1; TUS
Dillard, R(ichard) H(enry) W(ilde)
1937- .... **CLC 5**
See also CA 21-24R; CAAS 7; CANR 10; CP 2, 3, 4, 5, 6, 7; CSW; DLB 5, 244
Dillon, Eilis 1920-1994 .... **CLC 17**
See also CA 9-12R, 182; 147; CAAE 182; CAAS 3; CANR 4, 38, 78; CLR 26; MAICYA 1, 2; MAICYAS 1; SATA 2, 74; SATA-Essay 105; SATA-Obit 83; YAW
Dimont, Penelope
See Mortimer, Penelope (Ruth)
Dinesen, Isak ..... **CLC 10, 29, 95; SSC 7, 75**
See Blixen, Karen (Christentze Dinesen)
See also EW 10; EWL 3; EXPS; FW; GL 2; HGG; LAIT 3; MTCW 1; NCFS 2; NFS 9; RGSF 2; RGWL 2, 3; SSFS 3, 6, 13; WLIT 2
Ding Ling .... **CLC 68**
See Chiang, Pin-chin
See also RGWL 3
Diphusa, Patty
See Almodovar, Pedro
Disch, Thomas M(ichael) 1940- ... **CLC 7, 36**
See Disch, Tom
See also AAYA 17; BPFB 1; CA 21-24R; CAAS 4; CANR 17, 36, 54, 89; CLR 18; CP 7; DA3; DLB 8; HGG; MAICYA 1, 2; MTCW 1, 2; MTFW 2005; SAAS 15; SATA 92; SCFW 1, 2; SFW 4; SUFW 2
Disch, Tom
See Disch, Thomas M(ichael)
See also DLB 282
d'Isly, Georges
See Simenon, Georges (Jacques Christian)
Disraeli, Benjamin 1804-1881 ... **NCLC 2, 39, 79**
See also BRW 4; DLB 21, 55; RGEL 2
Ditcum, Steve
See Crumb, R(obert)
Dixon, Paige
See Corcoran, Barbara (Asenath)
Dixon, Stephen 1936- .... **CLC 52; SSC 16**
See also AMWS 12; CA 89-92; CANR 17, 40, 54, 91; CN 4, 5, 6, 7; DLB 130; MAL 5
Dixon, Thomas, Jr. 1864-1946 ..... **TCLC 163**
See also RHW
Djebar, Assia 1936- .... **CLC 182**
See also CA 188; EWL 3; RGWL 3; WLIT 2
Doak, Annie
See Dillard, Annie
Dobell, Sydney Thompson
1824-1874 .... **NCLC 43**
See also DLB 32; RGEL 2
Doblin, Alfred .... **TCLC 13**
See Doeblin, Alfred
See also CDWLB 2; EWL 3; RGWL 2, 3
Dobroliubov, Nikolai Aleksandrovich
See Dobrolyubov, Nikolai Alexandrovich
See also DLB 277
Dobrolyubov, Nikolai Alexandrovich
1836-1861 .... **NCLC 5**
See Dobroliubov, Nikolai Aleksandrovich
Dobson, Austin 1840-1921 .... **TCLC 79**
See also DLB 35, 144
Dobyns, Stephen 1941- .... **CLC 37**
See also AMWS 13; CA 45-48; CANR 2, 18, 99; CMW 4; CP 4, 5, 6, 7; PFS 23
Doctorow, E(dgar) L(aurence)
1931- .... **CLC 6, 11, 15, 18, 37, 44, 65, 113, 214**
See also AAYA 22; AITN 2; AMWS 4; BEST 89:3; BPFB 1; CA 45-48; CANR 2, 33, 51, 76, 97, 133; CDALB 1968-1988; CN 3, 4, 5, 6, 7; CPW; DA3; DAM NOV, POP; DLB 2, 28, 173; DLBY 1980; EWL 3; LAIT 3; MAL 5; MTCW 1, 2; MTFW 2005; NFS 6; RGAL 4; RHW; TCLE 1:1; TCWW 1, 2; TUS
Dodgson, Charles L(utwidge) 1832-1898
See Carroll, Lewis
See also CLR 2; DA; DA3; DAB; DAC; DAM MST, NOV, POET; MAICYA 1, 2; SATA 100; YABC 2
Dodsley, Robert 1703-1764 .... **LC 97**
See also DLB 95; RGEL 2
Dodson, Owen (Vincent) 1914-1983 .. **BLC 1; CLC 79**
See also BW 1; CA 65-68; 110; CANR 24; DAM MULT; DLB 76
Doeblin, Alfred 1878-1957 .... **TCLC 13**
See Doblin, Alfred
See also CA 110; 141; DLB 66
Doerr, Harriet 1910-2002 .... **CLC 34**
See also CA 117; 122; 213; CANR 47; INT CA-122; LATS 1:2
Domecq, H(onorio Bustos)
See Bioy Casares, Adolfo
Domecq, H(onorio) Bustos
See Bioy Casares, Adolfo; Borges, Jorge Luis
Domini, Rey
See Lorde, Audre (Geraldine)
See also GLL 1
Dominique
See Proust, (Valentin-Louis-George-Eugene) Marcel
Don, A
See Stephen, Sir Leslie
Donaldson, Stephen R(eeder)
1947- .... **CLC 46, 138**
See also AAYA 36; BPFB 1; CA 89-92; CANR 13, 55, 99; CPW; DAM POP; FANT; INT CANR-13; SATA 121; SFW 4; SUFW 1, 2
Donleavy, J(ames) P(atrick) 1926- .... **CLC 1, 4, 6, 10, 45**
See also AITN 2; BPFB 1; CA 9-12R; CANR 24, 49, 62, 80, 124; CBD; CD 5, 6; CN 1, 2, 3, 4, 5, 6, 7; DLB 6, 173; INT CANR-24; MAL 5; MTCW 1, 2; MTFW 2005; RGAL 4
Donnadieu, Marguerite
See Duras, Marguerite
Donne, John 1572-1631 ... **LC 10, 24, 91; PC 1, 43; WLC**
See also AAYA 67; BRW 1; BRWC 1; BRWR 2; CDBLB Before 1660; DA; DAB; DAC; DAM MST, POET; DLB 121, 151; EXPP; PAB; PFS 2, 11; RGEL 3; TEA; WLIT 3; WP
Donnell, David 1939(?)- .... **CLC 34**
See also CA 197
Donoghue, Denis 1928- .... **CLC 209**
See also CA 17-20R; CANR 16, 102
Donoghue, P. S.
See Hunt, E(verette) Howard, (Jr.)
Donoso (Yanez), Jose 1924-1996 ... **CLC 4, 8, 11, 32, 99; HLC 1; SSC 34; TCLC 133**
See also CA 81-84; 155; CANR 32, 73; CDWLB 3; CWW 2; DAM MULT; DLB 113; EWL 3; HW 1, 2; LAW; LAWS 1; MTCW 1, 2; MTFW 2005; RGSF 2; WLIT 1
Donovan, John 1928-1992 .... **CLC 35**
See also AAYA 20; CA 97-100; 137; CLR 3; MAICYA 1, 2; SATA 72; SATA-Brief 29; YAW
Don Roberto
See Cunninghame Graham, Robert (Gallnigad) Bontine
Doolittle, Hilda 1886-1961 . **CLC 3, 8, 14, 31, 34, 73; PC 5; WLC**
See H. D.
See also AAYA 66; AMWS 1; CA 97-100; CANR 35, 131; DA; DAC; DAM MST, POET; DLB 4, 45; EWL 3; FW; GLL 1; LMFS 2; MAL 5; MAWW; MTCW 1, 2; MTFW 2005; PFS 6; RGAL 4
Doppo, Kunikida .... **TCLC 99**
See Kunikida Doppo
Dorfman, Ariel 1942- .... **CLC 48, 77, 189; HLC 1**
See also CA 124; 130; CANR 67, 70, 135; CWW 2; DAM MULT; DFS 4; EWL 3; HW 1, 2; INT CA-130; WLIT 1
Dorn, Edward (Merton)
1929-1999 .... **CLC 10, 18**
See also CA 93-96; 187; CANR 42, 79; CP 1, 2, 3, 4, 5, 6, 7; DLB 5; INT CA-93-96; WP
Dor-Ner, Zvi .... **CLC 70**
Dorris, Michael (Anthony)
1945-1997 .... **CLC 109; NNAL**
See also AAYA 20; BEST 90:1; BYA 12; CA 102; 157; CANR 19, 46, 75; CLR 58; DA3; DAM MULT, NOV; DLB 175; LAIT 5; MTCW 2; MTFW 2005; NFS 3; RGAL 4; SATA 75; SATA-Obit 94; TCWW 2; YAW
Dorris, Michael A.
See Dorris, Michael (Anthony)
Dorsan, Luc
See Simenon, Georges (Jacques Christian)
Dorsange, Jean
See Simenon, Georges (Jacques Christian)
Dorset
See Sackville, Thomas
Dos Passos, John (Roderigo)
1896-1970 ... **CLC 1, 4, 8, 11, 15, 25, 34, 82; WLC**
See also AMW; BPFB 1; CA 1-4R; 29-32R; CANR 3; CDALB 1929-1941; DA; DA3; DAB; DAC; DAM MST, NOV; DLB 4, 9, 274, 316; DLBD 1, 15; DLBY 1996; EWL 3; MAL 5; MTCW 1, 2; MTFW 2005; NFS 14; RGAL 4; TUS
Dossage, Jean
See Simenon, Georges (Jacques Christian)
Dostoevsky, Fedor Mikhailovich
1821-1881 .. **NCLC 2, 7, 21, 33, 43, 119, 167; SSC 2, 33, 44; WLC**
See Dostoevsky, Fyodor
See also AAYA 40; DA; DA3; DAB; DAC; DAM MST, NOV; EW 7; EXPN; NFS 3, 8; RGSF 2; RGWL 2, 3; SSFS 8; TWA
Dostoevsky, Fyodor
See Dostoevsky, Fedor Mikhailovich
See also DLB 238; LATS 1:1; LMFS 1, 2
Doty, M. R.
See Doty, Mark (Alan)
Doty, Mark
See Doty, Mark (Alan)
Doty, Mark (Alan) 1953(?)- .... **CLC 176; PC 53**
See also AMWS 11; CA 161, 183; CAAE 183; CANR 110
Doty, Mark A.
See Doty, Mark (Alan)
Doughty, Charles M(ontagu)
1843-1926 .... **TCLC 27**
See also CA 115; 178; DLB 19, 57, 174
Douglas, Ellen .... **CLC 73**
See Haxton, Josephine Ayres; Williamson, Ellen Douglas
See also CN 5, 6, 7; CSW; DLB 292

MST, POP; DLB 191; GL 2; HGG; LAIT 3; MSW; MTCW 1, 2; NFS 12; RGEL 2; RGSF 2; RHW; SATA 27; SATA-Obit 60; SSFS 14, 16; TEA

Du Maurier, George 1834-1896 ..... **NCLC 86**
See also DLB 153, 178; RGEL 2

Dunbar, Paul Laurence 1872-1906 ... **BLC 1; PC 5; SSC 8; TCLC 2, 12; WLC**
See also AFAW 1, 2; AMWS 2; BW 1, 3; CA 104; 124; CANR 79; CDALB 1865-1917; DA; DA3; DAC; DAM MST, MULT, POET; DLB 50, 54, 78; EXPP; MAL 5; RGAL 4; SATA 34

Dunbar, William 1460(?)-1520(?) .... **LC 20; PC 67**
See also BRWS 8; DLB 132, 146; RGEL 2

Dunbar-Nelson, Alice .... **HR 1:2**
See Nelson, Alice Ruth Moore Dunbar

Duncan, Dora Angela
See Duncan, Isadora

Duncan, Isadora 1877(?)-1927 .... **TCLC 68**
See also CA 118; 149

Duncan, Lois 1934- .... **CLC 26**
See also AAYA 4, 34; BYA 6, 8; CA 1-4R; CANR 2, 23, 36, 111; CLR 29; JRDA; MAICYA 1, 2; MAICYAS 1; MTFW 2005; SAAS 2; SATA 1, 36, 75, 133, 141; SATA-Essay 141; WYA; YAW

Duncan, Robert (Edward) 1919-1988 .... **CLC 1, 2, 4, 7, 15, 41, 55; PC 2**
See also BG 1:2; CA 9-12R; 124; CANR 28, 62; CP 1, 2, 3, 4; DAM POET; DLB 5, 16, 193; EWL 3; MAL 5; MTCW 1, 2; MTFW 2005; PFS 13; RGAL 4; WP

Duncan, Sara Jeannette 1861-1922 .... **TCLC 60**
See also CA 157; DLB 92

Dunlap, William 1766-1839 .... **NCLC 2**
See also DLB 30, 37, 59; RGAL 4

Dunn, Douglas (Eaglesham) 1942- .... **CLC 6, 40**
See also BRWS 10; CA 45-48; CANR 2, 33, 126; CP 1, 2, 3, 4, 5, 6, 7; DLB 40; MTCW 1

Dunn, Katherine (Karen) 1945- .... **CLC 71**
See also CA 33-36R; CANR 72; HGG; MTCW 2; MTFW 2005

Dunn, Stephen (Elliott) 1939- .. **CLC 36, 206**
See also AMWS 11; CA 33-36R; CANR 12, 48, 53, 105; CP 3, 4, 5, 6, 7; DLB 105; PFS 21

Dunne, Finley Peter 1867-1936 ...... **TCLC 28**
See also CA 108; 178; DLB 11, 23; RGAL 4

Dunne, John Gregory 1932-2003 ..... **CLC 28**
See also CA 25-28R; 222; CANR 14, 50; CN 5, 6, 7; DLBY 1980

Dunsany, Lord .... **TCLC 2, 59**
See Dunsany, Edward John Moreton Drax Plunkett
See also DLB 77, 153, 156, 255; FANT; IDTP; RGEL 2; SFW 4; SUFW 1

Dunsany, Edward John Moreton Drax Plunkett 1878-1957
See Dunsany, Lord
See also CA 104; 148; DLB 10; MTCW 2

Duns Scotus, John 1266(?)-1308 ... **CMLC 59**
See also DLB 115

du Perry, Jean
See Simenon, Georges (Jacques Christian)

Durang, Christopher (Ferdinand) 1949- .... **CLC 27, 38**
See also CA 105; CAD; CANR 50, 76, 130; CD 5, 6; MTCW 2; MTFW 2005

Duras, Claire de 1777-1832 .... **NCLC 154**

Duras, Marguerite 1914-1996 . **CLC 3, 6, 11, 20, 34, 40, 68, 100; SSC 40**
See also BPFB 1; CA 25-28R; 151; CANR 50; CWW 2; DFS 21; DLB 83, 321; EWL 3; FL 1:5; GFL 1789 to the Present; IDFW 4; MTCW 1, 2; RGWL 2, 3; TWA

Durban, (Rosa) Pam 1947- .... **CLC 39**
See also CA 123; CANR 98; CSW

Durcan, Paul 1944- .... **CLC 43, 70**
See also CA 134; CANR 123; CP 1, 7; DAM POET; EWL 3

Durfey, Thomas 1653-1723 .... **LC 94**
See also DLB 80; RGEL 2

Durkheim, Emile 1858-1917 .... **TCLC 55**

Durrell, Lawrence (George) 1912-1990 ..... **CLC 1, 4, 6, 8, 13, 27, 41**
See also BPFB 1; BRWS 1; CA 9-12R; 132; CANR 40, 77; CDBLB 1945-1960; CN 1, 2, 3, 4; CP 1, 2, 3, 4; DAM NOV; DLB 15, 27, 204; DLBY 1990; EWL 3; MTCW 1, 2; RGEL 2; SFW 4; TEA

Durrenmatt, Friedrich
See Duerrenmatt, Friedrich
See also CDWLB 2; EW 13; EWL 3; RGWL 2, 3

Dutt, Michael Madhusudan 1824-1873 .... **NCLC 118**

Dutt, Toru 1856-1877 .... **NCLC 29**
See also DLB 240

Dwight, Timothy 1752-1817 .... **NCLC 13**
See also DLB 37; RGAL 4

Dworkin, Andrea 1946-2005 ..... **CLC 43, 123**
See also CA 77-80; 238; CAAS 21; CANR 16, 39, 76, 96; FL 1:5; FW; GLL 1; INT CANR-16; MTCW 1, 2; MTFW 2005

Dwyer, Deanna
See Koontz, Dean R.

Dwyer, K. R.
See Koontz, Dean R.

Dybek, Stuart 1942- .... **CLC 114; SSC 55**
See also CA 97-100; CANR 39; DLB 130

Dye, Richard
See De Voto, Bernard (Augustine)

Dyer, Geoff 1958- .... **CLC 149**
See also CA 125; CANR 88

Dyer, George 1755-1841 .... **NCLC 129**
See also DLB 93

Dylan, Bob 1941- .... **CLC 3, 4, 6, 12, 77; PC 37**
See also CA 41-44R; CANR 108; CP 1, 2, 3, 4, 5, 6, 7; DLB 16

Dyson, John 1943- .... **CLC 70**
See also CA 144

Dzyubin, Eduard Georgievich 1895-1934
See Bagritsky, Eduard
See also CA 170

E. V. L.
See Lucas, E(dward) V(errall)

Eagleton, Terence (Francis) 1943- .. **CLC 63, 132**
See also CA 57-60; CANR 7, 23, 68, 115; DLB 242; LMFS 2; MTCW 1, 2; MTFW 2005

Eagleton, Terry
See Eagleton, Terence (Francis)

Early, Jack
See Scoppettone, Sandra
See also GLL 1

East, Michael
See West, Morris L(anglo)

Eastaway, Edward
See Thomas, (Philip) Edward

Eastlake, William (Derry) 1917-1997 .... **CLC 8**
See also CA 5-8R; 158; CAAS 1; CANR 5, 63; CN 1, 2, 3, 4, 5, 6; DLB 6, 206; INT CANR-5; MAL 5; TCWW 1, 2

Eastman, Charles A(lexander) 1858-1939 .... **NNAL; TCLC 55**
See also CA 179; CANR 91; DAM MULT; DLB 175; YABC 1

Eaton, Edith Maude 1865-1914 .... **AAL**
See Far, Sui Sin
See also CA 154; DLB 221, 312; FW

Eaton, (Lillie) Winnifred 1875-1954 .... **AAL**
See also CA 217; DLB 221, 312; RGAL 4

Eberhart, Richard 1904-2005 ...... **CLC 3, 11, 19, 56**
See also AMW; CA 1-4R; 240; CANR 2, 125; CDALB 1941-1968; CP 1, 2, 3, 4, 5, 6, 7; DAM POET; DLB 48; MAL 5; MTCW 1; RGAL 4

Eberhart, Richard Ghormley
See Eberhart, Richard

Eberstadt, Fernanda 1960- .... **CLC 39**
See also CA 136; CANR 69, 128

Echegaray (y Eizaguirre), Jose (Maria Waldo) 1832-1916 .... **HLCS 1; TCLC 4**
See also CA 104; CANR 32; EWL 3; HW 1; MTCW 1

Echeverria, (Jose) Esteban (Antonino) 1805-1851 .... **NCLC 18**
See also LAW

Echo
See Proust, (Valentin-Louis-George-Eugene) Marcel

Eckert, Allan W. 1931- .... **CLC 17**
See also AAYA 18; BYA 2; CA 13-16R; CANR 14, 45; INT CANR-14; MAICYA 2; MAICYAS 1; SAAS 21; SATA 29, 91; SATA-Brief 27

Eckhart, Meister 1260(?)-1327(?) .. **CMLC 9, 80**
See also DLB 115; LMFS 1

Eckmar, F. R.
See de Hartog, Jan

Eco, Umberto 1932- .... **CLC 28, 60, 142**
See also BEST 90:1; BPFB 1; CA 77-80; CANR 12, 33, 55, 110, 131; CPW; CWW 2; DA3; DAM NOV, POP; DLB 196, 242; EWL 3; MSW; MTCW 1, 2; MTFW 2005; NFS 22; RGWL 3; WLIT 7

Eddison, E(ric) R(ucker) 1882-1945 .... **TCLC 15**
See also CA 109; 156; DLB 255; FANT; SFW 4; SUFW 1

Eddy, Mary (Ann Morse) Baker 1821-1910 .... **TCLC 71**
See also CA 113; 174

Edel, (Joseph) Leon 1907-1997 .. **CLC 29, 34**
See also CA 1-4R; 161; CANR 1, 22, 112; DLB 103; INT CANR-22

Eden, Emily 1797-1869 .... **NCLC 10**

Edgar, David 1948- .... **CLC 42**
See also CA 57-60; CANR 12, 61, 112; CBD; CD 5, 6; DAM DRAM; DFS 15; DLB 13, 233; MTCW 1

Edgerton, Clyde (Carlyle) 1944- ...... **CLC 39**
See also AAYA 17; CA 118; 134; CANR 64, 125; CN 7; CSW; DLB 278; INT CA-134; TCLE 1:1; YAW

Edgeworth, Maria 1768-1849 ... **NCLC 1, 51, 158; SSC 86**
See also BRWS 3; DLB 116, 159, 163; FL 1:3; FW; RGEL 2; SATA 21; TEA; WLIT 3

Edmonds, Paul
See Kuttner, Henry

Edmonds, Walter D(umaux) 1903-1998 .... **CLC 35**
See also BYA 2; CA 5-8R; CANR 2; CWRI 5; DLB 9; LAIT 1; MAICYA 1, 2; MAL 5; RHW; SAAS 4; SATA 1, 27; SATA-Obit 99

Edmondson, Wallace
See Ellison, Harlan (Jay)

Gelbart, Larry
See Gelbart, Larry (Simon)
See also CAD; CD 5, 6
Gelbart, Larry (Simon) 1928- .... **CLC 21, 61**
See Gelbart, Larry
See also CA 73-76; CANR 45, 94
Gelber, Jack 1932-2003 ...... **CLC 1, 6, 14, 79**
See also CA 1-4R; 216; CAD; CANR 2; DLB 7, 228; MAL 5
Gellhorn, Martha (Ellis) 1908-1998 .... **CLC 14, 60**
See also CA 77-80; 164; CANR 44; CN 1, 2, 3, 4, 5, 6 7; DLBY 1982, 1998
Genet, Jean 1910-1986 .. **CLC 1, 2, 5, 10, 14, 44, 46; DC 25; TCLC 128**
See also CA 13-16R; CANR 18; DA3; DAM DRAM; DFS 10; DLB 72, 321; DLBY 1986; EW 13; EWL 3; GFL 1789 to the Present; GLL 1; LMFS 2; MTCW 1, 2; MTFW 2005; RGWL 2, 3; TWA
Gent, Peter 1942- .... **CLC 29**
See also AITN 1; CA 89-92; DLBY 1982
Gentile, Giovanni 1875-1944 .... **TCLC 96**
See also CA 119
Gentlewoman in New England, A
See Bradstreet, Anne
Gentlewoman in Those Parts, A
See Bradstreet, Anne
Geoffrey of Monmouth c. 1100-1155 .... **CMLC 44**
See also DLB 146; TEA
George, Jean
See George, Jean Craighead
George, Jean Craighead 1919- .... **CLC 35**
See also AAYA 8; BYA 2, 4; CA 5-8R; CANR 25; CLR 1; 80; DLB 52; JRDA; MAICYA 1, 2; SATA 2, 68, 124; WYA; YAW
George, Stefan (Anton) 1868-1933 . **TCLC 2, 14**
See also CA 104; 193; EW 8; EWL 3
Georges, Georges Martin
See Simenon, Georges (Jacques Christian)
Gerald of Wales c. 1146-c. 1223 ... **CMLC 60**
Gerhardi, William Alexander
See Gerhardie, William Alexander
Gerhardie, William Alexander 1895-1977 .... **CLC 5**
See also CA 25-28R; 73-76; CANR 18; CN 1, 2; DLB 36; RGEL 2
Gerson, Jean 1363-1429 .... **LC 77**
See also DLB 208
Gersonides 1288-1344 .... **CMLC 49**
See also DLB 115
Gerstler, Amy 1956- .... **CLC 70**
See also CA 146; CANR 99
Gertler, T. .... **CLC 34**
See also CA 116; 121
Gertsen, Aleksandr Ivanovich
See Herzen, Aleksandr Ivanovich
Ghalib .... **NCLC 39, 78**
See Ghalib, Asadullah Khan
Ghalib, Asadullah Khan 1797-1869
See Ghalib
See also DAM POET; RGWL 2, 3
Ghelderode, Michel de 1898-1962 ..... **CLC 6, 11; DC 15**
See also CA 85-88; CANR 40, 77; DAM DRAM; DLB 321; EW 11; EWL 3; TWA
Ghiselin, Brewster 1903-2001 .... **CLC 23**
See also CA 13-16R; CAAS 10; CANR 13; CP 1, 2, 3, 4, 5, 6, 7
Ghose, Aurabinda 1872-1950 .... **TCLC 63**
See Ghose, Aurobindo
See also CA 163
Ghose, Aurobindo
See Ghose, Aurabinda
See also EWL 3
Ghose, Zulfikar 1935- .... **CLC 42, 200**
See also CA 65-68; CANR 67; CN 1, 2, 3, 4, 5, 6, 7; CP 1, 2, 3, 4, 5, 6, 7; EWL 3
Ghosh, Amitav 1956- .... **CLC 44, 153**
See also CA 147; CANR 80; CN 6, 7; WWE 1
Giacosa, Giuseppe 1847-1906 .... **TCLC 7**
See also CA 104
Gibb, Lee
See Waterhouse, Keith (Spencer)
Gibbon, Edward 1737-1794 .... **LC 97**
See also BRW 3; DLB 104; RGEL 2
Gibbon, Lewis Grassic .... **TCLC 4**
See Mitchell, James Leslie
See also RGEL 2
Gibbons, Kaye 1960- .... **CLC 50, 88, 145**
See also AAYA 34; AMWS 10; CA 151; CANR 75, 127; CN 7; CSW; DA3; DAM POP; DLB 292; MTCW 2; MTFW 2005; NFS 3; RGAL 4; SATA 117
Gibran, Kahlil 1883-1931 . **PC 9; TCLC 1, 9**
See also CA 104; 150; DA3; DAM POET, POP; EWL 3; MTCW 2; WLIT 6
Gibran, Khalil
See Gibran, Kahlil
Gibson, Mel 1956- .... **CLC 215**
Gibson, William 1914- .... **CLC 23**
See also CA 9-12R; CAD; CANR 9, 42, 75, 125; CD 5, 6; DA; DAB; DAC; DAM DRAM, MST; DFS 2; DLB 7; LAIT 2; MAL 5; MTCW 2; MTFW 2005; SATA 66; YAW
Gibson, William (Ford) 1948- ... **CLC 39, 63, 186, 192; SSC 52**
See also AAYA 12, 59; BPFB 2; CA 126; 133; CANR 52, 90, 106; CN 6, 7; CPW; DA3; DAM POP; DLB 251; MTCW 2; MTFW 2005; SCFW 2; SFW 4
Gide, Andre (Paul Guillaume) 1869-1951 ...... **SSC 13; TCLC 5, 12, 36, 177; WLC**
See also CA 104; 124; DA; DA3; DAB; DAC; DAM MST, NOV; DLB 65, 321; EW 8; EWL 3; GFL 1789 to the Present; MTCW 1, 2; MTFW 2005; NFS 21; RGSF 2; RGWL 2, 3; TWA
Gifford, Barry (Colby) 1946- .... **CLC 34**
See also CA 65-68; CANR 9, 30, 40, 90
Gilbert, Frank
See De Voto, Bernard (Augustine)
Gilbert, W(illiam) S(chwenck) 1836-1911 .... **TCLC 3**
See also CA 104; 173; DAM DRAM, POET; RGEL 2; SATA 36
Gilbreth, Frank B(unker), Jr. 1911-2001 .... **CLC 17**
See also CA 9-12R; SATA 2
Gilchrist, Ellen (Louise) 1935- .. **CLC 34, 48, 143; SSC 14, 63**
See also BPFB 2; CA 113; 116; CANR 41, 61, 104; CN 4, 5, 6, 7; CPW; CSW; DAM POP; DLB 130; EWL 3; EXPS; MTCW 1, 2; MTFW 2005; RGAL 4; RGSF 2; SSFS 9
Giles, Molly 1942- .... **CLC 39**
See also CA 126; CANR 98
Gill, Eric .... **TCLC 85**
See Gill, (Arthur) Eric (Rowton Peter Joseph)
Gill, (Arthur) Eric (Rowton Peter Joseph) 1882-1940
See Gill, Eric
See also CA 120; DLB 98
Gill, Patrick
See Creasey, John
Gillette, Douglas .... **CLC 70**
Gilliam, Terry (Vance) 1940- .... **CLC 21, 141**
See Monty Python
See also AAYA 19, 59; CA 108; 113; CANR 35; INT CA-113
Gillian, Jerry
See Gilliam, Terry (Vance)
Gilliatt, Penelope (Ann Douglass) 1932-1993 .... **CLC 2, 10, 13, 53**
See also AITN 2; CA 13-16R; 141; CANR 49; CN 1, 2, 3, 4, 5; DLB 14
Gilligan, Carol 1936- .... **CLC 208**
See also CA 142; CANR 121; FW
Gilman, Charlotte (Anna) Perkins (Stetson) 1860-1935 ...... **SSC 13, 62; TCLC 9, 37, 117**
See also AMWS 11; BYA 11; CA 106; 150; DLB 221; EXPS; FL 1:5; FW; HGG; LAIT 2; MAWW; MTCW 2; MTFW 2005; RGAL 4; RGSF 2; SFW 4; SSFS 1, 18
Gilmour, David 1946- .... **CLC 35**
Gilpin, William 1724-1804 .... **NCLC 30**
Gilray, J. D.
See Mencken, H(enry) L(ouis)
Gilroy, Frank D(aniel) 1925- .... **CLC 2**
See also CA 81-84; CAD; CANR 32, 64, 86; CD 5, 6; DFS 17; DLB 7
Gilstrap, John 1957(?)- .... **CLC 99**
See also AAYA 67; CA 160; CANR 101
Ginsberg, Allen 1926-1997 .... **CLC 1, 2, 3, 4, 6, 13, 36, 69, 109; PC 4, 47; TCLC 120; WLC**
See also AAYA 33; AITN 1; AMWC 1; AMWS 2; BG 1:2; CA 1-4R; 157; CANR 2, 41, 63, 95; CDALB 1941-1968; CP 1, 2, 3, 4, 5, 6; DA; DA3; DAB; DAC; DAM MST, POET; DLB 5, 16, 169, 237; EWL 3; GLL 1; LMFS 2; MAL 5; MTCW 1, 2; MTFW 2005; PAB; PFS 5; RGAL 4; TUS; WP
Ginzburg, Eugenia .... **CLC 59**
See Ginzburg, Evgeniia
Ginzburg, Evgeniia 1904-1977
See Ginzburg, Eugenia
See also DLB 302
Ginzburg, Natalia 1916-1991 .... **CLC 5, 11, 54, 70; SSC 65; TCLC 156**
See also CA 85-88; 135; CANR 33; DFS 14; DLB 177; EW 13; EWL 3; MTCW 1, 2; MTFW 2005; RGWL 2, 3
Giono, Jean 1895-1970 .... **CLC 4, 11; TCLC 124**
See also CA 45-48; 29-32R; CANR 2, 35; DLB 72, 321; EWL 3; GFL 1789 to the Present; MTCW 1; RGWL 2, 3
Giovanni, Nikki 1943- ...... **BLC 2; CLC 2, 4, 19, 64, 117; PC 19; WLCS**
See also AAYA 22; AITN 1; BW 2, 3; CA 29-32R; CAAS 6; CANR 18, 41, 60, 91, 130; CDALBS; CLR 6, 73; CP 2, 3, 4, 5, 6, 7; CSW; CWP; CWRI 5; DA; DA3; DAB; DAC; DAM MST, MULT, POET; DLB 5, 41; EWL 3; EXPP; INT CANR-18; MAICYA 1, 2; MAL 5; MTCW 1, 2; MTFW 2005; PFS 17; RGAL 4; SATA 24, 107; TUS; YAW
Giovene, Andrea 1904-1998 .... **CLC 7**
See also CA 85-88
Gippius, Zinaida (Nikolaevna) 1869-1945
See Hippius, Zinaida (Nikolaevna)
See also CA 106; 212
Giraudoux, Jean(-Hippolyte) 1882-1944 .... **TCLC 2, 7**
See also CA 104; 196; DAM DRAM; DLB 65, 321; EW 9; EWL 3; GFL 1789 to the Present; RGWL 2, 3; TWA
Gironella, Jose Maria (Pous) 1917-2003 .... **CLC 11**
See also CA 101; 212; EWL 3; RGWL 2, 3

Author Index

Harris, John (Wyndham Parkes Lucas) Beynon 1903-1969
See Wyndham, John
See also CA 102; 89-92; CANR 84; SATA 118; SFW 4
Harris, MacDonald .... **CLC 9**
See Heiney, Donald (William)
Harris, Mark 1922- .... **CLC 19**
See also CA 5-8R; CAAS 3; CANR 2, 55, 83; CN 1, 2, 3, 4, 5, 6, 7; DLB 2; DLBY 1980
Harris, Norman .... **CLC 65**
Harris, (Theodore) Wilson 1921- .... **CLC 25, 159**
See also BRWS 5; BW 2, 3; CA 65-68; CAAS 16; CANR 11, 27, 69, 114; CDWLB 3; CN 1, 2, 3, 4, 5, 6, 7; CP 1, 2, 3, 4, 5, 6, 7; DLB 117; EWL 3; MTCW 1; RGEL 2
Harrison, Barbara Grizzuti 1934-2002 .... **CLC 144**
See also CA 77-80; 205; CANR 15, 48; INT CANR-15
Harrison, Elizabeth (Allen) Cavanna 1909-2001
See Cavanna, Betty
See also CA 9-12R; 200; CANR 6, 27, 85, 104, 121; MAICYA 2; SATA 142; YAW
Harrison, Harry (Max) 1925- .... **CLC 42**
See also CA 1-4R; CANR 5, 21, 84; DLB 8; SATA 4; SCFW 2; SFW 4
Harrison, James (Thomas) 1937- ...... **CLC 6, 14, 33, 66, 143; SSC 19**
See Harrison, Jim
See also CA 13-16R; CANR 8, 51, 79, 142; DLBY 1982; INT CANR-8
Harrison, Jim
See Harrison, James (Thomas)
See also AMWS 8; CN 5, 6; CP 1, 2, 3, 4, 5, 6, 7; RGAL 4; TCWW 2; TUS
Harrison, Kathryn 1961- .... **CLC 70, 151**
See also CA 144; CANR 68, 122
Harrison, Tony 1937- .... **CLC 43, 129**
See also BRWS 5; CA 65-68; CANR 44, 98; CBD; CD 5, 6; CP 2, 3, 4, 5, 6, 7; DLB 40, 245; MTCW 1; RGEL 2
Harriss, Will(ard Irvin) 1922- .... **CLC 34**
See also CA 111
Hart, Ellis
See Ellison, Harlan (Jay)
Hart, Josephine 1942(?)- .... **CLC 70**
See also CA 138; CANR 70; CPW; DAM POP
Hart, Moss 1904-1961 .... **CLC 66**
See also CA 109; 89-92; CANR 84; DAM DRAM; DFS 1; DLB 7, 266; RGAL 4
Harte, (Francis) Bret(t) 1836(?)-1902 ... **SSC 8, 59; TCLC 1, 25; WLC**
See also AMWS 2; CA 104; 140; CANR 80; CDALB 1865-1917; DA; DA3; DAC; DAM MST; DLB 12, 64, 74, 79, 186; EXPS; LAIT 2; RGAL 4; RGSF 2; SATA 26; SSFS 3; TUS
Hartley, L(eslie) P(oles) 1895-1972 ... **CLC 2, 22**
See also BRWS 7; CA 45-48; 37-40R; CANR 33; CN 1; DLB 15, 139; EWL 3; HGG; MTCW 1, 2; MTFW 2005; RGEL 2; RGSF 2; SUFW 1
Hartman, Geoffrey H. 1929- .... **CLC 27**
See also CA 117; 125; CANR 79; DLB 67
Hartmann, Sadakichi 1869-1944 ... **TCLC 73**
See also CA 157; DLB 54
Hartmann von Aue c. 1170-c. 1210 .... **CMLC 15**
See also CDWLB 2; DLB 138; RGWL 2, 3
Hartog, Jan de
See de Hartog, Jan
Haruf, Kent 1943- .... **CLC 34**
See also AAYA 44; CA 149; CANR 91, 131
Harvey, Caroline
See Trollope, Joanna
Harvey, Gabriel 1550(?)-1631 .... **LC 88**
See also DLB 167, 213, 281
Harwood, Ronald 1934- .... **CLC 32**
See also CA 1-4R; CANR 4, 55; CBD; CD 5, 6; DAM DRAM, MST; DLB 13
Hasegawa Tatsunosuke
See Futabatei, Shimei
Hasek, Jaroslav (Matej Frantisek) 1883-1923 .... **SSC 69; TCLC 4**
See also CA 104; 129; CDWLB 4; DLB 215; EW 9; EWL 3; MTCW 1, 2; RGSF 2; RGWL 2, 3
Hass, Robert 1941- ... **CLC 18, 39, 99; PC 16**
See also AMWS 6; CA 111; CANR 30, 50, 71; CP 3, 4, 5, 6, 7; DLB 105, 206; EWL 3; MAL 5; MTFW 2005; RGAL 4; SATA 94; TCLE 1:1
Hastings, Hudson
See Kuttner, Henry
Hastings, Selina .... **CLC 44**
Hathorne, John 1641-1717 .... **LC 38**
Hatteras, Amelia
See Mencken, H(enry) L(ouis)
Hatteras, Owen .... **TCLC 18**
See Mencken, H(enry) L(ouis); Nathan, George Jean
Hauptmann, Gerhart (Johann Robert) 1862-1946 .... **SSC 37; TCLC 4**
See also CA 104; 153; CDWLB 2; DAM DRAM; DLB 66, 118; EW 8; EWL 3; RGSF 2; RGWL 2, 3; TWA
Havel, Vaclav 1936- ..... **CLC 25, 58, 65, 123; DC 6**
See also CA 104; CANR 36, 63, 124; CDWLB 4; CWW 2; DA3; DAM DRAM; DFS 10; DLB 232; EWL 3; LMFS 2; MTCW 1, 2; MTFW 2005; RGWL 3
Haviaras, Stratis .... **CLC 33**
See Chaviaras, Strates
Hawes, Stephen 1475(?)-1529(?) .... **LC 17**
See also DLB 132; RGEL 2
Hawkes, John (Clendennin Burne, Jr.) 1925-1998 .. **CLC 1, 2, 3, 4, 7, 9, 14, 15, 27, 49**
See also BPFB 2; CA 1-4R; 167; CANR 2, 47, 64; CN 1, 2, 3, 4, 5, 6; DLB 2, 7, 227; DLBY 1980, 1998; EWL 3; MAL 5; MTCW 1, 2; MTFW 2005; RGAL 4
Hawking, S. W.
See Hawking, Stephen W(illiam)
Hawking, Stephen W(illiam) 1942- . **CLC 63, 105**
See also AAYA 13; BEST 89:1; CA 126; 129; CANR 48, 115; CPW; DA3; MTCW 2; MTFW 2005
Hawkins, Anthony Hope
See Hope, Anthony
Hawthorne, Julian 1846-1934 .... **TCLC 25**
See also CA 165; HGG
Hawthorne, Nathaniel 1804-1864 ... **NCLC 2, 10, 17, 23, 39, 79, 95, 158; SSC 3, 29, 39, 89; WLC**
See also AAYA 18; AMW; AMWC 1; AMWR 1; BPFB 2; BYA 3; CDALB 1640-1865; CLR 103; DA; DA3; DAB; DAC; DAM MST, NOV; DLB 1, 74, 183, 223, 269; EXPN; EXPS; GL 2; HGG; LAIT 1; NFS 1, 20; RGAL 4; RGSF 2; SSFS 1, 7, 11, 15; SUFW 1; TUS; WCH; YABC 2
Hawthorne, Sophia Peabody 1809-1871 .... **NCLC 150**
See also DLB 183, 239
Haxton, Josephine Ayres 1921-
See Douglas, Ellen
See also CA 115; CANR 41, 83
Hayaseca y Eizaguirre, Jorge
See Echegaray (y Eizaguirre), Jose (Maria Waldo)
Hayashi, Fumiko 1904-1951 .... **TCLC 27**
See Hayashi Fumiko
See also CA 161
Hayashi Fumiko
See Hayashi, Fumiko
See also DLB 180; EWL 3
Haycraft, Anna (Margaret) 1932-2005
See Ellis, Alice Thomas
See also CA 122; 237; CANR 90, 141; MTCW 2; MTFW 2005
Hayden, Robert E(arl) 1913-1980 ..... **BLC 2; CLC 5, 9, 14, 37; PC 6**
See also AFAW 1, 2; AMWS 2; BW 1, 3; CA 69-72; 97-100; CABS 2; CANR 24, 75, 82; CDALB 1941-1968; CP 1, 2, 3; DA; DAC; DAM MST, MULT, POET; DLB 5, 76; EWL 3; EXPP; MAL 5; MTCW 1, 2; PFS 1; RGAL 4; SATA 19; SATA-Obit 26; WP
Haydon, Benjamin Robert 1786-1846 .... **NCLC 146**
See also DLB 110
Hayek, F(riedrich) A(ugust von) 1899-1992 .... **TCLC 109**
See also CA 93-96; 137; CANR 20; MTCW 1, 2
Hayford, J(oseph) E(phraim) Casely
See Casely-Hayford, J(oseph) E(phraim)
Hayman, Ronald 1932- .... **CLC 44**
See also CA 25-28R; CANR 18, 50, 88; CD 5, 6; DLB 155
Hayne, Paul Hamilton 1830-1886 . **NCLC 94**
See also DLB 3, 64, 79, 248; RGAL 4
Hays, Mary 1760-1843 .... **NCLC 114**
See also DLB 142, 158; RGEL 2
Haywood, Eliza (Fowler) 1693(?)-1756 .... **LC 1, 44**
See also DLB 39; RGEL 2
Hazlitt, William 1778-1830 ...... **NCLC 29, 82**
See also BRW 4; DLB 110, 158; RGEL 2; TEA
Hazzard, Shirley 1931- .... **CLC 18, 218**
See also CA 9-12R; CANR 4, 70, 127; CN 1, 2, 3, 4, 5, 6, 7; DLB 289; DLBY 1982; MTCW 1
Head, Bessie 1937-1986 ...... **BLC 2; CLC 25, 67; SSC 52**
See also AFW; BW 2, 3; CA 29-32R; 119; CANR 25, 82; CDWLB 3; CN 1, 2, 3, 4; DA3; DAM MULT; DLB 117, 225; EWL 3; EXPS; FL 1:6; FW; MTCW 1, 2; MTFW 2005; RGSF 2; SSFS 5, 13; WLIT 2; WWE 1
Headon, (Nicky) Topper 1956(?)- ..... **CLC 30**
Heaney, Seamus (Justin) 1939- ..... **CLC 5, 7, 14, 25, 37, 74, 91, 171; PC 18; WLCS**
See also AAYA 61; BRWR 1; BRWS 2; CA 85-88; CANR 25, 48, 75, 91, 128; CDBLB 1960 to Present; CP 1, 2, 3, 4, 5, 6, 7; DA3; DAB; DAM POET; DLB 40; DLBY 1995; EWL 3; EXPP; MTCW 1, 2; MTFW 2005; PAB; PFS 2, 5, 8, 17; RGEL 2; TEA; WLIT 4
Hearn, (Patricio) Lafcadio (Tessima Carlos) 1850-1904 .... **TCLC 9**
See also CA 105; 166; DLB 12, 78, 189; HGG; MAL 5; RGAL 4
Hearne, Samuel 1745-1792 .... **LC 95**
See also DLB 99
Hearne, Vicki 1946-2001 .... **CLC 56**
See also CA 139; 201

Author Index

Author Index

Jones, Terence Graham Parry 1942- .... **CLC 21**
See Jones, Terry; Monty Python
See also CA 112; 116; CANR 35, 93; INT CA-116; SATA 127
Jones, Terry
See Jones, Terence Graham Parry
See also SATA 67; SATA-Brief 51
Jones, Thom (Douglas) 1945(?)- ..... **CLC 81; SSC 56**
See also CA 157; CANR 88; DLB 244
Jong, Erica 1942- .... **CLC 4, 6, 8, 18, 83**
See also AITN 1; AMWS 5; BEST 90:2; BPFB 2; CA 73-76; CANR 26, 52, 75, 132; CN 3, 4, 5, 6, 7; CP 2, 3, 4, 5, 6, 7; CPW; DA3; DAM NOV, POP; DLB 2, 5, 28, 152; FW; INT CANR-26; MAL 5; MTCW 1, 2; MTFW 2005
Jonson, Ben(jamin) 1572(?)-1637 . **DC 4; LC 6, 33, 110; PC 17; WLC**
See also BRW 1; BRWC 1; BRWR 1; CDBLB Before 1660; DA; DAB; DAC; DAM DRAM, MST, POET; DFS 4, 10; DLB 62, 121; LMFS 1; PFS 23; RGEL 2; TEA; WLIT 3
Jordan, June (Meyer) 1936-2002 .. **BLCS; CLC 5, 11, 23, 114; PC 38**
See also AAYA 2, 66; AFAW 1, 2; BW 2, 3; CA 33-36R; 206; CANR 25, 70, 114; CLR 10; CP 3, 4, 5, 6, 7; CWP; DAM MULT, POET; DLB 38; GLL 2; LAIT 5; MAICYA 1, 2; MTCW 1; SATA 4, 136; YAW
Jordan, Neil (Patrick) 1950- .... **CLC 110**
See also CA 124; 130; CANR 54; CN 4, 5, 6, 7; GLL 2; INT CA-130
Jordan, Pat(rick M.) 1941- .... **CLC 37**
See also CA 33-36R; CANR 121
Jorgensen, Ivar
See Ellison, Harlan (Jay)
Jorgenson, Ivar
See Silverberg, Robert
Joseph, George Ghevarughese .... **CLC 70**
Josephson, Mary
See O'Doherty, Brian
Josephus, Flavius c. 37-100 .... **CMLC 13**
See also AW 2; DLB 176
Josiah Allen's Wife
See Holley, Marietta
Josipovici, Gabriel (David) 1940- ...... **CLC 6, 43, 153**
See also CA 37-40R, 224; CAAE 224; CAAS 8; CANR 47, 84; CN 3, 4, 5, 6, 7; DLB 14, 319
Joubert, Joseph 1754-1824 .... **NCLC 9**
Jouve, Pierre Jean 1887-1976 .... **CLC 47**
See also CA 65-68; DLB 258; EWL 3
Jovine, Francesco 1902-1950 .... **TCLC 79**
See also DLB 264; EWL 3
Joyce, James (Augustine Aloysius) 1882-1941 .... **DC 16; PC 22; SSC 3, 26, 44, 64; TCLC 3, 8, 16, 35, 52, 159; WLC**
See also AAYA 42; BRW 7; BRWC 1; BRWR 1; BYA 11, 13; CA 104; 126; CDBLB 1914-1945; DA; DA3; DAB; DAC; DAM MST, NOV, POET; DLB 10, 19, 36, 162, 247; EWL 3; EXPN; EXPS; LAIT 3; LMFS 1, 2; MTCW 1, 2; MTFW 2005; NFS 7; RGSF 2; SSFS 1, 19; TEA; WLIT 4
Jozsef, Attila 1905-1937 .... **TCLC 22**
See also CA 116; 230; CDWLB 4; DLB 215; EWL 3
Juana Ines de la Cruz, Sor 1651(?)-1695 ...... **HLCS 1; LC 5; PC 24**
See also DLB 305; FW; LAW; RGWL 2, 3; WLIT 1
Juana Inez de La Cruz, Sor
See Juana Ines de la Cruz, Sor
Judd, Cyril
See Kornbluth, C(yril) M.; Pohl, Frederik
Juenger, Ernst 1895-1998 .... **CLC 125**
See Junger, Ernst
See also CA 101; 167; CANR 21, 47, 106; DLB 56
Julian of Norwich 1342(?)-1416(?) . **LC 6, 52**
See also DLB 146; LMFS 1
Julius Caesar 100B.C.-44B.C.
See Caesar, Julius
See also CDWLB 1; DLB 211
Junger, Ernst
See Juenger, Ernst
See also CDWLB 2; EWL 3; RGWL 2, 3
Junger, Sebastian 1962- .... **CLC 109**
See also AAYA 28; CA 165; CANR 130; MTFW 2005
Juniper, Alex
See Hospital, Janette Turner
Junius
See Luxemburg, Rosa
Junzaburo, Nishiwaki
See Nishiwaki, Junzaburo
See also EWL 3
Just, Ward (Swift) 1935- .... **CLC 4, 27**
See also CA 25-28R; CANR 32, 87; CN 6, 7; INT CANR-32
Justice, Donald (Rodney) 1925-2004 .... **CLC 6, 19, 102; PC 64**
See also AMWS 7; CA 5-8R; 230; CANR 26, 54, 74, 121, 122; CP 1, 2, 3, 4, 5, 6, 7; CSW; DAM POET; DLBY 1983; EWL 3; INT CANR-26; MAL 5; MTCW 2; PFS 14; TCLE 1:1
Juvenal c. 60-c. 130 .... **CMLC 8**
See also AW 2; CDWLB 1; DLB 211; RGWL 2, 3
Juvenis
See Bourne, Randolph S(illiman)
K., Alice
See Knapp, Caroline
Kabakov, Sasha .... **CLC 59**
Kabir 1398(?)-1448(?) .... **LC 109; PC 56**
See also RGWL 2, 3
Kacew, Romain 1914-1980
See Gary, Romain
See also CA 108; 102
Kadare, Ismail 1936- .... **CLC 52, 190**
See also CA 161; EWL 3; RGWL 3
Kadohata, Cynthia (Lynn) 1956(?)- .... **CLC 59, 122**
See also CA 140; CANR 124; SATA 155
Kafka, Franz 1883-1924 ... **SSC 5, 29, 35, 60; TCLC 2, 6, 13, 29, 47, 53, 112; WLC**
See also AAYA 31; BPFB 2; CA 105; 126; CDWLB 2; DA; DA3; DAB; DAC; DAM MST, NOV; DLB 81; EW 9; EWL 3; EXPS; LATS 1:1; LMFS 2; MTCW 1, 2; MTFW 2005; NFS 7; RGSF 2; RGWL 2, 3; SFW 4; SSFS 3, 7, 12; TWA
Kahanovitsch, Pinkhes
See Der Nister
Kahn, Roger 1927- .... **CLC 30**
See also CA 25-28R; CANR 44, 69; DLB 171; SATA 37
Kain, Saul
See Sassoon, Siegfried (Lorraine)
Kaiser, Georg 1878-1945 .... **TCLC 9**
See also CA 106; 190; CDWLB 2; DLB 124; EWL 3; LMFS 2; RGWL 2, 3
Kaledin, Sergei .... **CLC 59**
Kaletski, Alexander 1946- .... **CLC 39**
See also CA 118; 143
Kalidasa fl. c. 400-455 .... **CMLC 9; PC 22**
See also RGWL 2, 3
Kallman, Chester (Simon) 1921-1975 .... **CLC 2**
See also CA 45-48; 53-56; CANR 3; CP 1, 2
Kaminsky, Melvin 1926-
See Brooks, Mel
See also CA 65-68; CANR 16; DFS 21
Kaminsky, Stuart M(elvin) 1934- ..... **CLC 59**
See also CA 73-76; CANR 29, 53, 89; CMW 4
Kamo no Chomei 1153(?)-1216 .... **CMLC 66**
See also DLB 203
Kamo no Nagaakira
See Kamo no Chomei
Kandinsky, Wassily 1866-1944 .... **TCLC 92**
See also AAYA 64; CA 118; 155
Kane, Francis
See Robbins, Harold
Kane, Henry 1918-
See Queen, Ellery
See also CA 156; CMW 4
Kane, Paul
See Simon, Paul (Frederick)
Kanin, Garson 1912-1999 .... **CLC 22**
See also AITN 1; CA 5-8R; 177; CAD; CANR 7, 78; DLB 7; IDFW 3, 4
Kaniuk, Yoram 1930- .... **CLC 19**
See also CA 134; DLB 299
Kant, Immanuel 1724-1804 ..... **NCLC 27, 67**
See also DLB 94
Kantor, MacKinlay 1904-1977 .... **CLC 7**
See also CA 61-64; 73-76; CANR 60, 63; CN 1, 2; DLB 9, 102; MAL 5; MTCW 2; RHW; TCWW 1, 2
Kanze Motokiyo
See Zeami
Kaplan, David Michael 1946- .... **CLC 50**
See also CA 187
Kaplan, James 1951- .... **CLC 59**
See also CA 135; CANR 121
Karadzic, Vuk Stefanovic 1787-1864 .... **NCLC 115**
See also CDWLB 4; DLB 147
Karageorge, Michael
See Anderson, Poul (William)
Karamzin, Nikolai Mikhailovich 1766-1826 .... **NCLC 3**
See also DLB 150; RGSF 2
Karapanou, Margarita 1946- .... **CLC 13**
See also CA 101
Karinthy, Frigyes 1887-1938 .... **TCLC 47**
See also CA 170; DLB 215; EWL 3
Karl, Frederick R(obert) 1927-2004 .... **CLC 34**
See also CA 5-8R; 226; CANR 3, 44, 143
Karr, Mary 1955- .... **CLC 188**
See also AMWS 11; CA 151; CANR 100; MTFW 2005; NCFS 5
Kastel, Warren
See Silverberg, Robert
Kataev, Evgeny Petrovich 1903-1942
See Petrov, Evgeny
See also CA 120
Kataphusin
See Ruskin, John
Katz, Steve 1935- .... **CLC 47**
See also CA 25-28R; CAAS 14, 64; CANR 12; CN 4, 5, 6, 7; DLBY 1983
Kauffman, Janet 1945- .... **CLC 42**
See also CA 117; CANR 43, 84; DLB 218; DLBY 1986
Kaufman, Bob (Garnell) 1925-1986 . **CLC 49**
See also BG 1:3; BW 1; CA 41-44R; 118; CANR 22; CP 1; DLB 16, 41

MST, NOV, POP; DLB 2, 16, 206; EWL 3; EXPN; LAIT 4; MAL 5; MTCW 1, 2; MTFW 2005; NFS 2; RGAL 4; SATA 66; SATA-Obit 131; TUS; YAW
Kesselring, Joseph (Otto) 1902-1967 .... **CLC 45**
See also CA 150; DAM DRAM, MST; DFS 20
Kessler, Jascha (Frederick) 1929- ...... **CLC 4**
See also CA 17-20R; CANR 8, 48, 111; CP 1
Kettelkamp, Larry (Dale) 1933- .... **CLC 12**
See also CA 29-32R; CANR 16; SAAS 3; SATA 2
Key, Ellen (Karolina Sofia) 1849-1926 .... **TCLC 65**
See also DLB 259
Keyber, Conny
See Fielding, Henry
Keyes, Daniel 1927- .... **CLC 80**
See also AAYA 23; BYA 11; CA 17-20R, 181; CAAE 181; CANR 10, 26, 54, 74; DA; DA3; DAC; DAM MST, NOV; EXPN; LAIT 4; MTCW 2; MTFW 2005; NFS 2; SATA 37; SFW 4
Keynes, John Maynard 1883-1946 .... **TCLC 64**
See also CA 114; 162, 163; DLBD 10; MTCW 2; MTFW 2005
Khanshendel, Chiron
See Rose, Wendy
Khayyam, Omar 1048-1131 .... **CMLC 11; PC 8**
See Omar Khayyam
See also DA3; DAM POET; WLIT 6
Kherdian, David 1931- .... **CLC 6, 9**
See also AAYA 42; CA 21-24R, 192; CAAE 192; CAAS 2; CANR 39, 78; CLR 24; JRDA; LAIT 3; MAICYA 1, 2; SATA 16, 74; SATA-Essay 125
Khlebnikov, Velimir .... **TCLC 20**
See Khlebnikov, Viktor Vladimirovich
See also DLB 295; EW 10; EWL 3; RGWL 2, 3
Khlebnikov, Viktor Vladimirovich 1885-1922
See Khlebnikov, Velimir
See also CA 117; 217
Khodasevich, Vladislav (Felitsianovich) 1886-1939 .... **TCLC 15**
See also CA 115; DLB 317; EWL 3
Kielland, Alexander Lange 1849-1906 .... **TCLC 5**
See also CA 104
Kiely, Benedict 1919- ... **CLC 23, 43; SSC 58**
See also CA 1-4R; CANR 2, 84; CN 1, 2, 3, 4, 5, 6, 7; DLB 15, 319; TCLE 1:1
Kienzle, William X(avier) 1928-2001 .... **CLC 25**
See also CA 93-96; 203; CAAS 1; CANR 9, 31, 59, 111; CMW 4; DA3; DAM POP; INT CANR-31; MSW; MTCW 1, 2; MTFW 2005
Kierkegaard, Soren 1813-1855 ..... **NCLC 34, 78, 125**
See also DLB 300; EW 6; LMFS 2; RGWL 3; TWA
Kieslowski, Krzysztof 1941-1996 .... **CLC 120**
See also CA 147; 151
Killens, John Oliver 1916-1987 .... **CLC 10**
See also BW 2; CA 77-80; 123; CAAS 2; CANR 26; CN 1, 2, 3, 4; DLB 33; EWL 3
Killigrew, Anne 1660-1685 .... **LC 4, 73**
See also DLB 131
Killigrew, Thomas 1612-1683 .... **LC 57**
See also DLB 58; RGEL 2
Kim
See Simenon, Georges (Jacques Christian)
Kincaid, Jamaica 1949- ...... **BLC 2; CLC 43, 68, 137; SSC 72**
See also AAYA 13, 56; AFAW 2; AMWS 7; BRWS 7; BW 2, 3; CA 125; CANR 47, 59, 95, 133; CDALBS; CDWLB 3; CLR 63; CN 4, 5, 6, 7; DA3; DAM MULT, NOV; DLB 157, 227; DNFS 1; EWL 3; EXPS; FW; LATS 1:2; LMFS 2; MAL 5; MTCW 2; MTFW 2005; NCFS 1; NFS 3; SSFS 5, 7; TUS; WWE 1; YAW
King, Francis (Henry) 1923- .... **CLC 8, 53, 145**
See also CA 1-4R; CANR 1, 33, 86; CN 1, 2, 3, 4, 5, 6, 7; DAM NOV; DLB 15, 139; MTCW 1
King, Kennedy
See Brown, George Douglas
King, Martin Luther, Jr. 1929-1968 . **BLC 2; CLC 83; WLCS**
See also BW 2, 3; CA 25-28; CANR 27, 44; CAP 2; DA; DA3; DAB; DAC; DAM MST, MULT; LAIT 5; LATS 1:2; MTCW 1, 2; MTFW 2005; SATA 14
King, Stephen 1947- .... **CLC 12, 26, 37, 61, 113; SSC 17, 55**
See also AAYA 1, 17; AMWS 5; BEST 90:1; BPFB 2; CA 61-64; CANR 1, 30, 52, 76, 119, 134; CN 7; CPW; DA3; DAM NOV, POP; DLB 143; DLBY 1980; HGG; JRDA; LAIT 5; MTCW 1, 2; MTFW 2005; RGAL 4; SATA 9, 55, 161; SUFW 1, 2; WYAS 1; YAW
King, Stephen Edwin
See King, Stephen
King, Steve
See King, Stephen
King, Thomas 1943- .... **CLC 89, 171; NNAL**
See also CA 144; CANR 95; CCA 1; CN 6, 7; DAC; DAM MULT; DLB 175; SATA 96
Kingman, Lee .... **CLC 17**
See Natti, (Mary) Lee
See also CWRI 5; SAAS 3; SATA 1, 67
Kingsley, Charles 1819-1875 .... **NCLC 35**
See also CLR 77; DLB 21, 32, 163, 178, 190; FANT; MAICYA 2; MAICYAS 1; RGEL 2; WCH; YABC 2
Kingsley, Henry 1830-1876 .... **NCLC 107**
See also DLB 21, 230; RGEL 2
Kingsley, Sidney 1906-1995 .... **CLC 44**
See also CA 85-88; 147; CAD; DFS 14, 19; DLB 7; MAL 5; RGAL 4
Kingsolver, Barbara 1955- .... **CLC 55, 81, 130, 216**
See also AAYA 15; AMWS 7; CA 129; 134; CANR 60, 96, 133; CDALBS; CN 7; CPW; CSW; DA3; DAM POP; DLB 206; INT CA-134; LAIT 5; MTCW 2; MTFW 2005; NFS 5, 10, 12; RGAL 4; TCLE 1:1
Kingston, Maxine (Ting Ting) Hong 1940- .... **AAL; CLC 12, 19, 58, 121; WLCS**
See also AAYA 8, 55; AMWS 5; BPFB 2; CA 69-72; CANR 13, 38, 74, 87, 128; CDALBS; CN 6, 7; DA3; DAM MULT, NOV; DLB 173, 212, 312; DLBY 1980; EWL 3; FL 1:6; FW; INT CANR-13; LAIT 5; MAL 5; MAWW; MTCW 1, 2; MTFW 2005; NFS 6; RGAL 4; SATA 53; SSFS 3; TCWW 2
Kinnell, Galway 1927- ..... **CLC 1, 2, 3, 5, 13, 29, 129; PC 26**
See also AMWS 3; CA 9-12R; CANR 10, 34, 66, 116, 138; CP 1, 2, 3, 4, 5, 6, 7; DLB 5; DLBY 1987; EWL 3; INT CANR-34; MAL 5; MTCW 1, 2; MTFW 2005; PAB; PFS 9; RGAL 4; TCLE 1:1; WP
Kinsella, Thomas 1928- .... **CLC 4, 19, 138; PC 69**
See also BRWS 5; CA 17-20R; CANR 15, 122; CP 1, 2, 3, 4, 5, 6, 7; DLB 27; EWL 3; MTCW 1, 2; MTFW 2005; RGEL 2; TEA
Kinsella, W(illiam) P(atrick) 1935- . **CLC 27, 43, 166**
See also AAYA 7, 60; BPFB 2; CA 97-100, 222; CAAE 222; CAAS 7; CANR 21, 35, 66, 75, 129; CN 4, 5, 6, 7; CPW; DAC; DAM NOV, POP; FANT; INT CANR-21; LAIT 5; MTCW 1, 2; MTFW 2005; NFS 15; RGSF 2
Kinsey, Alfred C(harles) 1894-1956 .... **TCLC 91**
See also CA 115; 170; MTCW 2
Kipling, (Joseph) Rudyard 1865-1936 . **PC 3; SSC 5, 54; TCLC 8, 17, 167; WLC**
See also AAYA 32; BRW 6; BRWC 1, 2; BYA 4; CA 105; 120; CANR 33; CDBLB 1890-1914; CLR 39, 65; CWRI 5; DA; DA3; DAB; DAC; DAM MST, POET; DLB 19, 34, 141, 156; EWL 3; EXPS; FANT; LAIT 3; LMFS 1; MAICYA 1, 2; MTCW 1, 2; MTFW 2005; NFS 21; PFS 22; RGEL 2; RGSF 2; SATA 100; SFW 4; SSFS 8, 21; SUFW 1; TEA; WCH; WLIT 4; YABC 2
Kircher, Athanasius 1602-1680 .... **LC 121**
See also DLB 164
Kirk, Russell (Amos) 1918-1994 .. **TCLC 119**
See also AITN 1; CA 1-4R; 145; CAAS 9; CANR 1, 20, 60; HGG; INT CANR-20; MTCW 1, 2
Kirkham, Dinah
See Card, Orson Scott
Kirkland, Caroline M. 1801-1864 . **NCLC 85**
See also DLB 3, 73, 74, 250, 254; DLBD 13
Kirkup, James 1918- .... **CLC 1**
See also CA 1-4R; CAAS 4; CANR 2; CP 1, 2, 3, 4, 5, 6, 7; DLB 27; SATA 12
Kirkwood, James 1930(?)-1989 .... **CLC 9**
See also AITN 2; CA 1-4R; 128; CANR 6, 40; GLL 2
Kirsch, Sarah 1935- .... **CLC 176**
See also CA 178; CWW 2; DLB 75; EWL 3
Kirshner, Sidney
See Kingsley, Sidney
Kis, Danilo 1935-1989 .... **CLC 57**
See also CA 109; 118; 129; CANR 61; CDWLB 4; DLB 181; EWL 3; MTCW 1; RGSF 2; RGWL 2, 3
Kissinger, Henry A(lfred) 1923- ..... **CLC 137**
See also CA 1-4R; CANR 2, 33, 66, 109; MTCW 1
Kivi, Aleksis 1834-1872 .... **NCLC 30**
Kizer, Carolyn (Ashley) 1925- ... **CLC 15, 39, 80; PC 66**
See also CA 65-68; CAAS 5; CANR 24, 70, 134; CP 1, 2, 3, 4, 5, 6, 7; CWP; DAM POET; DLB 5, 169; EWL 3; MAL 5; MTCW 2; MTFW 2005; PFS 18; TCLE 1:1
Klabund 1890-1928 .... **TCLC 44**
See also CA 162; DLB 66
Klappert, Peter 1942- .... **CLC 57**
See also CA 33-36R; CSW; DLB 5
Klein, A(braham) M(oses) 1909-1972 .... **CLC 19**
See also CA 101; 37-40R; CP 1; DAB; DAC; DAM MST; DLB 68; EWL 3; RGEL 2
Klein, Joe
See Klein, Joseph
Klein, Joseph 1946- .... **CLC 154**
See also CA 85-88; CANR 55

Author Index

Krumgold, Joseph (Quincy) 1908-1980 .... **CLC 12**
See also BYA 1, 2; CA 9-12R; 101; CANR 7; MAICYA 1, 2; SATA 1, 48; SATA-Obit 23; YAW

Krumwitz
See Crumb, R(obert)

Krutch, Joseph Wood 1893-1970 ..... **CLC 24**
See also ANW; CA 1-4R; 25-28R; CANR 4; DLB 63, 206, 275

Krutzch, Gus
See Eliot, T(homas) S(tearns)

Krylov, Ivan Andreevich 1768(?)-1844 .... **NCLC 1**
See also DLB 150

Kubin, Alfred (Leopold Isidor) 1877-1959 .... **TCLC 23**
See also CA 112; 149; CANR 104; DLB 81

Kubrick, Stanley 1928-1999 .... **CLC 16; TCLC 112**
See also AAYA 30; CA 81-84; 177; CANR 33; DLB 26

Kumin, Maxine (Winokur) 1925- ..... **CLC 5, 13, 28, 164; PC 15**
See also AITN 2; AMWS 4; ANW; CA 1-4R; CAAS 8; CANR 1, 21, 69, 115, 140; CP 2, 3, 4, 5, 6, 7; CWP; DA3; DAM POET; DLB 5; EWL 3; EXPP; MTCW 1, 2; MTFW 2005; PAB; PFS 18; SATA 12

Kundera, Milan 1929- . **CLC 4, 9, 19, 32, 68, 115, 135; SSC 24**
See also AAYA 2, 62; BPFB 2; CA 85-88; CANR 19, 52, 74, 144; CDWLB 4; CWW 2; DA3; DAM NOV; DLB 232; EW 13; EWL 3; MTCW 1, 2; MTFW 2005; NFS 18; RGSF 2; RGWL 3; SSFS 10

Kunene, Mazisi (Raymond) 1930- ... **CLC 85**
See also BW 1, 3; CA 125; CANR 81; CP 1, 7; DLB 117

Kung, Hans .... **CLC 130**
See Kung, Hans

Kung, Hans 1928-
See Kung, Hans
See also CA 53-56; CANR 66, 134; MTCW 1, 2; MTFW 2005

Kunikida Doppo 1869(?)-1908
See Doppo, Kunikida
See also DLB 180; EWL 3

Kunitz, Stanley (Jasspon) 1905- .. **CLC 6, 11, 14, 148; PC 19**
See also AMWS 3; CA 41-44R; CANR 26, 57, 98; CP 1, 2, 3, 4, 5, 6, 7; DA3; DLB 48; INT CANR-26; MAL 5; MTCW 1, 2; MTFW 2005; PFS 11; RGAL 4

Kunze, Reiner 1933- .... **CLC 10**
See also CA 93-96; CWW 2; DLB 75; EWL 3

Kuprin, Aleksander Ivanovich 1870-1938 .... **TCLC 5**
See Kuprin, Aleksandr Ivanovich; Kuprin, Alexandr Ivanovich
See also CA 104; 182

Kuprin, Aleksandr Ivanovich
See Kuprin, Aleksander Ivanovich
See also DLB 295

Kuprin, Alexandr Ivanovich
See Kuprin, Aleksander Ivanovich
See also EWL 3

Kureishi, Hanif 1954- .. **CLC 64, 135; DC 26**
See also BRWS 11; CA 139; CANR 113; CBD; CD 5, 6; CN 6, 7; DLB 194, 245; GLL 2; IDFW 4; WLIT 4; WWE 1

Kurosawa, Akira 1910-1998 ..... **CLC 16, 119**
See also AAYA 11, 64; CA 101; 170; CANR 46; DAM MULT

Kushner, Tony 1956- .... **CLC 81, 203; DC 10**
See also AAYA 61; AMWS 9; CA 144; CAD; CANR 74, 130; CD 5, 6; DA3; DAM DRAM; DFS 5; DLB 228; EWL 3; GLL 1; LAIT 5; MAL 5; MTCW 2; MTFW 2005; RGAL 4; SATA 160

Kuttner, Henry 1915-1958 .... **TCLC 10**
See also CA 107; 157; DLB 8; FANT; SCFW 1, 2; SFW 4

Kutty, Madhavi
See Das, Kamala

Kuzma, Greg 1944- .... **CLC 7**
See also CA 33-36R; CANR 70

Kuzmin, Mikhail (Alekseevich) 1872(?)-1936 .... **TCLC 40**
See also CA 170; DLB 295; EWL 3

Kyd, Thomas 1558-1594 .. **DC 3; LC 22, 125**
See also BRW 1; DAM DRAM; DFS 21; DLB 62; IDTP; LMFS 1; RGEL 2; TEA; WLIT 3

Kyprianos, Iossif
See Samarakis, Antonis

L. S.
See Stephen, Sir Leslie

Laȝamon
See Layamon
See also DLB 146

Labe, Louise 1521-1566 .... **LC 120**

Labrunie, Gerard
See Nerval, Gerard de

La Bruyere, Jean de 1645-1696 .... **LC 17**
See also DLB 268; EW 3; GFL Beginnings to 1789

Lacan, Jacques (Marie Emile) 1901-1981 .... **CLC 75**
See also CA 121; 104; DLB 296; EWL 3; TWA

Laclos, Pierre-Ambroise Francois 1741-1803 .... **NCLC 4, 87**
See also DLB 313; EW 4; GFL Beginnings to 1789; RGWL 2, 3

Lacolere, Francois
See Aragon, Louis

La Colere, Francois
See Aragon, Louis

La Deshabilleuse
See Simenon, Georges (Jacques Christian)

Lady Gregory
See Gregory, Lady Isabella Augusta (Persse)

Lady of Quality, A
See Bagnold, Enid

La Fayette, Marie-(Madelaine Pioche de la Vergne) 1634-1693 .... **LC 2**
See Lafayette, Marie-Madeleine
See also GFL Beginnings to 1789; RGWL 2, 3

Lafayette, Marie-Madeleine
See La Fayette, Marie-(Madelaine Pioche de la Vergne)
See also DLB 268

Lafayette, Rene
See Hubbard, L(afayette) Ron(ald)

La Flesche, Francis 1857(?)-1932 ...... **NNAL**
See also CA 144; CANR 83; DLB 175

La Fontaine, Jean de 1621-1695 .... **LC 50**
See also DLB 268; EW 3; GFL Beginnings to 1789; MAICYA 1, 2; RGWL 2, 3; SATA 18

Laforet, Carmen 1921-2004 .... **CLC 219**
See also CWW 2; DLB 322; EWL 3

Laforgue, Jules 1860-1887 . **NCLC 5, 53; PC 14; SSC 20**
See also DLB 217; EW 7; GFL 1789 to the Present; RGWL 2, 3

Lagerkvist, Paer (Fabian) 1891-1974 ..... **CLC 7, 10, 13, 54; TCLC 144**
See Lagerkvist, Par
See also CA 85-88; 49-52; DA3; DAM DRAM, NOV; MTCW 1, 2; MTFW 2005; TWA

Lagerkvist, Par .... **SSC 12**
See Lagerkvist, Paer (Fabian)
See also DLB 259; EW 10; EWL 3; RGSF 2; RGWL 2, 3

Lagerloef, Selma (Ottiliana Lovisa) .... **TCLC 4, 36**
See Lagerlof, Selma (Ottiliana Lovisa)
See also CA 108; MTCW 2

Lagerlof, Selma (Ottiliana Lovisa) 1858-1940
See Lagerloef, Selma (Ottiliana Lovisa)
See also CA 188; CLR 7; DLB 259; RGWL 2, 3; SATA 15; SSFS 18

La Guma, (Justin) Alex(ander) 1925-1985 . **BLCS; CLC 19; TCLC 140**
See also AFW; BW 1, 3; CA 49-52; 118; CANR 25, 81; CDWLB 3; CN 1, 2, 3; CP 1; DAM NOV; DLB 117, 225; EWL 3; MTCW 1, 2; MTFW 2005; WLIT 2; WWE 1

Laidlaw, A. K.
See Grieve, C(hristopher) M(urray)

Lainez, Manuel Mujica
See Mujica Lainez, Manuel
See also HW 1

Laing, R(onald) D(avid) 1927-1989 . **CLC 95**
See also CA 107; 129; CANR 34; MTCW 1

Laishley, Alex
See Booth, Martin

Lamartine, Alphonse (Marie Louis Prat) de 1790-1869 .... **NCLC 11; PC 16**
See also DAM POET; DLB 217; GFL 1789 to the Present; RGWL 2, 3

Lamb, Charles 1775-1834 ..... **NCLC 10, 113; WLC**
See also BRW 4; CDBLB 1789-1832; DA; DAB; DAC; DAM MST; DLB 93, 107, 163; RGEL 2; SATA 17; TEA

Lamb, Lady Caroline 1785-1828 ... **NCLC 38**
See also DLB 116

Lamb, Mary Ann 1764-1847 .... **NCLC 125**
See also DLB 163; SATA 17

Lame Deer 1903(?)-1976 .... **NNAL**
See also CA 69-72

Lamming, George (William) 1927- ... **BLC 2; CLC 2, 4, 66, 144**
See also BW 2, 3; CA 85-88; CANR 26, 76; CDWLB 3; CN 1, 2, 3, 4, 5, 6, 7; CP 1; DAM MULT; DLB 125; EWL 3; MTCW 1, 2; MTFW 2005; NFS 15; RGEL 2

L'Amour, Louis (Dearborn) 1908-1988 .... **CLC 25, 55**
See also AAYA 16; AITN 2; BEST 89:2; BPFB 2; CA 1-4R; 125; CANR 3, 25, 40; CPW; DA3; DAM NOV, POP; DLB 206; DLBY 1980; MTCW 1, 2; MTFW 2005; RGAL 4; TCWW 1, 2

Lampedusa, Giuseppe (Tomasi) di .... **TCLC 13**
See Tomasi di Lampedusa, Giuseppe
See also CA 164; EW 11; MTCW 2; MTFW 2005; RGWL 2, 3

Lampman, Archibald 1861-1899 ... **NCLC 25**
See also DLB 92; RGEL 2; TWA

Lancaster, Bruce 1896-1963 .... **CLC 36**
See also CA 9-10; CANR 70; CAP 1; SATA 9

Lanchester, John 1962- .... **CLC 99**
See also CA 194; DLB 267

Landau, Mark Alexandrovich
See Aldanov, Mark (Alexandrovich)

Author Index

Author Index

Maillet, Antonine 1929- .... **CLC 54, 118**
See also CA 115; 120; CANR 46, 74, 77, 134; CCA 1; CWW 2; DAC; DLB 60; INT CA-120; MTCW 2; MTFW 2005
Maimonides, Moses 1135-1204 ..... **CMLC 76**
See also DLB 115
Mais, Roger 1905-1955 .... **TCLC 8**
See also BW 1, 3; CA 105; 124; CANR 82; CDWLB 3; DLB 125; EWL 3; MTCW 1; RGEL 2
Maistre, Joseph 1753-1821 .... **NCLC 37**
See also GFL 1789 to the Present
Maitland, Frederic William 1850-1906 .... **TCLC 65**
Maitland, Sara (Louise) 1950- .... **CLC 49**
See also BRWS 11; CA 69-72; CANR 13, 59; DLB 271; FW
Major, Clarence 1936- ... **BLC 2; CLC 3, 19, 48**
See also AFAW 2; BW 2, 3; CA 21-24R; CAAS 6; CANR 13, 25, 53, 82; CN 3, 4, 5, 6, 7; CP 2, 3, 4, 5, 6, 7; CSW; DAM MULT; DLB 33; EWL 3; MAL 5; MSW
Major, Kevin (Gerald) 1949- .... **CLC 26**
See also AAYA 16; CA 97-100; CANR 21, 38, 112; CLR 11; DAC; DLB 60; INT CANR-21; JRDA; MAICYA 1, 2; MAICYAS 1; SATA 32, 82, 134; WYA; YAW
Maki, James
See Ozu, Yasujiro
Makine, Andrei 1957- .... **CLC 198**
See also CA 176; CANR 103; MTFW 2005
Malabaila, Damiano
See Levi, Primo
Malamud, Bernard 1914-1986 .. **CLC 1, 2, 3, 5, 8, 9, 11, 18, 27, 44, 78, 85; SSC 15; TCLC 129; WLC**
See also AAYA 16; AMWS 1; BPFB 2; BYA 15; CA 5-8R; 118; CABS 1; CANR 28, 62, 114; CDALB 1941-1968; CN 1, 2, 3, 4; CPW; DA; DA3; DAB; DAC; DAM MST, NOV, POP; DLB 2, 28, 152; DLBY 1980, 1986; EWL 3; EXPS; LAIT 4; LATS 1:1; MAL 5; MTCW 1, 2; MTFW 2005; NFS 4, 9; RGAL 4; RGSF 2; SSFS 8, 13, 16; TUS
Malan, Herman
See Bosman, Herman Charles; Bosman, Herman Charles
Malaparte, Curzio 1898-1957 .... **TCLC 52**
See also DLB 264
Malcolm, Dan
See Silverberg, Robert
Malcolm, Janet 1934- .... **CLC 201**
See also CA 123; CANR 89; NCFS 1
Malcolm X .... **BLC 2; CLC 82, 117; WLCS**
See Little, Malcolm
See also LAIT 5; NCFS 3
Malherbe, Francois de 1555-1628 .... **LC 5**
See also GFL Beginnings to 1789
Mallarme, Stephane 1842-1898 ...... **NCLC 4, 41; PC 4**
See also DAM POET; DLB 217; EW 7; GFL 1789 to the Present; LMFS 2; RGWL 2, 3; TWA
Mallet-Joris, Francoise 1930- .... **CLC 11**
See also CA 65-68; CANR 17; CWW 2; DLB 83; EWL 3; GFL 1789 to the Present
Malley, Ern
See McAuley, James Phillip
Mallon, Thomas 1951- .... **CLC 172**
See also CA 110; CANR 29, 57, 92
Mallowan, Agatha Christie
See Christie, Agatha (Mary Clarissa)
Maloff, Saul 1922- .... **CLC 5**
See also CA 33-36R
Malone, Louis
See MacNeice, (Frederick) Louis
Malone, Michael (Christopher) 1942- .... **CLC 43**
See also CA 77-80; CANR 14, 32, 57, 114
Malory, Sir Thomas 1410(?)-1471(?) . **LC 11, 88; WLCS**
See also BRW 1; BRWR 2; CDBLB Before 1660; DA; DAB; DAC; DAM MST; DLB 146; EFS 2; RGEL 2; SATA 59; SATA-Brief 33; TEA; WLIT 3
Malouf, (George Joseph) David 1934- .... **CLC 28, 86**
See also CA 124; CANR 50, 76; CN 3, 4, 5, 6, 7; CP 1, 3, 4, 5, 6, 7; DLB 289; EWL 3; MTCW 2; MTFW 2005
Malraux, (Georges-)Andre 1901-1976 .... **CLC 1, 4, 9, 13, 15, 57**
See also BPFB 2; CA 21-22; 69-72; CANR 34, 58; CAP 2; DA3; DAM NOV; DLB 72; EW 12; EWL 3; GFL 1789 to the Present; MTCW 1, 2; MTFW 2005; RGWL 2, 3; TWA
Malthus, Thomas Robert 1766-1834 .... **NCLC 145**
See also DLB 107, 158; RGEL 2
Malzberg, Barry N(athaniel) 1939- ... **CLC 7**
See also CA 61-64; CAAS 4; CANR 16; CMW 4; DLB 8; SFW 4
Mamet, David (Alan) 1947- .. **CLC 9, 15, 34, 46, 91, 166; DC 4, 24**
See also AAYA 3, 60; AMWS 14; CA 81-84; CABS 3; CAD; CANR 15, 41, 67, 72, 129; CD 5, 6; DA3; DAM DRAM; DFS 2, 3, 6, 12, 15; DLB 7; EWL 3; IDFW 4; MAL 5; MTCW 1, 2; MTFW 2005; RGAL 4
Mamoulian, Rouben (Zachary) 1897-1987 .... **CLC 16**
See also CA 25-28R; 124; CANR 85
Mandelshtam, Osip
See Mandelstam, Osip (Emilievich)
See also EW 10; EWL 3; RGWL 2, 3
Mandelstam, Osip (Emilievich) 1891(?)-1943(?) .... **PC 14; TCLC 2, 6**
See Mandelshtam, Osip
See also CA 104; 150; MTCW 2; TWA
Mander, (Mary) Jane 1877-1949 ... **TCLC 31**
See also CA 162; RGEL 2
Mandeville, Bernard 1670-1733 .... **LC 82**
See also DLB 101
Mandeville, Sir John fl. 1350- ...... **CMLC 19**
See also DLB 146
Mandiargues, Andre Pieyre de .... **CLC 41**
See Pieyre de Mandiargues, Andre
See also DLB 83
Mandrake, Ethel Belle
See Thurman, Wallace (Henry)
Mangan, James Clarence 1803-1849 .... **NCLC 27**
See also RGEL 2
Maniere, J.-E.
See Giraudoux, Jean(-Hippolyte)
Mankiewicz, Herman (Jacob) 1897-1953 .... **TCLC 85**
See also CA 120; 169; DLB 26; IDFW 3, 4
Manley, (Mary) Delariviere 1672(?)-1724 .... **LC 1, 42**
See also DLB 39, 80; RGEL 2
Mann, Abel
See Creasey, John
Mann, Emily 1952- .... **DC 7**
See also CA 130; CAD; CANR 55; CD 5, 6; CWD; DLB 266
Mann, (Luiz) Heinrich 1871-1950 ... **TCLC 9**
See also CA 106; 164, 181; DLB 66, 118; EW 8; EWL 3; RGWL 2, 3
Mann, (Paul) Thomas 1875-1955 . **SSC 5, 80, 82; TCLC 2, 8, 14, 21, 35, 44, 60, 168; WLC**
See also BPFB 2; CA 104; 128; CANR 133; CDWLB 2; DA; DA3; DAB; DAC; DAM MST, NOV; DLB 66; EW 9; EWL 3; GLL 1; LATS 1:1; LMFS 1; MTCW 1, 2; MTFW 2005; NFS 17; RGSF 2; RGWL 2, 3; SSFS 4, 9; TWA
Mannheim, Karl 1893-1947 .... **TCLC 65**
See also CA 204
Manning, David
See Faust, Frederick (Schiller)
Manning, Frederic 1882-1935 .... **TCLC 25**
See also CA 124; 216; DLB 260
Manning, Olivia 1915-1980 .... **CLC 5, 19**
See also CA 5-8R; 101; CANR 29; CN 1, 2; EWL 3; FW; MTCW 1; RGEL 2
Mannyng, Robert, of Brunne c. 1264-c. 1340 .... **CMLC 83**
See also CA 5-8R; 101; CANR 29; CN 1, 2; EWL 3; FW; MTCW 1; RGEL 2
Mano, D. Keith 1942- .... **CLC 2, 10**
See also CA 25-28R; CAAS 6; CANR 26, 57; DLB 6
Mansfield, Katherine .... **SSC 9, 23, 38, 81; TCLC 2, 8, 39, 164; WLC**
See Beauchamp, Kathleen Mansfield
See also BPFB 2; BRW 7; DAB; DLB 162; EWL 3; EXPS; FW; GLL 1; RGEL 2; RGSF 2; SSFS 2, 8, 10, 11; WWE 1
Manso, Peter 1940- .... **CLC 39**
See also CA 29-32R; CANR 44
Mantecon, Juan Jimenez
See Jimenez (Mantecon), Juan Ramon
Mantel, Hilary (Mary) 1952- .... **CLC 144**
See also CA 125; CANR 54, 101; CN 5, 6, 7; DLB 271; RHW
Manton, Peter
See Creasey, John
Man Without a Spleen, A
See Chekhov, Anton (Pavlovich)
Manzano, Juan Franciso 1797(?)-1854 .... **NCLC 155**
Manzoni, Alessandro 1785-1873 ... **NCLC 29, 98**
See also EW 5; RGWL 2, 3; TWA; WLIT 7
Map, Walter 1140-1209 .... **CMLC 32**
Mapu, Abraham (ben Jekutiel) 1808-1867 .... **NCLC 18**
Mara, Sally
See Queneau, Raymond
Maracle, Lee 1950- .... **NNAL**
See also CA 149
Marat, Jean Paul 1743-1793 .... **LC 10**
Marcel, Gabriel Honore 1889-1973 . **CLC 15**
See also CA 102; 45-48; EWL 3; MTCW 1, 2
March, William .... **TCLC 96**
See Campbell, William Edward March
See also CA 216; DLB 9, 86, 316; MAL 5
Marchbanks, Samuel
See Davies, (William) Robertson
See also CCA 1
Marchi, Giacomo
See Bassani, Giorgio
Marcus Aurelius
See Aurelius, Marcus
See also AW 2
Marguerite
See de Navarre, Marguerite
Marguerite d'Angouleme
See de Navarre, Marguerite
See also GFL Beginnings to 1789
Marguerite de Navarre
See de Navarre, Marguerite
See also RGWL 2, 3

Author Index

Massinger, Philip 1583-1640 .... **LC 70**
See also BRWS 11; DLB 58; RGEL 2

Master Lao
See Lao Tzu

Masters, Edgar Lee 1868-1950 ...... **PC 1, 36; TCLC 2, 25; WLCS**
See also AMWS 1; CA 104; 133; CDALB 1865-1917; DA; DAC; DAM MST, POET; DLB 54; EWL 3; EXPP; MAL 5; MTCW 1, 2; MTFW 2005; RGAL 4; TUS; WP

Masters, Hilary 1928- .... **CLC 48**
See also CA 25-28R, 217; CAAE 217; CANR 13, 47, 97; CN 6, 7; DLB 244

Mastrosimone, William 1947- .... **CLC 36**
See also CA 186; CAD; CD 5, 6

Mathe, Albert
See Camus, Albert

Mather, Cotton 1663-1728 .... **LC 38**
See also AMWS 2; CDALB 1640-1865; DLB 24, 30, 140; RGAL 4; TUS

Mather, Increase 1639-1723 .... **LC 38**
See also DLB 24

Matheson, Richard (Burton) 1926- .. **CLC 37**
See also AAYA 31; CA 97-100; CANR 88, 99; DLB 8, 44; HGG; INT CA-97-100; SCFW 1, 2; SFW 4; SUFW 2

Mathews, Harry (Burchell) 1930- ..... **CLC 6, 52**
See also CA 21-24R; CAAS 6; CANR 18, 40, 98; CN 5, 6, 7

Mathews, John Joseph 1894-1979 .. **CLC 84; NNAL**
See also CA 19-20; 142; CANR 45; CAP 2; DAM MULT; DLB 175; TCWW 1, 2

Mathias, Roland (Glyn) 1915- .... **CLC 45**
See also CA 97-100; CANR 19, 41; CP 1, 2, 3, 4, 5, 6, 7; DLB 27

Matsuo Basho 1644(?)-1694 ...... **LC 62; PC 3**
See Basho, Matsuo
See also DAM POET; PFS 2, 7, 18

Mattheson, Rodney
See Creasey, John

Matthews, (James) Brander 1852-1929 .... **TCLC 95**
See also CA 181; DLB 71, 78; DLBD 13

Matthews, Greg 1949- .... **CLC 45**
See also CA 135

Matthews, William (Procter III) 1942-1997 .... **CLC 40**
See also AMWS 9; CA 29-32R; 162; CAAS 18; CANR 12, 57; CP 2, 3, 4; DLB 5

Matthias, John (Edward) 1941- .... **CLC 9**
See also CA 33-36R; CANR 56; CP 4, 5, 6, 7

Matthiessen, F(rancis) O(tto) 1902-1950 .... **TCLC 100**
See also CA 185; DLB 63; MAL 5

Matthiessen, Peter 1927- ... **CLC 5, 7, 11, 32, 64**
See also AAYA 6, 40; AMWS 5; ANW; BEST 90:4; BPFB 2; CA 9-12R; CANR 21, 50, 73, 100, 138; CN 1, 2, 3, 4, 5, 6, 7; DA3; DAM NOV; DLB 6, 173, 275; MAL 5; MTCW 1, 2; MTFW 2005; SATA 27

Maturin, Charles Robert 1780(?)-1824 .... **NCLC 6, 169**
See also BRWS 8; DLB 178; GL 3; HGG; LMFS 1; RGEL 2; SUFW

Matute (Ausejo), Ana Maria 1925- .. **CLC 11**
See also CA 89-92; CANR 129; CWW 2; DLB 322; EWL 3; MTCW 1; RGSF 2

Maugham, W. S.
See Maugham, W(illiam) Somerset

Maugham, W(illiam) Somerset 1874-1965 .. **CLC 1, 11, 15, 67, 93; SSC 8; WLC**
See also AAYA 55; BPFB 2; BRW 6; CA 5-8R; 25-28R; CANR 40, 127; CDBLB 1914-1945; CMW 4; DA; DA3; DAB; DAC; DAM DRAM, MST, NOV; DFS 22; DLB 10, 36, 77, 100, 162, 195; EWL 3; LAIT 3; MTCW 1, 2; MTFW 2005; RGEL 2; RGSF 2; SATA 54; SSFS 17

Maugham, William Somerset
See Maugham, W(illiam) Somerset

Maupassant, (Henri Rene Albert) Guy de 1850-1893 . **NCLC 1, 42, 83; SSC 1, 64; WLC**
See also BYA 14; DA; DA3; DAB; DAC; DAM MST; DLB 123; EW 7; EXPS; GFL 1789 to the Present; LAIT 2; LMFS 1; RGSF 2; RGWL 2, 3; SSFS 4, 21; SUFW; TWA

Maupin, Armistead (Jones, Jr.) 1944- .... **CLC 95**
See also CA 125; 130; CANR 58, 101; CPW; DA3; DAM POP; DLB 278; GLL 1; INT CA-130; MTCW 2; MTFW 2005

Maurhut, Richard
See Traven, B.

Mauriac, Claude 1914-1996 .... **CLC 9**
See also CA 89-92; 152; CWW 2; DLB 83; EWL 3; GFL 1789 to the Present

Mauriac, Francois (Charles) 1885-1970 .... **CLC 4, 9, 56; SSC 24**
See also CA 25-28; CAP 2; DLB 65; EW 10; EWL 3; GFL 1789 to the Present; MTCW 1, 2; MTFW 2005; RGWL 2, 3; TWA

Mavor, Osborne Henry 1888-1951
See Bridie, James
See also CA 104

Maxwell, William (Keepers, Jr.) 1908-2000 .... **CLC 19**
See also AMWS 8; CA 93-96; 189; CANR 54, 95; CN 1, 2, 3, 4, 5, 6, 7; DLB 218, 278; DLBY 1980; INT CA-93-96; SATA-Obit 128

May, Elaine 1932- .... **CLC 16**
See also CA 124; 142; CAD; CWD; DLB 44

Mayakovski, Vladimir (Vladimirovich) 1893-1930 .... **TCLC 4, 18**
See Maiakovskii, Vladimir; Mayakovsky, Vladimir
See also CA 104; 158; EWL 3; MTCW 2; MTFW 2005; SFW 4; TWA

Mayakovsky, Vladimir
See Mayakovski, Vladimir (Vladimirovich)
See also EW 11; WP

Mayhew, Henry 1812-1887 .... **NCLC 31**
See also DLB 18, 55, 190

Mayle, Peter 1939(?)- .... **CLC 89**
See also CA 139; CANR 64, 109

Maynard, Joyce 1953- .... **CLC 23**
See also CA 111; 129; CANR 64

Mayne, William (James Carter) 1928- .... **CLC 12**
See also AAYA 20; CA 9-12R; CANR 37, 80, 100; CLR 25; FANT; JRDA; MAICYA 1, 2; MAICYAS 1; SAAS 11; SATA 6, 68, 122; SUFW 2; YAW

Mayo, Jim
See L'Amour, Louis (Dearborn)

Maysles, Albert 1926- .... **CLC 16**
See also CA 29-32R

Maysles, David 1932-1987 .... **CLC 16**
See also CA 191

Mazer, Norma Fox 1931- .... **CLC 26**
See also AAYA 5, 36; BYA 1, 8; CA 69-72; CANR 12, 32, 66, 129; CLR 23; JRDA; MAICYA 1, 2; SAAS 1; SATA 24, 67, 105; WYA; YAW

Mazzini, Guiseppe 1805-1872 .... **NCLC 34**

McAlmon, Robert (Menzies) 1895-1956 .... **TCLC 97**
See also CA 107; 168; DLB 4, 45; DLBD 15; GLL 1

McAuley, James Phillip 1917-1976 .. **CLC 45**
See also CA 97-100; CP 1, 2; DLB 260; RGEL 2

McBain, Ed
See Hunter, Evan
See also MSW

McBrien, William (Augustine) 1930- .... **CLC 44**
See also CA 107; CANR 90

McCabe, Patrick 1955- .... **CLC 133**
See also BRWS 9; CA 130; CANR 50, 90; CN 6, 7; DLB 194

McCaffrey, Anne 1926- .... **CLC 17**
See also AAYA 6, 34; AITN 2; BEST 89:2; BPFB 2; BYA 5; CA 25-28R, 227; CAAE 227; CANR 15, 35, 55, 96; CLR 49; CPW; DA3; DAM NOV, POP; DLB 8; JRDA; MAICYA 1, 2; MTCW 1, 2; MTFW 2005; SAAS 11; SATA 8, 70, 116, 152; SATA-Essay 152; SFW 4; SUFW 2; WYA; YAW

McCaffrey, Anne Inez
See McCaffrey, Anne

McCall, Nathan 1955(?)- .... **CLC 86**
See also AAYA 59; BW 3; CA 146; CANR 88

McCann, Arthur
See Campbell, John W(ood, Jr.)

McCann, Edson
See Pohl, Frederik

McCarthy, Charles, Jr. 1933-
See McCarthy, Cormac
See also CANR 42, 69, 101; CPW; CSW; DA3; DAM POP; MTCW 2; MTFW 2005

McCarthy, Cormac ...... **CLC 4, 57, 101, 204**
See McCarthy, Charles, Jr.
See also AAYA 41; AMWS 8; BPFB 2; CA 13-16R; CANR 10; CN 6, 7; DLB 6, 143, 256; EWL 3; LATS 1:2; MAL 5; TCLE 1:2; TCWW 2

McCarthy, Mary (Therese) 1912-1989 .. **CLC 1, 3, 5, 14, 24, 39, 59; SSC 24**
See also AMW; BPFB 2; CA 5-8R; 129; CANR 16, 50, 64; CN 1, 2, 3, 4; DA3; DLB 2; DLBY 1981; EWL 3; FW; INT CANR-16; MAL 5; MAWW; MTCW 1, 2; MTFW 2005; RGAL 4; TUS

McCartney, (James) Paul 1942- . **CLC 12, 35**
See also CA 146; CANR 111

McCauley, Stephen (D.) 1955- .... **CLC 50**
See also CA 141

McClaren, Peter .... **CLC 70**

McClure, Michael (Thomas) 1932- ... **CLC 6, 10**
See also BG 1:3; CA 21-24R; CAD; CANR 17, 46, 77, 131; CD 5, 6; CP 1, 2, 3, 4, 5, 6, 7; DLB 16; WP

McCorkle, Jill (Collins) 1958- .... **CLC 51**
See also CA 121; CANR 113; CSW; DLB 234; DLBY 1987

McCourt, Frank 1930- .... **CLC 109**
See also AAYA 61; AMWS 12; CA 157; CANR 97, 138; MTFW 2005; NCFS 1

McCourt, James 1941- .... **CLC 5**
See also CA 57-60; CANR 98

McCourt, Malachy 1931- .... **CLC 119**
See also SATA 126

McCoy, Horace (Stanley) 1897-1955 .... **TCLC 28**
See also AMWS 13; CA 108; 155; CMW 4; DLB 9

McCrae, John 1872-1918 .... **TCLC 12**
See also CA 109; DLB 92; PFS 5

McCreigh, James
See Pohl, Frederik
McCullers, (Lula) Carson (Smith) 1917-1967 .... **CLC 1, 4, 10, 12, 48, 100; SSC 9, 24; TCLC 155; WLC**
See also AAYA 21; AMW; AMWC 2; BPFB 2; CA 5-8R; 25-28R; CABS 1, 3; CANR 18, 132; CDALB 1941-1968; DA; DA3; DAB; DAC; DAM MST, NOV; DFS 5, 18; DLB 2, 7, 173, 228; EWL 3; EXPS; FW; GLL 1; LAIT 3, 4; MAL 5; MAWW; MTCW 1, 2; MTFW 2005; NFS 6, 13; RGAL 4; RGSF 2; SATA 27; SSFS 5; TUS; YAW
McCulloch, John Tyler
See Burroughs, Edgar Rice
McCullough, Colleen 1937- ...... **CLC 27, 107**
See also AAYA 36; BPFB 2; CA 81-84; CANR 17, 46, 67, 98, 139; CPW; DA3; DAM NOV, POP; MTCW 1, 2; MTFW 2005; RHW
McCunn, Ruthanne Lum 1946- .... **AAL**
See also CA 119; CANR 43, 96; DLB 312; LAIT 2; SATA 63
McDermott, Alice 1953- .... **CLC 90**
See also CA 109; CANR 40, 90, 126; CN 7; DLB 292; MTFW 2005
McElroy, Joseph (Prince) 1930- ... **CLC 5, 47**
See also CA 17-20R; CN 3, 4, 5, 6, 7
McEwan, Ian (Russell) 1948- .... **CLC 13, 66, 169**
See also BEST 90:4; BRWS 4; CA 61-64; CANR 14, 41, 69, 87, 132; CN 3, 4, 5, 6, 7; DAM NOV; DLB 14, 194, 319; HGG; MTCW 1, 2; MTFW 2005; RGSF 2; SUFW 2; TEA
McFadden, David 1940- .... **CLC 48**
See also CA 104; CP 1, 2, 3, 4, 5, 6, 7; DLB 60; INT CA-104
McFarland, Dennis 1950- .... **CLC 65**
See also CA 165; CANR 110
McGahern, John 1934- ... **CLC 5, 9, 48, 156; SSC 17**
See also CA 17-20R; CANR 29, 68, 113; CN 1, 2, 3, 4, 5, 6, 7; DLB 14, 231, 319; MTCW 1
McGinley, Patrick (Anthony) 1937- . **CLC 41**
See also CA 120; 127; CANR 56; INT CA-127
McGinley, Phyllis 1905-1978 .... **CLC 14**
See also CA 9-12R; 77-80; CANR 19; CP 1, 2; CWRI 5; DLB 11, 48; MAL 5; PFS 9, 13; SATA 2, 44; SATA-Obit 24
McGinniss, Joe 1942- .... **CLC 32**
See also AITN 2; BEST 89:2; CA 25-28R; CANR 26, 70; CPW; DLB 185; INT CANR-26
McGivern, Maureen Daly
See Daly, Maureen
McGrath, Patrick 1950- .... **CLC 55**
See also CA 136; CANR 65; CN 5, 6, 7; DLB 231; HGG; SUFW 2
McGrath, Thomas (Matthew) 1916-1990 .... **CLC 28, 59**
See also AMWS 10; CA 9-12R; 132; CANR 6, 33, 95; CP 1, 2, 3, 4; DAM POET; MAL 5; MTCW 1; SATA 41; SATA-Obit 66
McGuane, Thomas (Francis III) 1939- .... **CLC 3, 7, 18, 45, 127**
See also AITN 2; BPFB 2; CA 49-52; CANR 5, 24, 49, 94; CN 2, 3, 4, 5, 6, 7; DLB 2, 212; DLBY 1980; EWL 3; INT CANR-24; MAL 5; MTCW 1; MTFW 2005; TCWW 1, 2
McGuckian, Medbh 1950- .... **CLC 48, 174; PC 27**
See also BRWS 5; CA 143; CP 4, 5, 6, 7; CWP; DAM POET; DLB 40
McHale, Tom 1942(?)-1982 .... **CLC 3, 5**
See also AITN 1; CA 77-80; 106; CN 1, 2, 3
McHugh, Heather 1948- .... **PC 61**
See also CA 69-72; CANR 11, 28, 55, 92; CP 4, 5, 6, 7; CWP
McIlvanney, William 1936- .... **CLC 42**
See also CA 25-28R; CANR 61; CMW 4; DLB 14, 207
McIlwraith, Maureen Mollie Hunter
See Hunter, Mollie
See also SATA 2
McInerney, Jay 1955- .... **CLC 34, 112**
See also AAYA 18; BPFB 2; CA 116; 123; CANR 45, 68, 116; CN 5, 6, 7; CPW; DA3; DAM POP; DLB 292; INT CA-123; MAL 5; MTCW 2; MTFW 2005
McIntyre, Vonda N(eel) 1948- .... **CLC 18**
See also CA 81-84; CANR 17, 34, 69; MTCW 1; SFW 4; YAW
McKay, Claude .... **BLC 3; HR 1:3; PC 2; TCLC 7, 41; WLC**
See McKay, Festus Claudius
See also AFAW 1, 2; AMWS 10; DAB; DLB 4, 45, 51, 117; EWL 3; EXPP; GLL 2; LAIT 3; LMFS 2; MAL 5; PAB; PFS 4; RGAL 4; WP
McKay, Festus Claudius 1889-1948
See McKay, Claude
See also BW 1, 3; CA 104; 124; CANR 73; DA; DAC; DAM MST, MULT, NOV, POET; MTCW 1, 2; MTFW 2005; TUS
McKuen, Rod 1933- .... **CLC 1, 3**
See also AITN 1; CA 41-44R; CANR 40; CP 1
McLoughlin, R. B.
See Mencken, H(enry) L(ouis)
McLuhan, (Herbert) Marshall 1911-1980 .... **CLC 37, 83**
See also CA 9-12R; 102; CANR 12, 34, 61; DLB 88; INT CANR-12; MTCW 1, 2; MTFW 2005
McManus, Declan Patrick Aloysius
See Costello, Elvis
McMillan, Terry (L.) 1951- . **BLCS; CLC 50, 61, 112**
See also AAYA 21; AMWS 13; BPFB 2; BW 2, 3; CA 140; CANR 60, 104, 131; CN 7; CPW; DA3; DAM MULT, NOV, POP; MAL 5; MTCW 2; MTFW 2005; RGAL 4; YAW
McMurtry, Larry 1936- .... **CLC 2, 3, 7, 11, 27, 44, 127**
See also AAYA 15; AITN 2; AMWS 5; BEST 89:2; BPFB 2; CA 5-8R; CANR 19, 43, 64, 103; CDALB 1968-1988; CN 2, 3, 4, 5, 6, 7; CPW; CSW; DA3; DAM NOV, POP; DLB 2, 143, 256; DLBY 1980, 1987; EWL 3; MAL 5; MTCW 1, 2; MTFW 2005; RGAL 4; TCWW 1, 2
McNally, T. M. 1961- .... **CLC 82**
McNally, Terrence 1939- ... **CLC 4, 7, 41, 91; DC 27**
See also AAYA 62; AMWS 13; CA 45-48; CAD; CANR 2, 56, 116; CD 5, 6; DA3; DAM DRAM; DFS 16, 19; DLB 7, 249; EWL 3; GLL 1; MTCW 2; MTFW 2005
McNamer, Deirdre 1950- .... **CLC 70**
McNeal, Tom .... **CLC 119**
McNeile, Herman Cyril 1888-1937
See Sapper
See also CA 184; CMW 4; DLB 77
McNickle, (William) D'Arcy 1904-1977 .... **CLC 89; NNAL**
See also CA 9-12R; 85-88; CANR 5, 45; DAM MULT; DLB 175, 212; RGAL 4; SATA-Obit 22; TCWW 1, 2
McPhee, John (Angus) 1931- .... **CLC 36**
See also AAYA 61; AMWS 3; ANW; BEST 90:1; CA 65-68; CANR 20, 46, 64, 69, 121; CPW; DLB 185, 275; MTCW 1, 2; MTFW 2005; TUS
McPherson, James Alan 1943- . **BLCS; CLC 19, 77**
See also BW 1, 3; CA 25-28R; CAAS 17; CANR 24, 74, 140; CN 3, 4, 5, 6; CSW; DLB 38, 244; EWL 3; MTCW 1, 2; MTFW 2005; RGAL 4; RGSF 2
McPherson, William (Alexander) 1933- .... **CLC 34**
See also CA 69-72; CANR 28; INT CANR-28
McTaggart, J. McT. Ellis
See McTaggart, John McTaggart Ellis
McTaggart, John McTaggart Ellis 1866-1925 .... **TCLC 105**
See also CA 120; DLB 262
Mead, George Herbert 1863-1931 . **TCLC 89**
See also CA 212; DLB 270
Mead, Margaret 1901-1978 .... **CLC 37**
See also AITN 1; CA 1-4R; 81-84; CANR 4; DA3; FW; MTCW 1, 2; SATA-Obit 20
Meaker, Marijane (Agnes) 1927-
See Kerr, M. E.
See also CA 107; CANR 37, 63, 145; INT CA-107; JRDA; MAICYA 1, 2; MAICYAS 1; MTCW 1; SATA 20, 61, 99, 160; SATA-Essay 111; YAW
Medoff, Mark (Howard) 1940- .... **CLC 6, 23**
See also AITN 1; CA 53-56; CAD; CANR 5; CD 5, 6; DAM DRAM; DFS 4; DLB 7; INT CANR-5
Medvedev, P. N.
See Bakhtin, Mikhail Mikhailovich
Meged, Aharon
See Megged, Aharon
Meged, Aron
See Megged, Aharon
Megged, Aharon 1920- .... **CLC 9**
See also CA 49-52; CAAS 13; CANR 1, 140; EWL 3
Mehta, Deepa 1950- .... **CLC 208**
Mehta, Gita 1943- .... **CLC 179**
See also CA 225; CN 7; DNFS 2
Mehta, Ved (Parkash) 1934- .... **CLC 37**
See also CA 1-4R, 212; CAAE 212; CANR 2, 23, 69; MTCW 1; MTFW 2005
Melanchthon, Philipp 1497-1560 .... **LC 90**
See also DLB 179
Melanter
See Blackmore, R(ichard) D(oddridge)
Meleager c. 140B.C.-c. 70B.C. ...... **CMLC 53**
Melies, Georges 1861-1938 .... **TCLC 81**
Melikow, Loris
See Hofmannsthal, Hugo von
Melmoth, Sebastian
See Wilde, Oscar (Fingal O'Flahertie Wills)
Melo Neto, Joao Cabral de
See Cabral de Melo Neto, Joao
See also CWW 2; EWL 3
Meltzer, Milton 1915- .... **CLC 26**
See also AAYA 8, 45; BYA 2, 6; CA 13-16R; CANR 38, 92, 107; CLR 13; DLB 61; JRDA; MAICYA 1, 2; SAAS 1; SATA 1, 50, 80, 128; SATA-Essay 124; WYA; YAW
Melville, Herman 1819-1891 ..... **NCLC 3, 12, 29, 45, 49, 91, 93, 123, 157; SSC 1, 17, 46; WLC**
See also AAYA 25; AMW; AMWR 1; CDALB 1640-1865; DA; DA3; DAB; DAC; DAM MST, NOV; DLB 3, 74, 250, 254; EXPN; EXPS; GL 3; LAIT 1, 2; NFS 7, 9; RGAL 4; RGSF 2; SATA 59; SSFS 3; TUS

Miller, Walter M(ichael, Jr.) 1923-1996 .... **CLC 4, 30**
See also BPFB 2; CA 85-88; CANR 108; DLB 8; SCFW 1, 2; SFW 4
Millett, Kate 1934- .... **CLC 67**
See also AITN 1; CA 73-76; CANR 32, 53, 76, 110; DA3; DLB 246; FW; GLL 1; MTCW 1, 2; MTFW 2005
Millhauser, Steven (Lewis) 1943- .... **CLC 21, 54, 109; SSC 57**
See also CA 110; 111; CANR 63, 114, 133; CN 6, 7; DA3; DLB 2; FANT; INT CA-111; MAL 5; MTCW 2; MTFW 2005
Millin, Sarah Gertrude 1889-1968 ... **CLC 49**
See also CA 102; 93-96; DLB 225; EWL 3
Milne, A(lan) A(lexander) 1882-1956 .... **TCLC 6, 88**
See also BRWS 5; CA 104; 133; CLR 1, 26; CMW 4; CWRI 5; DA3; DAB; DAC; DAM MST; DLB 10, 77, 100, 160; FANT; MAICYA 1, 2; MTCW 1, 2; MTFW 2005; RGEL 2; SATA 100; WCH; YABC 1
Milner, Ron(ald) 1938-2004 ..... **BLC 3; CLC 56**
See also AITN 1; BW 1; CA 73-76; 230; CAD; CANR 24, 81; CD 5, 6; DAM MULT; DLB 38; MAL 5; MTCW 1
Milnes, Richard Monckton 1809-1885 .... **NCLC 61**
See also DLB 32, 184
Milosz, Czeslaw 1911-2004 .... **CLC 5, 11, 22, 31, 56, 82; PC 8; WLCS**
See also AAYA 62; CA 81-84; 230; CANR 23, 51, 91, 126; CDWLB 4; CWW 2; DA3; DAM MST, POET; DLB 215; EW 13; EWL 3; MTCW 1, 2; MTFW 2005; PFS 16; RGWL 2, 3
Milton, John 1608-1674 ..... **LC 9, 43, 92; PC 19, 29; WLC**
See also AAYA 65; BRW 2; BRWR 2; CDBLB 1660-1789; DA; DA3; DAB; DAC; DAM MST, POET; DLB 131, 151, 281; EFS 1; EXPP; LAIT 1; PAB; PFS 3, 17; RGEL 2; TEA; WLIT 3; WP
Min, Anchee 1957- .... **CLC 86**
See also CA 146; CANR 94, 137; MTFW 2005
Minehaha, Cornelius
See Wedekind, (Benjamin) Frank(lin)
Miner, Valerie 1947- .... **CLC 40**
See also CA 97-100; CANR 59; FW; GLL 2
Minimo, Duca
See D'Annunzio, Gabriele
Minot, Susan (Anderson) 1956- ...... **CLC 44, 159**
See also AMWS 6; CA 134; CANR 118; CN 6, 7
Minus, Ed 1938- .... **CLC 39**
See also CA 185
Mirabai 1498(?)-1550(?) .... **PC 48**
Miranda, Javier
See Bioy Casares, Adolfo
See also CWW 2
Mirbeau, Octave 1848-1917 .... **TCLC 55**
See also CA 216; DLB 123, 192; GFL 1789 to the Present
Mirikitani, Janice 1942- .... **AAL**
See also CA 211; DLB 312; RGAL 4
Mirk, John (?)-c. 1414 .... **LC 105**
See also DLB 146
Miro (Ferrer), Gabriel (Francisco Victor) 1879-1930 .... **TCLC 5**
See also CA 104; 185; DLB 322; EWL 3
Misharin, Alexandr .... **CLC 59**
Mishima, Yukio ... **CLC 2, 4, 6, 9, 27; DC 1; SSC 4; TCLC 161**
See Hiraoka, Kimitake
See also AAYA 50; BPFB 2; GLL 1; MJW; RGSF 2; RGWL 2, 3; SSFS 5, 12
Mistral, Frederic 1830-1914 .... **TCLC 51**
See also CA 122; 213; GFL 1789 to the Present
Mistral, Gabriela
See Godoy Alcayaga, Lucila
See also DLB 283; DNFS 1; EWL 3; LAW; RGWL 2, 3; WP
Mistry, Rohinton 1952- ... **CLC 71, 196; SSC 73**
See also BRWS 10; CA 141; CANR 86, 114; CCA 1; CN 6, 7; DAC; SSFS 6
Mitchell, Clyde
See Ellison, Harlan (Jay)
Mitchell, Emerson Blackhorse Barney 1945- .... **NNAL**
See also CA 45-48
Mitchell, James Leslie 1901-1935
See Gibbon, Lewis Grassic
See also CA 104; 188; DLB 15
Mitchell, Joni 1943- .... **CLC 12**
See also CA 112; CCA 1
Mitchell, Joseph (Quincy) 1908-1996 .... **CLC 98**
See also CA 77-80; 152; CANR 69; CN 1, 2, 3, 4, 5, 6; CSW; DLB 185; DLBY 1996
Mitchell, Margaret (Munnerlyn) 1900-1949 .... **TCLC 11, 170**
See also AAYA 23; BPFB 2; BYA 1; CA 109; 125; CANR 55, 94; CDALBS; DA3; DAM NOV, POP; DLB 9; LAIT 2; MAL 5; MTCW 1, 2; MTFW 2005; NFS 9; RGAL 4; RHW; TUS; WYAS 1; YAW
Mitchell, Peggy
See Mitchell, Margaret (Munnerlyn)
Mitchell, S(ilas) Weir 1829-1914 .... **TCLC 36**
See also CA 165; DLB 202; RGAL 4
Mitchell, W(illiam) O(rmond) 1914-1998 .... **CLC 25**
See also CA 77-80; 165; CANR 15, 43; CN 1, 2, 3, 4, 5, 6; DAC; DAM MST; DLB 88; TCLE 1:2
Mitchell, William (Lendrum) 1879-1936 .... **TCLC 81**
See also CA 213
Mitford, Mary Russell 1787-1855 ... **NCLC 4**
See also DLB 110, 116; RGEL 2
Mitford, Nancy 1904-1973 .... **CLC 44**
See also BRWS 10; CA 9-12R; CN 1; DLB 191; RGEL 2
Miyamoto, (Chujo) Yuriko 1899-1951 .... **TCLC 37**
See Miyamoto Yuriko
See also CA 170, 174
Miyamoto Yuriko
See Miyamoto, (Chujo) Yuriko
See also DLB 180
Miyazawa, Kenji 1896-1933 .... **TCLC 76**
See Miyazawa Kenji
See also CA 157; RGWL 3
Miyazawa Kenji
See Miyazawa, Kenji
See also EWL 3
Mizoguchi, Kenji 1898-1956 .... **TCLC 72**
See also CA 167
Mo, Timothy (Peter) 1950- .... **CLC 46, 134**
See also CA 117; CANR 128; CN 5, 6, 7; DLB 194; MTCW 1; WLIT 4; WWE 1
Modarressi, Taghi (M.) 1931-1997 ... **CLC 44**
See also CA 121; 134; INT CA-134
Modiano, Patrick (Jean) 1945- .... **CLC 18, 218**
See also CA 85-88; CANR 17, 40, 115; CWW 2; DLB 83, 299; EWL 3
Mofolo, Thomas (Mokopu) 1875(?)-1948 .... **BLC 3; TCLC 22**
See also AFW; CA 121; 153; CANR 83; DAM MULT; DLB 225; EWL 3; MTCW 2; MTFW 2005; WLIT 2
Mohr, Nicholasa 1938- .... **CLC 12; HLC 2**
See also AAYA 8, 46; CA 49-52; CANR 1, 32, 64; CLR 22; DAM MULT; DLB 145; HW 1, 2; JRDA; LAIT 5; LLW; MAICYA 2; MAICYAS 1; RGAL 4; SAAS 8; SATA 8, 97; SATA-Essay 113; WYA; YAW
Moi, Toril 1953- .... **CLC 172**
See also CA 154; CANR 102; FW
Mojtabai, A(nn) G(race) 1938- ..... **CLC 5, 9, 15, 29**
See also CA 85-88; CANR 88
Moliere 1622-1673 ..... **DC 13; LC 10, 28, 64, 125, 127; WLC**
See also DA; DA3; DAB; DAC; DAM DRAM, MST; DFS 13, 18, 20; DLB 268; EW 3; GFL Beginnings to 1789; LATS 1:1; RGWL 2, 3; TWA
Molin, Charles
See Mayne, William (James Carter)
Molnar, Ferenc 1878-1952 .... **TCLC 20**
See also CA 109; 153; CANR 83; CDWLB 4; DAM DRAM; DLB 215; EWL 3; RGWL 2, 3
Momaday, N(avarre) Scott 1934- ...... **CLC 2, 19, 85, 95, 160; NNAL; PC 25; WLCS**
See also AAYA 11, 64; AMWS 4; ANW; BPFB 2; BYA 12; CA 25-28R; CANR 14, 34, 68, 134; CDALBS; CN 2, 3, 4, 5, 6, 7; CPW; DA; DA3; DAB; DAC; DAM MST, MULT, NOV, POP; DLB 143, 175, 256; EWL 3; EXPP; INT CANR-14; LAIT 4; LATS 1:2; MAL 5; MTCW 1, 2; MTFW 2005; NFS 10; PFS 2, 11; RGAL 4; SATA 48; SATA-Brief 30; TCWW 1, 2; WP; YAW
Monette, Paul 1945-1995 .... **CLC 82**
See also AMWS 10; CA 139; 147; CN 6; GLL 1
Monroe, Harriet 1860-1936 .... **TCLC 12**
See also CA 109; 204; DLB 54, 91
Monroe, Lyle
See Heinlein, Robert A(nson)
Montagu, Elizabeth 1720-1800 .... **NCLC 7, 117**
See also FW
Montagu, Mary (Pierrepont) Wortley 1689-1762 .... **LC 9, 57; PC 16**
See also DLB 95, 101; FL 1:1; RGEL 2
Montagu, W. H.
See Coleridge, Samuel Taylor
Montague, John (Patrick) 1929- ..... **CLC 13, 46**
See also CA 9-12R; CANR 9, 69, 121; CP 1, 2, 3, 4, 5, 6, 7; DLB 40; EWL 3; MTCW 1; PFS 12; RGEL 2; TCLE 1:2
Montaigne, Michel (Eyquem) de 1533-1592 .... **LC 8, 105; WLC**
See also DA; DAB; DAC; DAM MST; EW 2; GFL Beginnings to 1789; LMFS 1; RGWL 2, 3; TWA
Montale, Eugenio 1896-1981 ... **CLC 7, 9, 18; PC 13**
See also CA 17-20R; 104; CANR 30; DLB 114; EW 11; EWL 3; MTCW 1; PFS 22; RGWL 2, 3; TWA; WLIT 7
Montesquieu, Charles-Louis de Secondat 1689-1755 .... **LC 7, 69**
See also DLB 314; EW 3; GFL Beginnings to 1789; TWA
Montessori, Maria 1870-1952 ...... **TCLC 103**
See also CA 115; 147
Montgomery, (Robert) Bruce 1921(?)-1978
See Crispin, Edmund
See also CA 179; 104; CMW 4
Montgomery, L(ucy) M(aud) 1874-1942 .... **TCLC 51, 140**
See also AAYA 12; BYA 1; CA 108; 137; CLR 8, 91; DA3; DAC; DAM MST; DLB 92; DLBD 14; JRDA; MAICYA 1, 2; MTCW 2; MTFW 2005; RGEL 2; SATA 100; TWA; WCH; WYA; YABC 1

Morton, Thomas 1579(?)-1647(?) .... **LC 72**
See also DLB 24; RGEL 2
Mosca, Gaetano 1858-1941 .... **TCLC 75**
Moses, Daniel David 1952- .... **NNAL**
See also CA 186
Mosher, Howard Frank 1943- .... **CLC 62**
See also CA 139; CANR 65, 115
Mosley, Nicholas 1923- .... **CLC 43, 70**
See also CA 69-72; CANR 41, 60, 108; CN 1, 2, 3, 4, 5, 6, 7; DLB 14, 207
Mosley, Walter 1952- .... **BLCS; CLC 97, 184**
See also AAYA 57; AMWS 13; BPFB 2; BW 2; CA 142; CANR 57, 92, 136; CMW 4; CN 7; CPW; DA3; DAM MULT, POP; DLB 306; MSW; MTCW 2; MTFW 2005
Moss, Howard 1922-1987 . **CLC 7, 14, 45, 50**
See also CA 1-4R; 123; CANR 1, 44; CP 1, 2, 3, 4; DAM POET; DLB 5
Mossgiel, Rab
See Burns, Robert
Motion, Andrew (Peter) 1952- .... **CLC 47**
See also BRWS 7; CA 146; CANR 90, 142; CP 4, 5, 6, 7; DLB 40; MTFW 2005
Motley, Willard (Francis)
1909-1965 .... **CLC 18**
See also BW 1; CA 117; 106; CANR 88; DLB 76, 143
Motoori, Norinaga 1730-1801 .... **NCLC 45**
Mott, Michael (Charles Alston)
1930- .... **CLC 15, 34**
See also CA 5-8R; CAAS 7; CANR 7, 29
Mountain Wolf Woman 1884-1960 . **CLC 92; NNAL**
See also CA 144; CANR 90
Moure, Erin 1955- .... **CLC 88**
See also CA 113; CP 7; CWP; DLB 60
Mourning Dove 1885(?)-1936 .... **NNAL**
See also CA 144; CANR 90; DAM MULT; DLB 175, 221
Mowat, Farley (McGill) 1921- .... **CLC 26**
See also AAYA 1, 50; BYA 2; CA 1-4R; CANR 4, 24, 42, 68, 108; CLR 20; CPW; DAC; DAM MST; DLB 68; INT CANR-24; JRDA; MAICYA 1, 2; MTCW 1, 2; MTFW 2005; SATA 3, 55; YAW
Mowatt, Anna Cora 1819-1870 ..... **NCLC 74**
See also RGAL 4
Moyers, Bill 1934- .... **CLC 74**
See also AITN 2; CA 61-64; CANR 31, 52
Mphahlele, Es'kia
See Mphahlele, Ezekiel
See also AFW; CDWLB 3; CN 4, 5, 6; DLB 125, 225; RGSF 2; SSFS 11
Mphahlele, Ezekiel 1919- ... **BLC 3; CLC 25, 133**
See Mphahlele, Es'kia
See also BW 2, 3; CA 81-84; CANR 26, 76; CN 1, 2, 3; DA3; DAM MULT; EWL 3; MTCW 2; MTFW 2005; SATA 119
Mqhayi, S(amuel) E(dward) K(rune Loliwe)
1875-1945 .... **BLC 3; TCLC 25**
See also CA 153; CANR 87; DAM MULT
Mrozek, Slawomir 1930- .... **CLC 3, 13**
See also CA 13-16R; CAAS 10; CANR 29; CDWLB 4; CWW 2; DLB 232; EWL 3; MTCW 1
Mrs. Belloc-Lowndes
See Lowndes, Marie Adelaide (Belloc)
Mrs. Fairstar
See Horne, Richard Henry Hengist
M'Taggart, John M'Taggart Ellis
See McTaggart, John McTaggart Ellis
Mtwa, Percy (?)- .... **CLC 47**
See also CD 6
Mueller, Lisel 1924- .... **CLC 13, 51; PC 33**
See also CA 93-96; CP 7; DLB 105; PFS 9, 13
Muggeridge, Malcolm (Thomas)
1903-1990 .... **TCLC 120**
See also AITN 1; CA 101; CANR 33, 63; MTCW 1, 2
Muhammad 570-632 .... **WLCS**
See also DA; DAB; DAC; DAM MST; DLB 311
Muir, Edwin 1887-1959 . **PC 49; TCLC 2, 87**
See Moore, Edward
See also BRWS 6; CA 104; 193; DLB 20, 100, 191; EWL 3; RGEL 2
Muir, John 1838-1914 .... **TCLC 28**
See also AMWS 9; ANW; CA 165; DLB 186, 275
Mujica Lainez, Manuel 1910-1984 ... **CLC 31**
See Lainez, Manuel Mujica
See also CA 81-84; 112; CANR 32; EWL 3; HW 1
Mukherjee, Bharati 1940- ..... **AAL; CLC 53, 115; SSC 38**
See also AAYA 46; BEST 89:2; CA 107, 232; CAAE 232; CANR 45, 72, 128; CN 5, 6, 7; DAM NOV; DLB 60, 218; DNFS 1, 2; EWL 3; FW; MAL 5; MTCW 1, 2; MTFW 2005; RGAL 4; RGSF 2; SSFS 7; TUS; WWE 1
Muldoon, Paul 1951- .... **CLC 32, 72, 166**
See also BRWS 4; CA 113; 129; CANR 52, 91; CP 2, 3, 4, 5, 6, 7; DAM POET; DLB 40; INT CA-129; PFS 7, 22; TCLE 1:2
Mulisch, Harry (Kurt Victor)
1927- .... **CLC 42**
See also CA 9-12R; CANR 6, 26, 56, 110; CWW 2; DLB 299; EWL 3
Mull, Martin 1943- .... **CLC 17**
See also CA 105
Muller, Wilhelm .... **NCLC 73**
Mulock, Dinah Maria
See Craik, Dinah Maria (Mulock)
See also RGEL 2
Multatuli 1820-1887 .... **NCLC 165**
See also RGWL 2, 3
Munday, Anthony 1560-1633 .... **LC 87**
See also DLB 62, 172; RGEL 2
Munford, Robert 1737(?)-1783 .... **LC 5**
See also DLB 31
Mungo, Raymond 1946- .... **CLC 72**
See also CA 49-52; CANR 2
Munro, Alice (Anne) 1931- .... **CLC 6, 10, 19, 50, 95, 222; SSC 3; WLCS**
See also AITN 2; BPFB 2; CA 33-36R; CANR 33, 53, 75, 114; CCA 1; CN 1, 2, 3, 4, 5, 6, 7; DA3; DAC; DAM MST, NOV; DLB 53; EWL 3; MTCW 1, 2; MTFW 2005; RGEL 2; RGSF 2; SATA 29; SSFS 5, 13, 19; TCLE 1:2; WWE 1
Munro, H(ector) H(ugh) 1870-1916 .... **WLC**
See Saki
See also AAYA 56; CA 104; 130; CANR 104; CDBLB 1890-1914; DA; DA3; DAB; DAC; DAM MST, NOV; DLB 34, 162; EXPS; MTCW 1, 2; MTFW 2005; RGEL 2; SSFS 15
Murakami, Haruki 1949- .... **CLC 150**
See Murakami Haruki
See also CA 165; CANR 102, 146; MJW; RGWL 3; SFW 4
Murakami Haruki
See Murakami, Haruki
See also CWW 2; DLB 182; EWL 3
Murasaki, Lady
See Murasaki Shikibu
Murasaki Shikibu 978(?)-1026(?) .. **CMLC 1, 79**
See also EFS 2; LATS 1:1; RGWL 2, 3
Murdoch, (Jean) Iris 1919-1999 ... **CLC 1, 2, 3, 4, 6, 8, 11, 15, 22, 31, 51; TCLC 171**
See also BRWS 1; CA 13-16R; 179; CANR 8, 43, 68, 103, 142; CBD; CDBLB 1960 to Present; CN 1, 2, 3, 4, 5, 6; CWD; DA3; DAB; DAC; DAM MST, NOV; DLB 14, 194, 233; EWL 3; INT CANR-8; MTCW 1, 2; MTFW 2005; NFS 18; RGEL 2; TCLE 1:2; TEA; WLIT 4
Murfree, Mary Noailles 1850-1922 .. **SSC 22; TCLC 135**
See also CA 122; 176; DLB 12, 74; RGAL 4
Murnau, Friedrich Wilhelm
See Plumpe, Friedrich Wilhelm
Murphy, Richard 1927- .... **CLC 41**
See also BRWS 5; CA 29-32R; CP 1, 2, 3, 4, 5, 6, 7; DLB 40; EWL 3
Murphy, Sylvia 1937- .... **CLC 34**
See also CA 121
Murphy, Thomas (Bernard) 1935- ... **CLC 51**
See Murphy, Tom
See also CA 101
Murphy, Tom
See Murphy, Thomas (Bernard)
See also DLB 310
Murray, Albert L. 1916- .... **CLC 73**
See also BW 2; CA 49-52; CANR 26, 52, 78; CN 7; CSW; DLB 38; MTFW 2005
Murray, James Augustus Henry
1837-1915 .... **TCLC 117**
Murray, Judith Sargent
1751-1820 .... **NCLC 63**
See also DLB 37, 200
Murray, Les(lie Allan) 1938- .... **CLC 40**
See also BRWS 7; CA 21-24R; CANR 11, 27, 56, 103; CP 1, 2, 3, 4, 5, 6, 7; DAM POET; DLB 289; DLBY 2001; EWL 3; RGEL 2
Murry, J. Middleton
See Murry, John Middleton
Murry, John Middleton
1889-1957 .... **TCLC 16**
See also CA 118; 217; DLB 149
Musgrave, Susan 1951- .... **CLC 13, 54**
See also CA 69-72; CANR 45, 84; CCA 1; CP 2, 3, 4, 5, 6, 7; CWP
Musil, Robert (Edler von)
1880-1942 .... **SSC 18; TCLC 12, 68**
See also CA 109; CANR 55, 84; CDWLB 2; DLB 81, 124; EW 9; EWL 3; MTCW 2; RGSF 2; RGWL 2, 3
Muske, Carol .... **CLC 90**
See Muske-Dukes, Carol (Anne)
Muske-Dukes, Carol (Anne) 1945-
See Muske, Carol
See also CA 65-68, 203; CAAE 203; CANR 32, 70; CWP
Musset, (Louis Charles) Alfred de
1810-1857 .... **DC 27; NCLC 7, 150**
See also DLB 192, 217; EW 6; GFL 1789 to the Present; RGWL 2, 3; TWA
Mussolini, Benito (Amilcare Andrea)
1883-1945 .... **TCLC 96**
See also CA 116
Mutanabbi, Al-
See al-Mutanabbi, Ahmad ibn al-Husayn Abu al-Tayyib al-Jufi al-Kindi
See also WLIT 6
My Brother's Brother
See Chekhov, Anton (Pavlovich)
Myers, L(eopold) H(amilton)
1881-1944 .... **TCLC 59**
See also CA 157; DLB 15; EWL 3; RGEL 2
Myers, Walter Dean 1937- .. **BLC 3; CLC 35**
See also AAYA 4, 23; BW 2; BYA 6, 8, 11; CA 33-36R; CANR 20, 42, 67, 108; CLR 4, 16, 35; DAM MULT, NOV; DLB 33;

Author Index

Niedecker, Lorine 1903-1970 ..... **CLC 10, 42; PC 42**
See also CA 25-28; CAP 2; DAM POET; DLB 48
Nietzsche, Friedrich (Wilhelm) 1844-1900 .... **TCLC 10, 18, 55**
See also CA 107; 121; CDWLB 2; DLB 129; EW 7; RGWL 2, 3; TWA
Nievo, Ippolito 1831-1861 .... **NCLC 22**
Nightingale, Anne Redmon 1943-
See Redmon, Anne
See also CA 103
Nightingale, Florence 1820-1910 ... **TCLC 85**
See also CA 188; DLB 166
Nijo Yoshimoto 1320-1388 .... **CMLC 49**
See also DLB 203
Nik. T. O.
See Annensky, Innokenty (Fyodorovich)
Nin, Anais 1903-1977 ..... **CLC 1, 4, 8, 11, 14, 60, 127; SSC 10**
See also AITN 2; AMWS 10; BPFB 2; CA 13-16R; 69-72; CANR 22, 53; CN 1, 2; DAM NOV, POP; DLB 2, 4, 152; EWL 3; GLL 2; MAL 5; MAWW; MTCW 1, 2; MTFW 2005; RGAL 4; RGSF 2
Nisbet, Robert A(lexander) 1913-1996 .... **TCLC 117**
See also CA 25-28R; 153; CANR 17; INT CANR-17
Nishida, Kitaro 1870-1945 .... **TCLC 83**
Nishiwaki, Junzaburo 1894-1982 .... **PC 15**
See Junzaburo, Nishiwaki
See also CA 194; 107; MJW; RGWL 3
Nissenson, Hugh 1933- .... **CLC 4, 9**
See also CA 17-20R; CANR 27, 108; CN 5, 6; DLB 28
Nister, Der
See Der Nister
See also EWL 3
Niven, Larry .... **CLC 8**
See Niven, Laurence Van Cott
See also AAYA 27; BPFB 2; BYA 10; DLB 8; SCFW 1, 2
Niven, Laurence Van Cott 1938-
See Niven, Larry
See also CA 21-24R, 207; CAAE 207; CAAS 12; CANR 14, 44, 66, 113; CPW; DAM POP; MTCW 1, 2; SATA 95; SFW 4
Nixon, Agnes Eckhardt 1927- .... **CLC 21**
See also CA 110
Nizan, Paul 1905-1940 .... **TCLC 40**
See also CA 161; DLB 72; EWL 3; GFL 1789 to the Present
Nkosi, Lewis 1936- .... **BLC 3; CLC 45**
See also BW 1, 3; CA 65-68; CANR 27, 81; CBD; CD 5, 6; DAM MULT; DLB 157, 225; WWE 1
Nodier, (Jean) Charles (Emmanuel) 1780-1844 .... **NCLC 19**
See also DLB 119; GFL 1789 to the Present
Noguchi, Yone 1875-1947 .... **TCLC 80**
Nolan, Christopher 1965- .... **CLC 58**
See also CA 111; CANR 88
Noon, Jeff 1957- .... **CLC 91**
See also CA 148; CANR 83; DLB 267; SFW 4
Norden, Charles
See Durrell, Lawrence (George)
Nordhoff, Charles Bernard 1887-1947 .... **TCLC 23**
See also CA 108; 211; DLB 9; LAIT 1; RHW 1; SATA 23
Norfolk, Lawrence 1963- .... **CLC 76**
See also CA 144; CANR 85; CN 6, 7; DLB 267
Norman, Marsha (Williams) 1947- . **CLC 28, 186; DC 8**
See also CA 105; CABS 3; CAD; CANR 41, 131; CD 5, 6; CSW; CWD; DAM DRAM; DFS 2; DLB 266; DLBY 1984; FW; MAL 5
Normyx
See Douglas, (George) Norman
Norris, (Benjamin) Frank(lin, Jr.) 1870-1902 .... **SSC 28; TCLC 24, 155**
See also AAYA 57; AMW; AMWC 2; BPFB 2; CA 110; 160; CDALB 1865-1917; DLB 12, 71, 186; LMFS 2; NFS 12; RGAL 4; TCWW 1, 2; TUS
Norris, Leslie 1921- .... **CLC 14**
See also CA 11-12; CANR 14, 117; CAP 1; CP 1, 2, 3, 4, 5, 6, 7; DLB 27, 256
North, Andrew
See Norton, Andre
North, Anthony
See Koontz, Dean R.
North, Captain George
See Stevenson, Robert Louis (Balfour)
North, Captain George
See Stevenson, Robert Louis (Balfour)
North, Milou
See Erdrich, (Karen) Louise
Northrup, B. A.
See Hubbard, L(afayette) Ron(ald)
North Staffs
See Hulme, T(homas) E(rnest)
Northup, Solomon 1808-1863 ...... **NCLC 105**
Norton, Alice Mary
See Norton, Andre
See also MAICYA 1; SATA 1, 43
Norton, Andre 1912-2005 .... **CLC 12**
See Norton, Alice Mary
See also AAYA 14; BPFB 2; BYA 4, 10, 12; CA 1-4R; 237; CANR 68; CLR 50; DLB 8, 52; JRDA; MAICYA 2; MTCW 1; SATA 91; SUFW 1, 2; YAW
Norton, Caroline 1808-1877 .... **NCLC 47**
See also DLB 21, 159, 199
Norway, Nevil Shute 1899-1960
See Shute, Nevil
See also CA 102; 93-96; CANR 85; MTCW 2
Norwid, Cyprian Kamil 1821-1883 .... **NCLC 17**
See also RGWL 3
Nosille, Nabrah
See Ellison, Harlan (Jay)
Nossack, Hans Erich 1901-1978 .... **CLC 6**
See also CA 93-96; 85-88; DLB 69; EWL 3
Nostradamus 1503-1566 .... **LC 27**
Nosu, Chuji
See Ozu, Yasujiro
Notenburg, Eleanora (Genrikhovna) von
See Guro, Elena (Genrikhovna)
Nova, Craig 1945- .... **CLC 7, 31**
See also CA 45-48; CANR 2, 53, 127
Novak, Joseph
See Kosinski, Jerzy (Nikodem)
Novalis 1772-1801 .... **NCLC 13**
See also CDWLB 2; DLB 90; EW 5; RGWL 2, 3
Novick, Peter 1934- .... **CLC 164**
See also CA 188
Novis, Emile
See Weil, Simone (Adolphine)
Nowlan, Alden (Albert) 1933-1983 ... **CLC 15**
See also CA 9-12R; CANR 5; CP 1, 2, 3; DAC; DAM MST; DLB 53; PFS 12
Noyes, Alfred 1880-1958 ...... **PC 27; TCLC 7**
See also CA 104; 188; DLB 20; EXPP; FANT; PFS 4; RGEL 2
Nugent, Richard Bruce 1906(?)-1987 .... **HR 1:3**
See also BW 1; CA 125; DLB 51; GLL 2
Nunn, Kem .... **CLC 34**
See also CA 159
Nussbaum, Martha Craven 1947- .. **CLC 203**
See also CA 134; CANR 102
Nwapa, Flora (Nwanzuruaha) 1931-1993 .... **BLCS; CLC 133**
See also BW 2; CA 143; CANR 83; CDWLB 3; CWRI 5; DLB 125; EWL 3; WLIT 2
Nye, Robert 1939- .... **CLC 13, 42**
See also BRWS 10; CA 33-36R; CANR 29, 67, 107; CN 1, 2, 3, 4, 5, 6, 7; CP 1, 2, 3, 4, 5, 6, 7; CWRI 5; DAM NOV; DLB 14, 271; FANT; HGG; MTCW 1; RHW; SATA 6
Nyro, Laura 1947-1997 .... **CLC 17**
See also CA 194
Oates, Joyce Carol 1938- .. **CLC 1, 2, 3, 6, 9, 11, 15, 19, 33, 52, 108, 134; SSC 6, 70; WLC**
See also AAYA 15, 52; AITN 1; AMWS 2; BEST 89:2; BPFB 2; BYA 11; CA 5-8R; CANR 25, 45, 74, 113, 129; CDALB 1968-1988; CN 1, 2, 3, 4, 5, 6, 7; CP 7; CPW; CWP; DA; DA3; DAB; DAC; DAM MST, NOV, POP; DLB 2, 5, 130; DLBY 1981; EWL 3; EXPS; FL 1:6; FW; GL 3; HGG; INT CANR-25; LAIT 4; MAL 5; MAWW; MTCW 1, 2; MTFW 2005; NFS 8; RGAL 4; RGSF 2; SATA 159; SSFS 1, 8, 17; SUFW 2; TUS
O'Brian, E. G.
See Clarke, Arthur C(harles)
O'Brian, Patrick 1914-2000 .... **CLC 152**
See also AAYA 55; CA 144; 187; CANR 74; CPW; MTCW 2; MTFW 2005; RHW
O'Brien, Darcy 1939-1998 .... **CLC 11**
See also CA 21-24R; 167; CANR 8, 59
O'Brien, Edna 1932- ..... **CLC 3, 5, 8, 13, 36, 65, 116; SSC 10, 77**
See also BRWS 5; CA 1-4R; CANR 6, 41, 65, 102; CDBLB 1960 to Present; CN 1, 2, 3, 4, 5, 6, 7; DA3; DAM NOV; DLB 14, 231, 319; EWL 3; FW; MTCW 1, 2; MTFW 2005; RGSF 2; WLIT 4
O'Brien, Fitz-James 1828-1862 ..... **NCLC 21**
See also DLB 74; RGAL 4; SUFW
O'Brien, Flann .... **CLC 1, 4, 5, 7, 10, 47**
See O Nuallain, Brian
See also BRWS 2; DLB 231; EWL 3; RGEL 2
O'Brien, Richard 1942- .... **CLC 17**
See also CA 124
O'Brien, (William) Tim(othy) 1946- . **CLC 7, 19, 40, 103, 211; SSC 74**
See also AAYA 16; AMWS 5; CA 85-88; CANR 40, 58, 133; CDALBS; CN 5, 6, 7; CPW; DA3; DAM POP; DLB 152; DLBD 9; DLBY 1980; LATS 1:2; MAL 5; MTCW 2; MTFW 2005; RGAL 4; SSFS 5, 15; TCLE 1:2
Obstfelder, Sigbjoern 1866-1900 .... **TCLC 23**
See also CA 123
O'Casey, Sean 1880-1964 .... **CLC 1, 5, 9, 11, 15, 88; DC 12; WLCS**
See also BRW 7; CA 89-92; CANR 62; CBD; CDBLB 1914-1945; DA3; DAB; DAC; DAM DRAM, MST; DFS 19; DLB 10; EWL 3; MTCW 1, 2; MTFW 2005; RGEL 2; TEA; WLIT 4
O'Cathasaigh, Sean
See O'Casey, Sean
Occom, Samson 1723-1792 .... **LC 60; NNAL**
See also DLB 175
Ochs, Phil(ip David) 1940-1976 .... **CLC 17**
See also CA 185; 65-68

Ortiz, Simon J(oseph) 1941- ... **CLC 45, 208; NNAL; PC 17**
See also AMWS 4; CA 134; CANR 69, 118; CP 3, 4, 5, 6, 7; DAM MULT, POET; DLB 120, 175, 256; EXPP; MAL 5; PFS 4, 16; RGAL 4; TCWW 2
Orton, Joe ...... **CLC 4, 13, 43; DC 3; TCLC 157**
See Orton, John Kingsley
See also BRWS 5; CBD; CDBLB 1960 to Present; DFS 3, 6; DLB 13, 310; GLL 1; RGEL 2; TEA; WLIT 4
Orton, John Kingsley 1933-1967
See Orton, Joe
See also CA 85-88; CANR 35, 66; DAM DRAM; MTCW 1, 2; MTFW 2005
Orwell, George ...... **SSC 68; TCLC 2, 6, 15, 31, 51, 128, 129; WLC**
See Blair, Eric (Arthur)
See also BPFB 3; BRW 7; BYA 5; CDBLB 1945-1960; CLR 68; DAB; DLB 15, 98, 195, 255; EWL 3; EXPN; LAIT 4, 5; LATS 1:1; NFS 3, 7; RGEL 2; SCFW 1, 2; SFW 4; SSFS 4; TEA; WLIT 4; YAW
Osborne, David
See Silverberg, Robert
Osborne, George
See Silverberg, Robert
Osborne, John (James) 1929-1994 .... **CLC 1, 2, 5, 11, 45; TCLC 153; WLC**
See also BRWS 1; CA 13-16R; 147; CANR 21, 56; CBD; CDBLB 1945-1960; DA; DAB; DAC; DAM DRAM, MST; DFS 4, 19; DLB 13; EWL 3; MTCW 1, 2; MTFW 2005; RGEL 2
Osborne, Lawrence 1958- .... **CLC 50**
See also CA 189
Osbourne, Lloyd 1868-1947 .... **TCLC 93**
Osgood, Frances Sargent 1811-1850 .... **NCLC 141**
See also DLB 250
Oshima, Nagisa 1932- .... **CLC 20**
See also CA 116; 121; CANR 78
Oskison, John Milton 1874-1947 .... **NNAL; TCLC 35**
See also CA 144; CANR 84; DAM MULT; DLB 175
Ossian c. 3rd cent. - .... **CMLC 28**
See Macpherson, James
Ossoli, Sarah Margaret (Fuller) 1810-1850 .... **NCLC 5, 50**
See Fuller, Margaret; Fuller, Sarah Margaret
See also CDALB 1640-1865; FW; LMFS 1; SATA 25
Ostriker, Alicia (Suskin) 1937- .... **CLC 132**
See also CA 25-28R; CAAS 24; CANR 10, 30, 62, 99; CWP; DLB 120; EXPP; PFS 19
Ostrovsky, Aleksandr Nikolaevich
See Ostrovsky, Alexander
See also DLB 277
Ostrovsky, Alexander 1823-1886 .. **NCLC 30, 57**
See Ostrovsky, Aleksandr Nikolaevich
Otero, Blas de 1916-1979 .... **CLC 11**
See also CA 89-92; DLB 134; EWL 3
O'Trigger, Sir Lucius
See Horne, Richard Henry Hengist
Otto, Rudolf 1869-1937 .... **TCLC 85**
Otto, Whitney 1955- .... **CLC 70**
See also CA 140; CANR 120
Otway, Thomas 1652-1685 ... **DC 24; LC 106**
See also DAM DRAM; DLB 80; RGEL 2
Ouida .... **TCLC 43**
See De la Ramee, Marie Louise (Ouida)
See also DLB 18, 156; RGEL 2
Ouologuem, Yambo 1940- .... **CLC 146**
See also CA 111; 176
Ousmane, Sembene 1923- ... **BLC 3; CLC 66**
See Sembene, Ousmane
See also BW 1, 3; CA 117; 125; CANR 81; CWW 2; MTCW 1
Ovid 43B.C.-17 .... **CMLC 7; PC 2**
See also AW 2; CDWLB 1; DA3; DAM POET; DLB 211; PFS 22; RGWL 2, 3; WP
Owen, Hugh
See Faust, Frederick (Schiller)
Owen, Wilfred (Edward Salter) 1893-1918 ... **PC 19; TCLC 5, 27; WLC**
See also BRW 6; CA 104; 141; CDBLB 1914-1945; DA; DAB; DAC; DAM MST, POET; DLB 20; EWL 3; EXPP; MTCW 2; MTFW 2005; PFS 10; RGEL 2; WLIT 4
Owens, Louis (Dean) 1948-2002 .... **NNAL**
See also CA 137, 179; 207; CAAE 179; CAAS 24; CANR 71
Owens, Rochelle 1936- .... **CLC 8**
See also CA 17-20R; CAAS 2; CAD; CANR 39; CD 5, 6; CP 1, 2, 3, 4, 5, 6, 7; CWD; CWP
Oz, Amos 1939- ...... **CLC 5, 8, 11, 27, 33, 54; SSC 66**
See also CA 53-56; CANR 27, 47, 65, 113, 138; CWW 2; DAM NOV; EWL 3; MTCW 1, 2; MTFW 2005; RGSF 2; RGWL 3; WLIT 6
Ozick, Cynthia 1928- .... **CLC 3, 7, 28, 62, 155; SSC 15, 60**
See also AMWS 5; BEST 90:1; CA 17-20R; CANR 23, 58, 116; CN 3, 4, 5, 6, 7; CPW; DA3; DAM NOV, POP; DLB 28, 152, 299; DLBY 1982; EWL 3; EXPS; INT CANR-23; MAL 5; MTCW 1, 2; MTFW 2005; RGAL 4; RGSF 2; SSFS 3, 12
Ozu, Yasujiro 1903-1963 .... **CLC 16**
See also CA 112
Pabst, G. W. 1885-1967 .... **TCLC 127**
Pacheco, C.
See Pessoa, Fernando (Antonio Nogueira)
Pacheco, Jose Emilio 1939- .... **HLC 2**
See also CA 111; 131; CANR 65; CWW 2; DAM MULT; DLB 290; EWL 3; HW 1, 2; RGSF 2
Pa Chin .... **CLC 18**
See Li Fei-kan
See also EWL 3
Pack, Robert 1929- .... **CLC 13**
See also CA 1-4R; CANR 3, 44, 82; CP 1, 2, 3, 4, 5, 6, 7; DLB 5; SATA 118
Padgett, Lewis
See Kuttner, Henry
Padilla (Lorenzo), Heberto 1932-2000 .... **CLC 38**
See also AITN 1; CA 123; 131; 189; CWW 2; EWL 3; HW 1
Page, James Patrick 1944-
See Page, Jimmy
See also CA 204
Page, Jimmy 1944- .... **CLC 12**
See Page, James Patrick
Page, Louise 1955- .... **CLC 40**
See also CA 140; CANR 76; CBD; CD 5, 6; CWD; DLB 233
Page, P(atricia) K(athleen) 1916- ...... **CLC 7, 18; PC 12**
See Cape, Judith
See also CA 53-56; CANR 4, 22, 65; CP 1, 2, 3, 4, 5, 6, 7; DAC; DAM MST; DLB 68; MTCW 1; RGEL 2
Page, Stanton
See Fuller, Henry Blake
Page, Stanton
See Fuller, Henry Blake
Page, Thomas Nelson 1853-1922 .... **SSC 23**
See also CA 118; 177; DLB 12, 78; DLBD 13; RGAL 4
Pagels, Elaine Hiesey 1943- .... **CLC 104**
See also CA 45-48; CANR 2, 24, 51; FW; NCFS 4
Paget, Violet 1856-1935
See Lee, Vernon
See also CA 104; 166; GLL 1; HGG
Paget-Lowe, Henry
See Lovecraft, H(oward) P(hillips)
Paglia, Camille (Anna) 1947- .... **CLC 68**
See also CA 140; CANR 72, 139; CPW; FW; GLL 2; MTCW 2; MTFW 2005
Paige, Richard
See Koontz, Dean R.
Paine, Thomas 1737-1809 .... **NCLC 62**
See also AMWS 1; CDALB 1640-1865; DLB 31, 43, 73, 158; LAIT 1; RGAL 4; RGEL 2; TUS
Pakenham, Antonia
See Fraser, Antonia (Pakenham)
Palamas, Costis
See Palamas, Kostes
Palamas, Kostes 1859-1943 .... **TCLC 5**
See Palamas, Kostis
See also CA 105; 190; RGWL 2, 3
Palamas, Kostis
See Palamas, Kostes
See also EWL 3
Palazzeschi, Aldo 1885-1974 .... **CLC 11**
See also CA 89-92; 53-56; DLB 114, 264; EWL 3
Pales Matos, Luis 1898-1959 .... **HLCS 2**
See Pales Matos, Luis
See also DLB 290; HW 1; LAW
Paley, Grace 1922- .... **CLC 4, 6, 37, 140; SSC 8**
See also AMWS 6; CA 25-28R; CANR 13, 46, 74, 118; CN 2, 3, 4, 5, 6, 7; CPW; DA3; DAM POP; DLB 28, 218; EWL 3; EXPS; FW; INT CANR-13; MAL 5; MAWW; MTCW 1, 2; MTFW 2005; RGAL 4; RGSF 2; SSFS 3, 20
Palin, Michael (Edward) 1943- .... **CLC 21**
See Monty Python
See also CA 107; CANR 35, 109; SATA 67
Palliser, Charles 1947- .... **CLC 65**
See also CA 136; CANR 76; CN 5, 6, 7
Palma, Ricardo 1833-1919 .... **TCLC 29**
See also CA 168; LAW
Pamuk, Orhan 1952- .... **CLC 185**
See also CA 142; CANR 75, 127; CWW 2; WLIT 6
Pancake, Breece Dexter 1952-1979
See Pancake, Breece D'J
See also CA 123; 109
Pancake, Breece D'J .... **CLC 29; SSC 61**
See Pancake, Breece Dexter
See also DLB 130
Panchenko, Nikolai .... **CLC 59**
Pankhurst, Emmeline (Goulden) 1858-1928 .... **TCLC 100**
See also CA 116; FW
Panko, Rudy
See Gogol, Nikolai (Vasilyevich)
Papadiamantis, Alexandros 1851-1911 .... **TCLC 29**
See also CA 168; EWL 3
Papadiamantopoulos, Johannes 1856-1910
See Moreas, Jean
See also CA 117
Papini, Giovanni 1881-1956 .... **TCLC 22**
See also CA 121; 180; DLB 264
Paracelsus 1493-1541 .... **LC 14**
See also DLB 179
Parasol, Peter
See Stevens, Wallace

Author Index

Pardo Bazan, Emilia 1851-1921 .... **SSC 30**
See also EWL 3; FW; RGSF 2; RGWL 2, 3
Pareto, Vilfredo 1848-1923 .... **TCLC 69**
See also CA 175
Paretsky, Sara 1947- .... **CLC 135**
See also AAYA 30; BEST 90:3; CA 125; 129; CANR 59, 95; CMW 4; CPW; DA3; DAM POP; DLB 306; INT CA-129; MSW; RGAL 4
Parfenie, Maria
See Codrescu, Andrei
Parini, Jay (Lee) 1948- .... **CLC 54, 133**
See also CA 97-100, 229; CAAE 229; CAAS 16; CANR 32, 87
Park, Jordan
See Kornbluth, C(yril) M.; Pohl, Frederik
Park, Robert E(zra) 1864-1944 ..... **TCLC 73**
See also CA 122; 165
Parker, Bert
See Ellison, Harlan (Jay)
Parker, Dorothy (Rothschild)
1893-1967 . **CLC 15, 68; PC 28; SSC 2; TCLC 143**
See also AMWS 9; CA 19-20; 25-28R; CAP 2; DA3; DAM POET; DLB 11, 45, 86; EXPP; FW; MAL 5; MAWW; MTCW 1, 2; MTFW 2005; PFS 18; RGAL 4; RGSF 2; TUS
Parker, Robert B(rown) 1932- .... **CLC 27**
See also AAYA 28; BEST 89:4; BPFB 3; CA 49-52; CANR 1, 26, 52, 89, 128; CMW 4; CPW; DAM NOV, POP; DLB 306; INT CANR-26; MSW; MTCW 1; MTFW 2005
Parkin, Frank 1940- .... **CLC 43**
See also CA 147
Parkman, Francis, Jr. 1823-1893 .. **NCLC 12**
See also AMWS 2; DLB 1, 30, 183, 186, 235; RGAL 4
Parks, Gordon (Alexander Buchanan)
1912- .... **BLC 3; CLC 1, 16**
See also AAYA 36; AITN 2; BW 2, 3; CA 41-44R; CANR 26, 66, 145; DA3; DAM MULT; DLB 33; MTCW 2; MTFW 2005; SATA 8, 108
Parks, Suzan-Lori 1964(?)- .... **DC 23**
See also AAYA 55; CA 201; CAD; CD 5, 6; CWD; DFS 22; RGAL 4
Parks, Tim(othy Harold) 1954- ...... **CLC 147**
See also CA 126; 131; CANR 77, 144; CN 7; DLB 231; INT CA-131
Parmenides c. 515B.C.-c. 450B.C. .... **CMLC 22**
See also DLB 176
Parnell, Thomas 1679-1718 .... **LC 3**
See also DLB 95; RGEL 2
Parr, Catherine c. 1513(?)-1548 .... **LC 86**
See also DLB 136
Parra, Nicanor 1914- ... **CLC 2, 102; HLC 2; PC 39**
See also CA 85-88; CANR 32; CWW 2; DAM MULT; DLB 283; EWL 3; HW 1; LAW; MTCW 1
Parra Sanojo, Ana Teresa de la
1890-1936 .... **HLCS 2**
See de la Parra, (Ana) Teresa (Sonojo)
See also LAW
Parrish, Mary Frances
See Fisher, M(ary) F(rances) K(ennedy)
Parshchikov, Aleksei 1954- .... **CLC 59**
See Parshchikov, Aleksei Maksimovich
Parshchikov, Aleksei Maksimovich
See Parshchikov, Aleksei
See also DLB 285
Parson, Professor
See Coleridge, Samuel Taylor
Parson Lot
See Kingsley, Charles
Parton, Sara Payson Willis
1811-1872 .... **NCLC 86**
See also DLB 43, 74, 239
Partridge, Anthony
See Oppenheim, E(dward) Phillips
Pascal, Blaise 1623-1662 .... **LC 35**
See also DLB 268; EW 3; GFL Beginnings to 1789; RGWL 2, 3; TWA
Pascoli, Giovanni 1855-1912 .... **TCLC 45**
See also CA 170; EW 7; EWL 3
Pasolini, Pier Paolo 1922-1975 .. **CLC 20, 37, 106; PC 17**
See also CA 93-96; 61-64; CANR 63; DLB 128, 177; EWL 3; MTCW 1; RGWL 2, 3
Pasquini
See Silone, Ignazio
Pastan, Linda (Olenik) 1932- .... **CLC 27**
See also CA 61-64; CANR 18, 40, 61, 113; CP 3, 4, 5, 6, 7; CSW; CWP; DAM POET; DLB 5; PFS 8
Pasternak, Boris (Leonidovich)
1890-1960 ...... **CLC 7, 10, 18, 63; PC 6; SSC 31; WLC**
See also BPFB 3; CA 127; 116; DA; DA3; DAB; DAC; DAM MST, NOV, POET; DLB 302; EW 10; MTCW 1, 2; MTFW 2005; RGSF 2; RGWL 2, 3; TWA; WP
Patchen, Kenneth 1911-1972 .... **CLC 1, 2, 18**
See also BG 1:3; CA 1-4R; 33-36R; CANR 3, 35; CN 1; CP 1; DAM POET; DLB 16, 48; EWL 3; MAL 5; MTCW 1; RGAL 4
Pater, Walter (Horatio) 1839-1894 . **NCLC 7, 90, 159**
See also BRW 5; CDBLB 1832-1890; DLB 57, 156; RGEL 2; TEA
Paterson, A(ndrew) B(arton)
1864-1941 .... **TCLC 32**
See also CA 155; DLB 230; RGEL 2; SATA 97
Paterson, Banjo
See Paterson, A(ndrew) B(arton)
Paterson, Katherine (Womeldorf)
1932- .... **CLC 12, 30**
See also AAYA 1, 31; BYA 1, 2, 7; CA 21-24R; CANR 28, 59, 111; CLR 7, 50; CWRI 5; DLB 52; JRDA; LAIT 4; MAICYA 1, 2; MAICYAS 1; MTCW 1; SATA 13, 53, 92, 133; WYA; YAW
Patmore, Coventry Kersey Dighton
1823-1896 .... **NCLC 9; PC 59**
See also DLB 35, 98; RGEL 2; TEA
Paton, Alan (Stewart) 1903-1988 ...... **CLC 4, 10, 25, 55, 106; TCLC 165; WLC**
See also AAYA 26; AFW; BPFB 3; BRWS 2; BYA 1; CA 13-16; 125; CANR 22; CAP 1; CN 1, 2, 3, 4; DA; DA3; DAB; DAC; DAM MST, NOV; DLB 225; DLBD 17; EWL 3; EXPN; LAIT 4; MTCW 1, 2; MTFW 2005; NFS 3, 12; RGEL 2; SATA 11; SATA-Obit 56; TWA; WLIT 2; WWE 1
Paton Walsh, Gillian 1937- .... **CLC 35**
See Paton Walsh, Jill; Walsh, Jill Paton
See also AAYA 11; CANR 38, 83; CLR 2, 65; DLB 161; JRDA; MAICYA 1, 2; SAAS 3; SATA 4, 72, 109; YAW
Paton Walsh, Jill
See Paton Walsh, Gillian
See also AAYA 47; BYA 1, 8
Patterson, (Horace) Orlando (Lloyd)
1940- .... **BLCS**
See also BW 1; CA 65-68; CANR 27, 84; CN 1, 2, 3, 4, 5, 6
Patton, George S(mith), Jr.
1885-1945 .... **TCLC 79**
See also CA 189
Paulding, James Kirke 1778-1860 ... **NCLC 2**
See also DLB 3, 59, 74, 250; RGAL 4
Paulin, Thomas Neilson 1949-
See Paulin, Tom
See also CA 123; 128; CANR 98
Paulin, Tom .... **CLC 37, 177**
See Paulin, Thomas Neilson
See also CP 3, 4, 5, 6, 7; DLB 40
Pausanias c. 1st cent. - .... **CMLC 36**
Paustovsky, Konstantin (Georgievich)
1892-1968 .... **CLC 40**
See also CA 93-96; 25-28R; DLB 272; EWL 3
Pavese, Cesare 1908-1950 .... **PC 13; SSC 19; TCLC 3**
See also CA 104; 169; DLB 128, 177; EW 12; EWL 3; PFS 20; RGSF 2; RGWL 2, 3; TWA; WLIT 7
Pavic, Milorad 1929- .... **CLC 60**
See also CA 136; CDWLB 4; CWW 2; DLB 181; EWL 3; RGWL 3
Pavlov, Ivan Petrovich 1849-1936 . **TCLC 91**
See also CA 118; 180
Pavlova, Karolina Karlovna
1807-1893 .... **NCLC 138**
See also DLB 205
Payne, Alan
See Jakes, John (William)
Payne, Rachel Ann
See Jakes, John (William)
Paz, Gil
See Lugones, Leopoldo
Paz, Octavio 1914-1998 . **CLC 3, 4, 6, 10, 19, 51, 65, 119; HLC 2; PC 1, 48; WLC**
See also AAYA 50; CA 73-76; 165; CANR 32, 65, 104; CWW 2; DA; DA3; DAB; DAC; DAM MST, MULT, POET; DLB 290; DLBY 1990, 1998; DNFS 1; EWL 3; HW 1, 2; LAW; LAWS 1; MTCW 1, 2; MTFW 2005; PFS 18; RGWL 2, 3; SSFS 13; TWA; WLIT 1
p'Bitek, Okot 1931-1982 .... **BLC 3; CLC 96; TCLC 149**
See also AFW; BW 2, 3; CA 124; 107; CANR 82; CP 1, 2, 3; DAM MULT; DLB 125; EWL 3; MTCW 1, 2; MTFW 2005; RGEL 2; WLIT 2
Peabody, Elizabeth Palmer
1804-1894 .... **NCLC 169**
See also DLB 1, 223
Peacham, Henry 1578-1644(?) .... **LC 119**
See also DLB 151
Peacock, Molly 1947- .... **CLC 60**
See also CA 103; CAAS 21; CANR 52, 84; CP 7; CWP; DLB 120, 282
Peacock, Thomas Love
1785-1866 .... **NCLC 22**
See also BRW 4; DLB 96, 116; RGEL 2; RGSF 2
Peake, Mervyn 1911-1968 .... **CLC 7, 54**
See also CA 5-8R; 25-28R; CANR 3; DLB 15, 160, 255; FANT; MTCW 1; RGEL 2; SATA 23; SFW 4
Pearce, Philippa
See Christie, Philippa
See also CA 5-8R; CANR 4, 109; CWRI 5; FANT; MAICYA 2
Pearl, Eric
See Elman, Richard (Martin)
Pearson, T(homas) R(eid) 1956- .... **CLC 39**
See also CA 120; 130; CANR 97; CSW; INT CA-130
Peck, Dale 1967- .... **CLC 81**
See also CA 146; CANR 72, 127; GLL 2
Peck, John (Frederick) 1941- .... **CLC 3**
See also CA 49-52; CANR 3, 100; CP 4, 5, 6, 7

Peck, Richard (Wayne) 1934- .... **CLC 21**
See also AAYA 1, 24; BYA 1, 6, 8, 11; CA 85-88; CANR 19, 38, 129; CLR 15; INT CANR-19; JRDA; MAICYA 1, 2; SAAS 2; SATA 18, 55, 97, 110, 158; SATA-Essay 110; WYA; YAW
Peck, Robert Newton 1928- .... **CLC 17**
See also AAYA 3, 43; BYA 1, 6; CA 81-84, 182; CAAE 182; CANR 31, 63, 127; CLR 45; DA; DAC; DAM MST; JRDA; LAIT 3; MAICYA 1, 2; SAAS 1; SATA 21, 62, 111, 156; SATA-Essay 108; WYA; YAW
Peckinpah, (David) Sam(uel) 1925-1984 .... **CLC 20**
See also CA 109; 114; CANR 82
Pedersen, Knut 1859-1952
See Hamsun, Knut
See also CA 104; 119; CANR 63; MTCW 1, 2
Peele, George 1556-1596 .... **DC 27; LC 115**
See also BRW 1; DLB 62, 167; RGEL 2
Peeslake, Gaffer
See Durrell, Lawrence (George)
Peguy, Charles (Pierre) 1873-1914 .... **TCLC 10**
See also CA 107; 193; DLB 258; EWL 3; GFL 1789 to the Present
Peirce, Charles Sanders 1839-1914 .... **TCLC 81**
See also CA 194; DLB 270
Pellicer, Carlos 1897(?)-1977 .... **HLCS 2**
See also CA 153; 69-72; DLB 290; EWL 3; HW 1
Pena, Ramon del Valle y
See Valle-Inclan, Ramon (Maria) del
Pendennis, Arthur Esquir
See Thackeray, William Makepeace
Penn, Arthur
See Matthews, (James) Brander
Penn, William 1644-1718 .... **LC 25**
See also DLB 24
PEPECE
See Prado (Calvo), Pedro
Pepys, Samuel 1633-1703 ... **LC 11, 58; WLC**
See also BRW 2; CDBLB 1660-1789; DA; DA3; DAB; DAC; DAM MST; DLB 101, 213; NCFS 4; RGEL 2; TEA; WLIT 3
Percy, Thomas 1729-1811 .... **NCLC 95**
See also DLB 104
Percy, Walker 1916-1990 .... **CLC 2, 3, 6, 8, 14, 18, 47, 65**
See also AMWS 3; BPFB 3; CA 1-4R; 131; CANR 1, 23, 64; CN 1, 2, 3, 4; CPW; CSW; DA3; DAM NOV, POP; DLB 2; DLBY 1980, 1990; EWL 3; MAL 5; MTCW 1, 2; MTFW 2005; RGAL 4; TUS
Percy, William Alexander 1885-1942 .... **TCLC 84**
See also CA 163; MTCW 2
Perec, Georges 1936-1982 .... **CLC 56, 116**
See also CA 141; DLB 83, 299; EWL 3; GFL 1789 to the Present; RGWL 3
Pereda (y Sanchez de Porrua), Jose Maria de 1833-1906 .... **TCLC 16**
See also CA 117
Pereda y Porrua, Jose Maria de
See Pereda (y Sanchez de Porrua), Jose Maria de
Peregoy, George Weems
See Mencken, H(enry) L(ouis)
Perelman, S(idney) J(oseph) 1904-1979 .. **CLC 3, 5, 9, 15, 23, 44, 49; SSC 32**
See also AITN 1, 2; BPFB 3; CA 73-76; 89-92; CANR 18; DAM DRAM; DLB 11, 44; MTCW 1, 2; MTFW 2005; RGAL 4
Peret, Benjamin 1899-1959 .... **PC 33; TCLC 20**
See also CA 117; 186; GFL 1789 to the Present
Peretz, Isaac Leib
See Peretz, Isaac Loeb
See also CA 201
Peretz, Isaac Loeb 1851(?)-1915 ...... **SSC 26; TCLC 16**
See Peretz, Isaac Leib
See also CA 109
Peretz, Yitzkhok Leibush
See Peretz, Isaac Loeb
Perez Galdos, Benito 1843-1920 ..... **HLCS 2; TCLC 27**
See Galdos, Benito Perez
See also CA 125; 153; EWL 3; HW 1; RGWL 2, 3
Peri Rossi, Cristina 1941- .... **CLC 156; HLCS 2**
See also CA 131; CANR 59, 81; CWW 2; DLB 145, 290; EWL 3; HW 1, 2
Perlata
See Peret, Benjamin
Perloff, Marjorie G(abrielle) 1931- .... **CLC 137**
See also CA 57-60; CANR 7, 22, 49, 104
Perrault, Charles 1628-1703 .... **LC 2, 56**
See also BYA 4; CLR 79; DLB 268; GFL Beginnings to 1789; MAICYA 1, 2; RGWL 2, 3; SATA 25; WCH
Perry, Anne 1938- .... **CLC 126**
See also CA 101; CANR 22, 50, 84; CMW 4; CN 6, 7; CPW; DLB 276
Perry, Brighton
See Sherwood, Robert E(mmet)
Perse, St.-John
See Leger, (Marie-Rene Auguste) Alexis Saint-Leger
Perse, Saint-John
See Leger, (Marie-Rene Auguste) Alexis Saint-Leger
See also DLB 258; RGWL 3
Persius 34-62 .... **CMLC 74**
See also AW 2; DLB 211; RGWL 2, 3
Perutz, Leo(pold) 1882-1957 .... **TCLC 60**
See also CA 147; DLB 81
Peseenz, Tulio F.
See Lopez y Fuentes, Gregorio
Pesetsky, Bette 1932- .... **CLC 28**
See also CA 133; DLB 130
Peshkov, Alexei Maximovich 1868-1936
See Gorky, Maxim
See also CA 105; 141; CANR 83; DA; DAC; DAM DRAM, MST, NOV; MTCW 2; MTFW 2005
Pessoa, Fernando (Antonio Nogueira) 1888-1935 ..... **HLC 2; PC 20; TCLC 27**
See also CA 125; 183; DAM MULT; DLB 287; EW 10; EWL 3; RGWL 2, 3; WP
Peterkin, Julia Mood 1880-1961 ...... **CLC 31**
See also CA 102; DLB 9
Peters, Joan K(aren) 1945- .... **CLC 39**
See also CA 158; CANR 109
Peters, Robert L(ouis) 1924- .... **CLC 7**
See also CA 13-16R; CAAS 8; CP 1, 7; DLB 105
Petofi, Sandor 1823-1849 .... **NCLC 21**
See also RGWL 2, 3
Petrakis, Harry Mark 1923- .... **CLC 3**
See also CA 9-12R; CANR 4, 30, 85; CN 1, 2, 3, 4, 5, 6, 7
Petrarch 1304-1374 .... **CMLC 20; PC 8**
See also DA3; DAM POET; EW 2; LMFS 1; RGWL 2, 3; WLIT 7
Petronius c. 20-66 .... **CMLC 34**
See also AW 2; CDWLB 1; DLB 211; RGWL 2, 3
Petrov, Evgeny .... **TCLC 21**
See Kataev, Evgeny Petrovich
Petry, Ann (Lane) 1908-1997 .. **CLC 1, 7, 18; TCLC 112**
See also AFAW 1, 2; BPFB 3; BW 1, 3; BYA 2; CA 5-8R; 157; CAAS 6; CANR 4, 46; CLR 12; CN 1, 2, 3, 4, 5, 6; DLB 76; EWL 3; JRDA; LAIT 1; MAICYA 1, 2; MAICYAS 1; MTCW 1; RGAL 4; SATA 5; SATA-Obit 94; TUS
Petursson, Halligrimur 1614-1674 .... **LC 8**
Peychinovich
See Vazov, Ivan (Minchov)
Phaedrus c. 15B.C.-c. 50 .... **CMLC 25**
See also DLB 211
Phelps (Ward), Elizabeth Stuart
See Phelps, Elizabeth Stuart
See also FW
Phelps, Elizabeth Stuart 1844-1911 .... **TCLC 113**
See Phelps (Ward), Elizabeth Stuart
See also DLB 74
Philips, Katherine 1632-1664 . **LC 30; PC 40**
See also DLB 131; RGEL 2
Philipson, Morris H. 1926- .... **CLC 53**
See also CA 1-4R; CANR 4
Phillips, Caryl 1958- .... **BLCS; CLC 96**
See also BRWS 5; BW 2; CA 141; CANR 63, 104, 140; CBD; CD 5, 6; CN 5, 6, 7; DA3; DAM MULT; DLB 157; EWL 3; MTCW 2; MTFW 2005; WLIT 4; WWE 1
Phillips, David Graham 1867-1911 .... **TCLC 44**
See also CA 108; 176; DLB 9, 12, 303; RGAL 4
Phillips, Jack
See Sandburg, Carl (August)
Phillips, Jayne Anne 1952- .... **CLC 15, 33, 139; SSC 16**
See also AAYA 57; BPFB 3; CA 101; CANR 24, 50, 96; CN 4, 5, 6, 7; CSW; DLBY 1980; INT CANR-24; MTCW 1, 2; MTFW 2005; RGAL 4; RGSF 2; SSFS 4
Phillips, Richard
See Dick, Philip K(indred)
Phillips, Robert (Schaeffer) 1938- .... **CLC 28**
See also CA 17-20R; CAAS 13; CANR 8; DLB 105
Phillips, Ward
See Lovecraft, H(oward) P(hillips)
Philostratus, Flavius c. 179-c. 244 .... **CMLC 62**
Piccolo, Lucio 1901-1969 .... **CLC 13**
See also CA 97-100; DLB 114; EWL 3
Pickthall, Marjorie L(owry) C(hristie) 1883-1922 .... **TCLC 21**
See also CA 107; DLB 92
Pico della Mirandola, Giovanni 1463-1494 .... **LC 15**
See also LMFS 1
Piercy, Marge 1936- .... **CLC 3, 6, 14, 18, 27, 62, 128; PC 29**
See also BPFB 3; CA 21-24R, 187; CAAE 187; CAAS 1; CANR 13, 43, 66, 111; CN 3, 4, 5, 6, 7; CP 1, 2, 3, 4, 5, 6, 7; CWP; DLB 120, 227; EXPP; FW; MAL 5; MTCW 1, 2; MTFW 2005; PFS 9, 22; SFW 4
Piers, Robert
See Anthony, Piers
Pieyre de Mandiargues, Andre 1909-1991
See Mandiargues, Andre Pieyre de
See also CA 103; 136; CANR 22, 82; EWL 3; GFL 1789 to the Present
Pilnyak, Boris 1894-1938 . **SSC 48; TCLC 23**
See Vogau, Boris Andreyevich
See also EWL 3

Author Index

Radcliffe, Ann (Ward) 1764-1823 ... **NCLC 6, 55, 106**
See also DLB 39, 178; GL 3; HGG; LMFS 1; RGEL 2; SUFW; WLIT 3
Radclyffe-Hall, Marguerite
See Hall, (Marguerite) Radclyffe
Radiguet, Raymond 1903-1923 ...... **TCLC 29**
See also CA 162; DLB 65; EWL 3; GFL 1789 to the Present; RGWL 2, 3
Radnoti, Miklos 1909-1944 .... **TCLC 16**
See also CA 118; 212; CDWLB 4; DLB 215; EWL 3; RGWL 2, 3
Rado, James 1939- .... **CLC 17**
See also CA 105
Radvanyi, Netty 1900-1983
See Seghers, Anna
See also CA 85-88; 110; CANR 82
Rae, Ben
See Griffiths, Trevor
Raeburn, John (Hay) 1941- .... **CLC 34**
See also CA 57-60
Ragni, Gerome 1942-1991 .... **CLC 17**
See also CA 105; 134
Rahv, Philip .... **CLC 24**
See Greenberg, Ivan
See also DLB 137; MAL 5
Raimund, Ferdinand Jakob 1790-1836 .... **NCLC 69**
See also DLB 90
Raine, Craig (Anthony) 1944- .. **CLC 32, 103**
See also CA 108; CANR 29, 51, 103; CP 3, 4, 5, 6, 7; DLB 40; PFS 7
Raine, Kathleen (Jessie) 1908-2003 .. **CLC 7, 45**
See also CA 85-88; 218; CANR 46, 109; CP 1, 2, 3, 4, 5, 6, 7; DLB 20; EWL 3; MTCW 1; RGEL 2
Rainis, Janis 1865-1929 .... **TCLC 29**
See also CA 170; CDWLB 4; DLB 220; EWL 3
Rakosi, Carl .... **CLC 47**
See Rawley, Callman
See also CA 228; CAAS 5; CP 1, 2, 3, 4, 5, 6, 7; DLB 193
Ralegh, Sir Walter
See Raleigh, Sir Walter
See also BRW 1; RGEL 2; WP
Raleigh, Richard
See Lovecraft, H(oward) P(hillips)
Raleigh, Sir Walter 1554(?)-1618 .... **LC 31, 39; PC 31**
See Ralegh, Sir Walter
See also CDBLB Before 1660; DLB 172; EXPP; PFS 14; TEA
Rallentando, H. P.
See Sayers, Dorothy L(eigh)
Ramal, Walter
See de la Mare, Walter (John)
Ramana Maharshi 1879-1950 .... **TCLC 84**
Ramoacn y Cajal, Santiago 1852-1934 .... **TCLC 93**
Ramon, Juan
See Jimenez (Mantecon), Juan Ramon
Ramos, Graciliano 1892-1953 .... **TCLC 32**
See also CA 167; DLB 307; EWL 3; HW 2; LAW; WLIT 1
Rampersad, Arnold 1941- .... **CLC 44**
See also BW 2, 3; CA 127; 133; CANR 81; DLB 111; INT CA-133
Rampling, Anne
See Rice, Anne
See also GLL 2
Ramsay, Allan 1686(?)-1758 .... **LC 29**
See also DLB 95; RGEL 2
Ramsay, Jay
See Campbell, (John) Ramsey
Ramuz, Charles-Ferdinand 1878-1947 .... **TCLC 33**
See also CA 165; EWL 3
Rand, Ayn 1905-1982 ...... **CLC 3, 30, 44, 79; WLC**
See also AAYA 10; AMWS 4; BPFB 3; BYA 12; CA 13-16R; 105; CANR 27, 73; CDALBS; CN 1, 2, 3; CPW; DA; DA3; DAC; DAM MST, NOV, POP; DLB 227, 279; MTCW 1, 2; MTFW 2005; NFS 10, 16; RGAL 4; SFW 4; TUS; YAW
Randall, Dudley (Felker) 1914-2000 . **BLC 3; CLC 1, 135**
See also BW 1, 3; CA 25-28R; 189; CANR 23, 82; CP 1, 2, 3, 4; DAM MULT; DLB 41; PFS 5
Randall, Robert
See Silverberg, Robert
Ranger, Ken
See Creasey, John
Rank, Otto 1884-1939 .... **TCLC 115**
Ransom, John Crowe 1888-1974 .. **CLC 2, 4, 5, 11, 24; PC 61**
See also AMW; CA 5-8R; 49-52; CANR 6, 34; CDALBS; CP 1, 2; DA3; DAM POET; DLB 45, 63; EWL 3; EXPP; MAL 5; MTCW 1, 2; MTFW 2005; RGAL 4; TUS
Rao, Raja 1909- .... **CLC 25, 56**
See also CA 73-76; CANR 51; CN 1, 2, 3, 4, 5, 6; DAM NOV; EWL 3; MTCW 1, 2; MTFW 2005; RGEL 2; RGSF 2
Raphael, Frederic (Michael) 1931- ... **CLC 2, 14**
See also CA 1-4R; CANR 1, 86; CN 1, 2, 3, 4, 5, 6, 7; DLB 14, 319; TCLE 1:2
Ratcliffe, James P.
See Mencken, H(enry) L(ouis)
Rathbone, Julian 1935- .... **CLC 41**
See also CA 101; CANR 34, 73
Rattigan, Terence (Mervyn) 1911-1977 .... **CLC 7; DC 18**
See also BRWS 7; CA 85-88; 73-76; CBD; CDBLB 1945-1960; DAM DRAM; DFS 8; DLB 13; IDFW 3, 4; MTCW 1, 2; MTFW 2005; RGEL 2
Ratushinskaya, Irina 1954- .... **CLC 54**
See also CA 129; CANR 68; CWW 2
Raven, Simon (Arthur Noel) 1927-2001 .... **CLC 14**
See also CA 81-84; 197; CANR 86; CN 1, 2, 3, 4, 5, 6; DLB 271
Ravenna, Michael
See Welty, Eudora (Alice)
Rawley, Callman 1903-2004
See Rakosi, Carl
See also CA 21-24R; 228; CANR 12, 32, 91
Rawlings, Marjorie Kinnan 1896-1953 .... **TCLC 4**
See also AAYA 20; AMWS 10; ANW; BPFB 3; BYA 3; CA 104; 137; CANR 74; CLR 63; DLB 9, 22, 102; DLBD 17; JRDA; MAICYA 1, 2; MAL 5; MTCW 2; MTFW 2005; RGAL 4; SATA 100; WCH; YABC 1; YAW
Ray, Satyajit 1921-1992 .... **CLC 16, 76**
See also CA 114; 137; DAM MULT
Read, Herbert Edward 1893-1968 ..... **CLC 4**
See also BRW 6; CA 85-88; 25-28R; DLB 20, 149; EWL 3; PAB; RGEL 2
Read, Piers Paul 1941- .... **CLC 4, 10, 25**
See also CA 21-24R; CANR 38, 86; CN 2, 3, 4, 5, 6, 7; DLB 14; SATA 21
Reade, Charles 1814-1884 .... **NCLC 2, 74**
See also DLB 21; RGEL 2
Reade, Hamish
See Gray, Simon (James Holliday)
Reading, Peter 1946- .... **CLC 47**
See also BRWS 8; CA 103; CANR 46, 96; CP 7; DLB 40
Reaney, James 1926- .... **CLC 13**
See also CA 41-44R; CAAS 15; CANR 42; CD 5, 6; CP 1, 2, 3, 4, 5, 6, 7; DAC; DAM MST; DLB 68; RGEL 2; SATA 43
Rebreanu, Liviu 1885-1944 .... **TCLC 28**
See also CA 165; DLB 220; EWL 3
Rechy, John (Francisco) 1934- ...... **CLC 1, 7, 14, 18, 107; HLC 2**
See also CA 5-8R, 195; CAAE 195; CAAS 4; CANR 6, 32, 64; CN 1, 2, 3, 4, 5, 6, 7; DAM MULT; DLB 122, 278; DLBY 1982; HW 1, 2; INT CANR-6; LLW; MAL 5; RGAL 4
Redcam, Tom 1870-1933 .... **TCLC 25**
Reddin, Keith 1956- .... **CLC 67**
See also CAD; CD 6
Redgrove, Peter (William) 1932-2003 .... **CLC 6, 41**
See also BRWS 6; CA 1-4R; 217; CANR 3, 39, 77; CP 1, 2, 3, 4, 5, 6, 7; DLB 40; TCLE 1:2
Redmon, Anne .... **CLC 22**
See Nightingale, Anne Redmon
See also DLBY 1986
Reed, Eliot
See Ambler, Eric
Reed, Ishmael (Scott) 1938- . **BLC 3; CLC 2, 3, 5, 6, 13, 32, 60, 174; PC 68**
See also AFAW 1, 2; AMWS 10; BPFB 3; BW 2, 3; CA 21-24R; CANR 25, 48, 74, 128; CN 1, 2, 3, 4, 5, 6, 7; CP 1, 2, 3, 4, 5, 6, 7; CSW; DA3; DAM MULT; DLB 2, 5, 33, 169, 227; DLBD 8; EWL 3; LMFS 2; MAL 5; MSW; MTCW 1, 2; MTFW 2005; PFS 6; RGAL 4; TCWW 2
Reed, John (Silas) 1887-1920 .... **TCLC 9**
See also CA 106; 195; MAL 5; TUS
Reed, Lou .... **CLC 21**
See Firbank, Louis
Reese, Lizette Woodworth 1856-1935 . **PC 29**
See also CA 180; DLB 54
Reeve, Clara 1729-1807 .... **NCLC 19**
See also DLB 39; RGEL 2
Reich, Wilhelm 1897-1957 .... **TCLC 57**
See also CA 199
Reid, Christopher (John) 1949- .... **CLC 33**
See also CA 140; CANR 89; CP 4, 5, 6, 7; DLB 40; EWL 3
Reid, Desmond
See Moorcock, Michael (John)
Reid Banks, Lynne 1929-
See Banks, Lynne Reid
See also AAYA 49; CA 1-4R; CANR 6, 22, 38, 87; CLR 24; CN 1, 2, 3, 7; JRDA; MAICYA 1, 2; SATA 22, 75, 111, 165; YAW
Reilly, William K.
See Creasey, John
Reiner, Max
See Caldwell, (Janet Miriam) Taylor (Holland)
Reis, Ricardo
See Pessoa, Fernando (Antonio Nogueira)
Reizenstein, Elmer Leopold
See Rice, Elmer (Leopold)
See also EWL 3
Remarque, Erich Maria 1898-1970 . **CLC 21**
See also AAYA 27; BPFB 3; CA 77-80; 29-32R; CDWLB 2; DA; DA3; DAB; DAC; DAM MST, NOV; DLB 56; EWL 3; EXPN; LAIT 3; MTCW 1, 2; MTFW 2005; NFS 4; RGWL 2, 3
Remington, Frederic S(ackrider) 1861-1909 .... **TCLC 89**
See also CA 108; 169; DLB 12, 186, 188; SATA 41; TCWW 2
Remizov, A.
See Remizov, Aleksei (Mikhailovich)

Sheed, Wilfrid (John Joseph) 1930- . **CLC 2, 4, 10, 53**
See also CA 65-68; CANR 30, 66; CN 1, 2, 3, 4, 5, 6, 7; DLB 6; MAL 5; MTCW 1, 2; MTFW 2005
Sheehy, Gail 1937- .... **CLC 171**
See also CA 49-52; CANR 1, 33, 55, 92; CPW; MTCW 1
Sheldon, Alice Hastings Bradley
1915(?)-1987
See Tiptree, James, Jr.
See also CA 108; 122; CANR 34; INT CA-108; MTCW 1
Sheldon, John
See Bloch, Robert (Albert)
Sheldon, Walter J(ames) 1917-1996
See Queen, Ellery
See also AITN 1; CA 25-28R; CANR 10
Shelley, Mary Wollstonecraft (Godwin)
1797-1851 ...... **NCLC 14, 59, 103; WLC**
See also AAYA 20; BPFB 3; BRW 3; BRWC 2; BRWS 3; BYA 5; CDBLB 1789-1832; DA; DA3; DAB; DAC; DAM MST, NOV; DLB 110, 116, 159, 178; EXPN; FL 1:3; GL 3; HGG; LAIT 1; LMFS 1, 2; NFS 1; RGEL 2; SATA 29; SCFW 1, 2; SFW 4; TEA; WLIT 3
Shelley, Percy Bysshe 1792-1822 .. **NCLC 18, 93, 143; PC 14, 67; WLC**
See also AAYA 61; BRW 4; BRWR 1; CDBLB 1789-1832; DA; DA3; DAB; DAC; DAM MST, POET; DLB 96, 110, 158; EXPP; LMFS 1; PAB; PFS 2; RGEL 2; TEA; WLIT 3; WP
Shepard, James R. .... **CLC 36**
See also CA 137; CANR 59, 104; SATA 90, 164
Shepard, Jim
See Shepard, James R.
Shepard, Lucius 1947- .... **CLC 34**
See also CA 128; 141; CANR 81, 124; HGG; SCFW 2; SFW 4; SUFW 2
Shepard, Sam 1943- .... **CLC 4, 6, 17, 34, 41, 44, 169; DC 5**
See also AAYA 1, 58; AMWS 3; CA 69-72; CABS 3; CAD; CANR 22, 120, 140; CD 5, 6; DA3; DAM DRAM; DFS 3, 6, 7, 14; DLB 7, 212; EWL 3; IDFW 3, 4; MAL 5; MTCW 1, 2; MTFW 2005; RGAL 4
Shepherd, Jean Parker
1921-1999 .... **TCLC 177**
See also AITN 2; CA 77-80, 187
Shepherd, Michael
See Ludlum, Robert
Sherburne, Zoa (Lillian Morin)
1912-1995 .... **CLC 30**
See also AAYA 13; CA 1-4R; 176; CANR 3, 37; MAICYA 1, 2; SAAS 18; SATA 3; YAW
Sheridan, Frances 1724-1766 .... **LC 7**
See also DLB 39, 84
Sheridan, Richard Brinsley
1751-1816 .... **DC 1; NCLC 5, 91; WLC**
See also BRW 3; CDBLB 1660-1789; DA; DAB; DAC; DAM DRAM, MST; DFS 15; DLB 89; WLIT 3
Sherman, Jonathan Marc 1968- .... **CLC 55**
See also CA 230
Sherman, Martin 1941(?)- .... **CLC 19**
See also CA 116; 123; CAD; CANR 86; CD 5, 6; DFS 20; DLB 228; GLL 1; IDTP
Sherwin, Judith Johnson
See Johnson, Judith (Emlyn)
See also CANR 85; CP 2, 3, 4; CWP
Sherwood, Frances 1940- .... **CLC 81**
See also CA 146, 220; CAAE 220
Sherwood, Robert E(mmet)
1896-1955 .... **TCLC 3**
See also CA 104; 153; CANR 86; DAM DRAM; DFS 11, 15, 17; DLB 7, 26, 249; IDFW 3, 4; MAL 5; RGAL 4
Shestov, Lev 1866-1938 .... **TCLC 56**
Shevchenko, Taras 1814-1861 .... **NCLC 54**
Shiel, M(atthew) P(hipps)
1865-1947 .... **TCLC 8**
See Holmes, Gordon
See also CA 106; 160; DLB 153; HGG; MTCW 2; MTFW 2005; SCFW 1, 2; SFW 4; SUFW
Shields, Carol (Ann) 1935-2003 ...... **CLC 91, 113, 193**
See also AMWS 7; CA 81-84; 218; CANR 51, 74, 98, 133; CCA 1; CN 6, 7; CPW; DA3; DAC; MTCW 2; MTFW 2005
Shields, David (Jonathan) 1956- ...... **CLC 97**
See also CA 124; CANR 48, 99, 112
Shiga, Naoya 1883-1971 .... **CLC 33; SSC 23; TCLC 172**
See Shiga Naoya
See also CA 101; 33-36R; MJW; RGWL 3
Shiga Naoya
See Shiga, Naoya
See also DLB 180; EWL 3; RGWL 3
Shilts, Randy 1951-1994 .... **CLC 85**
See also AAYA 19; CA 115; 127; 144; CANR 45; DA3; GLL 1; INT CA-127; MTCW 2; MTFW 2005
Shimazaki, Haruki 1872-1943
See Shimazaki Toson
See also CA 105; 134; CANR 84; RGWL 3
Shimazaki Toson .... **TCLC 5**
See Shimazaki, Haruki
See also DLB 180; EWL 3
Shirley, James 1596-1666 .... **DC 25; LC 96**
See also DLB 58; RGEL 2
Sholokhov, Mikhail (Aleksandrovich)
1905-1984 .... **CLC 7, 15**
See also CA 101; 112; DLB 272; EWL 3; MTCW 1, 2; MTFW 2005; RGWL 2, 3; SATA-Obit 36
Shone, Patric
See Hanley, James
Showalter, Elaine 1941- .... **CLC 169**
See also CA 57-60; CANR 58, 106; DLB 67; FW; GLL 2
Shreve, Susan
See Shreve, Susan Richards
Shreve, Susan Richards 1939- .... **CLC 23**
See also CA 49-52; CAAS 5; CANR 5, 38, 69, 100; MAICYA 1, 2; SATA 46, 95, 152; SATA-Brief 41
Shue, Larry 1946-1985 .... **CLC 52**
See also CA 145; 117; DAM DRAM; DFS 7
Shu-Jen, Chou 1881-1936
See Lu Hsun
See also CA 104
Shulman, Alix Kates 1932- .... **CLC 2, 10**
See also CA 29-32R; CANR 43; FW; SATA 7
Shuster, Joe 1914-1992 .... **CLC 21**
See also AAYA 50
Shute, Nevil .... **CLC 30**
See Norway, Nevil Shute
See also BPFB 3; DLB 255; NFS 9; RHW; SFW 4
Shuttle, Penelope (Diane) 1947- .... **CLC 7**
See also CA 93-96; CANR 39, 84, 92, 108; CP 3, 4, 5, 6, 7; CWP; DLB 14, 40
Shvarts, Elena 1948- .... **PC 50**
See also CA 147
Sidhwa, Bapsi
See Sidhwa, Bapsy (N.)
See also CN 6, 7
Sidhwa, Bapsy (N.) 1938- .... **CLC 168**
See Sidhwa, Bapsi
See also CA 108; CANR 25, 57; FW
Sidney, Mary 1561-1621 .... **LC 19, 39**
See Sidney Herbert, Mary
Sidney, Sir Philip 1554-1586 . **LC 19, 39; PC 32**
See also BRW 1; BRWR 2; CDBLB Before 1660; DA; DA3; DAB; DAC; DAM MST, POET; DLB 167; EXPP; PAB; RGEL 2; TEA; WP
Sidney Herbert, Mary
See Sidney, Mary
See also DLB 167
Siegel, Jerome 1914-1996 .... **CLC 21**
See Siegel, Jerry
See also CA 116; 169; 151
Siegel, Jerry
See Siegel, Jerome
See also AAYA 50
Sienkiewicz, Henryk (Adam Alexander Pius)
1846-1916 .... **TCLC 3**
See also CA 104; 134; CANR 84; EWL 3; RGSF 2; RGWL 2, 3
Sierra, Gregorio Martinez
See Martinez Sierra, Gregorio
Sierra, Maria (de la O'LeJarraga) Martinez
See Martinez Sierra, Maria (de la O'LeJarraga)
Sigal, Clancy 1926- .... **CLC 7**
See also CA 1-4R; CANR 85; CN 1, 2, 3, 4, 5, 6, 7
Siger of Brabant 1240(?)-1284(?) . **CMLC 69**
See also DLB 115
Sigourney, Lydia H.
See Sigourney, Lydia Howard (Huntley)
See also DLB 73, 183
Sigourney, Lydia Howard (Huntley)
1791-1865 .... **NCLC 21, 87**
See Sigourney, Lydia H.; Sigourney, Lydia Huntley
See also DLB 1
Sigourney, Lydia Huntley
See Sigourney, Lydia Howard (Huntley)
See also DLB 42, 239, 243
Siguenza y Gongora, Carlos de
1645-1700 .... **HLCS 2; LC 8**
See also LAW
Sigurjonsson, Johann
See Sigurjonsson, Johann
Sigurjonsson, Johann 1880-1919 ... **TCLC 27**
See also CA 170; DLB 293; EWL 3
Sikelianos, Angelos 1884-1951 .... **PC 29; TCLC 39**
See also EWL 3; RGWL 2, 3
Silkin, Jon 1930-1997 .... **CLC 2, 6, 43**
See also CA 5-8R; CAAS 5; CANR 89; CP 1, 2, 3, 4, 5, 6; DLB 27
Silko, Leslie (Marmon) 1948- .... **CLC 23, 74, 114, 211; NNAL; SSC 37, 66; WLCS**
See also AAYA 14; AMWS 4; ANW; BYA 12; CA 115; 122; CANR 45, 65, 118; CN 4, 5, 6, 7; CP 4, 5, 6, 7; CPW 1; CWP; DA; DA3; DAC; DAM MST, MULT, POP; DLB 143, 175, 256, 275; EWL 3; EXPP; EXPS; LAIT 4; MAL 5; MTCW 2; MTFW 2005; NFS 4; PFS 9, 16; RGAL 4; RGSF 2; SSFS 4, 8, 10, 11; TCWW 1, 2
Sillanpaa, Frans Eemil 1888-1964 ... **CLC 19**
See also CA 129; 93-96; EWL 3; MTCW 1
Sillitoe, Alan 1928- .. **CLC 1, 3, 6, 10, 19, 57, 148**
See also AITN 1; BRWS 5; CA 9-12R, 191; CAAE 191; CAAS 2; CANR 8, 26, 55, 139; CDBLB 1960 to Present; CN 1, 2, 3, 4, 5, 6; CP 1, 2, 3, 4; DLB 14, 139; EWL 3; MTCW 1, 2; MTFW 2005; RGEL 2; RGSF 2; SATA 61

Stebnitsky, M.
See Leskov, Nikolai (Semyonovich)
Steele, Richard 1672-1729 .... **LC 18**
See also BRW 3; CDBLB 1660-1789; DLB 84, 101; RGEL 2; WLIT 3
Steele, Timothy (Reid) 1948- .... **CLC 45**
See also CA 93-96; CANR 16, 50, 92; CP 7; DLB 120, 282
Steffens, (Joseph) Lincoln 1866-1936 .... **TCLC 20**
See also CA 117; 198; DLB 303; MAL 5
Stegner, Wallace (Earle) 1909-1993 .. **CLC 9, 49, 81; SSC 27**
See also AITN 1; AMWS 4; ANW; BEST 90:3; BPFB 3; CA 1-4R; 141; CAAS 9; CANR 1, 21, 46; CN 1, 2, 3, 4, 5; DAM NOV; DLB 9, 206, 275; DLBY 1993; EWL 3; MAL 5; MTCW 1, 2; MTFW 2005; RGAL 4; TCWW 1, 2; TUS
Stein, Gertrude 1874-1946 .... **DC 19; PC 18; SSC 42; TCLC 1, 6, 28, 48; WLC**
See also AAYA 64; AMW; AMWC 2; CA 104; 132; CANR 108; CDALB 1917-1929; DA; DA3; DAB; DAC; DAM MST, NOV, POET; DLB 4, 54, 86, 228; DLBD 15; EWL 3; EXPS; FL 1:6; GLL 1; MAL 5; MAWW; MTCW 1, 2; MTFW 2005; NCFS 4; RGAL 4; RGSF 2; SSFS 5; TUS; WP
Steinbeck, John (Ernst) 1902-1968 ... **CLC 1, 5, 9, 13, 21, 34, 45, 75, 124; SSC 11, 37, 77; TCLC 135; WLC**
See also AAYA 12; AMW; BPFB 3; BYA 2, 3, 13; CA 1-4R; 25-28R; CANR 1, 35; CDALB 1929-1941; DA; DA3; DAB; DAC; DAM DRAM, MST, NOV; DLB 7, 9, 212, 275, 309; DLBD 2; EWL 3; EXPS; LAIT 3; MAL 5; MTCW 1, 2; MTFW 2005; NFS 1, 5, 7, 17, 19; RGAL 4; RGSF 2; RHW; SATA 9; SSFS 3, 6; TCWW 1, 2; TUS; WYA; YAW
Steinem, Gloria 1934- .... **CLC 63**
See also CA 53-56; CANR 28, 51, 139; DLB 246; FW; MTCW 1, 2; MTFW 2005
Steiner, George 1929- .... **CLC 24, 221**
See also CA 73-76; CANR 31, 67, 108; DAM NOV; DLB 67, 299; EWL 3; MTCW 1, 2; MTFW 2005; SATA 62
Steiner, K. Leslie
See Delany, Samuel R(ay), Jr.
Steiner, Rudolf 1861-1925 .... **TCLC 13**
See also CA 107
Stendhal 1783-1842 .. **NCLC 23, 46; SSC 27; WLC**
See also DA; DA3; DAB; DAC; DAM MST, NOV; DLB 119; EW 5; GFL 1789 to the Present; RGWL 2, 3; TWA
Stephen, Adeline Virginia
See Woolf, (Adeline) Virginia
Stephen, Sir Leslie 1832-1904 .... **TCLC 23**
See also BRW 5; CA 123; DLB 57, 144, 190
Stephen, Sir Leslie
See Stephen, Sir Leslie
Stephen, Virginia
See Woolf, (Adeline) Virginia
Stephens, James 1882(?)-1950 .... **SSC 50; TCLC 4**
See also CA 104; 192; DLB 19, 153, 162; EWL 3; FANT; RGEL 2; SUFW
Stephens, Reed
See Donaldson, Stephen R(eeder)
Stephenson, Neal 1959- .... **CLC 220**
See also AAYA 38; CA 122; CANR 88, 138; CN 7; MTCW 2005; SFW 4
Steptoe, Lydia
See Barnes, Djuna
See also GLL 1
Sterchi, Beat 1949- .... **CLC 65**
See also CA 203
Sterling, Brett
See Bradbury, Ray (Douglas); Hamilton, Edmond
Sterling, Bruce 1954- .... **CLC 72**
See also CA 119; CANR 44, 135; CN 7; MTFW 2005; SCFW 2; SFW 4
Sterling, George 1869-1926 .... **TCLC 20**
See also CA 117; 165; DLB 54
Stern, Gerald 1925- .... **CLC 40, 100**
See also AMWS 9; CA 81-84; CANR 28, 94; CP 3, 4, 5, 6, 7; DLB 105; RGAL 4
Stern, Richard (Gustave) 1928- ... **CLC 4, 39**
See also CA 1-4R; CANR 1, 25, 52, 120; CN 1, 2, 3, 4, 5, 6, 7; DLB 218; DLBY 1987; INT CANR-25
Sternberg, Josef von 1894-1969 .... **CLC 20**
See also CA 81-84
Sterne, Laurence 1713-1768 .... **LC 2, 48; WLC**
See also BRW 3; BRWC 1; CDBLB 1660-1789; DA; DAB; DAC; DAM MST, NOV; DLB 39; RGEL 2; TEA
Sternheim, (William Adolf) Carl 1878-1942 .... **TCLC 8**
See also CA 105; 193; DLB 56, 118; EWL 3; IDTP; RGWL 2, 3
Stevens, Margaret Dean
See Aldrich, Bess Streeter
Stevens, Mark 1951- .... **CLC 34**
See also CA 122
Stevens, Wallace 1879-1955 . **PC 6; TCLC 3, 12, 45; WLC**
See also AMW; AMWR 1; CA 104; 124; CDALB 1929-1941; DA; DA3; DAB; DAC; DAM MST, POET; DLB 54; EWL 3; EXPP; MAL 5; MTCW 1, 2; PAB; PFS 13, 16; RGAL 4; TUS; WP
Stevenson, Anne (Katharine) 1933- .. **CLC 7, 33**
See also BRWS 6; CA 17-20R; CAAS 9; CANR 9, 33, 123; CP 3, 4, 5, 6, 7; CWP; DLB 40; MTCW 1; RHW
Stevenson, Robert Louis (Balfour) 1850-1894 ...... **NCLC 5, 14, 63; SSC 11, 51; WLC**
See also AAYA 24; BPFB 3; BRW 5; BRWC 1; BRWR 1; BYA 1, 2, 4, 13; CDBLB 1890-1914; CLR 10, 11; DA; DA3; DAB; DAC; DAM MST, NOV; DLB 18, 57, 141, 156, 174; DLBD 13; GL 3; HGG; JRDA; LAIT 1, 3; MAICYA 1, 2; NFS 11, 20; RGEL 2; RGSF 2; SATA 100; SUFW; TEA; WCH; WLIT 4; WYA; YABC 2; YAW
Stewart, J(ohn) I(nnes) M(ackintosh) 1906-1994 .... **CLC 7, 14, 32**
See Innes, Michael
See also CA 85-88; 147; CAAS 3; CANR 47; CMW 4; CN 1, 2, 3, 4, 5; MTCW 1, 2
Stewart, Mary (Florence Elinor) 1916- .... **CLC 7, 35, 117**
See also AAYA 29; BPFB 3; CA 1-4R; CANR 1, 59, 130; CMW 4; CPW; DAB; FANT; RHW; SATA 12; YAW
Stewart, Mary Rainbow
See Stewart, Mary (Florence Elinor)
Stifle, June
See Campbell, Maria
Stifter, Adalbert 1805-1868 .. **NCLC 41; SSC 28**
See also CDWLB 2; DLB 133; RGSF 2; RGWL 2, 3
Still, James 1906-2001 .... **CLC 49**
See also CA 65-68; 195; CAAS 17; CANR 10, 26; CSW; DLB 9; DLBY 01; SATA 29; SATA-Obit 127
Sting 1951-
See Sumner, Gordon Matthew
See also CA 167
Stirling, Arthur
See Sinclair, Upton (Beall)
Stitt, Milan 1941- .... **CLC 29**
See also CA 69-72
Stockton, Francis Richard 1834-1902
See Stockton, Frank R.
See also AAYA 68; CA 108; 137; MAICYA 1, 2; SATA 44; SFW 4
Stockton, Frank R. .... **TCLC 47**
See Stockton, Francis Richard
See also BYA 4, 13; DLB 42, 74; DLBD 13; EXPS; SATA-Brief 32; SSFS 3; SUFW; WCH
Stoddard, Charles
See Kuttner, Henry
Stoker, Abraham 1847-1912
See Stoker, Bram
See also CA 105; 150; DA; DA3; DAC; DAM MST, NOV; HGG; MTFW 2005; SATA 29
Stoker, Bram . **SSC 62; TCLC 8, 144; WLC**
See Stoker, Abraham
See also AAYA 23; BPFB 3; BRWS 3; BYA 5; CDBLB 1890-1914; DAB; DLB 304; GL 3; LATS 1:1; NFS 18; RGEL 2; SUFW; TEA; WLIT 4
Stolz, Mary (Slattery) 1920- .... **CLC 12**
See also AAYA 8; AITN 1; CA 5-8R; CANR 13, 41, 112; JRDA; MAICYA 1, 2; SAAS 3; SATA 10, 71, 133; YAW
Stone, Irving 1903-1989 .... **CLC 7**
See also AITN 1; BPFB 3; CA 1-4R; 129; CAAS 3; CANR 1, 23; CN 1, 2, 3, 4; CPW; DA3; DAM POP; INT CANR-23; MTCW 1, 2; MTFW 2005; RHW; SATA 3; SATA-Obit 64
Stone, Oliver (William) 1946- .... **CLC 73**
See also AAYA 15, 64; CA 110; CANR 55, 125
Stone, Robert (Anthony) 1937- ... **CLC 5, 23, 42, 175**
See also AMWS 5; BPFB 3; CA 85-88; CANR 23, 66, 95; CN 4, 5, 6, 7; DLB 152; EWL 3; INT CANR-23; MAL 5; MTCW 1; MTFW 2005
Stone, Ruth 1915- .... **PC 53**
See also CA 45-48; CANR 2, 91; CP 7; CSW; DLB 105; PFS 19
Stone, Zachary
See Follett, Ken(neth Martin)
Stoppard, Tom 1937- ... **CLC 1, 3, 4, 5, 8, 15, 29, 34, 63, 91; DC 6; WLC**
See also AAYA 63; BRWC 1; BRWR 2; BRWS 1; CA 81-84; CANR 39, 67, 125; CBD; CD 5, 6; CDBLB 1960 to Present; DA; DA3; DAB; DAC; DAM DRAM, MST; DFS 2, 5, 8, 11, 13, 16; DLB 13, 233; DLBY 1985; EWL 3; LATS 1:2; MTCW 1, 2; MTFW 2005; RGEL 2; TEA; WLIT 4
Storey, David (Malcolm) 1933- ..... **CLC 2, 4, 5, 8**
See also BRWS 1; CA 81-84; CANR 36; CBD; CD 5, 6; CN 1, 2, 3, 4, 5, 6; DAM DRAM; DLB 13, 14, 207, 245; EWL 3; MTCW 1; RGEL 2
Storm, Hyemeyohsts 1935- ... **CLC 3; NNAL**
See also CA 81-84; CANR 45; DAM MULT
Storm, (Hans) Theodor (Woldsen) 1817-1888 .... **NCLC 1; SSC 27**
See also CDWLB 2; DLB 129; EW; RGSF 2; RGWL 2, 3
Storni, Alfonsina 1892-1938 . **HLC 2; PC 33; TCLC 5**
See also CA 104; 131; DAM MULT; DLB 283; HW 1; LAW
Stoughton, William 1631-1701 .... **LC 38**
See also DLB 24

Swenson, May 1919-1989 ...... **CLC 4, 14, 61, 106; PC 14**
See also AMWS 4; CA 5-8R; 130; CANR 36, 61, 131; CP 1, 2, 3, 4; DA; DAB; DAC; DAM MST, POET; DLB 5; EXPP; GLL 2; MAL 5; MTCW 1, 2; MTFW 2005; PFS 16; SATA 15; WP

Swift, Augustus
See Lovecraft, H(oward) P(hillips)

Swift, Graham (Colin) 1949- ...... **CLC 41, 88**
See also BRWC 2; BRWS 5; CA 117; 122; CANR 46, 71, 128; CN 4, 5, 6, 7; DLB 194; MTCW 2; MTFW 2005; NFS 18; RGSF 2

Swift, Jonathan 1667-1745 ..... **LC 1, 42, 101; PC 9; WLC**
See also AAYA 41; BRW 3; BRWC 1; BRWR 1; BYA 5, 14; CDBLB 1660-1789; CLR 53; DA; DA3; DAB; DAC; DAM MST, NOV, POET; DLB 39, 95, 101; EXPN; LAIT 1; NFS 6; RGEL 2; SATA 19; TEA; WCH; WLIT 3

Swinburne, Algernon Charles 1837-1909 ... **PC 24; TCLC 8, 36; WLC**
See also BRW 5; CA 105; 140; CDBLB 1832-1890; DA; DA3; DAB; DAC; DAM MST, POET; DLB 35, 57; PAB; RGEL 2; TEA

Swinfen, Ann .... **CLC 34**
See also CA 202

Swinnerton, Frank (Arthur) 1884-1982 .... **CLC 31**
See also CA 202; 108; CN 1, 2, 3; DLB 34

Swinnerton, Frank Arthur 1884-1982 .... **CLC 31**
See also CA 108; DLB 34

Swithen, John
See King, Stephen

Sylvia
See Ashton-Warner, Sylvia (Constance)

Symmes, Robert Edward
See Duncan, Robert (Edward)

Symonds, John Addington 1840-1893 .... **NCLC 34**
See also DLB 57, 144

Symons, Arthur 1865-1945 .... **TCLC 11**
See also CA 107; 189; DLB 19, 57, 149; RGEL 2

Symons, Julian (Gustave) 1912-1994 .... **CLC 2, 14, 32**
See also CA 49-52; 147; CAAS 3; CANR 3, 33, 59; CMW 4; CN 1, 2, 3, 4, 5; CP 1, 3, 4; DLB 87, 155; DLBY 1992; MSW; MTCW 1

Synge, (Edmund) J(ohn) M(illington) 1871-1909 .... **DC 2; TCLC 6, 37**
See also BRW 6; BRWR 1; CA 104; 141; CDBLB 1890-1914; DAM DRAM; DFS 18; DLB 10, 19; EWL 3; RGEL 2; TEA; WLIT 4

Syruc, J.
See Milosz, Czeslaw

Szirtes, George 1948- .... **CLC 46; PC 51**
See also CA 109; CANR 27, 61, 117; CP 4, 5, 6, 7

Szymborska, Wislawa 1923- ... **CLC 99, 190; PC 44**
See also CA 154; CANR 91, 133; CDWLB 4; CWP; CWW 2; DA3; DLB 232; DLBY 1996; EWL 3; MTCW 2; MTFW 2005; PFS 15; RGWL 3

T. O., Nik
See Annensky, Innokenty (Fyodorovich)

Tabori, George 1914- .... **CLC 19**
See also CA 49-52; CANR 4, 69; CBD; CD 5, 6; DLB 245

Tacitus c. 55-c. 117 .... **CMLC 56**
See also AW 2; CDWLB 1; DLB 211; RGWL 2, 3

Tagore, Rabindranath 1861-1941 .... **PC 8; SSC 48; TCLC 3, 53**
See also CA 104; 120; DA3; DAM DRAM, POET; EWL 3; MTCW 1, 2; MTFW 2005; PFS 18; RGEL 2; RGSF 2; RGWL 2, 3; TWA

Taine, Hippolyte Adolphe 1828-1893 .... **NCLC 15**
See also EW 7; GFL 1789 to the Present

Talayesva, Don C. 1890-(?) .... **NNAL**

Talese, Gay 1932- .... **CLC 37**
See also AITN 1; CA 1-4R; CANR 9, 58, 137; DLB 185; INT CANR-9; MTCW 1, 2; MTFW 2005

Tallent, Elizabeth (Ann) 1954- .... **CLC 45**
See also CA 117; CANR 72; DLB 130

Tallmountain, Mary 1918-1997 .... **NNAL**
See also CA 146; 161; DLB 193

Tally, Ted 1952- .... **CLC 42**
See also CA 120; 124; CAD; CANR 125; CD 5, 6; INT CA-124

Talvik, Heiti 1904-1947 .... **TCLC 87**
See also EWL 3

Tamayo y Baus, Manuel 1829-1898 .... **NCLC 1**

Tammsaare, A(nton) H(ansen) 1878-1940 .... **TCLC 27**
See also CA 164; CDWLB 4; DLB 220; EWL 3

Tam'si, Tchicaya U
See Tchicaya, Gerald Felix

Tan, Amy (Ruth) 1952- . **AAL; CLC 59, 120, 151**
See also AAYA 9, 48; AMWS 10; BEST 89:3; BPFB 3; CA 136; CANR 54, 105, 132; CDALBS; CN 6, 7; CPW 1; DA3; DAM MULT, NOV, POP; DLB 173, 312; EXPN; FL 1:6; FW; LAIT 3, 5; MAL 5; MTCW 2; MTFW 2005; NFS 1, 13, 16; RGAL 4; SATA 75; SSFS 9; YAW

Tandem, Felix
See Spitteler, Carl (Friedrich Georg)

Tanizaki, Jun'ichiro 1886-1965 ... **CLC 8, 14, 28; SSC 21**
See Tanizaki Jun'ichiro
See also CA 93-96; 25-28R; MJW; MTCW 2; MTFW 2005; RGSF 2; RGWL 2

Tanizaki Jun'ichiro
See Tanizaki, Jun'ichiro
See also DLB 180; EWL 3

Tannen, Deborah F(rances) 1945- .. **CLC 206**
See also CA 118; CANR 95

Tanner, William
See Amis, Kingsley (William)

Tao Lao
See Storni, Alfonsina

Tapahonso, Luci 1953- .... **NNAL; PC 65**
See also CA 145; CANR 72, 127; DLB 175

Tarantino, Quentin (Jerome) 1963- .... **CLC 125**
See also AAYA 58; CA 171; CANR 125

Tarassoff, Lev
See Troyat, Henri

Tarbell, Ida M(inerva) 1857-1944 . **TCLC 40**
See also CA 122; 181; DLB 47

Tarkington, (Newton) Booth 1869-1946 .... **TCLC 9**
See also BPFB 3; BYA 3; CA 110; 143; CWRI 5; DLB 9, 102; MAL 5; MTCW 2; RGAL 4; SATA 17

Tarkovskii, Andrei Arsen'evich
See Tarkovsky, Andrei (Arsenyevich)

Tarkovsky, Andrei (Arsenyevich) 1932-1986 .... **CLC 75**
See also CA 127

Tartt, Donna 1964(?)- .... **CLC 76**
See also AAYA 56; CA 142; CANR 135; MTFW 2005

Tasso, Torquato 1544-1595 .... **LC 5, 94**
See also EFS 2; EW 2; RGWL 2, 3; WLIT 7

Tate, (John Orley) Allen 1899-1979 .. **CLC 2, 4, 6, 9, 11, 14, 24; PC 50**
See also AMW; CA 5-8R; 85-88; CANR 32, 108; CN 1, 2; CP 1, 2; DLB 4, 45, 63; DLBD 17; EWL 3; MAL 5; MTCW 1, 2; MTFW 2005; RGAL 4; RHW

Tate, Ellalice
See Hibbert, Eleanor Alice Burford

Tate, James (Vincent) 1943- ..... **CLC 2, 6, 25**
See also CA 21-24R; CANR 29, 57, 114; CP 1, 2, 3, 4, 5, 6, 7; DLB 5, 169; EWL 3; PFS 10, 15; RGAL 4; WP

Tate, Nahum 1652(?)-1715 .... **LC 109**
See also DLB 80; RGEL 2

Tauler, Johannes c. 1300-1361 ...... **CMLC 37**
See also DLB 179; LMFS 1

Tavel, Ronald 1940- .... **CLC 6**
See also CA 21-24R; CAD; CANR 33; CD 5, 6

Taviani, Paolo 1931- .... **CLC 70**
See also CA 153

Taylor, Bayard 1825-1878 .... **NCLC 89**
See also DLB 3, 189, 250, 254; RGAL 4

Taylor, C(ecil) P(hilip) 1929-1981 .... **CLC 27**
See also CA 25-28R; 105; CANR 47; CBD

Taylor, Edward 1642(?)-1729 . **LC 11; PC 63**
See also AMW; DA; DAB; DAC; DAM MST, POET; DLB 24; EXPP; RGAL 4; TUS

Taylor, Eleanor Ross 1920- .... **CLC 5**
See also CA 81-84; CANR 70

Taylor, Elizabeth 1912-1975 ..... **CLC 2, 4, 29**
See also CA 13-16R; CANR 9, 70; CN 1, 2; DLB 139; MTCW 1; RGEL 2; SATA 13

Taylor, Frederick Winslow 1856-1915 .... **TCLC 76**
See also CA 188

Taylor, Henry (Splawn) 1942- .... **CLC 44**
See also CA 33-36R; CAAS 7; CANR 31; CP 7; DLB 5; PFS 10

Taylor, Kamala (Purnaiya) 1924-2004
See Markandaya, Kamala
See also CA 77-80; 227; MTFW 2005; NFS 13

Taylor, Mildred D(elois) 1943- .... **CLC 21**
See also AAYA 10, 47; BW 1; BYA 3, 8; CA 85-88; CANR 25, 115, 136; CLR 9, 59, 90; CSW; DLB 52; JRDA; LAIT 3; MAICYA 1, 2; MTFW 2005; SAAS 5; SATA 135; WYA; YAW

Taylor, Peter (Hillsman) 1917-1994 .. **CLC 1, 4, 18, 37, 44, 50, 71; SSC 10, 84**
See also AMWS 5; BPFB 3; CA 13-16R; 147; CANR 9, 50; CN 1, 2, 3, 4, 5; CSW; DLB 218, 278; DLBY 1981, 1994; EWL 3; EXPS; INT CANR-9; MAL 5; MTCW 1, 2; MTFW 2005; RGSF 2; SSFS 9; TUS

Taylor, Robert Lewis 1912-1998 .... **CLC 14**
See also CA 1-4R; 170; CANR 3, 64; CN 1, 2; SATA 10; TCWW 1, 2

Tchekhov, Anton
See Chekhov, Anton (Pavlovich)

Tchicaya, Gerald Felix 1931-1988 .. **CLC 101**
See Tchicaya U Tam'si
See also CA 129; 125; CANR 81

Tchicaya U Tam'si
See Tchicaya, Gerald Felix
See also EWL 3

Teasdale, Sara 1884-1933 .... **PC 31; TCLC 4**
See also CA 104; 163; DLB 45; GLL 1; PFS 14; RGAL 4; SATA 32; TUS

Tecumseh 1768-1813 .... **NNAL**
See also DAM MULT

Author Index

Thurman, Wallace (Henry) 1902-1934 ..... **BLC 3; HR 1:3; TCLC 6**
See also BW 1, 3; CA 104; 124; CANR 81; DAM MULT; DLB 51
Tibullus c. 54B.C.-c. 18B.C. .... **CMLC 36**
See also AW 2; DLB 211; RGWL 2, 3
Ticheburn, Cheviot
See Ainsworth, William Harrison
Tieck, (Johann) Ludwig 1773-1853 .... **NCLC 5, 46; SSC 31**
See also CDWLB 2; DLB 90; EW 5; IDTP; RGSF 2; RGWL 2, 3; SUFW
Tiger, Derry
See Ellison, Harlan (Jay)
Tilghman, Christopher 1946- .... **CLC 65**
See also CA 159; CANR 135; CSW; DLB 244
Tillich, Paul (Johannes) 1886-1965 .... **CLC 131**
See also CA 5-8R; 25-28R; CANR 33; MTCW 1, 2
Tillinghast, Richard (Williford) 1940- .... **CLC 29**
See also CA 29-32R; CAAS 23; CANR 26, 51, 96; CP 2, 3, 4, 5, 6, 7; CSW
Timrod, Henry 1828-1867 .... **NCLC 25**
See also DLB 3, 248; RGAL 4
Tindall, Gillian (Elizabeth) 1938- ...... **CLC 7**
See also CA 21-24R; CANR 11, 65, 107; CN 1, 2, 3, 4, 5, 6, 7
Tiptree, James, Jr. .... **CLC 48, 50**
See Sheldon, Alice Hastings Bradley
See also DLB 8; SCFW 1, 2; SFW 4
Tirone Smith, Mary-Ann 1944- .... **CLC 39**
See also CA 118; 136; CANR 113; SATA 143
Tirso de Molina 1580(?)-1648 .... **DC 13; HLCS 2; LC 73**
See also RGWL 2, 3
Titmarsh, Michael Angelo
See Thackeray, William Makepeace
Tocqueville, Alexis (Charles Henri Maurice Clerel Comte) de 1805-1859 .. **NCLC 7, 63**
See also EW 6; GFL 1789 to the Present; TWA
Toer, Pramoedya Ananta 1925- ...... **CLC 186**
See also CA 197; RGWL 3
Toffler, Alvin 1928- .... **CLC 168**
See also CA 13-16R; CANR 15, 46, 67; CPW; DAM POP; MTCW 1, 2
Toibin, Colm 1955- .... **CLC 162**
See also CA 142; CANR 81; CN 7; DLB 271
Tolkien, J(ohn) R(onald) R(euel) 1892-1973 .... **CLC 1, 2, 3, 8, 12, 38; TCLC 137; WLC**
See also AAYA 10; AITN 1; BPFB 3; BRWC 2; BRWS 2; CA 17-18; 45-48; CANR 36, 134; CAP 2; CDBLB 1914-1945; CLR 56; CN 1; CPW 1; CWRI 5; DA; DA3; DAB; DAC; DAM MST, NOV, POP; DLB 15, 160, 255; EFS 2; EWL 3; FANT; JRDA; LAIT 1; LATS 1:2; LMFS 2; MAICYA 1, 2; MTCW 1, 2; MTFW 2005; NFS 8; RGEL 2; SATA 2, 32, 100; SATA-Obit 24; SFW 4; SUFW; TEA; WCH; WYA; YAW
Toller, Ernst 1893-1939 .... **TCLC 10**
See also CA 107; 186; DLB 124; EWL 3; RGWL 2, 3
Tolson, M. B.
See Tolson, Melvin B(eaunorus)
Tolson, Melvin B(eaunorus) 1898(?)-1966 .... **BLC 3; CLC 36, 105**
See also AFAW 1, 2; BW 1, 3; CA 124; 89-92; CANR 80; DAM MULT, POET; DLB 48, 76; MAL 5; RGAL 4
Tolstoi, Aleksei Nikolaevich
See Tolstoy, Alexey Nikolaevich
Tolstoi, Lev
See Tolstoy, Leo (Nikolaevich)
See also RGSF 2; RGWL 2, 3
Tolstoy, Aleksei Nikolaevich
See Tolstoy, Alexey Nikolaevich
See also DLB 272
Tolstoy, Alexey Nikolaevich 1882-1945 .... **TCLC 18**
See Tolstoy, Aleksei Nikolaevich
See also CA 107; 158; EWL 3; SFW 4
Tolstoy, Leo (Nikolaevich) 1828-1910 . **SSC 9, 30, 45, 54; TCLC 4, 11, 17, 28, 44, 79, 173; WLC**
See Tolstoi, Lev
See also AAYA 56; CA 104; 123; DA; DA3; DAB; DAC; DAM MST, NOV; DLB 238; EFS 2; EW 7; EXPS; IDTP; LAIT 2; LATS 1:1; LMFS 1; NFS 10; SATA 26; SSFS 5; TWA
Tolstoy, Count Leo
See Tolstoy, Leo (Nikolaevich)
Tomalin, Claire 1933- .... **CLC 166**
See also CA 89-92; CANR 52, 88; DLB 155
Tomasi di Lampedusa, Giuseppe 1896-1957
See Lampedusa, Giuseppe (Tomasi) di
See also CA 111; DLB 177; EWL 3; WLIT 7
Tomlin, Lily .... **CLC 17**
See Tomlin, Mary Jean
Tomlin, Mary Jean 1939(?)-
See Tomlin, Lily
See also CA 117
Tomline, F. Latour
See Gilbert, W(illiam) S(chwenck)
Tomlinson, (Alfred) Charles 1927- .... **CLC 2, 4, 6, 13, 45; PC 17**
See also CA 5-8R; CANR 33; CP 1, 2, 3, 4, 5, 6, 7; DAM POET; DLB 40; TCLE 1:2
Tomlinson, H(enry) M(ajor) 1873-1958 .... **TCLC 71**
See also CA 118; 161; DLB 36, 100, 195
Tonna, Charlotte Elizabeth 1790-1846 .... **NCLC 135**
See also DLB 163
Tonson, Jacob fl. 1655(?)-1736 .... **LC 86**
See also DLB 170
Toole, John Kennedy 1937-1969 ..... **CLC 19, 64**
See also BPFB 3; CA 104; DLBY 1981; MTCW 2; MTFW 2005
Toomer, Eugene
See Toomer, Jean
Toomer, Eugene Pinchback
See Toomer, Jean
Toomer, Jean 1894-1967 .. **BLC 3; CLC 1, 4, 13, 22; HR 1:3; PC 7; SSC 1, 45; TCLC 172; WLCS**
See also AFAW 1, 2; AMWS 3, 9; BW 1; CA 85-88; CDALB 1917-1929; DA3; DAM MULT; DLB 45, 51; EWL 3; EXPP; EXPS; LMFS 2; MAL 5; MTCW 1, 2; MTFW 2005; NFS 11; RGAL 4; RGSF 2; SSFS 5
Toomer, Nathan Jean
See Toomer, Jean
Toomer, Nathan Pinchback
See Toomer, Jean
Torley, Luke
See Blish, James (Benjamin)
Tornimparte, Alessandra
See Ginzburg, Natalia
Torre, Raoul della
See Mencken, H(enry) L(ouis)
Torrence, Ridgely 1874-1950 .... **TCLC 97**
See also DLB 54, 249; MAL 5
Torrey, E(dwin) Fuller 1937- .... **CLC 34**
See also CA 119; CANR 71
Torsvan, Ben Traven
See Traven, B.
Torsvan, Benno Traven
See Traven, B.
Torsvan, Berick Traven
See Traven, B.
Torsvan, Berwick Traven
See Traven, B.
Torsvan, Bruno Traven
See Traven, B.
Torsvan, Traven
See Traven, B.
Tourneur, Cyril 1575(?)-1626 .... **LC 66**
See also BRW 2; DAM DRAM; DLB 58; RGEL 2
Tournier, Michel (Edouard) 1924- .... **CLC 6, 23, 36, 95; SSC 88**
See also CA 49-52; CANR 3, 36, 74; CWW 2; DLB 83; EWL 3; GFL 1789 to the Present; MTCW 1, 2; SATA 23
Tournimparte, Alessandra
See Ginzburg, Natalia
Towers, Ivar
See Kornbluth, C(yril) M.
Towne, Robert (Burton) 1936(?)- ..... **CLC 87**
See also CA 108; DLB 44; IDFW 3, 4
Townsend, Sue .... **CLC 61**
See Townsend, Susan Lilian
See also AAYA 28; CA 119; 127; CANR 65, 107; CBD; CD 5, 6; CPW; CWD; DAB; DAC; DAM MST; DLB 271; INT CA-127; SATA 55, 93; SATA-Brief 48; YAW
Townsend, Susan Lilian 1946-
See Townsend, Sue
Townshend, Pete
See Townshend, Peter (Dennis Blandford)
Townshend, Peter (Dennis Blandford) 1945- .... **CLC 17, 42**
See also CA 107
Tozzi, Federigo 1883-1920 .... **TCLC 31**
See also CA 160; CANR 110; DLB 264; EWL 3; WLIT 7
Tracy, Don(ald Fiske) 1905-1970(?)
See Queen, Ellery
See also CA 1-4R; 176; CANR 2
Trafford, F. G.
See Riddell, Charlotte
Traherne, Thomas 1637(?)-1674 .. **LC 99; PC 70**
See also BRW 2; BRWS 11; DLB 131; PAB; RGEL 2
Traill, Catharine Parr 1802-1899 .. **NCLC 31**
See also DLB 99
Trakl, Georg 1887-1914 .... **PC 20; TCLC 5**
See also CA 104; 165; EW 10; EWL 3; LMFS 2; MTCW 2; RGWL 2, 3
Trambley, Estela Portillo .... **TCLC 163**
See Portillo Trambley, Estela
See also CA 77-80; RGAL 4
Tranquilli, Secondino
See Silone, Ignazio
Transtroemer, Tomas Gosta
See Transtromer, Tomas (Goesta)
Transtromer, Tomas (Gosta)
See Transtromer, Tomas (Goesta)
See also CWW 2
Transtromer, Tomas (Goesta) 1931- .... **CLC 52, 65**
See Transtromer, Tomas (Gosta)
See also CA 117; 129; CAAS 17; CANR 115; DAM POET; DLB 257; EWL 3; PFS 21
Transtromer, Tomas Gosta
See Transtromer, Tomas (Goesta)

Author Index

Author Index

Wells-Barnett, Ida B(ell) 1862-1931 .... **TCLC 125**
See also CA 182; DLB 23, 221

Welsh, Irvine 1958- .... **CLC 144**
See also CA 173; CANR 146; CN 7; DLB 271

Welty, Eudora (Alice) 1909-2001 .. **CLC 1, 2, 5, 14, 22, 33, 105, 220; SSC 1, 27, 51; WLC**
See also AAYA 48; AMW; AMWR 1; BPFB 3; CA 9-12R; 199; CABS 1; CANR 32, 65, 128; CDALB 1941-1968; CN 1, 2, 3, 4, 5, 6, 7; CSW; DA; DA3; DAB; DAC; DAM MST, NOV; DLB 2, 102, 143; DLBD 12; DLBY 1987, 2001; EWL 3; EXPS; HGG; LAIT 3; MAL 5; MAWW; MTCW 1, 2; MTFW 2005; NFS 13, 15; RGAL 4; RGSF 2; RHW; SSFS 2, 10; TUS

Wen I-to 1899-1946 .... **TCLC 28**
See also EWL 3

Wentworth, Robert
See Hamilton, Edmond

Werfel, Franz (Viktor) 1890-1945 ... **TCLC 8**
See also CA 104; 161; DLB 81, 124; EWL 3; RGWL 2, 3

Wergeland, Henrik Arnold 1808-1845 .... **NCLC 5**

Wersba, Barbara 1932- .... **CLC 30**
See also AAYA 2, 30; BYA 6, 12, 13; CA 29-32R, 182; CAAE 182; CANR 16, 38; CLR 3, 78; DLB 52; JRDA; MAICYA 1, 2; SAAS 2; SATA 1, 58; SATA-Essay 103; WYA; YAW

Wertmueller, Lina 1928- .... **CLC 16**
See also CA 97-100; CANR 39, 78

Wescott, Glenway 1901-1987 .. **CLC 13; SSC 35**
See also CA 13-16R; 121; CANR 23, 70; CN 1, 2, 3, 4; DLB 4, 9, 102; MAL 5; RGAL 4

Wesker, Arnold 1932- .... **CLC 3, 5, 42**
See also CA 1-4R; CAAS 7; CANR 1, 33; CBD; CD 5, 6; CDBLB 1960 to Present; DAB; DAM DRAM; DLB 13, 310, 319; EWL 3; MTCW 1; RGEL 2; TEA

Wesley, John 1703-1791 .... **LC 88**
See also DLB 104

Wesley, Richard (Errol) 1945- .... **CLC 7**
See also BW 1; CA 57-60; CAD; CANR 27; CD 5, 6; DLB 38

Wessel, Johan Herman 1742-1785 .... **LC 7**
See also DLB 300

West, Anthony (Panther) 1914-1987 .... **CLC 50**
See also CA 45-48; 124; CANR 3, 19; CN 1, 2, 3, 4; DLB 15

West, C. P.
See Wodehouse, P(elham) G(renville)

West, Cornel (Ronald) 1953- .... **BLCS; CLC 134**
See also CA 144; CANR 91; DLB 246

West, Delno C(loyde), Jr. 1936- .... **CLC 70**
See also CA 57-60

West, Dorothy 1907-1998 ...... **HR 1:3; TCLC 108**
See also BW 2; CA 143; 169; DLB 76

West, (Mary) Jessamyn 1902-1984 ... **CLC 7, 17**
See also CA 9-12R; 112; CANR 27; CN 1, 2, 3; DLB 6; DLBY 1984; MTCW 1, 2; RGAL 4; RHW; SATA-Obit 37; TCWW 2; TUS; YAW

West, Morris L(anglo) 1916-1999 ..... **CLC 6, 33**
See also BPFB 3; CA 5-8R; 187; CANR 24, 49, 64; CN 1, 2, 3, 4, 5, 6; CPW; DLB 289; MTCW 1, 2; MTFW 2005

West, Nathanael 1903-1940 .. **SSC 16; TCLC 1, 14, 44**
See also AMW; AMWR 2; BPFB 3; CA 104; 125; CDALB 1929-1941; DA3; DLB 4, 9, 28; EWL 3; MAL 5; MTCW 1, 2; MTFW 2005; NFS 16; RGAL 4; TUS

West, Owen
See Koontz, Dean R.

West, Paul 1930- .... **CLC 7, 14, 96**
See also CA 13-16R; CAAS 7; CANR 22, 53, 76, 89, 136; CN 1, 2, 3, 4, 5, 6, 7; DLB 14; INT CANR-22; MTCW 2; MTFW 2005

West, Rebecca 1892-1983 ... **CLC 7, 9, 31, 50**
See also BPFB 3; BRWS 3; CA 5-8R; 109; CANR 19; CN 1, 2, 3; DLB 36; DLBY 1983; EWL 3; FW; MTCW 1, 2; MTFW 2005; NCFS 4; RGEL 2; TEA

Westall, Robert (Atkinson) 1929-1993 .... **CLC 17**
See also AAYA 12; BYA 2, 6, 7, 8, 9, 15; CA 69-72; 141; CANR 18, 68; CLR 13; FANT; JRDA; MAICYA 1, 2; MAICYAS 1; SAAS 2; SATA 23, 69; SATA-Obit 75; WYA; YAW

Westermarck, Edward 1862-1939 . **TCLC 87**

Westlake, Donald E(dwin) 1933- . **CLC 7, 33**
See also BPFB 3; CA 17-20R; CAAS 13; CANR 16, 44, 65, 94, 137; CMW 4; CPW; DAM POP; INT CANR-16; MSW; MTCW 2; MTFW 2005

Westmacott, Mary
See Christie, Agatha (Mary Clarissa)

Weston, Allen
See Norton, Andre

Wetcheek, J. L.
See Feuchtwanger, Lion

Wetering, Janwillem van de
See van de Wetering, Janwillem

Wetherald, Agnes Ethelwyn 1857-1940 .... **TCLC 81**
See also CA 202; DLB 99

Wetherell, Elizabeth
See Warner, Susan (Bogert)

Whale, James 1889-1957 .... **TCLC 63**

Whalen, Philip (Glenn) 1923-2002 .... **CLC 6, 29**
See also BG 1:3; CA 9-12R; 209; CANR 5, 39; CP 1, 2, 3, 4, 5, 6, 7; DLB 16; WP

Wharton, Edith (Newbold Jones) 1862-1937 ... **SSC 6, 84; TCLC 3, 9, 27, 53, 129, 149; WLC**
See also AAYA 25; AMW; AMWC 2; AMWR 1; BPFB 3; CA 104; 132; CDALB 1865-1917; DA; DA3; DAB; DAC; DAM MST, NOV; DLB 4, 9, 12, 78, 189; DLBD 13; EWL 3; EXPS; FL 1:6; GL 3; HGG; LAIT 2, 3; LATS 1:1; MAL 5; MAWW; MTCW 1, 2; MTFW 2005; NFS 5, 11, 15, 20; RGAL 4; RGSF 2; RHW; SSFS 6, 7; SUFW; TUS

Wharton, James
See Mencken, H(enry) L(ouis)

Wharton, William (a pseudonym) 1925- .... **CLC 18, 37**
See also CA 93-96; CN 4, 5, 6, 7; DLBY 1980; INT CA-93-96

Wheatley (Peters), Phillis 1753(?)-1784 ... **BLC 3; LC 3, 50; PC 3; WLC**
See also AFAW 1, 2; CDALB 1640-1865; DA; DA3; DAC; DAM MST, MULT, POET; DLB 31, 50; EXPP; FL 1:1; PFS 13; RGAL 4

Wheelock, John Hall 1886-1978 .... **CLC 14**
See also CA 13-16R; 77-80; CANR 14; CP 1, 2; DLB 45; MAL 5

Whim-Wham
See Curnow, (Thomas) Allen (Monro)

White, Babington
See Braddon, Mary Elizabeth

White, E(lwyn) B(rooks) 1899-1985 .... **CLC 10, 34, 39**
See also AAYA 62; AITN 2; AMWS 1; CA 13-16R; 116; CANR 16, 37; CDALBS; CLR 1, 21; CPW; DA3; DAM POP; DLB 11, 22; EWL 3; FANT; MAICYA 1, 2; MAL 5; MTCW 1, 2; MTFW 2005; NCFS 5; RGAL 4; SATA 2, 29, 100; SATA-Obit 44; TUS

White, Edmund (Valentine III) 1940- .... **CLC 27, 110**
See also AAYA 7; CA 45-48; CANR 3, 19, 36, 62, 107, 133; CN 5, 6, 7; DA3; DAM POP; DLB 227; MTCW 1, 2; MTFW 2005

White, Hayden V. 1928- .... **CLC 148**
See also CA 128; CANR 135; DLB 246

White, Patrick (Victor Martindale) 1912-1990 ...... **CLC 3, 4, 5, 7, 9, 18, 65, 69; SSC 39, TCLC 176**
See also BRWS 1; CA 81-84; 132; CANR 43; CN 1, 2, 3, 4; DLB 260; EWL 3; MTCW 1; RGEL 2; RGSF 2; RHW; TWA; WWE 1

White, Phyllis Dorothy James 1920-
See James, P. D.
See also CA 21-24R; CANR 17, 43, 65, 112; CMW 4; CN 7; CPW; DA3; DAM POP; MTCW 1, 2; MTFW 2005; TEA

White, T(erence) H(anbury) 1906-1964 .... **CLC 30**
See also AAYA 22; BPFB 3; BYA 4, 5; CA 73-76; CANR 37; DLB 160; FANT; JRDA; LAIT 1; MAICYA 1, 2; RGEL 2; SATA 12; SUFW 1; YAW

White, Terence de Vere 1912-1994 ... **CLC 49**
See also CA 49-52; 145; CANR 3

White, Walter
See White, Walter F(rancis)

White, Walter F(rancis) 1893-1955 ... **BLC 3; HR 1:3; TCLC 15**
See also BW 1; CA 115; 124; DAM MULT; DLB 51

White, William Hale 1831-1913
See Rutherford, Mark
See also CA 121; 189

Whitehead, Alfred North 1861-1947 .... **TCLC 97**
See also CA 117; 165; DLB 100, 262

Whitehead, E(dward) A(nthony) 1933- .... **CLC 5**
See Whitehead, Ted
See also CA 65-68; CANR 58, 118; CBD; CD 5; DLB 310

Whitehead, Ted
See Whitehead, E(dward) A(nthony)
See also CD 6

Whiteman, Roberta J. Hill 1947- ...... **NNAL**
See also CA 146

Whitemore, Hugh (John) 1936- .... **CLC 37**
See also CA 132; CANR 77; CBD; CD 5, 6; INT CA-132

Whitman, Sarah Helen (Power) 1803-1878 .... **NCLC 19**
See also DLB 1, 243

Whitman, Walt(er) 1819-1892 .. **NCLC 4, 31, 81; PC 3; WLC**
See also AAYA 42; AMW; AMWR 1; CDALB 1640-1865; DA; DA3; DAB; DAC; DAM MST, POET; DLB 3, 64, 224, 250; EXPP; LAIT 2; LMFS 1; PAB; PFS 2, 3, 13, 22; RGAL 4; SATA 20; TUS; WP; WYAS 1

Whitney, Phyllis A(yame) 1903- .... **CLC 42**
See also AAYA 36; AITN 2; BEST 90:3; CA 1-4R; CANR 3, 25, 38, 60; CLR 59; CMW 4; CPW; DA3; DAM POP; JRDA; MAICYA 1, 2; MTCW 2; RHW; SATA 1, 30; YAW

Wilson, A(ndrew) N(orman) 1950- .. **CLC 33**
See also BRWS 6; CA 112; 122; CN 4, 5, 6, 7; DLB 14, 155, 194; MTCW 2
Wilson, Angus (Frank Johnstone) 1913-1991 . **CLC 2, 3, 5, 25, 34; SSC 21**
See also BRWS 1; CA 5-8R; 134; CANR 21; CN 1, 2, 3, 4; DLB 15, 139, 155; EWL 3; MTCW 1, 2; MTFW 2005; RGEL 2; RGSF 2
Wilson, August 1945-2005 .. **BLC 3; CLC 39, 50, 63, 118, 222; DC 2; WLCS**
See also AAYA 16; AFAW 2; AMWS 8; BW 2, 3; CA 115; 122; CAD; CANR 42, 54, 76, 128; CD 5, 6; DA; DA3; DAB; DAC; DAM DRAM, MST, MULT; DFS 3, 7, 15, 17; DLB 228; EWL 3; LAIT 4; LATS 1:2; MAL 5; MTCW 1, 2; MTFW 2005; RGAL 4
Wilson, Brian 1942- .... **CLC 12**
Wilson, Colin (Henry) 1931- .... **CLC 3, 14**
See also CA 1-4R; CAAS 5; CANR 1, 22, 33, 77; CMW 4; CN 1, 2, 3, 4, 5, 6; DLB 14, 194; HGG; MTCW 1; SFW 4
Wilson, Dirk
See Pohl, Frederik
Wilson, Edmund 1895-1972 .. **CLC 1, 2, 3, 8, 24**
See also AMW; CA 1-4R; 37-40R; CANR 1, 46, 110; CN 1; DLB 63; EWL 3; MAL 5; MTCW 1, 2; MTFW 2005; RGAL 4; TUS
Wilson, Ethel Davis (Bryant) 1888(?)-1980 .... **CLC 13**
See also CA 102; CN 1, 2; DAC; DAM POET; DLB 68; MTCW 1; RGEL 2
Wilson, Harriet
See Wilson, Harriet E. Adams
See also DLB 239
Wilson, Harriet E.
See Wilson, Harriet E. Adams
See also DLB 243
Wilson, Harriet E. Adams 1827(?)-1863(?) .... **BLC 3; NCLC 78**
See Wilson, Harriet; Wilson, Harriet E.
See also DAM MULT; DLB 50
Wilson, John 1785-1854 .... **NCLC 5**
Wilson, John (Anthony) Burgess 1917-1993
See Burgess, Anthony
See also CA 1-4R; 143; CANR 2, 46; DA3; DAC; DAM NOV; MTCW 1, 2; MTFW 2005; NFS 15; TEA
Wilson, Lanford 1937- .. **CLC 7, 14, 36, 197; DC 19**
See also CA 17-20R; CABS 3; CAD; CANR 45, 96; CD 5, 6; DAM DRAM; DFS 4, 9, 12, 16, 20; DLB 7; EWL 3; MAL 5; TUS
Wilson, Robert M. 1941- .... **CLC 7, 9**
See also CA 49-52; CAD; CANR 2, 41; CD 5, 6; MTCW 1
Wilson, Robert McLiam 1964- .... **CLC 59**
See also CA 132; DLB 267
Wilson, Sloan 1920-2003 .... **CLC 32**
See also CA 1-4R; 216; CANR 1, 44; CN 1, 2, 3, 4, 5, 6
Wilson, Snoo 1948- .... **CLC 33**
See also CA 69-72; CBD; CD 5, 6
Wilson, William S(mith) 1932- .... **CLC 49**
See also CA 81-84
Wilson, (Thomas) Woodrow 1856-1924 .... **TCLC 79**
See also CA 166; DLB 47
Wilson and Warnke eds. .... **CLC 65**
Winchilsea, Anne (Kingsmill) Finch 1661-1720
See Finch, Anne
See also RGEL 2
Windham, Basil
See Wodehouse, P(elham) G(renville)
Wingrove, David (John) 1954- .... **CLC 68**
See also CA 133; SFW 4
Winnemucca, Sarah 1844-1891 .... **NCLC 79; NNAL**
See also DAM MULT; DLB 175; RGAL 4
Winstanley, Gerrard 1609-1676 .... **LC 52**
Wintergreen, Jane
See Duncan, Sara Jeannette
Winters, Arthur Yvor
See Winters, Yvor
Winters, Janet Lewis .... **CLC 41**
See Lewis, Janet
See also DLBY 1987
Winters, Yvor 1900-1968 .... **CLC 4, 8, 32**
See also AMWS 2; CA 11-12; 25-28R; CAP 1; DLB 48; EWL 3; MAL 5; MTCW 1; RGAL 4
Winterson, Jeanette 1959- .... **CLC 64, 158**
See also BRWS 4; CA 136; CANR 58, 116; CN 5, 6, 7; CPW; DA3; DAM POP; DLB 207, 261; FANT; FW; GLL 1; MTCW 2; MTFW 2005; RHW
Winthrop, John 1588-1649 .... **LC 31, 107**
See also DLB 24, 30
Wirth, Louis 1897-1952 .... **TCLC 92**
See also CA 210
Wiseman, Frederick 1930- .... **CLC 20**
See also CA 159
Wister, Owen 1860-1938 .... **TCLC 21**
See also BPFB 3; CA 108; 162; DLB 9, 78, 186; RGAL 4; SATA 62; TCWW 1, 2
Wither, George 1588-1667 .... **LC 96**
See also DLB 121; RGEL 2
Witkacy
See Witkiewicz, Stanislaw Ignacy
Witkiewicz, Stanislaw Ignacy 1885-1939 .... **TCLC 8**
See also CA 105; 162; CDWLB 4; DLB 215; EW 10; EWL 3; RGWL 2, 3; SFW 4
Wittgenstein, Ludwig (Josef Johann) 1889-1951 .... **TCLC 59**
See also CA 113; 164; DLB 262; MTCW 2
Wittig, Monique 1935-2003 .... **CLC 22**
See also CA 116; 135; 212; CANR 143; CWW 2; DLB 83; EWL 3; FW; GLL 1
Wittlin, Jozef 1896-1976 .... **CLC 25**
See also CA 49-52; 65-68; CANR 3; EWL 3
Wodehouse, P(elham) G(renville) 1881-1975 . **CLC 1, 2, 5, 10, 22; SSC 2; TCLC 108**
See also AAYA 65; AITN 2; BRWS 3; CA 45-48; 57-60; CANR 3, 33; CDBLB 1914-1945; CN 1, 2; CPW 1; DA3; DAB; DAC; DAM NOV; DLB 34, 162; EWL 3; MTCW 1, 2; MTFW 2005; RGEL 2; RGSF 2; SATA 22; SSFS 10
Woiwode, L.
See Woiwode, Larry (Alfred)
Woiwode, Larry (Alfred) 1941- ... **CLC 6, 10**
See also CA 73-76; CANR 16, 94; CN 3, 4, 5, 6, 7; DLB 6; INT CANR-16
Wojciechowska, Maia (Teresa) 1927-2002 .... **CLC 26**
See also AAYA 8, 46; BYA 3; CA 9-12R, 183; 209; CAAE 183; CANR 4, 41; CLR 1; JRDA; MAICYA 1, 2; SAAS 1; SATA 1, 28, 83; SATA-Essay 104; SATA-Obit 134; YAW
Wojtyla, Karol (Jozef)
See John Paul II, Pope
Wojtyla, Karol (Josef)
See John Paul II, Pope
Wolf, Christa 1929- .... **CLC 14, 29, 58, 150**
See also CA 85-88; CANR 45, 123; CDWLB 2; CWW 2; DLB 75; EWL 3; FW; MTCW 1; RGWL 2, 3; SSFS 14
Wolf, Naomi 1962- .... **CLC 157**
See also CA 141; CANR 110; FW; MTFW 2005
Wolfe, Gene 1931- .... **CLC 25**
See also AAYA 35; CA 57-60; CAAS 9; CANR 6, 32, 60; CPW; DAM POP; DLB 8; FANT; MTCW 2; MTFW 2005; SATA 118, 165; SCFW 2; SFW 4; SUFW 2
Wolfe, Gene Rodman
See Wolfe, Gene
Wolfe, George C. 1954- .... **BLCS; CLC 49**
See also CA 149; CAD; CD 5, 6
Wolfe, Thomas (Clayton) 1900-1938 ...... **SSC 33; TCLC 4, 13, 29, 61; WLC**
See also AMW; BPFB 3; CA 104; 132; CANR 102; CDALB 1929-1941; DA; DA3; DAB; DAC; DAM MST, NOV; DLB 9, 102, 229; DLBD 2, 16; DLBY 1985, 1997; EWL 3; MAL 5; MTCW 1, 2; NFS 18; RGAL 4; SSFS 18; TUS
Wolfe, Thomas Kennerly, Jr. 1931- .... **CLC 147**
See Wolfe, Tom
See also CA 13-16R; CANR 9, 33, 70, 104; DA3; DAM POP; DLB 185; EWL 3; INT CANR-9; MTCW 1, 2; MTFW 2005; TUS
Wolfe, Tom .... **CLC 1, 2, 9, 15, 35, 51**
See Wolfe, Thomas Kennerly, Jr.
See also AAYA 8, 67; AITN 2; AMWS 3; BEST 89:1; BPFB 3; CN 5, 6, 7; CPW; CSW; DLB 152; LAIT 5; RGAL 4
Wolff, Geoffrey (Ansell) 1937- .... **CLC 41**
See also CA 29-32R; CANR 29, 43, 78
Wolff, Sonia
See Levitin, Sonia (Wolff)
Wolff, Tobias (Jonathan Ansell) 1945- .... **CLC 39, 64, 172; SSC 63**
See also AAYA 16; AMWS 7; BEST 90:2; BYA 12; CA 114; 117; CAAS 22; CANR 54, 76, 96; CN 5, 6, 7; CSW; DA3; DLB 130; EWL 3; INT CA-117; MTCW 2; MTFW 2005; RGAL 4; RGSF 2; SSFS 4, 11
Wolfram von Eschenbach c. 1170-c. 1220 .... **CMLC 5**
See Eschenbach, Wolfram von
See also CDWLB 2; DLB 138; EW 1; RGWL 2
Wolitzer, Hilma 1930- .... **CLC 17**
See also CA 65-68; CANR 18, 40; INT CANR-18; SATA 31; YAW
Wollstonecraft, Mary 1759-1797 .... **LC 5, 50, 90**
See also BRWS 3; CDBLB 1789-1832; DLB 39, 104, 158, 252; FL 1:1; FW; LAIT 1; RGEL 2; TEA; WLIT 3
Wonder, Stevie .... **CLC 12**
See Morris, Steveland Judkins
Wong, Jade Snow 1922- .... **CLC 17**
See also CA 109; CANR 91; SATA 112
Woodberry, George Edward 1855-1930 .... **TCLC 73**
See also CA 165; DLB 71, 103
Woodcott, Keith
See Brunner, John (Kilian Houston)
Woodruff, Robert W.
See Mencken, H(enry) L(ouis)
Woolf, (Adeline) Virginia 1882-1941 .. **SSC 7, 79; TCLC 1, 5, 20, 43, 56, 101, 123, 128; WLC**
See also AAYA 44; BPFB 3; BRW 7; BRWC 2; BRWR 1; CA 104; 130; CANR 64, 132; CDBLB 1914-1945; DA; DA3; DAB; DAC; DAM MST, NOV; DLB 36, 100, 162; DLBD 10; EWL 3; EXPS; FL 1:6; FW; LAIT 3; LATS 1:1; LMFS 2; MTCW 1, 2; MTFW 2005; NCFS 2; NFS 8, 12; RGEL 2; RGSF 2; SSFS 4, 12; TEA; WLIT 4

Literary Criticism Series Cumulative Topic Index

This index lists all topic entries in Thompson Gale's *Children's Literature Review* (CLR), *Classical and Medieval Literature Criticism* (CMLC), *Contemporary Literary Criticism* (CLC), *Drama Criticism* (DC), *Literature Criticism from 1400 to 1800* (LC), *Nineteenth-Century Literature Criticism* (NCLC), *Short Story Criticism* (SSC), and *Twentieth-Century Literary Criticism* (TCLC). The index also lists topic entries in the Gale Critical Companion Collection, which includes the following publications: *The Beat Generation* (BG), *Feminism in Literature* (FL), *Gothic Literature* (GL), and *Harlem Renaissance* (HR).

Topic Index

SSC Cumulative Nationality Index

JAPANESE

Abe, Kobo **61**
Akutagawa, Ryunosuke **44**
Dazai Osamu **41**
Endo, Shūsaku **48**
Kawabata, Yasunari **17**
Oe, Kenzaburo **20**
Shiga, Naoya **23**
Tanizaki, Junichirō **21**

MEXICAN

Arreola, Juan José **38**
Castellanos, Rosario **39, 68**
Fuentes, Carlos **24**
Rulfo, Juan **25**

NEW ZEALANDER

Frame, Janet **29**
Mansfield, Katherine **9, 23, 38, 81**

POLISH

Agnon, S(hmuel) Y(osef Halevi) **30**
Borowski, Tadeusz **48**
Conrad, Joseph **9, 71**
Peretz, Isaac Loeb **26**
Schulz, Bruno **13**
Singer, Isaac Bashevis **3, 53, 80**

PUERTO RICAN

Ferré, Rosario **36**

RUSSIAN

Babel, Isaak (Emmanuilovich) **16, 78**
Bulgakov, Mikhail (Afanas'evich) **18**
Bunin, Ivan Alexeyevich **5**
Chekhov, Anton (Pavlovich) **2, 28, 41, 51, 85**
Dostoevsky, Fedor Mikhailovich **2, 33, 44**
Gogol, Nikolai (Vasilyevich) **4, 29, 52**
Gorky, Maxim **28**
Kazakov, Yuri Pavlovich **43**
Leskov, Nikolai (Semyonovich) **34**
Nabokov, Vladimir (Vladimirovich) **11, 86**
Olesha, Yuri **69**
Pasternak, Boris (Leonidovich) **31**
Pilnyak, Boris **48**
Platonov, Andrei (Klimentov, Andrei Platonovich) **42**
Pushkin, Alexander (Sergeyevich) **27, 55**
Solzhenitsyn, Aleksandr I(sayevich) **32**
Tolstoy, Leo (Nikolaevich) **9, 30, 45, 54**
Turgenev, Ivan (Sergeevich) **7, 57**
Zamyatin, Yevgeny **89**
Zoshchenko, Mikhail (Mikhailovich) **15**

SCOTTISH

Davie, Elspeth **52**
Doyle, Arthur Conan **12**
Oliphant, Margaret (Oliphant Wilson) **25**
Scott, Walter **32**
Spark, Muriel (Sarah) **10**
Stevenson, Robert Louis (Balfour) **11, 51**

SOUTH AFRICAN

Gordimer, Nadine **17, 80**
Head, Bessie **52**

SPANISH

Alarcón, Pedro Antonio de **64**
Cela, Camilo José **71**
Cervantes (Saavedra), Miguel de **12**
Pardo Bazán, Emilia **30**
Unamuno (y Jugo), Miguel de **11, 69**

SWEDISH

Lagervist, Par **12**

SWISS

Hesse, Hermann **9, 49**
Meyer, Conrad Ferdinand **30**
Keller, Gottfried **26**
Walser, Robert **20**

TRINIDADIAN

Naipaul, V(idiadhar) S(urajprasad) **38**

UKRAINIAN

Aleichem, Sholom **33**

URUGUAYAN

Onetti, Juan Carlos **23**
Quiroga, Horacio **89**

WELSH

Evans, Caradoc **43**
Lewis, Alun **40**
Machen, Arthur **20**
Thomas, Dylan (Marlais) **3, 44**

YUGOSLAVIAN

Andrić, Ivo **36**

SSC-91 Title Index

ISBN 0-7876-8888-6

	DATE DUE		